THE OXFORD
ITALIAN
DICTIONARY

Italian–English   Italiano–Inglese
English–Italian   Inglese–Italiano

Debora Mazza

BERKLEY BOOKS, NEW YORK

Most Berkley Books are available at special quantity discounts for bulk purchases for sales promotions, premiums, fund-raising or educational use. Special books, or book excerpts, can also be created to fit specific needs.

For details, write: Special Markets, The Berkley Publishing Group, 375 Hudson Street, New York, New York 10014.

THE OXFORD ITALIAN DICTIONARY

A Berkley Book / published in mass-market paperback by arrangement with Oxford University Press, Inc.

PRINTING HISTORY
Oxford University Press edition published 1989
Berkley edition / August 1997

Copyright © 1986, 1997 by Oxford University Press.
First published in 1986 as *The Oxford Italian Minidictionary*.
First published (with corrections) in 1989 as *The Oxford Paperback Italian Dictionary*.
Reissued 1994.
Second edition 1997.
Oxford is a registered trademark of Oxford University Press.
All rights reserved. No part of this publication may be reproduced, stored in a retrieval system, or transmitted, in any form or by any means, electronic, mechanical, photocopying, recording, or otherwise, without the prior permission of Oxford University Press.
For information, contact: Oxford University Press, 198 Madison Avenue, New York, New York 10016.

The Penguin Putnam Inc. World Wide Web site address is
http://www.penguinputnam.com

ISBN: 0-425-16012-2

BERKLEY®
Berkley Books are published by The Berkley Publishing Group,
a division of Penguin Putnam Inc.,
375 Hudson Street, New York, New York 10014.
BERKLEY and the "B" design
are trademarks belonging to Penguin Putnam Inc.

PRINTED IN THE UNITED STATES OF AMERICA

14   13   12   11   10   9   8

Contents/Indice

Preface/Prefazione	iv
Introduction/Introduzione	v
Pronunciation of English/Pronuncia inglese	vi
Pronunciation of Italian/Pronuncia italiana	vi
Abbreviations/Abbreviazioni	vii - viii
Italian-English/Italiano-inglese	1 - 240
English-Italian/Inglese-italiano	1 - 258
Italian verb tables/Verbi italiani	259-262
English verb tables/Verbi inglesi	263-264

Editors/Redazione

Debora Mazza   Jane Goldie

Donatella Boi   Francesca Logi   Sonia Tinagli-Baxter

Peter Terrell   Carla Zipoli

Copy editors/Segreteria di redazione

Jacqueline Gregan   Daphne Trotter

Project management by/A cura di

LEXUS

Preface

This new edition of the Oxford Italian-English Minidictionary is an updated and expanded version of the dictionary edited by Joyce Andrews. Colloquial words and phrases figure largely, as do neologisms. Noteworthy additions include terms from special areas such as computers and business that have become a familiar feature of everyday language.

Prefazione

Questa nuova edizione del mini dizionario Oxford Italiano-Inglese è il risultato di un lavoro di ampliamento e aggiornamento della precedente edizione curata da Joyce Andrews. Un'attenzione particolare è stata rivolta a vocaboli ed espressioni colloquiali di coniazione recente e a termini relativi a settori specifici, quali l'informatica e il commercio, divenuti ricorrenti nella lingua di tutti i giorni.

Proprietary terms

This dictionary includes some words which are, or are asserted to be, proprietary names or trademarks. Their inclusion does not imply that they have acquired for legal purposes a non-proprietary or general significance, nor is any other judgment implied concerning their legal status. In cases where the editor has some evidence that a word is used as a proprietary name or trademark this is indicated by the symbol ®, but no judgment concerning the legal status of such words is made or implied thereby.

Marche depositate

Questo dizionario include alcune parole che sono o vengono considerate nomi di marche depositate. La loro presenza non implica che abbiano acquisito legalmente un significato generale, né si suggerisce alcun altro giudizio riguardo il loro stato giuridico. Qualora il redattore abbia trovato testimonianza dell'uso di una parola come marca depositata, quest'ultima è stata contrassegnata dal simbolo ®, ma nessun giudizio riguardo la stato giuridico di tale parola viene espresso o suggerito in tal modo.

Introduction

In order to give the maximum information about English and Italian in the space available, this new dictionary uses certain space-saving conventions.

A swung dash ~ is used to replace the headword within the entry.

Where the headword contains a vertical bar | the swung dash replaces only the part of the headword that comes in front of the |. For example: **efficien|te** *a* efficient. **~za** *nf* efficiency (the second bold word reads **efficienza**).

Indicators are provided to guide the user to the best translation for a specific sense of a word. Types of indicator are:

field labels (see the list on pp vii-viii), which indicate a general area of usage (commercial, computing, photography etc);

sense indicators, eg: **bore** *n* (*of gun*) calibro *m*; (*person*) seccatore, -trice *mf*;

typical subjects of verbs, eg: **bond** *vt* ⟨*glue*:⟩ attaccare;

typical objects of verbs, placed after the translation of the verb, eg: **boost** *vt* stimolare ⟨*sales*⟩; sollevare ⟨*morale*⟩;

nouns that typically go together with certain adjectives, eg: **rich** *a* ricco; ⟨*food*⟩ pesante.

A solid black circle means that the same word is being translated as a different part of speech, eg. **partition** *n* ... ● *vt* ...

English pronunciation is given for the Italian user in the International Phonetic Alphabet.

Italian stress is shown by a ' placed in front of the stressed syllable in a word.

Square brackets are used around parts of an expression which can be omitted without altering the sense.

Introduzione

Allo scopo di fornire il maggior numero possibile di informazioni in inglese e in italiano, questo nuovo dizionario ricorre ad alcune convenzioni per sfruttare al massimo lo spazio disponibile.

Un trattino ondulato ~ è utilizzato al posto del lemma all'interno della voce.

Qualora il lemma contenga una barra verticale |, il trattino ondulato sostituisce solo la parte del lemma che precede |. Ad esempio: **dark|en** *vt* oscurare. **~ness** *n* buio *m* (la seconda parola in neretto va letta **darkness**).

Degli indicatori vengono forniti per indirizzare l'utilizzatore verso la traduzione corrispondente al senso voluto di una parola. I tipi di indicatori sono:

etichette semantiche (vedi la lista a pp vii-viii), indicanti l'ambito specifico in cui la parola viene generalmente usata in quel senso (commercio, informatica, fotografia ecc);

indicatori di significato, es.: **redazione** *nf* (*ufficio*) editorial office; (*di testi*) editing;

soggetti tipici di verbi, es.: **trovarsi** *vr* ⟨*luogo:*⟩ be;

complementi oggetti tipici di verbi, collocati dopo la traduzione dello stesso verbo, es: **superare** *vt* overtake ⟨*veicolo*⟩; pass ⟨*esame*⟩;

sostantivi che ricorrono tipicamente con certi aggettivi, es.: **solare** *a* ⟨*energia, raggi*⟩ solar; ⟨*crema*⟩ sun.

Un cerchio nero pieno indica che la stessa parola viene tradotta come una diversa parte del discorso, es. **calcolatore** *a* ... ● *nm* ...

La pronuncia inglese è data usando l'Alfabetico Fonetico Internazionale.

L'accento tonico nelle parole italiane è indicato dal segno ' collocato davanti alla sillaba accentata.

Delle parentesi quadre racchiudono parti di espressioni che possono essere omesse senza alterazioni di senso.

Pronunciation of Italian

Vowels:

a is broad like *a* in *father*: **casa**.

e has two sounds: closed like *ey* in *they*: **sera**; open like *e* in *egg*: **sette**.

i is like *ee* in *feet*: **venire**.

o has two sounds: closed like *o* in *show*: **bocca**; open like *o* in *dog*: **croma**.

u is like *oo* in *moon*: **luna**.

When two or more vowels come together each vowel is pronounced separately: **buono**; **baia**.

Consonants:

b, d, f, l, m, n, p, t, v are pronounced as in English. When these are double they are sounded distinctly: **bello**.

c before **a, o** or **u** and before consonants is like *k* in *king*: **cane**.
before **e** or **i** is like *ch* in *church*: **cena**.

ch is also like *k* in *king*: **chiesa**.

g before **a, o,** or **u** is hard like *g* in *got*: **gufo**.
before **e** or **i** is like *j* in *jelly*: **gentile**.

gh is like *g* in *gun*: **ghiaccio**.

gl when followed by **a, e, o, u** is like *gl* in *glass*: **gloria**.

gli is like *lli* in *million*: **figlio**.

gn is like *ni* in *onion*: **bagno**.

h is silent.

ng is like *ng* in *finger* (not *singer*): **ringraziare**.

r is pronounced distinctly.

s between two vowels is like *s* in *rose*: **riso**.
at the beginning of a word it is like *s* in *soap*: **sapone**.

sc before **e** or **i** is like *sh* in *shell*: **scienza**.

z sounds like *ts* within a word: **fazione**; like *dz* at the beginning: **zoo**.

The stress is shown by the sign ' printed before the stressed syllable.

Pronuncia inglese

SIMBOLI FONETICI

Vocali e dittonghi

æ bad	ʊ put	aʊ now
ɑ: ah	u: too	aʊə flour
e wet	ə ago	ɔɪ coin
ɪ sit	ɜ: work	ɪə here
i: see	eɪ made	eə hair
ɒ got	əʊ home	ʊə poor
ɔ: door	aɪ five	
ʌ cup	aɪə fire	

Consonanti

b boy	l leg	t ten
d day	m man	tʃ chip
dʒ page	n new	θ three
f foot	ŋ sing	ð this
g go	p pen	v verb
h he	r run	w wet
j yes	s speak	z his
k coat	ʃ ship	ʒ pleasure

Note: ' precede la sillaba accentata.
La vocale nasale in parole quali *nuance* è indicata nella trascrizione fonetica come ɔ̃: nju:ɔ̃s.

Abbreviations/Abbreviazioni

adjective	*a*	aggettivo
abbreviation	*abbr*	abbreviazione
administration	*Admin*	amministrazione
adverb	*adv*	avverbio
aeronautics	*Aeron*	aeronautica
American	*Am*	americano
anatomy	*Anat*	anatomia
archaeology	*Archaeol*	archeologia
architecture	*Archit*	architettura
attributive	*attrib*	attributo
astrology	*Astr*	astrologia
automobiles	*Auto*	automobile
auxiliary	*aux*	ausiliario
biology	*Biol*	biologia
botany	*Bot*	botanica
British English	*Br*	inglese britannico
Chemistry	*Chem*	chimica
commerce	*Comm*	commercio
computers	*Comput*	informatica
conjunction	*conj*	congiunzione
cooking	*Culin*	cucina
definite article	*def art*	articolo determinativo
	ecc	eccetera
electricity	*Electr*	elettricità
et cetera	*etc*	
feminine	*f*	femminile
familiar	*fam*	familiare
figurative	*fig*	figurato
formal	*fml*	formale
geography	*Geog*	geografia
geology	*Geol*	geologia
grammar	*Gram*	grammatica
humorous	*hum*	umoristico
indefinite article	*indef art*	articolo indeterminativo
interjection	*int*	interiezione
interrogative	*inter*	interrogativo
invariable	*inv*	invariabile
(*no plural form*)		
law	*Jur*	legge/giuridico
literary	*liter*	letterario
masculine	*m*	maschile
mathematics	*Math*	matematica
mechanics	*Mech*	meccanica
medicine	*Med*	medicina
masculine or feminine	*mf*	maschile o femminile
military	*Mil*	militare
music	*Mus*	musica
noun	*n*	sostantivo

nautical	*Naut*	nautica
pejorative	*pej*	peggiorativo
personal	*pers*	personale
photography	*Phot*	fotografia
physics	*Phys*	fisica
plural	*pl*	plurale
politics	*Pol*	politica
possessive	*poss*	possessivo
past participle	*pp*	participio passato
prefix	*pref*	prefisso
preposition	*prep*	preposizione
present tense	*pres*	presente
pronoun	*pron*	pronome
psychology	*Psych*	psicologia
past tense	*pt*	tempo passato
	qcno	qualcuno
	qcsa	qualcosa
proprietary term	®	marca depositata
rail	*Rail*	ferrovia
reflexive	*refl*	riflessivo
religion	*Relig*	religione
relative pronoun	*rel pron*	pronome relativo
somebody	*sb*	
school	*Sch*	scuola
singular	*sg*	singolare
slang	*sl*	gergo
something	*sth*	
technical	*Techn*	tecnico
telephone	*Teleph*	telefono
theatrical	*Theat*	teatrale
television	*TV*	televisione
typography	*Typ*	tipografia
university	*Univ*	università
auxiliary verb	*v aux*	verbo ausiliare
intransitive verb	*vi*	verbo intransitivo
reflexive verb	*vr*	verbo riflessivo
transitive verb	*vt*	verbo transitivo
transitive and intransitive	*vt/i*	verbo transitivo e intransitivo
vulgar	*vulg*	volgare
cultural equivalent	≈	equivalenza culturale

a (*ad* before vowel) *prep* to; (*stato in luogo, tempo, età*) at; (*con mese, città*) in; (*mezzo, modo*) by; **dire qcsa a qcno** tell sb sth; **alle tre** at three o'clock; **a vent'anni** at the age of twenty; **a Natale** at Christmas; **a dicembre** in December; **ero al cinema** I was at the cinema; **vivo a Londra** I live in London; **a due a due** two by two; **a piedi** on *o* by foot; **maglia a maniche lunghe** long-sleeved sweater; **casa a tre piani** house with three floors; **giocare a tennis** play tennis; **50 km all'ora** 50 km an hour; **2 000 lire al chilo** 2,000 lire a kilo; **al mattino/alla sera** in the morning/evening; **a venti chilometri/due ore da qui** twenty kilometres/two hours away

a'bate *nm* abbot

abbacchi'ato *a* downhearted

ab'bacchio *nm* [young] lamb

abbagli'ante *a* dazzling ● *nm* headlight, high beam

abbagli'are *vt* dazzle. **ab'baglio** *nm* blunder; **prendere un ~** make a blunder

abbai'are *vi* bark

abba'ino *nm* dormer window

abbando'na|re *vt* abandon; leave ⟨*luogo*⟩; give up ⟨*piani ecc*⟩. **~rsi** *vr* let oneself go; **~rsi a** give oneself up to ⟨*ricordi ecc*⟩. **~to** *a* abandoned. **abban'dono** *nm* abandoning; *fig* abandon; (*stato*) neglect

abbassa'mento *nm* (*di temperatura, acqua, prezzi*) drop

abbas'sar|e *vt* lower; turn down ⟨*radio, TV*⟩; **~e i fari** dip the headlights. **~si** *vr* stoop; ⟨*sole ecc*⟩ sink; *fig* demean oneself

ab'basso *adv* below ● *int* down with

abba'stanza *adv* enough; (*alquanto*) quite

ab'batter|e *vt* demolish; shoot down ⟨*aereo*⟩; put down ⟨*animale*⟩; topple ⟨*regime*⟩; (*fig: demoralizzare*) dishearten. **~si** *vr* (*cadere*) fall; *fig* be discouraged

abbatti'mento *nm* (*morale*) despondency

abbat'tuto *a* despondent, down-in-the-mouth

abba'zia *nf* abbey

abbel'lir|e *vt* embellish. **~si** *vr* adorn oneself

abbeve'ra|re *vt* water. **~'toio** *nm* drinking trough

abbi'ente *a* well-to-do

abbiglia'mento *nm* clothes *pl*; (*industria*) clothing industry, rag trade

abbigli'ar|e *vt* dress. **~si** *vr* dress up

abbina'mento *nm* combining

abbi'nare *vt* combine; match ⟨*colori*⟩

abbindo'lare *vt* cheat

abbocca'mento *nm* interview; (*conversazione*) talk

abboc'care *vi* bite; ⟨*tubi:*⟩ join; *fig* swallow the bait

abboc'cato *a* ⟨*vino*⟩ fairly sweet

abbof'farsi *vr* stuff oneself

abbona'mento *nm* subscription; (*ferroviario ecc*) season-ticket; **fare l'~** take out a subscription

abbo'na|re *vt* make a subscriber. **~rsi** *vr* subscribe (**a** to); take out a season-ticket (**a** for) ⟨*teatro, stadio*⟩. **~to, -a** *nmf* subscriber

abbon'dan|te *a* abundant; ⟨*quantità*⟩ copious; ⟨*nevicata*⟩ heavy; ⟨*vestiario*⟩ roomy. **~te di** abounding in. **~te'mente** *adv* ⟨*mangiare*⟩ copiously. **~za** *nf* abundance

abbon'dare *vi* abound

abbor'da|bile *a* ⟨*persona*⟩ approachable; ⟨*prezzo*⟩ reasonable. **~ggio** *nm* *Mil* boarding. **~re** *vt* board ⟨*nave*⟩; approach ⟨*persona*⟩; (*fam: attaccar bottone a*) chat up; tackle ⟨*compito ecc*⟩

abbotto'na|re *vt* button up. **~'tura** *nf* [row of] buttons. **~to** *a fig* tight-lipped

abboz'zare *vt* sketch [out]; **~ un sorriso** give a hint of a smile. **ab'bozzo** *nm* sketch

abbracci'are *vt* embrace; hug, embrace ⟨*persona*⟩; take up ⟨*professione*⟩; *fig* include. **ab'braccio** *nm* hug

abbrevi'a|re *vt* shorten; (*ridurre*) curtail; abbreviate ⟨*parola*⟩. **~zi'one** *nf* abbreviation

abbron'za|re *nm* sun-tan lotion

abbron'za|re *vt* bronze; tan ⟨*pelle*⟩. **~rsi** *vr* get a tan. **~to** *a* tanned. **~'tura** *nf* [sun-]tan

abbrus'to'lire *vt* toast; roast ⟨*caffè ecc*⟩

abbruti'mento *nm* brutalization. **abbru'tire** *vt* brutalize. **abbru'tirsi** *vr* become brutalized

abbuf'fa|rsi *vr fam* stuff oneself. **~ta** *nf* blowout

abbuo'nare *vt* reduce

abbu'ono *nm* allowance; *Sport* handicap

abdi'ca|re *vi* abdicate. **~zi'one** *nf* abdication

aber'rante *a* aberrant

aberrazi'one *nf* aberration

a'bete *nm* fir

abi'etto *a* despicable

'abi|le *a* able; ⟨*idoneo*⟩ fit; ⟨*astuto*⟩ clever. **~ità** *nf inv* ability; ⟨*idoneità*⟩ fitness; ⟨*astuzia*⟩ cleverness. **~'mente** *adv* ably; ⟨*con astuzia*⟩ cleverly

abili'ta|re *vt* qualify. **~to** *a* qualified. **~zi'one** *nf* qualification; ⟨*titolo*⟩ diploma

abis'sale *a* abysmal. **a'bisso** *nm* abyss

abi'tabile *a* inhabitable

abi'tacolo *nm Auto* passenger compartment

abi'tante *nmf* inhabitant

abi'ta|re *vi* live. **~to** *a* inhabited ● *nm* built-up area. **~zi'one** *nf* house

'abito *nm* ⟨*da donna*⟩ dress; ⟨*da uomo*⟩ suit. **~ da cerimonia/da sera** formal/evening dress

abitu'al|e *a* usual, habitual. **~'mente** *adv* usually

abitu'ar|e *vt* accustom. **~si** *a vr* get used to

abitudi'nario, -a *a* of fixed habits ● *nmf* person of fixed habits

abi'tudine *nf* habit; **d'~** usually; **per ~** out of habit; **avere l'~ di fare qcsa** be in the habit of doing sth

abnegazi'one *nf* self-sacrifice

ab'norme *a* abnormal

abo'li|re *vt* abolish; repeal ⟨*legge*⟩. **~zi'one** *nf* abolition; repeal

abomi'nevole *a* abominable

abo'rigeno, -a *a* & *nmf* aboriginal

abor'rire *vt* abhor

abor'ti|re *vi* miscarry; ⟨*volontariamente*⟩ have an abortion; *fig* fail. **~vo** *a* abortive. **a'borto** *nm* miscarriage; ⟨*volontario*⟩ abortion. **~sta** *a* pro-choice

abrasi|'one *nf* abrasion. **abra'sivo** *a* & *nm* abrasive

abro'ga|re *vt* repeal. **~zi'one** *nf* repeal

'abside *nf* apse

abu'lia *nf* apathy. **a'bulico** *a* apathetic

abu's|are *vi* **~ di** abuse; over-indulge in ⟨*alcol*⟩; ⟨*approfittare di*⟩ take advantage of; ⟨*violentare*⟩ rape. **~ivo** *a* illegal

a'buso *nm* abuse. **~ di confidenza** breach of confidence

a.C. *abbr* **(avanti Cristo)** BC

'acca *nf fam* **non ho capito un'~** I understood damn all

acca'demi|a *nf* academy. **A~a di Belle Arti** Academy of Fine Arts. **~co, -a** *a* academic ● *nmf* academician

acca'd|ere *vi* happen; **accada quel che accada** come what may. **~uto** *nm* event

accalappi'are *vt* catch; *fig* allure

accal'carsi *vr* crowd

accal'da|rsi *vr* get overheated; *fig* get excited. **~to** *a* overheated

accalo'rarsi *vr* get excited

accampa'mento *nm* camp. **accam'pare** *vt fig* put forth. **accam'parsi** *vr* camp

accani'mento *nm* tenacity; ⟨*odio*⟩ rage

acca'ni|rsi *vr* persist; ⟨*infierire*⟩ rage. **~to** *a* persistent; ⟨*odio*⟩ fierce; *fig* inveterate

ac'canto *adv* near; **~ a** *prep* next to

accanto'nare *vt* set aside; *Mil* billet

accaparra'mento *nm* hoarding; *Comm* cornering

accapar'ra|re *vt* hoard. **~rsi** *vr* grab; corner ⟨*mercato*⟩. **~'tore, ~'trice** *nmf* hoarder

accapigli'arsi *vr* scuffle; ⟨*litigare*⟩ squabble

accappa'toio *nm* bathrobe; ⟨*per spiaggia*⟩ beachrobe

accappo'nare *vt* **fare ~ la pelle a** qcno make sb's flesh creep

accarez'zare *vt* caress, stroke; *fig* cherish

accartocci'ar|e *vt* scrunch up. **~si** *vr* curl up

acca'sarsi *vr* get married

accasci'arsi *vr* flop down; *fig* lose heart

accata'stare *vt* pile up

accat'tivante *a* beguiling

accatti'varsi *vr* **~ le simpatie/la stima/l'affetto di** qcno gain sb's sympathy/respect/affection

accatto'naggio *nm* begging. **accat'tone, -a** *nmf* beggar

accaval'lar|e *vt* cross *(gambe)*. **~si** *vr* pile up; *fig* overlap

acce'cante *a* *(luce)* blinding

acce'care *vt* blind ● *vi* go blind

ac'cedere *vi* **~ a** enter; *(acconsentire)* comply with

accele'ra|re *vi* accelerate ● *vt* speed up, accelerate; **~re il passo** quicken one's pace. **~to** *a* rapid. **~'tore** *nm* accelerator. **~zi'one** *nf* acceleration

ac'cender|e *vt* light; turn on *(luce, TV ecc)*; *fig* inflame; **ha da ~e?** have you got a light? **~si** *vr* catch fire; *(illuminarsi)* light up; *fig* become inflamed

accendi'gas *nm inv* gas lighter; *(su cucina)* automatic ignition

accen'dino *nm* lighter

accendi'sigari *nm* cigar-lighter

accen'nare *vt* indicate; hum *(melodia)* ● *vi* **~ a** beckon to; *fig* hint at; *(far l'atto di)* make as if to; **accenna a piovere** it looks like rain. **ac'cenno** *nm* gesture; *(con il capo)* nod; *fig* hint

accensi'one *nf* lighting; *(di motore)* ignition

accen'ta|re *vt* accent; *(con accento tonico)* stress. **~zi'one** *nf* accentuation. **ac'cento** *nm* accent; *(tonico)* stress

accentra'mento *nm* centralizing

accen'trare *vt* centralize

accentu'a|re *vt* accentuate. **~rsi** *vr* become more noticeable. **~to** *a* marked

accerchia'mento *nm* surrounding

accerchi'are *vt* surround

accerta'mento *nm* check

accer'tare *vt* ascertain; *(controllare)* check; assess *(reddito)*

ac'ceso *a* lighted; *(radio, TV ecc)* on; *(colore)* bright

acces'sibile *a* accessible; *(persona)* approachable; *(spesa)* reasonable

ac'cesso *nm* access; *(Med: di rabbia)* fit; **vietato l'~** no entry

acces'sorio *a* accessory; *(secondario)* of secondary importance ● *nm* accessory; **accessori** *pl* *(rifiniture)* fittings

ac'cetta *nf* hatchet

accet'tabile *a* acceptable

accet'tare *vt* accept; *(aderire a)* agree to

accettazi'one *nf* acceptance; *(luogo)* reception. **~ [bagagli]** check-in. **[banco] ~** check-in [desk]

ac'cetto *a* agreeable; **essere bene ~** be very welcome

accezi'one *nf* meaning

acchiap'pare *vt* catch

acchito *nm* **di primo ~** at first

acciac'ca|re *vt* crush; *fig* prostrate. **~to, -a** *a* **essere ~to** ache all over. **acci'acco** *nm* infirmity; *(pl: afflizioni)* aches and pains

acciaie'ria *nf* steelworks

acci'aio *nm* steel; **~ inossidabile** stainless steel

acciden'ta|le *a* accidental. **~l'mente** *adv* accidentally. **~to** *a* *(terreno)* uneven

acci'dente *nm* accident; *Med* stroke; **non capisce/non vede un ~** *fam* he doesn't understand/can't see a damn thing. **acci'denti!** *int* damn!

accigli'a|rsi *vr* frown. **~to** *a* frowning

ac'cingersi *vr* **~ a** be about to

acci'picchia *int* good Lord!

acciuf'fare *vt* catch

acci'uga *nf* anchovy

accla'ma|re *vt* applaud; *(eleggere)* acclaim. **~zi'one** *nf* applause

acclima'tar|e *vt* acclimatize. **~si** *vr* get acclimatized

ac'clu|dere *vt* enclose. **~so** *a* enclosed

accocco'larsi *vr* squat

accogli'en|te *a* welcoming; *(confortevole)* cosy. **~za** *nf* welcome

ac'cogliere *vt* receive; *(conpiacere)* welcome; *(contenere)* hold

accol'larsi *vr* take on *(responsabilità, debiti, doveri)*. **accol'lato** *a* high-necked

accoltel'lare *vt* knife

accomia'tar|e *vt* dismiss. **~si** *vr* take one's leave *(da of)*

accomo'dante *a* accommodating

accomo'dar|e *vt* *(riparare)* mend; *(disporre)* arrange. **~si** *vr* make oneself at home; **si accomodi!** come in!; *(si sieda)* take a seat!

accompagna'mento *nm* accompaniment; *(seguito)* retinue

accompa'gna|re *vt* accompany; **~re qcno a casa** see sb home; **~re qcno alla porta** show sb out. **~'tore, ~'trice** *nmf* companion; *(di comitiva)* escort; *Mus* accompanist

accomu'nare *vt* pool

acconci'a|re *vt* arrange. **~'tura** *nf* hair-style; *(ornamento)* head-dress

accondiscen'den|te *a* too obliging. **~za** *nf* excessive desire to please

accondi'scendere *vi* **~ a** condescend; comply with *(desiderio)*; *(acconsentire)* consent to

acconsen'tire *vi* consent

acconten'tar|e *vt* satisfy. ~**si** *vr* be content (**di** with)

ac'cònto *nm* instalment; **in** ~ on account; **lasciare un** ~ leave a deposit

accop'pare *vt fam* bump off

accoppia'mento *nm* coupling; (*di animali*) mating

accoppi'a|re *vt* couple; mate (*animali*). ~**rsi** *vr* pair off; mate. ~**ta** *nf* (*scommessa*) bet placed on two horses for first and second place

acco'rato *a* sorrowful

accorci'ar|e *vt* shorten. ~**si** *vr* get shorter

accor'dar|e *vt* concede; match (*colori ecc*); *Mus* tune. ~**si** *vr* agree

ac'cordo *nm* agreement; *Mus* chord; (*armonia*) harmony; **andare d'~** get on well; **d'~!** agreed!; **essere d'~** agree; **prendere accordi con qcno** make arrangements with sb

ac'corgersi *vr* ~ **di** notice; (*capire*) realize

accorgi'mento *nm* shrewdness; (*espediente*) device

ac'correre *vi* hasten

accor'tezza *nf* (*previdenza*) forethought

ac'corto *a* shrewd; **mal** ~ incautious

accosta'mento *nm* (*di colori*) combination

acco'star|e *vt* draw close to; approach (*persona*); set ajar (*porta ecc*). ~**si** *vr* ~**si a** come near to

accovacci'a|rsi *vr* crouch, squat down. ~**to a** squatting

accoz'zaglia *nf* jumble; (*di persone*) mob

accozzare *vt* ~ **colori** mix colours that clash

accredita'mento *nm* credit; ~ **tramite bancogiro** Bank Giro Credit

accredi'tare *vt* give credit to; *Comm* credit

ac'cresc|ere *vt* increase. ~**ersi** *vr* grow larger. ~**i'tivo** *a* augmentative

accucci'arsi *vr* (*cane:*) lie down; (*persona:*) crouch

accu'dire *vi* ~ **a** attend to

accumu'la|re *vt* accumulate. ~**rsi** *vr* pile up, accumulate. ~**tore** *nm* accumulator; *Auto* battery. ~**zi'one** *nf* accumulation. **ac'cumulo** *nm* (*di merce*) build-up

accura'tezza *nf* care

accu'rato *a* careful

ac'cusa *nf* accusation; *Jur* charge; **essere in stato di** ~ *Jur* have been charged; **la Pubblica A~** *Jur* the public prosecutor

accu'sa|re *vt* accuse; *Jur* charge; complain of (*dolore*); ~**re ricevuta di** *Comm* acknowledge receipt of. ~**to, -a** *nmf* accused. ~**'tore** *nm* *Jur* prosecutor

a'cerbo *a* sharp; (*immaturo*) unripe

'acero *nm* maple

a'cerrimo *a* implacable

ace'tone *nm* nail polish remover

a'ceto *nm* vinegar

A.C.I. *abbr* (**Automobile Club d'Italia**) Italian Automobile Association

acidità *nf* acidity. ~ **di stomaco** acid stomach

'acido *a* acid; (*persona*) sour ● *nm* acid

a'cidulo *a* slightly sour

'acino *nm* berry; (*chicco*) grape

'acne *nf* acne

'acqua *nf* water; **fare** ~ *Naut* leak; ~ **in bocca!** *fig* mum's the word!. ~ **di Colonia** eau de Cologne. ~ **corrente** running water. ~ **dolce** fresh water. ~ **minerale** mineral water. ~ **minerale gassata** fizzy mineral water. ~ **naturale** still mineral water. ~ **potabile** drinking water. ~ **salata** salt water. ~ **tonica** tonic water

acqua'forte *nf* etching

ac'quaio *nm* sink

acquama'rina *a* aquamarine

acqua'rello *nm* = **acquerello**

a'cquario *nm* aquarium; *Astr* Aquarius

acqua'santa *nf* holy water

acqua'scooter *nm inv* water-scooter

a'cquatico *a* aquatic

acquat'tarsi *vr* crouch

acqua'vite *nf* brandy

acquaz'zone *nm* downpour

acque'dotto *nm* aqueduct

'acqueo *a* **vapore** ~ water vapour

acque'rello *nm* water-colour

acqui'rente *nmf* purchaser

acqui'si|re *vt* acquire. ~**to a** acquired. ~**zi'one** *nf* attainment

acqui'st|are *vt* purchase; (*ottenere*) acquire. **a'cquisto** *nm* purchase; **uscire per** ~**i** go shopping; **fare** ~**i** shop

acqui'trino *nm* marsh

acquo'lina *nf* **far venire l'~ in bocca a qcno** make sb's mouth water

a'cquoso *a* watery

'acre *a* acrid; (*fig: suono*) harsh

a'crilico *nm* acrylic

a'croba|ta *nmf* acrobat. ~**'zia** *nf* acrobatics *pl*

a'cronimo *nm* acronym

acu'ir|e *vt* sharpen. **~si** *vr* become more intense

a'culeo *nm* sting; *Bot* prickle

a'cume *nm* acumen

acumi'nato *a* pointed

a'custic|a *nf* acoustics *pl.* **~o** *a* acoustic

acu'tezza *nf* acuteness

acutiz'zarsi *vr* become worse

a'cuto *a* sharp; ⟨*suono*⟩ shrill; ⟨*freddo, odore*⟩ intense; *Gram, Math, Med* acute ● *nm Mus* high note

adagi'ar|e *vt* lay down. **~si** *vr* lie down

a'dagio *adv* slowly ● *nm Mus* adagio; ⟨*proverbio*⟩ adage

adattabilità *nf* adaptability

adatta'mento *nm* adaptation; **avere spirito di ~** be adaptable

adat'ta|re *vt* adapt; ⟨*aggiustare*⟩ fit. **~rsi** *vr* adapt. **~'tore** *nm* adaptor. **a'datto** *a* suitable (**a** for); ⟨*giusto*⟩ right

addebita'mento *nm* debit. **~ diretto** direct debit

addebi'tare *vt* debit; *fig* blame

ad'debito *nm* charge

addensa'mento *nm* thickening, gathering

adden'sar|e *vt* thicken. **~si** *vr* thicken; ⟨*affollarsi*⟩ gather

adden'tare *vt* bite

adden'trarsi *vr* penetrate

ad'dentro *adv* deeply; **essere ~ in** be in on

addestra'mento *nm* training

adde'strar|e *vt* train. **~si** *vr* train

ad'detto *a* assigned ● *nm* employee; ⟨*diplomatico*⟩ attaché; **addetti** *pl* **ai lavori** persons involved in the work. **~ stampa** information officer, press officer

addiaccio *nm* **dormire all'~** sleep in the open

addi'etro *adv* ⟨*indietro*⟩ back; ⟨*nel passato*⟩ before

ad'dio *nm* & *int* goodbye. **~ al celibato** stag night, stag party

addirit'tura *adv* ⟨*perfino*⟩ even; ⟨*assolutamente*⟩ absolutely; **~!** really!

ad'dirsi *vr* **~ a** suit

addi'tare *vt* point at; ⟨*in mezzo a un gruppo*⟩ point out; *fig* point to

addi'tivo *a* & *nm* additive

addizio'nal|e *a* additional. **~'mente** *adv* additionally

addizio'nare *vt* add [up]. **addizi'one** *nf* addition

addob'bare *vt* decorate. **ad'dobbo** *nm* decoration

addol'cir|e *vt* sweeten; tone down ⟨*colore*⟩; *fig* soften. **~si** *vr fig* mellow

addolo'ra|re *vt* grieve. **~rsi** *vr* be upset (**per** by). **~to** *a* pained, distressed

ad'dom|e *nm* abdomen. **~i'nale** *a* abdominal; [**muscoli**] **addominali** *pl* abdominals

addomesti'ca|re *vt* tame. **~'tore** *nm* tamer

addormen'ta|re *vt* put to sleep. **~rsi** *vr* go to sleep. **~to** *a* asleep; *fig* slow

addos'sar|e *vt* **~e a** ⟨*appoggiare*⟩ lean against; ⟨*attribuire*⟩ lay on. **~si** *vr* ⟨*ammassarsi*⟩ crowd; shoulder ⟨*responsabilità ecc*⟩

ad'dosso *adv* on; **~ a** *prep* on; ⟨*molto vicino*⟩ right next to; **mettere gli occhi ~ a** *qcno/qcsa* hanker after sb/sth; **non mettermi le mani ~!** keep your hands off me!; **stare ~ a** *qcno fig* be on sb's back

ad'durre *vt* produce ⟨*prova, documento*⟩; give ⟨*pretesto, esempio*⟩

adegua'mento *nm* adjustment

adegu'a|re *vt* adjust. **~rsi** *vr* conform. **~to** *a* adequate; ⟨*conforme*⟩ consistent

a'dempi|ere *vt* fulfil. **~'mento** *nm* fulfilment

ade'noidi *nfpl* adenoids

ade'ren|te *a* adhesive; ⟨*vestito*⟩ tight ● *nmf* follower. **~za** *nf* adhesion. **~ze** *npl* connections

ade'rire *vi* **~ a** stick to, adhere to; support ⟨*sciopero, petizione*⟩; agree to ⟨*richiesta*⟩

adesca'mento *nm Jur* soliciting

ade'scare *vt* bait; *fig* entice

adesi'one *nf* adhesion; *fig* agreement

ade'sivo *a* adhesive ● *nm* sticker; *Auto* bumper sticker

a'desso *adv* now; ⟨*poco fa*⟩ just now; ⟨*tra poco*⟩ any moment now; **da ~ in poi** from now on; **per ~** for the moment

adia'cente *a* adjacent; **~ a** next to

adi'bire *vt* **~ a** put to use as

'adipe *nm* obesity

adi'ra|rsi *vr* get irate. **~to** *a* irate

a'dire *vt* resort to; **~ le vie legali** take legal proceedings

'adito *nm* **dare ~ a** give rise to

adocchi'are *vt* eye; ⟨*con desiderio*⟩ covet

adole'scen|te *a* & *nmf* adolescent. **~za** *nf* adolescence. **~zi'ale** *a* adolescent

adom'brar|e vt darken; fig veil. **~si** vr (offendersi) take offence

adope'rar|e vt use. **~si** vr take trouble

ado'rabile a adorable

ado'ra|re vt adore. **~zi'one** nf adoration

ador'nare vt adorn

adot't|are vt adopt. **~ivo** a adoptive. **adozi'one** nf adoption

ad prep = a (davanti a vocale)

adrena'lina nf adrenalin

adri'atico a Adriatic ● nm **l'A~** the Adriatic

adu'la|re vt flatter. **~'tore**, **~'trice** nmf flatterer. **~zi'one** nf flattery

adulte'ra|re vt adulterate. **~to** a adulterated

adul'terio nm adultery. **a'dultero, -a** a adulterous ● nm adulterer ● nf adulteress

a'dulto, -a a & nmf adult; (maturo) mature

adu'nanza nf assembly

adu'na|re vt gather. **~ta** nf Mil parade

a'dunco a hooked

ae'rare vt air (stanza)

a'ereo a aerial; (dell'aviazione) air attrib ● nm aeroplane, plane

ae'robic|a nf aerobics. **~o** a aerobic

aerodi'namic|a nf aerodynamics sg. **~o** a aerodynamic

aero'nautic|a nf aeronautics sg; Mil Air Force. **~o** a aeronautical

aero'plano nm aeroplane

aero'porto nm airport

aero'scalo nm cargo and servicing area

aero'sol nm inv aerosol

'afa nf sultriness

af'fabil|e a affable. **~ità** nf affability

affaccen'da|rsi vr busy oneself (a with). **~to** a busy

affacci'arsi vr show oneself; **~ alla finestra** appear at the window

affa'ma|re vt starve [out]. **~to** a starving

affan'na|re vt leave breathless. **~rsi** vr busy oneself; (agitarsi) get worked up. **~to** a breathless; **dal respiro ~to** wheezy. **af'fanno** nm breathlessness; fig worry

af'fare nm matter; Comm transaction, deal; (occasione) bargain; **affari** pl business; **non sono affari tuoi** fam it's none of your business. **affa'rista** nmf wheeler-dealer

affasci'nante a fascinating; (persona, sorriso) bewitching

affasci'nare vt bewitch; fig charm

affatica'mento nm fatigue

affati'car|e vt tire; (sfinire) exhaust. **~si** vr tire oneself out; (affannarsi) strive

af'fatto adv completely; **non... ~** not... at all; **niente ~!** not at all!

affer'ma|re vt affirm; (sostenere) assert. **~rsi** vr establish oneself

affermativa'mente adv in the affirmative

afferma'tivo a affirmative

affermazi'one nf assertion; (successo) achievement

affer'rar|e vt seize; catch (oggetto); (capire) grasp; **~e a volo** be quick on the uptake. **~si** vr **~si a** grasp at

affet'ta|re vt slice; (ostentare) affect. **~to** a sliced; (sorriso, maniere) affected ● nm cold meat, sliced meat. **~zi'one** nf affectation

affet'tivo a affective; **rapporto ~** emotional tie

af'fetto[1] nm affection; **con ~** affectionately

af'fetto[2] a suffering (da from)

affettuosità nf inv (gesto) affectionate gesture

affettu'oso a affectionate

affezio'na|rsi vr grow fond of. **~to** a devoted (a to)

affian'car|e vt put side by side; Mil flank; fig support. **~si** vr come side by side; fig stand together; **~si a qcno** fig help sb out

affiata'mento nm harmony

affia'ta|rsi vr get on well together. **~to** a close-knit; **una coppia ~ta** a very close couple

affibbi'are vt **~ qcsa a qcno** saddle sb with sth; **~ un pugno a qcno** let fly at sb

affi'dabil|e a established. **~ità** nf dependability

affida'mento nm (Jur: dei minori) custody; **fare ~ su qcno** rely on sb; **non dare ~** not inspire confidence

affi'dar|e vt entrust. **~si** vr **~si a** rely on

affievo'lirsi vr grow weak

af'figgere vt affix

affi'lare vt sharpen

affili'ar|e vt affiliate. **~si** vr become affiliated

affi'nare vt sharpen; (perfezionare) refine

affinché *conj* so that, in order that

af'fin|e *a* similar. **~ità** *nf* affinity

affiora'mento *nm* emergence; *Naut* surfacing

affio'rare *vi* emerge; *fig* come to light

af'fisso *nm* bill; *Gram* affix

affitta'camere *nm inv* landlord ● *nf inv* landlady

affit'tare *vt* ⟨dare in affitto⟩ let; ⟨prendere in affitto⟩ rent; **'af'fittasi'** 'to let', 'for rent'

af'fitt|o *nm* rent; **contratto d'~o** lease; **dare in ~o** let; **prendere in ~o** rent. **~u'ario, -a** *nmf Jur* lessee

af'flligger|e *vt* torment. **~si** *vr* distress oneself

af'fli|tto *a* distressed; **~tto da** suffering from. **~zi'one** *nf* distress; *fig* affliction

afflosci'arsi *vr* become floppy; ⟨accasciarsi⟩ flop down; ⟨morale:⟩ decline

afflu'en|te *a & nm* tributary. **~za** *nf* flow; ⟨di gente⟩ crowd

afflu'ire *vi* flow; *fig* pour in

af'flusso *nm* influx

affo'ga|re *vt/i* drown; *Culin* poach; **~re in** *fig* be swamped with. **~to** *a* ⟨persona⟩ drowned; ⟨uova⟩ poached. **~to al caffè** *nm* ice cream with hot espresso poured over it

affol'la|re *vt*, **~rsi** *vr* crowd. **~to** *a* crowded

affonda'mento *nm* sinking

affon'dare *vt/i* sink

affossa'mento *nm* pothole

affran'ca|re *vt* redeem ⟨bene⟩; stamp ⟨lettera⟩; free ⟨schiavo⟩. **~rsi** *vr* free oneself. **~'tura** *nf* stamping; ⟨di spedizione⟩ postage

af'franto *a* prostrated; ⟨esausto⟩ worn out

af'fresco *nm* fresco

affret'ta|re *vt* speed up. **~rsi** *vr* hurry. **~ta'mente** *adv* hastily. **~to** *a* hasty

affron'tar|e *vt* face; confront ⟨il nemico⟩; meet ⟨le spese⟩. **~si** *vr* clash

af'fronto *nm* affront, insult; **fare un ~ a qcno** insult sb

affumi'ca|re *vt* fill with smoke; *Culin* smoke. **~to** *a* ⟨prosciutto, formaggio⟩ smoked

affuso'la|re *vt* taper [off]. **~to** *a* tapering

afo'risma *nm* aphorism

a'foso *a* sultry

'Africa *nf* Africa. **afri'cano, -a** *a & nmf* African

afrodi'siaco *a & nm* aphrodisiac

a'genda *nf* diary

agen'dina *nf* pocket-diary

a'gente *nm* agent; **agenti** *pl* **atmosferici** atmospheric agents. **~ di cambio** stockbroker. **~ di polizia** policeman

agen'zia *nf* agency; ⟨filiale⟩ branch office; ⟨di banca⟩ branch. **~ di viaggi** travel agency. **~ immobiliare** estate agency

agevo'la|re *vt* facilitate. **~zi'one** *nf* facilitation

a'gevol|e *a* easy; ⟨strada⟩ smooth. **~'mente** *adv* easily

agganci'ar|e *vt* hook up; *Rail* couple. **~si** *vr* ⟨vestito:⟩ hook up

ag'geggio *nm* gadget

agget'tivo *nm* adjective

agghiacci'ante *a* terrifying

agghiacci'ar|e *vt fig* **~ qcno** make sb's blood run cold. **~si** *vr* freeze

agghin'da|re *vt fam* dress up. **~rsi** *vr fam* doll oneself up. **~to** *a* dressed up

aggiorna'mento *nm* up-date

aggior'na|re *vt* ⟨rinviare⟩ postpone; ⟨mettere a giorno⟩ bring up to date. **~rsi** *vr* get up to date. **~to** *a* up-to-date; ⟨versione⟩ updated

aggi'rar|e *vt* surround; ⟨fig: ingannare⟩ trick. **~si** *vr* hang about; **~si su** ⟨discorso ecc:⟩ be about; ⟨approssimarsi⟩ be around

aggiudi'car|e *vt* award; ⟨all'asta⟩ knock down. **~si** *vr* win

aggi'un|gere *vt* add. **~ta** *nf* addition. **~'tivo** *a* supplementary. **~to** *a* added ● *a & nm* ⟨assistente⟩ assistant

aggiu'star|e *vt* mend; ⟨sistemare⟩ settle; ⟨fam: mettere a posto⟩ fix. **~si** *vr* adapt; ⟨mettersi in ordine⟩ tidy oneself up; ⟨decidere⟩ sort things out; ⟨tempo:⟩ clear up

agglomera'mento *nm* conglomeration

agglome'rato *nm* built-up area

aggrap'par|e *vt* grasp. **~si** *vr* **~si a** cling to

aggra'vante *Jur nf* aggravation ● *a* aggravating

aggra'var|e *vt* ⟨peggiorare⟩ make worse; increase ⟨pena⟩; ⟨appesantire⟩ weigh down. **~si** *vr* worsen

aggrazi'ato *a* graceful

aggre'dire *vt* attack

aggre'ga|re *vt* add; ⟨associare a un gruppo ecc⟩ admit. **~rsi** *vr* **~rsi a** join. **~to** *a* associated ● *nm* aggregate; ⟨di case⟩ block

aggressi'one *nf* aggression; (*atto*) attack

aggres's|ivo *a* aggressive. **~ività** *nf* aggressiveness. **·'ore** *nm* aggressor

aggrin'zare, aggrin'zire *vt* wrinkle

aggrot'tare *vt* **~ le ciglia/la fronte** frown

aggrovigli'a|re *vt* tangle. **~rsi** *vr* get entangled; *fig* get complicated, **~to** *a* entangled; *fig* confused

agguan'tare *vt* catch

aggu'ato *nm* ambush; (*tranello*) trap; **stare in ~** lie in wait

agguer'rito *a* fierce

agia'tezza *nf* comfort

agi'ato *a* ⟨*persona*⟩ well off; ⟨*vita*⟩ comfortable

a'gibil|e *a* ⟨*palazzo*⟩ fit for human habitation. **~ità** *nf* fitness for human habitation

'agil|e *a* agile. **~ità** *nf* agility

'agio *nm* ease; **mettersi a proprio ~** make oneself at home

a'gire *vi* act; (*comportarsi*) behave; (*funzionare*) work; **~ su** affect

agi'ta|re *vt* shake; wave ⟨*mano*⟩; (*fig: turbare*) trouble. **~rsi** *vr* toss about; (*essere inquieto*) be restless; ⟨*mare:*⟩ get rough. **~to** *a* restless; ⟨*mare*⟩ rough. **~'tore, ~'trice** *nmf* ⟨*persona*⟩ agitator. **~zi'one** *nf* agitation; **mettere in ~zione** qcno make sb worried

'agli = **a + gli**

'aglio *nm* garlic

a'gnello *nm* lamb

agno'lotti *nmpl* ravioli *sg*

a'gnostico, -a *a & nmf* agnostic

'ago *nm* needle

ago'ni|a *nf* agony. **~z'zare** *vi* be on one's deathbed

ago'nistic|a *nf* athletics *sg*. **~o** *a* sporting

agopun'tura *nf* acupuncture

a'gosto *nm* August

a'grari|a *nf* agriculture. **~o** *a* agricultural ● *nm* landowner

a'gricol|o *a* agricultural. **~'tore** *nm* farmer. **~'tura** *nf* agriculture

agri'foglio *nm* holly

agritu'rismo *nm* farm holidays, agrotourism

'agro *a* sour

agroalimen'tare *a* food *attrib*

agro'dolce *a* bitter-sweet; *Culin* sweet-and-sour; **in ~** sweet and sour

agrono'mia *nf* agronomy

a'grume *nm* citrus fruit; (*pianta*) citrus tree

aguz'zare *vt* sharpen; **~ le orecchie** prick up one's ears; **~ la vista** look hard

aguz'zino *nm* slave-driver; (*carceriere*) jailer

ahimè *int* alas

'ai = **a + i**

'Aia *nf* **L'~** The Hague

'aia *nf* threshing-floor

Aids *nmf* Aids

ai'rone *nm* heron

ai'tante *a* sturdy

aiu'ola *nf* flower-bed

aiu'tante *nmf* assistant ● *nm Mil* adjutant. **~ di campo** aide-de-camp

aiu'tare *vt* help

ai'uto *nm* help, aid; (*assistente*) assistant

aiz'zare *vt* incite; **~ contro** set on

al = **a + il**

'ala *nf* wing; **fare ~** make way

ala'bastro *nm* alabaster

'alacre *a* brisk

a'lano *nm* Great Dane

'alba *nf* dawn

Alba'n|ia *nf* Albania. **a~ese** *a & nmf* Albanian

albeggi'are *vi* dawn

albe'ra|to *a* wooded; ⟨*viale*⟩ tree-lined. **~tura** *nf Naut* masts *pl*. **albe'rello** *nm* sapling

al'berg|o *nm* hotel. **~o diurno** *hotel where rooms are rented during the daytime*. **~a'tore, ~a'trice** *nmf* hotel-keeper. **~hi'ero** *a* hotel *attrib*

'albero *nm* tree; *Naut* mast; *Mech* shaft. **~ genealogico** family tree. **~ maestro** *Naut* mainmast. **~ di Natale** Christmas tree

albi'cocc|a *nf* apricot. **~o** *nm* apricot-tree

al'bino *nm* albino

'albo *nm* register; (*libro ecc*) album; (*per avvisi*) notice board

'album *nm* album. **~ da disegno** sketch-book

al'bume *nm* albumen

'alce *nm* elk

'alcol *nm* alcohol; *Med* spirit; (*liquori forti*) spirits *pl*; **darsi all'~** take to drink. **al'colici** *nmpl* alcoholic drinks. **al'colico** *a* alcoholic. **alco'lismo** *nm* alcoholism. **~iz'zato, -a** *a & nmf* alcoholic

alco'test® *nm inv* Breathalyser®

al'cova *nf* alcove

al'cun, al'cuno *a & pron* any; **non ha ~ amico** he hasn't any friends, he has no friends. **alcuni** *pl* some, a few; **~i suoi amici** some of his friends

alea'torio *a* unpredictable

a'letta *nf Mech* fin

alfa'betico *a* alphabetical

alfabetizzazi'one *nf* ~ **della popolazione** teaching people to read and write

alfa'beto *nm* alphabet

alfi'ere *nm* (*scacchi*) bishop

al'fine *adv* eventually, in the end

'alga *nf* seaweed

'algebra *nf* algebra

Alge'ri|a *nf* Algeria. **a~no, -a** *a & nmf* Algerian

ali'ante *nm* glider

'alibi *nm inv* alibi

alie'na|re *vt* alienate. **~rsi** *vr* become estranged; **~rsi le simpatie di qcno** lose sb's good will. **~to, -a** *a* alienated ● *nmf* lunatic

a'lieno, -a *nmf* alien ● *a* **è ~ da invidia** envy is foreign to him

alimen'ta|re *vt* feed; *fig* foment ● *a* food *attrib*; (*abitudine*) dietary. **~ri** *nmpl* food-stuffs. **~'tore** *nm* power unit. **~zi'one** *nf* feeding

ali'mento *nm* food; **alimenti** *pl* food; *Jur* alimony

a'liquota *nf* share; (*di imposta*) rate

ali'scafo *nm* hydrofoil

'alito *nm* breath

'alla = a + la

allaccia'mento *nm* connection

allacci'ar|e *vt* fasten (*cintura*); lace up (*scarpe*); do up (*vestito*); (*collegare*) connect; form (*amicizia*). **~si** *vr* do up, fasten (*vestito, cintura*)

allaga'mento *nm* flooding

alla'gar|e *vt* flood. **~si** *vr* become flooded

allampa'nato *a* lanky

allarga'mento *nm* (*di una strada, delle ricerche*) widening

allar'gar|e *vt* widen; open (*braccia, gambe*); let out (*vestito ecc*); *fig* extend. **~si** *vr* widen

allar'mante *a* alarming

allar'ma|re *vt* alarm. **~to** *a* panicky

al'larme *nm* alarm; **dare l'~** raise the alarm; **falso ~** *fig* false alarm. **~ aereo** air raid warning

allar'mis|mo *nm* alarmism. **~ta** *nmf* alarmist

allatta'mento *nm* (*di animale*) suckling; (*di neonato*) feeding

allat'tare *vt* suckle (*animale*); feed (*neonato*)

'alle = a + le

alle'a|nza *nf* alliance. **~to, -a** *a* allied ● *nmf* ally

alle'ar|e *vt* unite. **~si** *vr* form an alliance

alle'gare[1] *vt Jur* allege

alle'ga|re[2] *vt* (*accludere*) enclose; set on edge (*denti*). **~to** *a* enclosed ● *nm* enclosure; **in ~to** attached, appended. **~zi'one** *nf Jur* allegation

allegge'rir|e *vt* lighten; *fig* alleviate. **~si** *vr* become lighter; (*vestirsi leggero*) put on lighter clothes

allego'ria *nf* allegory. **alle'gorico** *a* allegorical

allegra'mente *adv* breezily

alle'gria *nf* gaiety

al'legro *a* cheerful; (*colore*) bright; (*brillo*) tipsy ● *nm Mus* allegro

alle'luia *int* hallelujah!

allena'mento *nm* training

alle'na|re *vt*, **~rsi** *vr* train. **~'tore, ~'trice** *nmf* trainer, coach

allen'tar|e *vt* loosen; *fig* relax. **~si** *vr* become loose; *Mech* work loose

aller'gia *nf* allergy. **al'lergico** *a* allergic

al'lerta *nf o nm inv* **stare ~** be on the alert

allesti'mento *nm* preparation. **~ scenico** *Theat* set

alle'stire *vt* prepare; stage (*spettacolo*); *Naut* fit out

allet'tante *a* alluring

allet'tare *vt* entice

alleva'mento *nm* breeding; (*processo*) bringing up; (*luogo*) farm; (*per piante*) nursery; **pollo di ~** battery hen *or* chicken

alle'vare *vt* bring up (*bambini*); breed (*animali*); grow (*piante*)

allevi'are *vt* alleviate; *fig* lighten

alli'bito *a* astounded

allibra'tore *nm* bookmaker

allie'tar|e *vt* gladden. **~si** *vr* rejoice

alli'evo, -a *nmf* pupil ● *nm Mil* cadet

alliga'tore *nm* alligator

allinea'mento *nm* alignment

alline'ar|e *vt* line up; *Typ* align; *Fin* adjust. **~si** *vr* fall into line

'allo = a + lo

al'locco *nm* tawny owl; *fig* dunce

al'lodola *nf* [sky]lark

alloggi'are *vt* (*persona:*) put up; (*casa:*) provide accommodation for; *Mil* billet ● *vi* put up, stay; *Mil* be billeted.

al'loggio *nm* (*appartamento*) flat; *Mil* billet

allonta'mento *nm* removal

allonta'nar|e *vt* move away; (*licenziare*) dismiss; avert (*pericolo*). ~si *vr* go away

al'lo̱ra *adv* then; (*in quel tempo*) at that time; (*in tal caso*) in that case; **d'~ in poi** from then on; **e ~?** what now?; (*e con ciò?*) so what?; **fino ~** until then

al'loro *nm* laurel; *Culin* bay

'alluce *nm* big toe

alluci'na|nte *a fam* incredible; **sostanza ~nte** hallucinogen. **~to, -a** *nmf fam* space cadet. **~zi'one** *nf* hallucination

allucino'geno *a* (*sostanza*) hallucinatory

al'ludere *vi* ~ a allude to

allu'minio *nm* aluminium

allun'gar|e *vt* lengthen; stretch [out] (*gamba*); extend (*tavolo*); (*diluire*) dilute; ~e il collo crane one's neck. ~e le mani su qcno touch sb up. ~e il passo quicken one's step. ~si *vr* grow longer; (*crescere*) grow taller; (*sdraiarsi*) lie down

allusi'one *nf* allusion

allu'sivo *a* allusive

alluvio'nale *a* alluvial

alluvi'one *nf* flood

al'meno *adv* at least; [se] ~ venisse il sole! if only the sun would come out!

a'logeno *nm* halogen ● *a* lampada alogena halogen lamp

a'lone *nm* halo

'Alpi *nfpl* le ~ the Alps

alpi'nis|mo *nm* mountaineering. ~ta *nmf* mountaineer

al'pino *a* Alpine ● *nm Mil* gli alpini the Alpine troops

al'quanto *a* a certain amount of ● *adv* rather

alt *int* stop

alta'lena *nf* swing; (*tavola in bilico*) see-saw

altale'nare *vi fig* vacillate

alta'mente *adv* highly

al'tare *nm* altar

alta'rino *nm* scoprire gli altarini di qcno reveal sb's guilty secrets

alte'ra|re *vt* alter; adulterate (*cibo*); (*falsificare*) falsify. ~rsi *vr* be altered; (*cibo:*) go bad; (*merci:*) deteriorate; (*arrabbiarsi*) get angry. ~to *a* (*vino*) spoilt. ~zi'one *nf* alteration; (*di cibo*) adulteration

al'terco *nm* altercation

alter'nanza *nf* alternation

alter'na|re *vt*, ~rsi *vr* alternate. ~'tiva *nf* alternative. ~'tivo *a* alternate. ~to *a* alternating. ~'tore *nm Electr* alternator

al'tern|o *a* alternate; **a giorni ~i** every other day

al'tero *a* haughty

al'tezza *nf* height; (*profondità*) depth; (*suono*) pitch; (*di tessuto*) width; (*titolo*) Highness; **essere all'~ di** be on a level with; *fig* be up to

altezzos|a'mente *adv* haughtily. ~ità *nf* haughtiness

altez'zoso *a* haughty

al'ticcio *a* tipsy, merry

alti'piano *nm* plateau

alti'tudine *nf* altitude

'alto *a* high; (*di statura*) tall; (*profondo*) deep; (*suono*) high-pitched; (*tessuto*) wide; *Geog* northern; **a notte alta** in the middle of the night; **avere degli alti e bassi** have some ups and downs; **ad alta fedeltà** high-fidelity; **a voce alta, ad alta voce** in a loud voice; (*leggere*) aloud; **essere in ~ mare** be on the high seas. **alta finanza** *nf* high finance. **alta moda** *nf* high fashion. **alta tensione** *nf* high voltage ● *adv* high; **in ~** at the top; **mani in ~!** hands up!

alto'forno *nm* blast-furnace

altolà *int* halt there!

altolo'cato *a* highly placed

altopar'lante *nm* loudspeaker

altopi'ano *nm* plateau

altret'tanto *a & pron* as much; (*pl*) as many ● *adv* likewise; **buona fortuna! grazie, ~** good luck! thank you, the same to you

altri'menti *adv* otherwise

'altr|o *a* other; **un ~, un'altra** another; **l'altr'anno** last year; **domani l'~** the day after tomorrow; **l'ho visto l'~ giorno** I saw him the other day ● *pron* other [one]; **un ~, un'altra** another [one]; **ne vuoi dell'~?** would you like some more?; **l'un l'~** one another; **nessun ~** nobody else; **gli altri** (*la gente*) other people ● *nm* something else; **non fa ~ che lavorare** he does nothing but work; **desidera ~?** (*in negozio*) anything else?; **più che ~, sono stanco** I'm tired more than anything; **se non ~** at least; **senz'~** certainly; **tra l'~** what's more; **~ che!** and how!

altroi'eri *nm* l'~ the day before yesterday

al'tronde *adv* **d'~** on the other hand

al'trove *adv* elsewhere

al'trui *a* other people's ● *nm* other people's belongings *pl*

altru'is|mo *nm* altruism. **~ta** *nmf* altruist

al'tura *nf* high ground; *Naut* deep sea

a'lunno, -a *nmf* pupil

alve'are *nm* hive

al'za|re *vt* lift, raise; ⟨*costruire*⟩ build; *Naut* hoist; **~re le spalle** shrug one's shoulders; **~re i tacchi** *fig* take to one's heels. **~rsi** *vr* rise; ⟨*in piedi*⟩ stand up; ⟨*da letto*⟩ get up; **~rsi in piedi** get to one's feet. **~ta** *nf* lifting; ⟨*aumento*⟩ rise; ⟨*da letto*⟩ getting up; *Archit* elevation. **~to a** up

a'mabile *a* lovable; ⟨*vino*⟩ sweet

a'maca *nf* hammock

amalga'mar|e *vt, e*, **~si** *vr* amalgamate

a'mante *a* **~ di** fond of ● *nm* lover ● *nf* mistress, lover

ama'rena *nf* sour black cherry

ama'retto *nm* macaroon

a'ma|re *vt* love; be fond of, like ⟨*musica, sport ecc*⟩. **~to, -a** *a* loved ● *nmf* beloved

ama'rezza *nf* bitterness; ⟨*dolore*⟩ sorrow

a'maro *a* bitter ● *nm* bitterness; ⟨*liquore*⟩ bitters *pl*

ama'rognolo *a* rather bitter

ama'tore, -'trice *nmf* lover

ambasci'a|ta *nf* embassy; ⟨*messaggio*⟩ message. **~'tore,** **~'trice** *nm* ambassador ● *nf* ambassadress

ambe'due *a & pron* both

ambien'ta|le *a* environmental. **~'lista** *a & nmf* environmentalist

ambien'tar|e *vt* acclimatize; set ⟨*personaggio, film ecc*⟩. **~si** *vr* get acclimatized

ambi'ente *nm* environment; ⟨*stanza*⟩ room; *fig* milieu

ambiguità *nf inv* ambiguity; ⟨*di persona*⟩ shadiness

am'biguo *a* ambiguous; ⟨*persona*⟩ shady

am'bire *vt* **~ a** aspire to

'ambito *nm* sphere

ambiva'len|te *a* ambivalent. **~za** *nf* ambivalence

ambizi'o|ne *nf* ambition. **~so** *a* ambitious

'ambra *nf* amber. **am'brato** *a* amber

ambu'lante *a* wandering; **venditore ~** hawker

ambu'lanza *nf* ambulance

ambula'torio *nm* ⟨*di medico*⟩ surgery; ⟨*di ospedale*⟩ out-patients' [department]

a'meba *nf* amoeba

'amen *int* amen

a'meno *a* pleasant

A'merica *nf* America. **~ del Sud** South America. **ameri'cano, -a** *a & nmf* American

ame'tista *nf* amethyst

ami'anto *nm* asbestos

ami'chevole *a* friendly

ami'cizia *nf* friendship; **fare ~ con qcno** make friends with sb; **amicizie** *pl* ⟨*amici*⟩ friends

a'mico, -a *nmf* friend; **~ del cuore** bosom friend

'amido *nm* starch

ammac'ca|re *vt* dent. **~rsi** *vr* ⟨*metallo:*⟩ get dented. **~to** *a* ⟨*frutto*⟩ bruised. **~'tura** *nf* dent; ⟨*livido*⟩ bruise

ammae'stra|re *vt* ⟨*istruire*⟩ teach; train ⟨*animale*⟩. **~to** *a* trained

ammai'nare *vt* lower ⟨*bandiera*⟩; furl ⟨*vele*⟩

amma'la|rsi *vr* fall ill. **~to, -a** *a* ill ● *nmf* sick person; ⟨*paziente*⟩ patient

ammali'are *vt* bewitch

am'manco *nm* deficit

ammanet'tare *vt* handcuff

ammani'cato *a* **essere ~** have connections

amma'raggio *nm* splashdown

amma'rare *vi* put down on the sea; ⟨*nave spaziale:*⟩ splash down

ammas'sar|e *vt* amass. **~si** *vr* crowd together. **am'masso** *nm* mass; ⟨*mucchio*⟩ pile

ammat'tire *vi* go mad

ammaz'zar|e *vt* kill. **~si** *vr* ⟨*suicidarsi*⟩ kill oneself; ⟨*rimanere ucciso*⟩ be killed

am'menda *nf* amends *pl*; ⟨*multa*⟩ fine; **fare ~ di qcsa** make amends for sth

am'messo *pp di* **ammettere** ● *conj* **~ che** supposing that

am'mettere *vt* admit; ⟨*riconoscere*⟩ acknowledge; ⟨*supporre*⟩ suppose

ammic'care *vi* wink

ammini'stra|re *vt* administer; ⟨*gestire*⟩ run. **~'tivo** *a* administrative. **~'tore, ~'trice** *nmf* administrator; ⟨*di azienda*⟩ manager; ⟨*di società*⟩ director. **~tore delegato** managing director. **~zi'one** *nf* administration; **fatti di ordinaria ~zione** *fig* routine matters

ammi'ragli|o *nm* admiral. **~'ato** *nm* admiralty

ammi'ra|re *vt* admire. **~to a restare/**

essere ~**to** be full of admiration. ~**'tore**, ~**'trice** *nmf* admirer. ~**zi'one** *nf* admiration. **ammi'revole** *a* admirable

ammis'sibile *a* admissible

ammissi'one *nf* admission; (*approvazione*) acknowledgement

ammobili'a|re *vt* furnish. ~**to** *a* furnished

am'modo *a* proper ● *adv* properly

am'mollo *nm* **in** ~ soaking

ammo'niaca *nf* ammonia

ammoni'mento *nm* warning; (*di rimprovero*) admonishment

ammo'ni|re *vt* warn; (*rimproverare*) admonish; *Jur* caution. ~**'tore** *a* admonishing. ~**zi'one** *nf Sport* warning

ammon'tare *vi* ~ **a** amount to ● *nm* amount

ammonticchi'are *vt* heap up

ammorbi'dente *nm* (*per panni*) softener

ammorbi'dir|e *vt*, ~**si** *vr* soften

ammorta'mento *nm Comm* amortization

ammor'tare *vt* pay off (*spesa*); *Comm* amortize (*debito*)

ammortiz'za|re *vt Comm* = **ammortare**; *Mech* damp. ~**'tore** *nm* shock-absorber

ammosci'ar|e *vt* make flabby. ~**si** *vi* get flabby

ammucchi'a|re *vt*, ~**rsi** *vr* pile up. ~**ta** *nf* (*sl: orgia*) orgy

ammuf'fi|re *vi* go mouldy. ~**to** *a* mouldy

ammutina'mento *nm* mutiny

ammuti'narsi *vr* mutiny

ammuto'lire *vi* be struck dumb

amne'sia *nf* amnesia

amni'stia *nf* amnesty

'amo *nm* hook; *fig* bait

amo'rale *a* amoral

a'more *nm* love; **fare l'**~ make love; **per l'amor di Dio/del cielo!** for heaven's sake!; **andare d'**~ **e d'accordo** get on like a house on fire; ~ **proprio** self-respect; **è un** ~ (*persona*) he/she is a darling; **per** ~ **di** for the sake of; **amori** *pl* love affairs. ~**ggi'are** *vi* flirt. **amo'revole** *a* loving

a'morfo *a* shapeless; (*persona*) colourless, grey

amo'roso *a* loving; (*sguardo ecc*) amorous; (*lettera, relazione*) love

ampi'ezza *nf* (*di esperienza*) breadth; (*di stanza*) spaciousness; (*di gonna*) fullness; (*importanza*) scale

'ampio *a* ample; (*esperienza*) wide; (*stanza*) spacious; (*vestito*) loose; (*gonna*) full; (*pantaloni*) baggy

am'plesso *nm* embrace

amplia'mento *nm* (*di casa, porto*) enlargement; (*di strada*) widening

ampli'are *vt* broaden (*conoscenze*)

amplifi'ca|re *vt* amplify; *fig* magnify. ~**'tore** *nm* amplifier. ~**zi'one** *nf* amplification

am'polla *nf* cruet

ampol'loso *a* pompous

ampu'ta|re *vt* amputate. ~**zi'one** *nf* amputation

amu'leto *nm* amulet

anabbagli'ante *a Auto* dipped ● *nmpl* **anabbaglianti** dipped headlights

anacro'nis|mo *nm* anachronism. ~**tico** *a* **essere** ~ be an anachronism

a'nagrafe *nf* (*ufficio*) registry office; (*registro*) register of births, marriages and deaths

ana'grafico *a* **dati** *nmpl* **anagrafici** personal data

ana'gramma *nm* anagram

anal'colico *a* non-alcoholic ● *nm* soft drink, non-alcoholic drink

a'nale *a* anal

analfa'be|ta *a* & *nmf* illiterate. ~**tismo** *nm* illiteracy

anal'gesico *nm* painkiller

a'nalisi *nf inv* analysis; *Med* test. ~ **grammaticale/del periodo/logica** parsing. ~ **del sangue** blood test

ana'li|sta *nmf* analyst. ~**tico** *a* analytical. ~**z'zare** *vt* analyse; *Med* test

anal'lergico *a* hypoallergenic

analo'gia *nf* analogy. **a'nalogo** *a* analogous

'ananas *nm inv* pineapple

anar'chi|a *nf* anarchy. **a'narchico, -a** *a* anarchic ● *nmf* anarchist. ~**smo** *nm* anarchism

A.N.A.S. *nf abbr* (**Azienda Nazionale Autonoma delle Strade**) *national road maintenance authority*

anato'mia *nf* anatomy. **ana'tomico** *a* anatomical; (*sedia*) contoured, ergonomic

'anatra *nf* duck

ana'troccolo *nm* duckling

'anca *nf* hip; (*di animale*) flank

ance'strale *a* ancestral

'anche *conj* also, too; (*persino*) even; ~ **se** even if; ~ **domani** tomorrow also o too, also tomorrow

anchilo'sato *a fig* stiff

an'cora *adv* still, yet; (*di nuovo*) again; (*di più*) some more; ~ **una volta** once more

'anco|ra *nf* anchor; **gettare l'~ra** drop anchor. **~'raggio** *nm* anchorage. **~'rare** *vt* anchor

anda'mento *nm* (*del mercato, degli affari*) trend

an'dante *a* (*corrente*) current; (*di poco valore*) cheap ● *nm Mus* andante

an'da|re *vi* go; (*funzionare*) work; ~ **via** (*partire*) leave; ⟨*macchia:*⟩ come out; ~ [**bene**] (*confarsi*) suit; ⟨*taglia:*⟩ fit; **ti va bene alle tre?** does three o'clock suit you?; **non mi va da mangiare** I don't feel like eating; ~ **di fretta** be in a hurry; ~ **fiero di** be proud of; ~ **di moda** be in fashion; **va per i 20 anni** he's nearly 20; **ma va' [là]!** come on!; **come va?** how are things?; ~ **a male** go off; ~ **a fuoco** go up in flames; **va spedito** [**entro**] **stamattina** it must be sent this morning; **ne va del mio lavoro** my job is at stake; **come è andata a finire?** how did it turn out?; **cosa vai dicendo?** what are you talking about?. **~rsene** go away; (*morire*) pass away ● *nm* going; a **lungo ~re** eventually

'andito *nm* passage

an'drone *nm* entrance

a'neddoto *nm* anecdote

ane'lare *vt* ~ **a** long for. **a'nelito** *nm* longing

a'nello *nm* ring; (*di catena*) link

ane'mia *nf* anaemia. **a'nemico** *a* anaemic

a'nemone *nm* anemone

aneste'si|a *nf* anaesthesia; (*sostanza*) anaesthetic. **~'sta** *nmf* anaesthetist. **ane'stetico** *a* & *nm* anaesthetic

an'fibi *nmpl* (*stivali*) army boots

an'fibio *nm* (*animale*) amphibian ● *a* amphibious

anfite'atro *nm* amphitheatre

'anfora *nf* amphora

an'fratto *nm* ravine

an'gelico *a* angelic

'angelo *nm* angel. ~ **custode** guardian angel

angli'c|ano *a* Anglican. **~ismo** *nm* Anglicism

an'glofilo, -a *a* & *nmf* Anglophile

an'glofono, -a *nmf* English-speaker

anglo'sassone *a* & *nmf* Anglo-Saxon

ango'la|re *a* angular. **~zi'one** *nf* angle shot

'angolo *nm* corner; *Math* angle. ~ [**di**] **cottura** kitchenette

ango'loso *a* angular

an'gosci|a *nf* anguish. **~'are** *vt* torment. **~'ato** *a* agonized. **~'oso** *a* (*disperato*) anguished; (*che dà angoscia*) distressing

angu'illa *nf* eel

an'guria *nf* water-melon

an'gusti|a *nf* (*ansia*) anxiety; (*penuria*) poverty. **~'are** *vt* distress. **~'arsi** *vr* be very worried (**per** about)

an'gusto *a* narrow

'anice *nm* anise; *Culin* aniseed; (*liquore*) anisette

ani'dride *nf* ~ **carbonica** carbon dioxide

'anima *nf* soul; **non c'era ~ viva** there was not a soul about; **all'~!** good grief!; **un'~ in pena** a soul in torment. ~ **gemella** soul mate

ani'ma|le *a* & *nm* animal; **~li domestici** *pl* pets. **~'lesco** *a* animal

ani'ma|re *vt* give life to; (*ravvivare*) enliven; (*incoraggiare*) encourage. **~rsi** *vr* come to life; (*accalorarsi*) become animated. **~to a** animate; (*vivace*) animated. **~'tore**, **~'trice** *nmf* leading spirit; *Cinema* animator. **~zi'one** *nf* animation

'animo *nm* (*mente*) mind; (*indole*) disposition; (*cuore*) heart; **perdersi d'~** lose heart; **farsi ~** take heart. **~sità** *nf* animosity

ani'moso *a* brave; (*ostile*) hostile

'anitra *nf* = **anatra**

anna'cqua|re *vt* anche *fig* water down. **~to** *a* watered down

annaffi'a|re *vt* water. **~'toio** *nm* watering-can

an'nali *nmpl* annals

anna'spare *vi* flounder

an'nata *nf* year; (*importo annuale*) annual amount; (*di vino*) vintage

annebbia'mento *nm* fog build-up; *fig* clouding

annebbi'ar|e *vt* cloud ⟨*vista, mente*⟩. **~si** *vr* become foggy; ⟨*vista, mente:*⟩ grow dim

annega'mento *nm* drowning

anne'ga|re *vt/i* drown

anne'rir|e *vt/i* blacken. **~si** *vr* become black

annessi'one *nf* (*di nazione*) annexation

an'nesso *pp di* **annettere** ● *a* attached

an'nettere vt add; (accludere) enclose; annex ‹uno stato›

annichi'lire vt annihilate

anni'darsi vr nest

annienta'mento nm annihilation

annien'tar|e vt annihilate. **~si** vr abase oneself

anniver'sario a & nm anniversary. **~ di matrimonio** wedding anniversary

anno'dar|e vt knot; do up ‹cintura›; fig form. **~si** vr become knotted

annoi'a|re vt bore; (recare fastidio) annoy. **~rsi** vr get bored; (condizione) be bored. **~to** a bored

'anno nm year; **Buon A~!** Happy New Year!; **quanti anni ha?** how old are you?; **Tommaso ha dieci anni** Thomas is ten [years old]. **~ bisestile** leap year

anno'ta|re vt note down; annotate ‹testo›. **~zi'one** nf note

annove'rare vt number

annu'a|le a annual, yearly. **~rio** nm year-book

annu'ire vi nod; (acconsentire) agree

annulla'mento nm annulment; (di appuntamento) cancellation

annul'lar|e vt annul; cancel ‹appuntamento›; (togliere efficacia a) undo; disallow ‹gol›; (distruggere) destroy. **~si** vr cancel each other out

annunci'a|re vt announce; (preannunciare) foretell. **~'tore**, **~'trice** nmf announcer. **~zi'one** nf Annunciation

an'nuncio nm announcement; (pubblicitario) advertisement; (notizia) news. **annunci** pl **economici** classified advertisements

'annuo a annual, yearly

annu'sare vt sniff

annuvo'lar|e vt cloud. **~si** vr cloud over

'ano nm anus

anoma'lia nf anomaly

a'nomalo a anomalous

anoni'mato nm **mantenere l'~** remain anonymous

a'nonimo a anonymous ● nm (pittore, scrittore) anonymous painter/writer

anores'sia nf Med anorexia

ano'ressico, -a nmf anorexic

anor'mal|e a abnormal ● nmf deviant, abnormal person. **~ità** nf inv abnormality

'ansa nf handle; (di fiume) bend

an'sare vi pant

'ansia, ansietà nf anxiety; **stare/essere in ~ per** be anxious about

ansi'oso a anxious

antago'nis|mo nm antagonism. **~ta** nmf antagonist

an'tartico a & nm Antarctic

antece'dente a preceding ● nm precedent

ante'fatto nm prior event

ante'guerra a pre-war ● nm pre-war period

ante'nato, -a nmf ancestor

an'tenna nf Radio, TV aerial; (di animale) antenna; Naut yard. **~ parabolica** satellite dish

ante'porre vt put before

ante'prima nf preview; **vedere qcsa in ~** have a sneak preview of sth

anteri'ore a front attrib; (nel tempo) previous

antiade'rente a ‹padella› nonstick

antia'ereo a anti-aircraft attrib

antial'lergico a hypoallergenic

antia'tomico a **rifugio ~** fallout shelter

antibi'otico a & nm antibiotic

anti'caglia nf (oggetto) piece of old junk

antica'mente adv in ancient times, long ago

anti'camera nf ante-room; **far ~** be kept waiting

antichità nf inv antiquity; (oggetto) antique

antici'clone nm anticyclone

antici'pa|re vt advance; Comm pay in advance; (prevedere) anticipate; (prevenire) forestall ● vi be early. **~ta'mente** adv in advance. **~zi'one** nf anticipation; (notizia) advance news

an'ticipo nm advance; (caparra) deposit; **in ~** early; (nel lavoro) ahead of schedule

an'tico a ancient; ‹mobile ecc› antique; (vecchio) old; **all'antica** old-fashioned ● nmpl **gli antichi** the ancients

anticoncezio'nale a & nm contraceptive

anticonfor'mis|mo nm unconventionality. **~ta** nmf nonconformist. **~tico** a unconventional, nonconformist

anticonge'lante a & nm anti-freeze

anti'corpo nm antibody

anticostituzio'nale a unconstitutional

anti'crimine a inv ‹squadra› crime attrib

antidemo'cratico a undemocratic

antidolo'rifico nm painkiller

an'tidoto nm antidote

anti'droga *a inv* ‹campagna› anti-drugs; ‹squadra› drug *attrib*

antie'stetico *a* ugly

antifa'scismo *nm* anti-fascism

antifa'scista *a & nmf* anti-fascist

anti'forfora *a inv* dandruff *attrib*

anti'furto *nm* anti-theft device; (allarme) alarm ● *a inv* ‹sistema› anti-theft

anti'gelo *nm* antifreeze; (parabrezza) defroster

antigi'enico *a* unhygienic

An'tille *nfpl* le ~ the West Indies

an'tilope *nf* antelope

antin'cendio *a inv* allarme ~ fire alarm; **porta** ~ fire door

anti'nebbia *nm inv* Auto [faro] ~ foglamp, foglight

antinfiamma'torio *a & nm* anti-inflammatory

antinucle'are *a* anti-nuclear

antio'rario *a* anti-clockwise

anti'pasto *nm* hors d'oeuvre, starter

antipa'tia *nf* antipathy. **anti'patico** *a* unpleasant

an'tipodi *nmpl* antipodes; **essere agli** ~ *fig* be poles apart

antiquari'ato *nm* antique trade

anti'quario, -a *nmf* antique dealer

anti'quato *a* antiquated

anti'ruggine *nm inv* rust-inhibitor

anti'rughe *a inv* anti-wrinkle *attrib*

anti'scippo *a inv* theft-proof

antise'mita *a* anti-Semitic

anti'settico *a & nm* antiseptic

antisoci'ale *a* anti-social

antista'minico *nm* antihistamine

anti'stante *a prep* in front of

anti'tarlo *nm inv* woodworm treatment

antiterro'ristico *a* antiterrorist *attrib*

an'titesi *nf* antithesis

antolo'gia *nf* anthology

'antro *nm* cavern

antropolo'gia *nf* anthropology. **antro'pologo, -a** *nmf* anthropologist

anu'lare *nm* ring-finger

'anzi *conj* in fact; (o meglio) or better still; (al contrario) on the contrary

anzianità *nf* old age; (di servizio) seniority

anzi'ano, -a *a* old, elderly; (di grado ecc) senior ● *nmf* elderly person

anziché *conj* rather than

anzi'tempo *adv* prematurely

anzi'tutto *adv* first of all

a'orta *nf* aorta

apar'titico *a* unaligned

apa'tia *nf* apathy. **a'patico** *a* apathetic

'ape *nf* bee; **nido** *nm* **di api** honeycomb

aperi'tivo *nm* aperitif

aperta'mente *adv* openly

a'perto *a* open; **all'aria aperta** in the open air; **all'**~ open-air

aper'tura *nf* opening; (inizio) beginning; (ampiezza) spread; (di arco) span; Pol overtures *pl*; Phot aperture; ~ **mentale** openness

'apice *nm* apex

apicol'tura *nf* beekeeping

ap'nea *nf* **immersione in** ~ free diving

a'polide *a* stateless ● *nmf* stateless person

a'postolo *nm* apostle

apostro'fare *vt* (mettere un apostrofo a) write with an apostrophe; reprimand ‹persona›

a'postrofo *nm* apostrophe

appaga'mento *nm* fulfilment

appa'ga|re *vt* satisfy. ~rsi *vr* ~rsi di be satisfied with

appai'are *vt* pair; mate ‹animali›

appallotto'lare *vt* roll into a ball

appalta'tore *nm* contractor

ap'palto *nm* contract; **dare in** ~ contract out

appan'naggio *nm* (in denaro) annuity; *fig* prerogative

appan'nar|e *vt* mist ‹vetro›; dim ‹vista›. ~**si** *vr* mist over; ‹vista:› grow dim

appa'rato *nm* apparatus; (pompa) display

apparecchi'a|re *vt* prepare ● *vi* lay the table. ~'**tura** *nf* (impianti) equipment

appa'recchio *nm* apparatus; (congegno) device; (radio, TV ecc) set; (aeroplano) aircraft. ~ **acustico** hearing aid

appa'ren|te *a* apparent. ~**te'mente** *adv* apparently. ~**za** *nf* appearance; **in** ~**za** apparently.

appa'ri|re *vi* appear; (sembrare) look. ~'**scente** *a* striking; *pej* gaudy. ~**zi'one** *nf* apparition

apparta'mento *nm* flat, apartment *Am*

appar'ta|rsi *vr* withdraw. ~**to** *a* secluded

apparte'nenza *nf* membership

apparte'nere *vi* belong

appassio'nante *a* ‹storia, argomento› exciting

appassio'na|re *vt* excite; (commuovere) move. ~**rsi** *vr* ~**rsi a** become excited by. **~to** a passionate; **~to di** (*entusiastico*) fond of

appas'sir|e vi wither. **~si** vr fade

appel'larsi vr **~ a** appeal to

ap'pello nm appeal; (*chiamata per nome*) rollcall; (*esami*) exam session; **fare l'~** call the roll

ap'pena adv just; (*a fatica*) hardly ● conj [**non**] **~** as soon as, no sooner... than

ap'pendere vt.hang [up]

appendi'abiti nm inv hat-stand, hallstand

appen'dice nf appendix. **appendi-'cite** nf appendicitis

Appen'nini nmpl **gli ~** the Apennines

appesan'tir|e vt weigh down. **~si** vr become heavy

ap'peso pp di **appendere** ● a hanging; (*impiccato*) hanged

appe'ti|to nm appetite; **aver ~to** be hungry; **buon ~to!** enjoy your meal!. **~toso** a appetizing; *fig* tempting

appezza'mento nm plot of land

appia'nar|e vt level; *fig* smooth. **~si** vr improve

appiat'tir|e vt flatten. **~si** vr flatten oneself

appic'care vt **~ il fuoco a** set fire to

appicci'car|e vt stick; **~e a** (*fig: appioppare*) palm off on ● vi be sticky. **~si** vr stick together; **~si a qcno** *fig* stick to sb like glue

appiccica'ticcio a sticky; *fig* clingy

appicci'coso a sticky; *fig* clingy

appie'dato a **sono ~** I don't have the car; **sono rimasto ~** I was stranded

appi'eno adv fully

appigli'arsi vr **~ a** get hold of; *fig* stick to sth. **ap'piglio** nm foothold; *fig* pretext

appiop'pare vt **~ a** palm off on; (*fam: dare*) give

appiso'larsi vr doze off

applau'dire vt/i applaud. **ap'plauso** nm applause

appli'cabile a applicable

appli'ca|re vt apply; enforce ‹*legge ecc*›. **~rsi** vr apply oneself. **~'tore** nm applicator. **~zi'one** nf application; (*di legge*) enforcement

appoggi'ar|e vt put; (*sostenere*) back. **~si** vr **~si a** lean against; *fig* rely on. **ap'poggio** nm support

appollai'arsi vr *fig* perch

ap'porre vt affix

appor'tare vt bring; (*causare*) cause. **ap'porto** nm contribution

apposita'mente adv (*specialmente*) especially

ap'posito a proper

ap'posta adv on purpose; (*espressamente*) specially

apposta'mento nm ambush; (*caccia*) lying in wait

appo'star|e vt post ‹*soldati*›. **~si** vr lie in wait

ap'prend|ere vt understand; (*imparare*) learn. **~i'mento** nm learning

appren'di|sta nmf apprentice. **~'stato** nm apprenticeship

apprensi'one nf apprehension; **essere in ~ per** be anxious about. **appren'sivo** a apprehensive

ap'presso adv & prep (*vicino*) near; (*dietro*) behind; **come ~** as follows

appre'star|e vt prepare. **~si** vr get ready

apprez'za|bile a appreciable. **~'mento** nm appreciation; (*giudizio*) opinion

apprez'za|re vt appreciate. **~to** a appreciated

ap'proccio nm approach

appro'dare vi land; **~ a** *fig* come to; **non ~ a nulla** come to nothing. **ap'prodo** nm landing; (*luogo*) landing-stage

approfit'ta|re vi take advantage (**di** of), profit (**di** by). **~'tore**, **~'trice** nmf chancer

approfondi'mento nm deepening; **di ~** ‹*fig: esame*› further

approfon'di|re vt deepen. **~rsi** vr ‹*divario:*› widen. **~to** a ‹*studio, ricerca*› in-depth

appropri'a|rsi vr take possession; (*essere adatto*) suit. **~to** a appropriate. **~zi'one** nf Jur appropriation. **~zione indebita** Jur embezzlement

approssi'ma|re vt **~re per eccesso/difetto** round up/down. **~rsi** vr draw near. **~tiva'mente** adv approximately. **~'tivo** a approximate. **~zi'one** nf approximation

appro'va|re vt approve of; approve ‹*legge*›. **~zi'one** nf approval

approvvigiona'mento nm supplying; **approvvigionamenti** pl provisions

approvvigio'nar|e vt supply. **~si** vr stock up

appunta'mento nm appointment, date *fam*; **fissare un ~** make an appointment; **darsi ~** decide to meet

appun'tar|e vt (*annotare*) take notes; (*fissare*) fix; (*con spillo*) pin; (*appuntire*) sharpen. **~si** *vr* **~si su** ⟨*teoria*⟩ be based on

appun'ti|re *vt* sharpen. **~to** *a* ⟨*mento*⟩ pointed

ap'punto[1] *nm* note; (*piccola critica*) niggle

ap'punto[2] *adv* exactly; **per l'~!** exactly!; **stavo ~ dicendo...** I was just saying...

appu'rare *vt* verify

a'pribile *a* that can be opened

apribot'tiglie *nm inv* bottle-opener

a'prile *nm* April; **il primo d'~** April Fools' Day

a'prir|e *vt* open; turn on ⟨*luce, acqua ecc*⟩; (*con chiave*) unlock; open up ⟨*ferita ecc*⟩. **~si** *vr* open; (*spaccarsi*) split; (*confidarsi*) confide (**con** in)

apri'scatole *nf inv* tin-opener

aqua'planing *nm* **andare in ~** aquaplane

'aquil|a *nf* eagle; **non è un'~a!** he is no genius!. **~'lino** *a* aquiline

aqui'lone *nm* (*giocattolo*) kite

ara'besco *nm* arabesque; *hum* scribble

A'rabia Sau'dita *nf* **l'~** Saudi Arabia

'arabo, -a *a* Arab; ⟨*lingua*⟩ Arabic ● *nmf* Arab ● *nm* (*lingua*) Arabic

a'rachide *nf* peanut

ara'gosta *nf* lobster

a'ranci|a *nf* orange. **~'ata** *nf* orangeade. **~'o** *nm* orange-tree; (*colore*) orange. **~'one** *a & nm* orange

a'ra|re *vt* plough. **~tro** *nm* plough

ara'tura *nf* ploughing

a'razzo *nm* tapestry

arbi'trar|e *vt* arbitrate in; *Sport* referee. **~ietà** *nf* arbitrariness. **~io** *a* arbitrary

ar'bitrio *nm* will; **è un ~** it's very high-handed

'arbitro *nm* arbiter; *Sport* referee; (*nel baseball*) umpire

ar'busto *nm* shrub

'arca *nf* ark; (*cassa*) chest

ar'ca|ico *a* archaic. **~'ismo** *nm* archaism

ar'cangelo *nm* archangel

ar'cata *nf* arch; (*serie di archi*) arcade

arche|olo'gia *nf* archaeology. **~o'lo-gico** *a* archaeological. **~'ologo, -a** *nmf* archaeologist

ar'chetto *nm Mus* bow

architet'tare *vt fig* devise; **cosa state architettando?** *fig* what are you plotting?

archi'tet|to *nm* architect. **~'tonico** *a* architectural. **~'tura** *nf* architecture

archivi'are *vt* file; *Jur* close

ar'chivio *nm* archives *pl*; *Comput* file

archi'vista *nmf* filing clerk

ar'cigno *a* grim

arci'pelago *nm* archipelago

arci'vescovo *nm* archbishop

'arco *nm* arch; *Math* arc; (*arma, Mus*) bow; **nell'~ di una giornata/due mesi** in the space of a day/two months

arcoba'leno *nm* rainbow

arcu'a|re *vt* bend. **~rsi** *vr* bend. **~to** *a* bent, curved; ⟨*schiena di gatto*⟩ arched

ar'dente *a* burning; *fig* ardent. **~'mente** *adv* ardently

'ardere *vt/i* burn

ar'desia *nf* slate

ar'di|re *vi* dare. **~to** *a* daring; (*coraggioso*) bold; (*sfacciato*) impudent

ar'dore *nm* (*calore*) heat; *fig* ardour

'arduo *a* arduous; (*ripido*) steep

'area *nf* area. **~ di rigore** (*in calcio*) penalty area. **~ di servizio** service area

a'rena *nf* arena

are'narsi *vr* run aground; ⟨*fig: trattative*⟩ reach deadlock; **mi sono arenato** I'm stuck

'argano *nm* winch

argen'tato *a* silver-plated

argente'ria *nf* silver[ware]

ar'gento *nm* silver

ar'gil|la *nf* clay. **~'loso** *a* ⟨*terreno*⟩ clayey

argi'nare *vt* embank; *fig* hold in check, contain

'argine *nm* embankment; (*diga*) dike

argomen'tare *vi* argue

argo'mento *nm* argument; (*motivo*) reason; (*soggetto*) subject

argu'ire *vt* deduce

ar'gu|to *a* witty. **~zia** *nf* wit; (*battuta*) witticism

'aria *nf* air; (*aspetto*) appearance; *Mus* tune; **andare all'~** *fig* come to nothing; **avere l'~...** look...; **corrente** *nf* **d'~** draught; **mandare all'~ qcsa** *fig* ruin sth

aridità *nf* dryness

'arido *a* arid

arieggi'a|re *vt* air. **~to** *a* airy

ari'ete *nm* ram. **A~** *Astr* Aries

ari'etta *nf* (*brezza*) breeze

a'ringa *nf* herring

ari'oso *a* (*locale*) light and airy

aristo'cra|tico, -a *a* aristocratic ● *nmf* aristocrat. **~'zia** *nf* aristocracy arit'metica *nf* arithmetic

arlec'chino *nm* Harlequin; *fig* buffoon

'arma *nf* weapon; armi *pl* arms; (*forze armate*) [armed] forces; chiamare alle armi call up; sotto le armi in the army; alle prime armi *fig* inexperienced, fledg[e]ling. ~ da fuoco firearm. ~ impropria makeshift weapon. ~ a doppio taglio *fig* double-edged sword

armadi'etto *nm* locker, cupboard

ar'madio *nm* cupboard; (*guardaroba*) wardrobe

armamen'tario *nm* tools *pl*; *fig* paraphernalia

arma'mento *nm* armament; *Naut* fitting out

ar'ma|re *vt* arm; (*equipaggiare*) fit out; *Archit* reinforce. ~rsi *vr* arm oneself (di with). ~ta *nf* army; (*flotta*) fleet. ~'tore *nm* shipowner. ~'tura *nf* framework; (*impalcatura*) scaffolding; (*di guerriero*) armour

armeggi'are *vi fig* manoeuvre

armi'stizio *nm* armistice

armo'ni|a *nf* harmony. ar'monica *nf* ~ [a bocca] mouth organ. ar'monico *a* harmonic. ~'oso *a* harmonious

armoniz'zar|e *vt* harmonize ● *vi* match. ~si *vr* (*colori:*) go together, match

ar'nese *nm* tool; (*oggetto*) thing; (*congegno*) gadget; male in ~ in bad condition

'arnia *nf* beehive

a'roma *nm* aroma; aromi *pl* herbs. ~tera'pia *nf* aromatherapy

aro'matico *a* aromatic

aromatiz'zare *vt* flavour

'arpa *nf* harp

ar'peggio *nm* arpeggio

ar'pia *nf* harpy

arpi'one *nm* hook; (*pesca*) harpoon

arrabat'tarsi *vr* do all one can

arrabbi'a|rsi *vr* get angry. ~to *a* angry. ~'tura *nf* rage; prendersi un'~tura fly into a rage

arraf'fare *vt* grab

arrampi'ca|rsi *vr* climb [up]. ~ta *nf* climb. ~'tore, ~'trice *nmf* climber. ~'tore sociale social climber

arran'care *vi* limp, hobble; *fig* struggle, limp along

arrangia'mento *nm* arrangement

arrangi'ar|e *vt* arrange. ~si *vr* manage; ~si alla meglio get by; ar'rangiati! get on with it!

arra'parsi *vr fam* get randy

arre'care *vt* bring; (*causare*) cause

arreda'mento *nm* interior decoration; (*l'arredare*) furnishing; (*mobili ecc*) furnishings *pl*

arre'da|re *vt* furnish. ~'tore, ~'trice *nmf* interior designer. ar'redo *nm* furnishings *pl*

ar'rendersi *vr* surrender

arren'devo|le *a* (*persona*) yielding. ~'lezza *nf* softness

arre'star|e *vt* arrest; (*fermare*) stop. ~si *vr* halt. ar'resto *nm* stop; *Med, Jur* arrest; la dichiaro in [stato d']arresto you are under arrest; mandato di arresto warrant. arresti *pl* domiciliari *Jur* house arrest

arre'tra|re *vt/i* withdraw; pull back (*giocatore*). ~to *a* (*paese ecc*) backward; (*Mil: posizione*) rear; numero ~to (*di rivista*) back number; del lavoro ~to a backlog of work ● *nm* (*di stipendio*) back pay

arre'trati *nmpl* arrears

arricchi'mento *nm* enrichment

arric'chi|re *vt* enrich. ~rsi *vr* get rich. ~to, -a *nmf* nouveau riche

arricci'are *vt* curl; ~ il naso turn up one's nose

ar'ringa *nf* harangue; *Jur* closing address

arrischi'a|rsi *vr* dare. ~to *a* risky; (*imprudente*) rash

arri'va|re *vi* arrive; ~re a (*raggiungere*) reach; (*ridursi*) be reduced to. ~to, -a *a* successful; ben ~to! welcome! ● *nmf* successful person

arrive'derci *int* goodbye; ~ a domani see you tomorrow

arri'vis|mo *nm* social climbing; (*nel lavoro*) careerism. ~ta *nmf* social climber; (*nel lavoro*) careerist

ar'rivo *nm* arrival; *Sport* finish

arro'gan|te *a* arrogant. ~za *nf* arrogance

arro'garsi *vr* ~ il diritto di fare qcsa take it upon oneself to do sth

arrossa'mento *nm* reddening

arros'sar|e *vt* make red, redden (*occhi*). ~si *vr* go red

arros'sire *vi* blush, go red

arro'stire *vt* roast; toast (*pane*); (*ai ferri*) grill. ar'rosto *a & nm* roast

arroto'lare *vt* roll up

arroton'dar|e *vt* round; *Math ecc* round off. ~si *vr* become round; (*persona:*) get plump

arrovel'larsi *vr* ~ **il cervello** rack one's brains

arroven'ta|re *vt* make red-hot. **~rsi** *vr* become red-hot. **~to** *a* red-hot

arruffa|re *vt* ruffle; *fig* confuse. **~to** *a* ⟨*capelli*⟩ ruffled

arruffianarsi *vr* ~ **qcno** *fig* butter sb up

arruggi'ni|re *vt* rust. **~rsi** *vr* go rusty; *fig* ⟨*fisicamente*⟩ stiffen up; ⟨*conoscenze:*⟩ go rusty. **~to** *a* rusty

arruola'mento *nm* enlistment

arruo'lar|e *vt/i.* **~si** *vr* enlist

arse'nale *nm* arsenal; ⟨*cantiere*⟩ [naval] dockyard

ar'senico *nm* arsenic

'arso *pp di* **ardere** ● *a* burnt; ⟨*arido*⟩ dry. **ar'sura** *nf* burning heat; ⟨*sete*⟩ parching thirst

'arte *nf* art; ⟨*abilità*⟩ craftsmanship; **le belle arti** the fine arts. **arti figurative** figurative arts

arte'fa|re *vt* adulterate ⟨*vino*⟩; disguise ⟨*voce*⟩. **~tto** *a* fake; ⟨*vino*⟩ adulterated

ar'tefice *nmf* craftsman; craftswoman; *fig* author

ar'teria *nf* artery. ~ **[stradale]** arterial road

arterioscle'rosi *nf* arteriosclerosis, hardening of the arteries

'artico *a & nm* Arctic

artico'la|re *a* articular ● *vt* articulate; ⟨*suddividere*⟩ divide. **~rsi** *vr* *fig* **~rsi in** consist of. **~to** *a* *Auto* articulated; *fig* well-constructed. **~zi'one** *nf Anat* articulation

ar'ticolo *nm* article. ~ **di fondo** leader

artifici'ale *a* artificial

arti'fici|o *nm* artifice; ⟨*affettazione*⟩ affectation. **~'oso** *a* artful; ⟨*affettato*⟩ affected

artigia'nal|e *a* made by hand; *hum* amateurish. **~'mente** *adv* with craftsmanship; *hum* amateurishly

artigi|a'nato *nm* craftsmanship; ⟨*ceto*⟩ craftsmen *pl.* **~'ano, -a** *nm* craftsman ● *nf* craftswoman

artigli'ere *nm* artilleryman. **~e'ria** *nf* artillery

ar'tiglio *nm* claw; *fig* clutch

ar'tist|a *nmf* artist. **~ica'mente** *adv* artistically. **~ico** *a* artistic

'arto *nm* limb

ar'trite *nf* arthritis

ar'trosi *nf* rheumatism

arzigogo'lato *a* fantastic, bizarre

ar'zillo *a* sprightly

a'scella *nf* armpit

ascen'den|te *a* ascending ● *nm* ⟨*antenato*⟩ ancestor; ⟨*influenza*⟩ ascendancy; *Astr* ascendant

ascensi'one *nf* ascent; **l'A~** the Ascension

ascen'sore *nm* lift, elevator *Am*

a'scesa *nf* ascent; ⟨*al trono*⟩ accession; ⟨*al potere*⟩ rise

a'scesso *nm* abscess

'sceta *nmf* ascetic

'ascia *nf* axe

asciugabianche'ria *nm inv* ⟨*stenditoio*⟩ clothes horse

asciugaca'pelli *nm inv* hair dryer, hairdresser

asciuga'mano *nm* towel

asciu'gar|e *vt* dry. **~si** *vr* dry oneself; ⟨*diventare asciutto*⟩ dry up

asci'utto *a* dry; ⟨*magro*⟩ wiry; ⟨*risposta*⟩ curt; **essere all'~** *fig* be hard up

ascol'ta|re *vt* listen to ● *vi* listen. **~'tore, ~'trice** *nmf* listener

a'scolto *nm* listening; **dare** ~ **a** pay attention to; **mettersi in** ~ *Radio* tune in

asfal'tare *vt* asphalt

a'sfalto *nm* asphalt

asfis'si|a *nf* asphyxia. **~'ante** *a* ⟨*caldo*⟩ oppressive; ⟨*fig: persona*⟩ annoying. **~'are** *vt* asphyxiate; *fig* annoy

'Asia *nf* Asia. **asi'atico, -a** *a & nmf* Asian

a'silo *nm* shelter; ⟨*d'infanzia*⟩ nursery school. ~ **nido** day nursery. ~ **politico** political asylum

asim'metrico *a* asymmetrical

a'sino *nm* donkey; ⟨*fig: persona stupida*⟩ ass

'asma *nf* asthma. **a'smatico** *a* asthmatic

asoci'ale *a* asocial

'asola *nf* buttonhole

a'sparagi *nmpl* asparagus *sg*

a'sparago *nm* asparagus spear

asperità *nf inv* harshness; ⟨*di terreno*⟩ roughness

aspet'ta|re *vt* wait for; ⟨*prevedere*⟩ expect; **~re un bambino** be expecting [a baby]; **fare ~re qcno** keep sb waiting ● *vi* wait. **~rsi** *vr* expect. **~'tiva** *nf* expectation

a'spetto[1] *nm* appearance; ⟨*di problema*⟩ aspect; **di bell'~** good-looking

a'spetto[2] *nm* **sala** *nf* **d'~** waiting room

aspi'rante *a* aspiring; ⟨*pompa*⟩ suction *attrib* ● *nmf* ⟨*a un posto*⟩ applicant;

(*al trono*) aspirant; **gli aspiranti al titolo** the contenders for the title

aspira'polvere *nm inv* vacuum cleaner

aspi'ra|re *vt* inhale; *Mech* suck in ● *vi* ~**re a** aspire to. ~**'tore** *nm* extractor fan. ~**zi'one** *nf* inhalation; *Mech* suction; (*ambizione*) ambition

aspi'rina *nf* aspirin

aspor'tare *vt* take away

aspra'mente *adv* (*duramente*) severely

a'sprezza *nf* (*al gusto*) sourness; (*di clima*) severity; (*di suono*) harshness; (*di odore*) pungency

'aspro *a* (*al gusto*) sour; ‹*clima*› severe; ‹*suono, parole*› harsh; ‹*odore*› pungent; ‹*litigio*› bitter

assag|gi'are *vt* taste. ~**'gini** *nmpl Culin* samples. **as'saggio** *nm* tasting; (*piccola quantità*) taste

as'sai *adv* very; (*moltissimo*) very much; (*abbastanza*) enough

assa'li|re *vt* attack. ~**'tore**, ~**'trice** *nmf* assailant

as'salto *nm* attack; **prendere d'~** · storm ‹*città*›; *fig* mob ‹*persona*›; hold up ‹*banca*›

assapo'rare *vt* savour

assassi'nare *vt* murder, assassinate; *fig* murder

assas'sin|io *nm* murder, assassination. ~**o, -a** *a* murderous ● *nm* murderer ● *nf* murderess

'asse *nf* board ● *nm Techn* axle; *Math* axis. ~ **da stiro** ironing board

assecon'dare *vt* satisfy; (*favorire*) support

assedi'are *vt* besiege. **as'sedio** *nm* siege

assegna'mento *nm* allotment; **fare ~ su** rely on

asse'gna|re *vt* allot; award ‹*premio*›. ~**'tario** *nmf* recipient. ~**zi'one** *nf* (*di alloggio, denaro, borsa di studio*) allocation

as'segno *nm* allowance; (*bancario*) cheque; **contro ~** cash on delivery. ~ **circolare** bank draft. **assegni** *pl* **familiari** family allowance. ~ **non trasferibile** cheque made out to 'account payee only'

assem'blea *nf* assembly; (*adunanza*) gathering

assembra'mento *nm* gathering

assen'nato *a* sensible

as'senso *nm* assent

assen'tarsi *vr* go away; (*da stanza*) leave the room

as'sen|te *a* absent; (*distratto*) absent-minded ● *nmf* absentee. ~**te'ismo** *nm* absenteeism. ~**te'ista** *nmf* frequent absentee. ~**za** *nf* absence; (*mancanza*) lack

asse'r|ire *vt* assert. ~**'tivo** *a* assertive. ~**zi'one** *nf* assertion

assesso'rato *nm* department

asses'sore *nm* councillor

assesta'mento *nm* settlement

asse'star|e *vt* arrange; ~**e un colpo** deal a blow. ~**si** *vr* settle oneself

asse'tato *a* parched

as'setto *nm* order; *Naut, Aeron* trim

assicu'ra|re *vt* assure; *Comm* insure; register ‹*posta*›; (*fissare*) secure; (*accertare*) ensure. ~**rsi** *vr* (*con contratto*) insure oneself; (*legarsi*) fasten oneself; ~**rsi che** make sure that. ~**'tivo** *a* insurance *attrib*. ~**'to** ~ **'trice** *nmf* insurance agent ● *a* insurance *attrib*. ~**zi'one** *nf* assurance; (*contratto*) insur-a. ?

assidera'mento *nm* exposure. **asside'rato** *a Med* suffering from exposure; *fam* frozen

assidu|a'mente *adv* assiduously. ~**ità** *nf* assiduity

as'siduo *a* assiduous; ‹*cliente*› regular

assil'lante *a* ‹*persona, pensiero*› nagging

assil'lare *vt* pester

as'sillo *nm* worry

assimi'la|re *vt* assimilate. ~**zi'one** *nf* assimilation

as'sise *nfpl* assizes; **Corte d'A~** Court of Assize[s]

assi'sten|te *nmf* assistant. ~**te sociale** social worker. ~**te di volo** flight attendant. ~**za** *nf* assistance; (*presenza*) presence. ~**za sociale** social work

assistenzi'a|le *a* welfare *attrib*. ~**'lismo** *nm* welfare

as'sistere *vt* assist; ‹*curare*› nurse ● *vi* ~ **a** (*essere presente*) be present at; watch ‹*spettacolo ecc*›

'asso *nm* ace; **piantare in ~** leave in the lurch

associ'a|re *vt* join; (*collegare*) associate. ~**rsi** *vr* join forces; *Comm* enter into partnership. ~**rsi a** join; subscribe to ‹*giornale ecc*›. ~**zi'one** *nf* association

assogget'tar|e *vt* subject. ~**si** *vr* submit

asso'lato *a* sunny

assol'dare *vt* recruit

as'solo *nm Mus* solo

as'solto *pp di* **assolvere**

assoluta'mente *adv* absolutely

assolu'tismo *nm* absolutism

asso'lu|to *a* absolute. **~zi'one** *nf* acquittal; *Relig* absolution

as'solvere *vt* perform ‹*compito*›; *Jur* acquit; *Relig* absolve

assomigli'ar|e *vi* **~e a** be like, resemble. **~si** *vr* resemble each other

assom'marsi *vr* combine; **~ a qcsa** add to sth

asso'nanza *nf* assonance

asson'nato *a* drowsy

asso'pirsi *vr* doze off

assor'bente *a & nm* absorbent. **~ igienico** sanitary towel

assor'bire *vt* absorb

assor'da|re *vt* deafen. **~nte** *a* deafening

assorti'mento *nm* assortment

assor'ti|re *vt* match ‹*colori*›. **~to** *a* assorted; ‹*colori, persone*› matched

as'sorto *a* engrossed

assottigli'ar|e *vt* make thin; (*aguzzare*) sharpen; (*ridurre*) reduce. **~si** *vr* grow thin; ‹*finanze:*› be whittled away

assue'fa|re *vt* accustom. **~rsi** *vr* **~rsi a** get used to. **~tto** *a* (*a caffè, aspirina*) immune to the effects; (*a droga*) addicted. **~zi'one** *nf* (*a caffè, aspirina*) immunity to the effects; (*a droga*) addiction

as'sumere *vt* assume; take on ‹*impiegato*›; **~** informazioni make inquiries

as'sunto *pp di* **assumere** ● *nm* task. **assunzi'one** *nf* (*di impiegato*) employment

assurdità *nf inv* absurdity; **~ pl** nonsense

as'surdo *a* absurd

'asta *nf* pole; *Mech* bar; *Comm* auction; **a mezz'~** at half-mast

a'stemio *a* abstemious

aste'n|ersi *vr* abstain (**da** from). **~si'one** *nf* abstention

aste'nuto, -a *nmf* abstainer

aste'risco *nm* asterisk

astig'ma|tico *a* astigmatic. **~'tismo** *nm* astigmatism

asti'nenza *nf* abstinence; **crisi di ~** cold turkey

'asti|o *nm* rancour; **avere ~o contro qcno** bear sb a grudge. **~'oso** *a* resentful

a'stratto *a* abstract

astrin'gente *a & nm* astringent

'astro *nm* star

astrolo'gia *nf* astrology. **a'strologo, -a** *nmf* astrologer

astro'nauta *nmf* astronaut

astro'nave *nf* spaceship

astrono'mia *nf* astronomy. **~o'nomico** *a* astronomical. **a'stronomo** *nm* astronomer

astrusità *nf* abstruseness

a'stuccio *nm* case

a'stu|to *a* shrewd; (*furbo*) cunning. **~zia** *nf* shrewdness; (*azione*) trick

ate'ismo *nm* atheism

A'tene *nf* Athens

'ateo, -a *a & nmf* atheist

a'tipico *a* atypical

at'lan|te *nm* atlas. **~ico** *a* Atlantic; **l'[Oceano] A~ico** the Atlantic [Ocean]

at'let|a *nmf* athlete. **~ica** *nf* athletics *sg*. **~ica leggera** track and field events. **~ica pesante** *weight-lifting, boxing, wrestling, etc*. **~ico** *a* athletic

atmo'sfer|a *nf* atmosphere. **~ico** *a* atmospheric

a'tomic|a *nf* atom bomb. **~o** *a* atomic

'atomo *nm* atom

'atrio *nm* entrance hall

a'troc|e *a* atrocious; (*terrible*) dreadful. **~ità** *nf inv* atrocity

atrofiz'zarsi *vr Med, fig* atrophy

attaccabot'toni *nmf inv* [crashing] bore

attacca'brighe *nmf inv* troublemaker

attacca'mento *nm* attachment

attacca'panni *nm inv* [coat-]hanger; (*a muro*) clothes hook

attac'car|e *vt* attach; (*legare*) tie; (*appendere*) hang; (*cucire*) sew on; (*contagiare*) pass on; (*assalire*) attack; (*iniziare*) start ● *vi* stick; (*diffondersi*) catch on. **~si** *vr* cling; (*affezionarsi*) become attached; (*litigare*) quarrel

attacca'ticcio *a* sticky

at'tacco *nm* attack; (*punto d'unione*) junction

attar'darsi *vr* stay late; (*indugiare*) linger

attec'chire *vi* take; ‹*moda ecc:*› catch on

atteggia'mento *nm* attitude

atteggi'ar|e *vt* assume. **~si** *vr* **~si a** pose as

attem'pato *a* elderly

at'tender|e *vt* wait for ● *vi* **~e a** attend to. **~si** *vr* expect

atten'dibil|e *a* reliable. **~ità** *nf* reliability

atte'nersi *vr* **~ a** stick to

attenta'mente *adv* attentively

atten'ta|re *vi* ~re a make an attempt on. ~to *nm* act of violence; (*contro politico ecc*) assassination attempt. ~'tore, ~'trice *nmf* (*a scopo politico*) terrorist

at'tento *a* attentive; (*accurato*) careful; ~! look out!; **stare** ~ pay attention

attenu'ante *nf* extenuating circumstance

attenu'a|re *vt* attenuate; (*minimizzare*) minimize; subdue (*colori ecc*); calm (*dolore*); soften (*colpo*). ~rsi *vr* diminish. ~zi'one *nf* lessening

attenzi'one *nf* attention; ~! watch out!

atter'ra|ggio *nm* landing. ~re ● vi knock down ● *vi* land

atter'rir|e *vt* terrorize. ~si *vr* be terrified

at'tes|a *nf* waiting; (*aspettativa*) expectation; **in** ~**a di** waiting for. ~o *pp di* **attendere**

atte'sta|re *vt* state; (*certificare*) certify. ~to *nm* certificate. ~zi'one *nf* certificate; (*dichiarazione*) declaration

'attico *nm* attic

at'tiguo *a* adjacent

attil'lato *a* (*vestito*) close-fitting; (*elegante*) dressed up

'attimo *nm* moment

atti'nente *a* ~ a pertaining to

at'tingere *vt* draw; *fig* obtain

atti'rare *vt* attract

atti'tudine *nf* (*disposizione*) aptitude; (*atteggiamento*) attitude

atti'v|are *vt* activate. ~ismo *nm* activism. ~ista *nmf* activist. **attività** *nf inv* activity; *Comm* assets *pl*. ~o *a* active; *Comm* productive ● *nm* assets *pl*

attiz'za|re *vt* poke; *fig* stir up. ~'toio *nm* poker

'atto *nm* act; (*azione*) action; *Comm, Jur* deed; (*certificato*) certificate; **atti** *pl* (*di società ecc*) proceedings; **mettere in** ~ put into effect

at'tonito *a* astonished

attorcigli'ar|e *vt* twist. ~si *vr* get twisted

at'tore *nm* actor

attorni'ar|e *vt* surround. ~si *vr* ~si di surround oneself with

at'torno *adv* around, about ● *prep* ~ a around, about

attrac'care *vt/i* dock

attra'ente *a* attractive

at'tra|rre *vt* attract. ~rsi *vr* be attracted to each other. ~t'tiva *nf* charm.

~zi'one *nf* attraction. ~zioni turisti-che tourist attractions

attraversa'mento *nm* (*di strada*) crossing. ~ **pedonale** pedestrian crossing, crosswalk *Am*

attraver'sare *vt* cross; (*passare*) go through

attra'verso *prep* through; (*obliquamente*) across

attrez'za|re *vt* equip; *Naut* rig. ~rsi *vr* kit oneself out; ~'tura *nf* equipment; *Naut* rigging

at'trezzo *nm* tool; **attrezzi** *pl* equipment; *Sport* appliances *pl*; *Theat* props *pl*

attribu'ir|e *vt* attribute. ~si *vr* ascribe to oneself; ~si il merito di claim credit for

attri'bu|to *nm* attribute. ~zi'one *nf* attribution

at'trice *nf* actress

at'trito *nm* friction

attu'abile *a* feasible

attu'al|e *a* present; (*di attualità*) topical; (*effettivo*) actual. ~ità *nf* topicality; (*avvenimento*) news; **programma di** ~ità current affairs programme. ~iz'zare *vt* update. ~'mente *adv* at present

attu'a|re *vt* carry out. ~rsi *vr* be realized. ~zi'one *nf* carrying out

attu'tire *vt* deaden; ~ il colpo soften the blow

au'dac|e *a* daring, bold; (*insolente*) audacious;. ~ia *nf* daring, boldness; (*insolenza*) audacity

'audience *nf inv* (*telespettatori*) audience

'audio *nm* audio

audiovi'sivo *a* audiovisual

audi'torio *nm* auditorium

audizi'one *nf* audition; *Jur* hearing

'auge *nm* height; **essere in** ~ be popular

augu'rar|e *vt* wish. ~si *vr* hope. **au'gurio** *nm* wish; (*presagio*) omen; auguri! all the best!; (*a Natale*) Happy Christmas!; **tanti auguri** best wishes

'aula *nf* classroom; (*università*) lecture-hall; (*sala*) hall. ~ **magna** (*in università*) great hall. ~ **del tribunale** courtroom

aumen'tare *vt/i* increase. **au'mento** *nm* increase; (*di stipendio*) [pay] rise

au'reola *nf* halo

au'rora *nf* dawn

auscul'tare *vt Med* auscultate

ausili'are *a* & *nmf* auxiliary

auspicabile *a* **è ~ che...** it is to be hoped that...

auspi'care *vt* hope for

au'spicio *nm* omen; **auspici** (*pl: protezione*) auspices

austerità *nf* austerity

au'stero *a* austere.

Au'strali|a *nf* Australia. **a~'ano, -a** *a* & *nmf* Australian

'Austria *nf* Austria. **au'striaco, -a** *a* & *nmf* Austrian

autar'chia *nf* autarchy. **au'tarchico** *a* autarchic

autentic|are *vt* authenticate. **~ità** *nf* authenticity

au'tentico *a* authentic; (*vero*) true

au'tista *nm* driver

'auto *nf inv* car

autoabbron'zante *nm* self-tan ● *a* self-tanning

autoambu'lanza *nf* ambulance

autoartico'lato *nm* articulated lorry

autobio|gra'fia *nf* autobiography. **~'grafico** *a* autobiographical

auto'botte *nf* tanker

'autobus *nm inv* bus

auto'carro *nm* lorry

autocommiserazi'one *nf* self-pity

autoconcessio'nario *nm* car dealer

auto'critica *nf* self-criticism

autodi'datta *nmf* self-educated person, autodidact

autodi'fesa *nf* self-defence

auto'gol *nm inv* own goal

au'tografo *a* & *nm* autograph

autolesio'nis|mo *nm fig* selfdestruction. **~tico** *a* self-destructive

auto'linea *nf* bus line

au'toma *nm* robot

automatica'mente *adv* automatically

auto'matico *a* automatic ● *nm* (*bottone*) press-stud; (*fucile*) automatic

automatiz'za|re *vt* automate. **~zi'one** *nf* automation

auto'mezzo *nm* motor vehicle

auto'mobi|le *nf* [motor] car. **~'lismo** *nm* motoring. **~'lista** *nmf* motorist. **~'listico** *a* ⟨*industria*⟩ automobile attrib

autonoma'mente *adv* autonomously

autono'mia *nf* autonomy; *Auto* range; (*di laptop, cellulare*) battery life. **au'tonomo** *a* autonomous

'auto+ *pref* self+

autop'sia *nf* autopsy

auto'radio *nf inv* car radio; (*veicolo*) radio car

au'tore, -'trice *nmf* author; (*di pitture*) painter; (*di furto ecc*) perpetrator; **quadro d'~** genuine master

auto'revo|le *a* authoritative; (*che ha influenza*) influential. **~'lezza** *nf* authority

autori'messa *nf* garage

autori|tà *nf inv* authority. **~'tario** *a* autocratic. **~ta'rismo** *nm* authoritarianism

autori'tratto *nm* self-portrait

autoriz'za|re *vt* authorize. **~zi'one** *nf* authorization

auto'scontro *nm inv* bumper car

autoscu'ola *nf* driving school

auto'stop *nm* hitch-hiking; **fare l'~** hitch-hike. **~'pista** *nmf* hitch-hiker

auto'strada *nf* motorway

autostra'dale *a* motorway *attrib*

autosuffici'en|te *a* self-sufficient. **~za** *nf* self-sufficiency

autotrasporta'|tore, ~'trice *nmf* haulier, carrier

auto'treno *nm* articulated lorry, roadtrain

autove'icolo *nm* motor vehicle

auto'velox *nm inv* speed camera

autovet'tura *nf* motor vehicle

autun'nale *a* autumn[al]

au'tunno *nm* autumn

aval'lare *vt* endorse, back ⟨*cambiale*⟩; *fig* endorse

a'vallo *nm* endorsement

avam'braccio *nm* forearm

avangu'ardia *nf* vanguard; *fig* avant-garde; **essere all'~** be in the forefront; *Techn* be at the leading edge

a'vanti *adv* (*in avanti*) forward; (*davanti*) in front; (*prima*) before; **~!** (*entrate*) come in!; (*suvvia*) come on!; (*su semaforo*) cross now, walk *Am*; **va'~!** go ahead!; **andare ~** (*precedere*) go ahead; ⟨*orologio:*⟩ be fast; **~ e indietro** backwards and forwards ● *a* ⟨*precedente*⟩ before ● *prep* **~ a** before; (*in presenza di*) in the presence of

avanti'eri *adv* the day before yesterday

avanza'mento *nm* progress; (*promozione*) promotion

avan'za|re *vi* advance; (*progredire*) progress; (*essere d'avanzo*) be left [over] ● *vt* advance; (*superare*) surpass; (*promuovere*) promote. **~rsi** *vr* advance; (*avvicinarsi*) approach. **~ta** *nf* advance. **~to** *a* advanced; (*nella notte*) late; **in**

età ~ta elderly. **a'vanzo** nm remainder; Comm surplus; **avanzi** pl ⟨rovine⟩ remains; ⟨di cibo⟩ left-overs

ava'ri|a nf ⟨di motore⟩ engine failure. **~'ato** a ⟨frutta, verdura⟩ rotten; ⟨carne⟩ tainted

ava'rizia nf avarice. **a'varo, -a** a stingy ● nmf miser

a'vena nf oats pl

a'vere vt have; ⟨ottenere⟩ get; ⟨indossare⟩ wear; ⟨provare⟩ feel; **ho trent'anni** I'm thirty; **ha avuto il posto** he got the job; **~ fame/freddo** be hungry/cold; **ho mal di denti** I've got toothache; **cos'ha a che fare con lui?** what has it got to do with him?; **~ da fare** be busy; **che hai?** what's the matter with you?; **nei hai per molto?** will you be long?; **quanti ne abbiamo oggi?** what date is it today?; **avercela con qcno** have it in for sb ● v aux have; **non l'ho visto** I haven't seen him; **lo hai visto?** have you seen him?; **l'ho visto ieri** I saw him yesterday. **averi** nmpl wealth sg

avia'|tore nm flyer, aviator. **~zi'one** nf aviation; Mil Air Force

avidità nf avidness. **'avido** a avid

avio'getto nm jet

'avo, -a nmf ancestor

avo'cado nm avocado

a'vorio nm ivory

Avv. abbr **avvocato**

avva'lersi vr avail oneself (**of** di)

avvalla'mento nm depression

avvalo'rare vt bear out ⟨tesi⟩; endorse ⟨documento⟩; ⟨accrescere⟩ enhance

avvam'pare vi flare up; ⟨arrossire⟩ blush

avvantaggi'ar|e vt favour. **~si** vr **~si di** benefit from; ⟨approfittare⟩ take advantage of

avve'd|ersi vr ⟨accorgersi⟩ notice; ⟨capire⟩ realize. **~uto** a shrewd

avvelena'mento nm poisoning

avvele'na|re vt poison. **~rsi** vr poison oneself. **~to** a poisoned

avve'nente a attractive

avveni'mento nm event

avve'nire[1] vi happen; ⟨aver luogo⟩ take place

avve'ni|re[2] nm future. **~'ristico** a futuristic

avven'ta|rsi vr fling oneself. **~to** a ⟨decisione⟩ rash

av'vento nm advent; Relig Advent

avven'tore nm regular customer

avven'tu|ra nf adventure; ⟨amorosa⟩ affair; **d'~** ⟨film⟩ adventure attrib.

~'rarsi vr venture. **~ri'ero, -a** nm adventurer ● nf adventuress. **~'roso** a adventurous

avve'ra|bile a ⟨previsione⟩ that may come true. **~rsi** vr come true

av'verbio nm adverb

avver'sar|e vt oppose. **~io, -a** a opposing ● nmf opponent

avversi|'one nf aversion. **~tà** nf inv adversity

av'verso a ⟨sfavorevole⟩ adverse; ⟨contrario⟩ averse

avver'tenza nf ⟨cura⟩ care; ⟨avvertimento⟩ warning; ⟨avviso⟩ notice; ⟨premessa⟩ foreword; **avvertenze** pl ⟨istruzioni⟩ instructions

avverti'mento nm warning

avver'tire vt warn; ⟨informare⟩ inform; ⟨sentire⟩ feel

avvez'zar|e vt accustom. **~si** vr accustom oneself. **av'vezzo** a **avvezzo a** used to

avvia'mento nm starting; Comm goodwill

avvi'a|re vt start. **~rsi** vr set out. **~to** a under way; **bene ~to** thriving

avvicenda'mento nm ⟨in agricoltura⟩ rotation; ⟨nel lavoro⟩ replacement

avvicen'darsi vr take turns, alternate

avvicina'mento nm approach

avvici'nar|e vt bring near; approach ⟨persona⟩. **~si** vr come nearer, approach; **~si a** come nearer to, approach

avvi'lente a demoralizing; ⟨umiliante⟩ humiliating

avvili'mento nm despondency; ⟨degradazione⟩ degradation

avvi'li|re vt dishearten; ⟨degradare⟩ degrade. **~rsi** vr lose heart; ⟨degradarsi⟩ degrade oneself. **~to** a disheartened; ⟨degradato⟩ degraded

avvilup'par|e vt envelop. **~si** vr wrap oneself up; ⟨aggrovigliarsi⟩ get entangled

avvinaz'zato a drunk

avvin'cente a charming; ⟨libro ecc⟩ enthralling. **av'vincere** vt charm

avvinghi'ar|e vt clutch. **~si** vr cling

av'vio nm start-up; **dare l'~ a qcsa** get sth under way; **prendere l'~** get under way

avvi'sare vt inform; ⟨mettere in guardia⟩ warn

av'viso nm notice; ⟨annuncio⟩ announcement; ⟨avvertimento⟩ warning; ⟨pubblicitario⟩ advertisement; **a mio ~**

in my opinion. **~ di garanzia** *Jur* notification that one is to be the subject of a legal enquiry

avvi'stare *vt* catch sight of

avvi'tare *vt* screw in; screw down ⟨coperchio⟩

avviz'zire *vi* wither

avvo'cato *nm* lawyer; *fig* advocate. **~'tura** *nf* legal profession

av'volger|e *vt* wrap [up]. **~si** *vr* wrap oneself up

avvol'gibile *nm* roller blind

avvol'toio *nm* vulture

aza'lea *nf* azalea

azi'en|da *nf* business, firm. **~ agricola** farm. **~ di soggiorno** tourist bureau. **~'dale** *a* ⟨politica, dirigente⟩ company *attrib*; ⟨giornale⟩ in-house

aziona'mento *nm* operation

azio'nare *vt* operate

azio'nario *a* share *attrib*

azi'one *nf* action; *Fin* share; **d'~** ⟨romanzo, film⟩ action[-packed]. **azio'nista** *nmf* shareholder

a'zoto *nm* nitrogen

azzan'nare *vt* seize with its teeth; sink its teeth into ⟨gamba⟩

azzar'd|are *vt* risk. **~arsi** *vr* dare. **~ato** *a* risky; ⟨precipitoso⟩ rash. **az'zardo** *nm* hazard; **gioco d'azzardo** game of chance

azzec'care *vt* hit; ⟨fig: indovinare⟩ guess

azzuf'farsi *vr* come to blows

az'zur|ro *a & nm* blue; **il principe ~** Prince Charming. **~'rognolo** *a* bluish

Bb

bab'beo *a* foolish ● *nm* idiot

'babbo *nm fam* dad, daddy. **B~ Natale** Father Christmas

bab'buccia *nf* slipper

babbu'ino *nm* baboon

ba'bordo *nm Naut* port side

'babysitter *nf inv* baby-sitter; **fare la ~** babysit

ba'cato *a* wormeaten

'bacca *nf* berry

baccalà *nm inv* dried salted cod

bac'cano *nm* din

bac'cello *nm* pod

bac'chetta *nf* rod; ⟨magica⟩ wand; ⟨di direttore d'orchestra⟩ baton; ⟨di tamburo⟩ drumstick

ba'checa *nf* showcase; ⟨in ufficio⟩ notice board. **~ elettronica** *Comput* bulletin board

bacia'mano *nm* kiss on the hand; **fare il ~ a qcno** kiss sb's hand

baci'ar|e *vt* kiss. **~si** *vr* kiss [each other]

ba'cillo *nm* bacillus

baci'nella *nf* basin

ba'cino *nm* basin; *Anat* pelvis; ⟨di porto⟩ dock; ⟨di minerali⟩ field

'bacio *nm* kiss

'baco *nm* worm. **~ da seta** silkworm

ba'cucco *a* **un vecchio ~** a senile old man

'bada *nf* **tenere qcno a ~** keep sb at bay

ba'dare *vi* take care (**a** of); ⟨fare attenzione⟩ look out; **bada ai fatti tuoi!** mind your own business!

ba'dia *nf* abbey

ba'dile *nm* shovel

'badminton *nm inv* badminton

'baffi *nmpl* moustache *sg*; ⟨di animale⟩ whiskers; **mi fa un baffo** I don't give a damn; **ridere sotto i ~** laugh up one's sleeve

baf'futo *a* moustached

ba'gagli *nmpl* luggage, baggage. **~'aio** *nm Rail* luggage van; *Auto* boot

ba'gaglio *nm* luggage; **un ~** a piece of luggage. **~ a mano** hand luggage, hand baggage

baggia'nata *nf* **non dire baggianate** don't talk nonsense

bagli'ore *nm* glare; ⟨improvviso⟩ flash; ⟨fig: di speranza⟩ glimmer

ba'gnante *nmf* bather

ba'gna|re *vt* wet; ⟨inzuppare⟩ soak; ⟨immergere⟩ dip; ⟨innaffiare⟩ water; ⟨mare, lago:⟩ wash; ⟨fiume:⟩ flow through. **~rsi** *vr* get wet; ⟨al mare ecc⟩ swim, bathe. **~to** *a* wet

ba'gnino, -a *nmf* life guard

'bagno *nm* bath; (*stanza*) bathroom; (*gabinetto*) toilet; (*in casa*) toilet, bathroom; (*al mare*) swim, bathe; **bagni** *pl* (*stabilimento*) lido; **fare il ~** have a bath; (*nel mare ecc*) [have a] swim *or* bathe; **andare in ~** go to the bathroom *or* toilet; **mettere a ~** soak. **~ turco** Turkish bath

bagna'sciuga *nm inv* edge of the water, waterline

bagnoma'ria *nm* **cuocere a ~** cook in a double saucepan

bagnoschi'uma *nm inv* bubble bath

'baia *nf* bay

baio'netta *nf* bayonet

'baita *nf* mountain chalet

bala'ustra, balaus'trata *nf* balustrade

balbet't|are *vt/i* stammer; (*bambino:*) babble. **~io** *nm* stammering; babble

bal'buzi|e *nf* stutter. **~'ente** *a* stuttering ● *nmf* stutterer

Bal'can|i *nmpl* Balkans. **b~ico** *a* Balkan

balco'nata *nf* *Theat* balcony, dress circle

balcon'cino *nm* **reggiseno a ~** underwired bra

bal'cone *nm* balcony

baldac'chino *nm* canopy; **letto a ~** four-poster bed

bal'dan|za *nf* boldness. **~'zoso** *a* bold

bal'doria *nf* revelry; **far ~** have a riotous time

Bale'ari *nfpl* **le [isole] ~** the Balearics, the Balearic Islands

ba'lena *nf* whale

bale'nare *vi* lighten; *fig* flash; **mi è balenata un'idea** I've just had an idea

bale'niera *nf* whaler

ba'leno *nm* **in un ~** in a flash

ba'lera *nf* dance hall

'balia[1] *nf* wetnurse

ba'lia[2] *nf* **in ~ di** at the mercy of

ba'listico *a* ballistic; **perito ~** ballistics expert

'balla *nf* bale; (*fam: frottola*) tall story

bal'labile *a* good for dancing to

bal'la|re *vi* dance. **~ta** *nf* ballad

balla'toio *nm* (*nelle scale*) landing

balle'rino, -a *nmf* dancer; (*classico*) ballet dancer; **ballerina** (*classica*) ballet dancer, ballerina

bal'letto *nm* ballet

bal'lista *nmf* *fam* bull-shitter

'ballo *nm* dance; (*il ballare*) dancing; **sala da ~** ballroom; **essere in ~** (*la-*

voro, vita:) be at stake; (*persona:*) be committed; **tirare qcno in ~** involve sb

ballonzo'lare *vi* skip about

ballo'taggio *nm* second count (*of votes*)

balne'a|re *a* bathing *attrib*. **stagione ~** swimming season. **stazione ~** seaside resort. **~zi'one** *nf* **è vietata la ~zione** no swimming

ba'lordo *a* foolish; (*stordito*) stunned; **tempo ~** nasty weather

'balsamo *nm* balsam; (*per capelli*) conditioner; (*lenimento*) remedy

'baltico *a* Baltic. **il [mar] B~** the Baltic [Sea]

balu'ardo *nm* bulwark

'balza *nf* crag; (*di abito*) flounce

bal'zano *a* (*idea*) weird

bal'zare *vi* bounce; (*saltare*) jump; **~ in piedi** leap to one's feet. **'balzo** *nm* bounce; (*salto*) jump; **prendere la palla al balzo** seize an opportunity

bam'bagia *nf* cotton wool; **vivere nella ~** *fig* be in clover

bambi'nata *nf* childish thing to do/say

bam'bi|no, -a *nmf* child; (*appena nato*) baby; **avere un ~no** have a baby. **~'none** *pej* big *or* overgrown child

bam'boccio *nm* chubby child; (*sciocco*) simpleton; (*fantoccio*) rag doll

'bambo|la *nf* doll. **~'lotto** *nm* male doll

bambù *nm* bamboo

ba'nal|e *a* banal; **~ità** *nf inv* banality; **~iz'zare** *vt* trivialize

ba'nan|a *nf* banana. **~o** *nm* banana-tree

'banca *nf* bank. **~ [di] dati** databank

banca'rella *nf* stall

ban'cario, -a *a* banking *attrib*; **trasferimento ~** bank transfer ● *nmf* bank employee

banca'rotta *nf* bankruptcy; **fare ~** go bankrupt

banchet'tare *vi* banquet. **ban'chetto** *nm* banquet

banchi'ere *nm* banker

ban'china *nf* *Naut* quay; (*in stazione*) platform; (*di strada*) path; **~ non transitabile** soft verge

ban'chisa *nf* floe

'banco *nm* (*di scuola*) desk; (*di negozio*) counter; (*di officina*) bench; (*di gioco, banca*) bank; (*di mercato*) stall; (*degli imputati*) dock; **sotto ~** under the counter; **medicinale da ~** over the counter medicines. **~ informazioni** information desk. **~ di nebbia** fog bank

'bancomat® nm inv autobank, cashpoint; (carta) bank card, cash card

ban'cone nm counter; (in bar) bar

banco'nota nf banknote, bill Am; **banco'note** pl paper currency

'banda nf band; (di delinquenti) gang. **~ d'atterraggio** Aeron landing strip. **~ rugosa** rumble strip

banderu'ola nf weathercock; Naut pennant

bandi'e|ra nf flag; **cambiare ~ra** change sides, switch allegiances. **~'rina** nf (nel calcio) corner flag. **~'rine** pl bunting sg

ban'di|re vt banish; (pubblicare) publish; fig dispense with (formalità, complimenti). **~ to** nm bandit. **~'tore** nm (di aste) auctioneer

'bando nm proclamation; **~ di concorso** job advertisement (published in an official gazette for a job for which a competitive examination has to be taken)

bar nm inv bar

'bara nf coffin

ba'rac|ca nf hut; (catapecchia) hovel; **mandare avanti la ~ca** keep the ship afloat. **~'cato** nm person living in a makeshift shelter. **~'chino** nm (di gelati, giornali) kiosk; Radio CB radio. **~'cone** nm (roulotte) circus caravan; (in luna park) booth. **~'copoli** nf inv shanty town

bara'onda nf chaos; **non fare ~** don't make a mess

ba'rare vi cheat

ba'ratro nm chasm

barat'tare vt barter. **ba'ratto** nm barter

ba'rattolo nm jar; (di latta) tin

'barba nf beard; (fam: noia) bore; **farsi la ~** shave; **è una ~** (noia) it's boring

barbabi'etola nf beetroot. **~ da zucchero** sugar-beet

bar'barico a barbaric. **bar'barie** nf barbarity. **'barb|aro** a barbarous ● nm barbarian

'barbecue nm inv barbecue

bar'biere nm barber; (negozio) barber's

barbi'turico nm barbiturate

bar'bone nm (vagabondo) vagrant; (cane) poodle

bar'boso a fam boring

barbu'gliare vi mumble

bar'buto a bearded

'barca nf boat; **una ~ di** fig a lot of. **~ a motore** motorboat. **~ da pesca** fishing boat. **~ a remi** rowing boat, rowboat Am. **~ di salvataggio** lifeboat. **~ a vela** sailing boat, sailboat Am. **~'iolo** nm boatman

barcame'narsi vr manage

barcol'lare vi stagger

bar'cone nm barge; (di ponte) pontoon

bar'dar|e vt harness. **~si** vr hum dress up

ba'rel|la nf stretcher. **~'liere** nm stretcher-bearer

'Barents: mare di ~ Barents Sea

bari'centro nm centre of gravity

ba'ri|le nm barrel. **~'lotto** nm fig tub of lard

ba'rista nm barman ● nf barmaid

ba'ritono nm baritone

bar'lume nm glimmer; **un ~ di speranza** a glimmer of hope

'barman nm inv barman

'baro, -a nmf cardsharper

ba'rocco a & nm baroque

ba'rometro nm barometer

ba'rone nm baron; **i baroni** fig the top brass. **baro'nessa** nf baroness

'barra nf bar; (lineetta) oblique; Naut tiller. **~ spazio** Comput space bar. **~ strumenti** Comput tool bar

bar'rare vt block off (strada)

barri'ca|re vt barricade. **~ta** nf barricade

barri'era nf barrier; (stradale) roadblock; Geol reef. **~ razziale** colour bar

bar'ri|re vi trumpet. **~to** nm trumpeting

barzel'letta nf joke; **~ sporca** o **spinta** dirty joke

basa'mento nm base

ba'sar|e vt base. **~si** vr **~si su** be based on; **mi baso su ciò che ho visto** I'm going on [the basis of] what I saw

'basco, -a nmf & a Basque ● nm (copricapo) beret

'base nf basis; (fondamento) foundation; Mil base; Pol rank and file; **a ~ di** containing; **in ~ a** on the basis of. **~ dati** database

'baseball nm inv baseball

ba'setta nf sideburn

basi'lare a basic

ba'silica nf basilica

ba'silico nm basil

ba'sista nm grass roots politician; (di un crimine) mastermind

'basket nm basketball

bas'sezza *nf* lowness; *(di statura)* shortness; *(viltà)* vileness

bas'sista *nmf* bassist

'basso *a* low; *(di statura)* short; *(acqua)* shallow; *(televisione)* quiet; *(vile)* despicable; **parlare a bassa voce** speak quietly, speak in a low voice; **la bassa Italia** southern Italy ● *nm* lower part; *Mus* bass. **guardare in ~** look down

basso'fondo *nm* *(pl* **bassi'fondi)** shallows *pl*; **bassifondi** *pl* *(quartieri poveri)* slums

bassori'lievo *nm* bas-relief

bas'sotto *nm* dachshund

ba'stardo, -a *a* bastard; *(di animale)* mongrel ● *nmf* bastard; *(animale)* mongrel

ba'stare *vi* be enough; *(durare)* last; **basta!** that's enough!, that'll do!; **basta che** *(purchè)* provided that; **basta così** that's enough; **basta così?** is that enough?, will that do?; *(in negozio)* will there be anything else?; **basta andare alla posta** you only have to go to the post office

Basti'an con'trario *nm* contrary old so-and-so

basti'one *nm* bastion

basto'nare *vt* beat

baston'cino *nm* *(da sci)* ski pole. **~ di pesce** fish finger, fish stick *Am*

ba'stone *nm* stick; *(da golf)* club; *(da passeggio)* walking stick

ba'tosta *nf* blow

bat'tagli|a *nf* battle; *(lotta)* fight. **~'are** *vi* battle; *fig* fight

bat'taglio *nm* *(di campana)* clapper; *(di porta)* knocker

battagli'one *nm* battalion

bat'tello *nm* boat; *(motonave)* steamer

bat'tente *nm* *(di porta)* wing; *(di finestra)* shutter; *(battaglio)* knocker

'batter|e *vt* beat; *(percorrere)* scour; thresh *(grano)*; break *(record)* ● *vi* *(bussare, urtare)* knock; *(cuore:)* beat; *(ali ecc:)* flap; *Tennis* serve; **~e a macchina** type; **~e gli occhi** blink; **~e le mani** clap [one's hands]; **~e le ore** strike the hours. **~si** *vr* fight

bat'teri *nmpl* bacteria

batte'ria *nf* battery; *Mus* drums *pl*

bat'terio *nm* bacterium. **~'logico** *a* bacteriological

batte'rista *nmf* drummer

bat'tesimo *nm* baptism, christening

battez'zare *vt* baptize, christen

battiba'leno *nm* **in un ~** in a flash

batti'becco *nm* squabble

batticu'ore *nm* palpitation; **mi venne il ~** I was scared

bat'tigia *nf* water's edge

batti'mano *nm* applause

batti'panni *nm inv* carpetbeater

batti'stero *nm* baptistery

batti'strada *nm inv* outrider; *(di pneumatico)* tread; *Sport* pacesetter

battitap'peto *nm inv* carpet sweeper

'battito *nm* *(del cuore)* [heart]beat; *(alle tempie)* throbbing; *(di orologio)* ticking; *(della pioggia)* beating

bat'tuta *nf* beat; *(colpo)* knock; *(spiritosaggine)* wisecrack; *(osservazione)* remark; *Mus* bar; *Tennis* service; *Theat* cue; *(dattilografia)* stroke

ba'tuffolo *nm* flock

ba'ule *nm* trunk

'bava *nf* dribble; *(di cane ecc)* slobber; **aver la ~ alla bocca** foam at the mouth

bava'glino *nm* bib

ba'vaglio *nm* gag

'bavero *nm* collar

ba'zar *nm inv* bazaar

baz'zecola *nf* trifle

bazzi'care *vt/i* haunt

be'arsi *vr* delight *(di* in)

beati'tudine *nf* bliss. **be'ato** *a* blissful; *Relig* blessed; **beato te!** lucky you!

beauty-'case *nm inv* toilet bag

bebè *nm inv* baby

bec'caccia *nf* woodcock

bec'ca|re *vt* peck; *fig* catch. **~rsi** *vr* *(litigare)* quarrel. **~ta** *nf* peck

beccheggi'are *vi* pitch

bec'chino *nm* grave-digger

'bec|co *nm* beak; *(di caffettiera ecc)* spout. **~'cuccio** *nm* spout

be'fana *nf* Epiphany; *(donna brutta)* old witch

'beffa *nf* hoax; **farsi beffe di qcno** mock sb. **bef'fardo** *a* derisory; *(persona)* mocking

beffar|e *vt* mock. **~si** *vr* **~si di** make fun of

'bega *nf* quarrel; **è una bella ~** it's really annoying

be'gonia *nf* begonia

'beige *a & nm* beige

be'la|re *vi* bleat. **~to** *nm* bleating

'belga *a & nmf* Belgian

'Belgio *nm* Belgium

'bella *nf* *(in carte, Sport)* decider

bel'lezza *nf* beauty; **che ~!** how lovely!; **chiudere/finire in ~** end on a high note

'**belli|co** *a* war *attrib.* ~'**coso** *a* warlike. ~**ge'rante** *a & nmf* belligerent

'**bello** *a* nice; (*di aspetto*) beautiful; ‹*uomo*› handsome; (*moralmente*) good; **cosa fai di ~ stasera?** what are you up to tonight?; **oggi fa ~** it's a nice day; **una bella cifra** a lot; **un bel piatto di pasta** a big plate of pasta; **nel bel mezzo** right in the middle; **un bel niente** absolutely nothing; **bell'e fatto** over and done with; **bell'amico!** [a] fine friend he is/you are!; **questa è bella!** that's a good one!; **scamparla bella** have a narrow escape ● *nm* (*bellezza*) beauty; (*innamorato*) sweetheart; **sul più ~** at the crucial moment; **il ~ è che...** the funny thing is that...

'**belva** *nf* wild beast

be'molle *nm Mus* flat

ben *vedi* **bene**

benché *conj* though, although

'**benda** *nf* bandage; (*per occhi*) blindfold. **ben'dare** *vt* bandage; blindfold ‹*occhi*›

'**bene** *adv* well; **ben ~** thoroughly; ~**!** good!; **star ~** (*di salute*) be well; ‹*vestito, stile:*› suit; (*finanziariamente*) be well off; **non sta ~** (*non è educato*) it's not nice; **sta/va ~!** all right!; **ti sta ~!** [it] serves you right!; **ti auguro ~** I wish you well; **di ~ in meglio** better and better; **fare ~** (*aver ragione*) do the right thing; **fare ~ a** ‹*cibo:*› be good for; **una persona per ~** a good person; **per ~** ‹*fare*› properly; **è ben difficile** it's very difficult; **come tu ben sai** as you well know; **lo credo ~!** I can well believe it! ● *nm* good; **per il tuo ~** for your own good. **beni** *nmpl* (*averi*) property *sg*; **un ~ di famiglia** a family heirloom

bene'detto *a* blessed

bene'di|re *vt* bless. ~**zi'one** *nf* blessing

benedu'cato *a* well-mannered

benefat'|tore, -'trice *nm* benefactor ● *nf* benefactress

benefi'care *vt* help

benefi'cenza *nf* charity

benefici'ar|e *vi* ~**e di** profit by. ~**io, -a** *a & nmf* beneficiary. **bene'ficio** *nm* benefit. **be'nefico** *a* beneficial; (*di beneficenza*) charitable

bene'placito *nm* consent, approval

be'nessere *nm* well-being

bene'stante *a* well-off ● *nmf* well-off person

bene'stare *nm* consent

benevo'lenza *nf* benevolence. **be'nevolo** *a* benevolent

ben'fatto *a* well-made

'**beni** *nmpl* property *sg; Fin* assets; ~ **di consumo** consumer goods

benia'mino *nm* favourite

be'nigno *a* kindly; *Med* benign

beninfor'mato *a* well-informed

benintenzio'nato, -a *a* well-meaning ● *nmf* well-meaning person

benin'teso *adv* needless to say, of course

benpen'sante *a & nmf* self-righteous

benser'vito *nm* **dare il ~ a qcno** give sb the sack

bensi *conj* but rather

benve'nuto *a & nm* welcome

ben'visto *a* **essere ~** go down well (da with)

benvo'lere *vt* **farsi ~ da qcno** win sb's affection; **prendere qcno in ~** take a liking to sb; **essere benvoluto da tutti** to be well-liked by everyone

ben'zina *nf* petrol, gas *Am*; **far ~** get petrol. ~ **verde** unleaded petrol. **benzi'naio, -a** *nmf* petrol station attendant

'**bere** *vt* drink; (*assorbire*) absorb; *fig* swallow ● *nm* drinking; (*bevande*) drinks *pl*

berga'motto *nm* bergamot

ber'lina *nf Auto* saloon

Ber'lino *nm* Berlin

ber'muda *nfpl* (*pantaloni*) Bermuda shorts

ber'noccolo *nm* bump; (*disposizione*) flair

ber'retto *nm* beret, cap

bersagli'are *vt fig* bombard. **ber'saglio** *nm* target

be'stemmi|a *nf* swear-word; (*maledizione*) oath; (*sproposito*) blasphemy. ~'**are** *vi* swear

'**besti|a** *nf* animal; (*persona brutale*) beast; (*persona sciocca*) fool; **andare in ~a** *fam* blow one's top. ~'**ale** *a* bestial; ‹*espressione, violenza*› brutal; ‹*fam: freddo, fame*› terrible. ~**alità** *nf inv* bestiality; *fig* nonsense. ~'**ame** *nm* livestock

'**bettola** *nf fig* dive

be'tulla *nf* birch

be'vanda *nf* drink

bevi'|tore, -'trice *nmf* drinker

be'vut|a *nf* drink. ~**o** *pp di* **bere**

bi'ada *nf* fodder

bianche'ria *nf* linen. ~ **intima** underwear

bi'anco *a* white; ‹*foglio*› blank ● *nm*

white; (*foglio, pagina*) blank; **mangia-re in** ~ not eat fried or heavy foods; **andare in** ~ *fam* not score; **in** ~ **e nero** (*film, fotografia*) black and white, monochrome; **passare una notte in** ~ have a sleepless night

bian'core *nm* (*bianchezza*) whiteness

bianco'spino *nm* hawthorn

biasci'care *vt* (*mangiare*) eat noisily; (*parlare*) mumble

biasi'mare *vt* blame. **bi'asimo** *nm* blame

'Bibbia *nf* Bible

bibe'ron *nm inv* [baby's] bottle

'bibita *nf* [soft] drink

'biblico *a* biblical

bibliogra'fia *nf* bibliography

biblio'te|ca *nf* library; (*mobile*) bookcase. ~**'cario, -a** *nmf* librarian

bicarbo'nato *nm* bicarbonate. ~ **di sodio** bicarbonate of soda

bicchi'ere *nm* glass

bicchie'rino *nm fam* tipple

bici'cletta *nf* bicycle; **andare in** ~ ride a bicycle

bico'lore *a* two-coloured

bidè *nm inv* bidet

bi'dello, -a *nmf* janitor, [school] caretaker

bido'nata *nf fam* swindle

bi'done *nm* bin; (*fam: truffa*) swindle; **fare un** ~ **a qcno** *fam* stand sb up

bien'nale *a* biennial

bi'ennio *nm* two-year period

bi'etola *nf* beet

bifo'cale *a* bifocal

bi'folco, -a *nmf fig* boor

bifor'c|arsi *vr* fork. ~**azi'one** *nf* fork. ~**uto** *a* forked

biga'mia *nf* bigamy. **'bigamo, -a** *a* bigamous ● *nmf* bigamist

bighello'nare *vi* loaf around. **bighel'lone** *nm* loafer

bigiotte'ria *nf* costume jewellery; (*negozio*) jeweller's

bigliet't|aio *nm* booking clerk; (*sui treni*) ticket-collector. ~**e'ria** *nf* ticket-office; *Theat* box-office

bigli'et|to *nm* ticket; (*lettera breve*) note; (*cartoncino*) card; (*di banca*) banknote. ~**to da visita** business card. ~**'tone** *nm* (*fam: soldi*) big one

bignè *nm inv* cream puff

bigo'dino *nm* roller

bi'gotto *nm* bigot

bi'kini *nm inv* bikini

bi'lanci|a *nf* scales *pl*; (*di orologio, Comm*) balance. **B~a** *Astr* Libra. ~**'are** *vt* balance; *fig* weigh. ~**o** *nm* budget; *Comm* balance sheet; **fare il** ~**o** balance the books; *fig* take stock

'bil|e *nf* bile; *fig* rage

bili'ardo *nm* billiards *sg*

'bilico *nm* equilibrium; **in** ~ in the balance

bi'lingue *a* bilingual

bili'one *nm* billion

bilo'cale *a* two-room

'bimbo, -a *nmf* child

bimen'sile *a* fortnightly

bime'strale *a* bimonthly

bi'nario *nm* track; (*piattaforma*) platform

bi'nocolo *nm* binoculars *pl*

bio'chimica *nf* biochemistry

biodegra'dabile *a* biodegradable

bio'etica *nf* bioethics

bio'fisica *nf* biophysics

biogra'fia *nf* biography. **bio'grafico** *a* biographical. **bi'ografo, -a** *nmf* biographer

biolo'gia *nf* biology. **bio'logico** *a* biological. **bi'ologo, -a** *nmf* biologist

bi'ond|a *nf* blonde. ~**o** *a* blond ● *nm* fair colour; (*uomo*) fair-haired man

bio'sfera *nf* biosphere

bi'ossido *nm* ~ **di carbonio** carbon dioxide

biparti'tismo *nm* two-party system

'birba *nf*, **bir'bante** *nm* rascal, rogue. **bir'bone** *a* wicked

biri'chino, -a *a* naughty ● *nmf* little devil

bi'rillo *nm* skittle

'birr|a *nf* beer; **a tutta** ~**a** *fig* flat out. ~**a chiara** lager. ~**a scura** brown ale. ~**e'ria** *nf* beer-house; (*fabbrica*) brewery

bis *nm inv* encore

bi'saccia *nf* haversack

bi'sbetic|a *nf* shrew. ~**o** *a* bad-tempered

bisbigli'are *vt/i* whisper. **bi'sbiglio** *nm* whisper

'bisca *nf* gambling-house

'biscia *nf* snake

bi'scotto *nm* biscuit

bisessu'ale *a* & *nmf* bisexual

bise'stile *a* **anno** ~ leap year

bisettima'nale *a* fortnightly

bi'slacco *a* peculiar

bis'nonno, -a *nmf* great-grandfather; great-grandmother

biso'gn|are *vi* ~**a agire subito** we must act at once; ~**a farlo** it is necessary to do it; **non** ~**a venire** you don't have to come. **~o** nm need; (povertà) poverty; **aver ~o di** need. **~oso** a needy; (povero) poor; **~oso di** in need of

bi'sonte nm bison

bi'stecca nf steak

bisticci'are vi quarrel. **bi'sticcio** nm quarrel; (gioco di parole) pun

bistrat'tare vt mistreat

'bisturi nm inv scalpel

bi'torzolo nm lump

'bitter nm inv (bitter) aperitif

bi'vacco nm bivouac

'bivio nm crossroads; (di strada) fork

bizan'tino a Byzantine

'bizza nf tantrum; **fare le bizze** ‹bambini:› play up

biz'zarro a bizarre

biz'zeffe adv **a ~** galore

blan'dire vt soothe; (allettqre) flatter. **'blando** a mild

bla'sone nm coat of arms

blate'rare vi blether, blather

'blatta nf cockroach

blin'da|re vt armour-plate. **~to** a armoured

'blitz nm inv blitz

bloc'car|e vt block; (isolare) cut off; Mil blockade; Comm freeze. **~si** vr Mech jam

blocca'sterzo nm steering lock

'blocco nm block; Mil blockade; (dei fitti) restriction; (di carta) pad; (unione) coalition; **in ~** Comm in bulk. **~ stradale** road-block

bloc-'notes nm inv writing pad

blu a & nm blue

blue-'jeans nmpl jeans

'bluff nm inv (carte, fig) bluff. **bluf'fare** vi (carte, fig) bluff

'blusa nf blouse

'boa nm boa [constrictor]; (sciarpa) [feather] boa ● nf Naut buoy

bo'ato nm rumbling

bo'bina nf spool; (di film) reel; Electr coil

'bocca nf mouth; **a ~ aperta** fig dumbfounded; **in ~ al lupo!** break a leg!; **fare la respirazione ~ a ~ a** qcno give sb mouth to mouth resuscitation or the kiss of life

boc'caccia nf grimace; **far boccacce** make faces

boc'caglio nm nozzle

boc'cale nm jug; (da birra) tankard

bocca'porto nm Naut hatch

boc'cata nf (di fumo) puff; **prendere una ~ d'aria** get a breath of fresh air

boc'cetta nf small bottle

boccheggi'are vi gasp

boc'chino nm cigarette holder; (di pipa, Mus) mouthpiece

'bocc|ia nf (palla) bowl; **~e** pl (gioco) bowls sg

bocci'a|re vt (agli esami) fail; (respingere) reject; (alle bocce) hit; **essere ~to** fail; (ripetere) repeat a year. **~'tura** nf failure

bocci'olo nm bud

boccon'cino nm morsel

boc'cone nm mouthful; (piccolo pasto) snack

boc'coni adv face downwards

'boia nm executioner

boi'ata nf fam rubbish

boicot'tare vt boycott

bo'lero nm bolero

'bolgia nf (caos) bedlam

'bolide nm meteor; **passare come un ~** shoot past [like a rocket]

Bo'livi|a nf Bolivia. **b~'ano, -a** a & nmf Bolivian

'bolla nf bubble; (pustola) blister

bol'la|re vt stamp; fig brand. **~to** a fig branded; **carta ~ta** paper with stamp showing payment of duty

bol'lente a boiling [hot]

bol'let|ta nf bill; **essere in ~ta** be hard up. **~'tino** nm bulletin; Comm list

bol'lino nm coupon

bol'li|re vt/i boil. **~to** nm boiled meat. **~'tore** nm boiler; (per l'acqua) kettle. **~'tura** nf boiling

'bollo nm stamp

bol'lore nm boil; (caldo) intense heat; fig ardour

'bomba nf bomb; **a prova di ~** bombproof

bombarda'mento nm shelling; (con aerei) bombing; fig bombardment. **~ aereo** air raid

bombar'd|are vt shell; (con aerei) bomb; fig bombard. **~i'ere** nm bomber

bom'betta nf bowler [hat].

'bombola nf cylinder. **~ di gas** gas bottle, gas cylinder

bombo'lone nm doughnut

bomboni'era nf wedding keep-sake

bo'naccia nf Naut calm

bonacci'one, -a nmf good-natured person ● a good-natured

bo'nario a kindly

bo'nifica nf land reclamation. **bonifi-'care** vt reclaim

bo'nifico nm Comm discount; (bancario) [credit] transfer

bontà nf goodness; (gentilezza) kindness

'**bora** nf bora (cold north-east wind in the upper Adriatic)

borbott|are vi mumble; ⟨stomaco:⟩ rumble. ~**io** nm mumbling; (di stomaco) rumbling

'**borchi|a** nf stud. ~'**ato** a studded

bor'da|re vt border. ~'**tura** nf border

bor'deaux a inv (colore) claret

bor'dello nm brothel; fig bedlam; (disordine) mess

'**bordo** nm border; (estremità) edge; **a ~** Naut, Aeron on board

bor'gata nf hamlet

bor'ghese a bourgeois; ⟨abito⟩ civilian; **in ~** in civilian dress; ⟨poliziotto⟩ in plain clothes

borghe'sia nf middle classes pl

'**borgo** nm village; (quartiere) district

'**bori|a** nf conceit. ~'**oso** a conceited

bor'lotto nm [**fagiolo**] ~ borlotto bean

boro'talco nm talcum powder

bor'raccia nf flask

'**bors|a** nf bag; (borsetta) handbag; (valori) Stock Exchange. ~**a dell'acqua calda** hot-water bottle. ~**a frigo** coolbox. ~**a della spesa** shopping bag. ~**a di studio** scholarship. ~**ai'olo** nm pickpocket. ~**el'lino** nm purse. **bor-'sista** nmf Fin speculator; Sch scholarship holder

bor'se|llo nm (portamonete) purse; (borsetto) man's handbag. ~**tta** nf handbag. ~**tto** nm man's handbag

bo'scaglia nf woodlands pl

boscai'olo nm woodman; (guardaboschi) forester

'**bosco** nm wood. **bo'scoso** a wooded

'**bossolo** nm cartridge case

bo'tanic|a nf botany. ~**o** a botanical ● nm botanist

'**botola** nf trapdoor

'**botta** nf blow; (rumore) bang; **fare a botte** come to blows. ~ **e risposta** fig thrust and counter-thrust

'**botte** nf barrel

bot'te|ga nf shop; (di artigiano) workshop. ~'**gaio, -a** nmf shopkeeper. ~'**ghino** nm Theatr box-office; (del lotto) lottery-shop

bot'tigli|a nf bottle; **in ~a** bottled. ~**e'ria** nf wine shop

bot'tino nm loot; Mil booty

'**botto** nm bang; **di ~** all of a sudden

bot'tone nm button; Bot bud

bo'vino a bovine; **bovini** pl cattle

box nm inv (per cavalli) loosebox; (recinto per bambini) play-pen

'**boxe** nf boxing

'**bozza** nf draft; Typ proof; (bernoccolo) bump. **boz'zetto** nm sketch

'**bozzolo** nm cocoon

brac'care vt hunt

brac'cetto nm **a ~** arm in arm

bracci'a|le nm bracelet; (fascia) armband. ~'**letto** nm bracelet; (di orologio) watch-strap

bracci'ante nm day labourer

bracci'ata nf (nel nuoto) stroke

'**bracci|o** nm (pl nf **braccia**) arm; (di fiume, pl **bracci**) arm. ~'**olo** nm (di sedia) arm[rest]; (da nuoto) armband

'**bracco** nm hound

bracconi'ere nm poacher

'**brac|e** nf embers pl; **alla ~e** chargrilled. ~'**iere** nm brazier. ~'**ola** nf chop

'**brado** a **allo stato ~** in the wild

'**brama** nf longing. **bra'mare** vt long for. **bramo'sia** nf yearning

'**branca** nf branch

'**branchia** nf gill

'**branco** nm (di cani) pack; (pej: di persone) gang

branco'lare vi grope

'**branda** nf camp-bed

bran'dello nm scrap; **a brandelli** in tatters

bran'dire vt brandish

'**brano** nm piece; (di libro) passage

Bra'sil|e nm' Brazil. **b~i'ano, -a** a & nmf Brazilian

bra'vata nf bragging

'**bravo** a good; (abile) clever; (coraggioso) brave; ~**!** well done!. **bra'vura** nf skill

'**breccia** nf breach; **sulla ~** fig very successful, at the top

bre'saola nf dried, salted beef sliced thinly and eaten cold

bre'tella nf shoulder-strap; **bretelle** pl (di calzoni) braces

'**breve** a brief, short; **in ~** briefly; **tra ~** shortly

brevet'tare vt patent. **bre'vetto** nm patent; (attestato) licence

brevità nf shortness

'**brezza** nf breeze

'**bricco** nm jug

bric'cone nm blackguard; hum rascal

'briciol|a nf crumb; fig grain. ~**o** nm fragment

'**briga** nf (fastidio) trouble; (lite) quarrel; **attaccar ~** pick a quarrel;

prendersi la ~ di fare qcsa go to the trouble of doing sth

brigadi'ere *nm* (*dei carabinieri*) sergeant

bri'gante *nm* bandit; *hum* rogue

bri'gare *vi* intrigue

bri'gata *nf* brigade; (*gruppo*) group

briga'tista *nmf Pol* member of the Red Brigades

'briglia *nf* rein; **a ~ sciolta** at breakneck speed

bril'lante *a* brilliant; (*scintillante*) sparkling ● *nm* diamond

bril'lare *vi* shine; (*metallo:*) glitter; (*scintillare*) sparkle

'brillo *a* tipsy

'brina *nf* hoar-frost

brin'dare *vi* toast; **~ a qcno** drink a toast to sb

'brindisi *nm inv* toast

bri'tannico *a* British

'brivido *nm* shiver; (*di paura ecc*) shudder; (*di emozione*) thrill

brizzo'lato *a* greying

'brocca *nf* jug

broc'cato *nm* brocade

'broccolo *nm* broccoli *sg*

bro'daglia *nf pej* dishwater

'brodo *nm* broth; (*per cucinare*) stock. **~ ristretto** consommé

'broglio *nm* **~ elettorale** gerrymandering

bron'chite *nf* bronchitis

'broncio *nm* sulk; **fare il ~** sulk

bronto'l|are *vi* grumble; (*tuono ecc:*) rumble. **~io** *nm* grumbling; (*di tuono*) rumbling. **~one, -a** *nmf* grumbler

'bronzo *nm* bronze

bros'sura *nf* **edizione in ~** paperback

bru'care *vt* (*pecora:*) graze

bruciacchi'are *vt* scorch

brucia'pelo *adv* **a ~** point-blank

bruci'a|re *vt* burn; (*scottare*) scald; (*incendiare*) set fire to ● *vi* burn; (*scottare*) scald. **~rsi** *vr* burn oneself. **~to a** burnt; *fig* burnt-out. **~tore** *nm* burner. **~'tura** *nf* burn. **bruci'ore** *nm* burning sensation

'bruco *nm* grub

'brufolo *nm* spot

brughi'era *nf* heath

bruli'c|are *vi* swarm. **~hio** *nm* swarming

'brullo *a* bare

'bruma *nf* mist

'bruno *a* brown; (*occhi, capelli*) dark

brusca'mente *adv* (*di colpo*) suddenly

bru'schetta *nf* toasted bread rubbed with garlic and sprinkled with olive oil

'brusco *a* sharp; (*persona*) brusque, abrupt; (*improvviso*) sudden

bru'sio *nm* buzzing

bru'tal|e *a* brutal. **~ità** *nf inv* brutality. **~iz'zare** *vt* brutalize. **'bruto** *a* & *nm* brute

brut'tezza *nf* ugliness

'brut|to *a* ugly; (*tempo, tipo, situazione, affare*) nasty; (*cattivo*) bad; **~ta copia** rough copy; **~to tiro** dirty trick. **~'tura** *nf* ugly thing

'buca *nf* hole; (*avvallamento*) hollow. **~ delle lettere** post-box; (*a casa*) letter-box

buca'neve *nm inv* snowdrop

bu'car|e *vt* make a hole in; (*pungere*) prick; punch ⟨*biglietti*⟩ ● *vi* have a puncture. **~si** *vr* prick oneself; (*con droga*) shoot up

bu'cato *nm* washing

'buccia *nf* peel, skin

bucherel'lare *vt* riddle

'buco *nm* hole

bu'dello *nm* (*pl nf* **budella**) bowel

bu'dino *nm* pudding

'bue *nm* (*pl* **buoi**) ox; **carne di ~** beef

'bufalo *nm* buffalo

bu'fera *nf* storm; (*di neve*) blizzard

buf'fetto *nm* cuff

'buffo *a* funny; *Theat* comic ● *nm* funny thing. **~'nata** *nf* (*scherzo*) joke. **buf'fone** *nm* buffoon; **fare il buffone** play the fool

bu'gi|a *nf* lie; **~a pietosa** white lie. **~'ardo, -a** *a* lying ● *nmf* liar

bugi'gattolo *nm* cubby-hole

'buio *a* dark ● *nm* darkness; **al ~** in the dark; **~ pesto** pitch dark

'bulbo *nm* bulb; (*dell'occhio*) eyeball

Bulga'ria *nf* Bulgaria. **'bulgaro, -a** *a* & *nmf* Bulgarian

buli'mia *nf* bulimia. **bu'limico** *a* bulimic

'bullo *nm* bully

bul'lone *nm* bolt

'bunker *nm inv* bunker

buona'fede *nf* good faith

buona'notte *int* good night

buona'sera *int* good evening

buon'giorno *int* good morning; (*di pomeriggio*) good afternoon

buon'grado: di ~ *adv* willingly

buongu'staio, -a *nmf* gourmet. **buon'gusto** *nm* good taste

bu'ono *a* good; ⟨*momento*⟩ right; **dar ~** ⟨*convalidare*⟩ accept; **alla buona** easy-going; ⟨*cena*⟩ informal; **buona notte/ sera** good night/evening; **buon compleanno/Natale!** happy birthday/ merry Christmas!; **~ senso** common sense; **di buon'ora** early; **una buona volta** once and for all; **buona parte di** the best part of; **tre ore buone** three good hours ● *nm* good; ⟨*in film*⟩ goody; ⟨*tagliando*⟩ voucher; ⟨*titolo*⟩ bond; **con le buone** gently; **~ sconto** money-off coupon ● *nmf* **buono, -a a nulla** dead loss

buontem'pone, -a *nmf* happy-go-lucky person

buonu'more *nm* good temper

buonu'scita *nf* retirement bonus; ⟨*di dirigente*⟩ golden handshake

burat'tino *nm* puppet

'burbero *a* surly; ⟨*nei modi*⟩ rough

bu'rocra|te *nm* bureaucrat. **buro'cra-tico** *a* bureaucratic. **~'zia** *nf* bureaucracy

bur'ra|sca *nf* storm. **~'scoso** *a* stormy

'burro *nm* butter

bur'rone *nm* ravine

bu'scar|e *vt*, **~si** *vr* catch; **~le** *fam* get a hiding

bus'sare *vt* knock

'bussola *nf* compass; **perdere la ~** lose one's bearings

'busta *nf* envelope; ⟨*astuccio*⟩ case. **~ paga** pay packet. **~'rella** *nf* bribe. **bu'stina** *nf* ⟨*di tè*⟩ tea bag; ⟨*per medicine*⟩ sachet

'busto *nm* bust; ⟨*indumento*⟩ girdle

but'tar|e *vt* throw; **~e giù** ⟨*demolire*⟩ knock down; ⟨*inghiottire*⟩ gulp down; scribble down ⟨*scritto*⟩; *fam* put on ⟨*pasta*⟩; ⟨*scoraggiare*⟩ dishearten; **~e via** throw away. **~si** *vr* throw oneself; ⟨*saltare*⟩ jump

butte'rato *a* pock-marked

buz'zurro *nm fam* yokel

Cc

caba'ret *nm inv* cabaret

ca'bina *nf Naut, Aeron* cabin; ⟨*balneare*⟩ beach hut. **~ elettorale** polling booth. **~ di pilotaggio** cockpit. **~ telefonica** telephone box. **cabi'nato** *nm* cabin cruiser

ca'cao *nm* cocoa

'cacca *nf fam* pooh

'caccia *nf* hunt; ⟨*con fucile*⟩ shooting; ⟨*inseguimento*⟩ chase; ⟨*selvaggina*⟩ game ● *nm inv Aeron* fighter; *Naut* destroyer

cacciabombardi'ere *nm* fighter-bomber

cacciagi'one *nf* game

cacci'a|re *vt* hunt; ⟨*mandar via*⟩ chase away; ⟨*scacciare*⟩ drive out; ⟨*ficcare*⟩ shove ● *vi* go hunting. **~rsi** *vr* ⟨*nascondersi*⟩ hide; ⟨*andare a finire*⟩ get to; **~rsi nei guai** get into trouble; **alla ~'tora** *a Culin* chasseur. **~'tore, ~'trice** *nmf* hunter. **~tore di frodo** poacher

caccia'vite *nm inv* screwdriver

ca'chet *nm inv Med* capsule; ⟨*colorante*⟩ colour rinse; ⟨*stile*⟩ cachet

'cachi *nm inv* ⟨*albero, frutta*⟩ persimmon

'cacio *nm* ⟨*formaggio*⟩ cheese

'caco *nm fam* ⟨*frutto*⟩ persimmon

'cactus *nm inv* cactus

ca'da|vere *nm* corpse. **~'verico** *a fig* deathly pale

ca'dente *a* falling; ⟨*casa*⟩ crumbling

ca'denza *nf* cadence; ⟨*ritmo*⟩ rhythm; *Mus* cadenza

ca'dere *vi* fall; ⟨*capelli ecc:*⟩ fall out; ⟨*capitombolare*⟩ tumble; ⟨*vestito ecc:*⟩ hang; **far ~** ⟨*di mano*⟩ drop; **~ dal sonno** feel very sleepy; **lasciar ~** drop; **~ dalle nuvole** *fig* be taken aback

ca'detto *nm* cadet

ca'duta *nf* fall; ⟨*di capelli*⟩ loss; *fig* downfall

caffè *nm inv* coffee; ⟨*locale*⟩ café. **~ corretto** espresso coffee with a dash of liqueur. **~ lungo** weak black coffee. **~ macchiato** coffee with a dash of milk.

~ ristretto extra-strong espresso coffee. **~ solubile** instant coffee. **~'ina** nf caffeine. **~l'latte** nm inv white coffee.

caffetti'era nf coffee-pot

cafo'naggine nf boorishness

cafo'nata nf boorishness

ca'fone, -a nmf boor

ca'gare vi fam crap

cagio'nare vt cause

cagio'nevole a delicate

cagli'ar|e vi, **~si** vr curdle

'cagna nf bitch

ca'gnara nf fam din

ca'gnesco a **guardare qcno in ~** scowl at sb

'cala nf creek

cala'brone nm hornet

cala'maio nm inkpot

cala'mari nmpl squid

cala'mita nf magnet

calamità nf inv calamity

ca'lar|e vi come down; ⟨vento:⟩ drop; (diminuire) fall; (tramontare) set ● vt (abbassare) lower; (nei lavori a maglia) decrease ● nm (di luna) waning. **~si** vr lower oneself

'calca nf throng

cal'cagno nm heel

cal'care¹ nm limestone

cal'care² vt tread; (premere) press [down]; **~ la mano** exaggerate; **~ le orme di qcno** fig follow in sb's footsteps

'calce¹ nf lime

'calce² nm **in ~** at the foot of the page

calce'struzzo nm concrete

cal'cetto nm Sport five-a-side [football]

calci'a|re vt kick. **~'tore** nm footballer

cal'cina nf mortar

calci'naccio nm (pezzo di intonaco) flake of plaster

'calcio¹ nm kick; Sport football; (di arma da fuoco) butt; **dare un ~** a kick. **~ d'angolo** corner [kick]

'calcio² nm (chimica) calcium

'calco nm (con carta) tracing; (arte) cast

calco'la|re vt calculate; (considerare) consider. **~'tore** a calculating ● nm calculator; (macchina elettronica) computer

'calcolo nm calculation; Med stone

cal'daia nf boiler

caldar'rosta nf roast chestnut

caldeggi'are vt support

'caldo a warm; (molto caldo) hot ● nm heat; **avere ~** be warm/hot; **fa ~** it is warm/hot

calen'dario nm calendar

'calibro nm calibre; (strumento) callipers pl; **di grosso ~** ⟨persona⟩ top attrib

'calice nm goblet; Relig chalice

ca'ligine nm fog; (industriale) smog

calligra'fia nf handwriting; ⟨cinese⟩ calligraphy

cal'lista nmf chiropodist. **'callo** nm corn; **fare il callo a** become hardened to. **cal'loso** a callous

'calma nf calm. **cal'mante** a calming ● nm sedative. **cal'mare** vt calm [down]; (lenire) soothe. **cal'marsi** vr calm down; ⟨vento:⟩ drop; ⟨dolore:⟩ die down. **calmo** a calm

'calo nm Comm fall; (di volume) shrinkage; (di peso) loss

calorosa'mente adv (cordialmente) warmly

ca'lore nm heat; (moderato) warmth; **in ~** ⟨animale⟩ on heat. **calo'roso** a warm

calo'ria nf calorie

ca'lorico a calorific

calo'rifero nm radiator

calpe'stare vt trample [down]; fig trample on ⟨diritti, sentimenti⟩; **vietato ~ l'erba** keep off the grass

calpe'stio nm (passi) footsteps

ca'lunni|a nf slander. **~'are** vt slander. **~'oso** a slanderous

ca'lura nf heat

cal'vario nm Calvary; fig trial

cal'vizie nf baldness. **'calvo** a bald

'calz|a nf (da donna) stocking; (da uomo) sock. **~a'maglia** nf tights pl; (per danza) leotard

cal'zante a fig fitting

cal'za|re vt (indossare) wear; (mettersi) put on ● vi fit

calza'scarpe nm inv shoehorn

calza'tura nf footwear

calzatu'rificio nm shoe factory

cal'zetta nf **è una mezza ~** fig he's no use

calzet'tone nm knee-length woollen sock. **cal'zino** nm sock

calzo'l|aio nm shoemaker. **~e'ria** nf (negozio) shoe shop

calzon'cini nmpl shorts. **~ da bagno** swimming trunks

cal'zone nm Culin folded pizza with tomato and mozzarella or ricotta inside

cal'zoni nmpl trousers, pants Am

camale'onte nm chameleon

cambi'ale nf bill of exchange

cambia'mento nm change

cambi'ar|e vt/i change; move (casa); (fare cambio di) exchange; **~e rotta** Naut alter course. **~si** vr change.

'cambio nm change; (Comm, scambio) exchange; Mech gear; **dare il cambio a qcno** relieve sb; **in cambio di** in exchange for

'camera nf room; (mobili) [bedroom] suite; Phot camera; **C~** Pol, Comm Chamber. **~ ardente** funeral parlour. **~ d'aria** inner tube. **C~ di Commercio** Chamber of Commerce. **C~ dei Deputati** Pol ≈ House of Commons. **~ doppia** double room. **~ da letto** bedroom. **~ matrimoniale** double room. **~ oscura** darkroom. **~ singola** single room

came'rata¹ nf (dormitorio) dormitory; Mil barrack room

came'ra|ta² nmf (amico) mate; Pol comrade. **~'tismo** nm comradeship

cameri'era nf maid; (di ristorante) waitress; (in albergo) chamber-maid; (di bordo) stewardess

cameri'ere nm manservant; (di ristorante) waiter; (di bordo) steward

came'rino nm dressing-room

'camice nm overall. **cami'cetta** nf blouse. **ca'micia** nf shirt; **uovo in camicia** poached egg. **camicia da notte** nightdress

cami'netto nm fireplace

ca'mino nm chimney; (focolare) fireplace

'camion nm inv lorry Br, truck

camion'cino nm van

camio'netta nf jeep

camio'nista nm lorry driver Br, truck driver

cam'mello nm camel; (tessuto) camel-hair ● a inv (colore) camel

cam'meo nm cameo

cammi'na|re vi walk; (auto, orologio) go. **cam'mino** nm way; **essere in cammino** be on the way; **mettersi in cammino** set out. **~ta** nf walk; **fare una ~ta** go for a walk

camo'milla nf camomile; (bevanda) camomile tea

ca'morra nf Camorra

ca'moscio nm chamois; (pelle) suede

cam'pagna nf country; (paesaggio) countryside; Comm, Mil campaign; **in ~** in the country. **● elettorale** election campaign. **~ pubblicitaria** marketing campaign. **campa'gnolo, -a** a rustic ● nm countryman ● nf countrywoman

cam'pale a field attrib; **giornata ~** fig strenuous day

cam'pa|na nf bell; (di vetro) belljar. **~'nella** nf (di tenda) curtain ring. **~'nello** nm door-bell; (cicalino) buzzer

campa'nile nm belfry

campani'lismo nm parochialism

campani'lista nmf person with a parochial outlook

campa'nula nf Bot campanula

cam'pare vi live; (a stento) get by

cam'pato a **~ in aria** unfounded

campeggi'a|re vi camp; (spiccare) stand out. **cam'peggio** nm camping; (terreno) campsite. **~'tore, ~'trice** nmf camper

cam'pestre a rural

'camping nm inv campsite

campio'nari|o nm [set of] samples ● a samples; **fiera ~a** a trade fair

campio'nato nm championship

campiona'tura nf (di merce) range of samples

campi'on|e nm champion; Comm sample; (esemplare) specimen. **~'essa** nf ladies' champion

'campo nm field; (accampamento) camp. **~ da calcio** football pitch. **~ di concentramento** concentration camp. **~ da golf** golf course. **~ da tennis** tennis court

campo'santo nm cemetery

camuf'far|e vt disguise. **~si** vr disguise oneself

'Cana|da nm Canada. **~'dese** a & nmf Canadian

ca'naglia nf scoundrel; (plebaglia) rabble

ca'nal|e nm channel; (artificiale) canal. **~iz'zare** vt channel (acque). **~iz-zazi'one** nf channelling; (rete) pipes pl

'canapa nf hemp

cana'rino nm canary

cancel'la|re vt cross out; (con la gomma) rub out; fig wipe out; (annullare) cancel; Comput delete, erase. **~'tura** nf erasure. **~zi'one** nf cancellation; Comput deletion

cancelle'ria nf chancellery; (articoli per scrivere) stationery

cancelli'ere nm chancellor; (di tribunale) clerk

can'cello nm gate

cance'ro|geno nm carcinogen ● a carcinogenic. **~'roso** a cancerous

can'crena nf gangrene

'cancro nm cancer. **C~** Astr Cancer

candeg'gi|na nf bleach. **~'are** vt bleach. **can'deggio** nm bleaching

can'de|la nf candle; Auto spark plug; **~'labro** nm candelabra. **~li'ere** nm candlestick

cande'lotto nm (di dinamite) stick

candida'mente adv candidly

candi'da|rsi vr stand as a candidate. **~to, -a** nmf candidate. **~'tura** nf Pol candidacy; (per lavoro) application

'candido a snow-white; (sincero) candid; (puro) pure

can'dito a candied

can'dore nm whiteness; fig innocence

'cane nm dog; (di arma da fuoco) cock; **un tempo da cani** foul weather. **~ da caccia** hunting dog

ca'nestro nm basket

cangi'ante a iridescent; **seta ~** shot silk

can'guro nm kangaroo

ca'nile nm kennel; (di allevamento) kennels pl. **~ municipale** dog pound

ca'nino a & nm canine

'canna nf reed; (da zucchero) cane; (di fucile) barrel; (bastone) stick; (di bicicletta) crossbar; (asta) rod; (fam: hascish) joint. **povero in ~** destitute. **~ da pesca** fishing-rod

can'nella nf cinnamon

can'neto nm bed of reeds

can'niba|le nm cannibal. **~'lismo** nm cannibalism

cannocchi'ale nm telescope

canno'nata nf cannon shot; **è una ~** fig it's brilliant

cannon'cino nm (dolce) cream horn

can'none nm cannon; fig ace

can'nuccia nf [drinking] straw; (di pipa) stem

ca'noa nf canoe

'canone nm canon; (affitto) rent; **equo ~** fair rents act

ca'noni|co nm canon. **~z'zare** vt canonize. **~zzazi'one** nf canonization

ca'noro a melodious

ca'notta nf (estiva) vest top

canot'taggio nm canoeing; (voga) rowing

canotti'era nf singlet

canotti'ere nm oarsman

ca'notto nm [rubber] dinghy

cano'vaccio nm (trama) plot; (straccio) duster

can'tante nmf singer

cant|'are vt/i sing. **~au'tore, ~a-'trice** nmf singer-songwriter. **~icchi'a-re** vt sing softly; (a bocca chiusa) hum

canti'ere nm yard; Naut shipyard; (di edificio) construction site. **~ navale** naval dockyard

canti'lena nf singsong; (ninna-nanna) lullaby

can'tina nf cellar; (osteria) wine shop

'canto¹ nm singing; (canzone) song; Relig chant; (poesia) poem

'canto² nm (angolo) corner; (lato) side; **dal ~ mio** for my part; **d'altro ~** on the other hand

canto'nata nf **prendere una ~** fig be sadly mistaken

can'tone nm canton; (angolo) corner

can'tuccio nm nook

canzo'na|re vt tease. **~'torio** a teasing. **~'tura** nf teasing

can'zo|ne nf song. **~'netta** nf fam pop song. **~ni'ere** nm songbook

'caos nm chaos. **ca'otico** a chaotic

C.A.P. nm abbr (**Codice di Avviamento Postale**) post code, zip code Am

ca'pac|e a able; (esperto) skilled; ⟨stadio, contenitore⟩ big; **~e di** (disposto a) capable of. **~ità** nf inv ability; (attitudine) skill; (capienza) capacity

capaci'tarsi vr **~ di** (rendersi conto) understand; (accorgersi) realize

ca'panna nf hut

capan'nello nm **fare ~ intorno a qcno/qcsa** gather round sb/sth

capan'none nm shed; Aeron hangar

ca'parbio a obstinate

ca'parra nf deposit

capa'tina nf short visit; **fare una ~ in città/da qcno** pop into town/in on sb

ca'pel|lo nm hair; **~li** pl (capigliatura) hair sg. **~'lone** nm hippie. **~'luto** a hairy

capez'zale nm bolster; fig bedside

ca'pezzolo nm nipple

capi'en|te a capacious. **~za** nf capacity

capiglia'tura nf hair

ca'pire vt understand; **~ male** misunderstand; **si capisce!** naturally!; **sì, ho capito** yes, I see

capi'ta|le a Jur capital; (principale) main ●nf (città) capital ●nm Comm capital. **~'lismo** nm capitalism. **~'lista** nmf capitalist. **~'listico** a capitalist

capitane'ria nf **~ di porto** port authorities pl

capi'tano nm captain

capi'tare vi (giungere per caso) come; (accadere) happen

capi'tello nm Archit capital

capito'la|re *vi* capitulate. **~zi'one** *nf* capitulation

ca'pitolo *nm* chapter

capi'tombolo *nm* headlong fall; **fare un ~** tumble down

'capo *nm* head; *(chi comanda)* boss *fam*; *(di vestiario)* item; *Geog* cape; *(in tribù)* chief; *(parte estrema)* top; **a ~** *(in dettato)* new paragraph; **da ~** over again; **in ~ a un mese** within a month; **giramento di ~** dizziness; **mal di ~** headache; **~ d'abbigliamento** item of clothing. **~ d'accusa** *Jur* charge, count. **~ di bestiame** head of cattle

capo'banda *nm Mus* bandmaster; *(di delinquenti)* ringleader

ca'poccia *nm (fam: testa)* nut

capocci'one *nm fam* brainbox

capo'danno *nm* New Year's Day

capofa'miglia *nm* head of the family

capo'fitto *nm* **a ~** headlong

capo'giro *nm* giddiness

capola'voro *nm* masterpiece

capo'linea *nm* terminus

capo'lino *nm* **fare ~** peep in

capolu'ogo *nm* main town

capo'rale *nm* lance-corporal

capo'squadra *nmf Sport* team captain

capo'stipite *nmf (di famiglia)* progenitor

capo'tavola *nmf* head of the table

capo'treno *nm* guard

capouff'icio *nmf* head clerk

capo'verso *nm* first line

capo'vol|gere *vt* overturn; *fig* reverse. **~gersi** *vr* overturn; ‹barca:› capsize; *fig* be reversed. **~to** *pp di* **capovolgere ● a** upside-down

'cappa *nf* cloak; *(di camino)* cowl; *(di cucina)* hood

cap'pel|la *nf* chapel. **~'lano** *nm* chaplain

cap'pello *nm* hat. **~ a cilindro** top hat

'cappero *nm* caper

'cappio *nm* noose

cap'pone *nm* capon

cap'potto *nm* [over]coat

cappuc'cino *nm (frate)* Capuchin; *(bevanda)* white coffee

cap'puccio *nm* hood; *(di penna stilografica)* cap

'capra *nf* goat. **ca'pretto** *nm* kid

ca'pricci|o *nm* whim; *(bizzarria)* freak; **fare i capricci** have tantrums. **~'oso** *a* capricious; ‹bambino› naughty

Capri'corno *nm Astr* Capricorn

capri'ola *nf* somersault

capri'olo *nm* roe-deer

'capro *nm* [billy-]goat. **~ espiatorio** scapegoat. **ca'prone** *nm* [billy] goat

'capsula *nf* capsule; *(di proiettile)* cap; *(di dente)* crown

cap'tare *vt Radio, TV* pick up; catch ‹attenzione›

cara'bina *nf* carbine

carabini'ere *nm* carabiniere; **carabini'eri** *pl* Italian police force *(which is a branch of the army)*

ca'raffa *nf* carafe

Ca'raibi *nmpl (zona)* Caribbean *sg*; *(isole)* Caribbean Islands; **il mar dei ~** the Caribbean [Sea]

cara'mella *nf* sweet

cara'mello *nm* caramel

ca'rato *nm* carat

ca'ratte|re *nm* character; *(caratteristica)* characteristic; *Typ* type; **di buon ~re** good-natured. **~'ristico, -a** *a* characteristic; *(pittoresco)* quaint ● *nf* characteristic. **~riz'zare** *vt* characterize

carbon'cino *nm (per disegno)* charcoal

car'bone *nm* coal

carboniz'zare *vt* burn to a cinder

carbu'rante *nm* fuel

carbura'tore *nm* carburettor

car'cassa *nf* carcass; *fig* old wreck

carce'ra|rio *a* prison. **~to, -a** *nmf* prisoner. **~zi'one** *nf* imprisonment. **~zione preventiva** preventive detention

'carcer|e *nm* prison; *(punizione)* imprisonment. **~i'ere, -a** *nmf* gaoler

carci'ofo *nm* artichoke

car'diaco *a* cardiac

cardi'nale *a & nm* cardinal

'cardine *nm* hinge

cardio|chi'rurgo *nm* heart surgeon. **~lo'gia** *nf* cardiology. **cardi'ologo** *nm* heart specialist. **~'tonico** *nm* heart stimulant

'cardo *nm* thistle

ca'rena *nf Naut* bottom

ca'ren|te *a* **~te di** lacking in. **~za** *nf* lack; *(scarsità)* scarcity

care'stia *nf* famine; *(mancanza)* dearth

ca'rezza *nf* caress; **fare una ~** a caress

cari'a|rsi *vi* decay. **~to** *a* decayed

'carica *nf* office; *Mil, Electr* charge; *fig* drive. **cari'care** *vt* load; *Mil, Electr* charge; wind up ‹orologio›. **~'tore** *nm (per proiettile)* magazine

carica'tu|ra *nf* caricature. **~'rale** *a* grotesque. **~'rista** *nmf* caricaturist

'carico *a* loaded (**di** with); *‹colore›* strong; *‹orologio›* wound [up]; *‹batteria›* charged ● *nm* load; *(di nave)* cargo; *(il caricare)* loading; **a ~ di** *Comm* to be charged to; *‹persona›* dependent on

'carie *nf* [tooth] decay

ca'rino *a* pretty; *(piacevole)* agreeable

ca'risma *nm* charisma. **cari'smatico** *a* charismatic

carit|à *nf* charity; **per ~à!** *(come rifiuto)* God forbid!. **~a'tevole** *a* charitable

carnagi'one *nf* complexion

car'naio *nm fig* shambles

car'nale *a* carnal; **cugino ~** first cousin

'carne *nf* flesh; *(alimento)* meat; **~ di manzo/maiale/vitello** beef/pork/veal

car'nefi|ce *nm* executioner. **~'cina** *nf* slaughter

carne'va|le *nm* carnival. **~'lesco** *a* carnival

car'nivoro *nm* carnivore ● *a* carnivorous

car'noso *a* fleshy

'caro, -a *a* dear; **cari saluti** kind regards ● *nmf fam* darling, dear; **i miei cari** my nearest and dearest

ca'rogna *nf* carcass; *fig* bastard

caro'sello *nm* merry-go-round

ca'rota *nf* carrot

caro'vana *nf* caravan; *(di veicoli)* convoy

caro'vita *nm* high cost of living

'carpa *nf* carp

carpenti'ere *nm* carpenter

car'pire *vt* seize; *(con difficoltà)* extort

car'pone, car'poni *adv* on all fours

car'rabile *a* suitable for vehicles; **passo ~** *vedi* **carraio**

car'raio *a* **passo ~** *nm* **~** *entrance to driveway, garage etc where parking is forbidden*

carreggi'ata *nf* roadway; **doppia ~** dual carriageway, divided highway *Am*

carrel'lata *nf TV* pan

car'rello *nm* trolley; *(di macchina da scrivere)* carriage; *Aeron* undercarriage; *Cinema, TV* dolly. **~ d'atterraggio** *Aeron* landing gear

car'retto *nm* cart

carri'e|ra *nf* career; **di gran ~ra** at full speed; **fare ~ra** get on. **~'rismo** *nm* careerism

carri'ola *nf* wheelbarrow

'carro *nm* cart. **~ armato** tank. **~**

attrezzi breakdown vehicle, wrecker *Am*. **~ funebre** hearse. **~ merci** truck

car'rozza *nf* carriage; *Rail* car, coach. **~ cuccette** sleeping car. **~ ristorante** restaurant car

carroz'zella *nf* (*per bambini*) pram; (*per invalidi*) wheelchair

carrozze'ria *nf* bodywork; *(officina)* bodyshop

carroz'zina *nf* pram; *(pieghevole)* push-chair, stroller *Am*

carroz'zone *nm* (*di circo*) caravan

'carta *nf* paper; *(da gioco)* card; *(statuto)* charter; *Geog* map. **~ d'argento** ≈ senior citizens' railcard. **~ assorbente** blotting-paper. **~ geografica** map. **~ d'identità** identity card. **~ d'imbarco** boarding card. **~ da lettere** writing-paper. **~ da parati** wallpaper. **~ di credito** credit card. **~ igienica** toilet-paper. **~ stagnola** silver paper; *Culin* aluminium foil. **~ straccia** waste paper. **~ stradale** road map. **~ velina** tissue-paper. **~ verde** *Auto* green card. **~ vetrata** sandpaper

cartacar'bone *nf* carbon paper

car'taccia *nf* waste paper

carta'modello *nm* pattern

cartamo'neta *nf* paper money

carta'pesta *nf* papier mâché

carta'straccia *nf* waste paper

cartave'trare *vt* sand [down]

car'tel|la *nf* (*per documenti ecc*) briefcase; *(di cartone)* folder; *(di scolaro)* satchel. **~la clinica** medical record. **~'lina** *nf* document wallet, folder

cartel'lino *nm* (*etichetta*) label; (*dei prezzi*) price-tag; (*di presenza*) time-card; **timbrare il ~** clock in

car'tel|lo *nm* sign; (*pubblicitario*) poster; (*stradale*) road sign; (*di protesta*) placard; *Comm* cartel. **~'lone** *nm* poster; *Theat* bill

carti'era *nf* paper-mill

carti'lagine *nf* cartilage

car'tina *nf* map

car'toccio *nm* paper bag; **al ~** *Culin* baked in foil

carto'|laio, -a *nmf* stationer. **~le'ria** *nf* stationer's [shop]. **~libre'ria** *nf* stationer's and book shop

carto'lina *nf* postcard. **~ postale** postcard

carto'mante *nmf* fortune-teller

carton'cino *nm* (*materiale*) card

car'tone *nm* cardboard; (*arte*) cartoon. **~ animato** [animated] cartoon

car'tuccia *nf* cartridge

'**casa** nf house; (abitazione propria) home; (ditta) firm; **amico di ~** family friend; **andare a ~** go home; **essere di ~** be like one of the family; **fatto in ~** home-made; **padrone di ~** (di pensione ecc) landlord; (proprietario) house owner. **~ di cura** nursing home. **~ popolare** council house. **~ dello studente** hall of residence

ca'**sacca** nf military coat; (giacca) jacket

ca'**saccio** adv **a ~** at random

casa'**ling|a** nf housewife. **~o** a domestic; (fatto in casa) home-made; (amante della casa) home-loving; (semplice) homely

ca'**scante** a falling; (floscio) flabby

ca'**sca|re** vi fall [down]. **~ta** nf (di acqua) waterfall

ca'**schetto** nm **[capelli a] ~** bob

ca'**scina** nf farm building

'**casco** nm crash-helmet; (asciuga-capelli) [hair-]drier; **~ di banane** bunch of bananas

caseggi'**ato** nm block of flats Br, apartment block

casei'**ficio** nm dairy

ca'**sella** nf pigeon-hole. **~ postale** post office box; Comput mailbox

casel'**lante** nmf (per treni) signalman

casel'**lario** nm **~ giudiziario** record of convictions; **avere il ~ giudiziario vergine** have no criminal record

ca'**sello [autostra'dale]** nm [motorway] toll booth

case'**reccio** a home-made

ca'**serma** nf barracks pl; (dei carabinieri) [police] station

casi'**nista** nmf fam muddler. ca'**sino** nm fam (bordello) brothel; (fig: confusione) racket; (disordine) mess; **un casino di** loads of

casi'**nò** nm inv casino

ca'**sistica** nf (classificazione) case records pl

'**caso** nm chance; (fatto, circostanza, Med, Gram) case; **a ~** at random; **~ mai** if need be; **far ~ a** pay attention to; **non far ~ a** take no account of; **per ~** by chance. **~ [giudiziario]** [legal] case

caso'**lare** nm farmhouse

'**caspita** int good gracious!

'**cassa** nf case; Comm cash; (luogo di pagamento) cash desk; (mobile) chest; (istituto bancario) bank. **~ automatica prelievi** cash dispenser, automatic teller. **~ da morto** coffin. **~ toracica** chest

cassa'**forte** nf safe

cassa'**panca** nf linen chest

casseru'**ola** nf saucepan

cas'**setta** nf case; (per registratore) cassette. **~ delle lettere** postbox, letterbox. **~ di sicurezza** strong-box

cas'**set|to** nm drawer. **~tone** nm chest of drawers

cassi'**ere, -a** nmf cashier; (di supermercato) checkout assistant, checkout operator; (di banca) teller

'**casta** nf caste

ca'**stagn|a** nf chestnut. **casta'gneto** nm chestnut grove. **~o** nm chestnut[tree]

ca'**stano** a chestnut

ca'**stello** nm castle; (impalcatura) scaffold

casti'**gare** vt punish

casti'**gato** a (casto) chaste

ca'**stigo** nm punishment

casti**tà** nf chastity. '**casto** a chaste

ca'**storo** nm beaver

ca'**strare** vt castrate

casu'**al|e** a chance attrib. **~'mente** adv by chance

ca'**supola** nf little house

cata'**clisma** nm fig upheaval

cata'**comba** nf catacomb

cata'**fascio** nm **andare a ~** go to rack and ruin

cata'**litico** a **marmitta ~** Auto catalytic converter

cataliz'**za|re** vt fig heighten. **~tore** nm Auto catalytic converter

catalo'**gare** vt catalogue. ca'**talogo** nm catalogue

catama'**rano** nm (da diporto) catamaran

cata'**pecchia** nf hovel; fam dump

catapul'**tar|e** vt (scaraventare fuori) eject. **~si** vr (precipitarsi) dive

catarifran'**gente** nm reflector

ca'**tarro** nm catarrh

ca'**tasta** nf pile

ca'**tasto** nm land register

ca'**tastrofe** nf catastrophe. cata'**strofico** a catastrophic

cate'**chismo** nm catechism

cate**go'ria** nf category. **~'gorico** a categorical

ca'**tena** nf chain. **~ montuosa** mountain range. **catene** pl **da neve** tyre-chains. **cate'naccio** nm bolt

cate'**|nella** nf (collana) chain. **~'nina** nf chain

cate'**ratta** nf cataract

ca'**terva** nf **una ~ di** heaps of

cati'nell|a *nf* basin; **piovere a ~e**
bucket down

ca'tino *nm* basin

ca'torcio *nm fam* old wreck

ca'trame *nm* tar

'**cattedra** *nf* (*tavolo di insegnante*)
desk; (*di università*) chair

catte'drale *nf* cathedral

catti'veria *nf* wickedness; (*azione*)
wicked action

cattività *nf* captivity

cat'tivo *a* bad; ‹*bambino*› naughty

cattoli'cesimo *nm* Catholicism

cat'tolico, -a *a & nmf* [Roman] Catholic

cat'tu|ra *nf* capture. **~'rare** *vt* capture

caucciù *nm* rubber

'**causa** *nf* cause; *Jur* lawsuit; **far ~ a
qcno** sue sb. **cau'sare** *vt* cause

'**caustico** *a* caustic

cauta'mente *adv* cautiously

cau'tela *nf* caution

caute'lar|e *vt* protect. **~si** *vr* take pre-
cautions

cauteriz'z|are *vt* cauterize. **~i'one** *nf*
cauterization

'**cauto** *a* cautious

cauzi'one *nf* security; (*per libertà
provvisoria*) bail

'**cava** *nf* quarry; *fig* mine

caval'ca|re *vt* ride; (*stare a cavalcioni*)
sit astride. **~ta** *nf* ride; (*corteo*) caval-
cade. **~'via** *nm* flyover

cavalci'oni *adv* **a ~** astride

cavali'ere *nm* rider; (*titolo*) knight;
(*accompagnatore*) escort; (*al ballo*)
partner

cavalle'|resco *a* chivalrous. **~'ria** *nf*
chivalry; *Mil* cavalry. **~'rizzo, -a** *nm*
horseman ● *nf* horsewoman

caval'letta *nf* grasshopper

caval'letto *nm* trestle; (*di macchina
fotografica*) tripod; (*di pittore*) easel

caval'lina *nf* (*ginnastica*) horse

ca'vallo *nm* horse; (*misura di potenza*)
horsepower; (*scacchi*) knight; (*dei pantaloni*) crotch; **a ~** on horseback; **andare a ~** go horse-riding. **~ a dondolo**
rocking-horse

caval'lone *nm* (*ondata*) roller

caval'luccio ma'rino *nm* sea horse

ca'var|e *vt* take out; (*di dosso*) take off;
~sela get away with it; **se la cava
bene** she's doing all right

cava'tappi *nm inv* corkscrew

ca'ver|na *nf* cave. **~'noso** *a* (*voce*)
deep

'**cavia** *nf* guinea-pig

cavi'ale *nm* caviar

ca'viglia *nf* ankle

cavil'lare *vi* quibble. **ca'villo** *nm* quibble

cavità *nf inv* cavity

'**cavo** *a* hollow ● *nm* cavity; (*di metallo*)
cable; *Naut* rope

cavo'lata *nf fam* rubbish

cavo'letto *nm* **~ di Bruxelles** Brussels sprout

cavolfi'ore *nm* cauliflower

'**cavolo** *nm* cabbage; **~! fam** sugar!

caz'zo *int vulg* fuck!

caz'zott|o *nm* punch; **prendere qcno
a ~i** beat sb up

cazzu'ola *nf* trowel

c/c *abbr* (**conto corrente**) c/a

CD-Rom *nm inv* CD-Rom

ce *pron pers* (*a noi*) (to) us ● *adv* there;
~ ne sono molti there are many

'**cece** *nm* chick-pea

cecità *nf* blindness

ceco, -a *a & nmf* Czech; **la
Repubblica Ceca** the Czech Republic

Cecoslo'vacc|hia *nf* Czechoslova-
kia. **c~o, -a** *a & nmf* Czechoslovak

'**cedere** *vi* (*arrendersi*) surrender;
(*concedere*) yield; (*sprofondare*) subside
● *vt* give up; make over ‹*proprietà ecc*›.
ce'devole *a* ‹*terreno ecc*› soft; *fig* yield-
ing. **cedi'mento** *nm* (*di terreno*) subsid-
ence

'**cedola** *nf* coupon

'**cedro** *nm* (*albero*) cedar; (*frutto*)
citron

C.E.E. *nf abbr* (**Communità Economica Europea**) E[E]C

'**ceffo** *nm* (*muso*) snout; (*pej: persona*)
mug

cef'fone *nm* slap

ce'lar|e *vt* conceal. **~si** *vr* hide

cele'bra|re *vt* celebrate. **~zi'one** *nf*
celebration

'**celebr|e** *a* famous. **~ità** *nf inv* celeb-
rity

'**celere** *a* swift

ce'leste *a* (*divino*) heavenly ● *a & nm*
(*colore*) sky-blue

celi'bato *nm* celibacy

'**celibe** *a* single ● *nm* bachelor

'**cella** *nf* cell

cello'fan *nm inv* cellophane; *Culin*
cling film

'**cellula** *nf* cell. **~ fotoelettrica** electronic eye

cellu'lare *nm* (*telefono*) cellular phone
● *a* **furgone ~** police van; **telefono ~**
cellular phone

cellu'lite nf cellulite
cellu'loide a celluloid
cellu'losa nf cellulose
'celt|a nm Celt. **~ico** a Celtic
cemen'tare vt cement. **ce'mento** nm cement. **cemento armato** reinforced concrete
'cena nf dinner; (leggera) supper
ce'nacolo nm circle
ce'nare vi have dinner
'cenci|o nm rag; (per spolverare) duster. **~'oso** a in rags
'cenere nf ash; (di carbone ecc) cinders
ce'netta nf (cena semplice) informal dinner
'cenno nm sign; (col capo) nod; (con la mano) wave; (allusione) hint; (breve resoconto) mention
ce'none nm il **~ di Capodanno/ Natale** special New Year's Eve/Christmas Eve dinner
censi'mento nm census
cen's|ore nm censor. **~ura** nf censorship. **~u'rare** vt censor
centelli'nare vt sip
cente'n|ario, -a a & nmf centenarian ● nm (commemorazione) centenary. **~'nale** a centennial
cen'tesimo a hundredth ● nm (di dollaro) cent; **non avere un ~** be penniless
cen'ti|grado a centigrade. **~metro** nm centimetre
centi'naio nm hundred
'cento a & nm a o one hundred; **per ~** per cent
centome'trista nmf Sport one hundred metres runner
cento'mila nm a o one hundred thousand
cen'trale a central ● nf (di società ecc) head office. **~ atomica** atomic power station. **~ elettrica** power station. **~ nucleare** nuclear power station. **~ telefonica** [telephone] exchange
centra'li|na nf Teleph switchboard. **~'nista** nmf operator
centra'lino nm Teleph exchange; (di albergo ecc) switchboard
centra'li|smo nm centralism. **~z'zare** vt centralize
cen'trare vt **~ qcsa** hit sth in the centre; (fissare nel centro) centre; fig hit on the head (idea)
cen'trifu|ga nf spin-drier. **~ [asciugaverdure]** shaker. **~'gare** vt Techn centrifuge; (lavatrice:) spin
cen'trino nm doily

'centro nm centre. **~ [città]** city centre. **~ commerciale** shopping centre, mall. **~ sociale** community centre
'ceppo nm (di albero) stump; (da ardere) log; (fig: gruppo) stock
'cera nf wax; (aspetto) look. **~ per il pavimento** floor-polish
ce'ramica nf (arte) ceramics; (materia) pottery; (oggetto) piece of pottery
ce'rato a (tela) waxed
cer'biatto nm fawn
'cerca nf andare in **~ di** look for
cercaper'sone nm inv beeper
cer'care vt look for ● vi **~ di** try to
'cerchi|a nf circle. **~'are** vt circle (parola). **~'ato** a (occhi) black-ringed. **~'etto** nm (per capelli) hairband
'cerchi|o nm circle; (giocattolo) hoop. **~'one** nm alloy wheel
cere'ale nm cereal
cere'brale a cerebral
'cereo a waxen
ce'retta nf depilatory wax
ceri'moni|a nf ceremony. **~'ale** nm ceremonial. **~'oso** a ceremonious
ce'rino nm [wax] match
cerni'era nf hinge; (di borsa) clasp. **~ lampo** zip[-fastener], zipper Am
'cernita nf selection
'cero nm candle
ce'rone nm grease-paint
ce'rotto nm [sticking] plaster
certa'mente adv certainly
cer'tezza nf certainty
certifi'ca|re vt certify. **~to** nm certificate
'certo a certain; (notizia) definite; (indeterminativo) some; **sono ~ di riuscire** I am certain to succeed; **a una certa età** at a certain age; **certi giorni** some days; **un ~ signor Giardini** a Mr Giardini; **una certa Anna** somebody called Anna; **certa gente** pej some people; **ho certi dolori!** I'm in such pain!. **certi** pron pl some; (alcune persone) some people ● adv of course; **sapere per ~** know for certain, know for sure; **di ~** surely; **~ che sì!** of course!
cer'vel|lo nm brain. **~'lone, -a** nmf hum genius. **~'lotico** a (macchinoso) over-elaborate
'cervo nm deer
ce'sareo a Med Caesarean
cesel'la|re vt chisel. **~to** a chiselled. **ce'sello** nm chisel
ce'soie nfpl shears
ce'spugli|o nm bush. **~'oso** a (terreno) bushy

ces'sa|re vi stop, cease ● vt stop. **~re nm il fuoco** ceasefire. **~zi'one** nf cessation

cessi'one nf handover

'cesso nm sl (gabinetto) bog, john Am; (fig: locale, luogo) dump

'cesta nf [large] basket. **ce'stello** nm (per lavatrice) drum

cesti'nare vt throw away. **ce'stino** nm [small] basket; (per la carta straccia) waste-paper basket. **'cesto** nm basket

'ceto nm [social] class

'cetra nf lyre

cetri'olino nm gherkin. **cetri'olo** nm cucumber

cfr abbr (confronta) cf.

che pron rel (persona: soggetto) who; (persona: oggetto) that, who, whom fml; (cosa, animale) that, which; **questa è la casa ~ ho comprato** this is the house [that] I've bought; **il ~ mi sorprende** which surprises me; **dal ~ deduco che...** from which I gather that...; **avere di ~ vivere** have enough to live on; **grazie! – non c'è di!** thank you! – don't mention it!; **il giorno ~ ti ho visto** fam the day I saw you ● a inter what; (esclamativo: con aggettivo) how; (con nome) what a; **~ macchina prendiamo, la tua o la mia?** which car are we taking, yours or mine?; **~ bello!** how nice!; **~ ideal** what an idea!; **~ bella giornata!** what a lovely day! ● pron inter what; **a ~ pensi?** what are you thinking about? ● conj that; (con comparazioni) than; **credo ~ abbia ragione** I think [that] he is right; **era così commosso ~ non riusciva a parlare** he was so moved [that] he couldn't speak; **aspetto ~ telefoni** I'm waiting for him to phone; **è da un po' ~ non lo vedo** it's been a while since I saw him; **mi piace più Roma ~ Milano** I like Rome better than Milan; **~ ti piaccia o no** whether you like it or not; **~ io sappia** as far as I know

checché pron indef whatever

chemiotera'pia nf chemotherapy

chero'sene nm paraffin

cheru'bino nm cherub

cheti'chella: alla ~ adv silently

'cheto a quiet

chi pron rel whoever; (coloro che) people who; **ho trovato ~ ti può aiutare** I found somebody who can help you; **c'è ~ dice che...** some people say that...; **senti ~ parla!** listen to who's talking! ● pron inter (soggetto) who; (oggetto, con preposizione) who, whom fml; (possessivo) **di ~** whose; **~ sei?** who are you?; **~ hai incontrato?** who did you meet?; **di ~ sono questi libri?** whose books are these?; **con ~ parli?** who are you talking to?; **a ~ lo dici!** tell me about it!

chi'acchie|ra nf chat; (pettegolezzo) gossip. **~'rare** vi chat; (far pettegolezzi) gossip. **~'rato** a essere **~rato** (persona:) be the subject of gossip; **~re** pl chitchat; **far quattro ~re** have a chat. **~'rone, -a** a talkative ● nmf chatterer

chia'ma|re vt call; (far venire) send for; **come ti chiami?** what's your name?; **mi chiamo Roberto** my name is Robert; **~re alle armi** call up. **~rsi** vr be called. **~ta** nf call; Mil call-up

chi'appa nf fam cheek

chiara'mente adv clearly

chia'rezza nf clarity; (limpidezza) clearness

chiarifi'ca|re vt clarify. **~'tore** a clarificatory. **~zi'one** nf clarification

chiari'mento nm clarification

chia'rir|e vt make clear; (spiegare) clear up. **~si** vr become clear

chi'aro a clear; (luminoso) bright; (colore) light. **chia'rore** nm glimmer

chiaroveg'gente a clear-sighted ● nmf clairvoyant

chi'as|so nm din. **~'soso** a rowdy

chi'av|e nf key; **chiudere a ~e** lock. **~e inglese** monkey-wrench. **~i'stello** nm latch

chiaz|za nf stain. **~'zare** vt stain

chic a inv chic

chicches'sia pron anybody

'chicco nm grain; (di caffè) bean; (d'uva) grape

chi'eder|e vt ask; (per avere) ask for; (esigere) demand. **~si** vr wonder

chi'esa nf church

chi'esto pp di chiedere

'chiglia nf keel

'chilo nm kilo

chilo'grammo nm kilogram[me]

chilome'traggio nm Auto ≈ mileage

chilo'metrico a in kilometres

chi'lometro nm kilometre

chi'mera nf fig illusion

'chimic|a nf chemistry. **~o, -a** a chemical ● nmf chemist

'china nf (declivio) slope; **inchiostro di ~** Indian ink

chi'nar|e vt lower. **~si** vr stoop

chincaglie'rie nfpl knick-knacks

chinesitera'pia *nf* physiotherapy

chi'nino *nm* quinine

'chino *a* bent

chi'notto *nm sparkling soft drink*

chi'occia *nf* sitting hen

chi'occiola *nf* snail; **scala a ~** spiral staircase

chi'odo *nm* nail; (*idea fissa*) obsession. **~ di garofano** clove

chi'oma *nf* head of hair; (*fogliame*) foliage

chi'osco *nm* kiosk; (*per giornali*) news-stand

chi'ostro *nm* cloister

chiro'man|te *nmf* palmist. **~'zia** *nf* palmistry

chirur'gia *nf* surgery. **chi'rurgico** *a* surgical. **chi'rurgo** *nm* surgeon

chissà *adv* who knows; **~ quando arriverà** I wonder when he will arrive

chi'tar|ra *nf* guitar. **~'rista** *nmf* guitarist

chi'uder|e *vt* shut, close; (*con la chiave*) lock; turn off (*luce, acqua ecc*); (*per sempre*) close down (*negozio, fabbrica ecc*); (*recingere*) enclose ● *vi* shut, close. **~si** *vr* shut; (*tempo:*) cloud over; (*ferita:*) heal over; *fig* withdraw into oneself

chi'unque *pron indef* anyone, anybody ● *pron rel* whoever

chi'usa *nf* enclosure; (*di canale*) lock; (*conclusione*) close

chi'u|so *pp di* **chiudere** ● *a* shut; (*tempo*) overcast; (*persona*) reserved. **~'sura** *nf* closing; (*sistema*) lock; (*allacciatura*) fastener. **~sura lampo** zip, zipper *Am*

ci *pron* (*personale*) us; (*riflessivo*) ourselves; (*reciproco*) each other; (*a ciò, di ciò ecc*) about it; **non ci disturbare** don't disturb us; **aspettateci** wait for us; **ci ha detto tutto** he told us everything; **ce lo manderanno** they'll send it to us; **ci consideriamo...** we consider ourselves...; **ci laviamo le mani** we wash our hands; **ci odiamo** we hate each other; **non ci penso mai** I never think about it; **pensaci!** think about it! ● *adv* (*qui*) here; (*lì*) there; (*moto per luogo*) through it; **ci siamo** we are here; **ci siete?** are you there?; **ci siamo passati tutti** we all went through it; **c'è** there is; **ce ne sono molti** there are many; **ci vuole pazienza** it takes patience; **non ci vedo/sento** I can't see/hear

cia'bat|ta *nf* slipper. **~'tare** *vi* shuffle

ciabat'tino *nm* cobbler

ci'alda *nf* wafer

cial'trone *nm* (*mascalzone*) scoundrel

ciam'bella *nf Culin* ring-shaped cake; (*salvagente*) lifebelt; (*gonfiabile*) rubber ring

cianci'are *vi* gossip

cianfru'saglie *nfpl* knick-knacks

cia'notico *a* (*colorito*) puce

ci'ao *int fam* (*all' arrivo*) hello!, hi!; (*alla partenza*) bye-bye!, cheerio!

ciar'la|re *vi* chat. **~'tano** *nm* charlatan

cias'cuno *a* each ● *pron* everyone, everybody; (*distributivo*) each [one]; **per ~** each

ci'bar|e *vt* feed. **~ie** *nfpl* provisions. **~si** *vr* eat; **~si di** live on

ciber'netico *a* cybernetic

'cibo *nm* food

ci'cala *nf* cicada

cica'lino *nm* buzzer

cica'tri|ce *nf* scar. **~z'zante** *nm* ointment

cicatriz'zarsi *vr* heal [up]. **cicatrizzazi'one** *nf* healing

'cicca *nf* cigarette end; (*fam: sigaretta*) fag; (*fam: gomma*) [chewing] gum

cic'chetto *nm* (*bicchierino*) nip; (*rimprovero*) telling-off

'cicci|a *nf fam* fat, flab. **~'one, -a** *nmf fam* fatty, fatso

cice'rone *nm* guide

cicla'mino *nm* cyclamen

ci'clis|mo *nm* cycling. **~ta** *nmf* cyclist

'ciclo *nm* cycle; (*di malattia*) course

ciclomo'tore *nm* moped

ci'clone *nm* cyclone

ci'cogna *nf* stork

ci'coria *nf* chicory

ci'eco, -a *a* blind ● *nm* blind man ● *nf* blind woman

ci'elo *nm* sky; *Relig* heaven; **santo ~!** good heavens!

'cifra *nf* figure; (*somma*) sum; (*monogramma*) monogram; (*codice*) code

ci'fra|re *vt* embroider with a monogram; (*codificare*) code. **~to** *a* monogrammed; coded

'ciglio *nm* (*bordo*) edge; (*pl nf* **ciglia**: *delle palpebre*) eyelash

'cigno *nm* swan

cigo'l|are *vt* squeak. **~io** *nm* squeak

'Cile *nm* Chile

ci'lecca *nf* far **~** miss

ci'leno, -a *a & nmf* Chilean

cili'egi|a *nf* cherry. **~o** *nm* cherry [tree]

cilin'drata *nf* cubic capacity, c.c.; **macchina di alta ~** highpowered car

ci'lindro *nm* cylinder; (*cappello*) top hat

'cima *nf* top; (*fig: persona*) genius; **da ~ a fondo** from top to bottom

ci'melio *nm* relic

cimen'tar|e *vt* put to the test. **~si** *vr* (*provare*) try one's hand

'cimice *nf* bug; (*puntina*) drawing pin, thumbtack *Am*

cimini'era *nf* chimney; *Naut* funnel

cimi'tero *nm* cemetery

ci'murro *nm* distemper

'Cina *nf* China

cin cin! *int* cheers!

cincischi'are *vi* fiddle

'cine *nm fam* cinema

cine'asta *nmf* film maker

'cinema *nm inv* cinema. **cine'presa** *nf* cine-camera

ci'nese *a & nmf* Chinese

cine'teca *nf* (*raccolta*) film collection

ci'netico *a* kinetic

'cingere *vt* (*circondare*) surround

'cinghia *nf* strap; (*cintura*) belt

cinghi'ale *nm* wild boar; **pelle di ~** pigskin

cinguet't|are *vi* twitter. **~io** *nm* twittering

'cinico *a* cynical

ci'niglia *nf* (*tessuto*) chenille

ci'nismo *nm* cynicism

ci'nofilo *a* (*unità*) dog-loving

cin'quanta *a & nm* fifty. **cinquan'tenne** *a & nmf* fifty-year-old. **cinquan'tesimo** *a* fiftieth. **cinquan'tina** *nf* **una cinquantina** about fifty

'cinque *a & nm* five

cinquecen'tesco *a* sixteenth-century

cinque'cento *a* five hundred ● *nm* **il C~** the sixteenth century

cinque'mila *a & nm* five thousand

'cinta *nf* (*di pantaloni*) belt; **muro di ~** [boundary] wall. **cin'tare** *vt* enclose

'cintola *nf* (*di pantaloni*) belt

cin'tura *nf* belt. **~ di salvataggio** lifebelt. **~ di sicurezza** *Aeron, Auto* seat-belt

cintu'rino *nm* **~ dell'orologio** watchstrap

ciò *pron* this; that; **~ che** what; **~ nondimeno** nevertheless

ci'occa *nf* lock

ciocco'la|ta *nf* chocolate; (*bevanda*) [hot] chocolate. **~'tino** *nm* chocolate.

~to *nm* chocolate. **~to al latte/ fondente** milk/plain chocolate

cioè *adv* that is

ciondo'l|are *vi* dangle. **ci'ondolo** *nm* pendant. **~oni** *adv fig* hanging about

cionono'stante *adv* nonetheless

ci'otola *nf* bowl

ci'ottolo *nm* pebble

ci'polla *nf* onion; (*bulbo*) bulb

ci'presso *nm* cypress

'cipria *nf* [face] powder

'Cipro *nm* Cyprus. **cipri'ota** *a & nmf* Cypriot

'circa *adv & prep* about

'circo *nm* circus

circo'la|re *a* circular ● *nf* circular; (*di metropolitana*) circle line ● *vi* circulate. **~'torio** *a Med* circulatory. **~zi'one** *nf* circulation; (*traffico*) traffic

'circolo *nm* circle; (*società*) club

circon'ci|dere *vt* circumcise. **~si'one** *nf* circumcision

circon'dar|e *vt* surround. **~io** *nm* (*amministrativo*) administrative district. **~si di** *vr* surround oneself with

circonfe'renza *nf* circumference. **~ dei fianchi** hip measurement

circonvallazi'one *nf* ring road

circo'scritto *a* limited

circoscrizi'one *nf* area. **~ elettorale** constituency

circo'spetto *a* wary

circospezi'one *nf* **con ~** warily

circo'stante *a* surrounding

circo'stanza *nf* circumstance; (*occasione*) occasion

circu'ire *vt* (*ingannare*) trick

cir'cuito *nm* circuit

circumnavi'ga|re *vt* circumnavigate. **~zi'one** *nf* circumnavigation

'ciste *nf inv* cyst

ci'sterna *nf* cistern; (*serbatoio*) tank

'cisti *nf inv* cyst

ci'ta|re *vt* (*riportare brani ecc*) quote; (*come esempio*) cite; *Jur* summons. **~zi'one** *nf* quotation; *Jur* summons *sg*

citofo'nare *vt* buzz. **ci'tofono** *nm* entry phone; (*in ufficio, su aereo ecc*) intercom

ci'trullo *nmf fam* dimwit

città *nf inv* town; (*grande*) city

citta'della *nf* citadel

citta'di|nanza *nf* citizenship; (*popolazione*) citizens *pl*. **~'dino, -a** *nmf* citizen; (*abitante di città*) city dweller

ciucci'are *vt fam* suck. **ci'uccio** *nm fam* dummy

ci'uco *nm* ass

ci'uffo *nm* tuft

ci'urma *nf* Naut crew

ci'vet|ta *nf* owl; (*fig: donna*) flirt; [auto] **~ta** unmarked police car. **~'tare** *vi* flirt. **~te'ria** *nf* coquettishness

'civico *a* civic

ci'vil|e *a* civil. **~iz'zare** *vt* civilize. **~iz'zato** *a* (*paese*) civilized. **~izzazi'one** *nf* civilization. **~'mente** *adv* civilly

civiltà *nf inv* civilization; (*cortesia*) civility

'clacson *nm inv* horn. **clacso'nare** *vi* beep the horn, hoot

cla'mo|re *nm* clamour; **fare ~re** cause a sensation. **~rosa'mente** *adv* (*sbagliare*) sensationally. **~'roso** *a* noisy; (*sbaglio*) sensational

clan *nm inv* clan; *fig* clique

clandestin|a'mente *adv* secretly. **~ità** *nf* secrecy

clande'stino *a* clandestine; **movimento ~** underground movement; **passeggero ~** stowaway

clari'netto *nm* clarinet

'classe *nf* class. **~ turistica** tourist class

classi'cis|mo *nm* classicism. **~ta** *nmf* classicist

'classico *a* classical; (*tipico*) classic ● *nm* classic

clas'sifi|ca *nf* classification; *Sport* results *pl.* **~'care** *vt* classify. **~'carsi** *vr* be placed. **~ca'tore** *nm* (*cartella*) folder. **~cazi'one** *nf* classification

clas'sista *nmf* class-conscious person

'clausola *nf* clause

claustro|fo'bia *nf* claustrophobia. **~'fobico** *a* claustrophobic

clau'sura *nf* Relig enclosed order

clavi'cembalo *nm* harpsichord

cla'vicola *nf* collar-bone

cle'men|te *a* merciful; (*tempo*) mild. **~za** *nf* mercy

cleri'cale *a* clerical. **'clero** *nm* clergy

clic *nm* Comput click; **fare ~ su** click on

cli'en|te *nmf* client; (*di negozio*) customer. **~'tela** *nf* customers *pl*

'clima *nm* climate. **cli'matico** *a* climatic; **stazione climatica** health resort

'clinica *nf* clinic. **clinico** *a* clinical ● *nm* clinician

clo'aca *nf* sewer

'cloro *nm* chlorine. **~'formio** *nm* chloroform

clou *a inv* **momenti ~** highlights

coabi'ta|re *vi* live together. **~zi'one** *nf* cohabitation

coagu'la|re *vt*, **~rsi** *vr* coagulate. **~zi'one** *nf* coagulation

coalizi'one *nf* coalition. **~'zarsi** *vr* unite

co'atto *a* Jur compulsory

'cobra *nm inv* cobra

coca'ina *nf* cocaine. **cocai'nomane** *nmf* cocaine addict

cocci'nella *nf* ladybird

'coccio *nm* earthenware; (*frammento*) fragment

cocci|u'taggine *nf* stubbornness. **~'uto** *a* stubborn

'cocco *nm* coconut palm; *fam* love; **noce di ~** coconut

cocco'drillo *nm* crocodile

cocco'lare *vt* cuddle

co'cente *a* (*sole*) burning

'cocktail *nm inv* (*ricevimento*) cocktail party

co'comero *nm* watermelon

co'cuzzolo *nm* top; (*di testa, cappello*) crown

'coda *nf* tail; (*di abito*) train; (*fila*) queue; **fare la ~** queue [up], stand in line *Am.* **~ di cavallo** (*acconciatura*) ponytail. **~ dell'occhio** corner of one's eye **~ di paglia** guilty conscience

co'dardo, -a *a* cowardly ● *nmf* coward

'codice *nm* code. **~ di avviamento postale** postal code, zip code *Am.* **~ a barre** bar-code. **~ fiscale** tax code. **~ della strada** highway code.

codifi'care *vt* codify

coe'ren|te *a* coherent. **~za** *nf* coherence

coesi'one *nf* cohesion

coe'sistere *vi* coexist

coe'taneo, -a *a & nmf* contemporary

cofa'netto *nm* casket. **'cofano** *nm* (*forziere*) chest; *Auto* bonnet, hood *Am*

'cogliere *vt* pick; (*sorprendere*) catch; (*afferrare*) seize; (*colpire*) hit

co'gnato, -a *nmf* brother-in-law; sister-in-law

cognizi'one *nf* knowledge

co'gnome *nm* surname

'coi = con + i

coinci'denza *nf* coincidence; (*di treno ecc*) connection

coin'cidere *vi* coincide

coinqui'lino *nm* flatmate

coin'vol|gere *vt* involve. **~gi'mento** *nm* involvement. **~to** *a* involved

'coito *nm* coitus

col = con + il

colà *adv* there

cola|'brodo *nm inv* strainer; **ridotto a un ~brodo** *fam* full of holes. **~'pasta** *nm inv* colander

co'la|re *vt* strain; *(versare lentamente)* drip ● *vi (gocciolare)* drip; *(perdere)* leak; **~re a picco** *Naut* sink. **~ta** *nf (di metallo)* casting; *(di lava)* flow·

colazi'one *nf (del mattino)* breakfast; *(di mezzogiorno)* lunch; **prima ~** breakfast; **far ~** have breakfast/lunch. **~ al sacco** packed lunch

co'lei *pron f* the one

co'lera *nm* cholera

coleste'rolo *nm* cholesterol

colf *nf abbr* **(collaboratrice familiare)** home help

'colica *nf* colic

co'lino *nm* [tea] strainer

'colla *nf* glue; *(di farina)* paste. **~ di pesce** gelatine

collabo'ra|re *vi* collaborate. **~'tore, ~'trice** *nmf* collaborator. **~zi'one** *nf* collaboration

col'lana *nf* necklace; *(serie)* series

col'lant *nm* tights *pl*

col'lare *nm* collar

col'lasso *nm* collapse

collau'dare *vt* test. **col'laudo** *nm* test

'colle *nm* hill

col'lega *nmf* colleague

collega'mento *nm* connection; *Mil* liaison; *Radio ecc* link. **colle'gar|e** *vt* connect. **~si** *vr TV, Radio* link up

collegi'ale *nmf* boarder ● *a (responsabilità, decisione)* collective

col'legio *nm (convitto)* boarding-school. **~ elettorale** constituency

'collera *nf* anger; **andare in ~** get angry. **col'lerico** *a* irascible

col'letta *nf* collection

collet|tivi'tà *nf inv* community. **~'tivo** *a* collective; *(interesse)* general; **biglietto ~tivo** group ticket

col'letto *nm* collar

collezi|o'nare *vt* collect. **~'one** *nf* collection. **~o'nista** *nmf* collector

colli'mare *vi* coincide

col'li|na *nf* hill. **~'noso** *a (terreno)* hilly

col'lirio *nm* eyewash

collisi'one *nf* collision

'collo *nm* neck; *(pacco)* package; **a ~ alto** high-necked. **~ del piede** instep

colloca'mento *nm* placing; *(impiego)* employment

collo'ca|re *vt* place. **~rsi** *vr* take one's place. **~zi'one** *nf* placing

colloqui'ale *a (termine)* colloquial.

col'loquio *nm* conversation; *(udienza ecc)* interview; *(esame)* oral [exam]

collusi'one *nf* collusion

colluttazi'one *nf* scuffle

col'mare *vt* fill [to the brim]; **~ qcn di gentilezze** overwhelm sb with kindness. **'colmo** *a* full ● *nm* top; *fig* height; **al colmo della disperazione** in the depths of despair; **questo è il colmo!** *(con indignazione)* this is the last straw!; *(con stupore)* I don't believe it!

col'mare *vt* bridge *(divario)*

co'lomb|a *nf* dove. **~o** *nm* pigeon

co'loni|a[1] *nf* colony; **~a [estiva]** *(per bambini)* holiday camp. **~'ale** *a* colonial

co'lonia[2] *nf* **[acqua di] ~** [eau de] Cologne

co'lonico *a (terreno, casa)* farm

coloniz'za|re *vt* colonize. **~'tore, ~'trice** *nmf* colonizer

co'lon|na *nf* column. **~ sonora** soundtrack. **~ vertebrale** spine. **~'nato** *nm* colonnade

colon'nello *nm* colonel

co'lono *nm* tenant farmer

colo'rante *nm* colouring

colo'rare *vt* colour; colour in *(disegno)*

co'lore *nm* colour; **a colori** in colour; **di ~** coloured. **colo'rito** *a* coloured; *(viso)* rosy; *(racconto)* colourful ● *nm* complexion

co'loro *pron pl* the ones

colos'sale *a* colossal. **co'losso** *nm* colossus

'colpa *nf* fault; *(biasimo)* blame; *(colpevolezza)* guilt; *(peccato)* sin; **dare la ~ a** blame; **essere in ~** be at fault; **per ~ di** because of. **col'pevole** *a* guilty ● *nmf* culprit

col'pire *vt* hit, strike; **~ nel segno** hit the nail on the head

'colpo *nm* blow; *(di arma da fuoco)* shot; *(urto)* knock; *(emozione)* shock; *Med, Sport* stroke; *(furto)* raid; **di ~** suddenly; **far ~** make a strong impression; **far venire un ~ a qcno** *fig* give sb a fright; **perdere colpi** *(motore:)* keep missing; **a ~ d'occhio** at a glance; **a ~ sicuro** for certain. **~ d'aria** chill. **~ basso** blow below the belt. **~ di scena** coup de théâtre. **~ di sole** sunstroke; **colpi di sole** *pl* highlights. **~ di stato** coup [d'état]. **~ di telefono** ring;

dare un ~ **di telefono a qn** give sb a
ring. ~ **di testa** [sudden] impulse. ~ **di
vento** gust of wind

col'poso a omicidio ~ manslaughter

coltel'lata nf stab. **col'tello** nm knife

colti'va|re vt cultivate. ~**'tore,
~'trice** nmf farmer. ~**zi'one** nf farming; (di piante) growing

'colto pp di **cogliere** ● a cultured

'coltre nf blanket

col'tura nf cultivation

co'lui pron inv m the one

'coma nm inv coma; **in** ~ in a coma

comanda'mento nm commandment

coman'dante nm commander; Naut,
Aeron captain

coman'dare vt command; Mech control ● vi be in charge. **co'mando** nm
command; (di macchina) control

co'mare nf (madrina) godmother

combaci'are vi fit together; (testi-
monianze) concur

combat'tente a fighting ● nm com-
batant. **ex** ~ ex-serviceman

com'bat|tere vt/i fight. ~**ti'mento**
nm fight; Mil battle; **fuori** ~**timento**
(pugilato) knocked out. ~**'tuto** (gara)
hard fought

combi'na|re vt/i arrange; (mettere
insieme) combine; (fam: fare) do; **cosa
stai** ~**ndo?** what are you doing?. ~**rsi**
vr combine; (mettersi d'accordo) come to
an agreement. ~**zi'one** nf combination;
(caso) coincidence; **per** ~**zione** by
chance

com'briccola nf gang

combu'sti|bile a combustible ● nm
fuel. ~**'one** nf combustion

com'butta nf gang; **in** ~ in league

'come adv like; (in qualità di) as; (interrogativo, esclamativo) how; **questo vestito è** ~ **il tuo** this dress is like yours;
~ **stai?** how are you?; ~ **va?** how are
things?; ~ **mai?** how come?; ~**?** what?;
non sa ~ **fare** he doesn't know what to
do; ~ **sta bene!** how well he looks!; ~
no! that will be right!; ~ **tu sai** as you
know; **fa** ~ **vuoi** do as you like; ~ **se** as
if ● conj (non appena) as soon as

co'meta nf comet

'comico, -a a comic[al]; (teatro) comic
● nm funny side ● nmf (attore) comedian, comic actor ● nf (a torte in faccia)
slapstick sketch

co'mignolo nm chimney-pot

cominci'are vt/i begin, start; **a** ~ **da
oggi** from today; **per** ~ to begin with

comi'tato nm committee

comi'tiva nf party, group

co'mizio nm meeting

com'mando nm inv commando

com'medi|a nf comedy; (opera teatra-
le) play; fig sham. ~**a musicale** musical. ~**'ante** nmf comedian; fig pej
phoney. ~**'ografo, -a** nmf playwright

commemo'ra|re vt commemorate.
~**zi'one** nf commemoration

commen'sale nmf fellow diner

commen't|are vt comment on; (anno-
tare) annotate. ~**ario** nm commentary.
~**a'tore,** ~**a'trice** nmf commentator.
com'mento nm comment

commerci'a|le a commercial; (rela-
zioni, trattative) trade; (attività) business. **centro** ~**le** shopping centre.
~**'lista** nmf business consultant;
(contabile) accountant. ~**liz'zare** vt
market. ~**lizzazi'one** nf marketing

commerci'ante nmf trader, merchant; (negoziante) shopkeeper. ~
all'ingrosso wholesaler

commerci'are vi ~ **in** deal in

com'mercio nm commerce; (internazionale) trade; (affari) business; **in** ~
(prodotto) on sale. ~ **all'ingrosso**
wholesale trade. ~ **al minuto** retail
trade

com'messo, -a pp di **commettere**
● nmf shop assistant. ~ **viaggiatore**
commercial traveller ● nf (ordine) order

comme'stibile a edible. **commesti-
bili** nmpl groceries

com'mettere vt commit; make (sbaglio)

commi'ato nm leave; **prendere** ~ **da**
take leave of

commise'rar|e vt commiserate. ~**si**
vr feel sorry for oneself

commissari'ato nm (di polizia) police station

commis's|ario nm ≈ [police] super-
intendent; (membro di commissione)
commissioner; Sport steward; Comm
commission agent. ~**ario d'esame** ex-
aminer. ~**i'one** nf (incarico) errand;
(comitato ecc) commission; (Comm: di
merce) order; ~**ioni** pl (acquisti) **fare**
~**ioni** go shopping. ~**ione d'esame**
board of examiners. **C**~**ione Europea**
European Commission

commit'tente nmf purchaser

com'mo|sso pp di **commuovere** ● a
moved. ~**'vente** a moving

commozi'one nf emotion. ~ **cerebrale** concussion

commu'over|e *vt* touch, move. **~si** *vr* be touched

commu'tare *vt* change; *Jur* commute

comò *nm inv* chest of drawers

comoda'mente *adv* comfortably

como'dino *nm* bedside table

comodità *nf inv* comfort; *(convenienza)* convenience

'comodo *a* comfortable; *(conveniente)* convenient; *(spazioso)* roomy; *(facile)* easy; **stia ~!** don't get up!; **far ~** be useful ● *nm* comfort; **fare il proprio ~** do as one pleases

compae'sano, -a *nmf* fellow countryman

com'pagine *nf (squadra)* team

compa'gnia *nf* company; *(gruppo)* party; **fare ~ a qcno** keep sb company; **essere di ~** be sociable. **~ aerea** airline

com'pagno, -a *nmf* companion, mate; *Comm, Sport* partner; *Pol* comrade. **~ di scuola** schoolmate

compa'rabile *a* comparable

compa'ra|re *vt* compare. **~'tivo** *a* & *nm* comparative. **~zi'one** *nf* comparison

com'pare *nm (padrino)* godfather; *(testimone di matrimonio)* witness

compa'rire *vi* appear; *(spiccare)* stand out; **~ in giudizio** appear in court

com'parso, -a *pp di* **comparire** ● *nf* appearance; *Cinema* extra; *Theat* walk-on

compartecipazi'one *nf* sharing; *(quota)* share

comparti'mento *nm* compartment; *(amministrativo)* department

compas'sato *a* calm and collected

compassi'o|ne *nf* compassion; **aver ~ per** feel pity for; **far ~** arouse pity. **~'nevole** *a* compassionate

com'passo *nm* [pair of] compasses *pl*

compa'tibil|e *a (conciliabile)* compatible; *(scusabile)* excusable. **~ità** *nf* compatibility. **~'mente** *adv* **~mente con i miei impegni** if my commitments allow

compa'tire *vt* pity; *(scusare)* make allowances for

compatri'ota *nmf* compatriot

compat'tezza *nf (di materia)* compactness. **com'patto** *a* compact; *(denso)* dense; *(solido)* solid; *fig* united

compene'trare *vt* pervade

compen'sar|e *vt* compensate; *(supplire)* make up for. **~si** *vr* balance each other out

compen'sato *nm (legno)* plywood

compensazi'one *nf* compensation

com'penso *nm* compensation; *(retribuzione)* remuneration; **in ~** *(in cambio)* in return; *(d'altra parte)* on the other hand; *(invece)* instead

'comper|a *nf* purchase; **far ~e** do some shopping

compe'rare *vt* buy

compe'ten|te *a* competent. **~za** *nf* competence; *(responsabilità)* responsibility

com'petere *vi* compete; **~ a** *(competi-to:)* be the responsibility of

competi|tività *nf* competitiveness. **~'tivo** *a (prezzo, carattere)* competitive. **~'tore, ~'trice** *nmf* competitor. **~zi'one** *nf* competition

compiacen|te *a* obliging. **~za** *nf* obligingness

compia'c|ere *vt/i* please. **~ersi** *vr* *(congratularsi)* congratulate. **~ersi di** *(degnarsi)* condescend. **~i'mento** *nm* satisfaction. **~i'uto** *a (aria, sorriso)* smug

compi'an|gere *vt* pity; *(per lutto ecc)* sympathize with. **~to** *a* lamented ● *nm* grief

'compier|e *vt (concludere)* complete; commit *(delitto)*; **~e gli anni** have one's birthday. **~si** *vr* end; *(avverarsi)* come true

compi'la|re *vt* compile; fill in *(modulo)*. **~zi'one** *nf* compilation

compi'mento *nm* **portare a ~ qcsa** conclude sth

com'pire *vt* = **compiere**

compi'tare *vt* spell

com'pito[1] *a* polite

'compito[2] *nm* task; *Sch* homework

compi'ut|o *a* **avere 30 anni ~i** be over 30

comple'anno *nm* birthday

complemen'tare *a* complementary; *(secondario)* subsidiary

comple'mento *nm* complement; *Mil* draft. **~ oggetto** direct object

comples|sità *nf* complexity. **~siva'mente** *adv* on the whole. **~'sivo** *a* comprehensive; *(totale)* total. **com'plesso** *a* complex; *(difficile)* complicated ● *nm* complex; *(di cantanti ecc)* group; *(di circostanze, fattori)* combination; **in ~so** on the whole

completa'mente *adv* completely

comple'tare *vt* complete

com'pleto *a* complete; *(pieno)* full [up]; **essere al ~** *(teatro:)* be sold out;

la **famiglia al** ~ the whole family ● *nm* (*vestito*) suit; (*insieme di cose*) set

compli'ca|re *vt* complicate. ~**rsi** *vr* become complicated. ~**to** complicated. ~**zi'one** *nf* complication; **salvo** ~**zioni** all being well

'**complic|e** *nmf* accomplice ● *a* (*sguardo*) knowing. ~**ità** *nf* complicity

complimen'tar|e *vt* compliment. ~**si** *vr* ~**si con** congratulate

compli'menti *nmpl* (*ossequi*) regards; (*congratulazioni*) congratulations; **far** ~ stand on ceremony

compli'mento *nm* compliment

complot'tare *vi* plot. **com'plotto** *nm* plot

compo'nente *a & nm* component ● *nmf* member

compo'nibile *a* (*cucina*) fitted; (*mobili*) modular

componi'mento *nm* composition; (*letterario*) work

com'por|re *vt* compose; (*ordinare*) put in order; *Typ* set. ~**si** *vr* ~**si di** be made up of

comporta'mento *nm* behaviour

compor'tar|e *vt* involve; (*consentire*) allow. ~**si** *vr* behave

composi'|tore, -'trice *nmf* composer; *Typ* compositor. ~**zi'one** *nf* composition

com'posta *nf* stewed fruit; (*concime*) compost

compo'stezza *nf* composure

com'posto *pp di* **comporre** ● *a* composed; (*costituito*) comprising; **stai** ~! sit properly! ● *nm Chem* compound

com'pra|re *vt* buy. ~'**tore**, ~'**trice** *nmf* buyer

compra'vendita *nf* buying and selling

com'pren|dere *vt* understand; (*includere*) comprise. ~'**sibile** *a* understandable. ~**sibil'mente** *adv* understandably. ~**si'one** *nf* understanding. ~'**sivo** *a* understanding; (*che include*) inclusive. **com'preso** *pp di* **comprendere** ● *a* included; **tutto compreso** (*prezzo*) all-in

com'pressa *nf* compress; (*pastiglia*) tablet

compressi'one *nf* compression. **com'presso** *pp di* **comprimere** ● *a* compressed

com'primere *vt* press; (*reprimere*) repress

compro'me|sso *pp di* **compromet-**

tere ● *nm* compromise. ~**t'tente** *a* compromising. ~**ttere** *vt* compromise

comproprietà *nf* multiple ownership

compro'vare *vt* prove

com'punto *a* contrite

compu'tare *vt* calculate

com'puter *nm* computer. ~**iz'zare** *vt* computerize. ~**iz'zato** *a* computerized

computiste'ria *nf* book-keeping. '**computo** *nm* calculation

comu'nale *a* municipal

co'mune *a* common; (*condiviso*) mutual; (*ordinario*) ordinary ● *nm* borough, council; (*amministrativo*) commune; **fuori del** ~ out of the ordinary. ~'**mente** *adv* commonly

comuni'ca|re *vt* communicate; pass on (*malattia*); *Relig* administer Communion to. ~**rsi** *vr* receive Communion. ~'**tiva** *nf* communicativeness. ~'**tivo** *a* communicative. ~**to** *nm* communiqué. ~**to stampa** press release. ~**zi'one** *nf* communication; *Teleph* [phone] call; **avere la** ~**zione** get through; **dare la** ~**zione a qcno** put sb through

comuni'one *nf* communion; *Relig* [Holy] Communion

comu'nis|mo *nm* communism. ~**ta** *a & nmf* communist

comunità *nf inv* community. **C~** **[Economica] Europea** European [Economic] Community

co'munque *conj* however ● *adv* anyhow

con *prep* with; (*mezzo*) by; ~ **facilità** easily; ~ **mia grande gioia** to my great delight; **è gentile** ~ **tutti** he is kind to everyone; **col treno** by train; ~ **questo tempo** in this weather

co'nato *nm* ~ **di vomito** retching

'**conca** *nf* basin; (*valle*) dell

concate'na|re *vt* link together. ~**zi'one** *nf* connection

'**concavo** *a* concave

con'ceder|e *vt* grant; award (*premio*); (*ammettere*) admit. ~**si** *vr* allow oneself (*pausa*)

concentra'mento *nm* concentration

concen'tra|re *vt*, ~**rsi** *vr* concentrate. ~**to** *a* concentrated ● *nm* ~**to di pomodoro** tomato purée. ~**zi'one** *nf* concentration

concepi'mento *nm* conception

conce'pire *vt* conceive (*bambino*); (*capire*) understand; (*figurarsi*) conceive of; devise (*piano ecc*)

con'cernere *vt* concern

concer'tar|e *vt Mus* harmonize; (*organizzare*) arrange. **~si** *vr* agree

concer'tista *nmf* concert performer. **con'certo** *nm* concert; (*composizione*) concerto

concessio'nario *nm* agent

concessi'one *nf* concession

con'cesso *pp di* concedere

con'cetto *nm* concept; (*opinione*) opinion

concezi'one *nf* conception; (*idea*) concept

con'chiglia *nf* [sea] shell

'concia *nf* tanning; (*di tabacco*) curing

conci'a|re *vt* tan; cure (*tabacco*); **~re qcno per le feste** give sb a good hiding. **~rsi** *vr* (*sporcarsi*) get dirty; (*vestirsi male*) dress badly. **~to** *a* (*pelle, cuoio*) tanned

concili'abile *a* compatible

concili'ante *a* conciliatory

concili'a|re *vt* reconcile; settle (*contravvenzione*); (*favorire*) induce. **~rsi** *vr* go together; (*mettersi d'accordo*) become reconciled. **~zi'one** *nf* reconciliation; *Jur* settlement

con'cilio *nm Relig* council; (*riunione*) assembly

conci'mare *vt* feed (*pianta*). **con'cime** *nm* manure; (*chimico*) fertilizer

concisi'one *nf* conciseness. **con'ciso** *a* concise

conci'tato *a* excited

concitta'dino, -a *nmf* fellow citizen

con'clu|dere *vt* conclude; (*finire con successo*) achieve. **~dersi** *vr* come to an end. **~si'one** *nf* conclusion; **in ~sione** (*insomma*) in short. **~'sivo** *a* conclusive. **~so** *pp di* concludere

concomi'tanza *nf* (*di circostanze, fatti*) combination

concor'da|nza *nf* agreement. **~re** *vt* agree; *Gram* make agree. **~to** *nm* agreement; *Jur, Comm* arrangement

con'cord|e *a* in agreement; (*unanime*) unanimous

concor'ren|te *a* concurrent; (*rivale*) competing ● *nmf Comm, Sport* competitor; (*candidato*) candidate. **~za** *nf* competition. **~zi'ale** *a* competitive

con'cor|rere *vi* (*contribuire*) concur; (*andare insieme*) go together; (*competere*) compete. **~so** *pp di* concorrere ● *nm* competition; **fuori ~so** not in the official competition. **~so di bellezza** beauty contest

concreta'mente *adv* concretely

concre|'tare *vt* (*concludere*) achieve.

~tiz'zare *vt* put into concrete form (*idea, progetto*)

con'creto *a* concrete; **in ~** in concrete terms

concussi'one *nf* extortion

con'danna *nf* sentence; **pronunziare una ~** pass a sentence. **condan'nare** *vt* condemn; *Jur* sentence. **condan'nato, -a** *nmf* convict

conden'sa|re *vt*, **~rsi** *vr* condense. **~zi'one** *nf* condensation

condi'mento *nm* seasoning; (*salsa*) dressing. **con'dire** *vt* flavour; dress (*insalata*)

condiscen'den|te *a* indulgent; *pej* condescending. **~za** *nf* indulgence; *pej* condescension

condi'videre *vt* share

condizio'na|le *a & nm* conditional ● *nf Jur* suspended sentence. **~'mento** *nm Psych* conditioning

condizio'na|re *vt* condition. **~to** *a* conditional. **~'tore** *nm* air conditioner

condizi'one *nf* condition; **a ~ che** on condition that

condogli'anze *nfpl* condolences; **fare le ~** a offer condolences to

condomini'ale *a* (*spese*) common. **condo'minio** *nm* joint ownership; (*edificio*) condominium

condo'nare *vt* remit. **con'dono** *nm* remission

con'dotta *nf* conduct, (*circoscrizione di medico*) district; (*di gara ecc*) management; (*tubazione*) piping

con'dotto *pp di* condurre ● *a* **medico ~** district doctor ● *nm* pipe; *Anat* duct

condu'cente *nm* driver

con'du|rre *vt* lead; drive (*veicoli*); (*accompagnare*) take; conduct (*gas, elettricità ecc*); (*gestire*) run. **~rsi** *vr* behave. **~'tore, ~'trice** *nmf* TV presenter; (*di veicolo*) driver ● *nm Electr* conductor. **~t'tura** *nf* duct

confabu'lare *vi* have a confab

confa'cente *a* suitable. **con'farsi** *vr* confarsi a suit

confederazi'one *nf* confederation

confe'renz|a *nf* (*discorso*) lecture; (*congresso*) conference. **~a stampa** news conference. **~i'ere, -a** *nmf* lecturer

confe'rire *vt* (*donare*) give ● *vi* confer

con'ferma *nf* confirmation. **confer'mare** *vt* confirm

confes's|are *vt*, **~arsi** *vr* confess.

~io'nale *a* & *nm* confessional. **~i'one**
nf confession. **~ore** *nm* confessor
con'fetto *nm* sugared almond
confet'tura *nf* jam
confezio'na|re *vt* manufacture; make
⟨*abiti*⟩; package ⟨*merci*⟩. **~to** *a* ⟨*vestiti*⟩
off-the-peg; ⟨*gelato*⟩ wrapped
confezi'one *nf* manufacture; ⟨*di abiti*⟩
tailoring; ⟨*di pacchi*⟩ packaging; **con-
fezioni** *pl* clothes. **~ regalo** gift pack
confic'car|e *vt* thrust. **~si** *vr* run into
confi'd|are *vi* **~are in** trust ● *vt* con-
fide. **~arsi** *vr* **~arsi con** confide in.
~ente *a* confident ● *nmf* confidant
confi'denz|a *nf* confidence; ⟨*familia-
rità*⟩ familiarity; **prenders|i delle ~e**
take liberties. **~i'ale** *a* confidential;
⟨*rapporto, tono*⟩ familiar
configu'ra|re *vt* *Comput* configure.
~zi'one *nf* configuration
confi'nante *a* neighbouring
confi'na|re *vi* ⟨*relegare*⟩ confine ● *vi*
~re con border on. **~rsi** *vr* withdraw.
~to *a* confined
con'fin|e *nm* border; ⟨*tra terreni*⟩
boundary. **~o** *nm* political exile
con'fi|sca *nf* ⟨*di proprietà*⟩ forfeiture.
~'scare *vt* confiscate
con'flitt|o *nm* conflict. **~u'ale** *a*
adversarial
conflu'enza *nf* confluence; ⟨*di strade*⟩
junction
conflu'ire *vi* ⟨*fiumi:*⟩ flow together;
⟨*strade:*⟩ meet
con'fonder|e *vt* confuse; ⟨*turbare*⟩
confound; ⟨*imbarazzare*⟩ embarrass.
~si *vr* ⟨*mescolarsi*⟩ mingle; ⟨*turbarsi*⟩
become confused; *vr* ⟨*sbagliarsi*⟩ be mistaken
confor'ma|re *vt*, **~rsi** *vr* conform.
~zi'one *nf* conformity (**a** with); ⟨*del
terreno*⟩ composition
con'forme *a* according. **~'mente** *adv*
accordingly
confor'mi|smo *nm* conformity. **~sta**
nmf conformist. **~tà** *nf* ⟨*a norma*⟩ conformity
confor'tante *a* comforting
confor't|are *vt* comfort. **~evole** *a*
⟨*comodo*⟩ comfortable. **con'forto** *nm*
comfort
confron'tare *vt* compare
con'fronto *nm* comparison; **in ~ a** by
comparison with; **nei tuoi confronti**
towards you; **senza ~** far and away
confusi|o'nario *a* ⟨*a persona*⟩ muddle-
headed. **~'one** *nf* confusion; ⟨*baccano*⟩
racket; ⟨*disordine*⟩ mess; ⟨*imbarazzo*⟩

embarrassment. **con'fuso** *pp di* **confondere** ● *a* confused; ⟨*indistinto*⟩ indistinct; ⟨*imbarazzato*⟩ embarrassed
confu'tare *vt* confute
conge'dar|e *vt* dismiss; *Mil* dis-
charge. **~si** *vr* take one's leave
con'gedo *nm* leave; **essere in ~** be on
leave. **~ malattia** sick leave. **~
maternità** maternity leave
conge'gnare *vt* devise; ⟨*mettere insieme*⟩ assemble. **con'gegno** *nm* device
congela'mento *nm* freezing; *Med*
frost-bite
conge'la|re *vt* freeze. **~to** *a* ⟨*cibo*⟩
deep-frozen. **~'tore** *nm* freezer
congeni'ale *a* congenial
con'genito *a* congenital
congestio'na|re *vt* congest. **~to** *a*
⟨*traffico*⟩ congested; ⟨*viso*⟩ flushed.
congesti'one *nf* congestion
conget'tura *nf* conjecture
con'giunger|e *vt* join; ⟨*collegare*⟩ con-
nect. **~si** *vr* join
congiunti'vite *nf* conjunctivitis
congiun'tivo *nm* subjunctive
congi'unto *pp di* **congiungere** ● *a*
joined ● *nm* relative
congiun'tu|ra *nf* joint; ⟨*circostanza*⟩
juncture; ⟨*situazione*⟩ situation. **~'rale**
a economic
congiunzi'one *nf* *Gram* conjunction
congi'u|ra *nf* conspiracy. **~'rare** *vi*
conspire
conglome'rato *nm* conglomerate; *fig*
conglomeration; ⟨*da costruzione*⟩ concrete
congratu'la|rsi *vr* **~rsi con** qcno
per congratulate sb on. **~zi'oni** *nfpl*
congratulations
con'grega *nf* band
congre'ga|re *vt*, **~rsi** *vr* congregate.
~zi'one *nf* congregation
con'gresso *nm* congress
'congruo *a* proper; ⟨*giusto*⟩ fair
conguagli'are *vt* balance. **con-
gu'aglio** *nm* balance
coni'are *vt* coin
'conico *a* conical
co'nifera *nf* conifer
co'niglio *nm* rabbit
coniu'gale *a* marital; ⟨*vita*⟩ married
coniu'ga|re *vt* conjugate. **~rsi** *vr* get
married. **~zi'one** *nf* conjugation
'coniuge *nmf* spouse
connazio'nale *nmf* compatriot
connessi'one *nf* connection. **con-
'nesso** *pp di* **connettere**

con'nettere vt connect ● vi think rationally

conni'vente a conniving

conno'ta|re vt connote. **~to** nm distinguishing feature; **~ti** pl description

con'nubio nm fig union

'cono nm cone

cono'scen|te nmf acquaintance. **~za** nf knowledge; (persona) acquaintance; (sensi) consciousness; **perdere ~za** lose consciousness; **riprendere ~za** regain consciousness, come to

co'nosc|ere vt know; (essere a conoscenza di) be acquainted with; (fare la conoscenza di) meet. **~i'tore, ~i'trice** nmf connoisseur. **~i'uto** pp di **conoscere** ● a well-known

con'quist|a nf conquest. **conqui'stare** vt conquer; fig win

consa'cra|re vt consecrate; ordain ‹sacerdote›; (dedicare) dedicate. **~rsi** vr devote oneself. **~zi'one** nf consecration

consangu'ineo, -a nmf blood-relation

consa'pevo|le a conscious. **~'lezza** nf consciousness. **~l'mente** adv consciously

'conscio a conscious

consecu'tivo a consecutive; (seguente) next

con'segna nf delivery; (merce) consignment; (custodia) care; (di prigioniero) handover; (Mil: ordine) orders pl; (Mil: punizione) confinement; **pagamento alla ~** cash on delivery

conse'gnare vt deliver; (affidare) give in charge; Mil confine to barracks

consegu'en|te a consequent. **~za** nf consequence; **di ~za** (perciò) consequently

consegui'mento nm achievement

consegu'ire vt achieve ● vi follow

con'senso nm consent

consensu'ale a consensus-based

consen'tire vi consent ● vt allow

con'serto a **a braccia conserte** with one's arms folded

con'serva nf preserve; (di frutta) jam; (di agrumi) marmalade. **~ di pomodoro** tomato sauce

conser'var|e vt preserve; (mantenere) keep. **~si** vr keep; **~si in salute** keep well

conserva|'tore, -'trice nmf Pol conservative

conserva'torio nm conservatory

conservazi'one nf preservation; **a lunga ~** long-life

conside'ra|re vt consider; (stimare) regard. **~to** a (stimato) esteemed. **~zi'one** nf consideration; (osservazione, riflessione) remark

conside'revole a considerable

consigli'abile a advisable

consigli|'are vt advise; (raccomandare) recommend. **~'arsi** vr **~arsi con qcno** ask sb's advice. **~'ere, -a** nmf adviser; (membro di consiglio) councillor

con'siglio nm advice; (ente) council. **~ d'amministrazione** board of directors. **C~ dei Ministri** Cabinet

consi'sten|te a substantial; (spesso) thick; (fig: argomento) valid. **~za** nf consistency; (spessore) thickness

con'sistere vi **~ in** consist of

consoci'ata nf (azienda) associate company

conso'lar|e[1] vt console; (rallegrare) cheer. **~si** vr console oneself

conso'la|re[2] a consular. **~to** nm consulate

consolazi'one nf consolation; (gioia) joy

con'sole nf inv (tastiera) console

'console nm consul

consoli'dar|e vt, **~si** vr consolidate

conso'nante nf consonant

'consono a consistent

con'sorte nmf consort

con'sorzio nm consortium

con'stare vi **~ di** consist of; (risultare) appear; **a quanto mi consta** as far as I know; **mi consta che** it appears that

consta'ta|re vt ascertain. **~zi'one** nf observation

consu'e|to a & nm usual. **~tudi'nario** a (diritto) common; (persona) set in one's ways. **~'tudine** nf habit; (usanza) custom

consu'len|te nmf consultant. **~za** nf consultancy

consul'ta|re vt consult. **~rsi con** consult with. **~zi'one** nf consultation

consul't|ivo a consultative. **~orio** nm clinic

consu'ma|re vt (usare) consume; wear out (abito, scarpe); consummate (matrimonio); commit (delitto). **~rsi** vr consume; (abito, scarpe:) wear out; (struggersi) pine

consu'mato a (politico) seasoned; (scarpe, tappeto) worn

consuma|'tore, -'trice nmf consumer. **~zi'one** nf (bibita) drink; (spuntino) snack

consu'mis|mo *nm* consumerism. **~ta** *nmf* consumerist

con'sumo *nm* consumption; (*di abito, scarpe*) wear; (*uso*) use; **generi di ~** consumer goods. **~ [di carburante]** [fuel] consumption

consun'tivo *nm* **[bilancio]** ~ final statement

conta'balle *nmf fam* storyteller

con'tabil|e *a* book-keeping ● *nmf* accountant. **~ità** *nf* accounting; **tenere la ~ità** keep the accounts

contachi'lometri *nm inv* mileometer, odometer *Am*

conta'dino, -a *nmf* farm-worker; (*medievale*) peasant

contagi|'are *vt* infect. **con'tagio** *nm* infection. **~'oso** *a* infectious

conta'gocce *nm inv* dropper

contami'na|re *vt* contaminate. **~zi'one** *nf* contamination

con'tante *nm* cash; **pagare in contanti** pay cash

con'tare *vt/i* count; (*tenere conto di*) take into account; (*proporsi*) intend

conta'scatti *nm inv Teleph* time-unit counter

conta'tore *nm* meter

contat'tare *vt* contact. **con'tatto** *nm* contact

'conte *nm* count

conteggi'are *vt* put on the bill ● *vi* calculate. **con'teggio** *nm* calculation. **conteggio alla rovescia** countdown

con'te|gno *nm* behaviour; (*atteggiamento*) attitude. **~'gnoso** *a* dignified

contemp'la|re *vt* contemplate; (*fissare*) gaze at. **~zi'one** *nf* contemplation

con'tempo *nm* **nel ~** in the meantime

contempo|ranea'mente *adv* at once. **~'raneo, -a** *a* & *nmf* contemporary

conten'dente *nmf* competitor. **con'tendere** *vi* compete; (*litigare*) quarrel ● *vt* contend

conte'n|ere *vt* contain; (*reprimere*) repress. **~ersi** *vr* contain oneself. **~i'tore** *nm* container

conten'tarsi *vr* **~ di** be content with

conten'tezza *nf* joy

conten'tino *nm* placebo

con'tento *a* glad; (*soddisfatto*) contented

conte'nuto *nm* contents *pl*; (*soggetto*) content

contenzi'oso *nm* legal department

con'tes|a *nf* disagreement; *Sport* contest. **~o** *pp di* **contendere** ● *a* contested

con'tessa *nf* countess

conte'sta|re *vt* contest; *Jur* notify. **~'tario** *a* anti-establishment. **~'tore, ~'trice** *nmf* protester. **~zi'one** *nf* (*disputa*) dispute

con'testo *nm* context

con'tiguo *a* adjacent

continen'tale *a* continental. **conti'nente** *nm* continent

conti'nenza *nf* continence

contin'gen|te *nm* contingent; (*quota*) quota. **~za** *nf* contingency

continua'mente *adv* (*senza interruzione*) continuously; (*frequentemente*) continually

continu|'are *vt/i* continue; (*riprendere*) resume. **~a'tivo** *a* permanent. **~azi'one** *nf* continuation. **~ità** *nf* continuity

con'tinu|o *a* continuous; (*molto frequente*) continual. **corrente ~a** direct current; **di ~o** continually

'conto *nm* calculation; (*in banca, negozio*) account; (*di ristorante ecc*) bill; (*stima*) consideration; **a conti fatti** all things considered; **far ~ di** (*supporre*) suppose; (*proporsi*) intend; **far ~ su** rely on; **in fin dei conti** when all is said and done; **per ~ di** on behalf of; **per ~ mio** (*a mio parere*) in my opinion; (*da solo*) on my own; **starsene per ~ proprio** be on one's own; **rendersi ~ di** qcsa realize sth; **sul ~ di** qcno (*voci, informazioni*) about sb; **tener ~ di** qcsa take sth into account; **tenere da ~ qcsa** look after sth; **fare i conti con** qcno *fig* sort sb out. **~ corrente** current account, checking account *Am*. **~ alla rovescia** countdown

con'torcer|e *vt* twist. **~si** *vr* twist about

contor'nare *vt* surround

con'torno *nm* contour; *Culin* vegetables *pl*

contorsi'one *nf* contortion. **con'torto** *pp di* **contorcere** ● *a* twisted

contrabban|'dare *vt* smuggle. **~di'ere, -a** *nmf* smuggler. **contrab'bando** *nm* contraband

contrab'basso *nm* double bass

contraccambi'are *vt* return. **contrac'cambio** *nm* return

contracce|t'tivo *nm* contraceptive. **~zi'one** *nf* contraception

contrac'col|po *nm* rebound; (*di arma da fuoco*) recoil; *fig* repercussion

con'trada *nf* (*rione*) district

contrad'detto *pp di* **contraddire**

contrad'di|re *vt* contradict. **~t'torio** *a* contradictory. **~zi'one** *nf* contradiction

contraddi'stin|guere *vt* differentiate. **~to** *a* distinct

contra'ente *nmf* contracting party

contra'ereo *a* anti-aircraft

contraf'fa|re *vt* disguise; (*imitare*) imitate; (*falsificare*) forge. **~tto** *a* forged. **~zi'one** *nf* disguising; (*imitazione*) imitation; (*falsificazione*) forgery

con'tralto *nm* countertenor ● *nf* contralto

contrap'peso *nm* counterbalance

contrap'por|re *vt* counter; (*confrontare*) compare. **~si** *vr* contrast; **~si a** be opposed to

contraria'mente *adv* contrary (**a** to)

contrari|'are *vt* oppose; (*infastidire*) annoy. **~'arsi** *vr* get annoyed. **~età** *nf inv* adversity; (*ostacolo*) set-back

con'trario *a* contrary, opposite; (*direzione*) opposite; (*sfavorevole*) unfavourable ● *nm* contrary, opposite; **al ~** on the contrary

con'trarre *vt* contract

contras|se'gnare *vt* mark. **~'segno** *nm* mark; [**in**] **~segno** (*spedizione*) cash on delivery, COD

contra'stante *a* contrasting

contra'stare *vt* oppose; (*contestare*) contest ● *vi* clash. **con'trasto** *nm* contrast; (*litigio*) dispute

contrattac'care *vt* counter-attack. **contrat'tacco** *nm* counter-attack

contrat'ta|re *vt/i* negotiate; (*mercanteggiare*) bargain. **~zi'one** *nf* (*salariale*) bargaining

contrat'tempo *nm* hitch

con'tratt|o *pp di* **contrarre** ● *nm* contract. **~o a termine** fixed-term contract. **~u'ale** *a* contractual

contravve'n|ire *vi* contravene. **~zi'one** *nf* contravention; (*multa*) fine

contrazi'one *nf* contraction; (*di prezzi*) reduction

contribu'ente *nmf* contributor; (*del fisco*) taxpayer

contribu|'ire *vi* contribute. **contri'buto** *nm* contribution

'contro *prep* against; **~ di me** against me ● *nm* **il pro e il ~** the pros and cons *pl*

contro'battere *vt* counter

controbilanci'are *vt* counterbalance

controcor'rente *a* (*idee, persona*) non-conformist ● *adv* upriver; *fig* upstream

controffen'siva *nf* counter-offensive

controfi'gura *nf* stand-in

controfir'mare *vt* countersign

controindicazi'one *nf Med* contraindication

control'la|re *vt* control; (*verificare*) check; (*collaudare*) test. **~rsi** *vr* have self-control. **~to** *a* controlled

con'troll|o *nm* control; (*verifica*) check; *Med* check-up. **~lo delle nascite** birth control. **~'lore** *nm* controller; (*sui treni ecc*) [ticket] inspector. **~lore di volo** air-traffic controller

contro'luce *nf* **in ~** against the light

contro'mano *adv* in the wrong direction

contromi'sura *nf* countermeasure

contropi'ede *nm* **prendere in ~** catch off guard

controprodu'cente *a* self-defeating

con'trordin|e *nm* counter order; **salvo ~i** unless I/you hear to the contrary

contro'senso *nm* contradiction in terms

controspio'naggio *nm* counterespionage

contro'vento *adv* against the wind

contro'vers|ia *nf* controversy; *Jur* dispute. **~o** *a* controversial

contro'voglia *adv* unwillingly

contu'macia *nf* default; **in ~** in one's absence

contun'dente *a* (*corpo, arma*) blunt

contur'ba|nte *a* perturbing

contusi'one *nf* bruise

convale'scen|te *a* convalescent. **~za** *nf* convalescence; **essere in ~za** be convalescing

con'vali|da *nf* validation. **~'dare** *vt* confirm; validate (*atto, biglietto*)

con'vegno *nm* meeting; (*congresso*) congress

conve'nevol|e *a* suitable; **~i** *pl* pleasantries

conveni'en|te *a* convenient; (*prezzo*) attractive; (*vantaggioso*) advantageous. **~za** *nf* convenience; (*interesse*) advantage; (*di prezzo*) attractiveness

conve'nire *vi* (*riunirsi*) gather; (*concordare*) agree; (*ammettere*) admit; (*essere opportuno*) be convenient ● *vt* agree on; **ci conviene andare** it is better to go; **non mi conviene stancarmi** I'd better not tire myself out

con'vento *nm* (*di suore*) convent; (*di frati*) monastery

conve'nuto *a* fixed

convenzi|o'nale *a* conventional. **~'one** *nf* convention

conver'gen|te *a* converging. **~za** *nf* *fig* confluence

con'vergere *vi* converge

conver'sa|re *vi* converse. **~zi'one** *nf* conversation

conversi'one *nf* conversion

con'verso *pp di* **convergere**

conver'tibile *nf Auto* convertible

conver'ti|re *vt* convert. **~rsi** *vr* be converted. **~to, -a** *nmf* convert

con'vesso *a* convex

convin'cente *a* convincing

con'vin|cere *vt* convince. **~to** *a* convinced. **~zi'one** *nf* conviction

con'vitto *nm* boarding school

convi'ven|te *nm* common-law husband ● *nf* common-law wife. **~za** *nf* cohabitation. **con'vivere** *vi* live together

convivi'ale *a* convivial

convo'ca|re *vt* convene. **~zi'one** *nf* convening

convogli'are *vt* convey; ⟨navi:⟩ convoy. **con'voglio** *nm* convoy; (*ferroviario*) train

convulsi'one *nf* convulsion. **con'vulso** *a* convulsive; (*febbrile*) feverish

coope'ra|re *vi* co-operate. **~'tiva** *nf* co-operative. **~zi'one** *nf* co-operation

coordina'mento *nm* co-ordination

coordi'na|re *vt* co-ordinate. **~ta** *nf* *Math* coordinate. **~zi'one** *nf* co-ordination

co'perchio *nm* lid; (*copertura*) cover

co'perta *nf* blanket; (*copertura*) cover; *Naut* deck

coper'tina *nf* cover; (*di libro*) dust-jacket

co'perto *pp di* **coprire** ● *a* covered; ⟨cielo⟩ overcast ● *nm* (*a tavola*) place; (*prezzo del coperto*) cover charge; **al ~** under cover

coper'tone *nm* tarpaulin; (*gomma*) tyre

coper'tura *nf* covering; *Comm, Fin* cover

'copia *nf* copy; **bella/brutta ~** fair/rough copy. **~ su carta** hardcopy. **copi'are** *vt* copy

copi'one *nm* script

copi'oso *a* plentiful

'coppa *nf* (*calice*) goblet; (*per gelato*

ecc) dish; *Sport* cup. **~ [di] gelato** ice-cream (*served in a dish*)

cop'petta *nf* (*di ceramica, vetro*) bowl; (*di gelato*) small tub

'coppia *nf* couple; (*in carte*) pair

co'prente *a* (*cipria, vernice*) covering

copri'capo *nm* headgear

copri'fuoco *nm* curfew

copri'letto *nm* bedspread

copripiu'mino *nm* duvet cover

co'prir|e *vt* cover; drown ⟨suono⟩; hold ⟨carica⟩. **~si** *vr* (*vestirsi*) cover up; *fig* cover oneself; ⟨cielo:⟩ become overcast

coque *sf alla ~* ⟨uovo⟩ soft-boiled

co'raggi|o *nm* courage; (*sfacciataggine*) nerve; **~o!** come on. **~'oso** *a* courageous

co'rale *a* choral

co'rallo *nm* coral

co'rano *nm* Koran

co'raz|za *nf* armour; (*di animali*) shell. **~'zata** *nf* battleship. **~'zato** *a* ⟨nave⟩ armour-clad

corbelle'ria *nf* nonsense; (*sproposito*) blunder

'corda *nf* cord; (*spago, Mus*) string; (*fune*) rope; (*cavo*) cable; **essere giù di ~** be depressed; **dare ~ a qcno** encourage sb. **corde** *pl* **vocali** vocal cords

cor'data *nf* roped party

cordi'al|e *a* cordial ● *nm* (*bevanda*) cordial; **saluti ~i** best wishes. **~ità** *nf* cordiality

cor'doglio *nm* grief; (*lutto*) mourning

cor'done *nm* cord; (*schieramento*) cordon. **~ ombelicale** umbilical cord

core|ogra'fia *nf* choreography. **~'ografo, -a** *nmf* choreographer

cori'andoli *nmpl* confetti *sg*

cori'andolo *nm* (*spezia*) coriander

cori'car|e *vt* put to bed. **~si** *vr* go to bed

co'rista *nmf* choir member

cor'nacchia *nf* crow

corna *vedi* **corno**

corna'musa *nf* bagpipes *pl*

'cornea *nf* cornea

cor'nett|a *nf Mus* cornet; (*del telefono*) receiver. **~o** *nm* (*brioche*) croissant

cor'ni|ce *nf* frame. **~ci'one** *nm* cornice

'corno *nm* (*pl nf* **corna**) horn; **fare le corna a qcno** be unfaithful to sb; **fare le corna** (*per scongiuro*) touch wood. **cor'nuto** *a* horned ● *nm* (*fam: marito tradito*) cuckold; (*insulto*) bastard

'coro *nm* chorus; *Relig* choir

co'rolla *nf* corolla

co'rona *nf* crown; (*di fiori*) wreath; (*rosario*) rosary. ~'mento *nm* (*di impresa*) crowning. coro'nare *vt* crown; (*sogno*) fulfil

cor'petto *nm* bodice

'corpo *nm* body; (*Mil, diplomatico*) corps *inv*; a ~ a ~ man to man; andare di ~ move one's bowels. ~ di ballo corps de ballet. ~ insegnante teaching staff. ~ del reato incriminating item

corpo'rale *a* corporal

corporati'vismo *nm* corporatism

corpora'tura *nf* build

corporazi'one *nf* corporation

cor'poreo *a* bodily

cor'poso *a* full-bodied

corpu'lento *a* stout

cor'puscolo *nm* corpuscle

corre'dare *vt* equip

corre'dino *nm* (*per neonato*) layette

cor'redo *nm* (*nuziale*) trousseau

cor'reggere *vt* correct; lace (*bevanda*)

corre'lare *vt* correlate

cor'rente *a* running; (*in vigore*) current; (*frequente*) everyday; (*inglese ecc*) fluent ● *nf* current; (*d'aria*) draught; essere al ~ be up to date. ~'mente *adv* (*parlare*) fluently

'correre *vi* run; (*affrettarsi*) hurry; *Sport* race; (*notizie:*) circulate; ~ dietro a run after ● *vt* run; ~ un pericolo run a risk; lascia ~! don't bother!

corre|tta'mente *adv* correctly. cor'retto *pp di* correggere ● *a* correct; (*caffè*) with a drop of alcohol. ~'zi'one *nf* correction. ~zione di bozze proofreading

cor'rida *nf* bullfight

corri'doio *nm* corridor; *Aeron* aisle

corri|'dore, -'trice *nmf* racer; (*a piedi*) runner

corri'era *nf* coach, bus

corri'ere *nm* courier; (*posta*) mail; (*spedizioniere*) carrier

corri'mano *nm* bannister

corrispet'tivo *nm* amount due

corrispon'den|te *a* corresponding ● *nmf* correspondent. ~za *nf* correspondence; scuola/corsi per ~za correspondence course; vendite per ~za mail-order [shopping]. corri'spondere *vi* correspond; (*stanza:*) communicate; corrispondere a (*contraccambiare*) return

corri'sposto *a* (*amore*) reciprocated

corrobo'rare *vt* strengthen; *fig* corroborate

cor'roder|e *vt*, ~si *vr* corrode

cor'rompere *vt* corrupt; (*con denaro*) bribe

corrosi'one *nf* corrosion. corro'sivo *a* corrosive

cor'roso *pp di* corrodere

cor'rotto *pp di* corrompere ● *a* corrupt

corrucci'a|rsi *vr* be vexed. ~to *a* upset

corru'gare *vt* wrinkle; ~ la fronte knit one's brows

corruzi'one *nf* corruption; (*con denaro*) bribery

'corsa *nf* running; (*rapida*) dash; *Sport* race; (*di treno ecc*) journey; di ~ at a run; fare una ~ run

cor'sia *nf* gangway; (*di ospedale*) ward; *Auto* lane; (*di supermercato*) aisle

cor'sivo *nm* italics *pl*

'corso *pp di* correre ● *nm* course; (*strada*) main street; *Comm* circulation; lavori in ~ work in progress; nel ~ di during. ~ d'acqua watercourse

'corte *nf* [court]yard; (*Jur, regale*) court; fare la ~ a qcno court sb. ~ d'appello court of appeal

cor'teccia *nf* bark

corteggia'mento *nm* courtship

coreggi'a|re *vt* court. ~'tore *nm* admirer

cor'teo *nm* procession

cor'te|se *a* courteous. ~'sia *nf* courtesy; per ~sia please

cortigi'ano, -a *nmf* courtier ● *nf* courtesan

cor'tile *nm* courtyard

cor'tina *nf* curtain; (*schermo*) screen

'corto *a* short; per farla corta in short; essere a ~ di be short of. ~ circuito *nm* short [circuit]

cortome'traggio *nm* *Cinema* short

cor'vino *a* jet-black

'corvo *nm* raven

'cosa *nf* thing; (*faccenda*) matter; *inter, rel* what; [che] ~ what; nessuna ~ nothing; ogni ~ everything; per prima ~ first of all; tante cose so many things; (*augurio*) all the best

'cosca *nf* clan

'coscia *nf* thigh; *Culin* leg

cosci'en|te *a* conscious. ~za *nf* conscience; (*consapevolezza*) consciousness

co'scri|tto *nm* conscript. ~zi'one *nf* conscription

così adv so; (in questo modo) like this, like that; (perciò) therefore; **le cose stanno ~** that's how things stand; **fermo ~!** hold it; **proprio ~!** exactly!; **basta ~!** that will do!; **ah, è ~?** it's like that, is it?; **~ ~** so-so; **e ~ via** and so on; **per ~ dire** so to speak; **più in ~** any more; **una ~ cara ragazza!** such a nice girl!; **è stato ~ generoso da aiutarti** he was kind enough to help you ● conj (allora) so ● a inv (tale) like that, such; **una ragazza ~ a** girl like that, such a girl

cosicché conj and so

cosid'detto a so-called

co'smesi nf cosmetics

co'smetico a & nm cosmetic

'cosmico a cosmic

'cosmo nm cosmos

cosmopo'lita a cosmopolitan

co'spargere vt sprinkle; (disseminare) scatter

co'spetto nm **al ~ di** in the presence of

co'spicuo a conspicuous; (somma ecc) considerable

cospi'ra|re vi conspire. **~'tore, ~'trice** nmf conspirator. **~zi'one** nf conspiracy

'costa nf coast, coastline; Anat rib

co'stà adv there

co'stan|te a & nf constant. **~za** nf constancy

co'stare vi cost; **quanto costa?** how much is it?

co'stata nf chop

costeggi'are vt (per mare) coast; (per terra) skirt

co'stei pron vedi **costui**

costellazi'one nf constellation

coster'na|to a dismayed. **~zi'one** nf consternation

costi'er|a nf stretch of coast. **~o** a coastal

costi'pa|to a constipated. **~zi'one** nf constipation; (raffreddore) bad cold

costitu'ir|e vt constitute; (formare) form; (nominare) appoint. **~si** vr Jur give oneself up

costituzio'nale a constitutional. **costituzi'one** nf constitution; (fondazione) setting up

'costo nm cost; **ad ogni ~** at all costs; **a nessun ~** on no account

'costola nf rib; (di libro) spine

costo'letta nf cutlet

co'storo pron vedi **costui**

co'stoso a costly

co'stretto pp di **costringere**

co'stri|ngere vt compel; (stringere) constrict. **~t'tivo** a coercive. **~zi'one** nf constraint

costru'|ire vt build, construct. **~t'tivo** a constructive. **~zi'one** nf building, construction

co'stui, co'stei, pl **co'storo** prons (soggetto) he, she, pl they; (complemento) him, her, pl them

co'stume nm (usanza) custom; (condotta) morals pl; (indumento) costume. **~ da bagno** swim-suit; (da uomo) swimming trunks

co'tenna nf pigskin; (della pancetta) rind

coto'letta nf cutlet

co'tone nm cotton. **~ idrofilo** cotton wool, absorbent cotton Am

'cotta nf (fam: innamoramento) crush

'cottimo nm **lavorare a ~** do piecework

'cotto pp di **cuocere** ● a done; (infatuato) in love; (sbronzo) drunk; **ben ~** (carne) well done

cotton fi'oc® nm inv cotton bud

cot'tura nf cooking

co'vare vt hatch; sicken for (malattia); harbour (odio) ● vi smoulder

'covo nm den

co'vone nm sheaf

'cozza nf mussel

coz'zare vi **~ contro** bump into. **'cozzo** nm fig clash

C.P. abbr (Casella Postale) PO Box

'crampo nm cramp

'cranio nm skull

cra'tere nm crater

cra'vatta nf tie; (a farfalla) bow-tie

cre'anza nf politeness; **mala ~** bad manners

cre'a|re vt create; (causare) cause. **~tività** nf creativity. **~'tivo** a creative. **~to** nm creation. **~'tore, ~'trice** nmf creator. **~zi'one** nf creation

crea'tura nf creature; (bambino) baby; **povera ~!** poor thing!

cre'den|te nmf believer. **~za** nf belief; Comm credit; (mobile) sideboard. **~zi'ali** nfpl credentials

'creder|e vt believe; (pensare) think ● vi **~e in** believe in; **credo di sì** I think so; **non ti credo** I don't believe you. **~si** vr think oneself to be; **si crede uno scrittore** he flatters himself he is a writer. **cre'dibile** a credible. **credibilità** nf credibility

'credi|to nm credit; (stima) esteem;

comprare a ~**to** buy on credit.
~'**tore**, ~'**trice** nmf creditor

'**credo** nm inv credo

credulità nf credulity

'**credu|lo** a credulous. ~'**lone, -a** nmf
simpleton

'**crema** nf cream; (di uova e latte) custard. ~ **idratante** moisturizer. ~ **pasticciera** egg custard. ~ **solare**
suntan lotion

cre'ma|re vt cremate. ~'**torio** nm cre-
matorium. ~**zi'one** nf cremation

crème cara'mel nf crème caramel

creme'ria nf dairy (also selling ice
cream and cakes)

Crem'lino nm Kremlin

'**crepa** nf crack

cre'paccio nm cleft; (di ghiacciaio)
crevasse

crepacu'ore nm heart-break

crepa'pelle adv a ~ fit to burst;
ridere a ~ split one's sides with laughter

cre'pare vi crack; (fam: morire) kick
the bucket; ~ **dal ridere** laugh fit to
burst

crepa'tura nf crevice

crêpe nf inv pancake

crepi'tare vi crackle

cre'puscolo nm twilight

cre'scendo nm crescendo

'**cresc|ere** vi grow; (aumentare) in-
crease ● vt (allevare) bring up; (aumentare) raise. ~**ita** nf growth; (aumento)
increase. ~**i'uto** pp di crescere

'**cresi|ma** nf confirmation. ~'**mare** vt
confirm

'**crespo** a (capelli) frizzy ● nm crêpe

'**cresta** nf crest; (cima) peak

'**creta** nf clay

'**Creta** nf Crete

cre'tino, -a a stupid ● nmf idiot

cric nm jack

'**cricca** nf gang

cri'ceto nm hamster

crimi'nal|e a & nmf criminal. ~**ità** nf
crime. '**crimine** nm crime

crimi'noso a criminal

'**crin|e** nm horsehair. ~**i'era** nf mane

'**cripta** nf crypt

crisan'temo nm chrysanthemum

'**crisi** nf inv crisis; Med fit

cristal'lino nm crystalline

cristalliz'zar|e vt, ~**si** vr crystallize;
(fig: parola, espressione:) become part
of the language

cri'stallo nm crystal

Cristia'nesimo nm Christianity

cristi'ano, -a a & nmf Christian

'**Cristo** nm Christ; **un povero c~** a
poor beggar

cri'terio nm criterion; (buon senso)
[common] sense

'**criti|ca** nf criticism; (recensione) re-
view. **criti'care** vt criticize. ~**co** a criti-
cal ● nm critic. ~**cone, -a** nmf
faultfinder

crivel'lare vt riddle (**di** with)

cri'vello nm sieve

croc'cante a crisp ● nm type of
crunchy nut biscuit

croc'chetta nf croquette

'**croce** nf cross; **a occhio e** ~ roughly;
fare testa e ~ spin a coin. **C~ Rossa**
Red Cross

croce'via nm inv crossroads sg

croci'ata nf crusade

cro'cicchio nm crossroads sg

croci'era nf cruise; Archit crossing

croci'fi|ggere vt crucify. ~**ssi'one** nf
crucifixion. ~**sso** pp di crocifiggere
● a crucified ● nm crucifix

crogio'larsi vr bask

crogi[u]'olo nm crucible; fig melting
pot

crol'lare vi collapse; (prezzi:) slump.
'**crollo** nm collapse; (dei prezzi) slump

cro'mato a chromium-plated. '**cromo**
nm chrome. **cromo'soma** nm chromosome

'**cronaca** nf chronicle; (di giornale)
news; TV, Radio commentary; **fatto di**
~ news item. ~ **nera** crime news

'**cronico** a chronic

cro'nista nmf reporter

crono'logico a chronological

cronome'traggio nm timing

cronome'trare vt time

cro'nometro nm chronometer

'**crosta** nf crust; (di formaggio) rind;
(di ferita) scab; (quadro) daub

cro'staceo nm shellfish

cro'stata nf tart

cro'stino nm croûton

crucci'arsi vr worry. '**cruccio** nm
worry

cruci'ale a crucial

cruci'verba nm inv crossword [puz-
zle]

cru'del|e a cruel. ~**tà** nf inv cruelty

'**crudo** a raw; (rigido) harsh

cru'ento a bloody

cru'miro nm blackleg, scab

'**crusca** nf bran

cru'scotto nm dashboard

'**Cuba** nf Cuba

cu'betto *nm* ~ di ghiaccio ice cube

'cubico *a* cubic

cubi'tal|e *a* a caratteri ~i in enormous letters

'cubo *nm* cube

cuc'cagna *nf* abundance; (*baldoria*) merry-making; paese della ~ land of plenty

cuc'cetta *nf* (*su un treno*) couchette; *Naut* berth

cucchi'aino *nm* teaspoon

cucchi'a|io *nm* spoon; al ~io (*dolce*) creamy. ~i'ata *nf* spoonful

'cuccia *nf* dog's bed; fa la ~! lie down!

cuccio'lata *nf* litter

'cucciolo *nm* puppy

cu'cina *nf* kitchen; (*il cucinare*) cooking; (*cibo*) food; (*apparecchio*) cooker; far da ~ cook; libro di ~ cook[ery] book. ~ a gas gas cooker

cuci'n|are *vt* cook. ~ino *nm* kitchenette

cu'ci|re *vt* sew; macchina per ~re sewing-machine. ~to *nm* sewing. ~'tura *nf* seam

cucù *nm inv* cuckoo

cu'culo *nm* cuckoo

'cuffia *nf* bonnet; (*da bagno*) bathing-cap; (*ricevitore*) headphones *pl*

cu'gino, -a *nmf* cousin

'cui *pron rel* (*persona: con prep*) who, whom *fml*; (*cose, animali: con prep*) which; (*tra articolo e nome*) whose; la persona con ~ ho parlato the person [who] I spoke to; la ditta per ~ lavoro the company I work for, the company for which I work; l'amico il ~ libro è stato pubblicato the friend whose book was published; in ~ (*dove*) where; (*quando*) that; per ~ (*perciò*) so; la città in ~ vivo the city I live in, the city where I live; il giorno in ~ l'ho visto the day [that] I saw him

culi'nari|a *nf* cookery. ~o *a* culinary

'culla *nf* cradle. cul'lare *vt* rock

culmi'na|nte *a* culminating. ~re *vi* culminate. 'culmine *nm* peak

'culo *nm vulg* arse; (*fortuna*) luck

'culto *nm* cult; *Relig* religion; (*adorazione*) worship

cul'tu|ra *nf* culture. ~ra generale general knowledge. ~'rale *a* cultural

cultu'ris|mo *nm* body-building. ~ta *nmf* body builder

cumula'tivo *a* cumulative; biglietto ~ group ticket

'cumulo *nm* pile; (*mucchio*) heap; (*nuvola*) cumulus

'cuneo *nm* wedge

cu'netta *nf* gutter

cu'ocere *vt/i* cook; fire (*ceramica*)

cu'oco, -a *nmf* cook

cu'oio *nm* leather. ~ capelluto scalp

cu'ore *nm* heart; cuori *pl* (*carte*) hearts; nel profondo del ~ in one's heart of hearts; di [buon] ~ (*persona*) kind-hearted; nel ~ della notte in the middle of the night; stare a ~ a qcno be very important to sb

cupi'digia *nf* greed

'cupo *a* gloomy; (*suono*) deep

'cupola *nf* dome

'cura *nf* care; (*amministrazione*) management; *Med* treatment; a ~ di edited by; in ~ under treatment. ~ dimagrante [slimming] diet. cu'rante *a* medico curante GP, doctor

cu'rar|e *vt* take care of; *Med* treat; (*guarire*) cure; edit (*testo*). ~si *vr* take care of oneself; *Med* follow a treatment; ~si di (*badare a*) mind

cu'rato *nm* parish priest

cura'tore, -'trice *nmf* trustee; (*di testo*) editor

'curia *nf* curia

curio's|are *vi* be curious; (*mettere il naso*) pry (in into); (*nei negozi*) look around. ~ità *nf inv* curiosity. curi'oso *a* curious; (*strano*) odd

cur'sore *nm Comput* cursor

'curva *nf* curve; (*stradale*) bend. ~ a gomito U-bend. cur'vare *vt* curve; (*strada:*) bend. cur'varsi *vr* bend. 'curvo *a* curved; (*piegato*) bent

cusci'netto *nm* pad; *Mech* bearing

cu'scino *nm* cushion; (*guanciale*) pillow. ~ d'aria air cushion

'cuspide *nf* spire

cu'stod|e *nm* caretaker. ~e giudiziario official receiver. ~ia *nf* care; *Jur* custody; (*astuccio*) case. ~ia cautelare remand. custo'dire *vt* keep; (*badare*) look after

cu'taneo *a* skin

'cute *nf* skin

cu'ticola *nf* cuticle

Dd

da *prep* from; (*con verbo passivo*) by; (*moto a luogo*) to; (*moto per luogo*) through; (*stato in luogo*) at; (*temporale*) since; (*continuativo*) for; (*causale*) with; (*in qualità di*) as; (*con caratteristica*) with; (*come*) like; **da Roma a Milano** from Rome to Milan; **staccare un quadro dalla parete** take a picture off the wall; **i bambini dai 5 ai 10 anni** children between 5 and 10; **vedere qcsa da vicino/lontano** see sth from up close/from a distance; **scritto da** written by; **andare dal panettiere** go to the baker's; **passo da te più tardi** I'll come over to your place later; **passiamo da qui** let's go this way; **un appuntamento dal dentista** an appointment at the dentist's; **il treno passa da Venezia** the train goes through Venice; **dall'anno scorso** since last year; **vivo qui da due anni** I've been living here for two years; **da domani** from tomorrow; **piangere dal dolore** cry with pain; **ho molto da fare** I have a lot to do; **occhiali da sole** sunglasses; **qualcosa da mangiare** something to eat; **un uomo dai capelli scuri** a man with dark hair; **è un oggetto da poco** it's not worth much; **l'ho fatto da solo** I did it by myself; **si è fatto da sé** he is a self-made man; **non è da lui** it's not like him

dac'capo *adv* again; (*dall'inizio*) from the beginning

dacchè *conj* since

'dado *nm* dice; *Culin* stock cube; *Techn* nut

daf'fare *nm* work

'dagli = da + gli. **'dai** = da + i

'dai *int* come on!

'daino *nm* deer; (*pelle*) buckskin

dal = da + il. **'dalla** = da + la. **'dalle** = da + le. **'dallo** = da + lo

'dalia *nf* dahlia

dal'tonico *a* colour-blind

'dama *nf* lady; (*nei balli*) partner; (*gioco*) draughts *sg*

dami'gella *nf* (*di sposa*) bridesmaid

damigi'ana *nf* demijohn

dam'meno *adv* **non essere ~ (di qcno)** be no less good (than sb)

da'naro *nm* = denaro

dana'roso *a* (*fam: ricco*) loaded

da'nese *a* Danish ● *nmf* Dane ● *nm* (*lingua*) Danish

Dani'marca *nf* Denmark

dan'na|re *vt* damn; **far ~re qcno** drive sb mad. **~to** *a* damned. **~zi'one** *nf* damnation

danneggi|a'mento *nm* damage. **~'are** *vt* damage; (*nuocere*) harm

'danno *nm* damage; (*a persona*) harm. **dan'noso** *a* harmful

Da'nubio *nm* Danube

'danza *nf* dance; (*il danzare*) dancing. **dan'zare** *vi* dance

dapper'tutto *adv* everywhere

dap'poco *a* worthless

dap'prima *adv* at first

'dardo *nm* dart

'dar|e *vt* give; sit (*esame*); have (*festa*); **~ qcsa a qcno** give sb sth; **~ da mangiare a qcno** give sb something to eat; **~ il benvenuto a qcno** welcome sb; **~ la buonanotte a qcno** say good night to sb; **~ del tu/del lei a qcno** address sb as "tu"/"lei"; **~ del cretino a qcno** call sb an idiot; **~ qcsa per scontato** take sth for granted; **cosa danno alla TV stasera?** what's on TV tonight? ● *vi* **~ nell'occhio** be conspicuous; **~ alla testa** go to one's head; **~e su** (*finestra, casa:*) look on to; **~ sui o ai nervi a qcno** get on sb's nerves ● *nm Comm* debit. **~si** *vr* (*scambiarsi*) give each other; **~si da fare** get down to it; **si è dato tanto da fare!** he went to so much trouble!; **~si a** (*cominciare*) take up; **~si al bere** take to drink; **~si per** (*malato, assente*) pretend to be; **~si per vinto** give up; **può ~si** maybe

'darsena *nf* dock

'data *nf* date. **~ di emissione** date of issue. **~ di nascita** date of birth. **~ di scadenza** cut-off date

da'ta|re *vt* date; **a ~re da** as from. **~to** *a* dated

'**dato** *a* given; (*dedito*) addicted; ~ **che** seeing that, given that ● *nm* datum. ~ **di fatto** well-established fact; **dati** *pl* data. **da'tore** *nm* giver. **datore, datrice** *nmf* **di lavoro** employer

'**dattero** *nm* date

dattilogra'f|are *vt* type. ~**ia** *nf* typing. **datti'lografo, -a** *nmf* typist

dattilo'scritto *a* ⟨*copia*⟩ typewritten

dat'torno *adv* **togliersi** ~ clear off

da'vanti *adv* before; (*dirimpetto*) opposite; (*di fronte*) in front ● *a* front ● *nm* front; ~ **a** *prep* before, in front of

davan'zale *nm* window sill

da'vanzo *adv* more than enough

dav'vero *adv* really; **per** ~ in earnest; **dici** ~? honestly?

'**dazio** *nm* duty; (*ufficio*) customs *pl*

d.C. *abbr* (**dopo Cristo**) AD

'**dea** *nf* goddess

debel'lare *vt* defeat

debili'ta|nte *a* weakening. ~**re** *vt* weaken. ~**rsi** *vr* become debilitated. ~**zi'one** *nf* debilitation

debita'mente *adv* duly

'**debi|to** *a* due; **a tempo** ~ in due course ● *nm* debt. ~'**tore**, ~'**trice** *nmf* debtor

'**debo|le** *a* weak; ⟨*luce*⟩ dim; ⟨*suono*⟩ faint ● *nm* weak point; (*preferenza*) weakness. ~'**lezza** *nf* weakness

debor'dare *vi* overflow

debosci'ato *a* debauched

debut'ta|nte *nm* (*attore*) actor making his début ● *nf* actress making her début. ~**re** *vi* make one's début. **de'butto** *nm* début

deca'den|te *a* decadent. ~'**tismo** *nm* decadence. ~**za** *nf* decline; *Jur* loss. **deca'dere** *vi* lapse. **decadi'mento** *nm* (*delle arti*) decline

decaffei'nato *a* decaffeinated ● *nm* decaffeinated coffee, decaf *fam*

decan'tare *vt* (*lodare*) praise

decapi'ta|re *vt* decapitate; behead ⟨*condannato*⟩. ~**zi'one** *nf* decapitation; beheading

decappot'tabile *a* convertible

de'ce|dere *vi* (*morire*) die. ~'**duto** *a* deceased

decele'rare *vt* decelerate, slow down

decen'nale *a* ten-yearly. **de'cennio** *nm* decade

de'cen|te *a* decent. ~**te'mente** *adv* decently. ~**za** *nf* decency

decentra'mento *nm* decentralization

de'cesso *nm* death; **atto di** ~ death certificate

de'cider|e *vt* decide; settle ⟨*questione*⟩. ~**si** *vr* make up one's mind

deci'frare *vt* decipher; (*documenti cifrati*) decode

deci'male *a* decimal

deci'mare *vt* decimate

'**decimo** *a* tenth

de'cina *nf* *Math* ten; **una** ~ (*circa dieci*) about ten

decisa'mente *adv* definitely, decidedly

decisio'nale *a* decision-making

deci|si'one *nf* decision. ~'**sivo** *a* decisive. **de'ciso** *pp di* **decidere** ● *a* decided

decla'ma|re *vt/i* declaim. ~'**torio** *a* ⟨*stile*⟩ declamatory

declas'sare *vt* downgrade

decli'na|re *vt* decline; ~**re ogni responsabilità** disclaim all responsibility ● *vi* go down; (*tramontare*) set. ~**zi'one** *nf* *Gram* declension. **de'clino** *nm* decline; **in declino** ⟨*popolarità*⟩ on the decline

decodificazi'one *nf* decoding

decol'lare *vi* take off

décolle'té *nm inv* décolleté, low neckline

de'collo *nm* take-off

decolo'ra|nte *nm* bleach. ~**re** *vt* bleach

decolorazi'one *nf* bleaching

decom'po|rre *vt*, ~**rsi** *vr* decompose. ~**sizi'one** *nf* decomposition

deconcen'trarsi *vr* become distracted

deconge'lare *vt* defrost

decongestio'nare *vt* *Med*, *fig* relieve congestion in

deco'ra|re *vt* decorate. ~'**tivo** *a* decorative. ~**to** *a* (*ornato*) decorated. ~'**tore**, ~'**trice** *nmf* decorator. ~**zi'one** *nf* decoration

de'coro *nm* decorum

decorosa'mente *adv* decorously. **decoroso** *a* dignified

decor'renza *nf* ~ **dal...** starting from...

de'correre *vi* pass; **a** ~ **da** with effect from. **de'corso** *pp di* **decorrere** ● *nm* passing; *Med* course

de'crepito *a* decrepit

decre'scente *a* decreasing. **de'crescere** *vi* decrease; ⟨*prezzi*⟩ go down; ⟨*acque*⟩ subside

decre'tare *vt* decree. **de'creto** *nm* decree. **decreto legge** *decree which has the force of law*

'dedalo *nm* maze

'dedica *nf* dedication

dedi'car|e *vt* dedicate. **~si** *vr* dedicate oneself

'dedi|to *a* **~ a** given to; (*assorto*) engrossed in; addicted to (*vizi*). **~zi'one** *nf* dedication

de'dotto *pp di* dedurre

dedu'cibile *a* (*tassa*) allowable

de'du|rre *vt* deduce; (*sottrarre*) deduct. **~t'tivo** *a* deductive. **~zi'one** *nf* deduction

defal'care *vt* deduct

defe'rire *vt* Jur remit

defezi|o'nare *vi* (*abbandonare*) defect. **~'one** *nf* defection

defici'en|te *a* (*mancante*) deficient; Med mentally deficient ● *nmf* mental defective; *pej* half-wit. **~za** *nf* deficiency; (*lacuna*) gap; Med mental deficiency

'defici|t *nm inv* deficit. **~'tario** *a* (*bilancio*) deficit

defi'larsi *vr* (*scomparire*) slip away

défilé *nm inv* fashion show

defi'ni|re *vt* define; (*risolvere*) settle. **~tiva'mente** *adv* for good. **~'tivo** *a* definitive. **~to** *a* definite. **~zi'one** *nf* definition; (*soluzione*) settlement

deflazi'one *nf* deflation

deflet'tore *nm* Auto quarterlight

deflu'ire *vi* (*liquidi:*) flow away; (*persone:*) stream out

de'flusso *nm* (*di marea*) ebb

defor'mar|e *vt* deform (*arto*); *fig* distort. **~si** *vr* lose its shape. **de'form|e** *a* deformed. **~ità** *nf* deformity

defor'ma|to *a* warped. **~zi'one** *nf* (*di fatti*) distortion; è una **~zione profes-sionale** put it down to the job

defrau'dare *vt* defraud

de'funto, -a *a* & *nmf* deceased

degene'ra|re *vi* degenerate. **~to** *a* degenerate. **~zi'one** *nf* degeneration. **de'genere** *a* degenerate

de'gen|te *a* bedridden ● *nmf* patient. **~za** *nf* confinement

'degli = di + gli

deglu'tire *vt* swallow

de'gnar|e *vt* **~e** qcno di uno sguar-do deign to look at sb. **~si** *vr* deign, condescend

'degno *a* worthy; (*meritevole*) deserving

degrada'mento *nm* degradation

degra'dante *a* demeaning

degra'da|re *vt* degrade. **~rsi** *vr* lower oneself; (*città:*) fall into a state of disrepair. **~zi'one** *nf* degradation

de'grado *nm* damage; **~ ambientale** *nm* environmental damage

degu'sta|re *vt* taste. **~zi'one** *nf* tasting

'dei = di + i. **'del** = di + il

dela|'tore, -'trice *nmf* [police] informer. **~zi'one** *nf* informing

'delega *nf* proxy

dele'ga|re *vt* delegate. **~to** *ɹm* delegate. **~zi'one** *nf* delegation

dele'terio *a* harmful

del'fino *nm* dolphin; (*stile di nuoto*) butterfly [stroke]

de'libera *nf* bylaw

delibe'ra|re *vt/i* deliberate; **~ su/in** rule on/in. **~to** *a* deliberate

delicata'mente *adv* daintily

delica'tezza *nf* delicacy; (*fragilità*) frailty; (*tatto*) tact

deli'cato *a* delicate; (*salute*) frail; (*suono, colore*) soft

delimi'tare *vt* delimit

deline'a|re *vt* outline. **~rsi** *vr* be outlined; *fig* take shape. **~to** *a* defined

delin'quen|te *nmf* delinquent. **~za** *nf* delinquency

deli'rante *a* Med delirious; (*assurdo*) insane

deli'rare *vi* be delirious. **de'lirio** *nm* delirium; *fig* frenzy

de'litt|o *nm* crime. **~u'oso** *a* criminal

de'lizi|a *nf* delight. **~'are** *vt* delight. **~'oso** *a* delightful; (*cibo*) delicious

'della = di + la. **'delle** = di + le. **'dello** = di + lo

'delta *nm inv* delta

delta'plano *nm* hang-glider; **fare ~** go hang-gliding

delucidazi'one *nf* clarification

delu'dente *a* disappointing

de'lu|dere *vt* disappoint. **~si'one** *nf* disappointment. **de'luso** *a* disappointed

dema'gogico *a* popularity-seeking, demagogic

demar'ca|re *vt* demarcate. **~zi'one** *nf* demarcation

de'men|te *a* demented. **~za** *nf* dementia. **~zi'ale** *a* (*assurdo*) zany

demilitariz'za|re *vt* demilitarize. **~zi'one** *nf* demilitarization

demistificazi'one *nf* debunking

demo'cra|tico *a* democratic. **~'zia** *nf* democracy

democristi'ano, -a *a & nmf* Christian Democrat

demogra'fia *nf* demography. **demo'grafico** *a* demographic

demoli're *vt* demolish. **~zi'one** *nf* demolition

'demone *nm* demon. **de'monio** *nm* demon

demoraliz'zar|e *vt* demoralize. **~si** *vr* become demoralized

de'mordere *vi* give up

demoti'vato *a* demotivated

de'nari *nmpl* (*nelle carte*) diamonds

de'naro *nm* money

deni'gra|re *vt* denigrate. **~'torio** *a* denigratory

denomi'na|re *vt* name. **~'tore** *nm* denominator. **~zi'one** *nf* denomination; **~zione di origine controllata** mark guaranteeing the quality of a wine

deno'tare *vt* denote

densità *nf inv* density. **'denso** *a* thick, dense

den'ta|le *a* dental. **~rio** *a* dental. **~ta** *nf* bite. **~'tura** *nf* teeth *pl*

'dente *nm* tooth; (*di forchetta*) prong; **al ~** *Culin* just slightly firm. **~ del giudizio** wisdom tooth. **~ di latte** milk tooth. **denti'era** *nf* dentures *pl*, false teeth *pl*

denti'fricio *nm* toothpaste

den'tista *nmf* dentist

'dentro *adv* in, inside; (*in casa*) indoors; **da ~** from within; **qui ~** in here ● *prep* in, inside; (*di tempo*) within, by ● *nm* inside

denuclearizzazi'one *nf* denuclearization

denu'dar|e *vt* bare. **~si** *vr* strip

de'nunci|a, de'nunzia *nf* denunciation; (*alla polizia*) reporting; (*dei redditi*) [income] tax return. **~'are** *vt* denounce; (*accusare*) report

denu'tri|to *a* underfed. **~zi'one** *nf* malnutrition

deodo'rante *a & nm* deodorant

dépendance *nf inv* outbuilding

depe'ri|bile *a* perishable. **~'mento** *nm* wasting away; (*di merci*) deterioration. **~re** *vi* waste away

depi'la|re *vt* depilate. **~rsi** *vr* shave (*gambe*); pluck (*sopracciglia*). **~'torio** *nm* depilatory

deplo'rabile *a* deplorable

deplo'r|are *vt* deplore; (*dolersi di*) grieve over. **~evole** *a* deplorable

de'porre *vt* put down; lay down (*armi*); lay (*uova*); (*togliere da una carica*) depose; (*testimoniare*) testify

depor'ta|re *vt* deport. **~to, -a** *nmf* deportee. **~zi'one** *nf* deportation

deposi'tar|e *vt* deposit; (*lasciare in custodia*) leave; (*in magazzino*) store. **~io, -a** *nmf* (*di segreto*) repository. **~si** *vr* settle

de'posi|to *nm* deposit; (*luogo*) warehouse; *Mil* depot. **~to bagagli** left-luggage office. **~zi'one** *nf* deposition; (*da una carica*) removal

depra'va|re *vt* deprave. **~to** *a* depraved. **~zi'one** *nf* depravity

depre'ca|bile *a* appalling. **~re** *vt* deprecate

depre'dare *vt* plunder

depressi'one *nf* depression. **de'presso** *pp di* **deprimere** ● *a* depressed

deprez'zar|e *vt* depreciate. **~si** *vr* depreciate

depri'mente *a* depressing

de'primer|e *vt* depress. **~si** *vr* become depressed

depu'ra|re *vt* purify. **~'tore** *nm* purifier

depu'ta|re *vt* delegate. **~to, -a** *nmf* deputy, Member of Parliament

deraglia'mento *nm* derailment

deragli'are *vi* go off the lines; **far ~** derail

'derby *nm inv Sport* local Derby

deregolamentazi'one *nf* deregulation

dere'litto *a* derelict

dere'tano *nm* backside, bottom

de'ri|dere *vt* deride. **~si'one** *nf* derision. **~'sorio** *a* derisory

de'riva *nf* drift; **andare alla ~** drift

deri'va|re *vi* **~re da** (*provenire*) derive from ● *vt* derive; (*sviare*) divert. **~zi'one** *nf* derivation; (*di fiume*) diversion

dermato|lo'gia *nf* dermatology. **~'logico** *a* dermatological. **derma'tologo, -a** *nmf* dermatologist

'deroga *nf* dispensation. **dero'gare** *vi* **derogare a** depart from

der'ra|ta *nf* merchandise. **~e alimentari** foodstuffs

deru'bare *vt* rob

descrit'tivo *a* descriptive. **des'critto** *pp di* **descrivere**

des'cri|vere *vt* describe. **~'vibile** *a* describable. **~zi'one** *nf* description

de'serto *a* uninhabited ● *nm* desert

deside'rabile *a* desirable

deside'rare *vt* wish; (*volere*) want;

(*intensamente*) long for; (*bramare*) desire; **desidera?** what would you like?, can I help you?; **lasciare a ~** leave a lot to be desired

desi'de|rio *nm* wish; (*brama*) desire; (*intenso*) longing. **~'roso** *a* desirous; (*bramoso*) longing

desi'gnare *vt* designate; (*fissare*) fix

desi'nenza *nf* ending

de'sistere *vi* **~ da** desist from

desktop publishing *nm inv* desktop publishing

deso'lante *a* distressing

deso'la|re *vt* distress. **~to** desolate; (*spiacente*) sorry. **~zi'one** *nf* desolation

'despota *nm* despot

de'sta|re *vt* waken; *fig* awaken. **~si** *vr* waken; *fig* awaken

desti'na|re *vt* destine; (*nominare*) appoint; (*assegnare*) assign; (*indirizzare*) address. **~'tario** *nm* (*di lettera, pacco*) addressee. **~zi'one** *nf* destination; *fig* purpose

de'stino *nm* destiny; (*fato*) fate

destitu'|ire *vt* dismiss. **~zi'one** *nf* dismissal

'desto *a liter* awake

'destra *nf* (*parte*) right; (*mano*) right hand; **prendere a ~** turn right

destreggi'ar|e *vi*, **~si** *vr* manoeuvre

de'strezza *nf* dexterity; (*abilità*) skill

'destro *a* right; (*abile*) skilful

detei'nato *a* tannin-free

dete'n|ere *vt* hold; (*polizia:*) detain. **~uto, -a** *nmf* prisoner. **~zi'one** *nf* detention

deter'gente *a* cleaning; (*latte, crema*) cleansing ● *nm* detergent; (*per la pelle*) cleanser

deteriora'mento *nm* deterioration

deterio'rar|e *vt*, **~si** *vr* deteriorate

determi'nante *a* decisive

determi'na|re *vt* determine. **~rsi** *vr* **~rsi a** resolve to. **~'tezza** *nf* determination. **~'tivo** *a Gram* definite. **~to** *a* (*risoluto*) determined; (*particolare*) specific. **~zi'one** *nf* determination; (*decisione*) decision

deter'rente *a & nm* deterrent

deter'sivo *nm* detergent. **~ per i piatti** washing-up liquid

dete'stare *vt* detest, hate

deto'nare *vi* detonate

de'tra|rre *vt* deduct (**da** from). **~zi'one** *nf* deduction

detri'mento *nm* detriment; **a ~ di** to the detriment of

de'trito *nm* debris

'detta *nf* **a ~ di** according to

dettagli'ante *nmf Comm* retailer

dettagli'a|re *vt* detail. **~ta'mente** *adv* in detail

det'taglio *nm* detail; **al ~** *Comm* retail

det'ta|re *vt* dictate; **~re legge** *fig* lay down the law. **~to** *nm*, **~'tura** *nf* dictation

'detto *a* said; (*chiamato*) called; (*soprannominato*) nicknamed; **~ fatto** no sooner said than done ● *nm* saying

detur'pare *vt* disfigure

deva'sta|re *vt* devastate. **~to** *a* devastated. **~zi'one** *nf* devastation; *fig* ravages *pl*

devi'a|re *vi* deviate ● *vt* divert. **~zi'one** *nf* deviation; (*stradale*) diversion

devitaliz'zare *vt* deaden (*dente*)

devo'lu|to *pp di* **devolvere** ● *a* devolved. **~zi'one** *nf* devolution

de'volvere *vt* devolve

de'vo|to *a* devout; (*affezionato*) devoted. **~zi'one** *nf* devotion

di *prep* of; (*partitivo*) some; (*scritto da*) by; (*parlare, pensare ecc*) about; (*con causa, mezzo*) with; (*con provenienza*) from; (*in comparazioni*) than; (*con infinito*) to; **la casa di mio padre/dei miei genitori** my father's house/my parents' house; **compra del pane** buy some bread; **hai del pane?** do you have any bread?; **un film di guerra** a war film; **piangere di dolore** cry with pain; **coperto di neve** covered with snow; **sono di Genova** I'm from Genoa; **uscire di casa** leave one's house; **più alto di te** taller than you; **è ora di partire** it's time to go; **crede di aver ragione** he thinks he's right; **dire di sì** say yes; **di domenica** on Sundays; **di sera** in the evening; **una pausa di un'ora** an hour's break; **un corso di due mesi** a two-month course

dia'bet|e *nm* diabetes. **~ico, -a** *a & nmf* diabetic

dia'bolico *a* diabolical

dia'dema *nm* diadem; (*di donna*) tiara

di'afano *a* diaphanous

dia'framma *nm* diaphragm; (*divisione*) screen

di'agnos|i *nf* diagnosis. **~ti'care** *vt* diagnose

diago'nale *a & nf* diagonal

dia'gramma *nm* diagram

dia'let'tale *a* dialect. **dia'letto** *nm* dialect

dialo'gante *a* **unità ~** *Comput* interactive terminal

di'alogo *nm* dialogue

dia'mante *nm* diamond

di'ametro *nm* diameter

di'amine *int* **che ~...** what on earth...

diaposi'tiva *nf* slide

di'ario *nm* diary

diar'rea *nf* diarrhoea

di'avolo *nm* devil; **va al ~** go to hell!; **che ~ fai?** what the hell are you doing?

di'batt|ere *vt* debate. **~ersi** *vr* struggle. **~ito** *nm* debate; (*meno formale*) discussion

dica'stero *nm* office

di'cembre *nm* December

dice'ria *nf* rumour

dichia'ra|re *vt* state; (*ufficialmente*) declare. **~rsi** *vr* **si dichiara innocente** he says he's innocent. **~zi'one** *nf* statement; (*documento, di guerra*) declaration

dician'nove *a & nm* nineteen

dicias'sette *a & nm* seventeen

dici'otto *a & nm* eighteen

dici'tura *nf* wording

didasca'lia *nf* (*di film*) subtitle; (*di illustrazione*) caption

di'dattic|a *nf* didactics *sg*. **~o** *a* didactic; (*televisione*) educational

di'dentro *adv* inside

didi'etro *adv* behind ● *nm* *hum* hindquarters *pl*

di'eci *a & nm* ten

die'cina = **decina**

'diesel *a & nf inv* diesel

di'esis *nm inv* sharp

di'eta *nf* diet; **essere a ~** be on a diet. **die'tetico** *a* diet. **die'tista** *nmf* dietician. **die'tologo** *nmf* dietician

di'etro *adv* behind ● *prep* behind; (*dopo*) after ● *a* back; (*di zampe*) hind ● *nm* back; **le stanze di ~** the back rooms; **le zampe di ~** the hind legs

dietro'front *nm inv* about-turn; *fig* U-turn

di'fatti *adv* in fact

di'fen|dere *vt* defend. **~dersi** *vr* defend oneself. **~'siva** *nf* **stare sulla ~siva** be on the defensive. **~'sivo** *a* defensive. **~'sore** *nm* defender; **avvocato ~sore** defence counsel

di'fes|a *nf* defence; **prendere le ~e di qcno** come to sb's defence. **~o** *pp di* **difendere**

difet't|are *vi* be defective; **~are di** lack. **~ivo** *a* defective

di'fet|to *nm* defect; (*morale*) fault, flaw; (*mancanza*) lack; (*in tessuto, abito*) flaw; **essere in ~to** be at fault; **far ~to** be

lacking. **~'toso** *a* defective; (*abito*) flawed

diffa'ma|re *vt* (*con parole*) slander; (*per iscritto*) libel. **~'torio** *a* slanderous; (*per iscritto*) libellous. **~zi'one** *nf* slander; (*scritta*) libel

diffe'ren|te *a* different. **~za** *nf* difference; **a ~za di** unlike; **non fare ~za** make no distinction (**fra** between). **~zi'ale** *a & nm* differential

differenzi'ar|e *vt* differentiate. **~si** *vr* **~si da** differ from

diffe'ri|re *vt* postpone ● *vi* be different. **~ta** *nf* **in ~ta** *TV* prerecorded

dif'ficil|e *a* difficult; (*duro*) hard; (*improbabile*) unlikely ● *nm* difficulty. **~'mente** *adv* with difficulty

difficoltà *nf inv* difficulty

dif'fida *nf* warning

diffi'd|are *vi* **~are di** distrust ● *vt* warn. **~ente** *a* mistrustful. **~enza** *nf* mistrust

dif'fonder|e *vt* spread; diffuse (*calore, luce ecc*). **~si** *vr* spread. **diffusi'one** *nf* diffusion; (*di giornale*) circulation

dif'fu|so *pp di* **diffondere** ● *a* common; (*malattia*) widespread; (*luce*) diffuse. **~'sore** *nm* (*per asciugacapelli*) diffuser

difi'lato *adv* straight; (*subito*) straight-away

'diga *nf* dam; (*argine*) dike

dige'ribile *a* digestible

dige'rire *vt* digest; *fam* stomach. **~sti'one** *nf* digestion. **~'stivo** *a* digestive ● *nm* digestive; (*dopo cena*) liqueur

digi'tale *a* digital; (*delle dita*) finger *attrib* ● *nf* (*fiore*) foxglove

digi'tare *vt* key in

digiu'nare *vi* fast

digi'uno *a* **essere ~** have an empty stomach ● *nm* fast; **a ~** on an empty stomach

digni|tà *nf* dignity. **~'tario** *nm* dignitary. **~'toso** *a* dignified

digressi'one *nf* digression

digri'gnare *vi* **~ i denti** grind one's teeth

dila'gare *vi* flood; *fig* spread

dilani'are *vt* tear to pieces

dilapi'dare *vt* squander

dila'ta|re *vt*, **~rsi** *vr* dilate; (*metallo, gas*) expand. **~zi'one** *nf* dilation

dilazio'nabile *a* postponable

dilazi|o'nare *vt* delay. **~'one** *nf* delay

dilegu'ar|e *vt* disperse. **~si** *vr* disappear

di'lemma *nm* dilemma

dilet'tan|te *nmf* amateur. **~'tistico** *a* amateurish

dilet'tare *vt* delight

di'letto, -a *a* beloved ● *nm* (*piacere*) delight ● *nmf* (*persona*) beloved

dili'gen|te *a* diligent; ⟨*lavoro*⟩ accurate. **~za** *nf* diligence

dilu'ire *vt* dilute

dilun'gar|e *vt* prolong. **~si** *vr* **~si su** dwell on ⟨*argomento*⟩

diluvi'are *vi* pour [down]. **di'luvio** *nm* downpour; *fig* flood

dima'gr|ante *a* slimming, diet. **~i'mento** *nm* loss of weight. **~ire** *vi* slim

dime'nar|e *vt* wave; wag ⟨*coda*⟩. **~si** *vr* be agitated

dimensi'one *nf* dimension; (*misura*) size

dimenti'canza *nf* forgetfulness; (*svista*) oversight

dimenti'car|e *vt*, **~si** *vr* ~ [di] forget. **dimentico** *a* **dimentico di** (*che non ricorda*) forgetful of

di'messo *pp di* **dimettere** ● *a* humble; (*trasandato*) shabby; ⟨*voce*⟩ low

dimesti'chezza *nf* familiarity

di'metter|e *vt* dismiss; (*da ospedale ecc*) discharge. **~si** *vr* resign

dimez'zare *vt* halve

diminu'|ire *vt/i* diminish; (*in maglia*) decrease. **~'tivo** *a & nm* diminutive. **~zi'one** *nf* decrease; (*riduzione*) reduction

dimissi'oni *nfpl* resignation *sg*; **dare le ~** resign

di'mo|ra *nf* residence. **~'rare** *vi* reside

dimo'strante *nmf* demonstrator

dimo'stra|re *vt* demonstrate; (*provare*) prove; (*mostrare*) show. **~rsi** *vr* prove [to be]. **~'tivo** *a* demonstrative. **~zi'one** *nf* demonstration; *Math* proof

di'namico, -a *a* dynamic ● *nf* dynamics *sg*. **dina'mismo** *nm* dynamism

dinami'tardo *a* **attentato ~** bomb attack

dina'mite *nf* dynamite

'dinamo *nf inv* dynamo

di'nanzi *adv* in front ● *prep* **~ a** in front of

dina'stia *nf* dynasty

dini'ego *nm* denial

dinocco'lato *a* lanky

dino'sauro *nm* dinosaur

din'torn|i *nmpl* outskirts; **nei ~i di** in the vicinity of. **~o** *adv* around

'dio *nm* (*pl* **'dei**) god; **D~** God

di'ocesi *nf inv* diocese

dipa'nare *vt* wind into a ball; *fig* unravel

diparti'mento *nm* department

dipen'den|te *a* depending ● *nmf* employee. **~za** *nf* dependence; (*edificio*) annexe

di'pendere *vi* ~ **da** depend on; (*provenire*) derive from; **dipende** it depends

di'pinger|e *vt* paint; (*descrivere*) describe. **~si** *vr* (*truccarsi*) make up. **di'pinto** *pp di* **dispingere** ● *a* painted ● *nm* painting

di'plo|ma *nm* diploma. **~'marsi** *vr* graduate

diplo'matico *a* diplomatic ● *nm* diplomat; (*pasticcino*) millefeuille (*with alcohol*)

diplo'mato *nmf person with school qualification* ● *a* qualified

diploma'zia *nf* diplomacy

di'porto *nm* **imbarcazione da ~** pleasure craft

dira'dar|e *vt* thin out; make less frequent ⟨*visite*⟩. **~si** *vr* thin out; ⟨*nebbia:*⟩ clear

dira'ma|re *vt* issue ● *vi*, **~rsi** *vr* branch out; (*diffondersi*) spread. **~zi'one** *nf* (*di strada*) fork

'dire *vt* say; (*raccontare, riferire*) tell; ~ **quello che si pensa** speak one's mind; **voler ~** mean; **volevo ben ~!** I wondered!; **~ di sì/no** say yes/no; **si dice che...** rumour has it that...; **come si dice "casa" in inglese?** what's the English for "casa"?; **questo nome mi dice qualcosa** the name rings a bell; **che ne dici di...?** how about...?; **non c'è che ~** there's no disputing that; **e ~ che...** to think that...; **a dir poco/tanto** at least/most ● *vi* ~ **bene/male di** speak highly/ill of sb; **dica pure** (*in negozio*) how can I help you?; **dici sul serio?** are you serious?; **per modo di ~** in a manner of speaking

diretta'mente *adv* directly

diret'tissima *nf* **processare per ~** *Jur* try as speedily as possible

diret'tissimo *nm* fast train

diret'tiva *nf* directive

di'retto *pp di* **dirigere** ● *a* direct. ~ **a** (*inteso*) meant for. **essere ~ a** be heading for. **in diretta** ⟨*trasmissione*⟩ live ● *nm* (*treno*) through train

diret|'tore, -'trice *nmf* manager; manageress; (*di scuola*) headmaster; headmistress. **~tore d'orchestra** conductor

direzi'one *nf* direction; (*di società*)

management; *Sch* headmaster's/head-mistress's office (*primary school*)

diri'gen|te *a* ruling ● *nmf* executive; *Pol* leader. **~za** *nf* management. **~zi'ale** *a* management *attrib*, managerial

di'riger|e *vt* direct; conduct (*orchestra*); run (*impresa*). **~si** *vr* **~si verso** head for

dirim'petto *adv* opposite ● *prep* **~ a** facing

di'ritto¹, dritto *a* straight; (*destro*) right ● *adv* straight; **andare ~** go straight on ● *nm* right side; *Tennis* forehand; **fare un ~** (*a maglia*) knit one

di'ritt|o² *nm* right; *Jur* law. **~i d'autore** royalties

dirit'tura *nf* straight line; *fig* honesty. **~ d'arrivo** *Sport* home straight

diroc'cato *a* tumbledown

dirom'pente *a fig* explosive

dirot'ta|re *vt* reroute (*treno, aereo*); (*illegalmente*) hijack; divert (*traffico*) ● *vi* alter course. **~'tore, ~'trice** *nmf* hijacker

di'rotto *a* (*pioggia*) pouring; (*pianto*) uncontrollable; **piovere a ~** rain heavily

di'rupo *nm* precipice

dis'abile *nmf* disabled person

disabi'tato *a* uninhabited

disabitu'arsi *vr* **~ a** get out of the habit of

disac'cordo *nm* disagreement

disadat'tato, -a *a* maladjusted ● *nmf* misfit

disa'dorno *a* unadorned

disa'gevole *a* (*scomodo*) uncomfortable

disagi'ato *a* poor; (*vita*) hard

di'sagio *nm* discomfort; (*difficoltà*) inconvenience; (*imbarazzo*) embarrassment; **sentirsi a ~** feel uncomfortable; **disagi** *pl* (*privazioni*) hardships

disappro'va|re *vt* disapprove of. **~zi'one** *nf* disapproval

disap'punto *nm* disappointment

disar'mante *a fig* disarming

disar'mare *vt/i* disarm. **di'sarmo** *nm* disarmament

disa'strato, -a *a* devastated ● *nmf* victim

di'sastro *nm* disaster; (*fam: grande confusione*) mess; (*fig: persona*) disaster area. **disa'stroso** *a* disastrous

disat'ten|to *a* inattentive. **~zi'one** *nf* inattention; (*svista*) oversight

disatti'vare *vt* de-activate

disa'vanzo *nm* deficit

disavven'tura *nf* misadventure

dis'brigo *nm* dispatch

dis'capito *nm* **a ~ di** to the detriment of

dis'carica *nf* scrap-yard

discen'den|te *a* descending ● *nmf* descendant. **~za** *nf* descent; (*discendenti*) descendants *pl*

di'scendere *vt/i* descend; (*dal treno*) get off; (*da cavallo*) dismount; (*sbarcare*) land. **~ da** (*trarre origine da*) be a descendant of

di'scepolo, -a *nmf* disciple

di'scernere *vt* discern

di'sces|a *nf* descent; (*pendio*) slope; **~a in picchiata** (*di aereo*) nosedive; **essere in ~a** (*strada:*) go downhill. **~a libera** (*in sci*) downhill race. **disce-'sista** *nmf* (*sciatore*) downhill skier. **~o** *pp di* **discendere**

dis'chetto *nm Comput* diskette

dischi'uder|e *vt* open; (*svelare*) disclose. **~si** *vr* open up

disci'oglier|e *vt*, **~si** *vr* dissolve; (*neve:*) thaw; (*fondersi*) melt. **disci'olto** *pp di* **disciogliere**

disci'pli|na *nf* discipline. **~'nare** *a* disciplinary ● *vt* discipline. **~'nato** *a* disciplined

'disco *nm* disc; *Comput* disk; *Sport* discus; *Mus* record; **ernia del ~** slipped disc. **~ fisso** *Comput* hard disk. **~ volante** flying saucer

discogra'fia *nf* (*insieme di incisioni*) discography. **disco'grafico** *a* (*industria*) record, recording; **casa discografica** record company, recording company

'discolo *nmf* rascal ● *a* unruly

discol'par|e *vt* clear. **~si** *vr* clear oneself

disco'noscere *vt* disown (*figlio*)

discontinuità *nf* (*nel lavoro*) irregularity. **discon'tinuo** *a* intermittent; (*fig: impegno, rendimento*) uneven

discor'dan|te *a* discordant. **~za** *nf* mismatch

discor'dare *vi* (*opinioni:*) conflict. **dis'corde** *a* clashing. **dis'cordia** *nf* discord; (*dissenso*) dissension

dis'cor|rere *vi* talk (**di** about). **~'sivo** *a* colloquial. **dis'corso** *pp di* **discorrere** ● *nm* speech; (*conversazione*) talk

dis'costo *a* distant ● *adv* far away; **stare ~** stand apart

disco'te|ca *nf* disco; (*raccolta*) record library. **~'caro** *nmf pej* disco freak

discre'pan|te *a* contradictory. **~za** *nf* discrepancy

dis'cre|to *a* discreet; (*moderato*) moderate; (*abbastanza buono*) fairly good. **~zi'one** *nf* discretion; (*giudizio*) judgement; **a ~zione di** at the discretion of

discrimi'nante *a* extenuating

discrimi'na|re *vt* discriminate. **~'to-rio** *a* (*atteggiamento*) discriminatory. **~zi'one** *nf* discrimination

discussi'one *nf* discussion; (*alterco*) argument. **dis'cusso** *pp di* **discutere** ● *a* controversial

dis'cutere *vt* discuss; (*formale*) debate; (*litigare*) argue; **~ sul prezzo** bargain. **discu'tibile** *a* debatable; (*gusto*) questionable

disde'gnare *vt* disdain. **dis'degno** *nm* disdain

dis'dett|a *nf* retraction; (*sfortuna*) bad luck; *Comm* cancellation. **~o** *pp di* **disdire**

disdi'cevole *a* unbecoming

dis'dire *vt* retract; (*annullare*) cancel

diseduca'tivo *a* boorish, uncouth

dise'gna|re *vt* draw; (*progettare*) design. **~'tore, ~'trice** *nmf* designer. **di'segno** *nm* drawing; (*progetto, linea*) design

diser'bante *nm* herbicide, weed-killer ● *a* herbicidal, weed-killing

disere'da|re *vt* disinherit. **~to** *a* dispossessed ● *nmf i* **~ti** the dispossessed

diser|'tare *vt/i* desert; **~'tare la scuola** stay away from school. **~'tore** *nm* deserter. **~zi'one** *nf* desertion

disfaci'mento *nm* decay

dis'fa|re *vt* undo; strip (*letto*); (*smantellare*) take down; (*annientare*) defeat; **~re le valigie** unpack [one's bags]. **~rsi** *vr* fall to pieces; (*sciogliersi*) melt; **~rsi di** (*liberarsi di*) get rid of; **~rsi in lacrime** dissolve into tears. **~tta** *nf* defeat. **~tto** *a fig* worn out

disfat'tis|mo *nm* defeatism. **~ta** *a & nmf* defeatist

disfunzi'one *nf* disorder

dis'gelo *nm* thaw

dis'grazi|a *nf* misfortune; (*incidente*) accident; (*sfavore*) disgrace. **~ata'mente** *adv* unfortunately. **~'ato, -a** *a* unfortunate ● *nmf* wretch

disgre'gar|e *vt* break up. **~si** *vr* disintegrate

disgu'ido *nm* **~ postale** mistake in delivery

disgu'st|are *vt* disgust. **~arsi** *vr*

~arsi di be disgusted by. **dis'gusto** *nm* disgust. **~oso** *a* disgusting

disidra'ta|re *vt* dehydrate. **~to** *a* dehydrated

disil'lu|dere *vt* disenchant. **~si'one** *nf* disenchantment. **~so** *a* disillusioned

disimbal'lare *vt* unpack

disimpa'rare *vt* forget

disimpe'gnar|e *vt* release; (*compiere*) fulfil; redeem (*oggetto dato in pegno*). **~si** *vr* disengage oneself; (*cavarsela*) manage. **disim'pegno** *nm* (*locale*) vestibule

disincan'tato *a* (*disilluso*) disillusioned

disinfe'sta|re *vt* disinfest. **~zi'one** *nf* disinfestation

disinfet'tante *a & nm* disinfectant

disinfe|t'tare *vt* disinfect. **~zi'one** *nf* disinfection

disinfor'mato *a* uninformed

disini'bito *a* uninhibited

disinne'scare *vt* defuse (*mina*). **disin'nesco** *nm* (*di bomba*) bomb disposal

disinse'rire *vt* disconnect

disinte'gra|re *vt*, **~rsi** *vr* disintegrate. **~zi'one** *nf* disintegration

disinteres'sarsi *vr* **~ di** take no interest in. **disinte'resse** *nm* indifference; (*oggettività*) disinterestedness

disintossi'ca|re *vt* detoxify. **~rsi** *vr* come off drugs. **~zi'one** *nf* giving up alcohol/drugs

disin'volto *a* natural. **disinvol'tura** *nf* confidence

disles'sia *nf* dyslexia. **dis'lessico** *a* dyslexic

disli'vello *nm* difference in height; *fig* inequality

dislo'care *vt Mil* post

dismenor'rea *nf* dysmenorrhoea

dismi'sura *nf* excess; **a ~** excessively

disobbedi'ente *a* disobedient

disobbe'dire *vt* disobey

disoccu'pa|to, -a *a* unemployed ● *nmf* unemployed person. **~zi'one** *nf* umemployment

disonestà *nf* dishonesty. **diso'nesto** *a* dishonest

disono'rare *vt* dishonour. **diso'nore** *nm* dishonour

di'sopra *adv* above ● *a* upper ● *nm* top

disordi'na|re *vt* disarrange. **~ta-'mente** *adv* untidily. **~to** *a* untidy; (*sregolato*) immoderate. **di'sordine** *nm* disorder, untidiness; (*sregolatezza*) debauchery

disorganiz'za|re vt disorganize. **~to** a disorganized. **~zi'one** nf disorganization

disorienta'mento nm disorientation

disorien'ta|re vt disorientate. **~rsi** vr lose one's bearings. **~to** a fig bewildered

di'sotto adv below ● a lower ● nm bottom

dis'paccio nm dispatch

dispa'rato a disparate

'dispari a odd, uneven. **~tà** nf inv disparity

dis'parte adv in **~** apart; **stare in ~** stand aside

dis'pendi|o nm (spreco) waste. **~'oso** a expensive

dis'pen|sa nf pantry; (distribuzione) distribution; (mobile) cupboard; Jur exemption; Relig dispensation; (pubblicazione periodica) number. **~'sare** vt distribute; (esentare) exonerate

dispe'ra|re vi despair (di of). **~rsi** vr despair. **~ta'mente** (piangere) desperately. **~to** a desperate. **~zi'one** nf despair

dis'per|dere vt, **~dersi** vr scatter, disperse. **~si'one** nf dispersion; (di truppe) dispersal. **~'sivo** a disorganized. **~so** pp di **disperdere** ● a scattered; (smarrito) lost ● nm missing soldier

dis'pet|to nm spite; **a ~to di** in spite of; **fare un ~to a qcno** spite sb. **~'toso** a spiteful

dispia'c|ere nm upset; (rammarico) regret; (dolore) sorrow; (preoccupazione) worry ● vi **mi dispiace** I'm sorry; **non mi dispiace** I don't dislike it; **se non ti dispiace** if you don't mind. **~i'uto** a upset; (dolente) sorry

dispo'nibil|e a available; (gentile) helpful. **~ità** nf availability; (gentilezza) helpfulness

dis'por|re vt arrange ● vi dispose; (stabilire) order; **~re di** have at one's disposal. **~si** vr (in fila) line up

disposi'tivo nm device

disposizi'one nf disposition; (ordine) order; (libera disponibilità) disposal. **dis'posto** pp di **disporre** ● a ready; (incline) disposed; **essere ben disposto verso** be favourably disposed towards

di'spotico a despotic. **dispo'tismo** nm despotism

dispregia'tivo a disparaging

dispez'zare vt despise. **dis'prezzo** nm contempt

'disputa nf dispute

dispu'tar|e vi dispute; (gareggiare) compete. **~si** vr contend with each other

dissacra'torio a debunking

dissangua'mento nm loss of blood

dissangu'a|re vt, **~rsi** vr bleed. **~rsi** vr fig become impoverished. **~to** a bloodless; fig impoverished

dissa'pore nm disagreement

dissec'car|e vt, **~si** vr dry up

dissemi'nare vt disseminate; (notizie) spread

dis'senso nm dissent; (disaccordo) disagreement

dissente'ria nf dysentery

dissen'tire vi disagree (da with)

dissertazi'one nf dissertation

disser'vizio nm poor service

disse'sta|re vt upset; Comm damage. **~to** a (strada) uneven. **dis'sesto** nm ruin

disse'tante a thirst-quenching

disse'ta|re vt **~re qcno** quench sb's thirst

dissi'dente a & nmf dissident

dis'sidio nm disagreement

dis'simile a unlike, dissimilar

dissimu'lare vt conceal; (fingere) dissimulate

dissi'pa|re vt dissipate; (sperperare) squander. **~rsi** vr (nebbia:) clear; (dubbio:) disappear. **~to** a dissipated. **~zi'one** nf squandering

dissoci'ar|e vt, **~si** vr dissociate

disso'dare vt till

dis'solto pp di **dissolvere**

disso'luto a dissolute

dis'solver|e vt, **~si** vr dissolve; (disperdere) dispel

disso'nanza nf dissonance

dissu'a|dere vt dissuade. **~si'one** nf dissuasion. **~'siva** a dissuasive

distac'car|e vt detach; Sport leave behind. **~si** vr be detached. **di'stacco** nm detachment; (separazione) separation; Sport lead

di'stan|te a far away; (fig: person) detached ● adv far away. **~za** nf distance. **~zi'are** vt space out; Sport outdistance

di'stare vi be distant; **quanto dista?** how far is it?

di'sten|dere vt stretch out (parte del corpo); (spiegare) spread; (deporre) lay. **~dersi** vr stretch; (sdraiarsi) lie down; (rilassarsi) relax. **~si'one** nf stretching; (*rilassamento*) relaxation; *Pol* détente. **~'sivo** *a* relaxing

di'steso, -a *pp di* **distendere ●** *nf* expanse

distil'l|are *vt/i* distil. **~azi'one** *nf* distillation. **~e'ria** *nf* distillery

di'stinguer|e *vt* distinguish. **~si** *vr* distinguish oneself. **distin'guibile** *a* distinguishable

di'stinta *nf* *Comm* list. **~ di pagamento** receipt. **~ di versamento** paying-in slip

distinta'mente *adv* (*separatamente*) individually, separately; (*chiaramente*) clearly

distin'tivo *a* distinctive **●** *nm* badge

di'stin|to, -a *pp di* **distinguere ●** *a* distinct; (*signorile*) distinguished; **~ti saluti** Yours faithfully. **~zi'one** *nf* distinction

di'stogliere *vt* **~ da** (*allontanare*) remove from; (*dissuadere*) dissuade from. **di'stolto** *pp di* **distogliere**

di'storcere *vt* twist

distorsi'one *nf* *Med* sprain; (*alterazione*) distortion

di'stra|rre *vt* distract; (*divertire*) amuse. **~rsi** *vr* get distracted; (*svagarsi*) amuse oneself; **non ti distrarre!** pay attention!. **~rsi** *vr* (*deconcentrarsi*) be distracted. **~tta'mente** *adv* absently. **~tto** *pp di* **distrarre ●** *a* absentminded; (*disattento*) inattentive. **~zi'one** *nf* absent-mindedness; (*errore*) inattention; (*svago*) amusement

di'stretto *nm* district

distribu'|ire *vt* distribute; (*disporre*) arrange; deal ‹*carte*›. **~'tore** *nm* distributor; (*di benzina*) petrol pump; (*automatico*) slot-machine. **~zi'one** *nf* distribution

distri'car|e *vt* disentangle; **~si** *vr fig* get out of it

di'stru|ggere *vt* destroy. **~t'tivo** *a* destructive; ‹*critica*› negative. **~tto** *pp di* **distruggere ●** *a* destroyed; **un uomo ~tto** a broken man. **~zi'one** *nf* destruction

distur'bar|e *vt* disturb; (*sconvolgere*) upset. **~si** *vr* trouble oneself. **di'sturbo** *nm* bother; (*indisposizione*) trouble; *Med* problem; *Radio, TV* interference; **disturbi** *pl Radio, TV* static. **disturbi di stomaco** stomach trouble

disubbidi'en|te *a* disobedient. **~za** *nf* disobedience

disubbi'dire *vi* **~ a** disobey

disugu|agli'anza *nf* disparity. **~'ale** *a* unequal; (*irregolare*) irregular

disu'mano *a* inhuman

di'suso *nm* **cadere in ~** fall into disuse

di'tale *nm* thimble

di'tata *nf* poke; (*impronta*) finger-mark

'dito *nm* (*pl nf* **dita**) finger; (*di vino, acqua*) finger. **~ del piede** toe

'ditta *nf* firm

dit'tafono *nm* dictaphone

ditta'tor|e *nm* dictator. **~i'ale** *a* dictatorial. **ditta'tura** *nf* dictatorship

dit'tongo *nm* diphthong

di'urno *a* daytime; **spettacolo ~** matinée

'diva *nf* diva

diva'ga|re *vi* digress. **~zi'one** *nf* digression

divam'pare *vi* burst into flames; *fig* spread like wildfire

di'vano *nm* settee, sofa. **~ letto** sofa bed

divari'care *vt* open

di'vario *nm* discrepancy; **un ~ di opinioni** a difference of opinion

dive'n|ire *vi* **= diventare. ~uto** *pp di* **divenire**

diven'tare *vi* become; (*lentamente*) grow; (*rapidamente*) turn

di'verbio *nm* squabble

diver'gen|te *a* divergent. **~za** *nf* divergence; **~za di opinioni** difference of opinion. **di'vergere** *vi* diverge

diversa'mente *adv* (*altrimenti*) otherwise; (*in modo diverso*) differently

diversifi'car|e *vt* diversify. **~rsi** *vr* differ, be different. **~zi'one** *nf* diversification

diver|si'one *nf* diversion. **~sità** *nf inv* difference. **~'sivo** *nm* diversion. **di'verso** *a* different; **diversi** *pl* (*parecchi*) several **●** *pron* several [people]

diver'tente *a* amusing. **diverti'mento** *nm* amusement

diver'tir|e *vt* amuse. **~si** *vr* enjoy oneself

divi'dendo *nm* dividend

di'vider|e *vt* divide; (*condividere*) share. **~si** *vr* (*separarsi*) separate

divi'eto *nm* prohibition; **~ di sosta** no parking

divinco'larsi *vr* wriggle

divinità *nf inv* divinity. **di'vino** *a* divine

di'visa *nf* uniform; *Comm* currency

divisi'one *nf* division

di'vismo *nm* worship; (*atteggiamento*) superstar mentality

di'vi|so *pp di* **dividere.** ~'**sore** *nm* divisor. ~'**sorio** *a* dividing; **muro ~sorio** partition wall

'**divo, -a** *nmf* star

divo'rar|e *vt* devour. ~**si** *vr* ~**si da** be consumed with

divorzi'a|re *vi* divorce. ~**to, -a** *nmf* divorcee. **di'vorzio** *nm* divorce

divul'ga|re *vt* divulge; (*rendere popolare*) popularize. ~**rsi** *vr* spread. ~'**tivo** *a* popular. ~**zi'one** *nf* popularization

dizio'nario *nm* dictionary

dizi'one *nf* diction

do *nm Mus* (*chiave, nota*) C

'**doccia** *nf* shower; (*grondaia*) gutter; **fare la** ~ have a shower

do'cen|te *a* teaching ● *nmf* teacher; (*di università*) lecturer. ~**za** *nf* university teacher's qualification

'**docile** *a* docile

documen'tar|e *vt* document. ~**si** *vr* gather information (**su** about)

documen'tario *a & nm* documentary

documen'ta|to *a* well-documented; (*persona*) well-informed. ~**zi'one** *nf* documentation

docu'mento *nm* document

dodi'cesimo *a & nm* twelfth. '**dodici** *a & nm* twelve

do'gan|a *nf* customs *pl*; (*dazio*) duty. **doga'nale** *a* customs. ~'**iere** *nm* customs officer

'**doglie** *nfpl* labour pains

'**dogma** *nm* dogma. **dog'matico** *a* dogmatic. ~'**tismo** *nm* dogmatism

'**dolce** *a* sweet; (*clima*) mild; (*voce, fonetica*) soft; (*acqua*) fresh ● *nm* (*portata*) dessert; (*torta*) cake; **non mangio dolci** I don't eat sweet things. ~'**mente** *adv* sweetly. **dol'cezza** *nf* sweetness; (*di clima*) mildness

dolce'vita *a inv* (*maglione*) rollneck

dolci'ario *a* confectionery

dolci'astro *a* sweetish

dolcifi'cante *nm* sweetener ● *a* sweetening

dolci'umi *nmpl* sweets

do'lente *a* painful; (*spiacente*) sorry

do'le|re *vi* ache, hurt; (*dispiacere*) regret. ~**rsi** *vr* regret; (*protestare*) complain; ~**rsi di** be sorry for

'**dollaro** *nm* dollar

'**dolo** *nm Jur* malice; (*truffa*) fraud

Dolo'miti *nfpl* **le** ~ the Dolomites

do'lore *nm* pain; (*morale*) sorrow. **dolo'roso** *a* painful

do'loso *a* malicious

do'manda *nf* question; (*richiesta*) request; (*scritta*) application; *Comm* demand; **fare una** ~ (**a qcno**) ask (sb) a question. ~ **di impiego** job application

doman'dar|e *vt* ask; (*esigere*) demand; ~**e qcsa a qcno** ask sb for sth. ~**si** *vr* wonder

do'mani *adv* tomorrow; ~ **sera** tomorrow evening ● *nm* **il** ~ the future; **a** ~ see you tomorrow

do'ma|re *vt* tame; *fig* control (*emozioni*). ~'**tore** *nm* tamer

domat'tina *adv* tomorrow morning

do'meni|ca *nf* Sunday. ~'**cale** *a* Sunday *attrib*

do'mestico, -a *a* domestic ● *nm* servant ● *nf* maid

domicili'are *a* **arresti domiciliari** *Jur* house arrest

domicili'arsi *vr* settle

domi'cilio *nm* domicile; (*abitazione*) home; **recapitiamo a** ~ we do home deliveries

domi'na|re *vt* dominate; (*controllare*) control ● *vi* rule over; (*prevalere*) be dominant. ~**rsi** *vr* control onself. ~'**tore**, ~'**trice** *nmf* ruler ~**zi'one** *nf* domination

do'minio *nm* control; *Pol* dominion; (*ambito*) field; **di** ~ **pubblico** common knowledge

don *nm* (*ecclesiastico*) Father

do'na|re *vt* give; donate (*sangue, organo*) ● *vi* ~**re a** (*giovare esteticamente*) suit. ~'**tore**, ~'**trice** *nmf* donor. ~**zi'one** *nf* donation

dondo'l|are *vt* swing; (*cullare*) rock ● *vi* sway. ~**arsi** *vr* swing. ~**io** *nm* rocking. '**dondolo** *nm* swing; **cavallo/ sedia a dondolo** rocking-horse/chair

dongio'vanni *nm inv* Romeo

'**donna** *nf* woman. ~ **di servizio** domestic help

don'naccia *nf pej* whore

donnai'olo *nm* philanderer

don'nola *nf* weasel

'**dono** *nm* gift

'**dopo** *prep* after; (*a partire da*) since ● *adv* after, afterwards; (*più tardi*) later; (*in seguito*) later on; ~ **di me** after me

dopo'barba *nm inv* aftershave

dopo'cena *nm inv* evening

dopodi'ché *adv* after which

dopodo'mani *adv* the day after tomorrow

dopogu'erra *nm inv* post-war period

dopo'pranzo *nm inv* afternoon
dopo'sci *a & nm inv* après-ski
doposcu'ola *nm inv* after-school activities *pl*
dopo-'shampoo *nm inv* conditioner ● *a inv* conditioning
dopo'sole *nm inv* aftersun cream ● *a inv* aftersun
dopo'tutto *adv* after all
doppi'aggio *nm* dubbing
doppia'mente *adv* (*in misura doppia*) doubly
doppi'a|re *vt Naut* double; *Sport* lap; *Cinema* dub. **~'tore**, **~'trice** *nmf* dubber
'doppio *a & adv* double. **~ clic** *nm Comput* double click. **~ fallo** *nm Tennis* double fault. **~ gioco** *nm* double-dealing. **~ mento** *nm* double chin. **~ misto** *nm Tennis* mixed doubles. **~ senso** *nm* double entendre. **doppi vetri** *nmpl* double glazing ● *nm* double, twice the quantity; *Tennis* doubles *pl* ● *adv* double
doppi'one *nm* duplicate
doppio'petto *a* double-breasted
dop'pista *nmf Tennis* doubles player
do'ra|re *vt* gild; *Culin* brown. **~to** *a* gilt; (*color oro*) golden. **~'tura** *nf* gilding
dormicchi'are *vi* doze
dormigli'one, -a *nmf* sleepyhead; *fig* lazy-bones
dor'mi|re *vi* sleep; (*essere addormentato*) be asleep; *fig* be asleep. **~ta** *nf* good sleep. **~'tina** *nf* nap. **~'torio** *nm* dormitory
dormi'veglia *nm* **essere in ~** be half asleep
dor'sale *a* dorsal ● *nf* (*di monte*) ridge
'dorso *nm* back; (*di libro*) spine; (*di monte*) crest; (*nel nuoto*) backstroke
do'saggio *nm* dosage
do'sare *vt* dose; *fig* measure; **~ le parole** weigh one's words
dosa'tore *nm* measuring jug
'dose *nf* dose; **in buona ~** *fig* in good measure. **~ eccessiva** overdose
dossi'er *nm inv* (*raccolta di dati, fascicolo*) file
'dosso *nm* (*dorso*) back; **levarsi di ~ gli abiti** take off one's clothes
do'ta|re *vt* endow; (*di accessori*) equip. **~to** *a* (*persona*) gifted; (*fornito*) equipped. **~zi'one** *nf* (*attrezzatura*) equipment; **in ~zione** at one's disposal
'dote *nf* dowry; (*qualità*) gift

'dotto *a* learned ● *nm* scholar; *Anat* duct
dotto'rato *nm* doctorate. **dot'tore**, **~'ressa** *nmf* doctor
dot'trina *nf* doctrine
'dove *adv* where; **di ~ sei?** where do you come from; **fin ~?** how far?; **per ~?** which way?
do'vere *vi* (*obbligo*) have to, must; **devo andare** I have to go, I must go; **devo venire anch'io?** do I have to come too?; **avresti dovuto dirmelo** you should have told me, you ought to have told me; **devo sedermi un attimo** I must sit down for a minute, I need to sit down for a minute; **dev'essere successo qualcosa** something must have happened; **come si deve** properly ● *vt* (*essere debitore di, derivare*) owe; **essere dovuto a** be due to ● *nm* duty; **per ~** out of duty.
dove'roso *a* only right and proper
do'vunque *adv* (*dappertutto*) everywhere; (*in qualsiasi luogo*) anywhere ● *conj* wherever
do'vuto *a* due; (*debito*) proper
doz'zi|na *nf* dozen. **~'nale** *a* cheap
dra'gare *vt* dredge
'drago *nm* dragon
'dramm|a *nm* drama. **dram'matico** *a* dramatic. **~atiz'zare** *vt* dramatize. **~a'turgo** *nm* playwright. **dram'mone** *nm* (*film*) tear-jerker
drappeggi'are *vt* drape. **drap'peggio** *nm* drapery
drap'pello *nm Mil* squad; (*gruppo*) band
'drastico *a* drastic
dre'na|ggio *nm* drainage. **~re** *vt* drain
drib'blare *vt* (*in calcio*) dribble. **'dribbling** *nm inv* (*in calcio*) dribble
'dritta *nf* (*mano destra*) right hand; *Naut* starboard; (*informazione*) pointer, tip; **a ~ e a manca** (*dappertutto*) left, right and centre
'dritto *a* = **diritto**[1] ● *nmf fam* crafty so-and-so
driz'zar|e *vt* straighten; (*rizzare*) prick up. **~si** *vr* straighten [up]; (*alzarsi*) raise
dro'ga *nf* drug. **~'gare** *vt* drug. **~'garsi** *vr* take drugs. **~'gato, -a** *nmf* drug addict
drogh|e'ria *nf* grocery. **~i'ere, -a** *nmf* grocer
drome'dario *nm* dromedary
'dubbi|o *a* doubtful; (*ambiguo*) dubious ● *nm* doubt; (*sospetto*) suspicion; **met-**

tere in ~o doubt; **essere fuori** ~o be beyond doubt; **essere in** ~o be doubtful. ~'**oso** *a* doubtful

dubi'ta|re *vi* doubt; ~**re di** doubt; ⟨*diffidare*⟩ mistrust; **dubito che venga** I doubt whether he'll come. ~'**tivo** *a* ⟨*ambiguo*⟩ ambiguous

'**duca|du'chessa** *nmf* duke; duchess

'**due** *a & nm* two

due'cento *a & nm* two hundred

du'ello *nm* duel

due'mila *a & nm* two thousand

due'pezzi *nm inv* ⟨*bikini*⟩ bikini

du'etto *nm* duo; *Mus* duet

'**duna** *nf* dune

'**dunque** *conj* therefore; ⟨*allora*⟩ well [then]

'**duo** *nm inv* duo; *Mus* duet

du'omo *nm* cathedral

'**duplex** *nm Teleph* party line

dupli'ca|re *vt* duplicate. ~**to** *nm* duplicate. '**duplice** *a* double; **in duplice** in duplicate

dura'mente *adv* ⟨*lavorare*⟩ hard; ⟨*rimproverare*⟩ harshly

du'rante *prep* during

du'r|are *vi* last; ⟨*cibo:*⟩ keep; ⟨*resistere*⟩ hold out. ~**ata** *nf* duration. ~**a'turo**, ~**evole** *a* lasting, enduring

du'rezza *nf* hardness; ⟨*di carne*⟩ toughness; ⟨*di voce, padre*⟩ harshness

'**duro, -a** *a* hard; ⟨*persona, carne*⟩ tough; ⟨*voce*⟩ harsh; ⟨*pane*⟩ stale; **tieni** ~! ⟨*resistere*⟩ hang in there! ● *nmf* ⟨*persona*⟩ tough person, toughie *fam*

du'rone *nm* hardened skin

'**duttile** *a* ⟨*materiale*⟩ ductile; ⟨*carattere*⟩ malleable

e, ed *conj* and

'**ebano** *nm* ebony

eb'bene *conj* well [then]

eb'brezza *nf* inebriation; ⟨*euforia*⟩ elation; **guida in stato di** ~ drink-driving. '**ebbro** *a* inebriated; **ebbro di gioia** delirious with joy

'**ebete** *a* stupid

ebollizi'one *nf* boiling

e'braico *a* Hebrew ● *nm* ⟨*lingua*⟩ Hebrew. **e'br|eo, -a** *a* Jewish ● *nmf* Jew; Jewess

'**Ebridi** *nfpl* **le** ~ the Hebrides

eca'tombe *nf* **fare un'**~ wreak havoc

ecc *abbr* ⟨*eccetera*⟩ etc

ecce'den|te *a* ⟨*peso, bagaglio*⟩ excess. ~**za** *nf* excess; ⟨*d'avanzo*⟩ surplus; **avere qcsa in** ~**za** have an excess of sth; **bagagli in** ~**za** excess baggage. ~**za di cassa** surplus. **ec'cedere** *vt* exceed ● *vi* go too far; **eccedere nel mangiare** overeat; **eccedere nel bere** drink to excess

eccel'len|te *a* excellent. ~**za** *nf* excellence; ⟨*titolo*⟩ Excellency; **per** ~**za** par excellence. **ec'cellere** *vi* excel (**in** at)

eccentricità *nf* eccentricity. **ec'centrico, -a** *a & nmf* eccentric

eccessiva'mente *adv* excessively. **ecces'sivo** *a* excessive

ec'cesso *nm* excess; **andare agli eccessi** go to extremes; **all'**~ to excess. ~ **di velocità** speeding

ec'cetera *adv* et cetera

ec'cetto *prep* except; ~ **che** ⟨*a meno che*⟩ unless. **eccettu'are** *vt* except

eccezio'nal|e *a* exceptional. ~**men-te** *adv* exceptionally; ⟨*contrariamente alla regola*⟩ as an exception

eccezi'one *nf* exception; *Jur* objection; **a** ~ **di** with the exception of

ecci'ta'mento *nm* excitement. **ec-ci'tante** *a* exciting; ⟨*sostanza*⟩ stimulant ● *nm* stimulant

ecci'ta|re *vt* excite. ~**rsi** *vr* get excited. ~**to** *a* excited

eccitazi'one *nf* excitement

ecclesi'astico *a* ecclesiastical ● *nm* priest

'**ecco** *adv* ⟨*qui*⟩ here; ⟨*là*⟩ there; ~! exactly!; ~ **fatto** there we are; ~ **la tua borsa** here is your bag; ~ **[li] mio figlio** there is my son; ~**mi** here I am; ~ **tutto** that is all

ec'come *adv & int* and how!

echeggi'are *vi* echo

e'clissi *nf inv* eclipse

'**eco** *nmf* (*pl m* **echi**) echo
ecogra'fia *nf* scan
ecolo'gia *nf* ecology. **eco'logico** *a*
ecological; ⟨*prodotto*⟩ environmentally
friendly
e commerci'ale *nf* ampersand
econo'm|ia *nf* economy; (*scienza*) eco-
nomics *sg*; **fare ~ia** economize (**di** on).
eco'nomico *a* economic; ⟨*a buon
prezzo*⟩ cheap. **~ista** *nmf* economist.
~iz'zare *vt/i* economize; save ⟨*tempo,
denaro*⟩. **e'conomo, -a** *a* thrifty ● *nmf*
(*di collegio*) bursar
écru *a inv* raw
'**Ecu** *nm inv* ECU, ecu
ec'zema *nm* eczema
ed *conj vedi* **e**
'**edera** *nf* ivy
e'dicola *nf* [newspaper] kiosk
edifi'cabile *a* ⟨*area, terreno*⟩ classified
as suitable for development
edifi'cante *a* edifying
edifi'care *vt* build; (*indurre al bene*)
edify
edi'ficio *nm* building; *fig* structure
'**edile** *a* building *attrib*
edi'lizi|a *nf* building trade. **~o** *a* build-
ing *attrib*
edi'|tore, -'trice *a* publishing ● *nmf*
publisher; (*curatore*) editor. **~to'ria** *nf*
publishing. **~tori'ale** *a* publishing
● *nm* (*articolo*) editorial, leader
edizi'one *nf* edition; (*di manifestazione*) performance. **~ ridotta** abridg[e]-
ment. **~ della sera** (*del telegiornale*)
evening news
edu'ca|re *vt* educate; (*allevare*) bring
up. **~'tivo** *a* educational. **~to** *a* polite.
~'tore, ~'trice *nmf* educator. **~zi'one**
nf education; (*di bambini*) upbringing;
(*buone maniere*) [good] manners *pl*.
~zione fisica physical education
e'felide *nf* freckle
effemi'nato *a* effeminate
efferve'scente *a* effervescent; (*frizzante*) fizzy; ⟨*aspirina*⟩ soluble
effettiva'mente *adv* è troppo tardi
– ~ it's too late – so it is
effet'tivo *a* actual; (*efficace*) effective;
(*personale*) permanent; *Mil* regular
● *nm* (*somma totale*) sum total
ef'fett|o *nm* effect; (*impressione*) im-
pression; **in ~i** in fact; **a tutti gli ~i** to
all intents and purposes; **~i personali**
personal belongings. **~u'are** *vt* effect;
carry out ⟨*controllo, sondaggio*⟩.
~u'arsi *vr* take place

effi'cac|e *a* effective. **~ia** *nf* effective-
ness
effici'en|te *a* efficient. **~za** *nf* effi-
ciency
ef'fimero *a* ephemeral
effusi'one *nf* effusion
E'geo *nm* **l'~** the Aegean [Sea]
E'gitto *nm* Egypt. **egizi'ano, -a** *a* &
nmf Egyptian
'**egli** *pron* he; **~ stesso** he himself
ego'centrico, -a *a* egocentric ● *nmf*
egocentric person
ego'is|mo *nm* selfishness. **~ta** *a* self-
ish ● *nmf* selfish person. **~tico** *a* selfish
e'gregio *a* distinguished; **E~ Signore**
Dear Sir
eguali'tario *a* & *nm* egalitarian
eiaculazi'one *nf* ejaculation
elabo'ra|re *vt* elaborate; process
⟨*dati*⟩. **~to** *a* elaborate. **~zi'one** *nf*
elaboration; (*di dati*) processing. **~zio-
ne testi** word processing
elar'gire *vt* lavish
elastici|tà *nf* elasticity. **~z'zato** *a*
⟨*stoffa*⟩ elasticated. **e'lastico** *a* elastic;
(*tessuto*) stretch; ⟨*orario, mente*⟩ flexible; ⟨*persona*⟩ easy-going ● *nm* elastic;
(*fascia*) rubber band
ele'fante *nm* elephant
ele'gan|te *a* elegant. **~za** *nf* elegance
e'leggere *vt* elect. **eleg'gibile** *a* eligible
elemen'tare *a* elementary; **scuola ~**
primary school
ele'mento *nm* element; **elementi** *pl*
(*fatti*) data; (*rudimenti*) elements
ele'mosina *nf* charity; **chiedere l'~**
beg. **elemosi'nare** *vt/i* beg
elen'care *vt* list
e'lenco *nm* list. **~ abbonati** telephone
directory. **~ telefonico** telephone directory
elet'tivo *a* ⟨*carica*⟩ elective. **e'letto, -a**
pp di **eleggere** ● *a* chosen ● *nmf* (*no-
minato*) elected member; **per pochi
eletti** for the chosen few
eletto'ra|le *a* electoral. **~to** *nm* elec-
torate
elet'|tore, -'trice *nmf* voter
elet'trauto *nm* garage for electrical repairs
elettri'cista *nm* electrician
elettri|cità *nf* electricity. **e'lettrico** *a*
electric. **~z'zante** *a* ⟨*notizia, gara*⟩
electrifying. **~z'zare** *vt fig* electrify.
~z'zato *a fig* electrified

elettrocardio'gramma *nm* electro-cardiogram

e'lettrodo *nm* electrode

elettrodo'mestico *nm* [electrical] household appliance

elet'trone *nm* electron

elet'tronico, -a *a* electronic ● *nf* electronics *sg*

ele'va|re *vt* raise; (*promuovere*) promote; (*erigere*) erect; (*fig: migliorare*) better; **~ al quadrato/cubo** square/ cube. **~rsi** *vr* rise; (*edificio:*) stand. **~to** *a* high. **~zi'one** *nf* elevation

elezi'one *nf* election

'elica *nf* Naut screw, propeller; Aeron propeller; (*del ventilatore*) blade

eli'cottero *nm* helicopter

elimi'na|re *vt* eliminate. **~'toria** *nf* Sport preliminary heat. **~zi'or,e** *nf* elimination

éli|te *nf inv* élite. **~'tista** *a* élitist

'ella *pron* she

ellepì *nm inv* LP

el'metto *nm* helmet

elogi'are *vt* praise. **e'logio** *nm* praise; (*discorso, scritto*) eulogy

elo'quen|te *a* eloquent; *fig* tell-tale. **~za** *nf* eloquence

e'lu|dere *vt* elude; evade (*sorveglianza, controllo*). **~'sivo** *a* elusive

el'vetico *a* Swiss

emaci'ato *a* emaciated

E-mail *nf* e-mail

ema'na|re *vt* give off; pass (*legge*) ● *vi* emanate. **~zi'one** *nf* giving off; (*di legge*) enactment

emanci'pa|re *vt* emancipate. **~rsi** *vr* become emancipated. **~to** *a* emancipated. **~zi'one** *nf* emancipation

emargi'na|to *nm* marginalized person. **~zi'one** *nf* marginalization

ema'toma *nm* haematoma

em'bargo *nm* embargo

em'ble|ma *nm* emblem. **~'matico** *a* emblematic

embo'lia *nf* embolism

embrio'nale *a* Biol, fig embryonic. **embri'one** *nm* embryo

emen|da'mento *nm* amendment. **~'dare** *vt* amend

emer'gen|te *a* emergent. **~za** *nf* emergency; **in caso di ~za** in an emergency

e'mergere *vi* emerge; (*sottomarino:*) surface; (*distinguersi*) stand out

e'merito *a* (*professore*) emeritus; **un ~ imbecille** a prize idiot

e'merso *pp di* emergere

e'messo *pp di* emettere

e'mettere *vt* emit; give out (*luce, suono*); let out (*grido*); (*mettere in circolazione*) issue

emi'crania *nf* migraine

emi'gra|re *vi* emigrate. **~to, -a** *nmf* immigrant. **~zi'one** *nf* emigration

emi'nen|te *a* eminent. **~za** *nf* eminence

e'miro *nm* emir

emis'fero *nm* hemisphere

emis'sario *nm* emissary

emissi'one *nf* emission; (*di denaro*) issue; (*trasmissione*) broadcast

emit'tente *a* issuing; (*trasmittente*) broadcasting ● *nf* Radio transmitter

emorra'gia *nf* haemorrhage

emor'roidi *nfpl* piles

emotività *nf* emotional make-up. **emo'tivo** *a* emotional

emozio'na|nte *a* exciting; (*commovente*) moving. **~re** *vt* excite; (*commuovere*) become excited; (*commuoversi*) be moved. **~to** *a* excited; (*commosso*) moved. **emozi'one** *nf* emotion; (*agitazione*) excitement

'empio *a* impious; (*spietato*) pitiless; (*malvagio*) wicked

em'pirico *a* empirical

em'porio *nm* emporium; (*negozio*) general store

emu'la|re *vt* emulate. **~zi'one** *nf* emulation

emulsi'one *nf* emulsion

en'ciclica *nf* encyclical

enciclope'dia *nf* encyclopaedia

encomi'are *vt* commend. **en'comio** *nm* commendation

en'demico *a* endemic

endo've|na *nf* intravenous injection. **~'noso** *a* intravenous; **per via ~nosa** intravenously

E.N.I.T. *nm abbr* (**Ente Nazionale Italiano per il Turismo**) Italian State Tourist Office

e'nergetico *a* (*risorse, crisi*) energy; (*alimento*) energy-giving

ener'gia *nf* energy. **e'nergico** *a* energetic; (*efficace*) strong

ener'gumeno *nm* Neanderthal

'enfasi *nf* emphasis

en'fati|co *a* emphatic. **~z'zare** *vt* emphasize

e'nigma *nm* enigma. **enig'matico** *a* enigmatic. **enig'mistica** *nf* puzzles *pl*

en'nesimo *a* Math nth; *fam* umpteenth

e'norm|e *a* enormous. **~e'mente** *adv*

massively. **~ità** *nf inv* enormity; *(assurdità)* absurdity

eno'teca *nf* wine-tasting shop

'ente *nm* board; *(società)* company; *(filosofia)* being

entità *nf inv* *(filosofia)* entity; *(gravità)* seriousness; *(dimensione)* extent

entou'rage *nm inv* entourage

en'trambi *a & pron* both

en'tra|re *vi* go in, enter; **~re in** go into; *(stare, trovar posto)* fit into; *(arruolarsi)* join; **~rci** *(avere a che fare)* have to do with; **tu che c'entri?** what has it got to do with you? **~ta** *nf* entry, entrance; **~te** *pl Comm* takings; *(reddito)* income *sg*

'entro *prep* *(tempo)* within

entro'terra *nm inv* hinterland

entusias'mante *a* fascinating, exciting

entusias'mar|e *vt* arouse enthusiasm in. **~si** *vr* be enthusiastic (**per** about)

entusi'as|mo *nm* enthusiasm. **~ta** *a* enthusiastic ● *nmf* enthusiast. **~tico** *a* enthusiastic

enume'ra|re *vt* enumerate. **~zi'one** *nf* enumeration

enunci'a|re *vt* enunciate. **~zi'one** *nf* enunciation

epa'tite *nf* hepatitis

'epico *a* epic

epide'mia *nf* epidemic

epi'dermide *nf* epidermis

Epifa'nia *nf* Epiphany

epi'gramma *nm* epigram

epil|es'sia *nf* epilepsy. **epi'lettico, -a** *a & nmf* epileptic

e'pilogo *nm* epilogue

epi'sodi|co *a* episodic; **caso ~co** one-off case. **~o** *nm* episode

e'piteto *nm* epithet

'epoca *nf* age; *(periodo)* period; **a quell'~** in those days; **auto d'~** vintage car

ep'pure *conj* [and] yet

epu'rare *vt* purge

equa'tore *nm* equator. **equatori'ale** *a* equatorial

equazi'one *nf* equation

e'questre *a* equestrian; **circo ~** circus

equi'latero *a* equilateral

equili'bra|re *vt* balance. **~to** *a* *(persona)* well-balanced. **equi'librio** *nm* balance; *(buon senso)* common sense; *(di bilancia)* equilibrium

equili'brismo *nm* **fare ~** do a balancing act

e'quino *a* horse *attrib*

equi'nozio *nm* equinox

equipaggia'mento *nm* equipment

equipaggi'are *vt* equip; *(di persone)* man

equi'paggio *nm* crew; *Aeron* cabin crew

equipa'rare *vt* make equal

équipe *nf inv* team

equità *nf* equity

equitazi'one *nf* riding

equiva'len|te *a & nm* equivalent. **~za** *nf* equivalence

equiva'lere *vi* **~ a** be equivalent to

equivo'care *vi* misunderstand

e'quivoco *a* equivocal; *(sospetto)* suspicious; **un tipo ~** a shady character ● *nm* misunderstanding

'equo *a* fair, just

'era *nf* era

'erba *nf* grass; *(aromatica, medicinale)* herb. **~ cipollina** chives *pl*. **er'baccia** *nf* weed. **er'baceo** *a* herbaceous

erbi'cida *nm* weed-killer

erbo'rist|a *nmf* herbalist. **~e'ria** *nf* herbalist's shop

er'boso *a* grassy

er'culeo *a* *(forza)* herculean

e'red|e *nmf* heir; heiress. **~ità** *nf inv* inheritance; *Biol* heredity. **~i'tare** *vt* inherit. **~itarietà** *nf* heredity. **~i'tario** *a* hereditary

ere'mita *nm* hermit

ere'sia *nf* heresy. **e'retico, -a** *a* heretical ● *nmf* heretic

e're|tto *pp di* **erigere** ● *a* erect. **~zi'one** *nf* erection; *(costruzione)* building

er'gastolo *nm* life sentence; *(luogo)* prison

'erica *nf* heather

e'rigere *vt* erect; *(fig: fondare)* found

eri'tema *nm* *(cutaneo)* inflammation; *(solare)* sunburn

ermel'lino *nm* ermine

ermetica'mente *adv* hermetically. **er'metico** *a* hermetic; *(a tenuta d'aria)* airtight

'ernia *nf* hernia

e'rodere *vi* erode

e'ro|e *nm* hero. **~ico** *a* heroic. **~'ismo** *nm* heroism

ero'ga|re *vt* distribute; *(fornire)* supply. **~zi'one** *nf* supply

ero'ina *nf* heroine; *(droga)* heroin

erosi'one *nf* erosion

e'rotico *a* erotic. **ero'tismo** *nm* eroticism

er'rante *a* wandering. **er'rare** *vi* wander; (*sbagliare*) be mistaken

er'rato *a* (*sbagliato*) mistaken

'erre *nf* ~ **moscia** burr

erronea'mente *adv* mistakenly

er'rore *nm* error, mistake; (*di stampa*) misprint; **essere in** ~ be wrong

'erta *nf* **stare all'**~ be on the alert

eru'di|rsi *vr* get educated. **~to** *a* learned

erut'tare *vt* (*vulcano:*) erupt ● *vi* (*ruttare*) belch. **eruzi'one** *nf* eruption; *Med* rash

esacer'bare *vt* exacerbate

esage'ra|re *vt* exaggerate ● *vi* exaggerate; (*nel comportamento*) go over the top; **~re nel mangiare** eat too much. **~ta'mente** *adv* excessively. **~to** *a* exaggerated; (*prezzo*) exorbitant ● *nm* person who goes to extremes. **~zi'one** *nf* exaggeration; **è costato un'**~**zione** it cost the earth

esa'lare *vt/i* exhale

esal'ta|re *vt* exalt; (*entusiasmare*) elate. **~to** *a* (*fanatico*) fanatical ● *nm* fanatic. **~zi'one** *nf* exaltation; (*in discorso*) fervour

e'same *nm* examination, exam; **dare un** ~ take an exam; **prendere in** ~ examine. ~ **del sangue** blood test. **esami** *pl* **di maturità** ≈ A-levels

esami'na|re *vt* examine. **~'tore**, **~'trice** *nmf* examiner

e'sangue *a* bloodless

e'sanime *a* lifeless

esaspe'rante *a* exasperating

esaspe'ra|re *vt* exasperate. **~rsi** *vr* get exasperated. **~zi'one** *nf* exasperation

esat|ta'mente *adv* exactly. **~'tezza** *nf* exactness; (*precisione*) precision; (*di risposta, risultato*) accuracy

e'satto *pp di* **esigere** ● *a* exact; (*risposta, risultato*) correct; (*orologio*) right; **hai l'ora esatta?** do you have the right time?; **sono le due esatte** it's two o'clock exactly

esat'tore *nm* collector

esau'dire *vt* grant; fulfil (*speranze*)

esauri'ente *a* exhaustive

esau'ri|re *vt* exhaust. **~rsi** *vr* exhaust oneself; (*merci ecc:*) run out. **~to** *a* exhausted; (*merci*) sold out; (*libro*) out of print; **fare il tutto ~to** (*spettacolo:*) play to a full house

'esca *nf* bait

escande'scenz|a *nf* outburst; **dare in ~e** lose one's temper

escla'ma|re *vi* exclaim. **~'tivo** *a* exclamatory. **~zi'one** *nf* exclamation

es'clu|dere *vt* exclude; rule out (*possibilità, ipotesi*). **~si'one** *nf* exclusion. **~'siva** *nf* exclusive right, sole right; **in ~siva** exclusive. **~siva'mente** *adv* exclusively. **~'sivo** *a* exclusive. **~so** *pp di* **escludere** ● *a* **non è ~so che ci sia** it's not out of the question that he'll be there

escogi'tare *vt* contrive

escre'mento *nm* excrement

escursi'one *nf* excursion; (*scorreria*) raid; (*di temperatura*) range

ese'cra|bile *a* abominable. **~re** *vt* abhor

esecu|'tivo *a* & *nm* executive. **~'tore**, **~'trice** *nmf* executor; *Mus* performer. **~zi'one** *nf* execution; *Mus* performance

esegu'ire *vt* carry out; *Jur* execute; *Mus* perform

e'sempio *nm* example; **ad** *o* **per** ~ for example; **dare l'**~ *a* qcno set sb an example; **fare un** ~ give an example. **esem'plare** *a* examplary ● *nm* specimen; (*di libro*) copy. **esemplifi'care** *vt* exemplify

esen'tar|e *vt* exempt. **~si** *vr* free oneself. **e'sente** *a* exempt. **esente da imposta** duty-free. **esente da IVA** VAT-exempt

esen'tasse *a* duty-free

e'sequie *nfpl* funeral rites

eser'cente *nmf* shopkeeper

eserci'ta|re *vt* exercise; (*addestrare*) train; (*fare uso di*) exert; (*professione*) practise. **~rsi** *vr* practise. **~zi'one** *nf* exercise; *Mil* drill

e'sercito *nm* army

eser'cizio *nm* exercise; (*pratica*) practice; *Comm* financial year; (*azienda*) business; **essere fuori** ~ be out of practice

esi'bi|re *vt* show off; produce (*documenti*). **~rsi** *vr Theat* perform; *fig* show off. **~zi'one** *nf* production; *Theat* performance

esibizio'nis|mo *nm* showing off. **~ta** *nmf* exhibitionist

esi'gen|te *a* exacting; (*pignolo*) fastidious. **~za** *nf* demand; (*bisogno*) need. **e'sigere** *vt* demand; (*riscuotere*) collect

e'siguo *a* meagre

esila'ra|nte *a* exhilarating

'esile *a* slender; (*voce*) thin

esili'a|re *vt* exile. **~'rsi** *vr* go into exile. **~to, -a** *a* exiled ● *nmf* exile. **e'silio** *nm* exile

e'simer|e *vt* release. **~si** *vr* **~si da** get out of

esi'sten|te *a* existing. **~za** *nf* existence. **~zi'ale** *a* existential. **~zia'lismo** *nm* existentialism

e'sistere *vi* exist

esi'tante *a* hesitating; ⟨*voce*⟩ faltering

esi'ta|re *vi* hesitate. **~zi'one** *nf* hesitation

'esito *nm* result; **avere buon ~** be a success

'esodo *nm* exodus

e'sofago *nm* oesophagus

esone'rare *vt* exempt. **e'sonero** *nm* exemption

esorbi'tante *a* exorbitant

esorciz'zare *vt* exorcize

esordi'ente *nmf* person making his/her début. **e'sordio** *nm* opening; ⟨*di attore*⟩ début. **esor'dire** *vi* debut

esor'tare *vt* ⟨*pregare*⟩ beg; ⟨*incitare*⟩ urge

eso'terico *a* esoteric

e'sotico *a* exotic

espa'drillas *nfpl* espadrilles

es'pan|dere *vt* expand. **~dersi** *vr* expand; ⟨*diffondersi*⟩ extend. **~si'one** *nf* expansion. **~'sivo** *a* expansive; ⟨*persona*⟩ friendly

espatri'are *vi* leave one's country. **es'patrio** *nm* expatriation

espedi'ent|e *nm* expedient; **vivere di ~i** live by one's wits

es'pellere *vt* expel

esperi|'enza *nf* experience; **parlare per ~enza** speak from experience. **~'mento** *nm* experiment

es'perto, -a *a & nmf* expert

espi'a|re *vt* atone for. **~'torio** *a* expiatory

espi'rare *vt/i* breathe out

espli'care *vt* carry on

esplicita'mente *adv* explicitly. **es'plicito** *a* explicit

es'plodere *vi* explode ● *vt* fire

esplo'ra|re *vt* explore. **~'tore, ~'trice** *nmf* explorer; **giovane ~tore** boy scout. **~zi'one** *nf* exploration

esplosi'one *nf* explosion. **~'sivo** *a & nm* explosive

espo'nente *nm* exponent

es'por|re *vt* expose; display ⟨*merci*⟩; ⟨*spiegare*⟩ expound; exhibit ⟨*quadri ecc*⟩. **~si** *vr* ⟨*compromettersi*⟩ compromise

oneself; ⟨*al sole*⟩ expose oneself; ⟨*alle critiche*⟩ lay oneself open

espor'ta|re *vt* export. **~'tore, ~'trice** *nmf* exporter. **~zi'one** *nf* export

esposizi'one *nf* ⟨*mostra*⟩ exhibition; ⟨*in vetrina*⟩ display; ⟨*spiegazione ecc*⟩ exposition; ⟨*posizione, fotografia*⟩ exposure. **es'posto** *pp di* **esporre** ● *a* exposed; **esposto a** ⟨*rivolto*⟩ facing ● *nm Jur ecc* statement

espressa'mente *adv* expressly; **non l'ha detto ~** he didn't put it in so many words

espres|si'one *nf* expression. **~'sivo** *a* expressive

es'presso *pp di* **esprimere** ● *a* express ● *nm* ⟨*lettera*⟩ express letter; ⟨*treno*⟩ express train; ⟨*caffè*⟩ espresso; **per ~** ⟨*spedire*⟩ [by] express [post]

es'primer|e *vt* express. **~si** *vr* express oneself

espropri'a|re *vt* dispossess. **~zi'one** *nf Jur* expropriation. **es'proprio** *nm* expropriation

espulsi'one *nf* expulsion. **es'pulso** *pp di* **espellere**

es'senz|a *nf* essence. **~i'ale** *a* essential ● *nm* important thing. **~ial'mente** *a* essentially

'essere *vi* be; **c'è** there is; **ci sono** there are; **che ora è? – sono le dieci** what time is it? – it's ten o'clock; **chi è? – sono io** who is it? – it's me; **ci sono!** ⟨*ho capito*⟩ I've got it!; **ci siamo!** ⟨*siamo arrivati*⟩ here we are at last!; **è stato detto che** it has been said that; **siamo in due** there are two of us; **questa camicia è da lavare** this shirt is to be washed; **non è da te** it's not like you; **~ di** ⟨*provenire da*⟩ be from; **~ per** ⟨*favorevole*⟩ be in favour of; **se fossi in te,...** if I were you,...; **sarà!** if you say so!; **come sarebbe a dire?** what are you getting at? ● *v aux* have; ⟨*in passivi*⟩ be; **siamo arrivati** we have arrived; **ci sono stato ieri** I was there yesterday; **sono nato a Torino** I was born in Turin; **è riconosciuto come...** he is recognized as... ● *nm* being. **~ umano** human being. **~ vivente** living creature

essic'cato *a Culin* desiccated

'esso, -a *pron* he, she; ⟨*cosa, animale*⟩ it

est *nm* east

'estasi *nf* ecstasy; **andare in ~ per** go into raptures over. **~'are** *vt* enrapture

e'state *nf* summer

e'sten|dere *vt* extend. **~dersi** *vr*

spread; (*allungarsi*) stretch. **~si'one** *nf* extention; (*ampiezza*) expanse; *Mus* range. **~'sivo** *a* extensive

estenu'ante *a* exhausting

estenu'a|re *vt* wear out; deplete ⟨*risorse, casse*⟩. **~rsi** *vr* wear oneself out

esteri'or|e *a* & *nm* exterior. **~'mente** *adv* externally; (*di persone*) outwardly

esterna'mente *adv* on the outside

ester'nare *vt* express, show

e'sterno *a* external; **per uso ~** for external use only ● *nm* (*allievo*) day-boy; *Archit* exterior; (*scala*) outside; (*in film*) location shot

'estero *a* foreign ● *nm* foreign countries *pl*; **all'~** abroad

esterre'fatto *a* horrified

e'steso *pp di* **estendere** ● *a* extensive; (*diffuso*) widespread; **per ~** ⟨*scrivere*⟩ in full

e'stetic|a *nf* aesthetics *sg*. **~a'mente** *adv* aesthetically. **~o, -a** *a* aesthetic; ⟨*chirurgia, chirurgo*⟩ plastic. **este'tista** *nf* beautician

e'stimo *nm* estimate

e'stin|guere *vt* extinguish. **~guersi** *vr* die out. **~to, -a** *pp di* ● **'inguere** ● *nmf* deceased. **~'tore** *nm* [fire] extinguisher. **~zi'one** *nf* extinction; (*di incendio*) putting out

estir'pa|re *vt* uproot; extract ⟨*dente*⟩; *fig* eradicate ⟨*crimine, malattia*⟩. **~zi'one** *nf* eradication; (*di dente*) extraction

e'stivo *a* summer

e'stor|cere *vt* extort. **~si'one** *nf* extortion. **~to** *pp di* **estorcere**

estradizi'one *nf* extradition

e'straneo, -a *a* extraneous; (*straniero*) foreign ● *nmf* stranger

estrani'ar|e *vt* estrange. **~si** *vr* become estranged

e'stra|rre *vt* extract; (*sorteggiare*) draw. **~tto** *pp di* **estrarre** ● *nm* extract; (*brano*) excerpt; (*documento*) abstract. **~tto conto** statement [of account], bank statement. **~zi'one** *nf* extraction; (*a sorte*) draw

estrema'mente *adv* extremely

estre'mis|mo *nm* extremism. **~ta** *nmf* extremist

estremità *nf inv* extremity; (*di una corda*) end ● *nfpl Anat* extremities

e'stremo *a* extreme; (*ultimo*) last; **misure estreme** drastic measures; **l'E~ Oriente** the Far East ● *nm* (*limite*) extreme. **estremi** *pl* (*di documento*) main points; (*di reato*) essential ele-

ments; **essere agli estremi** be at the end of one's tether

'estro *nm* (*disposizione artistica*) talent; (*ispirazione*) inspiration; (*capriccio*) whim. **e'stroso** *a* talented; (*capriccioso*) unpredictable

estro'mettere *vt* expel

estro'verso *a* extroverted ● *nm* extrovert

estu'ario *nm* estuary

esube'ran|te *a* exuberant. **~za** *nf* exuberance

'esule *nmf* exile

esul'tante *a* exultant

esul'tare *vi* rejoice

esu'mare *vt* exhume

età *nf inv* age; **raggiungere la maggiore ~** come of age; **un uomo di mezz'~** a middle-aged man

'etere *nm* ether. **e'tereo** *a* ethereal

eterna'mente *adv* eternally

eternità *nf* eternity; **è un'~ che non la vedo** I haven't seen her for ages

e'te™ ;o *a* eternal; ⟨*questione, problema*⟩ age-old; **in ~** *fam* for ever

etero'geneo *a* diverse, heterogeneous

eterosessu'ale *nmf* heterosexual

'etic|a *nf* ethics *sg*. **~o** *a* ethical

eti'chetta[1] *nf* label; (*con il prezzo*) price-tag

eti'chetta[2] *nf* (*cerimoniale*) etiquette

etichet'tare *vt* label

eti'lometro *nm* Breathalyzer®

etimolo'gia *nf* etymology

Eti'opia *nf* Ethiopia

'etnico *a* ethnic. **etnolo'gia** *nf* ethnology

e'trusco *a* & *nmf* Etruscan

'ettaro *nm* hectare

'etto, etto'grammo *nm* hundred grams, ≈ quarter pound

euca'lipto *nm* eucalyptus

eucari'stia *nf* Eucharist

eufe'mismo *nm* euphemism

eufo'ria *nf* elation; *Med* euphoria. **eu'forico** *a* elated; *Med* euphoric

Euro'city *nm* international Intercity

eurodepu'tato *nm* Euro MP, MEP

Eu'ropa *nf* Europe. **euro'peo, -a** *a* & *nmf* European

eutana'sia *nf* euthanasia

evacu'a|re *vt* evacuate. **~zi'one** *nf* evacuation

e'vadere *vt* evade; (*sbrigare*) deal with ● *vi* **~ da** escape from

evane'scente a vanishing

evan'gel|ico a evangelical. **evange'- lista** nm evangelist. **~o** nm = **vangelo**

evapo'ra|re vi evaporate. **~zi'one** nf evaporation

evasi'one nf escape; (fiscale) evasion; fig escapism. **eva'sivo** a evasive

e'vaso pp di **evadere** ● nm fugitive

eva'sore nm **~ fiscale** tax evader

eveni'enza nf eventuality

e'vento nm event

eventu'al|e a possible. **~ità** nf inv eventuality

evi'den|te a evident; **è ~te che** it is obvious that. **~te'mente** adv evidently. **~za** nf evidence; **mettere in ~za** emphasize; **mettersi in ~za** make oneself conspicuous

evidenzi'a|re vt highlight. **~'tore** nm (penna) highlighter

evi'tare vt avoid; (risparmiare) spare

evo'care vt evoke

evo'lu|to pp di **evolvere** ● a evolved; (progredito) progressive; ⟨civiltà, nazione⟩ advanced; **una donna evoluta** a modern woman. **~zi'one** nf evolution; (di ginnasta, aereo) circle

e'volver|e vt develop. **~si** vr evolve

ev'viva int hurray; **~ il Papa!** long live the Pope!; **gridare ~** cheer

ex+ pref ex+, former

'extra a inv extra; ⟨qualità⟩ first-class ● nm inv extra

extracomuni'tario a non-EC

extraconiu'gale a extramarital

extrater'restre nmf extra-terrestrial

Ff

---

fa¹ nm inv Mus (chiave, nota) F

fa² adv ago; **due mesi ~** two months ago

fabbi'sogno nm requirements pl, needs pl

'fabbri|ca nf factory

fabbri'cabile a ⟨area, terreno⟩ that can be built on

fabbri'cante nm manufacturer

fabbri'ca|re vt build; (produrre) manufacture; (fig: inventare) fabricate. **~to** nm building. **~zi'one** nf manufacturing; (costruzione) building

'fabbro nm blacksmith

fac'cend|a nf matter; **~e** pl (lavori domestici) housework sg. **~i'ere** nm wheeler-dealer

fac'chino nm porter

'facci|a nf face; (di foglio) side; **~a a ~a** face to face; **~a tosta** cheek; **voltar ~a** change sides; **di ~a** ⟨palazzo⟩ opposite; **alla ~a di** (fam: a dispetto di) in spite of. **~'ata** nf façade; (di foglio) side; (fig: esteriorità) outward appearance

fa'ceto a facetious; **tra il serio e il ~** half joking

fa'chiro nm fakir

'facil|e a easy; (affabile) easy-going; **essere ~e alle critiche** be quick to criticize; **essere ~e al riso** laugh a lot; **~e a farsi** easy to do; **è ~e che piova** it's likely to rain. **~ità** nf inv ease; (disposizione) aptitude; **avere ~ità di parola** express oneself well

facili'ta|re vt facilitate. **~zi'one** nf facility; **~zioni** pl special terms

facil'mente adv (con facilità) easily; (probabilmente) probably

faci'lone a slapdash. **~'ria** nf slapdash attitude

facino'roso a violent

facoltà nf inv faculty; (potere) power. **~'tivo** a optional; **fermata ~tiva** request stop

facol'toso a wealthy

fac'simile nm facsimile

fac'totum nmf man/girl Friday, factotum

'faggio nm beech

fagi'ano nm pheasant

fagio'lino nm French bean

fagi'olo nm bean; **a ~** ⟨arrivare, capitare⟩ at the right time

fagoci'tare vt gobble up ⟨società⟩

fa'gotto nm bundle; Mus bassoon

'faida nf feud

fai da te nm do-it-yourself, DIY

fal'cata nf stride

'falc|e nf scythe. **fal'cetto** nm sickle.

~**i'are** vt cut; fig mow down. ~**ia'trice** nf [lawn-]mower

'**falco** nm hawk

fal'cone nm falcon

'**falda** nf stratum; (di neve) flake; (di cappello) brim; (pendìo) slope

fale'gname nm carpenter. ~'**ria** nf carpentry

'**falla** nf leak

fal'lace a deceptive

'**fallico** a phallic

fallimen'tare a disastrous; Jur bankruptcy. **falli'mento** nm Fin bankruptcy; fig failure

fal'li|re vi Fin go bankrupt; fig fail ● vt miss ‹colpo›. ~**to, -a** a unsuccessful; Fin bankrupt ● nmf failure; Fin bankrupt

'**fallo** nm fault; (errore) mistake; Sport foul; (imperfezione) flaw; **senza ~** without fail

falò nm inv bonfire

fal'sar|e vt alter; (falsificare) falsify. ~**io, -a** nmf forger; (di documenti) counterfeiter

falsifi'ca|re vt fake; (contraffare) forge. ~**zi'one** nf (di documento) falsification

falsità nf falseness

'**falso** a false; (sbagliato) wrong; ‹opera d'arte ecc› fake; ‹gioielli, oro› imitation ● nm forgery; **giurare il ~** commit perjury

'**fama** nf fame; (reputazione) reputation

'**fame** nf hunger; **aver ~** be hungry; **fare la ~** barely scrape a living.

fa'melico a ravenous

famige'rato a infamous

fa'miglia nf family

famili'ar|e a family attrib; (ben noto) familiar; (senza cerimonie) informal ● nmf relative, relation ~**ità** nf familiarity; (informalità) informality. ~**iz'zarsi** vr familiarize oneself

fa'moso a famous

fa'nale nm lamp; Auto ecc light. **fanali** pl **posteriori** Auto rear lights

fa'natico, -a a fanatical; **essere ~ di** calcio/cinema be a football/cinema fanatic ● nmf fanatic. **fana'tismo** nm fanaticism

fanciul'l|a nf young girl. ~'**lezza** nf childhood. ~**lo** nm young boy

fan'donia nf lie; **fandonie!** nonsense!

fan'fara nf fanfare; (complesso) brass band

fanfaro'nata nf brag. **fanfa'rone, -a** nmf braggart

fan'ghiglia nf mud. '**fango** nm mud. **fan'goso** a muddy

fannul'lone, -a nmf idler

fantasci'enza nf science fiction

fanta'si|a nf fantasy; (immaginazione) imagination; (capriccio) fancy; (di tessuto) pattern. ~'**oso** a ‹stilista, ragazzo› imaginative; ‹resoconto› improbable

fan'tasma nm ghost

fantasti'c|are vi day-dream. ~**he'ria** nf day-dream. **fan'tastico** a fantastic; ‹racconto› fantasy

'**fante** nm infantryman; (carte) jack. ~'**ria** nf infantry

fan'tino nm jockey

fan'toccio nm puppet

fanto'matico a (inafferrabile) phantom attrib

fara'butto nm trickster

fara'ona nf (uccello) guinea-fowl

far'ci|re vt stuff; fill ‹torta›. ~**to** a stuffed; ‹dolce› filled

far'dello nm bundle; fig burden

'**fare** vt do; make ‹dolce, letto ecc›; (recitare la parte di) play; (trascorrere) spend; **~ una pausa/un sogno** have a break/a dream; **~ colpo su** impress; **~ paura** a frighten; **~ piacere** a please; **farla finita** put an end to it; **~ l'insegnante** be a teacher; **~ lo scemo** play the idiot; **~ una settimana al mare** spend a week at the seaside; **3 più 3 fa 6** 3 and 3 makes 6; **quanto fa?** – **fanno 10 000 lira** how much is it? – it's 10,000 lire; **far ~ qcsa a qcno** get sb to do sth; (costringere) make sb do sth; **~ vedere** show; **fammi parlare** let me speak; **niente a che ~ con** nothing to do with; **non c'è niente da ~** (per problema) there is nothing we/you/etc. can do; **fa caldo/buio** it's warm/dark; **non fa niente** it doesn't matter; **strada facendo** on the way. **farcela** (riuscire) manage ● vi **fai in modo di venire** try and come; **~ da** act as; **~ per** make as if to; **~ presto** be quick; **non fa per me** it's not for me ● nm way; **sul far del giorno** at daybreak. **farsi** vr (diventare) get; (sl: drogarsi) shoot up; **farsi avanti** come forward; **farsi i fatti propri** mind one's own business; **farsi la barba** shave; **farsi la villa** fam buy a villa; **farsi il ragazzo** fam find a boyfriend; **farsi due risate** have a laugh; **farsi male** hurt oneself; **farsi strada** (aver succe.s.o) make one's way in the world

fa'retto nm spot[light]

far'falla nf butterfly

farfal'lino nm (cravatta) bow tie
farfugli'are vt mutter
fa'rina nf flour. **fari'nacei** nmpl starchy food sg
fa'ringe nf pharynx
fari'noso a (neve) powdery; (mela) soft; (patata) floury
farma|'ceutico a pharmaceutical. **~'cia** nf pharmacy; (negozio) chemist's [shop]. **~cia di turno** duty chemist. **~'cista** nmf chemist. **'farmaco** nm drug
'faro nm Auto headlight; Aeron beacon; (costruzione) lighthouse
'farsa nf farce
'fasci|a nf band; (zona) area; (ufficiale) sash; (benda) bandage. **~'are** vt bandage; cling to (fianchi). **~a'tura** nf dressing; (azione) bandaging
fa'scicolo nm file; (di rivista) issue; (libretto) booklet
'fascino nm fascination
'fascio nm bundle; (di fiori) bunch
fa'scis|mo nm fascism. **~ta** nmf fascist
'fase nf phase
fa'stidi|o nm nuisance; (scomodo) inconvenience; **dar ~o a qcno** bother sb; **~i** pl (preoccupazioni) worries; (disturbi) troubles. **~'oso** a tiresome
'fasto nm pomp. **fa'stoso** a sumptuous
fa'suilo a bogus
'fata nf fairy
fa'ta|le a fatal; (inevitabile) fated
fata'l|ismo nm fatalism. **~ista** nmf fatalist. **~ità** nf inv fate; (caso sfortunato) misfortune. **~'mente** adv inevitably
fa'tica nf effort; (lavoro faticoso) hard work; (stanchezza) fatigue; **a ~** with great difficulty; **è ~ sprecata** it's a waste of time; **fare ~ a fare qcsa** find it difficult to do sth; **fare ~ a finire qcsa** struggle to finish sth. **fati'caccia** nf pain
fati'ca|re vi toil; **~re a** (stentare) find it difficult to. **~ta** nf effort; (sfacchinata) grind. **fati'coso** a tiring; (difficile) difficult
'fato nm fate
fat'taccio nm hum foul deed
fat'tezze nfpl features
fat'tibile a feasible
'fatto pp di **fare** ● a done, made; **~ a mano/in casa** handmade/home-made ● nm fact; (azione) action; (avvenimento) event; **bada ai fatti tuoi** mind your own business; **sa il ~ suo** he knows his

business; **di ~** in fact; **in ~ di** as regards
fat'to|re nm (causa, Math) factor; (di fattoria) farm manager. **~'ria** nf farm; (casa) farmhouse
fatto'rino nm messenger [boy]
fattucchi'era nf witch
fat'tura nf (stile) cut; (lavorazione) workmanship; Comm invoice
fattu'ra|re vt invoice; (adulterare) adulterate. **~to** nm turnover, sales pl. **~zi'one** nf invoicing, billing
'fatuo a fatuous
'fauna nf fauna
fau'tore nm supporter
'fava nf broad bean
fa'vella nf speech
fa'villa nf spark
'favo|la nf fable; (fiaba) story; (oggetto di pettegolezzi) laughing-stock; (meraviglia) dream. **~'loso** a fabulous
fa'vore nm favour; **essere a ~ di** be in favour of; **per ~** please; **di ~** (condizioni, trattamento) preferential. **~ggia- 'mento** nm Jur aiding and abetting. **favo'revole** a favourable. **~vol'mente** adv favourably
favo'ri|re vt favour; (promuovere) promote; **vuol ~re?** (accettare) will you have some?; (entrare) will you come in?. **~to, -a** a & nmf favourite
fax nm inv fax. **fa'xare** vt fax
fazi'one nf faction
faziosità nf bias. **fazi'oso** nm sectarian
fazzolet'tino nm **~ [di carta]** [paper] tissue
fazzo'letto nm handkerchief; (da testa) headscarf
feb'braio nm February
'febbre nf fever; **avere la ~** have o run a temperature. **~ da fieno** hay fever. **febbrici'tante** a fevered. **feb'brile** a feverish
'feccia nf dregs pl
'fecola nf potato flour
fecon'da|re vt fertilize. **~'tore** nm fertilizer. **~zi'one** nf fertilization. **~zione artificiale** artificial insemination. **fe'condo** a fertile
'fede nf faith; (fiducia) trust; (anello) wedding-ring; **in buona/mala ~** in good/bad faith; **prestar ~ a** believe; **tener ~ alla parola** keep one's word. **fe'dele** a faithful ● nmf believer; (seguace) follower. **~l'mente** adv faithfully. **~ltà** nf faithfulness; **alta ~ltà** high fidelity

'**federa** nf pillowcase
fede'ra|le a federal. ~'**lismo** nm federalism. ~**zi'one** nf federation
fe'dina nf avere la ~ **penale sporca/pulita** have a/no criminal record
'**fegato** nm liver; fig guts pl
'**felce** nf fern
fe'lic|e a happy; (fortunato) lucky. ~**ità** nf happiness
felici'ta|rsi vr ~**rsi con** congratulate. ~**zi'oni** nfpl congratulations
fe'lino a feline
'**felpa** nf (indumento) sweatshirt
fel'pato a brushed; (passo) stealthy
'**feltro** nm felt; (cappello) felt hat
'**femmin|a** nf female. **femmi'nile** a feminine; (rivista, abbigliamento) women's; (sesso) female ● nm feminine. ~**ilità** nf femininity. **femmi'nismo** nm feminism
'**femore** nm femur
'**fend|ere** vt split. ~**itura** nf split; (nella roccia) crack
feni'cottero nm flamingo
fenome'nale a phenomenal. **fe'nomeno** nm phenomenon
'**feretro** nm coffin
feri'ale a weekday; **giorno** ~ weekday
'**ferie** nfpl holidays; (di università, tribunale ecc) vacation sg; **andare in** ~ go on holiday
feri'mento nm wounding
fe'ri|re vt wound; (in incidente) injure; fig hurt. ~**rsi** vr injure oneself. ~**ta** nf wound. ~**to** a wounded ● nm wounded person; Mil casualty
'**ferma** nf Mil period of service
fermaca'pelli nm inv hairslide
ferma'carte nm inv paperweight
fermacra'vatta nm inv tiepin
fer'maglio nm clasp; (spilla) brooch; (per capelli) hair slide
ferma'mente adv firmly
fer'ma|re vt stop; (fissare) fix; Jur detain ● vi stop. ~**rsi** vr stop. ~**ta** nf stop. ~**ta dell'autobus** bus-stop. ~**ta a richiesta** request stop
fermen'ta|re vi ferme. ~**zi'one** nf fermentation. **fer'mento** nm ferment; (lievito) yeast
fer'mezza nf firmness
'**fermo** a still; (veicolo) stationary; (stabile) steady; (orologio) not working ● nm Jur detention; Mech catch; **in stato di** ~ in custody
fe'roc|e a ferocious; (bestia) wild; (freddo, dolore) unbearable. ~**e'mente** adv fiercely, ferociously. ~**ia** nf ferocity

fer'ragia nf scrap iron
ferra'gosto nm 15 August (bank holiday in Italy); (periodo) August holidays pl
ferra'menta nfpl ironmongery sg; **negozio di** ~ ironmonger's
fer'ra|re vt shoe (cavallo). ~**to a** ~**to in** (preparato in) well up in
'**ferreo** a iron
'**ferro** nm iron; (attrezzo) tool; (di chirurgo) instrument; **bistecca ai ferri** grilled steak; **di** ~ (memoria) excellent; (alibi) cast-iron; **salute di** ~ iron constitution. ~ **battuto** wrought iron. ~ **da calza** knitting needle. ~ **di cavallo** horseshoe. ~ **da stiro** iron
ferro'vecchio nm scrap merchant
ferro'vi|a nf railway. ~'**ario** a railway. ~'**ere** nm railwayman
'**fertil|e** a fertile. ~**ità** nf fertility. ~**iz'zante** nm fertilizer
fer'vente a blazing; fig fervent
'**fervere** vi (preparativi:) be well under way
'**fervid|o** a fervent; ~**i auguri** best wishes
fer'vore nm fervour
fesse'ria nf nonsense
'**fesso** pp di **fendere** ● a cracked; (sciocca) foolish ● nm (idiota) fool; **far** ~ **qcno** fam con sb
fes'sura nf crack; (per gettone ecc) slot
'**festa** nf feast; (giorno festivo) holiday; (compleanno) birthday; (ricevimento) party; fig joy; **fare** ~ **a qcno** welcome sb; **essere in** ~ be on holiday; **far** ~ celebrate. ~'**olo** a festive
festeggia'mento nm celebration; (manifestazione) festivity
festeggi'are vt celebrate; (accogliere festosamente) give a hearty welcome to
fe'stino nm party
festività nfpl festivities. **fe'stivo** a holiday; (lieto) festive. **festivi** nmpl public holidays
fe'stone nm (nel cucito) scallop, scollop
fe'stoso a merry
fe'tente a evil smelling; fig revolting ● nmf fam bastard
fe'ticcio nm fetish
'**feto** nm foetus
fe'tore nm stench
'**fetta** nf slice; **a fette** sliced. ~ **biscottata** slices of crispy toast-like bread
fet'tuccia nf tape; (con nome) name tape
feu'dale a feudal. '**feudo** nm feud

FFSS *abbr* (**Ferrovie dello Stato**) Italian state railways

fi'aba *nf* fairy-tale. **fia'besco** *a* fairy-tale

fi'acc|a *nf* weariness; (*indolenza*) laziness; **battere la ~a** be sluggish. **fiac-'care** *vt* weaken. **~o** *a* weak; (*indolente*) slack; (*stanco*) weary; (*partita*) dull

fi'acco|la *nf* torch. **~'lata** *nf* torchlight procession

fi'ala *nf* phial

fi'amma *nf* flame; *Naut* pennant; **in fiamme** aflame. **andare in fiamme** go up in flames. **~ ossidrica** blowtorch

fiam'ma|nte *a* flaming; **nuovo ~nte** brand new. **~ta** *nf* blaze

fiammeggi'are *vi* blaze

fiam'mifero *nm* match

fiam'mingo, -a *a* Flemish ●*nmf* Fleming ●*nm* (*lingua*) Flemish

fiancheggi'are *vt* border; *fig* support

fi'anco *nm* side; (*di persona*) hip; (*di animale*) flank; *Mil* wing; **al mio ~** by my side; **~ a ~** ⟨*lavorare*⟩ side by side

fi'asco *nm* flask; *fig* fiasco; **fare ~** be a fiasco

fia'tare *vi* breathe; (*parlare*) breathe a word

fi'ato *nm* breath; (*vigore*) stamina; **strumenti a ~** wind instruments; **senza ~** breathlessly; **tutto d'un ~** ⟨*bere, leggere*⟩ all in one go

'fibbia *nf* buckle

'fibra *nf* fibre; **fibre** *pl* (*alimentari*) roughage. **~ ottica** optical fibre

ficca'naso *nmf* nosey parker

fic'car|e *vt* thrust; drive ⟨*chiodo ecc*⟩; (*fam: mettere*) shove. **~si** *vr* thrust oneself; (*nascondersi*) hide; **~si nei guai** get oneself into trouble

fiche *nf* (*gettone*) chip

'fico *nm* (*albero*) fig-tree; (*frutto*) fig. **~ d'India** prickly pear

'fico, -a *fam nmf* cool sort ●*a* cool

fidanza'mento *nm* engagement

fidan'za|rsi *vr* become engaged. **~to, -a** *nmf* fiancé; fiancée

fi'da|rsi *vr* **~rsi di** trust. **~to** *a* trustworthy

'fido *nm* devoted follower; *Comm* credit

fi'duci|a *nf* confidence; **degno di ~a** trustworthy; **di ~a** ⟨*fornitore, banca*⟩ regular, usual; **persona di ~a** reliable person. **~'oso** *a* trusting

fi'ele *nm* bile; *fig* bitterness

fie'nile *nm* barn. **fi'eno** *nm* hay

fi'era *nf* fair

fie'rezza *nf* (*dignità*) pride. **fi'ero** *a* proud

fi'evole *a* faint; ⟨*luce*⟩ dim

'fifa *nf fam* jitters; **aver ~** have the jitters. **fi'fone, -a** *nmf fam* chicken

'figli|a *nf* daughter; **~a unica** only child. **~'astra** *nf* stepdaughter. **~'astro** *nm* stepson. **~o** *nm* son; (*generico*) child. **~o di papà** spoilt brat. **~o unico** only child

figli'occi|a *nf* goddaughter. **~o** *nm* godson

figli'o|la *nf* girl. **~'lanza** *nf* offspring. **~lo** *nm* boy

'figo, -a *vedi* **fico, -a**

fi'gura *nf* figure; (*aspetto esteriore*) shape; (*illustrazione*) illustration; **far bella/brutta ~** make a good/bad impression; **mi hai fatto fare una brutta ~** you made me look a fool; **che ~!** how embarrassing!. **figu'raccia** *nf* bad impression

figu'ra|re *vt* represent; (*simboleggiare*) symbolize; (*immaginare*) imagine ●*vi* (*far figura*) cut a fine figure; (*in lista*) appear, figure. **~rsi** *vr* (*immaginarsi*) imagine; **~ti!** imagine that!; **posso? – [ma] ~ti!** may I? – of course!. **~'tivo** *a* figurative

figu'rina *nf* (*da raccolta*) ≈ cigarette card

figu|ri'nista *nmf* dress designer. **~'rino** *nm* fashion sketch. **~'rone** *nm* **fare un ~rone** make an excellent impression

'fila *nf* line; (*di soldati ecc*) file; (*di oggetti*) row; (*coda*) queue; **di ~** in succession; **fare la ~** queue [up], stand in line *Am*; **in ~ indiana** single file

fila'mento *nm* filament

filantro'pia *nf* philanthropy

fi'lare *vt* spin; *Naut* pay out ●*vi* (*andarsene*) run away; ⟨*liquido:*⟩ trickle; **fila!** scram!; **~ con** (*fam: amoreggiare*) go out with; **~ dritto** toe the line

filar'monica *nf* (*orchestra*) orchestra

fila'strocca *nf* rigmarole; (*per bambini*) nursery rhyme

filate'lia *nf* philately

fi'la|to *a* spun; (*ininterrotto*) running; (*continuato*) uninterrupted; **di ~to** (*subito*) immediately ●*nm* yarn. **~'tura** *nf* spinning; (*filanda*) spinning mill

fil di 'ferro *nm* wire

fi'letto *nm* (*bordo*) border; (*di vite*) thread; *Culin* fillet

fili'ale *a* filial ●*nf Comm* branch

fili'grana *nf* filigree; (*su carta*) watermark

film *nm inv* film. **~ giallo** thriller. **~ a lungo metraggio** feature film

fil'ma|re *vt* film. **~to** *nm* short film. **fil'mino** *nm* cine film

'filo *nm* thread; (*tessile*) yarn; (*metallico*) wire; (*di lama*) edge; (*venatura*) grain; (*di perle*) string; (*d'erba*) blade; (*di luce*) ray; **con un ~ di voce** in a whisper; **per ~ e per segno** in detail; **fare il ~ a qcno** fancy sb; **perdere il ~** lose the thread. **~ spinato** barbed wire

'filobus *nm inv* trolleybus

filodiffusi'one *nf* rediffusion

fi'lone *nm* vein; (*di pane*) French

filoso'fia *nf* philosophy. **fi'losofo, -a** *nmf* philosopher

fil'trare *vt* filter. **'filtro** *nm* filter

'filza *nf* string

fin *vedi* **fine, fino¹**

fi'nal|e *a* final ● *nm* end ● *nf* Sport final. **fina'lista** *nmf* finalist. **~ità** *nf inv* finality; (*scopo*) aim. **~'mente** *adv* at last; (*in ultimo*) finally

fi'nanz|a *nf* finance; **~i'ario** *a* financial. **~i'ere** *nm* financier; (*guardia di finanza*) customs officer. **~ia'mento** *nm* funding

finanzi'a|re *vt* fund, finance. **~'tore, ~'trice** *nmf* backer

finché *conj* until; (*per tutto il tempo che*) as long as

'fine *a* fine; (*sottile*) thin; (*udito, vista*) keen; (*raffinato*) refined ● *nf* end; **alla ~** in the end; **alla fin ~** after all; **in fin dei conti** when all's said and done; **te lo dico a fin di bene** I'm telling you for your own good; **senza ~** endless ● *nm* aim. **~ settimana** weekend

fi'nestra *nf* window. **fine'strella** *nf* **di aiuto** Comput help window, help box. **fine'strino** *nm* Rail, Auto window

fi'nezza *nf* fineness; (*sottigliezza*) thinness; (*raffinatezza*) refinement

'finger|e *vt* pretend; feign (*affetto ecc*). **~si** *vr* pretend to be

fini'menti *nmpl* finishing touches; (*per cavallo*) harness *sg*

fini'mondo *nm* end of the world; *fig* pandemonium

fi'ni|re *vt/i* finish, end; (*smettere*) stop; (*diventare, andare a finire*) end up; **~scila** stop it!. **~to** *a* finished; (*abile*) accomplished. **~'tura** *nf* finish

finlan'dese *a* Finnish ● *nmf* Finn ● *nm* (*lingua*) Finnish

Fin'landia *nf* Finland

'fino¹ *prep* **~ a** till, until; (*spazio*) as far as; **~ all'ultimo** to the last; **fin da** (*tempo*) since; (*spazio*) from; **fin qui** as far as here; **fin troppo** too much; **~ a che punto** how far

'fino² *a* fine; (*acuto*) subtle; (*puro*) pure

fi'nocchio *nm* fennel; (*fam: omosessuale*) poof

fi'nora *adv* so far, up till now

'finta *nf* pretence, sham; *Sport* feint; **far ~ di** pretend to; **far ~ di niente** act as if nothing had happened; **per ~** (*per scherzo*) for a laugh

'fint|o, -a *pp di* **fingere** ● *a* false; (*artificiale*) artificial; **fare il ~o tonto** act dumb

finzi'one *nf* pretence

fi'occo *nm* bow; (*di neve*) flake; (*nappa*) tassel; **coi fiocchi** *fig* excellent. **~ di neve** snowflake

fi'ocina *nf* harpoon

fi'oco *a* weak; (*luce*) dim

fi'onda *nf* catapult

fio'raio, -a *nmf* florist

fiorda'liso *nm* cornflower

fi'ordo *nm* fiord

fi'ore *nm* flower; (*parte scelta*) cream; **fiori** *pl* (*nelle carte*) clubs; **a fior d'acqua** on the surface of the water; **~ di** (*abbondanza*) a lot of; **ha i nervi a fior di pelle** his nerves are on edge; **a fiori** flowery

fioren'tino *a* Florentine

fio'retto *nm* (*scherma*) foil; *Relig* act of mortification

fio'rire *vi* flower; (*albero:*) blossom; *fig* flourish

fio'rista *nmf* florist

fiori'tura *nf* (*di albero*) blossoming

fi'otto *nm* **scorrere a fiotti** pour out; **piove a fiotti** the rain is pouring down

Fi'renze *nf* Florence

'firma *nf* signature; (*nome*) name

fir'ma|re *vt* sign. **~'tario, -a** *nmf* signatory. **~to** (*abito, borsa*) designer *attrib*

fisar'monica *nf* accordion

fi'scale *a* fiscal

fischi'are *vi* whistle ● *vt* whistle; (*in segno di disapprovazione*) boo

fischiet't|are *vt* whistle. **~io** *nm* whistling

fischi'etto *nm* whistle. **'fischio** *nm* whistle

'fisco *nm* treasury; (*tasse*) taxation; **il ~** the taxman

'fisica *nf* physics

fisica'mente *adv* physically

'fisico, -a *a* physical ● *nmf* physicist ● *nm* physique

'fisima *nf* whim

fisio|lo'gia *nf* physiology. **~'logico** *a* physiological

fisiono'mia *nf* features, face; *(di paesaggio)* appearance

fisiotera'pi|a *nf* physiotherapy. **~sta** *nmf* physiotherapist

fis'sa|re *vt* fix, fasten; *(guardare fissamente)* stare at; arrange *(appuntamento, ora)*. **~rsi** *vr* *(stabilirsi)* settle; *(fissare lo sguardo)* stare; **~rsi su** *(ostinarsi)* set one's mind on; **~rsi di fare qcsa** become obsessed with doing sth. **~to** *nm* *(persona)* person with an obsession. **~zi'one** *nf* fixation; *(ossessione)* obsession

'fisso *a* fixed; **un lavoro ~** a regular job; **senza fissa dimora** of no fixed abode

'fitta *nf* sharp pain

fit'tizio *a* fictitious

'fitto¹ *a* thick; **~ di** full of ● *nm* depth

fitto² *nm* *(affitto)* rent; **dare a ~** let; **prendere a ~** rent; *(noleggiare)* hire

fiu'mana *nf* swollen river; *fig* stream

fi'ume *nm* river; *fig* stream

fiu'tare *vt* smell. **fi'uto** *nm* [sense of] smell; *fig* nose

'flaccido *a* flabby

fla'cone *nm* bottle

fla'gello *nm* scourge

fla'grante *a* flagrant; **in ~** in the act

fla'nella *nf* flannel

'flash *nm inv Journ* newsflash

'flauto *nm* flute

'flebile *a* feeble

'flemma *nf* calm; *Med* phlegm. **flem'matico** *a* phlegmatic

fles'sibil|e *a* flexible. **~ità** *nf* flexibility

flessi'one *nf* *(ginnastica, del busto in avanti)* forward bend

'flesso *pp di* **flettere**

flessu'oso *a* supple

'flettere *vt* bend

flir'tare *vi* flirt

F.lli *abbr* **(fratelli)** Bros

floppy disk *nm inv* floppy disk

'flora *nf* flora

'florido *a* flourishing

'floscio *a* limp; *(flaccido)* flabby

'flotta *nf* fleet. **flot'tiglia** *nf* flotilla

flu'ente *a* fluent

'fluido *nm* fluid

flu'ire *vi* flow

fluore'scente *a* fluorescent

flu'oro *nm* fluorine

'flusso *nm* flow; *Med* flux; *(del mare)* flood[-tide]; **~ e riflusso** ebb and flow

fluttu'ante *a* fluctuating

fluttu'a|re *vi* *(prezzi, moneta:)* fluctuate. **~zi'one** *nf* fluctuation

fluvi'ale *a* river

fo'bia *nf* phobia

'foca *nf* seal

fo'caccia *nf* *(pane)* flat bread; *(dolce)* ≈ raisin bread

fo'cale *(distanza, punto)* focal. **focaliz'zare** *vt* get into focus *(fotografia)*; focus *(attenzione)*; define *(problema)*

'foce *nf* mouth

foco'laio *nm Med* focus; *fig* centre

foco'lare *nm* hearth; *(caminetto)* fireplace; *Techn* furnace

fo'coso *a* fiery

'foder|a *nf* lining; *(di libro)* dust-jacket; *(di poltrona ecc)* loose cover. **fode'rare** *vt* line; cover *(libro)*. **~o** *nm* sheath

'foga *nf* impetuosity

'foggi|a *nf* fashion; *(maniera)* manner; *(forma)* shape. **~'are** *vt* mould

'fogli|a *nf* leaf; *(di metallo)* foil. **~'ame** *nm* foliage

fogli'etto *nm* *(pezzetto di carta)* piece of paper

'foglio *nm* sheet; *(pagina)* leaf. **~ elettronico** *Comput* spreadsheet. **~ rosa** ≈ provisional driving licence

'fogna *nf* sewer. **~'tura** *nf* sewerage

fo'lata *nf* gust

fol'clo|re *nm* folklore. **~'ristico** *a* folk; *(bizzarro)* weird

folgo'ra|re *vi* *(splendere)* shine ● *vt* *(con un fulmine)* strike. **~zi'one** *nf* *(da fulmine, elettrica)* electrocution; *(idea)* brainwave

fol'gore *nf* thunderbolt

'folla *nf* crowd

'folle *a* mad; **in ~** *Auto* in neutral; **andare in ~** *Auto* coast

folle'mente *adv* madly

fol'lia *nf* madness; **alla ~** *(amare)* to distraction

'folto *a* thick

fomen'tare *vt* stir up

fond'ale *nm Theat* backcloth

fonda'men|ta *nfpl* foundations. **~'tale** *a* fundamental. **~to** *nm* *(di principio, teoria)* foundation

fon'da|re *vt* establish; base *(ragionamento, accusa)*. **~to** *a* *(ragionamento)* well-founded. **~zi'one** *nf* establishment; **~zioni** *pl* *(di edificio)* foundations

fon'delli *nmpl* **prendere qcno per i ~** pull sb's leg

fon'dente *a* ⟨cioccolato⟩ dark

'fonder|e *vt/i* melt; ⟨colori:⟩ blend. **~si** *vr* melt; *Comm* merge. **fonde'ria** *nf* foundry

'fondi *nmpl* ⟨denaro⟩ funds; ⟨di caffè⟩ grounds

'fondo *a* deep; **è notte fonda** it's the middle of the night ● *nm* bottom; ⟨fine⟩ end; ⟨sfondo⟩ background; ⟨indole⟩ nature; ⟨somma di denaro⟩ fund; ⟨feccia⟩ dregs *pl*; **andare a ~** ⟨nave:⟩ sink; **da cima a ~** from beginning to end; **in ~** after all; **in ~ in ~** deep down; **fino in ~** right to the end; ⟨capire⟩ thoroughly. **~ d'investimento** investment trust

fondo'tinta *nm* foundation cream

fon'duta *nf* fondue *made with cheese, milk and eggs*

fo'netic|a *nf* phonetics *sg*. **~o** *a* phonetic

fon'tana *nf* fountain

'fonte *nf* spring; *fig* source ● *nm* font

fo'raggio *nm* forage

fo'rar|e *vt* pierce; punch ⟨biglietto⟩ ● *vi* puncture. **~si** *vr* ⟨gomma, pallone:⟩ go soft

'forbici *nfpl* scissors

forbi'cine *nfpl* ⟨per le unghie⟩ nail scissors

for'bito *a* erudite

'forca *nf* fork; ⟨patibolo⟩ gallows *pl*

for'cella *nf* fork; ⟨per capelli⟩ hairpin

for'chet|ta *nf* fork. **~'tata** *nf* ⟨quantità⟩ forkful

for'cina *nf* hairpin

'forcipe *nm* forceps *pl*

for'cone *nm* pitchfork

fo'resta *nf* forest. **fore'stale** *a* forest *attrib*

foresti'ero, -a *a* foreign ● *nmf* foreigner

for'fait *nm inv* fixed price; **dare ~** ⟨abbandonare⟩ give up

'forfora *nf* dandruff

'forgi|a *nf* forge. **~'are** *vt* forge

'forma *nf* form; ⟨sagoma⟩ shape; *Culin* mould; ⟨da calzolaio⟩ last; **essere in ~** be in good form: **a ~ di** in the shape of; **forme** *pl* ⟨del corpo⟩ figure *sg*; ⟨convenzioni⟩ appearances

formag'gino *nm* processed cheese. **for'maggio** *nm* cheese

for'mal|e *a* formal. **~ità** *nf inv* formality. **~iz'zarsi** *vr* stand on ceremony. **~'mente** *adv* formally

for'ma|re *vt* form. **~rsi** *vr* form;

⟨svilupparsi⟩ develop. **~to** *nm* size; ⟨di libro⟩ format; **~to tessera** ⟨fotografia⟩ passport-size

format'tare *vt* format

formazi'one *nf* formation; *Sport* line-up. **~ professionale** vocational training

for'mi|ca *nf* ant. **~'caio** *nm* anthill

'formica® *nf* ⟨laminato plastico⟩ Formica®

formico'l|are *vi* ⟨braccio ecc:⟩ tingle; **~are di** be swarming with; **mi ~a la mano** I have pins and needles in my hand. **~io** *nm* swarming; ⟨di braccio ecc⟩ pins and needles *pl*

formi'dabile *a* ⟨tremendo⟩ formidable; ⟨eccezionale⟩ tremendous

for'mina *nf* mould

for'moso *a* shapely

'formula *nf* formula. **formu'lare** *vt* formulate; ⟨esprimere⟩ express

for'nace *nf* furnace; ⟨per laterizi⟩ kiln

for'naio *nm* baker; ⟨negozio⟩ bakery

for'nello *nm* stove; ⟨di pipa⟩ bowl

for'ni|re *vt* supply (**di** with). **~'tore** *nm* supplier. **~'tura** *nf* supply

'forno *nm* oven; ⟨panetteria⟩ bakery; **al ~** roast. **~ a microonde** microwave [oven]

'foro *nm* hole; ⟨romano⟩ forum; ⟨tribunale⟩ [law] court

'forse *adv* perhaps, maybe; **essere in ~** be in doubt

forsen'nato, -a *a* mad ● *nmf* madman; madwoman

'forte *a* strong; ⟨colore⟩ bright; ⟨suono⟩ loud; ⟨resistente⟩ tough; ⟨spesa⟩ considerable; ⟨dolore⟩ severe; ⟨pioggia⟩ heavy; ⟨a tennis, calcio⟩ good; ⟨fam: simpatico⟩ great; ⟨taglia⟩ large ● *adv* strongly; ⟨parlare⟩ loudly; ⟨velocemente⟩ fast; ⟨piovere⟩ heavily ● *nm* ⟨fortezza⟩ fort; ⟨specialità⟩ strong point

for'tezza *nf* fortress; ⟨forza morale⟩ fortitude

fortifi'care *vt* fortify

for'tino *nm Mil* blockhouse

for'tuito *a* fortuitous; **incontro ~** chance encounter

for'tuna *nf* fortune; ⟨successo⟩ success; ⟨buona sorte⟩ luck. **atterraggio di ~** forced landing; **aver ~** be lucky; **buona ~!** good luck!; **di ~** makeshift; **per ~** luckily. **fortu'nato** *a* lucky, fortunate; ⟨impresa⟩ successful. **~ta'mente** *adv* fortunately

fo'runcolo *nm* pimple; ⟨grosso⟩ boil

'forza *nf* strength; ⟨potenza⟩ power;

(*fisica*) force; **di** ~ by force; **a** ~ **di** by dint of; **con** ~ hard; ~**!** come on!; ~ **di volontà** will-power; ~ **maggiore** circumstances beyond one's control; **la** ~ **pubblica** the police; **per** ~ against one's will; (*naturalmente*) of course; **farsi** ~ bear up; **mare** ~ **8** force 8 gale; **bella** ~**!** *fam* big deal!. ~ **di gravità** [force of] gravity. **le forze armate** the armed forces

for'za|re *vt* force; (*scassare*) break open; (*sforzare*) strain. ~**to** *a* forced; (*sorriso*) strained ● *nm* convict

forzi'ere *nm* coffer

for'zuto *a* strong

fo'schia *nf* haze

'fosco *a* dark

fo'sfato *nm* phosphate

'fosforo *nm* phosphorus

'fossa *nf* pit; (*tomba*) grave. ~ **biologica** cesspool. **fos'sato** *nm* (*di fortificazione*) moat

fos'setta *nf* dimple

'fossile *nm* fossil

'fosso *nm* ditch; *Mil* trench

'foto *nf inv fam* photo; **fare delle** ~ take some photos

foto'cellula *nf* photocell

fotocomposizi'one *nf* filmsetting, photocomposition

foto'copi|a *nf* photocopy. ~**'are** *vt* photocopy. ~**a'trice** *nf* photocopier

foto'finish *nm inv* photo finish

foto'genico *a* photogenic

fotogra|'fare *vt* photograph. ~**'fia** *nf* (*arte*) photography; (*immagine*) photograph; **fare** ~**fie** take photographs. **foto'grafico** *a* photographic; **macchina fotografica** camera. **fo'tografo, -a** *nmf* photographer

foto'gramma *nm* frame

fotomo'dello *nm* [photographer's] model

fotomon'taggio *nm* photomontage

foto'romanzo *nm* photo story

'fotter|e *vt* (*fam: rubare*) nick; *vulg* fuck, screw. ~**sene** *vr vulg* not give a fuck

fot'tuto *a* (*fam: maledetto*) bloody

fou'lard *nm inv* scarf

fra *prep* (*in mezzo a due*) between; (*in un insieme*) among; (*tempo, distanza*) in; **detto** ~ **noi** between you and me; ~ **sé e sé** to oneself; ~ **l'altro** what's more; ~ **breve** soon; ~ **quindici giorni** in two weeks' time; ~ **tutti, siamo in venti** there are twenty of us altogether

fracas'sar|e *vt* smash. ~**si** *vr* shatter

fra'casso *nm* din; (*di cose che cadono*) crash

'fradicio *a* (*bagnato*) soaked; (*guasto*) rotten; **ubriaco** ~ blind drunk

'fragil|e *a* fragile; *fig* frail. ~**ità** *nf* fragility; *fig* frailty

'fragola *nf* strawberry

fra'go|re *nm* uproar; (*di cose rotte*) clatter; (*di tuono*) rumble. ~**'roso** *a* uproarious; (*tuono*) rumbling; (*suono*) clanging

fra'gran|te *a* fragrant. ~**za** *nf* fragrance

frain'ten|dere *vt* misunderstand. ~**dersi** *vr* be at cross-purposes. ~**so** *pp di* **fraintendere**

frammen'tario *a* fragmentary. **fram'mento** *nm* fragment

'frana *nf* landslide; (*fam: persona*) walking disaster area. **fra'nare** *vi* slide down

franca'mente *adv* frankly

fran'cese *a* French ● *nmf* Frenchman; Frenchwoman ● *nm* (*lingua*) French

fran'chezza *nf* frankness

'Francia *nf* France

'franco[1] *a* frank; *Comm* free; **farla franca** get away with sth

'franco[2] *nm* (*moneta*) franc

franco'bollo *nm* stamp

fran'gente *nm* (*onda*) breaker; (*scoglio*) reef; (*fig: momento difficile*) crisis; **in quel** ~ given the situation

'frangia *nf* fringe

fra'noso *a* subject to landslides

fran'toio *nm* olive-press

frantu'mar|e *vt, ~si vr* shatter. **fran'tumi** *nmpl* splinters; **andare in frantumi** be smashed to smithereens

frappé *nm inv* milkshake

frap'por|re *vt* interpose. ~**si** *vr* intervene

fra'sario *nm* vocabulary; (*libro*) phrase book

'frase *nf* sentence; (*espressione*) phrase. ~ **fatta** cliché

'frassino *nm* ash[-tree]

frastagli'a|re *vt* make jagged. ~**to** *a* jagged

frastor'na|re *vt* daze. ~**to** *a* dazed

frastu'ono *nm* racket

'frate *nm* friar; (*monaco*) monk

fratel'la|nza *nf* brotherhood. ~**stro** *nm* half-brother

fra'tel|li *nmpl* (*fratello e sorella*) brother and sister. ~**o** *nm* brother

fraterniz'zare *vi* fraternize. **fra'terno** *a* brotherly

frat'taglie *nfpl (di pollo ecc)* giblets

frat'tanto *adv* in the meantime

frat'tempo *nm* **nel** ~ meanwhile, in the meantime

frat'tu|ra *nf* fracture. ~'**rare** *vt*, ~'**rarsi** *vr* break

fraudo'lento *a* fraudulent

frazi'one *nf* fraction; *(borgata)* hamlet

'frecci|a *nf* arrow; *Auto* indicator. ~'**ata** *nf (osservazione pungente)* cutting remark

fredda'mente *adv* coldly

fred'dare *vt* cool; *(fig: con sguardo, battuta)* cut down; *(uccidere)* kill

fred'dezza *nf* coldness

'freddo *a & nm* cold; **aver** ~ be cold; **fa** ~ it's cold

freddo'loso *a* sensitive to cold, chilly

fred'dura *nf* pun

fre'ga|re *vt* rub; *(fam: truffare)* cheat; *(fam: rubare)* swipe. ~**rsene** *fam* not give a damn; **chi se ne frega!** what the heck!. ~**si** *vr* rub *(occhi)*. ~**ta** *nf* rub. ~'**tura** *nf fam (truffa)* swindle; *(delusione)* letdown

'fregio *nm Archit* frieze; *(ornamento)* decoration

fre'mente *a* quivering

'frem|ere *vi* quiver. ~**ito** *nm* quiver

fre'na|re *vt* brake; *fig* restrain; hold back *(lacrime, impazienza)* ● *vi* brake. ~**rsi** *vr* check oneself. ~**ta** *nf* **fare una** ~**ta brusca** hit the brakes

frene'sia *nf* frenzy; *(desiderio smodato)* craze. **fre'netico** *a* frenzied

'freno *nm* brake; *fig* check; **togliere il** ~ release the brake; **usare il** ~ apply the brake; **tenere a** ~ restrain. ~ **a mano** handbrake

frequen'tare *vt* frequent; attend *(scuola ecc)*; mix with *(persone)*

fre'quen|te *a* frequent; **di** ~**te** frequently. ~**za** *nf* frequency; *(assiduità)* attendance

fre'schezza *nf* freshness; *(di temperatura)* coolness

'fresco *a* fresh; *(temperatura)* cool; **stai** ~! you're for it! ● *nm* coolness; **far** ~ be cool; **mettere/tenere in** ~ put/keep in a cool place

'fretta *nf* hurry, haste; **aver** ~ be in a hurry; **far** ~ **a qcno** hurry sb; **in** ~ **e furia** in a great hurry. **frettolosa'mente** *adv* hurriedly. **fretto'loso** *a (persona)* in a hurry; *(lavoro)* rushed, hurried

fri'abile *a* crumbly

'friggere *vt* fry; **vai a farti** ~! get lost! ● *vi* sizzle

friggi'trice *nf* chip pan

frigidità *nf* frigidity. **'frigido** *a* frigid

fri'gnare *vi* whine

'frigo *nm* fridge

frigo'bar *nm inv* minibar

frigo'rifero *a* refrigerating ● *nm* refrigerator

fringu'ello *nm* chaffinch

frit'tata *nf* omelette

frit'tella *nf* fritter; *(fam: macchia d'unto)* grease stain

'fritto *pp di* **friggere** ● *a* fried; **essere** ~ be done for ● *nm* fried food. ~ **misto** mixed fried fish/vegetables. **frit'tura** *nf (pietanza)* fried dish

frivo'lezza *nf* frivolity. **'frivolo** *a* frivolous

frizio'nare *vt* rub. **frizi'one** *nf* friction; *Mech* clutch; *(di pelle)* rub

friz'zante *a* fizzy; *(vino)* sparkling; *(aria)* bracing

'frizzo *nm* gibe

fro'dare *vt* defraud

'frode *nf* fraud. ~ **fiscale** tax evasion

'frollo *a* tender; *(selvaggina)* high; *(persona)* spineless; **pasta frolla** short[crust] pastry

'fronda *nf* [leafy] branch; *fig* rebellion. **fron'doso** *a* leafy

fron'tale *a* frontal; *(scontro)* head-on

'fronte *nf* forehead; *(di edificio)* front; **di** ~ opposite; **di** ~ **a** opposite, facing; *(a paragone)* compared with; **far** ~ **a** face ● *nm Mil, Pol* front. ~**ggi'are** *vt* face

fronte'spizio *nm* title page

fronti'era *nf* frontier, border

fron'tone *nm* pediment

'fronzolo *nm* frill

'frotta *nf* swarm; *(di animali)* flock

'frottola *nf* fib; **frottole** *pl* nonsense *sg*

fru'gale *a* frugal

fru'gare *vi* rummage ● *vt* search

frul'la|re *vt Culin* whisk ● *vi (ali:)* whirr. ~**to** *nm* ~**to di frutta** fruit drink with milk and crushed ice. ~'**tore** *nm* [electric] mixer. **frul'lino** *nm* whisk

fru'mento *nm* wheat

frusci'are *vi* rustle

fru'scio *nm* rustle; *(radio, giradischi)* ground noise; *(di acque)* murmur

'frusta *nf* whip; *(frullino)* whisk

fru'sta|re *vt* whip. ~**ta** *nf* lash. **fru'stino** *nm* riding crop

fru'stra|re *vt* frustrate. ~**to** *a* frustrated. ~**zi'one** *nf* frustration

'frutt|a *nf* fruit; *(portata)* dessert. **frutt'tare** *vi* bear fruit ● *vt* yield. **frut'teto**

nm orchard. **~i'vendolo, -a** *nmf* greengrocer. **~o** *nm anche fig* fruit; *Fin* yield; **~i di bosco** fruits of the forest. **~i di mare** seafood *sg*. **~u'oso** *a* profitable

f.to *abbr* (**firmato**) signed

fu *a* (*defunto*) late; **il ~ signor Rossi** the late Mr Rossi

fuci'la|re *vt* shoot. **~ta** *nf* shot

fu'cile *nm* rifle

fu'cina *nf* forge

'fucsia *nf* fuchsia

'fuga *nf* escape; (*perdita*) leak; *Mus* fugue; **darsi alla ~** take to flight

fu'gace *a* fleeting

fug'gevole *a* short-lived

fuggi'asco, -a *nmf* fugitive

fuggi'fuggi *nm* stampede

fug'gi|re *vi* flee; (*innamorati:*) elope; *fig* fly. **~'tivo, -a** *nmf* fugitive

'fulcro *nm* fulcrum

ful'gore *nm* splendour

fu'liggine *nf* soot

fulmi'nar|e *vt* strike by lightning; (*con sguardo*) look daggers at; (*con scarica elettrica*) electrocute. **~si** *vr* burn out. **'fulmine** *nm* lightning. **ful'mineo** *a* rapid

'fulvo *a* tawny

fumai'olo *nm* funnel; (*di casa*) chimney

fu'ma|re *vt/i* smoke; (*in ebollizione*) steam. **~'tore, ~'trice** *nmf* smoker; **non fumatori** non-smoker, non-smoking

fu'metto *nm* comic strip; **fumetti** *pl* comics

'fumo *nm* smoke; (*vapore*) steam; *fig* hot air; **andare in ~** vanish. **fu'moso** *a* (*ambiente*) smoky; (*discorso*) vague

fu'nambolo, -a *nmf* tightrope walker

'fune *nf* rope; (*cavo*) cable

'funebre *a* funeral; (*cupa*) gloomy

fune'rale *nm* funeral

fu'nereo *a* (*aria*) funereal

fu'nesto *a* sad

'fungere *vi* **~ da** act as

'fungo *nm* mushroom; *Bot, Med* fungus

funico'lare *nf* funicular [railway]

funi'via *nf* cableway

funzio'nal|e *a* functional. **~ità** *nf* functionality

funziona'mento *nm* functioning

funzio'nare *vi* work, function; **~ da** (*fungere da*) act as

funzio'nario *nm* official

funzi'one *nf* function; (*carica*) office; *Relig* service; **entrare in ~** take up office

fu'oco *nm* fire; (*fisica, fotografia*) focus; **far ~** fire; **dar ~ a** set fire to; **prendere ~** catch fire. **fuochi** *pl* **d'artificio** fireworks. **~ di paglia** nine-days' wonder

fuorché *prep* except

fu'ori *adv* out; (*all'esterno*) outside; (*all'aperto*) outdoors; **andare di ~** (*traboccare*) spill over; **essere ~ di sé** be beside oneself; **essere in ~** (*sporgere*) stick out; **far ~** *fam* do in; **~ mano** out of the way; **~ moda** old-fashioned; **~ pasto** between meals; **~ pericolo** out of danger; **~ questione** out of the question; **~ uso** out of use ● *nm* outside

fuori'bordo *nm* speedboat (*with outboard motor*)

fuori'classe *nmf inv* champion

fuorigi'oco *nm* & *adv* offside

fuori'legge *nmf* outlaw

fuori'serie *a* custom-made ● *nf* custom-built model

fuori'strada *nm* off-road vehicle

fuorvi'are *vt* lead astray ● *vi* go astray

furbacchi'one *nm* crafty old devil

furbe'ria *nf* cunning. **fur'bizia** *nf* cunning

'furbo *a* cunning; (*intelligente*) clever; (*astuto*) shrewd; **bravo ~**! nice one!; **fare il ~** try to be clever

fu'rente *a* furious

fur'fante *nm* scoundrel

furgon'cino *nm* delivery van. **fur'gone** *nm* van

'furi|a *nf* fury; (*fretta*) haste; **a ~a di** by dint of. **~'bondo, ~'oso** *a* furious

fu'rore *nm* fury; (*veemenza*) frenzy; **far ~** be all the rage. **~ggi'are** *vi* be a great success

furtiva'mente *adv* covertly. **fur'tivo** *a* furtive

'furto *nm* theft; (*con scasso*) burglary

'fusa *nfpl* **fare le ~** purr

fu'scello *nm* (*di legno*) twig; (*di paglia*) straw; **sei un ~** you're as light as a feather

fu'seaux *mpl* leggings

fu'sibile *nm* fuse

fusi'one *nf* fusion; *Comm* merger

'fuso *pp di* **fondere** ● *a* melted ● *nm* spindle. **~ orario** time zone

fusoli'era *nf* fuselage

fu'stagno *nm* corduroy

fu'stino *nm* (*di detersivo*) box

'fusto *nm* stem; (*tronco*) trunk; (*di metallo*) drum; (*di legno*) barrel

'futile *a* futile

fu'turo *a* & *nm* future

Gg

gab'bar|e *vt* cheat. **~si** *vr* **~si di** make fun of

'gabbia *nf* cage; (*da imballaggio*) crate. **~ degli imputati** dock. **~ toracica** rib cage

gabbi'ano *nm* [sea]gull

gabi'netto *nm* (*di medico*) consulting room; *Pol* cabinet; (*toletta*) lavatory; (*laboratorio*) laboratory

'gaffe *nf inv* blunder

gagli'ardo *a* vigorous

gai'ezza *nf* gaiety. **'gaio** *a* cheerful

'gala *nf* gala

ga'lante *a* gallant. **~'ria** *nf* gallantry. **galantu'omo** *nm* (*pl* **galantuomini**) gentleman

ga'lassia *nf* galaxy

gala'teo *nm* [good] manners *pl*; (*trattato*) book of etiquette

gale'otto *nm* (*rematore*) galley-slave; (*condannato*) convict

ga'lera *nf* (*nave*) galley; *fam* prison

'galla *nf Bot* gall; **a ~** *adv* afloat; **venire a ~** surface

galleggi'ante *a* floating ● *nm* craft; (*boa*) float

galleggi'are *vi* float

galle'ria *nf* (*traforo*) tunnel; (*d'arte*) gallery; *Theat* circle; (*arcata*) arcade. **~ d'arte** art gallery

'Galles *nm* Wales. **gal'lese** *a* welsh ● *nm* Welshman; (*lingua*) Welsh ● *nf* Welshwoman

gal'letto *nm* cockerel; **fare il ~** show off

gal'lina *nf* hen

gal'lismo *nm* machismo

'gallo *nm* cock

gal'lone *nm* stripe; (*misura*) gallon

galop'pare *vi* gallop. **ga'loppo** *nm* gallop; **al galoppo** at a gallop

galvaniz'zare *vt* galvanize

'gamba *nf* leg; (*di lettera*) stem; **a quattro gambe** on all fours; **darsela a gambe** take to one's heels; **essere in ~** (*essere forte*) be strong; (*capace*) be smart

gamba'letto *nm* pop sock

gambe'retto *nm* shrimp. **'gambero** *nm* prawn; (*di fiume*) crayfish

'gambo *nm* stem; (*di pianta*) stalk

'gamma *nf Mus* scale; *fig* range

ga'nascia *nf* jaw; **ganasce** *pl* **del freno** brake shoes

'gancio *nm* hook

'ganghero *nm* **uscire dai gangheri** *fig* get into a temper

'gara *nf* competition; (*di velocità*) race; **fare a ~** compete. **~ d'appalto** call for tenders

ga'rage *nm inv* garage

ga'ran|te *nmf* guarantor. **~'tire** *vt* guarantee; (*rendersi garante*) vouch for; (*assicurare*) assure. **~'zia** *nf* guarantee; **in ~zia** under guarantee

gar'ba|re *vi* like; **non mi garba** I don't like it. **~to** *a* courteous

'garbo *nm* courtesy; (*grazia*) grace; **con ~** graciously

gareggi'are *vi* compete

garga'nella *nf* **a ~** from the bottle

garga'rismo *nm* gargle; **fare i gargarismi** gargle

ga'rofano *nm* carnation

gar'rire *vi* chirp

'garza *nf* gauze

gar'zone *nm* boy. **~ di stalla** stable-boy

gas *nm inv* gas; **dare ~** *Auto* accelerate; **a tutto ~** flat out. **~ lacrimogeno** tear gas. **~ di scarico** *pl* exhaust fumes

gas'dotto *nm* natural gas pipeline

ga'solio *nm* diesel oil

ga'sometro *nm* gasometer

gas's|are *vt* aerate; (*uccidere col gas*) gas. **~ato** *a* gassy. **~oso, -a** *a* gassy; ‹*bevanda*› fizzy ● *nf* lemonade

'gastrico *a* gastric. **ga'strite** *nf* gastritis

gastro|no'mia *nf* gastronomy. **~'nomico** *a* gastronomic. **ga'stronomo, -a** *nmf* gourmet

'gatta *nf* **una ~ da pelare** a headache

gatta'buia *nf hum* clink

gat'tino, -a *nmf* kitten

'gatto, -a *nmf* cat. **~ delle nevi** snowmobile

gat'toni *adv* on all fours

ga'vetta *nf* mess tin; **fare la ~** rise through the ranks

gay *a inv* gay

'gazza *nf* magpie

gaz'zarra *nf* racket

gaz'zella *nf* gazelle; *Auto* police car

gaz'zetta *nf* gazette

gaz'zosa *nf* clear lemonade

'geco *nm* gecko

ge'la|re *vt/i* freeze. **~ta** *nf* frost

gela't|aio, -a *nmf* ice-cream seller; (*negozio*) ice-cream shop. **~e'ria** *nf* ice-cream parlour. **~i'era** *nf* ice-cream maker

gela'ti|na *nf* gelatine; (*dolce*) jelly. **~na di frutta** fruit jelly. **~'noso** *a* gelatinous

ge'lato *a* frozen ● *nm* ice-cream

'gelido *a* freezing

'gelo *nm* (*freddo intenso*) freezing cold; (*brina*) frost; *fig* chill

ge'lone *nm* chilblain

gelosa'mente *adv* jealously

gelo'sia *nf* jealousy. **ge'loso** *a* jealous

'gelso *nm* mulberry[-tree]

gelso'mino *nm* jasmine

gemel'laggio *nm* twinning

ge'mello, -a *a* & *nmf* twin; (*di polsino*) cuff-link; **Gemelli** *pl Astr* Gemini *sg*

'gem|ere *vi* groan; (*tubare*) coo. **~ito** *nm* groan

'gemma *nf* gem; *Bot* bud

'gene *nm* gene

genealo'gia *nf* genealogy

gene'ral|e¹ *a* general; **spese ~i** overheads

gene'rale² *nm Mil* general

generalità *nf* (*qualità*) generality, general nature; **~ pl** (*dati personali*) particulars

generaliz'za|re *vt* generalize. **~zi'o-ne** *nf* generalization. **general'mente** *adv* generally

gene'ra|re *vt* give birth to; (*causare*) breed; *Techn* generate. **~'tore** *nm Techn* generator. **~zi'one** *nf* generation

'genere *nm* kind; *Biol* genus; *Gram* gender; (*letterario, artistico*) genre; (*prodotto*) product; **il ~ umano** mankind; **in ~** generally. **generi** *pl* **alimentari** provisions

generica'mente *adv* generically. **ge'nerico** *a* generic; **medico generico** general practitioner

'genero *nm* son-in-law

generosità *nf* generosity. **gene'roso** *a* generous

'genesi *nf* genesis

ge'netico, -a *a* genetic ● *nf* genetics *sg*

gen'giva *nf* gum

geni'ale *a* ingenious; (*congeniale*) congenial

'genio *nm* genius; **andare a ~** be to one's taste. **~ civile** civil engineering. **~ [militare]** Engineers

geni'tale *a* genital. **genitali** *nmpl* genitals

geni'tore *nm* parent

gen'naio *nm* January

'Genova *nf* Genoa

gen'taglia *nf* rabble

'gente *nf* people *pl*

gen'til|e *a* kind; **G~e Signore** Dear Sir. **genti'lezza** *nf* kindness; **per genti-lezza** (*per favore*) please. **~'mente** *adv* kindly. **~u'omo** (*pl* **~u'omini**) *nm* gentleman

genu'ino *a* genuine; (*cibo, prodotto*) natural

geogra'fia *nf* geography. **geo'grafico** *a* geographical. **ge'ografo** *nm* geographer

geolo'gia *nf* geology. **geo'logico** *a* geological. **ge'ologo, -a** *nmf* geologist

ge'ometra *nmf* surveyor

geome'tria *nf* geometry. **geo'metrico** *a* geometric[al]

ge'ranio *nm* geranium

gerar'chia *nf* hierarchy. **ge'rarchico** *a* hierarchic[al]

ge'rente *nm* manager ● *nf* manageress

'gergo *nm* slang; (*di professione ecc*) jargon

geria'tria *nf* geriatrics *sg*

Ger'mania *nf* Germany

'germe *nm* germ; (*fig: principio*) seed

germogli'are *vi* sprout. **ger'moglio** *nm* sprout

gero'glifico *nm* hieroglyph

'gesso *nm* chalk; (*Med, scultura*) plaster

gestazi'one *nf* gestation

gestico'lare *vi* gesticulate

gesti'one *nf* management

ge'stir|e *vi* manage. **~si** *vr* budget one's time and money

'gesto *nm* gesture; (*azione pl nf* **gesta**) deed

ge'store *nm* manager

Gesù *nm* Jesus. **~ bambino** baby Jesus

gesu'ita *nm* Jesuit

get'ta|re *vt* throw; (*scagliare*) fling; (*emettere*) spout; *Techn, fig* cast; **~re via** throw away. **~rsi** *vr* throw oneself; **~rsi in** 〈*fiume:*〉 flow into. **~ta** *nf* throw; *Techn* casting

get'tito *nm* **~ fiscale** tax revenue

'getto *nm* throw; (*di liquidi, gas*) jet; **a ~ continuo** in a continuous stream; **di ~** straight off

getto'nato *a* 〈*canzone*〉 popular. **get'tone** *nm* token; (*per giochi*) counter

ghe'pardo *nm* cheetah

ghettiz'zare *vt* ghettoize. **'ghetto** *nm* ghetto

ghiacci'aio *nm* glacier

ghiacci'a|re *vt/i* freeze. **~to** *a* frozen; (*freddissimo*) ice-cold

ghi'acci|o *nm* ice; *Auto* black ice. **~'olo** *nm* icicle; (*gelato*) ice lolly

ghi'aia *nf* gravel

ghi'anda *nf* acorn

ghi'andola *nf* gland

ghigliot'tina *nf* guillotine

ghi'gnare *vi* sneer. **'ghigno** *nm* sneer

ghi'ot|to *a* greedy, gluttonous; (*appetitoso*) appetizing. **~'tone, -a** *nmf* glutton. **~tone'ria** *nf* (*qualità*) gluttony; (*cibo*) tasty morsel

ghir'landa *nf* (*corona*) wreath; (*di fiori*) garland

'ghiro *nm* dormouse; **dormire come un ~** sleep like a log

'ghisa *nf* cast iron

già *adv* already; (*un tempo*) formerly; **~!** indeed!; **~ da ieri** since yesterday

gi'acca *nf* jacket. **~ a vento** windcheater

giacché *conj* since

giac'cone *nm* jacket

gia'cere *vi* lie

giaci'mento *nm* deposit. **~ di petrolio** oil deposit

gia'cinto *nm* hyacinth

gi'ada *nf* jade

giaggi'olo *nm* iris

giagu'aro *nm* jaguar

gial'lastro *a* yellowish

gi'allo *a & nm* yellow; [**libro**] **~** thriller

Giap'pone *nm* Japan. **giappo'nese** *a & nmf* Japanese

giardi'n|aggio *nm* gardening. **~i'ere, -a** *nmf* gardener ● *nf Auto* estate car; (*sottaceti*) pickles *pl*

giar'dino *nm* garden. **~ d'infanzia** kindergarten. **~ pensile** roof-garden. **~ zoologico** zoo

giarretti'era *nf* garter

giavel'lotto *nm* javelin

gi'gan|te *a* gigantic ● *nm* giant. **~'tesco** *a* gigantic

gigantogra'fia *nf* blow-up

'giglio *nm* lily

gilè *nm inv* waistcoat

gin *nm inv* gin

gineco|lo'gia *nf* gynaecology. **~'logico** *a* gynaecological. **gine'cologo, -a** *nmf* gynaecologist

gi'nepro *nm* juniper

gi'nestra *nf* broom

gingil'larsi *vr* fiddle; (*perder tempo*) potter. **gin'gillo** *nm* plaything; (*ninnolo*) knick-knack

gin'nasio *nm* (*scuola*) ≈ grammar school

gin'nast|a *nmf* gymnast. **~ica** *nf* gymnastics; (*esercizi*) exercises *pl*

ginocchi'ata *nf* **prendere una ~** bang one's knee

gi'nocchi|o *nm* (*pl nm* **ginocchi** *o nf* **ginocchia**) knee; **in ~o** on one's knees; **mettersi in ~o** kneel down; (*per supplicare*) go down on one's knees; **al ~o** (*gonna*) knee-length. **~'oni** *adv* kneeling

gio'ca|re *vt/i* play; (*giocherellare*) toy; (*d'azzardo*) gamble; (*puntare*) stake; (*ingannare*) trick. **~rsi la carriera** throw one's career away. **~'tore, ~'trice** *nmf* player; (*d'azzardo*) gambler

gio'cattolo *nm* toy

giocherel'l|are *vi* toy; (*nervosamente*) fiddle. **~one** *a* skittish

gi'oco *nm* game; (*di bambini, Techn*) play; (*d'azzardo*) gambling; (*scherzo*) joke; (*insieme di pezzi ecc*) set; **essere in ~** be at stake; **fare il doppio ~ con qcno** double-cross sb

giocoli'ere *nm* juggler

gio'coso *a* playful

gi'ogo *nm* yoke

gi'oia *nf* joy; (*gioiello*) jewel; (*appellativo*) sweetie

gioiell|e'ria *nf* jeweller's [shop]. **~i'ere, -a** *nmf* jeweller; (*negozio*) jeweller's. **gioi'ello** *nm* jewel; **gioielli** *pl* jewellery

gioi'oso *a* joyous

gio'ire *vi* **~ per** rejoice at

Gior'dania *nf* Jordan

giorna'laio, -a *nmf* newsagent, newsdealer

gior'nale *nm* [news]paper; (*diario*) journal. **~ di bordo** logbook. **~ radio** news bulletin

giornali'ero *a* daily ● *nm* (*per sciare*) day pass

giorna'lino *nm* comic

giorna'lis|mo *nm* journalism. **~ta** *nmf* journalist

giornal'mente *adv* daily

gior'nata *nf* day; **in ~** today; **vivere alla ~** live from day to day

gi'orno *nm* day; **al ~** per day; **al ~ d'oggi** nowadays; **di ~** by day; **in pieno ~** in broad daylight; **un ~ sì, un ~ no** every other day

gi'ostra *nf* merry-go-round

giova'mento *nm* **trarre ~ da** derive benefit from

gi'ova|ne *a* young; (*giovanile*) youthful ● *nm* youth, young man ● *nf* girl, young woman. **~'nile** *a* youthful. **~'notto** *nm* young man

gio'var|e *vi* **~e** *a* be useful to; (*far bene*) be good for. **~si** *vr* **~si di** avail oneself of

giovedì *nm inv* Thursday. **~ grasso** *last Thursday before Lent*

gioventù *nf* youth; (*i giovani*) young people *pl*

giovi'ale *a* jovial

giovi'nezza *nf* youth

gira'dischi *nm inv* record-player

gi'raffa *nf* giraffe; *Cinema* boom

gi'randola *nf* (*fuoco d'artificio*) Catherine wheel; (*giocattolo*) windmill; (*banderuola*) weathercock

gi'ra|re *vt* turn; (*andare intorno, visitare*) go round; *Comm* endorse; *Cinema* shoot ● *vi* turn; (*aerei, uccelli:*) circle; (*andare in giro*) wander; **far ~re le scatole a qcno** *fam* drive sb round the twist; **~re al largo** steer clear. **~rsi** *vr* turn [round]; **mi gira la testa** I feel dizzy. **~ta** *nf* turn; *Comm* endorsement; (*in macchina ecc*) ride; **fare una ~ta** (*a piedi*) go for a walk; (*in macchina*) go for a ride

girar'rosto *nm* spit

gira'sole *nm* sunflower

gira'volta *nf* spin; *fig* U-turn

gi'rello *nm* (*per bambini*) babywalker; *Culin* topside

gi'revole *a* revolving

gi'rino *nm* tadpole

'giro *nm* turn; (*circolo*) circle; (*percorso*) round; (*viaggio*) tour; (*passeggiata*) short walk; (*in macchina*) drive; (*in bicicletta*) ride; (*circolazione di denaro*) circulation; **nel ~ di un mese** within a month; **prendere in ~ qcno** pull sb's leg; **senza giri di parole** without beating about the bush; **a ~ di posta** by return mail. **~ d'affari** *Comm* turnover. **~ [della] manica** armhole. **giri pl al minuto** rpm. **~ turistico** sightseeing tour. **~ vita** waist measurement

giro'collo *nm* choker; **a ~** crewneck

gi'rone *nm* round

gironzo'lare *vi* wander about

giro'tondo *nm* ring-a-ring-o'-roses

girova'gare *vi* wander about. **gi'rovago** *nm* wanderer

'gita *nf* trip; **andare in ~** go on a trip. **~ scolastica** school trip. **gi'tante** *nmf* tripper

giù *adv* down; (*sotto*) below; (*dabbasso*) downstairs; **a testa in ~** (*a capofitto*) headlong; **essere ~** be down; (*di salute*) be run down; **~ di corda** down; **~ di lì, su per ~** more or less; **non andare ~ a qcno** stick in sb's craw

gi'ub|ba *nf* jacket; *Mil* tunic. **~'botto** *nm* bomber jacket, jerkin

giudi'care *vt* judge; (*ritenere*) consider

gi'udice *nm* judge. **~ conciliatore** justice of the peace. **~ di gara** umpire. **~ di linea** linesman

giu'dizi|o *nm* judg[e]ment; (*opinione*) opinion; (*senno*) wisdom; (*processo*) trial; (*sentenza*) sentence; **mettere ~o** become wise. **~'oso** *a* sensible

gi'ugno *nm* June

giu'menta *nf* mare

gi'unco *nm* reed

gi'ungere *vi* arrive; **~ a** (*riuscire*) succeed in ● *vt* (*unire*) join

gi'ungla *nf* jungle

gi'unta *nf* addition; *Mil* junta; **per ~** in addition. **~ comunale** district council

gi'unto *pp di* **giungere** ● *nm Mech* joint

giun'tura *nf* joint

giuo'care, giu'oco = **giocare, gioco**

giura'mento *nm* oath; **prestare ~** take the oath

giu'ra|re *vt/i* swear. **~to, -a** *a* sworn ● *nmf* juror

giu'ria *nf* jury

giu'ridico *a* legal

giurisdizi'one *nf* jurisdiction

giurispru'denza *nf* jurisprudence

giu'rista *nmf* jurist

giustifi'ca|re *vt* justify. **~zi'one** *nf* justification

giu'stizi|a *nf* justice. **~'are** *vt* execute. **~'ere** *nm* executioner

gi'usto *a* just, fair; (*adatto*) right; (*esatto*) exact ● *nm* (*uomo retto*) just

man; (*cosa giusta*) right ● *adv* exactly;
~ **ora** just now
glaci'ale *a* glacial
gla'diolo *nm* gladiolus
'glassa *nf Culin* icing
gli *def art mpl* (*before vowel and s + consonant, gn, ps, z*) the; *vedi* **il** ● *pron* (*a lui*) [to] him; (*a esso*) [to] it; (*a loro*) [to] them
glice'rina *nf* glycerine
'glicine *nm* wisteria
gli'elo, -a *pron* [to] him/her/them; (*forma di cortesia*) [to] you; ~ **chiedo** I'll ask him/her/them; **gliel'ho presta-to** I've lent it to him/her/them. ~**ne** *pron* (*di ciò*) [of] it; ~**ne ho dato un po'** I gave him/her/them some
glo'bal|e *a* global; *fig* overall. ~'**mente** *adv* globally
'globo *nm* globe. ~ **oculare** eyeball. ~ **terrestre** globe
'globulo *nm* globule; *Med* corpuscle. ~ **bianco** white cell, white corpuscle. ~ **rosso** red cell, red corpuscle
'glori|a *nf* glory. ~'**arsi** *vr* ~**arsi di** be proud of. ~'**oso** *a* glorious
glos'sario *nm* glossary
glu'cosio *nm* glucose
'gluteo *nm* buttock
'gnomo *nm* gnome
'gnoρρi *nm* **fare lo ~** play dumb
'gobb|a *nf* hump. ~**o, -a** *a* hunch-backed ● *nmf* hunchback
'gocci|a *nf* drop; (*di sudore*) bead; **è stata l'ultima ~a** it was the last straw. ~**o'lare** *vi* drip. ~**o'lio** *nm* dripping
go'der|e *vi* (*sessualmente*) come; ~**e di** enjoy. ~**sela** have a good time. ~**si** *vr* ~**si qcsa** enjoy sth
godi'mento *nm* enjoyment
goffa'mente *adv* awkwardly. '**goffo** *a* awkward
'gola *nf* throat; (*ingordigia*) gluttony; *Geog* gorge; (*di camino*) flue; **avere mal di** ~ have a sore throat; **far ~ a qcno** tempt sb
golf *nm inv* jersey; *Sport* golf
'golfo *nm* gulf
golo'sità *nf inv* greediness; (*cibo*) tasty morsel. **go'loso** *a* greedy
'golpe *nm inv* coup
gomi'tata *nf* nudge
'gomito *nm* elbow; **alzare il** ~ raise one's elbow
go'mitolo *nm* ball
'gomma *nf* rubber; (*colla, da mastica-re*) gum; (*pneumatico*) tyre. ~ **da masticare** chewing gum

gommapi'uma *nf* foam rubber
gom'mista *nm* tyre specialist
gom'mone *nm* [rubber] dinghy
gom'moso *a* chewy
'gondol|a *nf* gondola. ~**i'ere** *nm* gondolier
gonfa'lone *nm* banner
gon'fiabile *a* inflatable
gonfi'ar|e *vi* swell ● *vt* blow up; pump up (*pneumatico*); (*esagerare*) exagger-ate. ~**si** *vr* swell; (*acque:*) rise. '**gonfio** *a* swollen; (*pneumatico*) inflated; **a gonfie vele** splendidly. **gonfi'ore** *nm* swelling
gongo'la|nte *a* overjoyed. ~**re** *vi* be overjoyed
'gonna *nf* skirt. ~ **pantalone** culottes *pl*
'gonzo *nm* simpleton
gorgheggi'are *vi* warble. **gor'gheg-gio** *nm* warble
'gorgo *nm* whirlpool
gorgogli'are *vi* gurgle
go'rilla *nm inv* gorilla; (*guardia del corpo*) bodyguard, minder
'gotico *a & nm* Gothic
gover'nante *nf* housekeeper
gover'na|re *vt* govern; (*dominare*) rule; (*dirigere*) manage; (*curare*) look af-ter. ~'**tivo** *a* government. ~'**tore** *nm* governor
go'verno *nm* government; (*dominio*) rule; **al** ~ in power
gracchi'are *vi* caw; (*fig: persona:*) screech
graci'dare *vi* croak
'gracile *a* delicate
gra'dasso *nm* braggart
grada'mente *adv* gradually
gradazi'one *nf* gradation. ~ **alcooli-ca** alcohol[ic] content
gra'devol|e *a* agreeable. ~'**mente** *adv* pleasantly, agreeably
gradi'mento *nm* liking; **indice di** ~ *Radio, TV* popularity rating; **non è di mio** ~ it's not to my liking
gradi'nata *nf* flight of steps; (*di stadio*) stand; (*di teatro*) tiers *pl*
gra'dino *nm* step
gra'di|re *vt* like; (*desiderare*) wish. ~**to** *a* pleasant; (*bene accetto*) welcome
'grado *nm* degree; (*rango*) rank; **di buon** ~ willingly; **essere in** ~ **di fare qcsa** be in a position to do sth; (*essere capace a*) be able to do sth
gradu'ale *a* gradual
gradu'a|re *vt* graduate. ~**to** *a* graded; (*provvisto di scala graduata*) graduated

●*nm Mil* noncommissioned officer. ~**'toria** *nf* list. ~**zi'one** *nf* graduation

'graffa *nf* clip; (*segno grafico*) brace

graf'fetta *nf* staple

graffi'a|re *vt* scratch. ~**'tura** *nf* scratch

'graffio *nm* scratch

gra'fia *nf* [hand]writing; (*ortografia*) spelling

'grafic|a *nf* graphics; ~**a pubblicitaria** commercial art. ~**a'mente** *adv* in graphics, graphically. ~**o** *a* graphic ●*nm* graph; (*persona*) graphic designer

gra'migna *nf* weed

gram'mati|ca *nf* grammar. ~**'cale** *a* grammatical

'grammo *nm* gram[me]

gran *a vedi* **grande**

'grana *nf* grain; (*formaggio*) parmesan; (*fam: seccatura*) trouble; (*fam: soldi*) readies *pl*

gra'naio *nm* barn

gra'nat|a *nf Mil* grenade; (*frutto*) pomegranate. ~**i'ere** *nm Mil* grenadier

Gran Bre'tagna *nf* Great Britain

'granchio *nm* crab; (*fig: errore*) blunder; **prendere un** ~ make a blunder

grandango'lare *nm* wide-angle lens

'grande (*qualche volta* **gran** *a* (*ampio*) large; (*grosso*) big; (*alto*) tall; (*largo*) wide; (*fig: senso morale*) great; (*grandioso*) grand; (*adulto*) grown-up; **ho una gran fame** I'm very hungry; **fa un gran caldo** it is very hot; **in** ~ on a large scale; **in gran parte** to a great extent; **non è un gran che** it is nothing much; **un gran ballo** a grand ball ●*nmf* (*persona adulta*) grown-up; (*persona eminente*) great man/woman. ~**ggi'are** *vi* ~**ggiare su** tower over; (*darsi arie*) show off

gran'dezza *nf* greatness; (*ampiezza*) largeness; (*larghezza*) width, breadth; (*dimensione*) size; (*fasto*) grandeur; (*prodigalità*) lavishness; **a** ~ **naturale** life-size

grandi'nare *vi* hail; **grandina** it's hailing. **'grandine** *nf* hail

grandiosità *nf* grandeur. **grandi'oso** *a* grand

gran'duca *nm* grand duke

gra'nello *nm* grain; (*di frutta*) pip

gra'nita *nf* crushed ice drink

gra'nito *nm* granite

'grano *nm* grain; (*frumento*) wheat

gran'turco *nm* maize

'granulo *nm* granule

'grappa *nf* grappa; (*morsa*) cramp

'grappolo *nm* bunch. ~ **d'uva** bunch of grapes

gras'setto *nm* bold [type]

gras'sezza *nf* fatness; (*untuosità*) greasiness

'gras|so *a* fat; (*cibo*) fatty; (*unto*) greasy; (*terreno*) rich; (*grossolano*) coarse ●*nm* fat; (*sostanza*) grease. ~**'soccio** *a* plump

'grata *nf* grating. **gra'tella, gra'ticola** *nf Culin* grill

gra'tifica *nf* bonus. ~**zi'one** *nf* satisfaction

grati'na|re *vt* cook au gratin. ~**to** *a* au gratin

'gratis *adv* free

grati'tudine *nf* gratitude. **'grato** *a* grateful; (*gradito*) pleasant

gratta'capo *nm* trouble

grattaci'elo *nm* skyscraper

grat'tar|e *vt* scratch; (*raschiare*) scrape; (*grattugiare*) grate; (*fam: rubare*) pinch ●*vi* grate. ~**si** *vr* scratch oneself

grat'tugi|a *nf* grater. ~**'are** *vt* grate

gratuita'mente *adv* free [of charge]. **gra'tuito** *a* free [of charge]; (*ingiustificato*) gratuitous

gra'vare *vt* burden ●*vi* ~ **su** weigh on

'grave *a* (*pesante*) heavy; (*serio*) serious; (*difficile*) hard; (*voce, suono*) low; (*fonetica*) grave; **essere** ~ (*gravemente ammalato*) be seriously ill. ~**'mente** *adv* seriously, gravely

gravi'danza *nf* pregnancy. **'gravido** *a* pregnant

gravità *nf* seriousness; *Phys* gravity

gravi'tare *vi* gravitate

gra'voso *a* onerous

'grazi|a *nf* grace; (*favore*) favour; *Jur* pardon; **entrare nelle ~e di qcno** get into sb's good books. ~**'are** *vt* pardon

'grazie *int* thank you!, thanks!; ~ **mille!** many thanks!, thanks a lot!

grazi'oso *a* charming; (*carino*) pretty

'Grec|ia *nf* Greece. **g~o, -a** *a & nmf* Greek

'gregge *nm* flock

'greggio *a* raw ●*nm* (*petrolio*) crude [oil]

grembi'ale, grembi'ule *nm* apron

'grembo *nm* lap; (*utero*) womb; *fig* bosom

gre'mi|re *vt* pack. ~**rsi** *vr* become crowded (**di** with). ~**to** *a* packed

'gretto *a* stingy; (*di vedute ristrette*) narrow-minded

'grezzo *a* = **greggio**

gri'dare vi shout; (di dolore) scream; ⟨animale:⟩ cry ● vt shout

'**grido** nm (pl m gridi o f grida) shout, cry; (di animale) cry; **l'ultimo ~** the latest fashion; **scrittore di ~** celebrated writer

'**grigio** a & nm grey

'**griglia** nf grill; **alla ~** grilled

gril'letto nm trigger

'**grillo** nm cricket; (fig: capriccio) whim

grimal'dello nm picklock

grin'fia nf fig clutch

'**grin|ta** nf grit. **~'toso** a determined

'**grinza** nf wrinkle; (di stoffa) crease

grip'pare vi Mech seize

gris'sino nm bread-stick

'**gronda** nf eaves pl

gron'daia nf gutter

gron'dare vi pour; (essere bagnato fradicio) be dripping

'**groppa** nf back

'**groppo** nm knot; **avere un ~ alla gola** have a lump in one's throat

gros'sezza nf size; (spessore) thickness

gros'sista nmf wholesaler

'**grosso** a big, large; (spesso) thick; (grossolano) coarse; (grave) serious ● nm big part; (massa) bulk; **farla grossa** do a stupid thing

grosso|lanità nf inv (qualità) coarseness; (di errore) grossness; (azione, parola) coarse thing. **~'lano** a coarse; ⟨errore⟩ gross

grosso'modo adv roughly

'**grotta** nf cave, grotto

grot'tesco a & nm grotesque

grovi'era nmf Gruyère

gro'viglio nm tangle; fig muddle

'**gru** nf inv (uccello, edilizia) crane

'**gruccia** nf (stampella) crutch; (per vestito) hanger

gru'gni|re vi grunt. **~to** nm grunt

'**grugno** nm snout

'**grullo** a silly

'**grumo** nm clot; (di farina ecc) lump. **gru'moso** a lumpy

'**gruppo** nm group; (comitiva) party. **~ sanguigno** blood group

gru'viera nmf Gruyère

'**gruzzolo** nm nest-egg

guada'gnare vt earn; gain ⟨tempo, forza ecc⟩. **gua'dagno** nm gain; (profitto) profit; (entrate) earnings pl

gu'ado nm ford; **passare a ~** ford

gua'ina nf sheath; (busto) girdle

gu'aio nm trouble; **che ~!** that's just brilliant!; **essere nei guai** be in a fix;

guai a te se lo tocchi! don't you dare touch it!

gua'i|re vi yelp. **~to** nm yelp

gu'anci|a nf cheek. **~'ale** nm pillow

gu'anto nm glove. **guantoni pl [da boxe]** boxing gloves

guarda'coste nm inv coastguard

guarda'linee nm inv Sport linesman

guar'dar|e vt look at; (osservare) watch; (badare a) look after; (dare su) look out on ● vi look; (essere orientato verso) face. **~si** vr look at oneself; **~si da** beware of; (astenersi) refrain from

guarda'rob|a nm inv wardrobe; (di locale pubblico) cloakroom. **~i'ere, -a** nmf cloakroom attendant

gu'ardia nf guard; (poliziotto) policeman; (vigilanza) watch; **essere di ~** be on guard; ⟨medico:⟩ be on duty; **fare la ~ a** keep guard over; **mettere in ~** qcno warn sb; **stare in ~** be on one's guard. **~ carceraria** prison warder. **~ del corpo** bodyguard, minder. **~ di finanza** ≈ Fraud Squad. **~ forestale** forest ranger. **~ medica** duty doctor

guardi'ano, -a nmf caretaker. **~ notturno** night watchman

guar'dingo a cautious

guardi'ola nf gatekeeper's lodge

guarigi'one nf recovery

gua'rire vt cure ● vi recover; ⟨ferita:⟩ heal [up]

guarnigi'one nf garrison

guar'ni|re vt trim; Culin garnish. **~zi'one** nf trimming; Culin garnish; Mech gasket

guasta'feste nmf inv spoilsport

gua'star|e vt spoil; (rovinare) ruin; break ⟨meccanismo⟩. **~si** vr spoil; (andare a male) go bad; ⟨tempo:⟩ change for the worse; ⟨meccanismo:⟩ break down. **gu'asto** a broken; ⟨ascensore, telefono⟩ out of order; ⟨auto⟩ broken down; ⟨cibo, dente⟩ bad ● nm breakdown; (danno) damage

guazza'buglio nm muddle

guaz'zare vi wallow

gu'ercio a cross-eyed

gu'err|a nf war; (tecnica bellica) warfare. **~ fredda** Cold War. **~ mondiale** world war. **~afon'daio** nm warmonger. **~eggi'are** vi wage war. **guer'resco** a ⟨di guerra⟩ war; (bellicoso) warlike. **~i'ero** nm warrior

guer'rigli|a nf guerrilla warfare. **~'ero, -a** nmf guerrilla

'**gufo** nm owl

'**guglia** nf spire

gu'id|a *nf* guide; (*direzione*) guidance; (*comando*) leadership; *Auto* driving; (*tappeto*) runner; **~a a destra/sinistra** right-/left-hand drive. **~a telefonica** telephone directory. **~a turistica** tourist guide. **gui'dare** *vt* guide; *Auto* drive; steer ‹*nave*›. **~a'tore**, **~a'trice** *nmf* driver

guin'zaglio *nm* leash

guiz'zare *vi* dart; ‹*luce:*› flash. **gu'izzo** *nm* dart; (*di luce*) flash

'guscio *nm* shell

gu'stare *vt* taste ● *vi* like. **'gusto** *nm* taste; (*piacere*) liking; **mangiare di gusto** eat heartily; **prenderci gusto** come to enjoy it, develop a taste for it. **gu'stoso** *a* tasty; *fig* delightful

guttu'rale *a* guttural

Hh

---

habitué *nmf inv* regular [customer]
ham'burger *nm inv* hamburger
'handicap *nm inv Sport* handicap
handicap'pa|re *vt* handicap. **~to, -a** *nmf* disabled person ● *a* disabled
'harem *nm inv* harem
'hascisc *nm* hashish

henné *nm* henna
hi-fi *nm inv* hi-fi
'hippy *a* hippy
hockey *nm* hockey. **~ su ghiaccio** ice hockey. **~ su prato** hockey
hollywoodi'ano *a* Hollywood *attrib*
ho'tel *nm inv* hotel

Ii

---

i *def art mpl* the; *vedi* **il**
i'ato *nm* hiatus
iber'na|re *vi* hibernate. **~zi'one** *nf* hibernation
i'bisco *nm* hibiscus
'ibrido *a & nm* hybrid
'iceberg *nm inv* iceberg
i'cona *nf* icon
Id'dio *nm* God
i'dea *nf* idea; (*opinione*) opinion; (*ideale*) ideal; (*indizio*) inkling; (*piccola quantità*) hint; (*intenzione*) intention; **cambiare ~** change one's mind; **neanche per ~!** not on your life!; **chiarirsi le idee** get one's ideas straight. **~ fissa** obsession
ide'a|le *a & nm* ideal. **~'lista** *nmf* idealist. **~liz'zare** *vt* idealize
ide'a|re *vt* conceive. **~'tore**, **~'trice** *nmf* originator
'idem *adv* the same
i'dentico *a* identical

identifi'cabile *a* identifiable
identifi'ca|re *vt* identify. **~zi'one** *nf* identification
identi'kit *nm inv* identikit®
identità *nf inv* identity
ideolo'gia *nf* ideology. **ideo'logico** *a* ideological
i'dilli|co *a* idyllic. **~o** *nm* idyll
idi'oma *nm* idiom. **idio'matico** *a* idiomatic
idi'ota *a* idiotic ● *nmf* idiot. **idio'zia** *nf* (*cosa stupida*) idiocy
idola'trare *vt* worship
idoleggi'are *vt* idolize. **'idolo** *nm* idol
idoneità *nf* suitability; *Mil* fitness; **esame di ~** qualifying examination. **i'doneo** *a* **idoneo a** suitable for; *Mil* fit for
i'drante *nm* hydrant
idra'ta|re *vt* hydrate; ‹*cosmetico:*› moisturize. **~nte** *a* ‹*crema, gel*› moisturizing. **~zi'one** *nf* moisturizing

i'draulico *a* hydraulic ● *nm* plumber

'idrico *a* water *attrib*

idrocar'buro *nm* hydrocarbon

idroe'lettrico *a* hydroelectric

i'drofilo *a vedi* cotone

i'drogeno *nm* hydrogen

idromas'saggio *nm* (*sistema*) whirl-pool bath

idrovo'lante *nm* seaplane

i'ella *nf* bad luck; **portare ~** be bad luck. **iel'lato** *a* plagued by bad luck

i'ena *nf* hyena

i'eri *adv* yesterday; **~ l'altro, l'altro ~** the day before yesterday; **~ pomeriggio** yesterday afternoon; **il giornale di ~** yesterday's paper

ietta'tore, -'trice *nmf* jinx. **~'tura** *nf* (*sfortuna*) bad luck

igi'en|e *nf* hygiene. **~ico** *a* hygienic. **igie'nista** *nmf* hygienist

i'gnaro *a* unaware

i'gnobile *a* base; (*non onorevole*) dishonourable

igno'ran|te *a* ignorant ● *nmf* ignoramus. **~za** *nf* ignorance

igno'rare *vt* (*non sapere*) be unaware of; (*trascurare*) ignore

i'gnoto *a* unknown

il *def art m* the; **il latte fa bene** milk is good for you; **il signor Magnetti** Mr Magnetti; **il dottor Piazza** Dr Piazza; **ha il naso storto** he has a bent nose; **mettiti il cappello** put your hat on; **il lunedì** on Mondays; **il 1986** 1986; **5 000 lire il chilo** 5,000 lire the *o* a kilo

'ilar|e *a* merry. **~ità** *nf* hilarity

illazi'one *nf* inference

illecita'mente *adv* illicitly. **il'lecito** *a* illicit

ille'gal|e *a* illegal. **~ità** *nf* illegality. **~'mente** *adv* illegally

illeg'gibile *a* illegible; (*libro*) unreadable

illegittimità *nf* illegitimacy. **ille'gittimo** *a* illegitimate

il'leso *a* unhurt

illette'rato, -a *a* & *nmf* illiterate

illi'bato *a* chaste

illimi'tato *a* unlimited

illivi'dire *vt* bruise ● *vi* (*per rabbia*) turn livid

il'logico *a* illogical

il'luder|e *vt* deceive. **~si** *vr* deceive oneself

illumi'na|re *vt* light [up]; *fig* enlighten; **~re a giorno** floodlight. **~rsi** *vr* light up. **~zi'one** *nf* lighting; *fig* enlightenment

illumi'nismo *nm* Enlightenment

illusi'one *nf* illusion; **farsi illusioni** delude oneself

illusio'nis|mo *nm* conjuring. **~ta** *nmf* conjurer

il'lu|so, -a *pp di* illudere ● *a* deluded ● *nmf* day-dreamer. **~'sorio** *a* illusory

illu'stra|re *vt* illustrate. **~'tivo** *a* illustrative. **~'tore, ~'trice** *nmf* illustrator. **~zi'one** *nf* illustration

il'lustre *a* distinguished

imbacuc'ca|re *vt*, **~rsi** *vr* wrap up. **~to** *a* wrapped up

imbal'la|ggio *nm* packing. **~re** *vt* pack; *Auto* race

imbalsa'ma|re *vt* embalm; stuff ⟨*animale*⟩. **~to** *a* embalmed; ⟨*animale*⟩ stuffed

imbambo'lato *a* vacant

imbaraz'zante *a* embarrassing

imbaraz'za|re *vt* embarrass; (*ostacolare*) encumber. **~to** *a* embarrassed

imba'razzo *nm* embarrassment; (*ostacolo*) hindrance; **trarre qcno d'~** help sb out of a difficulty; **avere l'~ della scelta** be spoilt for choice. **~ di stomaco** indigestion

imbarca'dero *nm* landing-stage

imbar'ca|re *vt* embark; (*fam: rimorchiare*) score. **~rsi** *vr* embark, go on board. **~zi'one** *nf* boat. **~zione di salvataggio** lifeboat. **im'barco** *nm* embarkation, boarding; (*banchina*) landing-stage

imba'sti|re *vt* tack; *fig* sketch. **~'tura** *nf* tacking, basting

im'battersi *vr* **~ in** run into

imbat't|ibile *a* unbeatable. **~uto** *a* unbeaten

imbavagli'are *vt* gag

imbec'cata *nf Theat* prompt

imbe'cille *a* stupid ● *nmf Med* imbecile

imbel'lire *vt* embellish

im'berbe *a* beardless; *fig* inexperienced

imbestia'li|re *vi*, **~rsi** *vr* fly into a rage. **~to** *a* enraged

im'bever|e *vt* imbue (**di** with). **~si** *vr* absorb

imbe'v|ibile *a* undrinkable. **~uto** *a* **~uto di** ⟨*acqua*⟩ soaked in; ⟨*nozioni*⟩ imbued with

imbian'c|are *vt* whiten ● *vi* turn white. **~hino** *nm* house painter

imbizzar'rir|e *vi*, **~si** *vr* become restless; (*arrabbiarsi*) become angry

imboc'ca|re *vt* feed; (*entrare*) enter;

fig prompt. **~'tura** *nf* opening; (*ingresso*) entrance; (*Mus: di strumento*) mouthpiece. **im'bocco** *nm* entrance

imbo'scar|e *vt* hide. **~si** *vr Mil* shirk military service

imbo'scata *nf* ambush

imbottigli'a|re *vt* bottle. **~rsi** *vr* get snarled up in a traffic jam. **~to** *a* ⟨*vino, acqua*⟩ bottled

imbot'ti|re *vt* stuff; pad ⟨*giacca*⟩; *Culin* fill. **~rsi** *vr* **~rsi di** (*fig: di pasticche*) stuff oneself with. **~ta** *nf* quilt. **~to** *a* ⟨*spalle*⟩ padded; ⟨*cuscino*⟩ stuffed; ⟨*panino*⟩ filled. **~'tura** *nf* stuffing; (*di giacca*) padding; *Culin* filling

imbracci'are *vt* shoulder ⟨*fucile*⟩

imbra'nato *a* clumsy

imbrat'tar|e *vt* mark. **~si** *vr* dirty oneself

imbroc'car|e *vt* hit; **~la giusta** hit the nail on the head

imbrogli|'are *vt* muddle; (*raggirare*) cheat. **~arsi** *vr* get tangled; (*confondersi*) get confused. **im'broglio** *nm* tangle; (*pasticcio*) mess; (*inganno*) trick. **~'one, -a** *nmf* cheat

imbronci'a|re *vi*, **~rsi** *vr* sulk. **~to** *a* sulky

imbru'nire *vi* get dark; **all'~** at dusk

imbrut'tire *vt* make ugly ● *vi* become ugly

imbu'care *vt* post, mail; (*nel biliardo*) pot

imbur'rare *vt* butter

im'buto *nm* funnel

imi'ta|re *vt* imitate. **~'tore**, **~'trice** *nmf* imitator, impersonator. **~zi'one** *nf* imitation

immaco'lato *a* immaculate, spotless

immagazzi'nare *vt* store

immagi'na|re *vt* imagine; (*supporre*) suppose; **s'immagini!** imagine that!. **~rio** *a* imaginary. **~zi'one** *nf* imagination. **im'magine** *nf* image; (*rappresentazione, idea*) picture

imman'cabi|le *a* unfailing. **~'mente** *adv* without fail

im'mane *a* huge; (*orribile*) terrible

imma'nente *a* immanent

immangi'abile *a* inedible

immatrico'la|re *vt* register. **~rsi** *vr* ⟨*studente:*⟩ matriculate. **~zi'one** *nf* registration; (*di studente*) matriculation

immaturità *nf* immaturity. **imma'turo** *a* unripe; ⟨*persona*⟩ immature; (*precoce*) premature

immedesi'ma|rsi *vr* **~rsi in** identify oneself with. **~zi'one** *nf* identification

immedia|ta'mente *adv* immediately. **~'tezza** *nf* immediacy. **immedi'ato** *a* immediate

immemo'rabile *a* immemorial

immens|a'mente *adv* enormously. **~ità** *nf* immensity. **im'menso** *a* immense

immensu'rabile *a* immeasurable

im'merger|e *vt* immerse. **~si** *vr* plunge; ⟨*sommergibile:*⟩ dive; **~si in** immerse oneself in

immeri't|ato *a* undeserved. **~evole** *a* undeserving

immersi'one *nf* immersion; (*di sommergibile*) dive. **im'merso** *pp di* **immergere**

immi'gra|nte *a* & *nmf* immigrant. **~re** *vi* immigrate. **~to, -a** *nmf* immigrant. **~zi'one** *nf* immigration

immi'nen|te *a* imminent. **~za** *nf* imminence

immischi'ar|e *vt* involve. **~si** *vr* **~si in** meddle in

immis'sario *nm* tributary

immissi'one *nf* insertion

im'mobile *a* motionless

im'mobili *nmpl* real estate. **~'are** *a* **società ~are** building society, savings and loan *Am*

immobili|tà *nf* immobility. **~z'zare** *vt* immobilize; *Comm* tie up

immo'desto *a* immodest

immo'lare *vt* sacrifice

immondez'zaio *nm* rubbish tip. **immon'dizia** *nf* filth; (*spazzatura*) rubbish. **im'mondo** *a* filthy

immo'ral|e *a* immoral. **~ità** *nf* immorality

immorta'lare *vt* immortalize. **immor'tale** *a* immortal

immoti'vato *a* ⟨*gesto*⟩ unjustified

im'mun|e *a* exempt; *Med* immune. **~ità** *nf* immunity. **~iz'zare** *vt* immunize. **~izzazi'one** *nf* immunization

immunodefi'cienza *nf* immunodeficiency

immuso'ni|rsi *vr* sulk. **~to** *a* sulky

immu'ta|bile *a* unchangeable. **~to** *a* unchanging

impacchet'tare *vt* wrap up

impacci'a|re *vt* hamper; (*disturbare*) inconvenience; (*imbarazzare*) embarrass. **~to** *a* embarrassed; (*goffo*) awkward. **im'paccio** *nm* embarrassment; (*ostacolo*) hindrance; (*situazione difficile*) awkward situation

im'pacco *nm* compress

impadro'nirsi vr ~ **di** take possession of; (fig: imparare) master

impa'gabile a priceless

impagi'na|re vt paginate. **~zi'one** nf pagination

impagli'are vt stuff (animale)

impa'lato a fig stiff

impalca'tura nf scaffolding; fig structure

impalli'dire vi turn pale; (fig: perdere d'importanza) pale into insignificance

impa'nare vt Culin roll in breadcrumbs

impanta'narsi vr get bogged down

impape'rarsi vr, **impappi'narsi** vr falter, stammer

impa'rare vt learn

impareggi'abile a incomparable

imparen'ta|rsi vr ~ **con** become related to. **~to** a related

'impari a unequal; (dispari) odd

impar'tire vt impart

imparzi'al|e a impartial. **~ità** nf impartiality

impas'sibile a impassive

impa'sta|re vt Culin knead; blend (colori). **~'tura** nf kneading. **im'pasto** nm Culin dough; (miscuglio) mixture

impastic'carsi vr pop pills

im'patto nm impact

impau'rir|e vt frighten. **~si** vr become frightened

im'pavido a fearless

impazi'en|te a impatient; **~te di fare qcsa** eager to do sth. **~'tirsi** vr lose patience. **~za** nf impatience

impaz'zata nf **all'~** at breakneck speed

impaz'zire vi go mad; (maionese:) separate; **far ~ qcno** drive sb mad; **~ per** be crazy about; **da ~** (mal di testa) blinding

impec'cabile a impeccable

impedi'mento nm hindrance; (ostacolo) obstacle

impe'dire vt ~ **di** prevent from; (impacciare) hinder; (ostruire) obstruct; **~ a qcno di fare qcsa** prevent sb [from] doing sth

impe'gna|re vt (dare in pegno) pawn; (vincolare) bind; (prenotare) reserve; (assorbire) take up. **~rsi** vr ~**rsi a** engage oneself in; (dedicarsi) devote oneself to. **~'tiva** nf referral. **~'tivo** a binding; (lavoro) demanding. **~ato** a engaged. **im'pegno** nm engagement; Comm commitment; (zelo) care

impel'lente a pressing

impene'trabile a impenetrable

impen'na|rsi vr (cavallo:) rear; fig bristle. **~ta** nf (di prezzi) sharp rise; (di cavallo) rearing; (di moto) wheelie

impen'sa|bile a unthinkable. **~to** a unexpected

impensie'rir|e vt, **~si** vr worry

impe'ra|nte a prevailing. **~re** vi reign; (tendenza:) prevail, hold sway

impera'tivo a & nm imperative

impera'tore, -'trice nm emperor ● nf empress

impercet'tibile a imperceptible

imperdo'nabile a unforgivable

imper'fe|tto a & nm imperfect. **~zi'one** nf imperfection

imperi'a|le a imperial. **~'lismo** nm imperialism. **~'lista** a imperialist. **~'listico** a imperialistic

imperi'oso a imperious; (impellente) urgent

impe'rizia nf lack of skill

imperme'abile a waterproof ● nm raincoat

imperni'ar|e vt pivot; (fondare) base. **~si** vr **~si su** be based on

im'pero nm empire; (potere) rule

imperscru'tabile a inscrutable

imperso'nale a impersonal

imperso'nare vt personify; (interpretare) act [the part of]

imper'territo a undaunted

imperti'nen|te a impertinent. **~za** nf impertinence

impertur'ba|bile a imperturbable. **~to** a unperturbed

imperver'sare vi rage

im'pervio a inaccessible

'impet|o nm impetus; (impulso) impulse; (slancio) transport. **~u'oso** a impetuous; (vento) blustering

impet'tito a stiff

impian'tare vt install; set up (azienda)

impi'anto nm plant; (sistema) system; (operazione) installation. **~ radio** Auto car stereo system

impia'strare vt plaster; (sporcare) dirty. **impi'astro** nm poultice; (persona noiosa) bore; (pasticcio) cack-handed person

impic'car|e vt hang. **~si** vr hang oneself

impicci'|arsi vr meddle. **im'piccio** nm hindrance; (seccatura) bother. **~'one, -a** nmf nosey parker

impie'ga|re vt employ; (usare) use; spend (tempo, denaro); Fin invest;

impiegatizio | improduttivo

l'autobus ha ~to un'ora it took the bus an hour. **~rsi** *vr* get [oneself] a job
impiega'tizio *a* clerical
impie'gato, -a *nmf* employee. **~ di banca** bank clerk. **impi'ego** *nm* employment; (*posto*) job; *Fin* investment
impieto'sir|e *vt* move to pity. **~si** *vr* be moved to pity
impie'trito *a* petrified
impigli'ar|e *vt* entangle. **~si** *vr* get entangled
impi'grir|e *vt* make lazy. **~si** *vr* get lazy
impla'cabile *a* implacable
impli'ca|re *vt* implicate; (*sottintendere*) imply. **~rsi** *vr* become involved. **~zi'one** *nf* implication
implicita'mente *adv* implicitly. **im'plicito** *a* implicit
implo'ra|re *vt* implore. **~zi'one** *nf* entreaty
impolve'ra|re *vt* cover with dust. **~rsi** *vr* get covered with dust. **~to** *a* dusty
imponde'rabile *a* imponderable; (*causa, evento*) unpredictable
impo'nen|te *a* imposing. **~za** *nf* impressiveness
impo'nibile *a* taxable ● *nm* taxable income
impopo'lar|e *a* unpopular. **~ità** *nf* unpopularity
im'por|re *vt* impose; (*ordinare*) order. **~si** *vr* assert oneself; (*aver successo*) be successful; **~si di** (*prefiggersi*) set oneself the task of
impor'tan|te *a* important ● *nm* important thing. **~za** *nf* importance
impor'ta|re *vt* Comm, Comput import; (*comportare*) cause ● *vi* matter; (*essere necessario*) be necessary. **non ~!** it doesn't matter!; **non me ne ~ niente!** I couldn't care less!. **~'tore, ~'trice** *nmf* importer. **~zi'one** *nf* importation; (*merce importata*) import
im'porto *nm* amount
importu'nare *vt* pester. **impor'tuno** *a* troublesome; (*inopportuno*) untimely
imposizi'one *nf* imposition; (*imposta*) tax
imposses'sarsi *vr* **~ di** seize
impos'sibil|e *a* impossible ● *nm* **fare l'~e** do absolutely all one can. **~ità** *nf* impossibility
im'posta[1] *nf* tax; **~ sul reddito** income tax; **~ sul valore aggiunto** value added tax
im'posta[2] *nf* (*di finestra*) shutter

impo'sta|re *vt* (*progettare*) plan; (*basare*) base; *Mus* pitch; (*imbucare*) post, mail; set out ⟨*domanda, problema*⟩. **~zi'one** *nf* planning; (*di voce*) pitching
im'posto *pp di* imporre
impo'store, -a *nmf* impostor
impo'ten|te *a* powerless; *Med* impotent. **~za** *nf* powerlessness; *Med* impotence
impove'rir|e *vt* impoverish. **~si** *vr* become poor
imprati'cabile *a* impracticable; ⟨*strada*⟩ impassable
imprati'chir|e *vt* train. **~si** *vr* **~si in o** *a* get practice in
impre'ca|re *vi* curse. **~zi'one** *nf* curse
impreci's|abile *a* indeterminable. **~ato** *a* indeterminate. **~i'one** *nf* inaccuracy. **impre'ciso** *a* inaccurate
impre'gnar|e *vt* impregnate; (*imbevere*) soak; *fig* imbue. **~si** *vr* become impregnated with
imprendi'tor|e, -'trice *nmf* entrepreneur. **~i'ale** *a* entrepreneurial
imprepa'rato *a* unprepared
im'presa *nf* undertaking; (*gesta*) exploit; (*azienda*) firm
impre'sario *nm* impresario; (*appaltatore*) contractor
imprescin'dibile *a* inescapable
impressio'na|bile *a* impressionable. **~nte** *a* impressive; (*spaventoso*) frightening
impressi|o'nare *vt* impress; (*spaventare*) frighten; expose ⟨*foto*⟩. **~o'narsi** *vr* be affected; (*spaventarsi*) be frightened. **~'one** *nf* impression; (*sensazione*) sensation; (*impronta*) mark; **far ~one a qcno** upset sb
impressio'nis|mo *nm* impressionism. **~ta** *nmf* impressionist
im'presso *pp di* **imprimere** ● *a* printed
impre'stare *vt* lend
impreve'dibile *a* unforeseeable; ⟨*persona*⟩ unpredictable
imprevi'dente *a* improvident
impre'visto *a* unforeseen ● *nm* unforeseen event; **salvo imprevisti** all being well
imprigio|na'mento *nm* imprisonment. **~'nare** *vt* imprison
im'primere *vt* impress; (*stampare*) print; (*comunicare*) impart
impro'babil|e *a* unlikely, improbable. **~ità** *nf* improbability
improdut'tivo *a* unproductive

im'pronta *nf* impression; *fig* mark. ~ **digitale** fingerprint. ~ **del piede** footprint

impro'perio *nm* insult; **improperi** *pl* abuse *sg*

im'proprio *a* improper

improvvisa'mente *adv* suddenly

improvvi'sa|re *vt/i* improvise. ~**rsi** *vr* turn oneself into a. ~**ta** *nf* surprise. ~**to** *a* ⟨*discorso*⟩ unrehearsed. ~**zi'one** *nf* improvisation

improv'viso *a* sudden; **all'~** unexpectedly

impru'den|te *a* imprudent. ~**za** *nf* imprudence

impu'gna|re *vt* grasp; *Jur* contest. ~'**tura** *nf* grip; ⟨*manico*⟩ handle

impulsività *nf* impulsiveness. **impul'sivo** *a* impulsive

im'pulso *nm* impulse; **agire d'~** act on impulse

impune'mente *adv* with impunity. **impu'nito** *a* unpunished

impun'tarsi *vr* dig one's heels in

impun'tura *nf* stitching

impurità *nf inv* impurity. **im'puro** *a* impure

impu'tabile *a* attributable (**a** to)

impu'ta|re *vt* attribute; ⟨*accusare*⟩ charge. ~**to, -a** *nmf* accused. ~**zi'one** *nf* charge

imputri'dire *vi* rot

in *prep* in; ⟨*moto a luogo*⟩ to; ⟨*su*⟩ on; ⟨*entro*⟩ within; ⟨*mezzo*⟩ by; ⟨*con materiale*⟩ made of; **essere in casa/ufficio** be at home/at the office; **in mano/tasca** in one's hand/pocket; **andare in Francia/campagna** go to France/the country; **salire in treno** get on the train; **versa la birra nel bicchiere** pour the beer into the glass; **in alto** up there; **in giornata** within the day; **nel 1997** in 1997; **una borsa in pelle** a bag made of leather, a leather bag; **in macchina** ⟨*viaggiare, venire*⟩ by car; **in contanti** [in] cash; **in vacanza** on holiday; **di giorno in giorno** from day to day; **se fossi in te** if I were you; **siamo in sette** there are seven of us

inabbor'dabile *a* unapproachable

i'nabil|e *a* incapable; ⟨*fisicamente*⟩ unfit. ~**ità** *nf* incapacity

inabi'tabile *a* uninhabitable

inacces'sibile *a* inaccessible; ⟨*persona*⟩ unapproachable

inaccet'tabil|e *a* unacceptable. ~**ità** *nf* unacceptability

inacer'bi|re *vt* embitter; exacerbate ⟨*rapporto*⟩. ~**si** *vr* grow bitter

inaci'dir|e *vt* turn sour. ~**si** *vr* go sour; ⟨*persona:*⟩ become embittered

ina'datto *a* unsuitable

inadegu'ato *a* inadequate

inadempi'|ente *nmf* defaulter. ~'**mento** *nm* non-fulfilment

inaffer'rabile *a* elusive

ina'la|re *vt* inhale. ~'**tore** *nm* inhaler. ~**zi'one** *nf* inhalation

inalbe'rar|e *vt* hoist. ~**si** *vr* ⟨*cavallo:*⟩ rear [up]; ⟨*adirarsi*⟩ lose one's temper

inalte'ra|bile *a* unchangeable; ⟨*colore*⟩ fast. ~**to** *a* unchanged

inami'da|re *vt* starch. ~**to** *a* starched

inammis'sibile *a* inadmissible

inamovi'bile *a* irremovable

inani'mato *a* inanimate; ⟨*senza vita*⟩ lifeless

inappa'ga|bile *a* unsatisfiable. ~**to** *a* unfulfilled

inappel'labile *a* final

inappe'tenza *nf* lack of appetite

inappli'cabile *a* inapplicable

inappun'tabile *a* faultless

inar'car|e *vt* arch; raise ⟨*sopracciglia*⟩. ~**si** *vr* ⟨*legno:*⟩ warp; ⟨*ripiano:*⟩ sag; ⟨*linea:*⟩ curve

inari'dir|e *vt* parch; empty of feelings ⟨*persona*⟩. ~**si** *vr* dry up; ⟨*persona:*⟩ become empty of feelings

inartico'lato *a* inarticulate

inaspettata'mente *adv* unexpectedly. **inaspet'tato** *a* unexpected

inaspri'mento *nm* ⟨*di carattere*⟩ embitterment; ⟨*di conflitto*⟩ worsening

ina'sprir|e *vt* embitter. ~**si** *vr* become embittered

inattac'cabile *a* unassailable; ⟨*irreprensibile*⟩ irreproachable

inatten'dibile *a* unreliable. **inat'teso** *a* unexpected

inattività *nf* inactivity. **inat'tivo** *a* inactive

inattu'abile *a* impracticable

inau'dito *a* unheard of

inaugu'rale *a* inaugural; **viaggio ~** maiden voyage

inaugu'ra|re *vt* inaugurate; open ⟨*mostra*⟩; unveil ⟨*statua*⟩; christen ⟨*lavastoviglie*⟩. ~**zi'one** *nf* inauguration; ⟨*di mostra*⟩ opening; ⟨*di statua*⟩ unveiling

inavver't|enza *nf* inadvertence. ~**ita'mente** *adv* inadvertently

incagli'ar|e *vi* ground ● *vt* hinder. ~**si** *vr* run aground

incalco'labile *a* incalculable

incal'li|rsi *vr* grow callous; ⟨*abituarsi*⟩ become hardened. ~**to** *a* callous; ⟨*abituato*⟩ hardened

incal'za|nte *a* ⟨*ritmo*⟩ driving; ⟨*richiesta*⟩ urgent. ~**re** *vt* pursue; *fig* press

incame'rare *vt* appropriate

incammi'nar|e *vt* get going; ⟨*fig: guidare*⟩ set off. ~**si** *vr* set out

incana'lar|e *vt* canalize; *fig* channel. ~**si** *vr* converge on

incande'scen|te *a* incandescent; ⟨*discussione*⟩ burning. ~**za** *nf* incandescence

incan'ta|re *vt* enchant. ~**rsi** *vr* stand spellbound; ⟨*incepparsi*⟩ jam. ~'**tore,** ~'**trice** *nmf* enchanter ● *nf* enchantress

incan'tesimo *nm* spell

incan'tevole *a* enchanting

in'canto *nm* spell; *fig* delight; ⟨*asta*⟩ auction; **come per** ~ as if by magic

incanu'ti|re *vt* turn white. ~**to** *a* white

inca'pac|e *a* incapable. ~**ità** *nf* incapability

incapo'nirsi *vr* be set

incap'pare *vi* ~ **in** run into

incappucci'arsi *vr* wrap up

incapricci'arsi *vr* ~ **di** take a fancy to

incapsu'lare *vt* seal; crown ⟨*dente*⟩

incarce'ra|re *vt* imprison. ~**zi'one** *nf* imprisonment

incari'ca|re *vt* charge. ~**rsi** *vr* take upon oneself; **me ne incarico io** I will see to it. ~**to, -a** *a* in charge ● *nmf* representative. **in'carico** *nm* charge; **per incarico di** on behalf of

incar'na|re *vt* embody. ~**rsi** *vr* become incarnate. ~**zi'one** *nf* incarnation

incarta'mento *nm* documents *pl.* **incar'tare** *vt* wrap [in paper]

incasi'nato *a fam* ⟨*vita*⟩ screwed up; ⟨*stanza*⟩ messed up

incas'sa|re *vt* pack; *Mech* embed; box in ⟨*mobile, frigo*⟩; ⟨*riscuotere*⟩ cash; take ⟨*colpo*⟩. ~**to** *a* set; ⟨*fiume*⟩ deeply embanked. **in'casso** *nm* collection; ⟨*introito*⟩ takings *pl*

incasto'na|re *vt* set. ~'**tura** *nf* setting. ~**to** *a* embedded; ⟨*anello*⟩ inset (**di** with)

inca'strar|e *vt* fit in; ⟨*fam: in situazione*⟩ corner. ~**si** *vr* fit. **in'castro** *nm* joint; **a incastro** ⟨*pezzi*⟩ interlocking

incate'nare *vt* chain

incatra'mare *vt* tar

incatti'vire *vt* turn nasty

in'cauto *a* imprudent

inca'va|re *vt* hollow out. ~**to** *a* hollow. ~'**tura** *nf* hollow. **in'cavo** *nm* hollow; ⟨*scanalatura*⟩ groove

incavo'la|rsi *vr fam* get shirty. ~**to** *a fam* shirty

incendi'ar|e *vt* set fire to; *fig* inflame. ~**si** *vr* catch fire. ~**io, -a** *a* incendiary; ⟨*fig: discorso*⟩ inflammatory; ⟨*fig: bellezza*⟩ sultry ● *nmf* arsonist. **in'cendio** *nm* fire. **incendio doloso** arson

incene'ri|re *vt* burn to ashes; ⟨*cremare*⟩ cremate. ~**rsi** *vr* be burnt to ashes. ~'**tore** *nm* incinerator

in'censo *nm* incense

incensu'rato *a* blameless; **essere** ~ *Jur* have a clean record

incenti'vare *vt* motivate. **incen'tivo** *nm* incentive

incen'trarsi *vr* ~ **su** centre on

incep'par|e *vt* block; *fig* hamper. ~**si** *vr* jam

ince'rata *nf* oilcloth

incerot'tato *a* with a plaster on

incer'tezza *nf* uncertainty. **in'certo** *a* uncertain ● *nm* uncertainty

inces'sante *a* unceasing. ~'**mente** *adv* incessantly

in'cest|o *nm* incest. ~**u'oso** *a* incestuous

in'cetta *nf* buying up; **fare** ~ **di** stockpile

inchi'esta *nf* investigation

inchi'nar|e *vt*, ~**si** *vr* bow. **in'chino** *nm* bow; ⟨*di donna*⟩ curtsy

inchio'dare *vt* nail; nail down ⟨*coperchio*⟩; ~ **a letto** ⟨*malattia:*⟩ confine to bed

inchi'ostro *nm* ink

inciam'pare *vi* stumble; ~ **in** ⟨*imbattersi*⟩ run into. **inci'ampo** *nm* hindrance

inciden'tale *a* incidental

inci'den|te *nm* ⟨*episodio*⟩ incident; ⟨*infortunio*⟩ accident. ~**za** *nf* incidence

in'cidere *vt* cut; ⟨*arte*⟩ engrave; ⟨*registrare*⟩ record ● *vi* ~ **su** ⟨*gravare*⟩ weigh upon

in'cinta *a* pregnant

incipi'ente *a* incipient

incipri'ar|e *vt* powder. ~**si** *vr* powder one's face

in'circa *adv* **all'**~ more or less

incisi'one *nf* incision; ⟨*arte*⟩ engraving; ⟨*acquaforte*⟩ etching; ⟨*registrazione*⟩ recording

inci'sivo *a* incisive ● *nm* ⟨*dente*⟩ incisor

in'ciso *nm* per ~ incidentally
incita'mento *nm* incitement. **inci'ta-re** *vt* incite
inci'vil|e *a* uncivilized; ⟨*maleducato*⟩ impolite. ~**tà** *nf* barbarism; ⟨*maleducazione*⟩ rudeness
incle'men|te *a* harsh. ~**za** *nf* harshness
incli'nabile *a* reclining
incli'na|re *vt* tilt ● *vi* ~**re a** be inclined to. ~**rsi** *vr* list. ~**to** *a* tilted; ⟨*terreno*⟩ sloping. ~**zi'one** *nf* slope, inclination. **in'cline** *a* inclined
in'clu|dere *vt* include; ⟨*allegare*⟩ enclose. ~**si'one** *nf* inclusion. ~**sivo** *a* inclusive. ~**so** *pp di* **includere** ● *a* included; ⟨*compreso*⟩ inclusive; ⟨*allegato*⟩ enclosed
incoe'ren|te *a* ⟨*contraddittorio*⟩ inconsistent. ~**za** *nf* inconsistency
in'cognit|a *nf* unknown quantity. ~**o** *a* unknown ● *nm* **in** ~**o** incognito
incol'lar|e *vt* stick; ⟨*con colla liquida*⟩ glue. ~**si** *vr* stick to; ~**si a qcno** stick close to sb
incolle'ri|rsi *vr* lose one's temper. ~**to** *a* enraged
incol'mabile *a* ⟨*differenza*⟩ unbridgeable; ⟨*vuoto*⟩ unfillable
incolon'nare *vt* line up
inco'lore *a* colourless
incol'pare *vt* blame
in'colto *a* uncultivated; ⟨*persona*⟩ uneducated
in'colume *a* unhurt
incom'ben|te *a* impending. ~**za** *nf* task
in'combere *vi* ~ **su** hang over; ~ **a** ⟨*spettare*⟩ be incumbent on
incominci'are *vt/i* begin, start
incomo'dar|e *vt* inconvenience. ~**si** *vr* trouble. **in'comodo** *a* uncomfortable; ⟨*inopportuno*⟩ inconvenient ● *nm* inconvenience
incompa'rabile *a* incomparable
incompa'tibil|e *a* incompatible. ~**ità** *nf* incompatibility
incompe'ten|te *a* incompetent. ~**za** *nf* incompetence
incompi'uto *a* unfinished
incom'pleto *a* incomplete
incompren'si|bile *a* incomprehensible. ~**one** *nf* lack of understanding; ⟨*malinteso*⟩ misunderstanding. **incom'preso** *a* misunderstood
inconce'pibile *a* inconceivable
inconcili'abile *a* irreconcilable

inconclu'dente *a* inconclusive; ⟨*persona*⟩ ineffectual
incondizio|nata'mente *adv* unconditionally. ~**'nato** *a* unconditional
inconfes'sabile *a* unmentionable
inconfon'dibile *a* unmistakable
inconfu'tabile *a* irrefutable
incongru'ente *a* inconsistent
in'congruo *a* inadequate
inconsa'pevol|e *a* unaware; ⟨*inconscio*⟩ unconscious. ~**'mente** *adv* unwittingly
inconscia'mente *adv* unconsciously. **in'conscio** *a* & *nm Psych* unconscious
inconsi'sten|te *a* insubstantial; ⟨*notizia ecc*⟩ unfounded. ~**za** *nf* ⟨*di ragionamento, prove*⟩ flimsiness
inconso'labile *a* inconsolable
inconsu'eto *a* unusual
incon'sulto *a* rash
incontami'nato *a* uncontaminated
inconte'nibile *a* irrepressible
inconten'tabile *a* insatiable; ⟨*esigente*⟩ hard to please
inconte'stabile *a* indisputable
inconti'nen|te *a* incontinent. ~**za** *nf* incontinence
incon'trar|e *vt* meet; encounter, meet with ⟨*difficoltà*⟩. ~**si** *vr* meet (**con** qcno sb)
incon'trario: **all'**~ *adv* the other way around; ⟨*in modo sbagliato*⟩ the wrong way around
incontra'sta|bile *a* incontrovertible. ~**to** *a* undisputed
in'contro *nm* meeting; *Sport* match. ~ **al vertice** summit meeting ● *prep* ~ **a** towards; **andare** ~ **a qn** go to meet sb; *fig* meet sb half way
inconveni'ente *nm* drawback
incoraggi|a'mento *nm* encouragement. ~**'ante** *a* encouraging. ~**'are** *vt* encourage
incornici'a|re *vt* frame. ~**'tura** *nf* framing
incoro'na|re *vt* crown. ~**zi'one** *nf* coronation
incorpo'rar|e *vt* incorporate; ⟨*mescolare*⟩ blend. ~**si** *vr* blend; ⟨*territori:*⟩ merge
incorreg'gibile *a* incorrigible
in'correre *vt* ~ **in** incur; ~ **nel pericolo di...** run the risk of...
incorrut'tibile *a* incorruptible
incosci'en|te *a* unconscious; ⟨*irresponsabile*⟩ reckless ● *nmf* irresponsi-

ble person. **~za** *nf* unconsciousness; recklessness

inco'stan|te *a* changeable; ⟨*persona*⟩ fickle. **~za** *nf* changeableness; ⟨*di persona*⟩ fickleness

incostituzio'nale *a* unconstitutional

incre'dibile *a* unbelievable, incredible

incredulità *nf* incredulity. **in'credulo** *a* incredulous

incremen'tare *vt* increase; ⟨*intensificare*⟩ step up. **incre'mento** *nm* increase. **incremento demografico** population growth

incresci'oso *a* regrettable

incre'spar|e *vt* ruffle; wrinkle ⟨*tessuto*⟩; make frizzy ⟨*capelli*⟩. **~e la fronte** frown. **~si** *vr* ⟨*acqua:*⟩ ripple; ⟨*tessuto*⟩ wrinkle; ⟨*capelli:*⟩ go frizzy

incrimi'na|re *vt* indict; *fig* incriminate. **~'zi'one** *nf* indictment

incri'na|re *vt* crack; *fig* affect ⟨*amicizia*⟩. **~rsi** *vr* crack; ⟨*amicizia:*⟩ be affected. **~'tura** *nf* crack

incroci'a|re *vt* cross ● *vi* Naut, Aeron cruise. **~rsi** *vr* cross. **~'tore** *nm* cruiser

in'crocio *nm* crossing; ⟨*di strade*⟩ crossroads *sg*

incrol'labile *a* indestructible

incro'sta|re *vt* encrust. **~zi'one** *nf* encrustation

incuba|'trice *nf* incubator. **~zi'one** *nf* incubation

'incubo *nm* nightmare

in'cudine *nf* anvil

incu'rabile *a* incurable

incu'rante *a* careless

incurio'sir|e *vt* make curious. **~si** *vr* become curious

incursi'one *nf* raid. **~ aerea** air raid

incurva'mento *nm* bending

incur'va|re *vt*, **~rsi** *vr* bend. **~'tura** *nf* bending

in'cusso *pp di* incutere

incusto'dito *a* unguarded

in'cutere *vt* arouse; **~ spavento a qcno** strike fear into sb

'indaco *nm* indigo

indaffa'rato *a* busy

inda'gare *vt/i* investigate

in'dagine *nf* research; ⟨*giudiziaria*⟩ investigation. **~ di mercato** market survey

indebi'tar|e *vt*, **~si** *vr* get into debt

in'debito *a* undue

indeboli'mento *nm* weakening

indebo'lir|e *vt*, **~si** *vr* weaken

inde'cen|te *a* indecent. **~za** *nf* indecency; ⟨*vergogna*⟩ disgrace

indeci'frabile *a* indecipherable

indecisi'one *nf* indecision. **inde'ciso** *a* undecided

inde'fesso *a* tireless

indefi'ni|bile *a* indefinable. **~to** *a* indefinite

indefor'mabile *a* crushproof

in'degno *a* unworthy

inde'lebile *a* indelible

indelica'tezza *nf* indelicacy; ⟨*azione*⟩ tactless act. **indeli'cato** *a* indiscreet; ⟨*grossolano*⟩ indelicate

indemoni'ato *a* possessed

in'denn|e *a* uninjured; ⟨*da malattia*⟩ unaffected. **~ità** *nf inv* allowance; ⟨*per danni*⟩ compensation. **~ità di trasferta** travel allowance. **~iz'zare** *vt* compensate. **~iz'zo** *nm* compensation

indero'gabile *a* binding

indescri'vibile *a* indescribable

indeside'ra|bile *a* undesirable. **~to** *a* ⟨*figlio, ospite*⟩ unwanted

indetermi'na|bile *a* indeterminable. **~'tezza** *nf* vagueness. **~to** *a* indeterminate

'Indi|a *nf* India. **i~'ano, -a** *a & nmf* Indian; **in fila i~ana** in single file

indiavo'lato *a* possessed; ⟨*vivace*⟩ wild

indi'ca|re *vt* show, indicate; ⟨*col dito*⟩ point at; ⟨*far notare*⟩ point out; ⟨*consigliare*⟩ advise. **~'tivo** *a* indicative ● *nm* Gram indicative. **~'tore** *nm* indicator; Techn gauge; ⟨*prontuario*⟩ directory. **~zi'one** *nf* indication; ⟨*istruzione*⟩ direction

'indice *nm* ⟨*dito*⟩ forefinger; ⟨*lancetta*⟩ pointer; ⟨*di libro, statistica*⟩ index; ⟨*fig: segno*⟩ sign

indi'cibile *a* inexpressible

indietreggi'are *vi* draw back; *Mil* retreat

indi'etro *adv* back, behind; **all'~** backwards; **avanti e ~** back and forth; **essere ~** be behind; ⟨*mentalmente*⟩ be backward; ⟨*con pagamenti*⟩ be in arrears; ⟨*di orologio*⟩ be slow; **fare marcia ~** reverse; **rimandare ~** send back; **rimanere ~** be left behind; **torna ~!** come back!

indi'feso *a* undefended; ⟨*inerme*⟩ helpless

indiffe'ren|te *a* indifferent; **mi è ~te** it is all the same to me. **~za** *nf* indifference

in'digeno, -a a indigenous ● nmf native

indi'gen|te a needy. **~za** nf poverty

indigesti'one nf indigestion. **indi'gesto** a indigestible

indi'gna|re vt make indignant. **~rsi** vr be indignant. **~to a** indignant. **~zi'one** nf indignation

indimenti'cabile a unforgettable

indipen'den|te a independent. **~te'mente** adv independently; **~temente dal tempo** regardless of the weather, whatever the weather. **~za** nf independence

in'dire vt announce

indiretta'mente adv indirectly. **indi'retto** a indirect

indiriz'zar|e vt address; (mandare) send; (dirigere) direct. **~si** vr direct one's steps. **indi'rizzo** nm address; (direzione) direction

indisci'pli|na nf lack of discipline. **~'nato** a undisciplined

indi'scre|to a indiscreet. **~zi'one** nf indiscretion

indiscrimi|nata'mente adv indiscriminately. **~'nato** a indiscriminate

indi'scusso a unquestioned

indiscu'tibil|e a unquestionable. **~'mente** adv unquestionably

indispen'sabile a essential, indispensable

indispet'tir|e vt irritate. **~si** vr get irritated

indi'spo|rre vt antagonize. **~sto** pp di **indisporre** ● a indisposed. **~sizi'one** nf indisposition

indisso'lubile a indissoluble

indissolubil'mente adv indissolubly

indistin'guibile a indiscernible

indistinta'mente adv without exception. **indi'stinto** a indistinct

indistrut'tibile a indestructible

indistur'bato a undisturbed

in'divia nf endive

individu'a|le a individual. **~'lista** nmf individualist. **~lità** nf individuality. **~re** vt individualize; (localizzare) locate; (riconoscere) single out

indi'viduo nm individual

indivi'sibile a indivisible. **indi'viso** a undivided

indizi'a|re vt throw suspicion on. **~to, -a** a suspected ● nmf suspect. **in'dizio** nm sign; Jur circumstantial evidence

'indole nf nature

indo'len|te a indolent. **~za** nf indolence

indolenzi'mento nm stiffness

indolen'zi|rsi vr go stiff. **~to** a stiff

indo'lore a painless

indo'mani nm **l'~** the following day

Indo'nesia nf Indonesia

indo'rare vt gild

indos'sa|re vt wear; (mettere addosso) put on. **~'tore, ~'trice** nmf model

in'dotto pp di **indurre**

indottri'nare vt indoctrinate

indovi'n|are vt guess; (predire) foretell. **~ato** a successful; (scelta) well-chosen. **~ello** nm riddle. **indo'vino, -a** nmf fortune-teller

indubbia'mente adv undoubtedly. **in'dubbio** a undoubted

indugi'ar|e vi, **~si** vr linger. **in'dugio** nm delay

indul'gen|te a indulgent. **~za** nf indulgence

in'dul|gere vi **~gere** a indulge in. **~to** pp di **indulgere** ● nm Jur pardon

indu'mento nm garment; **indumenti** pl clothes

induri'mento nm hardening

indu'rir|e vt, **~si** vr harden

in'durre vt induce

in'dustri|a nf industry. **~'ale** a industrial ● nm industrialist

industrializ'za|re vt industrialize. **~to** a industrialized. **~zi'one** nf industrialization

industrial'mente adv industrially

industri|'arsi vr try one's hardest. **~'oso** a industrious

induzi'one nf induction

inebe'tito a stunned

inebri'ante a intoxicating, exciting

inecce'pibile a unexceptionable

i'nedia nf starvation

i'nedito a unpublished

ineffi'cace a ineffective

ineffici'en|te a inefficient. **~za** nf inefficiency

ineguagli'abile a incomparable

inegu'ale a unequal; (superficie) uneven

inelut'tabile a inescapable

ine'rente a **~ a** concerning

i'nerme a unarmed; fig defenceless

inerpi'carsi vr **~ su** clamber up; (pianta:) climb up

i'ner|te a inactive; Phys inert. **~zia** nf inactivity; Phys inertia

inesat'tezza nf inaccuracy. **ine'satto**

a inaccurate; (*erroneo*) incorrect; (*non riscosso*) uncollected

inesau'ribile *a* inexhaustible

inesi'sten|te *a* non-existent. **~za** *nf* non-existence

ineso'rabile *a* inexorable

inesperi'enza *nf* inexperience. **ine-'sperto** *a* inexperienced

inespli'cabile *a* inexplicable

ine'sploso *a* unexploded

inespri'mibile *a* inexpressible

inesti'mabile *a* inestimable

inetti'tudine *nf* ineptitude. **i'netto** *a* inept; **inetto a** unsuited to

ine'vaso *a* ⟨*pratiche*⟩ pending; ⟨*corrispondenza*⟩ unanswered

inevi'tabil|e *a* inevitable. **~'mente** *adv* inevitably

i'nezia *nf* trifle

infagot'tar|e *vt* wrap up. **~si** *vr* wrap [oneself] up

infal'libile *a* infallible

infa'ma|re *vt* defame. **~'torio** *a* defamatory

in'fam|e *a* infamous; (*fam: orrendo*) awful, shocking. **~ia** *nf* infamy

infan'garsi *vr* get muddy

infan'tile *a* ⟨*letteratura, abbigliamento*⟩ children's; ⟨*ingenuità*⟩ childlike; *pej* childish

in'fanzia *nf* childhood; (*bambini*) children *pl*; **prima ~** infancy

infar'cire *vi* pepper ⟨*discorso*⟩ (*di* with)

infari'na|re *vt* flour; **~re di** sprinkle with. **~'tura** *nf fig* smattering

in'farto *nm* coronary

infasti'dir|e *vt* irritate. **~si** *vr* get irritated

infati'cabile *a* untiring

in'fatti *conj* as a matter of fact; (*veramente*) indeed

infatu'a|rsi *vr* become infatuated (**di** with). **~to** *a* infatuated. **~zi'one** *nf* infatuation

in'fausto *a* ill-omened

infe'condo *a* infertile

infe'del|e *a* unfaithful. **~tà** *nf* unfaithfulness; **~** *pl* affairs

infe'lic|e *a* unhappy; (*inappropriato*) unfortunate; (*cattivo*) bad. **~ità** *nf* unhappiness

infel'tri|rsi *vr* get matted. **~to** *a* matted

inferi'or|e *a* (*più basso*) lower; ⟨*qualità*⟩ inferior ● *nmf* inferior. **~ità** *nf* inferiority

inferme'ria *nf* infirmary; (*di nave*) sick-bay

infermi'er|a *nf* nurse. **~e** *nm* [male] nurse

infermità *nf* sickness. **~ mentale** mental illness. **in'fermo, -a** *a* sick ● *nmf* invalid

infer'nale *a* infernal; (*spaventoso*) hellish

in'ferno *nm* hell; **va all'~!** go to hell!

infero'cirsi *vr* become fierce

inferri'ata *nf* grating

infervo'rar|e *vt* arouse enthusiasm in. **~si** *vr* get excited

infe'stare *vt* infest

infet't|are *vt* infect. **~arsi** *vr* become infected. **~ivo** *a* infectious. **in'fetto** *a* infected. **infezi'one** *nf* infection

infiac'chir|e *vt/i*, **~si** *vr* weaken

infiam'mabile *a* [in]flammable

infiam'ma|re *vt* set on fire; *Med, fig* inflame. **~rsi** *vr* catch fire; *Med* become inflamed. **~zi'one** *nf Med* inflammation

in'fido *a* treacherous

infie'rire *vi* (*imperversare*) rage; **~ su** attack furiously

in'figger|e *vt* drive. **~si** *vr.* **~si in** penetrate

infi'lar|e *vt* thread; (*mettere*) insert; (*indossare*) put on. **~si** *vr* slip on ⟨*vestito*⟩; **~si in** (*introdursi*) slip into

infil'tra|rsi *vr* infiltrate. **~zi'one** *nf* infiltration; (*d'acqua*) seepage; (*Med: iniezione*) injection

infil'zare *vt* pierce; (*infilare*) string; (*conficcare*) stick

'infimo *a* lowest

in'fine *adv* finally; (*insomma*) in short

infinità *nf* infinity; **un'~ di** masses of. **~'mente** *adv* infinitely. **infi'nito** *a* infinite; *Gram* infinitive ● *nm* infinite; *Gram* infinitive; *Math* infinity; **all'infinito** endlessly

infinocchi'are *vt fam* hoodwink

infischi'arsi *vr* **~ di** not care about; **me ne infischio** *fam* I couldn't care less

in'fisso *pp di* **infiggere** ● *nm* fixture; (*di porta, finestra*) frame

infit'tir|e *vt/i*, **~si** *vr* thicken

inflazi'one *nf* inflation

infles'sibil|e *a* inflexible. **~ità** *nf* inflexibility

inflessi'one *nf* inflexion

in'fli|ggere *vt* inflict. **~tto** *pp di* **infliggere**

influ'en|te *a* influential. **~za** *nf* influence; *Med* influenza

influen'za|bile *a* ⟨mente, opinione⟩ impressionable. **~re** *vt* influence. **~to** *a* ⟨malato⟩ with the flu

influ'ire *vi* **~ su** influence

in'flusso *nm* influence

info'carsi *vr* catch fire; ⟨viso:⟩ go red; ⟨discussione:⟩ become heated

info'gnarsi *vr fam* get into a mess

infol'tire *vt/i* thicken

infon'dato *a* unfounded

in'fondere *vt* instil

infor'care *vt* fork up; get on ⟨bici⟩; put on ⟨occhiali⟩

infor'male *a* informal

infor'ma|re *vt* inform. **~rsi** *vr* inquire (**di** about). **~'tivo** *a* informative.

infor'matic|a *nf* computing, IT. **~o** *a* computer *attrib*

infor'ma|tivo *a* informative. **infor-'mato** *a* informed; **male informa** ill-informed. **~'tore**, **~'trice** *nmf* ⟨di polizia⟩ informer. **~zi'one** *nf* information ⟨solo sg⟩; **un'~zione** a piece of information

in'forme *a* shapeless

infor'nare *vt* put into the oven

infortu'narsi *vr* have an accident.

infor'tu|nio *nm* accident. **~nio sul lavoro** industrial accident. **~'nistica** *nf* study of industrial accidents

infos'sa|rsi *vr* sink; ⟨guance, occhi:⟩ become hollow. **~to** *a* sunken, hollow

infradici'ar|e *vt* drench. **~si** *vr* get drenched; ⟨diventare marcio⟩ rot

infra'dito *nm inv* ⟨scarpa⟩ flip-flop

in'frang|ere *vt* break; ⟨in mille pezzi⟩ shatter. **~ersi** *vr* break. **~'gibile** *a* unbreakable

in'franto *pp di* **infrangere** ● *a* shattered; ⟨fig: cuore⟩ broken

infra'rosso *a* infra-red

infrastrut'tura *nf* infrastructure

infrazi'one *nf* offence

infredda'tura *nf* cold

infreddo'li|rsi *vr* feel cold. **~to** *a* cold

infruttu'oso *a* fruitless

infuo'ca|re *vt* make red-hot. **~to** *a* burning

infu'ori *adv* **all'~** outwards; **all'~** except

infuri'a|re *vi* rage. **~rsi** *vr* fly into a rage. **~to** *a* blustering

infusi'one *nf* infusion. **in'fuso** *pp di* **infondere** ● *nm* infusion

Ing. *abbr* **ingegnere**

ingabbi'are *vt* cage; ⟨fig: mettere in prigione⟩ jail

ingaggi'are *vt* engage; sign up ⟨calciatori ecc⟩; begin ⟨lotta, battaglia⟩. **in'gaggio** *nm* engagement; ⟨di calciatore⟩ signing [up]

ingan'nar|e *vt* deceive; ⟨essere infedele a⟩ be unfaithful to. **~si** *vr* deceive oneself; **se non m'inganno** if I am not mistaken

ingan'nevole *a* deceptive. **in'ganno** *nm* deceit; ⟨frode⟩ fraud

ingarbugli'a|re *vt* entangle; ⟨confondere⟩ confuse. **~rsi** *vr* get entangled; ⟨confondersi⟩ become confused. **~to** *a* confused

inge'gnarsi *vr* do one's best

inge'gnere *nm* engineer. **ingegne'ria** *nf* engineering

in'gegno *nm* brains *pl*; ⟨genio⟩ genius; ⟨abilità⟩ ingenuity. **~sa'mente** *adv* ingeniously

ingegnosità *nf* ingenuity. **inge'gnoso** *a* ingenious

ingelo'sir|e *vt* make jealous. **~si** *vr* become jealous

in'gente *a* huge

ingenu|a'mente *adv* artlessly. **~ità** *nf* ingenuousness. **in'genuo** *a* ingenuous; ⟨credulone⟩ naïve

inge'renza *nf* interference

inge'rire *vt* swallow

inges'sa|re *vt* put in plaster. **~'tura** *nf* plaster

Inghil'terra *nf* England

inghiot'tire *vt* swallow

in'ghippo *nm* trick

ingial'li|re *vi*, **~rsi** *vr* turn yellow. **~to** *a* yellowed

ingigan'tir|e *vt* magnify ● *vi*, **~si** *vr* grow to enormous proportions

inginocchi'a|rsi *vr* kneel [down]. **~to** *a* kneeling. **~'toio** *nm* prie-dieu

ingioiel'larsi *vr* put on one's jewels

ingiù *adv* down; **all'~** downwards; **a testa ~** head downwards

ingi'un|gere *vt* order. **~zi'one** *nf* injunction. **~zione di pagamento** final demand

ingi'uri|a *nf* insult; ⟨torto⟩ wrong; ⟨danno⟩ damage. **~'are** *vt* insult; ⟨fare un torto a⟩ wrong. **~'oso** *a* insulting

ingiusta'mente *adv* unjustly, unfairly. **ingiu'stizia** *nf* injustice. **ingi'usto** *a* unjust, unfair

in'glese *a* English ● *nm* Englishman; ⟨lingua⟩ English ● *nf* Englishwoman

ingoi'are *vt* swallow

ingol'far|e vt flood ‹motore›. **~si** vr fig get involved; ‹motore:› flood

ingom'bra|nte a cumbersome. **~re** vt clutter up; fig cram ‹mente›

in'gombro nm encumbrance; **essere d'~** be in the way

ingor'digia nf greed. **in'gordo** a greedy

ingor'gar|e vt block. **~si** vr be blocked [up]. **in'gorgo** nm blockage; (del traffico) jam

ingoz'zar|e vt gobble up; (nutrire eccessivamente) stuff; fatten ‹animali›. **~si** vr stuff oneself (**di** with)

ingra'na|ggio nm gear; fig mechanism. **~re** vt engage ● vi be in gear

ingrandi'mento nm enlargement

ingran'di|re vt enlarge; (esagerare) magnify. **~rsi** vr become larger; (aumentare) increase

ingras'sar|e vt fatten up; Mech grease ● vi, **~si** vr put on weight

ingrati'tudine nf ingratitude. **in'grato** a ungrateful; (sgradevole) thankless

ingrazi'arsi vr ingratiate oneself with

ingredi'ente nm ingredient

in'gresso nm entrance; (accesso) admittance; (sala) hall; **~ gratuito/ libero** admission free; **vietato l'~** no entry; no admittance

ingros'sar|e vt make big; (gonfiare) swell ● vi, **~si** vr grow big; (gonfiare) swell

in'grosso adv **all'~** wholesale; (pressappoco) roughly

ingua'ribile a incurable

'inguine nm groin

ingurgi'tare vt gulp down

ini'bi|re vt inhibit; (vietare) forbid. **~to** a inhibited. **~zi'one** nf inhibition; (divieto) prohibition

iniet'tar|e vt inject. **~si** vr **~si di sangue** ‹occhi:› become bloodshot. **iniezi'one** nf injection

inimi'carsi vr make an enemy of. **inimi'cizia** nf enmity

inimi'tabile a inimitable

ininter|rotta'mente adv continuously. **~'rotto** a continuous

iniquità nf iniquity. **i'niquo** a iniquitous

inizi'al|e a & nf initial. **~'mente** adv initially

inizi'are vt begin; (avviare) open; **~ qcno a qcsa** initiate sb in sth ● vi begin

inizia'tiva nf initiative; **prendere l'~** take the initiative

inizi'a|to, -a a initiated ● nmf initiate; **gli ~ti** the initiated. **~'tore, ~'trice** nmf initiator. **~zi'one** nf initiation

i'nizio nm beginning, start; **dare ~ a** start; **avere ~** get under way

innaffi'a|re vt water. **~'toio** nm watering-can

innal'zar|e vt raise; (erigere) erect. **~si** vr rise

innamo'ra|rsi vr fall in love (**di** with). **~ta** nf girl-friend. **~to** a in love ● nm boy-friend

in'nanzi adv (stato in luogo) in front; (di tempo) ahead; (avanti) forward; (prima) before; **d'ora ~** from now on ● prep (prima) before; **~ a** in front of. **~'tutto** adv first of all; (soprattutto) above all

in'nato a innate

innatu'rale a unnatural

inne'gabile a undeniable

innervo'sir|e vt make nervous. **~si** vr get irritated

inne'scare vt prime. **in'nesco** nm primer

inne'stare vt graft; Mech engage; (inserire) insert. **in'nesto** nm graft; Mech clutch; Electr connection

inne'vato a covered in snow

'inno nm hymn. **~ nazionale** national anthem

inno'cen|te a innocent **~te'mente** adv innocently. **~za** nf innocence.

in'nocuo a innocuous

inno'va|re vt make changes in. **~'tivo** a innovative. **~'tore** a a trail-blazing. **~zi'one** nf innovation

innume'revole a innumerable

ino'doro a odourless

inoffen'sivo a harmless

inol'trar|e vt forward. **~si** vr advance

inol'trato a late

i'noltre adv besides

inon'da|re vt flood. **~zi'one** nf flood

inope'roso a idle

inoppor'tuno a untimely

inorgo'glir|e vt make proud. **~si** vr become proud

inorri'dire vt horrify ● vi be horrified

inospi'tale a inhospitable

inosser'vato a unobserved; (non rispettato) disregarded; **passare ~** go unnoticed

inossi'dabile a stainless

'inox a inv ‹acciaio› stainless

inqua'dra|re vt frame; fig put in context ⟨*scrittore, problema*⟩. **~rsi** *vr* fit into. **~'tura** *nf* framing

inqualifi'cabile *a* unspeakable

inquie'tar|e *vt* worry. **~si** get worried; (*impazientirsi*) get cross. **inqui'eto** *a* restless; (*preoccupato*) worried. **inquie'tudine** *nf* anxiety

inqui'lino, -a *nmf* tenant

inquina'mento *nm* pollution

inqui'na|re *vt* pollute. **~to** *a* polluted

inqui'rente *a* Jur ⟨*magistrato*⟩ examining; **commissione ~** commission of enquiry

inqui'si|re *vt/i* investigate. **~to** *a* under investigation. **~'tore, ~'trice** *a* inquiring ● *nmf* inquisitor. **~zi'one** *nf* inquisition

insabbi'are *vt* shelve

insa'lat|a *nf* salad. **~a belga** endive. **~i'era** *nf* salad bowl

insa'lubre *a* unhealthy

insa'nabile *a* incurable

insangui'na|re *vt* cover with blood. **~to** *a* bloody

insapo'nare *vt* soap

insa'po|re *a* tasteless. **~'rire** *vt* flavour

insa'puta *nf* **all'~ di** unknown to

insazi'abile *a* insatiable

insce'nare *vt* stage

inscin'dibile *a* inseparable

insedia'mento *nm* installation

insedi'ar|e *vt* install. **~si** *vr* install oneself

in'segna *nf* sign; (*bandiera*) flag; (*decorazione*) decoration; (*emblema*) insignia *pl*; (*stemma*) symbol. **~ luminosa** neon sign

insegna'mento *nm* teaching. **inse'gnante** *a* teaching ● *nmf* teacher

inse'gnare *vt/i* teach; **~ qcsa a qcno** teach sb sth

insegui'mento *nmf* pursuit

insegu'i|re *vt* pursue. **~'tore, ~'trice** *nmf* pursuer

inselvati'chir|e *vt* make wild ● *vi*, **~si** *vr* grow wild

insemi'na|re *vt* inseminate. **~zi'one** *nf* insemination. **~zione artificiale** artificial insemination

insena'tura *nf* inlet

insen'sato *a* senseless; (*folle*) crazy

insen'sibil|e *a* insensitive; ⟨*braccio ecc*⟩ numb. **~ità** *nf* insensitivity

insepa'rabile *a* inseparable

inseri'mento *nm* insertion

inse'rir|e *vt* insert; place ⟨*annuncio*⟩;

Electr connect. **~si** *vr* **~si in** get into. **in'serto** *nm* file; (*in un film ecc*) insert

inservi'ente *nmf* attendant

inserzi'o|ne *nf* insertion; (*avviso*) advertisement. **~'nista** *nmf* advertiser

insetti'cida *nm* insecticide

in'setto *nm* insect

insicu'rezza *nf* insecurity. **insi'curo** *a* insecure

in'sidi|a *nf* trick; (*tranello*) snare. **~'are** *vt/i* lay a trap for. **~'oso** *a* insidious

insi'eme *adv* together; (*contemporaneamente*) at the same time ● *prep* **~ a** [together] with ● *nm* whole; (*completo*) outfit; *Theat* ensemble; *Math* set; **nell'~** as a whole; **tutto ~** all together; ⟨*bere*⟩ at one go

in'signe *a* renowned

insignifi'cante *a* insignificant

insi'gnire *vt* decorate

insinda'cabile *a* final

insinu'ante *a* insinuating

insinu'a|re *vt* insinuate. **~rsi** *vr* penetrate; **~rsi in** *fig* creep into. **~zi'one** *nf* insinuation

in'sipido *a* insipid

insi'sten|te *a* insistent. **~te'mente** *adv* repeatedly. **~za** *nf* insistence. **in'sistere** *vi* insist; (*perseverare*) persevere

insoddisfa'cente *a* unsatisfactory

insoddi'sfa|tto *a* unsatisfied; (*scontento*) dissatisfied. **~zi'one** *nf* dissatisfaction

insoffe'ren|te *a* intolerant. **~za** *nf* intolerance

insolazi'one *nf* sunstroke

inso'len|te *a* rude, insolent. **~za** *nf* rudeness, insolence; (*commento*) insolent remark

in'solito *a* unusual

inso'lubile *a* insoluble

inso'luto *a* unsolved; (*non pagato*) unpaid

insol'v|enza *nf* insolvency

in'somma *adv* in short; **~!** well really!; (*così così*) so so

in'sonne *a* sleepless. **~ia** *nf* insomnia

insonno'lito *a* sleepy

insonoriz'zato *a* soundproofed

insoppor'tabile *a* unbearable

insor'genza *nf* onset

in'sorgere *vi* revolt, rise up; (*sorgere*) arise; (*difficoltà*) crop up

insormon'tabile *a* ⟨*ostacolo, difficoltà*⟩ insurmountable

in'sorto *pp di* **insorgere** ● *a* rebellious ● *nm* rebel

insospet'tabile *a* unsuspected

insospet'tir|e *vt* make suspicious ● *vi*, **~si** *vr* become suspicious

insoste'nibile *a* untenable; (*insopportabile*) unbearable

insostitu'ibile *a* irreplaceable

inspe'ra|bile *a* **una sua vittoria è ~bile** there is no hope of him winning. **~to** *a* unhoped-for

inspie'gabile *a* inexplicable

inspi'rare *vt* breathe in

in'stabi|le *a* unstable; ⟨*tempo*⟩ changeable. **~ità** *nf* instability; (*di tempo*) changeability

instal'la|re *vt* install. **~rsi** *vr* settle in. **~zi'one** *nf* installation

instan'cabile *a* untiring

instau'ra|re *vt* found. **~rsi** *vr* become established. **~zi'one** *nf* foundation

instra'dare *vt* direct

insù *adv* **all'~** upwards

insubordinazi'one *nf* insubordination

insuc'cesso *nm* failure

insudici'ar|e *vt* dirty. **~si** *vr* get dirty

insuffici'en|te *a* insufficient; (*inadeguato*) inadequate ● *nf Sch* fail. **~za** *nf* insufficiency; (*inadeguatezza*) inadequacy; *Sch* fail. **~za cardiaca** heart failure. **~za di prove** lack of evidence

insu'lare *a* insular

insu'lina *nf* insulin

in'sulso *a* insipid; (*sciocco*) silly

insul'tare *vt* insult. **in'sulto** *nm* insult

insupe'rabile *a* insuperable; (*eccezionale*) incomparable

insurrezi'one *nf* insurrection

insussi'stente *a* groundless

intac'care *vt* nick; (*corrodere*) corrode; draw on ⟨*un capitale*⟩; (*danneggiare*) damage

intagli'are *vt* carve. **in'taglio** *nm* carving

intan'gibile *a* untouchable

in'tanto *adv* meanwhile; (*per ora*) for the moment; (*avversativo*) but; **~ che** while

intarsi'a|re *vt* inlay. **~to** *a* **~to di** inset with. **in'tarsio** *nm* inlay

inta'sa|re *vt* clog; block ⟨*traffico*⟩. **~rsi** *vr* get blocked. **~to** *a* blocked

inta'scare *vt* pocket

in'tatto *a* intact

intavo'lare *vt* start

inte'gra|le *a* whole; **edizione ~le** unabridged edition; **pane ~le** whole-

meal bread. **~l'mente** *adv* fully. **~nte** *a* integral. **'integro** *a* complete; (*retto*) upright

inte'gra|re *vt* integrate; (*aggiungere*) supplement. **~rsi** *vr* integrate. **~'tivo** *a* ⟨*corso*⟩ supplementary. **~zi'one** *nf* integration

integrità *nf* integrity

intelaia'tura *nf* framework

intel'letto *nm* intellect

intellettu'al|e *a* & *nmf* intellectual. **~'mente** *adv* intellectually

intelli'gen|te *a* intelligent. **~te'mente** *adv* intelligently. **~za** *nf* intelligence

intelli'gibil|e *a* intelligible. **~'mente** *adv* intelligibly

intempe'ranza *nf* intemperance

intem'perie *nfpl* bad weather

inten'den|te *nm* superintendent. **~za** *nf* **~za di finanza** inland revenue office

in'tender|e *vt* (*comprendere*) understand; (*udire*) hear; (*avere intenzione*) intend; (*significare*) mean. **~si** *vr* (*capirsi*) understand each other; **~si di** (*essere esperto*) have a good knowledge of

intendi'|mento *nm* understanding; (*intenzione*) intention. **~'tore**, **~'trice** *nmf* connoisseur

intene'rir|e *vt* soften; (*commuovere*) touch. **~si** *vr* be touched

intensa'mente *adv* intensely

intensifi'car|e *vt*, **~si** *vr* intensify

intensità *nf inv* intensity. **inten'sivo** *a* intensive. **in'tenso** *a* intense

inten'tare *vt* start up; **~ causa contro** qcno bring *o* institute proceedings against sb

in'tento *a* engrossed (**a** in) ● *nm* purpose

intenzio'nato *a* **essere ~ a fare** qcsa have the intention of doing sth

intenzio'nale *a* intentional. **intenzi'one** *nf* intention; **senza ~ne** unintentionally; **avere ~ne di fare qcsa** intend to do sth, have the intention of doing sth.

intera'gire *vi* interact

intera'mente *adv* completely, entirely

intera|t'tivo *a* interactive. **~zi'one** *nf* interaction

interca'lare[1] *nm* stock phrase

interca'lare[2] *vt* insert

intercam'biabile *a* interchangeable

interca'pedine *nf* cavity

inter'ce|dere *vi* intercede. **~ssi'one** *nf* intercession

intercet'ta|re *vt* intercept; tap *‹telefono›*. **~zi'one** *nf* interception. **~zione telefonica** telephone tapping

inter'city *nm inv* inter-city

intercontinen'tale *a* intercontinental

inter'correre *vi* *‹tempo:›* elapse; *‹esistere›* exist

interco'stale *a* intercostal

inter'detto *pp di* **interdire** ● *a* astonished; *(proibito)* forbidden; **rimanere ~** be taken aback

inter'di|re *vt* forbid; *Jur* deprive of civil rights. **~zi'one** *nf* prohibition

interessa'mento *nm* interest

interes'sante *a* interesting; **essere in stato ~** be pregnant

interes'sa|re *vt* interest; *(riguardare)* concern ● *vi* **~re a** matter to. **~rsi** *vr* **~rsi a** take an interest in. **~rsi di** take care of. **~to, -a** *nmf* interested party ● *a* interested; **essere ~to** *pej* have an interest

inte'resse *nm* interest; **fare qcsa per ~** do sth out of self-interest

inter'faccia *nf* *Comput* interface

interfe'renza *nf* interference

interfe'r|ire *vi* interfere

interiezi'one *nf* interjection

interi'ora *nfpl* entrails

interi'ore *a* interior

inter'ludio *nm* interlude

intermedi'ario, -a *a & nmf* intermediary

inter'medio *a* in-between

inter'mezzo *nm* *Theat, Mus* intermezzo

intermi'nabile *a* interminable

intermit'ten|te *a* intermittent; *‹luce›* flashing. **~za** *nf* **luce a ~za** flashing light

interna'mento *nm* internment; *(in manicomio)* committal

inter'nare *vt* intern; *(in manicomio)* commit [to a mental institution]

in'terno *a* internal; *Geog* inland; *(interiore)* inner; *‹politica›* national; **alunno ~** boarder ● *nm* interior; *(di ‘condominio)* flat; *Teleph* extension; *Cinema* interior shot; **all'~** inside

internazio'nale *a* international

in'tero *a* whole, entire; *(intatto)* intact; *(completo)* complete; **per ~** in full

interpel'lare *vt* consult

inter'por|re *vt* place *‹ostacolo›*. **~si** *vr* come between

interpre'ta|re *vt* interpret; *Mus* perform. **~zi'one** *nf* interpretation; *Mus* performance. **in'terprete** *nmf* interpreter; *Mus* performer

inter'ra|re *vt* *(seppellire)* bury; plant *‹pianta, seme›*. **~to** *nm* basement

interro'ga|re *vt* question; *Sch* test; examine *‹studenti›*. **~tiva'mente** *adv* questioningly. **~'tivo** *a* interrogative; *(sguardo)* questioning ● *nm* question. **punto ~tivo** question mark. **~'torio** *a & nm* questioning. **~zi'one** *nf* question; *Sch* oral [test]

inter'romper|e *vt* interrupt; *(sospendere)* stop; cut off *‹collegamento›*. **~si** *vr* break off

interrut'tore *nm* switch

interruzi'one *nf* interruption; **senza ~** non-stop. **~ di gravidanza** termination of pregnancy

interse|'care *vt,* **~'carsi** *vr* intersect. **~zi'one** *nf* intersection

inter'stizio *nm* interstice

interur'ban|a *nf* long-distance call. **~o** *a* inter-city; **telefonata ~a** long-distance call

interval'lare *vt* space out. **inter'vallo** *nm* interval; *(spazio)* space; *Sch* break. **intervallo pubblicitario** commercial break

interve'nire *vi* intervene; *(Med: operare)* operate; **~ a** take part in. **inter'vento** *nm* intervention; *(presenza)* presence; *(chirurgico)* operation; **pronto intervento** emergency services

inter'vista *nf* interview

intervi'sta|re *vt* interview. **~'tore, ~'trice** *nmf* interviewer

in'tes|a *nf* understanding; **cenno d'~a** acknowledgement. **~o** *pp di* **intendere** ● *a* **resta ~o che...** needless to say,...; **~il** agreed!; **~o a** meant to; **non darsi per ~o** refuse to understand

inte'sta|re *vt* head; write one's name and address at the top of *‹lettera›*; *Comm* register. **~rsi** *vr* **~rsi a fare qcsa** take it into one's head to do sth. **~'tario, -a** *nmf* holder. **~zi'one** *nf* heading; *(su carta da lettere)* letterhead

intesti'nale *a* intestinal

inte'stino *a* *‹lotte›* internal ● *nm* intestine

intima'mente *adv* *‹conoscere›* intimately

inti'ma|re *vt* order; **~re l'alt a qcno** order sb to stop. **~zi'one** *nf* order

intimida|'torio *a* threatening. **~zi'one** *nf* intimidation

intimi'dire *vt* intimidate

intimità *nf* cosiness. **'intimo** *a* intimate; (*interno*) innermost; ⟨*amico*⟩ close ● *nm* (*amico*) close friend; (*dell'animo*) heart

intimo'ri|re *vt* frighten. ~**rsi** *vr* get frightened. ~**to** *a* frightened

in'tingere *vt* dip

in'tingolo *nm* sauce; (*pietanza*) stew

intiriz'zi|re *vt* numb. ~**rsi** *vr* grow numb. ~**to** *a* **essere** ~**to** (*dal freddo*) be perished

intito'lar|e *vt* entitle; (*dedicare*) dedicate. ~**si** *vr* be called

intolle'rabile *a* intolerable

intona'care *vt* plaster. **in'tonaco** *nm* plaster

into'na|re *vt* start to sing; tune ⟨*strumento*⟩; (*accordare*) match. ~**rsi** *vr* match. ~**to** *a* ⟨*persona*⟩ able to sing in tune; ⟨*colore*⟩ matching

intonazi'one *nf* (*inflessione*) intonation; (*ironico*) tone

inton'ti|re *vt* daze; ⟨*gas:*⟩ make dizzy ● *vi* be dazed. ~**to** *a* dazed

intop'pare *vi* ~ **in** run into

in'toppo *nm* obstacle

in'torno *adv* around ● *prep* ~ **a** around; (*circa*) about

intorpi'di|re *vt* numb. ~**rsi** *vr* become numb. ~**to** *a* torpid

intossi'ca|re *vt* poison. ~**rsi** *vr* be poisoned. ~**zi'one** *nf* poisoning

intralci'are *vt* hamper

in'tralcio *nm* hitch; **essere d'~** be a hindrance (**a** to)

intrallaz'zare *vi* intrigue. **intral'lazzo** *nm* racket

intramon'tabile *a* timeless

intramusco'lare *a* intramuscular

intransi'gen|te *a* intransigent, uncompromising. ~**za** *nf* intransigence

intransi'tivo *a* intransitive

intrappo'lato *a* **rimanere** ~ be trapped

intrapren'den|te *a* enterprising. ~**za** *nf* initiative

intra'prendere *vt* undertake

intrat'tabile *a* very difficult

intrat'te'n|ere *vt* entertain. ~**ersi** *vr* linger. ~**i'mento** *nm* entertainment

intrave'dere *vt* catch a glimpse of; (*presagire*) foresee

intrecci'ar|e *vt* interweave; plait ⟨*capelli, corda*⟩. ~**si** *vr* intertwine; (*aggrovigliarsi*) become tangled; ~**e le mani** clasp one's hands

in'treccio *nm* (*trama*) plot

in'trepido *a* intrepid

intri'cato *a* tangled

intri'gante *a* scheming; (*affascinante*) intriguing

intri'ga|re *vt* entangle; (*incuriosire*) intrigue ● *vi* intrigue, scheme. ~**rsi** *vr* meddle. **in'trigo** *nm* plot; **intrighi** *pl* intrigues

in'trinseco *a* intrinsic

in'triso *a* ~ **di** soaked in

intri'stirsi *vr* grow sad

intro'du|rre *vt* introduce; (*inserire*) insert; ~**rre a** (*iniziare a*) introduce to. ~**rsi** *vr* get in (**in** to). ~**t'tivo** *a* ⟨*pagine, discorso*⟩ introductory. ~**zi'one** *nf* introduction

in'troito *nm* income, revenue; (*incasso*) takings *pl*

intro'metter|e *vt* introduce. ~**si** *vr* interfere; (*interporsi*) intervene. **intromissi'one** *nf* intervention

intro'vabile *a* that can't be found; ⟨*prodotto*⟩ unobtainable

intro'verso, -a *a* introverted ● *nmf* introvert

intrufo'larsi *vr* sneak in

in'truglio *nm* concoction

intrusi'one *nf* intrusion. **in'truso, -a** *nmf* intruder

intu'i|re *vt* perceive

intui|tiva'mente *adv* intuitively. ~**'tivo** *a* intuitive. **in'tuito** *nm* intuition. ~**zi'one** *nf* intuition

inugua'glianza *nf* inequality

inu'mano *a* inhuman

inu'mare *vt* inter

inumi'dir|e *vt* dampen; moisten ⟨*labbra*⟩. ~**si** *vr* become damp

in'util|e *a* useless; (*superfluo*) unnecessary. ~**ità** *nf* uselessness

inutiliz'za|bile *a* unusable. ~**to** *a* unused

inutil'mente *adv* fruitlessly

inva'dente *a* intrusive

in'vadere *vt* invade; (*affollare*) overun

invali'd|are *vt* invalidate. ~**ità** *nf* disability; *Jur* invalidity. **in'valido, -a** *a* invalid; (*handicappato*) disabled ● *nmf* disabled person

in'vano *adv* in vain

invari'abil|e *a* invariable

invari'ato *a* unchanged

invasi'one *nf* invasion. **in'vaso** *pp di* **invadere**. **inva'sore** *a* invading ● *nm* invader

invecchia'mento *nm* (*di vino*) maturation

invecchi'are *vt/i* age

in'vece *adv* instead; (*anzi*) but; ~ **di** instead of

inve'ire *vi* ~ **contro** inveigh against

inven'd|ibile *a* unsaleable. **~uto** *a* unsold

inven'tare *vt* invent

inventari'are *vt* make an inventory of. **inven'tario** *nm* inventory

inven|'tivo, -a *a* inventive ● *nf* inventiveness. **~'tore, ~'trice** *nmf* inventor. **~zi'one** *nf* invention

inver'nale *a* wintry. **in'verno** *nm* winter

invero'simile *a* improbable

inversa'mente *adv* inversely; ~ **proporzionale** in inverse proportion

inversi'one *nf* inversion; *Mech* reversal. **in'verso** *a* inverse; (*opposto*) opposite ● *nm* opposite

inverte'brato *a & nm* invertebrate

inver'ti|re *vt* reverse; (*capovolgere*) turn upside down. **~to, -a** *nmf* homosexual

investi'ga|re *vt* investigate. **~'tore** *nm* investigator. **~zi'one** *nf* investigation

investi'mento *nm* investment; (*incidente*) crash

inve'sti|re *vt* invest; (*urtare*) collide with; (*travolgere*) run over; **~re qcno di** invest sb with. **~'tura** *nf* investiture

invet'tiva *nf* invective

invi'a|re *vt* send. **~to, -a** *nmf* envoy; (*di giornale*) correspondent

invidi|a *nf* envy. **~'are** *vt* envy. **~'oso** *a* envious

invigo'rir|e *vt* invigorate. **~si** *vr* become strong

invin'cibile *a* invincible

in'vio *nm* dispatch; *Comput* enter

invio'labile *a* inviolable

invipe'ri|rsi *vr* get nasty. **~to** *a* furious

invi'sibil|e *a* invisible. **~ità** *nf* invisibility

invi'tante *a* (*piatto, profumo*) enticing

invi'ta|re *vt* invite. **~to, -a** *nmf* guest. **in'vito** *nm* invitation

invo'ca|re *vt* invoke; (*implorare*) beg. **~zi'one** *nf* invocation

invogli'ar|e *vt* tempt; (*indurre*) induce. **~si** *vr* **~si di** take a fancy to

involon|taria'mente *adv* involuntarily. **~'tario** *a* involuntary

invol'tino *nm* *Culin* beef olive

in'volto *nm* parcel; (*fagotto*) bundle

in'volucro *nm* wrapping

invulne'rabile *a* invulnerable

inzacche'rare *vt* splash with mud

inzup'par|e *vt* soak; (*intingere*) dip. **~si** *vr* get soaked

'io *pron* I; **chi è?** – **[sono] io** who is it? – [it's] me; **l'ho fatto io [stesso]** I did it myself ● *nm* **l'~** the ego

i'odio *nm* iodine

l'onio *nm* **lo** ~ the Ionian [Sea]

i'osa: a ~ *adv* in abundance

iperat'tivo *a* hyperactive

ipermer'cato *nm* hypermarket

iper'metrope *a* long-sighted

ipersen'sibile *a* hypersensitive

ipertensi'one *nf* high blood pressure

ip'no|si *nf* hypnosis. **~tico** *a* hypnotic. **~'tismo** *nm* hypnotism. **~tiz'zare** *vt* hypnotize

ipoca'lorico *a* low-calorie

ipocon'driaco, -a *a & nmf* hypochondriac

ipocri'sia *nf* hypocrisy. **i'pocrita** *a* hypocritical ● *nmf* hypocrite

ipo'te|ca *nf* mortgage. **~'care** *vt* mortgage

i'potesi *nf inv* hypothesis; (*caso, eventualità*) eventuality. **ipo'tetico** *a* hypothetical. **ipotiz'zare** *vt* hypothesize

'ippico, -a *a* horse *attrib* ● *nf* riding

ippoca'stano *nm* horse-chestnut

ip'podromo *nm* racecourse

ippo'potamo *nm* hippopotamus

'ira *nf* anger. **~'scibile** *a* irascible

i'rato *a* irate

'iride *nf* *Anat* iris; (*arcobaleno*) rainbow

Ir'lan|da *nf* Ireland. **~da del Nord** Northern Ireland. **i~'dese** *a* Irish ● *nm* Irishman; (*lingua*) Irish ● *nf* Irishwoman

iro'nia *nf* irony. **i'ronico** *a* ironic[al]

irradi'a|re *vt/i* radiate. **~zi'one** *nf* radiation

irraggiun'gibile *a* unattainable

irragio'nevole *a* unreasonable; (*speranza, timore*) irrational; (*assurdo*) absurd

irrazio'nal|e *a* irrational. **~ità** *a* irrationality. **~'mente** *adv* irrationally

irre'a|le *a* unreal. **~'listico** *a* unrealistic. **~liz'zabile** *a* unattainable. **~ltà** *nf* unreality

irrecupe'rabile *a* irrecoverable

irrego'lar|e *a* irregular. **~ità** *nf inv* irregularity

irremo'vibile *a fig* adamant

irrepa'rabile *a* irreparable

irrepe'ribile *a* not to be found; **sarò** ~ I won't be contactable

irrepren'sibile *a* irreproachable

irrepri'mibile *a* irrepressible

irrequi'eto *a* restless

irresi'stibile *a* irresistible

irrespon'sabil|e *a* irresponsible. **~ità** *nf* irresponsibility

irrever'sibile *a* irreversible

irrevo'cabile *a* irrevocable

irricono'scibile *a* unrecognizable

irri'ga|re *vt* irrigate; ⟨*fiume:*⟩ flow through. **~zi'one** *nf* irrigation

irrigidi'mento *nm* stiffening

irrigi'dir|e *vt*, **~si** *vr* stiffen

irrile'vante *a* unimportant

irrimedi'abile *a* irreparable

irripe'tibile *a* unrepeatable

irri'sorio *a* derisive; ⟨*differenza, particolare, somma:*⟩ insignificant

irri'ta|bile *a* irritable. **~nte** *a* aggravating

irri'ta|re *vt* irritate. **~rsi** *vr* get annoyed. **~to** *a* irritated; ⟨*gola:*⟩ sore. **~zi'one** *nf* irritation

irrobu'stir|e *vt* fortify. **~si** *vr* get stronger

ir'rompere *vi* burst (**in** into)

irro'rare *vt* sprinkle

irru'ente *a* impetuous

irruzi'one *nf* **fare ~ in** burst into

i'scritto, -a *pp di* **iscrivere** ● *a* registered ● *nmf* member; **per ~** in writing

i'scriver|e *vt* register. **~si** *vr* **~si a** register at, enrol at ⟨*scuola*⟩; join ⟨*circolo ecc*⟩. **iscrizi'one** *nf* registration; ⟨*epigrafe*⟩ inscription

i'sla|mico *a* Islamic. **~'mismo** *nm* Islam

I'slan|da *nf* Iceland. **i~'dese** *a* Icelandic ● *nmf* Icelander

'isola *nf* island. **le isole britanniche** the British Isles. **~ pedonale** traffic island. **~ spartitraffico** traffic island. **iso'lano, -a** *a* insular ● *nmf* islander

iso'lante *a* insulating ● *nm* insulator

iso'la|re *vt* isolate; *Mech, Electr* insulate; ⟨*acusticamente*⟩ soundproof. **~to** *a* isolated ● *nm* ⟨*di appartamenti*⟩ block

ispes'sir|e *vt*, **~si** *vr* thicken

ispetto'rato *nm* inspectorate. **ispet-**

'tore *nm* inspector. **ispezio'nare** *vt* inspect. **ispezi'one** *nf* inspection

'ispido *a* bristly

ispi'ra|re *vt* inspire; suggest ⟨*idea, soluzione*⟩. **~rsi** *vr* **~rsi a** be based on. **~to** *a* inspired. **~zi'one** *nf* inspiration; ⟨*idea*⟩ idea

Isra'el|e *nm* Israel. **i~i'ano, -a** *a* & *nmf* Israeli

is'sare *vt* hoist

istan'taneo, -a *a* instantaneous ● *nf* snapshot

i'stante *nm* instant; **all'~** instantly

i'stanza *nf* petition

i'sterico *a* hysterical. **iste'rismo** *nm* hysteria

isti'ga|re *vt* instigate; **~re qcno al male** incite sb to evil. **~'tore**, **~'trice** *nmf* instigator. **~zi'one** *nf* instigation

istin|tiva'mente *adv* instinctively. **~'tivo** *a* instinctive. **i'stinto** *nm* instinct; **d'istinto** instinctively

istitu'ire *vt* institute; ⟨*fondare*⟩ found; initiate ⟨*manifestazione*⟩

isti'tu|to *nm* institute; ⟨*universitario*⟩ department; *Sch* secondary school. **~to di bellezza** beauty salon. **~'tore**, **~'trice** *nmf* ⟨*insegnante*⟩ tutor; ⟨*fondatore*⟩ founder

istituzio'nale *a* institutional. **istituzi'one** *nf* institution

'istmo *nm* isthmus

'istrice *nm* porcupine

istru'i|re *vt* instruct; ⟨*addestrare*⟩ train; ⟨*informare*⟩ inform; *Jur* prepare. **~to** *a* educated

istrut't|ivo *a* instructive. **~ore**, **~rice** *nmf* instructor; **giudice ~ore** examining magistrate. **~'oria** *nf Jur* investigation. **istruzi'one** *nf* education; ⟨*indicazione*⟩ instruction

I'tali|a *nf* Italy. **i~'ano, -a** *a* & *nmf* Italian

itine'rario *nm* route, itinerary

itte'rizia *nf* jaundice

'ittico *a* fishing *attrib*

I.V.A. *nf abbr* (**imposta sul valore aggiunto**) VAT

jack *nm inv* jack
jazz *nm* jazz. **jaz'zista** *nmf* jazz player
jeep *nf inv* jeep
'jolly *nm inv* (*carta da gioco*) joker

Jugo'slav|ia *nf* Yugoslavia. **j~o, -a** *a*
& *nmf* Yugoslav[ian]
ju'niores *nmfpl Sport* juniors

ka'jal *nm inv* kohl
kara'oke *nm inv* karaoke
karatè *nm* karate

kg *abbr* (**chilogrammo**) kg
km *abbr* (**chilometro**) km

l' *def art mf* (*before vowel*) the; *vedi* **il**
la *def art f* the; *vedi* **il** ● *pron* (*oggetto,
riferito a persona*) her; (*riferito a cosa,
animale*) it; (*forma di cortesia*) you
● *nm inv Mus* (*chiave, nota*) A
là *adv* there; **di là** (*in quel luogo*)
in there; (*da quella parte*) that
way; **eccolo là!** there he is!; **farsi
più in là** (*far largo*) make way; **là
dentro** in there; **là fuori** out there;
[ma] **va là!** come off it!; **più in là** (*nel
tempo*) later on; (*nello spazio*) further
on
'labbro *nm* (*pl nf Anat* **labbra**) lip
labi'rinto *nm* labyrinth; (*di sentieri
ecc*) maze
labora'torio *nm* laboratory; (*di negozio, officina ecc*) workshop
labori'oso *a* (*operoso*) industrious;
(*faticoso*) laborious
labu'rista *a* Labour ● *nmf* member of
the Labour Party

'lacca *nf* lacquer; (*per capelli*)
hairspray, lacquer. **lac'care** *vt* lacquer
'laccio *nm* noose; (*lazo*) lasso; (*trappola*) snare; (*stringa*) lace
lace'rante *a* (*grido*) earsplitting
lace'ra|re *vt* tear; lacerate (*carne*).
~rsi *vr* tear. **~zi'one** *nf* laceration.
'lacero *a* torn; (*cencioso*) ragged
la'conico *a* laconic
'lacri|ma *nf* tear; (*goccia*) drop.
~'mare *vi* weep. **~'mevole** *a* tear-jerk-
ing
lacri'mogeno *a* gas **~** tear gas
lacri'moso *a* tearful
la'cuna *nf* gap. **lacu'noso** *a* (*preparazione, resoconto*) incomplete
la'custre *a* lake *attrib*
lad'dove *conj* whereas
'ladro, -a *nmf* thief; **al ~!** stop thief!
~'cinio *nm* theft. **la'druncolo** *nm* petty
thief
'lager *nm inv* concentration camp

laggiù *adv* down there; (*lontano*) over there

'lagna *nf* (*fam: persona*) moaning Minnie; (*film*) bore

la'gna|nza *nf* complaint. **~rsi** *vr* moan; (*protestare*) complain (**di** about). **la'gnoso** *a* ⟨*persona*⟩ moaning

'lago *nm* lake

la'guna *nf* lagoon

'laico, -a *a* lay; ⟨*vita*⟩ secular ● *nm* layman ● *nf* laywoman

'lama *nf* blade ● *nm inv* (*animale*) llama

lambic'carsi *vr* **~ il cervello** rack one's brains

lam'bire *vt* lap

lamé *nm inv* lamé

lamen'tar|e *vt* lament. **~si** *vr* moan. **~si di** (*lagnarsi*) complain about

lamen'te|la *nf* complaint. **~vole** *a* mournful; (*pietoso*) pitiful. **la'mento** *nm* moan

la'metta *nf* **~ [da barba]** razor blade

lami'era *nf* sheet metal

'lamina *nf* foil. **~ d'oro** gold leaf

lami'na|re *vt* laminate. **~to** *a* laminated ● *nm* laminate; (*tessuto*) lamé

'lampa|da *nf* lamp. **~da abbronzante** sunlamp. **~da a pila** torch. **~'dario** *nm* chandelier. **~'dina** *nf* light bulb

lam'pante *a* clear

lampeggi'a|re *vi* flash. **~'tore** *nm* Auto indicator

lampi'one *nm* street lamp

'lampo *nm* flash of lightning; (*luce*) flash; **lampi** *pl* lightning *sg*. **~ di genio** stroke of genius. **[cerniera] ~** zip [fastener], zipper *Am*

lam'pone *nm* raspberry

'lana *nf* wool; **di ~** woollen. **~ d'acciaio** steel wool. **~ vergine** new wool. **~ di vetro** glass wool

lan'cetta *nf* pointer; (*di orologio*) hand

'lancia *nf* (*arma*) spear, lance; *Naut* launch

lanci'ar|e *vt* throw; (*da un aereo*) drop; launch ⟨*missile, prodotto*⟩; give ⟨*grido*⟩; **~e uno sguardo a** glance at. **~si** *vr* fling oneself; (*intraprendere*) launch out

lanci'nante *a* piercing

'lancio *nm* throwing; (*da aereo*) drop; (*di missile, prodotto*) launch. **~ del disco** discus [throwing]. **~ del giavellotto** javelin [throwing]. **~ del peso** putting the shot

'landa *nf* heath

'languido *a* languid

lani'ero *a* wool

lani'ficio *nm* woollen mill

lan'terna *nf* lantern; (*faro*) lighthouse

la'nugine *nf* down

lapi'dare *vt* stone; *fig* demolish

lapi'dario *a* (*conciso*) terse

'lapide *nf* tombstone; (*commemorativa*) memorial tablet

'lapis *nm inv* pencil

'lapsus *nm inv* lapse, error

'lardo *nm* lard

larga'mente *adv* (*ampiamente*) widely

lar'ghezza *nf* width, breadth; *fig* liberality. **~ di vedute** broadmindedness

'largo *a* wide; (*ampio*) broad; ⟨*abito*⟩ loose; (*liberale*) liberal; (*abbondante*) generous; **stare alla larga** keep away; **~ di manica** generous; **essere ~ di spalle/vedute** be broad-shouldered/minded ● *nm* width; **andare al ~** *Naut* go out to sea; **fare ~** make room; **farsi ~** make one's way; **al ~ di** off the coast of

'larice *nm* larch

la'ringe *nf* larynx. **larin'gite** *nf* laryngitis

'larva *nf* larva; (*persona emaciata*) shadow

la'sagne *nfpl* lasagna *sg*

lasciapas'sare *nm inv* pass

lasci'ar|e *vt* leave; (*rinunciare*) give up; (*rimetterci*) lose; (*smettere di tenere*) let go [of]; (*concedere*) let; **~e di fare qcsa** (*smettere*) stop doing sth; **lascia perdere!** forget it!; **lascialo venire, lascia che venga** let him come. **~si** *vr* (*reciproco*) leave each other, split up; **~si andare** let oneself go

'lascito *nm* legacy

'laser *a & nm inv* **[raggio] ~** laser [beam]

lassa'tivo *a & nm* laxative

'lasso *nm* **~ di tempo** period of time

lassù *adv* up there

'lastra *nf* slab; (*di ghiaccio*) sheet; (*di metallo, Phot*) plate; (*radiografia*) X-ray [plate]

lastri'ca|re *vt* pave. **~to, 'lastrico** *nm* pavement; **sul lastrico** on one's beam-ends

la'tente *a* latent

late'rale *a* side *attrib*; *Med, Techn ecc* lateral; **via ~** side street

late'rizi *nmpl* bricks

lati'fondo *nm* large estate

la'tino *a & nm* Latin

lati'tan|te *a* in hiding ● *nmf* fugitive [from justice]

lati'tudine *nf* latitude

'lato *a* (*ampio*) broad; **in senso ~** broadly speaking ● *nm* side; (*aspetto*) aspect; **a ~ di** beside; **dal ~ mio** (*punto di vista*) for my part; **d'altro ~** *fig* on the other hand

la'tra|re *vi* bark. **~to** *nm* barking

la'trina *nf* latrine

'latta *nf* tin, can

lat'taio *nm* milkman

lat'tante *a* breast-fed ● *nmf* suckling

'latt|e *nm* milk. **~e acido** sour milk. **~e condensato** condensed milk. **~e detergente** skin cleanser. **~e in polvere** powdered milk. **~e scremato** skimmed milk. **~eo** *a* milky. **~e'ria** *nf* dairy. **~i'cini** *nmpl* dairy products. **~i'era** *nf* milk jug

lat'tina *nf* can

lat'tuga *nf* lettuce

'laure|a *nf* degree; **prendere la ~a** graduate. **~'ando, -a** *nmf* final-year student

laure'a|rsi *vr* graduate. **~to, -a** *a* & *nmf* graduate

'lauro *nm* laurel

'lauto *a* lavish; **guadagno ~** handsome profit

'lava *nf* lava

la'vabile *a* washable

la'vabo *nm* wash-basin

la'vaggio *nm* washing. **~ automatico** (*per auto*) carwash. **~ del cervello** brainwashing. **~ a secco** dry-cleaning

la'vagna *nf* slate; *Sch* blackboard

la'van|da *nf* wash; *Bot* lavender; **fare una ~da gastrica** have one's stomach pumped. **~'daia** *nf* washerwoman. **~de'ria** *nf* laundry. **~deria automatica** launderette

lavan'dino *nm* sink; (*hum: persona*) bottomless pit

lavapi'atti *nmf inv* dishwasher

la'var|e *vt* wash; **~e i piatti** wash up. **~si** *vr* wash, have a wash; **~si i denti** brush one's teeth; **~si le mani** wash one's hands

lava'secco *nmf inv* dry-cleaner's

lavasto'viglie *nf inv* dishwasher

la'vata *nf* wash; **darsi una ~** have a wash; **~ di capo** *fig* scolding

lava'tivo, -a *nmf* idler

lava'trice *nf* washing-machine

lavo'rante *nmf* worker

lavo'ra|re *vi* work ● *vt* work; knead (*pasta ecc*); till (*la terra*); **~re a maglia** knit. **~'tivo** *a* working. **~to** *a* (*pietra, legno*) carved; (*cuoio*) tooled; (*metallo*) wrought. **~'tore, ~'trice** *nmf* worker

● *a* working. **~zi'one** *nf* manufacture; (*di terra*) working; (*artigianale*) workmanship; (*del terreno*) cultivation.

lavo'rio *nm* intense activity

la'voro *nm* work; (*faticoso, sociale*) labour; (*impiego*) job; *Theat* play; **mettersi al ~** set to work (**su** on). **~ a maglia** knitting. **~ nero** moonlighting. **~ straordinario** overtime. **~ a tempo pieno** full-time job. **lavori** *pl* **di casa** housework. **lavori** *pl* **in corso** roadworks. **lavori** *pl* **forzati** hard labour. **lavori** *pl* **stradali** roadworks

le *def art fpl* the; *vedi* **il** ● *pron* (*oggetto*) them; (*a lei*) her; (*forma di cortesia*) you

le'al|e *a* loyal. **~'mente** *adv* loyally. **~tà** *nf* loyalty

'lebbra *nf* leprosy

'lecca 'lecca *nm inv* lollipop

leccapi'edi *nmf inv pej* bootlicker

lec'ca|re *vt* lick; *fig* suck up to. **~rsi** *vr* lick; (*fig: agghindarsi*) doll oneself up; **da ~rsi i baffi** mouth-watering. **~ta** *nf* lick

leccor'nia *nf* delicacy

'lecito *a* lawful; (*permesso*) permissibile

'ledere *vt* damage; *Med* injure

'lega *nf* league; (*di metalli*) alloy; **far ~ con qcno** take up with sb

le'gaccio *nm* string; (*delle scarpe*) shoelace

le'gal|e *a* legal ● *nm* lawyer. **~ità** *nf* legality. **~iz'zare** *vt* authenticate; (*rendere legale*) legalize. **~'mente** *adv* legally

le'game *nm* tie; (*amoroso*) liaison; (*connessione*) link

lega'mento *nm* *Med* ligament

le'gar|e *vt* tie; tie up (*persona*); tie together (*due cose*); (*unire, rilegare*) bind; alloy (*metalli*); (*connettere*) connect; **~sela al dito** bear a grudge ● *vi* (*far lega*) get on well. **~si** *vr* bind oneself; **~si a qcno** become attached to sb

le'gato *nm* legacy; *Relig* legate

lega'tura *nf* tying; (*di libro*) binding

le'genda *nf* legend

'legge *nf* law; (*parlamentare*) act; **a norma di ~** by law

leg'genda *nf* legend; (*didascalia*) caption. **leggen'dario** *a* legendary

'leggere *vt/i* read

legge'r|ezza *nf* lightness; (*frivolezza*) frivolity; (*incostanza*) fickleness. **~'mente** *adv* slightly

leg'gero *a* light; (*bevanda*) weak; (*lieve*) slight; (*frivolo*) frivolous; (*incostante*) fickle; **alla leggera** frivolously

leg'gibile *a* ‹scrittura› legible; ‹stile› readable

leg'gio *nm* lectern; *Mus* music stand

legife'rare *vi* legislate

legio'nario *nm* legionary. **legi'one** *nf* legion

legisla'tivo *a* legislative. **~'tore** *nm* legislator. **~'tura** *nf* legislature. **~zi'one** *nf* legislation

legittimità *nf* legitimacy. **le'gittimo** *a* legitimate; ‹giusto› proper; **legittima difesa** self-defence

'legna *nf* firewood

le'gname *nm* timber

le'gnata *nf* blow with a stick

'legno *nm* wood; **di ~** wooden. **~ compensato** plywood. **le'gnoso** *a* woody

le'gume *nm* pod

'lei *pron* ‹soggetto› she; ‹oggetto, con prep› her; ‹forma di cortesia› you; **lo ha fatto ~ stessa** she did it herself

'lembo *nm* edge; ‹di terra› strip

'lemma *nm* headword

'lena *nf* vigour

le'nire *vt* soothe

lenta'mente *adv* slowly

'lente *nf* lens. **~ a contatto** contact lens. **~ d'ingrandimento** magnifying glass

len'tezza *nf* slowness

len'ticchia *nf* lentil

len'tiggine *nf* freckle

'lento *a* slow; ‹allentato› slack; ‹abito› loose

'lenza *nf* fishing-line

len'zuolo *nm* (*pl f* **lenzuola**) *nm* sheet

le'one *nm* lion; *Astr* Leo

leo'pardo *nm* leopard

'lepre *nf* hare

'lercio *a* filthy

'lesbica *nf* lesbian

lesi'nare *vt* grudge ● *vi* be stingy

lesio'nare *vt* damage. **lesi'one** *nf* lesion

'leso *pp di* ledere ● *a* injured

les'sare *vt* boil

'lessico *nm* vocabulary

'lesso *a* boiled ● *nm* boiled meat

'lesto *a* quick; ‹mente› sharp

le'tale *a* lethal

leta'maio *nm* dunghill; *fig* pigsty. **le'tame** *nm* dung

le'targ|ico *a* lethargic. **~o** *nm* lethargy; ‹di animali› hibernation

le'tizia *nf* joy

'lettera *nf* letter; **alla ~** literally; **~ maiuscola** capital letter; **~ minuscola** small letter; **lettere** *pl* ‹letteratura› literature *sg*; *Univ* Arts; **dottore in lettere** BA, Bachelor of Arts

lette'rale *a* literal

lette'rario *a* literary

lette'rato *a* well-read

lettera'tura *nf* literature

let'tiga *nf* stretcher

let'tino *nm* cot; *Med* couch

'letto *nm* bed. **~ a castello** bunkbed. **~ a una piazza** single bed. **~ a due piazze** double bed. **~ matrimoniale** double bed

letto'rato *nm* ‹corso› ≈ tutorial

let'tore, -'trice *nmf* reader; *Univ* language assistant ● *nm* *Comput* disk drive. **~ di CD-ROM** CD-Rom drive

let'tura *nf* reading

leuce'mia *nf* leukaemia

'leva *nf* lever; *Mil* call-up; **far ~** lever. **~ del cambio** gear lever

le'vante *nm* East; ‹vento› east wind

le'va|re *vt* ‹alzare› raise; ‹togliere› take away; ‹rimuovere› take off; ‹estrarre› pull out; **~re di mezzo** qcsa get sth out of the way. **~rsi** *vr* rise; ‹da letto› get up; ‹allontanarsi› get out of; **~rsi di mezzo** get out of the way. **~ta** *nf* rising; ‹di posta› collection

leva'taccia *nf* **fare una ~** get up at the crack of dawn

leva'toio *a* **ponte ~** drawbridge

levi'ga|re *vt* smooth; ‹con carta vetro› rub down. **~to** *a* ‹superficie› polished

levri'ero *nm* greyhound

lezi'one *nf* lesson; *Univ* lecture; ‹rimprovero› rebuke

lezi'oso *a* ‹stile, modi› affected

li *pron mpl* them

lì *adv* there; **fin lì** as far as there; **giù di lì** thereabouts; **lì per lì** there and then

Li'bano *nm* Lebanon

'libbra *nf* ‹peso› pound

li'beccio *nm* south-west wind

li'bellula *nf* dragon-fly

libe'rale *a* liberal; ‹generoso› generous ● *nmf* liberal

libe'ra|re *vt* free; release ‹prigioniero›; vacate ‹stanza›; ‹salvare› rescue. **~rsi** *vr* ‹stanza:› become vacant; *Teleph* become free; ‹da impegno› get out of it; **~rsi di** get rid of. **~'tore, ~'trice** *a* liberating ● *nmf* liberator. **~'torio** *a* liberating. **~zi'one** *nf* liberation; **la L~zione** ‹ricorrenza› Liberation Day

'liber|o *a* free; ‹strada› clear. **~o docente** qualified university lecturer. **~o professionista** self-employed person. **~tà** *nf inv* freedom; ‹di pri-

gioniero) release. **~tà provvisoria** *Jur* bail; **~tà** *pl* (*confidenze*) liberties

'liberty *nm & a inv* Art Nouveau

'Libi|a *nf* Libya. **l~co, -a** *a & nmf* Libyan

li'bidi|ne *nf* lust. **~'noso** *a* lustful. **li'bido** *nf* libido

libra'io *nm* bookseller

libre'ria *nf* (*negozio*) bookshop; (*mobile*) bookcase; (*biblioteca*) library

li'bretto *nm* booklet; *Mus* libretto. **~ degli assegni** cheque book. **~ di circolazione** logbook. **~ d'istruzioni** instruction booklet. **~ di risparmio** bankbook. **~ universitario** *book held by students which records details of their exam performances*

'libro *nm* book. **~ giallo** thriller. **~ paga** payroll

lice'ale *nmf* secondary-school student ● *a* secondary-school *attrib*

li'cenza *nf* licence; (*permesso*) permission; *Mil* leave; *Sch* school-leaving certificate; **essere in ~** be on leave

licenzia'mento *nm* dismissal

licenzi'a|re *vt* dismiss, sack *fam.* **~rsi** *vr* (*da un impiego*) resign; (*accomiatarsi*) take one's leave

li'ceo *nm* secondary school, high school. **~ classico** *secondary school with an emphasis on humanities.* **~ scientifico** *secondary school with an emphasis on sciences*

li'chene *nm* lichen

'lido *nm* beach

li'eto *a* glad; (*evento*) happy; **molto ~!** pleased to meet you!

li'eve *a* light; (*debole*) faint; (*trascurabile*) slight

lievi'tare *vi* rise ● *vt* leaven. **li'evito** *nm* yeast. **lievito in polvere** baking powder

'lifting *nm inv* face-lift

'ligio *a* **essere ~ al dovere** have a sense of duty

'lilla *nf Bot* lilac ● *nm* (*colore*) lilac

'lima *nf* file

limacci'oso *a* slimy

li'mare *vt* file

'limbo *nm* limbo

li'metta *nf* nail-file

limi'ta|re *nm* threshold ● *vt* limit. **~rsi** *vr* **~rsi a fare qcsa** restrict oneself to doing sth; **~rsi in qcsa** cut down on sth. **~'tivo** *a* limiting. **~to** *a* limited. **~zi'one** *nf* limitation

'limite *nm* limit; (*confine*) boundary. **~ di velocità** speed limit

li'mitrofo *a* neighbouring

limo'nata *nf* (*bibita*) lemonade; (*succo*) lemon juice

li'mone *nm* lemon; (*albero*) lemon tree

'limpido *a* clear; (*occhi*) limpid

'lince *nf* lynx

linci'are *vt* lynch

'lindo *a* neat; (*pulito*) clean

'linea *nf* line; (*di autobus, aereo*) route; (*di metro*) line; (*di abito*) cut; (*di auto, mobile*) design; (*fisico*) figure; **in ~ d'aria** as the crow flies; **è caduta la ~** I've been cut off; **in ~ di massima** as a rule; **a grandi linee** in outline; **mantenere la ~** keep one's figure; **in prima ~** in the front line; **mettersi in ~** line up; **nave di ~** liner; **volo di ~** scheduled flight. **~ d'arrivo** finishing line. **~ continua** unbroken line

linea'menti *nmpl* features

line'are *a* linear; (*discorso*) to the point; (*ragionamento*) consistent

line'etta *nf* (*tratto lungo*) dash; (*d'unione*) hyphen

lin'gotto *nm* ingot

'lingu|a *nf* tongue; (*linguaggio*) language. **~'accia** *nf* (*persona*) backbiter. **~'aggio** *nm* language. **~'etta** *nf* (*di scarpa*) tongue; (*di strumento*) reed; (*di busta*) flap

lingu'ist|a *nmf* linguist. **~ica** *nf* linguistics *sg.* **~ico** *a* linguistic

'lino *nm Bot* flax; (*tessuto*) linen

li'noleum *nm* linoleum

liofiliz'za|re *vt* freeze-dry. **~to** *a* freeze-dried

liposuzi'one *nf* liposuction

lique'far|e *vt*, **~si** *vr* liquefy; (*sciogliersi*) melt

liqui'da|re *vt* liquidate; settle (*conto*); pay off (*debiti*); clear (*merce*); (*fam: uccidere*) get rid of. **~zi'one** *nf* liquidation; (*di conti*) settling; (*di merce*) clearance sale

'liquido *a & nm* liquid

liqui'rizia *nf* liquorice

li'quore *nm* liqueur; **liquori** *pl* (*bevande alcooliche*) liquors

'lira *nf* lira; *Mus* lyre

'lirico, -a *a* lyrical; (*poesia*) lyric; (*cantante, musica*) opera *attrib* ● *nf* lyric poetry; *Mus* opera

'lisca *nf* fishbone; **avere la ~** (*fam: nel parlare*) have a lisp

lisci'are *vt* smooth; (*accarezzare*) stroke. **'liscio** *a* smooth; (*capelli*) straight; (*liquore*) neat; (*non gassato*) still; **passarla liscia** get away with it

'liso a worn [out]

'lista nf list; (striscia) strip; **in ~ di attesa** stand-by. **~ elettorale** electoral register. **~ di nozze** wedding list. **li'stare** vt edge; Comput list

li'stino nm list. **~ prezzi** price list

Lit. abbr (**lire italiane**) Italian lire

'lite nf quarrel; (baruffa) row; Jur lawsuit

liti'gare vi quarrel. **li'tigio** nm quarrel. **litigi'oso** a quarrelsome

lito'rale a coastal ● nm coast

'litro nm litre

li'turgico a liturgical

li'vella nf level. **~ a bolla d'aria** spirit level

livel'lar|e vt level. **~si** vr level out

li'vello nm level; **passaggio a ~** level crossing; **sotto/sul ~ del mare** below/above sea level

'livido a livid; (per il freddo) blue; (per una botta) black and blue ● nm bruise

Li'vorno nf Leghorn

'lizza nf lists pl; **essere in ~ per qcsa** be in the running for sth

lo def art m (before s + consonant, gn, ps, z) the; vedi **il** ● pron (riferito a persona) him; (riferito a cosa) it; **non lo so** I don't know

'lobo nm lobe

lo'cal|e a local ● nm (stanza) room; (treno) local train; **~i** pl (edifici) premises. **~e notturno** night-club. **~ità** nf inv locality

localiz'zare vt localize; (trovare) locate

lo'cand|a nf inn

locan'dina nf bill, poster

loca'|tario, -a nmf tenant. **~'tore, ~'trice** nm landlord ● nf landlady. **~zi'one** nf tenancy

locomo'|tiva nf locomotive. **~zi'one** nf locomotion; **mezzi di ~zione** means of transport

'loculo nm burial niche

lo'custa nf locust

locuzi'one nf expression

lo'dare vt praise. **'lode** nf praise; **laurea con lode** first-class degree

'loden nm inv (cappotto) loden coat

lo'devole a praiseworthy

'lodola nf lark

'loggia nf loggia; (massonica) lodge

loggi'one nm gallery, the gods

'logica nf logic

logica'mente adv (in modo logico) logically; (ovviamente) of course

'logico a logical

lo'gistica nf logistics sg

logo'rante a (esperienza) wearing

logo'ra|re vt wear out; (sciupare) waste. **~rsi** vr wear out; (persona) wear oneself out. **logo'rio** nm wear and tear. **'logoro** a worn-out

lom'baggine nf lumbago

Lombar'dia nf Lombardy

lom'bata nf loin. **'lombo** nm Anat loin

lom'brico nm earthworm

'Londra nf London

lon'gevo a long-lived

longi'lineo a tall and slim

longi'tudine nf longitude

lontana'mente adv distantly; (vagamente) vaguely; **neanche ~** not for a moment

lonta'nanza nf distance; (separazione) separation; **in ~** in the distance

lon'tano a far; (distante) distant; (nel tempo) far-off, distant; (parente) distant; (vago) vague; (assente) absent; **più ~** further ● adv far [away]; **da ~** from a distance; **tenersi ~ da** keep away from

'lontra nf otter

lo'quace a talkative

'lordo a dirty; (somma, peso) gross

'loro[1] pron pl (soggetto) they; (oggetto) them; (forma di cortesia) you; **sta a ~** it is up to them

'loro[2] (il ~ m, la ~ f, i ~ mpl, le ~ fpl) a their; (forma di cortesia) your; **un ~ amico** a friend of theirs; (forma di cortesia) a friend of yours ● pron theirs; (forma di cortesia) yours; **i ~** their folk

losanga nf lozenge; **a losanghe** diamond-shaped

'losco a suspicious

'loto nm lotus

'lott|a nf fight, struggle; (contrasto) conflict; Sport wrestling. **lot'tare** vi fight, struggle; Sport, fig wrestle. **~a'tore** nm wrestler

lotte'ria nf lottery

'lotto nm [national] lottery; (porzione) lot; (di terreno) plot

lozi'one nf lotion

lubrifi'ca|nte a lubricating ● nm lubricant. **~re** vt lubricate

luc'chetto nm padlock

lucci'ca|nte a sparkling. **~re** vi sparkle. **lucci'chio** nm sparkle

'luccio nm pike

'lucciola nf glow-worm

'luce nf light; **far ~ su** shed light on; **dare alla ~** give birth to. **~ della luna** moonlight. **luci pl di posizione** sidelights. **~ del sole** sunlight

lu'cen|te *a* shining. **~'tezza** *nf* shine

lucer'nario *nm* skylight

lu'certola *nf* lizard

lucida'labbra *nm inv* lip gloss

luci'da|re *vt* polish. **~'trice** *nf* [floor-]polisher. **'lucido** *a* shiny; ⟨*pavimento, scarpe*⟩ polished; ⟨*chiaro*⟩ clear; ⟨*persona, mente*⟩ lucid; ⟨*occhi*⟩ watery ● *nm* shine. **lucido [da scarpe]** [shoe] polish

lucra'tivo *a* lucrative. **'lucro** *nm* lucre

'luglio *nm* July

'lugubre *a* gloomy

'lui *pron* ⟨*soggetto*⟩ he; ⟨*oggetto, con prep*⟩ him; **lo ha fatto ~ stesso** he did it himself

lu'maca *nf* ⟨*mollusco*⟩ snail; *fig* slow-coach

'lume *nm* lamp; ⟨*luce*⟩ light; **a ~ di candela** by candlelight

luminosità *nf* brightness. **lumi'noso** *a* luminous; ⟨*stanza, cielo ecc*⟩ bright

'luna *nf* moon; **chiaro di ~** moonlight; **avere la ~ storta** be in a bad mood. **~ di miele** honeymoon

luna park *nm inv* fairground

lu'nare *a* lunar

lu'nario *nm* almanac; **sbarcare il ~** make both ends meet

lu'natico *a* moody

lunedì *nm inv* Monday

lu'netta *nf* half-moon [shape]

lun'gaggine *nf* slowness

lun'ghezza *nf* length. **~ d'onda** wavelength

'lungi *adv* ero **[ben] ~ dall'imma-ginare che...** I never dreamt for a moment that...

lungimi'rante *a* far-seeing

'lungo *a* long; ⟨*diluito*⟩ weak; ⟨*lento*⟩ slow; **saperla lunga** be shrewd ● *nm* length; **di gran lunga** by far; **andare per le lunghe** drag on ● *prep* ⟨*durante*⟩ throughout; ⟨*per la lunghezza di*⟩ along

lungofi'ume *nm* riverside

lungo'lago *nm* lakeside

lungo'mare *nm* sea front

lungome'traggio *nm* feature film

lu'notto *nm* rear window

lu'ogo *nm* place; ⟨*punto preciso*⟩ spot; ⟨*passo d'autore*⟩ passage; **aver ~** take place; **dar ~ a** give rise to; **del ~** ⟨*usanze*⟩ local. **~ comune** platitude. **~ pubblico** public place

luogote'nente *nm Mil* lieutenant

lu'petto *nm* Cub [Scout]

'lupo *nm* wolf

'luppolo *nm* hop

'lurido *a* filthy. **luri'dume** *nm* filth

lu'singa *nf* flattery

lusin'g|are *vt* flatter. **~arsi** *vr* flatter oneself; ⟨*illudersi*⟩ fool oneself. **~hi'ero** *a* flattering

lus'sa|re *vt*, **~rsi** *vr* dislocate. **~zi'one** *nf* dislocation

Lussem'burgo *nm* Luxembourg

'lusso *nm* luxury; **di ~** luxury

lussu'oso *a* luxurious

lussureggi'ante *a* luxuriant

lus'suria *nf* lust

lu'strare *vt* polish

lu'strino *nm* sequin

'lustro *a* shiny ● *nm* sheen; *fig* prestige; ⟨*quinquennio*⟩ five-year period

'lutt|o *nm* mourning; **~o stretto** deep mourning. **~u'oso** *a* mournful

Mm

m *abbr* ⟨**metro**⟩ m

ma *conj* but; ⟨*eppure*⟩ yet; **ma!** ⟨*dubbio*⟩ I don't know; ⟨*indignazione*⟩ really!; **ma davvero?** really?; **ma sì!** why not!; ⟨*certo che sì*⟩ of course!

'macabro *a* macabre

maccelle'ria *nf* butcher's [shop]

macché *int* of course not!

macche'roni *nmpl* macaroni *sg*

macche'ronico *a* ⟨*italiano*⟩ broken

'macchia¹ *nf* stain; ⟨*di diverso colore*⟩ spot; ⟨*piccola*⟩ speck; **senza ~** spotless

'macchia² *nf* ⟨*boscaglia*⟩ scrub; **darsi alla ~** take to the woods

macchi'a|re *vt*, **~rsi** *vr* stain. **~to a** ⟨*caffè*⟩ with a dash of milk; **~to di** ⟨*sporco*⟩ stained with

'macchina *nf* machine; ⟨*motore*⟩ engine; ⟨*automobile*⟩ car. **~ da cucire**

sewing machine. **~ da presa** cine camera. **~ da scrivere** typewriter

macchinal'mente adv mechanically

macchi'nare vt plot

macchi'nario nm machinery

macchi'netta nf (per i denti) brace

macchi'nista nm Rail engine-driver; Naut engineer; Theat stagehand

macchi'noso a complicated

mace'donia nf fruit salad

macel'la|io nm butcher. **~re** vt slaughter. **ma'cello** nm (mattatoio) slaughterhouse; fig shambles sg; **andare al macello** fig go to the slaughter; **mandare al macello** fig send to his/ her death

mace'rar|e vt macerate; fig distress. **~si** vr be consumed

ma'cerie nfpl rubble sg; (rottami) debris sg

ma'cigno nm boulder

maci'lento a emaciated

'macina nf millstone

macinacaffè nm inv coffee mill

macina'pepe nm inv pepper mill

maci'na|re vt mill. **~to** a ground ● nm (carne) mince. **maci'nino** nm mill; (hum: macchina) old banger

maciul'lare vt (stritolare) crush

macrobiotic|a nf **negozio di ~a** health-food shop. **~o** a macrobiotic

macro'scopico a macroscopic

macu'lato a spotted

'madido a **~ di** moist with

Ma'donna nf Our Lady

mador'nale a gross

madre nf mother. **~'lingua** a inv inglese **~lingua** English native speaker. **~'patria** nf native land. **~'perla** nf mother-of-pearl

ma'drina nf godmother

maestà nf majesty

maestosità nf majesty. **mae'stoso** a majestic

mae'strale nm northwest wind

mae'stranza nf workers pl

mae'stria nf mastery

ma'estro, -a nmf teacher ● nm master; Mus maestro. **~ di cerimonie** master of ceremonies ● a (principale) chief; (di grande abilità) skilful

'mafi|a nf Mafia. **~'oso** a of the Mafia ● nm member of the Mafia, Mafioso

'maga nf sorceress

ma'gagna nf fault

ma'gari adv (forse) maybe ● int I wish! ● conj (per esprimere desiderio) if only; (anche se) even if

magazzini'ere nm storesman, warehouseman. **magaz'zino** nm warehouse; (emporio) shop; **grande magazzino** department store

'maggio nm May

maggio'lino nm May bug

maggio'rana nf marjoram

maggio'ranza nf majority

maggio'rare vt increase

maggior'domo nm butler

maggi'ore a (di dimensioni, numero) bigger, larger; (superlativo) biggest, largest; (di età) older; (superlativo) oldest; (di importanza, Mus) major; (superlativo) greatest; **la maggior parte di** most; **la maggior parte del tempo** most of the time ● pron (di dimensioni) the bigger, the larger; (superlativo) the biggest, the largest; (di età) the older; (superlativo) the oldest; (di importanza) the major; (superlativo) the greatest ● nm Mil major; Aeron squadron leader. **maggio'renne** a of age ● nmf adult

maggior|i'tario a (sistema) first-past-the-post attrib. **~'mente** adv [all] the more; (più di tutto) most

'Magi nmpl **i re ~** the Magi

ma'gia nf magic; (trucco) magic trick **magica'mente** adv magically. **'magico** a magic

magi'stero nm (insegnamento) teaching; (maestria) skill; **facoltà di ~** arts faculty

magi'strale a masterly; **istituto ~e** teachers' training college

magi'stra|to nm magistrate. **~'tura** nf magistrature. **la ~tura** the Bench

'magli|a nf stitch; (lavoro ai ferri) knitting; (tessuto) jersey; (di rete) mesh; (di catena) link; (indumento) vest; **fare la ~a** knit. **~a diritta** knit. **~a rosa** (ciclismo) ≈ yellow jersey. **~a rovescia** purl. **~e'ria** nf knitwear. **~'etta** nf **~etta [a maniche corte]** tee-shirt. **~'ficio** nm knitwear factory. **ma'glina** nf (tessuto) jersey

magli'one nm sweater

'magma nm magma

ma'gnanimo a magnanimous

ma'gnate nm magnate

ma'gnesi|a nf magnesia. **~o** nm magnesium

ma'gne|te nm magnet. **~tico** a magnetic. **~'tismo** nm magnetism

magne'tofono nm tape recorder

magnifi|ca'mente adv magnificently. **~'cenza** nf magnificence;

(*generosità*) munificence. **ma'gnifico** *a* magnificent; (*generoso*) munificent

ma'gnolia *nf* magnolia

'mago *nm* magician

ma'gone *nm* **avere il ~** be down; **mi è venuto il ~** I had a lump in my throat

'magr|a *nf* low water. **ma'grezza** *nf* thinness. **~o** *a* thin; (*carne*) lean; (*scarso*) meagre

'mai *adv* never; (*inter, talvolta*) ever; **caso ~** if anything; **caso ~ tornasse** in case he comes back; **come ~?** why?; **cosa ~?** what on earth?; **~ più** never again; **più che ~** more than ever; **quando ~?** whenever?; **quasi ~** hardly ever

mai'ale *nm* pig; (*carne*) pork

mai'olica *nf* majolica

maio'nese *nf* mayonnaise

'mais *nm* maize

mai'uscol|a *nf* capital [letter]. **~o** *a* capital

mal *vedi* **male**

'mala *nf* **la ~** *sl* the underworld

mala'fede *nf* bad faith

malaf'fare *nm* **gente di ~** shady characters *pl*

mala'lingua *nf* backbiter

mala'mente *adv* (*ridotto*) badly

malan'dato *a* in bad shape; (*di salute*) in poor health

ma'lanimo *nm* ill will

ma'lanno *nm* misfortune; (*malattia*) illness; **prendersi un ~** catch something

mala'pena: a ~ *adv* hardly

ma'laria *nf* malaria

mala'ticcio *a* sickly

ma'lato, -a *a* ill, sick; (*pianta*) diseased ● *nmf* sick person. **~ di mente** mentally ill person. **malat'tia** *nf* disease, illness; **ho preso due giorni di malattia** I had two days off sick. **malattia venerea** venereal disease

malaugu'rato *a* ill-omened. **malau-'gurio** *nm* bad *o* ill omen

mala'vita *nf* underworld

mala'voglia *nf* unwillingness; **di ~** unwillingly

malcapi'tato *a* wretched

malce'lato *a* ill-concealed

mal'concio *a* battered

malcon'tento *nm* discontent

malco'stume *nm* immorality

mal'destro *a* awkward; (*inesperto*) inexperienced

maldi'cen|te *a* slanderous. **~za** *nf* slander

maldi'sposto *a* ill-disposed

'male *adv* badly; **funzionare ~** not work properly; **star ~** be ill; **star ~ a qcno** (*vestito ecc.*) not suit sb; **rimaner-ci ~** be hurt; **non c'è ~!** not bad at all! ● *nm* evil; (*dolore*) pain; (*malattia*) illness; (*danno*) harm. **distinguere il bene dal ~** know right from wrong; **andare a ~** go off; **aver ~ a** have a pain in; **dove hai ~?** where does it hurt?; **far ~ a qcno** (*provocare dolore*) hurt sb; (*cibo:*) be bad for sb; **le cipolle mi fanno ~** onions don't agree with me; **mi fa ~ la schiena** my back is hurting; **mal d'auto** car-sickness. **mal di denti** toothache. **mal di gola** sore throat. **mal di mare** sea-sickness; **avere il mal di mare** be sea-sick. **mal di pancia** stomach ache. **mal di testa** headache

male'detto *a* cursed; (*orribile*) awful

male'di|re *vt* curse. **~zi'one** *nf* curse; **~zione!** damn!

maledu|cata'mente *adv* rudely. **~'cato** *a* ill-mannered. **~cazi'one** *nf* rudeness

r ale'fatta *nf* misdeed

male'ficio *nm* witchcraft. **ma'lefico** *a* (*azione*) evil; (*nocivo*) harmful

maleodo'rante *a* foul-smelling

ma'lessere *nm* indisposition; *fig* uneasiness

ma'levolo *a* malevolent

malfa'mato *a* of ill repute

mal'fat|to *a* badly done; (*malformato*) ill-shaped. **~'tore** *nm* wrongdoer

mal'fermo *a* unsteady; (*salute*) poor

malfor'ma|to *a* misshapen. **~zi'one** *nf* malformation

malgo'verno *nm* misgovernment

mal'grado *prep* in spite of ● *conj* although

ma'lia *nf* spell

mali'gn|are *vi* malign. **~ità** *nf* malice; *Med* malignancy. **ma'ligno** *a* malicious; (*perfido*) evil; *Med* malignant

malinco'ni|a *nf* melancholy. **~ca-'mente** *adv* melancholically. **malin-'conico** *a* melancholy

malincu'ore: a ~ *adv* unwillingly, reluctantly

malinfor'mato *a* misinformed

malintenzio'nato, -a *nmf* miscreant

malin'teso *a* mistaken ● *nm* misunderstanding

ma'lizi|a *nf* malice; (*astuzia*) cunning; (*espediente*) trick. **~'oso** *a* malicious; (*birichino*) mischievous

malle'abile *a* malleable

mal'loppo *nm fam* loot

malme'nare vt ill-treat

mal'messo a (vestito male) shabbily dressed; (casa) poorly furnished; (fig: senza soldi) hard up

malnu'tri|to a undernourished. **~zi'one** nf malnutrition

'malo a **in ~ modo** badly

ma'locchio nm evil eye

ma'lora nf ruin; **della ~** awful; **andare in ~** go to ruin

ma'lore nm illness; **essere colto da ~** be suddenly taken ill

malri'dotto a (persona) in a sorry state

mal'sano a unhealthy

'malta nf mortar

mal'tempo nm bad weather

'malto nm malt

maltrat|ta'mento nm ill-treatment. **~'tare** vt ill-treat

malu'more nm bad mood; **di ~** in a bad mood

mal'vagi|o a wicked. **~tà** nf wickedness

malversazi'one nf embezzlement

mal'visto a unpopular (**da** with)

malvi'vente nm criminal

malvolenti'eri adv unwillingly

malvo'lere vt **farsi ~** make oneself unpopular

'mamma nf mummy, mum; **~ mia!** good gracious!

mam'mella nf breast

mam'mifero nm mammal

'mammola nf violet

ma'nata nf handful; (colpo) slap

'manca nf vedi **manco**

manca'mento nm **avere un ~** faint

man'can|te a missing. **~za** nf lack; (assenza) absence; (insufficienza) shortage; (fallo) fault; (imperfezione) defect; **in ~za d'altro** failing all else; **sento la sua ~za** I miss him

man'care vi be lacking; (essere assente) be missing; (venir meno) fail; (morire) pass away; **~ di** be lacking in; **~ a** fail to keep (promessa); **mi manca casa** I miss home; **mi manchi** I miss you; **mi è mancato il tempo** I didn't have [the] time; **mi mancano 1000 lire** I'm 1,000 lire short; **quanto manca alla partenza?** how long before we leave?; **è mancata la corrente** there was a power failure; **sentirsi ~** feel faint; **sentirsi ~ il respiro** be unable to breathe [properly] ● vt miss (bersaglio); **è mancato poco che cadesse** he nearly fell

'manche nf inv heat

man'chevole a defective

'mancia nf tip

manci'ata nf handful

man'cino a left-handed

'manco, -a a left ● nf left hand ● adv (nemmeno) not even

man'dante nmf (di delitto) instigator

manda'rancio nm clementine

man'dare vt send; (emettere) give off; utter (suono); **~ a chiamare** send for; **~ avanti la casa** run the house; **~ giù** (ingoiare) swallow

manda'rino nm Bot mandarin

man'data nf consignment; (di serratura) turn; **chiudere a doppia ~** double lock

man'dato nm (incarico) mandate; Jur warrant; (di pagamento) money order. **~ di comparizione [in giudizio]** subpoena. **~ di perquisizione** search warrant

man'dibola nf jaw

mando'lino nm mandolin

'mandor|la nf almond; **a ~la** (occhi) almond-shaped. **~'lato** nm nut brittle (type of nougat). **~lo** nm almond[-tree]

'mandria nf herd

maneg'gevole a easy to handle.

maneggi'are vt handle

ma'neggio nm handling; (intrigo) plot; (scuola di equitazione) riding school

ma'nesco a quick to hit out

ma'netta nf hand lever; **manette** pl handcuffs

man'forte nm **dare ~ a qcno** support sb

manga'nello nm truncheon

manga'nese nm manganese

mange'reccio a edible

mangia'dischi® nm inv type of portable record player

mangia'fumo a inv **candela** nf **~** air-purifying candle

mangia'nastri nm inv cassette player

mangi'a|re vt/i eat; (consumare) eat up; (corrodere) eat away; take (scacchi, carte ecc) ● nm eating; (cibo) food; (pasto) meal. **~rsi** vr **~rsi le parole** mumble; **~rsi le unghie** bite one's nails

mangi'ata nf big meal; **farsi una bella ~ di...** feast on...

mangia'toia nf manger

man'gime nm fodder

mangi'one, -a nmf fam glutton

mangiucchi'are vt nibble

'mango nm mango

ma'nia nf mania. **~ di grandezza** delu-

sions of grandeur. **~co, -a** a maniacal
● nmf maniac

'**manica** nf sleeve; (fam: gruppo) band;
a maniche lunghe long-sleeved; **essere in maniche di camicia** be in shirt
sleeves; **essere di ~ larga** be free with
one's money. **~ a vento** wind sock

'**Manica** nf **la ~** the [English] Channel

manica'retto nm tasty dish

mani'chetta nf hose

mani'chino nm (da sarto, vetrina)
dummy

'**manico** nm handle; Mus neck

mani'comio nm mental home; (fam:
confusione) tip

mani'cotto nm muff; Mech sleeve

mani'cure nf manicure ● nmf inv (persona) manicurist

mani'e|ra nf manner; **in ~ra che** so
that. **~'rato** a affected; (stile) mannered. **~'rismo** nm mannerism

manifat'tura nf manufacture;
(fabbrica) factory

manife'stante nmf demonstrator

manife'sta|re vt show; (esprimere) ex-
press ● vi demonstrate. **~rsi** vr show
oneself. **~zi'one** nf show; (espressione)
expression; (sintomo) manifestation;
(dimostrazione pubblica) demonstration

mani'festo a evident ● nm poster;
(dichiarazione pubblica) manifesto

ma'niglia nf handle; (sostegno, in autobus ecc) strap

manipo'la|re vt handle; (massaggiare)
massage; (alterare) adulterate; fig manipulate. **~'tore, ~'trice** nmf manipu-
lator. **~zi'one** nf handling; (massaggio)
massage; (alterazione) adulteration; fig
manipulation

mani'scalco nm smith

man'naia nf (scure) axe; (da macellaio)
cleaver

man'naro a lupo nm **~** werewolf

'**mano** nf hand; (strato di vernice ecc)
coat; **alla ~** informal; **fuori ~** out of the
way; **man ~** little by little; **man ~ che**
as; **sotto ~** to hand

mano'dopera nf labour

ma'nometro nm gauge

mano'mettere vt tamper with; (viola-
re) violate

ma'nopola nf (di apparecchio) knob;
(guanto) mitten; (su pullman) handle

mano'scritto a handwritten ● nm
manuscript

mano'vale nm labourer

mano'vella nf handle; Techn crank

ma'no|vra nf manoeuvre; Rail shunt-

ing; **fare le ~vre** manoeuvre. **~'vra-
bile** a fig easy to manipulate. **~'vrare** vt
(azionare) operate; fig manipulate
(persona) ● vi manoeuvre

manro'vescio nm slap

man'sarda nf attic

mansi'one nf task; (dovere) duty

mansu'eto a meek; (animale) do-cile

man'tell|a nf cape. **~o** nm cloak; (so-
prabito, di animale) coat; (di neve)
mantle

mante'ner|e vt (conservare) keep; (in
buono stato, sostentare) maintain. **~si**
vr **~si in forma** keep fit. **manteni-
'mento** nm maintenance

'**mantice** nm bellows pl; (di automobile) hood

'**manto** nm cloak; (coltre) mantle

manto'vana nf pelmet

manu'al|e a & nm manual. **~e d'uso**
user manual. **~'mente** adv manually

ma'nubrio nm handle; (di bicicletta)
handlebars pl; (per ginnastica) dumb-
bell

manu'fatto a manufactured

manutenzi'one nf maintenance

'**manzo** nm steer; (carne) beef

'**mappa** nf map

mappa'mondo nm globe

mar vedi mare

ma'rasma nm fig decline

mara'to|na nf marathon. **~'neta** nmf
marathon runner

'**marca** nf mark; Comm brand; (fabbricazione) make; (scontrino) ticket. **~
da bollo** revenue stamp

mar'ca|re vt mark; Sport score. **~ta-
'mente** adv markedly. **~to** a (tratto,
accento) strong, marked. **~'tore** nm (nel
calcio) scorer

mar'chese, -a nm marquis ● nf mar-
chioness

marchi'are vt brand

'**marchio** nm brand; (caratteristica)
mark. **~ di fabbrica** trademark. **~
registrato** registered trademark

'**marcia** nf march; Auto gear; Sport
walk; **mettere in ~** put into gear;
mettersi in ~ start off. **~ funebre** funeral march. **~ indietro** reverse gear;
fare ~ indietro reverse; fig back-pedal.
~ nuziale wedding march

marciapi'ede nm pavement; (di stazione) platform

marci'a|re vi march; (funzionare) go,
work. **~'tore, ~'trice** nmf walker

'**marcio** a rotten ● nm rotten part; fig
corruption. **mar'cire** vi go bad, rot

'**marco** nm (moneta) mark

'**mare** nm sea; (luogo di mare) seaside; **sul ~** ⟨casa⟩ at the seaside; ⟨città⟩ on the sea; **in alto ~** on the high seas; **essere in alto ~** fig not know which way to turn. **~ Adriatico** Adriatic Sea. **mar Ionio** Ionian Sea. **mar Mediterraneo** Mediterranean. **mar Tirreno** Tyrrhenian Sea

ma'rea nf tide; **una ~ di** hundreds of; **alta/bassa ~** high/low tide

mareggi'ata nf [sea] storm

mare'moto nm tidal wave, seaquake

maresci'allo nm (ufficiale) marshal; (sottufficiale) warrant-officer

marga'rina nf margarine

marghe'rita nf marguerite. **margheri'tina** nf daisy

margi'nal|e a marginal. **~'mente** adv marginally

'**margine** nm margin; (orlo) brink; (bordo) border. **~ di errore** margin of error. **~ di sicurezza** safety margin

ma'rina nf navy; (costa) seashore; (quadro) seascape. **~ mercantile** merchant navy. **~ militare** navy

mari'naio nm sailor

mari'na|re vt marinate; **~re la scuola** play truant. **~ta** nf marinade. **~to** a Culin soused and pickled

ma'rino a sea attrib, marine

mario'netta nf puppet

ma'rito nm husband

ma'rittimo a maritime

mar'maglia nf rabble

marmel'lata nf jam; (di agrumi) marmalade

mar'mitta nf pot; Auto silencer. **~ catalitica** catalytic converter

'**marmo** nm marble

mar'mocchio nm fam brat

mar'mor|eo a marble. **~iz'zato** a marbled

mar'motta nf marmot

Ma'rocco nm Morocco

ma'roso nm breaker

mar'rone a brown ● nm maroon; (castagna) chestnut; **marroni** pl **canditi** marrons glacés

mar'sina nf tails pl

mar'supio nm (borsa) bumbag

martedì nm inv Tuesday. **~ grasso** Shrove Tuesday

martel'lante a ⟨mal di testa⟩ pounding

martel'la|re vt hammer ● vi throb. **~ta** nf hammer blow

martel'letto nm (di giudice) gavel

mar'tello nm hammer; (di battente) knocker. **~ pneumatico** pneumatic drill

marti'netto nm Mech jack

'**martire** nmf martyr. **mar'tirio** nm martyrdom

'**martora** nf marten

martori'are vt torment

mar'xis|mo nm Marxism. **~ta** a & nmf Marxist

marza'pane nm marzipan

marzi'ale a martial

marzi'ano, -a nmf Martian

'**marzo** nm March

mascal'zone nm rascal

ma'scara nm inv mascara

mascar'pone nm full-fat cream cheese often used for desserts

ma'scella nf jaw

'**mascher|a** nf mask; (costume) fancy dress; Cinema, Theat usher m, usherette f; (nella commedia dell'arte) stock character. **~a antigas** gas mask. **~a di bellezza** face pack. **~a ad ossigeno** oxygen mask. **~a'mento** nm masking; Mil camouflage. **masche'rare** vt mask; fig camouflage. **~arsi** vr put on a mask; **~arsi da** dress up as. **~ata** nf masquerade

maschi'accio nm (ragazza) tomboy

ma'schi|le a masculine; ⟨sesso⟩ male ● nm masculine [gender]. **~'lista** a sexist. '**maschio** a male; (virile) manly ● nm male; (figlio) son. **masco'lino** a masculine

ma'scotte nf inv mascot

maso'chis|mo nm masochism. **~ta** a & nmf masochist

'**massa** nf mass; Electr earth, ground Am; **communicazioni di ~** mass media

massa'cra|nte a gruelling. **~re** vt massacre. **mas'sacro** nm massacre; fig mess

massaggi'a|re vt massage. **mas'saggio** nm massage. **~'tore**, **~'trice** nm masseur ● nf masseuse

mas'saia nf housewife

masse'rizie nfpl household effects

mas'siccio a massive; ⟨oro ecc⟩ solid; ⟨corporatura⟩ heavy ● nm massif

'**massim|a** nf maxim; (temperatura) maximum. **~o** a greatest; ⟨quantità⟩ maximum, greatest ● nm **il ~o** the maximum; **al ~o** at [the] most, as a maximum

'**masso** nm rock

mas'sone *nm* [Free]mason. **~'ria** Freemasonry

ma'stello *nm* wooden box for the grape or olive harvest

masti'care *vt* chew; (*borbottare*) mumble

'mastice *nm* mastic; (*per vetri*) putty

ma'stino *nm* mastiff

masto'dontico *a* gigantic

'mastro *nm* master; **libro ~** ledger

mastur'ba|rsi *vr* masturbate. **~zi'o-ne** *nf* masturbation

ma'tassa *nf* skein

mate'matic|a *nf* mathematics, maths. **~o, -a** *a* mathematical ● *nmf* mathematician

materas'sino *nm* **~ gonfiabile** air bed

mate'rasso *nm* mattress. **~ a molle** spring mattress

ma'teria *nf* matter; (*materiale*) material; (*di studio*) subject. **~ prima** raw material

materi'a|le *a* material; (*grossolano*) coarse ● *nm* material. **~'lismo** *nm* materialism. **~'lista** *a* materialistic ● *nmf* materialist. **~liz'zarsi** *vr* materialize. **~l'mente** *adv* physically

mater'nità *nf* motherhood; **ospedale di ~** maternity hospital

ma'terno *a* maternal; **lingua mater-na** mother tongue

ma'tita *nf* pencil

ma'trice *nf* matrix; (*origini*) roots *pl*; *Comm* counterfoil

ma'tricola *nf* (*registro*) register; *Univ* fresher

ma'trigna *nf* stepmother

matrimoni'ale *a* matrimonial; **vita ~** married life. **matri'monio** *nm* marriage; (*cerimonia*) wedding

ma'trona *nf* matron

'matta *nf* (*nelle carte*) joker

mattacchi'one, -a *nmf* rascal

matta'toio *nm* slaughterhouse

matte'rello *nm* rolling-pin

mat'ti|na *nf* morning; **la ~na** in the morning. **~'nata** *nf* morning; *Theat* matinée. **~ni'ero** *a* **essere ~niero** be an early riser. **~no** *nm* morning

'matto, -a *a* mad, crazy; *Med* insane; (*falso*) false; (*opaco*) matt; **~ da legare** barking mad; **avere una voglia matta di** be dying for ● *nmf* madman; madwoman

mat'tone *nm* brick; (*libro*) bore

matto'nella *nf* tile

mattu'tino *a* morning *attrib*

matu'rare *vt* ripen. **maturità** *nf* maturity; *Sch* school-leaving certificate. **ma-'turo** *a* mature; (*frutto*) ripe

ma'tusa *nm* old fogey

mauso'leo *nm* mausoleum

maxi+ *pref* maxi+

'mazza *nf* club; (*martello*) hammer; (*da baseball, cricket*) bat. **~ da golf** golf-club. **maz'zata** *nf* blow

maz'zetta *nf* (*di banconote*) bundle

'mazzo *nm* bunch; (*carte da gioco*) pack

me *pers pron* me; **me lo ha dato** he gave it to me; **fai come me** do as I do; **è più veloce di me** he is faster than me *o* faster than I am

me'andro *nm* meander

M.E.C. *nm abbr* (**Mercato Comune Europeo**) EEC

mec'canica *nf* mechanics *sg*

meccanica'mente *adv* mechanically

mec'canico *a* mechanical ● *nm* mechanic. **mecca'nismo** *nm* mechanism

mèche *nfpl* [farsi] **fare le ~** have one's hair streaked

me'dagli|a *nf* medal. **~'one** *nm* medallion; (*gioiello*) locket

me'desimo *a* same

'medi|a *nf* average; *Sch* average mark; *Math* mean; **essere nella ~a** be in the mid-range. **~'ano** *a* middle ● *nm* (*calcio*) half-back

medi'ante *prep* by

medi'a|re *vt* act as intermediary in. **~'tore**, **~'trice** *nmf* mediator; *Comm* middleman. **~zi'one** *nf* mediation

medica'mento *nm* medicine

medi'ca|re *vt* treat; dress (*ferita*). **~zi'one** *nf* medication; (*di ferita*) dressing

medi'c|ina *nf* medicine. **~ina legale** forensic medicine. **~i'nale** *a* medicinal ● *nm* medicine

'medico *a* medical ● *nm* doctor. **~ ge-nerico** general practitioner. **~ legale** forensic scientist. **~ di turno** duty doctor

medie'vale *a* medieval

'medio *a* average; (*punto*) middle; (*statura*) medium ● *nm* (*dito*) middle finger

medi'ocre *a* mediocre; (*scadente*) poor

medio'evo *nm* Middle Ages *pl*

medi'ta|re *vt* meditate; (*progettare*) plan; (*considerare attentamente*) think over ● *vi* meditate. **~zi'one** *nf* meditation

mediter'raneo *a* Mediterranean; **il [mare] M~** the Mediterranean [Sea]

me'dusa nf jellyfish

me'gafono nm megaphone

megaga'lattico a fam gigantic

mega'lomane nmf megalomaniac

me'gera nf hag

'meglio adv better; **tanto ~, ~ così** so much the better ● a better; (superlativo) best ● nm best ● nf **avere la ~ su** have the better of; **fare qcsa alla [bell'e] ~** do sth as best one can ● nm **fare del proprio ~** do one's best; **fare qcsa il ~ possibile** make an excellent job of sth; **al ~** to the best of one's ability; **per il ~** for the best

'mela nf apple. **~ cotogna** quince

mela'grana nf pomegranate

mela'nina nf melanin

melan'zana nf aubergine, eggplant Am

me'lassa nf molasses sg

me'lenso a (persona, film) dull

mel'ifluo a (parole) honeyed; (voce) sugary

'melma nf slime. **mel'moso** a slimy

melo nm apple[-tree]

melo'di|a nf melody. **me'lodico** a melodic. **~'oso** a melodious

melo'dram|ma nm melodrama. **~'matico** a melodramatic

melo'grano nm pomegranate tree

me'lone nm melon

mem'brana nf membrane

'membro nm member; (pl nf **membra** Anat) limb

memo'rabile a memorable

'memore a mindful; (riconoscente) grateful

me'mori|a nf memory; (oggetto ricordo) souvenir. **imparare a ~a** learn by heart. **~a permanente** Comput non-volatile memory. **~a tampone** Comput buffer. **~a volatile** Comput volatile memory; **memorie** pl (biografiche) memoirs. **~'ale** nm memorial. **~z'zare** vt memorize; Comput save, store

mena'dito: a ~ adv perfectly

me'nare vt lead; (fam: picchiare) hit

mendi'ca|nte nmf beggar. **~re** vt/i beg

menefre'ghista a devil-may-care

me'ningi nfpl **spremersi le ~** rack one's brains

menin'gite nf meningitis

me'nisco nm meniscus

'meno adv less; (superlativo) least; (in operazioni, con temperatura) minus; **far qcsa alla ~ peggio** do sth as best one can; **fare a ~ di qcsa** do without sth; **non posso fare a ~ di ridere** I can't help laughing; **~ male!** thank goodness!; **sempre ~** less and less; **venir ~** (svenire) faint; **venir ~ a qcno** ‹coraggio:› fail sb; **sono le tre ~ un quarto** it's a quarter to three; **che tu venga o ~** whether you're coming or not; **quanto ~** at least ● a inv less; (con nomi plurali) fewer ● nm least; Math minus sign; **il ~ possibile** as little as possible; **per lo ~** at least ● prep except [for] ● conj a ~ **che** unless

meno'ma|re vt (incidente:) maim. **~to** a disabled

meno'pausa nf menopause

'mensa nf table; Mil mess; Sch, Univ refectory

men'sil|e a monthly ● nm (stipendio) [monthly] salary; (rivista) monthly. **~ità** nf inv monthly salary. **~'mente** adv monthly

'mensola nf bracket; (scaffale) shelf

'menta nf mint. **~ peperita** peppermint

men'tal|e a mental. **~ità** nf inv mentality

'mente nf mind; **a ~ fredda** in cold blood; **venire in ~ a qcno** occur to sb; **mi è uscito di ~** it slipped my mind

men'tina nf mint

men'tire vi lie

'mento nm chin

'mentre conj (temporale) while; (invece) whereas

menù nm inv menu. **~ fisso** set menu. **~ a tendina** Comput pulldown menu

menzio'nare vt mention. **menzi'one** nf mention

men'zogna nf lie

mera'viglia nf wonder; **a ~** marvellously; **che ~!** how wonderful!; **con mia grande ~** much to my amazement; **mi fa ~ che...** I am surprised that...

meravigli'ar|e vt surprise. **~si** vr **~si di** be surprised at

meravigli|osa'mente adv marvellously. **~'oso** a marvellous

mer'can|te nm merchant. **~teggi'are** vi trade; (sul prezzo) bargain. **~'tile** a mercantile. **~'zia** nf merchandise, goods pl ● nm merchant ship

mer'cato nm market; Fin market [-place]. **a buon ~** ‹comprare› cheap[ly]; ‹articolo› cheap. **~ dei cambi** foreign exchange market. **M~ Comune [Europeo]** [European] Common Market. **~ coperto** covered market. **~ libero** free market. **~ nero** black market '**merce** *nf* goods *pl*

mercé *nf* **alla ~ di** at the mercy of

merce'nario *a & nm* mercenary

merce'ria *nf* haberdashery; (*negozio*) haberdasher's

mercoledì *nm inv* Wednesday. **~ delle Ceneri** Ash Wednesday

mer'curio *nm* mercury

me'renda *nf* afternoon snack; **far ~** have an afternoon snack

meridi'ana *nf* sundial

meridi'ano *a* midday ● *nm* meridian

meridio'nale *a* southern ● *nmf* southerner. **meridi'one** *nm* south

me'rin|ga *nf* meringue. **~'gata** *nf* meringue pie

meri'tare *vt* deserve. **meri'tevole** *a* deserving

'**meri|to** *nm* merit; (*valore*) worth; **in ~to a** as to; **per ~to di** thanks to. **~'torio** *a* meritorious

mer'letto *nm* lace

'**merlo** *nm* blackbird

mer'luzzo *nm* cod

'**mero** *a* mere

meschine'ria *nf* meanness. **me'schino** *a* wretched; (*gretto*) mean ● *nm* wretch

mesco|la'mento *nm* mixing. **~'lanza** *nf* mixture

mesco'la|re *vt* mix; shuffle ‹*carte*›; (*confondere*) mix up; blend ‹*tè, tabacco ecc*›. **~rsi** *vr* mix; (*immischiarsi*) meddle. **~ta** *nf* (*a carte*) shuffle; *Culin* stir

'**mese** *nm* month

me'setto *nm* **un ~** about a month

'**messa**[1] *nf* Mass

'**messa**[2] *nf* (*il mettere*) putting. **~ in moto** *Auto* starting. **~ in piega** (*di capelli*) set. **~ a punto** adjustment. **~ in scena** production. **~ a terra** earthing, grounding *Am*

messag'gero *nm* messenger. **mes-'saggio** *nm* message

mes'sale *nm* missal

'**messe** *nf* harvest

Mes'sia *nm* Messiah

messi'cano, -a *a & nmf* Mexican

'**Messico** *nm* Mexico

messin'scena *nf* staging; *fig* act

'**messo** *pp di* **mettere** ● *nm* messenger

mesti'ere *nm* trade; (*lavoro*) job; **essere del ~** be an expert, know one's trade

'**mesto** *a* sad

'**mestola** *nf* (*di cuoco*) ladle

mestru'a|le *a* menstrual. **~zi'one** *nf* menstruation. **~zi'oni** *pl* period

'**meta** *nf* destination; *fig* aim

metà *nf inv* half; (*centro*) middle; **a ~ strada** half-way; **fare a ~ con qcno** go halves with sb

metabo'lismo *nm* metabolism

meta'done *nm* methadone

meta'fisico *a* metaphysical

me'tafora *nf* metaphor. **meta'forico** *a* metaphorical

me'talli|co *a* metallic. **~z'zato** *a* ‹*grigio*› metallic

me'tall|o *nm* metal. **~ur'gia** *nf* metallurgy

metalmec'canico *a* engineering ● *nm* engineering worker

meta'morfosi *nf* metamorphosis

me'tano *nm* methane. **~'dotto** *nm* methane pipeline

meta'nolo *nm* methanol

me'teora *nf* meteor. **meteo'rite** *nm* meteorite

meteoro|lo'gia *nf* meteorology. **~'logico** *a* meteorological

me'ticcio, -a *nmf* half-caste

metico'loso *a* meticulous

me'tod|ico *a* methodical. '**metodo** *nm* method. **~olo'gia** *nf* methodology

me'traggio *nm* length (*in metres*)

'**metrico, -a** *a* metric; (*in poesia*) metrical ● *nf* metrics *sg*

'**metro** *nm* metre; (*nastro*) tape measure ● *nf* (*fam: metropolitana*) tube *Br*, subway

me'tronomo *nm* metronome

metro'notte *nmf inv* night security guard

me'tropoli *nf inv* metropolis. **~'tana** *nf* subway, underground *Br*. **~'tano** *a* metropolitan

'**metter|e** *vt* put; (*indossare*) put on; (*fam: installare*) put in; **~e al mondo** bring into the world; **~e da parte** set aside; **~e fiducia** inspire trust; **~e qcsa in chiaro** make sth clear; **~e in mostra** display; **~e a posto** tidy up; **~e in vendita** put up for sale; **~e su** set up ‹*casa, azienda*›; **metter su famiglia** start a family; **ci ho messo un'ora** it took me an hour; **mettiamo che...** let's suppose that... **~si** *vr* (*indossare*) put on; (*diventare*) turn out; **~si a** start to; **~si con qcno** (*fam: formare una coppia*) start to go out with sb; **~si a letto** go to bed; **~si a sedere** sit down; **~si in viaggio** set out

'**mezza** *nf* **è la ~** it's half past twelve; **sono le quattro e ~** it's half past four

mezza'luna *nf* half moon; (*simbolo*

mezzamanica | mina

islamico) crescent; *(coltello)* two-handled chopping knife; **a ~** half-moon shaped

mezza'manica *nf* **a ~** *(maglia)* short-sleeved

mez'zano *a* middle

mezza'notte *nf* midnight

mezz'asta: a ~ *adv* at half mast

'mezzo *a* half; **di mezza età** middle-aged; **~ bicchiere** half a glass; **una mezza idea** a vague idea; **siamo mezzi morti** we're half dead; **sono le quattro e ~** it's half past four. **mezz'ora** *nf* half an hour. **mezza pensione** *nf* half board. **mezza stagione** *nf* **una giacca di mezza stagione** a spring/autumn jacket ● *adv (a metà)* half ● *nm (metà)* half; *(centro)* middle; *(per raggiungere un fine)* means *sg*; **uno e ~** one and a half; **tre anni e ~** three and a half years; **in ~ a** in the middle of; **il giusto ~** the happy medium; **levare di ~** clear away; **per ~ di** by means of; **a ~ posta** by mail; **mezzi** *pl (denaro)* means *pl*. **mezzi pubblici** public transport. **mezzi di trasporto** [means of] transport. **via di ~** *fig* halfway house; *(soluzione)* middle way

mezzo'busto: a ~ *a (foto, ritratto)*, half-length

mezzo'fondo *nm* middle-distance running

mezzogi'orno *nm* midday; *(sud)* South. **il M~** Southern Italy. **~ in punto** high noon

mi *pers pron* me; *(refl)* myself; **mi ha dato un libro** he gave me a book; **mi lavo le mani** I wash my hands; **eccomi** here I am ● *nm Mus (chiave, nota)* E

miago'l|are *vi* miaow. **~io** *nm* miaowing

'mica[1] *nf* mica

'mica[2] *adv fam (per caso)* by any chance; **hai ~ visto Paolo?** have you seen Paul, by any chance?; **non è ~ bello** it is not at all nice; **~ male** not bad

'miccia *nf* fuse

micidi'ale *a* deadly

'micio *nm* pussy-cat

'microbo *nm* microbe

micro'cosmo *nm* microcosm

micro'fiche *nf inv* microfiche

micro'film *nm inv* microfilm

mi'crofono *nm* microphone

microorga'nismo *nm* microorganism

microproces'sore *nm* microprocessor

micro'scopi|o *nm* microscope. **~co** *a* microscopic

micro'solco *nm (disco)* long-playing record

mi'dollo *nm (pl nf* **midolla**, *Anat)* marrow; **fino al ~** through and through. **~ osseo** bone marrow. **~ spinale** spinal cord

'mie, mi'ei *vedi* mio

mi'ele *nm* honey

mi'et|ere *vt* reap. **~i'trice** *nf Mech* harvester. **~i'tura** *nf* harvest

migli'aio *nm (pl nf* **migliaia)** thousand. **a migliaia** in thousands

'miglio *nm Bot* millet; *(pl nf* **miglia**: *misura)* mile

migliora'mento *nm* improvement

miglio'rare *vt/i* improve

migli'ore *a* better; *(superlativo)* the best ● *nmf* **il/la ~** the best

'mignolo *nm* little finger; *(del piede)* little toe

mi'gra|re *vi* migrate. **~zi'one** *nf* migration

'mila *vedi* mille

Mi'lano *nf* Milan

miliar'dario, -a *nm* millionaire; *(plurimiliardario)* billionaire ● *nf* millionairess. **mili'ardo** *nm* billion

mili'are *a* **pietra** *nf* **~** milestone

milio'nario, -a *nm* millionaire ● *nf* millionairess

mili'one *nm* million

milio'nesimo *a* millionth

mili'tante *a & nmf* militant

mili'tare *vi* **~ in** be a member of *(partito ecc)* ● *a* military ● *nm* soldier; **fare il ~** do one's military service. **~ di leva** National Serviceman

mi'lite *nm* soldier. **mi'lizia** *nf* militia

'mille *a & nm (pl* **mila)** *a o* one thousand; **due/tre mila** two/three thousand; **~ grazie!** thanks a lot!

mille'foglie *nm inv Culin* vanilla slice

mil'lennio *nm* millennium

mille'piedi *nm inv* centipede

mil'lesimo *a & nm* thousandth

milli'grammo *nm* milligram

mil'limetro *nm* millimetre

'milza *nf* spleen

mi'mare *vt* mimic *(persona)* ● *vi* mime

mi'metico *a* camouflage *attrib*

mimetiz'zar|e *vt* camouflage. **~si** *vr* camouflage oneself

'mim|ica *nf* mime. **~ico** *a* mimic. **~o** *nm* mime

mi'mosa *nf* mimosa

'mina *nf* mine; *(di matita)* lead

mi'naccia *nf* threat

minacci|'are *vt* threaten. **~'oso** *a* threatening

mi'nare *vt* mine; *fig* undermine

mina'tor|e *nm* miner. **~io** *a* threatening

mine'ra|le *a & nm* mineral. **~rio** *a* mining *attrib*

mi'nestra *nf* soup. **mine'strone** *nm* vegetable soup; (*fam: insieme confuso*) hotchpotch

mingher'lino *a* skinny

mini+ *pref* mini+

minia'tura *nf* miniature. **miniaturiz-'zato** *a* miniaturized

mini'era *nf* mine

mini'golf *nm* miniature golf

mini'gonna *nf* miniskirt

minima'mente *adv* minimally

mini'market *nm inv* minimarket

minimiz'zare *vt* minimize

'minimo *a* least, slightest; (*il più basso*) lowest; (*salario, quantità ecc*) minimum ● *nm* minimum; **girare al ~** *Auto* idle

mini'stero *nm* ministry; (*governo*) government

mi'nistro *nm* minister. **M~ del Tesoro** Finance Minister, Chancellor of the Exchequer *Br*

mino'ranza *nf* minority *attrib*

mino'rato, -a *a* disabled ● *nmf* disabled person

mi'nore *a* (*gruppo, numero*) smaller; (*superlativo*) smallest; (*distanza*) shorter; (*superlativo*) shortest; (*prezzo*) lower; (*superlativo*) lowest; (*di età*) younger; (*superlativo*) youngest; (*di importanza*) minor; (*superlativo*) least important ● *nmf* younger; (*superlativo*) youngest; *Jur* minor; **il ~ dei mali** the lesser of two evils; **i minori di 14 anni** children under 14. **mino'renne** *a* under age ● *nmf* minor

minori'tario *a* minority *attrib*

minu'etto *nm* minuet

mi'nuscolo, -a *a* tiny ● *nf* small letter

mi'nuta *nf* rough copy

mi'nuto[1] *a* minute; (*persona*) delicate; (*ricerca*) detailed; (*pioggia, neve*) fine; **al ~** *Comm* retail

mi'nuto[2] *nm* (*di tempo*) minute; **spaccare il ~** be dead on time

mi'nuzi|a *nf* trifle. **~'oso** *a* detailed; (*persona*) meticulous

'mio (**il mio** *m*, **la mia** *f*, **i miei** *mpl*, **le mie** *fpl*) *a poss* my; **questa macchina è mia** this car is mine; **~ padre** my fa-

ther; **un ~ amico** a friend of mine ● *poss pron* mine; **i miei** (*genitori ecc*) my folks

'miope *a* short-sighted. **mio'pia** *nf* short-sightedness

'mira *nf* aim; (*bersaglio*) target; **prendere la ~** take aim; **prendere di ~ qcno** *fig* have it in for sb

mi'racolo *nm* miracle. **~sa'mente** *adv* miraculously. **miraco'loso** *a* miraculous

mi'raggio *nm* mirage

mi'rar|e *vi* [take] aim. **~si** *vr* (*guardarsi*) look at oneself

mi'riade *nf* myriad

mi'rino *nm* sight; *Phot* view-finder

mir'tillo *nm* blueberry

mi'santropo, -a *nmf* misanthropist

mi'scela *nf* mixture; (*di caffè, tabacco*) blend. **~'tore** *nm* (*di acqua*) mixer tap

miscel'lanea *nf* miscellany

'mischia *nf* scuffle; (*nel rugby*) scrum

mischi'ar|e *vt* mix; shuffle (*carte da gioco*). **~si** *vr* mix; (*immischiarsi*) interfere

misco'noscere *vt* not appreciate

mi'scuglio *nm* mixture; *fig* medley

mise'rabile *a* wretched

misera'mente *adv* (*finire*) miserably; (*vivere*) in abject poverty

mi'seria *nf* poverty; (*infelicità*) misery; **guadagnare una ~** earn a pittance; **porca ~!** hell!; **miserie** *pl* (*disgrazie*) misfortunes

miseri'cordi|a *nf* mercy. **~'oso** *a* merciful

'misero *a* (*miserabile*) wretched; (*povero*) poor; (*scarso*) paltry

mi'sfatto *nm* misdeed

mi'sogino *nm* misogynist

mis'saggio *nm* vision mixer

'missile *nm* missile

missio'nario, -a *nmf* missionary. **missi'one** *nf* mission

misteri|osa'mente *adv* mysteriously. **~'oso** *a* mysterious. **mi'stero** *nm* mystery

'misti|ca *nf* mysticism. **~'cismo** *nm* mysticism. **~co** *a* mystic[al] ● *nm* mystic

mistifi'ca|re *vt* distort (*verità*). **~zi'one** *nf* (*della verità*) distortion

'misto *a* mixed; **~ lana/cotone** wool/cotton-mix; **scuola mista** mixed *o* co-educational school ● *nm* mixture

mi'sura *nf* measure; (*dimensione*) measurement; (*taglia*) size; (*limite*) limit; **su ~** (*abiti*) made to measure;

⟨*mobile*⟩ custom-made; **a ~** ⟨*andare, calzare*⟩ perfectly; **a ~ che** as. **~ di sicurezza** safety measure. **misu'rare** *vt* measure; try on ⟨*indumenti*⟩; ⟨*limitare*⟩ limit. **misu'rarsi** *vr* **misurarsi con** ⟨*gareggiare*⟩ compete with. **misu'rato** *a* measured. **misu'rino** *nm* measuring spoon

'**mite** *a* mild; ⟨*prezzo*⟩ moderate

'**mitico** *a* mythical

miti'gar|e *vt* mitigate. **~si** *vr* calm down; ⟨*clima:*⟩ become mild

mitiz'zare *vt* mythicize

'**mito** *nm* myth. **~lo'gia** *nf* mythology. **~'logico** *a* mythological

mi'tomane *nmf* compulsive liar

'**mitra** *nf Relig* mitre ● *nm inv Mil* machine-gun

mitragli'a|re *vt* machine-gun; **~re di domande** fire questions at. **~'trice** *nf* machine-gun

mit'tente *nmf* sender

mne'monico *a* mnemonic

mo' *nm* **a ~ di** by way of ⟨*esempio, consolazione*⟩

'**mobile**[1] *a* mobile; ⟨*volubile*⟩ fickle; ⟨*che si può muovere*⟩ movable; **beni mobili** personal estate; **squadra ~** flying squad

'**mobi|le**[2] *nm* piece of furniture; **mobili** *pl* furniture *sg*. **mo'bilia** *nf* furniture. **~li'ficio** *nm* furniture factory

mo'bilio *nm* furniture

mobilità *nf* mobility

mobili'ta|re *vt* mobilize. **~zi'one** *nf* mobilization

mocas'sino *nm* moccasin

mocci'oso, -a *nmf* brat

'**moccolo** *nm* ⟨*di candela*⟩ candle-end; ⟨*moccio*⟩ snot

'**moda** *nf* fashion; **di ~** in fashion; **alla ~** ⟨*musica, vestiti*⟩ up-to-date; **fuori ~** unfashionable

modalità *nf inv* formality; **~ d'uso** instruction

mo'della *nf* model. **model'lare** *vt* model

model'li|no *nm* model. **~sta** *nmf* designer

mo'dello *nm* model; ⟨*stampo*⟩ mould; ⟨*di carta*⟩ pattern; ⟨*modulo*⟩ form

'**modem** *nm inv* modem; **mandare per ~ modem,** send by modem

mode'ra|re *vt* moderate; ⟨*diminuire*⟩ reduce. **~rsi** *vr* control oneself. **~ta'mente** *adv* moderately **~to** *a* moderate. **~'tore, ~'trice** *nmf* ⟨*in tavola*

rotonda⟩ moderator. **~zi'one** *nf* moderation

modern|a'mente *adv* ⟨*in modo moderno*⟩ in a modern style. **~iz'zare** *vt* modernize. **mo'derno** *a* modern

mo'dest|ia *nf* modesty. **~o** *a* modest

'**modico** *a* reasonable

mo'difica *nf* modification

modifi'ca|re *vt* modify. **~zi'one** *nf* modification

mo'dista *nf* milliner

'**modo** *nm* way; ⟨*garbo*⟩ manners *pl*; ⟨*occasione*⟩ chance; *Gram* mood; **ad ogni ~** anyhow; **di ~ che** so that; **fare in ~ di** try to; **in che ~** ⟨*inter*⟩ how; **in qualche ~** somehow; **in questo ~** like this; **~ di dire** idiom; **per ~ di dire** so to speak

modu'la|re *vt* modulate. **~zi'one** *nf* modulation. **~zione di frequenza** frequency modulation. **~'tore** *nm* **~tore di frequenza** frequency modulator

'**modulo** *nm* form; ⟨*lunare, di comando*⟩ module. **~ continuo** continuous paper

'**mogano** *nm* mahogany

'**mogio** *a* dejected

'**moglie** *nf* wife

'**mola** *nf* millstone; *Mech* grindstone

mo'lare *nm* molar

'**mole** *nf* mass; ⟨*dimensione*⟩ size

mo'lecola *nf* molecule

mole'stare *vt* bother; ⟨*più forte*⟩ molest. **mo'lestia** *nf* nuisance. **mo'lesto** *a* bothersome

'**molla** *nf* spring; **molle** *pl* tongs

mol'lare *vt* let go; ⟨*fam: lasciare*⟩ leave; *fam* give ⟨*ceffone*⟩; *Naut* cast off ● *vi* cease; **mollala!** *fam* stop that!

'**molle** *a* soft; ⟨*bagnato*⟩ wet

mol'letta *nf* ⟨*per capelli*⟩ hair-grip; ⟨*per bucato*⟩ clothes-peg; **mollette** *pl* ⟨*per ghiaccio ecc*⟩ tongs

mol'lezz|a *nf* softness; **~e** *pl fig* luxury

mol'lica *nf* crumb

mol'lusco *nm* mollusc

'**molo** *nm* pier; ⟨*banchina*⟩ dock

mol'teplic|e *a* manifold; ⟨*numeroso*⟩ numerous. **~ità** *nf* multiplicity

moltipli'ca|re *vt,* **~rsi** *vr* multiply. **~'tore** *nm* multiplier. **~'trice** *nf* calculating machine. **~zi'one** *nf* multiplication

molti'tudine *nf* multitude

'**molto** *a* a lot of; ⟨*con negazione e interrogazione*⟩ much, a lot of; ⟨*con nomi plurali*⟩ many, a lot of; **non ~ tempo** not much time, not a lot of time ● *adv* very; ⟨*con verbi*⟩ a lot; ⟨*con avverbi*⟩ much; **~ stupido** very stupid; **mangiare ~** eat a lot; ~ **più veloce** much faster; **non mangiare** ~ not eat a lot, not eat much ● *pron* a lot; (*molto tempo*) a lot of time; (*con negazione e interrogazione*) much, a lot; (*plurale*) many; **non ne ho** ~ I don't have much, I don't have a lot; **non ne ho molti** I don't have many, I don't have a lot; **non ci metterò** ~ I won't be long; **fra non** ~ before long; **molti** (*persone*) a lot of people; **eravamo in molti** there were a lot of us

momentanea'mente *adv* momentarily; **è ~ assente** he's not here at the moment. **momen'taneo** *a* momentary

mo'mento *nm* moment; **a momenti** (*a volte*) sometimes; (*fra un momento*) in a moment; **dal ~ che** since; **per il ~** for the time being; **da un ~ all'altro** (*cambiare idea ecc*) from one moment to the next; (*aspettare qcno ecc*) at any moment

'**monac|a** *nf* nun. ~**o** *nm* monk

'**Monaco** *nm* Monaco ● *nf* (*di Baviera*) Munich

mo'narc|a *nm* monarch. **monar'chia** *nf* monarchy. ~**hico, -a** *a* monarchic ● *nmf* monarchist

mona'stero *nm* (*di monaci*) monastery; (*di monache*) convent. **mo'nastico** *a* monastic

monche'rino *nm* stump

'**monco** *a* maimed; (*fig: troncato*) truncated; ~ **di un braccio** one-armed

mon'dano *a* worldly; **vita mondana** social life

mondi'ale *a* world *attrib*; **di fama ~** world-famous

'**mondo** *nm* world; **il bel ~** fashionable society; **un ~** (*molto*) a lot

mondovisi'one *nf* **in ~** transmitted worldwide

mo'nello, -a *nmf* urchin

mo'neta *nf* coin; (*denaro*) money; (*denaro spicciolo*) [small] change. ~ **estera** foreign currency. ~ **legale** legal tender. ~ **unica** single currency. **mone-'tario** *a* monetary

mongolfi'era *nf* hot air balloon

mo'nile *nm* jewel

'**monito** *nm* warning

moni'tore *nm* monitor

mo'nocolo *nm* monocle

monoco'lore *a Pol* one-party

mono'dose *a inv* individually packaged

monogra'fia *nf* monograph

mono'gramma *nm* monogram

mono'kini *nm inv* monokini

mono'lingue *a* monolingual

monolo'cale *nm* studio flat, studio apartment *Am*

mo'nologo *nm* monologue

mono'pattino *nm* [child's] scooter

mono'poli|o *nm* monopoly. ~**o di stato** state monopoly. ~**z'zare** *vt* monopolize

mono'sci *nm inv* monoski

monosil'labico *a* monosyllabic. **mono'sillabo** *nm* monosyllable

monoto'nia *nf* monotony. **mo'notono** *a* monotonous

mono'uso *a* disposable

monou'tente *a inv* single-user *attrib*

monsi'gnore *nm* monsignor

mon'sone *nm* monsoon

monta'carichi *nm inv* hoist

mon'taggio *nm Mech* assembly; *Cinema* editing; **catena di ~** production line

mon'ta|gna *nf* mountain; (*zona*) mountains *pl*; **montagne *pl* russe** big dipper. ~**'gnoso** *a* mountainous. ~**'naro, -a** *nmf* highlander. ~**no** *a* mountain *attrib*

mon'tante *nm* (*di finestra, porta*) upright

mon'ta|re *vt/i* mount; get on (*veicolo*); (*aumentare*) rise; *Mech* assemble; frame (*quadro*); *Culin* whip; edit (*film*); (*a cavallo*) ride; *fig* blow up; ~**rsi la testa** get big-headed. ~**to, -a** *nmf* poser. ~**'tura** *nf Mech* assembling; (*di occhiali*) frame; (*di gioiello*) mounting; *fig* exaggeration

'**monte** *nm anche fig* mountain; **a ~** upstream; **andare a ~** be ruined; **mandare a ~ qcsa** ruin sth; **~ di pietà** pawnshop

monte'premi *nm inv* jackpot

mont'gomery *nm inv* duffle coat

mon'tone *nm* ram; **carne di ~** mutton

montu'oso *a* mountainous

monumen'tale *a* monumental. **monu'mento** *nm* monument

mo'quette *nf* (*tappeto*) fitted carpet

'**mora** *nf* (*del gelso*) mulberry; (*del rovo*) blackberry

mo'ral|e *a* moral ● *nf* morals *pl*; (*di storia*) moral ● *nm* morale. **mora'lista** *nmf* moralist. ~**ità** *nf* morality; (*condotta*) morals *pl*. ~**iz'zare** *vt/i* moralize. ~**'mente** *adv* morally

morbi'dezza *nf* softness

'**morbido** *a* soft

mor'billo *nm* measles *sg*

'**morbo** *nm* disease. ~**sità** *nf* (*qualità*) morbidity

mor'boso a morbid

mor'dace a cutting

mor'dente a biting. **'mordere** vt bite; (corrodere) bite into. **mordicchi'are** vt gnaw

mor'fina nf morphine. **morfi'nomane** nmf morphine addict

mori'bondo a dying; (istituzione) moribund

morige'rato a moderate

mo'rire vi die; fig die out; **fa un freddo da ~** it's freezing cold, it's perishing; **~ di noia** be bored to death; **c'era da ~ dal ridere** it was hilariously funny

mor'mone nmf Mormon

mormo'r|are vt/i murmur; (brontolare) mutter. **~io** nm murmuring; (lamentela) grumbling

'moro a dark ● nm Moor

mo'roso a in arrears

'morsa nf vice; fig grip

'morse a alfabeto ~ Morse code

mor'setto nm clamp

morsi'care vt bite. **'morso** nm bite; (di cibo, briglia) bit; **i morsi della fame** hunger pangs

morta'della nf mortadella (type of salted pork)

mor'taio nm mortar

mor'tal|e a mortal; (simile a morte) deadly; **di una noia ~e** deadly. **~ità** nf mortality. **~'mente** adv (ferito) fatally; (offeso) mortally

morta'retto nm firecracker

'morte nf death

mortifi'cante a mortifying

mortifi'ca|re vt mortify. **~rsi** vr be mortified. **~to** a mortified. **~zi'one** nf mortification

'morto, -a pp di morire ● a dead; **~ di freddo** frozen to death; **stanco ~** dead tired ● nm dead man ● nf dead woman

mor'torio nm funeral

mo'saico nm mosaic

'Mosca nf Moscow

'mosca nf fly; (barba) goatee. **~ cieca** blindman's buff

mo'scato a muscat; **noce moscata** nutmeg ● nm muscatel

mosce'rino nm midge; (fam: persona) midget

mo'schea nf mosque

moschi'cida a fly attrib

'moscio a limp; **avere l'erre moscia** not be able to say one's r's properly

mo'scone nm bluebottle; (barca) pedalo

'moss|a nf movement; (passo) move.

~o pp di **muovere** ● a (mare) rough; (capelli) wavy; (fotografia) blurred

mo'starda nf mustard

'mostra nf show; (d'arte) exhibition; **far ~ di** pretend; **in ~** on show; **mettersi in ~** make oneself conspicuous

mo'stra|re vt show; (indicare) point out; (spiegare) explain. **~rsi** vr show oneself; (apparire) appear

'mostro nm monster; (fig: persona) genius; **~ sacro** fig sacred cow

mostru|osa'mente adv tremendously. **~'oso** a monstrous; (incredibile) enormous

mo'tel nm inv motel

moti'va|re vt cause; Jur justify. **~to** a (persona) motivated. **~zi'one** nf motivation; justification

mo'tivo nm reason; (movente) motive; (in musica, letteratura) theme; (disegno) motif

'moto nm motion; (esercizio) exercise; (gesto) movement; (sommossa) rising ● nf inv (motocicletta) motor bike; **mettere in ~** start (motore)

moto'carro nm three-wheeler

motoci'cl|etta nf motor cycle. **~ismo** nm motorcycling. **~ista** nmf motor-cyclist

moto'cros|s nm motocross. **~'sista** nmf scrambler

moto'lancia nf motor launch

moto'nave nf motor vessel

mo'tore a motor ● nm motor, engine. **moto'retta** nf motor scooter. **moto'rino** nm moped. **motorino d'avviamento** starter

motoriz'za|to a Mil motorized. **~zi'one** nf (ufficio) vehicle licensing office

moto'scafo nm motorboat

motove'detta nf patrol vessel

'motto nm motto; (facezia) witticism; (massima) saying

mountain bike nf inv mountain bike

mouse nm inv Comput mouse

mo'vente nm motive

movimen'ta|re vt enliven. **~to** a lively. **movi'mento** nm movement; **essere sempre in movimento** be always on the go

mozi'one nf motion

mozzafi'ato a inv nail-biting

moz'zare vt cut off; dock (coda); **~ il fiato a qcno** take sb's breath away

mozza'rella nf mozzarella, mild, white cheese

mozzi'cone nm (di sigaretta) stub

'mozzo nm Mech hub; Naut ship's boy ● a ⟨coda⟩ truncated; ⟨testa⟩ severed

'mucca nf cow. **morbo della ~ pazza** mad cow disease

'mucchio nm heap, pile; **un ~ di** fig lots of

'muco nm mucus

'muffa nf mould; **fare la ~** go mouldy. **muf'fire** vi go mouldy

muf'fole nfpl mittens

mug'gi|re vi ⟨mucca:⟩ moo, low; ⟨toro:⟩ bellow. **~to** nm moo; bellow; ⟨azione⟩ mooing; bellowing

mu'ghetto nm lily of the valley

mugo'lare vi whine; ⟨persona:⟩ moan. **mugo'lio** nm whining

mugu'gnare vt fam mumble

mulat'tiera nf mule track

mu'latto, -a nmf mulatto

muli'nello nm ⟨d'acqua⟩ whirl-pool; ⟨di vento⟩ eddy; ⟨giocattolo⟩ windmill

mu'lino nm mill. **~ a vento** windmill

'mulo nm mule

'multa nf fine. **mul'tare** vt fine

multico'lore a multicoloured

multi'lingue a multilingual

multi'media mpl multimedia

multimedi'ale a multimedia attrib

multimiliar'dario, -a nmf multi-millionaire

multinazio'nale nf multinational

'multiplo a & nm multiple

multiproprietà nf inv time-share

multi'uso a ⟨utensile⟩ all-purpose

'mummia nf mummy

'mungere vt milk

mungi'tura nf milking

munici'pal|e a municipal. **~ità** nf inv town council. **muni'cipio** nm town hall

mu'nifico a munificent

mu'nire vt fortify; **~ di** ⟨provvedere⟩ supply with

munizi'oni nfpl ammunition sg

'munto pp di **mungere**

mu'over|e vt move; ⟨suscitare⟩ arouse. **~si** vr move; **muoviti!** hurry up!, come on!

mura nfpl ⟨cinta di città⟩ walls

mu'raglia nf wall

mu'rale a mural; ⟨pittura⟩ wall attrib

mur'a|re vt wall up. **~'tore** nm bricklayer; ⟨con pietre⟩ mason; ⟨operaio edile⟩ builder. **~'tura** nf ⟨di pietra⟩ masonry, stonework; ⟨di mattoni⟩ brickwork

mu'rena nf moray eel

'muro nm wall; ⟨di nebbia⟩ bank; **a ~** ⟨armadio⟩ built-in. **~ portante** load-bearing wall. **~ del suono** sound barrier

'muschio nm Bot moss

musco'la|re a muscular. **~'tura** nf muscles pl. **'muscolo** nm muscle

mu'seo nm museum

museru'ola nf muzzle

'musi|ca nf music. **~cal** nm inv musical. **~'cale** a musical. **~'cista** nmf musician.

'muso nm muzzle; ⟨pej: di persona⟩ mug; ⟨di aeroplano⟩ nose; **fare il ~** sulk. **mu'sone, -a** nmf sulker

mussola nf muslin

musul'mano, -a nmf Moslem

'muta nf ⟨cambio⟩ change; ⟨di penne⟩ moult; ⟨di cani⟩ pack; ⟨per immersione subacquea⟩ wetsuit

muta'mento nm change

mu'tan|de nfpl pants; ⟨da donna⟩ knickers. **~'doni** nmpl ⟨da uomo⟩ long johns; ⟨da donna⟩ bloomers

mu'tare vt change

mu'tevole a changeable

muti'la|re vt mutilate. **~to, -a** nmf disabled person. **~to di guerra** disabled ex-serviceman. **~zi'one** nf mutilation

mu'tismo nm dumbness; fig obstinate silence

'muto a dumb; ⟨silenzioso⟩ silent; ⟨fonetica⟩ mute

'mutu|a nf [**cassa** nf] **~** sickness benefit fund. **~'ato, -a** nmf NHS patient

'mutuo[1] a mutual

'mutuo[2] nm loan; ⟨per la casa⟩ mortgage; **fare un ~** take out a mortgage. **~ ipotecario** mortgage

'nacchera nf castanet

'nafta nf naphtha; (per motori) diesel oil

'naia nf cobra; (sl: servizio militare) national service

'nailon nm nylon

'nanna nf (sl: infantile) byebyes; **andare a ~** go byebyes; **fare la ~** sleep

'nano, -a a & nmf dwarf

napole'tano, -a a & nmf Neapolitan

'Napoli nf Naples

'nappa nf tassel; (pelle) soft leather

narci'sis|mo nm narcissism. **~ta** a & nmf narcissist

nar'ciso nm narcissus

nar'cotico a & nm narcotic

na'rice nf nostril

nar'ra|re vt tell. **~'tivo, -a** a narrative • nf fiction. **~'tore, ~'trice** nmf narrator. **~zi'one** nf narration; (racconto) story

na'sale a nasal

'nasc|ere vi (venire al mondo) be born; (germogliare) sprout; (sorgere) rise; **~ere da** fig arise from. **~ita** nf birth. **~i'turo** nm unborn child

na'sconder|e vt hide. **~si** vr hide

nascon'di|glio nm hiding-place. **~no** nm hide-and-seek. **na'scosto** pp di nascondere • a hidden; **di nascosto** secretly

na'sello nm (pesce) hake

'naso nm nose

'nastro nm ribbon; (di registratore ecc) tape. **~ adesivo** adhesive tape. **~ isolante** insulating tape. **~ trasportatore** conveyor belt

na'tal|e a (paese) of one's birth. **N~e** nm Christmas; **~i** pl parentage. **~ità** nf [number of] births. **nata'lizio** a (del Natale) Christmas attrib; (di nascita) of one's birth

na'tante a floating • nm craft

'natica nf buttock

na'tio a native

Nativi'tà nf Nativity. **na'tivo, -a** a & nmf native

'nato pp di nascere • a born; **uno scrittore ~** a born writer; **nata Rossi** née Rossi

NATO nf Nato, NATO

na'tura nf nature; **pagare in ~** pay in kind. **~ morta** still life

natu'ra|le a natural; **al ~le** (alimento) plain, natural; **~le!** naturally, of course. **~'lezza** nf naturalness. **~liz'zare** vt naturalize. **~l'mente** adv (ovviamente) naturally, of course

natu'rista nmf naturalist

naufra'gare vi be wrecked; (persona:) be shipwrecked. **nau'fragio** nm shipwreck; fig wreck. **'naufrago, -a** nmf survivor

'nause|a nf nausea; **avere la ~a** feel sick. **~a'bondo** a nauseating. **~'ante** a nauseating. **~'are** vt nauseate

'nautic|a nf navigation. **~o** a nautical

na'vale a naval

na'vata nf (centrale) nave; (laterale) aisle

'nave nf ship. **~ cisterna** tanker. **~ da guerra** warship. **~ spaziale** spaceship

na'vetta nf shuttle

navicella nf **~ spaziale** nose cone

navi'gabile a navigable

navi'ga|re vi sail; **~re in Internet** surf the Net. **~'tore, ~'trice** mf navigator. **~zi'one** nf navigation

na'viglio nm fleet; (canale) canal

nazio'na|le a national • nf Sport national team. **~'lismo** nm nationalism. **~'lista** nmf nationalist **~lità** nf inv nationality. **~liz'zare** vt nationalize. **na-zi'one** nf nation

na'zista a nmf Nazi

N.B. abbr (nota bene) N.B.

ne pers pron (di lui) about him; (di lei) about her; (di loro) about them; (di ciò) about it; (da ciò) from that; (di un insieme) of it; (di un gruppo) of them; **non ne conosco nessuno** I don't know any of them; **ne ho** I have some; **non ne ho più** I don't have any left • adv from there; **ne vengo ora** I've just come from there; **me ne vado** I'm off

né conj **né... né...** neither... nor...; **non**

ne ho il tempo né la voglia I don't have either the time or the inclination; **né tu né io vogliamo andare** neither you nor I want to go; **né l'uno né l'altro** neither [of them/us]

ne'anche adv (peppure) not even; (senza peppure) neither... nor; **non parlo inglese, e lui ~** I don't speak English, neither does he o and he doesn't either

'nebbi|a nf mist; (in città, su strada) fog. **~'oso** a misty; foggy

necessaria'mente adv necessarily. **neces'sario** a necessary

necessità nf inv necessity; (bisogno) need

necessi'tare vi **~ di** need; (essere necessario) be necessary

necro'logio nm obituary

ne'cropoli nf inv necropolis

ne'fando a wicked

ne'fasto a ill-omened

ne'ga|re vt deny; (rifiutare) refuse; **essere ~to per qcsa** be no good at sth. **~'tivo, -a** a negative ● nf negative. **~zi'one** nf negation; (diniego) denial; Gram negative

ne'gletto a neglected

'negli = in + gli

negli'gen|te a negligent. **~za** nf negligence

negozi'abile a negotiable

negozi'ante nmf dealer; (bottegaio) shopkeeper

negozi'a|re vt negotiate ● vi **~re in** trade in. **~ti** nmpl negotiations

ne'gozio nm shop

'negro, -a a Negro, black ● nmf Negro, black; (scrittore) ghost writer

'nei = in + i. **nel** = in + il. **'nella** = in + la. **'nelle** = in + le. **'nello** = in + lo

'nembo nm nimbus

ne'mico, -a a hostile ● nmf enemy

nem'meno conj not even

'nenia nf dirge; (per bambini) lullaby; (piagnucolio) wail

'neo nm mole; (applicato) beauty spot

'neo+ pref neo+

neofa'scismo nm neofascism

neo'litico a Neolithic

neolo'gismo nm neologism

'neon nm neon

neo'nato, -a a newborn ● nmf newborn baby

neozelan'dese a New Zealand ● nmf New Zealander

nep'pure conj not even

'nerb|o nm (forza) strength; fig backbone. **~o'ruto** a brawny

ne'retto nm Typ bold [type]

'nero a black; (fam: arrabbiato) fuming ● nm black; **mettere ~ su bianco** put in writing

nerva'tura nf nerves pl; Bot veining; (di libro) band

'nervo nm nerve; Bot vein; **avere i nervi** be bad-tempered; **dare ai nervi a qcno** get on sb's nerves. **~'sismo** nm nerviness

ner'voso a nervous; (irritabile) bad-tempered; **avere il ~** be irritable; **esaurimento** nm **~** nervous breakdown

'nespol|a nf medlar. **~o** nm medlar[tree]

'nesso nm link

nes'suno a no, not... any; (qualche) any; **non ho nessun problema** I don't have any problems, I have no problems; **non lo trovo da nessuna parte** I can't find it anywhere; **in nessun modo** on no account; **nessuna notizia?** any news? ● pron nobody, no one, not... anybody, not... anyone; (qualcuno) anybody, anyone; **hai delle domande? – nessuna** do you have any questions? – none; **~ di voi** none of you; **~ dei due** (di voi due) neither of you; **non ho visto ~ dei tuoi amici** I haven't seen any of your friends; **c'è ~?** is anybody there?

'nettare[1] nm nectar

net'tare[2] vt clean

net'tezza nf cleanliness. **~ urbana** cleansing department

'netto a clean; (chiaro) clear; Comm net; **di ~** just like that

nettur'bino nm dustman

neu'tral|e a & nm neutral. **~ità** nf neutrality. **~iz'zare** vt neutralize. **'neutro** a neutral; Gram neuter ● nm Gram neuter

neu'trone nm neutron

'neve nf snow

nevi'care vi snow; **~ca** it is snowing. **~'cata** nf snowfall. **ne'vischio** nm sleet. **ne'voso** a snowy

nevral'gia nf neuralgia. **ne'vralgico a** neuralgic

ne'vro|si nf inv neurosis. **~tico** a neurotic

'nibbio nm kite

'nicchia nf niche

nicchi'are vi shilly-shally

'nichel nm nickel

nichi'lista a & nmf nihilist

nico'tina *nf* nicotine

nidi'ata *nf* brood. '**nido** *nm* nest; (*giardino d'infanzia*) crèche

ni'ente *pron* nothing, not... anything; (*qualcosa*) anything; **non ho fatto ~ di male** I didn't do anything wrong, I did nothing wrong; **grazie! – di ~!** thank you! – don't mention it!; **non serve a ~** it is no use; **vuoi ~?** do you want anything?; **da ~** (*poco importante*) minor; (*di poco valore*) worthless ● *a inv fam* **non ho ~ fame** I'm not the slightest bit hungry ● *adv* **non fa ~** (*non importa*) it doesn't matter; **per ~** at all; ⟨*litigare*⟩ over nothing; **~ affatto!** no way! ● *nm* **un bel ~** absolutely nothing

nientedi'meno, **niente'meno** *adv* **~ che** no less than ● *int* fancy that!

'**ninfa** *nf* nymph

nin'fea *nf* water-lily

ninna'nanna *nf* lullaby

'**ninnolo** *nm* plaything; (*fronzolo*) knick-knack

ni'pote *nm* (*di zii*) nephew; (*di nonni*) grandson, grandchild ● *nf* (*di zii*) niece; (*di nonni*) granddaughter, grandchild

'**nisba** *pron* (*sl: niente*) zilch

'**nitido** *a* neat; (*chiaro*) clear

ni'trato *nm* nitrate

ni'tri|re *vi* neigh. **~to** *nm* (*di cavallo*) neigh

n° *abbr* (**numero**) No

no *adv* no; (*con congiunzione*) not; **dire di no** say no; **credo di no** I don't think so; **perché no?** why not?; **io no** not me; **ha detto così, no?** he said so, didn't he?; **fa freddo, no?** it's cold, isn't it?

'**nobil|e** *a* noble ● *nm* noble, nobleman ● *nf* noble, noblewoman. **~i'are** *a* noble. **~tà** *nf* nobility

'**nocca** *nf* knuckle

nocci'ol|a *nf* hazel-nut. **~o** *nm* (*albero*) hazel

'**nocciolo** *nm* stone; *fig* heart

'**noce** *nf* walnut ● *nm* (*albero, legno*) walnut. **~ moscata** nutmeg. **~'pesca** *nf* nectarine

no'civo *a* harmful

'**nodo** *nm* knot; *fig* lump; *Comput* node; **fare il ~ della cravatta** do up one's tie. **~ alla gola** lump in the throat. **no'doso** *a* knotty. '**nodulo** *nm* nodule

'**noi** *pers pron* (*soggetto*) we; (*oggetto, con prep*) us; **chi è? – siamo ~** who is it? – it's us

'**noia** *nf* boredom; (*fastidio*) bother; (*persona*) bore; **dar ~** annoy

noi'altri *pers pron* we

noi'oso *a* boring; (*fastidioso*) tiresome

noleggi'are *vt* hire; (*dare a noleggio*) hire out; charter (*nave, aereo*). **no'leggio** *nm* hire; (*di nave, aereo*) charter. '**nolo** *nm* hire; *Naut* freight; **a nolo** for hire

'**nomade** *a* nomadic ● *nmf* nomad

'**nome** *nm* name; *Gram* noun; **a ~ di** in the name of; **di ~** by name; **farsi un ~** make a name for oneself. **~ di famiglia** surname. **~ da ragazza** maiden name. **no'mea** *nf* reputation

nomencla'tura *nf* nomenclature

no'mignolo *nm* nickname

no'mina *nf* appointment. **nomi'nale** *a* nominal; *Gram* noun *attrib*

nomi'na|re *vt* name; (*menzionare*) mention; (*eleggere*) appoint. **~'tivo** *a* nominative; *Comm* registered ● *nm* nominative; (*nome*) name

non *adv* not; **~ ti amo** I do not *o* don't love you; **~ c'è di che** not at all

nonché *conj* (*tanto meno*) let alone; (*e anche*) as well as

noncu'ran|te *a* nonchalant; (*negligente*) indifferent. **~za** *nf* nonchalance; (*negligenza*) indifference

nondi'meno *conj* nevertheless

'**nonna** *nf* grandmother, grandma *fam*

'**nonno** *nm* grandfather, grandpa *fam*; **nonni** *pl* grandparents

non'nulla *nm inv* trifle

'**nono** *a & nm* ninth

nono'stante *prep* in spite of ● *conj* although

nontiscordardimé *nm inv* forget-me-not

nonvio'lento *a* nonviolent

nord *nm* north; **del ~** northern

nor'd-est *nm* northeast; **a ~** north-easterly

'**nordico** *a* northern

nordoccidentale *a* northwestern

nordorien'tale *a* northeastern

nor'd-ovest *nm* northwest; **a ~** north-westerly

'**norma** *nf* rule; (*istruzione*) instruction; **a ~ di legge** according to law; **è buona ~** it's advisable

nor'mal|e *a* normal. **~ità** *nf* normality. **~iz'zare** *vt* normalize. **~'mente** *adv* normally

norve'gese *a & nmf* Norwegian. **Nor'vegia** *nf* Norway

nossi'gnore *adv* no way

nostal'gia *nf* (*di casa, patria*) homesickness; (*del passato*) nostalgia; **aver ~** be homesick; **aver ~ di qcno** miss sb.

no'stalgico, -a a nostalgic ● nmf reactionary

no'strano a local; (fatto in casa) homemade

'nostro (il nostro m, la nostra f, i nostri mpl, le nostre fpl) poss a our; quella macchina è nostra that car is ours; ~ padre our father; un ~ amico a friend of ours ● poss pron ours

'nota nf (segno) sign; (comunicazione, commento, Mus) note; (conto) bill; (lista) list; degno di ~ noteworthy; prendere ~ take note. note pl caratteristiche distinguishing marks

no'tabile a & nm notable

no'taio nm notary

no'ta|re vt (segnare) mark; (annotare) note down; (osservare) notice; far ~re qcsa point sth out; farsi ~re get oneself noticed. ~zi'one nf marking; (annotazione) notation

'notes nm inv notepad

no'tevole a (degno di nota) remarkable; (grande) considerable

no'tifica nf notification. notifi'care vt notify; Comm advise. ~zi'one nf notification

no'tizi|a nf una ~a a piece of news, some news; (informazione) a piece of information, some information; le ~e the news sg. ~'ario nm news sg

'noto a [well-]known; rendere ~ (far sapere) announce

notorietà nf fame; raggiungere la ~ become famous. no'torio a well-known; pej notorious

nott'tambulo nm night-bird

not'tata nf night; far ~ stay up all night

'notte nf night; di ~ at night; ~ bianca sleepless night; peggio che andar di ~ worse than ever. ~'tempo adv at night

not'turno a nocturnal; (servizio ecc) night

no'vanta a & nm ninety

novan't|enne a & nmf ninety-year-old. ~esimo a ninetieth. ~ina nf about ninety. 'nove a & nm nine. nove'cento a & nm nine hundred. il N~cento the twentieth century

no'vella nf short story

novel'lino, -a a inexperienced ● nmf novice, beginner. no'vello a new

no'vembre nm November

novità nf inv novelty; (notizie) news sg; l'ultima ~ (moda) the latest fashion

novizi'ato nm Relig novitiate; (tirocinio) apprenticeship

nozi'one nf notion; nozioni pl rudiments

'nozze nfpl marriage sg; (cerimonia) wedding sg. ~ d'argento silver wedding [anniversary]. ~ d'oro golden wedding [anniversary]

'nub|e nf cloud. ~e tossica toxic cloud. ~i'fragio nm cloudburst

'nubile a unmarried ● nf unmarried woman

'nuca nf nape

nucle'are a nuclear

'nucleo nm nucleus; (unità) unit

nu'di|smo nm nudism. ~sta nmf nudist. ~tà nf inv nudity, nakedness

'nudo a naked; (spoglio) bare; a occhio ~ to the naked eye

'nugolo nm large number

'nulla pron = niente; da ~ worthless

nulla'osta nm inv permit

nullate'nente nm i nullatenenti the have-nots

nullità nf inv (persona) nonentity

'nullo a Jur null and void

nume'ra|bile a countable. ~le a & nm numeral

nume'ra|re vt number. ~zi'one nf numbering. nu'merico a numerical

'numero nm number; (romano, arabo) numeral; (di scarpe ecc) size; dare i numeri be off one's head. ~ cardinale cardinal [number]. ~ decimale decimal. ~ ordinale ordinal [number]. ~ di telefono phone number. nume'roso a numerous

'nunzio nm nuncio

nu'ocere vi ~ a harm

nu'ora nf daughter-in-law

nuo'ta|re vi swim; fig wallow; ~re nell'oro be stinking rich, be rolling in it. nu'oto nm swimming. ~'tore, ~'trice nmf swimmer

nu'ov|a nf (notizia) news sg. ~a'mente adv again. ~o a new; di ~o again; rimettere a ~o give a new lease of life to

nutri'ente a nourishing. ~'mento nm nourishment

nu'tri|re vt nourish; harbour (sentimenti). ~rsi eat; ~rsi di fig live on. ~'tivo a nourishing. ~zi'one nf nutrition

'nuvola nf cloud. nuvo'loso a cloudy

nuzi'ale a nuptial; (vestito, anello ecc) wedding attrib

O *abbr* (**ovest**) W

o *conj* or; **~ l'uno ~ l'altro** one or the other, either

'oasi *nf inv* oasis

obbedi'ente ecc = **ubbidiente** ecc

obbli'ga|re *vt* force, oblige; **~rsi** *vr* **~rsi a** undertake to. **~to** *a* obliged. **~'torio** *a* compulsory. **~zi'one** *nf* obligation; *Comm* bond. **'obbligo** *nm* obligation; (*dovere*) duty; **avere obblighi verso** be under an obligation to; **d'obbligo** obligatory

obbligatoria'mente *adv* **fare qcsa ~** be obliged to do sth; **bisogna ~ farlo** you absolutely have to do it

ob'bro|brio *nm* disgrace. **~'brioso** *a* disgraceful

obe'lisco *nm* obelisk

obe'rare *vt* overburden

obesità *nf* obesity. **o'beso** *a* obese

obiet'tare *vt/i* object; **~ su** object to

obietti|va'mente *adv* objectively. **~vità** *nf* objectivity. **obiet'tivo** *a* objective ● *nm* objective; (*scopo*) object

obie|t'tore *nm* objector. **~ttore di coscienza** conscientious objector. **~zi'one** *nf* objection

obi'torio *nm* mortuary

o'blio *nm* oblivion

o'bliquo *a* oblique; *fig* underhand

oblite'rare *vt* obliterate

oblò *nm inv* porthole

'oboe *nm* oboe

obso'leto *a* obsolete

'oca *nf* (*pl* **oche**) goose; (*donna*) silly girl

occasio'nal|e *a* occasional. **~'mente** *adv* occasionally

occasi'one *nf* occasion; (*buon affare*) bargain; (*motivo*) cause; (*opportunità*) chance; **d'~** secondhand

occhi'aia *nf* eye socket; **occhiaie** *pl* shadows under the eyes

occhi'ali *nmpl* glasses, spectacles. **~ da sole** sunglasses. **~ da vista** glasses, spectacles

occhi'ata *nf* look; **dare un'~ a** have a look at

occhieggi'are *vt* ogle ● *vi* (*far capolino*) peep

occhi'ello *nm* buttonhole; (*asola*) eyelet

'occhio *nm* eye; **~!** watch out!; **a quattr'occhi** in private; **tenere d'~ qcno** keep an eye on sb; **a ~ [e croce]** roughly; **chiudere un'~** turn a blind eye; **dare nell'~** attract attention; **pagare o spendere un ~ [della testa]** pay an arm and a leg; **saltare agli occhi** be blindingly obvious. **~ nero** (*pesto*) black eye. **~ di pernice** (*callo*) corn. **~'lino** *nm* **fare l'~lino a qcno** wink at sb

occiden'tale *a* western ● *nmf* westerner. **occi'dente** *nm* west

oc'clu|dere *vt* obstruct. **~si'one** *nf* occlusion

occor'ren|te *a* necessary ● *nm* the necessary. **~za** *nf* need; **all'~za** if need be

oc'correre *vi* be necessary

occulta'mento *nm* **~ di prove** concealment of evidence

occul't|are *vt* hide. **~ismo** *nm* occult. **oc'culto** *a* hidden; (*magico*) occult

occu'pante *nmf* occupier; (*abusivo*) squatter

occu'pa|re *vt* occupy; spend (*tempo*); take up (*spazio*); (*dar lavoro a*) employ. **~rsi** *vr* occupy oneself; (*trovare lavoro*) find a job; **~rsi di** (*badare*) look after. **~to** *a* engaged; (*persona*) busy; (*posto*) taken. **~zi'one** *nf* occupation; **trovarsi un'~zione** (*interesse*) find oneself something to do

o'ceano *nm* ocean. **~ Atlantico** Atlantic [Ocean]. **~ Pacifico** Pacific [Ocean]

'ocra *nf* ochre

ocu'lare *a* ocular; (*testimone, bagno*) eye *attrib*

ocula'tezza *nf* care. **ocu'lato** *a* (*scelta*) wise

ocu'lista *nmf* optician; (*per malattie*) ophthalmologist

od *conj* or

'ode *nf* ode

odi'are *vt* hate

odi'erno *a* of today; (*attuale*) present

'odi|o *nm* hatred; **avere in ~o** hate. **~'oso** *a* hateful

odo'ra|re *vt* smell; (*profumare*) perfume ● *vi* **~re di** smell of. **~to** *nm* sense of smell. **o'dore** *nm* smell; (*profumo*) scent; **c'è odore di...** there's a smell of...; **sentire odore di** smell; **odori** *pl* Culin herbs. **odo'roso** *a* fragrant

of'fender|e *vt* offend; (*ferire*) injure. **~si** *vr* take offence

offen'siv|a *nf* Mil offensive. **~o** *a* offensive

offe'rente *nmf* offerer; (*in aste*) bidder

of'fert|a *nf* offer; (*donazione*) donation; Comm supply; (*nelle aste*) bid; **in ~a speciale** on special offer. **~o** *pp di* **offrire**

of'fes|a *nf* offence. **~o** *pp di* **offendere** ● *a* offended

offi'ciare *vt* officiate

offi'cina *nf* workshop; **~ [meccanica]** garage

of'frir|e *vt* offer. **~si** *vr* offer oneself; (*occasione:*) present itself; **~si di fare qcsa** offer to do sth

offu'scar|e *vt* darken; *fig* dull (*memoria, bellezza*); blur (*vista*). **~si** *vr* darken; (*fig: memoria, bellezza:*) fade away; (*vista:*) become blurred

of'talmico *a* ophthalmic

oggettività *nf* objectivity. **ogget'tivo** *a* objective

og'getto *nm* object; (*argomento*) subject; **oggetti** *pl* **smarriti** lost property, lost and found

'oggi *adv & nm* today; (*al giorno d'oggi*) nowadays; **da ~ in poi** from today on; **~ a otto** a week today; **dall'~ al domani** overnight; **il giornale di ~** today's paper; **al giorno d'~** these days, nowadays. **~gi'orno** *adv* nowadays

'ogni *a inv* every; (*qualsiasi*) any; **~ tre giorni** every three days; **ad ~ costo** at any cost; **ad ~ modo** anyway; **~ cosa** everything; **~ tanto** now and then; **~ volta che** every time, whenever

o'gnuno *pron* everyone, everybody; **~ di voi** each of you

ohimè *int* oh dear!

'ola *nf inv* Mexican wave

O'lan|da *nf* Holland. **~'dese** *a* Dutch ● *nm* Dutchman; (*lingua*) Dutch ● *nf* Dutchwoman

ole'andro *nm* oleander

ole'at|o *a* oiled; **carta ~a** grease-proof paper

oleo'dotto *nm* oil pipeline. **ole'oso** *a* oily

ol'fatto *nm* sense of smell

oli'are *vt* oil

oli'era *nf* cruet

olim'piadi *nfpl* Olympic Games. **o'limpico** *a* Olympic. **olim'pionico** *a* (*primato, squadra*) Olympic

'olio *nm* oil; **sott'~** in oil; **colori a ~** oils; **quadro a ~** oil painting. **~ di mais** corn oil. **~ d'oliva** olive oil. **~ di semi** vegetable oil. **~ solare** sun-tan oil

o'liv|a *nf* olive. **oli'vastro** *a* olive. **oli'veto** *nm* olive grove. **~o** *nm* olive tree

'olmo *nm* elm

olo'gramma *nm* hologram

oltraggi'are *vt* offend. **ol'traggio** *nm* offence

ol'tranza *nf* **ad ~** to the bitter end

'oltre *adv* (*di luogo*) further; (*di tempo*) longer ● *prep* (*di luogo*) over; (*di tempo*) later than; (*più di*) more than; (*in aggiunta*) besides; **~ a** (*eccetto*) except, apart from; **per ~ due settimane** for more than two weeks; **una settimana e ~** a week and more. **~'mare** *adv* overseas. **~'modo** *adv* extremely

oltrepas'sare *vt* go beyond; (*eccedere*) exceed

o'maggio *nm* homage; (*dono*) gift; **in ~ con** free with; **omaggi** *pl* (*saluti*) respects

ombeli'cale *a* umbilical; **cordone ~** umbilical cord. **ombe'lico** *nm* navel

'ombr|a *nf* (*zona*) shade; (*immagine oscura*) shadow; **all'~a** in the shade. **~eggi'are** *vt* shade

om'brello *nm* umbrella. **ombrel'lone** *nm* beach umbrella

om'bretto *nm* eye-shadow

om'broso *a* shady; (*cavallo*) skittish

ome'lette *nf inv* omelette

ome'lia *nf* Relig sermon

omeopa'tia *nf* homoeopathy. **omeo'patico** *a* homoeopathic ● *nm* homoeopath

omertà *nf* conspiracy of silence

o'messo *pp di* **omettere**

o'mettere *vt* omit

omi'cid|a *a* murderous ● *nmf* murderer. **~io** *nm* murder. **~io colposo** manslaughter

omissi'one *nf* omission

omogeneiz'zato *a* homogenized. **omo'geneo** *a* homogeneous

omolo'gare *vt* approve

o'monimo, -a *nmf* namesake ● *nm* (*parola*) homonym

omosessu'al|e *a & nmf* homosexual. **~ità** *nf* homosexuality

On. *abbr* (**onorevole**) M.P.

'oncia *nf* ounce

'onda *nf* wave; **andare in ~** *Radio* go on the air. **a ondate** in waves. **onde** *pl* **corte** short wave. **onde** *pl* **lunghe** long wave. **onde** *pl* **medie** medium wave. **on'data** *nf* wave

'onde *conj* so that ● *pron* whereby

ondeggi'are *vi* wave; ‹*barca:*› roll

ondula|'torio *a* undulating. **~zi'one** *nf* undulation; (*di capelli*) wave

'oner|e *nm* burden. **~'oso** *a* onerous

onestà *nf* honesty; (*rettitudine*) integrity. **o'nesto** *a* honest; (*giusto*) just

'onice *nf* onyx

onnipo'tente *a* omnipotent

onnipre'sente *a* ubiquitous; *Rel* omnipresent

ono'mastico *nm* name-day

ono'ra|bile *a* honourable. **~re** *vt* (*fare onore* a) be a credit to; honour ‹*promessa*›. **~rio** *a* honorary ● *nm* fee. **~rsi** *vr* **~rsi di** be proud of

o'nore *nm* honour; **in ~ di** ‹*festa, ricevimento*› in honour of; **fare ~ a** do justice to ‹*pranzo*›; **farsi ~ in** excel in; **fare gli onori di casa** do the honours

ono'revole *a* honourable ● *nmf* Member of Parliament

onorifi'cenza *nf* honour; (*decorazione*) decoration. **ono'rifico** *a* honorary

'onta *nf* shame

O.N.U. *nf abbr* (**Organizzazione delle Nazioni Unite**) UN

o'paco *a* opaque; ‹*colori ecc*› dull; ‹*fotografia, rossetto*› matt

o'pale *nf* opal

'opera *nf* (*lavoro*) work; (*azione*) deed; *Mus* opera; (*teatro*) opera house; (*ente*) institution; **mettere in ~** put into effect; **mettersi all'~** get to work; **opere** *pl* **pubbliche** public works. **~ d'arte** work of art. **~ lirica** opera

ope'raio, -a *a* working ● *nmf* worker; **~ specializzato** skilled worker

ope'ra|re *vt Med* operate on; **farsi ~re** have an operation ● *vi* operate; (*agire*) work. **~'tivo, ~'torio** *a* operating *attrib.* **~'tore, ~'trice** *nmf* operator; *TV* cameraman. **~tore turistico** tour operator. **~zi'one** *nf* operation; *Comm* transaction

ope'retta *nf* operetta

ope'roso *a* industrious

opini'one *nf* opinion; **rimanere della propria ~** still feel the same way. **~ pubblica** public opinion, vox pop

'oppio *nm* opium

oppo'nente *a* opposing ● *nmf* opponent

op'por|re *vt* oppose; (*obiettare*) object; **~re resistenza** offer resistance. **~si** *vr* **~si a** oppose

opportu'ni|smo *nm* expediency. **~sta** *nmf* opportunist. **~tà** *nf inv* opportunity; (*l'essere opportuno*) timeliness. **oppor'tuno** *a* opportune; (*adeguato*) appropriate; **ritenere opportuno fare qcsa** think it appropriate to do sth; **il momento opportuno** the right moment

opposi|'tore *nm* opposer. **~zi'one** *nf* opposition; **d'~zione** ‹*giornale, partito*› opposition

op'posto *pp di* **opporre** ● *a* opposite; ‹*opinioni*› opposing ● *nm* opposite; **all'~** on the contrary

oppres|si'one *nf* oppression. **~'sivo** *a* oppressive. **op'presso** *pp di* **opprimere** ● *a* oppressed. **~'sore** *nm* oppressor

oppri'me|nte *a* oppressive. **op'prime-re** *vt* oppress; (*gravare*) weigh down

op'pure *conj* otherwise, or [else]; **lunedì ~ martedì** Monday or Tuesday

op'tare *vi* **~ per** opt for

opu'lento *a* opulent

o'puscolo *nm* booklet; (*pubblicitario*) brochure

opzio'nale *a* optional. **opzi'one** *nf* option

'ora[1] *nf* time; (*unità*) hour; **di buon'~** early; **che ~ è?, che ore sono?** what time is it?; **mezz'~** half an hour; **a ore** ‹*lavorare, pagare*› by the hour; **50 km all'~** 50 km an hour; **a un'~ di macchina** one hour by car; **non vedo l'~ di vederti** I can't wait to see you; **fare le ore piccole** stay up until the small hours. **~ d'arrivo** arrival time. **l'~ esatta** *Teleph* speaking clock. **~ legale** daylight saving time. **~ di punta, ore** *pl* **di punta** peak time; (*per il traffico*) rush hour

'ora[2] *adv* now; (*tra poco*) presently; **~ come ~** just now, at the moment; **d'~ in poi** from now on; **per ~** for the time being, for now; **è ~ di finirla!** that's enough now! ● *conj* (*dunque*) now [then]; **~ che ci penso,...** now that I come to think about it,...

o'racolo *nm* oracle

'orafo *nm* goldsmith

o'rale *a & nm* oral; **per via ~** by mouth

ora'mai *adv* = **ormai**

o'rario *a* ⟨*tariffa*⟩ hourly; ⟨*segnale*⟩
time *attrib*; ⟨*velocità*⟩ per hour ● *nm*
time; ⟨*tabella dell'orario*⟩ timetable,
schedule *Am*; **essere in ~** be on time;
in senso ~ clockwise. **~ di chiusura**
closing time. **~ flessibile** flexitime. **~**
di sportello banking hours. **~ d'uf-**
ficio business hours. **~ di visita** *Med*
consulting hours

o'rata *nf* gilthead

ora'tore, -'trice *nmf* speaker

ora'torio, -a *a* oratorical ● *nm Mus*
oratorio ● *nmf* oratory. orazi'one *nf*
Relig prayer

'orbita *nf* orbit; *Anat* [eye-]socket

or'chestra *nf* orchestra; ⟨*parte del*
teatro⟩ pit

orche'stra|le *a* orchestral ● *nmf*
member of an/the orchestra. **~re** *vt* or-
chestrate

orchi'dea *nf* orchid

'orco *nm* ogre

'orda *nf* horde

or'digno *nm* device; ⟨*arnese*⟩ tool. **~**
esplosivo explosive device

ordi'nale *a & nm* ordinal

ordina'mento *nm* order; ⟨*leggi*⟩ rules
pl.

ordi'nanza *nf* ⟨*del sindaco*⟩ bylaw; **d'~**
⟨*soldato*⟩ on duty

ordi'na|re *vt* ⟨*sistemare*⟩ arrange;
⟨*comandare*⟩ order; ⟨*prescrivere*⟩ prescribe; *Relig* ordain

ordi'nario *a* ordinary; ⟨*grossolano*⟩
common; ⟨*professore*⟩ with a permanent
position; **di ordinaria amministra-**
zione routine ● *nm* ordinary; *Univ* professor

ordi'nato *a* ⟨*in ordine*⟩ tidy

ordinazi'one *nf* order; **fare un'~**
place an order

'ordine *nm* order; ⟨*di avvocati, medici*⟩
association; **mettere in ~** put in order;
tidy up ⟨*appartamento ecc*⟩; **di prim'~**
first-class; **di terz'~ e** ⟨*film, albergo*⟩
third- rate; **di ~ pratico/economico**
⟨*problema*⟩ of a practical/economic nature; **fino a nuovo ~** until further notice; **parola d'~** password. **~ del gior-**
no agenda. **ordini sacri** *pl* Holy Orders

or'dire *vt* ⟨*tramare*⟩ plot

orec'chino *nm* ear-ring

o'recchi|o *nm* ⟨*pl* **orecchie**⟩ ear;
avere ~o have a good ear; **mi è giunto**

all'~o che... I've heard that...; **parlare**
all'~o a qcno whisper in sb's ear;
suonare a ~o play by ear; **~'oni** *pl*
Med mumps *sg*

o'refice *nm* jeweller. **~'ria** *nf* ⟨*arte*⟩
goldsmith's art; ⟨*negozio*⟩ goldsmith's
[shop]

'orfano, -a *a* orphan ● *nmf* orphan.
~'trofio *nm* orphanage

orga'netto *nm* barrel-organ; ⟨*a bocca*⟩
mouth-organ; ⟨*fisarmonica*⟩ accordion

or'ganico *a* organic ● *nm* personnel

orga'nismo *nm* organism; ⟨*corpo uma-*
no⟩ body

orga'nista *nmf* organist

organiz'za|re *vt* organize. **~rsi** *vr* get
organized. **~'tore, -'trice** *nmf* organizer. **~zi'one** *nf* organization

'organo *nm* organ

or'gasmo *nm* orgasm; *fig* agitation

'orgia *nf* orgy

or'gogli|o *nm* pride. **~'oso** *a* proud

orien'tale *a* eastern; ⟨*cinese ecc*⟩ orien-
tal

orienta'mento *nm* orientation; **per-**
dere l'~ lose one's bearings; **senso**
dell'~ sense of direction

orien'ta|re *vt* orientate. **~rsi** *vr* find
one's bearings; ⟨*tendere*⟩ tend

ori'ente *nm* east. **l'Estremo O~** the
Far East. **il Medio O~** the Middle East

o'rigano *nm* oregano

origi'na|le *a* original; ⟨*eccentrico*⟩ odd
● *nm* original. **~lità** *nf* originality. **~re**
vt/i originate. **~rio** *a* ⟨*nativo*⟩ native

o'rigine *nf* origin; **in ~** originally; **aver**
~ da originate from; **dare ~ a** give rise
to

origli'are *vi* eavesdrop

o'rina *nf* urine. **ori'nale** *nm* chamber-
pot. **ori'nare** *vi* urinate

ori'undo *a* native

orizzon'tale *a* horizontal

orizzon'tare *vt* = **orientare**. **oriz'zon-**
te *nm* horizon

or'la|re *vt* hem. **~'tura** *nf* hem. **'orlo**
nm edge; ⟨*di vestito ecc*⟩ hem

'orma *nf* track; ⟨*di piede*⟩ footprint;
⟨*impronta*⟩ mark

or'mai *adv* by now; ⟨*passato*⟩ by then;
⟨*quasi*⟩ almost

ormeggi'are *vt* moor. **or'meggio** *nm*
mooring

ormo'nale *a* hormonal. **or'mone** *nm*
hormone

ornamen'tale *a* ornamental. **orna-**
'mento *nm* ornament

or'na|re *vt* decorate. **~rsi** *vr* deck oneself. **~to** *a ⟨stile⟩* ornate

ornitolo'gia *nf* ornithology

'oro *nm* gold; **d'~** gold; *fig* golden; **una persona d'~** a wonderful person

orolo'gia|io, -a *nmf* clockmaker, watchmaker

oro'logio *nm ⟨portatile⟩* watch; *⟨da tavolo, muro ecc⟩* clock. **~ a pendolo** grandfather clock. **~ da polso** wristwatch. **~ a sveglia** alarm clock

o'roscopo *nm* horoscope

or'rendo *a* awful, dreadful

or'ribile *a* horrible

orripi'lante *a* horrifying

or'rore *nm* horror; **avere qcsa in ~** hate sth

orsacchi'otto *nm* teddy bear

'orso *nm* bear; *⟨persona scontrosa⟩* hermit. **~ bianco** polar bear

or'taggio *nm* vegetable

or'tensia *nf* hydrangea

or'tica *nf* nettle. **orti'caria** *nf* nettlerash

orticol'tura *nf* horticulture. **'orto** *nm* vegetable plot

orto'dosso *a* orthodox

ortogo'nale *a* perpendicular

orto|gra'fia *nf* spelling. **~'grafico** *a* spelling *attrib*

orto'lano *nm* market gardener

orto|pe'dia *nf* orthopaedics *sg*. **~'pedico** *a* orthopaedic ● *nm* orthopaedist

orzai'olo *nm* sty

or'zata *nf* barley-water

osan'nato *a ⟨esaltato⟩* praised to the skies

o'sare *vt/i* dare; *⟨avere audacia⟩* be daring

oscenità *nf inv* obscenity. **o'sceno** *a* obscene

oscil'la|re *vi* swing; *⟨prezzi ecc:⟩* fluctuate; *Tech* oscillate; *⟨fig: essere indeciso⟩* vacillate. **~zi'one** *nf* swinging; *⟨di prezzi⟩* fluctuation; *Tech* oscillation

oscura'mento *nm* darkening; *⟨fig: di vista, mente⟩* dimming; *⟨totale⟩* black-out

oscu'r|are *vt* darken; *fig* obscure. **~arsi** *vr* get dark. **~ità** *nf* darkness. **o'scuro** *a* dark; *⟨triste⟩* gloomy; *⟨incomprensibile⟩* obscure

ospe'dal|e *nm* hospital. **~i'ero** *a* hospital *attrib*

ospi'ta|le *a* hospitable. **~lità** *nf* hospitality. **~re** *vt* give hospitality to. **'ospite** *nm ⟨chi ospita⟩* host; *⟨chi viene ospitato⟩* guest ● *nf* hostess; guest

o'spizio *nm ⟨per vecchi⟩* [old people's] home

ossa'tura *nf* bone structure; *⟨di romanzo⟩* structure, framework. **'osseo** *a* bone *attrib*

ossequi'are *vt* pay one's respects to. **os'sequio** *nm* homage; **ossequi** *pl* respects. **~'oso** *a* obsequious

osser'van|te *a ⟨cattolico⟩* practising. **~za** *nf* observance

osser'va|re *vt* observe; *⟨notare⟩* notice; keep *⟨ordine, silenzio⟩*. **~'tore, ~'trice** *nmf* observer. **~'torio** *nm Astr* observatory; *Mil* observation post. **~zi'one** *nf* observation; *⟨rimprovero⟩* reproach

ossessio'na|nte *a* haunting; *⟨persona⟩* nagging. **~re** *vt* obsess; *⟨infastidire⟩* nag. **ossessi'one** *nf* obsession; *⟨assillo⟩* pain in the neck. **osses'sivo** *a* obsessive. **os'sesso** *a* obsessed

os'sia *conj* that is

ossi'dabile *a* liable to tarnish

ossi'dar|e *vt*, **~si** *vr* oxidize

'ossido *nm* oxide. **~ di carbonio** carbon monoxide

os'sidrico *a* **fiamma ossidrica** blowlamp

ossige'nar|e *vt* oxygenate; *⟨decolorare⟩* bleach. **~si** *vr* **~si i capelli** dye one's hair blonde; *fig* put back on its feet *⟨azienda⟩*. **os'sigeno** *nm* oxygen

'osso *nm ⟨Anat: pl nf* ossa⟩ bone; *⟨di frutto⟩* stone

osso'buco *nm* marrowbone

os'suto *a* bony

ostaco'lare *vt* hinder, obstruct. **o'stacolo** *nm* obstacle; *Sport* hurdle

o'staggio *nm* hostage; **prendere in ~** take hostage

o'stello *nm* **~ della gioventù** youth hostel

osten'ta|re *vt* show off; **~re indifferenza** pretend to be indifferent. **~zi'one** *nf* ostentation

oste'ria *nf* inn

o'stetrico, -a *a* obstetric ● *nmf* obstetrician

'ostia *nf* host; *⟨cialda⟩* wafer

'ostico *a* tough

o'stil|e *a* hostile. **~ità** *nf inv* hostility

osti'na|rsi *vr* persist (**a** in). **~to** *a* obstinate. **~zi'one** *nf* obstinacy

ostra'cismo *nm* ostracism

'ostrica *nf* oyster

ostro'goto *nm* **parlare ~** talk double Dutch

ostru|'ire *vt* obstruct. **~zi'one** *nf* obstruction

otorinolaringoi'atra *nmf* ear, nose and throat specialist

ottago'nale *a* octagonal. **ot'tagono** *nm* octagon

ot'tan|ta *a & nm* eighty. **~'tenne** *a & nmf* eighty-year-old. **~'tesimo** *a* eightieth. **~'tina** *nf* about eighty

ot'tav|a *nf* octave. **~o** *a* eighth

otte'nere *vt* obtain; (*più comune*) get; (*conseguire*) achieve

'ottico, -a *a* optic[al] ● *nmf* optician ● *nf* (*scienza*) optics *sg* (*di lenti ecc*) optics *pl*

otti'ma|le *a* optimum. **~'mente** *adv* very well

otti'mis|mo *nm* optimism. **~ta** *nmf* optimist. **~tico** *a* optimistic

'ottimo *a* very good ● *nm* optimum

'otto *a & nm* eight

ot'tobre *nm* October

otto'cento *a & nm* eight hundred; **l'O~** the nineteenth century

ot'tone *nm* brass

ottuage'nario, -a *a & nmf* octogenarian

ottu'ra|re *vt* block; fill (*dente*). **~rsi** *vr* clog. **~'tore** *nm Phot* shutter. **~zi'one** *nf* stopping; (*di dente*) filling

ot'tuso *pp di* **ottundere** ● *a* obtuse

o'vaia *nf* ovary

o'vale *a & nm* oval

o'vat|ta *nf* cotton wool. **~'tato** *a* (*suono, passi*) muffled

ovazi'one *nf* ovation

over'dose *nf inv* overdose

'ovest *nm* west

o'vi|le *nm* sheep-fold. **~no** *a* sheep *attrib*

ovo'via *nf* two-seater cable car

ovulazi'one *nf* ovulation

o'vunque *adv* = **dovunque**

ov'vero *conj* or; (*cioè*) that is

ovvia'mente *adv* obviously

ovvi'are *vi* **~ a** qcsa counter sth. **'ovvio** *a* obvious

ozi'are *vi* laze around. **'ozio** *nm* idleness; **stare in ozio** idle about. **ozi'oso** *a* idle; (*questione*) pointless

o'zono *nm* ozone; **buco nell'~** hole in the ozone layer

#

pa'ca|re *vt* quieten. **~to** *a* quiet

pac'chetto *nm* packet; (*postale*) parcel, package; (*di sigarette*) pack, packet. **~ software** software package

'pacchia *nf* (*fam: situazione*) bed of roses

pacchia'nata *nf* **è una ~** it's so garish. **pacchi'ano** *a* garish

'pacco *nm* parcel; (*involto*) bundle. **~ regalo** gift-wrapped package

paccot'tiglia *nf* (*roba scadente*) junk, rubbish

'pace *nf* peace; **darsi ~** forget it; **fare ~ con** qcno make it up with sb; **lasciare in ~** qcno leave sb in peace

pachi'derma *nm* (*animale*) pachyderm

pachi'stano, -a *nmf & a* Pakistani

pacifi'ca|re *vt* reconcile; (*mettere pace*) pacify. **~zi'one** *nf* reconciliation

pa'cifico *a* pacific; (*calmo*) peaceful; **il P~** the Pacific

paci'fis|mo *nm* pacifism. **~ta** *nmf* pacifist

pacioc'cone, -a *nmf fam* chubby-chops

pa'dano *a* **pianura** *nf* **padana** Po Valley

pa'del|la *nf* frying-pan; (*per malati*) bedpan. **~'lata** *nf* **una ~lata di** a frying-panful of

padigli'one *nm* pavilion

'padr|e *nm* father; **~i** *pl* (*antenati*) forefathers. **pa'drino** *nm* godfather. **~e'nostro** *nm* **il ~enostro** the Lord's Prayer. **~e'terno** *nm* God Almighty

padro'nanza *nf* mastery. **~ di sé** self-control

pa'drone, -a *nmf* master; mistress; (*datore di lavoro*) boss; (*proprietario*) owner. **~ggi'are** *vt* master

pae'sag|gio *nm* scenery; (*pittura*) landscape. **~'gista** *nmf* landscape architect

pae'sano, -a *a* country ● *nmf* villager

pa'ese *nm* (*nazione*) country; (*territorio*) land; (*villaggio*) village; **il Bel P~** Italy; **va' a quel ~!** get lost!; **Paesi** *pl* **Bassi** Netherlands

paf'futo *a* plump

'paga *nf* pay, wages *pl*

pa'gabile *a* payable

pa'gaia *nf* paddle

paga'mento *nm* payment; **a ~** (*parcheggio*) which you have to pay to use. **~ anticipato** *Comm* advance payment. **~ alla consegna** cash on delivery, COD

paga'nesimo *nm* paganism

pa'gano, -a *a* & *nmf* pagan

pa'gare *vt/i* pay; **~ da bere a qcno** buy sb a drink; **te la faccio ~** you'll pay for this

pa'gella *nf* [school] report

'pagina *nf* page. **Pagine** *pl* **Gialle** Yellow Pages. **~ web** *Comput* web page

'paglia *nf* straw

pagliac'cetto *nm* (*per bambini*) rompers *pl*

pagliac'ciata *nf* farce

pagli'accio *nm* clown

pagli'aio *nm* haystack

paglie'riccio *nm* straw mattress

pagli'etta *nf* (*cappello*) boater; (*per pentole*) steel wool

pagli'uzza *nf* wisp of straw; (*di metallo*) particle

pa'gnotta *nf* [round] loaf

pa'goda *nf* pagoda

pail'lette *nf inv* sequin

'paio *nm* (*pl nf* **paia**) pair; **un ~** (*circa due*) a couple; **un ~ di** (*scarpe, forbici*) a pair of

'Pakistan *nm* Pakistan

'pala *nf* shovel; (*di remo, elica*) blade; (*di ruota*) paddle

pala'fitta *nf* pile-dwelling

pala'sport *nm inv* indoor sports arena

pa'late *nfpl* **a ~** (*fare soldi*) hand over fist

pa'lato *nm* palate

palaz'zetto *nm* **~ dello sport** indoor sports arena

palaz'zina *nf* villa

pa'lazzo *nm* palace; (*edificio*) building. **~ delle esposizioni** exhibition centre. **~ di giustizia** law courts *pl*, courthouse. **~ dello sport** indoor sports arena

'palco *nm* (*pedana*) platform; *Theat* box. **~['scenico]** *nm* stage

pale'sar|e *vt* disclose. **~si** *vr* reveal oneself. **pa'lese** *a* evident

Pale'sti|na *nf* Palestine. **~'nese** *nmf* Palestinian

pa'lestra *nf* gymnasium, gym; (*ginnastica*) gymnastics *pl*

pa'letta *nf* spade; (*per focolare*) shovel. **~ [della spazzatura]** dustpan

pa'letto *nm* peg

'palio *nm* (*premio*) prize. **il P~** horserace held at Siena

paliz'zata *nf* fence

'palla *nf* ball; (*proiettile*) bullet; (*fam: bugia*) porkie; **che palle!** *vulg* this 's a pain in the arse!. **~ di neve** snowball. **~ al piede** *fig* millstone round one's neck

pallaca'nestro *nf* basketball

palla'mano *nf* handball

pallanu'oto *nf* water polo

palla'volo *nf* volley-ball

palleggi'are *vi* (*calcio*) practise ball control; *Tennis* knock up

pallia'tivo *nm* palliative

'pallido *a* pale; **non ne ho la più pallida idea** I don't have the faintest idea

pal'lina *nf* (*di vetro*) marble

pal'lino *nm* **avere il ~ del calcio** be crazy about football

pallon'cino *nm* balloon; (*lanterna*) Chinese lantern; (*fam: etilometro*) Breathalyzer®

pal'lone *nm* ball; (*calcio*) football; (*aerostato*) balloon

pal'lore *nm* pallor

pal'loso *a sl* boring

pal'lottola *nf* pellet; (*proiettile*) bullet

'palm|a *nf Bot* palm. **~o** *nm Anat* palm; (*misura*) hand's-breadth; **restare con un ~o di naso** feel disappointed

'palo *nm* pole; (*di sostegno*) stake; (*in calcio*) goalpost; **fare il ~** (*di ladro:*) keep a lookout. **~ della luce** lamppost

palom'baro *nm* diver

pal'pare *vt* feel

'palpebra *nf* eyelid

palpi'ta|re *vi* throb; (*fremere*) quiver. **~zi'one** *nf* palpitation. **'palpito** *nm* throb; (*del cuore*) beat

pa'lude *nf* marsh, swamp

palu'doso *a* marshy

pa'lustre *a* marshy; (*piante, uccelli*) marsh *attrib*

'pampino *nm* vine leaf

pana'cea *nf* panacea

'panca *nf* bench; (*in chiesa*) pew

pancar'ré *nm* sliced bread

pan'cetta *nf Culin* bacon; (*di una certa età*) paunch

pan'chetto *nm* [foot]stool

pan'china *nf* garden seat; (*in calcio*) bench

'pancia *nf* belly, tummy *fam*; **mal di ~** stomach-ache; **metter su ~** develop a paunch; **a ~ in giù** lying face down. **panci'era** *nf* corset

panci'olle: stare in ~ lounge about

panci'one *nm* (*persona*) pot belly

panci'otto *nm* waistcoat

pande'monio *nm* pandemonium

pan'doro *nm* kind of sponge cake eaten at Christmas

'pane *nm* bread; (*pagnotta*) loaf; (*di burro*)· block. **~ a cassetta** sliced bread. **pan grattato** breadcrumbs *pl*. **~ di segale** rye bread. **pan di Spagna** sponge cake. **~ tostato** toast

panett|e'ria *nf* bakery; (*negozio*) baker's [shop]. **~'i'ere, -a** *nmf* baker

panet'tone *nf* dome-shaped cake with sultanas and candied fruit eaten at Christmas

'panfilo *nm* yacht

pan'forte *nm* nougat-like spicy delicacy from Siena

'panico *nm* panic; **lasciarsi prendere dal ~** panic

pani'ere *nm* basket; (*cesta*) hamper

pani'ficio *nm* bakery; (*negozio*) baker's [shop]

pani'naro *nm* *sl* ≈ preppie

pa'nino *nm* [bread] roll. **~ imbottito** filled roll. **~ al prosciutto** ham roll. **~'teca** *nf* sandwich bar

'panna *nf* cream. **~ da cucina** [single] cream. **~ montata** whipped cream

'panne *nf* Mech **in ~** broken down; **restare in ~** break down

pan'nello *nm* panel. **~ solare** solar panel

'panno *nm* cloth; **panni**· *pl* (*abiti*) clothes; **mettersi nei panni di qcno** *fig* put oneself in sb's shoes

pan'nocchia *nf* (*di granturco*) cob

panno'lino *nm* (*per bambini*) nappy; (*da donna*) sanitary towel

pano'ram|a *nm* panorama; *fig* overview. **~ico** *a* panoramic

pantacol'lant *nmpl* leggings

pantalon'cini *nmpl* **~** [*corti*] shorts

panta'loni *nmpl* trousers, pants *Am*

pan'tano *nm* bog

pan'tera *nf* panther; (*auto della polizia*) high-speed police car

pan'tofo|la *nf* slipper. **~'laio, -a** *nmf* *fig* stay-at-home

pan'zana *nf* fib

pao'nazzo *a* purple

'papa *nm* Pope

papà *nm inv* dad[dy]

pa'pale *a* papal

papa'lina *nf* skull-cap

papa'razzo *nm* paparazzo

pa'pato *nm* papacy

pa'pavero *nm* poppy

'paper|a *nf* (*errore*) slip of the tongue. **~o** *nm* gosling

papil'lon *nm inv* bow tie

pa'piro *nm* papyrus

'pappa *nf* (*per bambini*) pap

pappa'gallo *nm* parrot

pappa'molle *nmf* wimp

'para *nf* **suole** *nfpl* **di ~** crêpe soles

pa'rabola *nf* parable; (*curva*) parabola

para'bolico *a* parabolic

para'brezza *nm inv* windscreen, windshield *Am*

paracadu'tar|e *vt* parachute. **~si** *vr* parachute

paraca'du|te *nm inv* parachute. **~'tismo** *nm* parachuting. **~'tista** *nmf* parachutist

para'carro *nm* roadside post

paradi'siaco *a* heavenly

para'diso *nm* paradise. **~ terrestre** Eden, earthly paradise

parados'sale *a* paradoxical. **para'dosso** *nm* paradox

para'fango *nm* mudguard

paraf'fina *nf* paraffin

parafra'sare *vt* paraphrase

para'fulmine *nm* lightning-conductor

pa'raggi *nmpl* neighbourhood *sg*

parago'na|bile *a* comparable (**a** to). **~re** *vt* compare. **para'gone** *nm* comparison; **a paragone di** in comparison with

pa'ragrafo *nm* paragraph

pa'ra|lisi *nf inv* paralysis. **~'litico, -a** *a* & *nmf* paralytic. **~liz'zare** *vt* paralyse. **~liz'zato** *a* (*dalla paura*) transfixed

paral'lel|a *nf* parallel line. **~a'mente** *adv* in parallel. **~o** *a* & *nm* parallel; **~e** *pl* parallel bars. **~o'gramma** *nm* parallelogram

para'lume *nm* lampshade

para'medico *nm* paramedic

pa'rametro *nm* parameter

para'noi|a *nf* paranoia. **~co, -a** *a* & *nmf* paranoid

paranor'male *a* ⟨*fenomeno, facoltà*⟩ paranormal

para'occhi *nmpl* blinkers. **parao'rec-chie** *nm* earmuffs

para'petto *nm* parapet

para'piglia nm turmoil
para'plegico, -a a & nmf paraplegic
pa'rar|e vt (addobbare) adorn; (riparare) shield; save ⟨tiro, pallone⟩; ward off, parry ⟨schiaffo, pugno⟩ ● vi (mirare) lead up to. **~si** vr (abbigliarsi) dress up; (da pioggia, pugni) protect oneself; **~si dinanzi a qcno** appear in front of sb
para'sole nm inv parasol
paras'sita a parasitic ● nm parasite
parasta'tale a government-controlled
pa'rata nf parade; (in calcio) save; (in scherma, pugilato) parry
para'urti nm inv Auto bumper, fender Am
para'vento nm screen
par'cella nf bill
parcheggi'a|re vt park. **par'cheggio** nm parking; (posteggio) carpark, parking lot Am. **~'tore**, **~'trice** nmf parking attendant. **~tore abusivo** person who illegally earns money by looking after parked cars
par'chimetro nm parking-meter
'parco[1] a sparing; (moderato) moderate
'parco[2] nm park. **~ di divertimenti** fun-fair. **~ giochi** playground. **~ naturale** wildlife park. **~ nazionale** national park. **~ regionale** [regional] wildlife park
pa'recchi a a good many ● pron several
pa'recchio a quite a lot of ● pron quite a lot ● adv rather; (parecchio tempo) quite a time
pareggi'are vt level; (eguagliare) equal; Comm balance ● vi draw
pa'reggio nm Comm balance; Sport draw
paren'tado nm relatives pl; (vincolo di sangue) relationship
pa'rente nmf relative. **~ stretto** close relation
paren'tela nf relatives pl; (vincolo di sangue) relationship
pa'rentesi nf inv parenthesis; (segno grafico) bracket; (fig: pausa) break. **~ pl graffe** curly brackets. **~ quadre** square brackets. **~ tonde** round brackets
pa'reo nm (copricostume) sarong; **a** ⟨gonna⟩ wrap-around
pa'rere[1] nm opinion; **a mio ~** in my opinion
pa'rere[2] vi seem; (pensare) think; **che te ne pare?** what do you think of it?; **pare di sì** it seems so

pa'rete nf wall; (in alpinismo) face. **~ divisoria** partition wall
'pari a inv equal; ⟨numero⟩ even; **andare di ~ passo** keep pace; **essere ~** be even o quits; **arrivare ~** draw; **~** ⟨copiare, ripetere⟩ word for word; **fare ~ o dispari** ≈ toss a coin ● nmf inv equal, peer; **ragazza alla ~** au pair [girl]; **mettersi in ~ con qcsa** catch up with sth ● nm (titolo nobiliare) peer
Pa'rigi nf Paris
pa'riglia nf pair
pari'tà nf equality; Tennis deuce. **~'tario** a parity attrib
parlamen'tare a parliamentary ● nmf Member of Parliament ● vi discuss. **parla'mento** nm Parliament. **il Parlamento europeo** the European Parliament
parlan'tina nf **avere la ~** be a chatterbox
par'la|re vt/i speak, talk; (confessare) talk; **~ bene/male di qcno** speak well/ill of somebody; **non parliamone più** let's forget about it; **non se ne parla nemmeno** don't even mention it!. **~to** a ⟨lingua⟩ spoken. **~'torio** nm parlour; (in prigione) visiting room
parlot'tare vi mutter. **parlot'tio** nm muttering
parmigi'ano nm Parmesan
paro'dia nf parody
pa'rola nf word; (facoltà) speech; **è una ~!** it is easier said than done!; **parole** pl (di canzone) words, lyrics; **rivolgere la ~ a** address; **dare a qcno la propria ~** give sb one's word; **in parole povere** crudely speaking. **parole** pl **incrociate** crossword [puzzle] sg. **~ d'onore** word of honour. **~ d'ordine** password. **paro'laccia** nf swear-word
par'quet nm inv (pavimento) parquet flooring
par'rocchi|a nf parish. **~'ale** a parish attrib. **~'ano, -a** nmf parishioner. **'parr|oco** nm parish priest
par'rucca nf wig
parrucchi'ere, -a nmf hairdresser
parruc'chino nm toupée, hairpiece
parsi'moni|a nf thrift. **~'oso** a thrifty
'parso pp di **parere**
'parte nf part; (lato) side; (partito) party; (porzione) share; **a ~** apart from; **in ~** in part; **la maggior ~ di** the majority of; **d'altra ~** on the other hand; **da ~** aside; (in disparte) to one side; **farsi da ~** stand aside; **da ~ di** from; (per conto di) on behalf of; **è gentile da**

~ **tua** it is kind of you; **fare una brutta ~ a qcno** behave badly towards sb; **da che ~ è...?** whereabouts is...?; **da una ~..., dall'altra...** on the one hand..., on the other hand...; **dall'altra ~ di** on the other side of; **da nessuna ~** nowhere; **da tutte le parti** (essere) everywhere; **da questa ~** (in questa direzione) this way; **da un anno a questa ~** for about a year now; **essere dalla ~ di qcno** be on sb's side; **prendere le parti di qcno** take sb's side; **essere ~ in causa** be involved; **fare ~ di** (appartenere a) be a member of; **rendere ~ a** take part in. **~ civile** plaintiff

parteci'pante nmf participant

parteci'pa|re vi ~re a participate in, take part in; (condividere) share in. **~zi'one** nf participation; (annuncio) announcement; Fin shareholding; (presenza) presence. **par'tecipe** a participating

parteggi'are vi ~ **per** side with

par'tenza nf departure; Sport start; **in ~ per** leaving for

parti'cella nf particle

parti'cipio nm participle

partico'lar|e a particular; (privato) private ● nm detail, particular; **fin nei minimi ~i** down to the smallest detail. **~eggi'ato** a detailed. **~ità** nf inv particularity; (dettaglio) detail

partigi'ano, -a a & nmf partisan

par'tire vi leave; (aver inizio) start; **a ~ da** [beginning] from

par'tita nf game; (incontro) match; Comm lot; (contabilità) entry. **~ di calcio** football match. **~ a carte** game of cards

par'tito nm party; (scelta) choice; (occasione di matrimonio) match; **per ~ preso** out of sheer pig-headedness

'parto nm childbirth; **un ~ facile** an easy birth o labour; **dolori pl del ~** labour pains. **~ cesareo** Caesarian section. **~'rire** vt give birth to

par'venza nf appearance

parzi'al|e a partial. **~ità** nf partiality. **~'mente** adv (non completamente) partially; **~mente scremato** semi-skimmed

pasco'lare vt graze. **'pascolo** nm pasture

'Pasqua nf Easter. **pa'squale** a Easter attrib

'passa: e ~ adv (e oltre) plus

pas'sabile a passable

pas'saggio nm passage; (traversata) crossing; Sport pass; (su veicolo) lift; **essere di ~** be passing through. **~ a livello** level crossing, grade crossing Am. **~ pedonale** pedestrian crossing

passamon'tagna nm inv balaclava

pas'sante nmf passer-by ● nm (di cintura) loop ● a Tennis passing

passa'porto nm passport

pas'sa|re vi pass; (attraversare) pass through; (far visita) call; (andare) go; (essere approvato) be passed; **~re alla storia** go down in history; **mi è ~to di mente** it slipped my mind; **~re per un genio/idiota** be taken for a genius/an idiot; **farsi ~re per qcno** pass oneself off as sb ● vt (far scorrere) pass over; (sopportare) go through; (al telefono) put through; Culin strain; **~re di moda** go out of fashion; **le passo il signor Rossi** I'll put you through to Mr Rossi; **~rsela bene** be well off; **come te la passi?** how are you doing?. **~ta** nf (di vernice) coat; (spolverata) dusting; (occhiata) look

passa'tempo nm pastime

pas'sato a past; **l'anno ~** last year; **sono le tre passate** it's past o after three o'clock ● nm past; Culin purée; Gram past tense. **~ prossimo** Gram present perfect. **~ remoto** Gram [simple] past. **~ di verdure** cream of vegetable soup

passaver'dure nm inv food mill

passeg'gero, -a a passing ● nmf passenger

passeggi'a|re vi walk, stroll. **~ta** nf walk, stroll; (luogo) public walk; (in bicicletta) ride; **fare una ~ta** go for a walk

passeg'gino nm pushchair, stroller Am

pas'seggio nm walk; (luogo) promenade; **andare a ~** go for a walk; **scarpe da ~** walking shoes

passe-partout nm inv master-key

passe'rella nf gangway; Aeron boarding bridge; (per sfilate) catwalk

'passero nm sparrow. **passe'rotto** nm (passero) sparrow

pas'sibile a ~ **di** liable to

passio'nale a passionate. **passi'one** nf passion

pas'sivo a passive ● nm passive; Comm liabilities pl; **in ~** ‹bilancio› loss-making

'passo nm step; (orma) footprint; (andatura) pace; (brano) passage; (valico) pass; **a due passi da qui** a stone's throw away; **a ~ d'uomo** at walking pace; **di buon ~** at a spanking pace; **fare due passi** go for a stroll; **di pari ~** *fig* hand in hand. **~ carrabile, ~ carraio** driveway

'past|a *nf* (*impasto per pane ecc*) dough; (*per dolci, pasticcino*) pastry; (*pastasciutta*) pasta; (*massa molle*) paste; *fig* nature. **~a frolla** shortcrust pastry. **pa'stella** *nf* batter

pastasci'utta *nf* pasta

pa'stello *nm* pastel

pa'sticca *nf* pastille; (*fam: pastiglia*) pill

pasticc|e'ria *nf* cake shop, patisserie; (*pasticcini*) pastries *pl*; (*arte*) confectionery

pasticci'are *vi* make a mess ● *vt* make a mess of

pasticci'ere, -a *nmf* confectioner

pastic'cino *nm* little cake

pa'sticci|o *nm* Culin pie; (*lavoro disordinato*) mess; **mettersi nei pasticci** get into trouble. **~'one, -a** *nmf* bungler ● *a* bungling

pasti'ficio *nm* pasta factory

pa'stiglia *nf* Med pill, tablet; (*di menta*) sweet. **~ dei freni** brake pad

'pasto *nm* meal

pasto'rale *a* pastoral. **pa'store** *nm* shepherd; *Relig* pastor. **pastore tedesco** German shepherd, Alsatian

pastoriz'za|re *vt* pasteurize. **~to** *a* pasteurized. **~zi'one** *nf* pasteurization

pa'stoso *a* doughy; *fig* mellow

pa'stura *nf* pasture; (*per pesci*) bait

pa'tacca *nf* (*macchia*) stain; (*fig: oggetto senza valore*) piece of junk

pa'tata *nf* potato. **patate** *pl* **fritte** chips *Br*, French fries. **pata'tine** *nfpl* [potato] crisps, chips *Am*

pata'trac *nm inv* (*crollo*) crash

pâté *nm inv* pâté

pa'tella *nf* limpet

pa'tema *nm* anxiety

pa'tente *nf* licence. **~ di guida** driving licence, driver's license *Am*

pater'na|le *nf* scolding. **~'lista** *nm* paternalist

paternità *nf* paternity. **pa'terno** *a* paternal; (*affetto ecc*) fatherly

pa'tetico *a* pathetic. **'pathos** *nm* pathos

pa'tibolo *nm* gallows *sg*

'patina *nf* patina; (*sulla lingua*) coating

pa'ti|re *vt/i* suffer. **~to, -a** *a* suffering ● *nmf* fanatic. **~to della musica** music lover

patolo'gia *nf* pathology. **pato'logico** *a* pathological

'patria *nf* native land

patri'arca *nm* patriarch

pa'trigno *nm* stepfather

patrimoni'ale *a* property *attrib*. **patri'monio** *nm* estate

patri'o|ta *nmf* patriot. **~tico** *a* patriotic. **~'tismo** *nm* patriotism

pa'trizio, -a *a & nmf* patrician

patro|ci'nare *vt* support. **~'cinio** *nm* support

patro'nato *nm* patronage. **pa'trono** *nm* Relig patron saint; *Jur* counsel

'patta¹ *nf* (*di tasca*) flap

'patta² *nf* (*pareggio*) draw

patteggi|a'mento *nm* bargaining. **~'are** *vt/i* negotiate

patti'naggio *nm* skating. **~ su ghiaccio** ice skating. **~ a rotelle** roller skating

patti'na|re *vi* skate; ⟨*auto:*⟩ skid. **~'tore, ~'trice** *nmf* skater. **'pattino** *nm* skate; *Aeron* skid. **pattino da ghiaccio** iceskate. **pattino a rotelle** roller-skate

'patto *nm* deal; *Pol* pact; **a ~ che** on condition that

pat'tuglia *nf* patrol. **~ stradale** ≈ patrol car; police motorbike, highway patrol *Am*

pattu'ire *vt* negotiate

pattumi'era *nf* dustbin, trashcan *Am*

pa'ura *nf* fear; (*spavento*) fright; **aver ~** be afraid; **mettere ~ a** frighten. **pau'roso** *a* (*che fa paura*) frightening; (*che ha paura*) fearful; (*fam: enorme*) awesome

'pausa *nf* pause; (*nel lavoro*) break; **fare una ~** pause; (*nel lavoro*) have a break

pavimen'ta|re *vt* pave ⟨*strada*⟩. **~zi'one** *nf* (*operazione*) paving. **pavi'mento** *nm* floor

pa'vone *nm* peacock. **~ggi'arsi** *vr* strut

pazien'tare *vi* be patient

pazi'ente *a & nmf* patient. **~'mente** *adv* patiently. **pazi'enza** *nf* patience; **pazienza!** never mind!

'pazza *nf* madwoman. **~'mente** *adv* madly

paz'z|esco *a* foolish; (*esagerato*) crazy. **~ia** *nf* madness; (*azione*) [act of] folly. **'pazzo** *a* mad; *fig* crazy ● *nm* madman; **essere pazzo di/per** be crazy about; **pazzo di gioia** mad with joy; **da pazzi** *fam* crackpot; **darsi alla pazza gioia** live it up. **paz'zoide** *a* whacky

'**pecca** *nf* fault; **senza ~** flawless.
peccami'noso *a* sinful
pec'ca|re *vi* sin; **~re di** be guilty of
⟨*ingratitudine*⟩. **~to** *nm* sin; **~to che...**
it's a pity that...; [**che**] **~to!** [what a]
pity!. **~'tore**, **~'trice** *nmf* sinner
'**pece** *nf* pitch
'**peco|ra** *nf* sheep. **~ra nera** black
sheep. **~raio** *nm* shepherd. **~'rella** *nf*
cielo a ~relle sky full of fluffy white
clouds. **~'rino** *nm* (*formaggio*) sheep's
milk cheese
peculi'ar|e *a* **~ di** peculiar to. **~ità** *nf*
inv peculiarity
pe'daggio *nm* toll
pedago'gia *nf* pedagogy. **peda'gogico** *a* pedagogical
peda'lare *vi* pedal. **pe'dale** *nm* pedal.
pedalò *nm inv* pedalo
pe'dana *nf* footrest; *Sport* springboard
pe'dante *a* pedantic. **~'ria** *nf* pedantry.
pedan'tesco *a* pedantic
pe'data *nf* (*in calcio*) kick; (*impronta*)
footprint
pede'rasta *nm* pederast
pe'destre *a* pedestrian
pedi'atra *nmf* paediatrician. **pedia-
'tria** *nf* paediatrics *sg*
pedi'cure *nmf inv* chiropodist, podia-
trist *Am* ● *nm* (*cura dei piedi*) pedicure
pedi'gree *nm inv* pedigree
pe'dina *nf* (*alla dama*) piece; *fig* pawn.
~'mento *nm* shadowing. **pedi'nare** *vt*
shadow
pe'dofilo, **-a** *nmf* paedophile
pedo'nale *a* pedestrian. **pe'done**, **-a**
nmf pedestrian
peeling *nm inv* exfoliation treatment
'**peggio** *adv* worse; **~ per te!** too bad!;
~ di così any worse; **la persona ~
vestita** the worst dressed person ● *a*
worse; **niente di ~** nothing worse ● *nm*
il ~ è che... the worst of it is that...;
pensare al ~ think the worst ● *nf* **alla
~** at worst; **avere la ~** get the worst of
it; **alla meno ~** as best I can
peggiora'mento *nm* worsening
peggio'ra|re *vt* make worse, worsen
● *vi* get worse, worsen. **~'tivo** *a* pejorative
peggi'ore *a* worse; (*superlativo*) worst;
nella ~ delle ipotesi if the worst
comes to the worst ● *nmf* **il/la ~** the
worst
'**pegno** *nm* pledge; (*nei giochi di società*)
forfeit; *fig* token
pelan'drone *nm* slob
pe'la|re *vt* (*spennare*) pluck; (*spellare*)

skin; (*sbucciare*) peel; (*fam: spillare
denaro*) fleece. **~rsi** *vr fam* lose one's
hair. **~to** *a* bald. **~ti** *nmpl* (*pomodori*)
peeled tomatoes
pel'lame *nm* skins *pl*
'**pelle** *nf* skin; (*cuoio*) leather; (*buccia*)
peel; **avere la ~ d'oca** have goose-flesh
pellegri'naggio *nm* pilgrimage.
pelle'grino, **-a** *nmf* pilgrim
pelle'rossa *nmf* Red Indian, Redskin
pellette'ria *nf* leather goods *pl*
pelli'cano *nm* pelican
pellicc'e'ria *nf* furrier's [shop].
pel'licc|ia *nf* fur; (*indumento*) fur coat.
~i'aio, **-a** *nmf* furrier
pel'licola *nf* *Phot, Cinema* film. **~
[trasparente]** cling film
'**pelo** *nm* hair; (*di animale*) coat; (*di
lana*) pile; **per un ~** by the skin of one's
teeth; **cavarsela per un ~** have a narrow escape. **pe'loso** *a* hairy
'**peltro** *nm* pewter
pe'luche *nm inv* **giocattolo di ~** soft
toy
pe'luria *nf* down
'**pelvico** *a* pelvic
'**pena** *nf* (*punizione*) punishment; (*sofferenza*) pain; (*dispiacere*) sorrow; (*disturbo*) trouble; **a mala ~** hardly; **mi fa
~** I pity him; **vale la ~ andare** it is
worth [while] going. **~ di morte** death
sentence
pe'nal|e *a* criminal; **diritto** *nm* **~e**
criminal law. **~ità** *nf inv* penalty
penaliz'za|re *vt* penalize. **~zi'one** *nf*
(*penalità*) penalty
pe'nare *vi* suffer; (*faticare*) find it difficult
pen'daglio *nm* pendant
pen'dant *nm inv* **fare ~** [**con**] match
pen'den|te *a* hanging; *Comm* out-
standing ● *nm* (*ciondolo*) pendant; **~ti**
pl drop earrings. **~za** *nf* slope; *Comm*
outstanding account
'**pendere** *vi* hang; (*superficie*:) slope;
(*essere inclinato*) lean
pen'dio *nm* slope; **in ~** sloping
pendo'l|are *a* pendulum ● *nmf* com-
muter. **~ino** *nm* (*treno*) special, first
class only, fast train
'**pendolo** *nm* pendulum
'**pene** *nm* penis
pene'trante *a* penetrating; (*freddo*)
biting
pene'tra|re *vt/i* penetrate; (*trafiggere*)
pierce ● *vt* (*odore*:) get into ● *vi* (*entrare
furtivamente*) steal in. **~zi'one** *nf* pen-
etration

penicil'lina *nf* penicillin

pe'nisola *nf* peninsula

peni'ten|te *a & nmf* penitent. **~za** *nf* penitence; (*punizione*) penance; (*in gioco*) forfeit. **~zi'ario** *nm* penitentiary

'**penna** *nf* (*da scrivere*) pen; (*di uccello*) feather. **~ a feltro** felt-tip[ped pen]. **~ a sfera** ball-point [pen]. **~ stilografica** fountain-pen

pen'nacchio *nm* plume

penna'rello *nm* felt-tip[ped pen]

pennel'la|re *vt* paint. **~ta** *nf* brushstroke. **pen'nello** *nm* brush; **a pennello** (*a perfezione*) perfectly

pen'nino *nm* nib

pen'none *nm* (*di bandiera*) flagpole

pen'nuto *a* feathered

pe'nombra *nf* half-light

pe'noso *a* (*fam: pessimo*) painful

pen'sa|re *vi* think; **penso di sì** I think so; **~re a** think of; remember to ‹*chiudere il gas ecc*›; **pensa ai fatti tuoi!** mind your own business!; **ci penso io** I'll take care of it; **~re di fare qcsa** think of doing sth; **~re tra sé e sé** think to oneself ● *vt* think. **~ta** *nf* idea

pensi'e|ro *nm* thought; (*mente*) mind; (*preoccupazione*) worry; **stare in ~ro per** be anxious about. **~'roso** *a* pensive

'**pensi|le** *a* hanging; **giardino ~le** roof-garden ● *nm* (*mobile*) wall unit. **~'lina** *nf* (*di fermata d'autobus*) bus shelter

pensio'nante *nmf* boarder; (*ospite pagante*) lodger

pensio'nato, -a *nmf* pensioner ● *nm* (*per anziani*) [old folks'] home; (*per studenti*) hostel. **pensi'one** *nf* pension; (*albergo*) boarding-house; (*vitto e alloggio*) board and lodging; **andare in pensione** retire; **mezza pensione** half board. **pensione completa** full board

pen'soso *a* pensive

pen'tagono *nm* pentagon

Pente'coste *nf* Whitsun

penti'mento *nm* repentance

pen'ti|rsi *vr* **~rsi di** repent of; (*rammaricarsi*) regret. **~'tismo** *nm* turning informant. **~to** *nm* Mafioso turned informant

'**pentola** *nf* saucepan; (*contenuto*) potful. **~ a pressione** pressure cooker

pe'nultimo *a* last but one

pe'nuria *nf* shortage

penzo'l|are *vi* dangle. **~oni** *adv* dangling

pe'pa|re *vt* pepper. **~to** *a* peppery

'**pepe** *nm* pepper; **grano di ~** pepper-

corn. **~ in grani** whole peppercorns. **~ macinato** ground pepper

pepero'n|ata *nf* peppers cooked in olive oil with onion, tomato and garlic. **~'cino** *nm* chilli pepper. **pepe'rone** *nm* pepper. **peperone verde** green pepper

pe'pita *nf* nugget

per *prep* for; (*attraverso*) through; (*stato in luogo*) in, on; (*distributivo*) per; (*mezzo, entro*) by; (*causa*) with; (*in qualità di*) as; **~ strada** on the street; **~ la fine del mese** by the end of the month; **in fila ~ due** in double file; **l'ho sentito ~ telefono** I spoke to him on the phone; **~ iscritto** in writing; **~ caso** by chance; **ho aspettato ~ ore** I've been waiting for hours; **~ tempo** in time; **~ sempre** forever; **~ scherzo** as a joke; **gridare ~ il dolore** scream with pain; **vendere ~ 10 milioni** sell for 10 million; **uno ~ volta** one at a time; **uno ~ uno** one by one; **venti ~ cento** twenty per cent; **~ fare qcsa** [in order to] do sth; **stare ~** be about to; **è troppo bello ~ essere vero** it's too good to be true

'**pera** *nf* pear; **farsi una ~** (*sl: di eroina*) shoot up

perbe'nis|mo *nm* prissiness. **~ta** *a inv* prissy

per'cento *adv* per cent. **percentu'ale** *nf* percentage

perce'pibile *a* perceivable; ‹*somma*› payable

perce'pi|re *vt* perceive; (*riscuotere*) cash

perce|t'tibile *a* perceptible. **~zi'one** *nf* perception

perché *conj* (*in interrogazioni*) why; (*per il fatto che*) because; (*affinché*) so that; **~ non vieni?** why don't you come?; **dimmi ~** tell me why; **~ no/sì** because!; **la ragione ~ l'ho fatto** the reason [that] I did it, the reason why I did it; **è troppo difficile ~ lo possa capire** it's too difficult for me to understand ● *nm inv* reason [why]; **senza un ~** without any reason

perciò *conj* so

per'correre *vt* cover ‹*distanza*›; (*viaggiare*) travel. **per'corso** *pp di* **percorrere** ● *nm* (*tragitto*) course, route; (*distanza*) distance; (*viaggio*) journey

per'coss|a *nf* blow. **~o** *pp di* **percuotere. percu'otere** *vt* strike

percussi'o|ne *nf* percussion; **strumenti a ~ne** percussion instruments. **~'nista** *nmf* percussionist

per'dente *nmf* loser

'**perder|e** *vt* lose; (*sprecare*) waste; (*non prendere*) miss; ⟨*fig: vizio:*⟩ ruin; **~e tempo** waste time ● *vi* lose; ⟨*recipiente:*⟩ leak; **lascia ~e!** forget it!. **~si** *vr* get lost; (*reciproco*) lose touch

perdifi'ato: a ~ *adv* ⟨*gridare*⟩ at the top of one's voice

perdigi'orno *nmf inv* idler

'**perdita** *nf* loss; (*spreco*) waste; (*falla*) leak; **a ~ d'occhio** as far as the eye can see. **~ di tempo** waste of time. **perdi'tempo** *nm* waste of time

perdo'nare *vt* forgive; (*scusare*) excuse. **per'dono** *nm* forgiveness; *Jur* pardon

perdu'rare *vi* last; (*perseverare*) persist

perduta'mente *adv* hopelessly. **per'duto** *pp di* **perdere** ● *a* lost; (*rovinato*) ruined

pe'renne *a* everlasting; *Bot* perennial; **nevi perenni** perpetual snow. **~'mente** *adv* perpetually

peren'torio *a* peremptory

per'fetto *a* perfect ● *nm Gram* perfect [tense]

perfezio'nar|e *vt* perfect; (*migliorare*) improve. **~si** *vr* improve oneself; (*specializzarsi*) specialize

perfezi'o|ne *nf* perfection; **alla ~ne** to perfection. **~'nismo** *nm* perfectionism. **~'nista** *nmf* perfectionist

per'fidia *nf* wickedness; (*atto*) wicked act. '**perfido** *a* treacherous; (*malvagio*) perverse

per'fino *adv* even

perfo'ra|re *vt* pierce; punch ⟨*schede*⟩; *Mech* drill. **~'tore, ~'trice** *nmf* punchcard operator ● *nm* perforator. **~zi'one** *nf* perforation; (*di schede*) punching

per'formance *nf inv* performance

perga'mena *nf* parchment

perico'lante *a* precarious; ⟨*azienda*⟩ shaky

pe'rico|lo *nm* danger; (*rischio*) risk; **mettere in ~lo** endanger. **~lo pubblico** danger to society. **~'loso** *a* dangerous

perife'ria *nf* periphery; (*di città*) outskirts *pl*; *fig* fringes *pl*

peri'feric|a *nf* peripheral; (*strada*) ring road. **~o** ⟨*quartiere*⟩ outlying

pe'rifrasi *nf inv* circumlocution

pe'rimetro *nm* perimeter

peri'odico *nm* periodical ● *a* periodical; ⟨*vento, mal di testa, Math*⟩ recurring. **pe'riodo** *nm* period; *Gram* sentence. **periodo di prova** trial period

peripe'zie *nfpl* misadventures

pe'rire *vi* perish

peri'scopio *nm* periscope

pe'ri|to, -a *a* skilled ● *nmf* expert

perito'nite *nf* peritonitis

pe'rizia *nf* skill; (*valutazione*) survey

'**perla** *nf* pearl. **per'lina** *nf* bead

perlo'meno *adv* at least

perlu'stra|re *vt* patrol. **~zi'one** *nf* patrol; **andare in ~zione** go on patrol

perma'loso *a* touchy

perma'ne|nte *a* permanent ● *nf* perm; **farsi [fare] la ~nte** have a perm. **~nza** *nf* permanence; (*soggiorno*) stay; **in ~nza** permanently. **~re** *vi* remain

perme'are *vt* permeate

per'messo *pp di* **permettere** ● *nm* permission; (*autorizzazione*) permit; *Mil* leave; **[è] ~?** (*posso entrare?*) may I come in?; (*posso passare?*) excuse me. **~ di lavoro** work permit

per'mettere *vt* allow, permit; **potersi ~ qcsa** (*finanziariamente*) be able to afford sth; **come si permette?** how dare you?. **permis'sivo** *a* permissive

permutazi'one *nf* exchange; *Math* permutation

per'nacchia *nf* ⟨*sl: con la bocca*⟩ raspberry *sl*

per'nic|e *nf* partridge. **~i'oso** *a* pernicious

'**perno** *nm* pivot

pernot'tare *vi* stay overnight

'**pero** *nm* pear-tree

però *conj* but; (*tuttavia*) however

pero'rare *vt* plead

perpendico'lare *a* & *nf* perpendicular

perpe'trare *vt* perpetrate

perpetu'are *vt* perpetuate. **per'petuo** *a* perpetual

perplessità *nf inv* perplexity; (*dubbio*) doubt. **per'plesso** *a* perplexed

perqui'si|re *vt* search. **~zi'one** *nf* search. **~zione domiciliare** search of the premises

persecu'tore, -'trice *nmf* persecutor. **~zi'one** *nf* persecution

persegui're *vt* pursue

persegui'tare *vt* persecute

perseve'ra|nte *a* persevering. **~nza** *nf* perseverance. **~re** *vi* persevere

persi'ano, -a *a* Persian ● *nf* (*di finestra*) shutter. '**persico** *a* Persian

per'sino *adv* = **perfino**

persi'sten|te *a* persistent. **~za** *nf* persistence. **per'sistere** *vi* persist

'perso *pp di* perdere ● *a* lost; **a tempo ~** in one's spare time

per'sona *nf* person; (*un tale*) somebody; **di ~**, **in ~** in person, personally; **per ~** per person, a head; **per interposta ~** through an intermediary; **persone** *pl* people

perso'naggio *nm* (*persona di riguardo*) personality; *Theat ecc* character

perso'nal|e *a* personal ● *nm* staff. **~e di terra** ground crew. **~ità** *nf inv* personality. **~iz'zare** *vt* customize (*auto ecc*); personalize (*penna ecc*)

personifi'ca|re *vt* personify. **~zi'one** *nf* personification

perspi'cac|e *a* shrewd. **~ia** *nf* shrewdness

persu'a|dere *vt* convince; impress (*critici*); **~dere qcno a fare qcsa** persuade sb to do sth. **~si'one** *nf* persuasion. **~sivo** *a* persuasive. **persu'aso** *pp di* persuadere

per'tanto *conj* therefore

'pertica *nf* pole

perti'nente *a* relevant

per'tosse *nf* whooping cough

pertur'ba|re *vt* perturb. **~rsi** *vr* be perturbed. **~zi'one** *nf* disturbance. **~zione atmosferica** atmospheric disturbance

per'va|dere *vt* pervade. **~so** *pp di* pervadere

perven'ire *vi* reach; **far ~ qcsa a qcno** send sth to sb

pervers|'ione *nf* perversion. **~ità** *nf* perversity. **per'verso** *a* perverse

perver'ti|re *vt* pervert. **~to** *a* perverted ● *nm* pervert

per'vinca *nm* (*colore*) blue with a touch of purple

p. es. *abbr* (**per esempio**) e.g.

pesa *nf* weighing; (*bilancia*) weighing machine; (*per veicoli*) weighbridge

pe'sante *a* heavy; (*stomaco*) overfull ● *adv* (*vestirsi*) warmly. **~'mente** *adv* (*cadere*) heavily. **pesan'tezza** *nf* heaviness

pe'sar|e *vt/i* weigh; **~e su** *fig* lie heavy on; **~e le parole** weigh one's words. **~si** *vr* weigh oneself

'pesca[1] *nf* (*frutto*) peach

'pesca[2] *nf* fishing; **andare a ~** go fishing. **~ subacquea** underwater fishing. **pe'scare** *vt* (*andare a pesca di*) fish for; (*prendere*) catch; (*fig: trovare*) fish out. **~'tore** *nm* fisherman

'pesce *nm* fish. **~ d'aprile!** April Fool!. **~ grosso** *fig* big fish. **~ piccolo** *fig* small fry. **~ rosso** goldfish. **~ spada** swordfish. **Pesci** *Astr* Pisces

pesce'cane *nm* shark

pesche'reccio *nm* fishing boat

pesc|he'ria *nf* fishmonger's [shop]. **~i'era** *nf* fish-pond. **~i'vendolo** *nm* fishmonger

'pesco *nm* peach-tree

'peso *nm* weight; **essere di ~ per qcno** be a burden to sb; **di poco ~** (*senza importanza*) not very important; **non dare ~ a qcsa** not attach any importance to sth

pessi'mis|mo *nm* pessimism. **~ta** *nmf* pessimist ● *a* pessimistic. **'pessimo** *a* very bad

pe'staggio *nm* beating-up. **pe'stare** *vt* tread on; (*schiacciare*) crush; (*picchiare*) beat; crush (*aglio, prezzemolo*)

'peste *nf* plague; (*persona*) pest

pe'stello *nm* pestle

pesti'cida *nm* pesticide. **pe'stifero** *a* (*fastidioso*) pestilential

pesti'len|za *nf* pestilence; (*fetore*) stench. **~zi'ale** *a* (*odore aria*) noxious

'pesto *a* ground ● *nm* basil and garlic sauce; **occhio** *nm* **~** black eye

'petalo *nm* petal

pe'tardo *nm* banger

petizi'one *nf* petition; **fare una ~** draw up a petition

petro|li'era *nf* [oil] tanker. **~'lifero** *a* oil-bearing. **pe'trolio** *nm* oil

pettego|'lare *vi* gossip. **~'lezzo** *nm* gossip; **far ~lezzi** gossip

pet'tegolo, -a *a* gossipy ● *nmf* gossip

petti'na|re *vt* comb. **~rsi** *vr* comb one's hair. **~'tura** *nf* combing; (*acconciatura*) hair-style. **'pettine** *nm* comb

'petting *nm* petting

petti'nino *nm* (*fermaglio*) comb

petti'rosso *nm* robin [redbreast]

'petto *nm* chest; (*seno*) breast; **a doppio ~** double-breasted

petto|'rale *nm* (*in gare sportive*) number.. **~'rina** *nf* (*di salopette*) bib. **~'ruto** *a* (*donna*) full-breasted; (*uomo*) broad-chested

petu'lante *a* impertinent

'pezza *nf* cloth; (*toppa*) patch; (*rotolo di tessuto*) roll

pez'zente *nmf* tramp; (*avaro*) miser

'pezzo *nm* piece; (*parte*) part; **un bel ~ d'uomo** a fine figure of a man; **un ~** (*di tempo*) some time; (*di spazio*) a long way; **al ~** (*costare*) each; **essere a pezzi** (*stanco*) be shattered; **fare a pezzi** tear to shreds. **~ grosso** bigwig

pia'cente *a* attractive

pia'ce|re *nm* pleasure; (*favore*) favour; **a ~re** as much as one likes; **per ~re!** please!; **~re [di conoscerla]!** pleased to meet you!; **con ~re** with pleasure ● *vi* **la Scozia mi piace** I like Scotland; **mi piacciono i dolci** I like sweets; **faccio come mi pare e piace** I do as I please; **ti piace?** do you like it?; **lo spettacolo è piaciuto** the show was a success. **~vole** *a* pleasant

piaci'mento *nm* **a ~** as much as you like

pia'dina *nf unleavened focaccia bread*

pi'aga *nf* sore; *fig* scourge; (*fig: persona noiosa*) pain; (*fig: ricordo doloroso*) wound

piagni'steo *nm* whining

piagnuco'lare *vi* whimper

pi'alla *nf* plane. **pial'lare** *vt* plane

pi'ana *nf* (*pianura*) plane. **pianeg-gi'ante** *a* level

piane'rottolo *nm* landing

pia'neta *nm* planet

pi'angere *vi* cry; (*disperatamente*) weep ● *vt* (*lamentare*) lament; (*per un lutto*) mourn

pianifi'ca|re *vt* plan. **~zi'one** *nf* planning

pia'nista *nmf* *Mus* pianist

pi'ano *a* flat; (*a livello*) flush; (*regolare*) smooth; (*facile*) easy ● *adv* slowly; (*con cautela*) gently; **andarci ~** go carefully ● *nm* plain; (*di edificio*) floor; (*livello*) plane; (*progetto*) plan; *Mus* piano; **di primo ~** first-rate; **primo ~** *Phot* close-up; **in primo ~** in the foreground. **~ regolatore** town plan. **~ di studi** syllabus

piano'forte *nm* piano. **~ a coda** grand piano

piano'terra *nm inv* ground floor, first floor *Am*

pi'anta *nf* plant; (*del piede*) sole; (*disegno*) plan; **di sana ~** (*totalmente*) entirely; **in ~ stabile** permanently. **~ stradale** road map. **~gi'one** *nf* plantation

piantagrane *nmf fam* **è un/una ~** he's/she's bolshie

pian'tar|e *vt* plant; (*conficcare*) drive; (*fam: abbandonare*) dump; **piantala!** *fam* stop it!. **~si** *vr* plant oneself; (*fam: lasciarsi*) leave each other

pianter'reno *nm* ground floor, first floor *Am*

pi'anto *pp di* **piangere** ● *nm* crying; (*disperato*) weeping; (*lacrime*) tears *pl*

pian|to'nare *vt* guard. **~'tone** *nm* orderly

pia'nura *nf* plain

p'iastra *nf* plate; (*lastra*) slab; *Culin* griddle. **~ elettronica** circuit board. **~ madre** *Comput* motherboard

pia'strella *nf* tile

pia'strina *nf* *Mil* identity disc; *Med* platelet; *Comput* chip

piatta'forma *nf* platform. **~ di lancio** launch pad

piat'tino *nm* saucer

pi'atto *a* flat ● *nm* plate; (*da portata, vivanda*) dish; (*portata*) course; (*parte piatta*) flat; (*di giradischi*) turntable; **piatti** *pl* *Mus* cymbals; **lavare i piatti** do the dishes, do the washing-up. **~ fondo** soup plate. **~ piano** [ordinary] plate

pi'azza *nf* square; *Comm* market; **letto a una ~** single bed; **letto a due piazze** double bed; **far ~ pulita** make a clean sweep. **~'forte** *nf* stronghold. **piaz'zale** *nm* large square. **~'mento** *nm* (*in classifica*) placing

piaz'za|re *vt* place. **~rsi** *vr* *Sport* be placed; **~rsi secondo** come second. **~to** *a* (*cavallo*) placed; **ben ~to** (*robusto*) well built

piaz'zista *nm* salesman

piaz'zuola *nf* **~ di sosta** pull-in

pic'cante *a* hot; (*pungente*) sharp; (*salace*) spicy

pic'carsi *vr* (*risentirsi*) take offence; **~ di** (*vantarsi di*) claim to

'picche *nfpl* (*in carte*) spades

picchet'tare *vt* stake; (*scioperanti:*) picket. **pic'chetto** *nm* picket

picchi'a|re *vt* beat, hit ● *vi* (*bussare*) knock; *Aeron* nosedive; **~re in testa** (*motore:*) knock. **~ta** *nf* beating; *Aeron* nosedive; **scendere in ~ta** nosedive

picchiet'tare *vt* tap; (*punteggiare*) spot

picchiet'tio *nm* tapping

'picchio *nm* woodpecker

pic'cino *a* tiny; (*gretto*) mean; (*di poca importanza*) petty ● *nm* little one, child

picci'one *nm* pigeon

'picco *nm* peak; **a ~** vertically; **colare a ~** sink

'piccolo, -a *a* small, little; (*di età*) young; (*di statura*) short; (*gretto*) petty ● *nmf* child, little one; **da ~** as a child

pic'co|ne *nm* pickaxe. **~zza** *nf* ice axe

pic'nic *nm inv* picnic

pi'docchio *nm* louse

piè *nm inv* **a ~ di pagina** at the foot of the page; **saltare a ~ pari** skip

pi'ede nm foot; **a piedi** on foot; **andare a piedi** walk; **a piedi nudi** barefoot; **a ~ libero** free; **in piedi** standing; **alzarsi in piedi** stand up; **in punta di piedi** on tiptoe; **ai piedi di** ⟨montagna⟩ at the foot of; ⟨moda:⟩ catch on; **mettere in piedi** ⟨allestire⟩ set up; **togliti dai piedi!** get out of the way!. **~ di porco** ⟨strumento⟩ jemmy

pie'dino nm fare **~** a qcno fam play footsie with sb

piedi'stallo nm pedestal

pi'ega nf ⟨piegatura⟩ fold; ⟨di gonna⟩ pleat; ⟨di pantaloni⟩ crease; ⟨grinza⟩ wrinkle; ⟨andamento⟩ turn; **non fare una ~** ⟨ragionamento:⟩ be flawless

pie'ga|re vt fold; ⟨flettere⟩ bend ● vi bend. **~rsi** vr bend. **~rsi a** ⟨fig⟩ yield to. **~'tura** nf folding

pieghet'ta|re vt pleat. **~to** a pleated.

pie'ghevole a pliable; ⟨tavolo⟩ folding ● nm leaflet

piemon'tese a Piedmontese

pi'en|a nf ⟨di fiume⟩ flood; ⟨folla⟩ crowd. **~o** a full; ⟨massiccio⟩ solid; **in ~a estate** in the middle of summer; **a ~i voti** ⟨diplomarsi⟩ with A-grades, with first class honours ● nm ⟨colmo⟩ height; ⟨carico⟩ full load; **in ~o** ⟨completamente⟩ fully; **fare il ~o** ⟨di benzina⟩ fill up

pie'none nm **c'era il ~** the place was packed

pietà nf pity; ⟨misericordia⟩ mercy; **senza ~** ⟨persona⟩ pitiless; ⟨spietatamente⟩ pitilessly; **avere ~ di qcno** take pity on sb; **far ~** ⟨far pena⟩ be pitiful

pie'tanza nf dish

pie'toso a pitiful, merciful; ⟨fam: pessimo⟩ terrible

pi'etr|a nf stone. **~a dura** semi-precious stone. **~a preziosa** precious stone. **~a dello scandalo** cause of the scandal. **~a** fig stones pl. **~ifi'care** vt petrify. **pie'trina** nf ⟨di accendino⟩ flint. **pie'troso** a stony

'piffero nm fife

pigi'ama nm pyjamas pl

'pigia 'pigia nm inv crowd, crush. **pigi'are** vt press

pigi'one nf rent; **dare a ~** let, rent out; **prendere a ~** rent

pigli'are vt ⟨fam: afferrare⟩ catch. **'piglio** nm air

pig'mento nm pigment

pig'meo, -a a & nmf pygmy

'pigna nf cone

pi'gnolo a pedantic

pigo'lare vi chirp. **pigo'lio** nm chirping

pi'grizia nf laziness. **'pigro** a lazy; ⟨intelletto⟩ slow

'pila nf pile; Electr battery; ⟨fam: lampadina tascabile⟩ torch; ⟨vasca⟩ basin; **a pile** battery operated, battery powered

pi'lastro nm pillar

'pillola nf pill; **prendere la ~** be on the pill

pi'lone nm pylon; ⟨di ponte⟩ pier

pi'lota nmf pilot ● nm Auto driver. **pilo'tare** vt pilot; drive ⟨auto⟩

pinaco'teca nf art gallery

'Pinco Pallino nm so-and-so

pi'neta nf pine-wood

ping-'pong nm table tennis, ping-pong fam

'pingue a fat. **~'edine** nf fatness

pingu'ino nm penguin; ⟨gelato⟩ choc ice on a stick

'pinna nf fin; ⟨per nuotare⟩ flipper

'pino nm pine[-tree]. **pi'nolo** nm pine kernel. **~ marittimo** cluster pine

'pinta nf pint

'pinza nf pliers pl; Med forceps pl

pin'za|re vt ⟨con pinzatrice⟩ staple. **~'trice** nf stapler

pin'zette nfpl tweezers pl

pinzi'monio nm sauce for crudités

'pio a pious; ⟨benefico⟩ charitable

pi'oggia nf rain; ⟨fig: di pietre, insulti⟩ hail, shower; **sotto la ~** in the rain. **~ acida** acid rain

pi'olo nm ⟨di scala⟩ rung

piom'ba|re vi fall heavily; **~re su** fall upon ● vt fill ⟨dente⟩. **~'tura** nf ⟨di dente⟩ filling. **piom'bino** nm ⟨sigillo⟩ [lead] seal; ⟨da pesca⟩ sinker; ⟨in gonne⟩ weight

pi'ombo nm lead; ⟨sigillo⟩ [lead] seal; **a ~** plumb; **senza ~** ⟨benzina⟩ lead-free

pioni'ere, -a nmf pioneer

pi'oppo nm poplar

pio'vano a **acqua piovana** rainwater

pi'ov|ere vi rain; **~e** it's raining; **~iggi'nare** vi drizzle. **pio'voso** a rainy

'pipa nf pipe

pipi nf fare [la] **~** pee, piddle; **andare a fare [la] ~** go for a pee

pipi'strello nm bat

pi'ramide nf pyramid

pi'ranha nm inv piranha

pi'rat|a nm pirate. **~a della strada** road-hog ● a inv pirate. **~e'ria** nf piracy

piro'etta nf pirouette

pi'rofi|la nf ⟨tegame⟩ oven-proof dish. **~o** a heat-resistant

pi'romane nmf pyromaniac

pi'roscafo nm steamer. **~ di linea** liner

pisci'are vi vulg piss

pi'scina nf swimming pool. **~ coperta** indoor swimming pool. **~ scoperta** outdoor swimming pool

pi'sello nm pea; (fam: pene) willie

piso'lino nm nap; **fare un ~** have a nap

'pista nf track; Aeron runway; (orma) footprint; (sci) slope, piste. **~ d'atterraggio** airstrip. **~ da ballo** dance floor. **~ ciclabile** cycle track

pi'stacchio nm pistachio

pi'stola nf pistol; (per spruzzare) spray-gun. **~ a spruzzo** paint spray

pi'stone nm piston

pi'tone nm python

pit'to|re, -'trice nmf painter. **~'resco** a picturesque. **pit'torico** a pictorial

pit'tu|ra nf painting. **~'rare** vt paint

più adv more; (superlativo) most; Math plus; **~ importante** more important; **il ~ importante** the most important; **~ caro** dearer; **il ~ caro** the dearest; **di ~** more; **una coperta in ~** an extra blanket; **non ho ~ soldi** I don't have any more money; **non vive ~ a Milano** he no longer lives in Milan, he doesn't live in Milan any longer; **~ o meno** more or less; **il ~ lentamente possibile** as slow as possible; **per di ~** what's more; **mai ~!** never again!; **~ di** more than; **sempre ~** more and more ● a more; (superlativo) most; **~ tempo** more time; **la classe con ~ alunni** the class with most pupils; **~ volte** several times ● nm most; Math plus sign; **il ~ è fatto** the worst is over; **parlare del ~ e del meno** make small talk; **i ~** the majority

piuccheper'fetto nm pluperfect

pi'uma nf feather. **~'maggio** nm plumage. **piu'mino** nm (di cigni) down; (copriletto) eiderdown; (per cipria) powder-puff; (per spolverare) feather duster; (giacca) down jacket. **piu'mone®** nm duvet, continental quilt

piut'tosto adv rather; (invece) instead

pi'vello nm fam greenhorn

'pizza nf pizza; Cinema reel.

pizzai'ola nf slices of beef in tomato sauce, oregano and anchovies

pizze'ria nf pizza restaurant, pizzeria

pizzi'c|are vt pinch; (pungere) sting; (di sapore) taste sharp; (fam: sorprendere) catch; Mus pluck ● vi scratch; (cibo:) be spicy **'pizzico** nm, **~otto** nm pinch

'pizzo nm lace; (di montagna) peak

pla'car|e vt placate; assuage (fame, dolore). **~si** vr calm down

'placca nf plate; (commemorativa, dentale) plaque; Med patch

plac'ca|re vt plate. **~to a ~to d'argento** silver-plated. **~to d'oro** gold-plated. **~'tura** nf plating

pla'centa nf placenta

'placido a placid

plagi'are vt plagiarize; pressure (persona). **'plagio** nm plagiarism

plaid nm inv tartan rug

pla'nare vi glide

'plancia nf Naut bridge; (passerella) gangplank

plane'tario a planetary ● nm planetarium

pla'smare vt mould

'plastic|a nf (arte) plastic art; Med plastic surgery; (materia) plastic. **~o a** plastic ● nm plastic model

'platano nm plane[-tree]

pla'tea nf stalls pl; (pubblico) audience

'platino nm platinum

pla'tonico a platonic

plau'sibil|e a plausible. **~ità** nf plausibility

ple'baglia nf pej mob

pleni'lunio nm full moon

'plettro nm plectrum

pleu'rite nf pleurisy

'plico nm packet; **in ~ a parte** under separate cover

plissé a inv plissé; (gonna) accordeon-pleated

plo'tone nm platoon; (di ciclisti) group. **~ d'esecuzione** firing-squad

'plumbeo a leaden

plu'ral|e a & nm plural; **al ~e** in the plural. **~ità** nf (maggioranza) majority

pluridiscipli'nare a multi-disciplinary

plurien'nale a **~ esperienza** many years' experience

pluripar'titico a Pol multi-party

plu'tonio nm plutonium

pluvi'ale a rain attrib

pneu'matico a pneumatic ● nm tyre

pneu'monia nf pneumonia

po' vedi poco

po'chette nf inv clutch bag

po'chino nm **un ~** a little bit

'poco a little; (tempo) short; (con nomi plurali) few ● pron little; (poco tempo) a short time; (plurale) few ● nm little; **un po'** a little [bit]; **un po' di** a little, some; (con nomi plurali) a few; **a ~ a ~** little by little; **fra ~** soon; **per ~** (*a poco prezzo*) cheap; (*quasi*) nearly; **~ fa** a little while ago; **sono arrivato da ~** I have just arrived; **un bel po'** quite a lot; **un ~ di buono** a shady character ● *adv* (*con verbi*) not much; (*con avverbi*) not very; **parla ~** he doesn't speak much; **lo conosco ~** I don't know him very well; **~ spesso** not very often

po'dere *nm* farm

pode'roso *a* powerful

'podio *nm* dais; *Mus* podium

po'dis|mo *nm* walking. **~ta** *nmf* walker

po'e|ma *nm* poem. **~'sia** *nf* poetry; (*componimento*) poem. **~ta** *nm* poet. **~'tessa** *nf* poetess. **~tico** *a* poetic

poggia'piedi *nm inv* footrest

poggi'a|re *vt* lean; (*posare*) place ● *vi* **~re su** be based on. **~'testa** *nm inv* head-rest

'poggio *nm* hillock

poggi'olo *nm* balcony

'poi *adv* (*dopo*) then; (*più tardi*) later [on]; (*finalmente*) finally. **d'ora in ~** from now on; **questa ~I** well!

poiché *conj* since

pois *nm inv* **a ~** polka-dot

'poker *nm* poker

po'lacco, -a *a* Polish ● *nmf* Pole ● *nm* (*lingua*) Polish

po'lar|e *a* polar. **~iz'zare** *vt* polarize

'polca *nf* polka

po'lemi|ca *nf* controversy. **~ca'mente** *adv* controversially. **~co** *a* controversial. **~z'zare** *vi* engage in controversy

po'lenta *nf* cornmeal porridge

poli'clinico *nm* general hospital

poli'estere *nm* polyester

poliga'mia *nf* polygamy. **po'ligamo** *a* polygamous

polio[mie'lite] *nf* polio[myelitis]

'polipo *nm* polyp

polisti'rolo *nm* polystyrene

poli'tecnico *nm* polytechnic

po'litic|a *nf* politics *sg*; (*linea di condotta*) policy; **fare ~a** be in politics. **~iz'zare** *vt* politicize. **~o, -a** *a* political ● *nmf* politician

poliva'lente *a* catch-all

poli'zi|a *nf* police. **~a giudiziaria** ≈ Criminal Investigation Department, CID. **~a stradale** traffic police. **~'esco** a police *attrib*; (*romanzo, film*) detective. **~'otto** *nm* policeman

po'lizza *nf* policy

pol'la|io *nm* chicken run; (*fam: luogo chiassoso*) mad house. **~me** *nm* poultry.

~'strello *nm* spring chicken. **~stro** *nm* cockerel

'pollice *nm* thumb; (*unità di misura*) inch

'polline *nm* pollen; **allergia al ~** hay fever

polli'vendolo, -a *nmf* poulterer

'pollo *nm* chicken; (*fam: semplicione*) simpleton. **~ arrosto** roast chicken

polmo|'nare *a* pulmonary. **pol'mone** *nm* lung. **polmone d'acciaio** iron lung. **~'nite** *nf* pneumonia

'polo *nm* pole; *Sport* polo; (*maglietta*) polo top. **~ nord** North Pole. **~ sud** South Pole

Po'lonia *nf* Poland

'polpa *nf* pulp

pol'paccio *nm* calf

polpa'strello *nm* fingertip

pol'pet|ta *nf* meatball. **~'tone** *nm* meat loaf

'polpo *nm* octopus

pol'poso *a* fleshy

pol'sino *nm* cuff

'polso *nm* pulse; *Anat* wrist; *fig* authority; **avere ~** be strict

pol'tiglia *nf* mush

pol'trire *vi* lie around

pol'tron|a *nf* armchair; *Theat* seat in the stalls. **~e** *a* lazy

'polve|re *nf* dust; (*sostanza polverizzata*) powder; **in ~re** powdered; **sapone in ~re** soap powder. **~re da sparo** gun powder. **~'rina** *nf* (*medicina*) powder. **~riz'zare** *vt* pulverize; (*nebulizzare*) atomize. **~'rone** *nm* cloud of dust. **~'roso** *a* dusty

po'mata *nf* ointment, cream

po'mello *nm* knob; (*guancia*) cheek

pomeridi'ano *a* afternoon *attrib*; **alle tre pomeridiane** at three in the afternoon, at three p.m. **pome'riggio** *nm* afternoon

'pomice *nf* pumice

'pomo *nm* (*oggetto*) knob. **~ d'Adamo** Adam's apple

pomo'doro *nm* tomato

'pompa *nf* pump; (*sfarzo*) pomp. **pompe** *pl* **funebri** (*funzione*) funeral. **pom'pare** *vt* pump; (*gonfiare d'aria*) pump up; (*fig: esagerare*) exaggerate; **pompare fuori** pump out

pom'pelmo *nm* grapefruit

pompi'ere *nm* fireman; **i pompieri** the fire brigade

pom'pon *nm inv* pompom

pom'poso *a* pompous

ponde'rare *vt* ponder

po'nente *nm* west

'ponte *nm* bridge; *Naut* deck; (*impalca-tura*) scaffolding; **fare il ~** *fig* make a long weekend of it

pon'tefice *nm* pontiff

pontifi'ca|re *vi* pontificate. **~to** *nm* pontificate

ponti'ficio *a* papal

pon'tile *nm* jetty

popò *nf inv fam* pooh

popo'lano *a* of the [common] people

popo'la|re *a* popular; (*comune*) common ● *vt* populate. **~rsi** *vr* get crowded. **~rità** *nf* popularity. **~zi'one** *nf* population. **'popolo** *nm* people. **popo'loso** *a* populous

'poppa *nf Naut* stern; (*mammella*) breast; **a ~** astern

pop'pa|re *vt* suck. **~ta** *nf* (*pasto*) feed. **~'toio** *nm* [feeding-]bottle

popu'lista *nmf* populist

por'cata *nf* load of rubbish; **porcate** *pl* (*fam: cibo*) junk food

porcel'lana *nf* porcelain, china

porcel'lino *nm* piglet. **~ d'India** guinea-pig

porche'ria *nf* dirt; (*fig: cosa orrenda*) piece of filth; (*fam: robaccia*) rubbish

por'ci|le *nm* pigsty. **~no** *a* pig *attrib* ● *nm* (*fungo*) edible mushroom. **'porco** *nm* pig; (*carne*) pork

porco'spino *nm* porcupine

'porgere *vt* give; (*offrire*) offer; **porgo distinti saluti** (*in lettera*) I remain, yours sincerely

porno|gra'fia *nf* pornography. **~'grafico** *a* pornographic

'poro *nm* pore. **po'roso** *a* porous

'porpora *nf* purple

'por|re *vt* put; (*collocare*) place; (*suppor-re*) suppose; ask (*domanda*); present (*candidatura*); **poniamo il caso che...** let us suppose that...; **~re fine, ~re termine** a put an end to. **~si** *vr* put oneself; **~si a sedere** sit down; **~si in cammino** set out

'porro *nm Bot* leek; (*verruca*) wart

'porta *nf* door; *Sport* goal; (*di città*) gate; *Comput* port. **~ a ~** door-to-door; **mettere alla ~** show sb the door. **~ di servizio** tradesmen's entrance

portaba'gagli *nm inv* (*facchino*) porter; (*di treno ecc*) luggage rack; *Auto* boot, trunk *Am*; (*sul tetto di un'auto*) luggage rack

portabot'tiglie *nm inv* bottle rack, wine rack

porta'cenere *nm inv* ashtray

portachi'avi *nm inv* keyring

porta'cipria *nm inv* compact

portadocu'menti *nm inv* document wallet

porta'erei *nf inv* aircraft carrier

portafi'nestra *nf* French window

porta'foglio *nm* wallet; (*per documenti*) portfolio; (*ministero*) ministry

portafor'tuna *nm inv* lucky charm ● *a inv* lucky

portagi'oie *nm inv* jewellery box

por'tale *nm* door

portama'tite *nm inv* pencil case

porta'mento *nm* carriage; (*condotta*) behaviour

porta'mina *nm inv* propelling pencil

portamo'nete *nm inv* purse

por'tante *a* bearing *attrib*

portaom'brelli *nm inv* umbrella stand

porta'pacchi *nm inv* roof rack; (*su bicicletta*) luggage rack

porta'penne *nm inv* pencil case

por'ta|re *vt* (*verso chi parla*) bring; (*lontano da chi parla*) take; (*sorreggere, Math*) carry; (*condurre*) lead; (*indossa-re*) wear; (*avere*) bear. **~rsi** *vr* (*trasferir-si*) move; (*comportarsi*) behave; **~rsi bene/male gli anni** look young/old for one's age

portari'viste *nm inv* magazine rack

porta'sci *nm inv* ski rack

portasiga'rette *nm inv* cigarette-case

porta'spilli *nm inv* pin-cushion

por'ta|ta *nf* (*di pranzo*) course; *Auto* carrying capacity; (*di arma*) range; (*fig: abilità*) capability; **a ~ta di mano** within reach; **alla ~ta di tutti** accessible to all; (*finanziariamente*) within everybody's reach. **por'tatile** *a* & *nm* portable. **~to** *a* (*indumento*) worn; (*dotato*) gifted; **essere ~to per qcsa** have a gift for sth; **essere ~to a** (*tendere a*) be inclined to. **~'tore, ~'tri-ce** *nmf* bearer. **al ~tore** to the bearer. **~tore di handicap** disabled person

portatovagli'olo *nm* napkin ring

portau'ovo *nm inv* egg-cup

porta'voce *nm inv* spokesman ● *nf inv* spokeswoman

por'tento *nm* marvel; (*persona dotata*) prodigy

'portico *nm* portico

porti'er|a *nf* door; (*tendaggio*) door curtain. **~e** *nm* porter, doorman; *Sport* goalkeeper. **~e di notte** night porter

porti'n|aio, -a *nmf* caretaker, concierge. ~**e'ria** *nf* concierge's room; (*di ospedale*) porter's lodge

'**porto** *pp di* porgere ● *nm* harbour; (*complesso*) port; (*vino*) port [wine]; (*spesa di trasporto*) carriage; **andare in ~** succeed. ~ **d'armi** gun licence

Porto'g|allo *nm* Portugal. **p~hese** *a* & *nmf* Portuguese

por'tone *nm* main door

portu'ale *nm* dockworker, docker

porzi'one *nf* portion

'**posa** *nf* laying; (*riposo*) rest; *Phot* exposure; (*atteggiamento*) pose; **mettersi in ~** pose

po'sa|re *vt* put; (*giù*) put [down] ● *vi* (*poggiare*) rest; (*per un ritratto*) pose. ~**rsi** *vr* alight; (*sostare*) rest; *Aeron* land. ~**ta** *nf* piece of cutlery; ~**te** *pl* cutlery *sg*. ~**to** *a* sedate

po'scritto *nm* postscript

posi'tivo *a* positive

posizio'nare *vt* position

posizi'one *nf* position; **farsi una ~** get ahead

posolo'gia *nf* dosage

po'spo|rre *vt* place after; (*posticipare*) postpone. ~**sto** *pp di* posporre

posse'd|ere *vt* possess, own. ~**i'mento** *nm* possession

posses'sivo *a* possessive. **pos'sesso** *nm* ownership; (*bene*) possession. ~**'so-re** *nm* owner

pos'sibil|e *a* possible; **il più presto ~e** as soon as possible ● *nm* fare [**tutto**] **il ~e** do one's best. ~**ità** *nf inv* possibility; (*occasione*) chance ● *nfpl* (*mezzi*) means

possi'dente *nmf* land-owner

'**posta** *nf* post, mail; (*ufficio postale*) post office; (*al gioco*) stake; **spese di ~** postage; **per ~** by post, by mail; **la ~ in gioco è...** *fig* what's at stake is...; **a bella ~** on purpose; **Poste e Telecomunicazioni** *pl* [Italian] Post Office. **~ elettronica** electronic mail, e-mail. **~ elettronica vocale** voice-mail.

posta'giro *nm* postal giro

po'stale *a* postal

postazi'one *nf* position

postda'tare *vt* postdate (*assegno*)

posteggi'a|re *vt/i* park. ~**'tore**, ~**'trice** *nmf* parking attendant. **po'steggio** *nm* car-park, parking lot *Am*; (*di taxi*) taxi-rank

'**posteri** *nmpl* descendants. ~**'ore** *a* rear; (*nel tempo*) later ● *nm fam* posterior, behind. ~**tà** *nf* posterity

po'sticcio *a* artificial; (*baffi, barba*) false ● *nm* hair-piece

postici'pare *vt* postpone

po'stilla *nf* note; *Jur* rider

po'stino *nm* postman, mailman *Am*

'**posto** *pp di* porre ● *nm* place; (*spazio*) room; (*impiego*) job; *Mil* post; (*sedile*) seat; **a/fuori ~** in/out of place; **prendere ~** take up room; **sul ~** on-site; **essere a ~** (*casa, libri*) be tidy; **mettere a ~** tidy (*stanza*); **fare ~** a make room for; **al ~ di** (*invece di*) in place of, instead of. **~ di blocco** checkpoint. **~ di guida** driving seat. **~ di lavoro** workstation. **~ di polizia** police station. **posti** *pl* **in piedi** standing room. **posti** *pl* **a sedere** seating

post-partum *a* post-natal

'**postumo** *a* posthumous ● *nm* after-effect

po'tabile *a* drinkable; **acqua ~** drinking water

po'tare *vt* prune

po'tassio *nm* potassium

po'ten|te *a* powerful; (*efficace*) potent. ~**za** *nf* power; (*efficacia*) potency. ~**zi'ale** *a* & *nm* potential

po'tere *nm* power; **al ~** in power ● *vi* can, be able to; **posso entrare?** can I come in?; (*formale*) may I come in?; **posso fare qualche cosa?** can I do something?; **che tu possa essere felice!** may you be happy!; **non ne posso più** (*sono stanco*) I can't go on; (*sono stufo*) I can't take any more; **può darsi** perhaps; **può darsi che sia vero** perhaps it's true; **potrebbe aver ragione** he could be right, he might be right; **avresti potuto telefonare** you could have phoned, you might have phoned; **spero di poter venire** I hope to be able to come; **senza poter telefonare** without being able to phone

potestà *nf inv* power

'**pover|o, -a** *a* poor; (*semplice*) plain ● *nm* poor man ● *nf* poor woman; **i ~i** the poor. ~**tà** *nf* poverty

'**pozza** *nf* pool. **poz'zanghera** *nf* puddle

'**pozzo** *nm* well; (*minerario*) pit. **'~ petrolifero** oil-well

PP.TT. *abbr* (**Poste e Telegrafi**) [Italian] Post Office

prag'matico *a* pragmatic

prali'nato *a* (*mandorla, gelato*) praline-coated

pram'matica *nf* essere di **~** be customary

pran'zare *vi* dine; (*a mezzogiorno*)

lunch. '**pranzo** *nm* dinner; (*a mezzo-giorno*) lunch. **pranzo di nozze** wedding breakfast

'**prassi** *nf* standard procedure

prate'ria *nf* grassland

'**prati|ca** *nf* practice; (*esperienza*) experience; (*documentazione*) file; **avere ~ca di qcsa** be familiar with sth; **far ~ca** gain experience; **fare le pratiche per** gather the necessary papers for. ~'**cabile** *a* practicable; (*strada*) passable. ~**ca'mente** *adv* practically. ~'**cante** *nmf* apprentice; *Relig* [regular] church-goer

prati'ca|re *vt* practise; (*frequentare*) associate with; (*fare*) make

praticità *nf* practicality. '**pratico** *a* practical; (*esperto*) experienced; **essere pratico di qcsa** know about sth

'**prato** *nm* meadow; (*di giardino*) lawn

pre'ambolo *nm* preamble

preannunci'are *vt* give advance notice of

preavvi'sare *vt* forewarn. **preav'viso** *nm* warning

pre'cario *a* precarious

precauzi'one *nf* precaution; (*cautela*) care

prece'den|te *a* previous ● *nm* precedent. ~**te'mente** *adv* previously. ~**za** *nf* precedence; (*di veicoli*) right of way; **dare la ~za** give way. **pre'cedere** *vt* precede

pre'cetto *nm* precept

precipi'ta|re *vt* ~**re le cose** precipitate events; ~**re qcno nella disperazione** cast sb into a state of despair ● *vi* fall headlong; (*situazione, eventi:*) come to a head. ~**rsi** *vr* (*gettarsi*) throw oneself; (*affrettarsi*) rush; ~**rsi a fare qcsa** rush to do sth. ~**zi'one** *nf* (*fretta*) haste; (*atmosferica*) precipitation. **pre'cipi'toso** *a* hasty; (*avventato*) reckless; ⟨*caduta*⟩ headlong

preci'pizio *nm* precipice; **a ~** headlong

precisa'mente *adv* precisely

preci'sa|re *vt* specify; (*spiegare*) clarify. ~**zi'one** *nf* clarification

precisi'one *nf* precision. **pre'ciso** *a* precise; ⟨*ore*⟩ sharp; (*identico*) identical

pre'clu|dere *vt* preclude. ~**so** *pp di* **precludere**

pre'coc|e *a* precocious; (*prematuro*) premature. ~**ità** *nf* precociousness

precon'cetto *a* preconceived ● *nm* prejudice

pre'corr|ere *vt* ~**ere i tempi** be ahead of one's time

precur'sore *nm* forerunner, precursor

'**preda** *nf* prey; (*bottino*) booty; **essere in ~ al panico** be panic-stricken; **in ~ alle fiamme** engulfed in flames. **pre'dare** *vt* plunder. ~'**tore** *nm* predator

predeces'sore *nmf* predecessor

pre'del|la *nf* platform. ~'**lino** *nm* step

predesti'na|re *vt* predestine. ~**to a** *Relig* predestined, preordained

predetermi'nato *a* predetermined, preordained

pre'detto *pp di* **predire**

'**predica** *nf* sermon; *fig* lecture

predi'ca|re *vt* preach. ~**to** *nm* predicate

predi'le|tto, -a *pp di* **prediligere** ● *a* favourite ● *nmf* pet. ~**zi'one** *nf* predilection. **predi'ligere** *vt* prefer

pre'di|re *vt* foretell

predi'spo|rre *vt* arrange. ~**rsi** *vr* ~**rsi a** prepare oneself for. ~**sizi'one** *nf* predisposition; (*al disegno ecc*) bent (a for). ~**sto** *pp di* **predisporre**

predizi'one *nf* prediction

predomi'na|nte *a* predominant. ~**re** *vi* predominate. **predo'minio** *nm* predominance

pre'done *nm* robber

prefabbri'cato *a* prefabricated ● *nm* prefabricated building

prefazi'one *nf* preface

prefe'renz|a *nf* preference; **di ~a** preferably. ~**i'ale** *a* preferential; **corsia ~iale** bus and taxi lane

prefe'ribil|e *a* preferable. ~'**mente** *adv* preferably

prefe'ri|re *vt* prefer. ~**to, -a** *a* & *nmf* favourite

pre'fet|to *nm* prefect. ~'**tura** *nf* prefecture

pre'figgersi *vr* be determined

pre'fisso *pp di* **prefiggere** ● *nm* prefix; *Teleph* [dialling] code

pre'gare *vt/i* pray; (*supplicare*) beg; **farsi ~** need persuading

pre'gevole *a* valuable

preghi'era *nf* prayer; (*richiesta*) request

pregi'ato *a* esteemed; (*prezioso*) valuable. '**pregio** *nm* esteem; (*valore*) value; (*di persona*) good point; **di pregio** valuable

pregiudi'ca|re *vt* prejudice; (*danneggiare*) harm. ~**to** *a* prejudiced ● *nm* *Jur* previous offender

pregiu'dizio *nm* prejudice; *(danno)* detriment

'prego *int (non c'è di che)* don't mention it!; *(per favore)* please; **~?** I beg your pardon?

pregu'stare *vt* look forward to

prei'storia *nf* prehistory. **prei'storico** *a* prehistoric

pre'lato *nm* prelate

prela'vaggio *nm* prewash

preleva'mento *nm* withdrawal. **pre-le'vare** *vt* withdraw *(denaro)*; collect *(merci)*; *Med* take. **preli'evo** *nm (di soldi)* withdrawal. **prelievo di sangue** blood sample

prelimi'nare *a* preliminary ● *nm* **pre-liminari** *pl* preliminaries

pre'ludio *nm* prelude

prema'man *nm inv* maternity dress ● *a* maternity *attrib*

prematrimoni'ale *a* premarital

prema'turo, -a *a* premature ● *nmf* premature baby

premedi'ta|re *vt* premeditate. **~zi'one** *nf* premeditation

'premere *vt* press; *Comput* hit *(tasto)* ● *vi* **~ a** *(importare)* matter to; **mi pre-me sapere** I need to know; **~ su** press on; push *(pulsante)*

pre'messa *nf* introduction

pre'me|sso *pp di* **premettere. ~sso che** granted that. **~ttere** *vt* put forward; *(mettere prima)* put before.

premi'a|re *vt* give a prize to; *(ricompensare)* reward. **~zi'one** *nf* prize giving

premi'nente *a* pre-eminent

'premio *nm* prize; *(ricompensa)* reward; *Comm* premium. **~ di consolazione** booby prize

premoni'|tore *a (sogno, segno)* premonitory. **~zi'one** *nf* premonition

premu'nir|e *vt* fortify. **~si** *vr* take protective measures; **~si di** provide oneself with; **~si contro** protect oneself against

pre'mu|ra *nf (fretta)* hurry; *(cura)* care. **~'roso** *a* thoughtful

prena'tale *a* antenatal

'prender|e *vt* take; *(afferrare)* seize; catch *(treno, malattia, ladro, pesce)*; have *(cibo, bevanda)*; *(far pagare)* charge; *(assumere)* take on; *(ottenere)* get; *(occupare)* take up; **~e informa-zioni** make inquiries; **~e a calci/pu-gni** kick/punch; **che ti prende?** what's got into you?; **quanto prende?** what do you charge?; **~e una persona per**

un'altra mistake sb for sb else ● *vi (voltare)* turn; *(attecchire)* take root; *(rap-prendersi)* set; **~e a destra/sinistra** turn right/left; **~e a fare qcsa** start doing sth. **~si** *vr* **~si a pugni** come to blows; **~si cura di** take care of *(ammalato)*; **~sela** take it to heart

prendi'sole *nm* sundress

preno'ta|re *vt* book, reserve. **~to** *a* booked, reserved **~zi'one** *nf* booking, reservation

'prensile *a* prehensile

preoccu'pante *a* alarming

preoccu'pa|re *vt* worry. **~rsi** *vr* **~rsi** worry **(di** about); **~rsi di fare qcsa** take the trouble to do sth. **~to** *a (ansioso)* worried. **~zi'one** *nf* worry; *(apprensione)* concern

prepa'ra|re *vt* prepare **~rsi** *vr* get ready. **~'tivi** *nmpl* preparations. **~to** *nm (prodotto)* preparation. **~'torio** *a* preparatory. **~zi'one** *nf* preparation

prepensiona'mento *nm* early retirement

preponde'ran|te *a* predominant. **~za** *nf* prevalence

pre'porre *vt* place before

preposizi'one *nf* preposition

pre'posto *pp di* **preporre** ● *a* **~ a** *(addetto a)* in charge of

prepo'ten|te *a* overbearing ● *nmf* bully. **~za** *nf* high-handedness

preroga'tiva *nf* prerogative

'presa *nf* taking; *(conquista)* capture; *(stretta)* hold; *(di cemento ecc)* setting; *Electr* socket; *(pizzico)* pinch; **essere alle prese con** be struggling *o* grappling with; **a ~ rapida** *(cemento, colla)* quick-setting; **fare ~ su qcno** influence sb. **~ d'aria** air vent. **~ in giro** leg-pull. **~ multipla** adaptor

pre'sagio *nm* omen. **presa'gire** *vt* foretell

'presbite *a* long-sighted

presbiteri'ano, -a *a & nmf* Presbyterian. **presbi'terio** *nm* presbytery

pre'scelto *a* selected

pre'scindere *vi* **~ da** leave aside; **a ~ da** apart from

presco'lare *a* **in età ~** preschool

pre'scri|tto *pp di* **prescrivere**

pre'scri|vere *vt* prescribe. **~zi'one** *nf* prescription; *(norma)* rule

preselezi'one *nf* **chiamare qcno in ~** call sb via the operator

presen'ta|re *vt* present; *(far conoscere)* introduce; show *(documento)*; *(inoltrare)* submit. **~rsi** *vr* present oneself;

(*farsi conoscere*) introduce oneself; (*a ufficio*) attend; (*alla polizia ecc*) report; (*come candidato*) stand, run; ⟨*occasione:*⟩ occur; **~rsi bene/male** ⟨*persona:*⟩ make a good/bad impression; ⟨*situazione:*⟩ look good/bad. **~'tore**, **~'trice** *nmf* presenter; (*di notizie*) announcer. **~zi'one** *nf* presentation; (*per conoscersi*) introduction

pre'sente *a* present; (*attuale*) current; (*questo*) this; **aver ~** remember ● *nm* present; **i presenti** those present ● *nf* **allegato alla ~** (*in lettera*) enclosed

presenti'mento *nm* foreboding

pre'senza *nf* presence; (*aspetto*) appearance; **in ~ di**, **alla ~ di** in the presence of; **di bella ~** personable. **~ di spirito** presence of mind

presenzi'are *vi* **~ a** attend

pre'sepe *nm*, **pre'sepio** *nm* crib

preser'va|re *vt* preserve; (*proteggere*) protect (**da** from). **~'tivo** *nm* condom. **~zi'one** *nf* preservation

'preside *nm* headmaster; *Univ* dean ● *nf* headmistress; *Univ* dean

presi'den|te *nm* chairman; *Pol* president ● *nf* chairwoman; *Pol* president. **~ del consiglio [dei ministri]** Prime Minister. **~ della repubblica** President of the Republic. **~za** *nf* presidency; (*di assemblea*) chairmanship. **~zi'ale** *a* presidential

presidi'are *vt* garrison. **pre'sidio** *nm* garrison

presi'edere *vt* preside over

'preso *pp di* **prendere**

'pressa *nf Mech* press

pres'sante *a* urgent

pressap'poco *adv* about

pres'sare *vt* press

pressi'one *nf* pressure; **far ~ su** put pressure on. **~ del sangue** blood pressure

'presso *prep* near; (*a casa di*) with; (*negli indirizzi*) care of, c/o; ⟨*lavorare*⟩ for ● *pressi nmpl*: **nei pressi di...** in the neighbourhood o vicinity of...

pressoché *adv* almost

pressuriz'za|re *vt* pressurize. **~to** *a* pressurized

prestabi'li|re *vt* arrange in advance. **~to** *a* agreed

prestam'pato *a* printed ● *nm* (*modulo*) form

pre'stante *a* good-looking

pre'star|e *vt* lend; **~e attenzione** pay attention; **~e aiuto** lend a hand; **farsi ~e** borrow (**da** from). **~si** *vr* ⟨*frase:*⟩ lend itself; ⟨*persona:*⟩ offer

prestazi'one *nf* performance; **prestazioni** *pl* (*servizi*) services

prestigia'tore, **-'trice** *nmf* conjurer

pre'stigi|o *nm* prestige; **gioco di ~o** conjuring trick. **~'oso** *nm* prestigious

'prestito *nm* loan; **dare in ~** lend; **prendere in ~** borrow

'presto *adv* soon; (*di buon'ora*) early; (*in fretta*) quickly; **a ~** see you soon; **al più ~** as soon as possible; **~ o tardi** sooner or later; **far ~** be quick

pre'sumere *vt* presume; (*credere*) think

presu'mibile *a* **è ~ che...** presumably,...

pre'sunto *a* ⟨*colpevole*⟩ presumed

presun|tu'oso *a* presumptuous ● *nmf* presumptuous person. **~zi'one** *nf* presumption

presup'po|rre *vt* suppose; (*richiedere*) presuppose. **~sizi'one** *nf* presupposition. **~sto** *nm* essential requirement

'prete *nm* priest

preten'dente *nmf* pretender ● *nm* (*corteggiatore*) suitor

pre'ten|dere *vt* (*sostenere*) claim; (*esigere*) demand ● *vi* **~dere a** claim to; **~dere di** (*esigere*) demand to. **~si'one** *nf* pretension. **~zi'oso** *a* pretentious

pre'tes|a *nf* pretension; (*esigenza*) claim; **senza ~e** unpretentious. **~o** *pp di* **pretendere**

pre'testo *nm* pretext

pre'tore *nm* magistrate

pretta'mente *adv* decidedly

pre'tura *nf* magistrate's court

preva'le|nte *a* prevalent. **~nte'mente** *adv* primarily. **~nza** *nf* prevalence. **~re** *vi* prevail

pre'valso *pp di* **prevalere**

preve'dere *vt* foresee; forecast ⟨*tempo*⟩; ⟨*legge ecc:*⟩ provide for

preve'nire *vt* precede; (*evitare*) prevent; (*avvertire*) forewarn

preven|ti'vare *vt* estimate; (*aspettarsi*) budget for. **~'tivo** *a* preventive ● *nm Comm* estimate

preve'n|uto *a* forewarned; (*mal disposto*) prejudiced. **~zi'one** *nf* prevention; (*preconcetto*) prejudice

previ'den|te *a* provident. **~za** *nf* foresight. **~za sociale** social security, welfare *Am*. **~zi'ale** *a* provident

'previo *a* **~ pagamento** on payment

previsi'one *nf* forecast; **in ~ di** in anticipation of

pre'visto *pp di* **prevedere** ● *a* foreseen ● *nm* **più/meno/prima del ~** more/less/earlier than expected

prezi'oso *a* precious

prez'zemolo *nm* parsley

'prezzo *nm* price. **~ di fabbrica** factory price. **~ all'ingrosso** wholesale price. **[a] metà ~** half price

prigi'on|e *nf* prison; (*pena*) imprisonment. **prigio'nia** *nf* imprisonment. **~i'ero, -a** *a* imprisoned ● *nmf* prisoner

'prima *adv* before; (*più presto*) earlier; (*in primo luogo*) first; **~, finiamo questo** let's finish this first; **puoi venire ~?** (*di giorni*) can't you come any sooner?; (*di ore*) can't you come any earlier?; **~ o poi** sooner or later; **quanto ~** as soon as possible ● *prep* **~ di** before; **~ d'ora** before now ● *conj* **~ che** before ● *nf* first class; *Theat* first night; *Auto* first [gear]

pri'mario *a* primary; (*principale*) principal

pri'mat|e *nm* primate. **~o** *nm* supremacy; *Sport* record

prima've|ra *nf* spring. **~'rile** *a* spring *attrib*

primeggi'are *vi* excel

primi'tivo *a* primitive; (*originario*) original

pri'mizie *nfpl* early produce *sg*

'primo *a* first; (*fondamentale*) principal; (*precedente di due*) former; (*iniziale*) early; (*migliore*) best ● *nm* first; **primi** *pl* (*i primi giorni*) the beginning; **in un ~ tempo** at first. **prima copia** master copy

primo'genito, -a *a* & *nmf* first-born

primordi'ale *a* primordial

'primula *nf* primrose

princi'pale *a* main ● *nm* head, boss *fam*

princi|'pato *nm* principality. **'principe** *nm* prince. **principe ereditario** crown prince. **~'pesco** *a* princely. **~'pessa** *nf* princess

principi'ante *nmf* beginner

prin'cipio *nm* beginning; (*concetto*) principle; (*causa*) cause; **per ~** on principle

pri'ore *nm* prior

priori|tà *nf inv* priority. **~'tario** *a* having priority

'prisma *nm* prism

pri'va|re *vt* deprive. **~rsi** *vr* deprive oneself

privatizzazi'one *nf* privatization.

pri'vato, -a *a* private ● *nmf* private citizen

privazi'one *nf* deprivation

privilegi'are *vt* privilege; (*considerare più importante*) favour. **privi'legio** *nm* privilege

'privo *a* **~ di** devoid of; (*mancante*) lacking in

pro *prep* for ● *nm* advantage; **a che ~?** what's the point?; **il ~ e il contro** the pros and cons

pro'babil|e *a* probable. **~ità** *nf inv* probability. **~'mente** *adv* probably

pro'ble|ma *nm* problem. **~'matico** *a* problematic

pro'boscide *nf* trunk

procacci'ar|e *vt*, **~si** *vr* obtain

pro'cace *a* impudent

pro'ced|ere *vi* proceed; (*iniziare*) start; **~ere contro** *Jur* start legal proceedings against. **~i'mento** *nm* process; *Jur* proceedings *pl*. **proce'dura** *nf* procedure

proces'sare *vt Jur* try

processi'one *nf* procession

pro'cesso *nm* process; *Jur* trial

proces'sore *nm Comput* processor

processu'ale *a* trial

pro'cinto *nm* **essere in ~ di** be about to

pro'clama *nm* proclamation

procla'ma|re *vt* proclaim. **~zi'one** *nf* proclamation

procrasti'na|re *vt liter* postpone

procrezi'one *nf* procreation

pro'cura *nf* power of attorney; **per ~** by proxy

procu'ra|re *vt/i* procure; (*causare*) cause; (*cercare*) try. **~'tore** *nm* attorney. **P~tore Generale** Attorney General. **~tore legale** lawyer. **~tore della repubblica** public prosecutor

'prode *a* brave. **pro'dezza** *nf* bravery

prodi'gar|e *vt* lavish. **~si** *vr* do one's best

pro'digi|o *nm* prodigy. **~'oso** *a* prodigious

pro'dotto *pp di* **produrre** ● *nm* product. **prodotti agricoli** farm produce *sg*. **~ derivato** by-product. **~ interno lordo** gross domestic product. **~ nazionale lordo** gross national product

pro'du|rre *vt* produce. **~rsi** *vr* (*attore:*) play; (*accadere*) happen. **~ttività** *nf* productivity. **~t'tivo** *a* productive. **~t'tore, ~t'trice** *nmf* producer. **~zi'one** *nf* production

profa'na|re vt desecrate. **~zi'one** nf desecration. **pro'fano** a profane

profe'rire vt utter

Prof.essa abbr (**Professoressa**) Prof.

profes'sare vt profess; practise (professione)

professio'nale a professional

professi'o|ne nf profession; **libera ~ne** profession. **~'nismo** nm professionalism. **~'nista** nmf professional

profes'sor|e, -'essa nmf Sch teacher; Univ lecturer; (titolare di cattedra) professor

pro'fe|ta nm prophet. **~tico** a prophetic. **~tiz'zare** vt prophesy. **~'zia** nf prophecy

pro'ficuo a profitable

profi'lar|e vt outline; (ornare) border; Aeron streamline. **~si** vr stand out

profi'lattico a prophylactic ● nm condom

pro'filo nm profile; (breve studio) outline; **di ~** in profile

profit'tar|e vi **~ di** (avvantaggiarsi) profit by; (approfittare) take advantage of. **pro'fitto** nm profit; (vantaggio) advantage

profond|a'mente adv deeply, profoundly. **~ità** nf inv depth

pro'fondo a deep; fig profound; (cultura) great

'profugo, -a nmf refugee

profu'mar|e vt perfume. **~si** vr put on perfume

profumata'mente adv **pagare ~** pay through the nose

profu'mato a (fiore) fragrant; (fazzoletto ecc) scented

profume'ria nf perfumery. **pro'fumo** nm perfume, scent

profusi'one nf profusion; **a ~** in profusion. **pro'fuso** pp di **profondere** ● a profuse

proget'tar|e vt plan. **~'tista** nmf designer. **pro'getto** nm plan; (di lavoro importante) project. **progetto di legge** bill

prog'nosi nf inv prognosis; **in ~ riservata** on the danger list

pro'gramma nm programme; Comput program. **~ scolastico** syllabus

program'ma|re vt programme; Comput program. **~'tore, ~'trice** nmf [computer] programmer. **~zi'one** nf programming

progre'dire vi [make] progress

progres|si'one nf progression.

~'sivo a progressive. **pro'gresso** nm progress

proi'bi|re vt forbid. **~'tivo** a prohibitive. **~to** a forbidden. **~zi'one** nf prohibition

proiet'tare vt project; show (film). **~t'tore** nm projector; Auto headlight

proi'ettile nm bullet

proiezi'one nf projection

'prole nf offspring. **proletari'ato** nm proletariat. **prole'tario** a & nm proletarian

prolife'rare vi proliferate. **pro'lifico** a prolific

pro'lisso a verbose, prolix

'prologo nm prologue

pro'lunga nf Electr extension

prolun'gar|e vt prolong; (allungare) lengthen; extend (contratto, scadenza). **~si** vr continue; **~si su** (dilungarsi) dwell upon

prome'moria nm memo; (per se stessi) reminder, note; (formale) memorandum

pro'me|ssa nf promise. **~sso** pp di **promettere**. **~ttere** vt/i promise

promet'tente a promising

promi'nente a prominent

promiscuità nf promiscuity. **pro'miscuo** a promiscuous

promon'torio nm promontory

pro'mo|sso pp di **promuovere** ● a Sch who has/have gone up a year; Univ who has/have passed an exam. **~'tore, ~'trice** nmf promoter

promozio'nale a promotional. **promozi'one** nf promotion

promul'gare vt promulgate

promu'overe vt promote; Sch move up a class

proni'pote nm (di bisnonno) greatgrandson; (di prozio) great-nephew ● nf (di bisnonno) granddaughter; (di prozio) great-niece

pro'nome nm pronoun

pronosti'care vt forecast, predict. **pro'nostico** nm forecast

pron'tezza nf readiness; (rapidità) quickness

'pronto a ready; (rapido) quick; **~!** Teleph hallo!; **tenersi ~** be ready (per for); **pronti, via!** (in gare) ready! steady! go!. **~ soccorso** first aid; (in ospedale) accident and emergency

prontu'ario nm handbook

pro'nuncia nf pronunciation

pronunci'a|re vt pronounce; (dire) utter; deliver (discorso). **~rsi** vr (su un

169

argomento) give one's opinion. **~to** *a* pronounced; (*prominente*) prominent

pro'nunzia *ecc* = **pronuncia** *ecc*

propa'ganda *nf* propaganda

propa'ga|re *vt* propagate. **~rsi** *vr* spread. **~zi'one** *nf* propagation

prope'deutico *a* introductory

pro'pen|dere *vi* **~dere per** be in favour of. **~si'one** *nf* inclination, propensity. **~so** *pp di* **propendere** ● *a* **essere ~so a fare qcsa** be inclined to do sth

propi'nare *vt* administer

pro'pizio *a* favourable

proponi'mento *nm* resolution

pro'por|re *vt* propose; (*suggerire*) suggest. **~si** *vr* set oneself 〈*obiettivo, meta*〉; **~si di** intend to

proporzio'na|le *a* proportional. **~re** *vt* proportion. **~to** *a* proportioned. **proporzi'one** *nf* proportion

pro'posito *nm* purpose; **a ~** by the way; **a ~ di** with regard to; **di ~** (*apposta*) on purpose; **capitare a ~**, **giungere a ~** come at just the right time

proposizi'one *nf* clause; (*frase*) sentence

pro'post|a *nf* proposal. **~o** *pp di* **proporre**

proprietà *nf inv* property; (*diritto*) ownership; (*correttezza*) propriety. **~ immobiliare** property. **~ privata** private property. **proprie'taria** *nf* owner; (*di casa affittata*) landlady. **proprie'tario** *nm* owner; (*di casa affittata*) landlord

'proprio *a* one's [own]; (*caratteristico*) typical; (*appropriato*) proper ● *adv* just; (*veramente*) really; **non ~** not really, not exactly; (*affatto*) not... at all ● *pron* one's own ● *nm* one's [own]; **lavorare in ~** be one's own boss; **mettersi in ~** set up on one's own

propul|si'one *nf* propulsion. **~'sore** *nm* propeller

'proroga *nf* extension

proro'ga|bile *a* extendable. **~re** *vt* extend

pro'rompere *vi* burst out

'prosa *nf* prose. **pro'saico** *a* prosaic

pro'scio|gliere *vt* release; *Jur* acquit. **~lto** *pp di* **prosciogliere**

prosciu'gar|e *vt* dry up; (*bonificare*) reclaim. **~si** *vr* dry up

prosci'utto *nm* ham. **~ cotto** cooked ham. **~ crudo** type of dry-cured ham, Parma ham

pro'scri|tto, -a *pp di* **proscrivere** ● *nmf* exile

prosecuzi'one *nf* continuation

prosegui'mento *nm* continuation; **buon ~!** (*viaggio*) have a good journey!; (*festa*) enjoy the rest of the party!

prosegu'ire *vt* continue ● *vi* go on, continue

prospe'r|are *vi* prosper. **~ità** *nf* prosperity. **'prospero** *a* prosperous; (*favorevole*) favourable. **~oso** *a* flourishing; 〈*ragazza*〉 buxom

prospet'tar|e *vt* show. **~si** *vr* seem

prospet'tiva *nf* perspective; (*panorama*) view; *fig* prospect. **pro'spetto** *nm* (*vista*) view; (*facciata*) façade; (*tabella*) table

prospici'ente *a* facing

prossima'mente *adv* soon

prossimità *nf* proximity

'prossimo, -a *a* near; (*seguente*) next; (*molto vicino*) close; **l'anno** *nm* **~** next year ● *nmf* neighbour

prosti'tu|ta *nf* prostitute. **~zi'one** *nf* prostitution

pro'stra|re *vt* prostrate. **~rsi** *vr* prostrate oneself. **~to a** prostrate

protago'nista *nmf* protagonist

pro'te|ggere *vt* protect; (*favorire*) favour

prote'ina *nf* protein

pro'tender|e *vt* stretch out. **~si** *vr* (*in avanti*) lean out. **pro'teso** *pp di* **protendere**

pro'te|sta *nf* protest; (*dichiarazione*) protestation. **~'stante** *a & nmf* Protestant. **~'stare** *vt/i* protest

prote|t'tivo *a* protective. **~tto** *pp di* **proteggere**. **~t'tore**, **~t'trice** *nmf* protector; (*sostenitore*) patron ● *nm* (*di prostituta*) pimp. **~zi'one** *nf* protection

protocol'lare *a* 〈*visita*〉 protocol ● *vt* register

proto'collo *nm* protocol; (*registro*) register; **carta ~** official stamped paper

proto'tipo *nm* prototype

pro'tra|rre *vt* protract; (*differire*) postpone. **~rsi** *vr* go on, continue. **~tto** *pp di* **protrarre**

protuberan|te *a* protuberant. **~za** *nf* protuberance

'prova *nf* test; (*dimostrazione*) proof; (*tentativo*) try; (*di abito*) fitting; *Sport* heat; *Theat* rehearsal; (*bozza*) proof; **fino a ~ contraria** until I'm told otherwise; **in ~** (*assumere*) for a trial period;

mettere alla ~ put to the test. **~ generale** dress rehearsal

pro'var|e *vt* test; *(dimostrare)* prove; *(tentare)* try; try on *‹abiti ecc›*; *(sentire)* feel; *Theat* rehearse. **~si** *vr* try

proveni'enza *nf* origin. **prove'nire** *vi* **provenire da** come from

pro'vento *nm* proceeds *pl*

prove'nuto *pp di* provenire

pro'verbio *nm* proverb

pro'vetta *nf* test-tube; **bambino in ~** test-tube baby

pro'vetto *a* skilled

pro'vinci|a *nf* province; *(strada)* B road, secondary road. **~'ale** *a* provincial; **strada ~ale** B road, secondary road

pro'vino *nm* specimen; *Cinema* screen test

provo'ca|nte *a* provocative. **~re** *vt* provoke; *(causare)* cause. **~'tore**, **~'trice** *nmf* trouble-maker. **~'torio** *a* provocative. **~zi'one** *nf* provocation

provve'd|ere *vi* **~ere a** provide for. **~i'mento** *nm* measure; *(previdenza)* precaution

provvi'denz|a *nf* providence. **~i'ale** *a* providential

provvigi'one *nf Comm* commission

provvi'sorio *a* provisional

prov'vista *nf* supply

pro'zio, -a *nm* great-uncle ● *nf* great-aunt

'prua *nf* prow

pru'den|te *a* prudent. **~za** *nf* prudence; **per ~za** as a precaution

'prudere *vi* itch

'prugn|a *nf* plum. **~a secca** prune. **~o** *nm* plum[-tree]

prurigi'noso *a* itchy. **pru'rito** *nm* itch

pseu'donimo *nm* pseudonym

psica'na|lisi *nf* psychoanalysis. **~'lista** *nmf* psychoanalyst. **~liz'zare** *vt* psychoanalyse

'psiche *nf* psyche

psichi'a|tra *nmf* psychiatrist. **~'tria** *nf* psychiatry. **~'trico** *a* psychiatric

'psichico *a* mental

psico|lo'gia *nf* psychology. **~'logico** *a* psychological. **psi'cologo, -a** *nmf* psychologist

psico'patico, -a *a* psychopathic ● *nmf* psychopath

PT *abbr* **(Posta e Telecomunicazioni)** PO

pubbli'ca|re *vt* publish. **~zi'one** *nf* publication. **~zioni** *pl (di matrimonio)* banns

pubbli'cista *nmf Journ* correspondent

pubblicità *nf inv* publicity, advertising; *(annuncio)* advertisement, advert; **fare ~ a qcsa** advertise sth; **piccola ~** small advertisements. **pubblici'tario** *a* advertising

'pubblico *a* public; **scuola pubblica** state school ● *nm* public; *(spettatori)* audience; **grande ~** general public. **Pubblica Sicurezza** Police. **~ ufficiale** civil servant

'pube *nm* pubis

pubertà *nf* puberty

'pudico *a* modest. **pu'dore** *nm* modesty

pue'rile *a* children's; *pej* childish

pugi'lato *nm* boxing. **'pugile** *nm* boxer

pugna'la|re *vt* stab. **~ta** *nf* stab. **pu'gnale** *nm* dagger

'pugno *nm* fist; *(colpo)* punch; *(manciata)* fistful; *(fig: numero limitato)* handful; **dare un ~** a punch

'pulce *nf* flea; *(microfono)* bug

pul'cino *nm* chick; *(nel calcio)* junior

pu'ledra *nf* filly

pu'ledro *nm* colt

pu'li|re *vt* clean. **~re a secco** dry-clean. **~to** *a* clean. **~'tura** *nf* cleaning. **~'zia** *nf (il pulire)* cleaning; *(l'essere pulito)* cleanliness; **~zie** *pl* housework; **fare le ~zie** do the cleaning

'pu|llman *nm inv* bus, coach; *(urbano)* bus

pul'mino *nm* minibus

'pulpito *nm* pulpit

pul'sante *nm* button; *Electr* [push-]button. **~ di accensione** on/off switch

pul'sa|re *vi* pulsate. **~zi'one** *nf* pulsation

pul'viscolo *nm* dust

'puma *nm inv* puma

pun'gente *a* prickly; *‹insetto›* stinging; *‹odore ecc›* sharp

'punger|e *vt* prick; *‹insetto:›* sting. **~si** *vr* **~si un dito** prick one's finger

pungigli'one *nm* sting

pu'ni|re *vt* punish. **~'tivo** *a* punitive. **~zi'one** *nf* punishment; *Sport* free kick

'punta *nf* point; *(estremità)* tip; *(di monte)* peak; *(un po')* pinch; *Sport* forward; **doppie punte** *(di capelli)* split ends

pun'tare *vt* point; *(spingere con forza)* push; *(scommettere)* bet; *(fam: appuntare)* fasten ● *vi* **~ su** *fig* rely on; **~ verso** *(dirigersi)* head for; **~ a** aspire to

punta'spilli *nm inv* pincushion

pun'tat|a *nf (di una storia)* instalment;

(televisiva) episode; *(al gioco)* stake, bet; *(breve visita)* flying visit; **a ~e** serialized, in instalments; **fare una ~ a/in** pop over to ⟨*luogo*⟩

punteggia'tura *nf* punctuation

pun'teggio *nm* score

puntel'lare *vt* prop. **pun'tello** *nm* prop

pun'tigli|o *nm* spite; *(ostinazione)* obstinacy. **~'oso** *a* punctilious, pernickety *pej*

pun'tin|a *nf (da disegno)* drawing pin, thumb tack *Am*; *(di giradischi)* stylus. **~o** *nm* dot; **a ~o** perfectly; *(cotto)* to a T

'punto *nm* point; *(in cucito, Med)* stitch; *(in punteggiatura)* full stop; **in che ~?** where, exactly?; **di ~ in bianco** all of a sudden; **due punti** colon; **in ~** sharp; **mettere a ~** put right; *fig* fine tune; tune up *(motore)*; **essere sul ~ di fare qcsa** be about to do sth, be on the point of doing sth. **punti** *pl* **cardinali** points of the compass. **~ debole** blind spot. **~ esclamativo** exclamation mark. **~ interrogativo** question mark. **~ nero** *Med* blackhead. **~ di riferimento** landmark; *(per la qualità)* benchmark. **~ di vendita** point of sale. **~ e virgola** semicolon. **~ di vista** point of view

pun'tual|e *a* punctual. **~ità** *nf* punctuality. **~'mente** *adv* punctually, on time

pun'tura *nf (di insetto)* sting; *(di ago ecc)* prick; *Med* puncture; *(iniezione)* injection; *(fitta)* stabbing pain

punzecchi'are *vt* prick; *fig* tease

'pupa *nf* doll. **pu'pazzo** *nm* puppet. **pupazzo di neve** snowman

pup'illa *nf. Anat* pupil

pu'pillo, -a *nmf (di professore)* favourite

purché *conj* provided

'pure *adv* too, also; *(concessivo)* **fate ~!** please do! ● *conj (tuttavia)* yet; *(anche se)* even if; **pur di** just to

purè *nm inv* purée. **~ di patate** mashed potatoes, creamed potatoes

pu'rezza *nf* purity

'purga *nf* purge. **pur'gante** *nm* laxative. **pur'gare** *vt* purge

purga'torio *nm* purgatory

purifi'care *vt* purify

puri'tano, -a *a & nmf* Puritan

'puro *a* pure; *(vino ecc)* undiluted; **per ~ caso** by sheer chance, purely by chance

puro'sangue *a & nm* thoroughbred

pur'troppo *adv* unfortunately

pus *nm* pus. **'pustola** *nf* pimple

puti'ferio *nm* uproar

putre'far|e *vi*, **~si** *vr* putrefy

'putrido *a* putrid

put'tana *nf vulg* whore

'puzza *nf =* **puzzo**

puz'zare *vi* stink; **~ di bruciato** *fig* smell fishy

'puzzo *nm* stink, bad smell. **~la** *nf* polecat. **~'lente** *a* stinking

p.zza *abbr* **(piazza)** Sq.

Qq

qua *adv* here; **da un anno in ~** for the last year; **da quando in ~?** since when?; **di ~** this way; **di ~ di** on this side of; **~ dentro** in here; **~ sotto** under here; **~ vicino** near here; **~ e là** here and there

qua'derno *nm* exercise book; *(per appunti)* notebook

quadrango'lare *a (forma)* quadrangular. **qua'drangolo** *nm* quadrangle

qua'drante *nm* quadrant; *(di orologio)* dial

qua'dra|re *vt* square; *(contabilità)* balance ● *vi* fit in. **~to** *a* square; *(equilibrato)* levelheaded ● *nm* square; *(pugilato)* ring; **al ~to** squared

quadret'tato *a* squared; ⟨*carta*⟩ graph *attrib*. **qua'dretto** *nm* square; *(piccolo quadro)* small picture; **a quadretti** ⟨*tessuto*⟩ check

quadricro'mia *nf* four-colour printing

quadrien'nale *a (che dura quattro anni)* four-year

quadri'foglio *nm* four-leaf clover

quadri'latero *nm* quadrilateral

quadri'mestre *nm (periodo)* four-month period

'quadro nm picture, painting; (quadrato) square; (fig: scena) sight; (tabella) table; Theat scene; Comm executive **quadri** pl (carte) diamonds; **a quadri** (tessuto, giacca, motivo) check. **quadri** pl **direttivi** senior management

qua'drupede nm quadruped

quaggiù adv down here

'quaglia nf quail

'qualche a (alcuni) a few, some; (un certo) some; (in interrogazioni) any; **ho ~ problema** I have a few problems, I have some problems; **~ tempo fa** some time ago; **hai ~ libro italiano?** have you any Italian books?; **posso prendere ~ libro?** can I take some books?; **in ~ modo** somehow; **in ~ posto** somewhere; **~ volta** sometimes; **~ cosa = qualcosa**

qual'cos|a pron something; (in interrogazioni) anything; **~'altro** something else; **vuoi qualcos'altro?** would you like anything else?; **~a di strano** something strange; **vuoi ~a da mangiare?** would you like something to eat?

qual'cuno pron someone, somebody; (in interrogazioni) anyone, anybody; (alcuni) some; (in interrogazioni) any; **c'è ~?** is anybody in?; **qualcun altro** someone else, somebody else; **c'è qualcun altro che aspetta?** is anybody else waiting?; **ho letto ~ dei suoi libri** I've read some of his books; **conosci ~ dei suoi amici?** do you know any of his friends?

'quale a which; (indeterminato) what; (come) as, like; **~ macchina è la tua?** which car is yours?; **~ motivo avrà di parlare così?** what reason would he have to speak like that?; **~ onore!** what an honour!; **città quali Venezia** towns like Venice!; **~ che sia la tua opinione** whatever you may think ● pron inter which [one]; **~ preferisci?** which [one] do you prefer? ● pron rel **il/la ~** (persona) who; (animale, cosa) that, which; (oggetto: con prep) whom; (animale, cosa) which; **ho incontrato tua madre, la ~ mi ha detto...** I met your mother, who told me...; **l'ufficio nel ~ lavoro** the office in which I work; **l'uomo con il ~ parlavo** the man to whom I was speaking ● adv (come) as

qua'lifica nf qualification; (titolo) title

qualifi'ca|re vt qualify; (definire) define. **~rsi** vr be placed. **~'tivo** a qualifying. **~to** a (operaio) semiskilled. **~zi'one** nf qualification

qualità nf inv quality; (specie) kind; **in ~ di** in one's capacity as. **~tiva'mente** adv qualitatively. **~'tivo** a qualitative

qua'lora conj in case

qual'siasi, qua'lunque a any; (non importa quale) whatever; (ordinario) ordinary; **dammi una penna ~** give me any pen [whatsoever]; **farei ~ cosa** I would do anything; **~ cosa io faccia** whatever I do; **~ persona** anyone; **in ~ caso** in any case; **uno ~** any one, whichever; **l'uomo qualunque** the man in the street; **vivo in una casa ~** I live in an ordinary house

qualunqu'ismo nm lack of political views

'quando conj & adv when; **da ~ ti ho visto** since I saw you; **da ~ esci con lui?** how long have you been going out with him?; **da ~ in qua?** since when?; **~... ~...** sometimes..., sometimes...

quantifi'care vt quantify

quantità nf inv quantity; **una ~ di** (gran numero) a great deal of. **~tiva'mente** adv quantitatively. **~'tivo** nm amount ● a quantitative

'quanto a inter how much; (con nomi plurali) how many; (in esclamazione) what a lot of; (tempo) how long; **quanti anni hai?** how old are you? ● a rel as much... as; (tempo) as long as; (con nomi plurali) as many... as; **prendi ~ denaro ti serve** take as much money as you need; **prendi quanti libri vuoi** take as many books as you like ● pron inter how much; (quanto tempo) how long; (plurale) how many; **quanti ne abbiamo oggi?** what date is it today? ● pron rel as much as; (quanto tempo) as long as; (plurale) as many as; **prendine ~/quanti ne vuoi** take as much/as many as you like; **stai ~ vuoi** stay as long as you like; **questo è ~** that's it ● adv inter how much; (quanto tempo) how long; **~ sei alto?** how tall are you?; **~ hai aspettato?** how long did you wait for?; **~ costa?** how much is it?; **~ mi dispiace!** I'm so sorry!; **~ è bello!** how nice! ● adv rel as much as; **lavoro ~ posso** I work as much as I can; **è tanto intelligente ~ bello** he's as intelligent as he's good-looking; **in ~** (in qualità di) as; (poiché) since; **in ~ a me** as far as I'm concerned; **per ~** however; **per ~ ne sappia** as far as I know; **per ~ mi riguarda** as far as I'm concerned; **per ~ mi sia simpatico** much as I like him; ~ **a** as for; ~ **prima** (*al più presto*) as soon as possible

quan'tunque *conj* although

qua'ranta *a & nm* forty

quaran'tena *nf* quarantine

quaran'tenn|e *a* forty-year-old. **~io** *nm* period of forty years

quaran't|esimo *a* fortieth. **~ina** *nf* una **~ina** about forty

qua'resima *nf* Lent

quar'tetto *nm* quartet

quarti'ere *nm* district; *Mil* quarters *pl.* ~ **generale** headquarters

quarto *a* fourth ● *nm* fourth; (*quarta parte*) quarter; **le sette e un ~** a quarter past seven. **quarti** *pl* **di finale** quarterfinals. ~ **d'ora** quarter of an hour. **quar'tultimo, -a** *nmf* fourth from the end, fourth last

'quarzo *nm* quartz

'quasi *adv* almost, nearly; ~ **mai** hardly ever ● *conj* (*come se*) as if; ~ ~ **sto a casa** I'm tempted to stay home

quassù *adv* up here

'quatto *a* crouching; (*silenzioso*) silent; **starsene ~ ~** keep very quiet

quat'tordici *a & nm* fourteen

quat'trini *nmpl* money *sg*, dosh *sg fam*

'quattro *a & nm* four; **dirne ~ a** qcno give sb a piece of one's mind; **farsi in ~ (per** qcno/**per fare** qcsa) go to a lot of trouble (for sb/to do sth); **in ~ e quattr'otto** in a flash. ~ **per ~** *nm inv* *Auto* four-wheel drive [vehicle]

quat'trocchi: a ~ *adv* in private

quattro|'cento *a & nm* four hundred; **il ~cento** the fifteenth century

quattro'mila *a & nm* four thousand

'quell|o *a* that (*pl* those); **quell'albero** that tree; **quegli alberi** those trees; **quel cane** that dog; **quei cani** those dogs ● *pron* that [one] (*pl* those [ones]); ~**o** li that one over there; ~**o che** the one that; (*ciò che*) what; **quelli che** the ones that, those that; ~**o a destra** the one on the right

'quercia *nf* oak

que'rela *nf* [legal] action

quere'lare *vt* bring an action against

que'sito *nm* question

questio'nario *nm* questionnaire

quest'ione *nf* question; (*faccenda*)

matter; (*litigio*) quarrel; **in ~** in doubt; **è fuori ~** it's out of the question; **è ~ di vita o di morte** it's a matter of life and death

'quest|o *a* this (*pl* these) ● *pron* this [one] (*pl* these [ones]); ~**o qui, ~o qua** this one here; ~**o è quello che a detto** that's what he said; **per ~o** for this *or* that reason. **quest'oggi** today

que'store *nm* chief of police

que'stura *nf* police headquarters

qui *adv* here; **da ~ in poi** from now on; **fin ~** (*di tempo*) up till now, until now; ~ **dentro** in here; ~ **sotto** under here; ~ **vicino** *adv* near here ● *nm* ~ **pro quo** misunderstanding

quie'scienza *nf* **trattamento di ~** retirement package

quie'tanza *nf* receipt

quie'tar|e *vt* calm. **~si** *vr* quieten down

qui'et|e *nf* quiet; **disturbo della ~e pubblica** breach of the peace. **~o** *a* quiet

'quindi *adv* then ● *conj* therefore

'quindi|ci *a & nm* fifteen. **~'cina** *nf* una **~cina** about fifteen; **una ~cina di giorni** a fortnight *Br*, two weeks

quinquen'nale *a* (*che dura cinque anni*) five-year. **quin'quennio** *nm* [period of] five years

quin'tale *nm* a hundred kilograms

'quinte *nfpl* *Theat* wings

quin'tetto *nm* quintet

'quinto *a* fifth

quin'tuplo *a* quintuple

qui'squiglia *nf* **perdersi in quisquiglie** get bogged down in details

'quota *nf* quota; (*rata*) instalment; (*altitudine*) height; *Aeron* altitude, height; (*ippica*) odds *pl*; **perdere ~** lose altitude; **prendere ~** gain altitude. ~ **di iscrizione** entry fee

quo'ta|re *vt* *Comm* quote. **~to a** quoted; **essere ~to in Borsa** be quoted on the Stock Exchange. **~zi'one** *nf* quotation

quotidi|ana'mente *adv* daily. **~'ano** *a* daily; (*ordinario*) everyday ● *nm* daily [paper]

quozi'ente *nm* quotient. ~ **d'intelligenza** intelligence quotient, IQ

Rr

ra'barbaro *nm* rhubarb

'rabbia *nf* rage; (*ira*) anger; *Med* rabies *sg*; **che ~!** what a nuisance!; **mi fa ~** it makes me angry

rab'bino *nm* rabbi

rabbiosa'mente *adv* furiously. **rabbi'oso** *a* hot-tempered; *Med* rabid; (*violento*) violent

rabbo'nir|e *vt* pacify. **~si** *vr* calm down

rabbrivi'dire *vi* shudder; (*di freddo*) shiver

rabbui'arsi *vr* become dark

raccapez'zar|e *vt* put together. **~si** *vr* see one's way ahead

raccapricci'ante *a* horrifying

raccatta'palle *nm inv* ball boy ● *nf inv* ball girl

raccat'tare *vt* pick up

rac'chetta *nf* racket. **~ da ping pong** table-tennis bat. **~ da sci** ski stick, ski pole. **~ da tennis** tennis racket

'racchio *a fam* ugly

racchi'udere *vt* contain

rac'cogli|ere *vt* pick; (*da terra*) pick up; (*mietere*) harvest; (*collezionare*) collect; (*radunare*) gather; win (*voti ecc*); (*dare asilo a*) take in. **~ersi** *vr* gather; (*concentrarsi*) collect one's thoughts. **~'mento** *nm* concentration. **~'tore**, **~'trice** *nmf* collector ● *nm* (*cartella*) ring-binder

rac'colto, -a *pp di* **raccogliere** ● *a* (*rannicchiato*) hunched; (*intimo*) cosy; (*concentrato*) engrossed ● *nm* (*mietitura*) harvest ● *nf* collection; (*di scritti*) compilation; (*del grano ecc*) harvesting; (*adunata*) gathering

raccoman'dabile *a* recommendable; **poco ~** (*persona*) shady

raccoman'da|re *vt* recommend; (*affidare*) entrust. **~rsi** *vr* (*implorare*) beg. **~ta** *nf* registered letter; **~ta con ricevuta di ritorno** recorded delivery. **~-espresso** *nf guaranteed next-day delivery of recorded items*. **~zi'one** *nf* recommendation

raccon'tare *vt* tell. **rac'conto** *nm* story

raccorci'are *vt* shorten

raccor'dare *vt* join. **rac'cordo** *nm* connection; (*stradale*) feeder. **raccordo anulare** ring road. **raccordo ferroviario** siding

ra'chitico *a* rickety; (*poco sviluppato*) stunted

racimo'lare *vt* scrape together

racket *nm inv* racket

'radar *nm* radar

raddol'cir|e *vt* sweeten; *fig* soften. **~si** *vr* become milder; (*carattere:*) mellow

raddoppi'are *vt* double. **rad'doppio** *nm* doubling

raddriz'zare *vt* straighten

'rader|e *vt* shave; graze (*muro*); **~e al suolo** raze [to the ground]. **~si** *vr* shave

radi'are *vt* strike off; **~ dall'albo** strike off

radia|'tore *nm* radiator. **~zi'one** *nf* radiation

'radica *nf* briar

radi'cale *a* radical ● *nm* *Gram* root; *Pol* radical

ra'dicchio *nm* chicory

ra'dice *nf* root; **mettere [le] radici** *fig* put down roots. **~ quadrata** square root

'radio *nf inv* radio; **via ~** by radio. **~ a transistor** transistor radio ● *nm* *Chem* radium.

radioama'tore, -'trice *nmf* [radio] ham

radioascolta'tore, -'trice *nmf* listener

radioat|tività *nf* radioactivity. **~'tivo** *a* radioactive

radio'cro|naca *nf* radio commentary; **fare la ~naca di** commentate on. **~'nista** *nmf* radio reporter

radiodiffusi'one *nf* broadcasting

radiogra|'fare *vt* X-ray. **~'fia** *nf* X-ray [photograph]; (*radiologia*) radiography; **fare una ~fia** (*paziente:*) have an X-ray; (*dottore:*) take an X-ray

radio'fonico *a* radio *attrib*

radio'lina *nf* transistor

radi'ologo, -a *nmf* radiologist

radi'oso *a* radiant

radio'sveglia *nf* radio alarm

radio'taxi *nm inv* radio taxi

radiote'lefono *nm* radio-telephone; (*privato*) cordless [phone]

radiotelevi'sivo *a* broadcasting *attrib*

'rado *a* sparse; (*non frequente*) rare; **di ~** seldom

radu'nar|e *vt*, **~si** *vr* gather [together]. **ra'duno** *nm* meeting; *Sport* rally

ra'dura *nf* clearing

'rafano *nm* horseradish

raffazzo'nato *a* ⟨*discorso, lavoro*⟩ botched

raf'fermo *a* stale

'raffica *nf* gust; (*di armi da fuoco*) burst; (*di domande*) barrage

raffigu'ra|re *vt* represent. **~zi'one** *nf* representation

raffi'na|re *vt* refine. **~ta'mente** *adv* elegantly. **~'tezza** *nf* refinement. **~to** *a* refined. **raffine'ria** *nf* refinery

rafforza|'mento *nm* reinforcement; (*di muscolatura*) strengthening. **~re** *vt* reinforce. **~'tivo** *nm* *Gram* intensifier

raffredda|'mento *nm* (*processo*) cooling

raffred'd|are *vt* cool. **~arsi** *vr* get cold; (*prendere un raffreddore*) catch a cold. **~ore** *nm* cold. **~ore da fieno** hay fever

raf'fronto *nm* comparison

'rafia *nf* raffia

Rag. *abbr* **ragioniere**

ra'gaz|za *nf* girl; (*fidanzata*) girlfriend. **~za alla pari** au pair [girl]. **~'zata** *nf* prank. **~zo** *nm* boy; (*fidanzato*) boyfriend; **da ~zo** (*da giovane*) as a boy

ragge'lar|e *vt fig* freeze. **~si** *vr fig* turn to ice

raggi'ante *a* radiant; **~ di successo** flushed with success

raggi'era *nf* **a ~** with a pattern like spokes radiating from a centre

'raggio *nm* ray; *Math* radius; (*di ruota*) spoke; **~ d'azione** range. **~ laser** laser beam

raggi'rare *vt* trick. **rag'giro** *nm* trick

raggi'un|gere *vt* reach; (*conseguire*) achieve. **~'gibile** *a* ⟨*luogo*⟩ within reach

raggomito'lar|e *vt* wind. **~si** *vr* curl up

raggranel'lare *vt* scrape together

raggrin'zir|e *vt*, **~si** *vr* wrinkle

raggrup|pa'mento *nm* (*gruppo*) group; (*azione*) grouping. **~'pare** *vt* group together

ragguagli'are *vt* compare; (*informare*) inform. **raggu'aglio** *nm* comparison; (*informazione*) information

ragguar'devole *a* considerable

'ragia *nf* resin; **acqua** *nf* **~** turpentine

ragiona'mento *nm* reasoning; (*discussione*) discussion. **ragio'nare** *vi* reason; (*discutere*) discuss

ragi'one *nf* reason; (*ciò che è giusto*) right; **a ~ o a torto** rightly or wrongly; **aver ~** be right; **perdere la ~** go out of one's mind; **a ragion veduta** after due consideration

ragion|e'ria *nf* accountancy

ragio'nevol|e *a* reasonable. **~'mente** *adv* reasonably

ragioni'ere, -a *nmf* accountant

ragli'are *vi* bray

ragna'tela *nf* cobweb. **'ragno** *nm* spider

ragù *nm inv* meat sauce

RAI *nf abbr* (**Radio Audizioni Italiane**) *Italian public broadcasting company*

ralle'gra|re *vt* gladden. **~rsi** *vr* rejoice; **~rsi con qcno** congratulate sb. **~'menti** *nmpl* congratulations

rallenta'mento *nm* slowing down

rallen'ta|re *vt/i* slow down; (*allentare*) slacken. **~rsi** *vr* slow down. **~'tore** *nm* (*su strada*) speed bump; **al ~tore** in slow motion

raman'zina *nf* reprimand

ra'marro *nm* type of lizard

ra'mato *a* ⟨*capelli*⟩ copper[-coloured]

'rame *nm* copper

ramifi'ca|re *vi*, **~rsi** *vr* branch out; ⟨*strada:*⟩ branch. **~zi'one** *nf* ramification

rammari'carsi *vr* **~ di** regret; (*lamentarsi*) complain (**di** about). **ram'marico** *nm* regret

rammen'dare *vt* darn. **ram'mendo** *nm* darning

rammen'tar|e *vt* remember; **~e qcsa a qcno** (*richiamare alla memoria*) remind sb of sth. **~si** *vr* remember

rammol'li|re *vt* soften. **~rsi** *vr* go soft. **~to, -a** *nmf* wimp

'ramo *nm* branch. **~'scello** *nm* twig

'rampa *nf* (*di scale*) flight. **~ d'accesso** slip road. **~ di lancio** launch[ing] pad

ram'pante **a giovane ~** yuppie

rampi'cante *a* climbing ●*nm Bot* creeper

ram'pollo *nm hum* brat; *(discendente)* descendant

ram'pone *nm* harpoon; *(per scarpe)* crampon

'rana *nf* frog; *(nel nuoto)* breaststroke; **uomo ~** frogman

'rancido *a* rancid

ran'core *nm* resentment

ran'dagio *a* stray

'rango *nm* rank

rannicchi'arsi *vr* huddle up

rannuvola'mento *nm* clouding over. **rannuvo'larsi** *vr* cloud over

ra'nocchio *nm* frog

ranto'lare *vi* wheeze. **'rantolo** *nm* wheeze; *(di moribondo)* death-rattle

'rapa *nf* turnip

ra'pace *a* rapacious; *(uccello)* predatory

ra'pare *vt* crop

'rapida *nf* rapids *pl*. **~'mente** *adv* rapidly

rapidità *nf* speed

'rapido *a* swift ● *nm (treno)* express [train]

rapi'mento *nm (crimine)* kidnapping

ra'pina *nf* robbery; **~ a mano armata** armed robbery. **~ in banca** bank robbery. **rapi'nare** *vt* rob. **~'tore** *nm* robber

ra'pi|re *vt* abduct; *(a scopo di riscatto)* kidnap; *(estasiare)* ravish. **~'tore, ~'trice** *nmf* kidnapper

rappacifi'ca|re *vt* pacify. **~rsi** *vr* be reconciled, make it up. **~zi'one** *nf* reconciliation

rappor'tare *vt* reproduce *(disegno)*; *(confrontare)* compare

rap'porto *nm* report; *(connessione)* relation; *(legame)* relationship; *Math, Techn* ratio; **rapporti** *pl* relationship; **essere in buoni rapporti** be on good terms. **~ di amicizia** friendship. **~ di lavoro** working relationship. **rapporti** *pl* **sessuali** sexual intercourse

rap'prendersi *vr* set; *(latte:)* curdle

rappre'saglia *nf* reprisal

rappresen'tan|te *nmf* representative. **~te di classe** class representative. **~te di commercio** sales representative, [sales] rep *fam*. **~za** *nf* delegation; *Comm* agency; **spese** *nfpl* **di ~za** entertainment expenses; **di ~za** *(appartamento ecc)* company

rappresen'ta|re *vt* represent; *Theat* perform. **~'tivo** *a* representative. **~zi'one** *nf* representation; *(spettacolo)* performance

rap'preso *pp di* **rapprendersi**

rapso'dia *nf* rhapsody

'raptus *nm inv* fit of madness

rara'mente *adv* rarely, seldom

rare'fa|re *vt*, **~rsi** *vr* rarefy. **~tto** *a* rarefied

rarità *nf inv* rarity. **'raro** *a* rare

ra'sar|e *vt* shave; trim *(siepe ecc)*. **~si** *vr* shave

raschia'mento *nm Med* curettage

raschi'are *vt* scrape; *(togliere)* scrape off

rasen'tare *vt* go close to. **ra'sente** *prep* very close to

'raso *pp di* **radere** ● *a* smooth; *(colmo)* full to the brim; *(barba)* close-cropped; **~ terra** close to the ground; **un cucchiaio ~** a level spoonful ● *nm* satin

ra'soio *nm* razor

ras'segna *nf* review; *(mostra)* exhibition; *(musicale, cinematografica)* festival; **passare in ~** review; *Mil* inspect

rasse'gna|re *vt* present. **~rsi** *vr* resign oneself. **~to a** *(persona, aria, tono)* resigned. **~zi'one** *nf* resignation

rassere'nar|e *vt* clear; *fig* cheer up. **~si** *vr* become clear; *fig* cheer up

rasset'tare *vt* tidy up; *(riparare)* mend

rassicu'ra|nte *a* *(persona, parole, presenza)* reassuring. **~re** *vt* reassure. **~zi'one** *nf* reassurance

rasso'dare *vt* harden; *fig* strengthen

rassomigli'a|nza *nf* resemblance. **~re** *vi* **~re a** resemble

rastrella'mento *nm (di fieno)* raking; *(perlustrazione)* combing. **rastrel'lare** *vt* rake; *(perlustrare)* comb

rastrelli'era *nf* rack; *(per biciclette)* bicycle rack; *(scolapiatti)* [plate] rack. **ra'strello** *nm* rake

'rata *nf* instalment; **pagare a rate** pay by instalments; **comprare qcsa a rate** buy sth on hire purchase, buy sth on the installment plan *Am*. **rate'ale** *a* by instalments; **pagamento rateale** payment by instalments

rate'are, rateiz'zare *vt* divide into instalments

ra'tifica *nf Jur* ratification

ratifi'care *vt Jur* ratify

'ratto *nm* abduction; *(roditore)* rat

rattop'pare *vt* patch. **rat'toppo** *nm* patch

rattrap'pir|e *vt* make stiff. **~si** *vr* become stiff

rattri'star|e vt sadden. **~si** vr become sad

rau'cedine nf hoarseness. **'rauco** a hoarse

rava'nello nm radish

ravi'oli nmpl ravioli sg

ravve'dersi vr mend one's ways

ravvicina'mento nm (tra persone) reconciliation; Pol rapprochement

ravvici'nar|e vt bring closer; (riconciliare) reconcile. **~si** vr be reconciled

ravvi'sare vt recognize

ravvi'var|e vt revive; fig brighten up. **~si** vr revive

'rayon nm rayon

razio'cinio nm rational thought; (buon senso) common sense

razio'nal|e a rational. **~ità** nf (raziocinio) rationality; (di ambiente) functional nature. **~iz'zare** vt rationalize (programmi, metodi, spazio). **~'mente** adv (con raziocinio) rationally

razio'nare vt ration. **razi'one** nf ration

'razza nf race; (di cani ecc) breed; (genere) kind; **che ~ di idiota!** fam what an idiot!

raz'zia nf raid

razzi'ale a racial

raz'zis|mo nm racism. **~ta** a & nmf racist

'razzo nm rocket. **~ da segnalazione** flare

razzo'lare vi (polli:) scratch about

re nm inv king; Mus (chiave, nota) D

rea'gire vi react

re'ale a real; (di re) royal

rea'lis|mo nm realism. **~ta** nmf realist; (fautore del re) royalist

realistica'mente adv realistically. **rea'listico** a realistic

realiz'zabile a (programma) feasible

realiz'za|re vt (attuare) carry out, realize; Comm make; score (gol, canestro); (rendersi conto di) realize. **~rsi** vr come true; (nel lavoro ecc) fulfil oneself. **~zi'one** nf realization; (di sogno, persona) fulfilment. **~zione scenica** production

rea'lizzo nm (vendita) proceeds pl; (riscossione) yield

real'mente adv really

realtà nf inv reality. **~ virtuale** virtual reality

re'ato nm crime, criminal offence

reat'tivo a reactive

reat'tore nm reactor; Aeron jet [aircraft]

reazio'nario, -a a & nmf reactionary

reazi'one nf reaction. **~ a catena** chain reaction

'rebus nm inv rebus; (enigma) puzzle

recapi'tare vt deliver. **re'capito** nm address; (consegna) delivery. **recapito a domicilio** home delivery. **recapito telefonico** contact telephone number

re'car|e vt bear; (produrre) cause. **~si** vr go

re'cedere vi recede; fig give up

recensi'one nf review

recen's|ire vt review. **~ore** nm reviewer

re'cente a recent; **di ~** recently. **~'mente** adv recently

recessi'one nf recession

reces'sivo a Biol recessive. **re'cesso** nm recess

re'cidere vt cut off

reci'divo, -a a Med recurrent ● nmf repeat offender

recin|'tare vt close off. **re'cinto** nm enclosure; (per animali) pen; (per bambini) play-pen. **~zi'one** nf (muro) wall; (rete) wire fence; (cancellata) railings pl

recipi'ente nm container

re'ciproco a reciprocal

re'ciso pp di recidere

'recita nf performance. **reci'tare** vt recite; Theat act; play (ruolo). **~zi'one** nf recitation; Theat acting

recla'mare vi protest ● vt claim

ré'clame nf inv advertising; (avviso pubblicitario) advertisement

re'clamo nm complaint; **ufficio reclami** complaints department

recli'na|bile a reclining; **sedile ~bile** reclining seat. **~re** vt tilt (sedile); lean (capo)

reclusi'one nf imprisonment. **re'cluso, -a** a secluded ● nmf prisoner

'recluta nf recruit

reclu|ta'mento nm recruitment. **~'tare** vt recruit

'record nm inv record ● a inv (cifra) record attrib

recrimi'na|re vi recriminate. **~zi'one** nf recrimination

recupe'rare vt recover. **re'cupero** nm recovery; **corso di recupero** additional classes; **minuti di recupero** Sport injury time

redargu'ire vt rebuke

re'datto pp di redigere

redat'tore, -'trice *nmf* editor; *(di testo)* writer. **redazi'one** *nf (ufficio)* editorial office; *(di testi)* editing

reddi'tizio *a* profitable

'reddito *nm* income. **~ imponibile** taxable income

re'den|to *pp di* redimere. **~'tore** *nm* redeemer. **~zi'one** *nf* redemption

re'digere *vt* write; draw up *(documento)*

re'dimer|e *vt* redeem. **~si** *vr* redeem oneself

'redini *nfpl* reins

'reduce *a* **~ da** back from ● *nmf* survivor

refe'rendum *nm inv* referendum

refe'renza *nf* reference

refet'torio *nm* refectory

refrat'tario *a* refractory; **essere ~ a** have no aptitude for

refrige'ra|re *vt* refrigerate. **~zi'one** *nf* refrigeration

refur'tiva *nf* stolen goods *pl*

rega'lare *vt* give

re'gale *a* regal

re'galo *nm* present, gift

re'gata *nf* regatta

reg'gen|te *nmf* regent. **~za** *nf* regency

'regger|e *vt (sorreggere)* bear; *(tenere in mano)* hold; *(dirigere)* run; *(governare)* govern; *Gram* take ● *vi (resistere)* hold out; *(durare)* last; *fig* stand. **~si** *vr* stand

'reggia *nf* royal palace

reggi'calze *nm inv* suspender belt

reggi'mento *nm* regiment; *(fig: molte persone)* army

reggi'petto, reggi'seno *nm* bra

re'gia *nf Cinema* direction; *Theat* production

re'gime *nm* regime; *(dieta)* diet; *Mech* speed. **~ militare** military regime

re'gina *nf* queen

'regio *a* royal

regio'na|le *a* regional. **~'lismo** *nm (parola)* regionalism

regi'one *nf* region

re'gista *nmf Cinema* director; *Theat, TV* producer

regi'stra|re *vt* register; *Comm* enter; *(incidere su nastro)* tape, record; *(su disco)* record. **~'tore** *nm* recorder; *(magnetofono)* tape-recorder. **~tore di cassa** cash register. **~zi'one** *nf* registration; *Comm* entry; *(di programma)* recording

re'gistro *nm* register; *(ufficio)* registry. **~ di cassa** ledger

re'gnare *vi* reign

'regno *nm* kingdom; *(sovranità)* reign. **R~ Unito** United Kingdom

'regola *nf* rule; **essere in ~** be in order; *(persona:)* have one's papers in order. **rego'labile** *a (meccanismo)* adjustable. **~'mento** *nm* regulation; *Comm* settlement. **~mento di conti** settling of scores

rego'lar|e *a* regular ● *vt* regulate; *(ridurre, moderare)* limit; *(sistemare)* settle. **~si** *vr (agire)* act; *(moderarsi)* control oneself. **~ità** *nf inv* regularity. **~iz'zare** *vt* settle *(debito)*

rego'la|ta *nf* **darsi una ~ta** pull oneself together. **~'tore, ~'trice** *a* **piano ~tore** urban development plan

'regolo *nm* ruler

regre'dire *vi Biol, Psych* regress

regres|si'one *nf* regression. **~'sivo** *a* regressive. **re'gresso** *nm* decline

reinseri'mento *nm (di persona)* reintegration

reinser'irsi *vr (in ambiente)* reintegrate

reinte'grare *vt* restore

relativa'mente *adv* relatively; **~ a** as regards. **relatività** *nf* relativity. **rela'tivo** *a* relative

rela'tore, -'trice *nmf (in una conferenza)* speaker

re'lax *nm* relaxation

relazi'one *nf* relation[ship]; *(rapporto amoroso)* [love] affair; *(resoconto)* report; **pubbliche relazioni** *pl* public relations

rele'gare *vt* relegate

religi'o|ne *nf* religion. **~so, -a** *a* religious ● *nm* monk ● *nf* nun

re'liqui|a *nf* relic. **~'ario** *nm* reliquary

re'litto *nm* wreck

re'ma|re *vi* row. **~'tore, ~'trice** *nmf* rower

remini'scenza *nf* reminiscence

remissi'one *nf* remission; *(sottomissione)* submissiveness. **remis'sivo** *a* submissive

'remo *nm* oar

'remora *nf* **senza remore** without hesitation

re'moto *a* remote

remune'ra|re *vt* remunerate. **~'tivo** *a* remunerative. **~zi'one** *nf* remuneration

'render|e *vt (restituire)* return; *(esprimere)* render; *(fruttare)* yield; *(far diventare)* make. **~si** *vr* become; **~si**

conto di qcsa realize sth; **~si utile** make oneself useful

rendi'conto nm report

rendi'mento nm rendering; (*produzione*) yield

'**rendita** nf income; (*dello Stato*) revenue; **vivere di ~** *fig* rest on one's laurels

'**rene** nm kidney. **~ artificiale** kidney machine

'**reni** nfpl (*schiena*) back

reni'tente a **essere ~ a** ⟨*consigli di qcno*⟩ be unwilling to accept

'**renna** nf reindeer (*pl inv*); (*pelle*) buckskin

'**Reno** nm Rhine

'**reo, -a** a guilty ● nmf offender

re'parto nm department; *Mil* unit

repel'lente a repulsive

repen'taglio nm **mettere a ~** risk

repen'tino a sudden

reper'ibile a available; **non è ~** (*perduto*) it's not to be found

repe'rire vt trace ⟨*fondi*⟩

re'perto nm **~ archeologico** find

reper'torio nm repertory; (*elenco*) index; **immagini di ~** archive footage

'**replica** nf reply; (*obiezione*) objection; (*copia*) replica; *Theat* repeat performance. **repli'care** vt reply; *Theat* repeat

repor'tage nm inv report

repres|si'one nf repression. **~'sivo** a repressive. **re'presso** pp di **reprimere**.

re'primere vt repress

re'pubbli|ca nf republic. **~'cano, -a** a & nmf republican

repu'tare vt consider

reputazi'one nf reputation

requi'si|re vt requisition. **~to** nm requirement

requisi'toria nf (*arringa*) closing speech

requisizi'one nf requisition

'**resa** nf surrender; *Comm* rendering. **~ dei conti** rendering of accounts

'**residence** nm inv service flat

resi'den|te a & nmf resident. **~za** nf residence; (*soggiorno*) stay. **~zi'ale** a residential; **zona ~ziale** residential district

re'siduo a residual ● nm remainder

'**resina** nf resin

resi'sten|te a resistant; **~te all'acqua** water-resistant. **~za** nf resistance; (*fisica*) stamina; *Electr* resistor; **la R~za** the Resistance

re'sistere vi **~ [a]** resist; ⟨*a colpi,*

scosse⟩ stand up to; **~ alla pioggia/al vento** be rain-/wind-resistant

'**reso** pp di **rendere**

reso'conto nm report

respin'gente nm *Rail* buffer

re'spin|gere vt repel; (*rifiutare*) reject; (*bocciare*) fail. **~to** pp di **respingere**

respi'ra|re vt/i breathe. **~'tore** nm respirator. **~tore [a tubo]** snorkel **~'torio** a respiratory. **~zi'one** nf breathing; *Med* respiration. **~zione bocca a bocca** mouth to mouth rescuscitation, kiss of life. **re'spiro** nm breath; (*il respirare*) breathing; *fig* respite

respon'sabil|e a responsible (**di** for); *Jur* liable. **~ità** nf inv responsibility; *Jur* liability. **~ità civile** *Jur* civil liability. **~iz'zare** vt give responsibility to ⟨*dipendente*⟩

re'sponso nm response

'**ressa** nf crowd

re'stante a remaining ● nm remainder

re'stare vi = rimanere

restau'ra|re vt restore. **~'tore, ~'trice** nmf restorer. **~zi'one** nf restoration. **re'stauro** nm (*riparazione*) repair

re'stio a restive; **~ a** reluctant to

restitu'|ire vt return; (*reintegrare*) restore. **~zi'one** nf return; *Jur* restitution

'**resto** nm remainder; (*saldo*) balance; (*denaro*) change; **resti** pl (*avanzi*) remains; **del ~** besides

re'string|ere vt contract; take in ⟨*vestiti*⟩; (*limitare*) restrict; shrink ⟨*stoffa*⟩. **~si** vr contract; (*farsi più vicini*) close up; ⟨*stoffa*⟩ shrink. **restringi'mento** nm (*di tessuto*) shrinkage

restri|t'tivo a ⟨*legge, clausola*⟩ restrictive. **~zi'one** nf restriction

resurrezi'one nf resurrection

resusci'tare vt/i revive

re'tata nf round-up

'**rete** nf net; (*sistema*) network; (*televisiva*) channel; (*in calcio, hockey*) goal; *fig* trap; (*per la spesa*) string bag. **~ locale** *Comput* local [area] network, LAN. **~ stradale** road network. **~ televisiva** television channel

reti'cen|te a reticent. **~za** nf reticence

retico'lato nm grid; (*rete metallica*) wire netting. **re'ticolo** nm network '**retina** *nf* retina

re'tina *nf* (*per capelli*) hair net

re'torico, -a *a* rhetorical; **domanda retorica** rhetorical question ● *nf* rhetoric

retribu'ire *vt* remunerate. **~zi'one** *nf* remuneration

'**retro** *adv* behind; **vedi ~** see over ● *nm inv* back. **~ di copertina** outside back cover

retroat'tivo *a* retroactive

retro'ce|dere *vi* retreat ● *vt*. *Mil* demote; *Sport* relegate. **~ssi'one** *nf Sport* relegation

retroda'tare *vt* backdate

re'trogrado *a* retrograde; *fig* old-fashioned; *Pol* reactionary

retrogu'ardia *nf Mil* rearguard

retro'marcia *nf* reverse [gear]

retro'scena *nm inv Theat* backstage; *fig* background details *pl*

retrospet'tivo *a* retrospective

retro'stante *a* **il palazzo ~** the building behind

retrovi'sore *nm* rear-view mirror

'**retta**[1] *nf Math* straight line; (*di collegio, pensionato*) fee

'**retta**[2] *nf* **dar ~ a qcno** take sb's advice

rettango'lare *a* rectangular. **ret'tangolo** *a* right-angled ● *nm* rectangle

ret'tifi|ca *nf* rectification. **~'care** *vt* rectify

'**rettile** *nm* reptile

retti'lineo *a* rectilinear; (*retto*) upright ● *nm Sport* back straight

retti'tudine *nf* rectitude

'**retto** *pp di* **reggere** ● *a* straight; *fig* upright; (*giusto*) correct; **angolo ~** right angle

ret'tore *nm Relig* rector; *Univ* chancellor

reu'matico *a* rheumatic

reuma'tismi *nmpl* rheumatism

reve'rendo *a* reverend

rever'sibile *a* reversible

revisio'nare *vt* revise; *Comm* audit; *Auto* overhaul. **revisi'one** *nf* revision; *Comm* audit; *Auto* overhaul. **revi'sore** *nm* (*di conti*) auditor; (*di bozze*) proofreader; (*di traduzioni*) revisor

re'vival *nm inv* revival

'**revoca** *nf* repeal. **revo'care** *vt* repeal

riabili'ta|re *vt* rehabilitate. **~zi'one** *nf* rehabilitation

riabitu'ar|e *vt* reaccustom. **~si** *vr* reaccustom oneself

riac'cender|e *vt* rekindle (*fuoco*). **~si** *vr* (*luce:*) come back on

riacqui'stare *vt* buy back; regain (*libertà, prestigio*); recover (*vista, udito*)

riaggan'ciare *vt* replace (*ricevitore*); **~ la cornetta** hang up ● *vi* hang up

riallac'ciare *vt* refasten; reconnect (*corrente*); renew (*amicizia*)

rial'zare *vt* raise ● *vi* rise. **ri'alzo** *nm* rise

riani'mar|e *vt Med* resuscitate; (*ridare forza a*) revive; (*ridare coraggio a*) cheer up. **~si** *vr* regain consciousness; (*riprendere forza*) revive; (*riprendere coraggio*) cheer up

riaper'tura *nf* reopening

ria'prir|e *vt*, **~si** *vr* reopen

ri'armo *nm* rearmament

rias'sumere *vt* (*ricapitolare*) resume

riassun'tivo *a* summarizing. **rias'sunto** *pp di* **riassumere** ● *nm* summary

ria'ver|e *vt* get back; regain (*salute, vista*). **~si** *vr* recover

riavvicina'mento *nm* (*tra persone*) reconciliation

riavvici'nar|e *vt* reconcile (*paesi, persone*). **~si** *vr* (*riconciliarsi*) be reconciled, make it up

riba'dire *vt* (*confermare*) reaffirm

ri'balta *nf* flap; *Theat* footlights *pl*; *fig* limelight

ribal'tabile *a* tip-up

ribal'tar|e *vt/i*, **~si** *vr* tip over; *Naut* capsize

ribas'sare *vt* lower ● *vi* fall. **ri'basso** *nm* fall; (*sconto*) discount

ri'battere *vt* (*a macchina*) retype; (*controbattere*) deny ● *vi* answer back

ribel'l|arsi *vr* rebel. **ri'belle** *a* rebellious ● *nmf* rebel. **~'ione** *nf* rebellion

'**ribes** *nm inv* (*rosso*) redcurrant; (*nero*) blackcurrant

ribol'lire *vi* (*fermentare*) ferment; *fig* seethe

ri'brezzo *nm* disgust; **far ~ a** disgust

rica'dere *vi* fall back; (*nel peccato ecc*) lapse; (*pendere*) hang [down]; **~ su** (*riversarsi*) fall on. **rica'duta** *nf* relapse

rical'care *vt* trace

ricalci'trante *a* recalcitrant

rica'ma|re *vt* embroider. **~to** *a* embroidered

ri'cambi *nmpl* spare parts

ricambi'are *vt* return; reciprocate (*sentimento*); **~ qcsa a qcno** repay sb for sth. **ri'cambio** *nm* replacement; *Biol* metabolism; **pezzo di ricambio** spare [part]

ri'camo nm embroidery

ricapito'la|re vt sum up. **~zi'one** nf summary, recap fam

ri'carica nf (di sveglia) rewinding

ricari'care vt reload ⟨macchina fotografica, fucile, camion⟩; recharge ⟨batteria⟩; Comput reboot

ricat'ta|re vt blackmail. **~'tore**, **~'trice** nmf blackmailer. **ri'catto** nm blackmail

rica'va|re vt get; (ottenere) obtain; (dedurre) draw. **~to** nm proceeds pl. **ri'cavo** nm proceeds pl

'ricca nf rich woman. **~'mente** adv lavishly

ric'chezza nf wealth; fig richness; **ricchezze** pl riches

'riccio a curly ● nm curl; (animale) hedgehog. **~ di mare** sea-urchin. **~lo** nm curl. **~'luto** a curly. **ricci'uto** a ⟨barba⟩ curly

'ricco a rich ● nm rich man

ri'cerca nf search; (indagine) investigation; (scientifica) research; Sch project

ricer'ca|re vt search for; (fare ricerche su) research. **~ta** nf wanted woman. **~'tezza** nf refinement. **~to** a sought-after; (raffinato) refined; (affettato) affected ● nm (polizia) wanted man

ricetrasmit'tente nf transceiver

ri'cetta nf Med prescription; Culin recipe

ricet'tacolo nm receptacle

ricet'tario nm (di cucina) recipe book

ricetta'|tore, **-'trice** nmf fence, receiver of stolen goods. **~zi'one** nf receiving [stolen goods]

rice'vente a ⟨apparecchio, stazione⟩ receiving ● nmf receiver

ri'cev|ere vt receive; (dare il benvenuto) welcome; (di albergo) accommodate. **~i'mento** nm receiving; (accoglienza) welcome; (trattenimento) reception

ricevi'tor|e nm receiver. **~ia** nf **~ia del lotto** agency authorized to sell lottery tickets

rice'vuta nf receipt. **~ fiscale** tax receipt

ricezi'one nf Radio, TV reception

richia'mare vt (al telefono) call back; (far tornare) recall; (rimproverare) rebuke; (attirare) draw; **~ alla mente** call to mind. **richi'amo** nm recall; ⟨attrazione⟩ call

richi'edere vt ask for; (di nuovo) ask again for; **~ a qcno di fare qcsa** ask o request sb to do sth. **richi'esta** nf request; Comm demand

ri'chiuder|e vt shut again, close again. **~si** vr ⟨ferita:⟩ heal

rici'claggio nm recycling

rici'clar|e vt recycle. **~si** vr retrain; (cambiare lavoro) change one's line of work

'ricino nm olio di **~** castor oil

ricogni'zi'one nf Mil reconnaissance

ri'colmo a full

ricominci'are vt/i start again

ricompa'rire vi reappear

ricom'pen|sa nf reward. **~'sare** vt reward

ricom'por|re vt (riscrivere) rewrite; (ricostruire) reform; Typ reset. **~si** vr regain one's composure

riconcili'a|re vt reconcile. **~rsi** vr be reconciled. **~zi'one** nf reconciliation

ricono'scen|te a grateful. **~za** nf gratitude

rico'nosc|ere vt recognize; (ammettere) acknowledge. **~i'mento** nm recognition; (ammissione) acknowledgement; (per la polizia) identification. **~i'uto** a recognized

riconqui'stare vt Mil retake, reconquer

riconside'rare vt rethink

rico'prire vt recover; (rivestire) coat; (di insulti) shower (**di** with); hold ⟨carica⟩

ricor'dar|e vt remember; (richiamare alla memoria) recall; (far ricordare) remind; (rassomigliare) look like. **~si** vr **~si [di]** remember. **ri'cordo** nm memory; (oggetto) memento; (di viaggio) souvenir; **ricordi** pl (memorie) memoirs

ricor'ren|te a recurrent. **~za** nf recurrence; (anniversario) anniversary

ri'correre vi recur; (accadere) occur; ⟨data:⟩ fall; **~ a** have recourse to; (rivolgersi a) turn to. **ri'corso** pp di **ricorrere** ● nm recourse; Jur appeal

ricostitu'ente nm tonic

ricostitu'ire vt re-establish

ricostru'|ire vt reconstruct. **~zi'one** nf reconstruction

ricove'ra|re vt give shelter to; **~re in ospedale** admit to hospital, hospitalize. **~to**, **-a** nmf hospital patient. **ri'covero** nm shelter; (ospizio) home

ricre'a|re vt re-create; (ristorare) restore. **~rsi** vr amuse oneself. **~'tivo** a recreational. **~zi'one** nf recreation; Sch break

ri'credersi vr change one's mind

ricupe'rare vt recover; rehabilitate ‹tossicodipendente›; **~ il tempo perduto** make up for lost time. **ri'cupero** nm recovery; ‹di tossicodipendente› rehabilitation; ‹salvataggio› rescue; [**minuti** nmpl **di**] **ricupero** injury time

ri'curvo a bent

ridacchi'are vi giggle

ri'dare vt give back, return

ri'dente a ‹piacevole› pleasant

'ridere vi laugh; **~ di** ‹deridere› laugh at

ri'detto pp di **ridire**

ridicoliz'zare vt ridicule. **ri'dicolo** a ridiculous

ridimensio'nare vt reshape; fig see in the right perspective

ri'dire vt repeat; ‹criticare› find fault with; **trova sempre da ~** he's always finding fault

ridon'dante a redundant

ri'dotto pp di **ridurre** ● nm Theat foyer ● a reduced

ri'du|rre vt reduce. **~rsi** vr diminish. **~rsi a** be reduced to. **~t'tivo** a reductive. **~zi'one** nf reduction; ‹per cinema, teatro› adaptation

rieducazi'one nf ‹di malato› rehabilitation

riem'pi|re vt fill [up]; fill in ‹moduli ecc›. **~rsi** vr fill [up]. **~'tivo** a filling ● nm filler

rien'tranza nf recess

rien'trare vi go/come back in; ‹tornare› return; ‹piegare indentro› recede; **~ in** ‹far parte› fall within. **ri'entro** nm return; ‹di astronave› re-entry

riepilo'gare vt recapitulate. **rie'pilogo** nm roundup

riesami'nare vt reappraise

ri'essere vi **ci risiamo!** here we go again!

riesu'mare vt exhume

rievo'ca|re vt ‹commemorare› commemorate. **~zi'one** nf ‹commemorazione› commemoration

rifaci'mento nm remake

ri'fa|re vt do again; ‹creare› make again; ‹riparare› repair; ‹imitare› imitate; make ‹letto›. **~rsi** vr ‹rimettersi› recover; ‹vendicarsi› get even; **~rsi una vita/carriera** make a new life/career for oneself; **~rsi il trucco** touch up

one's makeup; **~rsi di** make up for. **~tto** pp di **rifare**

riferi'mento nm reference

rife'ri|re vt report; **~e a** attribute to ● vi make a report. **~si** vr **~si a** refer to

rifi'lare vt ‹tagliare a filo› trim; ‹fam: affibbiare› saddle

rifi'ni|re vt finish off. **~'tura** nf finish

riflo'rire vi blossom again; fig flourish again

rifiu'tare vt refuse. **rifi'uto** nm refusal; **rifiuti** pl ‹immondizie› rubbish. **rifiuti** pl **urbani** urban waste

riflessi'one nf reflection; ‹osservazione› remark. **rifles'sivo** a thoughtful; Gram reflexive

ri'flesso pp di **riflettere** ● nm ‹luce› reflection; Med reflex; **per ~** indirectly

ri'fletter|e vt reflect ● vi think. **~si** vr be reflected

riflet'tore nm reflector; ‹proiettore› searchlight

ri'flusso nm ebb

rifocil'lar|e vt restore. **~si** vr liter, hum take some refreshment

ri'fondere vt ‹rimborsare› refund

ri'forma nf reform; Relig reformation; Mil exemption on medical grounds

rifor'ma|re vt reform; ‹n.igliorare› reform; Mil declare unfit for military service. **~to a** ‹chiesa› Reformed. **~'tore**, **~'trice** nmf reformer. **~'torio** nm reformatory. **rifor'mista** a reformist

riforni'mento nm supply; ‹scorta› stock; ‹di combustibile› refuelling; **stazione** nf **di ~** petrol station

rifor'nir|e vt **~e di** provide with. **~si** vr restock, stock up ‹di with›

ri'fra|ngere vt refract. **~tto** pp di **rifangere**. **~zi'one** nf refraction

rifug'gire vi **~ da** fig shun

rifugi'a|rsi vr take refuge. **~to, -a** nmf refugee

ri'fugio nm shelter; ‹nascondiglio› hideaway

'riga nf line; ‹fila› row; ‹striscia› stripe; ‹scriminatura› parting; ‹regolo› rule; a **righe** ‹stoffa› striped; ‹quaderno› ruled; **mettersi in ~** line up

ri'gagnolo nm rivulet

ri'gare vt rule ‹foglio› ● vi **~ dritto** behave well

rigatti'ere nm junk dealer

rigene'rare vt regenerate

riget'tare vt ‹gettare indietro› throw back; ‹respingere› reject; ‹vomitare› throw up. **ri'getto** nm rejection

ri'ghello *nm* ruler

rigid|a'mente *adv* rigidly. **~ità** *nf* rigidity; (*di clima*) severity; (*severità*) strictness. **'rigido** *a* rigid; (*freddo*) severe; (*severo*) strict

rigi'rar|e *vt* turn again; (*ripercorrere*) go round; *fig* twist (*argomentazione*) ● *vi* walk about. **~si** *vr* turn round; (*nel letto*) turn over. **ri'giro** *nm* (*imbroglio*) trick

'rigo *nm* line; *Mus* staff

ri'gogli|o *nm* bloom. **~'oso** *a* luxuriant

ri'gonfio *a* swollen

ri'gore *nm* rigours *pl*; **a ~** strictly speaking; **calcio di ~** penalty [kick]; **area di ~** penalty area; **essere di ~** be compulsory

rigo|rosa'mente *adv* (*giudicare*) severely. **~'ros|o** *a* (*severo*) strict; (*scrupoloso*) rigorous.

riguada'gnare *vt* regain (*quota, velocità*)

riguar'dar|e *vt* look at again; (*considerare*) regard; (*concernere*) concern; **per quanto riguarda** with regard to. **~si** *vr* take care of oneself. **rigu'ardo** *nm* care; (*considerazione*) consideration; **nei riguardi di** towards; **riguardo a** with regard to

ri'gurgito *nm* regurgitation

rilanci'are *vt* throw back (*palla*); (*di nuovo*) throw again; increase (*offerta*); revive (*moda*); relaunch (*prodotto*) ● *vi* (*a carte*) raise the stakes

rilasci'ar|e *vt* (*concedere*) grant; (*liberare*) release; issue (*documento*). **~si** *vr* relax. **ri'lascio** *nm* release; (*di documento*) issue

rilassa'mento *nm* (*relax*) relaxation

rilas'sa|re *vt*, **~rsi** *vr* relax. **~to** *a* (*ambiente*) relaxed

rile'ga|re *vt* bind (*libro*). **~to** *a* bound. **~'tura** *nf* binding

ri'leggere *vt* reread

ri'lento: a ~ *adv* slowly

rileva'mento *nm* survey; *Comm* buyout

rile'van|te *a* considerable

rile'va|re *vt* (*trarre*) get; (*mettere in evidenza*) point out; (*notare*) notice; (*topografia*) survey; *Comm* take over; *Mil* relieve. **~zi'one** *nf* (*statistica*) survey

rili'evo *nm* relief; *Geog* elevation; (*topografia*) survey; (*importanza*) importance; (*osservazione*) remark; **mettere in ~** qcsa point sth out

rilut'tan|te *a* reluctant. **~za** *nf* reluctance

'rima *nf* rhyme; **far ~ con** qcsa rhyme with sth

riman'dare *vt* (*posporre*) postpone; (*mandare indietro*) send back; (*mandare di nuovo*) send again; (*far ridare un esame*) make resit an examination. **ri'mando** *nm* return; (*in un libro*) cross-reference

rima'nen|te *a* remaining ● *nm* remainder. **~za** *nf* remainder; **~ze** *pl* remnants

rima'ne|re *vi* stay, remain; (*essere d'avanzo*) be left; (*venirsi a trovare*) be; (*restare stupito*) be astonished; (*restare d'accordo*) agree

rimar'chevole *a* remarkable

ri'mare *vt/i* rhyme

rimargi'nar|e *vt*, **~si** *vr* heal

ri'masto *pp di* rimanere

rima'sugli *nmpl* (*di cibo*) leftovers

rimbal'zare *vi* rebound; (*proiettile*) ricochet; **far ~** bounce. **rim'balzo** *nm* rebound; (*di proiettile*) ricochet

rimbam'bi|re *vi* be in one's dotage ● *vt* stun. **~to** *a* in one's dotage

rimboc'care *vt* turn up; roll up (*maniche*); tuck in (*coperte*)

rimbom'bare *vi* resound

rimbor'sare *vt* reimburse, repay. **rim'borso** *nm* reimbursement, repayment. **rimborso spese** reimbursement of expenses

rimedi'are *vi* **~ a** remedy; make up for (*errore*); (*procurare*) scrape up. **ri'medio** *nm* remedy

rimesco'lare *vt* mix [up]; shuffle (*carte*); (*rivangare*) rake up

ri'messa *nf* (*locale per veicoli*) garage; (*per aerei*) hangar; (*per autobus*) depot; (*di denaro*) remittance; (*di merci*) consignment

ri'messo *pp di* rimettere

ri'metter|e *vt* (*a posto*) put back; (*restituire*) return; (*affidare*) entrust; (*perdonare*) remit; (*rimandare*) put off; (*vomitare*) bring up; **~ci** (*fam: perdere*) lose [out]. **~si** *vr* (*ristabilirsi*) recover; (*tempo*) clear up; **~si a** start again

'rimmel® *nm inv* mascara

rimoder'nare *vt* modernize

rimon'tare *vt* (*risalire*) go up; *Mech* reassemble ● *vi* remount; **~ a** (*risalire*) go back to

rimorchi'a|re *vt* tow; *fam* pick up (*ragazza*). **~'tore** *nm* tug[boat]. **ri'morchio** *nm* tow; (*veicolo*) trailer

ri'morso *nm* remorse

rimo'stranza *nf* complaint

rimozi'one *nf* removal; *(da un incarico)* dismissal. **~ forzata** *illegally parked vehicles removed at owner's expense*

rim'pasto *nm Pol* reshuffle

rimpatri'are *vt/i* repatriate. **rim'patrio** *nm* repatriation

rim'pian|gere *vt* regret. **~to** *pp di* **rimpiangere** ● *nm* regret

rimpiat'tino *nm* hide-and-seek

rimpiaz'zare *vt* replace

rimpiccio'lire *vi* become smaller

rimpinz'ar|e *vt* **~e di** stuff with. **~si** *vr* stuff oneself

rimprove'rare *vt* reproach; **~ qcsa a qcno** reproach sb for sth. **rim'provero** *nm* reproach

rimugi'nare *vt* rummage; *fig* **~ su** brood over

rimune'ra|re *vt* remunerate. **~'tivo** *a* remunerative. **~zi'one** *nf* remuneration

ri'muovere *vt* remove

ri'nascere *vi* be reborn, be born again

rinascimen'tale *a* Renaissance. **˙Rinasci'mento** *nm* Renaissance

ri'nascita *nf* rebirth

rincal'zare *vt (sostenere)* support; *(rimboccare)* tuck in. **rin'calzo** *nm* support; **rincalzi** *pl Mil* reserves

rincantucci'arsi *vr* hide oneself away in a corner

rinca'rare *vt* increase the price of ● *vi* become more expensive. **rin'caro** *nm* price increase

rinca'sare *vi* return home

rinchi'uder|e *vt* shut up. **~si** *vr* shut oneself up

rin'correre *vt* run after

rin'cors|a *nf* run-up. **~o** *pp di* **rincorrere**

rin'cresc|ere *vi* **mi rincresce di non…** I'm sorry *o* I regret that I can't…; **se non ti ~e** if you don't mind. **~i'mento** *nm* regret. **~i'uto** *pp di* **rincrescere**

rincreti'nire *vi* be stupid

rincu'lare *vi (arma:)* recoil; *(cavallo:)* shy. **rin'culo** *nm* recoil

rincuo'rar|e *vt* encourage. **~si** *vr* take heart

rinfacci'are *vt* **~ qcsa a qcno** throw sth in sb's face

rinfor'zar|e *vt* strengthen; *(rendere più saldo)* reinforce. **~si** *vr* become stronger. **rin'forzo** *nm* reinforcement; *fig* support

rinfran'care *vt* reassure

rinfre'scante *a* cooling

rinfre'scar|e *vt* cool; *(rinnovare)* freshen up ● *vi* get cooler. **~si** *vr* freshen [oneself] up. **rin'fresco** *nm* light refreshment; *(ricevimento)* party

rin'fusa *nf* **alla ~** at random

ringhi'are *vi* snarl

ringhi'era *nf* railing; *(di scala)* banisters *pl*

ringiova'nire *vt* rejuvenate *(pelle, persona)*; *(vestito:)* make look younger ● *vi* become young again; *(sembrare)* look young again

ringrazi|a'mento *nm* thanks *pl*. **~'are** *vt* thank

rinne'ga|re *vt* disown. **~to, -a** *nmf* renegade

rinnova'mento *nm* renewal; *(di edifici)* renovation

rinno'var|e *vt* renew; renovate *(edifici)*. **~si** *vr* be renewed; *(ripetersi)* recur, happen again. **rin'novo** *nm* renewal

rinoce'ronte *nm* rhinoceros

rino'mato *a* renowned

rinsal'dare *vt* consolidate

rinsa'vire *vi* come to one's senses

rinsec'chi|re *vi* shrivel up. **~to** *a* shrivelled up

rinta'narsi *vr* hide oneself away; *(animale:)* retreat into its den

rintoc'care *vi (campana:)* toll; *(orologio:)* strike. **rin'tocco** *nm* toll; *(di orologio)* stroke

rinton'ti|re *vt anche fig* stun. **~to** *a (stordito)* dazed

rintracci'are *vt* trace

rintro'nare *vt* stun ● *vi* boom

ri'nuncia *nf* renunciation

rinunci'a|re *vi* **~re a** renounce, give up. **~'tario** *a* defeatist

ri'nunzia, rinunzi'are = **rinuncia, rinunciare**

rinveni'mento *nm (di reperti)* discovery; *(di refurtiva)* recovery. **rinve'nire** *vt* find ● *vi (riprendere i sensi)* come round; *(ridiventare fresco)* revive

rinvi'are *vt* put off; *(mandare indietro)* return; *(in libro)* refer; **~ a giudizio** indict

rin'vio *nm Sport* goal kick; *(in libro)* cross-reference; *(di appuntamento)* postponement; *(di merce)* return

rio'nale *a* local. **ri'one** *nm* district

riordi'nare *vt* tidy [up]; *(ordinare di*

nuovo) reorder; (*riorganizzare*) reorganize

riorganiz'zare *vt* reorganize

ripa'gare *vt* repay

ripa'ra|re *vt* (*proteggere*) shelter, protect; (*aggiustare*) repair; (*porre rimedio*) remedy ● *vi* ~**re a** make up for. ~**rsi** *vr* take shelter. ~**to** *a* (*luogo*) sheltered. ~**zi'one** *nf* repair; *fig* reparation. **ri'paro** *nm* shelter; (*rimedio*) remedy

ripar'ti|re *vt* (*dividere*) divide ● *vi* leave again. ~**zi'one** *nf* division

ripas'sa|re *vt* recross; (*rivedere*) revise ● *vi* pass again. ~**ta** *nf* (*di vernice*) second coat. **ri'passo** *nm* (*di lezione*) revision

ripensa'mento *nm* second thoughts *pl*

ripen'sare *vi* (*cambiare idea*) change one's mind; ~ **a** think of; **ripensaci!** think again!

riper'correre *vt* (*con la memoria*) go back over

riper'cosso *pp di* **ripercuotere**

ripercu'oter|e *vt* strike again. ~**si** *vr* (*suono:*) reverberate; ~**si su** (*fig: avere conseguenze*) impact on. **ripercussi'one** *nf* repercussion

ripe'scare *vt* fish out (*oggetti*)

ripe'tente *nmf* student repeating a year

ri'pet|ere *vt* repeat. ~**ersi** *vr* (*evento:*) recur. ~**izi'one** *nf* repetition; (*di lezione*) revision; (*lezione privata*) private lesson. ~**uta'mente** *adv* repeatedly

ri'piano *nm* (*di scaffale*) shelf; (*terreno pianeggiante*) terrace

ri'picc|a *nf* **fare qcsa per** ~**a** do sth out of spite. ~**o** *nm* spite

'ripido *a* steep

ripie'gar|e *vt* refold; (*abbassare*) lower ● *vi* (*indietreggiare*) retreat. ~**si** *vr* bend; (*sedile:*) fold. **ripi'ego** *nm* expedient; (*via d'uscita*) way out

ripi'eno *a* full; *Culin* stuffed ● *nm* filling; *Culin* stuffing

ripopo'lar|e *vt* repopulate. ~**si** *vr* be repopulated

ri'porre *vt* put back; (*mettere da parte*) put away; (*collocare*) place; repeat (*domanda*)

ripor'tar|e *vt* (*restituire*) bring/take back; (*riferire*) report; (*subire*) suffer; *Math* carry; win (*vittoria*); transfer (*disegno*). ~**si** *vr* go back; (*riferirsi*) refer. **ri'porto** *nm* **cane da riporto** gun dog

ripo'sante *a* (*colore*) restful, soothing

ripo'sa|re *vi* rest ● *vt* put back. ~**rsi** *vr* rest. ~**to** *a* (*mente*) fresh. **ri'poso** *nm* rest; **andare a riposo** retire; **riposo!** *Mil* at ease!; **giorno di riposo** day off

ripo'stiglio *nm* cupboard

ri'posto *pp di* **riporre**

ri'prender|e *vt* take again; (*prendere indietro*) take back; (*riconquistare*) recapture; (*ricuperare*) recover; (*ricominciare*) resume; (*rimproverare*) reprimand; take in (*cucitura*); *Cinema* shoot. ~**si** *vr* recover; (*correggersi*) correct oneself

ri'presa *nf* resumption; (*ricupero*) recovery; *Theat* revival; *Cinema* shot; *Auto* acceleration; *Mus* repeat. ~ **aerea** bird's-eye view

ripresen'tar|e *vt* resubmit (*domanda, certificato*). ~**si** *vr* (*a ufficio*) go/come back again; (*come candidato*) stand *o* run again; (*occasione:*) arise again

ri'preso *pp di* **riprendere**

ripristi'nare *vt* restore

ripro'dotto *pp di* **riprodurre**

ripro'du|rre *vt*, ~**rsi** *vr* reproduce. ~**t'tivo** *a* reproductive. ~**zi'one** *nf* reproduction

ripro'mettersi *vr* (*intendere*) intend

ri'prova *nf* confirmation

ripudi'are *vt* repudiate

ripu'gnan|te *a* repugnant. ~**za** *nf* disgust. **ripu'gnare** *vi* **ripugnare a** disgust

ripu'li|re *vt* clean [up]; *fig* polish. ~**ta** *nf* **darsi una** ~**ta** have a wash and brushup

ripuls|i'one *nf* repulsion. ~**'ivo** *a* repulsive

ri'quadro *nm* square; (*pannello*) panel

ri'sacca *nf* undertow

ri'saia *nf* rice field, paddy field

risa'lire *vt* go back up ● *vi* ~ **a** (*nel tempo*) go back to; (*essere datato a*) date back to, go back to

risal'tare *vi* (*emergere*) stand out. **ri'salto** *nm* prominence; (*rilievo*) relief

risa'nare *vt* heal; (*bonificare*) reclaim

risa'puto *a* well-known

risarci'mento *nm* compensation. **risar'cire** *vt* indemnify

ri'sata *nf* laugh

riscalda'mento *nm* heating. ~ **autonomo** central heating (*for one apartment*)

riscal'dar|e *vt* heat; warm (*persona*). ~**si** *vr* warm up

riscat'tar|e *vt* ransom. ~**si** *vr* redeem

oneself. **ri'scatto** *nm* ransom; (*morale*) redemption

rischia'rar|e *vt* light up; brighten (*colore*). **~si** *vr* light up; (*cielo:*) clear up

rischi|'are *vt* risk ● *vi* run the risk. **'rischio** *nm* risk. **~'oso** *a* risky

risciac'quare *vt* rinse. **risci'acquo** *nm* rinse

riscon'trare *vt* (*confrontare*) compare; (*verificare*) check; (*rilevare*) find. **ri'scontro** *nm* comparison; check; (*Comm: risposta*) reply

ri'scossa *nf* revolt; (*riconquista*) recovery

riscossi'one *nf* collection

ri'scosso *pp di* **riscuotere**

riscu'oter|e *vt* shake; (*percepire*) draw; (*ottenere*) gain; cash (*assegno*). **~si** *vr* rouse oneself

risen'ti|re *vt* hear again; (*provare*) feel ● *vi* **~re di** feel the effect of. **~rsi** *vr* (*offendersi*) take offence. **~to** *a* resentful

ri'serbo *nm* reserve; **mantenere il ~** remain tight-lipped

ri'serva *nf* reserve; (*di caccia, pesca*) preserve; *Sport* substitute, reserve. **~ di caccia** game reserve. **~ indiana** Indian reservation. **~ naturale** wildlife reserve

riser'va|re *vt* reserve; (*prenotare*) book; (*per occasione*) keep. **~rsi** *vr* (*ripromettersi*) plan for oneself (*cambiamento*). **~'tezza** *nf* reserve. **~to** *a* reserved

ri'siedere *vi* **~ a** reside in

'riso[1] *pp di* **ridere** ● *nm* (*pl nf* **risa**) laughter; (*singolo*) laugh. **~'lino** *nm* giggle

'riso[2] *nm* (*cereale*) rice

ri'solto *pp di* **risolvere**

risolu|'tezza *nf* determination. **riso'luto** *a* resolute, determined. **~zi'one** *nf* resolution

ri'solver|e *vt* resolve; *Math* solve. **~si** *vr* (*decidersi*) decide; **~si in** turn into

riso'na|nza *nf* resonance; **aver ~nza** *fig* arouse great interest. **~re** *vi* resound; (*rimbombare*) echo

ri'sorgere *vi* rise again

risorgi'mento *nm* revival; (*storico*) Risorgimento

ri'sorsa *nf* resource; (*espediente*) resort

ri'sorto *pp di* **risorgere**

ri'sotto *nm* risotto

ri'sparmi *nmpl* (*soldi*) savings

risparmi'a|re *vt* save; (*salvare*) spare. **~'tore**, **~'trice** *nmf* saver **ri'sparmio** *nm* saving

rispecchi'are *vt* reflect

rispet'tabil|e *a* respectable. **~ità** *nf* respectability

rispet'tare *vt* respect; **farsi ~** command respect

rispet'tivo *a* respective

ri'spetto *nm* respect; **~ a** as regards; (*in paragone a*) compared to

rispet|tosa'mente *adv* respectfully. **~'toso** *a* respectful

risplen'dente *a* shining. **ri'splendere** *vi* shine

rispon'den|te *a* **~te a** in keeping with. **~za** *nf* correspondence

ri'spondere *vi* answer; (*rimbeccare*) answer back; (*obbedire*) respond; **~ a** reply to; **~ di** (*rendersi responsabile*) answer for

ri'spost|a *nf* answer, reply; (*reazione*) response. **~o** *pp di* **rispondere**

'rissa *nf* brawl. **ris'soso** *a* pugnacious

ristabi'lir|e *vt* re-establish. **~si** *vr* (*in salute*) recover

rista'gnare *vi* stagnate; (*sangue:*) coagulate. **ri'stagno** *nm* stagnation

ri'stampa *nf* reprint; (*azione*) reprinting. **ristam'pare** *vt* reprint

risto'rante *nm* restaurant

risto'ra|re *vt* refresh. **~rsi** *vr liter* take some refreshment; (*riposarsi*) take a rest. **~'tore**, **~'trice** *nmf* (*proprietario di ristorante*) restaurateur; (*fornitore*) caterer ● *a* refreshing. **ri'storo** *nm* refreshment; (*sollievo*) relief

ristret'tezza *nf* narrowness; (*povertà*) poverty; **vivere in ristrettezze** live in straitened circumstances

ri'stretto *pp di* **restringere** ● *a* narrow; (*condensato*) condensed; (*limitato*) restricted; **di idee ristrette** narrow-minded

ristruttu'rare *vt* restructure, reorganize (*ditta*); refurbish (*casa*)

risucchi'are *vt* suck in. **ri'succhio** *nm* whirlpool; (*di corrente*) undertow

risul'ta|re *vi* result; (*riuscire*) turn out. **~to** *nm* result

risuo'nare *vi* (*grida, parola:*) echo; *Phys* resonate

risurrezi'one *nf* resurrection

risusci'tare *vt* resuscitate; *fig* revive ● *vi* return to life

risvegli'ar|e *vt* reawaken (*interesse*). **~si** *vr* wake up; (*natura:*) awake; (*desiderio:*) be aroused. **ri'sveglio** *nm* waking up; (*dell'interesse*) revival; (*del desiderio*) arousal

ri'svolto *nm* (*di giacca*) lapel; (*di pantaloni*) turn-up, cuff *Am*; (*di manica*) cuff; (*di tasca*) flap; (*di libro*) inside flap

ritagli'are *vt* cut out. **ri'taglio** *nm* cutting; (*di stoffa*) scrap

ritar'da|re *vi* be late; ⟨*orologio:*⟩ be slow ● *vt* delay; slow down ⟨*progresso*⟩; (*differire*) postpone. **~'tario, -a** *nmf* late-comer. **~to** *a Psych* retarded

ri'tardo *nm* delay; **essere in ~** be late; ⟨*volo:*⟩ be delayed

ri'tegno *nm* reserve

rite'n|ere *vt* retain; deduct ⟨*somma*⟩; (*credere*) believe. **~uta** *nf* (*sul salario*) deduction

riti'ra|re *vt* throw back ⟨*palla*⟩; (*prelevare*) withdraw; (*riscuotere*) draw; collect ⟨*pacco*⟩. **~rsi** *vr* withdraw; ⟨*stoffa:*⟩ shrink; (*da attività*) retire; ⟨*marea:*⟩ recede. **~ta** *nf* retreat; (*WC*) toilet. **ri'tiro** *nm* withdrawal; *Relig* retreat; (*da attività*) retirement. **ritiro bagagli** baggage reclaim

'ritmo *nm* rhythm

'rito *nm* rite; **di ~** customary

ritoc'care *vt* (*correggere*) touch up. **ri'tocco** *nm* retouch

ritor'nare *vi* return; (*andare/venire indietro*) go/come back; (*ricorrere*) recur; (*ridiventare*) become again

ritor'nello *nm* refrain

ri'torno *nm* return

ritorsi'one *nf* retaliation

ri'trarre *vt* (*ritirare*) withdraw; (*distogliere*) turn away; (*rappresentare*) portray

ritrat'ta|re *vt* deal with again; retract ⟨*dichiarazione*⟩. **~zi'one** *nf* withdrawal, retraction

ritrat'tista *nmf* portrait painter. **ri'tratto** *pp di* **ritrarre** ● *nm* portrait

ritro'sia *nf* shyness. **ri'troso** *a* backward; (*timido*) shy; **a ritroso** backwards; **ritroso a** reluctant to

ritrova'mento *nm* (*azione*) finding

ritro'va|re *vt* find [again]; regain ⟨*salute*⟩. **~rsi** *vr* meet; (*di nuovo*) meet again; (*capitare*) find oneself; (*raccapezzarsi*) see one's way. **~to** *nm* discovery. **ri'trovo** *nm* meeting-place; (*notturno*) night-club

'ritto *a* upright; (*diritto*) straight

ritu'ale *a & nm* ritual

riunifi'ca|re *vt* reunify. **~rsi** *vr* be reunited. **~zi'one** *nf* reunification

riuni'one *nf* meeting; (*fra amici*) reunion

riu'nir|e *vt* (*unire*) join together;

(*radunare*) gather. **~si** *vr* be reunited; (*adunarsi*) meet

riusc'i|re *vi* (*aver successo*) succeed; (*in matematica ecc*) be good (**in** at); (*aver esito*) turn out; **le è riuscito simpatico** she found him likeable. **~ta** *nf* (*esito*) result; (*successo*) success

'riva *nf* (*di mare, lago*) shore; (*di fiume*) bank

ri'val|e *nmf* rival. **~ità** *nf inv* rivalry

rivalutazi'one *nf* revaluation

rivan'gare *vt* dig up again

rive'dere *vt* see again; revise ⟨*lezione*⟩; (*verificare*) check

rive'la|re *vt* reveal. **~rsi** *vr* (*dimostrarsi*) turn out. **~'tore** *a* revealing ● *nm Techn* detector. **~zi'one** *nf* revelation

ri'vendere *vt* resell

rivendi'ca|re *vt* claim. **~zi'one** *nf* claim

ri'vendi|ta *nf* (*negozio*) shop. **~'tore, ~'trice** *nmf* retailer. **~tore autorizzato** authorized dealer

ri'verbero *nm* reverberation; (*bagliore*) glare

rive'renza *nf* reverence; (*inchino*) curtsy; (*di uomo*) bow

rive'rire *vt* respect; (*ossequiare*) pay one's respects to

river'sar|e *vt* pour. **~si** *vr* ⟨*fiume:*⟩ flow

river'sibile *a* reversible

rivesti'mento *nm* covering

rive'sti|re *vt* (*rifornire di abiti*) clothe; (*ricoprire*) cover; (*internamente*) line; hold ⟨*carica*⟩. **~rsi** *vr* get dressed again; (*per una festa*) dress up

rivi'era *nf* coast; **la ~ ligure** the Italian Riviera

ri'vincita *nf Sport* return match; (*vendetta*) revenge

rivis'suto *pp di* **rivivere**

ri'vista *nf* review; (*pubblicazione*) magazine; *Theat* revue; **passare in ~** review

ri'vivere *vi* come to life again; (*riprendere le forze*) revive ● *vt* relive

ri'volger|e *vt* turn; (*indirizzare*) address; **~e da** (*distogliere*) turn away from. **~si** *vr* turn round; **~si a** (*indirizzarsi*) turn to

ri'volta *nf* revolt

rivol'tante *a* disgusting

rivol'tar|e *vt* turn [over]; (*mettendo l'interno verso l'esterno*) turn inside out; (*sconvolgere*) upset. **~si** *vr* (*ribellarsi*) revolt

rivol'tella *nf* revolver

ri'volto *pp di* rivolgere

rivoluzio'nar|e *vt* revolutionize. ~io, -a *a & nmf* revolutionary. rivoluzi'one *nf* revolution; (*fig: disordine*) chaos

riz'zar|e *vt* raise; (*innalzare*) erect; prick up ⟨*orecchie:*⟩. ~si *vr* stand up; ⟨*capelli:*⟩ stand on end; ⟨*orecchie:*⟩ prick up

'roba *nf* stuff; (*personale*) belongings *pl*, stuff; (*faccenda*) thing; (*sl: droga*) drugs *pl*; ~ da matti! absolute madness!. ~ da mangiare food, things to eat

ro'baccia *nf* rubbish

ro'bot *nm inv* robot. ~iz'zato *a* robotic

robu'stezza *nf* sturdiness, robustness; (*forza*) strength. ro'busto *a* sturdy, robust; (*forte*) strong

'rocca *nf* fortress. ~'forte *nf* stronghold

roc'chetto *nm* reel

'roccia *nf* rock

ro'da|ggio *nm* running in. ~re *vt* run in

'roder|e *vt* gnaw; (*corrodere*) corrode. ~si *vr* ~si da (*logorarsi*) be consumed with. rodi'tore *nm* rodent

rodo'dendro *nm* rhododendron

'rogna *nf* scabies *sg*; *fig* nuisance

ro'gnone *nm* Culin kidney

'rogo *nm* (*supplizio*) stake; (*per cadaveri*) pyre

'Roma *nf* Rome

Roma'nia *nf* Romania

ro'manico *a* Romanesque

ro'mano, -a *a & nmf* Roman

romanti'cismo *nm* romanticism. ro'mantico *a* romantic

ro'man|za *nf* romance. ~'zato *a* romanticized. ~'zesco *a* fictional; (*stravagante*) wild, unrealistic. ~zi'ere *nm* novelist

ro'manzo *a* Romance ● *nm* novel. ~ d'appendice serial story. ~ giallo thriller

'rombo *nm* rumble; *Math* rhombus; (*pesce*) turbot

'romper|e *vt* break; break off ⟨*relazione*⟩; non ~e [le scatole]! (*fam: seccare*) don't be a pain [in the neck]!. ~si *vr* break; ~si una gamba break one's leg

rompi'capo *nm* nuisance; (*indovinello*) puzzle

rompi'collo *nm* daredevil; a ~ at breakneck speed

rompighi'accio *nm* ice-breaker

rompi'scatole *nmf inv fam* pain

'ronda *nf* rounds *pl*

ron'della *nf* washer

'rondine *nf* swallow

ron'done *nm* swift

ron'fare *vi* (*russare*) snore

ron'zare *vi* buzz; ~ attorno a qcno *fig* hang about sb

ron'zino *nm* jade

ron'zio *nm* buzz

'rosa *nf* rose. ~ dei venti wind rose ● *a & nm* (*colore*) pink. ro'saio *nm* rosebush

ro'sario *nm* rosary

ro'sato *a* rosy ● *nm* (*vino*) rosé

'roseo *a* pink

ro'seto *nm* rose garden

rosicchi'are *vt* nibble; (*rodere*) gnaw

rosma'rino *nm* rosemary

'roso *pp di* rodere

roso'lare *vt* brown

roso'lia *nf* German measles

ro'sone *nm* rosette; (*apertura*) rose-window

'rospo *nm* toad

ros'setto *nm* (*per labbra*) lipstick

'rosso *a & nm* red; passare con il ~ jump a red light. ~ d'uovo [egg] yolk. ros'sore *nm* redness; (*della pelle*) flush

rosticce'ria *nf* shop selling cooked meat and other prepared food

ro'tabile *a* strada ~ carriageway

ro'taia *nf* rail; (*solco*) rut

ro'ta|re *vt/i* rotate. ~zi'one *nf* rotation

rote'are *vt/i* roll

ro'tella *nf* small wheel; (*di mobile*) castor

roto'lar|e *vt/i* roll. ~si *vr* roll [about]. 'rotolo *nm* roll; andare a rotoli go to rack and ruin

rotondità *nf* (*qualità*) roundness; ~ *pl* (*curve femminili*) curves. ro'tondo, -a *a* round ● *nf* (*spiazzo*) terrace

ro'tore *nm* rotor

'rotta[1] *nf* Naut, Aeron course; far ~ per make course for; fuori ~ off course

'rotta[2] *nf* a ~ di collo at breakneck speed; essere in ~ con be on bad terms with

rot'tame *nm* scrap; *fig* wreck

'rotto *pp di* rompere ● *a* broken; (*stracciato*) torn

rot'tura *nf* break; che ~ di scatole! *fam* what a pain!

'rotula *nf* kneecap

rou'lette *nf inv* roulette

rou'lotte *nf inv* caravan, trailer *Am*

rou'tine *nf inv* routine; di ~ ⟨*operazioni, controlli*⟩ routine

ro'vente *a* scorching

'rovere nm (legno) oak
rovesci'ar|e vt (buttare a terra) knock over; (sottosopra) turn upside down; (rivoltare) turn inside out; spill ‹liquido›; overthrow ‹governo›; reverse ‹situazione›. **~si** vr (capovolgersi) overturn; (riversarsi) pour. **ro'vescio** a (contrario) reverse; **alla rovescia** (capovolto) upside down; (con l'interno all'esterno) inside out ● nm reverse; (nella maglia) purl; (di pioggia) downpour; Tennis backhand
ro'vina nf ruin; (crollo) collapse
rovi'na|re vt ruin; (guastare) spoil ● vi crash. **~rsi** vr be ruined. **~to** a ‹oggetto› ruined. **rovi'noso** a ruinous
rovi'stare vt ransack
'rovo nm bramble
'rozzo a rough
R.R. abbr (ricevuta di ritorno) return receipt for registered mail
'ruba nf **andare a ~** sell like hot cakes
ru'bare vt steal
rubi'netto nm tap, faucet Am
ru'bino nm ruby
ru'brica nf (in giornale) column; (in programma televisivo) TV report; (quaderno con indice) address book. **~ telefonica** telephone and address book
'rude a rough
'rudere nm ruin
rudimen'tale a rudimentary. **rudi'menti** nmpl rudiments

ruffi'an|a nf procuress. **~o** nm pimp; (adulatore) bootlicker
'ruga nf wrinkle
'ruggine nf rust; **fare la ~** go rusty
rug'gi|re vi roar. **~to** nm roar
rugi'ada nf dew
ru'goso a wrinkled
rul'lare vi roll; Aeron taxi
rul'lino nm film
rul'lio nm rolling; Aeron taxiing
'rullo nm roll; Techn roller
rum nm inv rum
ru'meno, -a a & nmf Romanian
rumi'nare vt ruminate
ru'mor|e nm noise; fig rumour. **~eggi'are** vi rumble. **rumo'roso** a noisy; (sonoro) loud
ru'olo nm roll; Theat role; **di ~** on the staff
ru'ota nf wheel; **andare a ~ libera** free-wheel. **~ di scorta** spare wheel
'rupe nf cliff
ru'rale a rural
ru'scello nm stream
'ruspa nf bulldozer
rus'sare vi snore
'Russ|ia nf Russia. **r~o, -a** a & nmf Russian; (lingua) Russian
'rustico a rural; ‹carattere› rough
rut'tare vi belch. **'rutto** nm belch
'ruvido a coarse
ruzzo'l|are vi tumble down. **~one** nm tumble; **cadere a ruzzoloni** tumble down

#

'sabato nm Saturday
'sabbi|a nf sand. **~e** pl **mobili** quicksand sg. **~'oso** a sandy
sabo'ta|ggio nm sabotage. **~re** vt sabotage. **~'tore, ~'trice** nmf saboteur
'sacca nf bag. **~ da viaggio** travelling-bag
sacca'rina nf saccharin
sac'cente a pretentious ● nmf know-all
saccheggi'a|re vt sack; hum plunder ‹frigo›. **~'tore, ~'trice** nmf plunderer. **sac'cheggio** nm sack
sac'chetto nm bag

'sacco nm sack; Anat sac; **mettere nel ~** fig swindle; **un ~** (moltissimo) a lot; **un ~ di** (gran quantità) lots of. **~ a pelo** sleeping-bag
sacer'do|te nm priest. **~zio** nm priesthood
sacra'mento nm sacrament
sacrifi'ca|re vt sacrifice. **~rsi** vr sacrifice oneself. **~to** a (non valorizzato) wasted. **sacri'ficio** nm sacrifice
sacri'legio nm sacrilege. **sa'crilego** a sacrilegious
'sacro a sacred ● nm Anat sacrum
sacro'santo a sacrosanct

'sadico, -a *a* sadistic ● *nmf* sadist. **sa'dismo** *nm* sadism

sa'etta *nf* arrow

sa'fari *nm inv* safari

'saga *nf* saga

sa'gace *a* shrewd

sag'gezza *nf* wisdom

saggi'are *vt* test

'saggio¹ *nm* (*scritto*) essay; (*prova*) proof; (*di metallo*) assay; (*campione*) sample; (*esempio*) example

'saggio² *a* wise ● *nm* (*persona*) sage

sag'gistica *nf* non-fiction

Sagit'tario *nm Astr* Sagittarius

'sagoma *nf* shape; (*profilo*) outline; **che ~!** *fam* what a character!. **sa-go'mato** *a* shaped

'sagra *nf* festival

sagre|'stano *nm* sacristan. **~'stia** *nf* sacristy

'sala *nf* hall; (*stanza*) room; (*salotto*) living room. **~ d'attesa** waiting room. **~ da ballo** ballroom. **~ d'imbarco** departure lounge. **~ macchine** engine room. **~ operatoria** operating theatre *Br*, operating room *Am*. **~ parto** delivery room. **~ da pranzo** dining room

sa'lame *nm* salami

sala'moia *nf* brine

sa'lare *vt* salt

sa'lario *nm* wages *pl*

sa'lasso *nm* **essere un ~** *fig* cost a fortune

sala'tini *nmpl* savouries (*eaten with aperitifs*)

sa'lato *a* salty; (*costoso*) dear

sal'ciccia *nf* = **salsiccia**

sal'dar|e *vt* weld; set (*osso*); pay off (*debito*); settle (*conto*); **~e a stagno** solder. **~si** *vr* (*Med: osso:*) knit

salda'trice *nf* welder; (*a stagno*) soldering iron

salda'tura *nf* weld; (*azione*) welding; (*di osso*) knitting

'saldo *a* firm; (*resistente*) strong ● *nm* (*di conto*) settlement; (*svendita*) sale; *Comm* balance

'sale *nm* salt; **restare di ~** be struck dumb [with astonishment]. **~ fine** table salt. **~ grosso** cooking salt. **sali** *pl* **e tabacchi** tobacconist's shop

'salice *nm* willow. **~ piangente** weeping willow

sali'ente *a* outstanding; **i punti salienti di un discorso** the main points of a speech

sali'era *nf* salt-cellar

sa'lina *nf* salt-works *sg*

sa'li|re *vi* go/come up; (*levarsi*) rise; (*su treno ecc*) get on; (*in macchina*) get in ● *vt* go/come up (*scale*). **~ta** *nf* climb; (*aumento*) rise; **in ~ta** uphill

sa'liva *nf* saliva

'salma *nf* corpse

'salmo *nm* psalm

sal'mone *nm & a inv* salmon

sa'lone *nm* hall; (*salotto*) living room; (*di parrucchiere*) salon. **~ di bellezza** beauty parlour

salo'pette *nf inv* dungarees *pl*

salot'tino *nm* bower

sa'lotto *nm* drawing room; (*soggiorno*) sitting room; (*mobili*) [three-piece] suite; **fare ~** chat

sal'pare *vi* sail; **~ l'ancora** weigh anchor

'salsa *nf* sauce. **~ di pomodoro** tomato sauce

sal'sedine *nf* saltiness

sal'siccia *nf* sausage

salsi'era *nf* sauce-boat

sal'ta|re *vi* jump; (*venir via*) come off; (*balzare*) leap; (*esplodere*) blow up; **~r fuori** spring from nowhere; (*oggetto cercato:*) turn up; **è ~to fuori che...** it emerged that...; **~re fuori con...** come out with...; **~re in aria** blow up; **~re in mente** spring to mind ● *vt* jump [over]; skip (*pasti, lezioni*); *Culin* sauté. **~to** *a Culin* sautéed

saltel'lare *vi* hop; (*di gioia*) skip

saltim'banco *nm* acrobat

'salto *nm* jump; (*balzo*) leap; (*dislivello*) drop; (*fig: omissione, lacuna*) gap; **fare un ~ da** (*visitare*) drop in on; **in un ~ di** *fig* in a jiffy. **~ in alto** high jump. **~ con l'asta** pole-vault. **~ in lungo** long jump. **~ pagina** *Comput* page down

saltuaria'mente *adv* occasionally. **saltu'ario** *a* desultory; **lavoro saltuario** casual work

sa'lubre *a* healthy

salume'ria *nf* ≈ delicatessen. **sa'lumi** *nmpl* cold cuts

salu'tare *vt* greet; (*congedandosi*) say goodbye to; (*portare i saluti a*) give one's regards to; *Mil* salute ● *a* healthy

sa'lute *nf* health; **~!** (*dopo uno starnuto*) bless you!; (*a un brindisi*) cheers!

sa'luto *nm* greeting; (*di addio*) goodbye; *Mil* salute; **saluti** *pl* (*ossequi*) regards

'salva *nf* salvo; **sparare a salve** fire blanks

salvada'naio *nm* money box

salva'gente *nm* lifebelt; (*a giubbotto*) life-jacket; (*ciambella*) rubber ring; (*spartitraffico*) traffic island

salvaguar'dare *vt* safeguard. **salvagu'ardia** *nf* safeguard

sal'var|e *vt* save; (*proteggere*) protect. **~si** *vr* save oneself

salva'slip *nm inv* panty-liner

salva|'taggio *nm* rescue; *Naut* salvage; *Comput* saving; **battello di ~taggio** lifeboat. **~'tore**, **~'trice** *nmf* saviour

sal'vezza *nf* safety; *Relig* salvation

'salvia *nf* sage

salvi'etta *nf* serviette

'salvo *a* safe ● *prep* except [for] ● *conj* **~ che** (*a meno che*) unless; (*eccetto che*) except that

samari'tano, -a *a & nmf* Samaritan

sam'buco *nm* elder

san *nm* **S~ Francesco** Saint Francis

sa'nare *vt* heal

sana'torio *nm* sanatorium

san'cire *vt* sanction

'sandalo *nm* sandal; *Bot* sandalwood

'sangu|e *nm* blood; **al ~e** (*carne*) rare; **farsi cattivo ~e per** worry about; **occhi iniettati di ~e** bloodshot eyes. **~e freddo** composure; **a ~e freddo** in cold blood. **~'igno** *a* blood

sangui'naccio *nm Culin* black pudding

sangui'nante *a* bleeding

sangui'nar|e *vi* bleed **~io** *a* bloodthirsty

sangui'noso *a* bloody

sangui'suga *nf* leech

sanità *nf* soundness; (*salute*) health. **~ mentale** sanity, mental health

sani'tario *a* sanitary; **Servizio S~** National Health Service

'sano *a* sound; (*salutare*) healthy; **~ di mente** sane; **~ come un pesce** as fit as a fiddle

San Sil'vestro *nm* New Year's Eve

santifi'care *vt* sanctify

'santo *a* holy; (*con nome proprio*) saint ● *nm* saint. **san'tone** *nm* guru. **santu'ario** *nm* sanctuary

sanzi'one *nf* sanction

sa'pere *vt* know; (*essere capace di*) be able to; (*venire a sapere*) hear; **saperla lunga** know a thing or two ● *vi* **~ di** know about; (*aver sapore di*) taste of;

(*aver odore di*) smell of; **saperci fare** have the know-how ● *nm* knowledge

sapi'en|te *a* wise; (*esperto*) expert ● *nm* (*uomo colto*) sage. **~za** *nf* wisdom

sa'pone *nm* soap. **~ da bucato** washing soap. **sapo'netta** *nf* bar of soap

sa'pore *nm* taste. **saporita'mente** *adv* (*dormire*) soundly. **sapo'rito** *a* tasty

sapu'tello, -a *a & nm sl* know-all, know-it-all *Am*

saraci'nesca *nf* roller shutter

sar'cas|mo *nm* sarcasm. **~tico** *a* sarcastic

Sar'degna *nf* Sardinia

sar'dina *nf* sardine

'sardo, -a *a & nmf* Sardinian

sar'donico *a* sardonic

'sarto, -a *nm* tailor ● *nf* dressmaker. **~'ria** *nf* tailor's; dressmaker's; (*arte*) couture

sas'sata *nf* blow with a stone; **prendere a sassate** stone. **'sasso** *nm* stone; (*ciottolo*) pebble

sassofo'nista *nmf* saxophonist. **sas'sofono** *nm* saxophone

sas'soso *a* stony

'Satana *nm* Satan. **sa'tanico** *a* satanic

sa'tellite *a inv & nm* satellite

sati'nato *a* glossy

'satira *nf* satire. **sa'tirico** *a* satirical

satu'rar|e *vt* saturate. **~zi'one** *nf* saturation. **'saturo** *a* saturated; (*pieno*) full

'sauna *nf* sauna

savoi'ardo *nm* (*biscotto*) sponge finger

sazi'ar|e *vt* satiate. **~si** *vr* **~si di** *fig* grow tired of

sazietà *nf* **mangiare a ~** eat one's fill. **'sazio** *a* satiated

sbaciucchi'ar|e *vt* smother with kisses. **~si** *vr* kiss and cuddle

sbada'ta|ggine *nf* carelessness; **è stata una ~ggine** it was careless. **~'mente** *adv* carelessly. **sba'dato** *a* careless

sbadigli'are *vi* yawn. **sba'diglio** *nm* yawn

sba'fa|re *vt* sponge. **~ta** *nf sl* nosh

'sbafo *nm* sponging; **a ~** (*gratis*) without paying

sbagli'ar|e *vi* make a mistake; (*aver torto*) be wrong ● *vt* make a mistake in; **~e strada** go the wrong way; **~e numero** get the number wrong; *Teleph* dial a wrong number. **~si** *vr* make a mistake. **'sbaglio** *nm* mistake; **per sbaglio** by mistake

sbal'l|are *vt* unpack; *fam* screw up (*conti*) ● *vi fam* go crazy. **~ato** *a* (*squilibrato*) unbalanced. **'sballo** *nm fam* scream; (*per droga*) trip; **da sballo** *sl* terrific

sballot'tare *vt* toss about

sbalor'di|re *vt* stun ● *vi* be stunned. ~**'tivo** *a* amazing. ~**to** *a* stunned

sbal'zare *vt* throw; (*da una carica*) dismiss ● *vi* bounce; (*saltare*) leap. **'sbalzo** *nm* bounce; (*sussulto*) jolt; (*di temperatura*) sudden change; **a sbalzi** in spurts; **a sbalzo** (*lavoro a rilievo*) embossed

sban'care *vt* bankrupt; ~ **il banco** break the bank

sbanda'mento *nm Auto* skid; *Naut* list; *fig* going off the rails

sban'da|re *vi Auto* skid; *Naut* list. ~**rsi** *vr* (*disperdersi*) disperse. ~**ta** *nf* skid; *Naut* list; **prendere una ~ta per** get a crush on. ~**to, -a** *a* mixed-up ● *nmf* mixed-up person

sbandie'rare *vt* wave; *fig* display

sbarac'care *vt/i* clear up

sbaragli'are *vt* rout. **sba'raglio** *nm* rout; **mettere allo sbaraglio** rout

sbaraz'zar|e *vt* clear. ~**si** *vr* ~**si di** get rid of

sbaraz'zino, -a *a* mischievous ● *nmf* scamp

sbar'bar|e *vt*, ~**si** *vr* shave

sbar'care *vt/i* disembark; ~ **il lunario** make ends meet. **'sbarco** *nm* landing; (*di merci*) unloading

'sbarra *nf* bar; (*di passaggio a livello*) barrier. ~**'mento** *nm* barricade. **sbar'rare** *vt* bar; (*ostruire*) block; cross (*assegno*); (*spalancare*) open wide

sbatacchi'are *vt/i sl* bang, slam

'sbatter|e *vt* bang; slam, bang (*porta*); (*urtare*) knock; *Culin* beat; flap (*ali*); shake (*tappeto*) ● *vi* bang; (*porta:*) slam, bang. ~**si** *vr sl* rush around; ~**sene di qcsa** not give a damn about sth. **sbat'tuto** *a* tossed; *Culin* beaten; *fig* run down

sba'va|re *vi* dribble; (*colore:*) smear. ~**'tura** *nf* smear; **senza ~ture** *fig* faultless

sbelli'carsi *vr* ~ **dalle risa** split one's sides [with laughter]

'sberla *nf* slap

sbia'di|re *vt/i*, ~**rsi** *vr* fade. ~**to** *a* faded; *fig* colourless

sbian'car|e *vt/i*, ~**si** *vr* whiten

sbi'eco *a* slanting; **di ~** on the slant; (*guardare*) sidelong; **guardare qcno di ~** look askance at sb; **tagliare di ~** cut on the bias

sbigot'ti|re *vt* dismay ● *vi*, ~**rsi** *vr* be dismayed. ~**to** *a* dismayed

sbilanci'ar|e *vt* unbalance ● *vi* (*perdere l'equilibrio*) overbalance. ~**si** *vr* lose one's balance

sbirci'a|re *vt* cast sidelong glances at. ~**ta** *nf* furtive glance. ~**'tina** *nf* **dare una ~tina a** sneak a glance at

sbizzar'rirsi *vr* satisfy one's whims

sbloc'care *vt* unblock; *Mech* release; decontrol (*prezzi*)

sboc'care *vi* ~ **in** (*fiume:*) flow into; (*strada:*) lead to; (*folla:*) pour into

sboc'cato *a* foul-mouthed

sbocci'are *vi* blossom

'sbocco *nm* flowing; (*foce*) mouth; *Comm* outlet

sbolo'gnare *vt fam* get rid of

'sbornia *nf* **prendersi una ~** get drunk

sbor'sare *vt* pay out

sbot'tare *vi* burst out

sbotto'nar|e *vt* unbutton. ~**si** *vr* (*fam: confidarsi*) open up; ~**si la camicia** unbutton one's shirt

sbra'carsi *vr* put on something more comfortable; ~ **dalle risate** *fam* kill oneself laughing

sbracci'a|rsi *vr* wave one's arms. ~**to** *a* bare-armed; (*abito*) sleeveless

sbrai'tare *vi* bawl

sbra'nare *vt* tear to pieces

sbricio'lar|e *vt*, ~**si** *vr* crumble

sbri'ga|re *vt* expedite; (*occuparsi di*) attend to. ~**rsi** *vr* be quick. ~**'tivo** *a* quick

sbrindel'la|re *vt* tear to shreds. ~**to** *a* in rags

sbrodo'l|are *vt* stain. ~**one** *nm* messy eater, dribbler

'sbronz|a *nf* **prendersi una ~a** get tight. **sbron'zarsi** *vr* get tight. ~**o** *a* (*ubriaco*) tight

sbruffo'nata *nf* boast. **sbruf'fone, -a** *nmf* boaster

sbu'care *vi* come out

sbucci'ar|e *vt* peel; shell (*piselli*). ~**si** *vr* graze oneself

sbuf'fare *vi* snort; (*per impazienza*) fume. **'sbuffo** *nm* puff

'scabbia *nf* scabies *sg*

sca'broso *a* rough; *fig* difficult; (*scena*) indecent

scacci'are *vt* chase away

'scacc|o *nm* check; ~**hi** *pl* (*gioco*) chess; (*pezzi*) chessmen; **dare ~o matto** checkmate; **a ~hi** (*tessuto*) checked. ~**hi'era** *nf* chess-board

sca'dente *a* shoddy

sca'de|nza *nf* (*di contratto*) expiry;

Comm maturity; *(di progetto)* deadline; **a breve/lunga ~nza** short-/long-term. **~re** *vi* expire; *(valore:)* decline; *(debito:)* be due. **sca'duto** *a* *(biglietto)* out-of-date

sca'fandro *nm* diving suit; *(di astronauta)* spacesuit

scaf'fale *nm* shelf; *(libreria)* bookshelf

'scafo *nm* hull

scagion'are *vt* exonerate

'scaglia *nf* scale; *(di sapone)* flake; *(scheggia)* chip

scagli'ar|e *vt* fling. **~si** *vr* fling oneself; **~si contro** *fig* rail against

scagli|o'nare *vt* space out. **~'one** *nm* group; **a ~oni** in groups. **~one di reddito** tax bracket

'scala *nf* staircase; *(portatile)* ladder; *(Mus, misura, fig)* scale; **scale** *pl* stairs. **~ mobile** escalator; *(dei salari)* cost of living index

sca'la|re *vt* climb; layer *(capelli)*; *(detrarre)* deduct. **~ta** *nf* climb; *(dell'Everest ecc)* ascent; **fare delle ~te** go climbing. **~'tore**, **~'trice** *nmf* climber

scalca'gnato *a* down at heel

scalci'are *vi* kick

scalci'nato *a* shabby

scalda'bagno *nm* water heater

scalda'muscoli *nm inv* leg-warmer

scal'dar|e *vt* heat. **~si** *vr* warm up; *(eccitarsi)* get excited

scal'fi|re *vt* scratch. **~t'tura** *nf* scratch

scali'nata *nf* flight of steps. **sca'lino** *nm* step; *(di scala a pioli)* rung

scalma'narsi *vr* get worked up

'scalo *nm* slipway; *Aeron, Naut* port of call; **fare ~** a call at; **Aeron** land at

sca'lo|gna *nf* bad luck. **~'gnato** *a* unlucky

scalop'pina *nf* escalope

scal'pello *nm* chisel

scalpi'tare *vi* paw the ground; *fig* champ at the bit

'scalpo *nm* scalp

scal'pore *nm* noise; **far ~** *fig* cause a sensation

scal'trezza *nf* shrewdness. **scal'trirsi** *vr* get shrewder. **'scaltro** *a* shrewd

scal'zare *vt* bare the roots of *(albero)*; *fig* undermine; *(da una carica)* oust

'scalzo *a & adv* barefoot

scambi|'are *vt* exchange; **~are qcno per qualcun altro** mistake sb for somebody else. **~'evole** *a* reciprocal

'scambio *nm* exchange; *Comm* trade; **libero ~** free trade

scamosci'ato *a* suede

scampa'gnata *nf* trip to the country

scampa'nato *a* *(gonna)* flared

scampanel'lata *nf* [loud] ring

scam'pare *vt* save; *(evitare)* escape; **scamparla bella** have a lucky escape. **'scampo** *nm* escape

'scampolo *nm* remnant

scanala'tura *nf* groove

scandagli'are *vt* sound

scanda'listico *a* sensational

scandal|iz'zare *vt* scandalize. **~iz'zarsi** *vr* be scandalized

'scanda|lo *nm* scandal. **~'loso** *a* *(somma ecc)* scandalous; *(fortuna)* outrageous

Scand|i'navia *nf* Scandinavia. **scan'dinavo, -a** *a & nmf* Scandinavian

scan'dire *vt* scan *(verso)*; pronounce clearly *(parole)*

scan'nare *vt* slaughter

scanneriz'zare *vt Comput* scan

scansafa'tiche *nmf inv* lazybones *sg*

scan'sar|e *vt* shift; *(evitare)* avoid. **~si** *vr* get out of the way

scansi'one *nf Comput* scanning

'scanso *nm* **a ~ di** in order to avoid; **a ~ di equivoci** to avoid any misunderstanding

scanti'nato *nm* basement

scanto'nare *vi* turn the corner; *(svignarsela)* sneak off

scanzo'nato *a* easy-going

scapacci'one *nm* smack

scape'strato *a* dissolute

'scapito *nm* loss; **a ~ di** to the detriment of

'scapola *nf* shoulder-blade

'scapolo *nm* bachelor

scappa'mento *nm Auto* exhaust

scap'pa|re *vi* escape; *(andarsene)* dash [off]; *(sfuggire)* slip; **mi ~ da ridere!** I want to burst out laughing; **mi ~ la pipì** I'm bursting, I need a pee. **~ta** *nf* short visit. **~'tella** *nf* escapade; *(infedeltà)* fling. **~'toia** *nf* way out

scappel'lotto *nm* cuff

scara'bocchio *nm* scribble

scara'faggio *nm* cockroach

scara'mantico *a* *(gesto)* to ward off the evil eye

scara'muccia *nf* skirmish

scarabocchi'are *vt* scribble

scaraven'tare *vt* hurl

scarce'rare *vt* release [from prison]

scardi'nare *vt* unhinge

'scarica *nf* discharge; *(di arma da fuoco)* volley; *fig* shower

scari'ca|re vt discharge; unload ⟨arma, merci⟩; fig unburden. **~rsi** vr ⟨fiume:⟩ flow; ⟨orologio, batteria:⟩ run down; fig unwind. **~'tore** nm loader; (di porto) docker. **'scarico** a unloaded; (vuoto) empty; ⟨orologio⟩ run-down; ⟨batteria⟩ flat; fig untroubled ● nm unloading; (di rifiuti) dumping; (di acqua) draining; (di sostanze inquinanti) discharge; (luogo) [rubbish] dump; Auto exhaust; (idraulico) drain; (tubo) waste pipe

scarlat'tina nf scarlet fever

scar'latto a scarlet

'scarno a thin; ⟨fig: stile⟩ bare

sca'ro|gna nf fam bad luck. **~'gnato** a fam unlucky

'scarpa nf shoe; (fam: persona) dead loss. **scarpe** pl **da ginnastica** trainers, gym shoes

scar'pata nf slope; (burrone) escarpment

scarpi'nare vi hike

scar'pone nm boot. **scarponi** pl **da sci** ski boot. **scarponi** pl **da trekking** walking boots

scarroz'zare vt/i drive around

scarseggi'are vi be scarce; **~ di** (mancare) be short of

scar'sezza nf scarcity, shortage. **scarsità** nf shortage. **'scarso** a scarce; (manchevole) short

scarta'mento nm Rail gauge. **~ ridotto** narrow gauge

scar'tare vt discard; unwrap ⟨pacco⟩; (respingere) reject ● vi (deviare) swerve. **'scarto** nm scrap; (in carte) discard; (deviazione) swerve; (distacco) gap

scar'toffie nfpl bumf, bumph

scas'sa|re vt break. **~to** a fam clapped out

scassi'nare vt force open

scassina'tore, -'trice nmf burglar. **'scasso** nm (furto) house-breaking

scate'na|re vt fig stir up. **~rsi** vr break out; ⟨fig: temporale:⟩ break; (fam: infiammarsi) get excited. **~to** a crazy

'scatola nf box; (di latta) can, tin Br; **in ~** ⟨cibo⟩ canned, tinned Br; **rompere le scatole a qcno** fam get on sb's nerves

scat'tare vi go off; (balzare) spring up; (adirarsi) lose one's temper; take ⟨foto⟩. **'scatto** nm (balzo) spring; (d'ira) outburst; (di telefono) unit; (dispositivo) release; **a scatti** jerkily; **di scatto** suddenly

scatu'rire vi spring

scaval'care vt jump over ⟨muretto⟩;

climb over ⟨muro⟩; ⟨fig: superare⟩ overtake

sca'vare vt dig ⟨buca⟩; dig up ⟨tesoro⟩; excavate ⟨città sepolta⟩. **'scavo** nm excavation

scazzot'tata nf fam punch-up

'scegliere vt choose, select

scelle'rato a wicked

'scelt|a nf choice; (di articoli) range; **...a ~a** (in menù) choice of...; **prendine uno a ~a** take your choice o pick; **di prima ~a** top-grade, choice. **~o** pp di **scegliere** ● a select; (merce ecc) choice

sce'mare vt/i diminish

sce'menza nf silliness; (azione) silly thing to do/say. **'scemo** a silly

scempio nm havoc; (di paesaggio) ruination; **fare ~ di** play havoc with

'scena nf scene; (palcoscenico) stage; **entrare in ~** go/come on; fig enter the scene; **fare ~** put on an act; **fare una ~** make a scene; **andare in ~** Theat be staged, be put on. **sce'nario** nm scenery

sce'nata nf row, scene

'scendere vi go/come down; (da treno, autobus) get off; (da macchina) get out; ⟨strada:⟩ slope; ⟨notte, prezzi:⟩ fall ● vt go/come down ⟨scale⟩

sceneggi'a|re vt dramatize. **~to** nm television serial. **~'tura** nf screenplay

'scenico a scenic

scervel'la|rsi vr rack one's brains. **~to** a brainless

'sceso pp di **scendere**

scetti'cismo nm scepticism. **'scettico, -a** a sceptical ● nmf sceptic

'scettro nm sceptre

'scheda nf card. **~ elettorale** ballot-paper. **~ di espansione** Comput expansion card. **~ perforata** punch card. **~ telefonica** phonecard. **sche'dare** vt file. **sche'dario** nm file; (mobile) filing cabinet

sche'dina nf pools coupon; **giocare la ~** do the pools

'scheggi|a nf fragment; (di legno) splinter. **~'arsi** vr chip; ⟨legno:⟩ splinter

'scheletro nm skeleton

'schema nm diagram; (abbozzo) outline. **sche'matico** a schematic. **~tiz'zare** vt schematize

'scherma nf fencing

scher'mirsi vr protect oneself

'schermo nm screen; **grande ~** big screen

scher'nire vt mock. **'scherno** nm mockery

scher'zare *vi* joke; *(giocare)* play

'scherzo *nm* joke; *(trucco)* trick; *(effetto)* play; *Mus* scherzo; **fare uno ~ a qcno** play a joke on sb; **per ~** for fun; **stare allo ~** take a joke. **scher'zoso** *a* playful

schiaccia'noci *nm inv* nutcrackers *pl*

schiacci'ante *a* damning

schiacci'are *vt* crush; *Sport* smash; press *(pulsante)*; crack *(noce)*; **~ un pisolino** grab forty winks

schiaffeggi'are *vt* slap. **schi'affo** *nm* slap; **dare uno schiaffo a** slap

schiamaz'zare *vi* make a racket; *(galline:)* cackle

schian'tar|e *vt* break. **~si** *vr* crash ● *vi* **schianto dalla fatica** I'm wiped out. **'schianto** *nm* crash; *fam* knock-out; *(divertente)* scream

schia'rir|e *vt* clear; *(sbiadire)* fade ● *vi*, **~si** *vr* brighten up; **~si la gola** clear one's throat

schiavitù *nf* slavery. **schi'avo, -a** *nmf* slave

schi'ena *nf* back; **mal di ~** backache. **schie'nale** *nm (di sedia)* back

schi'er|a *nf Mil* rank; *(moltitudine)* crowd. **~a'mento** *nm* lining up

schie'rar|e *vt* draw up. **~si** *vr* draw up; **~si con** *(parteggiare)* side with

schiet'tezza *nf* frankness. **schi'etto** *a* frank; *(puro)* pure

schi'fezza *nf* **una ~** rubbish. **schi-fil'toso** *a* fussy. **'schifo** *nm* disgust; **mi fa schifo** it makes me sick. **schi'foso** *a* disgusting; *(di cattiva qualità)* rubbishy

schioc'care *vt* crack; snap *(dita)*. **schi'occo** *nm (di frusta)* crack; *(di bacio)* smack; *(di dita, lingua)* click

schi'oppo *nm* **ad un tiro di ~** a stone's throw away

schi'uder|e *vt*, **~si** *vr* open

schi'u|ma *nf* foam; *(di sapone)* lather; *(feccia)* scum. **~ma da barba** shaving foam. **~'mare** *vt* skim ● *vi* foam

schi'uso *pp di* **schiudere**

schi'vare *vt* avoid. **'schivo** *a* bashful

schizo'frenico *a* schizophrenic

schiz'zare *vt* squirt; *(inzaccherare)* splash; *(abbozzare)* sketch ● *vi* spurt; **~ via** scurry away

schiz'zato, -a *a & nmf sl* loony

schizzi'noso *a* squeamish

'schizzo *nm* squirt; *(di fango)* splash; *(abbozzo)* sketch

sci *nm inv* ski; *(sport)* skiing. **~ d'acqua** water-skiing

'scia *nf* wake; *(di fumo ecc)* trail

sci'abola *nf* sabre

sciabor'dare *vt/i* lap

scia'callo *nm* jackal; *fig* profiteer

sciac'quar|e *vt* rinse. **~si** *vr* rinse oneself. **sci'acquo** *nm* mouthwash

scia'gu|ra *nf* disaster. **~'rato** *a* unfortunate; *(scellerato)* wicked

scialac'quare *vt* squander

scia'lare *vi* spend money like water

sci'albo *a* pale; *fig* dull

sci'alle *nm* shawl

scia'luppa *nf* dinghy. **~ di salva-taggio** lifeboat

sci'ame *nm* swarm

sci'ampo *nm* shampoo

scian'cato *a* lame

sci'are *vi* ski

sci'arpa *nf* scarf

sci'atica *nf Med* sciatica

scia'tore, -'trice *nmf* skier

sci'atto *a* slovenly; *(stile)* careless. **sciat'tone, -a** *nmf* slovenly person

scienti'fico *a* scientific

sci'enz|a *nf* science; *(sapere)* knowledge. **~i'ato, -a** *nmf* scientist

'scimmi|a *nf* monkey. **~ot'tare** *vt* ape

scimpanzé *nm inv* chimpanzee, chimp

scimu'nito *a* idiotic

'scinder|e *vt*, **~si** *vr* split

scin'tilla *nf* spark. **scintil'lante** *a* sparkling. **scintil'lare** *vi* sparkle

scioc'ca|nte *a* shocking. **~re** *vt* shock

scioc'chezza *nf* foolishness; *(assurdità)* nonsense. **sci'occo** *a* foolish

sci'oglier|e *vt* untie; undo, untie *(nodo)*; *(liberare)* release; *(liquefare)* melt; dissolve *(contratto, qcsa nell'acqua)*; loosen up *(muscoli)*. **~si** *vr* release oneself; *(liquefarsi)* melt; *(contratto:)* be dissolved; *(pastiglia:)* dissolve

sciogli'lingua *nm inv* tongue-twister

scio'lina *nf* wax

sciol'tezza *nf* agility; *(disinvoltura)* ease

sci'olto *pp di* **sciogliere** ● *a* loose; *(agile)* agile; *(disinvolto)* easy; **versi sciolti** blank verse

sciope'ra|nte *nmf* striker. **~re** *vi* go on strike, strike. **sci'opero** *nm* strike. **sciopero a singhiozzo** on-off strike

sciori'nare *vt fig* show off

sci'pito *a* insipid

scip'pa|re *vt fam* snatch. **~'tore, ~'trice** *nmf* bag snatcher. **'scippo** *nm* bag-snatching

sci'rocco *nm* sirocco

scirop'pato *a* ⟨frutta⟩ in syrup. **sci'roppo** *nm* syrup

'scisma *nm* schism

scissi'one *nf* division

'scisso *pp di* **scindere**

sciu'par|e *vt* spoil; ⟨sperperare⟩ waste. **~si** *vr* get spoiled; ⟨deperire⟩ wear oneself out. **sciu'pio** *nm* waste

scivo'l|are *vi* slide; ⟨involontariamente⟩ slip. **'scivolo** *nm* slide; *Techn* chute. **~oso** *a* slippery

scle'rosi *nf* sclerosis

scoc'care *vt* shoot ●*vi* ⟨scintilla:⟩ shoot out; ⟨ora:⟩ strike

scocci'a|re *vt* ⟨dare noia⟩ bother. **~rsi** *vr* be bothered. **~to** *a fam* narked. **~'tore, ~'trice** *nmf* bore. **~'tura** *nf* nuisance

sco'della *nf* bowl

scodinzo'lare *vi* wag its tail

scogli'era *nf* cliff; ⟨a fior d'acqua⟩ reef. **'scoglio** *nm* rock; ⟨fig: ostacolo⟩ stumbling block

scoi'attolo *nm* squirrel

scola|'pasta *nm inv* colander. **~pi'atti** *nm inv* dish drainer

sco'lara *nf* schoolgirl

sco'lare *vt* drain; strain ⟨pasta, verdura⟩ ●*vi* drip

sco'la|ro *nm* schoolboy. **~'resca** *nf* pupils *pl*. **~stico** *a* school *attrib*

scoli'osi *nf* curvature of the spine

scol'la|re *vt* cut away the neck of ⟨abito⟩; ⟨staccare⟩ unstick. **~to** *a* ⟨abito⟩ low-necked. **~'tura** *nf* neckline

'scolo *nm* drainage

scolo'ri|re *vt*, **~rsi** *vr* fade. **~to** *a* faded

scol'pire *vt* carve; ⟨imprimere⟩ engrave

scombi'nare *vt* upset

scombusso'lare *vt* muddle up

scom'mess|a *nf* bet. **~o** *pp di* **scommettere**. **scom'mettere** *vt* bet

scomo'dar|e *vt*, **~si** *vr* trouble. **scomodità** *nf* discomfort. **'scomodo** *a* uncomfortable ●*nm* **essere di scomodo a qcno** be a trouble to sb

scompa'rire *vi* disappear; ⟨morire⟩ pass on. **scom'parsa** *nf* disappearance; ⟨morte⟩ passing, death. **scom'parso, -a** *pp di* **scomparire** ●*nmf* departed

scomparti'mento *nm* compartment. **scom'parto** *nf* compartment

scom'penso *nm* imbalance

scompigli'are *vt* disarrange. **scom'piglio** *nm* confusion

scom'po|rre *vt* take to pieces; ⟨fig: turbare⟩ upset. **~rsi** *vr* get flustered, lose one's composure. **~sto** *pp di* **scomporre** ●*a* ⟨sguaiato⟩ unseemly; ⟨disordinato⟩ untidy

sco'muni|ca *nf* excommunication. **~'care** *vt* excommunicate

sconcer'ta|re *vt* disconcert; ⟨rendere perplesso⟩ bewilder. **~to** *a* disconcerted; bewildered

scon'cezza *nf* obscenity. **'sconcio** *a* ⟨osceno⟩ dirty ●*nm* **è uno sconcio che...** it's a disgrace that...

sconclusio'nato *a* incoherent

scon'dito *a* unseasoned; ⟨insalata⟩ with no dressing

sconfes'sare *vt* disown

scon'figgere *vt* defeat

sconfi'na|re *vi* cross the border; ⟨in proprietà privata⟩ trespass. **~to** *a* unlimited

scon'fitt|a *nf* defeat. **~o** *pp di* **sconfiggere**

scon'forto *nm* dejection

sconge'lare *vt* thaw out ⟨cibo⟩, defrost

scongiu'rare *vt* beseech; ⟨evitare⟩ avert. **~'uro** *nm* **fare gli scongiuri** ≈ touch wood, knock on wood *Am*

scon'nesso *pp di* **sconnettere** ●*a fig* incoherent. **scon'nettere** *vt* disconnect

sconosci'uto, -a *a* unknown ●*nmf* stranger

sconquas'sare *vt* smash; ⟨sconvolgere⟩ upset

conside'rato *a* inconsiderate

sconsigli'a|bile *a* not advisable. **~re** *vt* advise against

sconso'lato *a* disconsolate

scon'ta|re *vt* discount; ⟨dedurre⟩ deduct; ⟨pagare⟩ pay off; serve ⟨pena⟩. **~to** *a* discount; ⟨ovvio⟩ expected; **~to del 10%** with 10% discount; **dare qcsa per ~to** take sth for granted

scon'tento *a* displeased ●*nm* discontent

'sconto *nm* discount; **fare uno ~** give a discount

scon'trarsi *vr* clash; ⟨urtare⟩ collide

scon'trino *nm* ticket; ⟨di cassa⟩ receipt

'scontro *nm* clash; ⟨urto⟩ collision

scon'troso *a* unsociable

sconveni'ente *a* unprofitable; ⟨scorretto⟩ unseemly

sconvol'gente *a* mind-blowing

scon'vol|gere *vt* upset; ⟨mettere in disordine⟩ disarrange. **~gi'mento** *nm* upheaval. **~to** *pp di* **sconvolgere** ●*a* distraught

'**scopa** *nf* broom. **sco'pare** *vt* sweep; *vulg* shag, screw

scoperchi'are *vt* take the lid off ⟨*pentola*⟩; take the roof off ⟨*casa*⟩

sco'pert|a *nf* discovery. **~o** *pp di* **scoprire** ● *a* uncovered; (*senza riparo*) exposed; (*conto*) overdrawn; (*spoglio*) bare

'**scopo** *nm* aim; **allo ~ di** in order to

scoppi'are *vi* burst; *fig* break out. **scoppiet'tare** *vi* crackle. '**scoppio** *nm* burst; (*di guerra*) outbreak; (*esplosione*) explosion

sco'prire *vt* discover; (*togliere la copertura a*) uncover

scoraggi'ante *a* discouraging

scoraggi'a|re *vt* discourage. **~rsi** *vr* lose heart

scor'butico *a* peevish

scorcia'toia *nf* short cut

'**scorcio** *nm* (*di epoca*) end; (*di cielo*) patch; (*in arte*) foreshortening; **di ~** ⟨*vedere*⟩ from an angle. **~ panoramico** panoramic view

scor'da|re *vt*, **~rsi** *vr* forget. **~to a** *Mus* out of tune

sco'reggi|a *nf fam* fart. **~'are** *vi fam* fart

'**scorgere** *vt* make out; (*notare*) notice

scoria *nf* waste; (*di metallo, carbone*) slag; **scorie** *pl* **radioattive** radioactive waste

scor'nato *a fig* hangdog. '**scorno** *nm* humiliation

scorpacci'ata *nf* bellyful; **fare una ~ di** stuff oneself with

scorpi'one *nm* scorpion; *Astr* Scorpio

scorraz'zare *vi* run about

'**scorrere** *vt* (*dare un'occhiata*) glance through ● *vi* run; (*scivolare*) slide; (*fluire*) flow; *Comput* scroll. **scor'revole** *a* **porta scorrevole** sliding door

scorre'ria *nf* raid

scorret'tezza *nf* (*mancanza di educazione*) bad manners *pl*. **scor'retto** *a* incorrect; (*sconveniente*) improper

scorri'banda *nf* raid; *fig* excursion

'**scors|a** *nf* glance. **~o** *pp di* **scorrere** ● *a* last

scor'soio *a* **nodo ~** noose

'**scor|ta** *nf* escort; (*provvista*) supply. **~'tare** *vt* escort

scor'te|se *a* discourteous. **~'sia** *nf* discourtesy

scorti'ca|re *vt* skin. **~'tura** *nf* graze

'**scorto** *pp di* **scorgere**

'**scorza** *nf* peel; (*crosta*) crust; (*corteccia*) bark

sco'sceso *a* steep

'**scossa** *nf* shake; *Electr, fig* shock; **prendere la ~** get an electric shock. **~ elettrica** electric shock. **~ sismica** earth tremor

'**scosso** *pp di* **scuotere** ● *a* shaken; (*sconvolto*) upset

sco'stante *a* off-putting

sco'sta|re *vt* push away. **~rsi** *vr* stand aside

scostu'mato *a* dissolute; (*maleducato*) ill-mannered

scot'tante *a* ⟨*argomento*⟩ dangerous

scot'ta|re *vt* scald ● *vi* burn; ⟨*bevanda:*⟩ be too hot; ⟨*sole, pentola:*⟩ be very hot. **~rsi** *vr* burn oneself; (*al sole*) get sunburnt; *fig* get one's fingers burnt. **~'tura** *nf* burn; (*da liquido*) scald; **~'tura solare** sunburn; *fig* painful experience

'**scotto** *a* overcooked

sco'vare *vt* (*scoprire*) discover

'**Scoz|ia** *nf* Scotland. **~'zese** *a* Scottish ● *nmf* Scot

scredi'tare *vt* discredit

scre'mare *vt* skim

screpo'la|re *vt*, **~rsi** *vr* crack. **~to** *a* ⟨*labbra*⟩ chapped. **~'tura** *nf* crack

screzi'ato *a* speckled

screzio *nm* disagreement

scribac|chi'are *vt* scribble. **~'chino, -a** *nmf* scribbler; (*impiegato*) penpusher

scricchio'l|are *vi* creak. **~io** *nm* creaking

'**scricciolo** *nm* wren

'**scrigno** *nm* casket

scrimina'tura *nf* parting

'**scrit|ta** *nf* writing; (*su muro*) graffiti. **~to** *pp di* **scrivere** ● *a* written ● *nm* writing; (*lettera*) letter. **~'toio** *nm* writing-desk. **~'tore, ~'trice** *nmf* writer. **~'tura** *nf* writing; *Relig* scripture

scrittu'rare *vt* engage

scriva'nia *nf* desk

'**scrivere** *vt* write; (*descrivere*) write about; **~ a macchina** type

scroc'c|are *vt* **~are a** sponge off. '**scrocco** *nm fam* **a scrocco** *fam* without paying; **vivere a scrocco** sponge off other people. **~one, -a** *nmf* sponger

'**scrofa** *nf* sow

scrol'lar|e *vt* shake; **~e le spalle** shrug one's shoulders. **~si** *vr* shake oneself; **~si qcsa di dosso** shake sth off

scrosci'are *vi* roar; ⟨*pioggia:*⟩ pelt down. '**scroscio** *nm* roar; (*di pioggia*) pelting; **uno scroscio di applausi** thunderous applause

scro'star|e vt scrape. **~si** vr peel off

'scrupo|lo nm scruple; (diligenza) care; **senza scrupoli** unscrupulous, without scruples. **~'loso** a scrupulous

scru'ta|re vt scan; (indagare) search. **~'tore** nm (alle elezioni) returning officer

scruti'nare vt scrutinize. **scru'tinio** nm (di voti alle elezioni) poll; Sch assessment of progress

scu'cire vt unstitch; **scuci i soldi!** fam cough up [the money]!

scude'ria nf stable

scu'detto nm Sport championship shield

'scudo nm shield

sculacci|'are vt spank. **~'ata** nf spanking. **~'one** nm spanking

sculet'tare vi wiggle one's hips

scul|'tore, -'trice nm sculptor ● nf sculptress. **~'tura** nf sculpture

scu'ola nf school. **~ elementare** primary school. **~ guida** driving school. **~ materna** day nursery. **~ media** secondary school. **~ media [inferiore]** secondary school (10-13). **~ [media] superiore** secondary school (13-18). **~ dell'obbligo** compulsory education

scu'oter|e vt shake. **~si** vr (destarsi) rouse oneself; **~si di dosso** shake off

'scure nf axe

scu'reggia nf fam fart. **scureggi'are** vi fam fart

scu'rire vt/i darken

'scuro a dark ● nm darkness; (imposta) shutter

scur'rile a scurrilous

'scusa nf excuse; (giustificazione) apology; **chiedere ~** apologize; **chiedo ~!** I'm sorry!

scu'sar|e vt excuse. **~si** vr **~si** apologize (di for); **[mi] scusi!** excuse me!; (chiedendo perdono) [I'm] sorry!

sdebi'tarsi vr (disobbligarsi) repay a kindness

sde'gna|re vt despise. **~rsi** vr get angry. **~to** a indignant. **'sdegno** nm disdain. **sde'gnoso** a disdainful

sden'tato a toothless

sdolci'nato a sentimental, schmaltzy

sdoppi'are vt halve

sdrai'arsi vr lie down. **'sdraio** nm **[sedia a] sdraio** deckchair

sdrammatiz'zare vi provide some comic relief

sdruccio'l|are vi slither. **~evole** a slippery

se conj if; (interrogativo) whether, if; **se mai** (caso mai) if need be; **se mai telefonasse,...** should he call,..., if he calls,...; **se no** otherwise, or else; **se non altro** at least, if nothing else; **se pure** (sebbene) even if; (anche se) even if; **non so se sia vero** I don't know whether it's true, I don't know if it's true; **come se** as if; **se lo avessi saputo prima!** if only I had known before!; **e se andassimo fuori a cena?** how about going out for dinner? ● nm inv if

sé pron oneself; (lui) himself; (lei) herself; (esso, essa) itself; (loro) themselves; **l'ha fatto da sé** he did it himself; **ha preso i soldi con sé** he took the money with him; **si sono tenuti le notizie per sé** they kept the news to themselves

seb'bene conj although

'secca nf shallows pl; **in ~** (nave) aground

sec'cante a annoying

sec'ca|re vt dry; (importunare) annoy ● vi dry up; **~rsi** vr dry up; (irritarsi) get annoyed; (annoiarsi) get bored. **~'tore, ~'trice** nmf nuisance. **~'tura** nf bother

secchi'ello nm pail

'secchio nm bucket. **~ della spazzatura** rubbish bin, trash can Am

'secco, -a a dry; (disseccato) dried; (magro) thin; (brusco) curt; (preciso) sharp; **restare a ~** be left penniless; **restarci ~** (fam: morire di colpo) be killed on the spot ● nm (siccità) drought; **lavare a ~** dry-clean

secessi'one nf secession

seco'lare a age-old; (laico) secular. **'secolo** nm century; (epoca) age; **è un secolo che non lo vedo** fam I haven't seen him for ages o yonks

se'cond|a nf Sch, Rail second class; Auto second [gear]. **~o** a second ● nm second; (secondo piatto) main course ● prep according to; **~o me** in my opinion

secondo'genito, -a a & nm secondborn

secrezi'one nf secretion

'sedano nm celery

seda'tivo a & nm sedative

'sede nf seat; (centro) centre; Relig see; Comm head office. **~ sociale** registered office

seden'tario a sedentary

se'der|e *vi* sit. **~si** *vr* sit down ● *nm* (*deretano*) bottom

'sedia *nf* chair. **~ a dondolo** rocking chair. **~ a rotelle** wheelchair

sedi'cente *a* self-styled

'sedici *a & nm* sixteen

se'dile *nm* seat

sedizi'o|ne *nf* sedition. **~so** *a* seditious

se'dotto *pp di* **sedurre**

sedu'cente *a* seductive; (*allettante*) enticing

se'durre *vt* seduce

se'duta *nf* session; (*di posa*) sitting. **~ stante** *adv* here and now

seduzi'one *nf* seduction

'sega *nf* saw; *vulg* wank

'segala *nf* rye

se'gare *vt* saw

sega'tura *nf* sawdust

'seggio *nm* seat. **~ elettorale** polling station

seggio|la *nf* chair. **~'lino** *nm* seat; (*da bambino*) child's seat. **~'lone** *nm* (*per bambini*) high chair

seggio'via *nf* chair lift

seghe'ria *nf* sawmill

se'ghetto *nm* hacksaw

seg'mento *nm* segment

segna'lar|e *vt* signal; (*annunciare*) announce; (*indicare*) point out. **~si** *vr* distinguish oneself

se'gna|le *nm* signal; (*stradale*) sign. **~le acustico** beep. **~le orario** time signal. **~'letica** *nf* signals *pl*. **~letica stradale** road signs *pl*

segna'libro *nm* bookmark

se'gnar|e *vt* mark; (*prendere nota*) note; (*indicare*) indicate; *Sport* score. **~si** *vr* cross oneself. **'segno** *nm* sign; (*traccia, limite*) mark; (*bersaglio*) target; **far segno** (*col capo*) nod; (*con la mano*) beckon. **segno zodiacale** birth sign

segre'ga|re *vt* segregate. **~zi'one** *nf* segregation

segretari'ato *nm* secretariat

segre'tario, -a *nmf* secretary. **~ comunale** town clerk

segre'te|ria *nf* (*uffico*) [administrative] office; (*segretariato*) secretariat. **~ telefonica** answering machine, answerphone

segre'tezza *nf* secrecy

se'greto *a & nm* secret; **in ~** in secret

segu'ace *nmf* follower

segu'ente *a* following, next

se'gugio *nm* bloodhound

segu'ire *vt/i* follow; (*continuare*) continue

segui'tare *vt/i* continue

'seguito *nm* retinue; (*sequela*) series; (*continuazione*) continuation; **di ~** in succession; **in ~** later on; **in ~ a** following; **al ~** in his/her wake; (*a causa di*) owing to; **fare ~ a** *Comm* follow up

'sei *a & nm* six. **sei'cento** *a & nm* six hundred; **il Seicento** the seventeenth century. **sei'mila** *a & nm* six thousand

sel'ciato *nm* paving

selet'tivo *a* selective. **selezio'nare** *vt* select. **selezi'one** *nf* selection

'sella *nf* saddle. **sel'lare** *vt* saddle

seltz *nm* soda water

'selva *nf* forest

selvag'gina *nf* game

sel'vaggio, -a *a* wild; (*primitivo*) savage ● *nmf* savage

sel'vatico *a* wild

se'maforo *nm* traffic lights *pl*

se'mantica *nf* semantics *sg*

sem'brare *vi* seem; (*assomigliare*) look like; **che te ne sembra?** what do you think?; **mi sembra che...** I think...

'seme *nm* seed; (*di mela*) pip; (*di carte*) suit; (*sperma*) semen

se'mestre *nm* half-year

semi'cerchio *nm* semicircle

semifi'nale *nf* semifinal

semi'freddo *nm* ice cream and sponge dessert

'semina *nf* sowing

semi'nare *vt* sow; *fam* shake off ‹*inseguitori*›

semi'nario *nm* seminar; *Relig* seminary

seminter'rato *nm* basement

se'mitico *a* Semitic

sem'mai *conj* in case ● *adv* è lui, **~, che...** if anyone, it's him who...

'semola *nf* bran. **semo'lino** *nm* semolina

'sempli|ce *a* simple; **in parole semplici** in plain words. **~'cemente** *adv* simply. **~ci'otto, -a** *nmf* simpleton. **~'cistico** *a* simplistic. **~cità** *nf* simplicity. **~fi'care** *vt* simplify

'sempre *adv* always; (*ancora*) still; **per ~** for ever

sempre'verde *a & nm* evergreen

'senape *nf* mustard

se'nato *nm* senate. **sena'tore** *nm* senator

se'nil|e *a* senile. **~ità** *nf* senility

'senno *nm* sense

'seno nm (petto) breast; Math sine; **in ~ a** in the bosom of

sen'sato a sensible

sensazi|o'nale a sensational. **~'one** nf sensation

sen'sibil|e a sensitive; (percepibile) perceptible; (notevole) considerable. **~ità** nf sensitivity. **~iz'zare** vt make more aware (**a** of)

sensi'tivo, -a a sensory ● nmf sensitive person; (medium) medium

'senso nm sense; (significato) meaning; (direzione) direction; **far ~ a qcno** make sb shudder; **non ha ~** it doesn't make sense; **senza ~** meaningless; **perdere i sensi** lose consciousness. **~ dell'umorismo** sense of humour. **~ unico** (strada) one-way; **~ vietato** no entry

sensu'al|e a sensual. **~ità** nf sensuality

sen'tenz|a nf sentence; (massima) saying. **~i'are** vi Jur pass judgment

senti'ero nm path

sentimen'tale a sentimental. **senti'mento** nm feeling

senti'nella nf sentry

sen'ti|re vt feel; (udire) hear; (ascoltare) listen to; (gustare) taste; (odorare) smell ● vi feel; (udire) hear; **~re caldo/freddo** feel hot/cold. **~rsi** vr feel; **~rsi di fare qcsa** feel like doing sth; **~rsi bene** feel well; **~rsi poco bene** feel unwell; **~rsela di fare qcsa** feel up to doing sth. **~to a** (sincero) sincere; **per ~to dire** by hearsay

sen'tore nm inkling

'senza prep without; **~ correre** without running; **senz'altro** certainly; **~ ombrello** without an umbrella

senza'tetto nm inv **i ~** the homeless

sepa'ra|re vt separate. **~rsi** vr separate; (amici:) part; **~rsi da** be separated from. **~ta'mente** adv separately. **~zi'one** nf separation

se'pol|cro nm sepulchre. **~to** pp di **seppellire**. **~'tura** nf burial

seppel'lire vt bury

'seppia nf cuttle fish; **nero di ~** sepia

sep'pure conj even if

se'quenza nf sequence

seque'strare vt (rapire) kidnap; Jur impound; (confiscare) confiscate. **se'questro** nm Jur impounding; (di persona) kidnap[ping]

'sera nf evening; **di ~** in the evening. **se'rale** a evening. **se'rata** nf evening; (ricevimento) party

ser'bare vt keep; harbour ⟨odio⟩; cherish ⟨speranza⟩

serba'toio nm tank. **~ d'acqua** water tank; (per una città) reservoir

'serbo, -a a & nmf Serbian ● nm (lingua) Serbian; **mettere in ~** put aside

sere'nata nf serenade

serenità nf serenity. **se'reno** a serene; ⟨cielo⟩ clear

ser'gente nm sergeant

seria'mente adv seriously

'serie nf inv series; (complesso) set; Sport division; **fuori ~** custom-built; **produzione in ~** mass production; **di ~ B** second-rate

serietà nf seriousness. **'serio** a serious; (degno di fiducia) reliable; **sul serio** seriously; (davvero) really

ser'mone nm sermon

'serpe nf liter viper. **~ggi'are** vi meander; (diffondersi) spread

ser'pente nm snake. **~ a sonagli** rattlesnake

'serra nf greenhouse; **effetto ~** greenhouse effect

ser'randa nf shutter

ser'ra|re vt shut; (stringere) tighten; (incalzare) press on. **~'tura** nf lock

ser'vir|e vt serve; (al ristorante) wait on ● vi serve; (essere utile) be of use; **non serve** it's no good. **~si** vr (di cibo) help oneself; **~si da** buy from; **~si di** use

servitù nf inv servitude; (personale di servizio) servants pl

servizi'evole a obliging

ser'vizio nm service; (da caffè ecc) set; (di cronaca, sportivo) report; **servizi** pl bathroom; **essere di ~** be on duty; **fare ~** ⟨autobus ecc:⟩ run; **fuori ~** ⟨bus⟩ not in service; ⟨ascensore⟩ out of order; **~ compreso** service charge included. **~ in camera** room service. **~ civile** civilian duties done instead of national service. **~ militare** military service. **~ pubblico** utility company. **~ al tavolo** waiter service

'servo, -a nmf servant

servo'sterzo nm power steering

ses'san|ta a & nm sixty. **~'tina** nf una **~tina** about sixty

sessi'one nf session

'sesso nm sex

sessu'al|e a sexual. **~ità** nf sexuality

'sesto¹ a sixth

'sesto² nm (ordine) order

'seta nf silk

setacci'are *vt* sieve. **se'taccio** *nm* sieve

'**sete** *nf* thirst; **avere ~** be thirsty

'**setola** *nf* bristle

'**setta** *nf* sect

set'tan|ta *a & nm* seventy. **~'tina** *nf* una **~tina** about seventy

'**sette** *a & nm* seven. **~'cento** *a & nm* seven hundred; **il S~cento** the eighteenth century

set'tembre *nm* September

settentri|o'nale *a* northern ● *nmf* northerner. **~'one** *nm* north

setti'ma|na *nf* week. **~'nale** *a & nm* weekly

'**settimo** *a* seventh

set'tore *nm* sector

severità *nf* severity. **se'vero** *a* severe; ⟨*rigoroso*⟩ strict

se'vizi|a *nf* torture; **se'vizie** *pl* torture *sg*. **~'are** *vt* torture

sezio'nare *vt* divide; *Med* dissect. **sezi'one** *nf* section; ⟨*reparto*⟩ department; *Med* dissection

sfaccen'dato *a* idle

sfacchi'na|re *vi* toil. **~ta** *nf* drudgery

sfacci|a'taggine *nf* cheek, insolence. **~'ato** *a* cheeky, fresh *Am*

sfa'celo *nm* ruin; **in ~** in ruins

sfal'darsi *vr* flake off

sfa'mar|e *vt* feed. **~si** *vr* satisfy one's hunger, eat one's fill

'**sfar|zo** *nm* pomp. **~'zoso** *a* sumptuous

sfa'sato *a fam* confused; ⟨*motore*⟩ which needs tuning

sfasci'a|re *vt* unbandage; ⟨*fracassare*⟩ smash. **~rsi** *vr* fall to pieces. **~to** *a* beat-up

sfa'tare *vt* explode

sfati'cato *a* lazy

sfavil'la|nte *a* sparkling. **~re** *vi* sparkle

sfavo'revole *a* unfavourable

sfavo'rire *vt* disadvantage, put at a disadvantage

'**sfer|a** *nf* sphere. **~ico** *a* spherical

sfer'rare *vt* unshoe ⟨*cavallo*⟩; ⟨*scagliare*⟩ land

sfer'zare *vt* whip

sfian'carsi *vr* wear oneself out

sfi'bra|re *vt* exhaust. **~to** *a* exhausted

'**sfida** *nf* challenge. **sfi'dare** *vt* challenge

sfi'duci|a *nf* mistrust. **~'ato** *a* discouraged

'**sfiga** *nf vulg* bloody bad luck

sfigu'rare *vt* disfigure ● *vi* ⟨*far cattiva figura*⟩ look out of place

sfilacci'ar|e *vt*, **~si** *vr* fray

sfi'la|re *vt* unthread; ⟨*togliere di dosso*⟩ take off ● *vi* ⟨*truppe:*⟩ march past; ⟨*in parata*⟩ parade. **~rsi** *vr* come unthreaded; ⟨*collant:*⟩ ladder; take off ⟨*pantaloni*⟩. **~ta** *nf* parade; ⟨*sfilza*⟩ series. **~ta di moda** fashion show

'**sfilza** *nf* ⟨*di errori, domande*⟩ string

'**sfinge** *nf* sphinx

sfi'nito *a* worn out

sfio'rare *vt* skim; touch on ⟨*argomento*⟩

sfio'rire *vi* wither; ⟨*bellezza:*⟩ fade

'**sfitto** *a* vacant

'**sfizio** *nm* whim, fancy; **togliersi uno ~** satisfy a whim

sfo'cato *a* out of focus

sfoci'are *vi* ~ **in** flow into

sfode'ra|re *vt* draw ⟨*pistola, spada*⟩. **~to** *a* unlined

sfo'gar|e *vt* vent. **~si** *vr* give vent to one's feelings

sfoggi'are *vt/i* show off. '**sfoggio** *nm* show, display; **fare sfoggio di** show off

'**sfoglia** *nf* sheet of pastry; **pasta ~** puff pastry

sfogli'are *vt* leaf through

'**sfogo** *nm* outlet; *fig* outburst; *Med* rash; **dare ~ a** give vent to

sfolgo'ra|nte *a* blazing. **~re** *vi* blaze

sfol'lare *vt* clear ● *vi Mil* be evacuated

sfol'tire *vt* thin [out]

sfon'dare *vt* break down ● *vi* ⟨*aver successo*⟩ make a name for oneself

'**sfondo** *nm* background

sfor'ma|re *vt* pull out of shape ⟨*tasche*⟩. **~rsi** *vr* lose its shape; ⟨*persona:*⟩ lose one's figure. **~to** *nm* Culin flan

sfor'nito *a* ~ **di** ⟨*negozio*⟩ out of

sfor'tuna *nf* bad luck. **~ta'mente** *adv* unfortunately. **sfortu'nato** *a* unlucky

sfor'zar|e *vt* force. **~si** *vr* try hard. '**sforzo** *nm* effort; ⟨*tensione*⟩ strain

'**sfottere** *vt sl* tease

sfracel'larsi *vr* smash

sfrat'tare *vt* evict. '**sfratto** *nm* eviction

sfrecci'are *vi* flash past

sfregi'a|re *vt* slash. **~to** *a* scarred

'**sfregio** *nm* slash

sfre'na|rsi *vr* run wild. **~to** *a* wild

sfron'tato *a* shameless

sfrutta'mento *nm* exploitation. **sfrut'tare** *vt* exploit

sfug'gente *a* elusive; ⟨*mento*⟩ receding

sfug'gi|re *vi* escape; **~re a** escape [from]; **mi sfugge** it escapes me; **mi è**

sfuggito di mano I lost hold of it ● *vt* avoid. **~ta** *nf* **di ~ta** in passing

sfu'ma|re *vi* (*svanire*) vanish; (*colore:*) shade off ● *vt* soften (*colore*). **~'tura** *nf* shade

sfuri'ata *nf* outburst [of anger]

sga'bello *nm* stool

sgabuz'zino *nm* cupboard

sgam'bato *a* (*costume da bagno*) high-cut

sgambet'tare *vi* kick one's legs; (*camminare*) trot. **sgam'betto** *nm* **fare lo sgambetto a qcno** trip sb up

sganasci'arsi *vr* **~ dalle risa** roar with laughter

sganci'ar|e *vt* unhook; *Rail* uncouple; drop (*bombe*); *fam* cough up (*denaro*). **~si** *vr* become unhooked; *fig* get away

sganghe'rato *a* ramshackle

sgar'bato *a* rude. **'sgarbo** *nm* discourtesy; **fare uno sgarbo** be rude

sgargi'ante *a* garish

sgar'rare *vi* be wrong; (*da regola*) stray from the straight and narrow. **'sgarro** *nm* mistake, slip

sgattaio'lare *vi* sneak away; **~ via** decamp

sghignaz'zare *vi* laugh scornfully, sneer

sgob'b|are *vi* slog; (*fam: studente:*) swot. **~one, -a** *nmf* slogger; (*fam: studente*) swot

sgoccio'lare *vi* drip

sgo'larsi *vr* shout oneself hoarse

sgomb[e]'rare *vt* clear [out]. **'sgombro** *a* clear ● *nm* (*trasloco*) removal; (*pesce*) mackerel

sgomen'tar|e *vt* dismay. **~si** *vr* be dismayed. **sgo'mento** *nm* dismay

sgomi'nare *vt* defeat

sgom'mata *nf* screech of tyres

sgonfi'ar|e *vt* deflate. **~si** *vr* go down. **'sgonfio** *a* flat

'sgorbio *nm* scrawl; (*fig: vista sgradevole*) sight

sgor'gare *vi* gush [out] ● *vt* flush out, unblock (*lavandino*)

sgoz'zare *vt* **~ qcno** cut sb's throat

sgra'd|evole *a* disagreeable. **~ito** *a* unwelcome

sgrammati'cato *a* ungrammatical

sgra'nare *vt* shell (*piselli*); open wide (*occhi*)

sgran'chir|e *vt*, **~si** *vr* stretch

sgranocchi'are *vt* munch

sgras'sare *vt* remove the grease from

sgrazi'ato *a* ungainly

sgreto'lar|e *vt*, **~si** *vr* crumble

sgri'da|re *vt* scold. **~ta** *nf* scolding

sgros'sare *vt* rough-hew (*marmo*); *fig* polish

sguai'ato *a* coarse

sgual'cire *vt* crumple

sgual'drina *nf* slut

sgu'ardo *nm* look; (*breve*) glance

'sguattero, -a *nmf* skivvy

sguaz'zare *vi* splash; (*nel fango*) wallow

sguinzagli'are *vt* unleash

sgusci'are *vt* shell ● *vi* (*sfuggire*) slip away; **~ fuori** slip out

shake'rare *vt* shake

si *pron* (*riflessivo*) oneself; (*lui*) himself; (*lei*) herself; (*esso, essa*) itself; (*loro*) themselves; (*reciproco*) each other; (*tra più di due*) one another; (*impersonale*) you, one; **lavarsi** wash [oneself]; **si è lavata** she washed [herself]; **lavarsi le mani** wash one's hands; **si è lavata le mani** she washed her hands; **si è mangiato un pollo intero** he ate an entire chicken by himself; **incontrarsi** meet each other; **la gente si aiuta a vicenda** people help one another; **non si sa mai** you never know, one never knows; **queste cose si dimenticano facilmente** these things are easily forgotten ● *nm* (*chiave, nota*) B

sì *adv* yes

'sia¹ *vedi* **essere**

'sia² *conj* **~ ...~...** (*entrambi*) both... and...; (*o l'uno o l'altro*) either...or...**~ che venga, ~ che non venga** whether he comes or not; **scegli ~ questo ~ quello** choose either this one or that one; **voglio ~ questo che quello** I want both this one and that one

sia'mese *a* Siamese

sibi'lare *vi* hiss. **'sibilo** *nm* hiss

si'cario *nm* hired killer

sicché *conj* (*perciò*) so [that]; (*allora*) then

siccità *nf* drought

sic'come *conj* as

Si'cili|a *nf* Sicily. **s~'ano, -a** *a & nmf* Sicilian

si'cura *nf* safety catch; (*di portiera*) child-proof lock. **~'mente** *adv* definitely

sicu'rezza *nf* (*certezza*) certainty; (*salvezza*) safety; **uscita di ~** emergency exit

si'curo *a* (*non pericoloso*) safe; (*certo*) sure; (*saldo*) steady; *Comm* sound ● *adv* certainly ● *nm* safety; **al ~** safe; **andare sul ~** play [it] safe; **di ~** definitely; **di ~, sarà arrivato** he must have arrived

siderur'gia *nf* iron and steel industry. **side'rurgico** *a* iron and steel *attrib*

'sidro *nm* cider

si'epe *nf* hedge

si'ero *nm* serum

sieroposi'tivo, -a *a* HIV positive ● *nmf* person who is HIV positive

si'esta *nf* afternoon nap, siesta

si'fone *nm* siphon

Sig. *abbr* (**signore**) Mr

Sig.a *abbr* (**signora**) Mrs, Ms

siga'retta *nf* cigarette; **pantaloni a ~** drainpipes

'sigaro *nm* cigar

Sigg. *abbr* (**signori**) Messrs

sigil'lare *vt* seal. **si'gillo** *nm* seal

'sigla *nf* initials *pl*. **~ musicale** signature tune. **si'glare** *vt* initial

Sig.na *abbr* (**signorina**) Miss, Ms

signifi'ca|re *vt* mean. **~'tivo** *a* significant. **~to** *nm* meaning

si'gnora *nf* lady; (*davanti a nome proprio*) Mrs; (*non sposata*) Miss; (*in lettere ufficiali*) Dear Madam; **il signor Vené e ~** Mr and Mrs Vené

si'gnore *nm* gentleman; *Relig* lord; (*davanti a nome proprio*) Mr; (*in lettere ufficiali*) Dear Sir. **signo'rile** *a* gentlemanly; (*di lusso*) luxury

signo'rina *nf* young lady; (*seguito da nome proprio*) Miss

silenzia'tore *nm* silencer

si'lenzi|o *nm* silence. **~'oso** *a* silent

silhou'ette *nf* silhouette, outline

si'licio *nm* **piastrina di ~** silicon chip

sili'cone *nm* silicone

'sillaba *nf* syllable

silu'rare *vt* torpedo. **si'luro** *nm* torpedo

simboleggi'are *vt* symbolize

sim'bolico *a* symbolic[al]

'simbolo *nm* symbol

similarità *nf inv* similarity

'simil|e *a* similar; (*tale*) such; **~e a** like ● *nm* (*il prossimo*) fellow man. **~'mente** *adv* similarly. **~'pelle** *nf* Leatherette®

simme'tria *nf* symmetry. **sim'metrico** *a* symmetric[al]

simpa'ti|a *nf* liking; (*compenetrazione*) sympathy; **prendere qcno in ~a** take a liking to sb. **sim'patico** *a* nice. **~iz'zante** *nmf* well-wisher. **~iz'zare** *vi* **~izzare con** take a liking to; **~izzare per qcsa/qcno** lean towards sth/sb

sim'posio *nm* symposium

simu'la|re *vt* simulate; feign ‹*amicizia, interesse*›. **~zi'one** *nf* simulation

simul'tane|a *nf* **in ~a** simultaneously. **~o** *a* simultaneous

sina'goga *nf* synagogue

sincerità *nf* sincerity. **sin'cero** *a* sincere

'sincope *nf* syncopation; *Med* fainting fit

sincron'ia *nf* synchronization; **in ~** with synchronized timing

sincroniz'za|re *vt* synchronize. **~zi'one** *nf* synchronization

sinda'ca|le *a* [trade] union, [labor] union *Am*. **~'lista** *nmf* trade unionist, labor union member *Am*. **~re** *vt* inspect. **~to** *nm* [trade] union, [labor] union *Am*; (*associazione*) syndicate

'sindaco *nm* mayor

'sindrome *nf* syndrome

sinfo'nia *nf* symphony. **sin'fonico** *a* symphonic

singhi|oz'zare *vi* (*di pianto*) sob. **~'ozzo** *nm* hiccup; (*di pianto*) sob; **avere il ~ozzo** have the hiccups

singo'lar|e *a* singular ● *nm* singular. **~'mente** *adv* individually; (*stranamente*) peculiarly

'singolo *a* single ● *nm* individual; *Tennis* singles *pl*

si'nistra *nf* left; **a ~** on the left; **girare a ~** turn to the left; **con la guida a ~** ‹*auto*› with left-hand drive

si'nistr|o, -a *a* left[-hand]; (*avverso*) sinister ● *nm* accident ● *nf* left [hand]; *Pol* left [wing]

'sino *prep* = **fino**[1]

si'nonimo *a* synonymous ● *nm* synonym

sin'ta|ssi *nf* syntax. **~ttico** *a* syntactic[al]

'sintesi *nf* synthesis; (*riassunto*) summary

sin'teti|co *a* synthetic; (*conciso*) summary. **~z'zare** *vt* summarize

sintetizza'tore *nm* synthesizer

sinto'matico *a* symptomatic. **'sintomo** *nm* symptom

sinto'nia *nf* tuning; **in ~** on the same wavelength

sinu'oso *a* (*strada*) winding

sinu'site *nf* sinusitis

si'pario *nm* curtain

si'rena *nf* siren

'Siri|a *nf* Syria. **s~'ano, -a** *a & nmf* Syrian

si'ringa *nf* syringe

'sismico *a* seismic

si'stem|a *nm* system. **S~a Monetario Europeo** European Monetary System. **~a operativo** *Comput* operating system

siste'ma|re *vt* (*mettere*) put; tidy up ⟨*casa, camera*⟩; (*risolvere*) sort out; (*procurare lavoro a*) fix up with a job; (*trovare alloggio a*) find accommodation for; (*sposare*) marry off; (*fam: punire*) sort out. **~rsi** *vr* settle down; (*trovare un lavoro*) find a job; (*trovare alloggio*) find accommodation; (*sposarsi*) marry. **~tico** *a* systematic. **~zi'one** *nf* arrangement; (*di questione*) settlement; (*lavoro*) job; (*alloggio*) accommodation; (*matrimonio*) marriage

'sito *nm* site. **~ web** *Comput* web site

situ'are *vt* place

situazi'one *nf* situation

ski-'lift *nm* ski tow

slacci'are *vt* unfasten

slanci'a|rsi *vr* hurl oneself. **~to** *a* slender. **'slancio** *nm* impetus; (*impulso*) impulse

sla'vato *a* ⟨*carnagione, capelli*⟩ fair

'slavo *a* Slav[onic]

sle'al|e *a* disloyal. **~tà** *nf* disloyalty

sle'gare *vt* untie

'slitta *nf* sledge, sleigh. **~'mento** *nm* (*di macchina*) skid; (*fig: di unione*) postponement

slit'ta|re *vi* Auto skid; ⟨*riunione:*⟩ be put off. **~ta** *nf* skid

slit'tino *nm* toboggan

'slogan *nm inv* slogan

slo'ga|re *vt* dislocate. **~rsi** *vr* **~rsi una caviglia** sprain one's ankle. **~'tura** *nf* dislocation

sloggi'are *vt* dislodge ● *vi* move out

Slo'vacchia *nf* Slovakia

Slo'venia *nf* Slovenia

smacchi'a|re *vt* clean. **~'tore** *nm* stain remover

'smacco *nm* humiliating defeat

smagli'ante *a* dazzling

smagli'a|rsi *vr* ⟨*calza:*⟩ ladder *Br*, run. **~'tura** *nf* ladder *Br*, run

smalizi'ato *a* cunning

smal'ta|re *vt* enamel; glaze ⟨*ceramica*⟩; varnish ⟨*unghie*⟩. **~to** *a* enamelled

smalti'mento *nm* disposal; (*di merce*) selling off. **~ rifiuti** waste disposal; (*di grassi*) burning off

smal'tire *vt* burn off; (*merce*) sell off; *fig* get through ⟨*corrispondenza*⟩; **~ la sbornia** sober up

'smalto *nm* enamel; (*di ceramica*) glaze; (*per le unghie*) nail varnish

'smani|a *nf* fidgets *pl*; (*desiderio*) longing. **~'are** *vi* have the fidgets; **~are per** long for. **~'oso** *a* restless

smantel|la'mento *nm* dismantling. **~'lare** *vt* dismantle

smarri'mento *nm* loss; (*psicologico*) bewilderment

smar'ri|re *vt* lose; (*temporaneamente*) mislay. **~rsi** *vr* get lost; (*turbarsi*) be bewildered

smasche'rar|e *vt* unmask. **~si** *vr* (*tradirsi*) give oneself away

SME *nm abbr* (**Sistema Monetario Europeo**) EMS

smemo'rato, -a *a* forgetful ● *nmf* scatterbrain

smen'ti|re *vt* deny. **~ta** *nf* denial

sme'raldo *nm & a* emerald

smerci'are *vt* sell off

smerigli'ato *a* emery; **vetro ~** frosted glass. **sme'riglio** *nm* emery

'smesso *pp di* **smettere** ● *a* ⟨*abiti*⟩ cast-off

'smett|ere *vt* stop; stop wearing ⟨*abiti*⟩; **~ila!** stop it!

smidol'lato *a* spineless

smin...'ir|e *vt* diminish. **~si** *vr fig* belittle oneself

sminuz'zare *vt* crumble; (*fig: analizzare*) analyse in detail

smista'mento *nm* clearing; (*postale*) sorting. **smi'stare** *vt* sort; *Mil* post

smisu'rato *a* boundless; (*esorbitante*) excessive

smobili'ta|re *vt* demobilize. **~zi'one** *nf* demobilization

smo'dato *a* immoderate

smog *nm* smog

smoking *nm inv* dinner jacket, tuxedo *Am*

smon'tabile *a* jointed

smon'tar|e *vt* take to pieces; (*scoraggiare*) dishearten ● *vi* (*da veicolo*) get off; (*da cavallo*) dismount; (*dal servizio*) go off duty. **~si** *vr* lose heart

'smorfi|a *nf* grimace; (*moina*) simper; **fare ~e** make faces. **~'oso** *a* affected

'smorto *a* pale; ⟨*colore*⟩ dull

smor'zare *vt* dim ⟨*luce*⟩; tone down ⟨*colori*⟩; deaden ⟨*suoni*⟩; quench ⟨*sete*⟩

'smosso *pp di* **smuovere**

smotta'mento *nm* landslide

'smunto *a* emaciated

smu'over|e *vt* shift; (*commuovere*) move. **~si** *vr* move; (*commuoversi*) be moved

smus'sar|e *vt* round off; (*fig: attenuare*) tone down. **~si** *vr* go blunt

snatu'rato *a* inhuman

snel'lir|e *vt* slim down. **~si** *vr* slim [down]. **'snello** *a* slim

sner'vante *a* enervating

sner'va|re *vt* enervate. **~rsi** *vr* get exhausted

sni'dare *vt* drive out

snif'fare *vt* snort

snob'bare *vt* snub. **sno'bismo** *nm* snobbery

snoccio'lare *vt* stone; *fig* blurt out

sno'da|re *vt* untie; ⟨*sciogliere*⟩ loosen. **~rsi** *vr* come untied; ⟨*strada:*⟩ wind. **~to** *a* ⟨*persona*⟩ double-jointed; ⟨*dita*⟩ flexible

so'ave *a* gentle

sobbal'zare *vi* jerk; ⟨*trasalire*⟩ start. **sob'balzo** *nm* jerk; ⟨*trasalimento*⟩ start

sobbar'carsi *vr* **~ a** undertake

sob'borgo *nm* suburb

sobil'la|re *vt* stir up

'sobrio *a* sober

socchi'u|dere *vt* half-close. **~so** *pp di* **socchiudere ● *a*** ⟨*occhi*⟩ half-closed; ⟨*porta*⟩ ajar

soc'combere *vi* succumb

soc'cor|rere *vt* assist. **~so** *pp di* **soccorrere ● *nm*** assistance; **soccorsi** *pl* rescuers; ⟨*dopo disastro*⟩ relief workers. **~so stradale** breakdown service

socialdemo'cra|tico, -a *a* Social Democratic **● *nmf*** Social Democrat. **~'zia** *nf* Social Democracy

soci'ale *a* social

socia'li|smo *nm* Socialism. **~sta** *a & nmf* Socialist. **~z'zare** *vi* socialize

società *nf inv* society; *Comm* company. **~ per azioni** plc. **~ a responsabilità limitata** limited liability company

soci'evole *a* sociable

'socio, -a *nmf* member; *Comm* partner

sociolo'gia *nf* sociology. **socio'logico** *a* sociological

'soda *nf* soda

soddisfa'cente *a* satisfactory

soddi'sfa|re *vt/i* satisfy; meet ⟨*richiesta*⟩; make amends for ⟨*offesa*⟩. **~tto** *pp di* **soddisfare ● *a*** satisfied. **~zi'one** *nf* satisfaction

'sodo *a* hard; *fig* firm; ⟨*uovo*⟩ hard-boiled **● *adv*** hard; **dormire ~** sleep soundly **● *nm* venire al ~** get to the point

sofà *nm inv* sofa

soffe'ren|te *a* ⟨*malato*⟩ ill. **~za** *nf* suffering

soffer'marsi *vr* pause; **~ su** dwell on

sof'ferto *pp di* **soffrire**

soffi'a|re *vt* blow; reveal ⟨*segreto*⟩; ⟨*rubare*⟩ pinch *fam* **● *vi* blow. ~ta** *nf fig sl* tip-off

'soffice *a* soft

'soffio *nm* puff; *Med* murmur

sof'fitt|a *nf* attic. **~o** *nm* ceiling

soffo|ca'mento *nm* suffocation

soffo'ca|re *a* suffocating. **~re** *vt/i* suffocate; ⟨*con cibo*⟩ choke; *fig* stifle

sof'friggere *vt* fry lightly

sof'frire *vt/i* suffer; ⟨*sopportare*⟩ bear; **~ di** suffer from

sof'fritto *pp di* **soffriggere**

sof'fuso *a* ⟨*luce*⟩ soft

sofisti'ca|re *vt* ⟨*adulterare*⟩ adulterate **● *vi*** ⟨*sottilizzare*⟩ quibble. **~to** *a* sophisticated

sogget|tiva'mente *adv* subjectively. **~'tivo** *a* subjective

sog'getto *nm* subject **● *a*** subject; **essere ~ a** be subject to

soggezi'one *nf* subjection; ⟨*rispetto*⟩ awe

sogghi'gnare *vi* sneer. **sog'ghigno** *nm* sneer

soggio'gare *vt* subdue

soggior'nare *vi* stay. **soggi'orno** *nm* stay; ⟨*stanza*⟩ living room

soggi'ungere *vt* add

'soglia *nf* threshold

sogliola *nf* sole

so'gna|re *vt/i* dream; **~re a occhi aperti** daydream. **~'tore, ~'trice** *nmf* dreamer. **'sogno** *nm* dream; **fare un sogno** have a dream; **neanche per sogno!** not at all!

'soia *nf* soya

sol *nm* *Mus* ⟨*chiave, nota*⟩ G

so'laio *nm* attic

sola'mente *adv* only

so'lar|e *a* ⟨*energia, raggi*⟩ solar; ⟨*crema*⟩ sun *attrib*. **~ium** *nm inv* solarium

sol'care *vt* plough. **'solco** *nm* furrow; ⟨*di ruota*⟩ track; ⟨*di nave*⟩ wake; ⟨*di disco*⟩ groove

sol'dato *nm* soldier

'soldo *nm* **non ha un ~** he hasn't got a penny to his name; **senza un ~** penniless; **soldi** *pl* ⟨*denaro*⟩ money *sg*

'sole *nm* sun; ⟨*luce del sole*⟩ sun[light]; **al ~** in the sun; **prendere il ~** sunbathe

soleggi'ato *a* sunny

so'lenn|e *a* solemn. **~ità** *nf* solemnity

so'lere *vi* be in the habit of; **come si suol dire** as they say

sol'fato *nm* sulphate

soli'da|le *a* in agreement. **~rietà** *nf* solidarity

solidifi'car|e *vt/i,* **~si** *vr* solidify

solidità *nf* solidity; *(di colori)* fastness. **'solido** *a* solid; *(robusto)* sturdy; *(colore)* fast ● *nm* solid

soli'loquio *nm* soliloquy

so'lista *a* solo ● *nmf* soloist

solita'mente *adv* usually

soli'tario *a* solitary; *(isolato)* lonely ● *nm* (*brillante*) solitaire; *(gioco di carte)* patience, solitaire

'solito *a* usual; **essere ~ fare qcsa** be in the habit of doing sth ● *nm* usual; **di ~** usually

soli'tudine *nf* solitude

solleci'ta|re *vt* speed up; urge *(persona)*. **~zi'one** *nf* (*richiesta*) request; (*preghiera*) entreaty

sol'leci|to *a* prompt ● *nm* reminder. **~'tudine** *nf* promptness; (*interessamento*) concern

solle'one *nm* noonday sun; *(periodo)* dog days of summer

solleti'care *vt* tickle. **sol'letico** *nm* tickling; **fare il solletico a qcno** tickle sb; **soffrire il solletico** be ticklish

solleva'mento *nm* **~ pesi** weightlifting

solle'var|e *vt* lift; (*elevare*) raise; (*confortare*) comfort. **~si** *vr* rise; (*riaversi*) recover

solli'evo *nm* relief

'solo, -a *a* alone; *(isolato)* lonely; *(unico)* only; *Mus* solo; **da ~** by myself/yourself/himself etc ● *nmf* **il ~, la sola** the only one ● *nm Mus* solo ● *adv* only

sol'stizio *nm* solstice

sol'tanto *adv* only

so'lubile *a* soluble; *(caffè)* instant

soluzi'one *nf* solution; *Comm* payment; **in unica ~** *Comm* as a lump sum

sol'vente *a & nm* solvent; **~ per unghie** nail polish remover

'soma *nf* **bestia da ~** beast of burden

so'maro *nm* ass; *Sch* dunce

so'matico *a* somatic

somigli'an|te *a* similar. **~za** *nf* resemblance

somigli'ar|e *vi* **~e a** resemble. **~si** *vr* be alike

'somma *nf* sum; *Math* addition

som'mare *vt* add; *(totalizzare)* add up

som'mario *a & nm* summary

som'mato *a* **tutto ~** all things considered

sommeli'er *nm inv* wine waiter

som'mer|gere *vt* submerge. **~'gibile**
nm submarine. **~so** *pp di* **sommergere**

som'messo *a* soft

sommini'stra|re *vt* administer. **~zi'one** *nf* administration

sommità *nf inv* summit

'sommo *a* highest; *fig* supreme ● *nm* summit

som'mossa *nf* rising

sommozza'tore *nm* frogman

so'naglio *nm* bell

so'nata *nf* sonata; *fig fam* beating

'sonda *nf Mech* drill; *(spaziale, Med)* probe. **son'daggio** *nm* drilling; *(spaziale, Med)* probe; *(indagine)* survey. **sondaggio d'opinioni** opinion poll. **son'dare** *vt* sound; *(investigare)* probe

so'netto *nm* sonnet

sonnambu'lismo *nm* sleepwalking. **son'nambulo, -a** *nmf* sleepwalker

sonnecchi'are *vi* doze

son'nifero *nm* sleeping-pill

'sonno *nm* sleep; **aver ~** be sleepy. **~'lenza** *nf* sleepiness

so'noro *a* resonant; *(rumoroso)* loud; *(onde, scheda)* sound *attrib*

sontu'oso *a* sumptuous

sopo'rifero *a* soporific

sop'palco *nm* platform

soppe'rire *vi* **~ a qcsa** provide for sth

soppe'sare *vt* weigh up *(situazione)*

soppi'atto: di ~ *adv* furtively

soppor'ta|re *vt* support; *(tollerare)* stand; bear *(dolore)*

soppressi'one *nf* removal; *(di legge)* abolition; *(di diritti, pubblicazione)* suppression; *(annullamento)* cancellation. **sop'presso** *pp di* **sopprimere**

sop'primere *vt* get rid of; abolish *(legge)*; suppress *(diritti, pubblicazione)*; *(annullare)* cancel

'sopra *adv* on top; *(più in alto)* higher [up]; *(al piano superiore)* upstairs; *(in testo)* above; **mettilo lì ~** put it up there; **di ~** upstairs; **dormirci ~** *fig* sleep on it; **pensarci ~** think about it; **vedi ~** see above ● *prep* **~ [a]** on; *(senza contatto, oltre)* over; *(riguardo a)* about; **è ~ al tavolo, è ~ il tavolo** it's on the table; **il quadro è appeso ~ al camino** the picture is hanging over the fireplace; **il ponte passa ~ all'autostrada** the bridge crosses over the motorway; **è caduto ~ il tetto** it fell on the roof; **l'uno ~ l'altro** one on top of the other; *(senza contatto)* one above the other; **abita ~ di me** he lives upstairs from me; **i bambini ~ i dieci**

anni children over ten; **20' ~ lo zero 20'** above zero; **~ il livello del mare** above sea level; **rifletti ~ quello che è successo** think about what happened; **non ha nessuno ~ di sé** he has nobody above him; **al di ~ di** over ● *nm* il [di] ~ the top

so'prabito *nm* overcoat

soprac'ciglio *nm* (*pl nf* **sopracciglia**) eyebrow

sopracco'per|ta *nf* (*di letto*) bedspread; (*di libro*) [dust-]jacket. **~'tina** *nf* book jacket

soprad'detto *a* above-mentioned

sopraele'vata *nf* elevated railway

sopraf'fa|re *vt* overwhelm. **~tto** *pp di* **sopraffare. ~zi'one** *nf* abuse of power

sopraf'fino *a* excellent; (*gusto, udito*) highly refined

sopraggi'ungere *vi* (*persona:*) turn up; (*accadere*) happen

soprallu'ogo *nm* inspection

sopram'mobile *nm* ornament

soprannatu'rale *a & nm* supernatural

sopran'nom|e *nm* nickname. **~i'nare** *vt* nickname

so'prano *nmf* soprano

soprappensi'ero *adv* lost in thought

sopras'salto *nm* di ~ with a start

soprasse'dere *vi* ~ a postpone

soprat'tutto *adv* above all

sopravvalu'tare *vt* overvalue

soprav|ve'nire *vi* turn up; (*accadere*) happen. **~'vento** *nm fig* upper hand

sopravvi|s'suto *pp di* **sopravvivere. ~'venza** *nf* survival. **soprav'vivere** *vi* survive; **sopravvivere a** outlive (*persona*)

soprinten'den|te *nmf* supervisor; (*di museo ecc*) keeper. **~za** *nf* supervision; (*ente*) board

so'pruso *nm* abuse of power

soq'quadro *nm* **mettere a ~** turn upside down

sor'betto *nm* sorbet

sor'bire *vt* sip; *fig* put up with

'sordido *a* sordid; (*avaro*) stingy

sor'dina *nf* mute; **in ~** *fig* on the quiet

sordità *nf* deafness. **'sordo, -a** *a* deaf; (*rumore, dolore*) dull ● *nmf* deaf person. **sordo'muto, -a** *a* deaf-and-dumb ● *nmf* deaf mute

so'rel|la *nf* sister. **~'lastra** *nf* stepsister

sor'gente *nf* spring; (*fonte*) source

'sorgere *vi* rise; *fig* arise

sormon'tare *vt* surmount

sorni'one *a* sly

sorpas'sa|re *vt* surpass; (*eccedere*) exceed; overtake, pass *Am* (*veicolo*). **~to** *a* old-fashioned. **sor'passo** *nm* overtaking, passing *Am*

sorpren'dente *a* surprising; (*straordinario*) remarkable

sor'prendere *vt* surprise; (*cogliere in flagrante*) catch

sor'pres|a *nf* surprise; **di ~a** by surprise. **~o** *pp di* **sorprendere**

sor're|ggere *vt* support; (*tenere*) hold up. **~ggersi** *vr* support oneself. **~tto** *pp di* **sorreggere**

sorri'dente *a* smiling

sor'ri|dere *vi* smile. **~so** *pp di* **sorridere** ● *nm* smile

sorseggi'are *vt* sip. **'sorso** *nm* sip; (*piccola quantità*) drop

'sorta *nf* sort; **di ~** whatever; **ogni ~ di** all sorts of

'sorte *nf* fate; (*caso imprevisto*) chance; **tirare a ~** draw lots. **~ggi'are** *vt* draw lots for. **sor'teggio** *nm* draw

sorti'legio *nm* witchcraft

sor'ti|re *vi* come out. **~ta** *nf Mil* sortie; (*battuta*) witticism

'sorto *pp di* **sorgere**

sorvegli'an|te *nmf* keeper; (*controllore*) overseer. **~za** *nf* watch; *Mil ecc* surveillance

sorvegli'are *vt* watch over; (*controllare*) oversee; (*polizia:*) watch, keep under surveillance

sorvo'lare *vt* fly over; *fig* skip

'sosia *nm inv* double

so'spen|dere *vt* hang; (*interrompere*) stop; (*privare di una carica*) suspend. **~si'one** *nf* suspension. **~'sorio** *nm Sport* jockstrap

so'speso *pp di* **sospendere** ● *a* (*impiegato, alunno*) suspended; **~ a** hanging from; **~ a un filo** *fig* hanging by a thread ● *nm* **in ~** pending; (*emozionato*) in suspense

sospet|'tare *vt* suspect. **so'spetto** *a* suspicious ● *nm* suspicion; (*persona*) suspect. **~'toso** *a* suspicious

so'spin|gere *vt* drive. **~to** *pp di* **sospingere**

sospi'rare *vi* sigh ● *vt* long for. **so'spiro** *nm* sigh

'sosta *nf* stop; (*pausa*) pause; **senza ~** non-stop; **"divieto di ~"** "no parking"

sostan'tivo *nm* noun

so'stanz|a *nf* substance; **~e** *pl* (*patrimonio*) property *sg*; **in ~a** to sum up. **~'oso** a substantial; ⟨cibo⟩ nourishing

so'stare vi stop; (fare una pausa) pause

so'stegno nm support

soste'ner|e vt support; (sopportare) bear; (resistere) withstand; (affermare) maintain; (nutrire) sustain; sit (esame). **~e le spese** meet the costs. **~si** vr support oneself

sosteni'tore, -'trice nmf supporter

sostenta'mento nm maintenance

soste'nuto a ⟨stile⟩ formal; ⟨prezzi, velocità⟩ high

sostitu'ir|e vt substitute (a for), replace (con with). **~si** vr **~si a** replace

sosti'tu|to, -a nmf replacement, stand-in ● nm (surrogato) substitute. **~zi'one** nf substitution

sotta'ceto a pickled; **sottaceti** pl pickles

sot'tana nf petticoat; (di prete) cassock

sotter'fugio nm subterfuge; **di ~** secretly

sotter'raneo a underground ● nm cellar

sotter'rare vt bury

sottigli'ezza nf slimness; fig subtlety

sot'til|e a thin; ⟨udito, odorato⟩ keen; ⟨osservazione, distinzione⟩ subtle. **~iz-'zare** vi split hairs

sottin'te|ndere vt imply. **~so** pp di **sottintendere** ● nm allusion; **senza ~si** openly ● a implied

'sotto adv below; (più in basso) lower [down]; (al di sotto) underneath; (al piano di sotto) downstairs; **è lì ~** it's underneath; **~ ~** deep down; (di nascosto) on the quiet; **di ~** downstairs; **mettersi ~** fig get down to it; **mettere ~** (fam: investire) knock down; **fatti ~!** fam get stuck in! ● prep **~** [a] under; (al di sotto di) under[neath]; **abita ~ di me** he lives downstairs from me; **i bambini ~ i dieci anni** children under ten; **20° ~ zero** 20° below zero; **~ il livello del mare** below sea level; **~ la pioggia** in the rain; **~ Elisabetta I** under Elizabeth I; **~ calmante** under sedation; **~ condizione che...** on condition that...; **~ giuramento** under oath; **~ sorveglianza** under surveillance; **~ Natale/gli esami** around Christmas/exam time; **al di ~ di** under; **andare ~ i 50 all'ora** do less than 50km an hour ● nm **il [di] ~** the bottom

sotto'banco adv under the counter

sottobicchi'ere nm coaster

sotto'bosco nm undergrowth

sotto'braccio adv arm in arm

sotto'fondo nm background

sottoline'are vt underline; fig stress

sot'tolio adv in oil

sotto'mano adv within reach

sottoma'rino a & nm submarine

sotto'messo pp di **sottomettere** ● a (remissivo) submissive

sotto'metter|e vt submit; subdue ⟨popolo⟩. **~si** vr submit. **sottomissi'one** nf submission

sottopa'gare vt underpay

sottopas'saggio nm underpass; (pedonale) subway

sotto'por|re vt submit; (costringere) subject. **~si** vr submit oneself; **~si a** undergo. **sotto'posto** pp di **sottoporre**

sotto'scala nm cupboard under the stairs

sotto'scritto pp di **sottoscrivere** ● nm undersigned

sotto'scri|vere vt sign; (approvare) sanction, subscribe to. **~zi'one** nf (petizione) petition; (approvazione) sanction; (raccolta di denaro) appeal

sottosegre'tario nm undersecretary

sotto'sopra adv upside down

sotto'stante a **la strada ~** the road below

sottosu'olo nm subsoil

sottosvi'lup'pato a underdeveloped. **~'luppo** nm underdevelopment

sotto'terra adv underground

sotto'titolo nm subtitle

sottovalu'tare vt underestimate

sotto'veste nf slip

sotto'voce adv in a low voice

sottovu'oto a vacuum-packed

sot'tra|rre vt remove; embezzle ⟨fondi⟩; Math subtract. **~rsi** vr escape from; avoid ⟨responsabilità⟩. **~tto** pp di **sottrarre**. **~zi'one** nf removal; (di fondi) embezzlement; Math subtraction

sottuffici'ale nm non-commissioned officer; Naut petty officer

sou'brette nf inv showgirl

so'vietico, -a a & nmf Soviet

sovraccari'care vt overload. **sovrac'carico** a overloaded (di with) ● nm overload

sovraffati'carsi vr overexert oneself

sovrannatu'rale a & nm = **soprannaturale**

so'vrano, -a a sovereign; fig supreme ● nmf sovereign

sovrap'por|re *vt* superimpose. **~si** *vr* overlap. **sovrapposizi'one** *nf* superimposition

sovra'stare *vt* dominate; *⟨fig: pericolo:⟩* hang over

sovrinten'den|te, ~za = soprintendente, soprintendenza

sovru'mano *a* superhuman

sovvenzi'one *nf* subsidy

sovver'sivo *a* subversive

'sozzo *a* filthy

S.p.A. *abbr* **(società per azioni)** plc

spac'ca|re *vt* split; chop *⟨legna⟩*. **~rsi** *vr* split. **~'tura** *nf* split

spacci'a|re *vt* deal in, push *⟨droga⟩*; **~re qcsa per qcsa** pass sth off as sth; **essere ~to** be done for, be a goner. **~rsi** *vr* **~rsi per** pass oneself off as. **~'tore, ~'trice** *nmf* *(di droga)* pusher; *(di denaro falso)* distributor of forged bank notes. **'spaccio** *nm* *(di droga)* dealer, pusher; *(negozio)* shop

'spacco *nm* split

spac'cone, -a *nmf* boaster

'spada *nf* sword. **~c'cino** *nm* swordsman

spadroneggi'are *vi* act the boss

spae'sato *a* disorientated

spa'ghetti *nmpl* spaghetti *sg*

spa'ghetto *nm* *(fam: spavento)* fright

'Spagna *nf* Spain

spa'gnolo, -a *a* Spanish ● *nmf* Spaniard ● *nm* *(lingua)* Spanish

'spago *nm* string; **dare ~ a qcno** encourage sb

spai'ato *a* odd

spalan'ca|re *vt*, **~rsi** *vr* open wide. **~to** *a* wide open

spa'lare *vt* shovel

'spall|a *nf* shoulder; *(di comico)* straight man; *(di letto)* **~e** *pl* *(schiena)* back; **alle ~e di qcno** *⟨ridere⟩* behind sb's back. **~eggi'are** *vt* back up

spal'letta *nf* parapet

spalli'era *nf* back; *(di letto)* headboard; *(ginnastica)* wall bars *pl*

spal'lina *nf* strap; *(imbottitura)* shoulder pad

spal'mare *vt* spread

'spander|e *vt* spread; *(versare)* spill. **~si** *vr* spread

spappo'lare *vt* crush

spa'ra|re *vt/i* shoot; **~rle grosse** talk big. **~ta** *nf* *fam* tall story. **~'toria** *nf* shooting

sparecchi'are *vt* clear

spa'reggio *nm* *Comm* deficit; *Sport* play-off

'sparg|ere *vt* scatter; *(diffondere)* spread; shed *⟨lacrime, sangue⟩*. **~ersi** *vr* spread. **~i'mento** *nm* scattering; *(di lacrime, sangue)* shedding; **~imento di sangue** bloodshed

spa'ri|re *vi* disappear; **~sci!** get lost!. **~zi'one** *nf* disappearance

spar'lare *vi* **~ di** run down

'sparo *nm* shot

sparpagli'ar|e *vt*, **~si** *vr* scatter

'sparso *pp* di **spargere** ● *a* scattered; *(sciolto)* loose

spar'tire *vt* share out; *(separare)* separate

sparti'traffico *nm inv* traffic island; *(di autostrada)* central reservation, median strip *Am*

spartizi'one *nf* division

spa'ruto *a* gaunt; *⟨gruppo⟩* small; *⟨peli, capelli⟩* sparse

sparvi'ero *nm* sparrow-hawk

spasi'ma|nte *nm hum* admirer. **~re** *vi* suffer agonies

'spasimo *nm* spasm

spa'smodico *a* spasmodic

spas'sar|si *vr* amuse oneself; **~sela** have a good time

spassio'nato *a* *⟨osservatore⟩* dispassionate, impartial

'spasso *nm* fun; **essere uno ~** be hilarious; **andare a ~** go for a walk. **spas'soso** *a* hilarious

'spatola *nf* spatula

spau'racchio *nm* scarecrow; *fig* bugbear. **spau'rire** *vt* frighten

spa'valdo *a* defiant

spaventa'passeri *nm inv* scarecrow

spaven'tar|e *vt* frighten, scare. **~si** *vr* be frightened, be scared. **spa'vento** *nm* fright. **spaven'toso** *a* frightening; *(fam: enorme)* incredible

spazi'ale *a* spatial; *(cosmico)* space *attrib*

spazi'are *vt* space out ● *vi* range

spazien'tirsi *vr* lose [one's] patience

'spazio *nm* space. **~'oso** *a* spacious

spazzaca'mino *nm* chimney sweep

spaz'z|are *vt* sweep; **~are via** sweep away; *(fam: mangiare)* devour. **~a'tura** *nf* *(immondizia)* rubbish. **~ino** *nm* road sweeper; *(netturbino)* dustman

'spazzo|la *nf* brush; *(di tergicristallo)* blade. **~'lare** *vt* brush. **~'lino** *nm* small brush. **~lino da denti** toothbrush. **~'lone** *nm* scrubbing brush

specchi'arsi *vr* look at oneself in a/ the mirror; *(riflettersi)* be mirrored; **~ in qcno** model oneself on sb

specchi'etto nm ~ retrovisore driving mirror, rearview mirror

'specchio nm mirror

speci'a|le a special ● nm TV special [programme]. ~**lista** nmf specialist. ~**lità** nf inv speciality, specialty Am

speci'aliz'za|re vt, ~**rsi** vr specialize. ~**to** a (di operaio) skilled

special'mente adv especially

'specie nf inv (scientifico) species; (tipo) kind; **fare ~ a** surprise

specifi'care vt specify. **spe'cifico** a specific

specu'lare[1] vi speculate; ~ **su** (indagare) speculate on; Fin speculate in

specu'lare[2] a mirror attrib

specula|'tore, -'trice nmf speculator. ~**zi'one** nf speculation

spe'di|re vt send. ~**to** pp di spedire ● a quick; (parlata) fluent. ~**zi'one** nf (di lettere ecc) dispatch; Comm consignment; (scientifica) expedition

'spegner|e vt put out; turn off (gas, luce); switch off (motore); slake (sete). ~**si** vr go out; (morire) pass away

spelacchi'ato a (tappeto) threadbare; (cane) mangy

spe'lar|e vt skin (coniglio). ~**si** vr (cane:) moult

speleolo'gia nf potholing, speleology

spel'lar|e vt skin; fig fleece. ~**si** vr peel off

spe'lonca nf cave; fig dingy hole

spendacci'one, -a nmf spendthrift

'spendere vt spend; ~ **fiato** waste one's breath

spen'nare vt pluck; fam fleece (cliente)

spennel'lare vt brush

spensie|ra'tezza nf lightheartedness. ~**'rato** a carefree

'spento pp di spegnere ● a off; (gas) out; (smorto) dull

spe'ranza nf hope; **pieno di ~** hopeful; **senza ~** hopeless

spe'rare vt hope for; (aspettarsi) expect ● vi ~ **in** trust in; **spero di sì** I hope so

'sper|dersi vr get lost. ~**'duto** a lost; (isolato) secluded

spergi'uro, -a nmf perjurer ● nm perjury

sperico'lato a swashbuckling

sperimen'ta|le a experimental. ~**re** vt experiment with; test (resistenza, capacità, teoria). ~**zi'one** nf experimentation

'sperma nm sperm

spe'rone nm spur

sperpe'rare vt squander. **'sperpero** nm waste

'spes|a nf expense; (acquisto) purchase; **andare a far ~e** go shopping; **fare la ~a** do the shopping; **fare le ~e di** pay for. ~**e** pl **bancarie** bank charges. ~**e a carico del destinatario** carriage forward. ~**e di spedizione** shipping costs. **spe'sato** a all-expenses-paid. ~**o** pp di **spendere**

'spesso[1] a thick

'spesso[2] adv often

spes'sore nm thickness; (fig: consistenza) substance

spet'tabile a (Comm abbr **Spett.**) **S~ ditta Rossi** Messrs Rossi

spettaco'lare a spectacular. **spet'tacolo** nm spectacle; (rappresentazione) show. ~**loso** a spectacular

spet'tare vi ~ **a** be up to; (diritto:) be due to

spetta'tore, -'trice nmf spectator; **spettatori** pl (di cinema ecc) audience sg

spettego'lare vi gossip

spetti'nar|e vt ~**e** qcno ruffle sb's hair. ~**si** vr ruffle one's hair

spet'trale a ghostly. **'spettro** nm ghost; Phys spectrum

'spezie nfpl spices

spez'zar|e vt, ~**si** vr break

spezza'tino nm stew

spez'zato nm coordinated jacket and trousers

spezzet'tare vt break into small pieces

'spia nf spy; (della polizia) informer; (di porta) peep-hole; **fare la ~** sneak. ~ **[luminosa]** light. ~ **dell'olio** oil [warning] light

spiacci'care vt squash

spia'ce|nte a sorry. ~**vole** a unpleasant

spi'aggia nf beach

spia'nare vt level; (rendere liscio) smooth; roll out (pasta); raze to the ground (edificio)

spi'ano nm **a tutto ~** flat out

splan'tato a fig penniless

spi'are vt spy on; wait for (occasione ecc)

spiattel'lare vt blurt out; shove (oggetto)

spiaz'zare vt wrong-foot

spi'azzo nm (radura) clearing

spic'ca|re vt ~**re un salto** jump; ~**re il volo** take flight ● vi stand out. ~**to** a marked

'spicchio *nm* ⟨*di agrumi*⟩ segment; ⟨*di aglio*⟩ clove

spicci'a|rsi *vr* hurry up. ~'tivo *a* speedy

'spicciolo *a* ⟨*comune*⟩ banal; ⟨*denaro, 10 000 lire*⟩ in change. **spiccioli** *pl* change *sg*

'spicco *nm* relief; **fare ~** stand out

'spider *nmf inv* open-top sports car

spie'dino *nm* kebab. **spi'edo** *nm* spit; **allo spiedo** on a spit, spit-roasted

spie'ga|re *vt* explain; open out ⟨*cartina*⟩; unfurl ⟨*vele*⟩. ~rsi *vr* explain oneself; ⟨*vele, bandiere:*⟩ unfurl. ~zi'one *nf* explanation

spiegaz'zato *a* crumpled

spie'tato *a* ruthless

spiffe'rare *vt* blurt out ● *vi* ⟨*vento:*⟩ whistle. 'spiffero *nm* ⟨*corrente d'aria*⟩ draught

'spiga *nf* spike; *Bot* ear

spigli'ato *a* self-possessed

'spigolo *nm* edge; ⟨*angolo*⟩ corner

'spilla *nf* ⟨*gioiello*⟩ brooch. **~ da balia** safety pin. **~ di sicurezza** safety pin

spil'lare *vt* tap

'spillo *nm* pin. **~ di sicurezza** safety pin; ⟨*in arma*⟩ safety catch

spi'lorcio *a* stingy

spilun'gone, -a *nmf* beanpole

'spina *nf* thorn; ⟨*di pesce*⟩ bone; *Electr* plug. **~ dorsale** spine

spi'naci *nmpl* spinach *sg*

spi'nale *a* spinal

spi'nato *a* ⟨*filo*⟩ barbed; ⟨*pianta*⟩ thorny

spi'nello *nm fam* joint

'spinger|e *vt* push; *fig* drive. ~si *vr* ⟨*andare*⟩ proceed

spi'noso *a* thorny

'spint|a *nf* push; ⟨*violenta*⟩ thrust; *fig* spur. ~o *pp di* spingere

spio'naggio *nm* espionage, spying

spio'vente *a* ⟨*tetto*⟩ sloping

spi'overe *vi liter* stop raining; ⟨*ricadere*⟩ fall; ⟨*scorrere*⟩ flow down

'spira *nf* coil

spi'raglio *nm* small opening; ⟨*soffio d'aria*⟩ breath of air; ⟨*raggio di luce*⟩ gleam of light

spi'rale *a* spiral ● *nf* spiral; ⟨*negli orologi*⟩ hairspring; ⟨*anticoncezionale*⟩ coil

spi'rare *vi* ⟨*soffiare*⟩ blow; ⟨*morire*⟩ pass away

spiri't|ato *a* possessed; ⟨*espressione*⟩ wild. ~ismo *nm* spiritualism. 'spirito *nm* spirit; ⟨*arguzia*⟩ wit; ⟨*intelletto*⟩

mind; **fare dello spirito** be witty; **sotto spirito** ≈ in brandy. ~o'saggine *nf* witticism. spiri'toso *a* witty

spiritu'ale *a* spiritual

splen'dente *a* shining

'splen|dere *vi* shine. ~dido *a* splendid. ~'dore *nm* splendour

spode'stare *vt* dispossess; depose ⟨*re*⟩

'spoglia *nf* ⟨*di animale*⟩ skin; **spoglie** *pl* ⟨*salma*⟩ mortal remains; ⟨*bottino*⟩ spoils

spogli'a|re *vt* strip; ⟨*svestire*⟩ undress; ⟨*fare lo spoglio di*⟩ go through. ~'rello *nm* strip-tease. ~rsi *vr* strip, undress. ~'toio *nm* dressing room; *Sport* changing room; ⟨*guardaroba*⟩ cloakroom, checkroom *Am*. 'spoglio *a* undressed; ⟨*albero, muro*⟩ bare ● *nm* ⟨*scrutinio*⟩ perusal

'spola *nf* shuttle; **fare la ~** shuttle

spol'pare *vt* take the flesh off; *fig* fleece

spolve'rare *vt* dust; *fam* devour ⟨*cibo*⟩

'sponda *nf* ⟨*di mare, lago*⟩ shore; ⟨*di fiume*⟩ bank; ⟨*bordo*⟩ edge

sponsoriz'zare *vt* sponsor

spon'taneo *a* spontaneous

spopo'lar|e *vt* depopulate ● *vi* ⟨*avere successo*⟩ draw the crowds. ~si *vr* become depopulated

sporadica'mente *adv* sporadically. spo'radico *a* sporadic

sporcacci'one, -a *nmf* dirty pig

spor'o|are *vt* dirty; ⟨*macchiare*⟩ soil. ~arsi *vr* get dirty. ~izia *nf* dirt. 'sporco *a* dirty; **avere la coscienza sporca** have a guilty conscience ● *nm* dirt

spor'gen|te *a* jutting. ~za *nf* projection

'sporger|e *vt* stretch out; ~e querela contro take legal action against ● *vi* jut out. ~si *vr* lean out

'sport *nm inv* sport

'sporta *nf* shopping basket

spor'tello *nm* door; ⟨*di banca ecc*⟩ window. **~ automatico** cash dispenser

spor'tivo, -a *a* sports *attrib*; ⟨*persona*⟩ sporty ● *nm* sportsman ● *nf* sportswoman

'sporto *pp di* sporgere

'sposa *nf* bride. ~'lizio *nm* wedding

spo'sa|re *vt* marry; *fig* espouse. ~rsi *vr* get married; ⟨*vino:*⟩ go ⟨**con** with⟩. ~to *a* married. 'sposo *nm* bridegroom; **sposi** *pl* ⟨**novelli**⟩ newlyweds

spossa'tezza *nf* exhaustion. spos'sato *a* exhausted, worn out

spo'sta|re *vt* move; ⟨*differire*⟩ postpone; (*cambiare*) change. **~rsi** *vr* move. **~to, -a** *a* ill-adjusted ● *nmf* (*disadattato*) misfit

'spranga *nf* bar. **spran'gare** *vt* bar

'sprazzo *nm* (*di colore*) splash; (*di luce*) flash; *fig* glimmer

spre'care *vt* waste. **'spreco** *nm* waste

spre'g|evole *a* despicable. **~ia'tivo** *a* pejorative. **'spregio** *nm* contempt

spregiudi'cato *a* unscrupulous

'sprem|ere *vt* squeeze. **~si** *vr* **~si le meningi** rack one's brains

spremia'grumi *nm* lemon squeezer

spre'muta *nf* juice. **~ d'arancia** fresh orange [juice]

sprez'zante *a* contemptuous

sprigio'nar|e *vt* emit. **~si** *vr* burst out

spriz'zare *vt/i* spurt; be bursting with ⟨*salute, gioia*⟩

sprofon'dar|e *vi* sink; (*crollare*) collapse. **~si** *vr* **~si in** sink into; *fig* be engrossed in

spro'nare *vt* spur on. **'sprone** *nm* spur; (*sartoria*) yoke

sproporzi|o'nato *a* disproportionate. **~'one** *nf* disproportion

spropo'sitato *a* full of blunders; (*enorme*) huge. **spro'posito** *nm* blunder; (*eccesso*) excessive amount; **a sproposito** inopportunely

sprovve'duto *a* unprepared; **~ di** lacking in

sprov'visto *a* **~ di** out of; lacking in ⟨*fantasia, pazienza*⟩; **alla sprovvista** unexpectedly

spruz'za|re *vt* sprinkle; (*vaporizzare*) spray; (*inzaccherare*) spatter. **~'tore** *nm* spray; **'spruzzo** *nm* spray; (*di fango*) splash

spudo|ra'tezza *nf* shamelessness. **~'rato** *a* shameless

'spugna *nf* sponge; (*tessuto*) towelling. **spu'gnoso** *a* spongy

'spuma *nf* foam; (*schiuma*) froth; *Culin* mousse. **spu'mante** *nm* sparkling wine, spumante. **spumeggi'are** *vi* foam

spun'ta|re *vt* (*rompere la punta di*) break the point of; trim ⟨*capelli*⟩; **~rla** *fig* win ● ⟨*pianta:*⟩ sprout; ⟨*capelli:*⟩ begin to grow; (*sorgere*) rise; (*apparire*) appear. **~rsi** *vr* get blunt. **~ta** *nf* trim

spun'tino *nm* snack

'spunto *nm* cue; *fig* starting point; **dare ~ a** give rise to

spur'gar|e *vt* purge. **~si** *vr* *Med* expectorate

spu'tare *vt/i* spit; **~ sentenze** pass judgment. **'sputo** *nm* spit

'squadra *nf* (*gruppo*) team, squad; (*di polizia ecc*) squad; (*da disegno*) square. **squa'drare** *vt* square; (*guardare*) look up and down

squa'dr|iglia *nf*, **~one** *nm* squadron

squagli'ar|e *vt*, **~si** *vr* melt; **~sela** (*fam: svignarsela*) steal out

squa'lifi|ca *nf* disqualification. **~'care** *vt* disqualify

'squallido *a* squalid. **squal'lore** *nm* squalor

'squalo *nm* shark

'squama *nf* scale; (*di pelle*) flake

squa'm|are *vt* scale. **~arsi** *vr* ⟨*pelle:*⟩ flake off. **~'moso** *a* scaly; ⟨*pelle*⟩ flaky

squarcia'gola: a ~ *adv* at the top of one's voice

squarci'are *vt* rip. **'squarcio** *nm* rip; (*di ferita, in nave*) gash; (*di cielo*) patch

squar'tare *vt* quarter; dismember ⟨*animale*⟩

squattri'nato *a* penniless

squilib'ra|re *vt* unbalance. **~to, -a** *a* unbalanced ● *nmf* lunatic. **squi'librio** *nm* imbalance

squil'la|nte *a* shrill. **~re** *vi* ⟨*campana:*⟩ peal; ⟨*tromba:*⟩ blare; ⟨*telefono:*⟩ ring. **'squillo** *nm* blare; *Teleph* ring; (*ragazza*) call girl

squi'sito *a* exquisite

squit'tire *vi* ⟨*pappagallo, fig:*⟩ squawk; ⟨*topo:*⟩ squeak

sradi'care *vt* uproot; eradicate ⟨*vizio, male*⟩

sragio'nare *vi* rave

srego|la'tezza *nf* dissipation. **~'lato** *a* inordinate; (*dissoluto*) dissolute

s.r.l. *abbr* (**società a responsabilità limitata**) Ltd

sroto'lare *vt* uncoil

SS *abbr* (**strada statale**) national road

'stabile *a* stable; (*permanente*) lasting; ⟨*saldo*⟩ steady; **compagnia ~** *Theat* repertory company ● *nm* (*edificio*) building

stabili'mento *nm* factory; (*industriale*) plant; (*edificio*) establishment. **~ balneare** lido

stabi'li|re *vt* establish; (*decidere*) decide. **~rsi** *vr* settle. **~tà** *nf* stability

stabiliz'za|re *vt* stabilize. **~rsi** *vr* stabilize. **~'tore** *nm* stabilizer

stac'car|e *vt* detach; pronounce clearly ⟨*parole*⟩; (*separare*) separate; turn off ⟨*corrente*⟩; **~e gli occhi da** take one's eyes off ● *vi* (*fam: finire di lavorare*) knock off. **~si** *vr* come off;

~si da break away from ⟨*partito, famiglia*⟩
staccio'nata *nf* fence
'stacco *nm* gap
'stadio *nm* stadium
'staffa *nf* stirrup
staf'fetta *nf* dispatch rider
stagio'nale *a* seasonal
stagio'na|re *vt* season ⟨*legno*⟩; mature ⟨*formaggio*⟩. **~to** *a* ⟨*legno*⟩ seasoned; ⟨*formaggio*⟩ matured
stagi'one *nf* season; **alta/bassa ~** high/low season
stagli'arsi *vr* stand out
sta'gna|nte *a* stagnant. **~re** *vt* ⟨*saldare*⟩ solder; ⟨*chiudere ermeticamente*⟩ seal ● *vi* ⟨*acqua:*⟩ stagnate. **'stagno** *a* ⟨*a tenuta d'acqua*⟩ watertight ● *nm* ⟨*acqua ferma*⟩ pond; ⟨*metallo*⟩ tin
sta'gnola *nf* tinfoil
stalag'mite *nf* stalagmite
stalat'tite *nf* stalactite
'stal|la *nf* stable; ⟨*per buoi*⟩ cowshed. **~i'ere** *nm* groom
stal'lone *nm* stallion
sta'mani, stamat'tina *adv* this morning
stam'becco *nm* ibex
stam'berga *nf* hovel
'stampa *nf* *Typ* printing; ⟨*giornali, giornalisti*⟩ press; ⟨*riproduzione*⟩ print
stam'pa|nte *nf* printer. **~nte ad aghi** dot matrix printer. **~nte laser** laser printer. **~re** *vt* print. **~'tello** *nm* block letters *pl*
stam'pella *nf* crutch
'stampo *nm* mould; **di vecchio ~** ⟨*persona*⟩ of the old school
sta'nare *vt* drive out
stan'car|e *vt* tire; ⟨*annoiare*⟩ bore. **~si** *vr* get tired
stan'chezza *nf* tiredness. **'stanco** *a* tired; **stanco di** ⟨*stufo*⟩ fed up with. **stanco morto** dead tired, knackered *fam*
'standard *a & nm* *inv* standard. **~iz'zare** *vt* standardize
'stan|ga *nf* bar; ⟨*persona*⟩ beanpole. **~'gata** *nf fig* blow; ⟨*fam: nel calcio*⟩ big kick; **prendere una ~gata** ⟨*fam: agli esami, economica*⟩ come a cropper. **stan'ghetta** *nf* ⟨*di occhiali*⟩ leg
sta'notte *nf* tonight; ⟨*la notte scorsa*⟩ last night
'stante *prep* on account of; **a sé ~** separate
stan'tio *a* stale
stan'tuffo *nm* piston

'stanza *nf* room; ⟨*metrica*⟩ stanza
stanzi'are *vt* allocate
stap'pare *vt* uncork
'stare *vi* ⟨*rimanere*⟩ stay; ⟨*abitare*⟩ live; ⟨*con gerundio*⟩ be; **sto solo cinque minuti** I'll stay only five minutes; **sto in piazza Peyron** I live in Peyron Square; **sta dormendo** he's sleeping; **~ a** ⟨*attenersi*⟩ keep to; ⟨*spettare*⟩ be up to; **~ bene** ⟨*economicamente*⟩ be well off; ⟨*di salute*⟩ be well; ⟨*addirsi*⟩ suit; **~ dietro a** ⟨*seguire*⟩ follow; ⟨*sorvegliare*⟩ keep an eye on; ⟨*corteggiare*⟩ run after; **~ in piedi** stand; **~ per** be about to; **ben ti sta!** it serves you right!; **come stai/ sta?** how are you?; **lasciar ~** leave alone; **starci** ⟨*essere contenuto*⟩ go into; ⟨*essere d'accordo*⟩ agree; **il 3 nel 12 ci sta 4 volte** 3 into 12 goes 4; **no sa ~ agli scherzi** he can't take a joke; **~ su** ⟨*con la schiena*⟩ sit up straight; **~ sulle proprie** keep oneself to oneself. **starsene** *vr* ⟨*rimanere*⟩ stay
starnu'tire *vi* sneeze. **star'nuto** *nm* sneeze
sta'sera *adv* this evening, tonight
sta'tale *a* state *attrib* ● *nmf* state employee ● *nf* ⟨*strada*⟩ main road, trunk road
'statico *a* static
sta'tista *nm* statesman
sta'tistic|a *nf* statistics *sg*. **~o** *a* statistical
'stato *pp di* essere, stare ● *nm* state; ⟨*posizione sociale*⟩ position; *Jur* status. **~ d'animo** frame of mind. **~ civile** marital status. **S~ Maggiore** *Mil* General Staff. **Stati** *pl* **Uniti** [**d'America**] United States [of America]
'statua *nf* statue
statuni'tense *a* United States *attrib*, US *attrib* ● *nmf* citizen of the United States, US citizen
sta'tura *nf* height; **di alta ~** tall; **di bassa ~** short
sta'tuto *nm* statute
stazio'nario *a* stationary
stazi'one *nf* station; ⟨*città*⟩ resort. **~ balneare** seaside resort. **~ ferroviaria** railway station *Br*, train station. **~ di servizio** petrol station *Br*, service station. **~ termale** spa
'stecca *nf* stick; ⟨*di ombrello*⟩ rib; ⟨*da biliardo*⟩ cue; *Med* splint; ⟨*di sigarette*⟩ carton; ⟨*di reggiseno*⟩ stiffener
stec'cato *nm* fence
stec'chito *a* skinny; ⟨*rigido*⟩ stiff; ⟨*morto*⟩ stone cold dead

'**stella** *nf* star; **salire alle stelle** ⟨*prezzi:*⟩ rise skyhigh. ~ **alpina** edelweiss. ~ **cadente** shooting star. ~ **filante** streamer. ~ **di mare** starfish

stel'la|re *a* star *attrib*; ⟨*grandezza*⟩ stellar. ~**to** *a* starry

'**stelo** *nm* stem; **lampada** *nf* a ~ standard lamp

'**stemma** *nm* coat of arms

stempi'ato *a* bald at the temples

sten'dardo *nm* standard

'**stender|e** *vt* spread out; ⟨*appendere*⟩ hang out; ⟨*distendere*⟩ stretch [out]; ⟨*scrivere*⟩ write down. ~**si** *vr* stretch out

stendibianche'ria *nm* *inv*, **stendi'toio** *nm* clothes horse

stenodatti|logra'fia *nf* shorthand typing. ~'**lografo, -a** *nmf* shorthand typist

stenogra'f|are *vt* take down in shorthand. ~**ia** *nf* shorthand

sten'ta|re *vi* ~**re a** find it hard to. ~**to** *a* laboured. '**stento** *nm* ⟨*fatica*⟩ effort; **a stento** with difficulty; **stenti** *pl* hardships, privations

'**sterco** *nm* dung

'**stereo**['**fonico**] *a* stereo[phonic]

stereoti'pato *a* stereotyped; ⟨*sorriso*⟩ insincere. **stere'otipo** *nm* stereotype

'**steril|e** *a* sterile; ⟨*terreno*⟩ barren. ~**ità** *nf* sterility. ~**iz'zare** *vt* sterilize. ~**izzazi'one** *nf* sterilization

ster'lina *nf* pound; **lira** ~ [pound] sterling

stermi'nare *vt* exterminate

stermi'nato *a* immense

ster'minio *nm* extermination

'**sterno** *nm* breastbone

ster'zare *vi* steer. '**sterzo** *nm* steering

'**steso** *pp di* **stendere**

'**stesso** *a* same; **io** ~ myself; **tu** ~ yourself; **me** ~ myself; **se** ~ himself; **in quel momento** ~ at that very moment; **dalla stessa regina** ⟨*in persona*⟩ by the Queen herself; **tuo fratello** ~ **dice che hai torto** even your brother says you're wrong; **coi miei stessi occhi** with my own eyes ● *pron* **lo** ~ the same one; ⟨*la stessa cosa*⟩ the same; **fa lo** ~ it's all the same; **ci vado lo** ~ I'll go just the same

ste'sura *nf* drawing up; ⟨*documento*⟩ draft

stick *nm* **colla a** ~ glue stick; **deodorante a** ~ stick deodorant

'**stigma** *nm* stigma. ~**te** *nfpl* stigmata

sti'lare *vt* draw up

'**stil|e** *nm* style. ~**e libero** ⟨*nel nuoto*⟩ freestyle, crawl. **sti'lista** *nmf* stylist. ~**iz'zato** *a* stylized

stil'lare *vi* ooze

stilo'grafic|a *nf* fountain pen. ~**o** *a* **penna** ~**a** fountain pen

'**stima** *nf* esteem; ⟨*valutazione*⟩ estimate. **sti'mare** *vt* esteem; ⟨*valutare*⟩ estimate; ⟨*ritenere*⟩ consider

stimo'la|nte *a* stimulating ● *nm* stimulant. ~**re** *vt* stimulate; ⟨*incitare*⟩ incite

'**stimolo** *nm* stimulus; ⟨*fitta*⟩ pang

'**stinco** *nm* shin

'**stinger|e** *vt/i* fade. ~**si** *vr* fade. '**stinto** *pp di* **stingere**

sti'par|e *vt* cram. ~**si** *vr* crowd together

stipendi'ato *a* salaried ● *nm* salaried worker. **sti'pendio** *nm* salary

sti'pite *nm* doorpost

stipu'la|re *vt* stipulate. ~**zi'one** *nf* stipulation; ⟨*accordo*⟩ agreement

stira'mento *nm* sprain

sti'ra|re *vt* iron; ⟨*distendere*⟩ stretch. ~**rsi** *vr* ⟨*distendersi*⟩ stretch; pull ⟨*muscolo*⟩. ~'**tura** *nf* ironing. '**stiro** *nm* **ferro da stiro** iron

'**stirpe** *nf* stock

stiti'chezza *nf* constipation. '**stitico** *a* constipated

'**stiva** *nf* *Naut* hold

sti'vale *nm* boot. **stivali** *pl* **di gomma** Wellington boots, Wellingtons

'**stizza** *nf* anger

stiz'zi|re *vt* irritate. ~**rsi** *vr* become irritated. ~**to** *a* irritated. **stiz'zoso** *a* peevish

stocca'fisso *nm* stockfish

stoc'cata *nf* stab; ⟨*battuta pungente*⟩ gibe

'**stoffa** *nf* material; *fig* stuff

'**stola** *nf* stole

'**stolto** *a* foolish

stoma'chevole *a* revolting

'**stomaco** *nm* stomach; **mal di** ~ stomach-ache

sto'na|re *vt/i* sing/play out of tune ● *vi* ⟨*non intonarsi*⟩ clash. ~**to** *a* out of tune; ⟨*discordante*⟩ clashing; ⟨*confuso*⟩ bewildered. ~'**tura** *nf* false note; ⟨*discordanza*⟩ clash

'**stoppia** *nf* stubble

stop'pino *nm* wick

stop'poso *a* tough

'**storcer|e** *vt*, ~**si** *vr* twist

stor'di|re *vt* stun; ⟨*intontire*⟩ daze. ~**rsi** *vr* dull one's senses. ~**to** *a* stunned; ⟨*intontito*⟩ dazed; ⟨*sventato*⟩ heedless

'**storia** *nf* history; (*racconto, bugia*) story; (*pretesto*) excuse; **senza storie!** no fuss!; **fare [delle] storie** make a fuss

'**storico, -a** *a* historical; (*di importanza storica*) historic ● *nmf* historian

stori'one *nm* sturgeon

'**stormo** *nm* flock

'**storno** *nm* starling

storpi'a|re *vt* cripple; mangle (*parole*). **~'tura** *nf* deformation. '**storpio, -a** *a* crippled ● *nmf* cripple

'**stort|a** *nf* (*distorsione*) sprain; **prendere una ~a alla caviglia** sprain one's ankle. **~o** *pp di* **storcere** ● *a* crooked; (*ritorto*) twisted; (*gambe*) bandy; *fig* wrong

sto'viglie *nfpl* crockery *sg*

'**strabico** *a* cross-eyed; **essere ~** be cross-eyed, have a squint

strabili'ante *a* astonishing

stra'bismo *nm* squint

straboc'care *vi* overflow

stra'carico *a* overloaded

stracci|'are *vt* tear; (*fam: vincere*) thrash. **~'ato** *a* torn; (*persona*) in rags; (*prezzi*) slashed; **a un prezzo ~ato** dirt cheap. '**straccio** *a* torn ● *nm* rag; (*strofinaccio*) cloth **~'one** *nm* tramp

stra'cotto *a* overdone; (*fam: innamorato*) head over heels ● *nm* stew

'**strada** *nf* road; (*di città*) street; (*fig: cammino*) way; **essere fuori ~** be on the wrong track; **fare ~** lead the way; **farsi ~** make one's way. **~ maestra** main road. **~ a senso unico** one-way street. **~ senza uscita** blind alley. **stra'dale** *a* road *attrib*

strafalci'one *nm* blunder

stra'fare *vi* overdo it, overdo things

stra'foro: di ~ *adv* on the sly

strafot'ten|te *a* arrogant. **~za** *nf* arrogance

'**strage** *nf* slaughter

'**stralcio** *nm* (*parte*) extract

stralu'na|re *vt* **~re gli occhi** open one's eyes wide. **~to** *a* (*occhi*) staring; (*persona*) distraught

stramaz'zare *vi* fall heavily

strambe'ria *nf* oddity. '**strambo** *a* strange

strampa'lato *a* odd

stra'nezza *nf* strangeness

strango'lare *vt* strangle

strani'ero, -a *a* foreign ● *nmf* foreigner

'**strano** *a* strange

straordi|naria'mente *adv* extraordinarily. **~'nario** *a* extraordinary; (*notevole*) remarkable; (*edizione*) special; **lavoro ~nario** overtime; **treno ~nario** special train

strapaz'zar|e *vt* ill-treat; scramble (*uova*). **~si** *vr* tire oneself out. **stra'pazzo** *nm* strain; **da strapazzo** *fig* worthless

strapi'eno *a* overflowing

strapi'ombo *nm* projection; **a ~** sheer

strap'par|e *vt* tear; (*per distruggere*) tear up; pull out (*dente, capelli*); (*sradicare*) pull up; (*estorcere*) wring. **~si** *vr* get torn; (*allontanarsi*) tear oneself away. '**strappo** *nm* tear; (*strattone*) jerk; (*fam: passaggio*) lift; **fare uno strappo alla regola** make an exception to the rule. **~ muscolare** muscle strain

strapun'tino *nm* folding seat

strari'pare *vi* flood

strasci'c|are *vt* trail; shuffle (*piedi*); drawl (*parole*). '**strascico** *nm* train; *fig* after-effect

'**strass** *nm inv* rhinestone

strata'gemma *nm* stratagem

strate'gia *nf* strategy. **stra'tegico** *a* strategic

'**strato** *nm* layer; (*di vernice ecc*) coat, layer; (*roccioso, sociale*) stratum. **~'sfera** *nf* stratosphere. **~'sferico** *a* stratospheric; *fig* sky-high

stravac'ca|rsi *vr fam* slouch. **~to** *a fam* slouching

strava'gan|te *a* extravagant; (*eccentrico*) eccentric. **~za** *nf* extravagance; (*eccentricità*) eccentricity

stra'vecchio *a* ancient

strave'dere *vt* **~ per** worship

stravizi'are *vi* indulge oneself. **stra'vizio** *nm* excess

stra'volg|ere *vt* twist; (*turbare*) upset. **~i'mento** *nm* twisting. **stra'volto** *a* distraught; (*fam: stanco*) done in

strazi'a|nte *a* heartrending; (*dolore*) agonizing. **~re** *vt* grate on (*orecchie*); break (*cuore*). '**strazio** *nm* agony; **essere uno strazio** be agony; **che strazio!** *fam* it's awful!

'**strega** *nf* witch. **stre'gare** *vt* bewitch. **stre'gone** *nm* wizard

'**stregua** *nf* **alla ~ di** like

stre'ma|re *vt* exhaust. **~to** *a* exhausted

'**stremo** *nm* **ridotto allo ~** at the end of one's tether

'**strenuo** *a* strenuous

strepi|'tare *vi* make a din. '**strepito**

nm noise. ~**'toso** *a* noisy; *fig* resounding

stres'sa|nte *a* ‹*lavoro, situazione*› stressful. ~**to** *a* stressed [out]

'stretta *nf* grasp; (*dolore*) pang; **essere alle strette** be in dire straits; **mettere alle strette qcno** have sb's back up against the wall. ~ **di mano** handshake

stret'tezza *nf* narrowness; **stret'tezze** *pl* (*difficoltà finanziarie*) financial difficulties

'stret|to *pp di* **stringere ●** *a* narrow; (*serrato*) tight; (*vicino*) close; ‹*dialetto*› broad; (*rigoroso*) strict; **lo** ~**to necessario** the bare minimum **●** *nm* *Geog* strait. ~**'toia** *nf* bottleneck; (*fam: difficoltà*) tight spot

stri'a|to *a* striped. ~**'tura** *nf* streak

stri'dente *a* strident

'stridere *vi* squeak; *fig* clash. **stri'dore** *nm* screech

'stridulo *a* shrill

strigli'a|re *vt* groom. ~**ta** *nf* grooming; *fig* dressing down

stril'l|are *vi/t* scream. **'strillo** *nm* scream

strimin'zito *a* skimpy; (*magro*) skinny

strimpel'lare *vt* strum

'strin|ga *nf* lace; *Comput* string. ~**'gato** *a fig* terse

'string|ere *vt* press; (*serrare*) squeeze; (*tenere stretto*) hold tight; take in ‹*abito*›; (*comprimere*) be tight; (*restringere*) tighten; ~**e la mano a** shake hands with **●** *vi* (*premere*) press. ~**si** *vr* (*accostarsi*) draw close (**a** to); (*avvicinarsi*) squeeze up

'striscia *nf* strip; (*riga*) stripe. **strisce** *pl* [**pedonali**] zebra crossing *sg*

strisci'ar|e *vi* crawl; (*sfiorare*) graze **●** *vt* drag ‹*piedi*›. ~**si** *vr* ~**si a** rub against. **'striscio** *nm* graze; *Med* smear; **colpire di striscio** graze

strisci'one *nm* banner

strito'lare *vt* grind

striz'zare *vt* squeeze; (*torcere*) wring [out]; ~ **l'occhio** wink

'strofa *nf* strophe

strofi'naccio *nm* cloth; (*per spolverare*) duster. ~ **da cucina** tea towel

strofi'nare *vt* rub

strombaz'zare *vt* boast about **●** *vi* hoot

strombaz'zata *nf* (*di clacson*) hoot

stron'care *vt* cut off; (*reprimere*) crush; (*criticare*) tear to shreds

'stronzo *nm vulg* shit

stropicci'are *vt* rub; crumple ‹*vestito*›

stroz'za|re *vt* strangle. ~**'tura** *nf* strangling; (*di strada*) narrowing

strozzi'naggio *nm* loan-sharking

stroz'zino *nm pej* usurer; (*truffatore*) shark

strug'gente *a* all-consuming

'struggersi *vr liter* pine [away]

strumen'tale *a* instrumental

strumentaliz'zare *vt* make use of

strumentazi'one *nf* instrumentation

stru'mento *nm* instrument; (*arnese*) tool. ~ **a corda** string instrument. ~ **musicale** musical instrument

strusci'are *vt* rub

'strutto *nm* lard

strut'tura *nf* structure. **struttu'rale** *a* structural

struttu'rare *vt* structure

strutturazi'one *nf* structuring

'struzzo *nm* ostrich

stuc'ca|re *vt* stucco

stuc'chevole *a* nauseating

'stucco *nm* stucco

stu'den|te, -'essa *nmf* student; (*di scuola*) schoolboy; schoolgirl. ~**'tesco** *a* student; (*di scolaro*) school *attrib*

studi'ar|e *vt* study. ~**si** *vr* ~**si di** try to

'studi|o *nm* studying; (*stanza, ricerca*) study; (*di artista, TV ecc*) studio; (*di professionista*) office. ~**'oso, -a** *a* studious **●** *nmf* scholar

'stufa *nf* stove. ~ **elettrica** electric fire

stu'fa|re *vt* *Culin* stew; (*dare fastidio*) bore. ~**rsi** *vr* get bored. ~**to** *nm* stew

'stufo *a* bored; **essere** ~ **di** be fed up with

stu'oia *nf* mat

stupefa'cente *a* amazing **●** *nm* drug

stu'pendo *a* stupendous

stupi'd|aggine *nf* (*azione*) stupid thing; (*cosa da poco*) nothing. ~**ata** *nf* stupid thing. ~**ità** *nf* stupidity. **'stupido** *a* stupid

stu'pir|e *vt* astonish **●** *vi*, ~**si** *vr* be astonished. **stu'pore** *nm* amazement

stu'pra|re *vt* rape. ~**'tore** *nm* rapist. **'stupro** *nm* rape

sturalavan'dini *nm inv* plunger

stu'rare *vt* uncork; unblock ‹*lavandino*›

stuzzica'denti *nm inv* toothpick

stuzzi'care *vt* prod [at]; pick ‹*denti*›; poke ‹*fuoco*›; (*molestare*) tease; whet ‹*appetito*›

stuzzi'chino *nm Culin* appetizer

su *prep* on; ⟨*senza contatto*⟩ over; ⟨*riguardo a*⟩ about; ⟨*circa, intorno a*⟩ about, around; **le chiavi sono sul tavolo** the keys are on the table; **il quadro è appeso sul camino** the picture is hanging over the fireplace; **un libro sull'antico Egitto** a book on *o* about Ancient Egypt; **costa sulle 50 000 lire** it costs about 50,000 lire; **decidere sul momento** decide at the time; **su commissione** on commission; **su due piedi** on the spot; **uno su dieci** one out of ten ● *adv* ⟨*sopra*⟩ up; ⟨*al piano di sopra*⟩ upstairs; ⟨*addosso*⟩ on; **ho su il cappotto** I've got my coat on; **in su** ⟨*guardare*⟩ up; **dalla vita in su** from the waist up; **su!** come on!

su'bacqueo *a* underwater
subaffit'tare *vt* sublet. **subaf'fitto** *nm* sublet
subal'terno *a & nm* subordinate
sub'buglio *nm* turmoil
sub'conscio *a & nm* subconscious
subdola'mente *adv* deviously. **'subdolo** *a* devious, underhand
suben'trare *vi* ⟨*circostanze:*⟩ come up; **~ a** take the place of
su'bire *vt* undergo; ⟨*patire*⟩ suffer
subis'sare *vt fig* **~ di** overwhelm with
'subito *adv* at once; **~ dopo** straight after
su'blime *a* sublime
subodo'rare *vt* suspect
subordi'nato, -a *a & nmf* subordinate
subur'bano *a* suburban
suc'ceder|e *vi* ⟨*accadere*⟩ happen; **~e a** succeed; ⟨*venire dopo*⟩ follow; **~e al trono** succeed to the throne. **~si** *vr* happen one after the other
successi'one *nf* succession; **in ~** in succession
succes|siva'mente *adv* subsequently. **~'sivo** *a* successive
suc'ces|so *pp di* **succedere** ● *nm* success; ⟨*esito*⟩ outcome; ⟨*disco ecc*⟩ hit. **~'sone** *nm* huge success
succes'sore *nm* successor
succhi'are *vt* suck [up]
suc'cinto *a* ⟨*conciso*⟩ concise; ⟨*abito*⟩ scanty
'succo *nm* juice; *fig* essence; **~ di frutta** fruit juice. **suc'coso** *a* juicy
'succube *nm* **essere ~ di qcno** be totally dominated by sb
succu'lento *a* succulent
succur'sale *nf* branch [office]
sud *nm* south; **del ~** southern

su'da|re *vi* sweat, perspire; ⟨*faticare*⟩ sweat blood; **~re freddo** be in a cold sweat. **~ta** *nf anche fig* sweat. **~'ticcio** *a* sweaty. **~to** *a* sweaty; ⟨*vittoria*⟩ hard-won; ⟨*pane*⟩ hard-earned
sud'detto *a* above-mentioned
'suddito, -a *nmf* subject
suddi'vi|dere *vt* subdivide. **~si'one** *nf* subdivision
su'd-est *nm* southeast
'sudici|o *a* dirty, filthy. **~'ume** *nm* dirt, filth
sudorazi'one *nf* perspiring. **su'dore** *nm* sweat, perspiration; *fig* sweat
su'd-ovest *nm* southwest
suffici'en|te *a* sufficient; ⟨*presuntuoso*⟩ conceited ● *nm* bare essentials *pl*; *Sch* pass mark. **~za** *nf* sufficiency; ⟨*presunzione*⟩ conceit; *Sch* pass; **a ~za** enough
suf'fisso *nm* suffix
suf'fragio *nm* ⟨*voto*⟩ vote. **~ universale** universal suffrage
suggeri'mento *nm* suggestion
sugge'ri|re *vt* suggest; *Theat* prompt. **~'tore, ~'trice** *nmf Theat* prompter
suggestiona'bile *a* suggestible
suggestio'na|re *vt* influence. **~to** *a* influenced. **suggesti'one** *nf* influence
sugge'stivo *a* suggestive; ⟨*musica ecc*⟩ evocative
'sughero *nm* cork
'sugli = **su + gli**
'sugo *nm* ⟨*di frutta*⟩ juice; ⟨*di carne*⟩ gravy; ⟨*salsa*⟩ sauce; ⟨*sostanza*⟩ substance
'sul = **su + i**
sui'cid|a *a* suicidal ● *nmf* suicide. **suici'darsi** *vr* commit suicide. **~io** *nm* suicide
su'ino *a* **carne suina** pork ● *nm* swine
sul = **su + il**. **'sullo** = **su + lo**. **'sulla** = **su + la**. **'sulle** = **su + le**
sul'ta|na *nf* sultana. **~'nina** *a* **uva ~nina** sultana. **~no** *nm* sultan
'sunto *nm* summary
'suo, -a *poss a* **il ~**, **i suoi** his; ⟨*di cosa, animale*⟩ its; ⟨*forma di cortesia*⟩ your; **la sua, le sue** her; ⟨*di cosa, animale*⟩ its; ⟨*forma di cortesia*⟩ your; **questa macchina è sua** this car is his/hers; **~ padre** his/her/your father; **un ~ amico** a friend of his/hers/yours ● *poss pron* **il ~**, **i suoi** his; ⟨*di cosa, animale*⟩ its; ⟨*forma di cortesia*⟩ yours; **la sua, le sue** hers; ⟨*di cosa animale*⟩ its; ⟨*forma di cortesia*⟩ yours; **i suoi** his/her folk
su'ocera *nf* mother-in-law

su'ocero nm father-in-law

su'ola nf sole

su'olo nm ground; (terreno) soil

suo'na|re vt/i Mus play; ring ‹campanello›; sound ‹allarme, clacson›; ‹orologio:› strike. **~'tore, ~'trice** nmf player. **suone'ria** nf alarm. **su'ono** nm sound

su'ora nf nun; **Suor Maria** Sister Maria

superal'colico nm spirit ● a **bevande superalcoliche** spirits

supera'mento nm (di timidezza) overcoming; (di esame) success (**di** in)

supe'rare vt surpass; (eccedere) exceed; (vincere) overcome; overtake, pass Am ‹veicolo›; pass ‹esame›

su'perb|ia nf haughtiness. **~o** a haughty; (magnifico) superb

superdo'tato a highly gifted

superfici'al|e a superficial ● nmf superficial person. **~ità** nf superficiality. **super'ficie** nf surface; (area) area

su'perfluo a superfluous

superi'or|e a superior; (di grado) senior; (più elevato) higher; (sovrastante) upper; (al di sopra) above ● nmf superior. **~ità** nf superiority

superla'tivo a & nm superlative

supermer'cato nm supermarket

super'sonico a supersonic

su'perstite a surviving ● nmf survivor

superstizi'o|ne nf superstition. **~so** a superstitious

super'strada nf toll-free motorway

supervi|si'one nf supervision. **~'sore** nm supervisor

su'pino a supine

suppel'lettili nfpl furnishings

supper'giù adv about

supplemen'tare a additional, supplementary

supple'mento nm supplement; **~ rapido** express train supplement

sup'plen|te a temporary ● nmf Sch supply teacher. **~za** nf temporary post

'suppli|ca nf plea; (domanda) petition. **~'care** vt beg. **~'chevole** a imploring

sup'plire vt replace ● vi **~ a** (compensare) make up for

sup'plizio nm torture

sup'porre vt suppose

sup'porto nm support

supposizi'one nf supposition

sup'posta nf suppository

sup'posto pp di **supporre**

suprema'zia nf supremacy. **su'premo** a supreme

sur'fare vi **~ in Internet** surf the Net

surge'la|re vt deep-freeze. **~ti** nmpl frozen food sg. **~to** a frozen

surrea'lis|mo nm surrealism. **~ta** nmf surrealist

surriscal'dare vt overheat

surro'gato nm substitute

suscet'tibil|e a touchy. **~ità** nf touchiness

susci'tare vt stir up; arouse ‹ammirazione ecc›

su'sin|a nf plum. **~o** nm plumtree

su'spense nf suspense

sussegu|'ente a subsequent. **~'irsi** vr follow one after the other

sussidi'ar|e vt subsidize. **~io** a subsidiary. **sus'sidio** nm subsidy; (aiuto) aid. **sussidio di disoccupazione** unemployment benefit

sussi'ego nm haughtiness

sussi'stenza nf subsistence. **sus'sistere** vi subsist; (essere valido) hold good

sussul'tare vi start. **sus'sulto** nm start

sussur'rare vt whisper. **sus'surro** nm whisper

su'tu|ra nf suture. **~'rare** vt suture

sva'gar|e vt amuse. **~si** vr amuse oneself. **'svago** nm relaxation; (divertimento) amusement

svaligi'are vt rob; burgle ‹casa›

svalu'ta|re vt devalue; fig underestimate. **~rsi** vr lose value. **~zi'one** nf devaluation

svam'pito a absent-minded

sva'nire vi vanish

svantaggi|'ato a at a disadvantage; ‹bambino, paese› disadvantaged. **svan'taggio** nm disadvantage; **essere in svantaggio** Sport be losing; **in svantaggio di tre punti** three points down; **~'oso** a disadvantageous

svapo'rare vi evaporate

svari'ato a varied

sva'sato a flared

'svastica nf swastika

sve'dese a & nm (lingua) Swedish ● nmf Swede

'sveglia nf (orologio) alarm [clock]; **~!** get up!; **mettere la ~** set the alarm [clock]

svegli'ar|e vt wake up; fig awaken. **~si** vr wake up. **'sveglio** a awake; (di mente) quick-witted

sve'lare vt reveal

svel'tezza nf speed; fig quick-wittedness

svel'tir|e vt quicken. **~si** vr ⟨persona:⟩ liven up. **'svelto** a quick; ⟨slanciato⟩ svelte; **alla svelta** quickly

'svend|ere vt undersell. **~ita** nf [clearance] sale

sveni'mento nm fainting fit. **sve'nire** vi faint

sven'ta|re vt foil. **~to** a thoughtless ● nmf thoughtless person

'sventola nf slap; **orecchie** nfpl **a ~** protruding ears

svento'lare vt/i wave

sven'trare vt disembowel; fig demolish ⟨edificio⟩

sven'tura nf misfortune. **sventu'rato** a unfortunate

sve'nuto pp di **svenire**

svergo'gnato a shameless

sver'nare vi winter

sve'stir|e vt undress. **~si** vr undress, get undressed

'Svezia nf Sweden

svezza'mento nm weaning. **svez'zare** vt wean

svi'ar|e vt divert; ⟨corrompere⟩ lead astray. **~si** vr fig go astray

svico'lare vi turn down a side street; ⟨fig: dalla questione ecc⟩ evade the issue; ⟨fig: da una persona⟩ dodge out of the way

svi'gnarsela vr slip away

svi'lire vt debase

svilup'par|e vt, **~si** vr develop. **svi'luppo** nm development; **paese in via di sviluppo** developing country

svinco'lar|e vt release; clear ⟨merce⟩. **~si** vr free oneself. **'svincolo** nm clearance; ⟨di autostrada⟩ exit

svisce'ra|re vt gut; fig dissect. **~to** a ⟨amore⟩ passionate; ⟨ossequioso⟩ obsequious

'svista nf oversight

svi'ta|re vt unscrew. **~to** a ⟨fam: matto⟩ cracked, nutty

'Svizzer|a nf Switzerland. **s~o, -a** a & nmf Swiss

svogli|a'tezza nf half-heartedness. **~'ato** a lazy

svolaz'za|nte a ⟨capelli⟩ wind-swept. **~re** vi flutter

'svolger|e vt unwind; unwrap ⟨pacco⟩; ⟨risolvere⟩ solve; ⟨portare a termine⟩ carry out; ⟨sviluppare⟩ develop. **~si** vr ⟨accadere⟩ take place. **svolgi'mento** nm course; ⟨sviluppo⟩ development

'svolta nf turning; fig turning-point. **svol'tare** vi turn

'svolto pp di **svolgere**

svuo'tare vt empty [out]

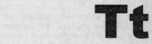

Tt

tabac'c|aio, -a nmf tobacconist. **~he'ria** nf tobacconist's (which also sells stamps, postcards etc). **ta'bacco** nm tobacco

ta'bel|la nf table; ⟨lista⟩ list. **~la dei prezzi** price list. **~'lina** nf Math multiplication table. **~'lone** nm wall chart. **~lone del canestro** backboard

taber'nacolo nm tabernacle

tabù a & nm inv taboo

tabu'lato nm Comput [data] printout

'tacca nf notch; **di mezza ~** ⟨attore, giornalista⟩ second-rate

tac'cagno a fam stingy

tac'cheggio nm shoplifting

tac'chetto nm Sport stud

tac'chino nm turkey

tacci'are vt **~ qcno di qcsa** accuse sb of sth

'tacco nm heel; **alzare i tacchi** take to one's heels; **scarpe senza ~** flat shoes. **tacchi** pl **a spillo** stiletto heels

tac'cuino nm notebook

ta'cere vi be silent ● vt say nothing about; **mettere a ~** qcsa ⟨scandalo⟩ hush sth up; **mettere a ~** qcno silence sb

ta'chimetro nm speedometer

'tacito a silent; ⟨inespresso⟩ tacit. **taci'turno** a taciturn

ta'fano nm horsefly

taffe'ruglio nm scuffle

'taglia nf ⟨riscatto⟩ ransom; ⟨ricompensa⟩ reward; ⟨statura⟩ height; ⟨misura⟩ size. **~ unica** one size

taglia'carte *nm inv* paperknife
taglia'erba *nm inv* lawn-mower
tagliafu'oco *a inv* **porta ~** fire door; **striscia ~** fire break
tagli'ando *nm* coupon; **fare il ~** ≈ put one's car in for its MOT
tagli'ar|e *vt* cut; *(attraversare)* cut across; *(interrompere)* cut off; *(togliere)* cut out; carve ⟨*carne*⟩; mow ⟨*erba*⟩; **farsi ~ i capelli** have a haircut ● *vi* cut. **~si** *vr* cut oneself; **~si i capelli** have a haircut
taglia'telle *nfpl* tagliatelle *sg*, *thin, flat strips of egg pasta*
taglieggi'are *vt* extort money from
tagli'ente *a* sharp ● *nm* cutting edge. **~re** *nm* chopping board
'taglio *nm* cut; *(il tagliare)* cutting; *(di stoffa)* length; *(parte tagliente)* edge; **a doppio ~** double-edged. **~ cesareo** Caesarean section
tagli'ola *nf* trap
tagli'one *nm* **legge del ~** an eye for an eye and a tooth for a tooth
tagliuz'zare *vt* cut into small pieces
tail'leur *nm inv* [lady's] suit
talassotera'pia *nf* thalassotherapy
'talco *nm* talcum powder
'tale *a* such a; *(con nomi plurali)* such; **c'è un ~ disordine** there is such a mess; **non accetto tali scuse** I won't accept such excuses; **il rumore era ~ che non si sentiva nulla** there was so much noise you couldn't hear yourself think; **il ~ giorno** on such and such a day; **quel tal signore** that gentleman; **~ quale** just like ● *pron* **un ~** someone; **quel ~** that man; **il tal dei tali** such and such a person
ta'lento *nm* talent
tali'smano *nm* talisman
tallo'nare *vt* be hot on the heels of
tallon'cino *nm* coupon
tal'lone *nm* heel
tal'mente *adv* so
ta'lora *adv* = **talvolta**
'talpa *nf* mole
tal'volta *adv* sometimes
tamburel'lare *vi* *(con le dita)* drum; *(pioggia:)* beat, drum. **tambu'rello** *nm* tambourine. **tambu'rino** *nm* drummer. **tam'buro** *nm* drum
Ta'migi *nm* Thames
tampona'mento *nm* Auto collision; *(di ferita)* dressing; *(di falla)* plugging. **~ a catena** pile-up. **tampo'nare** *vt* *(urtare)* crash into; *(otturare)* plug. **tam'pone** *nm* swab; *(per timbri)* pad;

(per mestruazioni) tampon; *(per treni, Comput)* buffer
'tana *nf* den
'tanfo *nm* stench
'tanga *nm inv* tanga
tan'gen|te *a* tangent ● *nf* tangent; *(somma)* bribe. **~'topoli** *nf* widespread corruption in Italy in the early 90s. **~zi'ale** *nf* orbital road
tan'gibile *a* tangible
'tango *nm* tango
tan'tino: un ~ *adv* a little [bit]
'tanto *a* [so] much; *(con nomi plurali)* [so] many, [such] a lot of; **~ tempo** [such] a long time; **non ha tanta pazienza** he doesn't have much patience; **~ tempo quanto ti serve** as much time as you need; **non è ~ intelligente quanto suo padre** he's not as intelligent as his father; **tanti amici quanti parenti** as many friends as relatives ● *pron* much; *(plurale)* many; *(tanto tempo)* a long time; **è un uomo come tanti** he's just an ordinary man; **tanti** *(molte persone)* many people; **non ci vuole così ~** it doesn't take that long; **~ quanto** as much as; **tanti quanti** as many as ● *conj* *(comunque)* anyway, in any case ● *adv* *(così)* so; *(con verbi)* so much; **~ debole** so weak; **è ~ ingenuo da crederle** he's naive enough to believe her; **di ~ in ~** every now and then; **~ l'uno come l'altro** both; **~ quanto** as much as; **tre volte ~** three times as much; **una volta ~** once in a while; **~ meglio così!** so much the better!; **tant'è** so much so; **~ per cambiare** for a change
'tappa *nf* stop; *(parte di viaggio)* stage
tappa'buchi *nm inv* stopgap
tap'par|e *vt* plug; cork ⟨*bottiglia*⟩; **~e la bocca a qcno** *fam* shut sb up. **~si** *vr* **~si gli occhi** cover one's eyes; **~si il naso** hold one's nose; **~si le orecchie** put one's fingers in one's ears
tappa'rella *nf fam* roller blind
tappe'tino *nm* mat; *Comput* mouse mat. **~ antiscivolo** safety bathmat
tap'peto *nm* carpet; *(piccolo)* rug; **andare al ~** *(pugilato:)* hit the canvas; **mandare qcno al ~** knock sb down
tappez'z|are *vt* paper *(pareti)*; *(rivestire)* cover. **~e'ria** *nf* tapestry; *(di carta)* wallpaper; *(arte)* upholstery. **~i'ere** *nm* upholsterer; *(imbianchino)* decorator
'tappo *nm* plug; *(di sughero)* cork; *(di*

metallo, per penna) top; (*fam: persona piccola*) dwarf. **~ di sughero** cork

'tara *nf* (*difetto*) flaw; (*ereditaria*) hereditary defect; (*peso*) tare

ta'rantola *nf* tarantula

ta'ra|re *vt* calibrate ‹*strumento*›. **~to a** *Comm* discounted; *Techn* calibrated; *Med* with a hereditary defect; *fam* crazy

tarchi'ato *a* stocky

tar'dare *vi* be late ● *vt* delay

'tard|i *adv* late; **al più ~i** at the latest; **più ~i** later [on]; **sul ~i** late in the day; **far ~i** (*essere in ritardo*) be late; (*con gli amici*) stay up late; **a più ~i** see you later. **tar'divo** *a* late; ‹*bambino*› retarded. **~o** *a* slow; ‹*tempo*› late

'targ|a *nf* plate; *Auto* numberplate. **~a di circolazione** numberplate. **tar'gato** *a* **un'auto targata...** a car with the registration number.... **~'hetta** *nf* (*su porta*) nameplate; (*sulla valigia*) name tag

ta'rif|fa *nf* rate, tariff. **~'fario** *nm* price list

tar'larsi *vr* get wormeaten. **'tarlo** *nm* woodworm

'tarma *nf* moth. **tar'marsi** *vr* get motheaten

ta'rocco *nm* tarot; **ta'rocchi** *pl* tarot

tartagli'are *vi* stutter

'tartaro *a & nm* tartar

tarta'ruga *nf* tortoise; (*di mare*) turtle; (*per pettine ecc*) tortoiseshell

tartas'sare *vt* (*angariare*) harass

tar'tina *nf* canapé

tar'tufo *nm* truffle

'tasca *nf* pocket; (*in borsa*) compartment; **da ~** pocket *attrib*; **avere le tasche piene di qcsa** *fam* have had a bellyful of sth. **~ da pasticciere** icing bag

ta'scabile *a* pocket *attrib* ● *nm* paperback

tasca'pane *nm inv* haversack

ta'schino *nm* breast pocket

'tassa *nf* tax; (*discrizione ecc*) fee; (*doganale*) duty. **~ di circolazione** road tax. **~ d'iscrizione** registration fee

tas'sametro *nm* taximeter

tas'sare *vt* tax

tassa|tiva'mente *adv* without question. **~'tivo** *a* peremptory

tassazi'one *nf* taxation

tas'sello *nm* wedge; (*di stoffa*) gusset

tassì *nm inv* taxi. **tas'sista** *nmf* taxi driver

'tasso¹ *nm* *Bot* yew; (*animale*) badger

'tasso² *nm* *Comm* rate. **~ di cambio** exchange rate. **~ di interesse** interest rate

ta'stare *vt* feel; (*sondare*) sound; **~ il terreno** *fig* test the ground, feel one's way

tasti'e|ra *nf* keyboard. **~'rista** *nmf* keyboarder

'tasto *nm* key; (*tatto*) touch. **~ delicato** *fig* touchy subject. **~ funzione** *Comput* function key. **~ tabulatore** tab key

ta'stoni **a ~** *adv* gropingly

'tattica *nf* tactics *pl*

'tattico *a* tactical

'tatto *nm* (*senso*) touch; (*accortezza*) tact; **aver ~** be tactful

tatu'a|ggio *nm* tattoo. **~re** *vt* tattoo

'tavola *nf* table; (*illustrazione*) plate; (*asse*) plank. **~ calda** snackbar

tavo'lato *nm* boarding; (*pavimento*) wood floor

tavo'letta *nf* bar; (*medicinale*) tablet; **andare a ~** *Auto* drive flat out

tavo'lino *nm* small table

'tavolo *nm* table. **~ operatorio** *Med* operating table

tavo'lozza *nf* palette

'tazza *nf* cup; (*del water*) bowl. **~ da caffè/tè** coffee-cup/teacup

taz'zina *nf* **~ da caffè** espresso coffee cup

T.C.I. *abbr* (**Touring Club Italiano**) Italian Touring Club

te *pers pron* you; **te l'ho dato** I gave it to you

tè *nm inv* tea

tea'trale *a* theatrical

te'atro *nm* theatre. **~ all'aperto** open-air theatre. **~ di posa** *Cinema* set. **~ tenda** *marquee for theatre performances*

'tecnico, -a *a* technical ● *nmf* technician ● *nf* technique

tec'nigrafo *nm* drawing board

tecno|lo'gia *nf* technology. **~'logico** *a* technological

te'desco, -a *a & nmf* German

'tedi|o *nm* tedium. **~'oso** *a* tedious

te'game *nm* saucepan

'teglia *nf* baking tin

'tegola *nf* tile; *fig* blow

tei'era *nf* teapot

tek *nm* teak

'tela *nf* cloth; (*per quadri, vele*) canvas; *Theat* curtain. **~ cerata** oilcloth. **~ di lino** linen

te'laio *nm* (*di bicicletta, finestra*) frame; *Auto* chassis; (*per tessere*) loom

tele'camera *nf* television camera

teleco|man'dato *a* remote-controlled, remote control *attrib*. **~'mando** *nm* remote control

Telecom Italia *nf* Italian State telephone company

telecomunicazi'oni *nfpl* telecommunications

tele'cro|naca *nf* [television] commentary. **~naca diretta** live [television] coverage. **~naca registrata** recording. **~'nista** *nmf* television commentator

tele'ferica *nf* cableway

telefonica'mente *adv* by [tele-]phone

telefo'nino *nm* mobile [phone]

telefo'na|re *vt/i* [tele]phone, ring. **~ta** *nf* call. **~ta interurbana** long-distance call

tele'fo|nico *a* [tele]phone *attrib*. **~'nista** *nmf* operator

te'lefono *nm* [tele]phone. **~ senza filo** cordless [phone]. **~ a gettoni** pay phone, coin-box. **~ interno** internal telephone. **~ a schede** cardphone

telegior'nale *nm* television news *sg*

telegra'fare *vt* telegraph. **tele'grafico** *a* telegraphic; ⟨*risposta*⟩ monosyllabic; **sii telegrafico** keep it brief

tele'gramma *nm* telegram

tele'matica *nf* data communications, telematics

teleno'vela *nf* soap opera

teleobiet'tivo *nm* telephoto lens

telepa'tia *nf* telepathy

telero'manzo *nm* television serial

tele'schermo *nm* television screen

tele'scopio *nm* telescope

teleselezi'one *nf* subscriber trunk dialling, STD; **chiamare in ~** dial direct

telespetta'tore, -'trice *nmf* viewer

tele'text® *nm* Teletext®

tele'video *nm* videophone

televisi'one *nf* television; **guardare la ~** watch television

televi'sivo *a* television *attrib*; **operatore ~** television cameraman; **apparecchio ~** television set

televi'sore *nm* television [set]

'tema *nm* theme; *Sch* essay. **te'matica** *nf* main theme

teme'rario *a* reckless

te'mere *vt* be afraid of, fear ● *vi* be afraid, fear

tem'paccio *nm* filthy weather

temperama'tite *nm inv* pencil-sharpener

tempera'mento *nm* temperament

tempe'ra|re *vt* temper; sharpen ⟨*matita*⟩. **~to** *a* temperate. **~'tura** *nf* temperature. **~tura ambiente** room temperature

tempe'rino *nm* penknife

tem'pe|sta *nf* storm. **~sta di neve** snowstorm. **~sta di sabbia** sandstorm **tempe|stiva'mente** *adv* quickly. **~'stivo** *a* timely. **~'stoso** *a* stormy

'tempia *nf Anat* temple

'tempio *nm Relig* temple

tem'pismo *nm* timing

'tempo *nm* time; ⟨*atmosferico*⟩ weather; *Mus* tempo; *Gram* tense; ⟨*di film*⟩ part; ⟨*di partita*⟩ half; **a suo ~** in due course; **~ fa** some time ago; **un ~** once; **ha fatto il suo ~** it's superannuated. **~ reale** real time. **~ supplementare** *Sport* extra time, overtime *Am*. **~'rale** *a* temporal ● *nm* [thunder]storm. **~ranea'mente** *adv* temporarily. **~'raneo** *a* temporary. **~reggi'are** *vi* play for time

tem'prare *vt* temper

te'nac|e *a* tenacious. **~ia** *nf* tenacity

te'naglia *nf* pincers *pl*

'tenda *nf* curtain; ⟨*per campeggio*⟩ tent; ⟨*tendone*⟩ awning. **~ a ossigeno** oxygen tent

ten'denz|a *nf* tendency. **~ial'mente** *adv* by nature. **~i'oso** *a* tendentious

'tendere *vt* ⟨*allargare*⟩ stretch [out]; ⟨*tirare*⟩ tighten; ⟨*porgere*⟩ hold out; *fig* lay ⟨*trappola*⟩ ● *vi* **~ a** aim at; ⟨*essere portato a*⟩ tend to

'tendine *nm* tendon

ten'do|ne *nm* awning; ⟨*di circo*⟩ tent. **~poli** *nf inv* tent city

'tenebre *nfpl* darkness *sg*. **tene'broso** *a* gloomy

te'nente *nm* lieutenant

tenera'mente *adv* tenderly

te'ner|e *vt* hold; ⟨*mantenere*⟩ keep; ⟨*gestire*⟩ run; ⟨*prendere*⟩ take; ⟨*seguire*⟩ follow; ⟨*considerare*⟩ consider ● *vi* hold; **~ci a**, **~e a** be keen on; **~e per** support ⟨*squadra*⟩. **~si** *vr* hold on ⟨**a ~ si**⟩; ⟨*in una condizione*⟩ keep oneself; ⟨*seguire*⟩ stick to; **~si indietro** stand back

tene'rezza *nf* tenderness. **'tenero** *a* tender

'tenia *nf* tapeworm

'tennis *nm* tennis. **~ da tavolo** table tennis. **ten'nista** *nmf* tennis player

te'nore *nm* standard; *Mus* tenor; **a ~ di**

legge by law. **~ di vita** standard of living

tensi'one *nf* tension; *Electr* voltage; **alta ~** high voltage

ten'tacolo *nm* tentacle

ten'ta|re *vt* attempt; *(sperimentare)* try; *(indurre in tentazione)* tempt. **~'tivo** *nm* attempt. **~zi'one** *nf* temptation

tenten|na'mento *nm* wavering. **~'nare** *vi* waver

'tenue *a* fine; *(debole)* weak; *(esiguo)* small; *(leggero)* slight

te'nuta *nf (capacità)* capacity; *(Sport: resistenza)* stamina; *(possedimento)* estate; *(divisa)* uniform; *(abbigliamento)* clothes *pl*; **a ~ d'aria** airtight. **~ di strada** road holding

teolo'gia *nf* theology. **teo'logico** *a* theological. **te'ologo** *nm* theologian

teo'rema *nm* theorem

teo'ria *nf* theory

teorica'mente *adv* theoretically. **te'orico** *a* theoretical

te'pore *nm* warmth

'teppa *nf* mob. **tep'pismo** *nm* hooliganism. **tep'pista** *nm* hooligan

tera'peutico *a* therapeutic. **tera'pia** *nf* therapy

tergicri'stallo *nm* windscreen wiper, windshield wiper *Am*

tergilu'notto *nm* rear windscreen wiper

tergiver'sare *vi* hesitate

'tergo *nm* **a ~** behind; **segue a ~** please turn over, PTO

ter'male *a* thermal; **stazione ~** spa. **'terme** *nfpl* thermal baths

'termico *a* thermal

termi'na|le *a & nm* terminal; **malato ~le** terminally ill person. **~re** *vt/i* finish, end. **'termine** *nm (limite)* limit; *(fine)* end; *(condizione, espressione)* term

terminolo'gia *nf* terminology

'termite *nf* termite

termoco'perta *nf* electric blanket

ter'mometro *nm* thermometer

'termos *nm inv* thermos®

termosi'fone *nm* radiator; *(sistema)* central heating

ter'mostato *nm* thermostat

'terra *nf* earth; *(regione)* land; *(terreno)* ground; *(argilla)* clay; *(cosmetico)* dark face powder *(which gives the impression of a tan)*; **a ~** *(sulla costa)* ashore; *(installazioni)* onshore; **per ~** on the ground; **sotto ~** underground. **~'cot-**

ta *nf* terracotta; **vasellame di ~cotta** earthenware. **~'ferma** *nf* dry land. **~pi'eno** *nm* embankment

ter'razz|a *nf*, **~o** *nm* balcony

terremo'tato, -a *a (zona)* affected by an earthquake ● *nmf* earthquake victim. **terre'moto** *nm* earthquake

ter'reno *a* earthly ● *nm* ground; *(suolo)* soil; *(proprietà terriera)* land; **perdere/guadagnare ~** lose/gain ground. **~ di gioco** playing field

ter'restre *a* terrestrial; **esercito ~** land forces *pl*

ter'ribil|e *a* terrible. **~'mente** *adv* terribly

ter'riccio *nm* potting compost

terrifi'cante *a* terrifying

territori'ale *a* territorial. **terri'torio** *nm* territory

ter'rore *nm* terror

terro'ris|mo *nm* terrorism. **~ta** *nmf* terrorist

terroriz'zare *vt* terrorize

'terso *a* clear

ter'zetto *nm* trio

terzi'ario *a* tertiary

'terzo *a* third; **di terz'ordine** *(locale, servizio)* third-rate; **fare il ~ grado a qn** give sb the third degree; **la terza età** the third age ● *nm* third; **terzi** *pl Jur* third party *sg*. **ter'zultimo, -a** *a & nmf* third from last

'tesa *nf* brim

'teschio *nm* skull

'tesi *nf inv* thesis

'teso *pp di* **tendere** ● *a* taut; *fig* tense

tesor|e'ria *nf* treasury. **~i'ere** *nm* treasurer

te'soro *nm* treasure; *(tesoreria)* treasury

'tessera *nf* card; *(abbonamento all'autobus)* season ticket

'tessere *vt* weave; hatch *(complotto)*

tesse'rino *nm* travel card

'tessile *a* textile. **tessili** *nmpl* textiles; *(operai)* textile workers

tessi|'tore, -'trice *nmf* weaver. **~'tura** *nf* weaving

tes'suto *nm* fabric; *Anat* tissue

'testa *nf* head; *(cervello)* brain; **essere in ~ a** be ahead of; in ~ *Sport* in the lead; **~ o croce?** heads or tails?; **fare ~ o croce** have a toss-up to decide

testa-coda *nm inv* **fare un ~** spin right round

testa'mento *nm* will; **T~** *Relig* Testament

testar'daggine *nf* stubbornness. **te'stardo** *a* stubborn

te'stata *nf* head; (*intestazione*) heading; (*colpo*) butt

'teste *nmf* witness

te'sticolo *nm* testicle

testi'mon|e *nmf* witness. **~e oculare** eye witness

testi'monial *nmf inv* celebrity who promotes a brand of cosmetics

testimoni|'anza *nf* testimony; **falsa ~anza** *Jur* perjury. **~'are** *vt* testify to ● *vi* testify, give evidence

'testo *nm* text; **far ~** be an authority

te'stone, -a *nmf* blockhead

testu'ale *a* textual

'tetano *nm* tetanus

'tetro *a* gloomy

tetta'rella *nf* teat

'tetto *nm* roof. **~ apribile** (*di auto*) sunshine roof. **tet'toia** *nf* roofing. **tet'tuccio** *nm* **tettuccio apribile** sunroof

'Tevere *nm* Tiber

ti *pers pron* you; (*riflessivo*) yourself; **ti ha dato un libro** he gave you a book; **lavati le mani** wash your hands; **eccoti!** here you are!; **sbrigati!** hurry up!

ti'ara *nf* tiara

tic *nm inv* tic

ticchet't|are *vi* tick. **~io** *nm* ticking

'ticchio *nm* tic; (*ghiribizzo*) whim

'ticket *nm inv* (*per farmaco, esame*) *amount paid by National Health patients*

tiepida'mente *adv* halfheartedly. **ti'epido** *a anche fig* lukewarm

ti'fare *vi* **~ per** shout for. **'tifo** *nm Med* typhus; **fare il tifo per** *fig* be a fan of

tifoi'dea *nf* typhoid

ti'fone *nm* typhoon

ti'foso, -a *nmf* fan

'tiglio *nm* lime

ti'grato *a* **gatto ~** tabby [cat]

'tigre *nf* tiger

'tilde *nmf* tilde

tim'ballo *nm Culin* pie

tim'brare *vt* stamp; **~ il cartellino** clock in/out

'timbro *nm* stamp; (*di voce*) tone

timida'mente *adv* timidly, shyly. **timi'dezza** *nf* timidity, shyness. **'timido** *a* timid, shy

'timo *nm* thyme

ti'mon|e *nm* rudder. **~i'ere** *nm* helmsman

ti'more *nm* fear; (*soggezione*) awe. **timo'roso** *a* timorous

'timpano *nm* eardrum; *Mus* kettledrum

ti'nello *nm* dining room

'tinger|e *vt* dye; (*macchiare*) stain. **~si** *vi* (*viso, cielo:*) be tinged (**di** with); **~si i capelli** have one's hair dyed; (*da solo*) dye one's hair

'tino *nm*, **ti'nozza** *nf* tub

'tint|a *nf* dye; (*colore*) colour; **in ~a unita** plain. **~a'rella** *nf fam* suntan

tintin'nare *vi* tinkle

'tinto *pp di* tingere. **~'ria** *nf* (*negozio*) cleaner's. **tin'tura** *nf* dyeing; (*colorante*) dye.

'tipico *a* typical

'tipo *nm* type; (*fam: individuo*) chap, guy

tipogra'fia *nf* printery; (*arte*) typography. **tipo'grafico** *a* typographic[al]. **ti'pografo** *nm* printer

tip tap *nm inv* tap dancing

ti'raggio *nm* draught

tiramisù *nm inv dessert made of coffee-soaked sponge, eggs, Marsala, cream and cocoa powder*

tiran|neggi'are *vt* tyrannize. **~'nia** *nf* tyranny. **ti'ranno, -a** *a* tyrannical ● *nmf* tyrant

tirapi'edi *nm inv pej* hanger-on

ti'rar|e *vt* pull; (*gettare*) throw; kick ‹*palla*›; (*sparare*) fire; (*tracciare*) draw; (*stampare*) print ● *vi* pull; ‹*vento:*› blow; ‹*abito:*› be tight; (*sparare*) fire; **~e avanti** get by; **~e su** (*crescere*) bring up; (*da terra*) pick up; **tirar su col naso** sniffle. **~si** *vr* **~si indietro** *fig* back out, pull out

tiras'segno *nm* target shooting; (*alla fiera*) rifle range

ti'rata *nf* (*strattone*) pull, tug; **in una ~** in one go

tira'tore *nm* shot. **~ scelto** marksman

tira'tura *nf* printing; (*di giornali*) circulation; (*di libri*) [print] run

tirchie'ria *nf* meanness. **'tirchio** *a* mean

tiri'tera *nf* spiel

'tiro *nm* (*traino*) draught; (*lancio*) throw; (*sparo*) shot; (*scherzo*) trick. **~ con l'arco** archery. **~ alla fune** tug-of-war. **~ a segno** rifle-range

tiro'cinio *nm* apprenticeship

ti'roide *nf* thyroid

Tir'reno *nm* **il [mar] ~** the Tyrrhenian Sea

ti'sana *nf* herb[al] tea

tito'lare *a* regular ● *nmf* principal; (*proprietario*) owner; (*calcio*) regular player

'titolo *nm* title; (*accademico*) qualification; *Comm* security; **a ~ di** as; **a ~ di favore** as a favour. **titoli** *pl* **di studio** qualifications

titu'ba|nte *a* hesitant. **~nza** *nf* hesitation. **~re** *vi* hesitate

tivù *nf inv fam* TV, telly

'tizio *nm* fellow

tiz'zone *nm* brand

toc'cante *a* touching

toc'ca|re *vt* touch; touch on (*argomento*); (*tastare*) feel; (*riguardare*) concern ● *vi* **~re a** (*capitare*) happen to; **mi tocca aspettare** I'll have to wait; **tocca a te** it's your turn; (*da pagare da bere*) it's your round

tocca'sana *nm inv* cure-all

'tocco *nm* touch; (*di pennello, orologio*) stroke; (*di pane ecc*) chunk ● *a fam* crazy, touched

'toga *nf* toga; (*accademica, di magistrato*) gown

'toglier|e *vt* take off (*coperta*); take away (*bambino da scuola, sete, Math*); take out, remove (*dente*); **~e qcsa di mano a qcno** take sth away from sb; **~e qcno dei guai** get sb out of trouble; **ciò non toglie che...** nevertheless... **~si** *vr* take off (*abito*); **~si la vita** take one's [own] life; **togliti dai piedi!** get out of here!

toilette *nf inv*, **to'letta** *nf* toilet; (*mobile*) dressing table

tolle'ra|nte *a* tolerant. **~nza** *nf* tolerance. **~re** *vt* tolerate

'tolto *pp di* **togliere**

to'maia *nf* upper

'tomba *nf* grave, tomb

tom'bino *nm* manhole cover

'tombola *nf* bingo; (*caduta*) tumble

'tomo *nm* tome

'tonaca *nf* habit

tonalità *nf inv Mus* tonality

'tondo *a* round ● *nm* circle

'tonfo *nm* thud; (*in acqua*) splash

'tonico *a & nm* tonic

tonifi'care *vt* brace

tonnel'la|ggio *nm* tonnage. **~ta** *nf* ton

'tonno *nm* tuna [fish]

'tono *nm* tone

ton'sil|la *nf* tonsil. **~'lite** *nf* tonsillitis

'tonto *a fam* thick

top *nm inv* (*indumento*) sun-top

to'pazio *nm* topaz

'topless *nm inv* **in ~** topless

'topo *nm* mouse. **~ di biblioteca** *fig* bookworm

topogra'fia *nf* topography. **topo'grafico** *a* topographic[al]

to'ponimo *nm* place name

'toppa *nf* (*rattoppo*) patch; (*serratura*) keyhole

to'race *nm* chest. **to'racico** *a* thoracic; **gabbia toracica** rib cage

'torba *nf* peat

'torbido *a* cloudy; *fig* troubled

'torcer|e *vt* twist; wring [out] (*biancheria*). **~si** *vr* twist

'torchio *nm* press

'torcia *nf* torch

torci'collo *nm* stiff neck

'tordo *nm* thrush

to'rero *nm* bullfighter

To'rino *nf* Turin

tor'menta *nf* snowstorm

tormen'tare *vt* torment. **tor'mento** *nm* torment

torna'conto *nm* benefit

tor'nado *nm* tornado

tor'nante *nm* hairpin bend

tor'nare *vi* return, go/come back; (*ridiventare*) become again; (*conto:*) add up; **~ a sorridere** become happy again

tor'neo *nm* tournament

'tornio *nm* lathe

'torno *nm* **togliersi di ~** get out of the way

'toro *nm* bull; *Astr* Taurus

tor'pedin|e *nf* torpedo. **~i'era** *nf* torpedo boat

tor'pore *nm* torpor

'torre *nf* tower; (*scacchi*) castle. **~ di controllo** control tower

torrefazi'one *nf* roasting

tor'ren|te *nm* torrent, mountain stream; (*fig: di lacrime*) flood. **~zi'ale** *a* torrential

tor'retta *nf* turret

'torrido *a* torrid

torri'one *nm* keep

tor'rone *nm* nougat

'torso *nm* torso; (*di mela, pera*) core; **a ~ nudo** bare-chested

'torsolo *nm* core

'torta *nf* cake; (*crostata*) tart

tortel'lini *nmpl* tortellini, *small packets of pasta stuffed with pork, ham, Parmesan and nutmeg*

torti'era *nf* baking tin

tor'tino *nm* pie

'torto pp di **torcere** ● a twisted ● nm wrong; (colpa) fault; **aver ~** be wrong; **a ~** wrongly

'tortora nf turtle-dove

tortu'oso a wınding; (ambiguo) tortuous

tor'tu|ra nf torture. **~'rare** vt torture

'torvo a grim

to'sare vt shear

tosa'tura nf shearing

To'scana nf Tuscany

'tosse nf cough

'tossico a toxic ● nm poison. **tossi'comane** nmf drug addict, drug user

tos'sire vi cough

tosta'pane nm inv toaster

to'stare vt toast ⟨pane⟩; roast ⟨caffè⟩

'tosto adv (subito) soon ● a fam cool

tot a inv **una cifra ~** such and such a figure ● nm **un ~** so much

to'tal|e a & nm total. **~ità** nf entirety; **la ~ità dei presenti** all those present

totali'tario a totalitarian

totaliz'zare vt total; score ⟨punti⟩

total'mente adv totally

'totano nm squid

toto'calcio nm ≈ [football] pools pl

tournée nf inv tour

to'vagli|a nf tablecloth. **~'etta** nf **~etta [all'americana]** place mat. **~'olo** nm napkin

'tozzo a squat ● nm **~ di pane** stale piece of bread

tra = **fra**

trabal'la|nte a staggering; ⟨sedia⟩ rickety, wonky. **~re** vi stagger; ⟨veicolo:⟩ jolt

tra'biccolo nm fam contraption; ⟨auto⟩ jalopy

traboc'care vi overflow

traboc'chetto nm trap

tracan'nare vt gulp down

'tracci|a nf track; (orma) footstep; (striscia) trail; (residuo) trace; fig sign. **~'are** vt trace; sketch out ⟨schema⟩; draw ⟨linea⟩. **~'ato** nm ⟨schema⟩ layout

tra'chea nf windpipe

tra'colla nf shoulder-strap; **borsa a ~** shoulder-bag

tra'collo nm collapse

tradi'mento nm betrayal; Pol treason

tra'di|re vt betray; be unfaithful to ⟨moglie, marito⟩. **~'tore, ~'trice** nmf traitor

tradizio'na|le a traditional. **~'lista** nmf traditionalist. **~l'mente** adv traditionally. **tradizi'one** nf tradition

tra'dotto pp di **tradurre**

tra'du|rre vt translate. **~t'tore, ~t'trice** nmf translator. **~ttore elettronico** electronic phrasebook. **~zi'one** nf translation

tra'ente nmf Comm drawer

trafe'lato a breathless

traffi'ca|nte nmf dealer. **~nte di droga** [drug] pusher. **~re** vi (affaccendarsi) busy oneself; **~re in** pej traffic in. **'traffico** nm traffic; Comm trade

tra'figgere vt stab; (straziare) pierce

tra'fila nf fig rigmarole

trafo'rare vt bore, drill. **tra'foro** nm boring; (galleria) tunnel

trafu'gare vt steal

tra'gedia nf tragedy

traghet'tare vt ferry. **tra'ghetto** nm ferrying; (nave) ferry

tragica'mente adv tragically. **'tragico** a tragic ● nm (autore) tragedian

tra'gitto nm journey; (per mare) crossing

tragu'ardo nm finishing post; (meta) goal

traiet'toria nf trajectory

trai'nare vt drag; (rimorchiare) tow

tralasci'are vt interrupt; (omettere) leave out

'tralcio nm Bot shoot

tra'liccio nm (graticcio) trellis

tram nm inv tram, streetcar Am

'trama nf weft; (di film ecc) plot

traman'dare vt hand down

tra'mare vt weave; (macchinare) plot

tram'busto nm turmoil, hullabaloo

trame'stio nm bustle

tramez'zino nm sandwich

tra'mezzo nm partition

'tramite prep through ● nm link; **fare da ~** act as go-between

tramon'tana nf north wind

tramon'tare vi set; (declinare) decline. **tra'monto** nm sunset; (declino) decline

tramor'tire vt stun ● vi faint

trampo'lino nm springboard; (per lo sci) ski-jump

'trampolo nm stilt

tramu'tare vt transform

'trancia nf shears pl; (fetta) slice

tra'nello nm trap

trangugi'are vt gulp down, gobble up

'tranne prep except

tranquilla'mente adv peacefully

tranquil'lante nm tranquillizer

tranquilli|tà nf calm; (di spirito) tranquillity. **~z'zare** vt reassure.

tran'quillo *a* quiet; (*pacifico*) peaceful; (*coscienza*) easy

transat'lantico *a* transatlantic ● *nm* ocean liner

tran'sa|tto *pp di* **transigere**. **~zi'one** *nf Comm* transaction

tran'senna *nf* (*barriera*) barrier

tran'sigere *vi* reach an agreement; (*cedere*) yield

transi'ta|bile *a* passable. **~re** *vi* pass

transi'tivo *a* transitive

'transi|to *nm* transit; **diritto di ~to** right of way; **"divieto di ~to"** "no thoroughfare". **~'torio** *a* transitory. **~zi'one** *nf* transition

tran'tran *nm fam* routine

tranvi'ere *nm* tram driver, streetcar driver *Am*

'trapano *nm* drill

trapas'sare *vt* go [right] through ● *vi* (*morire*) pass away

tra'passo *nm* passage

trape'lare *vi* (*liquido, fig:*) leak out

tra'pezio *nm* trapeze; *Math* trapezium

trapi|an'tare *vt* transplant. **~'anto** *nm* transplant

'trappola *nf* trap

tra'punta *nf* quilt

'trarre *vt* draw; (*ricavare*) obtain; **~ in inganno** deceive

trasa'lire *vi* start

trasan'dato *a* shabby

trasbor'dare *vt* transfer; *Naut* tran[s]ship ● *vi* change. **tra'sbordo** *nm* trans[s]hipment

tra'scendere *vt* transcend ● *vi* (*eccedere*) go too far

trasci'nar|e *vt* drag; (*fig: entusiasmo:*) carry away. **~si** *vr* drag oneself

tra'scorrere *vt* spend ● *vi* pass

tra'scri|vere *vt* transcribe. **~zi'one** *nf* transcription

trascu'ra|bile *a* negligible. **~re** *vt* neglect; (*non tenere conto di*) disregard. **~'tezza** *nf* negligence. **~to** *a* negligent; (*curato male*) neglected; (*nel vestire*) slovenly

traseco'lato *a* amazed

trasferi'mento *nm* transfer; (*trasloco*) move

trasfe'ri|re *vt* transfer. **~rsi** *vr* move

tra'sferta *nf* transfer; (*indennità*) subsistence allowance; *Sport* away match; **in ~** (*impiegato*) on secondment; **giocare in ~** play away

trasfigu'rare *vt* transfigure

trasfor'ma|re *vt* transform; (*in rugby*) convert. **~'tore** *nm* transformer.

~zi'one *nf* transformation; (*in rugby*) conversion

trasfor'mista *nmf* (*artista*) quickchange artist

trasfusi'one *nf* transfusion

trasgre'dire *vt* disobey; *Jur* infringe

trasgredi'trice *nf* transgressor

trasgres|si'one *nf* infringement. **~'sivo** *a* intended to shock. **~'sore** *nm* transgressor

tra'slato *a* metaphorical

traslo'car|e *vt* move ● *vi*, **~si** *vr* move house. **tra'sloco** *nm* removal

tra'smesso *pp di* **trasmettere**

tra'smett|ere *vt* pass on; *TV, Radio* broadcast; *Techn, Med* transmit. **~i'tore** *nm* transmitter

trasmis'si|bile *a* transmissible. **~'one** *nf* transmission; *TV, Radio* programme

trasmit'tente *nm* transmitter ● *nf* broadcasting station

traso'gna|re *vi* day-dream. **~to** *a* dreamy

traspa'ren|te *a* transparent. **~za** *nf* transparency; **in ~za** against the light. **traspa'rire** *vi* show [through]

traspi'ra|re *vi* perspire; *fig* transpire. **~zi'one** *nf* perspiration

tra'sporre *vt* transpose

traspor'tare *vt* transport; **lasciarsi ~ da** get carried away by. **tra'sporto** *nm* transport; (*passione*) passion

trastul'lar|e *vt* amuse. **~si** *vr* amuse oneself

trasu'dare *vt* ooze with ● *vi* sweat

trasver'sale *a* transverse

trasvo'la|re *vt* fly over ● *vi* **~re su** *fig* skim over. **~ta** *nf* crossing [by air]

'tratta *nf* (*traffico illegale*) trade; *Comm* draft

trat'tabile *a* or nearest offer, o.n.o.

tratta'mento *nm* treatment. **~ di riguardo** special treatment

trat'ta|re *vt* treat; (*commerciare in*) deal in; (*negoziare*) negotiate ● *vi* **~re di** deal with. **~rsi** *vr* **di che si tratta?** what is it about?; **si tratta di...** it's about... **~'tive** *nfpl* negotiations. **~to** *nm* treaty; (*opera scritta*) treatise

tratteggi'are *vt* outline; (*descrivere*) sketch

tratte'ner|e *vt* (*far restare*) keep; hold (*respiro, in questura*); hold back (*lacrime, riso*); (*frenare*) restrain; (*da paga*) withhold; **sono stato trattenuto** (*ritardato*) I was o got held up. **~si** *vr* restrain oneself; (*fermarsi*) stay;

~**si su** (*indugiare*) dwell on. **tratteni'mento** *nm* entertainment; (*ricevimento*) party

tratte'nuta *nf* deduction

trat'tino *nm* dash; (*in parole composte*) hyphen

'**tratto** *pp di* **trarre** ● *nm* (*di spazio, tempo*) stretch; (*di penna*) stroke; (*linea*) line; (*brano*) passage; **tratti** *pl* (*lineamenti*) features; **a tratti** at intervals; **ad un** ~ suddenly

trat'tore *nm* tractor

tratto'ria *nf* restaurant

'**trauma** *nm* trauma. **trau'matico** *a* traumatic. ~**tiz'zare** *vt* traumatize

tra'vaglio *nm* labour; (*angoscia*) anguish

trava'sare *vt* decant

'**trave** *nf* beam

tra'veggole *nfpl* **avere le** ~ be seeing things

tra'versa *nf* crossbar; **è una** ~ **di Via Roma** it's off Via Roma, it crosses via Roma

traver'sa|re *vt* cross. ~**ta** *nf* crossing

traver'sie *nfpl* misfortunes

traver'sina *nf* Rail sleeper

tra'vers|o *a* crosswise ● *adv* **di** ~**o** crossways; **andare di** ~**o** (*cibo:*) go down the wrong way; **camminare di** ~**o** not walk in a straight line; **guardare qcno di** ~**o** look askance at sb. ~**one** *nm* (*in calcio*) cross

travesti'mento *nm* disguise

trave'sti|re *vt* disguise. ~**rsi** *vr* disguise oneself. ~**to** *a* disguised ● *nm* transvestite

travi'are *vt* lead astray

travi'sare *vt* distort

travol'gente *a* overwhelming

tra'vol|gere *vt* sweep away; (*sopraffare*) overwhelm. ~**to** *pp di* **travolgere**

trazi'one *nf* traction. ~ **anteriore/ posteriore** front-/rear-wheel drive

tre *a & nm* three

trebbi'a|re *vt* thresh

'**treccia** *nf* plait, braid

tre'cento *a & nm* three hundred; **il T~** the fourteenth century

tredi'cesima *nf* extra month's salary paid as a Christmas bonus

'**tredici** *a & nm* thirteen

'**tregua** *nf* truce; *fig* respite

tre'mare *vi* tremble; (*di freddo*) shiver. **trema'rella** *nf fam* jitters *pl*

tremenda'mente *adv* terribly.

tre'mendo *a* terrible; **ho una fame tremenda** I'm terribly hungry

tremen'tina *nf* turpentine

tre'mila *a & nm* three thousand

'**tremito** *nm* tremble

tremo'lare *vi* shake; (*luce:*) flicker. **tre'more** *nm* trembling

tre'nino *nm* miniature railway

'**treno** *nm* train

'**tren|ta** *a & nm* thirty; ~**ta e lode** top marks. ~**tatré giri** *nm inv* LP. ~'**tenne** *a & nmf* thirty-year-old. ~'**tesimo** *a & nm* thirtieth. ~'**tina** *nf* **una** ~**tina di** about thirty

trepi'dare *vi* be anxious. '**trepido** *a* anxious

treppi'ede *nm* tripod

'**tresca** *nf* intrigue; (*amorosa*) affair

'**trespolo** *nm* perch

triango'lare *a* triangular. **tri'angolo** *nm* triangle

tri'bale *a* tribal

tribo'la|re *vi* (*soffrire*) suffer; (*fare fatica*) go through all kinds of trials and tribulations. ~**zi'one** *nf* tribulation

tribù *nf inv* tribe

tri'buna *nf* tribune; (*per uditori*) gallery; *Sport* stand. ~ **coperta** stand

tribu'nale *nm* court

tribu'tare *vt* bestow

tribu'tario *a* tax *attrib*. **tri'buto** *nm* tribute; (*tassa*) tax

tri'checo *nm* walrus

tri'ciclo *nm* tricycle

trico'lore *a* three-coloured ● *nm* (*bandiera*) tricolour

tri'dente *nm* trident

trien'nale *a* (*ogni tre anni*) three-yearly; (*lungo tre anni*) three-year. **tri'ennio** *nm* three-year period

tri'foglio *nm* clover

trifo'lato *a* sliced thinly and cooked with olive oil, parsley and garlic

'**triglia** *nf* mullet

trigonome'tria *nf* trigonometry

tril'lare *vi* trill

trilo'gia *nf* trilogy

tri'mestre *nm* quarter; *Sch* term

'**trina** *nf* lace

trin'ce|a *nf* trench. ~**rare** *vt* entrench

trincia'pollo *nm inv* poultry shears *pl*

trinci'are *vt* cut up

Trinità *nf* Trinity

'**trio** *nm* trio

trion'fa|le *a* triumphal. ~**nte** *a* triumphant. ~**re** *vi* triumph; ~**re su** triumph over. **tri'onfo** *nm* triumph

tripli'care *vt* triple. '**triplice** *a* triple;

in triplice [copia] in triplicate. **'triplo** *a* treble ● *nm* **il triplo (di)** three times as much (as)

'trippa *nf* tripe; ⟨*fam: pancia*⟩ belly

'trist|e *a* sad; ⟨*luogo*⟩ gloomy. **tri'stezza** *nf* sadness. **~o** *a* wicked; (*meschino*) miserable

trita|'carne *nm* *inv* mincer. **~ghi'accio** *nm* *inv* ice-crusher

tri'ta|re *vt* mince. **'trito** *a* trito e ritrito well-worn, trite

'trittico *nm* triptych

tritu'rare *vt* chop finely

triumvi'rato *nm* triumvirate

tri'vella *nf* drill. **trivel'lare** *vt* drill

trivi'ale *a* vulgar

tro'feo *nm* trophy

'trogolo *nm* (*per maiali*) trough

'troia *nf* sow; *vulg* bitch; (*sessuale*) whore

'tromba *nf* trumpet; *Auto* horn; (*delle scale*) well. **~ d'aria** whirlwind

trom'bare *vt* *vulg* screw; (*fam: in esame*) fail

trom'b|etta *nm* toy trumpet. **~one** *nm* trombone

trom'bosi *nf* thrombosis

tron'care *vt* sever; truncate ⟨*parola*⟩

'tronco *a* truncated; **licenziare in ~** fire on the spot ● *nm* trunk; (*di strada*) section. **tron'cone** *nm* stump

troneggi'are *vi* **~ su** tower over

'trono *nm* throne

tropi'cale *a* tropical. **'tropico** *nm* tropic

'troppo *a* too much; (*con nomi plurali*) too many ● *pron* too much; (*plurale*) too many; (*troppo tempo*) too long; **troppi** (*troppa gente*) too many people ● *adv* too; (*con verbi*) too much; **~ stanco** too tired; **ho mangiato ~** I ate too much; **hai fame? – non ~** are you hungry? – not very; **sentirsi di ~** feel unwanted

'trota *nf* trout

trot'tare *vi* trot. **trotterel'lare** *vi* trot along; ⟨*bimbo:*⟩ toddle

'trotto *nm* trot; **andare al ~** trot

'trottola *nf* [spinning] top; (*movimento*) spin

troupe *nf* *inv* **~ televisiva** camera crew

tro'va|re *vt* find; (*scoprire*) find out; (*incontrare*) meet; (*ritenere*) think; **andare a ~re** go and see. **~rsi** *vr* find oneself; ⟨*luogo:*⟩ be; (*sentirsi*) feel. **~ta** *nf* bright idea. **~ta pubblicitaria** advertising gimmick

truc'ca|re *vt* make up; (*falsificare*) fix

sl. **~rsi** *vr* make up. **~tore, ~'trice** *nmf* make-up artist

'trucco *nm* (*cosmetico*) make-up; (*imbroglio*) trick

'truce *a* fierce; ⟨*delitto*⟩ appalling

truci'dare *vt* slay

'truciolo *nm* shaving

trucu'lento *a* truculent

'truffa *nf* fraud. **truf'fare** *vt* swindle. **~'tore, ~trice** *nmf* swindler

'truppa *nf* troops *pl*; (*gruppo*) group

tu *pers pron* you; **sei tu?** is that you?; **l'hai fatto tu?** did you do it yourself?; **a tu per tu** in private; **darsi del tu** *use the familiar tu*

'tuba *nf* *Mus* tuba; (*cappello*) top hat

tu'bare *vi* coo

tuba'tura, tubazi'one *nf* piping

tubazi'oni *nfpl* piping *sg*, pipes

tuberco'losi *nf* tuberculosis

tu'betto *nm* tube

tu'bino *nm* (*vestito*) shift

'tubo *nm* pipe; *Anat* canal; **non ho capito un ~** *fam* I understood zilch. **~ di scappamento** exhaust [pipe]

tubo'lare *a* tubular

tuf'fa|re *vt* plunge. **~rsi** *vr* dive. **~'tore, ~'trice** *nmf* diver

'tuffo *nm* dive; (*bagno*) dip; **ho avuto un ~ al cuore** my heart missed a beat. **~ di testa** dive

'tufo *nm* tufa

tu'gurio *nm* hovel

tuli'pano *nm* tulip

'tulle *nm* tulle

tume'fa|tto *a* swollen. **~zi'one** *nf* swelling. **'tumido** *a* swollen

tu'more *nm* tumour

tumulazi'one *nf* burial

tu'mult|o *nm* turmoil; (*sommossa*) riot. **~u'oso** *a* uproarious

'tunica *nf* tunic

Tuni'sia *nf* Tunisia

'tunnel *nm* *inv* tunnel

'tuo (**il ~** *m*, **la tua** *f*, **i ~i** *mpl*, **le tue** *fpl*) *poss a* your; **è tua questa macchina?** is this car yours?; **un ~ amico** a friend of yours; **~ padre** your father ● *pers pron* yours; **i tuoi** your folks

tuo'nare *vi* thunder. **tu'ono** *nm* thunder

tu'orlo *nm* yolk

tu'racciolo *nm* stopper; (*di sughero*) cork

tu'rar|e *vt* stop; cork ⟨*bottiglia*⟩. **~si** *vr* become blocked; **~si le orecchie** stick one's fingers in one's ears; **~si il naso** hold one's nose

turba'mento *nm* disturbance; (*sconvolgimento*) upsetting. ~ **della quiete pubblica** breach of the peace

tur'bante *nm* turban

tur'ba|re *vt* upset. ~**rsi** *vr* get upset. ~**to** *a* upset

tur'bina *nf* turbine

turbi'nare *vi* whirl. **'turbine** *nm* whirl. **turbine di vento** whirlwind

turbo'len|to *a* turbulent. ~**za** *nf* turbulence

turboreat'tore *nm* turbo-jet

tur'chese *a & nmf* turquoise

Tur'chia *nf* Turkey

tur'chino *a & nm* deep blue

'turco, -a *a* Turkish ● *nmf* Turk ● *nm* (*lingua*) Turkish; *fig* double Dutch; **fumare come un** ~ smoke like a chimney; **bestemmiare come un** ~ swear like a trooper

tu'ris|mo *nm* tourism. ~**ta** *nmf* tourist. ~**tico** *a* tourist *attrib*

'turno *nm* turn; **a** ~ in turn; **di** ~ on duty; **fare a** ~ take turns. ~ **di notte** night shift

'turp|e *a* base. ~**i'loquio** *nm* foul language

'tuta *nf* overalls *pl*; *Sport* tracksuit. ~ **da ginnastica** tracksuit. ~ **da lavoro** overalls. ~ **mimetica** camouflage. ~ **spaziale** spacesuit. ~ **subacquea** wetsuit

tu'tela *nf* *Jur* guardianship; (*pro-* *tezione*) protection. **tute'lare** *vt* protect

tu'tina *nf* sleepsuit; (*da danza*) leotard

tu'tore, -'trice *nmf* guardian

'tutta *nf* **mettercela** ~ **per fare qcsa** go flat out for sth

tutta'via *conj* nevertheless, still

'tutto *a* whole; (*con nomi plurali*) all; (*ogni*) every; **tutta la classe** the whole class, all the class; **tutti gli alunni** all the pupils; **a tutta velocità** at full speed; **ho aspettato** ~ **il giorno** I waited all day [long]; **in** ~ **il mondo** all over the world; **noi tutti** all of us; **era tutta contenta** she was delighted; **tutti e due both; tutti e tre** all three ● *pron* all; (*tutta la gente*) everybody; (*tutte le cose*) everything; (*qualunque cosa*) anything; **l'ho mangiato** ~ I ate it all; **le ho lavate tutte** I washed them all; **raccontami** ~ tell me everything; **lo sanno tutti** everybody knows; **è capace di** ~ he's capable of anything; ~ **compreso** all in; **del** ~ quite; **in** ~ altogether ● *adv* completely; **tutt'a un tratto** all at once; **tutt'altro** not at all; **tutt'altro che** anything but ● *nm* whole; **tentare il** ~ **per** ~ go for broke. ~**'fare** *a inv & nmf* [impiegato] ~ general handyman; **donna** ~ general maid

tut'tora *adv* still

tutù *nm inv* tutu, ballet dress

tv *nf inv* TV

Uu

---

ubbidi'en|te *a* obedient. ~**za** *nf* obedience. **ubbi'dire** *vi* ~ (a) obey

ubi'ca|to *a* located. ~**zi'one** *nf* location

ubria'car|e *vt* get drunk. ~**si** *vr* get drunk; ~**si di** *fig* become intoxicated with

ubria'chezza *nf* drunkenness; **in stato di** ~ inebriated

ubri'aco, -a *a* drunk; ~ **fradicio** dead *o* blind drunk ● *nmf* drunk

ubria'cone *nm* drunkard

uccelli'era *nf* aviary. **uc'cello** *nm* bird; (*vulg: pene*) cock

uc'cider|e *vt* kill. ~**si** *vr* kill oneself

ucci|si'one *nf* killing. **uc'ciso** *pp di* **uccidere**. ~**'sore** *nm* killer

u'dente *a* **i non udenti** the hearing impaired

u'dibile *a* audible

udi'enza *nf* audience; (*colloquio*) interview; *Jur* hearing

u'di|re *vt* hear. ~**'tivo** *a* auditory. ~**to** *nm* hearing. ~**'tore**, ~**'trice** *nmf* listener; *Sch* unregistered student (*allowed to sit in on lectures*). ~**'torio** *nm* audience

'uffa *int* (*con impazienza*) come on!; (*con tono seccato*) damn!

uffici'al|e *a* official ● *nm* officer;

(*funzionario*) official; **pubblico ~e** public official. **~e giudiziario** clerk of the court. **~iz'zare** *vt* make official, officialize

uf'ficio *nm* office; (*dovere*) duty. **~ di collocamento** employment office. **~ informazioni** information office. **~ del personale** personnel department. **~sa'mente** *adv* unofficially. **uffici'oso** *a* unofficial

'ufo[1] *nm inv* UFO

'ufo[2]: **a ~** *adv* without paying

uggi'oso *a* boring

uguagli'a|nza *nf* equality. **~re** *vt* make equal; (*essere uguale*) equal; (*livellare*) level. **~rsi** *vr* **~rsi a** compare oneself to

ugu'al|e *a* equal; (*lo stesso*) the same; (*simile*) like. **~'mente** *adv* equally; (*malgrado tutto*) all the same

'ulcera *nf* ulcer

uli'veto *nm* olive grove

ulteri'or|e *a* further. **~'mente** *adv* further

ultima'mente *adv* lately

ulti'ma|re *vt* complete. **~tum** *nm inv* ultimatum

ulti'missime *nfpl Journ* stop press, latest news *sg*

'ultimo *a* last; (*notizie ecc*) latest; (*più lontano*) farthest; *fig* ultimate ● *nm* last; **fino all'~** to the last; **per ~** at the end; **l'~ piano** the top floor

ultrà *nmf inv Sport* fanatical supporter

ultramo'derno *a* ultramodern

ultra'rapido *a* extra-fast

ultrasen'sibile *a* ultrasensitive

ultra's|onico *a* ultrasonic. **~u'ono** *nm* ultrasound

ultrater'reno *a* after death

ultravio'letto *a* ultraviolet

ulu'la|re *vi* howl. **~to** *nm* howling; **gli ~ti** the howls, the howling

umana'mente *adv* (*trattare*) humanely; **~ impossibile** not humanly possible

uma'nesimo *nm* humanism

umani'tà *nf* humanity. **~'tario** *a* humanitarian. **u'mano** *a* human; (*benevolo*) humane

umidifica'tore *nm* humidifier

umidità *nf* dampness; (*di clima*) humidity. **'umido** *a* damp; (*clima*) humid; (*mani, occhi*) moist ● *nm* dampness; **in umido** *Culin* stewed

'umile *a* humble

umili'a|nte *a* humiliating. **~re** *vt* humiliate. **~rsi** *vr* humble oneself.

~zi'one *nf* humiliation. **umiltà** *nf* humility. **umil'mente** *adv* humbly

u'more *nm* humour; (*stato d'animo*) mood; **di cattivo/buon ~** in a bad/good mood

umo'ris|mo *nm* humour. **~ta** *nmf* humorist. **~tico** *a* humorous

un *indef art* a; (*davanti a vocale o h muta*) an; *vedi* **uno**

una *indef art f* a; *vedi* **un**

unanime'mente *adv* unanimously

u'nanim|e *a* unanimous. **~ità** *nf* unanimity; **all'~ità** unanimously

unci'nato *a* hooked; (*parentesi*) angle

unci'netto *nm* crochet hook

un'cino *nm* hook

'undici *a* & *nm* eleven

'unger|e *vt* grease; (*sporcare*) get greasy; *Relig* anoint; (*blandire*) flatter. **~si** *vr* (*con olio solare*) oil oneself; **~si le mani** get one's hands greasy

unghe'rese *a* & *nmf* Hungarian. **Unghe'ria** *nf* Hungary; (*lingua*) Hungarian

'unghi|a *nf* nail; (*di animale*) claw. **~'ata** *nf* (*graffio*) scratch

ungu'ento *nm* ointment

unica'mente *adv* only. **'unico** *a* only; (*singolo*) single; (*incomparabile*) unique

unifi'ca|re *vt* unify. **~zi'one** *nf* unification

unifor'mar|e *vt* level. **~si** *vr* conform (a to)

uni'form|e *a* & *nf* uniform. **~ità** *nf* uniformity

unilate'rale *a* unilateral

uni'one *nf* union; (*armonia*) unity. **U~ Europea** European Union. **U~ Monetaria Europea** European Monetary Union. **~ sindacale** trade union, labor union *Am*. **U~ Sovietica** Soviet Union

u'ni|re *vt* unite; (*collegare*) join; blend (*colori ecc*). **~rsi** *vr* unite; (*collegarsi*) join

'unisex *a inv* unisex

unità *nf inv* unity; *Math, Mil* unit; *Comput* drive. **~ di misura** unit of measurement. **~rio** *a* unitary

u'nito *a* united; (*tinta*) plain

univer'sal|e *a* universal. **~iz'zare** *vt* universalize. **~'mente** *adv* universally

università *nf inv* university. **~rio, -a** *a* university *attrib* ● *nmf* (*insegnante*) university lecturer; (*studente*) undergraduate

uni'verso *nm* universe

uno, -a *indef art* (*before s + consonant*,

gn, ps, z) a ● *pron* one; **a ~ a ~** one by one; **l'~ e l'altro** both [of them]; **né l'~ né l'altro** neither [of them]; **~ di noi** one of us; **~ fa quello che può** you do what you can ● *a a*, one ● *nm (numerale)* one; *(un tale)* some man ● *nf* some woman

'unt|o *pp di* ungere ● *a* greasy ● *nm* grease. **~u'oso** *a* greasy. **unzi'one** *nf* **l'Estrema Unzione** Extreme Unction

u'omo *nm (pl* uomini) man. **~ d'affari** business man. **~ di fiducia** right-hand man. **~ di Stato** statesman

u'ovo *nm (pl nf* uova) egg. **~ in camicia** poached egg. **~ alla coque** boiled egg. **~ di Pasqua** Easter egg. **~ sodo** hard-boiled egg. **~ strapazzato** scrambled egg

ura'gano *nm* hurricane

u'ranio *nm* uranium

urba'n|esimo *nm* urbanization. **~ista** *nmf* town planner. **~istica** *nf* town planning. **~istico** *a* urban. **urbanizzazi'one** *nf* urbanization. **ur'bano** *a* urban: *(cortese)* urbane

ur'gen|te *a* urgent. **~te'mente** *adv* urgently. **~za** *nf* urgency; **in caso d'~za** in an emergency; **d'~za** *(misura, chiamata)* emergency

'urgere *vi* be urgent

u'rina *nf* urine. **uri'nare** *vi* urinate

ur'lare *vi* shout, yell; *(cane, vento:)* howl. **'urlo** *nm (pl nm* urli, *nf* urla) shout; *(di cane, vento)* howling

'urna *nf* urn; *(elettorale)* ballot box; **andare alle urne** go to the polls

urrà *int* hurrah!

U.R.S.S. *nf abbr* **(Unione delle Repubbliche Socialiste Sovietiche)** USSR

ur'tar|e *vt* knock against; *(scontrarsi)* bump into; *fig* irritate. **~si** *vr* collide; *fig* clash

'urto *nm* knock; *(scontro)* crash; *(contrasto)* conflict; *fig* clash; **d'~** *(misure, terapia)* shock

usa e getta *a inv* *(rasoio, siringa)* throw-away, disposable

u'sanza *nf* custom; *(moda)* fashion

u'sa|re *vt* use; *(impiegare)* employ; *(esercitare)* exercise; **~re fare qcsa** be in the habit of doing sth ● *vi (essere di moda)* be fashionable; **non si usa più** it is out of fashion; *(attrezzatura, espressione:)* it's not used any more. **~to** *a* used; *(non nuovo)* second-hand

U.S.A. *nmpl* US[A] *sg*

u'scente *a (presidente)* outgoing

usci'ere *nm* usher. **'uscio** *nm* door

u'sci|re *vi* come out; *(andare fuori)* go out; *(sfuggire)* get out; *(essere sorteggiato)* come up; *(giornale:)* come out; **~re da** *Comput* exit from, quit; **~re di strada** leave the road. **~ta** *nf* exit, way out; *(spesa)* outlay; *(di autostrada)* junction; *(battuta)* witty remark; **essere in libera ~ta** be off duty. **~ta di servizio** back door. **~ta di sicurezza** emergency exit

usi'gnolo *nm* nightingale

'uso *nm* use; *(abitudine)* custom; *(usanza)* usage; **fuori ~** out of use; **per ~ esterno** *(medicina)* for external use only

U.S.S.L. *nf abbr* **(Unità Socio-Sanitaria Locale)** local health centre

ustio'na|rsi *vr* burn oneself. **~to, -a** *nmf* burns case ● *a* burnt. **usti'one** *nf* burn

usu'ale *a* usual

usufru'ire *vi* **~ di** take advantage of

u'sura *nf* usury. **usu'raio** *nm* usurer

usur'pare *vt* usurp

u'tensile *nm* tool; *Culin* utensil; **cassetta degli utensili** tool box

u'tente *nmf* user. **~ finale** end user

u'tenza *nf* use; *(utenti)* users *pl*

ute'rino *a* uterine. **'utero** *nm* womb

'util|e *a* useful ● *nm* *Comm* profit. **~ità** *nf* usefulness, utility; *Comput* utility. **~i'taria** *nf* *Auto* small car. **~i'tario** *a* utilitarian

utiliz'za|re *vt* utilize. **~zi'one** *nf* utilization. **uti'lizzo** *nm (utilizzazione)* use

uto'pistico *a* Utopian

'uva *nf* grapes *pl*; **chicco d'~** grape. **~ passa** raisins *pl*. **~ sultanina** currants *pl*

va'cante *a* vacant

va'canza *nf* holiday; (*posto vacante*) vacancy. **essere in ~** be on holiday

'vacca *nf* cow. **~ da latte** dairy cow

vacci|'nare *vt* vaccinate. **~inazi'one** *nf* vaccination. **vac'cino** *nm* vaccine

vacil'la|nte *a* tottering; (*oggetto*) wobbly; (*luce*) flickering; *fig* wavering. **~re** *vi* totter; (*oggetto:*) wobble; (*luce:*) flicker; *fig* waver

'vacuo *a* (*vano*) vain; *fig* empty ● *nm* vacuum

vagabon'dare *vi* wander. **vaga'bondo, -a** *a* (*cane*) stray; **gente vagabonda** tramps *pl* ● *nmf* tramp

va'gare *vi* wander

vagheggi'are *vt* long for

va'gi|na *nf* vagina. **~'nale** *a* vaginal

va'gi|re *vi* whimper. **~to** *nm* whimper

'vaglia *nm inv* money order. **~ bancario** bank draft. **~ postale** postal order

vagli'are *vt* sift; *fig* weigh

'vago *a* vague

vagon'cino *nm* (*di funivia*) car

va'gone *nm* (*per passeggeri*) carriage; (*per merci*) wagon. **~ letto** sleeper. **~ ristorante** restaurant car

vai'olo *nm* smallpox

va'langa *nf* avalanche

va'lente *a* skilful

va'ler|e *vi* be worth; (*contare*) count; (*regola:*) apply (**per** to); (*essere valido*) be valid; **far ~e i propri diritti** assert one's rights; **farsi ~e** assert oneself; **non vale!** that's not fair!; **tanto vale che me ne vada** I might as well go ● *vt* **~re qcsa a qcno** (*procurare*) earn sb sth; **~ne la pena** be worth it; **vale la pena di vederlo** it's worth seeing; **~si di** avail oneself of

valeri'ana *nf* valerian

va'levole *a* valid

vali'care *vt* cross. **'valico** *nm* pass

validità *nf* validity; **con ~ illimitata** valid indefinitely

'valido *a* valid; (*efficace*) efficient; (*contributo*) valuable

valige'ria *nf* (*fabbrica*) leather factory; (*negozio*) leather goods shop

va'ligia *nf* suitcase; **fare le valigie** pack; *fig* pack one's bags. **~ diplomatica** diplomatic bag

val'lata *nf* valley. **'valle** *nf* valley; **a valle** downstream

val'lett|a *nf* TV assistant. **~o** *nm* valet; TV assistant

val'lone *nm* (*valle*) deep valley

va'lor|e *nm* value, worth; (*merito*) merit; (*coraggio*) valour; **~i** *pl* Comm securities; **di ~e** (*oggetto*) valuable; **oggetti** *nmpl* **di ~e** valuables; **senza ~e** worthless. **~iz'zare** *vt* (*mettere in valore*) use to advantage; (*aumentare di valore*) increase the value of; (*migliorare l'aspetto di*) enhance

valo'roso *a* courageous

'valso *pp di* **valere**

va'luta *nf* currency. **~ estera** foreign currency

valu'ta|re *vt* value; weigh up (*situazione*). **~rio** *a* (*mercato, norme*) currency. **~zi'one** *nf* valuation

'valva *nf* valve. **'valvola** *nf* valve; *Electr* fuse

'valzer *nm inv* waltz

vam'pata *nf* blaze; (*di calore*) blast; (*al viso*) flush

vam'piro *nm* vampire; *fig* blood-sucker

vana'mente *adv* (*inutilmente*) in vain

van'da|lico *a* **atto ~lico** act of vandalism. **~'lismo** *nm* vandalism. **'vandalo** *nm* vandal

vaneggi'are *vi* rave

'vanga *nf* spade. **van'gare** *vt* dig

van'gelo *nm* Gospel; (*fam: verità*) gospel [truth]

vanifi'care *vt* nullify

va'nigli|a *nf* vanilla. **~'ato** *a* (*zucchero*) vanilla *attrib*

vanil'lina *nf* vanillin

vanità *nf* vanity. **vani'toso** *a* vain

'vano *a* vain ● *nm* (*stanza*) room; (*spazio vuoto*) hollow

van'taggi|o *nm* advantage; *Sport* lead; *Tennis* advantage; **trarre ~o da qcsa**

derive benefit from sth. ~'oso a advantageous

van't|are vt praise; (possedere) boast. ~arsi vr boast. ~e'ria nf boasting. 'vanto nm boast

'vanvera nf a ~ at random; parlare a ~ talk nonsense

va'por|e nm steam; (di benzina, cascata) vapour; a ~e steam; al ~e Culin steamed. ~e acqueo steam, water vapour; battello nm a ~e steamboat. vapo'retto nm ferry. ~i'era nf steam engine

vaporiz'za|re vt vaporize. ~'tore nm spray

vapo'roso a (vestito) filmy; capelli vaporosi big hair sg

va'rare vt launch

var'care vt cross. 'varco nm passage; aspettare al varco lie in wait

vari'abil|e a changeable, variable ● nf variable. ~ità nf changeableness, variability

vari'a|nte nf variant. ~re vt/i vary; ~re di umore change one's mood. ~zi'one nf variation

va'rice nf varicose vein

vari'cella nf chickenpox

vari'coso a varicose

varie'gato a variegated

varietà nf inv variety ● nm inv variety show

'vario a varied; (al pl, parecchi) various; vari pl (molti) several; varie ed eventuali any other business

vario'pinto a multicoloured

'varo nm launch

va'saio nm potter

'vasca nf tub; (piscina) pool; (lunghezza) length. ~ da bagno bath

va'scello nm vessel

va'schetta nf tub

vase'lina nf Vaseline®

vasel'lame nm china. ~ d'oro/d'argento gold/silver plate

'vaso nm pot; (da fiori) vase; Anat vessel; (per cibi) jar. ~ da notte chamber pot

vas'soio nm tray

vastità nf vastness. 'vasto a vast; di vaste vedute broad-minded

Vati'cano nm Vatican

vattela'pesca adv fam God knows!

ve pers pron you; ve l'ho dato I gave it to you

vecchia nf old woman. vecchi'aia nf old age. 'vecchio a old ● nmf old man; i vecchi old people

'vece nf in ~ di in place of; fare le veci di qcno take sb's place

ve'dente a i non vedenti the visually handicapped

ve'der|e vt/i see; far ~e show; farsi ~e show one's face; non ~e l'ora di fare qcsa be raring to go. ~si vr see oneself; (reciproco) see each other

ve'detta nf (luogo) lookout; Naut patrol vessel

'vedovo, -a nm widower ● nf widow

ve'duta nf view

vee'mente a vehement

vege'ta|le a & nm vegetable. ~li'ano a & nmf vegan. ~re vi vegetate. ~ri'ano, -a a & nmf vegetarian. ~zi'one nf vegetation

'vegeto a vedi vivo

veg'gente nmf clairvoyant

'veglia nf watch; fare la ~ keep watch. ~ funebre vigil

vegli'|are vi be awake; ~are su watch over. ~'one nm ~one di capodanno New Year's Eve celebration

ve'icolo nm vehicle

'vela nf sail; Sport sailing; far ~ set sail

ve'la|re vt veil; (fig: nascondere) hide. ~rsi vr (vista:) mist over; (voce:) go husky. ~ta'mente adv indirectly. ~to a veiled; (occhi) misty; (collant) sheer

'velcro® nm velcro®

veleggi'are vi sail

ve'leno nm poison. vele'noso a poisonous

veli'ero nm sailing ship

ve'lina nf (carta) ~ tissue paper; (copia) carbon copy

ve'lista nm yachtsman ● nf yachtswoman

ve'livolo nm aircraft

vellei|tà nf inv foolish ambition. ~'tario a unrealistic

'vello nm fleece

vellu'tato a velvety. vel'luto nm velvet. velluto a coste corduroy

'velo nm veil; (di zucchero, cipria) dusting; (tessuto) voile

ve'loc|e a fast. ~e'mente adv quickly. velo'cista nmf Sport sprinter. ~ità nf inv speed; (Auto: marcia) gear. ~ità di crociera cruising speed. ~iz'zare vt speed up

ve'lodromo nm cycle track

'vena nf vein; essere in ~ di be in the mood for

ve'nale a venal; (persona) mercenary, venal

ve'nato a grainy

vena'torio *a* hunting

vena'tura *nf* (*di legno*) grain; (*di foglia, marmo*) vein

ven'demmi|a *nf* grape harvest. **~'are** *vt* harvest

'vender|e *vt* sell. **~si** *vr* sell oneself; **vendesi** for sale

ven'detta *nf* revenge

vendi'ca|re *vt* avenge. **~rsi** *vr* get one's revenge. **~'tivo** *a* vindictive

'vendi|ta *nf* sale; **in ~ta** on sale. **~ta all'asta** sale by auction. **~ta al dettaglio** retailing. **~ta all'ingrosso** wholesaling. **~ta al minuto** retailing. **~ta porta a porta** door-to-door selling. **~'tore, ~'trice** seller. **~tore ambulante** hawker, pedlar

vene'ra|bile, ~ndo *a* venerable

vene'ra|re *vt* revere

venerdì *nm inv* Friday. **V~ Santo** Good Friday

'Venere *nf* Venus. **ve'nereo** *a* venereal

Ve'nezi|a *nf* Venice. **v~'ano, -a** *a & nmf* Venetian ● *nf* (*persiana*) Venetian blind; *Culin* sweet bun

veni'ale *a* venial

ve'nire *vi* come; (*riuscire*) turn out; (*costare*) cost; (*in passivi*) be; **~ a sapere** learn; **~ in mente** occur; **~ meno** (*svenire*) faint; **~ meno a un contratto** go back on a contract; **~ via** come away; (*staccarsi*) come off; **mi viene da piangere** I feel like crying; **vieni a prendermi** come and pick me up

ven'taglio *nm* fan

ven'tata *nf* gust [of wind]; *fig* breath

ven'te|nne *a & nmf* twenty-year-old. **~simo** *a & nm* twentieth. **'venti** *a & nm* twenty

venti'la|re *vt* air. **~'tore** *nm* fan. **~zi'one** *nf* ventilation

ven'tina *nf* **una ~** (*circa venti*) about twenty

ventiquat'trore *nf inv* (*valigia*) overnight case

'vento *nm* wind; **farsi ~** fan oneself

ven'tosa *nf* sucker

ven'toso *a* windy

'ventre *nm* stomach. **ven'triloquo** *nm* ventriloquist

ven'tura *nf* fortune; **andare alla ~** trust to luck

ven'turo *a* next

ve'nuta *nf* coming

vera'mente *adv* really

ve'randa *nf* veranda

ver'bal|e *a* verbal ● *nm* (*di riunione*) minutes *pl*. **~'mente** *adv* verbally

'verbo *nm* verb. **~ ausiliare** auxiliary [verb]

'verde *a* green ● *nm* green; (*vegetazione*) greenery; (*semaforo*) green light; **essere al ~** be broke. **~ oliva** olive green. **~ pisello** pea green. **~'rame** *nm* verdigris

ver'detto *nm* verdict

ver'dura *nf* vegetables *pl*; **una ~** a vegetable

'verga *nf* rod

vergi'n|ale *a* virginal. **'vergine** *nf* virgin; *Astr* Virgo ● *a* virgin; (*cassetta*) blank. **~ità** *nf* virginity

ver'gogna *nf* shame; (*timidezza*) shyness

vergo'gn|arsi *vr* feel ashamed; (*essere timido*) feel shy. **~oso** *a* ashamed; (*timido*) shy; (*disonorevole*) shameful

ve'rifica *nf* check. **verifi'cabile** *a* verifiable

verifi'car|e *vt* check. **~si** *vr* come true

ve'rismo *nm* realism

verit|à *nf* truth. **~i'ero** *a* truthful

'verme *nm* worm. **~ solitario** tapeworm

ver'miglio *a & nm* vermilion

'vermut *nm inv* vermouth

ver'nacolo *nm* vernacular

ver'nic|e *nf* paint; (*trasparente*) varnish; (*pelle*) patent leather; *fig* veneer; **"vernice fresca"** "wet paint". **~i'are** *vt* paint; (*con vernice trasparente*) varnish. **~ia'tura** *nf* painting; (*strato*) paintwork; *fig* veneer

'vero *a* true; (*autentico*) real; (*perfetto*) perfect; **è ~?** is that so?; **~ e proprio** full blown; **sei stanca, ~?** you're tired, aren't you ● *nm* truth; (*realtà*) life

verosimigli'anza *nf* probability. **vero'simile** *a* probable

ver'ruca *nf* wart; (*sotto la pianta del piede*) verruca

versa'mento *nm* (*pagamento*) payment; (*in banca*) deposit

ver'sante *nm* slope

ver'sa|re *vt* pour; (*spargere*) shed; (*rovesciare*) spill; pay (*denaro*). **~rsi** *vr* spill; (*sfociare*) flow

ver'satil|e *a* versatile. **~ità** *nf* versatility

ver'setto *nm* verse

versi'one *nf* version; (*traduzione*) translation; **"~ integrale"** "unabridged version"; **"~ ridotta"** "abridged version"

'verso[1] *nm* verse; (*grido*) cry; (*gesto*) gesture; (*senso*) direction; (*modo*) manner; **fare il ~ a** qcno ape sb; **non c'è ~ di** there is no way of

'verso² *prep* towards; *(nei pressi di)* round about; **~ dove?** which way?

'vertebra *nf* vertebra

'vertere *vi* **~ su** focus on

verti'cal|e *a* vertical; *(in parole crociate)* down ● *nm* vertical ● *nf* handstand. **~'mente** *adv* vertically

'vertice *nm* summit; *Math* vertex; **conferenza al ~** summit conference

ver'tigine *nf* dizziness; *Med* vertigo; **aver le vertigini** feel dizzy; **vertigini** *pl* giddy spells

vertigi|nosa'mente *adv* dizzily. **~'noso** *a* dizzy; *(velocità)* breakneck; *(prezzi)* sky-high; *(scollatura)* plunging

ve'scica *nf* bladder; *(sulla pelle)* blister

'vescovo *nm* bishop

'vespa *nf* wasp

vespasi'ano *nm* urinal

'vespro *nm* vespers *pl*

ves'sillo *nm* standard

ve'staglia *nf* dressing gown

'vest|e *nf* dress; *(rivestimento)* covering; **in ~e di** in the capacity of; **in ~e ufficiale** in an official capacity. **~i'ario** *nm* clothing

ve'stibolo *nm* hall

ve'stigio *nm* (*pl nm* **vestigi**, *pl nf* **vestigia**) trace

ve'sti|re *vt* dress. **~rsi** *vr* get dressed. **~ti** *pl* clothes. **~to** *a* dressed ● *nm* (*da uomo*) suit; *(da donna)* dress

vete'rano, **-a** *a* & *nmf* veteran

veteri'naria *nf* veterinary science

veteri'nario *a* veterinary ● *nm* veterinary surgeon

'veto *nm inv* veto

ve'tra|io *nm* glazier. **~ta** *nf* big window; *(in chiesa)* stained glass window; *(porta)* glass door. **~to** *a* glazed. **vetre'ria** *nf* glass works

ve'tri|na *nf* [shop-]window; *(mobile)* display cabinet. **~'nista** *nmf* window dresser

vetri'olo *nm* vitriol

'vetro *nm* glass; *(di finestra, porta)* pane. **~'resina** *nf* fibreglass

'vetta *nf* peak

vet'tore *nm* vector

vetto'vaglie *nfpl* provisions

vet'tura *nf* coach; *(ferroviaria)* carriage; *Auto* car. **vettu'rino** *nm* coachman

vezzeggi'a|re *vt* fondle. **~'tivo** *nm* pet name. **'vezzo** *nm* habit; *(attrattiva)* charm; **vezzi** *pl* *(moine)* affectation *sg*. **vez'zoso** *a* charming; *pej* affected

vi *pers pron* you; *(riflessivo)* yourselves; *(reciproco)* each other; *(tra più persone)* one another; **vi ho dato un libro** I gave you a book; **lavatevi le mani** wash your hands; **eccovi!** here you are! ● *adv* = **ci**

'via¹ *nf* street, road; *fig* way; *Anat* tract; **in ~** di in the course of; **per ~** di on account of; **~ ~ che** as; **per ~ aerea** by airmail

'via² *adv* away; *(fuori)* out; **andar ~** go away; **e così ~** and so on; **e ~ dicendo** and whatnot ● *int* **!** go away!; *Sport* go!; *(andiamo)* come on! ● *nm* starting signal

viabilità *nf* road conditions *pl*; *(rete)* road network; *(norme)* road and traffic laws *pl*

via'card *nf inv* motorway card

via'dotto *nm* viaduct

viaggi'a|re *vi* travel. **~'tore**, **~'trice** *nmf* traveller

vi'aggio *nm* journey; *(breve)* trip; **buon ~!** safe journey!, have a good trip!; **fare un ~** go on a journey. **~ di nozze** honeymoon

vi'ale *nm* avenue; *(privato)* drive

via'vai *nm* coming and going

vi'bra|nte *a* vibrant. **~re** *vi* vibrate; *(fremere)* quiver. **~zi'one** *nf* vibration

vi'cario *nm* vicar

'vice+ *pref* vice+

'vice *nmf* deputy. **~diret'tore** *nm* assistant manager

vi'cenda *nf* event; **a ~** *(fra due)* each other; *(a turno)* in turn[s]

vice'versa *adv* vice versa

vici'na|nza *nf* nearness; **~nze** *pl* *(paraggi)* neighbourhood. **~to** *nm* neighbourhood; *(vicini)* neighbours *pl*

vi'cino, **-a** *a* near; *(accanto)* next ● *adv* near, close. **~ a** *prep* near [to] ● *nmf* neighbour. **~ di casa** nextdoor neighbour

vicissi'tudine *nf* vicissitude

'vicolo *nm* alley

'video *nm* video. **~'camera** *nf* camcorder. **~cas'setta** *nf* video cassette

videoci'tofono *nm* video entry phone

video'clip *nm inv* video clip

videogi'oco *nm* video game

videoregistra'tore *nm* videorecorder

video'teca *nf* video library

video'tel® *nm* ≈ Videotex®

videotermi'nale *nm* visual display unit, VDU

vidi'mare *vt* authenticate

vie'ta|re *vt* forbid; **sosta ~ta** no parking; **~to fumare** no smoking; **~to ai**

minori di 18 anni prohibited to children under the age of 18

vi'gente *a* in force. **'vigere** *vi* be in force

vigi'la|nte *a* vigilant. **~nza** *nf* vigilance. **~re** *vt* keep an eye on ● *vi* keep watch

'vigile *a* watchful ● *nm* ~ **[urbano]** policeman. ~ **del fuoco** fireman

vi'gilia *nf* eve

vigliacche'ria *nf* cowardice. **vigli'acco, -a** *a* cowardly ● *nmf* coward

'vigna *nf*, **vi'gneto** *nm* vineyard

vi'gnetta *nf* cartoon

vi'gore *nm* vigour; **entrare in** ~ come into force. **vigo'roso** *a* vigorous

'vile *a* cowardly; (*abietto*) vile

'villa *nf* villa

vil'laggio *nm* village. ~ **turistico** holiday village

vil'lano *a* rude ● *nm* boor; (*contadino*) peasant

villeggia'|nte *nmf* holiday-maker. **~re** *vi* spend one's holidays. **~'tura** *nf* holiday[s] [*pl*], vacation *Am*

vil'l|etta *nf* small detached house. **~ino** *nm* detached house

viltà *nf* cowardice

'vimine *nm* wicker

'vinc|ere *vt* win; (*sconfiggere*) beat; (*superare*) overcome. **~ita** *nf* win; (*somma vinta*) winnings *pl*. **~i'tore**, **~i'trice** *nmf* winner

vinco'la|nte *a* binding. **~re** *vt* bind; *Comm* tie up. **'vincolo** *nm* bond

vi'nicolo *a* wine *attrib*

vinil'pelle® *nm* Leatherette®

'vino *nm* wine. ~ **spumante** sparkling wine. ~ **da taglio** blending wine. ~ **da tavola** table wine

'vinto *pp di* **vincere**

vi'ola *nf* Bot violet; *Mus* viola. **vio'laceo** *a* purplish; (*labbra*) blue

vio'la|re *vt* violate. **~zi'one** *nf* violation. **~zione di domicilio** breaking and entering

violen'tare *vt* rape

violente'mente *adv* violently

vio'len|to *a* violent. **~za** *nf* violence. **~za carnale** rape

vio'letta *nf* violet

vio'letto *a & nm* (*colore*) violet

violi'nista *nmf* violinist. **vio'lino** *nm* violin. **violon'cello** *nm* cello

vi'ottolo *nm* path

'vipera *nf* viper

vi'ra|ggio *nm* Phot toning; *Naut, Aeron* turn. **~re** *vi* turn; **~re di bordo** veer

'virgol|a *nf* comma. **~ette** *nfpl* inverted commas

vi'ril|e *a* virile; (*da uomo*) manly. **~ità** *nf* virility; manliness

virtù *nf inv* virtue; **in** ~ **di** (*legge*) under. **~'ale** *a* virtual. **~'oso** *a* virtuous ● *nm* virtuoso

viru'lento *a* virulent

'virus *nm inv* virus

visa'gista *nmf* beautician

visce'rale *a* visceral; (*odio*) deep-seated; (*reazione*) gut

'viscere *nm* internal organ ● *nfpl* guts

'vischi|o *nm* mistletoe. **~'oso** *a* viscous; (*appiccicoso*) sticky

'viscido *a* slimy

vi'scont|e *nm* viscount. **~'essa** *nf* viscountess

vi'scoso *a* viscous

vi'sibile *a* visible

visi'bilio *nm* profusion; **andare in** ~ go into ecstasies

visibilità *nf* visibility

visi'era *nf* (*di elmo*) visor; (*di berretto*) peak

visio'nare *vt* examine; *Cinema* screen. **visi'one** *nf* vision; **prima visione** *Cinema* first showing

'visit|a *nf* visit; (*breve*) call; *Med* examination; **fare ~a a** qcno pay sb a visit. **~a di controllo** *Med* checkup. **visi'tare** *vt* visit; (*brevemente*) call on; *Med* examine; **~a'tore**, **~a'trice** *nmf* visitor

vi'sivo *a* visual

'viso *nm* face

'visone *nm* mink

'vispo *a* lively

vis'suto *pp di* **vivere** ● *a* experienced

'vist|a *nf* sight; (*veduta*) view; **a ~a d'occhio** (*crescere*) visibly; (*estendersi*) as far as the eye can see; **in ~a di** in view of; **perdere di ~a** qcno lose sight of sb; *fig* lose touch with sb. **~o** *pp di* **vedere** ● *nm* visa. **vi'stoso** *a* showy; (*notevole*) considerable

visu'al|e *a* visual. **~izza'tore** *nm* Comput display, VDU. **~izzazi'one** *nf* Comput display

'vita *nf* life; (*durata della vita*) lifetime; *Anat* waist; **a** ~ for life; **essere in fin di** ~ be at death's door; **essere in** ~ be alive

vi'tal|e *a* vital. **~ità** *nf* vitality

vita'lizio *a* life *attrib* ● *nm* [life] annuity

vita'min|a *nf* vitamin. **~iz'zato** *a* vitamin-enriched

'vite *nf* Mech screw; *Bot* vine

vi'tello *nm* calf; *Culin* veal; (*pelle*) calfskin

vi'ticcio *nm* tendril

viticol't|ore *nm* wine grower. **~ura** *nf* wine growing

'vitreo *a* vitreous; *(sguardo)* glassy

'vittima *nf* victim

'vitto *nm* food; *(pasti)* board. **~ e alloggio** board and lodging

vit'toria *nf* victory

vittori'ano *a* Victorian

vittori'oso *a* victorious

vi'uzza *nf* narrow lane

'viva *int* hurrah!; **~ la Regina!** long live the Queen!

vi'vac|e *a* vivacious; *(mente)* lively; *(colore)* bright. **~ità** *nf* vivacity; *(di mente)* liveliness; *(di colore)* brightness. **~iz'zare** *vt* liven up

vi'vaio *nm* nursery; *(per pesci)* pond; *fig* breeding ground

viva'mente *adv* *(ringraziare)* warmly

vi'vanda *nf* food; *(piatto)* dish

vi'vente *a* living ● *nmpl* **i viventi** the living

'vivere *vi* live; **~ di** live on ● *vt (passare)* go through ● *nm* life

'viveri *nmpl* provisions

'vivido *a* vivid

vivisezi'one *nf* vivisection

'vivo *a* alive; *(vivente)* living; *(vivace)* lively; *(colore)* bright; **~ e vegeto** alive and kicking; **farsi ~** keep in touch; *(arrivare)* turn up ● *nm* **colpire qcno sul ~** cut sb to the quick; **dal ~** *(trasmissione)* live; *(disegnare)* from life; **i vivi** the living

vizi'|are *vt* spoil *(bambino ecc)*; *(guastare)* vitiate. **~'ato** *a* spoilt; *(aria)* stale. **'vizio** *nm* vice; *(cattiva abitudine)* bad habit; *(difetto)* flaw. **~'oso** *a* dissolute; *(difettoso)* faulty; **circolo ~oso** vicious circle

vocabo'lario *nm* dictionary; *(lessico)* vocabulary. **vo'cabolo** *nm* word

vo'cale *a* vocal ● *nf* vowel. **vo'calico** *a* *(corde)* vocal; *(suono)* vowel *attrib*

vocazi'one *nf* vocation

'voce *nf* voice; *(diceria)* rumour; *(di bilancio, dizionario)* entry

voci'are *vi* *(spettegolare)* gossip ● *nm* buzz of conversation

vocife'rare *vi* shout; **si vocifera che...** it is rumoured that...

'vog|a *nf* rowing; *(lena)* enthusiasm; *(moda)* vogue. **essere in ~a** be in fashion. **vo'gare** *vi* row. **~'a'tore** *nm* oarsman; *(attrezzo)* rowing machine

'vogli|a *nf* desire; *(volontà)* will; *(della pelle)* birthmark; **aver ~a di fare qcsa** feel like doing sth. **~'oso** *a* *(occhi, persona)* covetous

'voi *pers pron* you; **siete ~?** is that you?; **l'avete fatto ~?** did you do it yourself?. **~a'ltri** *pers pron* you

vo'lano *nm* shuttlecock; *Mech* flywheel

vo'lante *a* flying; *(foglio)* loose ● *nm* steering-wheel

volan'tino *nm* leaflet

vo'la|re *vi* fly. **~ta** *nf Sport* final sprint; **di ~ta** in a rush

vo'latile *a* *(liquido)* volatile ● *nm* bird

volée *nf inv* Tennis volley

vo'lente *a* **~ o nolente** whether you like it or not

volente'roso *a* willing

volenti'eri *adv* willingly; **~!** with pleasure!

vo'lere *vt* want; *(chiedere di)* ask for; *(aver bisogno di)* need; **vuole che lo faccia io** he wants me to do it; **fai come vuoi** do as you like; **se tuo padre vuole, ti porto al cinema** if your father agrees, I'll take you to the cinema; **vorrei un caffè** I'd like a coffee; **la leggenda vuole che...** legend has it that...; **la vuoi smettere?** will you stop that!; **senza ~** without meaning to; **voler bene/male a** qcno love/have something against sb; **voler dire** mean; **ci vuole il latte** we need milk; **ci vuole tempo/pazienza** it takes time/patience; **volerne a** have a grudge against; **vuoi...vuoi...** either...or... ● *nm* will; **voleri** *pl* wishes

vol'gar|e *a* vulgar; *(popolare)* common. **~ità** *nf inv* vulgarity. **~iz'zare** *vt* popularize. **~'mente** *adv* *(grossolanamente)* vulgarly, coarsely; *(comunemente)* commonly

'volger|e *vt/i* turn. **~si** *vr* turn [round]; **~si a** *(dedicarsi)* take up

voli'era *nf* aviary

voli'tivo *a* strong-minded

'volo *nm* flight; *al ~* *(fare qcsa)* quickly; *(prendere qcsa)* in mid-air; **alzarsi in ~** *(uccello:)* take off; **in ~** airborne. **~ di linea** scheduled flight. **~ nazionale** domestic flight. **~ a vela** gliding.

volontà *nf inv* will; *(desiderio)* wish; **a ~** *(mangiare)* as much as you like. **~ria'mente** *adv* voluntarily. **volonta'rio** *a* voluntary ● *nm* volunteer

volonte'roso *a* willing

'volpe *nf* fox

volt *nm inv* volt

'volta *nf* time; *(turno)* turn; *(curva)* bend; *Archit* vault; **4 volte** 4 4 times 4; **a volte** sometimes; **c'era una ~...** once upon a time, there was...; **una ~** once; **due volte** twice; **tre/quattro volte** three/four times; **una ~ per tutte** once and for all; **uno per ~** one at a time; **uno alla ~** one at a time; **alla ~ di** in the direction of

volta'faccia *nm inv* volte-face

vol'taggio *nm* voltage

vol'ta|re *vt/i* turn; *(rigirare)* turn round; *(rivoltare)* turn over; **~re pagina** *fig* forget the past. **~rsi** *vr* turn [round]

volta'stomaco *nm* nausea; *fig* disgust

volteggi'are *vi* circle; *(ginnastica)* vault

'volto *pp di* **volgere ● *nm* face; **mi ha mostrato il suo vero ~** he revealed his true colours

vo'lubile *a* fickle

vo'lum|e *nm* volume. **~i'noso** *a* voluminous

voluta'mente *adv* deliberately

voluttu|osità *nf* voluptuousness. **~'oso** *a* voluptuous

vomi'tare *vt* vomit, be sick. **vomi'tevole** *a* nauseating. **'vomito** *nm* vomit.

'vongola *nf* clam

vo'race *a* voracious. **~'mente** *adv* voraciously

vo'ragine *nf* abyss

'vortice *nm* whirl; *(gorgo)* whirlpool; *(di vento)* whirlwind

'vostro (**il ~** *m*, **la vostra** *f*, **i vostri** *mpl*, **le vostre** *fpl*) *poss a* your; **è vostra questa macchina?** is this car yours?; **un ~ amico** a friend of yours; **~ padre** your father ● *poss pron* yours; **i vostri** your folks

vo'ta|nte *nmf* voter. **~re** *vi* vote. **~zi'one** *nf* voting; *Sch* marks *pl*. **'voto** *nm* vote; *Sch* mark; *Relig* vow

vs. *abbr Comm* (**vostro**) yours

vul'canico *a* volcanic. **vul'cano** *nm* volcano

vulne'rabil|e *a* vulnerable. **~ità** *nf* vulnerability

vuo'tare *vt*, **vuo'tarsi** *vr* empty

vu'oto *a* empty; *(non occupato)* vacant; **~ di** *(sprovvisto)* devoid of ● *nm* empty space; *Phys* vacuum; *fig* void; **assegno a ~** dud cheque; **sotto ~** *(prodotto)* vacuum-packed; **~ a perdere** no deposit. **~ d'aria** air pocket

W *abbr* (**viva**) long live

'wafer *nm inv* (**biscotto**) wafer

walkie-'talkie *nm inv* walkie-talkie

water *nm inv* toilet, loo *fam*

watt *nm inv* watt

wat'tora *nm inv Phys* watt-hour

WC *nm* WC

'western *a inv* cowboy *attrib* ● *nm Cinema* western

X, x *a* **raggi** *nmpl* **X** X-rays; **il giorno X** D-day

xenofo'bia *nf* xenophobia. **xe'nofobo, -a** *a* xenophobic ● *nmf* xenophobe

'xeres *nm inv* sherry

xi'lofono *nm* xylophone

yacht *nm inv* yacht

yen *nm inv Fin* yen

'yeti *nm inv* yeti

'yoga *nm* yoga; *(praticante)* yogi

'yogurt *nm inv* yoghurt. **~i'era** *nf* yoghurt-maker

'yorkshire *nm inv* (**cane**) Yorkshire terrier

yo-yo *nm inv* yoyo®

Zz

zaba[gl]i'one *nm* zabaglione (*dessert made from eggs, wine or marsala and sugar*)

'zacchera *nf* (*schizzo*) splash of mud

zaf'fata *nf* whiff; (*di fumo*) cloud

zaffe'rano *nm* saffron

zaf'firo *nm* sapphire

'zaino *nm* rucksack

'zampa *nf* leg; **a quattro zampe** ⟨*animale*⟩ four-legged; (*carponi*) on all fours. **zampe** *pl* **di gallina** crow's feet

zampil'la|nte *a* spurting. **~re** *vi* spurt. **zam'pillo** *nm* spurt

zam'pogna *nf* bagpipe. **zampo'gnaro** *nm* piper

'zanna *nf* fang; (*di elefante*) tusk

zan'zar|a *nf* mosquito. **~i'era** *nf* (*velo*) mosquito net; (*su finestra*) insect screen

'zappa *nf* hoe. **zap'pare** *vt* hoe

'zattera *nf* raft

za'vorra *nf* ballast; *fig* dead wood

'zazzera *nf* mop of hair

'zebra *nf* zebra; **zebre** *pl* (*passaggio pedonale*) zebra crossing

'zecca [1] *nf* mint; **nuovo di ~** brand-new

'zecca [2] *nf* (*parassita*) tick

zec'chino *nm* sequin; **oro ~** pure gold

ze'lante *a* zealous. **'zelo** *nm* zeal

'zenit *nm* zenith

'zenzero *nm* ginger

'zeppa *nf* wedge

'zeppo *a* packed full; **pieno ~ di** crammed *o* packed with

zer'bino *nm* doormat

'zero *nm* zero, nought; (*in calcio*) nil; *Tennis* love; **due a ~** (*in partite*) two nil; **ricominciare da ~** *fig* start again from scratch

'zeta *nf* zed, zee *Am*

'zia *nf* aunt

zibel'lino *nm* sable

'zigomo *nm* cheek-bone

zigri'nato *a* ⟨*pelle*⟩ grained; ⟨*metallo*⟩ milled

zig'zag *nm inv* zigzag

zim'bello *nm* decoy; (*oggetto di scherno*) laughing-stock

'zinco *nm* zinc

'zingaro, -a *nmf* gypsy

'zio *nm* uncle

zi'tel|la *nf* spinster; *pej* old maid. **~'lona** *nf pej* old maid

zit'tire *vi* fall silent ● *vt* silence. **'zitto** *a* silent; **sta' zitto!** keep quiet!

ziz'zania *nf* (*discordia*) discord; **seminare ~** cause trouble

'zoccolo *nm* clog; (*di cavallo*) hoof; (*di terra*) clump; (*di parete*) skirting board, baseboard *Am*; (*di colonna*) base

zodia'cale *a* of the zodiac. **zo'diaco** *nm* zodiac

'zolfo *nm* sulphur

'zolla *nf* clod; (*di zucchero*) lump

zol'letta *nf* sugar cube, sugar lump

'zombi *nmf inv fig* zombi

'zona *nf* zone; (*area*) area. **~ di depressione** area of low pressure. **~ disco** area for parking discs only. **~ pedonale** pedestrian precinct. **~ verde** green belt

'zonzo *adv* **andare a ~** stroll about

zoo *nm inv* zoo

zoolo'gia *nf* zoology. **zoo'logico** *a* zoological. **zo'ologo, -a** *nmf* zoologist

zoo sa'fari *nm inv* safari park

zoppi'ca|nte *a* limping; *fig* shaky. **~re** *vi* limp; (*essere debole*) be shaky. **'zoppo, -a** *a* lame ● *nmf* cripple

zoti'cone *nm* boor

zu'ava *nf* **calzoni alla ~** plus-fours

'zucca *nf* marrow; (*fam: testa*) head; (*fam: persona*) thickie

zucche'r|are *vt* sugar. **~i'era** *nf* sugar bowl. **~i'ficio** *nm* sugar refinery. **zucche'rino** *a* sugary ● *nm* sugar lump

'zucchero *nm* sugar. **~ di canna** cane sugar. **~ a velo** icing sugar. **zuc-che'roso** *a fig* honeyed

zuc'chin|a *nf,* **~o** *nm* courgette, zucchini *Am*

zuc'cone *nm* blockhead

'zuffa *nf* scuffle

zufo'lare *vt/i* whistle

zu'mare *vi* zoom

'zuppa *nf* soup. **~ inglese** trifle

zup'petta *nf* **fare ~ [con]** dunk

zuppi'era *nf* soup tureen

'zuppo *a* soaked

Aa

A /eɪ/ n Mus la m inv

a /ə/, accentato /eɪ/ (davanti a una vocale an) indef art un m, una f; (before s + consonant, gn, ps and z) uno; (before feminine noun starting with a vowel) un'; (each) a; **I am a lawyer** sono avvocato; **a tiger is a feline** la tigre è un felino; **a knife and fork** un coltello e una forchetta; **a Mr Smith is looking for you** un certo signor Smith ti sta cercando; **£2 a kilo/a head** due sterline al chilo/a testa

aback /ə'bæk/ adv **be taken ~** essere preso in contropiede

abandon /ə'bændən/ vt abbandonare; (give up) rinunciare a ● n abbandono m. **~ed** a abbandonato

abashed /ə'bæʃt/ a imbarazzato

abate /ə'beɪt/ vi calmarsi

abattoir /'æbətwɑ:(r)/ n mattatoio m

abbey /'æbɪ/ n abbazia f

abbreviat|e /ə'bri:vɪeɪt/ vt abbreviare. **~ion** /-'eɪʃn/ n abbreviazione f

abdicat|e /'æbdɪkeɪt/ vi abdicare. ● vt rinunciare a. **~ion** /-'keɪʃn/ n abdicazione f

abdom|en /'æbdəmən/ n addome m. **~inal** /-'dɒmɪnl/ a addominale

abduct /əb'dʌkt/ vt rapire. **~ion** /-ʌkʃn/ n rapimento m

aberration /æbə'reɪʃn/ n aberrazione f

abet /ə'bet/ vt (pt/pp abetted) aid and **~** Jur essere complice di

abeyance /ə'beɪəns/ n **in ~** in sospeso; **fall into ~** cadere in disuso

abhor /əb'hɔ:(r)/ vt (pt/pp abhorred) aborrire. **~rence** /-'hɒrəns/ n orrore m

abid|e /ə'baɪd/ vt (pt/pp abided) (tolerate) sopportare ● **abide by** vi rispettare. **~ing** a perpetuo

ability /ə'bɪlətɪ/ n capacità f inv

abject /'æbdʒekt/ a (poverty) degradante; (apology) umile; (coward) abietto

ablaze /ə'bleɪz/ a in fiamme; **be ~ with light** risplendere di luci

able /'eɪbl/ a capace, abile; **be ~ to do sth** poter fare qcsa; **were you ~ to...?**

sei riuscito a...? ● **~-bodied** a robusto; Mil abile

ably /'eɪblɪ/ adv abilmente

abnormal /æb'nɔ:ml/ a anormale. **~ity** /-'mælətɪ/ n anormalità f inv. **~ly** adv in modo anormale

aboard /ə'bɔ:d/ adv & prep a bordo

abol|ish /ə'bɒlɪʃ/ vt abolire. **~ition** /æbə'lɪʃn/ n abolizione f

abomina|ble /ə'bɒmɪnəbl/ a abominevole

Aborigine /æbə'rɪdʒənɪ/ n aborigeno, -a mf d'Australia

abort /ə'bɔ:t/ vt fare abortire; fig annullare. **~ion** /-ɔ:ʃn/ n aborto m; **have an ~ion** abortire. **~ive** /-tɪv/ a (attempt) infruttuoso

abound /ə'baund/ vi abbondare; **~ in** abbondare di

about /ə'baut/ adv (here and there) [di] qua e [di] là; (approximately) circa; **be ~** (illness, tourists:) essere in giro; **be up and ~** essere alzato; **leave sth lying ~** lasciare in giro qcsa ● prep (concerning) su; (in the region of) intorno a; (here and there in) per; **what is the book/the film ~?** di cosa parla il libro/il film?; **he wants to see you - what ~?** ti vuole vedere - a che proposito?; **talk/know ~** parlare/sapere di; **I know nothing ~ it** non ne so niente; **~ 5 o'clock** intorno alle 5; **travel ~ the world** viaggiare per il mondo; **be ~ to do sth** stare per fare qcsa; **how ~ going to the cinema?** e se andassimo al cinema?

about: **~-'face** n, **~-'turn** n dietro front m inv

above /ə'bʌv/ adv & prep sopra; **~ all** soprattutto

above: **~-'board** a onesto. **~-'mentioned** a suddetto

abrasive /ə'breɪsɪv/ a abrasivo; (remark) caustico ● n abrasivo m

abreast /ə'brest/ adv fianco a fianco; **come ~ of** allinearsi con; **keep ~ of** tenersi al corrente di

abridged /ə'brɪdʒd/ a ridotto

abroad /ə'brɔ:d/ adv all'estero

abrupt /ə'brʌpt/ *a* brusco

abscess /'æbsɪs/ *n* ascesso *m*

abscond /əb'skɒnd/ *vi* fuggire

absence /'æbsəns/ *n* assenza *f*; (*lack*) mancanza *f*

absent[1] /'æbsənt/ *a* assente

absent[2] /æb'sent/ *vt* ~ oneself essere assente

absentee /æbsən'tiː/ *n* assente *mf*

absent-minded /æbsənt'maɪndɪd/ *a* distratto

absolute /'æbsəluːt/ *a* assoluto; **an ~ idiot** un perfetto idiota. **~ly** *adv* assolutamente; (*fam: indicating agreement*) esattamente

absolution /æbsə'luːʃn/ *n* assoluzione *f*

absolve /əb'zɒlv/ *vt* assolvere

absorb /əb'sɔːb/ *vt* assorbire; **~ed in** assorto in. **~ent** /-ənt/ *a* assorbente

absorption /əb'sɔːpʃn/ *n* assorbimento *m*; (*in activity*) concentrazione *f*

abstain /əb'steɪn/ *vi* astenersi (**from** da)

abstemious /əb'stiːmɪəs/ *a* moderato

abstention /əb'stenʃn/ *n* Pol astensione *f*

abstinence /'æbstɪnəns/ *n* astinenza *f*

abstract /'æbstrækt/ *a* astratto ● *n* astratto *m*; (*summary*) estratto *m*

absurd /əb'sɜːd/ *a* assurdo. **~ity** *n* assurdità *f* *inv*

abundan|ce /ə'bʌndəns/ *n* abbondanza *f*. **~t** *a* abbondante

abuse[1] /ə'bjuːz/ *vt* (*misuse*) abusare di; (*insult*) insultare; (*ill-treat*) maltrattare

abus|e[2] /ə'bjuːs/ *n* abuso *m*; (*verbal*) insulti *mpl*; (*ill-treatment*) maltrattamento *m*. **~ive** /-ɪv/ *a* offensivo

abut /ə'bʌt/ *vi* (*pt/pp* abutted) confinare (**onto** con)

abysmal /ə'bɪzml/ *a* fam pessimo; (*ignorance*) abissale

abyss /ə'bɪs/ *n* abisso *m*

academic /ækə'demɪk/ *a* teorico; (*qualifications, system*) scolastico; **be ~** (*person:*) avere predisposizione allo studio ● *n* docente *mf* universitario, -a

academy /ə'kædəmɪ/ *n* accademia *f*; (*of music*) conservatorio *m*

accede /ək'siːd/ *vi* ~ **to** accedere a (*request*); salire a (*throne*)

accelerat|e /ək'seləreɪt/ *vt/i* accelerare. **~ion** /-'reɪʃn/ *n* accelerazione *f*. **~or** *n* Auto acceleratore *m*

accent /'æksənt/ *n* accento *m*

accentuate /ək'sentjʊeɪt/ *vt* accentuare

accept /ək'sept/ *vt* accettare. **~able** /-əbl/ *a* accettabile. **~ance** *n* accettazione *f*

access /'ækses/ *n* accesso *m*. **~ible** /ək'sesɪbl/ *a* accessibile

accession /ək'seʃn/ *n* (*to throne*) ascesa *f* al trono

accessory /ək'sesərɪ/ *n* accessorio *m*; Jur complice *mf*

accident /'æksɪdənt/ *n* incidente *m*; (*chance*) caso *m*; **by ~** per caso; (*unintentionally*) senza volere; **I'm sorry, it was an ~** mi dispiace, non l'ho fatto apposta. **~al** /-'dentl/ *a* (*meeting*) casuale; (*death*) incidentale; (*unintentional*) involontario. **~ally** *adv* per caso; (*unintentionally*) inavvertitamente

acclaim /ə'kleɪm/ *n* acclamazione *f* ● *vt* acclamare (**as** come)

acclimatize /ə'klaɪmətaɪz/ *vt* **become ~d** acclimatarsi

accolade /'ækəleɪd/ *n* riconoscimento *m*

accommodat|e /ə'kɒmədeɪt/ *vt* ospitare; (*oblige*) favorire. **~ing** *a* accomodante. **~ion** /-'deɪʃn/ *n* (*place to stay*) sistemazione *f*

accompan|iment /ə'kʌmpənɪmənt/ *n* accompagnamento *m*. **~ist** *n* Mus accompagnatore, -trice *mf*

accompany /ə'kʌmpənɪ/ *vt* (*pt/pp* **-ied**) accompagnare

accomplice /ə'kʌmplɪs/ *n* complice *mf*

accomplish /ə'kʌmplɪʃ/ *vt* (*achieve*) concludere; realizzare (*aim*). **~ed** *a* dotato; (*fact*) compiuto. **~ment** *n* realizzazione *f*; (*achievement*) risultato *m*; (*talent*) talento *m*

accord /ə'kɔːd/ *n* (*treaty*) accordo *m*; **with one ~** tutti d'accordo; **of his own ~** di sua spontanea volontà. **~ance** *n* **in ~ance with** in conformità di o a

according /ə'kɔːdɪŋ/ *adv* ~ **to** secondo. **~ly** *adv* di conseguenza

accordion /ə'kɔːdɪən/ *n* fisarmonica *f*

accost /ə'kɒst/ *vt* abbordare

account /ə'kaʊnt/ *n* conto *m*; (*report*) descrizione *f*; (*of eye-witness*) resoconto *m*; **~s** *pl* Comm conti *mpl*; **on ~ of** a causa di; **on no ~** per nessun motivo; **on this ~** per questo motivo; **on my ~** per causa mia; **of no ~** di nessuna importanza; **take into ~** tener conto di ● **account for** *vi* (*explain*) spiegare; (*person:*) render conto di; (*constitute*) costituire. **~ability** *n* responsabilità *f* *inv*. **~able** *a* responsabile (**for** di)

accountant /ə'kaʊntənt/ n (book-keeper) contabile mf; (consultant) commercialista mf

accredited /ə'kredɪtɪd/ a accreditato

accrue /ə'kruː/ vi (interest:) maturare

accumulat|e /ə'kjuːmjʊleɪt/ vt accumulare ● vi accumularsi. **~ion** /-'leɪʃn/ n accumulazione f

accura|cy /'ækʊrəsɪ/ n precisione f. **~te** /-rət/ a preciso. **~tely** adv con precisione

accusation /ækjʊ'zeɪʃn/ n accusa f

accusative /ə'kjuːzətɪv/ a & n **~ [case]** Gram accusativo m

accuse /ə'kjuːz/ vt accusare; **~ sb of doing sth** accusare qcno di fare qcsa. **~d** n the **~d** l'accusato m, l'accusata f

accustom /ə'kʌstəm/ vt abituare (**to** a); **grow** or **get ~ed to** abituarsi a. **~ed** a abituato

ace /eɪs/ n Cards asso m; (tennis) ace m inv

ache /eɪk/ n dolore m ● vi dolere, far male; **~ all over** essere tutto indolenzito

achieve /ə'tʃiːv/ vt ottenere (success); realizzare (goal, ambition). **~ment** n (feat) successo m

acid /'æsɪd/ a acido ● n acido m. **~ity** /ə'sɪdətɪ/ n acidità f. **~ 'rain** n pioggia f acida

acknowledge /ək'nɒlɪdʒ/ vt riconoscere; rispondere a (greeting); far cenno di (sb's presence); far notare (sb's presence); **~ receipt of** accusare ricevuta di. **~ment** n riconoscimento m; **send an ~ment of a letter** confermare il ricevimento di una lettera

acne /'æknɪ/ n acne f

acorn /'eɪkɔːn/ n ghianda f

acoustic /ə'kuːstɪk/ a acustico. **~s** npl acustica fsg

acquaint /ə'kweɪnt/ vt **~ sb with** metter qcno al corrente di; **be ~ed with** conoscere (person); essere a conoscenza di (fact). **~ance** n (person) conoscente mf; **make sb's ~ance** fare la conoscenza di qcno

acquiesce /ækwɪ'es/ vi acconsentire (**to, in** a). **~nce** n acquiescenza f

acquire /ə'kwaɪə(r)/ vt acquisire

acquisit|ion /ækwɪ'zɪʃn/ n acquisizione f. **~ive** /ə'kwɪzətɪv/ a avido

acquit /ə'kwɪt/ vt (pt/pp acquitted) assolvere; **~ oneself well** cavarsela bene. **~tal** n assoluzione f

acre /'eɪkə(r)/ n acro m (= 4 047 m²)

acrid /'ækrɪd/ a acre

acrimon|ious /ækrɪ'məʊnɪəs/ a aspro. **~y** /'ækrɪmənɪ/ n asprezza f

acrobat /'ækrəbæt/ n acrobata mf. **~ic** /-'bætɪk/ a acrobatico

across /ə'krɒs/ adv dall'altra parte; (wide) in larghezza; (not lengthwise) attraverso; (in crossword) orizzontale; **come ~ sth** imbattersi in qcsa; **go ~** attraversare ● prep (crosswise) di traverso su; (on the other side of) dall'altra parte di

act /ækt/ n atto m; (in variety show) numero m; **put on an ~** fam fare scena ● vi agire; (behave) comportarsi; Theat recitare; (pretend) fingere; **~ as** fare da ● vt recitare (role). **~ing** a (deputy) provvisorio ● n Theat recitazione f; (profession) teatro m. **~ing profession** n professione f dell'attore

action /'ækʃn/ n azione f; Mil combattimento m; Jur azione f legale; **out of ~** (machine:) fuori uso; **take ~** agire. **~ 'replay** n replay m inv

activ|e /'æktɪv/ a attivo. **~ely** adv attivamente. **~ity** /-'tɪvətɪ/ n attività f inv

act|or /'æktə(r)/ n attore m. **~ress** n attrice f

actual /'æktʃʊəl/ a (real) reale. **~ly** adv in realtà

acumen /'ækjʊmən/ n acume m

acupuncture /'ækjʊ-/ n agopuntura f

acute /ə'kjuːt/ a acuto; (shortage, hardship) estremo

ad /æd/ n fam pubblicità f inv; (in paper) inserzione f, annuncio m

AD abbr (**Anno Domini**) d.C.

adamant /'ædəmənt/ a categorico (**that** sul fatto che)

adapt /ə'dæpt/ vt adattare (play) ● vi adattarsi. **~ability** /-ə'bɪlətɪ/ n adattabilità f. **~able** /-əbl/ a adattabile

adaptation /ædæp'teɪʃn/ n Theat adattamento m

adapter, adaptor /ə'dæptə(r)/ n adattatore m; (two-way) presa f multipla

add /æd/ vt aggiungere; Math addizionare ● vi addizionare; **~ to** (fig: increase) aggravare. **add up** vt addizionare (figures) ● vi addizionare; **~ up to** ammontare a; **it doesn't ~ up** fig non quadra

adder /'ædə(r)/ n vipera f

addict /'ædɪkt/ n tossicodipendente mf; fig fanatico, -a mf

addict|ed /ə'dɪktɪd/ a assuefatto (**to** a); **~ed to drugs** tossicodipendente; **he's ~ed to television** è videodipendente. **~ion** /-ɪkʃn/ n dipendenza f; (to drugs) tossicodipendenza f. ~ive /-ɪv/ a be ~ive dare assuefazione

addition /əˈdɪʃn/ n Math addizione f; (thing added) aggiunta f; in ~ in aggiunta. ~al a supplementare. ~ally adv in più

additive /ˈædɪtɪv/ n additivo m

address /əˈdres/ n indirizzo m; (speech) discorso m; **form of** ~ formula f di cortesia ● vt indirizzare; (speak to) rivolgersi a ⟨person⟩; tenere un discorso a ⟨meeting⟩. ~ee /ædreˈsiː/ n destinatario, -a mf

adenoids /ˈædənɔɪdz/ npl adenoidi fpl

adept /ˈædept/ a & n esperto, -a mf (at in)

adequate /ˈædɪkwət/ a adeguato. ~ly adv adeguatamente

adhere /ədˈhɪə(r)/ vi aderire; ~ to attenersi a ⟨principles, rules⟩

adhesive /ədˈhiːsɪv/ a adesivo ● n adesivo m

adjacent /əˈdʒeɪsənt/ a adiacente

adjective /ˈædʒɪktɪv/ n aggettivo m

adjoin /əˈdʒɔɪn/ vt essere adiacente a. ~ing a adiacente

adjourn /əˈdʒɜːn/ vt/i aggiornare (until a). ~ment n aggiornamento m

adjudicate /əˈdʒuːdɪkeɪt/ vi decidere; (in competition) giudicare

adjust /əˈdʒʌst/ vt modificare; regolare ⟨focus, sound etc⟩ ● vi adattarsi. ~able /-əbl/ a regolabile. ~ment n adattamento m; Techn regolamento m

ad lib /ædˈlɪb/ a improvvisato ● adv a piacere ● vi (pt/pp **ad libbed**) fam improvvisare

administer /ədˈmɪnɪstə(r)/ vt amministrare; somministrare ⟨medicine⟩

administrat|ion /ədmɪnɪˈstreɪʃn/ n amministrazione f; Pol governo m. ~or /ədˈmɪnɪstreɪtə(r)/ n amministratore, -trice mf

admirable /ˈædmərəbl/ a ammirevole

admiral /ˈædmərəl/ n ammiraglio m

admiration /ædməˈreɪʃn/ n ammirazione f

admire /ədˈmaɪə(r)/ vt ammirare. ~r n ammiratore, -trice mf

admissible /ədˈmɪsəbl/ a ammissibile

admission /ədˈmɪʃn/ n ammissione f; (to hospital) ricovero m; (entry) ingresso m

admit /ədˈmɪt/ vt (pt/pp **admitted**) (let in) far entrare; (to hospital) ricoverare; (acknowledge) ammettere ● vi ~ to sth ammettere qcsa. ~tance n ammissione

f; '**no** ~**tance**' 'vietato l'ingresso'. ~**tedly** adv bisogna riconoscerlo

admonish /ədˈmɒnɪʃ/ vt ammonire

ado /əˈduː/ n **without more** ~ senza ulteriori indugi

adolescen|ce /ædəˈlesns/ n adolescenza f. ~t a & n adolescente mf

adopt /əˈdɒpt/ vt adottare; Pol scegliere ⟨candidate⟩. ~ion /-ɒpʃn/ n adozione f. ~ive /-ɪv/ a adottivo

ador|able /əˈdɔːrəbl/ a adorabile. ~ation /ædəˈreɪʃn/ n adorazione f

adore /əˈdɔː(r)/ vt adorare

adrenalin /əˈdrenəlɪn/ n adrenalina f

Adriatic /eɪdrɪˈætɪk/ a & n the ~ [Sea] il mare Adriatico, l'Adriatico m

adrift /əˈdrɪft/ a alla deriva; be ~ andare alla deriva; come ~ staccarsi

adroit /əˈdrɔɪt/ a abile

adulation /ædjuˈleɪʃn/ n adulazione f

adult /ˈædʌlt/ n adulto, -a mf

adulterate /əˈdʌltəreɪt/ vt adulterare ⟨wine⟩

adultery /əˈdʌltərɪ/ n adulterio m

advance /ədˈvɑːns/ n avanzamento m; Mil avanzata f; (payment) anticipo m; in ~ in anticipo ● vi avanzare; (make progress) fare progressi ● vt avanzare ⟨theory⟩; promuovere ⟨cause⟩; anticipare ⟨money⟩. ~ **booking** n prenotazione f [in anticipo]. ~d a avanzato. ~ment n promozione f

advantage /ədˈvɑːntɪdʒ/ n vantaggio m; **take** ~ **of** approfittare di. ~ous /ædvənˈteɪdʒəs/ a vantaggioso

advent /ˈædvent/ n avvento m

adventur|e /ədˈventʃə(r)/ n avventura f. ~ous /-rəs/ a avventuroso

adverb /ˈædvɜːb/ n avverbio m

adversary /ˈædvəsərɪ/ n avversario, -a mf

advers|e /ˈædvɜːs/ a avverso. ~ity /ədˈvɜːsətɪ/ n avversità f

advert /ˈædvɜːt/ n fam = **advertisement**

advertise /ˈædvətaɪz/ vt reclamizzare; mettere un annuncio per ⟨job, flat⟩ ● vi fare pubblicità; (for job, flat) mettere un annuncio

advertisement /ədˈvɜːtɪsmənt/ n pubblicità f inv; (in paper) inserzione f, annuncio m

advertis|er /ˈædvətaɪzə(r)/ n (in newspaper) inserzionista mf. ~ing n pubblicità f ● attrib pubblicitario

advice /ədˈvaɪs/ n consigli mpl; **piece of** ~ consiglio m

advisable /ədˈvaɪzəbl/ a consigliabile

advis|e /əd'vaɪz/ *vt* consigliare; (*inform*) avvisare; **~e sb to do sth** consigliare a qcno di fare qcsa; **~e sb against sth** sconsigliare qcsa a qcno. **~er** *n* consulente *mf*. **~ory** *a* consultivo

advocate¹ /'ædvəkət/ *n* (*supporter*) fautore, -trice *mf*

advocate² /'ædvəkeɪt/ *vt* propugnare

aerial /'eərɪəl/ *a* aereo ● *n* antenna *f*

aerobics /eə'rəʊbɪks/ *n* aerobica *fsg*

aero|drome /'eərədrəʊm/ *n* aerodromo *m*. **~plane** *n* aeroplano *m*

aerosol /'eərəsɒl/ *n* bomboletta *f* spray

aesthetic /iːs'θetɪk/ *a* estetico

afar /ə'fɑː(r)/ *adv* **from ~** da lontano

affable /'æfəbl/ *a* affabile

affair /ə'feə(r)/ *n* affare *m*; (*scandal*) caso *m*; (*sexual*) relazione *f*

affect /ə'fekt/ *vt* influire su; (*emotionally*) colpire; (*concern*) riguardare. **~ation** /æfek'teɪʃn/ *n* affettazione *f*. **~ed** *a* affettato

affection /ə'fekʃn/ *n* affetto *m*. **~ate** /-ət/ *a* affettuoso

affiliated /ə'fɪlɪeɪtɪd/ *a* affiliato

affinity /ə'fɪnəti/ *n* affinità *f* inv

affirm /ə'fɜːm/ *vt* affermare; *Jur* dichiarare solennemente

affirmative /ə'fɜːmətɪv/ *a* affermativo ● *n* **in the ~** affermativamente

afflict /ə'flɪkt/ *vt* affliggere. **~ion** /-ɪkʃn/ *n* afflizione *f*

affluen|ce /'æflʊəns/ *n* agiatezza *f*. **~t** *a* agiato

afford /ə'fɔːd/ *vt* **be able to ~ sth** potersi permettere qcsa. **~able** /-əbl/ *a* abbordabile

affray /ə'freɪ/ *n* rissa *f*

affront /ə'frʌnt/ *n* affronto *m*

afield /ə'fiːld/ *adv* **further ~** più lontano

afloat /ə'fləʊt/ *a* a galla

afoot /ə'fʊt/ *a* **there's something ~** si sta preparando qualcosa

aforesaid /ə'fɔːsed/ *a* *Jur* suddetto

afraid /ə'freɪd/ *a* **be ~** aver paura; **I'm ~ not** purtroppo no; **I'm ~ so** temo di sì; **I'm ~ I can't help you** mi dispiace, ma non posso esserle d'aiuto

afresh /ə'freʃ/ *adv* da capo

Africa /'æfrɪkə/ *n* Africa *f*. **~n** *a* & *n* africano, -a *mf*

after /'ɑːftə(r)/ *adv* dopo; **the day ~** il giorno dopo; **be ~** cercare ● *prep* dopo; **~ all** dopotutto; **the day ~ tomorrow** dopodomani ● *conj* dopo che

after: ~-effect *n* conseguenza *f*. **~math** /-mɑːθ/ *n* conseguenze *fpl*; **the**

~math of war il dopoguerra; **in the ~math of** nel periodo successivo a. **~'noon** *n* pomeriggio *m*; **good ~noon!** buon giorno! **~-sales service** *n* servizio *m* assistenza clienti. **~shave** *n* [lozione *f*] dopobarba *m* inv. **~thought** *n* added as an **~thought** aggiunto in un secondo momento; **~wards** *adv* in seguito

again /ə'geɪn/ *adv* di nuovo; [**then**] **~** (*besides*) inoltre; (*on the other hand*) d'altra parte; **~ and ~** continuamente

against /ə'geɪnst/ *prep* contro

age /eɪdʒ/ *n* età *f* inv; (*era*) era *f*; **~s** *fam* secoli; **what ~ are you?** quanti anni hai?; **be under ~** non avere l'età richiesta; **he's two years of ~** ha due anni ● *vt/i* (*pres p* **ageing**) invecchiare

aged¹ /eɪdʒd/ *a* **~ two** di due anni

aged² /'eɪdʒɪd/ *a* anziano ● *npl* **the ~** gli anziani

ageless /'eɪdʒlɪs/ *a* senza età

agency /'eɪdʒənsɪ/ *n* agenzia *f*; **have the ~ for** essere un concessionario di

agenda /ə'dʒendə/ *n* ordine *m* del giorno; **on the ~** all'ordine del giorno; *fig* in programma

agent /'eɪdʒənt/ *n* agente *mf*

aggravat|e /'ægrəveɪt/ *vt* aggravare; (*annoy*) esasperare. **~ion** /-'veɪʃn/ *n* aggravamento *m*; (*annoyance*) esasperazione *f*

aggregate /'ægrɪgət/ *a* totale ● *n* totale *m*; **on ~** nel complesso

aggress|ion /ə'greʃn/ *n* aggressione *f*. **~ive** /-sɪv/ *a* aggressivo. **~iveness** *n* aggressività *f*. **~or** *n* aggressore *m*

aggro /'ægrəʊ/ *n* *fam* aggressività *f*; (*problems*) grane *fpl*

aghast /ə'gɑːst/ *a* inorridito

agil|e /'ædʒaɪl/ *a* agile. **~ity** /ə'dʒɪlətɪ/ *n* agilità *f*

agitat|e /'ædʒɪteɪt/ *vt* mettere in agitazione; (*shake*) agitare ● *vi* *fig* **~e for** creare delle agitazioni per. **~ed** *a* agitato. **~ion** /-'teɪʃn/ *n* agitazione *f*. **~or** *n* agitatore, -trice *mf*

agnostic /æg'nɒstɪk/ *n* agnostico, -a *mf*

ago /ə'gəʊ/ *adv* fa; **a long time/a month ~** molto tempo/un mese fa

agog /ə'gɒg/ *a* eccitato

agoniz|e /'ægənaɪz/ *vi* angosciarsi (*over* per). **~ing** *a* angosciante

agony /'ægənɪ/ *n* agonia *f*; (*mental*) angoscia *f*; **be in ~** avere dei dolori atroci

agree /ə'griː/ *vt* accordarsi su; **~ to do sth** accettare di fare qcsa; **~ that** essere d'accordo [sul fatto] che ● *vi* essere d'accordo; ⟨*figures:*⟩ concordare; ⟨*reach agreement*⟩ mettersi d'accordo; ⟨*get on*⟩ andare d'accordo; ⟨*consent*⟩ acconsentire (**to** a); **it doesn't ~ with me** mi fa male; **~ with sth** (*approve of*) approvare qcsa

agreeable /ə'griːəbl/ *a* gradevole; (*willing*) d'accordo

agreed /ə'griːd/ *a* convenuto

agreement /ə'griːmənt/ *n* accordo *m*; **in ~** d'accordo

agricultur|al /ægrɪ'kʌltʃərəl/ *a* agricolo. **~e** /'ægrɪkʌltʃə(r)/ *n* agricoltura *f*

aground /ə'graʊnd/ *adv* **run ~** ⟨*ship:*⟩ arenarsi

ahead /ə'hed/ *adv* avanti; **be ~ of** essere davanti a; *fig* essere avanti rispetto a; **draw ~** passare davanti (**of** a); **get ~** (*in life*) riuscire; **go ~!** fai pure!; **look ~** pensare all'avvenire; **plan ~** fare progetti per l'avvenire

aid /eɪd/ *n* aiuto *m*; **in ~ of** a favore di ● *vt* aiutare

aide /eɪd/ *n* assistente *mf*

Aids /eɪdz/ *n* AIDS *m*

ail|ing /'eɪlɪŋ/ *a* malato. **~ment** *n* disturbo *m*

aim /eɪm/ *n* mira *f*; *fig* scopo *m*; **take ~** prendere la mira ● *vt* puntare ⟨*gun*⟩ (**at** contro) ● *vi* mirare; **~ to do sth** aspirare a fare qcsa. **~less** *a*, **~lessly** *adv* senza scopo

air /eə(r)/ *n* aria *f*; **be on the ~** ⟨*programme:*⟩ essere in onda; **put on ~s** darsi delle arie; **by ~** in aereo; (*airmail*) per via aerea ● *vt* arieggiare; far conoscere ⟨*views*⟩

air: **~-bed** *n* materassino *m* [gonfiabile]. **~-conditioned** *a* con aria condizionata. **~-conditioning** *n* aria *f* condizionata. **~craft** *n* aereo *m*. **~craft carrier** *n* portaerei *f inv*. **~fare** *n* tariffa *f* aerea. **~field** *n* campo *m* d'aviazione. **~ force** *n* aviazione *f*. **~ freshener** *n* deodorante *m* per l'ambiente. **~gun** *n* fucile *m* pneumatico. **~ hostess** *n* hostess *f inv*. **~ letter** *n* aerogramma *m*. **~line** *n* compagnia *f* aerea. **~lock** *n* bolla *f* d'aria. **~mail** *n* posta *f* aerea. **~plane** *n Am* aereo *m*. **~ pocket** *n* vuoto *m* d'aria. **~port** *n* aeroporto *m*. **~-raid** *n* incursione *f* aerea. **~-raid shelter** *n* rifugio *m* antiaereo. **~ship** *n* dirigibile *m*. **~tight** *a* ermetico. **~ traffic** *n* traffico *m* aereo. **~-traffic controller** *n* controllore *m* di volo. **~worthy** *a* idoneo al volo

airy /'eərɪ/ *a* (**-ier**, **-iest**) arieggiato; ⟨*manner*⟩ noncurante

aisle /aɪl/ *n* corridoio *m*; (*in supermarket*) corsia *f*; (*in church*) navata *f*

ajar /ə'dʒɑː(r)/ *a* socchiuso

akin /ə'kɪn/ *a* **~ to** simile a

alacrity /ə'lækrətɪ/ *n* alacrità *f inv*

alarm /ə'lɑːm/ *n* allarme *m*; **set the ~** (*of alarm clock*) mettere la sveglia ● *vt* allarmare. **~ clock** *n* sveglia *f*

alas /ə'læs/ *int* ahimè

album /'ælbəm/ *n* album *m inv*

alcohol /'ælkəhɒl/ *n* alcool *m*. **~ic** /-'hɒlɪk/ *a* alcolico ● *n* alcolizzato, -a *mf*. **~ism** *n* alcolismo *m*

alcove /'ælkəʊv/ *n* alcova *f*

alert /ə'lɜːt/ *a* sveglio; (*watchful*) vigile ● *n* segnale *m* d'allarme; **be on the ~** stare allerta ● *vt* allertare

algae /'ældʒiː/ *npl* alghe *fpl*

algebra /'ældʒɪbrə/ *n* algebra *f*

Algeria /æl'dʒɪərɪə/ *n* Algeria *f*. **~n** *a & n* algerino, -a *mf*

alias /'eɪlɪəs/ *n* pseudonimo *m* ● *adv* alias

alibi /'ælɪbaɪ/ *n* alibi *m inv*

alien /'eɪlɪən/ *a* straniero; *fig* estraneo ● *n* straniero, -a *mf*; (*from space*) alieno, -a *mf*

alienat|e /'eɪlɪəneɪt/ *vt* alienare. **~ion** /-'neɪʃn/ *n* alienazione *f*

alight¹ /ə'laɪt/ *vi* scendere; ⟨*bird:*⟩ posarsi

alight² *a* **be ~** essere in fiamme; **set ~** dar fuoco a

align /ə'laɪn/ *vt* allineare. **~ment** *n* allineamento *m*; **out of ~ment** non allineato

alike /ə'laɪk/ *a* simile; **be ~** rassomigliarsi ● *adv* in modo simile; **look ~** rassomigliarsi; **summer and winter ~** sia d'estate che d'inverno

alimony /'ælɪmənɪ/ *n* alimenti *mpl*

alive /ə'laɪv/ *a* vivo; **~ with** brulicante di; **~ to** sensibile a

alkali /'ælkəlaɪ/ *n* alcali *m*

all /ɔːl/ *a* tutto; **~ the children, ~ children** tutti i bambini; **~ day** tutto il giorno; **he refused ~ help** ha rifiutato qualsiasi aiuto; **for ~ that** (*nevertheless*) ciononostante; **in ~ sincerity** in tutta sincerità; **be ~ for** essere favorevole a ● *pron* tutto; **~ of you/them** tutti voi/loro; **~ of it** tutto; **~ of the town** tutta la città; **in ~** in tutto; **in ~** tutto sommato; **most of ~** più di ogni altra cosa; **once and for ~** una

volta per tutte ● *adv* completamente; ~
but quasi; ~ **at once** (*at the same time*)
tutto in una volta; ~ **at once,** ~ **of a
sudden** all'improvviso; ~ **too soon**
troppo presto; ~ **the same** (*neverthe-less*) ciononostante; ~ **the better**
meglio ancora; **she's not** ~ **that good
an actress** non è poi così brava come
attrice; ~ **in** in tutto; *fam* esausto;
thirty/three ~ (*in sport*) trenta/tre
pari; ~ **over** (*finished*) tutto finito; (*eve-rywhere*) dappertutto; **it's** ~ **right** (*I
don't mind*) non fa niente; **I'm** ~ **right**
(*not hurt*) non ho niente; ~ **right!** va
bene!

allay /ə'leɪ/ *vt* placare ⟨suspicions,
anger⟩

allegation /ælɪ'geɪʃn/ *n* accusa *f*

allege /ə'ledʒ/ *vt* dichiarare. ~**d** *a* pre-sunto. ~**dly** /-ɪdlɪ/ *adv* a quanto si dice

allegiance /ə'liːdʒəns/ *n* fedeltà *f*

allegor|ical /ælɪ'gɒrɪkl/ *a* allegorico.
~**y** /'ælɪgərɪ/ *n* allegoria *f*

allerg|ic /ə'lɜːdʒɪk/ *a* allergico. ~**y**
/'ælədʒɪ/ *n* allergia *f*

alleviate /ə'liːvɪeɪt/ *vt* alleviare

alley /'ælɪ/ *n* vicolo *m*; (*for bowling*)
corsia *f*

alliance /ə'laɪəns/ *n* alleanza *f*

allied /'ælaɪd/ *a* alleato; (*fig: related*)
connesso (**to** a)

alligator /'ælɪgeɪtə(r)/ *n* alligatore *m*

allocat|e /'æləkeɪt/ *vt* assegnare; di-stribuire ⟨resources⟩. ~**ion** /-'keɪʃn/ *n*
assegnazione *f*; (*of resources*) distribu-zione *f*

allot /ə'lɒt/ *vt* (*pt/pp* **allotted**) distribu-ire. ~**ment** *n* distribuzione *f*; (*share*)
parte *f*; (*land*) piccolo lotto *m* di terreno

allow /ə'laʊ/ *vt* permettere; (*grant*) ac-cordare; (*reckon on*) contare; (*agree*)
ammettere; ~ **for** tener conto di; ~ **sb
to do sth** permettere a qcno di fare
qcsa; **you are not** ~**ed to...** è vietato...

allowance /ə'laʊəns/ *n* sussidio *m*;
(*Am: pocket money*) paghetta *f*; (*for
petrol etc*) indennità *f inv*; (*of luggage,
duty free*) limite *m*; **make** ~**s for** essere
indulgente verso ⟨sb⟩; tener conto di
⟨sth⟩

alloy /'ælɔɪ/ *n* lega *f*

allude /ə'luːd/ *vi* alludere

allusion /ə'luːʒn/ *n* allusione *f*

ally[1] /'ælaɪ/ *n* alleato, -a *mf*

ally[2] /ə'laɪ/ *vt* (*pt/pp* -**ied**) alleare; ~
oneself with allearsi con

almighty /ɔːl'maɪtɪ/ *a* (*fam: big*) mega
inv ● *n* **the A**~ l'Onnipotente *m*

almond /'ɑːmənd/ *n* mandorla *f*; (*tree*)
mandorlo *m*

almost /'ɔːlməʊst/ *adv* quasi

alone /ə'ləʊn/ *a* solo; **leave me** ~! la-sciami in pace!; **let** ~ (*not to mention*)
figurarsi ● *adv* da solo

along /ə'lɒŋ/ *prep* lungo ● *adv* ~ **with**
assieme a; **all** ~ tutto il tempo; **come**
~! (*hurry up*) vieni qui!; **I'll be** ~ **in a
minute** arrivo tra un attimo; **move** ~
spostarsi; **move** ~! circolare!

along'side *adv* lungo bordo ● *prep*
lungo; **work** ~ **sb** lavorare fianco a
fianco con qcno

aloof /ə'luːf/ *a* distante

aloud /ə'laʊd/ *adv* ad alta voce

alphabet /'ælfəbet/ *n* alfabeto *m*.
~**ical** /-'betɪkl/ *a* alfabetico

alpine /'ælpaɪn/ *a* alpino

Alps /ælps/ *npl* Alpi *fpl*

already /ɔːl'redɪ/ *adv* già

Alsatian /æl'seɪʃn/ *n* (*dog*) pastore *m*
tedesco

also /'ɔːlsəʊ/ *adv* anche; ~**, I need...** [e]
inoltre, ho bisogno di...

altar /'ɔːltə(r)/ *n* altare *m*

alter /'ɔːltə(r)/ *vt* cambiare; aggiustare
⟨clothes⟩ ● *vi* cambiare. ~**ation** /-'reɪʃn/
n modifica *f*

alternate[1] /'ɔːltəneɪt/ *vi* alternarsi
● *vt* alternare

alternate[2] /ɔːl'tɜːnət/ *a* alterno; **on** ~
days *a* giorni alterni

'alternating current *n* corrente *f* al-ternata

alternative /ɔːl'tɜːnətɪv/ *a* alternativo
● *n* alternativa *f*. ~**ly** *adv* alternativa-mente

although /ɔːl'ðəʊ/ *conj* benché, sebbe-ne

altitude /'æltɪtjuːd/ *n* altitudine *f*

altogether /ɔːltə'geðə(r)/ *adv* (*in all*)
in tutto; (*completely*) completamente;
I'm not ~ **sure** non sono del tutto sicu-ro

altruistic /æltrʊ'ɪstɪk/ *a* altruistico

aluminium /æljʊ'mɪnɪəm/ *n*, *Am*
aluminum /ə'luːmɪnəm/ *n* alluminio *m*

always /'ɔːlweɪz/ *adv* sempre

am /æm/ *see* **be**

a.m. *abbr* (**ante meridiem**) del matti-no

amalgamate /ə'mælgəmeɪt/ *vt* fonde-re ● *vi* fondersi

amass /ə'mæs/ *vt* accumulare

amateur /'æmətə(r)/ *n* non professio-nista *mf*; *pej* dilettante *mf* ● *attrib* dilet-

tante; ~ **dramatics** filodrammatica *f.*
~ish *a* dilettantesco
amaze /ə'meɪz/ *vt* stupire. **~d** *a* stupi-
to. **~ment** *n* stupore *m*
amazing /ə'meɪzɪŋ/ *a* incredibile
ambassador /æm'bæsədə(r)/ *n* amba-
sciatore, -trice *mf*
amber /'æmbə(r)/ *n* ambra *f* ● *a*
(*colour*) ambra *inv*
ambidextrous /æmbɪ'dekstrəs/ *a*
ambidestro
ambience /'æmbɪəns/ *n* atmosfera *f*
ambigu|ity /æmbɪ'gjuːətɪ/ *n* ambiguità
f inv. **~ous** /-'bɪgjʊəs/ *a* ambiguo
ambiti|on /æm'bɪʃn/ *n* ambizione *f*;
(*aim*) aspirazione *f.* **~ous** /-ʃəs/ *a* ambizioso
ambivalent /æm'bɪvələnt/ *a* ambiva-
lente
amble /'æmbl/ *vi* camminare senza
fretta
ambulance /'æmbjʊləns/ *n* ambulan-
za *f*
ambush /'æmbʊʃ/ *n* imboscata *f* ● *vt*
tendere un'imboscata a
amenable /ə'miːnəbl/ *a* conciliante; ~
to sensibile a
amend /ə'mend/ *vt* modificare. **~ment**
n modifica *f.* **~s** *npl* make **~s** fare am-
menda (**for** di, per)
amenities /ə'miːnətɪz/ *npl* comodità
fpl
America /ə'merɪkə/ *n* America *f.* **~n** *a*
& *n* americano, -a *mf*
amiable /'eɪmɪəbl/ *a* amabile
amicable /'æmɪkəbl/ *a* amichevole
amiss /ə'mɪs/ *a* **there's something ~**
c'è qualcosa che non va ● *adv* **take sth
~** prendersela [a male]; **it won't come
~** non sarebbe sgradito
ammonia /ə'məʊnɪə/ *n* ammoniaca *f*
ammunition /æmjʊ'nɪʃn/ *n* munizioni
fpl
amnesia /æm'niːzɪə/ *n* amnesia *f*
amnesty /'æmnəstɪ/ *n* amnistia *f*
among[st] /ə'mʌŋ[st]/ *prep* tra, fra
amoral /eɪ'mɒrəl/ *a* amorale
amorous /'æmərəs/ *a* amoroso
amount /ə'maʊnt/ *n* quantità *f inv*;
(*sum of money*) importo *m* ● *vi* ~ **to** ammontare a; *fig* equivalere a
amp /æmp/ *n* ampère *m inv*
amphibi|an /æm'fɪbɪən/ *n* anfibio *m.*
~ous /-ɪəs/ *a* anfibio
amphitheatre /'æmfɪ-/ *n* anfiteatro *m*
ample /'æmpl/ *a* (*large*) grande;
(*proportions*) ampio; (*enough*) largamente sufficiente

amplif|ier /'æmplɪfaɪə(r)/ *n* amplifica-
tore *m.* **~y** /-faɪ/ *vt* (*pt/pp* **-ied**) amplifi-
care (*sound*)
amputat|e /'æmpjʊteɪt/ *vt* amputare.
~ion /-'teɪʃn/ *n* amputazione *f*
amuse /ə'mjuːz/ *vt* divertire. **~ment** *n*
divertimento *m.* **~ment arcade** *n* sala
f giochi
amusing /ə'mjuːzɪŋ/ *a* divertente
an /ən/, *accentato* /æn/ *see* **a**
anaem|ia /ə'niːmɪə/ *n* anemia *f.* **~ic** *a*
anemico
anaesthetic /ænəs'θetɪk/ *n* anestesia *f*
anaesthet|ist /ə'niːsθətɪst/ *n* aneste-
sista *mf*
analog[ue] /'ænəlɒg/ *a* analogico
analogy /ə'nælədʒɪ/ *n* analogia *f*
analyse /'ænəlaɪz/ *vt* analizzare
analysis /ə'næləsɪs/ *n* analisi *f inv*
analyst /'ænəlɪst/ *n* analista *mf*
analytical /ænə'lɪtɪkl/ *a* analitico
anarch|ist /'ænəkɪst/ *n* anarchico, -a
mf. **~y** *n* anarchia *f*
anatom|ical /ænə'tɒmɪkl/ *a* anatomi-
co. **~ically** *adv* anatomicamente. **~y**
/ə'nætəmɪ/ *n* anatomia *f*
ancest|or /'ænsestə(r)/ *n* antenato, -a
mf. **~ry** *n* antenati *mpl*
anchor /'æŋkə(r)/ *n* ancora *f* ● *vi* get-
tar l'ancora ● *vt* ancorare
anchovy /'æntʃəvɪ/ *n* acciuga *f*
ancient /'eɪnʃənt/ *a* antico; *fam* vecchio
ancillary /æn'sɪlərɪ/ *a* ausiliario
and /ənd/, *accentato* /ænd/ *conj* e; **two
~ two** due più due; **six hundred ~
two** seicentodue; **more ~ more** sempre più; **nice ~ warm** bello caldo; **try
~ come** cerca di venire; **go ~ get** vai a
prendere
anecdote /'ænɪkdəʊt/ *n* aneddoto *m*
anew /ə'njuː/ *adv* di nuovo
angel /'eɪndʒl/ *n* angelo *m.* **~ic**
/æn'dʒelɪk/ *a* angelico
anger /'æŋgə(r)/ *n* rabbia *f* ● *vt* far arrabbiare
angle[1] /'æŋgl/ *n* angolo *m*; *fig* angolazione *f*; **at an ~** storto
angle[2] *vi* pescare con la lenza; ~ **for** *fig*
cercare di ottenere. **~r** *n* pescatore,
-trice *mf*
Anglican /'æŋglɪkən/ *a* & *n* anglicano,
-a *mf*
Anglo-Saxon /æŋgləʊ'sæksn/ *a* & *n*
anglo-sassone *mf*
angr|y /'æŋgrɪ/ *a* (**-ier, -iest**) arrabbia-
to; **get ~y** arrabbiarsi; **~y with** *or* **at
sb** arrabbiato con qcno; **~y at** *or*

about sth arrabbiato per qcsa. **~ily** *adv* rabbiosamente

anguish /'æŋgwɪʃ/ *n* angoscia *f*

angular /'æŋgjʊlə(r)/ *a* angolare

animal /'ænɪml/ *a & n* animale *m*

animate[1] /'ænɪmət/ *a* animato

animat|e[2] /'ænɪmeɪt/ *vt* animare. **~ed** *a* animato; ⟨person⟩ vivace. **~ion** /-'meɪʃn/ *n* animazione *f*

animosity /ænɪ'mɒsətɪ/ *n* animosità *f inv*

ankle /'æŋkl/ *n* caviglia *f*

annex /ə'neks/ *vt* annettere

annex[e] /'æneks/ *n* annesso *m*

annihilat|e /ə'naɪəleɪt/ *vt* annientare. **~ion** /-'leɪʃn/ *n* annientamento *m*

anniversary /ænɪ'vɜːsərɪ/ *n* anniversario *m*

announce /ə'naʊns/ *vt* annunciare. **~ment** *n* annuncio *m*. **~r** *n* annunciatore, -trice *mf*

annoy /ə'nɔɪ/ *vt* dare fastidio a; **get ~ed** essere infastidito. **~ance** *n* seccatura *f*; ⟨anger⟩ irritazione *f*. **~ing** *a* fastidioso

annual /'ænjʊəl/ *a* annuale; ⟨income⟩ annuo ● *n* *Bot* pianta *f* annua; ⟨children's book⟩ almanacco *m*

annuity /ə'njuːətɪ/ *n* annualità *f inv*

annul /ə'nʌl/ *vt* (*pt/pp* **annulled**) annullare

anomaly /ə'nɒməlɪ/ *n* anomalia *f*

anonymous /ə'nɒnɪməs/ *a* anonimo

anorak /'ænəræk/ *n* giacca *f* a vento

anorex|ia /ænə'reksɪə/ *n* anoressia *f*. **~ic** *a* anoressico

another /ə'nʌðə(r)/ *a & pron*; ~ [one] un altro, un'altra; **in ~ way** diversamente; **one ~** l'un l'altro

answer /'ɑːnsə(r)/ *n* risposta *f*; ⟨solution⟩ soluzione *f* ● *vt* rispondere a ⟨person, question, letter⟩; esaudire ⟨prayer⟩; ~ **the door** aprire la porta; ~ **the telephone** rispondere al telefono ● *vi* rispondere; **~ back** ribattere; **~ for** rispondere di. **~able** /-əbl/ *a* responsabile; **be ~able to sb** rispondere a qcno. **~ing machine** *n* Teleph segreteria *f* telefonica

ant /ænt/ *n* formica *f*

antagonis|m /æn'tægənɪzm/ *n* antagonismo *m*. **~tic** /-'nɪstɪk/ *a* antagonistico

antagonize /æn'tægənaɪz/ *vt* provocare l'ostilità di

Antarctic /æn'tɑːktɪk/ *n* Antartico *m* ● *a* antartico

antenatal /æntɪ'neɪtl/ *a* prenatale

antenna /æn'tenə/ *n* antenna *f*

anthem /'ænθəm/ *n* inno *m*

anthology /æn'θɒlədʒɪ/ *n* antologia *f*

anthropology /ænθrə'pɒlədʒɪ/ *n* antropologia *f*

anti-'aircraft /ænti-/ *a* antiaereo

antibiotic /æntɪbaɪ'ɒtɪk/ *n* antibiotico *m*

'antibody *n* anticorpo *m*

anticipat|e /æn'tɪsɪpeɪt/ *vt* prevedere; ⟨forestall⟩ anticipare. **~ion** /-'peɪʃn/ *n* anticipo *m*; ⟨excitement⟩ attesa *f*

anti'climax *n* delusione *f*

anti'clockwise *a & adv* in senso antiorario

antics /'æntɪks/ *npl* gesti *mpl* buffi

anti'cyclone *n* anticiclone *m*

antidote /'æntɪdəʊt/ *n* antidoto *m*

'antifreeze *n* antigelo *m*

antipathy /æn'tɪpəθɪ/ *n* antipatia *f*

antiquated /'æntɪkweɪtɪd/ *a* antiquato

antique /æn'tiːk/ *a* antico ● *n* antichità *f inv*. ~ **dealer** *n* antiquario, -a *mf*

antiquity /æn'tɪkwətɪ/ *n* antichità *f*

anti-Semitic /æntɪsɪ'mɪtɪk/ *a* antisemita

anti'septic *a & n* antisettico *m*

anti'social *a* ⟨behaviour⟩ antisociale; ⟨person⟩ asociale

anti'virus program *n* Comput programma *m* di antivirus

antlers /'æntləz/ *npl* corna *fpl*

anus /'eɪnəs/ *n* ano *m*

anxiety /æŋ'zaɪətɪ/ *n* ansia *f*

anxious /'æŋkʃəs/ *a* ansioso. **~ly** *adv* con ansia

any /'enɪ/ *a* ⟨no matter which⟩ qualsiasi, qualunque; **have we ~ wine/biscuits?** abbiamo del vino/dei biscotti?; **have we ~ jam/apples?** abbiamo della marmellata/delle mele?; ~ **colour/number you like** qualsiasi colore/numero ti piaccia; **we don't have ~ wine/biscuits** non abbiamo vino/biscotti; **I don't have ~ reason to lie** non ho nessun motivo per mentire; **for ~ reason** per qualsiasi ragione ● *pron* ⟨some⟩ ne; ⟨no matter which⟩ uno qualsiasi; **I don't want ~ [of it]** non ne voglio [nessuno]; **there aren't ~** non ce ne sono; **have we ~?** ne abbiamo?; **have you read ~ of her books?** hai letto qualcuno dei suoi libri? ● *adv* **I can't go ~ quicker** non posso andare più in fretta; **is it ~ better?** va un po' meglio?; **would you like ~ more?** ne vuoi ancora?; **I can't eat ~ more** non posso mangiare più niente

'**anybody** *pron* chiunque; (*after negative*) nessuno; **I haven't seen ~** non ho visto nessuno

'**anyhow** *adv* ad ogni modo, comunque; (*badly*) non importa come

'**anyone** *pron* = **anybody**

'**anything** *pron* qualche cosa, qualcosa; (*no matter what*) qualsiasi cosa; (*after negative*) niente; **take/ buy/ you like** prendi/compra quello che vuoi; **I don't remember ~** non mi ricordo niente; **he's ~ but stupid** è tutto, ma non stupido; **I'll do ~ but that** farò qualsiasi cosa, tranne quello

'**anyway** *adv* ad ogni modo, comunque

'**anywhere** *adv* dovunque; (*after negative*) da nessuna parte; **put it ~** mettilo dove vuoi; **I can't find it ~** non lo trovo da nessuna parte; **~ else** da qualch'altra parte; (*after negative*) da nessun'altra parte; **I don't want to go ~ else** non voglio andare da nessun'altra parte

a**part** /ə'pɑ:t/ *adv* lontano; **live ~** vivere separati; **100 miles ~** lontani 100 miglia; **~ from** a parte; **you can't tell them ~** non si possono distinguere; **joking ~** scherzi a parte

a**partment** /ə'pɑ:tmənt/ *n* (*Am: flat*) appartamento *m*; **in my ~** a casa mia

a**pathy** /'æpəθɪ/ *n* apatia *f*

a**pe** /eɪp/ *n* scimmia *f* ● *vt* scimmiottare

a**peritif** /ə'perətɪf/ *n* aperitivo *m*

a**perture** /'æpətʃə(r)/ *n* apertura *f*

a**pex** /'eɪpeks/ *n* vertice *m*

a**piece** /ə'pi:s/ *adv* ciascuno

a**pologetic** /əpɒlə'dʒetɪk/ *a* ⟨air, remark⟩ di scusa; **be ~** essere spiacente

a**pologize** /ə'pɒlədʒaɪz/ *vi* scusarsi (**for** per)

a**pology** /ə'pɒlədʒɪ/ *n* scusa *f*; *fig* **an ~ for a dinner** una sottospecie di cena

a**postle** /ə'pɒsl/ *n* apostolo *m*

a**postrophe** /ə'pɒstrəfɪ/ *n* apostrofo *m*

a**ppal** /ə'pɔ:l/ *vt* (*pt/pp* **appalled**) sconvolgere. **~ling** *a* sconvolgente

a**pparatus** /æpə'reɪtəs/ *n* apparato *m*

a**pparent** /ə'pærənt/ *a* evidente; (*seeming*) apparente. **~ly** *adv* apparentemente

a**pparition** /æpə'rɪʃn/ *n* apparizione *f*

a**ppeal** /ə'pi:l/ *n* appello *m*; (*attraction*) attrattiva *f* ● *vi* fare appello; **~ to** (*be attractive to*) attrarre. **~ing** *a* attraente

a**ppear** /ə'pɪə(r)/ *vi* apparire; (*seem*) sembrare; ⟨*publication:*⟩ uscire; *Theat* esibirsi. **~ance** *n* apparizione *f*; (*look*) aspetto *m*; **to all ~ances** a giudicare dalle apparenze; **keep up ~ances** salvare le apparenze

a**ppease** /ə'pi:z/ *vt* placare

a**ppendicitis** /əpendɪ'saɪtɪs/ *n* appendicite *f*

a**ppendix** /ə'pendɪks/ *n* (*pl* **-ices** /-ɪsi:z/) (*of book*) appendice *f*, (*pl* **-es**) *Anat* appendice *f*

a**ppetite** /'æpɪtaɪt/ *n* appetito *m*

a**ppetizer** /'æpɪtaɪzə(r)/ *n* stuzzichino *m*. **~ing** *a* appetitoso

a**pplaud** /ə'plɔ:d/ *vt/i* applaudire. **~se** *n* applauso *m*

a**pple** /'æpl/ *n* mela *f*. **~-tree** *n* melo *m*

a**ppliance** /ə'plaɪəns/ *n* attrezzo *m*; **[electrical] ~** elettrodomestico *m*

a**pplicable** /'æplɪkəbl/ *a* **be ~ to** essere valido per; **not ~** (*on form*) non applicabile

a**pplicant** /'æplɪkənt/ *n* candidato, -a *mf*

a**pplication** /æplɪ'keɪʃn/ *n* applicazione *f*; (*request*) domanda *f*; (*for job*) candidatura *f*. **~ form** *n* modulo *m* di domanda

a**pplied** /ə'plaɪd/ *a* applicato

a**pply** /ə'plaɪ/ *vt* (*pt/pp* **-ied**) applicare; **~ oneself** applicarsi ● *vi* applicarsi; ⟨*law:*⟩ essere applicabile; **~ to** (*ask*) rivolgersi a; **~ for** fare domanda per ⟨*job etc*⟩

a**ppoint** /ə'pɔɪnt/ *vt* nominare; fissare ⟨*time*⟩. **~ment** *n* appuntamento *m*; (*to job*) nomina *f*; (*job*) posto *m*

a**ppraisal** /ə'preɪz(ə)l/ *n* valutazione *f*

a**ppreciable** /ə'pri:ʃəbl/ *a* sensibile

a**ppreciate** /ə'pri:ʃɪeɪt/ *vt* apprezzare; (*understand*) comprendere ● *vi* (*increase in value*) aumentare di valore. **~ion** /-'eɪʃn/ *n* (*gratitude*) riconoscenza *f*, (*enjoyment*) apprezzamento *m*; (*understanding*) comprensione *f*; (*in value*) aumento *m*. **~ive** /-ətɪv/ *a* riconoscente

a**pprehend** /æprɪ'hend/ *vt* arrestare

a**pprehension** /æprɪ'henʃn/ *n* arresto *m*; (*fear*) apprensione *f*. **~ive** /-sɪv/ *a* apprensivo

a**pprentice** /ə'prentɪs/ *n* apprendista *mf*. **~ship** *n* apprendistato *m*

a**pproach** /ə'prəʊtʃ/ *n* avvicinamento *m*; (*to problem*) approccio *m*; (*access*) accesso *m*; **make ~es to** fare degli approcci con ● *vi* avvicinarsi ● *vt* avvicinarsi a; (*with request*) rivolgersi a; affrontare ⟨*problem*⟩. **~able** /-əbl/ *a* accessibile

appropriate¹ /ə'prəuprɪət/ a appropriato

appropriate² /ə'prəuprɪeɪt/ vt appropriarsi di

approval /ə'pru:vl/ n approvazione f; **on ~** in prova

approv|e /ə'pru:v/ vt approvare ● vi **~e of** approvare ⟨sth⟩; avere una buona opinione di ⟨sb⟩. **~ing** a ⟨smile, nod⟩ d'approvazione

approximate /ə'prɒksɪmət/ a approssimativo. **~ly** adv approssimativamente

approximation /əprɒksɪ'meɪʃn/ n approssimazione f

apricot /'eɪprɪkɒt/ n albicocca f

April /'eɪprəl/ n aprile m; **~ Fool's Day** il primo d'aprile

apron /'eɪprən/ n grembiule m

apt /æpt/ a appropriato; **be ~ to do sth** avere tendenza a fare qcsa

aptitude /'æptɪtju:d/ n disposizione f. **~ test** n test m inv attitudinale

aqualung /'ækwəlʌŋ/ n autorespiratore m

aquarium /ə'kweərɪəm/ n acquario m

Aquarius /ə'kweərɪəs/ n Astr Acquario m

aquatic /ə'kwætɪk/ a acquatico

Arab /'ærəb/ a & n arabo, -a mf. **~ian** /ə'reɪbɪən/ a arabo

Arabic /'ærəbɪk/ a arabo; **~ numerals** numeri mpl arabici ● n arabo m

arable /'ærəbl/ a coltivabile

arbitrary /'ɑ:bɪtrərɪ/ a arbitrario

arbitrat|e /'ɑ:bɪtreɪt/ vi arbitrare. **~ion** /-'treɪʃn/ n arbitraggio m

arc /ɑ:k/ n arco m

arcade /ɑ:'keɪd/ n portico m; ⟨shops⟩ galleria f

arch /ɑ:tʃ/ n arco m; ⟨of foot⟩ dorso m del piede

archaeological /ɑ:kɪə'lɒdʒɪkl/ a archeologico

archaeolog|ist /ɑ:kɪ'ɒlədʒɪst/ n archeologo, -a mf. **~y** n archeologia f

archaic /ɑ:'keɪɪk/ a arcaico

arch'bishop /ɑ:tʃ-/ n arcivescovo m

arch-'enemy n acerrimo nemico m

architect /'ɑ:kɪtekt/ n architetto m. **~ural** /ɑ:kɪ'tektʃərəl/ a architettonico

architecture /'ɑ:kɪtektʃə(r)/ n architettura f

archives /'ɑ:kaɪvz/ npl archivi mpl

archiving /'ɑ:kaɪvɪŋ/ n Comput archiviazione f

archway /'ɑ:tʃweɪ/ n arco m

Arctic /'ɑ:ktɪk/ a artico ● n **the ~** l'Artico

ardent /'ɑ:dənt/ a ardente

arduous /'ɑ:djʊəs/ a arduo

are /ɑ:(r)/ see be

area /'eərɪə/ n area f; ⟨region⟩ zona f; ⟨fig: field⟩ campo m. **~ code** n prefisso m [telefonico]

arena /ə'ri:nə/ n arena f

aren't /ɑ:nt/ = **are not** see be

Argentina /ɑ:dʒən'ti:nə/ n Argentina f

Argentinian /-'tɪnɪən/ a & n argentino, -a mf

argue /'ɑ:gju:/ vi litigare (**about** su); ⟨debate⟩ dibattere; **don't ~!** non discutere! ● vt ⟨debate⟩ dibattere; ⟨reason⟩ **~ that** sostenere che

argument /'ɑ:gjʊmənt/ n argomento m; ⟨reasoning⟩ ragionamento m; **have an ~** litigare. **~ative** /-'mentətɪv/ a polemico

aria /'ɑ:rɪə/ n aria f

arid /'ærɪd/ a arido

Aries /'eəri:z/ n Astr Ariete m

arise /ə'raɪz/ vi (pt arose, pp arisen) ⟨opportunity, need, problem⟩ presentarsi; ⟨result⟩ derivare

aristocracy /ærɪ'stɒkrəsɪ/ n aristocrazia f

aristocrat /'ærɪstəkræt/ n aristocratico, -a mf. **~ic** /-'krætɪk/ a aristocratico

arithmetic /ə'rɪθmətɪk/ n aritmetica f

arm /ɑ:m/ n braccio m; ⟨of chair⟩ bracciolo m; **~s** pl ⟨weapons⟩ armi fpl; **in ~** a braccetto; **up in ~s** fam furioso (**about** per) ● vt armare

armaments /'ɑ:məmənts/ npl armamenti mpl

'armchair n poltrona f

armed /ɑ:md/ a armato; **~ forces** forze fpl armate; **~ robbery** rapina f a mano armata

armistice /'ɑ:mɪstɪs/ n armistizio m

armour /'ɑ:mə(r)/ n armatura f. **~ed** a ⟨vehicle⟩ blindato

'armpit n ascella f

army /'ɑ:mɪ/ n esercito m; **join the ~** arruolarsi

aroma /ə'rəumə/ n aroma f. **~tic** /ærə'mætɪk/ a aromatico

arose /ə'rəuz/ see arise

around /ə'raʊnd/ adv intorno; **all ~** tutt'intorno; **he's not ~** non sono di qui; **he's not from ~ here** non sono di qui; **he's not ~** non c'è ● prep intorno a; in giro per ⟨room, shops, world⟩

arouse /ə'raʊz/ vt svegliare; ⟨sexually⟩ eccitare

arrange /ə'reɪndʒ/ vt sistemare ⟨furniture, books⟩; organizzare ⟨meeting⟩; fissare ⟨date, time⟩; ~ **to do sth** combinare di fare qcsa. ~**ment** ⟨of furniture⟩ sistemazione f; Mus arrangiamento m; ⟨agreement⟩ accordo; ⟨of flowers⟩ composizione f; **make** ~**ments** prendere disposizioni

arrears /ə'rɪəz/ npl arretrati mpl; **be in** ~ essere in arretrato; **paid in** ~ pagato a lavoro eseguito

arrest /ə'rest/ n arresto m; **under** ~ in stato d'arresto ● vt arrestare

arrival /ə'raɪvl/ n arrivo m; **new** ~**s** pl nuovi arrivati mpl

arrive /ə'raɪv/ vi arrivare; ~ **at** fig raggiungere

arrogan|ce /'ærəgəns/ n arroganza f. ~**t** a arrogante

arrow /'ærəʊ/ n freccia f

arse /ɑːs/ n vulg culo m

arsenic /'ɑːsənɪk/ n arsenico m

arson /'ɑːsn/ n incendio m doloso. ~**ist** /-sənɪst/ n incendiario, -a mf

art /ɑːt/ n arte f; ~**s and crafts** pl artigianato m; **the A**~**s** pl l'arte f; **A**~**s degree** Univ laurea f in Lettere

artery /'ɑːtərɪ/ n arteria f

artful /'ɑːtfl/ a scaltro

'art gallery n galleria f d'arte

arthritis /ɑː'θraɪtɪs/ n artrite f

artichoke /'ɑːtɪʃəʊk/ n carciofo m

article /'ɑːtɪkl/ n articolo m; ~ **of clothing** capo m d'abbigliamento

articulate¹ /ɑː'tɪkjʊlət/ a ⟨speech⟩ chiaro; **be** ~ esprimersi bene

articulate² /ɑː'tɪkjʊleɪt/ vt scandire ⟨words⟩. ~**d lorry** n autotreno m

artifice /'ɑːtɪfɪs/ n artificio m

artificial /ɑːtɪ'fɪʃl/ a artificiale. ~**ly** adv artificialmente; ⟨smile⟩ artificiosamente

artillery /ɑː'tɪlərɪ/ n artiglieria f

artist /'ɑːtɪst/ n artista mf

artiste /ɑː'tiːst/ n Theat artista mf

artistic /ɑː'tɪstɪk/ a artistico

as /æz/ conj come; siccome; ⟨since⟩ (while) mentre; **as he grew older** diventando vecchio; **as you get to know her** conoscendola meglio; **young as she is** per quanto sia giovane ● prep come; **as a friend** come amico; **as a child** da bambino; **as a foreigner** in quanto straniero; **disguised as** travestito da ● adv **as well** ⟨also⟩ anche; **as soon as I get home** [non] appena arrivo a casa; **as quick as you** veloce quanto te; **as quick as you can** più

veloce che puoi; **as far as** ⟨distance⟩ fino a; **as far as I'm concerned** per quanto mi riguarda; **as long as** finché; ⟨provided that⟩ purché

asbestos /æz'bestɒs/ n amianto m

ascend /ə'send/ vi salire ● vt salire a ⟨throne⟩

Ascension /ə'senʃn/ n Relig Ascensione f

ascent /ə'sent/ n ascesa f

ascertain /æsə'teɪn/ vt accertare

ascribe /ə'skraɪb/ vt attribuire

ash¹ /æʃ/ n ⟨tree⟩ frassino m

ash² n cenere f

ashamed /ə'ʃeɪmd/ a **be/feel** ~ vergognarsi

ashore /ə'ʃɔː(r)/ adv a terra; **go** ~ sbarcare

ash: ~**tray** n portacenere m. **A**~ '**Wednesday** n mercoledì m inv delle Ceneri

Asia /'eɪʒə/ n Asia f. ~**n** a & n asiatico, -a mf. ~**tic** /eɪʒɪ'ætɪk/ a asiatico

aside /ə'saɪd/ adv **take sb** ~ prendere qcno a parte; **put sth** ~ mettere qcsa da parte; ~ **from you** Am a parte te

ask /ɑːsk/ vt fare ⟨question⟩; ⟨invite⟩ invitare; ~ **sb sth** domandare or chiedere qcsa a qcno; ~ **sb to do sth** domandare or chiedere a qcno di fare qcsa ● vi ~ **about sth** informarsi su qcsa; ~ **after** chiedere [notizie] di; ~ **for** chiedere ⟨sth⟩; chiedere di ⟨sb⟩; ~ **for trouble** fam andare in cerca di guai. **ask in** vt ~ **sb in** invitare qcno ad entrare. **ask out** vt ~ **sb out** chiedere a qcno di uscire

askance /ə'skɑːns/ adv **look** ~ **at sb/sth** guardare qcno/qcsa di traverso

askew /ə'skjuː/ a & adv di traverso

asleep /ə'sliːp/ a **be** ~ dormire; **fall** ~ addormentarsi

asparagus /ə'spærəgəs/ n asparagi mpl

aspect /'æspekt/ n aspetto m

aspersions /ə'spɜːʃnz/ npl **cast** ~ **on** diffamare

asphalt /'æsfælt/ n asfalto m

asphyxia /əs'fɪksɪə/ n asfissia f. ~**te** /əs'fɪksɪeɪt/ vt asfissiare. ~**tion** /-'eɪʃn/ n asfissia f

aspirations /æspə'reɪʃnz/ npl aspirazioni fpl

aspire /ə'spaɪə(r)/ vi ~ **to** aspirare a

ass /æs/ n asino m

assailant /ə'seɪlənt/ n assalitore, -trice mf

assassin /ə'sæsɪn/ n assassino, -a mf.

~ate *vt* assassinare. **~ation** /-'neɪʃn/ *n* assassinio *m*

assault /ə'sɔːlt/ *n Mil* assalto *m*; *Jur* aggressione *f* ● *vt* aggredire

assemble /ə'sembl/ *vi* radunarsi ● *vt* radunare; *Techn* montare

assembly /ə'semblɪ/ *n* assemblea *f*; *Sch* assemblea *f* giornaliera di alunni e professori di una scuola; *Techn* montaggio *m*. **~ line** *n* catena *f* di montaggio

assent /ə'sent/ *n* assenso *m* ● *vi* acconsentire

assert /ə'sɜːt/ *vt* asserire; far valere ‹one's rights›; **~ oneself** farsi valere. **~ion** /-ɜːʃn/ *n* asserzione *f*. **~ive** /-tɪv/ *a* **be ~ive** farsi valere

assess /ə'ses/ *vt* valutare; (for tax purposes) stabilire l'imponibile di. **~ment** *n* valutazione *f*; (of tax) accertamento *m*

asset /'æset/ *n* (advantage) vantaggio *m*; (person) elemento *m* prezioso. **~s** *pl* beni *mpl*; (on balance sheet) attivo *msg*

assign /ə'saɪn/ *vt* assegnare. **~ment** *n* (task) incarico *m*

assimilate /ə'sɪmɪleɪt/ *vt* assimilare; integrare ‹person›

assist /ə'sɪst/ *vt*/*i* assistere; **~ sb to do sth** assistere qcno nel fare qcsa. **~ance** *n* assistenza *f*. **~ant** *a* **~ant manager** vicedirettore, -trice *mf* ● *n* assistente *mf*; (in shop) commesso, -a *mf*

associat|e[1] /ə'səʊʃɪeɪt/ *vt* associare (with a); **be ~ed with sth** (involved in) essere coinvolto in qcsa ● *vi* **~e with** frequentare. **~ion** /-'eɪʃn/ *n* associazione *f*. **A~ion 'Football** *n* [gioco *m* del] calcio *m*

associate[2] /ə'səʊʃɪət/ *a* associato ● *n* collega *mf*; (member) socio, -a *mf*

assort|ed /ə'sɔːtɪd/ *a* assortito. **~ment** *n* assortimento *m*

assum|e /ə'sjuːm/ *vt* presumere; assumere ‹control›; **~e office** entrare in carica; **~ing that you're right,...** ammettendo che tu abbia ragione,...

assumption /ə'sʌmpʃn/ *n* supposizione *f*; **on the ~ that** partendo dal presupposto che; **the A~** *Relig* l'Assunzione *f*

assurance /ə'ʃʊərəns/ *n* assicurazione *f*; (confidence) sicurezza *f*

assure /ə'ʃʊə(r)/ *vt* assicurare. **~d** *a* sicuro

asterisk /'æstərɪsk/ *n* asterisco *m*

astern /ə'stɜːn/ *adv* a poppa

asthma /'æsmə/ *n* asma *f*. **~tic** /-'mætɪk/ *a* asmatico

astonish /ə'stɒnɪʃ/ *vt* stupire. **~ing** *a* stupefacente. **~ment** *n* stupore *m*

astound /ə'staʊnd/ *vt* stupire

astray /ə'streɪ/ *adv* **go ~** smarrirsi; (morally) uscire dalla retta via; **lead ~** traviare

astride /ə'straɪd/ *adv* [a] cavalcioni ● *prep* a cavalcioni di

astrolog|er /ə'strɒlədʒə(r)/ *n* astrologo, -a *mf*. **~y** *n* astrologia *f*

astronaut /'æstrənɔːt/ *n* astronauta *mf*

astronom|er /ə'strɒnəmə(r)/ *n* astronomo, -a *mf*. **~ical** /æstrə'nɒmɪkl/ *a* astronomico. **~y** *n* astronomia *f*

astute /ə'stjuːt/ *a* astuto

asylum /ə'saɪləm/ *n* [**political**] **~** asilo *m* politico; [**lunatic**] **~** manicomio *m*

at /ət/, *accentato* /æt/ *prep* a; **at the station**/**the market** alla stazione/al mercato; **at the office**/**the bank** in ufficio/banca; **at the beginning** all'inizio; **at John's** da John; **at the hairdresser's** dal parrucchiere; **at home** a casa; **at work** al lavoro; **at school** a scuola; **at a party**/**wedding** a una festa/un matrimonio; **at 1 o'clock** all'una; **at 50 km an hour** ai 50 all'ora; **at Christmas**/**Easter** a Natale/Pasqua; **at times** talvolta; **two at a time** due alla volta; **good at languages** bravo nelle lingue; **at sb's request** su richiesta di qcno; **are you all worried?** sei preoccupato?

ate /et/ *see* eat

atheist /'eɪθɪɪst/ *n* ateo, -a *mf*

athlet|e /'æθliːt/ *n* atleta *mf*. **~ic** /-'letɪk/ *a* atletico. **~ics** /-'letɪks/ *n* atletica *fsg*

Atlantic /ət'læntɪk/ *a* & *n* **the ~** [**Ocean**] l'[Oceano *m*] Atlantico *m*

atlas /'ætləs/ *n* atlante *m*

atmospher|e /'ætməsfɪə(r)/ *n* atmosfera *f*. **~ic** /-'ferɪk/ *a* atmosferico

atom /'ætəm/ *n* atomo *m*. **~ bomb** *n* bomba *f* atomica

atomic /ə'tɒmɪk/ *a* atomico

atone /ə'təʊn/ *vi* **~ for** pagare per. **~ment** *n* espiazione *f*

atrocious /ə'trəʊʃəs/ *a* atroce; ‹fam: meal, weather› abominevole

atrocity /ə'trɒsətɪ/ *n* atrocità *f inv*

attach /ə'tætʃ/ *vt* attaccare; attribuire ‹importance›; **be ~ed to** *fig* essere attaccato a

attaché /ə'tæʃeɪ/ *n* addetto *m*. **~ case** *n* ventiquattrore *f inv*

attachment /ə'tætʃmənt/ n (affection) attaccamento m; (accessory) accessorio m

attack /ə'tæk/ n attacco m; (physical) aggressione f ● vt attaccare; (physically) aggredire. **~er** n assalitore, -trice mf; (critic) detrattore, -trice mf

attain /ə'teɪn/ vt realizzare (ambition); raggiungere (success, age, goal)

attempt /ə'tempt/ n tentativo m ● vt tentare

attend /ə'tend/ vt essere presente a; (go regularly to) frequentare; (doctor:) avere in cura ● vi essere presente; (pay attention) prestare attenzione. **attend to** vt occuparsi di; (in shop) servire. **~ance** n presenza f. **~ant** n guardiano, -a mf

attention /ə'tenʃn/ n attenzione f; **~!** Mil attenti!; **pay ~** prestare attenzione; **need ~** aver bisogno di attenzioni; (skin, hair, plant:) dover essere curato; (car, tyres:) dover essere riparato; **for the ~ of** all'attenzione di

attentive /ə'tentɪv/ a (pupil, audience) attento

attest /ə'test/ vt/i attestare

attic /'ætɪk/ n soffitta f

attitude /'ætɪtjuːd/ n atteggiamento m

attorney /ə'tɜːnɪ/ n (Am: lawyer) avvocato m; **power of ~** delega f

attract /ə'trækt/ vt attirare. **~ion** /-ækʃn/ n attrazione f; (feature) attrattiva f. **~ive** /-tɪv/ a (person) attraente; (proposal, price) allettante

attribute¹ /'ætrɪbjuːt/ n attributo m

attribute² /ə'trɪbjuːt/ vt attribuire

attrition /ə'trɪʃn/ n **war of ~** guerra f di logoramento

aubergine /'əʊbəʒiːn/ n melanzana f

auburn /'ɔːbən/ a castano ramato

auction /'ɔːkʃn/ n asta f ● vt vendere all'asta. **~eer** /-ʃə'nɪə(r)/ n banditore m

audaci|ous /ɔː'deɪʃəs/ a sfacciato; (daring) audace. **~ty** /-'dæsətɪ/ n sfacciataggine f; (daring) audacia f

audible /'ɔːdəbl/ a udibile

audience /'ɔːdɪəns/ n Theat pubblico m; TV telespettatori mpl; Radio ascoltatori mpl; (meeting) udienza f

audio /'ɔːdɪəʊ/: **~tape** n audiocassetta f. **~ typist** n dattilografo, -a mf (che trascrive registrazioni). **~'visual** a audiovisivo

audit /'ɔːdɪt/ n verifica f del bilancio ● vt verificare

audition /ɔː'dɪʃn/ n audizione f ● vi fare un'audizione

auditor /'ɔːdɪtə(r)/ n revisore m di conti

auditorium /ɔːdɪ'tɔːrɪəm/ n sala f

augment /ɔːg'ment/ vt aumentare

augur /'ɔːgə(r)/ vi **~ well/ill** essere di buon/cattivo augurio

August /'ɔːgəst/ n agosto m

aunt /ɑːnt/ n zia f

au pair /əʊ'peə(r)/ n **~ [girl]** ragazza f alla pari

aura /'ɔːrə/ n aura f

auspices /'ɔːspɪsɪz/ npl **under the ~ of** sotto l'egida di

auspicious /ɔː'spɪʃəs/ a di buon augurio

auster|e /ɒ'stɪə(r)/ a austero. **~ity** /-terətɪ/ n austerità f

Australia /ɒ'streɪlɪə/ n Australia f. **~n** a & n australiano, -a mf

Austria /'ɒstrɪə/ n Austria f. **~n** a & n austriaco, -a mf

authentic /ɔː'θentɪk/ a autentico. **~ate** vt autenticare. **~ity** /-'tɪsətɪ/ n autenticità f

author /'ɔːθə(r)/ n autore m

authoritarian /ɔːθɒrɪ'teərɪən/ a autoritario

authoritative /ɔː'θɒrɪtətɪv/ a autorevole; (manner) autoritario

authority /ɔː'θɒrətɪ/ n autorità f; (permission) autorizzazione f; **be in ~ over** avere autorità su

authorization /ɔːθəraɪ'zeɪʃn/ n autorizzazione f

authorize /'ɔːθəraɪz/ vt autorizzare

autobi'ography /ɔːtə-/ n autobiografia f

autocratic /ɔːtə'krætɪk/ a autocratico

autograph /'ɔːtəgrɑːf/ n autografo m

automate /'ɔːtəmeɪt/ vt automatizzare

automatic /ɔːtə'mætɪk/ a automatico ● n (car) macchina f col cambio automatico; (washing machine) lavatrice f automatica. **~ally** adv automaticamente

automation /ɔːtə'meɪʃn/ n automazione f

automobile /'ɔːtəməbiːl/ n automobile f

autonom|ous /ɔː'tɒnəməs/ a autonomo. **~y** n autonomia f

autopsy /'ɔːtɒpsɪ/ n autopsia f

autumn /'ɔːtəm/ n autunno m. **~al** /-'tʌmnl/ a autunnale

auxiliary /ɔːg'zɪlɪərɪ/ a ausiliario ● n ausiliare m

avail /ə'veɪl/ n **to no ~** invano ● vi **~ oneself of** approfittare di

available /ə'veɪləbl/ *a* disponibile; ‹*book, record etc*› in vendita

avalanche /'ævəlɑːnʃ/ *n* valanga *f*

avarice /'ævərɪs/ *n* avidità *f*

avenge /ə'vendʒ/ *vt* vendicare

avenue /'ævənjuː/ *n* viale *m*; *fig* strada *f*

average /'ævərɪdʒ/ *a* medio; (*mediocre*) mediocre ● *n* media *f*; **on ~** in media ● *vt* ‹*sales, attendance etc*› raggiungere una media di. **average out at** *vt* risultare in media

avers|e /ə'vɜːs/ *a* **not be ~e to sth** non essere contro qcsa. **~ion** /-ɜːʃn/ *n* avversione *f* (**to** per)

avert /ə'vɜːt/ *vt* evitare ‹*crisis*›; distogliere ‹*eyes*›

aviary /'eɪvɪərɪ/ *n* uccelliera *f*

aviation /eɪvɪ'eɪʃn/ *n* aviazione *f*

avid /'ævɪd/ *a* avido (**for** di); ‹*reader*› appassionato

avocado /ævə'kɑːdəʊ/ *n* avocado *m*

avoid /ə'vɔɪd/ *vt* evitare. **~able** /-əbl/ *a* evitabile

await /ə'weɪt/ *vt* attendere

awake /ə'weɪk/ *a* sveglio; **wide ~** completamente sveglio ● *vi* (*pt* **awoke**, *pp* **awoken**) svegliarsi

awaken /ə'weɪkn/ *vt* svegliare. **~ing** *n* risveglio *m*

award /ə'wɔːd/ *n* premio *m*; (*medal*) riconoscimento *m*; (*of prize*) assegnazio‹*time*› scomodo. **~ly** *adv* ‹*move*› goffamente; ‹*say*› con imbarazzo

awning /'ɔːnɪŋ/ *n* tendone *m*

awoke(n) /ə'wəʊk(ən)/ *see* **awake**

awry /ə'raɪ/ *adv* storto

axe /æks/ *n* scure *f* ● *vt* (*pres p* **axing**) fare dei tagli a ‹*budget*›; sopprimere ‹*jobs*›; annullare ‹*project*›

axis /'æksɪs/ *n* (*pl* **axes** /-siːz/) asse *m*

axle /'æksl/ *n* Techn asse *m*

ay[e] /aɪ/ *adv* sì ● *n* sì *m invar*

Bb

BA *n abbr* **Bachelor of Arts**

babble /'bæbl/ *vi* farfugliare; ‹*stream:*› gorgogliare

baby /'beɪbɪ/ *n* bambino, -a *mf*; (*fam: darling*) tesoro *m*

baby: **~ carriage** *n* Am carrozzina *f*. **~ish** *a* bambinesco. **~-sit** *vi* fare da baby-sitter. **~-sitter** *n* baby-sitter *mf*

bachelor /'bætʃələ(r)/ *n* scapolo *m*; **B~ of Arts/Science** laureato, -a *mf* in lettere/in scienze

back /bæk/ *n* schiena *f*; (*of horse, hand*) dorso *m*; (*of chair*) schienale *m*; (*of house, cheque, page*) retro *m*; (*in football*) difesa *f*; **at the ~** in fondo; **in the ~** Auto dietro; **~ to front** ‹*sweater*› il davanti di dietro; **at the ~ of beyond** in un posto sperduto ● *a* posteriore; ‹*taxes, payments*› arretrato ● *adv* indietro; (*returned*) di ritorno; **turn/ move ~** tornare/spostarsi indietro; **put it ~ here/there** rimettilo qui/là; **~ at home** di ritorno a casa; **I'll be ~ in five minutes** torno fra cinque minuti; **I'm just ~** sono appena tornato; **when do you want the book ~?**

quando rivuoi il libro?; **pay ~** ripagare ‹*sb*›; restituire ‹*money*›; **~ in power** di nuovo al potere ● *vt* (*support*) sostenere; (*with money*) finanziare; puntare su ‹*horse*›; (*cover the back of*) rivestire il retro di ● *vi* Auto fare retromarcia. **back down** *vi* battere in ritirata. **back in** *vi* Auto entrare in retromarcia; ‹*person:*› entrare camminando all'indietro. **back out** *vi* Auto uscire in retromarcia; ‹*person:*› uscire camminando all'indietro; *fig* tirarsi indietro (**of** da). **back up** *vt* sostenere; confermare ‹*person's alibi*›; Comput fare una copia di salvataggio di; **be ~ed up** ‹*traffic:*› essere congestionato ● *vi* Auto fare retromarcia

back: **~ache** *n* mal *m* di schiena. **~bencher** *n* parlamentare *mf* ordinario, -a. **~biting** *n* maldicenza *f*. **~bone** *n* spina *f* dorsale. **~chat** *n* risposta *f* impertinente. **~date** *vt* retrodatare ‹*cheque*›; **~dated to** valido a partire da. **~ 'door** *n* porta *f* di servizio

backer /'bækə(r)/ *n* sostenitore, -trice *mf*; (*with money*) finanziatore, -trice *mf*

back: **~'fire** *vi* Auto avere un ritorno di

fiamma; ⟨*fig: plan*⟩ fallire. **~ground** *n* sfondo *m*; ⟨*environment*⟩ ambiente *m*. **~hand** *n* ⟨*tennis*⟩ rovescio *m*. **~'handed** *a* ⟨*compliment*⟩ implicito. **~'hander** *n* ⟨*fam: bribe*⟩ bustarella *f*

backing /'bækɪŋ/ *n* ⟨*support*⟩ supporto *m*; ⟨*material*⟩ riserva *f*; *Mus* accompagnamento *m*; **~ group** gruppo *m* d'accompagnamento

back: **~lash** *n fig* reazione *f* opposta. **~log** *n* **~log of work** lavoro *m* arretrato. **~ 'seat** *n* sedile *m* posteriore. **~side** *n fam* fondoschiena *m inv*. **~slash** *n Typ* barra *f* retroversa. **~stage** *a & adv* dietro le quinte. **~stroke** *n* dorso *m*. **~up** *n* rinforzi *mpl*; *Comput* riserva *f*. **~up copy** *n Comput* copia *f* di riserva

backward /'bækwəd/ *a* ⟨*step*⟩ indietro; ⟨*child*⟩ lento nell'apprendimento; ⟨*country*⟩ arretrato ● *adv* **~s** ⟨*also Am:* **~**⟩ indietro; ⟨*fall, walk*⟩ all'indietro; **~s and forwards** avanti e indietro

back: **~water** *n fig* luogo *m* allo scarto. **~ 'yard** *n* cortile *m*

bacon /'beɪkn/ *n* pancetta *f*

bacteria /bæk'tɪərɪə/ *npl* batteri *mpl*

bad /bæd/ *a* ⟨**worse, worst**⟩ cattivo; ⟨*weather, habit, news, accident*⟩ brutto; ⟨*apple etc*⟩ marcio; **the light is ~** non c'è una buona luce; **use ~ language** dire delle parolacce; **feel ~** sentirsi male; ⟨*feel guilty*⟩ sentirsi in colpa; **have a ~ back** avere dei problemi alla schiena; **smoking is ~ for you** fumare fa male; **go ~** andare a male; **that's just too ~!** pazienza!; **not ~** niente male

bade /bæd/ *see* **bid**

badge /bædʒ/ *n* distintivo *m*

badger /'bædʒə(r)/ *n* tasso *m* ● *vt* tormentare

badly /'bædlɪ/ *adv* male; ⟨*hurt*⟩ gravemente; **~ off** povero; **~ behaved** maleducato; **need ~** aver estremamente bisogno di

bad-'mannered *a* maleducato

badminton /'bædmɪntən/ *n* badminton *m*

bad-'tempered *a* irascibile

baffle /'bæfl/ *vt* confondere

bag /bæg/ *n* borsa *f*; ⟨*of paper*⟩ sacchetto *m*; **old ~** *sl* megera *f*; **~s under the eyes** occhiaie *fpl*; **~s of** *fam* un sacco di

baggage /'bægɪdʒ/ *n* bagagli *mpl*

baggy /'bægɪ/ *a* ⟨*clothes*⟩ ampio

'bagpipes *npl* cornamusa *fsg*

Bahamas /bə'hɑ:məz/ *npl* **the ~** le Bahamas

bail /beɪl/ *n* cauzione *f*; **on ~** su cauzione ● **bail out** *vt Naut* aggottare; **~ sb out** *Jur* pagare la cauzione per qcno ● *vi Aeron* paracadutarsi

bait /beɪt/ *n* esca *f* ● *vt* innescare; ⟨*fig: torment*⟩ tormentare

bake /beɪk/ *vt* cuocere al forno; ⟨*make*⟩ fare ● *vi* cuocersi al forno

baker /'beɪkə(r)/ *n* fornaio, -a *mf*, panettiere, -a *mf*; **~'s** ⟨**shop**⟩ panetteria *f*. **~y** *n* panificio *m*, forno *m*

baking /'beɪkɪŋ/ *n* cottura *f* al forno. **~-powder** *n* lievito *m* in polvere. **~-tin** *n* teglia *f*

balance /'bæləns/ *n* equilibrio *m*; *Comm* bilancio *m*; ⟨*outstanding sum*⟩ saldo *m*; [**bank**] **~** saldo *m*; **be** *or* **hang in the ~** *fig* essere in sospeso ● *vt* bilanciare; equilibrare ⟨*budget*⟩; *Comm* fare il bilancio di ⟨*books*⟩ ● *vi* bilanciarsi; *Comm* essere in pareggio. **~d** *a* equilibrato. **~ sheet** *n* bilancio *m* [d'esercizio]

balcony /'bælkənɪ/ *n* balcone *m*

bald /bɔ:ld/ *a* ⟨*person*⟩ calvo; ⟨*tyre*⟩ liscio; ⟨*statement*⟩ nudo e crudo; **go ~** perdere i capelli

bald|ing /'bɔ:ldɪŋ/ *a* **be ~ing** stare perdendo i capelli. **~ness** *n* calvizie *f*

bale /beɪl/ *n* balla *f*

baleful /'beɪlfl/ *a* malvagio; ⟨*sad*⟩ triste

balk /bɔ:lk/ *vt* ostacolare ● *vi* **~ at** ⟨*horse:*⟩ impennarsi davanti a; *fig* tirarsi indietro davanti a

Balkans /'bɔ:lknz/ *npl* Balcani *mpl*

ball¹ /bɔ:l/ *n* palla *f*; ⟨*football*⟩ pallone *m*; ⟨*of yarn*⟩ gomitolo *m*; **on the ~** *fam* sveglio

ball² *n* ⟨*dance*⟩ ballo *m*

ballad /'bæləd/ *n* ballata *f*

ballast /'bæləst/ *n* zavorra *f*

ball-'bearing *n* cuscinetto *m* a sfera

ballerina /bælə'ri:nə/ *n* ballerina *f* [classica]

ballet /'bæleɪ/ *n* balletto *m*; ⟨*art form*⟩ danza *f*; **~ dancer** *n* ballerino, -a *mf* [classico, -a]

ballistic /bə'lɪstɪk/ *a* balistico. **~s** *n* balistica *fsg*

balloon /bə'lu:n/ *n* pallone *m*; *Aeron* mongolfiera *f*

ballot /'bælət/ *n* votazione *f*. **~-box** *n* urna *f*. **~-paper** *n* scheda *f* di votazione

ball: **~-point** [**'pen**] *n* penna *f* a sfera. **~room** *n* sala *f* da ballo

balm /bɑ:m/ *n* balsamo *m*

balmy /'bɑːmɪ/ a (-ier, -iest) mite; (fam: crazy) strampalato

Baltic /'bɔːltɪk/ a & n the ~ [Sea] il [mar] Baltico

bamboo /bæm'buː/ n bambù m inv

bamboozle /bæm'buːzl/ vt (fam: mystify) confondere

ban /bæn/ n proibizione f ● vt (pt/pp banned) proibire; ~ from espellere da ⟨club⟩; **she was ~ned from driving** le hanno ritirato la patente

banal /bə'nɑːl/ a banale. ~ity /-'nælətɪ/ n banalità f inv

banana /bə'nɑːnə/ n banana f

band /bænd/ n banda f; (stripe) nastro m; (Mus: pop group) complesso m; (Mus: brass ~) banda f; Mil fanfara f ● **band together** vi riunirsi

bandage /'bændɪdʒ/ n benda f ● vt fasciare ⟨limb⟩

b. & b. abbr bed and breakfast

bandit /'bændɪt/ n bandito m

band: ~**stand** n palco m coperto [dell'orchestra]. ~**wagon** n **jump on the** ~**wagon** fig seguire la corrente

bandy[1] /'bændɪ/ vt (pt/pp -ied) scambiarsi ⟨words⟩. **bandy about** vt far circolare

bandy[2] a (-ier, -iest) be ~ avere le gambe storte

bang /bæŋ/ n (noise) fragore m; (of gun, firework) scoppio m; (blow) colpo m ● adv ~ **in the middle of** fam proprio nel mezzo di; **go** ~ ⟨gun:⟩ sparare; ⟨balloon:⟩ esplodere ● int bum! ● vt battere ⟨fist⟩; battere su ⟨table⟩; sbattere ⟨door, head⟩ ● vi scoppiare; ⟨door:⟩ sbattere

banger /'bæŋə(r)/ n (firework) petardo m; (fam: sausage) salsiccia f; **old** ~ (fam: car) macinino m

bangle /'bæŋgl/ n braccialetto m

banish /'bænɪʃ/ vt bandire

banisters /'bænɪstəz/ npl ringhiera fsg

bank[1] /bæŋk/ n (of river) sponda f; (slope) scarpata f ● vi Aeron inclinarsi in virata

bank[2] n banca f ● vt depositare in banca ● vi ~ **with** avere un conto [bancario] presso. **bank on** vt contare su

'bank account n conto m in banca

'bank card n carta f assegno

banker /'bæŋkə(r)/ n banchiere m

bank: ~ **'holiday** n giorno m festivo. ~**ing** n bancario m. ~ **manager** n direttore, -trice mf di banca. ~**note** n banconota f

bankrupt /'bæŋkrʌpt/ a fallito; **go** ~ fallire ● n persona f che ha fatto fallimento ● vt far fallire. ~**cy** n bancarotta f

banner /'bænə(r)/ n stendardo m; (of demonstrators) striscione m

banns /bænz/ npl Relig pubblicazioni fpl [di matrimonio]

banquet /'bæŋkwɪt/ n banchetto m

banter /'bæntə(r)/ n battute fpl di spirito

baptism /'bæptɪzm/ n battesimo m

Baptist /'bæptɪst/ a & n battista mf

baptize /bæp'taɪz/ vt battezzare

bar /bɑː(r)/ n sbarra f; Jur ordine m degli avvocati; (of chocolate) tavoletta f; (café) bar m inv; (counter) banco m; Mus battuta f; (fig: obstacle) ostacolo m; ~ **of soap/gold** saponetta f/lingotto m; **behind** ~**s** fam dietro le sbarre ● vt (pt/pp barred) sbarrare ⟨way⟩; sprangare ⟨door⟩; escludere ⟨person⟩ ● prep tranne; ~ **none** in assoluto

barbarian /bɑː'beərɪən/ n barbaro, -a mf

barbar|ic /bɑː'bærɪk/ a barbarico. ~**ity** n barbarie f inv. ~**ous** /'bɑːbərəs/ a barbaro

barbecue /'bɑːbɪkjuː/ n barbecue m inv; (party) grigliata f, barbecue m inv ● vt arrostire sul barbecue

barbed /bɑːbd/ a ~ **wire** filo m spinato

barber /'bɑːbə(r)/ n barbiere m

barbiturate /bɑː'bɪtjʊrət/ n barbiturico m

'bar code n codice m a barre

bare /beə(r)/ a nudo; ⟨tree, room⟩ spoglio; ⟨floor⟩ senza moquette ● vt scoprire; mostrare ⟨teeth⟩

bare: ~**back** adv senza sella. ~**faced** a sfacciato. ~**foot** adv scalzo. ~**'headed** a a capo scoperto

barely /'beəlɪ/ adv appena

bargain /'bɑːgɪn/ n (agreement) patto m; (good buy) affare m; **into the** ~ per di più ● vi contrattare; (haggle) trattare. **bargain for** vt (expect) aspettarsi

barge /bɑːdʒ/ n barcone m ● **barge in** vi fam (to room) piombare dentro; (into conversation) interrompere bruscamente. ~ **into** vt piombare dentro a ⟨room⟩; venire addosso a ⟨person⟩

baritone /'bærɪtəʊn/ n baritono m

bark[1] /bɑːk/ n (of tree) corteccia f

bark[2] n abbaiamento m ● vi abbaiare

barley /'bɑːlɪ/ n orzo m

bar: ~**maid** n barista f. ~**man** n barista m

barmy /'bɑːmɪ/ a fam strampalato

barn /bɑːn/ n granaio m
barometer /bəˈrɒmɪtə(r)/ n barometro m
baron /ˈbærn/ n barone m. **~ess** n baronessa f
baroque /bəˈrɒk/ a & n barocco m
barracks /ˈbærəks/ npl caserma fsg
barrage /ˈbærɑːʒ/ n Mil sbarramento m; (fig: of criticism) sfilza f
barrel /ˈbærl/ n barile m, botte f; (of gun) canna f. **~-organ** n organetto m [a cilindro]
barren /ˈbærən/ a sterile; ⟨landscape⟩ brullo
barricade /bærɪˈkeɪd/ n barricata f ● vt barricare
barrier /ˈbærɪə(r)/ n barriera f; Rail cancello m; fig ostacolo m
barring /ˈbɑːrɪŋ/ prep **~ accidents** tranne imprevisti
barrister /ˈbærɪstə(r)/ n avvocato m
barrow /ˈbærəʊ/ n carretto m; (wheel~) carriola f
barter /ˈbɑːtə(r)/ vi barattare (**for** con)
base /beɪs/ n base f ● a vile ● vt basare; **be ~d on** basarsi su
base: ~ball n baseball m. **~less** a infondato. **~ment** n seminterrato m. **~ment flat** n appartamento m nel seminterrato
bash /bæʃ/ n colpo m [violento] ● vt colpire [violentemente]; (dent) ammaccare; **~ed in** ammaccato
bashful /ˈbæʃfl/ a timido
basic /ˈbeɪsɪk/ a di base; ⟨condition, requirement⟩ basilare; ⟨living conditions⟩ povero; **my Italian is pretty ~** il mio italiano è abbastanza rudimentale; **the ~s** (of language, science) i rudimenti; (essentials) l'essenziale m. **~ally** adv fondamentalmente
basil /ˈbæzɪl/ n basilico m
basilica /bəˈzɪlɪkə/ n basilica f
basin /ˈbeɪsn/ n bacinella f; (wash-hand ~) lavabo m; (for food) recipiente m; Geog bacino m
basis /ˈbeɪsɪs/ n (pl -ses /-siːz/) base f
bask /bɑːsk/ vi crogiolarsi
basket /ˈbɑːskɪt/ n cestino m. **~ball** n pallacanestro f
Basle /bɑːl/ n Basilea f
bass /beɪs/ a basso; **~ voice** voce f di basso ● n basso m
bastard /ˈbɑːstəd/ n (illegitimate child) bastardo, -a mf; sl figlio m di puttana
bastion /ˈbæstɪən/ n bastione m
bat[1] /bæt/ n mazza f; (for table tennis) racchetta f; **off one's own ~** fam tutto

da solo ● vt (pt/pp **batted**) battere; **she didn't ~ an eyelid** fig non ha battuto ciglio
bat[2] n Zool pipistrello m
batch /bætʃ/ n gruppo m; (of goods) partita f; (of bread) infornata f
bated /ˈbeɪtɪd/ a **with ~ breath** col fiato sospeso
bath /bɑːθ/ n (pl ~s /bɑːðz/) bagno m; (tub) vasca f da bagno; **~s** pl piscina f; **have a ~** fare un bagno ● vt fare il bagno a
bathe /beɪð/ n bagno m ● vi fare il bagno ● vt lavare ⟨wound⟩. **~r** n bagnante mf
bathing /ˈbeɪðɪŋ/ n bagni mpl. **~-cap** n cuffia f. **~-costume** n costume m da bagno
bath: ~-mat n tappetino m da bagno. **~robe** n accappatoio m. **~room** n bagno m. **~-towel** n asciugamano m da bagno
baton /ˈbætn/ n Mus bacchetta f
battalion /bəˈtælɪən/ n battaglione m
batter /ˈbætə(r)/ n Culin pastella f; **~ed** a ⟨car⟩ malandato; ⟨wife, baby⟩ maltrattato
battery /ˈbætərɪ/ n batteria f; (of torch, radio) pila f
battle /ˈbætl/ n battaglia f; fig lotta f ● vi fig lottare
battle: ~field n campo m di battaglia. **~ship** n corazzata f
bawdy /ˈbɔːdɪ/ a (-ier, -iest) piccante
bawl /bɔːl/ vt/i urlare
bay[1] /beɪ/ n Geog baia f
bay[2] n **keep at ~** tenere a bada
bay[3] n Bot alloro m. **~-leaf** n foglia f d'alloro
bayonet /ˈbeɪənɪt/ n baionetta f
bay 'window n bay window f inv (grande finestra sporgente)
bazaar /bəˈzɑː(r)/ n bazar m inv
BC abbr (before Christ) a.C.
be /biː/ vi (pres am, are, is, are; pt was, were; pp been) essere; **he is a teacher** è insegnante, fa l'insegnante; **what do you want to be?** cosa vuoi fare?; **be quiet!** sta' zitto!; **I am cold/hot** ho freddo/caldo; **it's cold/hot, isn't it?** fa freddo/caldo, vero?; **how are you?** come stai?; **I am well** sto bene; **there is** c'è; **there are** ci sono; **I have been to Venice** sono stato a Venezia; **has the postman been?** è passato il postino?; **you're coming too, aren't you?** vieni anche tu, no?; **it's yours, is it?** è tuo, vero?; **was**

John there? - yes, he was c'era John? - sì; **John wasn't there - yes he was!** John non c'era - sì che c'era!; **three and three are six** tre più tre fanno sei; **he is five** ha cinque anni; **that will be £10, please** fanno 10 sterline, per favore; **how much is it?** quanto costa?; **that's £5 you owe me** mi devi 5 sterline ● *v aux* **I am coming/reading** sto venendo/leggendo; **I'm staying** (*not leaving*) resto; **I am being lazy** sono pigro; **I was thinking of you** stavo pensando a te; **you are not to tell him** non devi dirgielo; **you are to do that immediately** devi farlo subito ● *passive* essere; **I have been robbed** sono stato derubato

beach /biːtʃ/ *n* spiaggia *f*. **~wear** *n* abbigliamento *m* da spiaggia

bead /biːd/ *n* perlina *f*

beak /biːk/ *n* becco *m*

beaker /'biːkə(r)/ *n* coppa *f*

beam /biːm/ *n* trave *f*; (*of light*) raggio *m* ● *vi* irradiare; ⟨*person:*⟩ essere raggiante. **~ing** *a* raggiante

bean /biːn/ *n* fagiolo *m*; (*of coffee*) chicco *m*

bear[1] /beə(r)/ *n* orso *m*

bear[2] *v* (*pt* **bore**, *pp* **borne**) ● *vt* (*endure*) sopportare; mettere al mondo ⟨*child*⟩; (*carry*) portare; **~ in mind** tenere presente ● *vi* **~ left/right** andare a sinistra/a destra. **bear with** *vt* aver pazienza con. **~able** /-əbl/ *a* sopportabile

beard /bɪəd/ *n* barba *f*. **~ed** *a* barbuto

bearer /'beərə(r)/ *n* portatore, -trice *mf*; (*of passport*) titolare *mf*

bearing /'beərɪŋ/ *n* portamento *m*; *Techn* cuscinetto *m* [a sfera]; **have a ~ on** avere attinenza con; **get one's ~s** orientarsi

bend /biːst/ *n* bestia *f*; (*fam: person*) animale *m*

beat /biːt/ *n* battito *m*; (*rhythm*) battuta *f*; (*of policeman*) giro *m* d'ispezione ● *v* (*pt* **beat**, *pp* **beaten**) ● *vt* battere; picchiare ⟨*person*⟩; **~ it!** *fam* darsela a gambe!; **it ~s me why...** *fam* non capisco proprio perché... **beat up** *vt* picchiare

beat|en /'biːtn/ *a* **off the ~en track** fuori mano. **~ing** *n* bastonata *f*; **get a ~ing** (*with fists*) essere preso a pugni; ⟨*team, player:*⟩ prendere una batosta

beautician /bjuː'tɪʃn/ *n* estetista *mf*

beauti|ful /'bjuːtɪfl/ *a* bello. **~fully** *adv* splendidamente

beauty /'bjuːtɪ/ *n* bellezza *f*. **~ parlour** *n* istituto *m* di bellezza. **~ spot** *n* neo *m*; (*place*) luogo *m* pittoresco

beaver /'biːvə(r)/ *n* castoro *m*

became /bɪ'keɪm/ *see* **become**

because /bɪ'kɒz/ *conj* perché; **~ you didn't tell me, I...** poiché non me lo hai detto,... ● *adv* **~ of** a causa di

beck /bek/ *n* **at the ~ and call of** a completa disposizione di

beckon /'bekn/ *vt/i* **~ [to]** chiamare con un cenno

becom|e /bɪ'kʌm/ *v* (*pt* **became**, *pp* **become**) ● *vt* diventare ● *vi* diventare; **what has ~e of her?** che ne è di lei? **~ing** *a* ⟨*clothes*⟩ bello

bed /bed/ *n* letto *m*; (*of sea, lake*) fondo *m*; (*layer*) strato *m*; (*of flowers*) aiuola *f*; **in ~** a letto; **go to ~** andare a letto; **~ and breakfast** pensione *f* familiare in cui il prezzo della camera comprende la prima colazione. **~clothes** *npl* lenzuola e coperte *fpl*. **~ding** *n* biancheria *f* per il letto, materasso e guanciali

bedlam /'bedləm/ *n* baraonda *f*

bedraggled /bɪ'drægld/ *a* inzaccherato

bed: ~ridden *a* costretto a letto. **~room** *n* camera *f* da letto

bedside *n* **at his ~** al suo capezzale. **~ 'lamp** *n* abat-jour *m inv*. **~ 'table** *n* comodino *m*

bed: ~'sit *n*, **~'sitter** *n*, **~'sitting-room** *n* = camera *f* ammobiliata fornita di cucina. **~spread** *n* copriletto *m*. **~time** *n* l'ora *f* di andare a letto

bee /biː/ *n* ape *f*

beech /biːtʃ/ *n* faggio *m*

beef /biːf/ *n* manzo *m*. **~burger** *n* hamburger *m inv*

bee: ~hive *n* alveare *m*. **~-line** *n* **make a ~line for** *fam* precipitarsi verso

been /biːn/ *see* **be**

beer /bɪə(r)/ *n* birra *f*

beetle /'biːtl/ *n* scarafaggio *m*

beetroot /'biːtruːt/ *n* barbabietola *f*

before /bɪ'fɔː(r)/ *prep* prima di; **the day ~ yesterday** ieri l'altro; **~ long** fra poco ● *adv* prima; **never ~ have I seen...** non ho mai visto prima...; **~ that** prima; **~ going** prima di andare ● *conj* (*time*) prima che; **~ you go** prima che tu vada. **~hand** *adv* in anticipo

befriend /bɪ'frend/ *vt* trattare da amico

beg /beg/ *v* (*pt/pp* **begged**) ● *vi* mendicare ● *vt* pregare; chiedere ⟨*favour, forgiveness*⟩

began /brˈgæn/ *see* **begin**

beggar /ˈbegə(r)/ *n* mendicante *mf*; **poor ~!** povero cristo!

begin /brˈgɪn/ *vt/i* (*pt* **began**, *pp* **begun**, *pres p* **beginning**) cominciare. **~ner** *n* principiante *mf*. **~ning** *n* principio *m*

begonia /brˈgəʊnɪə/ *n* begonia *f*

begrudge /brˈgrʌdʒ/ *vt* ⟨*envy*⟩ essere invidioso di; dare malvolentieri ⟨*money*⟩

begun /brˈgʌn/ *see* **begin**

behalf /brˈhɑːf/ *n* **on ~ of** a nome di; **on my ~** a nome mio

behave /brˈheɪv/ *vi* comportarsi; **~ [oneself]** comportarsi bene

behaviour /brˈheɪvjə(r)/ *n* comportamento *m*; ⟨*of prisoner, soldier*⟩ condotta *f*

behead /brˈhed/ *vt* decapitare

behind /brˈhaɪnd/ *prep* dietro; **be ~ sth** *fig* stare dietro qcsa ● *adv* dietro, indietro; ⟨*late*⟩ in ritardo; **a long way ~** molto indietro ● *n fam* didietro *m*. **~hand** *adv* indietro

beholden /brˈhəʊldn/ *a* obbligato (**to** verso)

beige /beɪʒ/ *a & n* beige *m inv*

being /ˈbiːɪŋ/ *n* essere *m*; **come into ~** nascere

belated /brˈleɪtɪd/ *a* tardivo

belch /beltʃ/ *vi* ruttare ● *vt* **~ [out]** eruttare ⟨*smoke*⟩

belfry /ˈbelfrɪ/ *n* campanile *m*

Belgian /ˈbeldʒən/ *a & n* belga *mf*

Belgium /ˈbeldʒəm/ *n* Belgio *m*

belief /brˈliːf/ *n* fede *f*; ⟨*opinion*⟩ convinzione *f*

believable /brˈliːvəbl/ *a* credibile

believe /brˈliːv/ *vt/i* credere. **~r** *n Relig* credente *mf*; **be a great ~r in** credere fermamente in

belittle /brˈlɪtl/ *vt* sminuire ⟨*person, achievements*⟩

bell /bel/ *n* campana *f*; ⟨*on door*⟩ campanello *m*

belligerent /brˈlɪdʒərənt/ *a* belligerante; ⟨*aggressive*⟩ bellicoso

bellow /ˈbeləʊ/ *vi* gridare a squarciagola; ⟨*animal:*⟩ muggire

bellows /ˈbeləʊz/ *npl* ⟨*for fire*⟩ soffietto *msg*

belly /ˈbelɪ/ *n* pancia *f*

belong /brˈlɒŋ/ *vi* appartenere (**to** a); ⟨*be member*⟩ essere socio (**to** di). **~ings** *npl* cose *fpl*

beloved /brˈlʌvɪd/ *a & n* amato, -a *mf*

below /brˈləʊ/ *prep* sotto; ⟨*with numbers*⟩ al di sotto di ● *adv* sotto, di sotto; *Naut* sotto coperta; **see ~** guardare qui di seguito

belt /belt/ *n* cintura *f*; ⟨*area*⟩ zona *f*; *Techn* cinghia *f* ● *vi* **~ along** ⟨*fam: rush*⟩ filare velocemente ● *vt* ⟨*fam: hit*⟩ picchiare

bemused /brˈmjuːzd/ *a* confuso

bench /bentʃ/ *n* panchina *f*; ⟨*work~*⟩ piano *m* da lavoro; **the B~** *Jur* la magistratura

bend /bend/ *n* curva *f*; ⟨*of river*⟩ ansa *f* ● *v* (*pt/pp* **bent**) ● *vt* piegare ● *vi* piegarsi; ⟨*road:*⟩ curvare; **~ [down]** chinarsi. **bend over** *vi* inchinarsi

beneath /brˈniːθ/ *prep* sotto, al di sotto di; **he thinks it's ~ him** *fig* pensa che sia sotto al suo livello ● *adv* giù

benediction /benɪˈdɪkʃn/ *n Relig* benedizione *f*

benefactor /ˈbenɪfæktə(r)/ *n* benefattore, -trice *mf*

beneficial /benɪˈfɪʃl/ *a* benefico

beneficiary /benɪˈfɪʃərɪ/ *n* beneficiario, -a *mf*

benefit /ˈbenɪfɪt/ *n* vantaggio *m*; ⟨*allowance*⟩ indennità *f inv* ● *v* (*pt/pp* **-fited**, *pres p* **-fiting**) ● *vt* giovare a ● *vi* trarre vantaggio (**from** da)

benevolen|ce /brˈnevələns/ *n* benevolenza *f*. **~t** *a* benevolo

benign /brˈnaɪn/ *a* benevolo; *Med* benigno

bent /bent/ *see* **bend** ● *a* ⟨*person*⟩ ricurvo; ⟨*distorted*⟩ curvato; ⟨*fam: dishonest*⟩ corrotto; **be ~ on doing sth** essere ben deciso a fare qcsa ● *n* predisposizione *f*

be|queath /brˈkwiːð/ *vt* lasciare in eredità. **~quest** /-ˈkwest/ *n* lascito *m*

bereave|d /brˈriːvd/ *n* **the ~d** *pl* i familiari del defunto. **~ment** *n* lutto *m*

bereft /brˈreft/ *a* **~ of** privo di

beret /ˈbereɪ/ *n* berretto *m*

berry /ˈberɪ/ *n* bacca *f*

berserk /bəˈsɜːk/ *a* **go ~** diventare una belva

berth /bɜːθ/ *n* ⟨*bed*⟩ cuccetta *f*; ⟨*anchorage*⟩ ormeggio *m* ● *vi* ormeggiare

beseech /brˈsiːtʃ/ *vt* (*pt/pp* **beseeched** *or* **besought**) supplicare

beside /brˈsaɪd/ *prep* accanto a; **~ oneself** fuori di sé

besides /brˈsaɪdz/ *prep* oltre a ● *adv* inoltre

besiege /brˈsiːdʒ/ *vt* assediare

besought /bɪˈsɔːt/ *see* **beseech**

best /best/ *a* migliore; **the ~ part of a year** la maggior parte dell'anno; **~ before** *Comm* preferibilmente prima di ● *n* **the ~** il meglio; (*person*) il/la migliore; **at ~** tutt'al più; **all the ~!** tanti auguri!; **do one's ~** fare del proprio meglio; **to the ~ of my knowledge** per quel che ne so; **make the ~ of it** cogliere il lato buono della cosa ● *adv* meglio, nel modo migliore; **as ~ I could** meglio che potevo. **~ 'man** *n* testimone *m*

bestow /bɪˈstəʊ/ *vt* conferire (**on** a)

best'seller *n* bestseller *m inv*

bet /bet/ *n* scommessa *f* ● *vt/i* (*pt/pp* **bet** *or* **betted**) scommettere

betray /bɪˈtreɪ/ *vt* tradire. **~al** *n* tradimento *m*

better /ˈbetə(r)/ *a* migliore, meglio; **get ~** migliorare; (*after illness*) rimettersi ● *adv* meglio; **~ off** meglio; (*wealthier*) più ricco; **all the ~** tanto meglio; **the sooner the ~** prima è, meglio è; **I've thought ~ of it** ci ho ripensato; **you'd ~ stay** faresti meglio a restare; **I'd not** è meglio che non lo faccia ● *vt* migliorare; **~ oneself** migliorare le proprie condizioni

'betting shop *n* ricevitoria *f* (*dell'allibratore*)

between /bɪˈtwiːn/ *prep* fra, tra; **~ you and me** detto fra di noi; **~ us** (*together*) tra me e te ● *adv* [**in**] **~** in mezzo; (*time*) frattempo

beverage /ˈbevərɪdʒ/ *n* bevanda *f*

beware /bɪˈweə(r)/ *vi* guardarsi (**of** da); **~ of the dog!** attenti al cane!

bewilder /bɪˈwɪldə(r)/ *vt* disorientare; **~ed** perplesso. **~ment** *n* perplessità *f*

beyond /bɪˈjɒnd/ *prep* oltre; **~ reach** irraggiungibile; **~ doubt** senza alcun dubbio; **~ belief** da non credere; **it's ~ me** *fam* non riesco proprio a capire ● *adv* più in là

bias /ˈbaɪəs/ *n* (*preference*) preferenza *f*; *pej* pregiudizio *m* ● *vt* (*pt/pp* **biased**) (*influence*) influenzare. **~ed** *a* parziale

bib /bɪb/ *n* bavaglino *m*

Bible /ˈbaɪbl/ *n* Bibbia *f*

biblical /ˈbɪblɪkl/ *a* biblico

bicarbonate /baɪˈkɑːbəneɪt/ *n* **~ of soda** bicarbonato *m* di sodio

biceps /ˈbaɪseps/ *n* bicipite *m*

bicker /ˈbɪkə(r)/ *vi* litigare

bicycle /ˈbaɪsɪkl/ *n* bicicletta *f* ● *vi* andare in bicicletta

bid¹ /bɪd/ *n* offerta *f*; (*attempt*) tentativo

m ● *vt/i* (*pt/pp* **bid**, *pres p* **bidding**) offrire; (*in cards*) dichiarare

bid² *vt* (*pt* **bade** *or* **bid**, *pp* **bidden** *or* **bid**, *pres p* **bidding**) *liter* (*command*) comandare; **~ sb welcome** dare il benvenuto a qcno

bidder /ˈbɪdə(r)/ *n* offerente *mf*

bide /baɪd/ *vt* **~ one's time** aspettare il momento buono

biennial /baɪˈenɪəl/ *a* biennale

bifocals /baɪˈfəʊklz/ *npl* occhiali *mpl* bifocali

big /bɪg/ *a* (**bigger, biggest**) grande; ⟨*brother, sister*⟩ più grande; (*fam: generous*) generoso ● *adv* **talk ~** *fam* spararle grosse

bigam|ist /ˈbɪgəmɪst/ *n* bigamo, -a *mf*. **~y** *n* bigamia *f*

'big-head *n fam* gasato, -a *mf*

big-'headed *a fam* gasato

bigot /ˈbɪgət/ *n* fanatico, -a *mf*. **~ed** *a* di mentalità ristretta

'bigwig *n fam* pezzo *m* grosso

bike /baɪk/ *n fam* bici *f inv*

bikini /bɪˈkiːnɪ/ *n* bikini *m inv*

bile /baɪl/ *n* bile *f*

bilingual /baɪˈlɪŋgwəl/ *a* bilingue

bill¹ /bɪl/ *n* fattura *f*; (*in restaurant etc*) conto *m*; (*poster*) manifesto *m*; *Pol* progetto *m* di legge; (*Am: note*) biglietto *m* di banca ● *vt* fatturare

bill² *n* (*beak*) becco *m*

'billfold *n Am* portafoglio *m*

billiards /ˈbɪljədz/ *n* biliardo *m*

billion /ˈbɪljən/ *n* (*thousand million*) miliardo *m*; (*old-fashioned Br: million million*) mille miliardi *mpl*

billy-goat /ˈbɪlɪ-/ *n* caprone *m*

bin /bɪn/ *n* bidone *m*

bind /baɪnd/ *vt* (*pt/pp* **bound**) legare (**to** a); (*bandage*) fasciare; *Jur* obbligare. **~ing** *a* ⟨*promise, contract*⟩ vincolante ● *n* (*of book*) rilegatura *f*; (*on ski*) attacco *m* [di sicurezza]

binge /bɪndʒ/ *n fam* **have a ~** fare baldoria; (*eat a lot*) abbuffarsi ● *vi* abbuffarsi (**on** di)

binoculars /bɪˈnɒkjʊləz/ *npl* [**pair of**] **~** binocolo *msg*

bio'chemist /baɪəʊ-/ *n* biochimico, -a *mf*. **~ry** *n* biochimica *f*

biodegradable /-dɪˈgreɪdəbl/ *a* biodegradabile

biograph|er /baɪˈɒgrəfə(r)/ *n* biografo, -a *mf*. **~y** *n* biografia *f*

biological /baɪəˈlɒdʒɪkl/ *a* biologico

biolog|ist /baɪˈɒlədʒɪst/ *n* biologo, -a *mf*. **~y** *n* biologia *f*

birch /bɜːtʃ/ n (tree) betulla f
bird /bɜːd/ n uccello m; (fam: girl) ragazza f
Biro® /'baɪrəʊ/ n biro f inv
birth /bɜːθ/ n nascita f
birth: ~ **certificate** n certificato m di nascita. ~-**control** n controllo m delle nascite. ~**day** n compleanno m. ~**mark** n voglia f. ~-**rate** n natalità f
biscuit /'bɪskɪt/ n biscotto m
bisect /baɪ'sekt/ vt dividere in due [parti]
bishop /'bɪʃəp/ n vescovo m; (in chess) alfiere m
bit¹ /bɪt/ n pezzo m; (smaller) pezzetto m; (for horse) morso m; Comput bit m inv; **a** ~ **of** un pezzo di (cheese, paper); un po' di (time, rain, silence); ~ **by** ~ poco a poco; **do one's** ~ fare la propria parte
bit² see **bite**
bitch /bɪtʃ/ n cagna f; sl stronza f. ~**y** a velenoso
bit|e /baɪt/ n morso m; (insect ~) puntura f; (mouthful) boccone m ● vt (pt **bit**, pp **bitten**) mordere; (insect:) pungere; ~**e one's nails** mangiarsi le unghie ● vi mordere; (insect:) pungere. ~**ing** a (wind, criticism) pungente; (remark) mordace
bitter /'bɪtə(r)/ a amaro ● n Br birra f amara. ~**ly** adv amaramente; **it's** ~**ly cold** c'è un freddo pungente. ~**ness** n amarezza f
bitty /'bɪtɪ/ a Br fam frammentario
bizarre /bɪ'zɑː(r)/ a bizzarro
blab /blæb/ vi (pt/pp **blabbed**) spifferare
black /blæk/ a nero; **be** ~ **and blue** essere pieno di lividi ● n negro, -a m f ● vt boicottare (goods). **black out** vt cancellare ● vi (lose consciousness) perdere coscienza
black: ~**berry** n mora f. ~**bird** n merlo m. ~**board** n Sch lavagna f. ~'**currant** n ribes m inv nero; ~ '**eye** n occhio m nero. ~ '**ice** n ghiaccio m (sulla strada). ~**leg** n Br crumiro m. ~**list** vt mettere sulla lista nera. ~**mail** n ricatto m ● vt ricattare. ~**mailer** n ricattatore, -trice mf. ~ '**market** n mercato m nero. ~-**out** n blackout m inv; **have a** ~-**out** Med perdere coscienza. ~**smith** n fabbro m
bladder /'blædə(r)/ n Anat vescica f
blade /bleɪd/ n lama f; (of grass) filo m
blame /bleɪm/ n colpa f ● vt dare la colpa a; ~ **sb for doing sth** dare la colpa a qcno per aver fatto qcsa; **no one is to**

~ non è colpa di nessuno. ~**less** a innocente
blanch /blɑːntʃ/ vi sbiancare ● vt Culin sbollentare
blancmange /blə'mɒnʒ/ n biancomangiare m inv
bland /blænd/ a (food) insipido; (person) insulso
blank /blæŋk/ a bianco; (look) vuoto ● n spazio m vuoto; (cartridge) a salve. ~ '**cheque** n assegno m in bianco
blanket /'blæŋkɪt/ n coperta f
blank 'verse n versi mpl sciolti
blare /bleə(r)/ vi suonare a tutto volume. **blare out** vt far risuonare ● vi (music, radio:) strillare
blasé /'blɑːzeɪ/ a vissuto, blasé inv
blaspheme /blæs'fiːm/ vi bestemmiare
blasphem|ous /'blæsfəməs/ a blasfemo. ~**y** n bestemmia f
blast /blɑːst/ n (gust) raffica f; (sound) scoppio m ● vt (with explosive) far saltare ● int sl maledizione!. ~**ed** a sl maledetto
blast: ~-**furnace** n altoforno m. ~-**off** n (of missile) lancio m
blatant /'bleɪtənt/ a sfacciato
blaze /bleɪz/ n incendio m; **a** ~ **of colour** un'esplosione f di colori ● vi ardere
blazer /'bleɪzə(r)/ n blazer m inv
bleach /bliːtʃ/ n decolorante m; (for cleaning) candeggina f ● vt sbiancare; ossigenare (hair)
bleak /bliːk/ a desolato; (fig: prospects, future) tetro
bleary-eyed /blɪərɪ'aɪd/ a **look** ~ avere gli occhi assonnati
bleat /bliːt/ vi belare ● n belato m
bleed /bliːd/ v (pt/pp **bled**) ● vi sanguinare ● vt spurgare (brakes, radiator)
bleep /bliːp/ n bip m ● vi suonare ● vt chiamare (col cercapersone) (doctor). ~**er** n cercapersone m inv
blemish /'blemɪʃ/ n macchia f
blend /blend/ n (of tea, coffee, whisky) miscela f; (of colours) insieme m ● vt mescolare ● vi (colours, sounds:) fondersi (with con). ~**er** n Culin frullatore m
bless /bles/ vt benedire. ~**ed** /'blesɪd/ a also sl benedetto. ~**ing** n benedizione f
blew /bluː/ see **blow²**
blight /blaɪt/ n Bot ruggine f ● vt far avvizzire (plants)
blind¹ /blaɪnd/ a cieco; ~ **man/woman** cieco/cieca ● npl **the** ~ i ciechi mpl; ● vt accecare

blind² n [**roller**] ~ avvolgibile m; [**Venetian**] ~ veneziana f

blind: ~ '**alley** n vicolo m cieco. ~**fold** a be ~**fold** avere gli occhi bendati ● n benda f ● vt bendare gli occhi a. ~**ly** adv ciecamente. ~**ness** n cecità f

blink /blɪŋk/ vi sbattere le palpebre; ⟨light:⟩ tremolare

blinkered /'blɪŋkəd/ adj fig be ~ avere i paraocchi

blinkers /'blɪŋkəz/ npl paraocchi mpl

bliss /blɪs/ n Rel beatitudine f; ⟨happiness⟩ felicità f. ~**ful** a beato; ⟨happy⟩ meraviglioso

blister /'blɪstə(r)/ n Med vescica f; ⟨in paint⟩ bolla f ● vi ⟨paint:⟩ formare una bolla/delle bolle

blitz /blɪts/ n bombardamento m aereo; **have a** ~ **on sth** fig darci sotto con qcsa

blizzard /'blɪzəd/ n tormenta f

bloated /'bləʊtɪd/ a gonfio

blob /blɒb/ n goccia f

bloc /blɒk/ n Pol blocco m

block /blɒk/ n blocco m; ⟨building⟩ isolato m; ⟨building ~⟩ cubo m ⟨per giochi di costruzione⟩; ~ **of flats** palazzo m ● vt bloccare. **block up** vt bloccare

blockade /blɒ'keɪd/ n blocco m ● vt bloccare

blockage /'blɒkɪdʒ/ n ostruzione f

block: ~**head** n fam testone, -a mf. ~'**letters** npl stampatello m

bloke /bləʊk/ n fam tizio m

blonde /blɒnd/ a biondo ● n bionda f

blood /blʌd/ n sangue m

blood: ~ **bath** n bagno m di sangue. ~ **count** n esame m emocromocitometrico. ~ **donor** n donatore m di sangue. ~ **group** n gruppo m sanguigno. ~**hound** n segugio m. ~-**poisoning** n setticemia f. ~-**pressure** n pressione f del sangue. ~**shed** n spargimento m di sangue. ~**shot** a iniettato di sangue. ~ **sports** npl sport mpl cruenti. ~-**stained** a macchiato di sangue. ~**stream** n sangue m. ~ **test** n analisi f del sangue. ~**thirsty** a assetato di sangue. ~ **transfusion** n trasfusione f del sangue

bloody /'blʌdɪ/ a (-**ier**, -**iest**) insanguinato; sl maledetto ● adv sl ~ **easy/difficult** facile/difficile da matti. ~-'**minded** a scorbutico

bloom /blu:m/ n fiore m; **in** ~ ⟨flower:⟩ sbocciato; ⟨tree:⟩ in fiore ● vi fiorire; fig essere in forma smagliante

bloom|er /'blu:mə(r)/ n fam papera f. ~**ing** a fam maledetto. ~**ers** npl mutandoni mpl ⟨da donna⟩

blossom /'blɒsəm/ n fiori mpl ⟨d'albero⟩; ⟨single one⟩ fiore m ● vi sbocciare

blot /blɒt/ n also fig macchia f ● **blot out** vt ⟨pt/pp blotted⟩ fig cancellare

blotch /blɒtʃ/ n macchia f. ~**y** a chiazzato

'**blotting-paper** n carta f assorbente

blouse /blaʊz/ n camicetta f

blow¹ /bləʊ/ n colpo m

blow² v ⟨pt blew, pp blown⟩ ● vi ⟨wind:⟩ soffiare; ⟨fuse:⟩ saltare ● vt ⟨fam: squander⟩ sperperare; ~ **one's nose** soffiarsi il naso. **blow away** vt far volar via ⟨papers⟩ ● vi ⟨papers:⟩ volare via. **blow down** vt abbattere ● vi abbattersi al suolo. **blow out** vt ⟨extinguish⟩ spegnere. **blow over** vi ⟨storm:⟩ passare; ⟨fuss, trouble:⟩ dissiparsi. **blow up** vt ⟨inflate⟩ gonfiare; ⟨enlarge⟩ ingrandire ⟨photograph⟩; ⟨by explosion⟩ far esplodere ● vi esplodere

blow: ~-**dry** vt asciugare col fon. ~**lamp** n fiamma f ossidrica

blown /bləʊn/ see **blow²**

'**blowtorch** n fiamma f ossidrica

blowy /'bləʊɪ/ a ventoso

blue /blu:/ a ⟨pale⟩ celeste; ⟨navy⟩ blu inv; ⟨royal⟩ azzurro; ~ **with cold** livido per il freddo ● n blu m inv; **have the** ~**s** essere giù [di tono]; **out of the** ~ inaspettatamente

blue: ~**bell** n giacinto m di bosco. ~**berry** n mirtillo m. ~**bottle** n moscone m. ~ **film** n film m inv a luci rosse. ~**print** n fig riferimento m

bluff /blʌf/ n bluff m inv ● vi bluffare

blunder /'blʌndə(r)/ n gaffe f inv ● vi fare una/delle gaffe

blunt /blʌnt/ a spuntato; ⟨person⟩ reciso. ~**ly** adv schiettamente

blur /blɜ:(r)/ n **it's all a** ~ fig è tutto un insieme confuso ● vt ⟨pt/pp blurred⟩ rendere confuso. ~**red** a ⟨vision, photo⟩ sfocato

blurb /blɜ:b/ n soffietto m editoriale

blurt /blɜ:t/ vt ~ **out** spifferare

blush /blʌʃ/ n rossore m ● vi arrossire

blusher /'blʌʃə(r)/ n fard m

bluster /'blʌstə(r)/ n sbruffonata f. ~**y** a ⟨wind⟩ furioso; ⟨day, weather⟩ molto ventoso

boar /bɔ:(r)/ n cinghiale m

board /bɔ:d/ n tavola f; ⟨for notices⟩ tabellone m; ⟨committee⟩ assemblea f; ⟨of directors⟩ consiglio m; **full** ~ Br pensione f completa; **half** ~ Br mezza pensione f; ~ **and lodging** vitto e alloggio m; **go by the ~** fam andare a monte ● vt Naut, Aeron salire a bordo di ● vi ⟨passengers:⟩ salire a bordo. **board up** vt sbarrare con delle assi. **board with** vt stare a pensione da.

boarder /'bɔːdə(r)/ n pensionante mf; Sch convittore, -trice mf

board: ~**game** n gioco m da tavolo. ~**ing-house** n pensione f. ~**ing-school** n collegio m

boast /bəʊst/ vi vantarsi (**about** di). ~**ful** a vanaglorioso

boat /bəʊt/ n barca f; ⟨ship⟩ nave f. ~**er** n ⟨hat⟩ paglietta f

bob /bɒb/ n ⟨hairstyle⟩ caschetto m ● vi (pt/pp **bobbed**) (also ~ **up and down**) andare su e giù

bob-sleigh n bob m inv

bode /bəʊd/ vi ~ **well/ill** essere di buono/cattivo augurio

bodily /'bɒdɪlɪ/ a fisico ● adv ⟨forcibly⟩ fisicamente

body /'bɒdɪ/ n corpo m; ⟨organization⟩ ente m; ⟨amount: of poems etc⟩ quantità f. ~**guard** n guardia f del corpo. ~**work** n Auto carrozzeria f

bog /bɒg/ n palude f ● vt (pt/pp **bogged**) **get** ~**ged down** impantanarsi

boggle /'bɒgl/ vi **the mind** ~**s** non posso neanche immaginarlo

bogus /'bəʊgəs/ a falso

boil[1] /bɔɪl/ n Med foruncolo m

boil[2] n **bring/come to the** ~ portare/arrivare ad ebollizione ● vt [far] bollire ● vi bollire; ⟨fig: with anger⟩ ribollire; **the water** or **kettle's** ~**ing** l'acqua bolle. **boil down to** vt fig ridursi a. **boil over** vi straboccare (bollendo). **boil up** vt far bollire

boiler /'bɔɪlə(r)/ n caldaia f. ~**suit** n tuta f

boiling point n punto m di ebollizione

boisterous /'bɔɪstərəs/ a chiassoso

bold /bəʊld/ a audace ● n Typ neretto m. ~**ness** n audacia f

bollard /'bɒlɑːd/ n colonnina m di sbarramento al traffico

bolster /'bəʊlstə(r)/ n cuscino m ⟨lungo e rotondo⟩ ● vt ~ [**up**] sostenere

bolt /bəʊlt/ n ⟨for door⟩ catenaccio m; ⟨for fixing⟩ bullone m ● vt fissare ⟨con i bulloni⟩ (**to** a); chiudere col chiavistello ⟨door⟩; ingurgitare ⟨food⟩ ● vi svignarsela; ⟨horse:⟩ scappar via ● adv ~ **upright** diritto come un fuso

bomb /bɒm/ n bomba f ● vt bombardare

bombard /bɒm'bɑːd/ vt also fig bombardare

bombastic /bɒm'bæstɪk/ a ampolloso

bomb|er /'bɒmə(r)/ n Aeron bombardiere m; ⟨person⟩ dinamitardo m. ~**er jacket** n giubbotto m, bomber m inv. ~**shell** n ⟨fig: news⟩ bomba f

bond /bɒnd/ n fig legame m; Comm obbligazione f ● vt ⟨glue:⟩ attaccare

bondage /'bɒndɪdʒ/ n schiavitù f

bone /bəʊn/ n osso m; ⟨of fish⟩ spina f ● vt disossare ⟨meat⟩; togliere le spine da ⟨fish⟩. ~'**dry** a secco

bonfire /'bɒn-/ n falò m inv. ~ **night** festa celebrata la notte del 5 novembre con fuochi d'artificio e falò

bonnet /'bɒnɪt/ n cuffia f; ⟨of car⟩ cofano m

bonus /'bəʊnəs/ n ⟨individual⟩ gratifica f; ⟨production ~⟩ premio m; ⟨life insurance⟩ dividendo m; **a** ~ fig qualcosa in più

bony /'bəʊnɪ/ a (-**ier**, -**iest**) ossuto; ⟨fish⟩ pieno di spine

boo /buː/ int ⟨to surprise or frighten⟩ bu! ● vt/i fischiare

boob /buːb/ n ⟨fam: mistake⟩ gaffe f inv; ⟨breast⟩ tetta f ● vi fam fare una gaffe

book /bʊk/ n libro m; ⟨of tickets⟩ blocchetto m; **keep the** ~**s** Comm tenere la contabilità; **be in sb's bad/good** ~**s** essere nel libro nero/nelle grazie di qcno ● vt ⟨reserve⟩ prenotare; ⟨for offence⟩ multare ● vi ⟨reserve⟩ prenotare

book: ~**case** n libreria f. ~**-ends** npl reggilibri mpl. ~**ing-office** n biglietteria f. ~**keeping** n contabilità f. ~**let** n opuscolo m. ~**maker** n allibratore m. ~**mark** n segnalibro m. ~**seller** n libraio, -a mf. ~**shop** n libreria f. ~**worm** n topo m di biblioteca

boom /buːm/ n Comm boom m inv; ⟨upturn⟩ impennata f; ⟨of thunder, gun⟩ rimbombo m ● vi ⟨thunder, gun:⟩ rimbombare; fig prosperare

boon /buːn/ n benedizione f

boor /bʊə(r)/ n zoticone m. ~**ish** a maleducato

boost /buːst/ n spinta f ● vt stimolare ⟨sales⟩; sollevare ⟨morale⟩; far crescere ⟨hopes⟩. ~**er** n Med dose f supplementare

boot /buːt/ n stivale m; ⟨up to ankle⟩ stivaletto m; ⟨football⟩ scarpetta f; ⟨climbing⟩ scarpone m; Auto portabagagli m inv ● vt Comput inizializzare

booth /buːð/ n (Teleph, voting) cabina f; (at market) bancarella f

'boot-up n Comput boot m inv

booty /'buːtɪ/ n bottino m

booze /buːz/ fam n alcolici mpl. ~-**up** n bella bevuta f

border /'bɔːdə(r)/ n bordo m; (frontier) frontiera f; (in garden) bordura f ● vi ~ **on** confinare con; fig essere ai confini di ⟨madness⟩. ~**line** n linea f di demarcazione; ~**line case** caso m dubbio

bore[1] /bɔː(r)/ see **bear**[2]

bore[2] vt Techn forare

bor|e[3] n (of gun) calibro m; (person) seccatore, -trice mf; (thing) seccatura f ● vt annoiare. ~**edom** n noia f. **be** ~**ed** (**to tears** or **to death**) annoiarsi (da morire). ~**ing** a noioso

born /bɔːn/ pp **be** ~ nascere; **I was** ~ **in 1966** sono nato nel 1966 ● a nato; **a** ~ **liar/actor** nato/attore nato

borne /bɔːn/ see **bear**[2]

borough /'bʌrə/ n municipalità f inv

borrow /'bɒrəʊ/ vt prendere a prestito (**from** da); **can I** ~ **your pen?** mi presti la tua penna?

bosom /'bʊzm/ n seno m

boss /bɒs/ n direttore, -trice mf ● vt (also ~ **about**) comandare a bacchetta. ~**y** a autoritario

botanical /bə'tænɪkl/ a botanico

botan|ist /'bɒtənɪst/ n botanico, -a mf. ~**y** n botanica f

botch /bɒtʃ/ vt fare un pasticcio con

both /bəʊθ/ a & pron tutti e due, entrambi ● adv ~ **men and women** entrambi uomini e donne; ~ [**of**] **the children** tutti e due i bambini; **they are** ~ **dead** sono morti entrambi; ~ **of them** tutti e due

bother /'bɒðə(r)/ n preoccupazione f; (minor trouble) fastidio m; **it's no** ~ non c'è problema ● int fam che seccatura! ● vt (annoy) dare fastidio a; (disturb) disturbare ● vi preoccuparsi (**about** di); **don't** ~ lascia perdere

bottle /'bɒtl/ n bottiglia f; (baby's) biberon m inv ● vt imbottigliare. **bottle up** vt fig reprimere

bottle: ~ **bank** n contenitore m per la raccolta del vetro. ~-**neck** n fig ingorgo m. ~-**opener** n apribottiglie m inv

bottom /'bɒtm/ a ultimo; **the** ~ **shelf** l'ultimo scaffale in basso ● n (of container) fondo m; (of river) fondale m; (of hill) piedi mpl; (buttocks) sedere m; **at the** ~ **of the page** in fondo alla pagina; **get to the** ~ **of** fig vedere cosa c'è sotto. ~**less** a senza fondo

bough /baʊ/ n ramoscello m

bought /bɔːt/ see **buy**

boulder /'bəʊldə(r)/ n masso m

bounce /baʊns/ vi rimbalzare; ⟨fam: cheque:⟩ essere respinto ● vt far rimbalzare ⟨ball⟩

bouncer /'baʊnsə(r)/ n fam buttafuori m inv

bound[1] /baʊnd/ n balzo m ● vi balzare

bound[2] see **bind** ● a ~ **for** ⟨ship⟩ diretto a; **be** ~ **to do** (likely) dovere fare per forza; (obliged) essere costretto a fare

boundary /'baʊndərɪ/ n limite m

'boundless a illimitato

bounds /baʊndz/ npl fig limiti mpl; **out of** ~ fuori dai limiti

bouquet /bʊ'keɪ/ n mazzo m di fiori; (of wine) bouquet m

bourgeois /'bʊəʒwɑː/ a pej borghese

bout /baʊt/ n Med attacco m; Sport incontro m

bow[1] /bəʊ/ n (weapon) arco m; Mus archetto m; (knot) nodo m

bow[2] /baʊ/ n inchino m ● vi inchinarsi ● vt piegare ⟨head⟩

bow[3] /baʊ/ n Naut prua f

bowel /'baʊəl/ n intestino m; ~**s** pl intestini mpl

bowl[1] /bəʊl/ n (for soup, cereal) scodella f; (of pipe) fornello m

bowl[2] n (ball) boccia f ● vt lanciare ● vi Cricket servire; (in bowls) lanciare. **bowl over** vt buttar giù; (fig: leave speechless) lasciar senza parole

bow-legged /bəʊ'legd/ a dalle gambe storte

bowler[1] /'bəʊlə(r)/ n Cricket lanciatore m; Bowls giocatore m di bocce

bowler[2] n ~ [**hat**] bombetta f

bowling /'bəʊlɪŋ/ n gioco m delle bocce. ~-**alley** n pista f da bowling

bowls /bəʊlz/ n gioco m delle bocce

bow-'tie /bəʊ-/ n cravatta f a farfalla

box[1] /bɒks/ n scatola f; Theat palco m

box[2] vi Sport fare il pugile ● vt ~ **sb's ears** dare uno scappaccione a qcno

box|er /'bɒksə(r)/ n pugile m. ~**ing** n pugilato m. **B**~**ing Day** n [giorno di] Santo Stefano m

box: ~-**office** n Theat botteghino m. ~-**room** n Br sgabuzzino m

boy /bɔɪ/ n ragazzo m; (younger) bambino m

boycott /'bɔɪkɒt/ n boicottaggio m ● vt boicottare

boy: ~**friend** n ragazzo m. ~**ish** a da ragazzino

bra /brɑː/ n reggiseno m

brace /breɪs/ n sostegno m; (dental) apparecchio m; ~**s** npl bretelle fpl ● vt ~ **oneself** fig farsi forza (**for** per affrontare)

bracelet /'breɪslɪt/ n braccialetto m

bracing /'breɪsɪŋ/ a tonificante

bracken /'brækn/ n felce f

bracket /'brækɪt/ n mensola f; (group) categoria f; Typ parentesi f inv ● vt mettere fra parentesi

brag /bræg/ vi (pt/pp **bragged**) vantarsi (**about** di)

braid /breɪd/ n (edging) passamano m

braille /breɪl/ n braille m

brain /breɪn/ n cervello m; ~**s** pl fig testa fsg

brain: ~**child** n invenzione f personale. ~ **dead** a Med celebralmente morto; fig fam senza cervello. ~**less** a senza cervello. ~**wash** vt fare il lavaggio del cervello a. ~**wave** n lampo m di genio

brainy /'breɪnɪ/ a (-ier, -iest) intelligente

braise /breɪz/ vt brasare

brake /breɪk/ n freno m ● vi frenare. ~-**light** n stop m inv

bramble /'bræmbl/ n rovo m; (fruit) mora f

bran /bræn/ n crusca f

branch /brɑːntʃ/ n also fig ramo m; Comm succursale f ● vi (road:) biforcarsi. **branch off** vi biforcarsi. **branch out** vi ~ **out into** allargare le proprie attività nel ramo di

brand /brænd/ n marca f; (on animal) marchio m ● vt marcare (animal); fig tacciare (**as** di)

brandish /'brændɪʃ/ vt brandire

brand-'new a nuovo fiammante

brandy /'brændɪ/ n brandy m inv

brash /bræʃ/ a sfrontato

brass /brɑːs/ n ottone m; **the** ~ Mus gli ottoni mpl; **top** ~ fam pezzi mpl grossi. ~ **band** n banda f (di soli ottoni)

brassiere /'bræzɪə(r)/ n fml, Am reggipetto m

brat /bræt/ n pej marmocchio, -a mf

bravado /brə'vɑːdəʊ/ n bravata f

brave /breɪv/ a coraggioso ● vt affrontare. ~**ry** /-ərɪ/ n coraggio m

brawl /brɔːl/ n rissa f ● vi azzuffarsi

brawn /brɔːn/ n Culin soppressata f

brawny /'brɔːnɪ/ a muscoloso

brazen /'breɪzn/ a sfrontato

brazier /'breɪzɪə(r)/ n braciere m

Brazil /brə'zɪl/ n Brasile m. ~**ian** a & n brasiliano, -a mf. ~ **nut** n noce f del Brasile

breach /briːtʃ/ n (of law) violazione f; (gap) breccia f; (fig: in party) frattura f; ~ **of contract** inadempienza f di contratto; ~ **of the peace** violazione f della quiete pubblica ● vt recedere (contract)

bread /bred/ n pane m; **a slice of** ~ **and butter** una fetta di pane imburrato

bread: ~ **bin** n cassetta f portapane inv. ~**crumbs** npl briciole fpl; Culin pangrattato m. ~**line** n **be on the** ~**line** essere povero in canna

breadth /bredθ/ n larghezza f

'bread-winner n quello, -a mf che porta i soldi a casa

break /breɪk/ n rottura f; (interval) intervallo m; (interruption) interruzione f; (fam: chance) opportunità f inv ● v (pt **broke**, pp **broken**) ● vt rompere; (interrupt) interrompere; ~ **one's arm** rompersi un braccio ● vi rompersi; (day:) spuntare; (storm:) scoppiare; (news:) diffondersi; (boy's voice:) cambiare. **break away** vi scappare; fig chiudere (**from** con). **break down** vi (machine, car:) guastarsi; (emotionally) cedere (psicologicamente) ● vt sfondare (door); ripartire (figures). **break into** vt introdursi (con la forza) in; forzare (car). **break off** vt rompere (engagement) ● vi (part of whole:) rompersi. **break out** vi (fight, war:) scoppiare. **break up** vt far cessare (fight); disperdere (crowd) ● vi (crowd:) disperdersi; (couple:) separarsi; Sch iniziare le vacanze

'break|able /'breɪkəbl/ a fragile. ~**age** /-ɪdʒ/ n rottura f. ~**down** n (of car, machine) guasto m; Med esaurimento m nervoso; (of figures) analisi f inv. ~**er** n (wave) frangente m

breakfast /'brekfəst/ n [prima] colazione f

break: ~**through** n scoperta f. ~**water** n frangiflutti m inv

breast /brest/ n seno m. ~-**feed** vt allattare [al seno]. ~-**stroke** n nuoto m a rana

breath /breθ/ n respiro m, fiato m; **out of** ~ senza fiato

breathalyse /'breθəlaɪz/ vt sottoporre alla prova [etilica] del palloncino. ~**r®** n Br alcoltest m inv

breathe /briːð/ vt/i respirare. **breathe in** vi inspirare ● vt respirare (scent, air). **breathe out** vt/i espirare

breath|er /'briːðə(r)/ n pausa f. ~**ing** n respirazione f

breath /breθ/: ~**less** a senza fiato. ~**-taking** a mozzafiato. ~ **test** n prova [etilica] f del palloncino

bred /bred/ see **breed**

breed /briːd/ n razza f ● v (pt/pp **bred**) ● vt allevare; (give rise to) generare ● vi riprodursi. ~**er** n allevatore, -trice mf. ~**ing** n allevamento m; fig educazione f

breez|e /briːz/ n brezza f. ~**y** a ventoso

brew /bruː/ n infuso m ● vt mettere in infusione ‹tea›; produrre ‹beer› ● vi fig ‹trouble:› essere nell'aria. ~**er** n birraio m. ~**ery** n fabbrica f di birra

bribe /braɪb/ n (money) bustarella f; (large sum of money) tangente f ● vt corrompere. ~**ry** /-ərɪ/ n corruzione f

brick /brɪk/ n mattone m. '~**layer** n muratore m ● **brick up** vt murare

bridal /'braɪdl/ a nuziale

bride /braɪd/ n sposa f. ~**groom** n sposo m. ~**smaid** n damigella f d'onore

bridge¹ /brɪdʒ/ n ponte m; (of nose) setto m nasale; (of spectacles) ponticello m ● vt fig colmare ‹gap›

bridge² n Cards bridge m

bridle /'braɪdl/ n briglia f

brief¹ /briːf/ a breve

brief² n istruzioni fpl; (Jur: case) causa f ● vt dare istruzioni a; Jur affidare la causa a. ~**case** n cartella f

brief|ing /'briːfɪŋ/ n briefing m inv. ~**ly** adv brevemente. ~**ly,...** in breve,... ~**ness** n brevità f

briefs /briːfs/ npl slip m inv

brigad|e /brɪ'geɪd/ n brigata f. ~**ier** /-ə'dɪə(r)/ n generale m di brigata

bright /braɪt/ a (metal, idea) brillante; (day, room, future) luminoso; (clever) intelligente; ~ **red** rosso m acceso

bright|en /'braɪtn/ v ~**en [up]** ● vt ravvivare; rallegrare ‹person› ● vi (weather:) schiarirsi; (face:) illuminarsi; (person:) rallegrarsi. ~**ly** adv (shine) intensamente; (smile) allegramente. ~**ness** n luminosità f; (intelligence) intelligenza f

brilliance /'brɪljəns/ n luminosità f; (of person) genialità f

brilliant /'brɪljənt/ a (very good) eccezionale; (very intelligent) brillante; (sunshine) splendente

brim /brɪm/ n bordo m; (of hat) tesa f ● **brim over** vi (pt/pp **brimmed**) traboccare

brine /braɪn/ n salamoia f

bring /brɪŋ/ vt (pt/pp **brought**) portare

‹person, object›. **bring about** vt causare. **bring along** vt portare [con sé]. **bring back** vt restituire ‹sth borrowed›; reintrodurre ‹hanging›; fare ritornare in mente ‹memories›. **bring down** vt portare giù; fare cadere ‹government›; fare abbassare ‹price›. **bring off** vt ~ **sth off** riuscire a fare qcsa. **bring on** vt (cause) provocare. **bring out** vt (emphasize) mettere in evidenza; pubblicare ‹book›. **bring round** vt portare; (persuade) convincere; far rinvenire ‹unconscious person›. **bring up** vt (vomit) rimettere; allevare ‹children›; tirare fuori ‹question, subject›

brink /brɪŋk/ n orlo m

brisk /brɪsk/ a svelto; ‹person› sbrigativo; ‹trade, business› redditizio; ‹walk› a passo spedito

brist|le /'brɪsl/ n setola f ● vi ~**ling with** pieno di. ~**ly** a ‹chin› ispido

Brit|ain /'brɪtn/ n Gran Bretagna f. ~**ish** a britannico; ‹ambassador› della Gran Bretagna ● npl **the** ~**ish** il popolo britannico. ~**on** n cittadino, -a britannico, -a mf

brittle /'brɪtl/ a fragile

broach /brəʊtʃ/ vt toccare ‹subject›

broad /brɔːd/ a ampio; ‹hint› chiaro; ‹accent› marcato. **two metres** ~ largo due metri; **in** ~ **daylight** in pieno giorno. ~ **beans** npl fave fpl

'**broadcast** n trasmissione f ● vt/i (pt/pp -**cast**) trasmettere. ~**er** n giornalista mf radiotelevisivo, -a. ~**ing** n diffusione f radiotelevisiva; **be in** ~**ing** lavorare per la televisione/radio

broaden /'brɔːdn/ vt allargare ● vi allargarsi

broadly /'brɔːdlɪ/ adv largamente; ~ [**speaking**] generalmente

broad'minded a di larghe vedute

broccoli /'brɒkəlɪ/ n inv broccoli mpl

brochure /'brəʊʃə(r)/ n opuscolo m; (travel ~) dépliant m inv

broke /brəʊk/ see **break** ● a fam al verde

broken /'brəʊkn/ see **break** ● a rotto; (fig: marriage) fallito. ~ **English** inglese m stentato. ~**-hearted** a affranto

broker /'brəʊkə(r)/ n broker m inv

brolly /'brɒlɪ/ n fam ombrello m

bronchitis /brɒŋ'kaɪtɪs/ n bronchite f

bronze /brɒnz/ n bronzo m ● attrib di bronzo

brooch /brəʊtʃ/ n spilla f

brood /bruːd/ n covata f; (hum: children) prole f ● vi fig rimuginare

brook /brʊk/ n ruscello m

broom /bruːm/ n scopa f. **~stick** n manico m di scopa

broth /brɒθ/ n brodo m

brothel /ˈbrɒθl/ n bordello m

brother /ˈbrʌðə(r)/ n fratello m

brother: **~-in-law** n (pl **~s-in-law**) cognato m. **~ly** a fraterno

brought /brɔːt/ see **bring**

brow /braʊ/ n fronte f; (of hill) cima f

'browbeat vt (pt **-beat**, pp **-beaten**) intimidire

brown /braʊn/ a marrone; castano ⟨hair⟩ ● n marrone m ● vt rosolare ⟨meat⟩ ● vi ⟨meat:⟩ rosolarsi. **~ 'paper** n carta f da pacchi

Brownie /ˈbraʊnɪ/ n coccinella f (negli scout)

browse /braʊz/ vi ⟨read⟩ leggicchiare; ⟨in shop⟩ curiosare

bruise /bruːz/ n livido m; (on fruit) ammaccatura f ● vt ammaccare ⟨fruit⟩; **~ one's arm** farsi un livido sul braccio. **~d** a contuso

brunette /bruːˈnet/ n bruna f

brunt /brʌnt/ n **bear the ~ of sth** subire maggiormente qcsa

brush /brʌʃ/ n spazzola f; ⟨with long handle⟩ spazzolone m; ⟨for paint⟩ pennello m; ⟨bushes⟩ boscaglia f; ⟨fig: conflict⟩ breve scontro m ● vt spazzolare ⟨hair⟩; lavarsi ⟨teeth⟩; scopare ⟨stairs, floor⟩. **brush against** vt sfiorare. **brush aside** vt fig ignorare. **brush off** vt spazzolare; ⟨with hands⟩ togliere; ignorare ⟨criticism⟩. **brush up** vt/i fig **~ up [on]** rinfrescare

brusque /brʊsk/ a brusco

Brussels /ˈbrʌslz/ n Bruxelles f. **~ sprouts** npl cavoletti mpl di Bruxelles

brutal /ˈbruːtl/ a brutale. **~ity** /-ˈtælətɪ/ n brutalità f inv

brute /bruːt/ n bruto m. **~ force** n forza f bruta

BSc n abbr **Bachelor of Science**

BSE n abbr (**bovine spongiform encephalitis**) encefalite f bovina spongiforme

bubble /ˈbʌbl/ n bolla f; ⟨in drink⟩ bollicina f

buck¹ /bʌk/ n maschio m del cervo; ⟨rabbit⟩ maschio m del coniglio ● vi ⟨horse:⟩ saltare a quattro zampe. **buck up** vi fam tirarsi su; ⟨hurry⟩ sbrigarsi

buck² n Am fam dollaro m

buck³ n **pass the ~** scaricare la responsabilità

bucket /ˈbʌkɪt/ n secchio m

buckle /ˈbʌkl/ n fibbia f ● vt allacciare ● vi ⟨shelf:⟩ piegarsi; ⟨wheel:⟩ storcersi

bud /bʌd/ n bocciolo m

Buddhis|m /ˈbʊdɪzm/ n buddismo m. **~t** a & n buddista mf

buddy /ˈbʌdɪ/ n fam amico, -a mf

budge /bʌdʒ/ vt spostare ● vi spostarsi

budgerigar /ˈbʌdʒərɪɡɑː(r)/ n cocorita f

budget /ˈbʌdʒɪt/ n bilancio m; ⟨allotted to specific activity⟩ budget m inv ● vi ⟨pt/pp **budgeted**⟩ prevedere le spese; **~ for sth** includere qcsa nelle spese previste

buff /bʌf/ a ⟨colour⟩ [color] camoscio ● n fam fanatico, -a mf

buffalo /ˈbʌfələʊ/ n (inv or pl **-es**) bufalo m

buffer /ˈbʌfə(r)/ n Rail respingente m; old — fam vecchio bacucco m. **~ zone** n zona f cuscinetto

buffet¹ /ˈbʊfeɪ/ n buffet m inv

buffet² /ˈbʌfɪt/ vt ⟨pt/pp **buffeted**⟩ sferzare

buffoon /bəˈfuːn/ n buffone, -a mf

bug /bʌg/ n ⟨insect⟩ insetto m; Comput bug m inv; ⟨fam: device⟩ cimice f ● vt ⟨pt/pp **bugged**⟩ fam installare delle microspie in ⟨room⟩; mettere sotto controllo ⟨telephone⟩; ⟨fam: annoy⟩ scocciare

buggy /ˈbʌgɪ/ n ⟨baby⟩ **~** passeggino m

bugle /ˈbjuːgl/ n tromba f

build /bɪld/ n ⟨of person⟩ corporatura f ● vt/i ⟨pt/pp **built**⟩ costruire. **build on** vt aggiungere ⟨extra storey⟩; sviluppare ⟨previous work⟩. **build up** vt **~ up one's strength** rimettersi in forza ● vi ⟨pressure, traffic:⟩ aumentare; ⟨excitement, tension:⟩ crescere

builder /ˈbɪldə(r)/ n ⟨company⟩ costruttore m; ⟨worker⟩ muratore m

building /ˈbɪldɪŋ/ n edificio m. **~ site** n cantiere m [di costruzione]. **~ society** n istituto m di credito immobiliare

'build-up n ⟨of gas etc⟩ accumulo m; fig battage m inv pubblicitario

built /bɪlt/ see **build**. **~-in** a ⟨unit⟩ a muro; ⟨fig: feature⟩ incorporato. **~-up area** n Auto centro m abitato

bulb /bʌlb/ n bulbo m; Electr lampadina f

bulg|e /bʌldʒ/ n rigonfiamento m ● vi esser gonfio (**with** di); ⟨stomach, wall:⟩ sporgere; ⟨eyes, with surprise:⟩ uscire dalle orbite. **~ing** a gonfio; ⟨eyes⟩ sporgente

bulk /bʌlk/ n volume m; ⟨greater part⟩ grosso m; **in ~** in grande quantità; ⟨loose⟩ sfuso. **~y** a voluminoso

bull /bʊl/ n toro m

'bulldog n bulldog m inv

bulldozer /'bʊldəʊzə(r)/ n bull-dozer m inv

bullet /'bʊlɪt/ n pallottola f

bulletin /'bʊlɪtɪn/ n bollettino m. **~ board** n Comput bacheca f elettronica

'bullet-proof a antiproiettile inv; ⟨vehicle⟩ blindato

'bullfight n corrida f. **~er** n torero m

bullion /'bʊlɪən/ n **gold ~** oro m in lingotti

bullock /'bʊlək/ n manzo m

bull: **~ring** n arena f. **~'s-eye** n centro m del bersaglio; **score a ~'s-eye** fare centro

bully /'bʊlɪ/ n prepotente mf ● vt fare il/la prepotente con. **~ing** n prepotenze fpl

bum¹ /bʌm/ n sl sedere m

bum² n Am fam vagabondo, -a mf ● **bum around** vi fam vagabondare

bumble-bee /'bʌmbl-/ n calabrone m

bump /bʌmp/ n botta f; ⟨swelling⟩ bozzo m, gonfiore m; ⟨in road⟩ protuberanza f ● vt sbattere. **bump into** vt sbattere contro; ⟨meet⟩ imbattersi in. **bump off** vt fam far fuori

bumper /'bʌmpə(r)/ n Auto paraurti m inv ● a abbondante

bumpkin /'bʌmpkɪn/ n **country ~** zoticone, -a mf

bumptious /'bʌmpʃəs/ a presuntuoso

bumpy /'bʌmpɪ/ a ⟨road⟩ accidentato; ⟨flight⟩ turbolento

bun /bʌn/ n focaccina f ⟨dolce⟩; ⟨hair⟩ chignon m inv

bunch /bʌntʃ/ n ⟨of flowers, keys⟩ mazzo m; ⟨of bananas⟩ casco m; ⟨of people⟩ gruppo m; **~ of grapes** grappolo m d'uva

bundle /'bʌndl/ n fascio m; ⟨of money⟩ mazzetta f; **a ~ of nerves** fam un fascio di nervi ● vt ~ [**up**] affastellare

bung /bʌŋ/ vt fam ⟨throw⟩ buttare. **bung up** vt ⟨block⟩ otturare

bungalow /'bʌŋgələʊ/ n bungalow m inv

bungle /'bʌŋgl/ vt fare un pasticcio di

bunion /'bʌnjən/ n Med callo m all'alluce

bunk /bʌŋk/ n cuccetta f. **~-beds** npl letti mpl a castello

bunny /'bʌnɪ/ n fam coniglietto m

buoy /bɔɪ/ n boa f

buoyan|cy /'bɔɪənsɪ/ n galleggiabilità f. **~t** a ⟨boat⟩ galleggiante; ⟨water⟩ che aiuta a galleggiare

burden /'bɜːdn/ n carico m ● vt caricare. **~some** /-səm/ a gravoso

bureau /'bjʊərəʊ/ n (pl -x /-əʊz/, or -s) ⟨desk⟩ scrivania f; ⟨office⟩ ufficio m

bureaucracy /bjʊə'rɒkrəsɪ/ n burocrazia f

bureaucrat /'bjʊərəkræt/ n burocrate mf. **~ic** /-'krætɪk/ a burocratico

burger /'bɜːgə(r)/ n hamburger m inv

burglar /'bɜːglə(r)/ n svaligiatore, -trice mf. **~ alarm** n antifurto m inv

burglar|ize /'bɜːgləraɪz/ vt Am svaligiare. **~y** n furto m con scasso

burgle /'bɜːgl/ vt svaligiare

Burgundy /'bɜːgəndɪ/ n Borgogna f

burial /'berɪəl/ n sepoltura f. **~ ground** n cimitero m

burlesque /bɜː'lesk/ n parodia f

burly /'bɜːlɪ/ a (-ier, -iest) corpulento

Burm|a /'bɜːmə/ n Birmania f. **~ese** /-'miːz/ a & n birmano, -a mf

burn /bɜːn/ n bruciatura f ● v (pt/pp **burnt** or **burned**) ● vt bruciare ● vi bruciare. **burn down** vt/i bruciare. **burn out** vi fig esaurirsi. **~er** n ⟨on stove⟩ bruciatore m

burnish /'bɜːnɪʃ/ vt lucidare

burnt /bɜːnt/ see **burn**

burp /bɜːp/ n fam rutto m ● vi fam ruttare

burrow /'bʌrəʊ/ n tana f ● vt scavare ⟨hole⟩

bursar /'bɜːsə(r)/ n economo, -a mf. **~y** n borsa f di studio

burst /bɜːst/ n ⟨of gunfire, energy, laughter⟩ scoppio m; ⟨of speed⟩ scatto m ● v (pt/pp **burst**) ● vi scoppiare; **~ into tears** scoppiare in lacrime; **she ~ into the room** ha fatto irruzione nella stanza. **burst out** vi **~ out laughing/crying** scoppiare a ridere/piangere

bury /'berɪ/ vt (pt/pp -**ied**) seppellire; ⟨hide⟩ nascondere

bus /bʌs/ n autobus m inv, pullman m inv; ⟨long distance⟩ pullman m inv, corriera f

bush /bʊʃ/ n cespuglio m; ⟨land⟩ boscaglia f. **~y** a (-ier, -iest) folto

busily /'bɪzɪlɪ/ adv con grande impegno

business /'bɪznɪs/ n affare m; Comm affari mpl; (establishment) attività f di commercio; **on ~** per affari; **he has no ~ to** non ha alcun diritto di; **mind one's own ~** farsi gli affari propri; **that's none of your ~** non sono affari tuoi. **~-like** a efficiente. **~man** n uomo m d'affari. **~woman** n donna f d'affari

busker /'bʌskə(r)/ n suonatore, -trice mf ambulante

'**bus station** n stazione f degli autobus

'**bus-stop** n fermata f d'autobus

bust[1] /bʌst/ n busto m; (chest) petto m

bust[2] a fam rotto; **go ~** fallire ● v (pt/pp **busted** or **bust**) fam ● vt far scoppiare ● vi scoppiare

bustl|e /'bʌsl/ n (activity) trambusto m ● **bustle about** vi affannarsi. **~ing** a animato

'**bust-up** n fam lite f

busy /'bɪzɪ/ a (-**ier**, -**iest**) occupato; ⟨day, time⟩ intenso; ⟨street⟩ affollato; ⟨with traffic⟩ pieno di traffico; **be ~ doing** essere occupato a fare ● vt ~ **oneself** darsi da fare

'**busybody** n ficcanaso mf inv

but /bʌt/, atono /bət/ conj ma ● prep eccetto, tranne; **nobody ~ you** nessuno tranne te; **~ for** (without) se non fosse stato per; **the last ~ one** il penultimo; **the next ~ one** il secondo ● adv (only) soltanto; **there were ~ two** ce n'erano soltanto due

butcher /'bʊtʃə(r)/ n macellaio m; **~'s** [**shop**] macelleria f ● vt macellare; fig massacrare

butler /'bʌtlə(r)/ n maggiordomo m

butt /bʌt/ n (of gun) calcio m; (of cigarette) mozzicone m; (for water) barile m; (fig: target) bersaglio m ● vt dare una testata a; ⟨goat:⟩ dare una cornata a. **butt in** vi interrompere

butter /'bʌtə(r)/ n burro m ● vt imburrare. **butter up** vt fam arruffianarsi

butter: **~cup** n ranuncolo m.

~fingers nsg fam **be a ~fingers** avere le mani di pasta frolla. **~fly** n farfalla f

buttocks /'bʌtəks/ npl natiche fpl

button /'bʌtn/ n bottone m ● vt ~ [**up**] abbottonare ● vi ~ [**up**] abbottonarsi. **~hole** n occhiello m, asola f

buttress /'bʌtrɪs/ n contrafforte m

buxom /'bʌksəm/ a formosa

buy /baɪ/ n **good/bad ~** buon/cattivo acquisto m ● vt (pt/pp **bought**) comprare; **~ sb a drink** pagare da bere a qcno; **I'll ~ this one** (drink) questo, lo offro io. **~er** n compratore, -trice mf

buzz /bʌz/ n ronzio m; **give sb a ~** fam (on phone) dare un colpo di telefono a qcno; (excite) mettere in fermento qcno ● vi ronzare ● vt ~ **sb** chiamare qcno col cicalino. **buzz off** vi fam levarsi di torno

buzzer /'bʌzə(r)/ n cicalino m

by /baɪ/ prep (near, next to) vicino a; (at the latest) per; **by Mozart** di Mozart; **he was run over by a bus** è stato investito da un autobus; **by oneself** da solo; **by the sea** al mare; **by sea** via mare; **by car/bus** in macchina/autobus; **by day/ night** di giorno/notte; **by the hour/metre** a ore/metri; **six metres by four** sei metri per quattro; **he won by six metres** ha vinto di sei metri; **I missed the train by a minute** ho perso il treno per un minuto; **I'll be home by six** sarò a casa per le sei; **by this time next week** a quest'ora tra una settimana; **he rushed by me** mi è passato accanto di corsa ● adv **she'll be here by and by** sarà qui fra poco; **by and large** in complesso

bye[-**bye**] /baɪ['baɪ]/ int fam ciao

by: **~-election** n elezione f straordinaria indetta per coprire una carica rimasta vacante in Parlamento. **~gone** a passato. **~-law** n legge f locale. **~pass** n circonvallazione f; Med by-pass m inv ● vt evitare. **~-product** n sottoprodotto m. **~stander** n spettatore, -trice mf. **~word** n **be a ~word for** essere sinonimo di

Cc

cab /kæb/ n taxi m inv; (of lorry, train) cabina f

cabaret /'kæbəreɪ/ n cabaret m inv

cabbage /'kæbɪdʒ/ n cavolo m

cabin /'kæbɪn/ n (of plane, ship) cabina f; (hut) capanna f

cabinet /'kæbɪnɪt/ n armadietto m; [display] ~ vetrina f; C~ Pol consiglio m dei ministri. ~-maker n ebanista mf

cable /'keɪbl/ n cavo m. ~ 'railway n funicolare f. ~ 'television n televisione f via cavo

cache /kæʃ/ n nascondiglio m; ~ of arms deposito m segreto di armi

cackle /'kækl/ vi ridacchiare

cactus /'kæktəs/ n (pl -ti /-taɪ/ or -tuses) cactus m inv

caddie /'kædɪ/ n portabastoni m inv

caddy /'kædɪ/ n [tea-]~ barattolo m del tè

cadet /kə'det/ n cadetto m

cadge /kædʒ/ vt/i fam scroccare

Caesarean /sɪ'zeərɪən/ n parto m cesareo

café /'kæfeɪ/ n caffè m inv

cafeteria /kæfə'tɪərɪə/ n tavola f calda

caffeine /'kæfi:n/ n caffeina f

cage /keɪdʒ/ n gabbia f

cagey /'keɪdʒɪ/ a fam riservato (about su)

cajole /kə'dʒəʊl/ vt persuadere con le lusinghe

cake /keɪk/ n torta f; (small) pasticcino m. ~d a incrostato (with di)

calamity /kə'læmətɪ/ n calamità f inv

calcium /'kælsɪəm/ n calcio m

calculate /'kælkjʊleɪt/ vt calcolare. ~ing a fig calcolatore. ~ion /-'leɪʃn/ n calcolo m. ~or n calcolatrice f

calendar /'kælɪndə(r)/ n calendario m

calf[1] /kɑ:f/ n (pl calves) vitello m

calf[2] n (pl calves) Anat polpaccio m

calibre /'kælɪbə(r)/ n calibro m

call /kɔ:l/ n grido m; Teleph telefonata f; (visit) visita f; be on ~ ⟨doctor:⟩ essere di guardia ● vt chiamare; indire ⟨strike⟩; be ~ed chiamarsi ● vi chiamare; ~ [in or round] passare. **call back** vt/i richiamare. **call for** vt (ask

for) chiedere; (require) richiedere; (fetch) passare a prendere. **call off** vt richiamare ⟨dog⟩; disdire ⟨meeting⟩; revocare ⟨strike⟩. **call on** vt chiamare; (appeal to) fare un appello a; (visit) visitare. **call out** vt chiamare ad alta voce ⟨names⟩ ● vi chiamare ad alta voce. **call together** vt riunire. **call up** vt Mil chiamare alle armi; Teleph chiamare

call: ~-box n cabina f telefonica. ~er n visitatore, -trice mf; Teleph persona f che telefona. ~ing n vocazione f

callous /'kæləs/ a insensibile

'call-up n Mil chiamata f alle armi

calm /kɑ:m/ a calmo ● n calma f. **calm down** vt calmare ● vi calmarsi. ~ly adv con calma

calorie /'kælərɪ/ n caloria f

calves /kɑ:vz/ npl see calf[1] &[2]

camber /'kæmbə(r)/ n curvatura f

Cambodia /kæm'bəʊdɪə/ n Cambogia f. ~n a & n cambogiano, -a mf

camcorder /'kæmkɔ:də(r)/ n videocamera f

came /keɪm/ see come

camel /'kæml/ n cammello m

camera /'kæmərə/ n macchina f fotografica; TV telecamera f. ~man n operatore m [televisivo], cameraman m inv

camouflage /'kæməflɑ:ʒ/ n mimetizzazione f ● vt mimetizzare

camp /kæmp/ n campeggio f; Mil campo m ● vi campeggiare; Mil accamparsi

campaign /kæm'peɪn/ n campagna f ● vi fare una campagna

camp: ~-bed n letto m da campo. ~er n campeggiatore, -trice mf; Auto camper m inv. ~ing n campeggio m. ~site n campeggio m

campus /'kæmpəs/ n (pl -puses) Univ città f universitaria, campus m inv

can[1] /kæn/ n (for petrol) latta f; (tin) scatola f; ~ of beer lattina f di birra ● vt mettere in scatola

can[2] /kæn/, atono /kən/ v aux (pres can; pt could) (be able to) potere; (know how to) sapere; **I cannot** or **can't go** non posso andare; **he could not** or **couldn't go** non poteva andare; **she**

can't swim non sa nuotare; **I ~ smell something burning** sento odor di bruciato

Canad|a /'kænədə/ n Canada m. **~ian** /kə'neɪdɪən/ a & n canadese mf

canal /kə'næl/ n canale m

Canaries /kə'neərɪz/ npl Canarie fpl

canary /kə'neərɪ/ n canarino m

cancel /'kænsl/ v (pt/pp **cancelled**) ● vt disdire ⟨meeting, newspaper⟩; revocare ⟨contract, order⟩; annullare ⟨reservation, appointment, stamp⟩. **~lation** /-ə'leɪʃn/ n (of meeting, contract) revoca f; (in hotel, restaurant, for flight) cancellazione f

cancer /'kænsə(r)/ n cancro m; **C~** Astr Cancro m. **~ous** /-rəs/ a canceroso

candelabra /kændə'lɑ:brə/ n candelabro m

candid /'kændɪd/ a franco

candidate /'kændɪdət/ n candidato, -a mf

candle /'kændl/ n candela f. **~stick** n portacandele m inv

candour /'kændə(r)/ n franchezza f

candy /'kændɪ/ n Am caramella f; **a [piece of] ~** una caramella. **~floss** /-flɒs/ n zucchero m filato

cane /keɪn/ n (stick) bastone m; Sch bacchetta f ● vt prendere a bacchettate ⟨pupil⟩

canine /'keɪnaɪn/ a canino. **~ tooth** n canino m

canister /'kænɪstə(r)/ n barattolo m (di metallo)

cannabis /'kænəbɪs/ n cannabis f

canned /kænd/ a in scatola; **~ music** fam musica f registrata

cannibal /'kænɪbl/ n cannibale mf. **~ism** n cannibalismo m

cannon /'kænən/ n inv cannone m. **~-ball** n palla f di cannone

cannot /'kænɒt/ see **can²**

canny /'kænɪ/ a astuto

canoe /kə'nu:/ n canoa f ● vi andare in canoa

'can-opener n apriscatole m inv

canopy /'kænəpɪ/ n baldacchino f; (of parachute) calotta f

can't /kɑ:nt/ = **cannot** see **can²**

cantankerous /kæn'tæŋkərəs/ a stizzoso

canteen /kæn'ti:n/ n mensa f; **~ of cutlery** servizio m di posate

canter /'kæntə(r)/ vi andare a piccolo galoppo

canvas /'kænvəs/ n tela f; (painting) dipinto m su tela

canvass /'kænvəs/ vi Pol fare propaganda elettorale. **~ing** n sollecitazione f di voti

canyon /'kænjən/ n canyon m inv

cap /kæp/ n berretto m; (nurse's) cuffia f; (top, lid) tappo m ● vt (pt/pp **capped**) (fig: do better than) superare

capability /keɪpə'bɪlətɪ/ n capacità f

capabl|e /'keɪpəbl/ a capace; (skilful) abile; **be ~e of doing sth** essere capace di fare qcsa. **~y** adv con abilità

capacity /kə'pæsətɪ/ n capacità f; (function) qualità f; **in my ~ as** in qualità di

cape¹ /keɪp/ n (cloak) cappa f

cape² n Geog capo m

caper¹ /'keɪpə(r)/ vi saltellare ● n fam birichinata f

caper² n Culin cappero m

capital /'kæpɪtl/ n (town) capitale f; (money) capitale m; (letter) lettera f maiuscola. **~ city** n capitale f

capital|ism /'kæpɪtəlɪzm/ n capitalismo m. **~ist** /-ɪst/ a & n capitalista mf. **~ize** /-aɪz/ vi **~ize on** fig trarre vantaggio da. **~ 'letter** n lettera f maiuscola. **~ 'punishment** n pena f capitale

capitulat|e /kə'pɪtjuleɪt/ vi capitolare. **~ion** /-'leɪʃn/ n capitolazione f

capricious /kə'prɪʃəs/ a capriccioso

Capricorn /'kæprɪkɔ:n/ n Astr Capricorno m

capsize /kæp'saɪz/ vi capovolgersi ● vt capovolgere

capsule /'kæpsjʊl/ n capsula f

captain /'kæptɪn/ n capitano m ● vt comandare ⟨team⟩

caption /'kæpʃn/ n intestazione f; (of illustration) didascalia f

captivate /'kæptɪveɪt/ vt incantare

captiv|e /'kæptɪv/ a prigioniero; **hold/take ~e** tenere/fare prigioniero ● n prigioniero, -a mf. **~ity** /-'tɪvətɪ/ n prigionia f; (animals) cattività f

capture /'kæptʃə(r)/ n cattura f ● vt catturare; attirare ⟨attention⟩

car /kɑ:(r)/ n macchina f; **by ~** in macchina

carafe /kə'ræf/ n caraffa f

caramel /'kærəmel/ n (sweet) caramella f al mou; Culin caramello m

carat /'kærət/ n carato m

caravan /'kærəvæn/ n roulotte f inv; (horse-drawn) carovana f

carbohydrate /kɑ:bə'haɪdreɪt/ n carboidrato m

carbon /'kɑ:bən/ n carbonio m

carbon: ~ copy n copia f in carta carbone; (*fig: person*) ritratto *m*. ~ **di'oxi**⸱**e** *n* anidride *f* carbonica. ~ **paper** *n* carta *f* carbone

carburettor /kɑːbjʊˈretə(r)/ *n* carburatore *m*

carcass /ˈkɑːkəs/ *n* carcassa *f*

card /kɑːd/ *n* (*for birthday, Christmas etc*) biglietto *m* di auguri; (*playing ~*) carta *f* [da gioco]; (*membership ~*) tessera *f*; (*business ~*) biglietto *m* da visita; (*credit ~*) carta *f* di credito; *Comput* scheda *f*

'**cardboard** *n* cartone *m*. ~ '**box** *n* scatola *f* di cartone; (*large*) scatolone *m*

'**card-game** *n* gioco *m* di carte

cardiac /ˈkɑːdɪæk/ *a* cardiaco

cardigan /ˈkɑːdɪgən/ *n* cardigan *m inv*

cardinal /ˈkɑːdɪnl/ *a* cardinale; ~ **number** numero *m* cardinale ● *n Relig* cardinale *m*

card 'index *n* schedario *m*

care /keə(r)/ *n* cura *f*; (*caution*) attenzione *f*; (*worry*) preoccupazione *f*; ~ **of** (*on letter abbr* **c/o**) presso; **take** ~ (*be cautious*) fare attenzione; **bye, take** ~ ciao, stammi bene; **take** ~ **of** occuparsi di; **be taken into** ~ essere preso in custodia da un ente assistenziale ● *vi* ~ **about** interessarsi di; ~ **for** (*feel affection for*) volere bene a; (*look after*) aver cura di; **I don't** ~ **for chocolate** non mi piace il cioccolato; **I don't** ~ non me ne importa; **who** ~**s?** chi se ne frega?

career /kəˈrɪə(r)/ *n* carriera *f*; (*profession*) professione *f* ● *vi* andare a tutta velocità

care: ~**free** *a* spensierato. ~**ful** *a* attento; (*driver*) prudente. ~**fully** *adv* con attenzione. ~**less** *a* irresponsabile; (*in work*) trascurato; (*work*) fatto con poca cura; (*driver*) distratto. ~**lessly** *adv* negligentemente. ~**lessness** *n* trascuratezza *f*. ~**r** *n* persona *f* che accudisce a un anziano o a un malato

caress /kəˈres/ *n* carezza *f* ● *vt* accarezzare

'**caretaker** *n* custode *mf*; (*in school*) bidello *m*

'**car ferry** *n* traghetto *m* (*per il trasporto di auto*)

cargo /ˈkɑːgəʊ/ *n* (*pl* -**es**) carico *m*

Caribbean /kærɪˈbiːən/ *n* **the** ~ (*sea*) il Mar dei Caraibi ● *a* caraibico

caricature /ˈkærɪkətjʊə(r)/ *n* caricatura *f*

caring /ˈkeərɪŋ/ *a* (*parent*) premuroso;

(*attitude*) altruista; **the** ~ **professions** le attività assistenziali

carnage /ˈkɑːnɪdʒ/ *n* carneficina *f*

carnal /ˈkɑːnl/ *a* carnale

carnation /kɑːˈneɪʃn/ *n* garofano *m*

carnival /ˈkɑːnɪvl/ *n* carnevale *m*

carnivorous /kɑːˈnɪvərəs/ *a* carnivoro

carol /ˈkærəl/ *n* [**Christmas**] ~ canzone *f* natalizia

carp[1] /kɑːp/ *n inv* carpa *f*

carp[2] *vi* ~ **at** trovare da ridire su

'**car park** *n* parcheggio *m*

carpent|er /ˈkɑːpɪntə(r)/ *n* falegname *m*. ~**ry** *n* falegnameria *f*

carpet /ˈkɑːpɪt/ *n* tappeto *m*; (*wall-to-wall*) moquette *f inv* ● *vt* méttere la moquette in (*room*)

'**car phone** *n* telefono *m* in macchina

carriage /ˈkærɪdʒ/ *n* carrozza *f*; (*of goods*) trasporto *m*; (*cost*) spese *fpl* di trasporto; (*bearing*) portamento *m*; ~**way** *n* strada *f* carrozzabile; **north-bound** ~**way** carreggiata *f* nord

carrier /ˈkærɪə(r)/ *n* (*company*) impresa *f* di trasporti; *Aeron* compagnia *f* di trasporto aereo; (*of disease*) portatore *m*. ~ [**bag**] *n* borsa *f* [per la spesa]

carrot /ˈkærət/ *n* carota *f*

carry /ˈkærɪ/ *v* (*pt/pp* -**ied**) ● *vt* portare; (*transport*) trasportare; **get carried away** *fam* lasciarsi prender la mano ● *vi* (*sound:*) trasmettersi. **carry off** *vt* portare via; vincere (*prize*). **carry on** *vi* continuare; (*fam: make scene*) fare delle storie; ~ **on with sth** continuare qcsa; ~ **on with sb** *fam* intendersela con qcno ● *vt* mantenere (*business*). **carry out** *vt* portare fuori; eseguire (*instructions, task*); mettere in atto (*threat*); effettuare (*experiment, survey*)

'**carry-cot** *n* porte-enfant *m inv*

cart /kɑːt/ *n* carretto *m* ● *vt* (*fam: carry*) portare

cartilage /ˈkɑːtɪlɪdʒ/ *n Anat* cartilagine *f*

carton /ˈkɑːtn/ *n* scatola *f* di cartone; (*for drink*) cartone *m*; (*of cream, yoghurt*) vasetto *m*; (*of cigarettes*) stecca *f*

cartoon /kɑːˈtuːn/ *n* vignetta *f*; (*strip*) vignette *fpl*; (*film*) cartone *m* animato; (*in art*) bozzetto *m*. ~**ist** *n* vignettista *mf*; (*for films*) disegnatore, -trice *mf* di cartoni animati

cartridge /ˈkɑːtrɪdʒ/ *n* cartuccia *f*; (*for film*) bobina *f*; (*of record player*) testina *f*

carve /kɑːv/ *vt* scolpire; tagliare (*meat*)

carving /'kɑːvɪŋ/ n scultura f. **~-knife** n trinciante m

'car wash n autolavaggio m inv

case¹ /keɪs/ n caso m; **in any ~** in ogni caso; **in that ~** in questo caso; **just in ~** per sicurezza; **in ~ he comes** nel caso in cui venisse

case² n (container) scatola f; (crate) cassa f; (for spectacles) astuccio m; (suitcase) valigia f; (for display) vetrina f

cash /kæʃ/ n denaro m contante; (fam: money) contanti mpl; **pay (in) ~** pagare in contanti; **~ on delivery** pagamento alla consegna ● vt incassare ⟨cheque⟩. **~ desk** n cassa f

cashier /kæ'ʃɪə(r)/ n cassiere, -a mf

'cash register n registratore m di cassa

casino /kə'siːnəʊ/ n casinò m inv

casket /'kɑːskɪt/ n scrigno m; (Am: coffin) bara f

casserole /'kæsərəʊl/ n casseruola f; (stew) stufato m

cassette /kə'set/ n cassetta f. **~ recorder** n registratore m (a cassette)

cast /kɑːst/ n (mould) forma f; Theat cast m inv; [plaster] **~** Med ingessatura f ● vt (pt/pp cast) dare ⟨vote⟩; Theat assegnare le parti di ⟨play⟩; fondere ⟨metal⟩; (throw) gettare; **~ an actor as** dare ad un attore il ruolo di; **~ a glance at** lanciare uno sguardo a. **cast -off** vi Naut sganciare gli ormeggi ● vt (in knitting) diminuire. **cast on** vt (in knitting) avviare

castaway /'kɑːstəweɪ/ n naufrago, -a mf

caste /kɑːst/ n casta f

caster /'kɑːstə(r)/ n (wheel) rotella f. **~ sugar** n zucchero m raffinato

cast 'iron n ghisa f

cast-'iron a di ghisa; fig solido

castle /'kɑːsl/ n castello m; (in chess) torre f

'cast-offs npl abiti mpl smessi

castor /'kɑːstə(r)/ n (wheel) rotella f. **~ oil** n olio m di ricino. **~ sugar** n zucchero m raffinato

castrat|e /kæ'streɪt/ vt castrare. **~ion** /-eɪʃn/ n castrazione f

casual /'kæʒʊəl/ a (chance) casuale; ⟨remark⟩ senza importanza; ⟨glance⟩ di sfuggita; ⟨attitude, approach⟩ disinvolto; ⟨chat⟩ informale; ⟨clothes⟩ casual inv; ⟨work⟩ saltuario; **~ wear** abbigliamento m casual. **~ly** adv ⟨dress⟩ casual; ⟨meet⟩ casualmente

casualty /'kæʒʊəltɪ/ n (injured person) ferito m; (killed) vittima f. **~ [department]** n pronto soccorso m

cat /kæt/ n gatto m; pej arpia f

catalogue /'kætəlɒg/ n catalogo m ● vt catalogare

catalyst /'kætəlɪst/ n Chem & fig catalizzatore m

catalytic /kætə'lɪtɪk/ a **~ converter** Auto marmitta f catalitica

catapult /'kætəpʌlt/ n catapulta f; (child's) fionda f ● vt fig catapultare

cataract /'kætərækt/ n Med cataratta f

catarrh /kə'tɑː(r)/ n catarro m

catastroph|e /kə'tæstrəfɪ/ n catastrofe f. **~ic** /kætə'strɒfɪk/ a catastrofico

catch /kætʃ/ n (of fish) pesca f; (fastener) fermaglio m; (on door) fermo m; (on window) gancio m; (fam: snag) tranello m ● v (pt/pp caught) ● vt acchiappare ⟨ball⟩; (grab) afferrare; prendere ⟨illness, fugitive, train⟩; **~ a cold** prendersi un raffreddore; **~ sight of** scorgere; **I caught him stealing** l'ho sorpreso mentre rubava; **~ one's finger in the door** chiudersi il dito nella porta; **~ sb's eye** or **attention** attirare l'attenzione di qcno ● vi ⟨fire:⟩ prendere; (get stuck) impigliarsi. **catch on** vi fam (understand) afferrare; (become popular) diventare popolare. **catch up** vt raggiungere ● vi recuperare; ⟨runner:⟩ riguadagnare terreno; **~ up with** raggiungere ⟨sb⟩; mettersi in pari con ⟨work⟩

catching /'kætʃɪŋ/ a contagioso

catch: ~-phrase n tormentone m. **~word** n slogan m inv

catchy /'kætʃɪ/ a (-ier, -iest) orecchiabile

categor|ical /kætɪ'gɒrɪkl/ a categorico. **~y** /'kætɪgərɪ/ n categoria f

cater /'keɪtə(r)/ vi **~ for** provvedere a ⟨needs⟩; fig venire incontro alle esigenze di. **~ing** n (trade) ristorazione f; (food) rinfresco m

caterpillar /'kætəpɪlə(r)/ n bruco m

cathedral /kə'θiːdrl/ n cattedrale f

Catholic /'kæθəlɪk/ a & n cattolico, -a mf. **~ism** /kə'θɒlɪsɪzm/ n cattolicesimo m

cat's eyes npl catarifrangente msg (inserito nell'asfalto)

cattle /'kætl/ npl bestiame msg

catty /'kætɪ/ a (-ier, -iest) dispettoso

catwalk /'kætwɔːk/ n passerella f

caught /kɔːt/ see **catch**

cauliflower /'kɒlɪ-/ n cavolfiore m

cause /kɔːz/ n causa f ● vt causare; **~ sb to do sth** far fare qcsa a qcno

'causeway n strada f sopraelevata

caustic /'kɔːstɪk/ a caustico

caution /'kɔːʃn/ n cautela f; (warning) ammonizione f ● vt mettere in guardia; Jur ammonire

cautious /'kɔːʃəs/ a cauto

cavalry /'kævəlrɪ/ n cavalleria f

cave /keɪv/ n caverna f ● **cave in** vi ‹roof:› crollare; ‹fig: give in› capitolare

cavern /'kævən/ n caverna f

caviare /'kævɪɑː(r)/ n caviale m

caving /'keɪvɪŋ/ n speleologia f

cavity /'kævətɪ/ n cavità f inv; (in tooth) carie f inv

cavort /kə'vɔːt/ vi saltellare

CD n CD m inv. **~ player** n lettore m [di] compact

CD-Rom /siːdiː'rɒm/ n CD-Rom m inv. **~ drive** n lettore m [di] CD-Rom

cease /siːs/ n **without ~** incessantemente ● vt/i cessare. **~-fire** n cessate il fuoco m inv. **~less** a incessante

cedar /'siːdə(r)/ n cedro m

cede /siːd/ vt cedere

ceiling /'siːlɪŋ/ n soffitto m; fig tetto m [massimo]

celebrat|e /'selɪbreɪt/ vt festeggiare ‹birthday, victory› ● vi far festa. **~ed** a celebre (**for** per). **~ion** /-'breɪʃn/ n celebrazione f

celebrity /sɪ'lebrətɪ/ n celebrità f inv

celery /'selərɪ/ n sedano m

celiba|cy /'selɪbəsɪ/ n celibato m. **~te** a ‹man› celibe; ‹woman› nubile

cell /sel/ n cella f; Biol cellula f

cellar /'selə(r)/ n scantinato m; (for wine) cantina f

cellist /'tʃelɪst/ n violoncellista mf

cello /'tʃeləʊ/ n violoncello m

Cellophane® /'seləfeɪn/ n cellofan m inv

cellular phone /seljʊlə'fəʊn/ n [telefono m] cellulare m

celluloid /'seljʊlɔɪd/ n celluloide f

Celsius /'selsɪəs/ a Celsius

Celt /kelt/ n celta mf. **~ic** a celtico

cement /sɪ'ment/ n cemento m; (adhesive) mastice m ● vt cementare; fig consolidare

cemetery /'semətrɪ/ n cimitero m

censor /'sensə(r)/ n censore m ● vt censurare. **~ship** n censura f

censure /'senʃə(r)/ vt biasimare

census /'sensəs/ n censimento m

cent /sent/ n (coin) centesimo m

centenary /sen'tiːnərɪ/ n, Am **centennial** /sen'tenɪəl/ n centenario m

center /'sentə(r)/ n Am = **centre**

centi|grade /'sentɪ-/ a centigrado. **~metre** n centimetro m. **~pede** /-piːd/ n centopiedi m inv

central /'sentrəl/ a centrale. **~ 'heating** n riscaldamento m autonomo. **~ize** vt centralizzare. **~ly** adv al centro; **~ly heated** con riscaldamento autonomo. **~ reser'vation** n Auto banchina f spartitraffico

centre /'sentə(r)/ n centro m ● v (pt/pp **centred**) ● vt centrare ● vi **~ on** fig incentrarsi su. **~-'forward** n centravanti m inv

centrifugal /sentrɪ'fjuːgl/ a **~ force** forza f centrifuga

century /'sentʃərɪ/ n secolo m

ceramic /sɪ'ræmɪk/ a ceramico. **~s** n (art) ceramica fsg; (objects) ceramiche fpl

cereal /'sɪərɪəl/ n cereale m

cerebral /'serɪbrl/ a cerebrale

ceremon|ial /serɪ'məʊnɪəl/ a da cerimonia ● n cerimoniale m. **~ious** /-ɪəs/ a cerimonioso

ceremony /'serɪmənɪ/ n cerimonia f

certain /'sɜːtn/ a certo; **for ~** di sicuro; **make ~** accertarsi; **he is ~ to win** è certo di vincere; **it's not ~ whether he'll come** non è sicuro che venga. **~ly** adv certamente; **~ly not!** no di certo! **~ty** n certezza f; **it's a ~ty** è una cosa certa

certificate /sə'tɪfɪkət/ n certificato m

certify /'sɜːtɪfaɪ/ vt (pt/pp **-ied**) certificare; (declare insane) dichiarare malato di mente

cessation /se'seɪʃn/ n cessazione f

cesspool /'ses-/ n pozzo m nero

cf abbr (compare) cf, cfr

chafe /tʃeɪf/ vt irritare

chain /tʃeɪn/ n catena f ● vt incatenare ‹prisoner›; attaccare con la catena ‹dog› (**to** a). **chain up** vt legare alla catena ‹dog›

chain: ~ re'action n reazione f a catena. **~-smoke** vi fumare una sigaretta dopo l'altra. **~-smoker** n fumatore, -trice mf accanito, -a. **~ store** n negozio m appartenente a una catena

chair /tʃeə(r)/ n sedia f; Univ cattedra f ● vt presiedere. **~-lift** n seggiovia f. **~man** n presidente m

chalet /'ʃæleɪ/ n chalet m inv; (in holiday camp) bungalow m inv

chalice /'tʃælɪs/ n Relig calice m

chalk /tʃɔːk/ n gesso m. **~y** a gessoso

challenge /'tʃælɪndʒ/ n sfida f; Mil intimazione f ● vt sfidare; Mil intimare il chi va là a; *fig* mettere in dubbio ⟨*statement*⟩. **~er** *n* sfidante *mf*. **~ing** *a* ⟨*job*⟩ impegnativo

chamber /'tʃeɪmbə(r)/ *n* **C~ of Commerce** camera *f* di commercio

chamber: **~maid** *n* cameriera *f* [d'albergo]. **~ music** *n* musica *f* da camera

chamois[1] /'ʃæmwɑ:/ *n inv* ⟨*animal*⟩ camoscio *m*

chamois[2] /'ʃæmɪ/ *n* **~[-leather]** [pelle *f* di] camoscio *m*

champagne /ʃæm'peɪn/ *n* champagne *m inv*

champion /'tʃæmpɪən/ *n* Sport campione *m*; (*of cause*) difensore, difenditrice *mf* ● *vt* (*defend*) difendere; (*fight for*) lottare per. **~ship** *n* Sport campionato *m*

chance /tʃɑːns/ *n* caso *m*; (*possibility*) possibilità *f inv*; (*opportunity*) occasione *f*; **by ~** per caso; **take a ~** provarci; **give sb a second ~** dare un'altra possibilità a qcno ● *attrib* fortuito ● *vt* **I'll ~ it** *fam* corro il rischio

chancellor /'tʃɑːnsələ(r)/ *n* cancelliere *m*; Univ rettore *m*; **C~ of the Exchequer** ministro *m* del tesoro

chancy /'tʃɑːnsɪ/ *a* rischioso

chandelier /ʃændə'lɪə(r)/ *n* lampadario *m*

change /tʃeɪndʒ/ *n* cambiamento *m*; (*money*) resto *m*; (*small coins*) spiccioli *mpl*; **for a ~** tanto per cambiare; **a ~ of clothes** un cambio di vestiti; **the ~ [of life]** la menopausa ● *vt* cambiare; (*substitute*) scambiare (**for** con); **~ one's clothes** cambiarsi [i vestiti]; **~ trains** cambiare treno ● *vi* cambiare; (**~** *clothes*) cambiarsi; **all ~!** stazione terminale!

changeable /'tʃeɪndʒəbl/ *a* mutevole; ⟨*weather*⟩ variabile

'**changing-room** *n* camerino *m*; (*for sports*) spogliatoio *m*

channel /'tʃænl/ *n* canale *m*; **the [English] C~** la Manica; **the C~ Islands** le Isole del Canale ● *vt* (*pt/pp* **channelled**) **~ one's energies into sth** convogliare le proprie energie in qcsa

chant /tʃɑːnt/ *n* cantilena *f*; (*of demonstrators*) slogan *m inv* di protesta ● *vt* cantare; ⟨*demonstrators:*⟩ gridare

chao|s /'keɪɒs/ *n* caos *m*. **~tic** /-'ɒtɪk/ *a* caotico

chap /tʃæp/ *n fam* tipo *m*

chapel /'tʃæpl/ *n* cappella *f*

chaperon /'ʃæpərəʊn/ *n* chaperon *f inv* ● *vt* fare da chaperon a ⟨*sb*⟩

chaplain /'tʃæplɪn/ *n* cappellano *m*

chapped /tʃæpt/ *a* ⟨*skin, lips*⟩ screpolato

chapter /'tʃæptə(r)/ *n* capitolo *m*

char[1] /tʃɑː(r)/ *n fam* donna *f* delle pulizie

char[2] *vt* (*pt/pp* **charred**) (*burn*) carbonizzare

character /'kærɪktə(r)/ *n* carattere *m*; (*in novel, play*) personaggio *m*; **quite a ~** *fam* un tipo particolare

characteristic /kærɪktə'rɪstɪk/ *a* caratteristico ● *n* caratteristica *f*. **~ally** *adv* tipicamente

characterize /'kærɪktəraɪz/ *vt* caratterizzare

charade /ʃə'rɑːd/ *n* farsa *f*

charcoal /'tʃɑː-/ *n* carbonella *f*

charge /tʃɑːdʒ/ *n* (*cost*) prezzo *m*; Electr, Mil carica *f*; Jur accusa *f*; **free of ~** gratuito; **be in ~ of** essere responsabile (**of** di); **take ~** assumersi la responsibilità; **take ~ of** occuparsi di ● *vt* far pagare ⟨*fee*⟩; far pagare a ⟨*person*⟩; Electr, Mil caricare; Jur accusare (**with** di); **~ sb for sth** far pagare qcsa a qcno; **~ it to my account** lo addebiti sul mio conto ● *vi* (*attack*) caricare

chariot /'tʃærɪət/ *n* cocchio *m*

charisma /kə'rɪzmə/ *n* carisma *m*. **~tic** /kærɪz'mætɪk/ *a* carismatico

charitable /'tʃærɪtəbl/ *a* caritatevole; (*kind*) indulgente

charity /'tʃærɪtɪ/ *n* carità *f*; (*organization*) associazione *f* di beneficenza; **concert given for ~** concerto *m* di beneficenza; **live on ~** vivere di elemosina

charm /tʃɑːm/ *n* fascino *m*; (*object*) ciondolo *m* ● *vt* affascinare. **~ing** *a* affascinante

chart /tʃɑːt/ *n* carta *f* nautica; (*table*) tabella *f*

charter /'tʃɑːtə(r)/ *n* **~ [flight]** [volo *m*] charter *m inv* ● *vt* noleggiare. **~ed accountant** *n* commercialista *mf*

charwoman /'tʃɑː-/ *n* donna *f* delle pulizie

chase /tʃeɪs/ *n* inseguimento *m* ● *vt* inseguire. **chase away** *or* **off** *vt* cacciare via

chasm /'kæz(ə)m/ *n* abisso *m*

chassis /'ʃæsɪ/ *n* (*pl chassis* /-sɪz/) telaio *m*

chaste /tʃeɪst/ *a* casto

chastity /'tʃæstətɪ/ *n* castità *f*

chat /tʃæt/ n chiacchierata f; **have a ~ with** fare quattro chiacchere con ● vi ⟨pt/pp **chatted**⟩ chiacchierare. **~ show** n talk show m inv

chatter /'tʃætə(r)/ n chiacchiere fpl ● vi chiacchierare; ⟨teeth:⟩ battere. **~box** n fam chiacchierone, -a mf

chatty /'tʃætɪ/ a (-ier, -iest) chiacchierone; ⟨style⟩ familiare

chauffeur /'ʃəʊfə(r)/ n autista mf

chauvin|ism /'ʃəʊvɪnɪzm/ n sciovinismo m. **~ist** n sciovinista mf. **male ~ist** n fam maschilista m

cheap /tʃi:p/ a a buon mercato; ⟨rate⟩ economico; ⟨vulgar⟩ grossolano; ⟨of poor quality⟩ scadente ● adv a buon mercato. **~ly** adv a buon mercato

cheat /tʃi:t/ n imbroglione, -a mf; ⟨at cards⟩ baro m ● vt imbrogliare; **~ sb out of sth** sottrarre qcsa a qcno con l'inganno ● vi imbrogliare; ⟨at cards⟩ barare. **cheat on** vt fam tradire ⟨wife⟩

check[1] /tʃek/ a ⟨pattern⟩ a quadri ● n disegno m a quadri

check[2] n verifica f; ⟨of tickets⟩ controllo m; ⟨in chess⟩ scacco m; ⟨Am: bill⟩ conto m; ⟨Am: cheque⟩ assegno m; ⟨Am: tick⟩ segnetto m; **keep a ~ on** controllare; **keep in ~** tenere sotto controllo ● vt verificare; controllare ⟨tickets⟩; ⟨restrain⟩ contenere; ⟨stop⟩ bloccare ● vi controllare; **~ on sth** controllare qcsa. **check in** vi registrarsi all'arrivo ⟨in albergo⟩; Aeron fare il check-in ● vt registrare all'arrivo ⟨in albergo⟩. **check out** vi ⟨of hotel⟩ saldare il conto ● vt ⟨fam: investigate⟩ controllare. **check up** vi accertarsi; **~ up on** prendere informazioni su

check|ed /tʃekt/ a a quadri. **~ers** n Am dama f

check: **~-in** n ⟨in airport: place⟩ banco m accettazione, check-in m inv; **~-in time** check-in m inv. **~ mark** n Am segnetto m. **~mate** int scacco matto! **~-out** n ⟨in supermarket⟩ cassa f. **~room** n Am deposito m bagagli. **~-up** n Med visita f di controllo, check-up m inv

cheek /tʃi:k/ n guancia f; ⟨impudence⟩ sfacciataggine f. **~y** a sfacciato

cheep /tʃi:p/ vi pigolare

cheer /tʃɪə(r)/ n evviva m inv; **three ~s** tre urrà; **~s!** salute!; ⟨goodbye⟩ arrivederci!; ⟨thanks⟩ grazie! ● vt/i acclamare. **cheer up** vt tirare su [di morale] ● vi tirarsi su [di morale]; **~ up!** su con

la vita!. **~ful** a allegro. **~fulness** n allegria f. **~ing** n acclamazione f

cheerio /tʃɪərɪ'əʊ/ int fam arrivederci

'cheerless a triste, tetro

cheese /tʃi:z/ n formaggio m. **~cake** n dolce m al formaggio

chef /ʃef/ n cuoco, -a mf, chef mf inv

chemical /'kemɪkl/ a chimico ● n prodotto m chimico

chemist /'kemɪst/ n ⟨pharmacist⟩ farmacista mf; ⟨scientist⟩ chimico, -a mf; **~'s** [shop] farmacia f. **~ry** n chimica f

cheque /tʃek/ n assegno m. **~-book** n libretto m degli assegni. **~ card** n carta f assegni

cherish /'tʃerɪʃ/ vt curare teneramente; ⟨love⟩ avere caro; nutrire ⟨hope⟩

cherry /'tʃerɪ/ n ciliegia f; ⟨tree⟩ ciliegio m

cherub /'tʃerəb/ n cherubino m

chess /tʃes/ n scacchi mpl

chess: **~board** n scacchiera f. **~-man** n pezzo m degli scacchi. **~player** n scacchista mf

chest /tʃest/ n petto m; ⟨box⟩ cassapanca f

chestnut /'tʃesnʌt/ n castagna f; ⟨tree⟩ castagno m

chest of 'drawers n cassettone m

chew /tʃu:/ vt masticare. **~ing-gum** n gomma f da masticare

chic /ʃi:k/ a chic inv

chick /tʃɪk/ n pulcino m; ⟨fam: girl⟩ ragazza f

chicken /'tʃɪkn/ n pollo m ● attrib ⟨soup, casserole⟩ di pollo ● a fam fifone ● **chicken out** vi fam **he ~ed out** gli è venuta fifa. **~pox** n varicella f

chicory /'tʃɪkərɪ/ n cicoria f

chief /tʃi:f/ a principale ● n capo m. **~ly** adv principalmente

chilblain /'tʃɪlbleɪn/ n gelone m

child /tʃaɪld/ n ⟨pl **~ren**⟩ bambino, -a mf; ⟨son/daughter⟩ figlio, -a mf

child: **~birth** n parto m. **~hood** n infanzia f. **~ish** a infantile. **~ishness** n puerilità f. **~less** a senza figli. **~like** a ingenuo. **~minder** n baby-sitter mf inv

children /'tʃɪldrən/ see **child**

Chile /'tʃɪlɪ/ n Cile m. **~an** a & n cileno, -a mf

chill /tʃɪl/ n freddo m; ⟨illness⟩ infreddatura f ● vt raffreddare

chilli /'tʃɪlɪ/ n ⟨pl -es⟩ **~** [**pepper**] peperoncino m

chilly /'tʃɪlɪ/ a freddo

chime /tʃaɪm/ vi suonare

chimney /'tʃɪmnɪ/ n camino m. **~-pot**

n comignolo *m*. **~-sweep** *n* spazzacamino *m*

chimpanzee /tʃɪmpæn'ziː/ *n* scimpanzé *m inv*

chin /tʃɪn/ *n* mento *m*

china /'tʃaɪnə/ *n* porcellana *f*

Chin|a *n* Cina *f*. **~ese** /-'niːz/ *a & n* cinese *mf*; (*language*) cinese *m*; **the ~ese** *pl* i cinesi

chink[1] /tʃɪŋk/ *n* (*slit*) fessura *f*

chink[2] *n* (*noise*) tintinnio *m*

chip /tʃɪp/ *n* (*fragment*) scheggia *f*; (*in china, paintwork*) scheggiatura *f*; *Comput* chip *m inv*; (*in gambling*) fiche *f inv*; **~s** *pl Br Culin* patatine *fpl* fritte; *Am Culin* patatine *fpl* ● *vt* (*pt/pp* **chipped**) (*damage*) scheggiare. **chip in** *vi fam* intromettersi; (*with money*) contribuire. **~ped** *a* (*damaged*) scheggiato

chiropod|ist /kɪ'rɒpədɪst/ *n* podiatra *mf inv*. **~y** *n* podiatria *f*

chirp /tʃɜːp/ *vi* cinguettare; ⟨cricket:⟩ fare cri cri. **~y** *a fam* pimpante

chisel /'tʃɪzl/ *n* scalpello *m*

chival|rous /'ʃɪvlrəs/ *a* cavalleresco. **~ry** *n* cavalleria *f*

chives /tʃaɪvz/ *npl* erba *f* cipollina

chlorine /'klɔːriːn/ *n* cloro *m*

chloroform /'klɒrəfɔːm/ *n* cloroformio *m*

chock-a-block /tʃɒkə'blɒk/, **chock-full** /tʃɒk'fʊl/ *a* pieno zeppo

chocolate /'tʃɒkələt/ *n* cioccolato *m*; (*drink*) cioccolata *f*; **a ~** un cioccolatino

choice /tʃɔɪs/ *n* scelta *f* ● *a* scelto

choir /'kwaɪə(r)/ *n* coro *m*. **~boy** *n* corista *m*

choke /tʃəʊk/ *n Auto* aria *f* ● *vt/i* soffocare

cholera /'kɒlərə/ *n* colera *m*

cholesterol /kə'lestərɒl/ *n* colesterolo *m*

choose /tʃuːz/ *vt/i* (*pt* **chose**, *pp* **chosen**) scegliere; **as you ~** come vuoi

choos[e]y /'tʃuːzɪ/ *a fam* difficile

chop /tʃɒp/ *n* (*blow*) colpo *m* (*d'ascia*); *Culin* costata *f* ● *vt* (*pt/pp* **chopped**) tagliare. **chop down** *vt* abbattere ⟨tree⟩. **chop off** *vt* spaccare

chop|per /'tʃɒpə(r)/ *n* accetta *f*; *fam* elicottero *m*. **~py** *a* increspato

'chopsticks *npl* bastoncini *mpl* cinesi

choral /'kɔːrəl/ *a* corale

chord /kɔːd/ *n Mus* corda *f*

chore /tʃɔː(r)/ *n* corvé *f inv*; [**household**] **~s** faccende *fpl* domestiche

choreograph|er /kɒrɪ'ɒgrəfə(r)/ *n* coreografo, -a *mf*. **~y** /-ɪ/ *n* coreografia *f*

chortle /'tʃɔːtl/ *vi* ridacchiare

chorus /'kɔːrəs/ *n* coro *m*; (*of song*) ritornello *m*

chose, chosen /tʃəʊz, 'tʃəʊzn/ *see* **choose**

Christ /kraɪst/ *n* Cristo *m*

christen /'krɪsn/ *vt* battezzare. **~ing** *n* battesimo *m*

Christian /'krɪstʃən/ *a & n* cristiano, -a *mf*. **~ity** /-stɪ'ænətɪ/ *n* cristianesimo *m*. **~ name** *n* nome *m* di battesimo

Christmas /'krɪsməs/ *n* Natale *m* ● *attrib* di Natale. '**~ card** *n* biglietto *m* d'auguri di Natale. **~ 'Day** *n* il giorno di Natale. '**~ Eve** *n* la vigilia di Natale. '**~ present** *n* regalo *m* di Natale. **~ 'pudding** *dolce m natalizio a base di frutta candita e liquore*. '**~ tree** *n* albero *m* di Natale

chrome /krəʊm/ *n*, **chromium** /'krəʊmɪəm/ *n* cromo *m*

chromosome /'krəʊməsəʊm/ *n* cromosoma *m*

chronic /'krɒnɪk/ *a* cronico

chronicle /'krɒnɪkl/ *n* cronaca *f*

chronological /krɒnə'lɒdʒɪkl/ *a* cronologico. **~ly** *adv* ⟨ordered⟩ in ordine cronologico

chrysanthemum /krɪ'sænθəməm/ *n* crisantemo *m*

chubby /'tʃʌbɪ/ *a* (**-ier, -iest**) paffuto

chuck /tʃʌk/ *vt fam* buttare. **chuck out** *vt fam* buttare via ⟨object⟩; buttare fuori ⟨person⟩

chuckle /'tʃʌkl/ *vi* ridacchiare

chug /tʃʌg/ *vi* (*pt/pp* **chugged**) **the train ~ged out of the station** il treno è uscito dalla stazione sbuffando

chum /tʃʌm/ *n* amico, -a *mf*. **~my** *a fam* **be ~my with** essere amico di

chunk /tʃʌŋk/ *n* grosso pezzo *m*

church /tʃɜːtʃ/ *n* chiesa *f*. **~yard** *n* cimitero *m*

churlish /'tʃɜːlɪʃ/ *a* sgarbato

churn /tʃɜːn/ *vt* **churn out** sfornare

chute /ʃuːt/ *n* scivolo *m*; (*for rubbish*) canale *m* di scarico

CID *n abbr* (**Criminal Investigation Department**) polizia *f* giudiziaria

cider /'saɪdə(r)/ *n* sidro *m*

cigar /sɪ'gɑː(r)/ *n* sigaro *m*

cigarette /sɪgə'ret/ *n* sigaretta *f*

cine-camera /'sɪnɪ-/ *n* cinepresa *f*

cinema /'sɪnɪmə/ *n* cinema *m inv*

cinnamon /'sɪnəmən/ *n* cannella *f*

circle /'sɜːkl/ *n* cerchio *m*; *Theat* galleria *f*; **in a** ~ in cerchio ● *vt* girare intorno a; cerchiare ‹*mistake*› ● *vi* descrivere dei cerchi

circuit /'sɜːkɪt/ *n* circuito *m*; (*lap*) giro *m*; ~ **board** *n* circuito *m* stampato. ~**ous** /səˈkjuːɪtəs/ *a* ~**ous route** percorso *m* lungo e indiretto

circular /'sɜːkjʊlə(r)/ *a* circolare ● *n* circolare *f*

circulat|e /'sɜːkjʊleɪt/ *vt* far circolare ● *vi* circolare. ~**ion** /-'leɪʃn/ *n* circolazione *f*; (*of newspaper*) tiratura *f*

circumcis|e /'sɜːkəmsaɪz/ *vt* circoncidere. ~**ion** /-'sɪʒn/ *n* circoncisione *f*

circumference /ʃəˈkʌmfərəns/ *n* conconferenza *f*

circumstance /'sɜːkəmstəns/ *n* circostanza *f*; ~**s** *pl* (*financial*) condizioni *fpl* finanziarie

circus /'sɜːkəs/ *n* circo *m*

CIS *n abbr* (**Commonwealth of Independent States**) CSI *f*

cistern /'sɪstən/ *n* (*tank*) cisterna *f*; (*of WC*) serbatoio *m*

cite /saɪt/ *vt* citare

citizen /'sɪtɪzn/ *n* cittadino, -a *mf*; (*of town*) abitante *mf*. ~**ship** *n* cittadinanza *f*

citrus /'sɪtrəs/ *n* ~ [**fruit**] agrume *m*

city /'sɪtɪ/ *n* città *f inv*; **the C**~ la City (*di Londra*)

civic /'sɪvɪk/ *a* civico

civil /'ʃɪvl/ *a* civile

civilian /sɪˈvɪljən/ *a* civile; **in** ~ **clothes** in borghese ● *n* civile *mf*

civiliz|ation /sɪvɪlaɪˈzeɪʃn/ *n* civiltà *f inv*. ~**e** /'sɪvɪlaɪz/ *vt* civilizzare

civil: ~ '**servant** *n* impiegato, -a *mf* statale. **C**~ '**Service** *n* pubblica amministrazione *f*

clad /klæd/ *a* vestito (**in** di)

claim /kleɪm/ *n* richiesta *f*; (*right*) diritto *m*; (*assertion*) dichiarazione *f*; **lay** ~ **to sth** rivendicare qcsa ● *vt* richiedere; reclamare ‹*lost property*›; rivendicare ‹*ownership*›; ~ **that** sostenere che. ~**ant** *n* richiedente *mf*

clairvoyant /kleəˈvɔɪənt/ *n* chiaroveggente *mf*

clam /klæm/ *n* Culin vongola *f* ● **clam up** *vi* (*pt/pp* **clammed**) zittirsi

clamber /'klæmbə(r)/ *vi* arrampicarsi

clammy /'klæmɪ/ *a* (**-ier, -iest**) appiccicaticcio

clamour /'klæmə(r)/ *n* (*protest*) rimostranza *f* ● *vi* ~ **for** chiedere a gran voce

clamp /klæmp/ *n* morsa *f* ● *vt*

ammorsare; *Auto* mettere i ceppi bloccaruote a. **clamp down** *vi fam* essere duro; ~ **down on** reprimere

clan /klæn/ *n* clan *m inv*

clandestine /klænˈdestɪn/ *a* clandestino

clang /klæŋ/ *n* suono *m* metallico. ~**er** *n fam* gaffe *f inv*

clank /klæŋk/ *n* rumore *m* metallico

clap /klæp/ *n* **give sb a** ~ applaudire qcno; ~ **of thunder** tuono *m* ● *vt/i* (*pt/pp* **clapped**) applaudire; ~ **one's hands** applaudire. ~**ping** *n* applausi *mpl*

clari|fication /klærɪfɪ'keɪʃn/ *n* chiarimento *m*. ~**fy** /'klærɪfaɪ/ *vt/i* (*pt/pp* **-ied**) chiarire

clarinet /klærɪ'net/ *n* clarinetto *m*

clarity /'klærətɪ/ *n* chiarezza *f*

clash /klæʃ/ *n* scontro *m*; (*noise*) fragore *m* ● *vi* scontrarsi; ‹*colours:*› stonare; ‹*events:*› coincidere

clasp /klɑːsp/ *n* chiusura *f* ● *vt* agganciare; (*hold*) stringere

class /klɑːs/ *n* classe *f*; (*lesson*) corso *m* ● *vt* classificare

classic /'klæsɪk/ *a* classico ● *n* classico *m*; ~**s** *pl Univ* lettere *fpl* classiche. ~**al** *a* classico

classi|fication /klæsɪfɪ'keɪʃn/ *n* classificazione *f*. ~**fy** /'klæsɪfaɪ/ *vt* (*pt/pp* **-ied**) classificare

classroom *n* aula *f*

classy /'klɑːsɪ/ *a* (**-ier, -iest**) *fam* d'alta classe

clatter /'klætə(r)/ *n* fracasso *m* ● *vi* far fracasso

clause /klɔːz/ *n* clausola *f*; *Gram* proposizione *f*

claustrophob|ia /klɔːstrəˈfəʊbɪə/ *n* claustrofobia *f*

claw /klɔː/ *n* artiglio *m*; (*of crab, lobster & Techn*) tenaglia *f* ● *vt* ‹*cat:*› graffiare

clay /kleɪ/ *n* argilla *f*

clean /kliːn/ *a* pulito, lindo ● *adv* completamente ● *vt* pulire ‹*shoes, windows*›; ~ **one's teeth** lavarsi i denti; **have a coat** ~**ed** portare un cappotto in lavanderia. **clean up** *vt* pulire ● *vi* far pulizia

cleaner /'kliːnə(r)/ *n* uomo *m*/donna *f* delle pulizie; (*substance*) detersivo *m*; [**dry**] ~'**s** lavanderia *f*, tintoria *f*

cleanliness /'klenlɪnɪs/ *n* pulizia *f*

cleanse /klenz/ *vt* pulire. ~**r** *n* detergente *m*

clean-shaven *a* sbarbato

cleansing cream /'klenz-/ n latte m detergente

clear /klɪə(r)/ a chiaro; ⟨conscience⟩ pulito; ⟨road⟩ libero; ⟨profit, advantage, majority⟩ netto; ⟨sky⟩ sereno; ⟨water⟩ limpido; ⟨glass⟩ trasparente; **make sth ~** mettere qcsa in chiaro; **have I made myself ~?** mi sono fatto capire?; **five ~ days** cinque giorni buoni ● adv **stand ~ of** allontanarsi da; **keep ~ of** tenersi alla larga da ● vt sgombrare ⟨room, street⟩; sparecchiare ⟨table⟩; ⟨acquit⟩ scagionare; ⟨authorize⟩ autorizzare; scavalcare senza toccare ⟨fence, wall⟩; guadagnare ⟨sum of money⟩; passare ⟨Customs⟩; **~ one's throat** schiarirsi la gola ● vi ⟨face, sky:⟩ rasserenarsi; ⟨fog:⟩ dissiparsi. **clear away** vt metter via. **clear off** vi fam filar via. **clear out** ● vt sgombrare ● vi fam filar via. **clear up** vt ⟨tidy⟩ mettere a posto; chiarire ⟨mystery⟩ ● vi ⟨weather:⟩ schiarirsi

clearance /'klɪərəns/ n ⟨space⟩ spazio m libero; ⟨authorization⟩ autorizzazione f; ⟨Customs⟩ sdoganamento m. **~ sale** n liquidazione f

clear|ing /'klɪərɪŋ/ n radura f. **~ly** adv chiaramente. **~ way** n Auto strada f con divieto di sosta

cleavage /'kli:vɪdʒ/ n ⟨woman's⟩ décolleté m inv

cleft /kleft/ n fenditura f

clench /klentʃ/ vt serrare

clergy /'klɜ:dʒɪ/ npl clero m. **~man** n ecclesiastico m

cleric /'klerɪk/ n ecclesiastico m. **~al** a impiegatizio; Relig clericale

clerk /klɑ:k/, Am /klɜ:k/ n impiegato, -a mf; (Am: shop assistant) commesso, -a mf

clever /'klevə(r)/ a intelligente; ⟨skilful⟩ abile

cliché /'kli:ʃeɪ/ n cliché m inv

click /klɪk/ vi scattare ● n Comput click m. **click on** vt Comput cliccare su

client /'klaɪənt/ n cliente mf

clientele /kli:ɒn'tel/ n clientela f

cliff /klɪf/ n scogliera f

climat|e /'klaɪmət/ n clima f. **~ic** /-'mætɪk/ a climatico

climax /'klaɪmæks/ n punto m culminante

climb /klaɪm/ n salita f ● vt scalare ⟨mountain⟩; arrampicarsi su ⟨ladder, tree⟩ ● vi arrampicarsi; ⟨rise⟩ salire; ⟨road:⟩ salire. **climb down** vi scendere; ⟨from ladder, tree⟩ scendere; fig tornare sui propri passi

climber /'klaɪmə(r)/ n alpinista mf; ⟨plant⟩ rampicante m

clinch /klɪntʃ/ vt fam concludere ⟨deal⟩ ● n ⟨in boxing⟩ clinch m inv

cling /klɪŋ/ vi ⟨pt/pp **clung**⟩ aggrapparsi; ⟨stick⟩ aderire. **~ film** n pellicola f trasparente

clinic /'klɪnɪk/ n ambulatorio m. **~al** a clinico

clink /klɪŋk/ n tintinnio m; ⟨fam: prison⟩ galera f ● vi tintinnare

clip[1] /klɪp/ n fermaglio m; ⟨jewellery⟩ spilla f ● vt ⟨pt/pp **clipped**⟩ attaccare

clip[2] n ⟨extract⟩ taglio m ● vt obliterare ⟨ticket⟩. **~board** n fermabloc m inv. **~pers** npl ⟨for hair⟩ rasoio m; ⟨for hedge⟩ tosasiepi m inv; ⟨for nails⟩ tronchesina f. **~ping** n ⟨from newspaper⟩ ritaglio m

clique /kli:k/ n cricca f

cloak /kləʊk/ n mantello m. **~room** n guardaroba m inv; ⟨toilet⟩ bagno m

clock /klɒk/ n orologio m; ⟨fam: speedometer⟩ tachimetro m ● **clock in** vi attaccare. **clock out** vi staccare

clock: ~ tower n torre f dell'orologio. **~wise** a & adv in senso orario. **~work** n meccanismo m

clod /klɒd/ n zolla f

clog /klɒg/ n zoccolo m ● vt ⟨pt/pp **clogged**⟩ ~ [up] intasare ⟨drain⟩; inceppare ⟨mechanism⟩ ● vi ⟨drain:⟩ intasarsi

cloister /'klɔɪstə(r)/ n chiostro m

clone /kləʊn/ n clone m

close[1] /kləʊs/ a vicino; ⟨friend⟩ intimo; ⟨weather⟩ afoso; **have a ~ shave** fam scamparla bella; **be ~ to sb** essere unito a qcno ● adv vicino; **~ by** vicino; **it's ~ on five o'clock** sono quasi le cinque

close[2] /kləʊz/ n fine f ● vt chiudere ● vi chiudersi; ⟨shop:⟩ chiudere. **close down** vt chiudere ● vi ⟨TV station:⟩ interrompere la trasmissione; ⟨factory:⟩ chiudere

closely /'kləʊslɪ/ adv da vicino; ⟨watch, listen⟩ attentamente

closet /'klɒzɪt/ n Am armadio m

close-up /'kləʊs-/ n primo piano m

closure /'kləʊʒə(r)/ n chiusura f

clot /klɒt/ n grumo m; ⟨fam: idiot⟩ tonto, -a mf ● vi ⟨pt/pp **clotted**⟩ ⟨blood:⟩ coagularsi

cloth /klɒθ/ n ⟨fabric⟩ tessuto m; ⟨duster etc⟩ straccio m

clothe /kləʊð/ vt vestire

clothes /kləʊðz/ npl vestiti mpl, abiti

mpl. **~-brush** *n* spazzola *f* per abiti.
~-line *n* corda *f* stendibiancheria

clothing /'kləʊðɪŋ/ *n* abbigliamento *m*

cloud /klaʊd/ *n* nuvola *f* ● **cloud over**
vi rannuvolarsi. **~burst** *n* acquazzone *m*

cloudy /'klaʊdɪ/ *a* (**-ier, -iest**) nuvoloso; ⟨*liquid*⟩ torbido

clout /klaʊt/ *n fam* colpo *m*; (*influence*)
impatto *m* (**with** su) ● *vt fam* colpire

clove /kləʊv/ *n* chiodo *m* di garofano; ~
of garlic spicchio *m* d'aglio

clover /'kləʊvə(r)/ *n* trifoglio *m*

clown /klaʊn/ *n* pagliaccio *m* ● *vi* ~
[**about**] fare il pagliaccio

club /klʌb/ *n* club *m inv*; (*weapon*) clava
f; *Sport* mazza *f*; ~**s** *pl* (*Cards*) fiori *mpl*
● *v* (*pt/pp* **clubbed**) ● *vt* bastonare.
club together *vi* unirsi

cluck /klʌk/ *vi* chiocciare

clue /kluː/ *n* indizio *m*; (*in crossword*)
definizione *f*; **I haven't a** ~ *fam* non ne
ho idea

clump /klʌmp/ *n* gruppo *m*

clumsiness /'klʌmzɪnɪs/ *n* goffaggine *f*

clumsy /'klʌmzɪ/ *a* (**-ier, -iest**) maldestro; ⟨*tool*⟩ scomodo; ⟨*remark*⟩ senza tatto

clung /klʌŋ/ *see* **cling**

cluster /'klʌstə(r)/ *n* gruppo *m* ● *vi*
raggrupparsi (**round** intorno a)

clutch /klʌtʃ/ *n* stretta *f*; *Auto* frizione
f; **be in sb's ~s** essere in balia di qcno
● *vt* stringere; (*grab*) afferrare ● *vi* ~
at afferrare

clutter /'klʌtə(r)/ *n* caos *m* ● *vt* ~ [**up**]
ingombrare

c/o *abbr* (**care of**) c/o, presso

coach /kəʊtʃ/ *n* pullman *m inv*; *Rail*
vagone *m*; (*horse-drawn*) carrozza *f*;
Sport allenatore, -trice *mf* ● *vt* fare esercitare; *Sport* allenare

coagulate /kəʊˈægjʊleɪt/ *vi* coagularsi

coal /kəʊl/ *n* carbone *m*

coalition /kəʊəˈlɪʃn/ *n* coalizione *f*

'coal-mine *n* miniera *f* di carbone

coarse /kɔːs/ *a* grossolano; ⟨*joke*⟩ spinto

coast /kəʊst/ *n* costa *f* ● *vi* (*freewheel*)
scendere a ruota libera; *Auto* scendere
in folle. **~al** *a* costiero. **~er** *n* (*mat*)
sottobicchiere *m inv*

coast: ~guard *n* guardia *f* costiera.
~line *n* litorale *m*

coat /kəʊt/ *n* cappotto *m*; ⟨*of animal*⟩
manto *m*; (*of paint*) mano *f*; ~ **of arms**
stemma *f* ● *vt* coprire; (*with paint*) ricoprire. **~-hanger** *n* gruccia *f*. **~-hook** *n*
gancio *m* [appendiabiti]

coating /'kəʊtɪŋ/ *n* rivestimento *m*; (*of
paint*) stato *m*

coax /kəʊks/ *vt* convincere con le moine

cob /kɒb/ *n* (*of corn*) pannocchia *f*

cobble /'kɒbl/ *vt* ~ **together** raffazzonare. **~r** *n* ciabattino *m*

'cobblestones *npl* ciottolato *msg*

cobweb /'kɒb-/ *n* ragnatela *f*

cocaine /kəˈkeɪn/ *n* cocaina *f*

cock /kɒk/ *n* gallo *m*; (*any male bird*)
maschio *m* ● *vt* sollevare il grilletto di
⟨*gun*⟩; ~ **its ears** ⟨*animal:*⟩ drizzare le
orecchie

cockerel /'kɒkərəl/ *n* galletto *m*

cock-'eyed *a fam* storto; (*absurd*) assurdo

cockle /'kɒkl/ *n* cardio *m*

cockney /'kɒknɪ/ *n* (*dialect*) dialetto *m*
londinese; (*person*) abitante *mf* dell'est
di Londra

cock: ~pit *n Aeron* cabina *f*. **~roach**
/-rəʊtʃ/ *n* scarafaggio *m*. **~tail** *n* cocktail *m inv*. **~-up** *n sl* **make a ~-up** fare
un casino (**of** con)

cocky /'kɒkɪ/ *a* (**-ier, -iest**) *fam* presuntuoso

cocoa /'kəʊkəʊ/ *n* cacao *m*

coconut /'kəʊkənʌt/ *n* noce *f* di cocco

cocoon /kəˈkuːn/ *n* bozzolo *m*

cod /kɒd/ *n inv* merluzzo *m*

COD *abbr* (**cash on delivery**) pagamento *m* alla consegna

code /kəʊd/ *n* codice *m*. **~d** *a* codificato

coedu'cational /kəʊ-/ *a* misto

coerc|e /kəʊˈɜːs/ *vt* costringere. **~ion**
/-ˈɜːʃn/ *n* coercizione *f*

coe'xist *vi* coesistere. **~ence** *n*
coesistenza *f*

coffee /'kɒfɪ/ *n* caffè *m inv*

coffee: ~-grinder *n* macinacaffè *m
inv*. **~-pot** *n* caffettiera *f*. **~-table** *n* tavolino *m*

coffin /'kɒfɪn/ *n* bara *f*

cog /kɒg/ *n Techn* dente *m* (*di ruota*)

cogent /'kəʊdʒənt/ *a* convincente

cog-wheel *n* ruota *f* dentata

cohabit /kəʊˈhæbɪt/ *vi Jur* convivere

coherent /kəʊˈhɪərənt/ *a* coerente;
(*when speaking*) logico

coil /kɔɪl/ *n* rotolo *m*; *Electr* bobina *f*;
~**s** *pl* spire *fpl* ● *vt* ~ [**up**] avvolgere

coin /kɔɪn/ *n* moneta *f* ● *vt* coniare
⟨*word*⟩

coincide /kəʊɪnˈsaɪd/ *vi* coincidere

coinciden|ce /kəʊˈɪnsɪdəns/ n coincidenza f. **~tal** /-ˈdentl/ a casuale. **~tally** adv casualmente

coke /kəʊk/ n [carbone m] coke m

Coke® n Coca[-cola]® f

cold /kəʊld/ a freddo; **I'm ~** ho freddo ● n freddo m; Med raffreddore m

cold: **~-ˈblooded** a spietato. **~-ˈhearted** a insensibile. **~ly** adv fig freddamente. **~ meat** n salumi mpl. **~ness** n freddezza f

coleslaw /ˈkəʊlslɔː/ n insalata f di cavolo crudo, cipolle e carote in maionese

colic /ˈkɒlɪk/ n colica f

collaborat|e /kəˈlæbəreɪt/ vi collaborare; **~e on sth** collaborare in qcsa. **~ion** /-ˈreɪʃn/ n collaborazione f; (with enemy) collaborazionismo m. **~or** n collaboratore, -trice mf; (with enemy) collaborazionista mf

collaps|e /kəˈlæps/ n crollo m ● vi ⟨person:⟩ svenire; ⟨roof, building:⟩ crollare. **~ible** a pieghevole

collar /ˈkɒlə(r)/ n colletto m; (for animal) collare m. **~-bone** n clavicola f

colleague /ˈkɒliːg/ n collega mf

collect /kəˈlekt/ vt andare a prendere ⟨person⟩; ritirare ⟨parcel, tickets⟩; riscuotere ⟨taxes⟩; raccogliere ⟨rubbish⟩; (as hobby) collezionare ● vi riunirsi ● adv **call ~** Am telefonare a carico del destinatario. **~ed** /-ɪd/ a controllato

collection /kəˈlekʃn/ n collezione f; (in church) questua f; (of rubbish) raccolta f; (of post) levata f

collective /kəˈlektɪv/ a collettivo

collector /kəˈlektə(r)/ n (of stamps etc) collezionista mf

college /ˈkɒlɪdʒ/ n istituto m parauniversitario; **C~ of...** Scuola f di...

collide /kəˈlaɪd/ vi scontrarsi

colliery /ˈkɒlɪərɪ/ n miniera f di carbone

collision /kəˈlɪʒn/ n scontro m

colloquial /kəˈləʊkwɪəl/ a colloquiale. **~ism** n espressione f colloquiale

cologne /kəˈləʊn/ n colonia f

colon /ˈkəʊlən/ n due punti mpl; Anat colon m inv

colonel /ˈkɜːnl/ n colonnello m

colonial /kəˈləʊnɪəl/ a coloniale

colon|ize /ˈkɒlənaɪz/ vt colonizzare. **~y** n colonia f

colossal /kəˈlɒsl/ a colossale

colour /ˈkʌlə(r)/ n colore m; (complexion) colorito m; **~s** pl (flag) bandiera fsg; **off ~** fam giù di tono ● vt

colorare; **~ [in]** colorare ● vi (blush) arrossire

colour: **~ bar** n discriminazione f razziale. **~-blind** a daltonico. **~ed** a colorato; ⟨person⟩ di colore ● n ⟨person⟩ persona f di colore. **~-fast** a dai colori resistenti. **~ film** n film m inv a colori. **~ful** a pieno di colore. **~less** a incolore. **~ television** n televisione f a colori

colt /kəʊlt/ n puledro m

column /ˈkɒləm/ n colonna ·f. **~ist** /-nɪst/ n giornalista mf che cura una rubrica

coma /ˈkəʊmə/ n coma m inv

comb /kəʊm/ n pettine m; (for wearing) pettinino m ● vt pettinare; (fig: search) setacciare; **~ one's hair** pettinarsi i capelli

combat /ˈkɒmbæt/ n combattimento m ● vt (pt/pp combated) combattere

combination /kɒmbɪˈneɪʃn/ n combinazione f

combine¹ /kəmˈbaɪn/ vt unire; **~ a job with being a mother** conciliare il lavoro con il ruolo di madre ● vi ⟨chemical elements:⟩ combinarsi

combine² /ˈkɒmbaɪn/ n Comm associazione f. **~ [harvester]** n mietitrebbia f

combustion /kəmˈbʌstʃn/ n combustione f

come /kʌm/ vi (pt came, pp come) venire; **where do you ~ from?** da dove vieni?; **~ to** (reach) arrivare a; **that ~s to £10** fanno 10 sterline; **~ into money** ricevere dei soldi; **~ true/open** verificarsi/aprirsi; **~ first** arrivare primo; fig venire prima di tutto; **~ in two sizes** esistere in due misure; **the years to ~** gli anni a venire; **how ~?** fam come mai? **come about** vi succedere. **come across** vi **~ across as being** fam dare l'impressione di essere ● vt (find) imbattersi in. **come along** vi venire; ⟨job, opportunity:⟩ presentarsi; (progress) andare bene. **come apart** vi smontarsi; (break) rompersi. **come away** vi venir via; ⟨button, fastener:⟩ staccarsi. **come back** vi ritornare. **come by** vi passare ● vt (obtain) avere. **come down** vi scendere; **~ down to** (reach) arrivare a. **come in** vi entrare; (in race) arrivare; ⟨tide:⟩ salire. **come in for** vt **~ in for criticism** essere criticato. **come off** vi staccarsi; (take place) esserci; (succeed) riuscire. **come on** vi (make progress) migliorare; **~ on!** (hurry) dai!; (indicating disbelief) ma va là!. **come out** vi venir fuori; ⟨book, *sun:*) uscire; (*stain:*) andar via. **come over** *vi* venire. **come round** *vi* venire; (*after fainting*) riaversi; (*change one's mind*) farsi convincere. **come to** *vi* (*after fainting*) riaversi. **come up** *vi* salire; (*sun:*) sorgere; (*plant:*) crescere; **something came up** (*I was prevented*) ho avuto un imprevisto. **come up with** *vt* tirar fuori

'**come-back** *n* ritorno *m*

comedian /kə'mi:dɪən/ *n* comico *m*

'**come-down** *n* passo *m* indietro

comedy /'kɒmədɪ/ *n* commedia *f*

comet /'kɒmɪt/ *n* cometa *f*

come-uppance /kʌm'ʌpəns/ *n* **get one's ~** *fam* avere quel che si merita

comfort /'kʌmfət/ *n* benessere *m*; (*consolation*) conforto *m* ● *vt* confortare

comfortabl|e /'kʌmfətəbl/ *a* comodo; **be ~e** (*person:*) stare comodo; (*fig: in situation*) essere a proprio agio; (*financially*) star bene. **~y** *adv* comodamente

'**comfort station** *n Am* bagno *m* pubblico

comfy /'kʌmfɪ/ *a fam* comodo

comic /'kɒmɪk/ *a* comico ● *n* comico, -a *mf*; (*periodical*) fumetto *m*. **~al** *a* comico. **~ strip** *n* striscia *f* di fumetti

coming /'kʌmɪŋ/ *n* venuta *f*; **~s and goings** viavai *m*

comma /'kɒmə/ *n* virgola *f*

command /kə'mɑ:nd/ *n* comando *m*; (*order*) ordine *m*; (*mastery*) padronanza *f* ● *vt* ordinare; comandare (*army*)

commandeer /kɒmən'dɪə(r)/ *vt* requisire

command|er /kə'mɑ:ndə(r)/ *n* comandante *m*. **~ing** a (*view*) imponente; (*lead*) dominante. **~ing officer** *n* comandante *m*. **~ment** *n* comandamento *m*

commemorat|e /kə'meməreɪt/ *vt* commemorare. **~ion** /-'reɪʃn/ *n* commemorazione *f*. **~ive** /-ətɪv/ *a* commemorativo

commence /kə'mens/ *vt/i* cominciare. **~ment** *n* inizio *m*

commend /kə'mend/ *vt* complimentarsi con (**on** per); (*recommend*) raccomandare (**to** a). **~able** /-əbl/ *a* lodevole

commensurate /kə'menʃərət/ *a* proporzionato (**with** a)

comment /'kɒment/ *n* commento *m* ● *vi* fare commenti (**on** su)

commentary /'kɒməntrɪ/ *n* commento *m*; **[running]** ~ (*on radio, TV*) cronaca *f* diretta

commentat|e /'kɒmənteɪt/ *vt* **~e on** *TV, Radio* fare la cronaca di. **~or** *n* cronista *mf*

commerce /'kɒmɜ:s/ *n* commercio *m*

commercial /kə'mɜ:ʃl/ *a* commerciale ● *n TV* pubblicità *f inv*. **~ize** *vt* commercializzare

commiserate /kə'mɪzəreɪt/ *vi* esprimere il proprio rincrescimento (**with** a)

commission /kə'mɪʃn/ *n* commissione *f*; **receive one's ~** *Mil* essere promosso ufficiale; **out of ~** fuori uso ● *vt* commissionare

commissionaire /kəmɪʃə'neə(r)/ *n* portiere *m*

commissioner /kə'mɪʃənə(r)/ *n* commissario *m*

commit /kə'mɪt/ *vt* (*pt/pp* **committed**) commettere; (*to prison, hospital*) affidare (**to** a); impegnare (*funds*); **~ oneself** impegnarsi. **~ment** *n* impegno *m*; (*involvement*) compromissione *f*. **~ted** *a* impegnato

committee /kə'mɪtɪ/ *n* comitato *m*

commodity /kə'mɒdətɪ/ *n* prodotto *m*

common /'kɒmən/ *a* comune; (*vulgar*) volgare ● *n* prato *m* pubblico; **have in ~** avere in comune; **House of C~s** Camera *f* dei Comuni. **~er** *n* persona *f* non nobile

common: ~'law *n* diritto *m* consuetudinario. **~ly** *adv* comunemente. **C~ 'Market** *n* Mercato *m* Comune. **~place** *a* banale. **~-room** *n* sala *f* dei professori/degli studenti. **~ 'sense** *n* buon senso *m*

commotion /kə'məʊʃn/ *n* confusione *f*

communal /'kɒmjʊnl/ *a* comune

communicate /kə'mju:nɪkeɪt/ *vt/i* comunicare

communication /kəmju:nɪ'keɪʃn/ *n* comunicazione *f*; (*of disease*) trasmissione *f*; **be in ~ with sb** essere in contatto con qcno; **~s** *pl* (*technology*) telecomunicazioni *fpl*. **~ cord** *n* fermata *f* d'emergenza

communicative /kə'mju:nɪkətɪv/ *a* comunicativo

Communion /kə'mju:nɪən/ *n* **[Holy] ~** comunione *f*

communiqué /kə'mju:nɪkeɪ/ *n* comunicato *m* stampa

Communis|m /'kɒmjʊnɪzm/ *n* comunismo *m*. **~t** /-ɪst/ *a* & *n* comunista *mf*

community /kə'mju:nətɪ/ *n* comunità *f*. **~ centre** *n* centro *m* sociale

commute /kə'mju:t/ *vi* fare il pendolare ● *vt Jur* commutare. **~r** *n* pendolare *mf*

compact¹ /kəm'pækt/ a compatto

compact² /'kɒmpækt/ n portacipria m inv. ~ **disc** n compact disc m inv

companion /kəm'pænjən/ n compagno, -a mf. ~**ship** n compagnia f

company /'kʌmpəni/ n compagnia f; (guests) ospiti mpl. ~ **car** n macchina f della ditta

comparable /'kɒmpərəbl/ a paragonabile

comparative /kəm'pærətɪv/ a comparativo; (relative) relativo ● n Gram comparativo m. ~**ly** adv relativamente

compare /kəm'peə(r)/ vt paragonare (**with/to** a) ● vi essere paragonato

comparison /kəm'pærɪsn/ n paragone m

compartment /kəm'pɑ:tmənt/ n compartimento m; Rail scompartimento m

compass /'kʌmpəs/ n bussola f. ~**es** npl, **pair of** ~**es** compasso msg

compassion /kəm'pæʃn/ n compassione f. ~**ate** /-ʃənət/ a compassionevole

compatible /kəm'pætəbl/ a compatibile

compatriot /kəm'pætrɪət/ n compatriota mf

compel /kəm'pel/ vt (pt/pp **compelled**) costringere. ~**ling** a (reason) inconfutabile

compensat|e /'kɒmpənseɪt/ vt risarcire ● vi ~**e for** fig compensare di. ~**ion** /-'seɪʃn/ n risarcimento m; (fig: comfort) consolazione f

compère /'kɒmpeə(r)/ n presentatore, -trice mf

compete /kəm'pi:t/ vi competere; (take part) gareggiare

competen|ce /'kɒmpɪtəns/ n competenza f. ~**t** a competente

competition /kɒmpə'tɪʃn/ n concorrenza f; (contest) gara f

competitive /kəm'petɪtɪv/ a competitivo; ~ **prices** prezzi mpl concorrenziali

competitor /kəm'petɪtə(r)/ n concorrente mf

complacen|cy /kəm'pleɪsənsɪ/ n compiacimento m. ~**t** a compiaciuto

complain /kəm'pleɪn/ vi lamentarsi (**about** di); (formally) reclamare; ~ **of** Med accusare. ~**t** n lamentela f; (formal) reclamo m; Med disturbo m

complement¹ /'kɒmplɪmənt/ n complemento m

complement² /'kɒmplɪment/ vt complementare; ~ **each other** complementarsi a vicenda. ~**ary** /-'mentərɪ/ a complementare

complete /kəm'pli:t/ a completo; (utter) finito ● vt completare; compilare (form). ~**ly** adv completamente

completion /kəm'pli:ʃn/ n fine f

complex /'kɒmpleks/ a complesso ● n complesso m

complexion /kəm'plekʃn/ n carnagione f

complexity /kəm'pleksətɪ/ n complessità f inv

compliance /kəm'plaɪəns/ n accettazione f; (with rules) osservanza f; **in** ~ **with** in osservanza a (law); conformemente a (request)

complicat|e /'kɒmplɪkeɪt/ vt complicare. ~**ed** a complicato. ~**ion** /-'keɪʃn/ n complicazione f

compliment /'kɒmplɪmənt/ n complimento m; ~**s** pl omaggi mpl ● vt complimentare. ~**ary** /-'mentərɪ/ a complimentoso; (given free) in omaggio

comply /kəm'plaɪ/ vi (pt/pp -**ied**) ~ **with** conformarsi a

component /kəm'pəʊnənt/ a & n ~ [**part**] componente m

compose /kəm'pəʊz/ vt comporre; ~ **oneself** ricomporsi; **be** ~**d of** essere composto da. ~**d** a (calm) composto. ~**r** n compositore, -trice mf

composition /kɒmpə'zɪʃn/ n composizione f; (essay) tema m

compost /'kɒmpɒst/ n composta f

composure /kəm'pəʊʒə(r)/ n calma f

compound /'kɒmpaʊnd/ a composto. ~ **fracture** n frattura f esposta. ~ '**interest** n interesse m composto ● n Chem composto m; Gram parola f composta; (enclosure) recinto m

comprehen|d /kɒmprɪ'hend/ vt comprendere. ~**sible** /-'hensəbl/ a comprensibile. ~**sion** /-'henʃn/ n comprensione f

comprehensive /kɒmprɪ'hensɪv/ a & n comprensivo; ~. [**school**] scuola f media in cui gli allievi hanno capacità d'apprendimento diverse. ~ **insurance** n Auto polizza f casco

compress¹ /'kɒmpres/ n compressa f

compress² /kəm'pres/ vt comprimere; ~**ed air** aria f compressa

comprise /kəm'praɪz/ vt comprendere; (form) costituire

compromise /'kɒmprəmaɪz/ n compromesso m ● vt compromettere ● vi fare un compromesso

compuls|ion /kəm'pʌlʃn/ *n* desiderio *m* irresistibile. **~ive** /-sɪv/ *a Psych* patologico. **~ive eating** voglia *f* ossessiva di mangiare. **~ory** /-sərɪ/ *a* obbligatorio

comput|er /kəm'pju:tə(r)/ *n* computer *m inv.* **~erize** *vt* computerizzare. **~ing** *n* informatica *f*

comrade /'kɒmreɪd/ *n* camerata *m*; *Pol* compagno, -a *mf*. **~ship** *n* cameratismo *m*

con[1] /kɒn/ *see* pro

con[2] *n fam* fregatura *f* ● *vt* (*pt/pp* **conned**) *fam* fregare

concave /'kɒnkeɪv/ *a* concavo

conceal /kən'si:l/ *vt* nascondere

concede /kən'si:d/ *vt* (*admit*) ammettere; (*give up*) rinunciare a; lasciar fare ⟨*goal*⟩

conceit /kən'si:t/ *n* presunzione *f*. **~ed** *a* presuntuoso

conceivable /kən'si:vəbl/ *a* concepibile

conceive /kən'si:v/ *vt Biol* concepire ● *vi* aver figli. **conceive of** *vt fig* concepire

concentrat|e /'kɒnsəntreɪt/ *vt* concentrare ● *vi* concentrarsi. **~ion** /-'treɪʃn/ *n* concentrazione *f*. **~ion camp** *n* campo *m* di concentramento

concept /'kɒnsept/ *n* concetto *m*. **~ion** /kən'sepʃn/ *n* concezione *f*; (*idea*) idea *f*

concern /kən'sɜ:n/ *n* preoccupazione *f*; *Comm* attività *f inv* ● *vt* (*be about, affect*) riguardare; (*worry*) preoccupare; **be ~ed about** essere preoccupato per; **~ oneself with** preoccuparsi di; **as far as I am ~ed** per quanto mi riguarda. **~ing** *prep* riguardo a

concert /'kɒnsət/ *n* concerto *m*. **~ed** /kən'sɜ:tɪd/ *a* collettivo

concertina /kɒnsə'ti:nə/ *n* piccola fisarmonica *f*

'concertmaster *n Am* primo violino *m*

concerto /kən'tʃeətəʊ/ *n* concerto *m*

concession /kən'seʃn/ *n* concessione *f*; (*reduction*) sconto *m*. **~ary** *a* (*reduced*) scontato

conciliation /kənsɪlɪ'eɪʃn/ *n* conciliazione *f*

concise /kən'saɪs/ *a* conciso

conclu|de /kən'klu:d/ *vt* concludere ● *vi* concludersi. **~ding** *a* finale

conclusion /kən'klu:ʒn/ *n* conclusione *f*; **in ~** per concludere

conclusive /kən'klu:sɪv/ *a* definitivo. **~ly** *adv* in modo definitivo

concoct /kən'kɒkt/ *vt* confezionare; *fig* inventare. **~ion** /-ɒkʃn/ *n* mistura *f*; (*drink*) intruglio *m*

concourse /'kɒŋkɔ:s/ *n* atrio *m*

concrete /'kɒŋkri:t/ *a* concreto ● *n* calcestruzzo *m*

concur /kən'kɜ:(r)/ *vi* (*pt/pp* **concurred**) essere d'accordo

concurrently /kən'kʌrəntlɪ/ *adv* contemporaneamente

concussion /kən'kʌʃn/ *n* commozione *f* cerebrale

condemn /kən'dem/ *vt* condannare; dichiarare inagibile ⟨*building*⟩. **~ation** /kɒndem'neɪʃn/ *n* condanna *f*

condensation /kɒnden'seɪʃn/ *n* condensazione *f*

condense /kən'dens/ *vt* condensare; *Phys* condensare ● *vi* condensarsi. **~d milk** *n* latte *m* condensato

condescend /kɒndɪ'send/ *vi* degnarsi. **~ing** *a* condiscendente

condition /kən'dɪʃn/ *n* condizione *f*; **on ~ that** a condizione che ● *vt Psych* condizionare; *a* ⟨*acceptance*⟩ condizionato; *Gram* condizionale ● *n Gram* condizionale *m*. **~er** *n* balsamo *m*; (*for fabrics*) ammorbidente *m*

condolences /kən'dəʊlənsɪz/ *npl* condoglianze *fpl*

condom /'kɒndəm/ *n* preservativo *m*

condo[minium] /'kɒndə('mɪnɪəm)/ *n Am* condominio *m*

condone /kən'dəʊn/ *vt* passare sopra a

conducive /kən'dju:sɪv/ *a* **be ~ to** contribuire a

conduct[1] /'kɒndʌkt/ *n* condotta *f*

conduct[2] /kən'dʌkt/ *vt* condurre; dirigere ⟨*orchestra*⟩. **~or** *n* direttore *m* d'orchestra; (*of bus*) bigliettaio *m*; *Phys* conduttore *m*. **~ress** *n* bigliettaia *f*

cone /kəʊn/ *n* cono *m*; *Bot* pigna *f*; *Auto* birillo *m* ● **cone off** *vt* **be ~d off** *Auto* essere chiuso da birilli

confectioner /kən'fekʃənə(r)/ *n* pasticciere, -a *mf*. **~y** *n* pasticceria *f*

confederation /kənfedə'reɪʃn/ *n* federazione *f*

confer /kən'fɜ:(r)/ *v* (*pt/pp* **conferred**) ● *vt* conferire (**on** a) ● *vi* (*discuss*) conferire

conference /'kɒnfərəns/ *n* conferenza *f*

confess /kən'fes/ *vt* confessare ● *vi* confessare; *Relig* confessarsi. **~ion** /-eʃn/ *n* confessione *f*. **~ional** /-eʃənəl/ *n* confessionale *m*. **~or** *n* confessore *m*

confetti /kən'fetɪ/ *n* coriandoli *mpl*

confide /kən'faɪd/ *vt* confidare. **confide in** *vt* ~ **in sb** fidarsi di qcno

confidence /'kɒnfɪdəns/ *n* (*trust*) fiducia *f*; (*self-assurance*) sicurezza *f* di sé; (*secret*) confidenza *f*; **in** ~ in confidenza. ~ **trick** *n* truffa *f*

confident /'kɒnfɪdənt/ *a* fiducioso; (*self-assured*) sicuro di sé. ~**ly** *adv* con aria fiduciosa

confidential /kɒnfɪ'denʃl/ *a* confidenziale

confine /kən'faɪn/ *vt* rinchiudere; (*limit*) limitare; **be** ~**d to bed** essere confinato a letto. ~**d** *a* (*space*) limitato. ~**ment** *n* detenzione *f*; *Med* parto *m*

confines /'kɒnfaɪnz/ *npl* confini *mpl*

confirm /kən'fɜːm/ *vt* confermare; *Relig* cresimare. ~**ation** /kɒnfə'meɪʃn/ *n* conferma *f*; *Relig* cresima *f*. ~**ed** *a* incallito; ~**ed bachelor** scapolo *m* impenitente

confiscat|e /'kɒnfɪskeɪt/ *vt* confiscare. ~**ion** /-'keɪʃn/ *n* confisca *f*

conflict[1] /'kɒnflɪkt/ *n* conflitto *m*

conflict[2] /kən'flɪkt/ *vi* essere in contraddizione. ~**ing** *a* contraddittorio

conform /kən'fɔːm/ *vi* (*person:*) conformarsi; (*thing:*) essere conforme (**to** a). ~**ist** *n* conformista *mf*

confounded /kən'faʊndɪd/ *a fam* maledetto

confront /kən'frʌnt/ *vt* affrontare; **the problems** ~**ing us** i problemi che dobbiamo affrontare. ~**ation** /kɒnfrʌn'teɪʃn/ *n* confronto *m*

confus|e /kən'fjuːz/ *vt* confondere. ~**ing** *a* che confonde. ~**ion** /-juːʒn/ *n* confusione *f*

congeal /kən'dʒiːl/ *vi* (*blood:*) coagularsi

congenial /kən'dʒiːnɪəl/ *a* congeniale

congenital /kən'dʒenɪtl/ *a* congenito

congest|ed /kən'dʒestɪd/ *a* congestionato. ~**ion** /-estʃn/ *n* congestione *f*

congratulat|e /kən'grætjuleɪt/ *vt* congratularsi con (**on** per). ~**ions** /-'eɪʃnz/ *npl* congratulazioni *fpl*

congregat|e /'kɒŋgrɪgeɪt/ *vi* radunarsi. ~**ion** /-'geɪʃn/ *n Relig* assemblea *f*

congress /'kɒŋgres/ *n* congresso *m*. ~**man** *n Am Pol* membro *m* del congresso

conical /'kɒnɪkl/ *a* conico

conifer /'kɒnɪfə(r)/ *n* conifera *f*

conjecture /kən'dʒektʃə(r)/ *n* congettura *f*

conjugal /'kɒndʒʊgl/ *a* coniugale

conjugat|e /'kɒndʒʊgeɪt/ *vt* coniugare. ~**ion** /-'geɪʃn/ *n* coniugazione *f*

conjunction /kən'dʒʌŋkʃn/ *n* congiunzione *f*; **in** ~ **with** insieme a

conjunctivitis /kəndʒʌŋktɪ'vaɪtɪs/ *n* congiuntivite *f*

conjur|e /'kʌndʒə(r)/ *vi* ~**ing tricks** *npl* giochi *mpl* di prestigio. ~**or** *n* prestigiatore, ·trice *mf*. **conjure up** *vt* evocare (*image*); tirar fuori dal nulla (*meal*)

conk /kɒŋk/ *vi* ~ **out** *fam* (*machine:*) guastarsi; (*person:*) crollare

'con-man *n fam* truffatore *m*

connect /kə'nekt/ *vt* collegare; **be** ~**ed with** avere legami con; (*be related to*) essere imparentato con; **be well** ~**ed** aver conoscenze influenti ● *vi* essere collegato (**with** a); (*train:*) fare coincidenza

connection /kə'nekʃn/ *n* (*between ideas*) nesso *m*; (*in travel*) coincidenza *f*; *Electr* collegamento *m*; **in** ~ **with** con riferimento a. ~**s** *pl* (*people*) conoscenze *fpl*

connoisseur /kɒnə'sɜː(r)/ *n* intenditore, ·trice *mf*

conquer /'kɒŋkə(r)/ *vt* conquistare; *fig* superare (*fear*). ~**or** *n* conquistatore *m*

conquest /'kɒŋkwest/ *n* conquista *f*

conscience /'kɒnʃəns/ *n* coscienza *f*

conscientious /kɒnʃɪ'enʃəs/ *a* coscienzioso. ~ **ob'jector** *n* obiettore *m* di coscienza

conscious /'kɒnʃəs/ *a* conscio; (*decision*) meditato; (**fully**) ~ cosciente; **be/become** ~ **of sth** rendersi conto di qcsa. ~**ly** *adv* consapevolmente. ~**ness** *n* consapevolezza *f*; *Med* conoscenza *f*

conscript[1] /'kɒnskrɪpt/ *n* coscritto *m*

conscript[2] /kən'skrɪpt/ *vt Mil* chiamare alle armi. ~**ion** /-ɪpʃn/ *n* coscrizione *f*, leva *f*

consecrat|e /'kɒnsɪkreɪt/ *vt* consacrare. ~**ion** /-'kreɪʃn/ *n* consacrazione *f*

consecutive /kən'sekjʊtɪv/ *a* consecutivo

consensus /kən'sensəs/ *n* consenso *m*

consent /kən'sent/ *n* consenso *m* ● *vi* acconsentire

consequen|ce /'kɒnsɪkwəns/ *n* conseguenza *f*; (*importance*) importanza *f*. ~**t** *a* conseguente. ~**tly** *adv* di conseguenza

conservation /kɒnsə'veɪʃn/ *n* conservazione *f*. ~**ist** *n* fautore, ·trice *mf* della tutela ambientale

conservative /kən'sɜːvətɪv/ *a*

conservativo; ⟨*estimate*⟩ ottimistico. **C~** *Pol a* conservatore ● *n* conservatore, -trice *mf*

conservatory /kən'sɜ:vətrɪ/ *n* spazio *m* chiuso da vetrate adiacente alla casa

conserve /kən'sɜ:v/ *vt* conservare

consider /kən'sɪdə(r)/ *vt* considerare; **~ doing sth** considerare la possibilità di fare qcsa. **~able** /-əbl/ *a* considerevole. **~ably** *adv* considerevolmente

consider|ate /kən'sɪdərət/ *a* pieno di riguardo. **~ately** *adv* con riguardo. **~ation** /-'reɪʃn/ *n* considerazione *f*; ⟨*thoughtfulness*⟩ attenzione *f*; ⟨*respect*⟩ riguardo *m*; ⟨*payment*⟩ compenso *m*; **take into ~ation** prendere in considerazione. **~ing** *prep* considerando

consign /kən'saɪn/ *vt* affidare. **~ment** *n* consegna *f*

consist /kən'sɪst/ *vi* **~ of** consistere di

consisten|cy /kən'sɪstənsɪ/ *n* coerenza *f*; ⟨*density*⟩ consistenza *f*. **~t** *a* coerente; ⟨*loyalty*⟩ costante. **~tly** *adv* coerentemente; ⟨*late, loyal*⟩ costantemente

consolation /kɒnsə'leɪʃn/ *n* consolazione *f*. **~ prize** *n* premio *m* di consolazione

console /kən'səʊl/ *vt* consolare

consolidate /kən'sɒlɪdeɪt/ *vt* consolidare

consonant /'kɒnsənənt/ *n* consonante *f*

consort /kən'sɔːt/ *vi* **~ with** frequentare

consortium /kən'sɔːtɪəm/ *n* consorzio *m*

conspicuous /kən'spɪkjʊəs/ *a* facilmente distinguibile

conspiracy /kən'spɪrəsɪ/ *n* cospirazione *f*

conspire /kən'spaɪə(r)/ *vi* cospirare

constable /'kʌnstəbl/ *n* agente *m* [di polizia]

constant /'kɒnstənt/ *a* costante. **~ly** *adv* costantemente

constellation /kɒnstə'leɪʃn/ *n* costellazione *f*

consternation /kɒnstə'neɪʃn/ *n* costernazione *f*

constipat|ed /'kɒnstɪpeɪtɪd/ *a* stitico. **~ion** /-'peɪʃn/ *n* stitichezza *f*

constituency /kən'stɪtjʊənsɪ/ *n area f* elettorale di un deputato nel Regno Unito

constituent /kən'stɪtjʊənt/ *n* costituente *m*; *Pol* elettore, -trice *mf*

constitute /'kɒnstɪtjuːt/ *vt* costituire. **~ion** /-'tjuːʃn/ *n* costituzione *f*. **~ional** /-'tjuːʃənl/ *a* costituzionale

constrain /kən'streɪn/ *vt* costringere.

~t *n* costrizione *f*; ⟨*restriction*⟩ restrizione *f*; ⟨*strained manner*⟩ disagio *m*

construct /kən'strʌkt/ *vt* costruire. **~ion** /-'ʌkʃn/ *n* costruzione *f*; **under ~ion** in costruzione. **~ive** /-ɪv/ *a* costruttivo

construe /kən'struː/ *vt* interpretare

consul /'kɒnsl/ *n* console *m*. **~ar** /'kɒnsjʊlə(r)/ *a* consolare. **~ate** /'kɒnsjʊlət/ *n* consolato *m*

consult /kən'sʌlt/ *vt* consultare. **~ant** *n* consulente *mf*; *Med* specialista *mf*. **~ation** /kɒnsl'teɪʃn/ *n* consultazione *f*; *Med* consulto *m*

consume /kən'sjuːm/ *vt* consumare. **~r** *n* consumatore, -trice *mf*. **~r goods** *npl* beni *mpl* di consumo. **~er organization** *n* organizzazione *f* per la tutela dei consumatori

consumerism /kən'sjuːmərɪzm/ *n* consumismo *m*

consummate /'kɒnsəmeɪt/ *vt* consumare

consumption /kən'sʌmpʃn/ *n* consumo *m*

contact /'kɒntækt/ *n* contatto *m*; ⟨*person*⟩ conoscenza *f* ● *vt* mettersi in contatto con. **~ 'lenses** *npl* lenti *fpl* a contatto

contagious /kən'teɪdʒəs/ *a* contagioso

contain /kən'teɪn/ *vt* contenere; **~ oneself** controllarsi. **~er** *n* recipiente *m*; ⟨*for transport*⟩ container *m inv*

contaminat|e /kən'tæmɪneɪt/ *vt* contaminare. **~ion** /-'neɪʃn/ *n* contaminazione *f*

contemplat|e /'kɒntəmpleɪt/ *vt* contemplare; ⟨*consider*⟩ considerare; **~e doing sth** considerare di fare qcsa. **~ion** /-'pleɪʃn/ *n* contemplazione *f*

contemporary /kən'tempərərɪ/ *a & n* contemporaneo, -a *mf*

contempt /kən'tempt/ *n* disprezzo *m*; **beneath ~** più che vergognoso; **~ of court** oltraggio *m* alla Corte. **~ible** /-əbl/ *a* spregevole. **~uous** /-tjʊəs/ *a* sprezzante

contend /kən'tend/ *vi* **~ with** occuparsi di ● *vt* ⟨*assert*⟩ sostenere. **~er** *n* concorrente *mf*

content¹ /'kɒntent/ *n* contenuto *m*

content² /kən'tent/ *a* soddisfatto ● *vt* **~ oneself** accontentarsi (**with** di). **~ed** *a* soddisfatto. **~edly** *adv* con aria soddisfatta

contention /kən'tenʃn/ *n* ⟨*assertion*⟩ opinione *f*

contentment /kən'tentmənt/ n soddisfazione f

contents /'kɒntents/ npl contenuto m

contest[1] /'kɒntest/ n gara f

contest[2] /kən'test/ vt contestare ‹statement›; impugnare ‹will›; Pol ‹candidates:› contendersi; ‹one candidate:› aspirare a. **~ant** n concorrente mf

context /'kɒntekst/ n contesto m

continent /'kɒntɪnənt/ n continente m; **the C~** l'Europa f continentale

continental /kɒntɪ'nentl/ a continentale. **~ breakfast** n prima colazione f a base di pane, burro, marmellata, croissant, ecc. **~ quilt** n piumone m

contingency /kən'tɪndʒənsɪ/ n eventualità f inv

continual /kən'tɪnjʊəl/ a continuo

continuation /kəntɪnjʊ'eɪʃn/ n continuazione f

continue /kən'tɪnju:/ vt continuare; **~ doing** or **to do sth** continuare a fare qcsa; **to be ~d** continua ● vi continuare. **~d** a continuo

continuity /kɒntɪ'nju:ətɪ/ n continuità f

continuous /kən'tɪnjʊəs/ a continuo

contort /kən'tɔ:t/ vt contorcere. **~ion** /-ɔ:ʃn/ n contorsione f. **~ionist** n contorsionista mf

contour /'kɒntʊə(r)/ n contorno m; ‹line› curva f di livello

contraband /'kɒntrəbænd/ n contrabbando m

contracep|tion /kɒntrə'sepʃn/ n contraccezione f. **~tive** /-tɪv/ n contraccettivo m

contract[1] /'kɒntrækt/ n contratto m

contract[2] /kən'trækt/ vi ‹get smaller› contrarsi ● vt contrarre ‹illness›. **~ion** /-ækʃn/ n contrazione f. **~or** n imprenditore, -trice mf

contradict /kɒntrə'dɪkt/ vt contraddire. **~ion** /-ɪkʃn/ n contraddizione f. **~ory** a contraddittorio

contra-flow /'kɒntrəfləʊ/ n utilizzazione f di una corsia nei due sensi di marcia durante lavori stradali

contralto /kən'træltəʊ/ n contralto m

contraption /kən'træpʃn/ n fam aggeggio m

contrary[1] /'kɒntrərɪ/ a contrario ● adv **~ to** contrariamente a ● n contrario m; **on the ~** al contrario

contrary[2] /kən'treərɪ/ a disobbediente

contrast[1] /'kɒntrɑ:st/ n contrasto m

contrast[2] /kən'trɑ:st/ vt confrontare ● vi contrastare. **~ing** a contrastante

contraven|e /kɒntrə'vi:n/ vt trasgredire. **~tion** /-'venʃn/ n trasgressione f

contribut|e /kən'trɪbju:t/ vt/i contribuire. **~ion** /kɒntrɪ'bju:ʃn/ n contribuzione f; ‹what is contributed› contributo m. **~or** n contributore, -trice mf

contrive /kən'traɪv/ vt escogitare; **~ to do sth** riuscire a fare sth

control /kən'trəʊl/ n controllo m; **~s** pl ‹of car, plane› comandi mpl; **get out of ~** sfuggire al controllo ● vt (pt/pp controlled) controllare; **~ oneself** controllarsi

controvers|ial /kɒntrə'vɜ:ʃl/ a controverso. **~y** /'kɒntrəvɜ:sɪ/ n controversia f

conurbation /kɒnɜ:'beɪʃn/ n conurbazione f

convalesce /kɒnvə'les/ vi essere in convalescenza

convalescent /kɒnvə'lesənt/ a convalescente. **~ home** n convalescenziario m

convector /kən'vektə(r)/ n **~ [heater]** convettore m

convene /kən'vi:n/ vt convocare ● vi riunirsi

convenience /kən'vi:nɪəns/ n convenienza f; [public] **~** gabinetti mpl pubblici; **with all modern ~s** con tutti i comfort

convenient /kən'vi:nɪənt/ a comodo; **be ~ for sb** andar bene per qcno; **if it is ~ [for you]** se ti va bene. **~ly** adv comodamente; **~ly located** in una posizione comoda

convent /'kɒnvənt/ n convento m

convention /kən'venʃn/ n convenzione f; ‹assembly› convegno m. **~al** a convenzionale

converge /kən'vɜ:dʒ/ vi convergere

conversant /kən'vɜ:sənt/ a **~ with** pratico di

conversation /kɒnvə'seɪʃn/ n conversazione f. **~al** a di conversazione. **~alist** n conversatore, -trice mf

converse[1] /kən'vɜ:s/ vi conversare

converse[2] /'kɒnvɜ:s/ n inverso m. **~ly** adv viceversa

conversion /kən'vɜ:ʃn/ n conversione f

convert[1] /'kɒnvɜ:t/ n convertito, -a mf

convert[2] /kən'vɜ:t/ vt convertire (**into** in); sconsacrare ‹church›. **~ible** /-əbl/ a convertibile ● n Auto macchina f decappottabile

convex /'kɒnveks/ a convesso

convey /kən'veɪ/ vt portare; trasmettere ⟨*idea, message*⟩. **~or belt** *n* nastro *m* trasportatore

convict¹ /'kɒnvɪkt/ *n* condannato, -a *mf*

convict² /kən'vɪkt/ *vt* giudicare colpevole. **~ion** /-ɪkʃn/ *n* condanna *f*; (*belief*) convinzione *f*; **previous ~ion** precedente *m* penale

convinc|e /kən'vɪns/ *vt* convincere. **~ing** *a* convincente

convivial /kən'vɪvɪəl/ *a* conviviale

convoluted /'kɒnvəlu:tɪd/ *a* contorto

convoy /'kɒnvɔɪ/ *n* convoglio *m*

convuls|e /kən'vʌls/ *vt* sconvolgere; **be ~ed with laughter** contorcersi dalle risa. **~ion** /-ʌlʃn/ *n* convulsione *f*

coo /ku:/ *vi* tubare

cook /kʊk/ *n* cuoco, -a *mf* ● *vt* cucinare; **is it ~ed?** è cotto?; **~ the books** *fam* truccare i libri contabili ● *vi* (*food:*) cuocere; (*person:*) cucinare. **~book** *n* libro *m* di cucina

cooker /'kʊkə(r)/ *n* cucina *f*; (*apple*) mela *f* da cuocere. **~y** *n* cucina *f*. **~y book** *n* libro *m* di cucina

cookie /'kʊkɪ/ *n Am* biscotto *m*

cool /ku:l/ *a* fresco; (*calm*) calmo; (*unfriendly*) freddo ● *n* fresco *m* ● *vt* rinfrescare ● *vi* rinfrescarsi. **~-box** *n* borsa *f* termica. **~ness** *n* freddezza *f*

coop /ku:p/ *n* stia *f* ● *vt* **~ up** rinchiudere

co-operat|e /kəʊ'ɒpəreɪt/ *vi* cooperare. **~ion** /-'reɪʃn/ *n* cooperazione *f*

co-operative /kəʊ'ɒpərətɪv/ *a* cooperativo ● *n* cooperativa *f*

co-opt /kəʊ'ɒpt/ *vt* eleggere

co-ordinat|e /kəʊ'ɔ:dɪneɪt/ *vt* coordinare. **~ion** /-'neɪʃn/ *n* coordinazione *f*

cop /kɒp/ *n fam* poliziotto *m*

cope /kəʊp/ *vi fam* farcela; **can she ~ by herself?** ce la fa da sola?; **~ with** farcela con

copious /'kəʊpɪəs/ *a* abbondante

copper¹ /'kɒpə(r)/ *n* rame *m*; **~s** *pl* monete *fpl* da uno o due pence ● *attrib* di rame

copper² *n fam* poliziotto *m*

coppice /'kɒpɪs/ *n*, **copse** /kɒps/ *n* boschetto *m*

copulat|e /'kɒpjʊleɪt/ *vi* accoppiarsi. **~ion** /-'leɪʃn/ *n* copulazione *f*

copy /'kɒpɪ/ *n* copia *f* ● *vt* (*pt/pp* -**ied**) copiare

copy: ~right *n* diritti *mpl* d'autore. **~writer** *n* copywriter *mf inv*

coral /'kɒrəl/ *n* corallo *m*

cord /kɔ:d/ *n* corda *f*; (*thinner*) cordon-

cino *m*; (*fabric*) velluto *m* a coste; **~s** *pl* pantaloni *mpl* di velluto a coste

cordial /'kɔ:dɪəl/ *a* cordiale ● *n* analcolico *m*

cordon /'kɔ:dn/ *n* cordone *m* (*di persone*) ● **cordon off** *vt* mettere un cordone (*di persone*) intorno a

corduroy /'kɔ:dərɔɪ/ *n* velluto *m* a coste

core /kɔ:(r)/ *n* (*of apple, pear*) torsolo *m*; (*fig: of organization*) cuore *m*; (*of problem, theory*) nocciolo *m*

cork /kɔ:k/ *n* sughero *m*; (*for bottle*) turacciolo *m*. **~screw** *n* cavatappi *m inv*

corn¹ /kɔ:n/ *n* grano *m*; (*Am: maize*) granturco *m*

corn² *n Med* callo *m*

cornea /'kɔ:nɪə/ *n* cornea *f*

corned beef /kɔ:nd'bi:f/ *n* manzo *m* sotto sale

corner /'kɔ:nə(r)/ *n* angolo *m*; (*football*) calcio *m* d'angolo, corner *m inv* ● *vt* fig bloccare; *Comm* accaparrarsi ⟨*market*⟩

cornet /'kɔ:nɪt/ *n Mus* cornetta *f*; (*for ice-cream*) cono *m*

corn: ~flour *n*, *Am* **~starch** *n* farina *f* di granturco

corny /'kɔ:nɪ/ *a* (**-ier, -est**) (*fam: joke, film*) scontato; ⟨*person*⟩ banale; (*sentimental*) sdolcinato

coronary /'kɒrənərɪ/ *a* coronario ● *n* **~ [thrombosis]** trombosi *f* coronarica

coronation /kɒrə'neɪʃn/ *n* incoronazione *f*

coroner /'kɒrənə(r)/ *n* coroner *m inv* (*nel diritto britannico, ufficiale incaricato delle indagini su morti sospette*)

corporal¹ /'kɔ:pərəl/ *n Mil* caporale *m*

corporal² *a* corporale; **~ punishment** punizione *f* corporale

corporate /'kɔ:pərət/ *a* ⟨*decision, policy, image*⟩ aziendale; **~ life** la vita in un'azienda

corporation /kɔ:pə'reɪʃn/ *n* ente *m*; (*of town*) consiglio *m* comunale

corps /kɔ:(r)/ *n* (*pl* **corps** /kɔ:z/) corpo *m*

corpse /kɔ:ps/ *n* cadavere *m*

corpulent /'kɔ:pjʊlənt/ *a* corpulento

corpuscle /'kɔ:pʌsl/ *n* globulo *m*

correct /kə'rekt/ *a* corretto; **be ~** ⟨*person:*⟩ aver ragione; **~!** esatto! ● *vt* correggere. **~ion** /-ekʃn/ *n* correzione *f*. **~ly** *adv* correttamente

correlation /kɒrə'leɪʃn/ *n* correlazione *f*

correspond /kɒrɪ'spɒnd/ *vi* corrispondere (**to** a); ⟨*two things:*⟩ corrispondere; (write) scriversi. ~**ence** n corrispondenza f. ~**ent** n corrispondente mf. ~**ing** a corrispondente. ~**ingly** adv in modo corrispondente

corridor /'kɒrɪdɔ:(r)/ n corridoio m

corroborate /kə'rɒbəreɪt/ vt corroborare

corro|de /kə'rəʊd/ vt corrodere ● vi corrodersi. ~**sion** /-'rəʊʒn/ n corrosione f

corrugated /'kɒrəgeɪtɪd/ a ondulato. ~ **iron** n lamiera f ondulata

corrupt /kə'rʌpt/ a corrotto ● vt corrompere. ~**ion** /-ʌpʃn/ n corruzione f

corset /'kɔ:sɪt/ n & -**s** pl busto m

Corsica /'kɔ:sɪkə/ n Corsica f. ~**n** a & n corso, -a mf

cortège /kɔ:'teɪʒ/ n [**funeral**] ~ corteo m funebre

cosh /kɒʃ/ n randello m

cosmetic /kɒz'metɪk/ a cosmetico ● n ~**s** pl cosmetici mpl

cosmic /'kɒzmɪk/ a cosmico

cosmonaut /'kɒzmənɔ:t/ n cosmonauta mf

cosmopolitan /kɒzmə'pɒlɪtən/ a cosmopolita

cosmos /'kɒzmɒs/ n cosmo m

cosset /'kɒsɪt/ vt coccolare

cost /kɒst/ n costo m; ~**s** pl Jur spese fpl processuali; **at all** ~**s** a tutti i costi; **I learnt to my** ~ ho imparato a mie spese ● vt (pt/pp **cost**) costare; **it** ~ **me £20** mi è costato 20 sterline ● vt (pt/pp **costed**) ~ [**out**] stabilire il prezzo di

costly /'kɒstlɪ/ a (-**ier, -iest**) costoso

cost: ~ **of 'living** n costo m della vita. ~ **price** n prezzo m di costo

costume /'kɒstju:m/ n costume m. ~ **jewellery** n bigiotteria f

cosy /'kəʊzɪ/ a (-**ier, -iest**) ⟨pub, chat⟩ intimo; **it's nice and** ~ **in here** si sta bene qui

cot /kɒt/ n lettino m; (Am: camp-bed) branda f

cottage /'kɒtɪdʒ/ n casetta f. ~ '**cheese** n fiocchi mpl di latte

cotton /'kɒtn/ n cotone m ● attrib di cotone ● **cotton on** vi fam capire

cotton 'wool n cotone m idrofilo

couch /kaʊtʃ/ n divano m. ~ **potato** n pantofolaio, -a mf

couchette /ku:'ʃet/ n cuccetta f

cough /kɒf/ n tosse f ● vi tossire. **cough up** vt/i sputare; (fam: pay) sborsare

'**cough mixture** n sciroppo m per la tosse

could /kʊd/, atono /kəd/ v aux (see also

can²) ~ **I have a glass of water?** potrei avere un bicchier d'acqua?; **I** ~**n't do it even if I wanted to** non potrei farlo nemmeno se lo volessi; **I** ~**n't care less** non potrebbe importarmene di meno; **he** ~**n't have done it without help** non avrebbe potuto farlo senza aiuto; **you** ~ **have phoned** avresti potuto telefonare

council /'kaʊnsl/ n consiglio m. ~ **house** n casa f popolare

councillor /'kaʊnsələ(r)/ n consigliere, -a mf

'**council tax** n imposta f locale sugli immobili

counsel /'kaʊnsl/ n consigli mpl; Jur avvocato m ● vt (pt/pp **counselled**) consigliare a ⟨person⟩. ~**lor** n consigliere, -a mf

count¹ /kaʊnt/ n (nobleman) conte m

count² n conto m; **keep** ~ tenere il conto ● vt/i contare. **count on** vt contare su

countdown /'kaʊntdaʊn/ n conto m alla rovescia

countenance /'kaʊntənəns/ n espressione f ● vt approvare

counter¹ /'kaʊntə(r)/ n banco m; (in games) gettone m

counter² adv ~ **to** contro, in contrasto a; **go** ~ **to sth** andare contro qcsa ● vt/i opporre ⟨measure, effect⟩; parare ⟨blow⟩

counter'act vt neutralizzare

'**counter-attack** n contrattacco m

counter-'espionage n controspionaggio m

'**counterfeit** /-fɪt/ a contraffatto ● n contraffazione f ● vt contraffare

'**counterfoil** n matrice f

'**counterpart** n equivalente mf

counter-pro'ductive a controproduttivo

'**countersign** vt controfirmare

countess /'kaʊntɪs/ n contessa f

countless /'kaʊntlɪs/ a innumerevole

country /'kʌntrɪ/ n nazione f, paese m; (native land) patria f; (countryside) campagna f; **in the** ~ in campagna; **go to the** ~ andare in campagna; Pol indire le elezioni politiche. ~**man** n uomo m di campagna; (fellow ~**man**) compatriota m. ~**side** n campagna f

county /'kaʊntɪ/ n contea f (unità amministrativa britannica)

coup /ku:/ n Pol colpo m di stato

couple /'kʌpl/ n coppia f; **a** ~ **of** un paio di

coupon /'ku:pɒn/ n tagliando m; (for discount) buono m sconto

courage /'kʌrɪdʒ/ n coraggio m. **~ous** /kə'reɪdʒəs/ a coraggioso

courgette /kʊə'ʒet/ n zucchino m

courier /'kʊrɪə(r)/ n corriere m; (for tourists) guida f

course /kɔːs/ n Sch corso m; Naut rotta f; Culin portata f; (for golf) campo m; **~ of treatment** Med serie f inv di cure; **of ~** naturalmente; **in the ~ of** durante; **in due ~** a tempo debito

court /kɔːt/ n tribunale m; Sport campo m; **take sb to ~** citare qcno in giudizio ● vt fare la corte a (woman); sfidare (danger); **~ing couples** coppiette fpl

courteous /'kɜːtɪəs/ a cortese

courtesy /'kɜːtəsɪ/ n cortesia f

court: ~ 'martial n (pl **~s martial**) corte f marziale ● **~-martial** vt (pt **~-martialled**) portare davanti alla corte marziale; **~yard** n cortile m

cousin /'kʌzn/ n cugino, -a mf

cove /kəʊv/ n insenatura f

cover /'kʌvə(r)/ n copertura f; (of cushion, to protect sth) fodera f; (of book, magazine) copertina f; **take ~** mettersi al riparo; **under separate ~** a parte ● vt coprire; foderare (cushion); Journ fare un servizio su. **cover up** vt coprire; fig soffocare (scandal)

coverage /'kʌvərɪdʒ/ n Journ **it got a lot of ~** i media gli hanno dedicato molto spazio

cover: ~ charge n coperto m. **~ing** n copertura f; (for floor) rivestimento m; **~ing letter** lettera f d'accompagnamento. **~-up** n messa f a tacere

covet /'kʌvɪt/ vt bramare

cow /kaʊ/ n vacca f, mucca f

coward /'kaʊəd/ n vigliacco, -a mf. **~ice** /-ɪs/ n vigliaccheria f. **~ly** a da vigliacco

'cowboy n cowboy m inv, buffone m fam

cower /'kaʊə(r)/ vi acquattarsi

'cowshed n stalla f

cox /kɒks/ n, **coxswain** /'kɒksn/ n timoniere, -a mf

coy /kɔɪ/ a falsamente timido; (flirtatiously) civettuolo; **be ~ about sth** essere evasivo su qcsa

crab /kræb/ n granchio m

crack /kræk/ n (in wall) crepa f; (in china, glass, bone) incrinatura f; (noise) scoppio m; (fam: joke) battuta f; **have a ~** (try) fare un tentativo ● a (fam: best) di prim'ordine ● vt incrinare (china, glass); schiacciare (nut); decifrare (code); fam risolvere (problem); **~ a joke** fam fare una battuta ● vi (china,

glass:) incrinarsi; (whip:) schioccare. **crack down** vi fam prendere seri provvedimenti. **crack down on** vt fam prendere seri provvedimenti contro

cracked /krækt/ a (plaster) crepato; (skin) screpolato; (rib) incrinato; (fam: crazy) svitato

cracker /'krækə(r)/ n (biscuit) cracker m inv; (firework) petardo m. **[Christmas] ~** tubo m di cartone colorato contenente una sorpresa

crackers /'krækəz/ a fam matto

crackle /'krækl/ vi crepitare

cradle /'kreɪdl/ n culla f

craft¹ /krɑːft/ n inv (boat) imbarcazione f

craft² n mestiere m; (technique) arte f. **~sman** n artigiano m

crafty /'krɑːftɪ/ a (-ier, -iest) astuto

crag /kræg/ n rupe f. **~gy** a scosceso; (face) dai lineamenti marcati

cram /kræm/ v (pt/pp **crammed**) ● vt stipare (**into** in) ● vi (for exams) sgobbare

cramp /kræmp/ n crampo m. **~ed** a (room) stretto; (handwriting) appiccicato

crampon /'kræmpən/ n rampone m

cranberry /'krænbərɪ/ n Culin mirtillo m rosso

crane /kreɪn/ n (at docks, bird) gru f inv ● vt **~ one's neck** allungare il collo

crank¹ /kræŋk/ n tipo, -a mf strampalato, -a

crank² n Techn manovella f. **~shaft** n albero m a gomiti

cranky /'kræŋkɪ/ a strampalato; (Am: irritable) irritabile

cranny /'krænɪ/ n fessura f

crash /kræʃ/ n (noise) fragore m; Auto, Aeron incidente m; Comm crollo m ● vi schiantarsi (**into** contro); (plane:) precipitare ● vt schiantare (car)

crash: ~ course n corso m intensivo. **~-helmet** n casco m. **~-landing** n atterraggio m di fortuna

crate /kreɪt/ n (for packing) cassa f

crater /'kreɪtə(r)/ n cratere m

crav|e /kreɪv/ vt morire dalla voglia di. **~ing** n voglia f smodata

crawl /krɔːl/ n (swimming) stile m libero; **do the ~** nuotare a stile libero; **at a ~** a passo di lumaca ● vi andare carponi; **~ with** brulicare di. **~er lane** n Auto corsia f riservata al traffico lento

crayon /'kreɪən/ n pastello m a cera; (pencil) matita f colorata

craze /kreɪz/ n mania f

crazy /'kreɪzɪ/ a (-ier, -iest) matto; be ~ **about** andar matto per

creak /kri:k/ n scricchiolio m ●vi scricchiolare

cream /kri:m/ n crema f; (fresh) panna f ●a (colour) [bianco] panna inv ●vt Culin sbattere. ~ **'cheese** n formaggio m cremoso. ~y a cremoso

crease /kri:s/ n piega f ●vt stropicciare ●vi stropicciarsi. ~-**resistant** a che non si stropiccia

creat|e /kri:'eɪt/ vt creare. ~**ion** /-'eɪʃn/ n creazione f. ~**ive** /-tɪv/ a creativo. ~**or** n creatore, -trice mf

creature /'kri:tʃə(r)/ n creatura f

crèche /kreʃ/ n asilo m nido

credentials /krɪ'denʃlz/ npl credenziali fpl

credibility /kredə'bɪlətɪ/ n credibilità f

credible /'kredəbl/ a credibile

credit /'kredɪt/ n credito m; (honour) merito m; take the ~ for prendersi il merito di ●vt (pt/pp credited) accreditare; ~ **sb with sth** Comm accreditare qcsa a qcno; fig attribuire qcsa a qcno. ~**able** /-əbl/ a lodevole

credit: ~ **card** n carta f di credito. ~**or** n creditore, -trice mf

creed /kri:d/ n credo m inv

creek /kri:k/ n insenatura f; (Am: stream) torrente m

creep /kri:p/ vi (pt/pp crept) muoversi furtivamente ●n fam tipo m viscido. ~**er** n pianta f rampicante. ~y a che fa venire i brividi

cremat|e /krɪ'meɪt/ vt cremare. ~**ion** /-'eɪʃn/ n cremazione f

crematorium /kremə'tɔ:rɪəm/ n crematorio m

crêpe /kreɪp/ n (fabric) crespo m

crept /krept/ see creep

crescent /'kresənt/ n mezzaluna f

cress /kres/ n crescione m

crest /krest/ n cresta f; (coat of arms) cimiero m

Crete /kri:t/ n Creta f

crevasse /krɪ'væs/ n crepaccio m

crevice /'krevɪs/ n crepa f

crew /kru:/ n equipaggio m; (gang) équipe f inv. ~ **cut** n capelli mpl a spazzola. ~ **neck** n girocollo m

crib¹ /krɪb/ n (for baby) culla f

crib² vt/i (pt/pp cribbed) fam copiare

crick /krɪk/ n ~ **in the neck** torcicollo m

cricket¹ /'krɪkɪt/ n (insect) grillo m

cricket² n cricket m. ~**er** n giocatore m di cricket

crime /kraɪm/ n crimine m; (criminality) criminalità f

criminal /'krɪmɪnl/ a criminale; (law, court) penale ●n criminale mf

crimson /'krɪmzn/ a cremisi inv

cringe /krɪndʒ/ vi (cower) acquattarsi; (at bad joke etc) fare una smorfia

crinkle /'krɪŋkl/ vt spiegazzare ●vi spiegazzarsi

cripple /'krɪpl/ n storpio, -a mf ●vt storpiare; fig danneggiare. ~**d** a (person) storpio; (ship) danneggiato

crisis /'kraɪsɪs/ n (pl -ses /-si:z/) crisi f inv

crisp /krɪsp/ a croccante; (air) frizzante; (style) incisivo. ~**bread** n crostini mpl di pane. ~**s** npl patatine fpl

criterion /kraɪ'tɪərɪən/ n (pl -ria /-rɪə/) criterio m

critic /'krɪtɪk/ n critico, -a mf. ~**al** a critico. ~**ally** adv in modo critico; ~**ally ill** gravemente malato

criticism /'krɪtɪsɪzm/ n critica f; he doesn't like ~ non ama le critiche

criticize /'krɪtɪsaɪz/ vt criticare

croak /krəʊk/ vi gracchiare; (frog:) gracidare

crochet /'krəʊʃeɪ/ n lavoro m all'uncinetto ●vt fare all'uncinetto. ~-**hook** n uncinetto m

crock /krɒk/ n fam old ~ (person) rudere m; (car) macinino m

crockery /'krɒkərɪ/ n terrecotte fpl

crocodile /'krɒkədaɪl/ n coccodrillo m. ~ **tears** lacrime fpl di coccodrillo

crocus /'krəʊkəs/ n (pl -es) croco m

crony /'krəʊnɪ/ n compare m

crook /krʊk/ n (fam: criminal) truffatore, -trice mf

crooked /'krʊkɪd/ a storto; (limb) storpiato; (fam: dishonest) disonesto

crop /krɒp/ n raccolto m; fig quantità f inv ●v (pt/pp cropped) ●vt coltivare. crop up vi fam presentarsi

croquet /'krəʊkeɪ/ n croquet m

croquette /krəʊ'ket/ n crocchetta f

cross /krɒs/ a (annoyed) arrabbiato; talk at ~ purposes fraintendersi ●n croce f; Bot, Zool incrocio m ●vt sbarrare (cheque); incrociare (road, animals); ~ **oneself** farsi il segno della croce; ~ **one's arms** incrociare le braccia; ~ **one's legs** accavallare le gambe; **keep one's fingers** ~**ed for sb** tenere le dita incrociate per qcno; it ~**ed my mind** mi è venuto in mente ●vi (go across) attraversare; (lines:) incrociarsi. **cross out** vt depennare

cross: **~bar** n (of goal) traversa f; (on bicycle) canna f. **~·'country** n Sport corsa f campestre. **~-ex'amine** vt sottoporre a controinterrogatorio. **~-exami'nation** n controinterrogatorio m. **~-'eyed** a strabico. **~fire** n fuoco m incrociato. **~ing** n (for pedestrians) passaggio m pedonale; (sea journey) traversata f. **~-'reference** n rimando m. **~roads** n incrocio m. **~-'section** n sezione f; (of community) campione m. **~wise** adv in diagonale. **~word** n **~word [puzzle]** parole fpl crociate

crotchet /'krɒtʃɪt/ n Mus semiminima f

crotchety /'krɒtʃɪti/ a irritabile

crouch /krautʃ/ vi accovacciarsi

crow /krəʊ/ n corvo m; **as the ~ flies** in linea d'aria ● vi cantare. **~bar** n piede m di porco

crowd /kraʊd/ n folla f ● vt affollare ● vi affollarsi. **~ed** /'kraʊdɪd/ a affollato

crown /kraʊn/ n corona f ● vt incoronare; incapsulare ⟨tooth⟩

crucial /'kru:ʃl/ a cruciale

crucifix /'kru:sɪfɪks/ n crocifisso m

crucif|ixion /kru:sɪ'fɪkʃn/ n crocifissione f. **~y** /'kru:sɪfaɪ/ vt (pt/pp -ied) crocifiggere

crude /kru:d/ a ⟨oil⟩ greggio; ⟨language⟩ crudo; ⟨person⟩ rozzo

cruel /'kru:əl/ a (**crueller, cruellest**) crudele (**to** verso). **~ly** adv con crudeltà. **~ty** n crudeltà f

cruis|e /kru:z/ n crociera f ● vi fare una crociera; ⟨car:⟩ andare a velocità di crociera. **~er** n Mil incrociatore m; (motor boat) motoscafo m. **~ing speed** n velocità m inv di crociera

crumb /krʌm/ n briciola f

crumb|le /'krʌmbl/ vt sbriciolare ● vi sbriciolarsi; ⟨building, society:⟩ sgretolarsi. **~ly** a friabile

crumple /'krʌmpl/ vt spiegazzare ● vi spiegazzarsi

crunch /krʌntʃ/ n fam **when it comes to the ~** quando si viene al dunque ● vt sgranocchiare ● vi ⟨snow:⟩ scricchiolare

crusade /kru:'seɪd/ n crociata f. **~r** n crociato m

crush /krʌʃ/ n (crowd) calca f; **have a ~ on** sb essersi preso una cotta per qcno ● vt schiacciare; sgualcire ⟨clothes⟩

crust /krʌst/ n crosta f

crutch /krʌtʃ/ n gruccia f; Anat inforcatura f

crux /krʌks/ n fig punto m cruciale

cry /kraɪ/ n grido m; **have a ~** farsi un pianto; **a far ~ from** fig tutta un'altra cosa rispetto a ● vi (pt/pp **cried**) ⟨weep⟩ piangere; (call) gridare

crypt /krɪpt/ n cripta f. **~ic** a criptico

crystal /'krɪstl/ n cristallo m; (glassware) cristalli mpl. **~lize** vi (become clear) concretizzarsi

cub /kʌb/ n (animal) cucciolo m; **C~** [**Scout**] lupetto m

Cuba /'kju:bə/ n Cuba f

cubby-hole /'kʌbɪ-/ n (compartment) scomparto m; (room) ripostiglio m

cub|e /kju:b/ n cubo m. **~ic** a cubico

cubicle /'kju:bɪkl/ n cabina f

cuckoo /'kʊku:/ n cuculo m. **~ clock** n orologio m a cucù

cucumber /'kju:kʌmbə(r)/ n cetriolo m

cuddl|e /'kʌdl/ vt coccolare ● vi **~e up to** starsene accoccolato insieme a ● vi **have a ~e** ⟨child:⟩ farsi coccolare; ⟨lovers:⟩ abbracciarsi. **~y** a tenerone; (wanting cuddles) coccolone. **~y 'toy** n peluche m inv

cudgel /'kʌdʒl/ n randello m

cue[1] /kju:/ n segnale m; Theat battuta f d'entrata

cue[2] n (in billiards) stecca f. **~ ball** n pallino m

cuff /kʌf/ n polsino m; (Am: turn-up) orlo m; (blow) scapaccione m; **off the ~** improvvisando ● vt dare una pacca a. **~-link** n gemello m

cul-de-sac /'kʌldəsæk/ n vicolo m cieco

culinary /'kʌlɪnərɪ/ a culinario

cull /kʌl/ vt scegliere ⟨flowers⟩; (kill) selezionare e uccidere

culminat|e /'kʌlmɪneɪt/ vi culminare. **~ion** /-'neɪʃn/ n culmine m

culottes /kju:'lɒts/ npl gonna fsg pantalone

culprit /'kʌlprɪt/ n colpevole mf

cult /kʌlt/ n culto m

cultivate /'kʌltɪveɪt/ vt coltivare; fig coltivarsi ⟨person⟩

cultural /'kʌltʃərəl/ a culturale

culture /'kʌltʃə(r)/ n cultura f. **~d** a colto

cumbersome /'kʌmbəsəm/ a ingombrante

cumulative /'kju:mjʊlətɪv/ a cumulativo

cunning /'kʌnɪŋ/ a astuto ● n astuzia f

cup /kʌp/ n tazza f; (prize, of bra) coppa f

cupboard /'kʌbəd/ n armadio m. **~ love** n fam amore m interessato

Cup 'Final n finale f di coppa

Cupid /'kjuːpɪd/ n Cupido m
curable /'kjʊərəbl/ a curabile
curate /'kjʊərət/ n curato m
curator /kjʊə'reɪtə(r)/ n direttore, -trice mf (di museo)
curb /kɜːb/ vt tenere a freno
curdle /'kɜːdl/ vi coagularsi
cure /kjʊə(r)/ n cura • vt curare; (salt) mettere sotto sale; (smoke) affumicare
curfew /'kɜːfjuː/ n coprifuoco m
curio /'kjʊərɪəʊ/ n curiosità f inv
curiosity /kjʊərɪ'ɒsətɪ/ n curiosità f
curious /'kjʊərɪəs/ a curioso. **~ly** adv curiosamente
curl /kɜːl/ n ricciolo m • vt arricciare • vi arricciarsi. **curl up** vi raggomitolarsi
curler /'kɜːlə(r)/ n bigodino m
curly /'kɜːlɪ/ a (-ier, -iest) riccio
currant /'kʌrənt/ n (dried) uvetta f
currency /'kʌrənsɪ/ n valuta f; (of word) ricorrenza f; **foreign ~** valuta f estera
current /'kʌrənt/ a corrente • n corrente f. **~ affairs or events** npl attualità fsg. **~ly** adv attualmente
curriculum /kə'rɪkjʊləm/ n programma m di studi. **~ vitae** /'viːtaɪ/ n curriculum vitae m inv
curry /'kʌrɪ/ n curry m inv; (meal) piatto m cucinato nel curry • vt (pt/pp -ied) **~ favour with sb** cercare d'ingraziarsi qcno
curse /kɜːs/ n maledizione f, (oath) imprecazione f • vt maledire • vi imprecare
cursor /'kɜːsə(r)/ n cursore m
cursory /'kɜːsərɪ/ a sbrigativo
curt /kɜːt/ a brusco
curtail /kɜː'teɪl/ vt ridurre
curtain /'kɜːtn/ n tenda f; Theat sipario m
curtsy /'kɜːtsɪ/ n inchino m • vi (pt/pp -ied) fare l'inchino
curve /kɜːv/ n curva f • vi curvare; **~ to the right/left** curvare a destra/ sinistra. **~d** a curvo
cushion /'kʊʃn/ n cuscino m • vt attutire; (protect) proteggere
cushy /'kʊʃɪ/ a (-ier, -iest) fam facile
custard /'kʌstəd/ n (liquid) crema f pasticciera
custodian /kʌ'stəʊdɪən/ n custode mf
custody /'kʌstədɪ/ n (of child) custodia f; (imprisoning) detenzione f preventiva
custom /'kʌstəm/ n usanza f; Jur consuetudine f; Comm clientela f. **~ary** a

(habitual) abituale; **it's ~ to...** è consuetudine.... **~er** n cliente mf
customs /'kʌstəmz/ npl dogana f. **~ officer** n guardia f di finanza
cut /kʌt/ n (with knife etc, of clothes) taglio m; (reduction) riduzione f; (in public spending) taglio m • vt/i (pt/pp **cut**, pres p **cutting**) tagliare; (reduce) ridurre; **~ one's finger** tagliarsi il dito; **~ sb's hair** tagliare i capelli a qcno • vi (with cards) alzare. **cut back** vt tagliare (hair); potare (hedge); (reduce) ridurre. **cut down** vt abbattere (tree); (reduce) ridurre. **cut off** vt tagliar via; (disconnect) interrompere; fig isolare; **I was ~ off** Teleph la linea è caduta. **cut out** vt ritagliare; (delete) eliminare; **be ~ out for** fam essere tagliato per; **~ it out!** fam dacci un taglio!. **cut up** vt (slice) tagliare a pezzi
'cut-back n riduzione f; (in government spending) taglio m
cute /kjuːt/ a fam (in appearance) carino; (clever) acuto
cuticle /'kjuːtɪkl/ n cuticola f
cutlery /'kʌtlərɪ/ n posate fpl
cutlet /'kʌtlɪt/ n cotoletta f
'cut-price a a prezzo ridotto; (shop) che fa prezzi ridotti
'cut-throat a spietato
cutting /'kʌtɪŋ/ a (remark) tagliente • n (from newspaper) ritaglio m; (of plant) talea f
CV n abbr curriculum vitae
cyanide /'saɪənaɪd/ n cianuro m
cybernetics /saɪbə'netɪks/ n cibernetica f
cycl|e /'saɪkl/ n ciclo m; (bicycle) bicicletta f, bici f inv fam • vi andare in bicicletta. **~ing** n ciclismo m. **~ist** n ciclista mf
cyclone /'saɪkləʊn/ n ciclone m
cylind|er /'sɪlɪndə(r)/ n cilindro m. **~rical** /-'lɪndrɪkl/ a cilindrico
cymbals /'sɪmblz/ npl Mus piatti mpl
cynic /'sɪnɪk/ n cinico, -a mf. **~al** a cinico. **~ism** /-sɪzm/ n cinismo m
cypress /'saɪprəs/ n cipresso m
Cypriot /'sɪprɪət/ n cipriota mf
Cyprus /'saɪprəs/ n Cipro m
cyst /sɪst/ n ciste f. **~itis** /-'staɪtɪs/ n cistite f
Czech /tʃek/ a ceco; **~ Republic** Repubblica f Ceca • n ceco, -a mf
Czechoslovak /tʃekə'sləʊvæk/ a cecoslovacco. **~ia** /-'vækɪə/ n Cecoslovacchia f

Dd

dab /dæb/ n colpetto m; **a ~ of** un pochino di ● vt (pt/pp **dabbed**) toccare leggermente ‹eyes›. **dab on** vt mettere un po' di ‹paint etc›

dabble /'dæbl/ vi ~ **in sth** fig occuparsi di qcsa a tempo perso

dachshund /'dækshund/ n bassotto m

dad[dy] /'dæd[ɪ]/ n fam papà m inv, babbo m

daddy-'long-legs n zanzarone m [dei boschi]; ‹Am: spider› ragno m

daffodil /'dæfədɪl/ n giunchiglia f

daft /dɑːft/ a sciocco

dagger /'dægə(r)/ n stiletto m

dahlia /'deɪlɪə/ n dalia f

daily /'deɪlɪ/ a giornaliero ● adv giornalmente ● n ‹newspaper› quotidiano m; ‹fam: cleaner› donna f delle pulizie

dainty /'deɪntɪ/ a (-ier, -iest) grazioso; ‹movement› delicato

dairy /'deərɪ/ n caseificio m; ‹shop› latteria f. ~ **cow** n mucca f da latte. ~ **products** npl latticini mpl

dais /'deɪɪs/ n pedana f

daisy /'deɪzɪ/ n margheritina f; ‹larger› margherita f

dale /deɪl/ n liter valle f

dam /dæm/ n diga f ● vt (pt/pp **dammed**) costruire una diga su

damage /'dæmɪdʒ/ n danno m (**to** a); ~es pl Jur risarcimento msg ● vt danneggiare; fig nuocere a. ~**ing** a dannoso

dame /deɪm/ n liter dama f; Am sl donna f

damn /dæm/ a fam maledetto ● adv ‹lucky, late› maledettamente ● n **I don't care** or **give a ~** fam non me ne frega un accidente ● vt dannare. ~**ation** /-'neɪʃn/ n dannazione f ● int fam accidenti!

damp /dæmp/ a umido ● n umidità f ● vt = **dampen**

damp|en /'dæmpən/ vt inumidire; fig raffreddare ‹enthusiasm›. ~**ness** n umidità f

dance /dɑːns/ n ballo m ● vt/i ballare. ~-**hall** n sala f da ballo. ~ **music** n musica f da ballo

dancer /'dɑːnsə(r)/ n ballerino, -a mf

dandelion /'dændɪlaɪən/ n dente m di leone

dandruff /'dændrʌf/ n forfora f

Dane /deɪn/ n danese mf; **Great ~** danese m

danger /'deɪndʒə(r)/ n pericolo m; **in/out of ~** in/fuori pericolo. ~**ous** /-rəs/ a pericoloso. ~**ously** adv pericolosamente; ~**ously ill** in pericolo di vita

dangle /'dæŋgl/ vi penzolare ● vt far penzolare

Danish /'deɪnɪʃ/ a & n danese. ~ '**pastry** n dolce m a base di pasta sfoglia contenente pasta di mandorle, mele ecc

dank /dæŋk/ a umido e freddo

Danube /'dænjuːb/ n Danubio m

dare /deə(r)/ vt/i osare; ‹challenge› sfidare (**to** a); ~ [**to**] **do sth** osare fare qcsa; **I ~ say!** molto probabilmente! ● n sfida f. ~-**devil** n spericolato, -a mf

daring /'deərɪŋ/ a audace ● n audacia f

dark /dɑːk/ a buio; ~ **blue/brown** blu/marrone scuro; **it's getting ~** sta cominciando a fare buio; ~ **horse** fig ‹in race, contest› vincitore m imprevisto; ‹not much known about› misterioso m; **keep sth ~** fig tenere qcsa nascosto ● n **after ~** col buio; **in the ~** al buio; **keep sb in the ~** fig tenere qcno all'oscuro

dark|en /'dɑːkn/ vt oscurare ● vi oscurarsi. ~**ness** n buio m

'**dark-room** n camera f oscura

darling /'dɑːlɪŋ/ a adorabile; **my ~ Joan** carissima Joan ● n tesoro m

darn /dɑːn/ vt rammendare. ~**ing-needle** n ago m da rammendo

dart /dɑːt/ n dardo m; ‹in sewing› pince f inv; ~**s** sg ‹game› freccette fpl ● vi lanciarsi

dartboard /'dɑːtbɔːd/ n bersaglio m [per freccette]

dash /dæʃ/ n Typ trattino m; ‹in Morse› linea f; **a ~ of milk** un goccio di latte; **make a ~ for** lanciarsi verso ● vi **I must ~** devo scappare ● vt far svanire ‹hopes›. **dash off** vi scappar via ● vt (*write quickly*) buttare giù. **dash out** *vi* uscire di corsa

'**dashboard** *n* cruscotto *m*

dashing /ˈdæʃɪŋ/ *a* (*bold*) ardito; (*in appearance*) affascinante

data /ˈdeɪtə/ *npl & sg* dati *mpl*. **~base** *n* base [di] dati *f*, database *m inv*. **~comms** /ˈkɒmz/ *n* telematica *f*. **~ processing** *n* elaborazione *f* [di] dati

date[1] /deɪt/ *n* (*fruit*) dattero *m*

date[2] *n* data *f*; (*meeting*) appuntamento *m*; **to ~** fino ad oggi; **out of ~** (*not fashionable*) fuori moda; (*expired*) scaduto; ‹*information*› non aggiornato; **make a ~ with sb** dare un appuntamento a qcno; **be up to ~** essere aggiornato ● *vt/i* datare; (*go out with*) uscire con. **date back to** *vi* risalire a

dated /ˈdeɪtɪd/ *a* fuori moda; ‹*language*› antiquato

'**date-line** *n* linea *f* [del cambiamento] di data

daub /dɔːb/ *vt* imbrattare ‹*walls*›

daughter /ˈdɔːtə(r)/ *n* figlia *f*. **~-in-law** *n* (*pl* **~s-in-law**) nuora *f*

daunt /dɔːnt/ *vt* scoraggiare; **nothing ~ed** per niente scoraggiato. **~less** *a* intrepido

dawdle /ˈdɔːdl/ *vi* bighellonare; (*over work*) cincischiarsi

dawn /dɔːn/ *n* alba *f*; **at ~** all'alba ● *vi* albeggiare; **it ~ed on me** *fig* mi è apparso chiaro

day /deɪ/ *n* giorno *m*; (*whole day*) giornata *f*, (*period*) epoca *f*; **these ~s** oggigiorno; **in those ~s** a quei tempi; **it's had its ~** *fam* ha fatto il suo tempo

day: ~break *n* **at ~break** allo spuntar del giorno. **~-dream** *n* sogno *m* ad occhi aperti ● *vi* sognare ad occhi aperti. **~light** *n* luce *f* del giorno. **~ re'turn** *n* (*ticket*) biglietto *m* di andata e ritorno con validità giornaliera. **~time** *n* giorno *m*; **in the ~time** di giorno

daze /deɪz/ *n* **in a ~** stordito; *fig* sbalordito. **~d** *a* stordito; *fig* sbalordito

dazzle /ˈdæzl/ *vt* abbagliare

deacon /ˈdiːkn/ *n* diacono *m*

dead /ded/ *a* morto; (*numb*) intorpidito; **~ body** morto *m*; **~ centre** pieno centro *m* ● *adv* **~ tired** stanco morto; **~ slow/easy** lentissimo/facilissimo; **you're ~ right** hai perfettamente ragione; **stop ~** fermarsi di colpo; **be ~ on time** essere in perfetto orario ● **the ~** *pl* i morti; **in the ~ of night** nel cuore della notte

deaden /ˈdedn/ *vt* attutire ‹*sound*›; calmare ‹*pain*›

dead: ~ 'end *n* vicolo *m* cieco. **~ 'heat** *n* **it was a ~ heat** è finita a pari merito. **~line** *n* scadenza *f*. **~lock** *n* **reach ~lock** *fig* giungere a un punto morto

deadly /ˈdedlɪ/ *a* (**-ier, -iest**) mortale; (*fam: dreary*) barboso; **~ sins** peccati *mpl* capitali

deadpan /ˈdedpæn/ *a* impassibile; ‹*humour*› all'inglese

deaf /def/ *a* sordo; **~ and dumb** sordomuto. **~-aid** *n* apparecchio *m* acustico

deaf|en /ˈdefn/ *vt* assordare; (*permanently*) render sordo. **~ening** *a* assordante. **~ness** *n* sordità *f*

deal /diːl/ *n* (*agreement*) patto *m*; (*in business*) accordo *m*; **whose ~?** (*in cards*) a chi tocca dare le carte?; **a good or great ~** molto; **get a raw ~** *fam* ricevere un trattamento ingiusto ● *vt* (*pt/pp* **dealt** /delt/) (*in cards*) dare; **~ sb a blow** dare un colpo a qcno. **deal in** *vt* trattare in. **deal out** *vt* ‹*hand out*› distribuire. **deal with** *vt* ‹*handle*› occuparsi di; trattare con ‹*company*›; (*be about*) trattare di; **that's been ~t with** è stato risolto

deal|er /ˈdiːlə(r)/ *n* commerciante *mf*; (*in drugs*) spacciatore, -trice *mf*. **~ings** *npl* **have ~ings with** avere a che fare con

dean /diːn/ *n* decano *m*; *Univ* preside *mf* di facoltà

dear /dɪə(r)/ *a* caro; (*in letter*) Caro; (*formal*) Gentile ● *n* caro, -a *mf* ● *int* **oh ~!** Dio mio!. **~ly** *adv* ‹*love*› profondamente; ‹*pay*› profumatamente

dearth /dɜːθ/ *n* penuria *f*

death /deθ/ *n* morte *f*. **~ certificate** *n* certificato *m* di morte. **~ duty** *n* tassa *f* di successione

deathly /ˈdeθlɪ/ *a* **~ silence** silenzio *m* di tomba ● *adv* **~ pale** di un pallore cadaverico

death: ~ penalty *n* pena *f* di morte. **~-trap** *n* trappola *f* mortale

debar /dɪˈbɑː(r)/ *vt* (*pt/pp* **debarred**) escludere

debase /dɪˈbeɪs/ *vt* degradare

debatable /dɪˈbeɪtəbl/ *a* discutibile

debate /dɪˈbeɪt/ *n* dibattito *m* ● *vt* discutere; (*in formal debate*) dibattere ● *vi* **~ whether to...** considerare se...

debauchery /dɪˈbɔːtʃərɪ/ *n* dissolutezza *f*

debility /dɪˈbɪlɪtɪ/ *n* debilitazione *f*

debit /'debɪt/ n debito m ● vt (pt/pp **debited**) Comm addebitare ‹sum›

debris /'debri:/ n macerie fpl

debt /det/ n debito m; **be in** ~ avere dei debiti. ~**or** n debitore, -trice mf

début /'deɪbu:/ n debutto m

decade /'dekeɪd/ n decennio m

decaden|ce /'dekədəns/ n decadenza f. ~**t** a decadente

decaffeinated /di:'kæfɪneɪtɪd/ a decaffeinato

decant /dɪ'kænt/ vt travasare. ~**er** n caraffa f (di cristallo)

decapitate /dɪ'kæpɪteɪt/ vt decapitare

decay /dɪ'keɪ/ n (also fig) decadenza f; (rot) decomposizione f; (of tooth) carie f inv ● vi imputridire; (rot) decomporsi; ‹tooth:› cariarsi

deceased /dɪ'si:st/ a defunto ● n the ~**d** il defunto; la defunta

deceit /dɪ'si:t/ n inganno m. ~**ful** a falso

deceive /dɪ'si:v/ vt ingannare

December /dɪ'sembə(r)/ n dicembre m

decency /'di:sənsɪ/ n decenza f

decent /'di:sənt/ a decente; (respectable) rispettabile; **very** ~ **of you** molto gentile da parte tua. ~**ly** adv decentemente; (kindly) gentilmente

decentralize /di:'sentrəlaɪz/ vt decentrare

decept|ion /dɪ'sepʃn/ n inganno m. ~**ive** /-tɪv/ a ingannevole. ~**ively** adv ingannevolmente; **it looks** ~**ively easy** sembra facile, ma non lo è

decibel /'desɪbel/ n decibel m inv

decide /dɪ'saɪd/ vt decidere ● vi decidere (**on** di)

decided /dɪ'saɪdɪd/ a risoluto. ~**ly** adv risolutamente; (without doubt) senza dubbio

deciduous /dɪ'sɪdjʊəs/ a a foglie decidue

decimal /'desɪml/ a decimale ● n numero m decimale. ~ '**point** n virgola f

decimate /'desɪmeɪt/ vt decimare

decipher /dɪ'saɪfə(r)/ vt decifrare

decision /dɪ'sɪʒn/ n decisione f

decisive /dɪ'saɪsɪv/ a decisivo

deck[1] /dek/ vt abbigliare

deck[2] n Naut ponte m; **on** ~ in coperta; **top** ~ (of bus) piano m di sopra; ~ **of cards** mazzo m. ~-**chair** n (sedia f a) sdraio f inv

declaration /deklə'reɪʃn/ n dichiarazione f

declare /dɪ'kleə(r)/ vt dichiarare; **anything to** ~? niente da dichiarare?

declension /dɪ'klenʃn/ n declinazione f

decline /dɪ'klaɪn/ n declino m ● vt also Gram declinare ● vi (decrease) diminuire; ‹health:› deperire; (say no) rifiutare

decode /di:'kəʊd/ vt decifrare; Comput decodificare

decompose /di:kəm'pəʊz/ vi decomporsi

décor /'deɪkɔ:(r)/ n decorazione f; (including furniture) arredamento m

decorat|e /'dekəreɪt/ vt decorare; (paint) pitturare; (wallpaper) tappezzare. ~**ion** /-'reɪʃn/ n decorazione f. ~**ive** /-rətɪv/ a decorativo. ~**or** n painter **and** ~**or** imbianchino m

decorum /dɪ'kɔ:rəm/ n decoro m

decoy[1] /'di:kɔɪ/ n esca f

decoy[2] /dɪ'kɔɪ/ vt adescare

decrease[1] /'di:kri:s/ n diminuzione f

decrease[2] /dɪ'kri:s/ vt/i diminuire

decree /dɪ'kri:/ n decreto m ● vt (pt/pp **decreed**) decretare

decrepit /dɪ'krepɪt/ a decrepito

dedicat|e /'dedɪkeɪt/ vt dedicare. ~**ed** a ‹person› scrupoloso. ~**ion** /-'keɪʃn/ n dedizione f; (in book) dedica f

deduce /dɪ'dju:s/ vt dedurre (**from** da)

deduct /dɪ'dʌkt/ vt dedurre

deduction /dɪ'dʌkʃn/ n deduzione f

deed /di:d/ n azione f; Jur atto m di proprietà

deem /di:m/ vt ritenere

deep /di:p/ a profondo; **go off the** ~ **end** fam arrabbiarsi. ~**ly** adv profondamente

deepen /'di:pn/ vt approfondire; scavare più profondamente (trench) ● vi approfondirsi; ⟨fig: mystery:⟩ infittirsi

deep-'freeze n congelatore m

deer /dɪə(r)/ n inv cervo m

deface /dɪ'feɪs/ vt sfigurare ⟨picture⟩; deturpare ⟨monument⟩

defamat|ion /defə'meɪʃn/ n diffamazione f. ~**ory** /dɪ'fæmətərɪ/ a diffamatorio

default /dɪ'fɔ:lt/ n (Jur: non-payment) morosità f; (failure to appear) contumacia f; **win by** ~ Sport vincere per abbandono dell'avversario; **in** ~ **of** per mancanza di ● a ~ **drive** Comput lettore m di default ● vi (not pay) venir meno a un pagamento

defeat /dɪ'fi:t/ n sconfitta f ● vt sconfiggere; (frustrate) vanificare ⟨attempts⟩; **that** ~**s the object** questo fa fallire l'obiettivo

defect[1] /dɪ'fekt/ vi Pol fare defezione

defect² /'di:fekt/ n difetto m. **~ive** /dɪ'fektɪv/ a difettoso

defence /dɪ'fens/ n difesa f. **~less** a indifeso

defend /dɪ'fend/ vt difendere; ⟨justify⟩ giustificare. **~ant** n Jur imputato, -a mf

defensive /dɪ'fensɪv/ a difensivo ● n difensiva f; **on the ~** sulla difensiva

defer /dɪ'fɜ:(r)/ v (pt/pp deferred) ● vt ⟨postpone⟩ rinviare ● vi **~ to sb** rimettersi a qcno

deferen|ce /'defərəns/ n deferenza f. **~tial** /-'renʃl/ a deferente

defian|ce /dɪ'faɪəns/ n sfida f; **in ~ce of** sfidando. **~t** a ⟨person⟩ ribelle; ⟨gesture, attitude⟩ di sfida. **~tly** adv con aria di sfida

deficien|cy /dɪ'fɪʃənsɪ/ n insufficienza f. **~t** a insufficiente; **be ~t in** mancare di

deficit /'defɪsɪt/ n deficit m inv

defile /dɪ'faɪl/ vt fig contaminare

define /dɪ'faɪn/ vt definire

definite /'defɪnɪt/ a definito; ⟨certain⟩ ⟨answer, yes⟩ definitivo; ⟨improvement, difference⟩ netto; **he was ~ about it** è stato chiaro in proposito. **~ly** adv sicuramente

definition /defɪ'nɪʃn/ n definizione f

definitive /dɪ'fɪnətɪv/ a definitivo

deflat|e /dɪ'fleɪt/ vt sgonfiare. **~ion** /-eɪʃn/ n Comm deflazione f

deflect /dɪ'flekt/ vt deflettere

deform|ed /dɪ'fɔ:md/ a deforme. **~ity** n deformità f inv

defraud /dɪ'frɔ:d/ vt defraudare

defrost /di:'frɒst/ vt sbrinare ⟨fridge⟩; scongelare ⟨food⟩

deft /deft/ a abile

defunct /dɪ'fʌŋkt/ a morto e sepolto; ⟨law⟩ caduto in disuso

defuse /di:'fju:z/ vt disinnescare; calmare ⟨situation⟩

defy /dɪ'faɪ/ vt (pt/pp -ied) ⟨challenge⟩ sfidare; resistere a ⟨attempt⟩; ⟨not obey⟩ disobbedire a

degenerate¹ /dɪ'dʒenəreɪt/ vi degenerare; **~ into** fig degenerare in

degenerate² /dɪ'dʒenərət/ a degenerato

degrading /dɪ'greɪdɪŋ/ a degradante

degree /dɪ'gri:/ n grado m; Univ laurea f; **20 ~s** 20 gradi; **not to the same ~** non allo stesso livello

dehydrate /di:'haɪdreɪt/ vt disidratare. **~d** /-ɪd/ a disidratato

de-ice /di:'aɪs/ vt togliere il ghiaccio da

deign /deɪn/ vi **~ to do sth** degnarsi di fare qcsa

deity /'di:ɪtɪ/ n divinità f inv

dejected /dɪ'dʒektɪd/ a demoralizzato

delay /dɪ'leɪ/ n ritardo m; **without ~** senza indugio ● vt ritardare; **be ~ed** ⟨person:⟩ essere trattenuto; ⟨train, aircraft:⟩ essere in ritardo ● vi indugiare

delegate¹ /'delɪgət/ n delegato, -a mf

delegat|e² /'delɪgeɪt/ vt delegare. **~ion** /-'geɪʃn/ n delegazione f

delet|e /dɪ'li:t/ vt cancellare. **~ion** /-i:ʃn/ n cancellatura f

deliberate¹ /dɪ'lɪbərət/ a deliberato; ⟨slow⟩ posato. **~ly** adv deliberatamente; ⟨slowly⟩ in modo posato

deliberat|e² /dɪ'lɪbəreɪt/ vt/i deliberare. **~ion** /-'reɪʃn/ n deliberazione f

delicacy /'delɪkəsɪ/ n delicatezza f; ⟨food⟩ prelibatezza f

delicate /'delɪkət/ a delicato

delicatessen /delɪkə'tesn/ n negozio m di specialità gastronomiche

delicious /dɪ'lɪʃəs/ a delizioso

delight /dɪ'laɪt/ n piacere m ● vt deliziare ● vi **~ in** dilettarsi con. **~ed** a lieto. **~ful** a delizioso

delinquen|cy /dɪ'lɪŋkwənsɪ/ n delinquenza f. **~t** a delinquente ● n delinquente mf

deli|rious /dɪ'lɪrɪəs/ a **be ~rious** delirare; ⟨fig: very happy⟩ essere pazzo di gioia. **~rium** /-rɪəm/ n delirio m

deliver /dɪ'lɪvə(r)/ vt consegnare; recapitare ⟨post, newspaper⟩; tenere ⟨speech⟩; dare ⟨message⟩; tirare ⟨blow⟩; ⟨set free⟩ liberare; **~ a baby** far nascere un bambino. **~ance** n liberazione f. **~y** n consegna f; ⟨of post⟩ distribuzione f; Med parto m; **cash on ~y** pagamento m alla consegna

delude /dɪ'lu:d/ vt ingannare; **~ oneself** illudersi

deluge /'delju:dʒ/ n diluvio m ● vt ⟨fig: with requests etc⟩ inondare

delusion /dɪ'lu:ʒn/ n illusione f

de luxe /də'lʌks/ a di lusso

delve /delv/ vi **~ into** ⟨into pocket etc⟩ frugare in; ⟨into notes, the past⟩ fare ricerche in

demand /dɪ'mɑ:nd/ n richiesta f; Comm domanda f; **in ~** richiesto; **on ~** a richiesta ● vt esigere (**of/from** da). **~ing** a esigente

demarcation /di:mɑ:'keɪʃn/ n demarcazione f

demean /dɪ'mi:n/ vt ~ **oneself** abbassarsi (**to** a)

demeanour /dɪ'mi:nə(r)/ n comportamento m

demented /dɪ'mentɪd/ a demente

demise /dɪ'maɪz/ n decesso m

demister /di:'mɪstə(r)/ n Auto sbrinatore m

demo /'deməʊ/ n (pl ~s) fam manifestazione f. ~ **disk** n Comput demodisk m inv

democracy /dɪ'mɒkrəsɪ/ n democrazia f

democrat /'deməkræt/ n democratico, -a mf. ~**ic** /-'krætɪk/ a democratico

demo|lish /dɪ'mɒlɪʃ/ vt demolire. ~**lition** /demə'lɪʃn/ n demolizione f

demon /'di:mən/ n demonio m

demonstrat|e /'demənstreɪt/ vt dimostrare; fare una dimostrazione sull'uso di ⟨appliance⟩ ● vi Pol manifestare. ~**ion** /-'streɪʃn/ n dimostrazione f; Pol manifestazione f

demonstrative /dɪ'mɒnstrətɪv/ a Gram dimostrativo; **be** ~ essere espansivo

demonstrator /'demənstreɪtə(r)/ n Pol manifestante mf, ⟨for product⟩ dimostratore, -trice mf

demoralize /dɪ'mɒrəlaɪz/ vt demoralizzare

demote /dɪ'məʊt/ vt retrocedere di grado; Mil degradare

demure /dɪ'mjʊə(r)/ a schivo

den /den/ n tana f; ⟨room⟩ rifugio m

denial /dɪ'naɪəl/ n smentita f

denim /'denɪm/ n [tessuto m] jeans m; ~**s** pl [blue]jeans mpl

Denmark /'denmɑ:k/ n Danimarca f

denomination /dɪnɒmɪ'neɪʃn/ n Relig confessione f; ⟨money⟩ valore f

denounce /dɪ'naʊns/ vt denunciare

dens|e /dens/ a denso; ⟨crowd, forest⟩ fitto; ⟨stupid⟩ ottuso. ~**ely** adv ⟨populated⟩ densamente; ~**ely wooded** fittamente ricoperto di alberi. ~**ity** n densità f inv; ⟨of forest⟩ fittezza f

dent /dent/ n ammaccatura f ● vt ammaccare; ~**ed** a ammaccato

dental /'dentl/ a dei denti; ⟨treatment⟩ dentistico; ⟨hygiene⟩ dentale. ~ **surgeon** n odontoiatra mf, medico m dentista

dentist /'dentɪst/ n dentista mf. ~**ry** n odontoiatria f

dentures /'dentʃəz/ npl dentiera fsg

denunciation /dɪnʌnsɪ'eɪʃn/ n denuncia f

deny /dɪ'naɪ/ vt (pt/pp -**ied**) negare; ⟨officially⟩ smentire; ~ **sb sth** negare qcsa a qcno

deodorant /di:'əʊdərənt/ n deodorante m

depart /dɪ'pɑ:t/ vi ⟨plane, train:⟩ partire; ⟨liter: person⟩ andare via; ⟨deviate⟩ allontanarsi (**from** da)

department /dɪ'pɑ:tmənt/ n reparto m; Pol ministero m; ⟨of company⟩ sezione f; Univ dipartimento m. ~ **store** n grande magazzino m

departure /dɪ'pɑ:tʃə(r)/ n partenza f, ⟨from rule⟩ allontanamento m; **new** ~ svolta f

depend /dɪ'pend/ vi dipendere (**on** da); ⟨rely⟩ contare (**on** su); **it all** ~**s** dipende; ~**ing on what he says** a seconda di quello che dice. ~**able** /-əbl/ a affidabile. ~**ant** n persona f a carico. ~**ence** n dipendenza f. ~**ent** a dipendente (**on** da)

depict /dɪ'pɪkt/ vt ⟨in writing⟩ dipingere; ⟨with picture⟩ rappresentare

depilatory /dɪ'pɪlətərɪ/ n ⟨cream⟩ crema f depilatoria

deplete /dɪ'pli:t/ vt ridurre; **totally** ~**d** completamente esaurito

deplor|able /dɪ'plɔ:rəbl/ a deplorevole. ~**e** vt deplorare

deploy /dɪ'plɔɪ/ vt Mil spiegare ● vi schierarsi

deport /dɪ'pɔ:t/ vt deportare. ~**ation** /di:pɔ:'teɪʃn/ n deportazione f

depose /dɪ'pəʊz/ vt deporre

deposit /dɪ'pɒzɪt/ n deposito m; ⟨against damage⟩ cauzione f; ⟨first instalment⟩ acconto m ● vt (pt/pp **deposited**) depositare. ~ **account** n libretto m di risparmio; ⟨without instant access⟩ conto m vincolato

depot /'depəʊ/ n deposito m; Am Rail stazione f ferroviaria

deprav|e /dɪ'preɪv/ vt depravare. ~**ed** a depravato. ~**ity** /-'prævətɪ/ n depravazione f

depreciat|e /dɪ'pri:ʃɪeɪt/ vi deprezzarsi. ~**ion** /-'eɪʃn/ n deprezzamento m

depress /dɪ'pres/ vt deprimere; ⟨press down⟩ premere. ~**ed** a depresso; ~**ed area** zona f depressa. ~**ing** a deprimente. ~**ion** /-eʃn/ n depressione f

deprivation /deprɪ'veɪʃn/ n privazione f

deprive /dɪ'praɪv/ vt ~ **sb of sth** privare qcno di qcsa. ~**d** a ⟨area, childhood⟩ disagiato

depth /depθ/ n profondità f inv; **in** ~ ⟨study, analyse⟩ in modo approfondito;

in the ~s of winter in pieno inverno; **be out of one's ~** (*in water*) non toccare il fondo; *fig* sentirsi in alto mare

deputation /depjʊ'teɪʃn/ n deputazione f

deputize /'depjʊtaɪz/ vi ~ **for** fare le veci di

deputy /'depjʊtɪ/ n vice mf; (*temporary*) sostituto, -a mf ● attrib ~ **leader** vicesegretario, -a mf; ~ **chairman** vicepresidente mf

derail /dɪ'reɪl/ vt **be ~ed** (*train:*) essere deragliato. **~ment** n deragliamento m

deranged /dɪ'reɪndʒd/ a squilibrato

derelict /'derəlɪkt/ a abbandonato

deri|de /dɪ'raɪd/ vt deridere. **~sion** /-'rɪʒn/ n derisione f

derisory /dɪ'raɪsərɪ/ a (*laughter*) derisorio; (*offer*) irrisorio

derivation /derɪ'veɪʃn/ n derivazione f

derivative /dɪ'rɪvətɪv/ a derivato ● n derivato m

derive /dɪ'raɪv/ vt (*obtain*) derivare; **be ~d from** (*word:*) derivare da

dermatologist /dɜ:mə'tɒlədʒɪst/ n dermatologo, -a mf

derogatory /dɪ'rɒgətrɪ/ a (*comments*) peggiorativo

descend /dɪ'send/ vi scendere ● vt scendere da; **be ~ed from** discendere da. **~ant** n discendente mf

descent /dɪ'sent/ n discesa f; (*lineage*) origine f

describe /dɪ'skraɪb/ vt descrivere

descrip|tion /dɪ'skrɪpʃn/ n descrizione f; **they had no help of any ~tion** non hanno avuto proprio nessun aiuto. **~tive** /-tɪv/ a descrittivo; (*vivid*) vivido

desecrat|e /'desɪkreɪt/ vt profanare. **~ion** /-'kreɪʃn/ n profanazione f

desert[1] /'dezət/ n deserto m ● a deserto; ~ **island** isola f deserta

desert[2] /dɪ'zɜ:t/ vt abbandonare ● vi disertare. **~ed** a deserto. **~er** n Mil disertore m. **~ion** /-'zɜ:ʃn/ n Mil diserzione f; (*of family*) abbandono m

deserts /dɪ'zɜ:ts/ npl **get one's just ~** ottenere ciò che ci si merita

deserv|e /dɪ'zɜ:v/ vt meritare. **~ing** a meritevole; **~ing cause** opera f meritoria

design /dɪ'zaɪn/ n progettazione f; (*fashion ~, appearance*) design m inv; (*pattern*) modello m; (*aim*) proposito m ● vt progettare; disegnare (*clothes, furniture, model*); **be ~ed for** essere fatto per

designat|e /'dezɪgneɪt/ vt designare. **~ion** /-'neɪʃn/ n designazione f

designer /dɪ'zaɪnə(r)/ n progettista mf; (*of clothes*) stilista mf; (*Theat: of set*) scenografo, -a mf

desirable /dɪ'zaɪərəbl/ a desiderabile

desire /dɪ'zaɪə(r)/ n desiderio m ● vt desiderare

desk /desk/ n scrivania f; (*in school*) banco m; (*in hotel*) reception f inv; (*cash ~*) cassa f. **~top 'publishing** n desktop publishing m, editoria f da tavolo

desolat|e /'desələt/ a desolato. **~ion** /-'leɪʃn/ n desolazione f

despair /dɪ'speə(r)/ n disperazione f; **in ~** disperato; (*say*) per disperazione ● vi **I ~ of that boy** quel ragazzo mi fa disperare

desperat|e /'despərət/ a disperato; **be ~e** (*criminal:*) essere un disperato; **be ~e for sth** morire dalla voglia di. **~ely** adv disperatamente; **he said ~ely** ha detto, disperato. **~ion** /-'reɪʃn/ n disperazione f; **in ~ion** per disperazione

despicable /dɪ'spɪkəbl/ a disprezzevole

despise /dɪ'spaɪz/ vt disprezzare

despite /dɪ'spaɪt/ prep malgrado

despondent /dɪ'spɒndənt/ a abbattuto

despot /'despɒt/ n despota m

dessert /dɪ'zɜ:t/ n dolce m. ~ **spoon** n cucchiaio m da dolce

destination /destɪ'neɪʃn/ n destinazione f

destine /'destɪn/ vt destinare; **be ~d for sth** essere destinato a qcsa

destiny /'destɪnɪ/ n destino m

destitute /'destɪtju:t/ a bisognoso

destroy /dɪ'strɔɪ/ vt distruggere. **~er** n Naut cacciatorpediniere m

destruc|tion /dɪ'strʌkʃn/ n distruzione f. **~tive** /-tɪv/ a distruttivo; (*fig: criticism*) negativo

detach /dɪ'tætʃ/ vt staccare. **~able** /-əbl/ a separabile. **~ed** a fig distaccato; **~ed house** villetta f

detachment /dɪ'tætʃmənt/ n distacco m; Mil distaccamento m

detail /'di:teɪl/ n particolare m, dettaglio m; **in ~** particolareggiatamente ● vt esporre con tutti i particolari; Mil assegnare. **~ed** a particolareggiato, dettagliato

detain /dɪ'teɪn/ vt (*police:*) trattenere; (*delay*) far ritardare. **~ee** /di:teɪ'ni:/ n detenuto, -a mf

detect /dɪ'tekt/ vt individuare;

(*perceive*) percepire. **~ion** /-ekʃn/ *n* scoperta *f*

detective /dɪˈtektɪv/ *n* investigatore, -trice *mf*. **~ story** *n* racconto *m* poliziesco

detector /dɪˈtektə(r)/ *n* (*for metal*) metal detector *m inv*

detention /dɪˈtenʃn/ *n* detenzione *f*; *Sch* punizione *f*

deter /dɪˈtɜː(r)/ *vt* (*pt/pp* **deterred**) impedire; **~ sb from doing sth** impedire a qcno di fare qcsa

detergent /dɪˈtɜːdʒənt/ *n* detersivo *m*

deteriorat|e /dɪˈtɪərɪəreɪt/ *vi* deteriorarsi. **~ion** /-ˈreɪʃn/ *n* deterioramento *m*

determination /dɪtɜːmɪˈneɪʃn/ *n* determinazione *f*

determine /dɪˈtɜːmɪn/ *vt* (*ascertain*) determinare; **~ to** (*resolve*) decidere di. **~d** *a* deciso

deterrent /dɪˈterənt/ *n* deterrente *m*

detest /dɪˈtest/ *vt* detestare. **~able** /-əbl/ *a* detestabile

detonat|e /ˈdetəneɪt/ *vt* far detonare ● *vi* detonare. **~or** *n* detonatore *m*

detour /ˈdiːtʊə(r)/ *n* deviazione *f*

detract /dɪˈtrækt/ *vi* **~ from** sminuire (*merit*); rovinare (*pleasure, beauty*)

detriment /ˈdetrɪmənt/ *n* **to the ~ of** a danno di. **~al** /-ˈmentl/ *a* dannoso

deuce /djuːs/ *n Tennis* deuce *m inv*

devaluation /diːvæljʊˈeɪʃn/ *n* svalutazione *f*

de'value *vt* svalutare (*currency*)

devastat|e /ˈdevəsteɪt/ *vt* devastare. **~ed** *a fam* sconvolto. **~ing** *a* devastante; (*news*) sconvolgente. **~ion** /-ˈsteɪʃn/ *n* devastazione *f*

develop /dɪˈveləp/ *vt* sviluppare; contrarre (*illness*); (*add to value of*) valorizzare (*area*) ● *vi* svilupparsi; **~ into** divenire. **~er** *n* [**property**] **~er** imprenditore, -trice *mf* edile

de'veloping country *n* paese *m* in via di sviluppo

development /dɪˈveləpmənt/ *n* sviluppo *m*; (*of vaccine etc*) messa *f* a punto

deviant /ˈdiːvɪənt/ *a* deviato

deviat|e /ˈdiːvɪeɪt/ *vi* deviare. **~ion** /-ˈeɪʃn/ *n* deviazione *f*

device /dɪˈvaɪs/ *n* dispositivo *m*

devil /ˈdevl/ *n* diavolo *m*

devious /ˈdiːvɪəs/ *a* (*person*) subdolo; (*route*) tortuoso

devise /dɪˈvaɪz/ *vt* escogitare

devoid /dɪˈvɔɪd/ *a* **~ of** privo di

devolution /diːvəˈluːʃn/ *n* (*of power*) decentramento *m*

devot|e /dɪˈvəʊt/ *vt* dedicare. **~ed** *a* (*daughter etc*) affezionato; **be ~ed to sth** consacrarsi a qcsa. **~ee** /devəˈtiː/ *n* appassionato, -a *mf*

devotion /dɪˈvəʊʃn/ *n* dedizione *f*; **~s** *pl Relig* devozione *fsg*

devour /dɪˈvaʊə(r)/ *vt* divorare

devout /dɪˈvaʊt/ *a* devoto

dew /djuː/ *n* rugiada *f*

dexterity /dekˈsterəti/ *n* destrezza *f*

diabet|es /daɪəˈbiːtiːz/ *n* diabete *m*. **~ic** /-ˈbetɪk/ *a* diabetico ● *n* diabetico, -a *mf*

diabolical /daɪəˈbɒlɪkl/ *a* diabolico

diagnose /daɪəgˈnəʊz/ *vt* diagnosticare

diagnosis /daɪəgˈnəʊsɪs/ *n* (*pl* **-oses** /-siːz/) diagnosi *f inv*

diagonal /daɪˈægənl/ *a* diagonale ● *n* diagonale *f*

diagram /ˈdaɪəgræm/ *n* diagramma *m*

dial /ˈdaɪəl/ *n* (*of clock, machine*) quadrante *m*; *Teleph* disco *m* combinatore ● *v* (*pt/pp* **dialled**) ● *vi Teleph* fare il numero; **~ direct** chiamare in teleselezione ● *vt* fare (*number*)

dialect /ˈdaɪəlekt/ *n* dialetto *m*

dialling **~ code** *n* prefisso *m*. **~ tone** *n* segnale *m* di linea libera

dialogue /ˈdaɪəlɒg/ *n* dialogo *m*

'dial tone *n Am Teleph* segnale *m* di linea libera

diameter /daɪˈæmɪtə(r)/ *n* diametro *m*

diametrically /daɪəˈmetrɪklɪ/ *adv* **~ opposed** diametralmente opposto

diamond /ˈdaɪəmənd/ *n* diamante *m*, brillante *m*; (*shape*) losanga *f*; **~s** *pl* (*in cards*) quadri *mpl*

diaper /ˈdaɪəpə(r)/ *n Am* pannolino *m*

diaphragm /ˈdaɪəfræm/ *n* diaframma *m*

diarrhoea /daɪəˈriːə/ *n* diarrea *f*

diary /ˈdaɪərɪ/ *n* (*for appointments*) agenda *f*; (*for writing in*) diario *m*

dice /daɪs/ *n inv* dadi *mpl* ● *vt Culin* tagliare a dadini

dicey /ˈdaɪsɪ/ *a fam* rischioso

dictat|e /dɪkˈteɪt/ *vt/i* dettare. **~ion** /-eɪʃn/ *n* dettato *m*

dictator /dɪkˈteɪtə(r)/ *n* dittatore *m*. **~ial** /-təˈtɔːrɪəl/ *a* dittatoriale. **~ship** *n* dittatura *f*

dictionary /ˈdɪkʃənrɪ/ *n* dizionario *m*

did /dɪd/ *see* **do**

didactic /dɪˈdæktɪk/ *a* didattico

diddle /ˈdɪdl/ *vt fam* gabbare

didn't /ˈdɪdnt/ = **did not**

die /daɪ/ *vi* (*pres p* **dying**) morire (**of** di); **be dying to do sth** *fam* morire dalla voglia di fare qcsa. **die down** vi calmarsi; ⟨fire, flames:⟩ spegnersi. **die out** vi estinguersi; ⟨custom:⟩ morire

diesel /'diːzl/ n diesel m

diet /'daɪət/ n regime m alimentare; ⟨restricted⟩ dieta f; **be on a ~** essere a dieta ● vi essere a dieta

differ /'dɪfə(r)/ vi differire; ⟨disagree⟩ non essere d'accordo

difference /'dɪfrəns/ n differenza f; ⟨disagreement⟩ divergenza f

different /'dɪfrənt/ a diverso, differente; ⟨various⟩ diversi; **be ~ from** essere diverso da

differential /dɪfə'renʃl/ a differenziale ● n differenziale m

differentiate /dɪfə'renʃɪeɪt/ vt distinguere (**between** fra); ⟨discriminate⟩ discriminare (**between** fra); ⟨make differ⟩ differenziare

differently /'dɪfrəntlɪ/ adv in modo diverso; **~ from** diversamente da

difficult /'dɪfɪkəlt/ a difficile. **~y** n difficoltà f inv; **with ~y** con difficoltà

diffuse[1] /dɪ'fjuːs/ a diffuso; ⟨wordy⟩ prolisso

diffuse[2] /dɪ'fjuːz/ vt Phys diffondere

dig /dɪg/ n ⟨poke⟩ spinta f; ⟨remark⟩ frecciata f; Archaeol scavo m; **~s** pl fam camera fsg ammobiliata ● vt/i ⟨pt/pp dug, pres p **digging**⟩ scavare ⟨hole⟩; vangare ⟨garden⟩; ⟨thrust⟩ conficcare; **~ sb in the ribs** dare una gomitata a qcno. **dig out** vt fig tirar fuori. **dig up** vt scavare ⟨garden, street, object⟩; sradicare ⟨tree, plant⟩; ⟨fig: find⟩ scovare

digest[1] /'daɪdʒest/ n compendio m

digest[2] /daɪ'dʒest/ vt digerire. **~ible** a digeribile. **~ion** /-estʃn/ n digestione f

digger /'dɪgə(r)/ n Techn scavatrice f

digit /'dɪdʒɪt/ n cifra f; ⟨finger⟩ dito m

digital /'dɪdʒɪtl/ a digitale; **~ clock** orologio m digitale

dignified /'dɪgnɪfaɪd/ a dignitoso

dignitary /'dɪgnɪtərɪ/ n dignitario m

dignity /'dɪgnɪtɪ/ n dignità f

digress /daɪ'gres/ vi divagare. **~ion** /-eʃn/ n digressione f

dike /daɪk/ n diga f

dilapidated /dɪ'læpɪdeɪtɪd/ a cadente

dilate /daɪ'leɪt/ vi dilatarsi

dilemma /dɪ'lemə/ n dilemma m

dilettante /dɪlɪ'tæntɪ/ n dilettante mf

dilly-dally /'dɪlɪdælɪ/ vi ⟨pt/pp **-ied**⟩ fam tentennare

dilute /daɪ'luːt/ vt diluire

dim /dɪm/ a (**dimmer, dimmest**) debole ⟨light⟩; ⟨dark⟩ scuro; ⟨prospect, chance⟩ scarso; ⟨indistinct⟩ impreciso; ⟨fam: stupid⟩ tonto ● vt/i ⟨pt/pp **dimmed**⟩ affievolire. **~ly** adv ⟨see, remember⟩ indistintamente; ⟨shine⟩ debolmente

dime /daɪm/ n Am moneta f da dieci centesimi

dimension /daɪ'menʃn/ n dimensione f

diminish /dɪ'mɪnɪʃ/ vt/i diminuire

diminutive /dɪ'mɪnjʊtɪv/ a minuscolo ● n diminutivo m

dimple /'dɪmpl/ n fossetta f

din /dɪn/ n baccano m

dine /daɪn/ vi pranzare. **~r** n ⟨Am: restaurant⟩ tavola f calda; **the last ~r in the restaurant** l'ultimo cliente nel ristorante

dinghy /'dɪŋgɪ/ n dinghy m; ⟨inflatable⟩ canotto m pneumatico

dingy /'dɪndʒɪ/ a (**-ier, -iest**) squallido e tetro

dining /'daɪnɪŋ/: **~-car** n carrozza f ristorante. **~-room** n sala f da pranzo. **~-table** n tavolo m da pranzo

dinner /'dɪnə(r)/ n cena f; ⟨at midday⟩ pranzo m. **~-jacket** n smoking m inv

dinosaur /'daɪnəsɔː(r)/ n dinosauro m

dint /dɪnt/ n **by ~ of** a forza di

diocese /'daɪəsɪs/ n diocesi f inv

dip /dɪp/ n ⟨in ground⟩ inclinazione f; Culin salsina f; **go for a ~** andare a fare una nuotata ● v ⟨pt/pp **dipped**⟩ ● vt ⟨in liquid⟩ immergere; abbassare ⟨head, headlights⟩ ● vi ⟨land:⟩ formare un avvallamento. **dip into** vt scorrere ⟨book⟩

diphtheria /dɪf'θɪərɪə/ n difterite f

diphthong /'dɪfθɒŋ/ n dittongo m

diploma /dɪ'pləʊmə/ n diploma m

diplomacy /dɪ'pləʊməsɪ/ n diplomazia f

diplomat /'dɪpləmæt/ n diplomatico, -a mf. **~ic** /-'mætɪk/ a diplomatico. **~ically** adv con diplomazia

'dip-stick n Auto astina f dell'olio

dire /'daɪə(r)/ a ⟨situation, consequences⟩ terribile

direct /dɪ'rekt/ a diretto ● adv direttamente ● vt ⟨aim⟩ rivolgere ⟨attention, criticism⟩; ⟨control⟩ dirigere; fare la regia di ⟨film, play⟩; **~ sb** ⟨show the way⟩ indicare la strada a qcno; **~ sb to do sth** ordinare a qcno di fare qcsa. **~ 'current** n corrente m continua

direction /dɪ'rekʃn/ n direzione f; ⟨of play, film⟩ regia f; **~s** pl indicazioni fpl

directly /dɪ'rektlɪ/ adv direttamente; ⟨at once⟩ immediatamente ● conj ⟨non⟩ appena

director /dɪˈrektə(r)/ n Comm direttore, -trice mf; (of play, film) regista mf

directory /dɪˈrektərɪ/ n elenco m; Teleph elenco m [telefonico]; (of streets) stradario m

dirt /dɜːt/ n sporco m; ~ **cheap** fam a [un] prezzo stracciato

dirty /ˈdɜːtɪ/ a (-ier, -iest) sporco; ~ **trick** brutto scherzo m; ~ **word** parolaccia f ● vt (pt/pp -ied) sporcare

dis|a'bility /dɪs-/ n infermità f inv. ~**abled** /dɪˈseɪbld/ a invalido

disad'van|tage n svantaggio m; **at a** ~**tage** in una posizione di svantaggio. ~**taged** a svantaggiato. ~'**tageous** a svantaggioso

disa'gree vi non essere d'accordo; ~ **with** ⟨food:⟩ far male a

disa'greeable a sgradevole

disa'greement n disaccordo m; (quarrel) dissidio m

disal'low vt annullare ⟨goal⟩

disap'pear vi scomparire. ~**ance** n scomparsa f

disap'point vt deludere; **I'm** ~**ed** sono deluso. ~**ing** a deludente. ~**ment** n delusione f

disap'proval n disapprovazione f

disap'prove vi disapprovare; ~ **of sb/sth** disapprovare qcno/qcsa

dis'arm vt disarmare ● vi Mil disarmarsi. ~**ament** n disarmo m. ~**ing** a ⟨frankness etc⟩ disarmante

disar'ray n **in** ~ in disordine

disast|er /dɪˈzɑːstə(r)/ n disastro m. ~**rous** /-rəs/ a disastroso

dis'band ● vt scogliere; smobilitare ⟨troops⟩ ● vi scogliersi; ⟨regiment:⟩ essere smobilitato

disbe'lief n incredulità f; **in** ~ con incredulità

disc /dɪsk/ n disco m; (CD) compact disc m inv

discard /dɪˈskɑːd/ vt scartare; (throw away) eliminare; scaricare ⟨boyfriend⟩

discern /dɪˈsɜːn/ vt discernere. ~**ible** a discernibile. ~**ing** a perspicace

'discharge¹ n Electr scarica f; (dismissal) licenziamento m; Mil congedo m; (Med: of blood) emissione f; (of cargo) scarico m

dis'charge² vt scaricare ⟨battery, cargo⟩; (dismiss) licenziare; Mil congedare; Jur assolvere ⟨accused⟩; dimettere ⟨patient⟩ ● vi Electr scaricarsi

disciple /dɪˈsaɪpl/ n discepolo m

disciplinary /ˈdɪsɪplɪnərɪ/ a disciplinare

discipline /ˈdɪsɪplɪn/ n disciplina f ● vt disciplinare; (punish) punire

'disc jockey n disc jockey m inv

dis'claim vt disconoscere. ~**er** n rifiuto m

dis'clos|e vt svelare. ~**ure** n rivelazione f

disco /ˈdɪskəʊ/ n discoteca f

dis'colour vt scolorire ● vi scolorirsi

dis'comfort n scomodità f; fig disagio m

disconcert /dɪskənˈsɜːt/ vt sconcertare

discon'nect vt disconnettere

disconsolate /dɪsˈkɒnsələt/ a sconsolato

discon'tent n scontentezza f. ~**ed** a scontento

discon'tinue vt cessare, smettere; Comm sospendere la produzione di; ~**d line** fine f serie

'discord n discordia f; Mus dissonanza f. ~**ant** /dɪˈskɔːdənt/ a ~**ant note** nota f discordante

discothèque /ˈdɪskətek/ n discoteca f

'discount¹ n sconto m

dis'count² vt (not believe) non credere a; (leave out of consideration) non tener conto di

dis'courage vt scoraggiare; (dissuade) dissuadere

'discourse n discorso m

dis'courteous a scortese

discover /dɪˈskʌvə(r)/ vt scoprire. ~**y** n scoperta f

dis'credit n discredito m ● vt (pt/pp **discredited**) screditare

discreet /dɪˈskriːt/ a discreto

discrepancy /dɪˈskrepənsɪ/ n discrepanza f

discretion /dɪˈskreʃn/ n discrezione f

discriminat|e /dɪˈskrɪmɪneɪt/ vi discriminare (**against** contro); ~**e between** distinguere tra. ~**ing** a esigente. ~**ion** /-ˈneɪʃn/ n discriminazione f; (quality) discernimento m

discus /ˈdɪskəs/ n disco m

discuss /dɪˈskʌs/ vt discutere; (examine critically) esaminare. ~**ion** /-ʌʃn/ n discussione f

disdain /dɪsˈdeɪn/ n sdegno f ● vt sdegnare. ~**ful** a sdegnoso

disease /dɪˈziːz/ n malattia f. ~**d** a malato

disem'bark vi sbarcare

disen'chant vt disincantare. ~**ment** n disincanto m

disen'gage vt disimpegnare; disinnestare ⟨clutch⟩

disen'tangle vt districare

dis'favour n sfavore m

dis'figure vt deformare

dis'grace n vergogna f; **I am in ~** sono caduto in disgrazia; **it's a ~** è una vergogna ● vt disonorare. **~ful** a vergognoso

disgruntled /dɪsˈgrʌntld/ a malcontento

disguise /dɪsˈgaɪz/ n travestimento m; **in ~** travestito ● vt contraffare ‹voice›; dissimulare ‹emotions›; **~d as** travestito da

disgust /dɪsˈgʌst/ n disgusto m; **in ~** con aria disgustata ● vt disgustare. **~ing** a disgustoso

dish /dɪʃ/ n piatto m; **do the ~es** lavare i piatti ● **dish out** vt ‹serve› servire; ‹distribute› distribuire. **dish up** vt servire

'dishcloth n strofinaccio m

dis'hearten vt scoraggiare

dishevelled /dɪˈʃevld/ a scompigliato

dis'honest a disonesto. **~y** n disonestà f

dis'honour n disonore m ● vt disonorare ‹family›; non onorare ‹cheque›. **~able** a disonorevole. **~ably** adv in modo disonorevole

'dishwasher n lavapiatti f inv

disil'lusion vt disilludere. **~ment** n disillusione f

disin'fect vt disinfettare. **~ant** n disinfettante m

disin'herit vt diseredare

dis'integrate vi disintegrarsi

dis'interested a disinteressato

dis'jointed a sconnesso

disk /dɪsk/ n Comput disco m; ‹diskette› dischetto m

dis'like n avversione f; **your likes and ~s** i tuoi gusti ● vt **I ~ him/it** non mi piace; **I don't ~ him/it** non mi dispiace

dislocate /'dɪsləkeɪt/ vt slogare; **~ one's shoulder** slogarsi una spalla

dis'lodge vt sloggiare

dis'loyal a sleale. **~ty** n slealtà f

dismal /'dɪzməl/ a ‹person› abbacchiato; ‹news, weather› deprimente; ‹performance› mediocre

dismantle /dɪsˈmæntl/ vt smontare ‹tent, machine›; fig smantellare

dis'may n sgomento m. **~ed** a sgomento

dis'miss vt licenziare ‹employee›; ‹reject› scartare ‹idea, suggestion›. **~al** n licenziamento m

dis'mount vi smontare

diso'bedien|ce n disubbidienza f. **~t** a disubbidiente

diso'bey vt disubbidire a ‹rule› ● vi disubbidire

dis'order n disordine m; Med disturbo m. **~ly** a disordinato; ‹crowd› turbolento; **~ly conduct** turbamento m della quiete pubblica

dis'organized a disorganizzato

dis'orientate vt disorientare

dis'own vt disconoscere

disparaging /dɪˈspærɪdʒɪŋ/ a sprezzante

disparity /dɪˈspærətɪ/ n disparità f inv

dispassionate /dɪˈspæʃənət/ a spassionato

dispatch /dɪˈspætʃ/ n Comm spedizione f; ‹Mil, report› dispaccio m; **with ~** con prontezza ● vt spedire; ‹kill› spedire al creatore

dispel /dɪˈspel/ vt (pt/pp **dispelled**) dissipare

dispensable /dɪˈspensəbl/ a dispensabile

dispensary /dɪˈspensərɪ/ n farmacia f

dispense /dɪˈspens/ vt distribuire; **~ with** fare a meno di; **dispensing chemist** farmacia mf; ‹shop› farmacia f. **~r** n ‹device› distributore m

dispers|al /dɪˈspɜːsl/ n disperzione f. **~e** /dɪˈspɜːs/ vt disperdere ● vi disperdersi

dispirited /dɪˈspɪrɪtɪd/ a scoraggiato

dis'place vt spostare; **~d person** profugo, -a mf

display /dɪˈspleɪ/ n mostra f; Comm esposizione f; ‹of feelings› manifestazione f; pej ostentazione f; Comput display m inv ● vt mostrare; esporre ‹goods›; manifestare ‹feelings›; Comput visualizzare

dis'please vt non piacere a; **be ~d with** essere scontento di

dis'pleasure n malcontento m

disposable /dɪˈspəʊzəbl/ a ‹throwaway› usa e getta; ‹income› disponibile

disposal /dɪˈspəʊzl/ n ‹getting rid of› eliminazione f; **be at sb's ~** essere a disposizione di qcno

dispose /dɪˈspəʊz/ vi **~ of** ‹get rid of› disfarsi di; **be well ~d** essere ben disposto (**to** verso)

disposition /dɪspəˈzɪʃn/ n disposizione f; ‹nature› indole f

disproportionate /dɪsprəˈpɔːʃənət/ a sproporzionato

dis'prove vt confutare

dispute /dɪˈspjuːt/ n disputa f;

(*industrial*) contestazione *f* ● *vt* contestare ⟨*statement*⟩

disqualifi'cation *n* squalifica *f*; (*from driving*) ritiro *m* della patente

dis'qualify *vt* (*pt/pp* **-ied**) escludere; *Sport* squalificare; ~ **sb from driving** ritirare la patente a qcno

disquieting /dɪs'kwaɪətɪŋ/ *a* allarmante

disre'gard *n* mancanza *f* di considerazione ● *vt* ignorare

disre'pair *n* **fall into** ~ deteriorarsi; **in a state of** ~ in cattivo stato

dis'reputable *a* malfamato

disre'pute *n* discredito *m*; **bring sb into** ~ rovinare la reputazione a qcno

disre'spect *n* mancanza *f* di rispetto. ~**ful** *a* irrispettoso

disrupt /dɪs'rʌpt/ *vt* creare scompiglio in; sconvolgere ⟨*plans*⟩. ~**ion** /-ʌpʃn/ *n* scompiglio *m*; (*of plans*) sconvolgimento *m*. ~**ive** /-tɪv/ *a* ⟨*person, behaviour*⟩ indisciplinato

dissatis'faction *n* malcontento *m*

dis'satisfied *a* scontento

dissect /dɪ'sekt/ *vt* sezionare. ~**ion** /-ekʃn/ *n* dissezione *f*

dissent /dɪ'sent/ *n* dissenso *m* ● *vi* dissentire

dissertation /dɪsə'teɪʃn/ *n* tesi *f inv*

dis'service *n* **do sb/oneself a** ~ rendere un cattivo servizio a qcno/se stesso

dissident /'dɪsɪdənt/ *n* dissidente *mf*

dis'similar *a* dissimile (**to** da)

dissociate /dɪ'səʊʃɪeɪt/ *vt* dissociare; ~ **oneself from** dissociarsi da

dissolute /'dɪsəluːt/ *a* dissoluto

dissolution /dɪsə'luːʃn/ *n* scioglimento *m*

dissolve /dɪ'zɒlv/ *vt* dissolvere ● *vi* dissolversi

dissuade /dɪ'sweɪd/ *vt* dissuadere

distance /'dɪstəns/ *n* distanza *f*; **it's a short** ~ **from here to the station** la stazione non è lontana da qui; **in the** ~ in lontananza; **from a** ~ da lontano

distant /'dɪstənt/ *a* distante; ⟨*relative*⟩ lontano

dis'taste *n* avversione *f*. ~**ful** *a* spiacevole

distil /dɪ'stɪl/ *vt* (*pt/pp* **distilled**) distillare. ~**lation** /-'leɪʃn/ *n* distillazione *f*. ~**lery** /-ərɪ/ *n* distilleria *f*

distinct /dɪ'stɪŋkt/ *a* chiaro; (*different*) distinto. ~**ion** /-ɪŋkʃn/ *n* distinzione *f*; *Sch* massimo *m* dei voti. ~**ive** /-tɪv/ *a* caratteristico. ~**ly** *adv* chiaramente

distinguish /dɪ'stɪŋgwɪʃ/ *vt/i* distin-

guere; ~ **oneself** distinguersi. ~**ed** *a* rinomato; ⟨*appearance*⟩ distinto; ⟨*career*⟩ brillante

distort /dɪ'stɔːt/ *vt* distorcere. ~**ion** /-ɔːʃn/ *n* distorsione *f*

distract /dɪ'strækt/ *vt* distrarre. ~**ed** /-ɪd/ *a* assente; (*fam: worried*) preoccupato. ~**ing** *a* che distoglie. ~**ion** /-ækʃn/ *n* distrazione *f*; ⟨*despair*⟩ disperazione *f*; **drive sb to** ~ portare qcno alla disperazione

distraught /dɪ'strɔːt/ *a* sconvolto

distress ~ /dɪ'stres/ *n* angoscia *f*; (*pain*) sofferenza *f*; (*danger*) difficoltà *f* ● *vt* sconvolgere; (*sadden*) affliggere. ~**ing** *a* penoso; (*shocking*) sconvolgente. ~**signal** *n* segnale *m* di richiesta di soccorso

distribut|e /dɪ'strɪbjuːt/ *vt* distribuire. ~**ion** /-'bjuːʃn/ *n* distribuzione *f*. ~**or** *n* distributore *m*

district /'dɪstrɪkt/ *n* regione *f*; *Admin* distretto *m*. ~ **nurse** *n* infermiere, -a *mf* che fa visite a domicilio

dis'trust *n* sfiducia *f* ● *vt* non fidarsi di. ~**ful** *a* diffidente

disturb /dɪ'stɜːb/ *vt* disturbare; (*emotionally*) turbare; spostare ⟨*papers*⟩. ~**ance** *n* disturbo *m*; ~**ances** (*pl: rioting etc*) disordini *mpl*. ~**ed** *a* turbato; [**mentally**] ~**ed** malato di mente. ~**ing** *a* inquietante

dis'used *a* non utilizzato

ditch /dɪtʃ/ *n* fosso *m* ● *vt* (*fam: abandon*) abbandonare ⟨*plan, car*⟩; piantare ⟨*lover*⟩

dither /'dɪðə(r)/ *vi* titubare

divan /dɪ'væn/ *n* divano *m*

dive /daɪv/ *n* tuffo *m*; *Aeron* picchiata *f*; (*fam: place*) bettola *f* ● *vi* tuffarsi; (*when in water*) immergersi; *Aeron* scendere in picchiata; (*fam: rush*) precipitarsi

diver /'daɪvə(r)/ *n* (*from board*) tuffatore, -trice *mf*; (*scuba*) sommozzatore, -trice *mf*; (*deep sea*) palombaro *m*

diver|ge /daɪ'vɜːdʒ/ *vi* divergere. ~**gent** /-ənt/ *a* divergente

diverse /daɪ'vɜːs/ *a* vario

diversify /daɪ'vɜːsɪfaɪ/ *vt/i* (*pt/pp* **-ied**) diversificare

diversion /daɪ'vɜːʃn/ *n* deviazione *f*; (*distraction*) diversivo *m*

diversity /daɪ'vɜːsətɪ/ *n* varietà *f*

divert /daɪ'vɜːt/ *vt* deviare ⟨*traffic*⟩; distogliere ⟨*attention*⟩

divest /daɪ'vest/ *vt* privare (**of** di)

divide /dɪˈvaɪd/ *vt* dividere (**by** per); **six ~d by two** sei diviso due ● *vi* dividersi

dividend /ˈdɪvɪdend/ *n* dividendo *m*; **pay ~s** *fig* ripagare

divine /dɪˈvaɪn/ *a* divino

diving /ˈdaɪvɪŋ/ *n* (*from board*) tuffi *mpl*; (*scuba*) immersione *f*. **~-board** *n* trampolino *m*. **~ mask** *n* maschera *f* [subacquea]. **~-suit** *n* muta *f*; (*deep sea*) scafandro *m*

divinity /dɪˈvɪnəti/ *n* divinità *f inv*; (*subject*) teologia *f*; (*at school*) religione *f*

divisible /dɪˈvɪzɪbl/ *a* divisibile (**by** per)

division /dɪˈvɪʒn/ *n* divisione *f*; (*in sports league*) serie *f*

divorce /dɪˈvɔːs/ *n* divorzio *m* ● *vt* divorziare da. **~d** *a* divorziato; **get ~d** divorziare

divorcee /dɪvɔːˈsiː/ *n* divorziato, -a *mf*

divulge /daɪˈvʌldʒ/ *vt* rendere pubblico

DIY *n abbr* **do-it-yourself**

dizziness /ˈdɪzɪnɪs/ *n* giramenti *mpl* di testa

dizzy /ˈdɪzɪ/ *a* (**-ier, -iest**) vertiginoso; **I feel ~** mi gira la testa

do /duː/ *n* (*pl* **dos** *or* **do's**) *fam* festa *f* ● *v* (*3 sg pres tense* **does**; *pt* **did**; *pp* **done**) ● *vt* fare; (*fam: cheat*) fregare; **be done** *Culin* essere cotto; **well done** bravo; *Culin* ben cotto; **do the flowers** sistemare i fiori; **do the washing up** lavare i piatti; **do one's hair** farsi i capelli ● *vi* (*be suitable*) andare; (*be enough*) bastare; **this will do** questo va bene; **that will do!** basta così!; **do well/badly** cavarsela bene/male; **how is he doing?** come sta? ● *v aux* **do you speak Italian?** parli italiano?; **you don't like him, do you?** non ti piace, vero?; (*expressing astonishment*) non dirmi che ti piace!; **yes, I do** sì; (*emphatic*) invece sì; **no, I don't** no; **I don't smoke** non fumo; **don't you/doesn't he?** vero?; **so do I** anch'io; **do come in, John** entra, John; **how do you do?** piacere. **do away with** *vt* abolire (*rule*). **do for** *vt* **done for** *fam* rovinato. **do in** *vt* (*fam: kill*) uccidere; farsi male a (*back*); **done in** *fam* esausto. **do up** *vt* (*fasten*) abbottonare; (*renovate*) rimettere a nuovo; (*wrap*) avvolgere. **do with** *vt* **I could do with a spanner** mi ci vorrebbe una chiave inglese. **do without** *vt* fare a meno di

docile /ˈdəʊsaɪl/ *a* docile

dock¹ /dɒk/ *n Jur* banco *m* degli imputati

dock² *n Naut* bacino *m* ● *vi* entrare in porto; (*spaceship:*) congiungersi. **~er** *n* portuale *m*. **~s** *npl* porto *m*. **~yard** *n* cantiere *m* navale

doctor /ˈdɒktə(r)/ *n* dottore *m*, dottoressa *f* ● *vt* alterare (*drink*); castrare (*cat*). **~ate** /-ət/ *n* dottorato *m*

doctrine /ˈdɒktrɪn/ *n* dottrina *f*

document /ˈdɒkjʊmənt/ *n* documento *m*. **~ary** /-ˈmentərɪ/ *a* documentario ● *n* documentario *m*

doddery /ˈdɒdərɪ/ *a fam* barcollante

dodge /dɒdʒ/ *n fam* trucco *m* ● *vt* schivare (*blow*); evitare (*person*) ● *vi* scansarsi; **~ out of the way** scansarsi

dodgems /ˈdɒdʒəmz/ *npl* auto-scontro *msg*

dodgy /ˈdɒdʒɪ/ *a* (**-ier, -iest**) (*fam: dubious*) sospetto

doe /dəʊ/ *n* femmina *f* (*di daino, renna, lepre*); (*rabbit*) coniglia *f*

does /dʌz/ *see* **do**

doesn't /ˈdʌznt/ = **does not**

dog /dɒg/ *n* cane *m* ● *vt* (*pt/pp* **dogged**) (*illness, bad luck:*) perseguitare

dog: ~-biscuit *n* biscotto *m* per cani. **~-collar** *n* collare *m* (*per cani*); *Relig fam* collare *m* del prete. **~-eared** *a* con le orecchie

dogged /ˈdɒgɪd/ *a* ostinato

'dog house *n* **in the ~** *fam* in disgrazia

dogma /ˈdɒgmə/ *n* dogma *m*. **~tic** /-ˈmætɪk/ *a* dogmatico

'dogsbody *n fam* tirapiedi *mf inv*

doily /ˈdɔɪlɪ/ *n* centrino *m*

do-it-yourself /duːɪtjəˈself/ *n* fai da te *m*, bricolage *m*. **~ shop** *n* negozio *m* di bricolage

doldrums /ˈdɒldrəmz/ *npl* **be in the ~** essere giù di corda; (*business:*) essere in fase di stasi

dole /dəʊl/ *n* sussidio *m* di disoccupazione; **be on the ~** essere disoccupato ● **dole out** *vt* distribuire

doleful /ˈdəʊlfl/ *a* triste

doll /dɒl/ *n* bambola *f* ● **doll oneself up** *vt fam* mettersi in ghingheri

dollar /ˈdɒlə(r)/ *n* dollaro *m*

dollop /ˈdɒləp/ *n fam* cucchiaiata *f*

dolphin /ˈdɒlfɪn/ *n* delfino *m*

dome /dəʊm/ *n* cupola *f*

domestic /dəˈmestɪk/ *a* domestico; *Pol* interno; *Comm* nazionale. **~ animal** *n* animale *m* domestico

domesticated /dəˈmestɪkeɪtɪd/ *a* (*animal*) addomesticato

domestic: ~ **flight** n volo m nazionale. ~ **'servant** n domestico, -a mf

dominant /'dɒmɪnənt/ a dominante

dominat|e /'dɒmɪneɪt/ vt/i dominare. **~ion** /-'neɪʃn/ n dominio m

domineering /dɒmɪ'nɪərɪŋ/ a autoritario

dominion /də'mɪnjən/ n Br Pol dominion m inv

domino /'dɒmɪnəʊ/ n (pl -es) tessera f del domino; **~es** sg (game) domino m

don[1] /dɒn/ vt (pt/pp **donned**) liter indossare

don[2] n docente mf universitario, -a

donat|e /dəʊ'neɪt/ vt donare. **~ion** /-'eɪʃn/ n donazione f

done /dʌn/ see do

donkey /'dɒŋkɪ/ n asino m; **~'s years** fam secoli mpl. **~-work** n sgobbata f

donor /'dəʊnə(r)/ n donatore, -trice mf

don't /dəʊnt/ = do not

doodle /'du:dl/ vi scarabocchiare

doom /du:m/ n fato m; (ruin) rovina f ● vt be **~ed [to failure]** essere destinato al fallimento; **~ed** ⟨ship⟩ destinato ad affondare

door /dɔ:(r)/ n porta f; (of car) portiera f; **out of ~s** all'aperto

door: **~man** n portiere m. **~mat** n zerbino m. **~step** n gradino m della porta. **~way** n vano m della porta

dope /dəʊp/ n fam (drug) droga f leggera; (information) indiscrezioni fpl; (idiot) idiota mf ● vt drogare; Sport dopare

dopey /'dəʊpɪ/ a fam addormentato

dormant /'dɔ:mənt/ a latente; ⟨volcano⟩ inattivo

dormer /'dɔ:mə(r)/ n ~ **[window]** abbaino m

dormitory /'dɔ:mɪtərɪ/ n dormitorio m

dormouse /'dɔ:-/ n ghiro m

dosage /'dəʊsɪdʒ/ n dosaggio m

dose /dəʊs/ n dose f

doss /dɒs/ vi sl accamparsi. **~er** n barbone, -a mf. **~-house** n dormitorio m pubblico

dot /dɒt/ n punto m; **at 8 o'clock on the ~** alle 8 in punto

dote /dəʊt/ vi **~ on** stravedere per

dotted /'dɒtɪd/ a ~ **line** linea f puntegggiata; **be ~ with** essere punteggiato di

dotty /'dɒtɪ/ a (-ier, -iest) fam tocco; ⟨idea⟩ folle

double /'dʌbl/ a doppio ● adv cost ~ costare il doppio; **see ~** vedere doppio; ~ **the amount** la quantità doppia ● n doppio m; (person) sosia m inv; **~s** pl Tennis doppio m; **at the ~** di corsa ● vt raddoppiare; (fold) piegare in due ● vi raddoppiare. **double back** vi (go back) fare dietro front. **double up** vi (bend over) piegarsi in due (**with** per); (share) dividere una stanza

double: **~-bass** n contrabbasso m. ~ **'bed** n letto m matrimoniale. **~-breasted** a a doppio petto. ~ **'chin** n doppio mento m. **~-'cross** vt ingannare. **~-'decker** n autobus m inv a due piani. ~ **'Dutch** n fam ostrogoto m. **~ 'glazing** n doppiovetro m. ~ **'room** n camera f doppia

doubly /'dʌblɪ/ adv doppiamente

doubt /daʊt/ n dubbio m ● vt dubitare di. **~ful** a dubbio; (having doubts) in dubbio. **~fully** adv con aria dubbiosa. **~less** adv indubbiamente

dough /dəʊ/ n pasta f; (for bread) impasto m; (fam: money) quattrini mpl. **~nut** n bombolone m, krapfen m inv

douse /daʊs/ vt spegnere

dove /dʌv/ n colomba f. **~tail** n Techn incastro m a coda di rondine

dowdy /'daʊdɪ/ a (-ier, -iest) trasandato

down[1] /daʊn/ n (feathers) piumino m

down[2] /daʊn/ adv giù; **go/come** ~ scendere; ~ **there** laggiù; **sales are** ~ le vendite sono diminuite; **£50 ~** 50 sterline d'acconto; ~ **10%** ridotto del 10%; ~ **with...!** abbasso...! ● prep walk ~ **the road** camminare per strada; ~ **the stairs** giù per le scale; **fall** ~ **the stairs** cadere giù dalle scale; **get that ~ you!** fam butta giù!; **be ~ the pub** fam essere al pub ● vt bere tutto d'un fiato ⟨drink⟩

down: **~-and-'out** n spiantato, -a mf. **~cast** a abbattuto. **~fall** n caduta f; (of person) rovina f. **~'grade** vt (in seniority) degradare. **~-'hearted** a scoraggiato. **~'hill** adv in discesa; **go ~hill** fig essere in declino. **~ payment** n deposito m. **~pour** n acquazzone m. **~right** a ⟨absolute⟩ totale; ⟨lie⟩ bell'e buono; ⟨idiot⟩ perfetto ● adv (completely) completamente. **~'stairs** adv al piano di sotto ● a /'-/ del piano di sotto. **~'stream** adv a valle. **~-to-'earth** a ⟨person⟩ con i piedi per terra. **~town** adv Am in centro. **~trodden** a oppresso. **~ward[s]** a verso il basso; ⟨slope⟩ in discesa ● adv verso il basso

dowry /'daʊrɪ/ n dote f

doze /dəʊz/ n sonnellino m ● vi sonnec

chiare. **doze off** vi assopirsi
dozen /'dʌzn/ n dozzina f; ~s of books libri a dozzine
Dr abbr doctor
drab /dræb/ a spento
draft[1] /drɑːft/ n abbozzo m; Comm cambiale f; Am Mil leva f ● vt abbozzare; Am Mil arruolare
draft[2] n Am = draught
drag /dræg/ n fam scocciatura f; in ~ fam ⟨man⟩ travestito da donna ● vt (pt/pp dragged) trascinare; dragare ⟨river⟩. **drag on** vi ⟨time, meeting:⟩ trascinarsi
dragon /'drægən/ n drago m. ~-fly n libellula f
drain /dreɪn/ n tubo m di scarico; ⟨grid⟩ tombino m; the ~s pl le fognature; be a ~ on sb's finances prosciugare le finanze di qcno ● vt drenare ⟨land, wound⟩; scolare ⟨liquid, vegetables⟩; svuotare ⟨tank, glass, person⟩ ● vi = [away] andar via
drain|age /'dreɪnɪdʒ/ n ⟨system⟩ drenaggio m; ⟨of land⟩ scolo m. ~ing board n scolapiatti m inv. ~-pipe n tubo m di scarico
drake /dreɪk/ n maschio m dell'anatra
drama /'drɑːmə/ n arte f drammatica; ⟨play⟩ opera f teatrale; ⟨event⟩ dramma m
dramatic /drə'mætɪk/ a drammatico
dramat|ist /'dræmətɪst/ n drammaturgo, -a mf. ~ize vt adattare per il teatro; fig drammatizzare
drank /dræŋk/ see drink
drape /dreɪp/ n Am tenda f ● vt appoggiare ⟨over su⟩
drastic /'dræstɪk/ a drastico; ~ally adv drasticamente
draught /drɑːft/ n corrente f [d'aria]; ~s sg ⟨game⟩ [gioco m della] dama f sg
draught: ~ beer n birra f alla spina. ~sman n disegnatore, -trice mf
draughty /'drɑːftɪ/ a pieno di correnti d'aria; it's ~ c'è corrente
draw /drɔː/ n ⟨attraction⟩ attrazione f; Sport pareggio m; ⟨in lottery⟩ sorteggio m ● v (pt drew, pp drawn) ● vt tirare; ⟨attract⟩ attirare; disegnare ⟨picture⟩; tracciare ⟨line⟩; ritirare ⟨money⟩; ~ lots tirare a sorte ● vi ⟨tea:⟩ essere in infusione; Sport pareggiare; ~ near avvicinarsi. **draw back** vt tirare indietro; ritirare ⟨hand⟩; tirare ⟨curtains⟩ ● vi ⟨recoil⟩ tirarsi indietro. **draw in** vt ritrarre ⟨claws etc⟩ ● vi ⟨train:⟩ arrivare; ⟨days:⟩ accorciarsi. **draw out** vt ⟨pull out⟩ tirar fuori; ritirare ⟨money⟩ ● vi

⟨train:⟩ partire; ⟨days:⟩ allungarsi.
draw up vt redigere ⟨document⟩; accostare ⟨chair⟩; ~ oneself up to one's full height farsi grande ● vi ⟨stop⟩ fermarsi
draw: ~back n inconveniente m. ~bridge n ponte m levatoio
drawer /drɔː(r)/ n cassetto m
drawing /'drɔːɪŋ/ n disegno m
drawing: ~-board n tavolo m da disegno; fig go back to the ~-board ricominciare da capo. ~-pin n puntina f. ~-room n salotto m
drawl /drɔːl/ n pronuncia f strascicata
drawn /drɔːn/ see draw
dread /dred/ n terrore m ● vt aver il terrore di
dreadful /'dredfʊl/ a terribile. ~ly adv terribilmente
dream /driːm/ n sogno m ● attrib di sogno ● vt/i (pt/pp dreamt /dremt/ or dreamed) sognare ⟨about/of di⟩
dreary /'drɪərɪ/ a (-ier, -iest) tetro; ⟨boring⟩ monotono
dredge /dredʒ/ vt/i dragare
dregs /dregz/ npl feccia f sg
drench /drentʃ/ vt get ~ed inzupparsi; ~ed zuppo
dress /dres/ n ⟨woman's⟩ vestito m; ⟨clothing⟩ abbigliamento m ● vt vestire; ⟨decorate⟩ adornare; Culin condire; Med fasciare; ~ oneself, get ~ed vestirsi ● vi vestirsi. **dress up** vi mettersi elegante; ⟨in disguise⟩ travestirsi ⟨as da⟩
dress: ~ circle n Theat prima galleria f. ~er n ⟨furniture⟩ credenza f; ⟨Am: dressing-table⟩ toilette f inv
dressing /'dresɪŋ/ n Culin condimento m; Med fasciatura f
dressing: ~-gown n vestaglia f. ~-room n ⟨in gym⟩ spogliatoio m; Theat camerino m. ~-table n toilette f inv
dress: ~maker n sarta f. ~ rehearsal n prova f generale
dressy /'dresɪ/ a (-ier, -iest) elegante
drew /druː/ see draw
dribble /'drɪbl/ vi gocciolare; ⟨baby:⟩ sbavare; Sport dribblare
dribs and drabs /drɪbzən'dræbz/ npl in ~ alla spicciolata
dried /draɪd/ a ⟨food⟩ essiccato
drier /'draɪə(r)/ n asciugabiancheria m inv
drift /drɪft/ n movimento m lento; ⟨of snow⟩ cumulo m; ⟨meaning⟩ senso m ● vi ⟨off course⟩ andare alla deriva; ⟨snow:⟩ accumularsi; ⟨fig: person:⟩ pro-

cedere senza meta. **drift apart** vi ⟨people:⟩ allontanarsi l'uno dall'altro

drill /drɪl/ n trapano m; Mil esercitazione f ● vt trapanare; Mil fare esercitare ● vi Mil esercitarsi; ~ **for oil** trivellare in cerca di petrolio

drily /'draɪlɪ/ adv seccamente

drink /drɪŋk/ n bevanda f; ⟨alcoholic⟩ bicchierino m; **have a** ~ bere qualcosa; **a** ~ **of water** un po' d'acqua ● vt/i ⟨pt **drank**, pp **drunk**⟩ bere. **drink up** vt finire re ● vi finire il bicchiere

drink|able /'drɪŋkəbl/ a potabile. ~**er** n bevitore, -trice mf

'drinking-water n acqua f potabile

drip /drɪp/ n gocciolamento m; ⟨drop⟩ goccia f; Med flebo f inv; ⟨fam: person⟩ mollaccione, -a mf ● vi ⟨pt/pp **dripped**⟩ gocciolare. ~**-'dry** a che non si stira. ~**ping** n ⟨from meat⟩ grasso m d'arrosto ● a ~**ping** [**wet**] fradicio

drive /draɪv/ n ⟨in car⟩ giro m; ⟨entrance⟩ viale m; ⟨energy⟩ grinta f; Psych pulsione f; ⟨organized effort⟩ operazione f; Techn motore m; Comput lettore m ● v ⟨pt **drove**, pp **driven**⟩ ● vt portare ⟨person by car⟩; guidare ⟨car⟩; ⟨Sport: hit⟩ mandare; far funzionare; ~ **sb mad** far diventare matto qcno ● vi guidare. **drive at** vt **what are you driving at?** dove vuoi arrivare? **drive away** vt portare via in macchina; ⟨chase⟩ cacciare ● vi andare via in macchina. **drive in** vt piantare ⟨nail⟩ ● vi arrivare [in macchina]. **drive off** vt portare via in macchina; ⟨chase⟩ cacciare ● vi andare via in macchina. **drive on** vi proseguire ⟨in macchina⟩. **drive up** vi arrivare ⟨in macchina⟩

drivel /'drɪvl/ n fam sciocchezze fpl

driven /'drɪvn/ see **drive**

driver /'draɪvə(r)/ n guidatore, -trice mf; ⟨of train⟩ conducente mf

driving /'draɪvɪŋ/ a ⟨rain⟩ violento; ⟨force⟩ motore ● n guida f

driving: ~ **lesson** n lezione f di guida. ~ **licence** n patente f di guida. ~ **school** n scuola f guida. ~ **test** n esame m di guida

drizzle /'drɪzl/ n pioggerella f ● vi piovigginare

drone /drəʊn/ n ⟨bee⟩ fuco m; ⟨sound⟩ ronzio m

droop /druːp/ vi abbassarsi; ⟨flowers:⟩ afflosciarsi

drop /drɒp/ n ⟨of liquid⟩ goccia f; ⟨fall⟩ caduta f; ⟨in price, temperature⟩ calo m ● v ⟨pt/pp **dropped**⟩ ● vt far cadere;

sganciare ⟨bomb⟩; ⟨omit⟩ omettere; ⟨give up⟩ abbandonare ● vi cadere; ⟨price, temperature, wind:⟩ calare; ⟨ground:⟩ essere in pendenza. **drop in** vi passare. **drop off** vt depositare ⟨person⟩ ● vi cadere; ⟨fall asleep⟩ assopirsi. **drop out** vi cadere; ⟨of race, society⟩ ritirarsi; ~ **out of school** lasciare la scuola

'drop-out n persona f contro il sistema sociale

droppings /'drɒpɪŋz/ npl sterco m

drought /draʊt/ n siccità f

drove /drəʊv/ see **drive**

droves /drəʊvz/ npl **in** ~ in massa

drown /draʊn/ vi annegare ● vt annegare; coprire ⟨noise⟩; **he was** ~**ed** è annegato

drowsy /'draʊzɪ/ a sonnolento

drudgery /'drʌdʒərɪ/ n lavoro m pesante e noioso

drug /drʌg/ n droga f; Med farmaco m; **take** ~**s** drogarsi ● vt ⟨pt/pp **drugged**⟩ drogare

drug: ~ **addict** n tossicomane, -a mf. ~ **dealer** n spacciatore, -trice mf [di droga]. ~**gist** n Am farmacista mf. ~**store** n Am negozio m di generi vari, inclusi medicinali, che funge anche da bar; ⟨dispensing⟩ farmacia f

drum /drʌm/ n tamburo m; ⟨for oil⟩ bidone m; ~**s** ⟨pl: in pop-group⟩ batteria f ● v ⟨pt/pp **drummed**⟩ ● vi suonare il tamburo; ⟨in pop-group⟩ suonare la batteria ● vt ~ **sth into sb** fam ripetere qcsa a qcno cento volte. ~**mer** n percussionista mf; ⟨in pop-group⟩ batterista mf. ~**stick** n bacchetta f; ⟨of chicken, turkey⟩ coscia f

drunk /drʌŋk/ see **drink** ● a ubriaco; **get** ~ ubriacarsi ● n ubriaco, -a mf

drunk|ard /'drʌŋkəd/ n ubriacone, -a mf. ~**en** a ubriaco; ~**en driving** guida f in stato di ebbrezza

dry /draɪ/ a ⟨**drier**, **driest**⟩ asciutto; ⟨climate, country⟩ secco ● vt/i ⟨pt/pp **dried**⟩ asciugare; ~ **one's eyes** asciugarsi le lacrime. **dry up** vi seccarsi; ⟨fig: source:⟩ prosciugarsi; ⟨fam: be quiet⟩ stare zitto; ⟨do dishes⟩ asciugare i piatti

dry: ~**-'clean** vt pulire a secco. ~**-'cleaner's** n ⟨shop⟩ tintoria f. ~**ness** n secchezza f

DTP n abbr (**desktop publishing**) desktop publishing m

dual /'djuːəl/ a doppio

dual: ~ **'carriageway** n strada f a due carreggiate. ~**-'purpose** a a doppio uso

dub /dʌb/ vt (pt/pp **dubbed**) doppiare ⟨film⟩; ⟨name⟩ soprannominare

dubious /ˈdjuːbɪəs/ a dubbio; **be ~ about** avere dei dubbi riguardo

duchess /ˈdʌtʃɪs/ n duchessa f

duck /dʌk/ n anatra f ● vt (in water) immergere; **~ one's head** abbassare la testa ● vi abbassarsi. **~ling** n anatroccolo m

duct /dʌkt/ n condotto m; Anat dotto m

dud /dʌd/ fam a Mil disattivato; ⟨coin⟩ falso; ⟨cheque⟩ a vuoto ● n ⟨banknote⟩ banconota f falsa

due /djuː/ a dovuto; **be ~** ⟨train:⟩ essere previsto; **the baby is ~ next week** il bambino dovrebbe nascere la settimana prossima; **~ to** (owing to) a causa di; **be ~ to** (causally) essere dovuto a; **I'm ~ to...** dovrei...; **in ~ course** a tempo debito ● adv **~ north** direttamente a nord

duel /ˈdjuːəl/ n duello m

dues /djuːz/ npl quota f [di iscrizione]

duet /djuːˈet/ n duetto m

dug /dʌg/ see **dig**

duke /djuːk/ n duca m

dull /dʌl/ a (overcast, not bright) cupo; (not shiny) opaco; ⟨sound⟩ soffocato; (boring) monotono; ⟨stupid⟩ ottuso ● vt intorpidire ⟨mind⟩; attenuare ⟨pain⟩

duly /ˈdjuːlɪ/ adv debitamente

dumb /dʌm/ a muto; (fam: stupid) ottuso. **~founded** /dʌmˈfaʊndɪd/ a sbigottito

dummy /ˈdʌmɪ/ n (tailor's) manichino m; (for baby) succhiotto m; (model) riproduzione f

dump /dʌmp/ n (for refuse) scarico m; (fam: town) mortorio m; **be down in the ~s** fam essere depresso ● vt scaricare; (fam: put down) lasciare; (fam: get rid of) liberarsi di

dumpling /ˈdʌmplɪŋ/ n gnocco m

dunce /dʌns/ n zuccone, -a mf

dune /djuːn/ n duna f

dung /dʌŋ/ n sterco m

dungarees /dʌŋgəˈriːz/ npl tuta fsg

dungeon /ˈdʌndʒən/ n prigione f sotterranea

duo /ˈdjuːəʊ/ n duo m inv; Mus duetto m

duplicate¹ /ˈdjuːplɪkət/ a doppio ● n duplicato m; ⟨document⟩ copia f; **in ~** in duplicato

duplicate² /ˈdjuːplɪkeɪt/ vt fare un duplicato di; ⟨research:⟩ essere una ripetizione di ⟨work⟩

durable /ˈdjʊərəbl/ a resistente; durevole ⟨basis, institution⟩

duration /djʊəˈreɪʃn/ n durata f

duress /djʊəˈres/ n costrizione f; **under ~** sotto minaccia

during /ˈdjʊərɪŋ/ prep durante

dusk /dʌsk/ n crepuscolo m

dust /dʌst/ n polvere f ● vt spolverare; (sprinkle) cospargere ⟨cake⟩ (**with** di) ● vi spolverare

dust: ~bin n pattumiera f. **~-cart** n camion m della nettezza urbana. **~er** n strofinaccio m. **~-jacket** n sopraccoperta f. **~man** n spazzino m. **~pan** n paletta f per la spazzatura

dusty /ˈdʌstɪ/ a (-ier, -iest) polveroso

Dutch /dʌtʃ/ a olandese; **go ~** fam fare alla romana ● n (language) olandese m; **the ~** pl gli olandesi. **~man** n olandese m

dutiable /ˈdjuːtɪəbl/ a soggetto a imposta

dutiful /ˈdjuːtɪfl/ a rispettoso

duty /ˈdjuːtɪ/ n dovere m; (task) compito m; (tax) dogana f; **be on ~** essere di servizio. **~-free** a esente da dogana

duvet /ˈduːveɪ/ n piumone m

dwarf /dwɔːf/ n (pl **-s** or **dwarves**) nano, -a mf ● vt rimpicciolire

dwell /dwel/ vi (pt/pp **dwelt**) liter dimorare. **dwell on** vt fig soffermarsi su. **~ing** n abitazione f

dwindle /ˈdwɪndl/ vi diminuire

dye /daɪ/ n tintura f ● vt (pres p **dyeing**) tingere

dying /ˈdaɪɪŋ/ see **die²**

dynamic /daɪˈnæmɪk/ a dinamico

dynamite /ˈdaɪnəmaɪt/ n dinamite f

dynamo /ˈdaɪnəməʊ/ n dinamo f inv

dynasty /ˈdɪnəstɪ/ n dinastia f

dysentery /ˈdɪsəntrɪ/ n dissenteria f

dyslex|ia /dɪsˈleksɪə/ n dislessia f. **~ic** a dislessico

Ee

each /iːtʃ/ *a* ogni ● *pron* ognuno; **£1 ~** una sterlina ciascuno; **they love/hate ~ other** si amano/odiano; **we lend ~ other money** ci prestiamo i soldi

eager /ˈiːgə(r)/ *a* ansioso ⟨*to do* di fare⟩; ⟨*pupil*⟩ avido di sapere. **~ly** *adv* ⟨*wait*⟩ ansiosamente; ⟨*offer*⟩ premurosamente. **~ness** *n* premura *f*

eagle /ˈiːgl/ *n* aquila *f*

ear[1] /ɪə(r)/ *n* ⟨*of corn*⟩ spiga *f*

ear[2] *n* orecchio *m*. **~ache** *n* mal *m* d'orecchi. **~drum** *n* timpano *m*

earl /ɜːl/ *n* conte *m*

early /ˈɜːlɪ/ *a* (**-ier, -iest**) (*before expected time*) in anticipo; ⟨*spring*⟩ prematuro; ⟨*reply*⟩ pronto; ⟨*works, writings*⟩ primo; **be here ~!** sii puntuale!; **you're ~!** sei in anticipo!; **~ morning walk** passeggiata *f* mattutina; **in the ~ morning** la mattina presto; **in the ~ spring** all'inizio della primavera; **~ retirement** prepensionamento *m* ● *adv* presto; (*ahead of time*) in anticipo; **~ in the morning** la mattina presto

ˈearmark *vt* riservare (**for** a)

earn /ɜːn/ *vt* guadagnare; ⟨*deserve*⟩ meritare

earnest /ˈɜːnɪst/ *a* serio ● *n* **in ~** sul serio. **~ly** *adv* con aria seria

earnings /ˈɜːnɪŋz/ *npl* guadagni *mpl*; ⟨*salary*⟩ stipendio *m*

ear: **~phones** *npl* cuffia *fsg*. **~ring** *n* orecchino *m*. **~shot** *n* **within ~shot** a portata d'orecchio; **he is out of ~shot** non può sentire

earth /ɜːθ/ *n* terra *f* **where/what on ~?** dove/che diavolo? ● *vt Electr* mettere a terra

earthenware /ˈɜːθn-/ *n* terraglia *f*

earthly /ˈɜːθlɪ/ *a* terrestre; **be no ~ use** *fam* essere perfettamente inutile

ˈearthquake *n* terremoto *m*

earthy /ˈɜːθɪ/ *a* terroso; ⟨*coarse*⟩ grossolano

earwig /ˈɪəwɪg/ *n* forbicina *f*

ease /iːz/ *n* **at ~** a proprio agio; **at ~!** *Mil* riposo!; **ill at ~** a disagio; **with ~** con facilità ● *vt* calmare ⟨*pain*⟩; allevia-

re ⟨*tension, shortage*⟩; ⟨*slow down*⟩ rallentare; ⟨*loosen*⟩ allentare ● *vi* ⟨*pain, situation, wind:*⟩ calmarsi

easel /ˈiːzl/ *n* cavalletto *m*

easily /ˈiːzɪlɪ/ *adv* con facilità; **~ the best** certamente il meglio

east /iːst/ *n* est *m*; **to the ~ of** a est di ● *a* dell'est ● *adv* verso est

Easter /ˈiːstə(r)/ *n* Pasqua *f*. **~ egg** *n* uovo *m* di Pasqua

east|erly /ˈiːstəlɪ/ *a* da levante. **~ern** *a* orientale. **~ward[s]** /-wəd[z]/ *adv* verso est

easy /ˈiːzɪ/ *a* (**-ier, -iest**) facile; **take it or things ~** prendersela con calma; **take it ~!** (*don't get excited*) calma!; **go ~ with** andarci piano con

easy: **~ chair** *n* poltrona *f*. **~ˈgoing** *a* conciliante; **too ~going** troppo accomodante

eat /iːt/ *vt/i* (*pt* **ate**, *pp* **eaten**) mangiare. **eat into** *vt* intaccare. **eat up** *vt* mangiare tutto ⟨*food*⟩; *fig* inghiottire ⟨*profits*⟩

eat|able /ˈiːtəbl/ *a* mangiabile. **~er** *n* ⟨*apple*⟩ mela *f* da tavola; **be a big ~er** ⟨*person:*⟩ essere una buona forchetta

eau-de-Cologne /əʊdəkəˈləʊn/ *n* acqua *f* di Colonia

eaves /iːvz/ *npl* cornicione *msg*. **~drop** *vi* (*pt/pp* **~dropped**) origliare; **~drop on** ascoltare di nascosto

ebb /eb/ *n* ⟨*tide*⟩ riflusso *m*; **at a low ~** *fig* a terra ● *vi* rifluire; *fig* declinare

ebony /ˈebənɪ/ *n* ebano *m*

EC *n abbr* (**European Community**) CE *f*

eccentric /ɪkˈsentrɪk/ *a & n* eccentrico, -a *mf*

ecclesiastical /ɪkliːzɪˈæstɪkl/ *a* ecclesiastico

echo /ˈekəʊ/ *n* (*pl* **-es**) eco *f* or *m* ● *v* (*pt/pp* **echoed**, *pres p* **echoing**) ● *vt* echeggiare; ripetere ⟨*words*⟩ ● *vi* risuonare (**with** di)

eclipse /ɪˈklɪps/ *n Astr* eclissi *f inv* ● *vt* *fig* eclissare

ecolog|ical /iːkəˈlɒdʒɪkl/ *a* ecologico. **~y** /ɪˈkɒlədʒɪ/ *n* ecologia *f*

economic /iːkəˈnɒmɪk/ *a* economico.

~al *a* economico. **~ally** *adv* economicamente; (*thriftily*) in economia. **~s** *n* economia *f*

economist /ɪˈkɒnəmɪst/ *n* economista *mf*

economize /ɪˈkɒnəmaɪz/ *vi* economizzare (**on** su)

economy /ɪˈkɒnəmɪ/ *n* economia *f*

ecstasy /ˈekstəsɪ/ *n* estasi *f inv*; (*drug*) ecstasy *f*

ecstatic /ɪkˈstætɪk/ *a* estatico

ecu /ˈeɪkjuː/ *n* ecu *m inv*

eczema /ˈeksɪmə/ *n* eczema *m*

edge /edʒ/ *n* bordo *m*; (*of knife*) filo *m*; (*of road*) ciglio *m*; **on ~** con i nervi tesi; **have the ~ on** *fam* avere un vantaggio su ● *vt* bordare. **edge forward** *vi* avanzare lentamente

edgeways /ˈedʒweɪz/ *adv* di fianco; **I couldn't get a word in ~** non ho potuto infilare neanche mezza parola nel discorso

edging /ˈedʒɪŋ/ *n* bordo *m*

edgy /ˈedʒɪ/ *a* nervoso

edible /ˈedɪbl/ *a* commestibile; **this pizza's not ~** questa pizza è immangiabile

edict /ˈiːdɪkt/ *n* editto *m*

edify /ˈedɪfaɪ/ *vt* (*pt/pp* **-ied**) edificare. **~ing** *a* edificante

edit /ˈedɪt/ *vt* (*pt/pp* **edited**) far la revisione di ‹*text*›; curare l'edizione di ‹*anthology, dictionary*›; dirigere ‹*newspaper*›; montare ‹*film*›; editare ‹*tape*›; **~ed by** ‹*book*› a cura di

edition /ɪˈdɪʃn/ *n* edizione *f*

editor /ˈedɪtə(r)/ *n* (*of anthology, dictionary*) curatore, -trice *mf*; (*of newspaper*) redattore, -trice *mf*; (*of film*) responsabile *mf* del montaggio

editorial /edɪˈtɔːrɪəl/ *a* redazionale ● *n Journ* editoriale *m*

educate /ˈedjʊkeɪt/ *vt* istruire; educare ‹*public, mind*›; **be ~d at Eton** essere educato a Eton. **~d** *a* istruito

education /edjʊˈkeɪʃn/ *n* istruzione *f*; (*culture*) cultura *f*, educazione *f*. **~al** *a* istruttivo; (*visit*) educativo; (*publishing*) didattico

eel /iːl/ *n* anguilla *f*

eerie /ˈɪərɪ/ *a* (**-ier, -iest**) inquietante

effect /ɪˈfekt/ *n* effetto *m*; **in ~** in effetti; **take ~** ‹*law:*› entrare in vigore; ‹*medicine:*› fare effetto ● *vt* effettuare

effective /ɪˈfektɪv/ *a* efficace; (*striking*) che colpisce; (*actual*) di fatto; **~ from** in vigore a partire da. **~ly** *adv*

efficacemente; (*actually*) di fatto. **~ness** *n* efficacia *f*

effeminate /ɪˈfemɪnət/ *a* effeminato

effervescent /efəˈvesnt/ *a* effervescente

efficiency /ɪˈfɪʃənsɪ/ *n* efficienza *f*; (*of machine*) rendimento *m*

efficient /ɪˈfɪʃənt/ *a* efficiente. **~ly** *adv* efficientemente

effort /ˈefət/ *n* sforzo *m*; **make an ~** sforzarsi. **~less** *a* facile. **~lessly** *adv* con facilità

effrontery /ɪˈfrʌntərɪ/ *n* sfrontatezza *f*

effusive /ɪˈfjuːsɪv/ *a* espansivo; ‹*speech*› caloroso

e.g. *abbr* (**exempli gratia**) per es.

egalitarian /ɪgælɪˈteərɪən/ *a* egalitario

egg¹ /eg/ *vt* **~ on** *fam* incitare

egg² *n* uovo *m*. **~-cup** *n* portauovo *m inv*. **~shell** *n* guscio *m* d'uovo. **~-timer** *n* clessidra *f* per misurare il tempo di cottura delle uova

ego /ˈiːgəʊ/ *n* ego *m*. **~centric** /-ˈsentrɪk/ *a* egocentrico. **~ism** *n* egoismo *m*. **~ist** *n* egoista *mf*. **~tism** *n* egotismo *m*. **~tist** *n* egotista *mf*

Egypt /ˈiːdʒɪpt/ *n* Egitto *m*. **~ian** /ɪˈdʒɪpʃn/ *a & n* egiziano, -a *mf*

eiderdown /ˈaɪdə-/ *n* (*quilt*) piumino *m*

eight /eɪt/ *a* otto ● *n* otto *m*. **~'teen** *a & n* diciotto *m*. **~'teenth** *a & n* diciottesimo, -a *mf*

eighth /eɪtθ/ *a* ottavo ● *n* ottavo *m*

eightieth /ˈeɪtɪɪθ/ *a & n* ottantesimo, -a *mf*

eighty /ˈeɪtɪ/ *a & n* ottanta *m*

either /ˈaɪðə(r)/ *a & pron* **~** [**of them**] l'uno o l'altro; **I don't like ~** [**of them**] non mi piace né l'uno né l'altro; **on ~ side** da tutte e due le parti ● *adv* **I don't ~** nemmeno io; **I don't like John or his brother ~** non mi piace John e nemmeno suo fratello ● *conj* **~ John or his brother will be there** ci saranno o John o suo fratello; **I don't like ~ John or his brother** non mi piacciono né John né suo fratello; **~ you go to bed or** [**else**]**...** o vai a letto o [altrimenti]..

eject /ɪˈdʒekt/ *vt* eiettare ‹*pilot*›; espellere ‹*tape, drunk*›

eke /iːk/ *vt* **~ out** far bastare; (*increase*) arrotondare; **~ out a living** arrangiarsi

elaborate¹ /ɪˈlæbərət/ *a* elaborato

elaborate² /ɪˈlæbəreɪt/ *vi* entrare nei particolari (**on** di)

elapse /ɪˈlæps/ *vi* trascorrere

elastic /ɪˈlæstɪk/ *a* elastico ● *n* elastico *m*. **~ 'band** *n* elastico *m*

elasticity /ɪlæs'tɪsətɪ/ *n* elasticità *f*

elated /ɪ'leɪtɪd/ *a* esultante

elbow /'elbəʊ/ *n* gomito *m*

elder[1] /'eldə(r)/ *n* (*tree*) sambuco *m*

eld|er[2] *a* maggiore ● **n the ~** il/la maggiore. **~erly** *a* anziano. **~est** *a* maggiore ● *n* **the ~est** il/la maggiore

elect /ɪ'lekt/ *a* **the president ~** il futuro presidente ● *vt* eleggere; **~ to do sth** decidere di fare qcsa. **~ion** /-ekʃn/ *n* elezione *f*

elector /ɪ'lektə(r)/ *n* elettore, -trice *mf*. **~al** *a* elettorale; **~al roll** liste *fpl* elettorali. **~ate** /-rət/ *n* elettorato *m*

electric /ɪ'lektrɪk/ *a* elettrico

electrical /ɪ'lektrɪkl/ *a* elettrico; **~ engineering** elettrotecnica *f*

electric: ~ 'blanket *n* termocoperta *f*. **~ 'fire** *n* stufa *f* elettrica

electrician /ɪlek'trɪʃn/ *n* elettricista *m*

electricity /ɪlek'trɪsətɪ/ *n* elettricità *f*

electrify /ɪ'lektrɪfaɪ/ *vt* (*pt/pp* **-ied**) elettrificare; *fig* elettrizzare. **~ing** *a fig* elettrizzante

electrocute /ɪ'lektrəkjuːt/ *vt* fulminare; (*execute*) giustiziare sulla sedia elettrica

electrode /ɪ'lektrəʊd/ *n* elettrodo *m*

electron /ɪ'lektrɒn/ *n* elettrone *m*

electronic /ɪlek'trɒnɪk/ *a* elettronico. **~ mail** *n* posta *f* elettronica. **~s** *n* elettronica *f*

elegance /'elɪgəns/ *n* eleganza *f*

elegant /'elɪgənt/ *a* elegante

elegy /'elɪdʒɪ/ *n* elegia *f*

element /'elɪmənt/ *n* elemento *m*. **~ary** /-'mentərɪ/ *a* elementare

elephant /'elɪfənt/ *n* elefante *m*

elevat|e /'elɪveɪt/ *vt* elevare. **~ion** /-'veɪʃn/ *n* elevazione *f*; (*height*) altitudine *f*; (*angle*) alzo *m*

elevator /'elɪveɪtə(r)/ *n Am* ascensore *m*

eleven /ɪ'levn/ *a* undici ● *n* undici *m*. **~th** *a & n* undicesimo, -a *mf*; **at the ~th hour** *fam* all'ultimo momento

elf /elf/ *n* (*pl* **elves**) elfo *m*

elicit /ɪ'lɪsɪt/ *vt* ottenere

eligible /'elɪdʒəbl/ *a* eleggibile; **~ young man** buon partito; **be ~ for** aver diritto a

eliminate /ɪ'lɪmɪneɪt/ *vt* eliminare

élite /eɪ'liːt/ *n* fior fiore *m*

ellip|se /ɪ'lɪps/ *n* ellisse *f*. **~tical** *a* ellittico

elm /elm/ *n* olmo *m*

elocution /elə'kjuːʃn/ *n* elocuzione *f*

elope /ɪ'ləʊp/ *vi* fuggire [per sposarsi]

eloquen|ce /'eləkwəns/ *n* eloquenza *f*. **~t** *a* eloquente. **~tly** *adv* con eloquenza

else /els/ *adv* altro; **who ~?** e chi altro?; **he did of course, who ~?** l'ha fatto lui e chi, se no?; **nothing ~** nient'altro; **or ~** altrimenti; **someone ~** qualcun altro; **somewhere ~** da qualche altra parte; **anyone ~** chiunque altro; (*as question*) nessun'altro?; **anything ~** qualunque altra cosa; (*as question*) altro?. **~where** *adv* altrove

elucidate /ɪ'luːsɪdeɪt/ *vt* delucidare

elude /ɪ'luːd/ *vt* eludere; (*avoid*) evitare; **the name ~s me** il nome mi sfugge

elusive /ɪ'luːsɪv/ *a* elusivo

emaciated /ɪ'meɪsɪeɪtɪd/ *a* emaciato

e-mail /'iːmeɪl/ *n* posta *f* elettronica ● *vt* spedire via posta elettronica

emanate /'eməneɪt/ *vi* emanare

emancipat|ed /ɪ'mænsɪpeɪtɪd/ *a* emancipato. **~ion** /-'peɪʃn/ *n* emancipazione *f*; (*of slaves*) liberazione *f*

embankment /ɪm'bæŋkmənt/ *n* argine *m*; *Rail* massicciata *f*

embargo /em'bɑːgəʊ/ *n* (*pl* **-es**) embargo *m*

embark /ɪm'bɑːk/ *vi* imbarcarsi; **~ on** intraprendere. **~ation** /embɑː'keɪʃn/ *n* imbarco *m*

embarrass /em'bærəs/ *vt* imbarazzare. **~ed** *a* imbarazzato. **~ing** *a* imbarazzante. **~ment** *n* imbarazzo *m*

embassy /'embəsɪ/ *n* ambasciata *f*

embedded /ɪm'bedɪd/ *a* (*in concrete*) cementato; (*traditions, feelings*) radicato

embellish /ɪm'belɪʃ/ *vt* abbellire

embers /'embəz/ *npl* braci *fpl*

embezzle /ɪm'bezl/ *vt* appropriarsi indebitamente di. **~ment** *n* appropriazione *f* indebita

embitter /ɪm'bɪtə(r)/ *vt* amareggiare

emblem /'embləm/ *n* emblema *m*

embody /ɪm'bɒdɪ/ *vt* (*pt/pp* **-ied**) incorporare; **~ what is best in...** rappresentare quanto c'è di meglio di...

emboss /ɪm'bɒs/ *vt* sbalzare (*metal*); stampare in rilievo (*paper*). **~ed** *a* in rilievo

embrace /ɪm'breɪs/ *n* abbraccio *m* ● *vt* abbracciare ● *vi* abbracciarsi

embroider /ɪm'brɔɪdə(r)/ *vt* ricamare (*design*); *fig* abbellire. **~y** *n* ricamo *m*

embryo /'embrɪəʊ/ *n* embrione *m*

emerald /'emərəld/ *n* smeraldo *m*

emer|ge /ɪ'mɜːdʒ/ *vi* emergere; (*come into being: nation*) nascere; (*sun,* *flowers*⟩ spuntare fuori. **~gence** /-əns/ *n* emergere *m*; (*of new country*) nascita *f*

emergency /ɪ'mɜ:dʒənsɪ/ *n* emergenza *f*; **in an ~** in caso di emergenza. **~ exit** *n* uscita *f* di sicurezza

emery /'emərɪ/: **~ board** *n* limetta *f* [per le unghie]

emigrant /'emɪgrənt/ *n* emigrante *mf*

emigrat|e /'emɪgreɪt/ *vi* emigrare. **~ion** /-'greɪʃn/ *n* emigrazione *f*

eminent /'emɪnənt/ *a* eminente. **~ly** *adv* eminentemente

emission /ɪ'mɪʃn/ *n* emissione *f*; (*of fumes*) esalazione *f*

emit /ɪ'mɪt/ *vt* (*pt/pp* **emitted**) emettere; esalare ⟨*fumes*⟩

emotion /ɪ'məʊʃn/ *n* emozione *f*. **~al** *a* denso di emozione; ⟨*person, reaction*⟩ emotivo; **become ~al** avere una reazione emotiva

emotive /ɪ'məʊtɪv/ *a* emotivo

empathize /'empəθaɪz/ *vi* **~ with sb** immedesimarsi nei problemi di qcno

emperor /'empərə(r)/ *n* imperatore *m*

emphasis /'emfəsɪs/ *n* enfasi *f*; **put the ~ on sth** accentuare qcsa

emphasize /'emfəsaɪz/ *vt* accentuare ⟨*word, syllable*⟩; sottolineare ⟨*need*⟩

emphatic /ɪm'fætɪk/ *a* categorico

empire /'empaɪə(r)/ *n* impero *m*

empirical /em'pɪrɪkl/ *a* empirico

employ /ɪm'plɔɪ/ *vt* impiegare; *fig* usare ⟨*tact*⟩. **~ee** /emplɔɪ'i:/ *n* impiegato, -a *mf*. **~er** *n* datore *m* di lavoro. **~ment** *n* occupazione *f*; (*work*) lavoro *m*. **~ment agency** *n* ufficio *m* di collocamento

empower /ɪm'paʊə(r)/ *vt* autorizzare; (*enable*) mettere in grado

empress /'emprɪs/ *n* imperatrice *f*

empties /'emptɪz/ *npl* vuoti *mpl*

emptiness /'emptɪnɪs/ *n* vuoto *m*

empty /'emptɪ/ *a* vuoto; ⟨*promise, threat*⟩ vano ● *v* (*pt/pp* **-ied**) ● *vt* vuotare ⟨*container*⟩ ● *vi* vuotarsi

emulate /'emjʊleɪt/ *vt* emulare

emulsion /ɪ'mʌlʃn/ *n* emulsione *f*

enable /ɪ'neɪbl/ *vt* **~ sb to** mettere qcno in grado di

enact /ɪ'nækt/ *vt* *Theat* rappresentare; decretare ⟨*law*⟩

enamel /ɪ'næml/ *n* smalto *m* ● *vt* (*pt/pp* **enamelled**) smaltare

enchant /ɪn'tʃɑːnt/ *vt* incantare. **~ing** *a* incantevole. **~ment** *n* incanto *m*

encircle /ɪn'sɜːkl/ *vt* circondare

enclave /'enkleɪv/ *n* enclave *f inv*; *fig* territorio *m*

enclos|e /ɪn'kləʊz/ *vt* circondare ⟨*land*⟩; (*in letter*) allegare (**with** a). **~ed** *a* ⟨*space*⟩ chiuso; (*in letter*) allegato. **~ure** /-ʒə(r)/ *n* (*at zoo*) recinto *m*; (*in letter*) allegato *m*

encompass /ɪn'kʌmpəs/ *vt* (*include*) comprendere

encore /'ɒŋkɔː(r)/ *n & int* bis *m inv*

encounter /ɪn'kaʊntə(r)/ *n* incontro *m*; (*battle*) scontro *m* ● *vt* incontrare

encourage /ɪn'kʌrɪdʒ/ *vt* incoraggiare; promuovere ⟨*the arts, independence*⟩. **~ment** *n* incoraggiamento *m*; (*of the arts*) promozione *f*. **~ing** *a* incoraggiante; ⟨*smile*⟩ di incoraggiamento

encroach /ɪn'krəʊtʃ/ *vt* **~ on** invadere ⟨*land, privacy*⟩; abusare di ⟨*time*⟩; interferire con ⟨*rights*⟩

encumb|er /ɪn'kʌmbə(r)/ *vt* **~ered with** essere carico di ⟨*children, suitcases*⟩; ingombro di ⟨*furniture*⟩. **~rance** /-rəns/ *n* peso *m*

encyclop[a]ed|ia /ɪnsaɪklə'piːdɪə/ *n* enciclopedia *f*. **~ic** *a* enciclopedico

end /end/ *n* fine *f*; (*of box, table, piece of string*) estremità *f*; (*of town, room*) parte *f*; (*purpose*) fine *m*; **in the ~** alla fine; **at the ~ of May** alla fine di maggio; **at the ~ of the street/garden** in fondo alla strada/al giardino; **on ~** (*upright*) in piedi; **for days on ~** per giorni e giorni; **for six days on ~** per sei giorni di fila; **put an ~ to sth** mettere fine a qcsa; **make ~s meet** *fam* sbarcare il lunario; **no ~ of** *fam* un sacco di ● *vt/i* finire. **end up** *vi* finire; **~ up doing sth** finire col fare qcsa

endanger /ɪn'deɪndʒə(r)/ *vt* rischiare ⟨*one's life*⟩; mettere a repentaglio ⟨*sb else, success of sth*⟩

endear|ing /ɪn'dɪərɪŋ/ *a* accattivante. **~ment** *n* term of **~ment** vezzeggiativo *m*

endeavour /ɪn'devə(r)/ *n* tentativo *m* ● *vi* sforzarsi (**to** di)

ending /'endɪŋ/ *n* fine *f*; *Gram* desinenza *f*

endive /'endaɪv/ *n* indivia *f*

endless /'endlɪs/ *a* interminabile; ⟨*patience*⟩ infinito. **~ly** *adv* continuamente; ⟨*patient*⟩ infinitamente

endorse /en'dɔːs/ *vt* girare ⟨*cheque*⟩; ⟨*sports personality:*⟩ fare pubblicità a ⟨*product*⟩; approvare ⟨*plan*⟩. **~ment** *n* (*of cheque*) girata *f*; (*of plan*) conferma *f*; (*on driving licence*) registrazione *f* su patente di un'infrazione

endow /ɪn'daʊ/ *vt* dotare

endur|able /ɪn'djʊərəbl/ *a* sopportabile. **~ance** /-rəns/ *n* resistenza *f*; **it is beyond ~ance** è insopportabile

endur|e /ɪn'djʊə(r)/ *vt* sopportare ● *vi* durare. **~ing** *a* duraturo

'end user *n* utente *m* finale

enemy /'enəmɪ/ *n* nemico, -a *mf* ● *attrib* nemico

energetic /enə'dʒetɪk/ *a* energico

energy /'enədʒɪ/ *n* energia *f*

enforce /ɪn'fɔːs/ *vt* far rispettare ⟨law⟩. **~d** *a* forzato

engage /ɪn'geɪdʒ/ *vt* assumere ⟨staff⟩; *Theat* ingaggiare; *Auto* ingranare ⟨gear⟩ ● *vi Techn* ingranare; **~ in** impegnarsi in. **~d** *a* ⟨in use, busy⟩ occupato; ⟨person⟩ impegnato; ⟨to be married⟩ fidanzato; **get ~d** fidanzarsi (**to** con); **~d tone** *Teleph* segnale *m* di occupato. **~ment** *n* fidanzamento *m*; ⟨appointment⟩ appuntamento *m*; *Mil* combattimento *m*; **~ment ring** anello *m* di fidanzamento

engaging /ɪn'geɪdʒɪŋ/ *a* attraente

engender /ɪn'dʒendə(r)/ *vt fig* generare

engine /'endʒɪn/ *n* motore *m*; *Rail* locomotrice *f*. **~-driver** *n* macchinista *m*

engineer /endʒɪ'nɪə(r)/ *n* ingegnere *m*; ⟨service, installation⟩ tecnico *m*; *Naut, Am Rail* macchinista *m* ● *vt fig* architettare. **~ing** *n* ingegneria *f*

England /'ɪŋglənd/ *n* Inghilterra *f*

English /'ɪŋglɪʃ/ *a* inglese; **the ~ Channel** la Manica ● *n* ⟨language⟩ inglese *m*; **the ~** *pl* gli inglesi. **~man** *n* inglese *m*. **~woman** *n* inglese *f*

engrav|e /ɪn'greɪv/ *vt* incidere. **~ing** *n* incisione *f*

engross /ɪn'grəʊs/ *vt* **~ed in** assorto in

engulf /ɪn'gʌlf/ *vt* ⟨fire, waves:⟩ inghiottire

enhance /ɪn'hɑːns/ *vt* accrescere ⟨beauty, reputation⟩; migliorare ⟨performance⟩

enigma /ɪ'nɪgmə/ *n* enigma *m*. **~tic** /enɪg'mætɪk/ *a* enigmatico

enjoy /ɪn'dʒɔɪ/ *vt* godere di ⟨good health⟩; **~ oneself** divertirsi; **I ~ cooking/painting** mi piace cucinare/dipingere; **~ your meal** buon appetito. **~able** /-əbl/ *a* piacevole. **~ment** *n* piacere *m*

enlarge /ɪn'lɑːdʒ/ *vt* ingrandire ● *vi* **~ upon** dilungarsi su. **~ment** *n* ingrandimento *m*

enlighten /ɪn'laɪtn/ *vt* illuminare.

~ed *a* progressista. **~ment** *n* **The E~ment** l'Illuminismo *m*

enlist /ɪn'lɪst/ *vt Mil* reclutare; **~ sb's help** farsi aiutare da qcno ● *vi Mil* arruolarsi

enliven /ɪn'laɪvn/ *vt* animare

enmity /'enmətɪ/ *n* inimicizia *f*

enormity /ɪ'nɔːmətɪ/ *n* enormità *f*

enormous /ɪ'nɔːməs/ *a* enorme. **~ly** *adv* estremamente; ⟨grateful⟩ infinitamente

enough /ɪ'nʌf/ *a* & *n* abbastanza; **I didn't bring ~ clothes** non ho portato abbastanza vestiti; **have you had ~?** ⟨to eat/drink⟩ hai mangiato/bevuto abbastanza?; **I've had ~!** *fam* ne ho abbastanza!; **is that ~?** basta?; **that's ~!** basta così!; **£50 isn't ~** 50 sterline non sono sufficienti ● *adv* abbastanza; **you're not working fast ~** non lavori in fretta; **funnily ~** stranamente

enquir|e /ɪn'kwaɪə(r)/ *vi* domandare; **~e about** chiedere informazioni su. **~y** *n* domanda *f*; ⟨investigation⟩ inchiesta *f*

enrage /ɪn'reɪdʒ/ *vt* fare arrabbiare

enrich /ɪn'rɪtʃ/ *vt* arricchire; ⟨improve⟩ migliorare ⟨vocabulary⟩

enrol /ɪn'rəʊl/ *vi* ⟨pt/pp -**rolled**⟩ ⟨for exam, in club⟩ iscriversi (**for, in** a). **~ment** *n* iscrizione *f*

ensemble /ɒn'sɒmbl/ *n* ⟨clothing & Mus⟩ complesso *m*

enslave /ɪn'sleɪv/ *vt* render schiavo

ensue /ɪn'sjuː/ *vi* seguire; **the ~ing discussion** la discussione che ne è seguita

ensure /ɪn'ʃʊə(r)/ *vt* assicurare; **~ that** ⟨person:⟩ assicurarsi che; ⟨measure:⟩ garantire che

entail /ɪn'teɪl/ *vt* comportare; **what does it ~?** in che cosa consiste?

entangle /ɪn'tæŋgl/ *vt* **get ~d in** rimanere impigliato in; *fig* rimanere coinvolto in

enter /'entə(r)/ *vt* entrare in; iscrivere ⟨horse, runner in race⟩; cominciare ⟨university⟩; partecipare a ⟨competition⟩; *Comput* immettere ⟨data⟩; ⟨write down⟩ scrivere ● *vi* entrare; *Theat* entrare in scena; ⟨register as competitor⟩ iscriversi; ⟨take part⟩ partecipare (**in** a)

enterpris|e /'entəpraɪz/ *n* impresa *f*; ⟨quality⟩ iniziativa *f*. **~ing** *a* intraprendente

entertain /entə'teɪn/ *vt* intrattenere;

(invite) ricevere; nutrire ‹*ideas, hopes*›; prendere in considerazione ‹*possibility*› ● *vi* intrattenersi; *(have guests)* ricevere. **~er** *n* artista *mf*. **~ing** *a* ‹*person*› di gradevole compagnia; ‹*evening, film, play*› divertente. **~ment** *n* (*amusement*) intrattenimento *m*

enthral /ɪnˈθrɔːl/ *vt* (*pt/pp* **enthralled**) **be ~led** essere affascinato (**by** da)

enthusias|m /ɪnˈθjuːzɪæzm/ *n* entusiasmo *m*. **~t** *n* entusiasta *mf*. **~tic** /-ˈæstɪk/ *a* entusiastico

entice /ɪnˈtaɪs/ *vt* attirare. **~ment** *n* (*incentive*) incentivo *m*

entire /ɪnˈtaɪə(r)/ *a* intero. **~ly** *adv* del tutto; **I'm not ~ly satisfied** non sono completamente soddisfatto. **~ty** /-rətɪ/ *n* **in its ~ty** nell'insieme

entitled /ɪnˈtaɪtld/ *a* ‹*book*› intitolato; **be ~ to sth** aver diritto a qcsa

entitlement /ɪnˈtaɪtlmənt/ *n* diritto *m*

entity /ˈentətɪ/ *n* entità *f*

entrance¹ /ˈentrəns/ *n* entrata *f*; *Theat* entrata *f* in scena; (*right to enter*) ammissione *f*; **'no ~'** 'ingresso vietato'. **~ examination** *n* esame *m* di ammissione. **~ fee** *n* **how much is the ~ fee?** quanto costa il biglietto di ingresso?

entrance² /ɪnˈtrɑːns/ *vt* estasiare

entrant /ˈentrənt/ *n* concorrente *mf*

entreat /ɪnˈtriːt/ *vt* supplicare

entrenched /ɪnˈtrentʃt/ *a* ‹*ideas, views*› radicato

entrust /ɪnˈtrʌst/ *vt* **~ sb with sth, ~ sth to sb** affidare qcsa a qcno

entry /ˈentrɪ/ *n* ingresso *m*; (*way in*) entrata *f*; (*in directory etc*) voce *f*; (*in appointment diary*) appuntamento *m*; **no ~** ingresso vietato; *Auto* accesso vietato. **~ form** *n* modulo *m* di ammissione. **~ visa** *n* visto *m* di ingresso

enumerate /ɪˈnjuːməreɪt/ *vt* enumerare

enunciate /ɪˈnʌnsɪeɪt/ *vt* enunciare

envelop /ɪnˈveləp/ *vt* (*pt/pp* **enveloped**) avviluppare

envelope /ˈenvələʊp/ *n* busta *f*

enviable /ˈenvɪəbl/ *a* invidiabile

envious /ˈenvɪəs/ *a* invidioso. **~ly** *adv* con invidia

environment /ɪnˈvaɪrənmənt/ *n* ambiente *m*

environmental /ɪnvaɪrənˈmentl/ *a* ambientale. **~ist** *n* ambientalista *mf*. **~ly** *adv* **~ly friendly** che rispetta l'ambiente

envisage /ɪnˈvɪzɪdʒ/ *vt* prevedere

envoy /ˈenvɔɪ/ *n* inviato, -a *mf*

envy /ˈenvɪ/ *n* invidia *f* ● *vt* (*pt/pp* **-ied**) **~ sb sth** invidiare qcno per qcsa

enzyme /ˈenzaɪm/ *n* enzima *m*

epic /ˈepɪk/ *a* epico ● *n* epopea *f*

epidemic /epɪˈdemɪk/ *n* epidemia *f*

epilep|sy /ˈepɪlepsɪ/ *n* epilessia *f*. **~tic** /-ˈleptɪk/ *a* & *n* epilettico, -a *mf*

epilogue /ˈepɪlɒg/ *n* epilogo *m*

episode /ˈepɪsəʊd/ *n* episodio *m*

epitaph /ˈepɪtɑːf/ *n* epitaffio *m*

epithet /ˈepɪθet/ *n* epiteto *m*

epitom|e /ɪˈpɪtəmɪ/ *n* epitome *f*. **~ize** *vt* essere il classico esempio di

epoch /ˈiːpɒk/ *n* epoca *f*

equal /ˈiːkwl/ *a* ‹*parts, amounts*› uguale; **of ~ height** della stessa altezza; **be ~ to the task** essere a l'altezza del compito ● *n* pari *m* *inv* ● *vt* (*pt/pp* **equalled**) (*be same in quantity as*) essere pari a; (*rival*) uguagliare; **5 plus 5 ~s 10** 5 più 5 [è] uguale a 10. **~ity** /ɪˈkwɒlətɪ/ *n* uguaglianza *f*

equalize /ˈiːkwəlaɪz/ *vi* *Sport* pareggiare. **~r** *n* *Sport* pareggio *m*

equally /ˈiːkwəlɪ/ *adv* ‹*divide*› in parti uguali; **~ intelligent** della stessa intelligenza; **~,...** allo stesso tempo...

equanimity /ekwəˈnɪmətɪ/ *n* equanimità *f*

equat|e /ɪˈkweɪt/ *vt* **~e sth with sth** equiparare qcsa a qcsa. **~ion** /-eɪʒn/ *n Math* equazione *f*

equator /ɪˈkweɪtə(r)/ *n* equatore *m*

equestrian /ɪˈkwestrɪən/ *a* equestre

equilibrium /iːkwɪˈlɪbrɪəm/ *n* equilibrio *m*

equinox /ˈiːkwɪnɒks/ *n* equinozio *m*

equip /ɪˈkwɪp/ *vt* (*pt/pp* **equipped**) equipaggiare; attrezzare ‹*kitchen, office*›. **~ment** *n* attrezzatura *f*

equitable /ˈekwɪtəbl/ *a* giusto

equity /ˈekwɪtɪ/ *n* (*justness*) equità *f*; *Comm* azioni *fpl*

equivalent /ɪˈkwɪvələnt/ *a* equivalente; **be ~ to** equivalere a ● *n* equivalente *m*

equivocal /ɪˈkwɪvəkl/ *a* equivoco

era /ˈɪərə/ *n* età *f*; (*geological*) era *f*

eradicate /ɪˈrædɪkeɪt/ *vt* eradicare

erase /ɪˈreɪz/ *vt* cancellare. **~r** *n* gomma *f* [da cancellare]; (*for blackboard*) cancellino *m*

erect /ɪˈrekt/ *a* eretto ● *vt* erigere. **~ion** /-ekʃn/ *n* erezione *f*

ero|de /ɪˈrəʊd/ *vt* ‹*water:*› erodere; ‹*acid:*› corrodere. **~sion** /-əʊʒn/ *n* erosione *f*; (*by acid*) corrosione *f*

erotic /ɪˈrɒtɪk/ *a* erotico. **~ism** /-tɪsɪzm/ *n* erotismo *m*

err /ɜː(r)/ vi errare; (sin) peccare

errand /'erənd/ n commissione f

erratic /ɪ'rætɪk/ a irregolare; ⟨person, moods⟩ imprevedibile; ⟨exchange rate⟩ incostante

erroneous /ɪ'rəʊnɪəs/ a erroneo

error /'erə(r)/ n errore m; **in ~** per errore

erudit|e /'erʊdaɪt/ a erudito. **~ion** /-'dɪʃn/ n erudizione f

erupt /ɪ'rʌpt/ vi eruttare; ⟨spots:⟩ spuntare; (fig: in anger) dare in escandescenze. **~ion** /-ʌpʃn/ n eruzione f; fig scoppio m

escalat|e /'eskəleɪt/ vi intensificarsi ● vt intensificare. **~ion** /-'leɪʃn/ n escalation f inv. **~or** n scala f mobile

escapade /'eskəpeɪd/ n scappatella f

escape /ɪ'skeɪp/ n fuga f; (from prison) evasione f; **have a narrow ~** cavarsela per un pelo ● vi ⟨prisoner:⟩ evadere (**from** da); sfuggire (**from sb** alla sorveglianza di qcno); ⟨animal:⟩ scappare; ⟨gas:⟩ fuoriuscire ● vt ~ **notice** passare inosservato; **the name ~s me** mi sfugge il nome

escapism /ɪ'skeɪpɪzm/ n evasione f [dalla realtà]

escort[1] /'eskɔːt/ n (of person) accompagnatore, -trice mf; Mil etc scorta f

escort[2] /ɪ'skɔːt/ vt accompagnare; Mil etc scortare

Eskimo /'eskɪməʊ/ n esquimese mf

esoteric /esə'terɪk/ a esoterico

especial /ɪ'speʃl/ a speciale. **~ly** adv specialmente; ⟨kind⟩ particolarmente

espionage /'espɪənɑːʒ/ n spionaggio m

essay /'eseɪ/ n saggio m; Sch tema f

essence /'esns/ n essenza f; **in ~** in sostanza

essential /ɪ'senʃl/ a essenziale ● n **the ~s** pl l'essenziale m. **~ly** adv essenzialmente

establish /ɪ'stæblɪʃ/ vt stabilire ⟨contact, lead⟩; fondare ⟨firm⟩; (prove) accertare; **~ oneself as** affermarsi come. **~ment** n (firm) azienda f; **the E~ment** l'ordine m costituito

estate /ɪ'steɪt/ n tenuta f; (possessions) patrimonio m; (housing) quartiere m residenziale. **~ agent** n agente m immobiliare. **~ car** n giardiniera f

esteem /ɪ'stiːm/ n stima f ● vt stimare; (consider) giudicare

estimate[1] /'estɪmət/ n valutazione f; Comm preventivo m; **at a rough ~** a occhio e croce

estimat|e[2] /'estɪmeɪt/ vt stimare. **~ion**

/-'meɪʃn/ n (esteem) stima f; **in my ~ion** (judgement) a mio giudizio

estuary /'estjʊərɪ/ n estuario m

etc /et'setərə/ abbr (et cetera) ecc

etching /'etʃɪŋ/ n acquaforte f

eternal /ɪ'tɜːnl/ a eterno

eternity /ɪ'tɜːnətɪ/ n eternità f

ethic /'eθɪk/ n etica f. **~al** a etico. **~s** n etica f

Ethiopia /iːθɪ'əʊpɪə/ n Etiopia f

ethnic /'eθnɪk/ a etnico

etiquette /'etɪket/ n etichetta f

EU n abbr (European Union) UE f

eucalyptus /juːkə'lɪptəs/ n eucalipto m

eulogy /'juːlədʒɪ/ n elogio m

euphemis|m /'juːfəmɪzm/ n eufemismo m. **~tic** /-'mɪstɪk/ a eufemistico

euphoria /juː'fɔːrɪə/ n euforia f

Euro+ /'jʊərəʊ-/ pref **~cheque** n eurochèque m inv. **~dollar** n eurodollaro m

Europe /'jʊərəp/ n Europa f

European /jʊərə'pɪən/ a europeo; **~ Community** Comunità f Europea; **~ Union** Unione f Europea ● n europeo, -a mf

evacuat|e /ɪ'vækjʊeɪt/ vt evacuare ⟨building, area⟩. **~ion** /-'eɪʃn/ n evacuazione f

evade /ɪ'veɪd/ vt evadere ⟨taxes⟩; evitare ⟨the enemy, authorities⟩; **~ the issue** evitare l'argomento

evaluate /ɪ'væljʊeɪt/ vt valutare

evange|lical /iːvæn'dʒelɪkl/ a evangelico. **~list** /ɪ'vændʒəlɪst/ n evangelista m

evaporat|e /ɪ'væpəreɪt/ vi evaporare; fig svanire. **~ion** /-'reɪʃn/ n evaporazione f

evasion /ɪ'veɪʒn/ n evasione f

evasive /ɪ'veɪsɪv/ a evasivo

eve /iːv/ n liter vigilia f

even /'iːvn/ a (level) piatto; (same, equal) uguale; (regular) regolare; ⟨number⟩ pari; **get ~ with** vendicarsi di; **now we're ~** adesso siamo pari ● adv anche, ancora; **~ if** anche se; **so** con tutto ciò; **not ~** nemmeno; **~ bigger/hotter** ancora più grande/caldo ● vt ~ **the score** Sport pareggiare. **even out** vi livellarsi. **even up** vt livellare

evening /'iːvnɪŋ/ n sera f; (whole evening) serata f; **this ~** stasera; **in the ~** la sera. **~ class** n corso m serale. **~ dress** n (man's) abito m scuro; (woman's) abito m da sera

evenly /'iːvnlɪ/ adv ⟨distributed⟩ uniformemente; ‹*breathe*› regolarmente; ‹*divided*› in uguali parti

event /ɪ'vent/ *n* avvenimento *m*; ‹*function*› manifestazione *f*; *Sport* gara *f*; **in the ~ of** nell'eventualità di; **in the ~** alla fine. **~ful** *a* movimentato

eventual /ɪ'ventjʊəl/ *a* **the ~ winner was...** alla fine il vincitore è stato.... **~ity** /-'ælətɪ/ *n* eventualità *f*. **~ly** *adv* alla fine; **~ly!** finalmente!

ever /'evə(r)/ *adv* mai; **I haven't ~...** non ho mai...; **for ~** per sempre; **hardly ~** quasi mai; **~ since** da quando; ‹*since that time*› da allora; **~ so** *fam* veramente

'evergreen *n* sempreverde *m*

ever'lasting *a* eterno

every /'evrɪ/ *a* ogni; **~ one** ciascuno; **~ other day** un giorno sì un giorno no

every: **~body** *pron* tutti *pl*. **~day** *a* quotidiano, di ogni giorno. **~one** *pron* tutti *pl*; **~one else** tutti gli altri. **~thing** *pron* tutto; **~thing else** tutto il resto. **~where** *adv* dappertutto; ‹*wherever*› dovunque

evict /ɪ'vɪkt/ *vt* sfrattare. **~ion** /-ɪkʃn/ *n* sfratto *m*

eviden|ce /'evɪdəns/ *n* evidenza *f*; *Jur* testimonianza *f*; **give ~ce** testimoniare. **~t** *a* evidente. **~tly** *adv* evidentemente

evil /'iːvl/ *a* cattivo ● *n* male *m*

evocative /ɪ'vɒkətɪv/ *a* evocativo; **be ~ of** evocare

evoke /ɪ'vəʊk/ *vt* evocare

evolution /iːvə'luːʃn/ *n* evoluzione *f*

evolve /ɪ'vɒlv/ *vt* evolvere ● *vi* evolversi

ewe /juː/ *n* pecora *f*

exacerbate /ɪg'zæsəbeɪt/ *vt* esacerbare ‹*situation*›

exact /ɪg'zækt/ *a* esatto ● *vt* esigere. **~ing** *a* esigente. **~itude** /-ɪtjuːd/ *n* esattezza *f*. **~ly** *adv* esattamente; **not ~ly** non proprio. **~ness** *n* precisione *f*

exaggerat|e /ɪg'zædʒəreɪt/ *vt/i* esagerare. **~ion** /-'reɪʃn/ *n* esagerazione *f*

exam /ɪg'zæm/ *n* esame *m*

examination /ɪgzæmɪ'neɪʃn/ *n* esame *m*; ‹*of patient*› visita *f*

examine /ɪg'zæmɪn/ *vt* esaminare; visitare ‹*patient*›. **~r** *n* *Sch* esaminatore, -trice *mf*

example /ɪg'zaːmpl/ *n* esempio *m*; **for ~** per esempio; **make an ~ of sb** punire qcno per dare un esempio; **be an ~ to sb** dare il buon esempio a qcno

exasperat|e /ɪg'zæspəreɪt/ *vt* esasperare. **~ion** /-'reɪʃn/ *n* esasperazione *f*

excavat|e /'ekskəveɪt/ *vt* scavare; *Archaeol* fare gli scavi di. **~ion** /-'veɪʃn/ *n* scavo *m*

exceed /ɪk'siːd/ *vt* eccedere. **~ingly** *adv* estremamente

excel /ɪk'sel/ *v* (*pt/pp* **excelled**) ● *vi* eccellere ● *vt* **~ oneself** superare se stessi

excellen|ce /'eksələns/ *n* eccellenza *f*. **E~cy** *n* (*title*) Eccellenza *f*. **~t** *a* eccellente

except /ɪk'sept/ *prep* eccetto, tranne; **~ for** eccetto, tranne; **~ that...** eccetto che... ● *vt* eccettuare. **~ing** *prep* eccetto, tranne

exception /ɪk'sepʃn/ *n* eccezione *f*; **take ~ to** fare obiezioni a. **~al** *a* eccezionale. **~ally** *adv* eccezionalmente

excerpt /'eksɜːpt/ *n* estratto *m*

excess /ɪk'ses/ *n* eccesso *m*; **in ~ of** oltre. **~ baggage** *n* bagaglio *m* in eccedenza. **~ 'fare** *n* supplemento *m*

excessive /ɪk'sesɪv/ *a* eccessivo. **~ly** *adv* eccessivamente

exchange /ɪks'tʃeɪndʒ/ *n* scambio *m*; *Teleph* centrale *f*; *Comm* cambio *m*; [**stock**] **~** borsa *f* valori; **in ~** in cambio (**for** di) ● *vt* scambiare (**for** con); cambiare ‹*money*›. **~ rate** *n* tasso *m* di cambio

exchequer /ɪks'tʃekə(r)/ *n* *Pol* tesoro *m*

excise[1] /'eksaɪz/ *n* dazio *m*; **~ duty** dazio *m*

excise[2] /ek'saɪz/ *vt* recidere

excitable /ɪk'saɪtəbl/ *a* eccitabile

excit|e /ɪk'saɪt/ *vt* eccitare. **~ed** *a* eccitato; **get ~ed** eccitarsi. **~edly** *adv* tutto eccitato. **~ement** *n* eccitazione *f*. **~ing** *a* eccitante; ‹*story, film*› appassionante; ‹*holiday*› entusiasmante

exclaim /ɪk'skleɪm/ *vt/i* esclamare

exclamation /eksklə'meɪʃn/ *n* esclamazione *f*. **~ mark** *n*, *Am* **~ point** *n* punto *m* esclamativo

exclu|de /ɪk'skluːd/ *vt* escludere. **~ding** *pron* escluso. **~sion** /-ʒn/ *n* esclusione *f*

exclusive /ɪk'skluːsɪv/ *a* ‹*rights, club*› esclusivo; ‹*interview*› in esclusiva; **~ of...** ...escluso. **~ly** *adv* esclusivamente

excommunicate /ekskə'mjuːnɪkeɪt/ *vt* scomunicare

excrement /'ekskrɪmənt/ *n* escremento *m*

excruciating /ɪk'skruːʃɪeɪtɪŋ/ *a* atroce ‹*pain*›; ‹*fam: very bad*› spaventoso

excursion /ɪk'skɜːʃn/ n escursione f

excusable /ɪk'skjuːzəbl/ a perdonabile

excuse¹ /ɪk'skjuːs/ n scusa f

excuse² /ɪk'skjuːz/ vt scusare; **~ from** esonerare da; **~ me!** (to get attention) scusi!; (to get past) permesso!, scusi!; (indignant) come ha detto?

ex-di'rectory a be **~** non figurare sull'elenco telefonico

execute /'eksɪkjuːt/ vt eseguire; (put to death) giustiziare; attuare ⟨plan⟩

execution /eksɪ'kjuːʃn/ n esecuzione f; (of plan) attuazione f. **~er** n boia m inv

executive /ɪg'zekjutɪv/ a esecutivo ● n dirigente mf; Pol esecutivo m

executor /ɪg'zekjutə(r)/ n Jur esecutore, -trice mf

exemplary /ɪg'zemplərɪ/ a esemplare

exemplify /ɪg'zemplɪfaɪ/ vt (pt/pp -ied) esemplificare

exempt /ɪg'zempt/ a esente ● vt esentare (from da). **~ion** /-empʃn/ n esenzione f

exercise /'eksəsaɪz/ n esercizio m; Mil esercitazione f; **physical ~s** ginnastica f; **take ~** fare del moto ● vt esercitare ⟨muscles, horse⟩; portare a spasso ⟨dog⟩; mettere in pratica ⟨skills⟩ ● vi esercitarsi. **~ book** n quaderno m

exert /ɪg'zɜːt/ vt esercitare; **~ oneself** sforzarsi. **~ion** /-ɜːʃn/ n sforzo m

exhale /eks'heɪl/ vt/i esalare

exhaust /ɪg'zɔːst/ n Auto scappamento m; (pipe) tubo m di scappamento; **~ fumes** fumi mpl di scarico m ● vt esaurire. **~ed** a esausto. **~ing** a estenuante; ⟨climate, person⟩ sfibrante. **~ion** /-ɔːstʃn/ n esaurimento m. **~ive** /-ɪv/ a fig esauriente

exhibit /ɪg'zɪbɪt/ n oggetto m esposto; Jur reperto m ● vt esporre; fig dimostrare

exhibition /eksɪ'bɪʃn/ n mostra f; (of strength, skill) dimostrazione f. **~ist** n esibizionista mf

exhibitor /ɪg'zɪbɪtə(r)/ n espositore, -trice mf

exhilarat|ed /ɪg'zɪləreɪtɪd/ a rallegrato. **~ing** a stimolante; ⟨mountain air⟩ tonificante. **~ion** /-'reɪʃn/ n allegria f

exhort /ɪg'zɔːt/ vt esortare

exhume /ɪg'zjuːm/ vt esumare

exile /'eksaɪl/ n esilio m; (person) esule mf ● vt esiliare

exist /ɪg'zɪst/ vi esistere. **~ence** /-əns/ n esistenza f; **in ~** esistente; **be in ~ence** esistere. **~ing** a attuale

exit /'eksɪt/ n uscita f; Theat uscita f di scena ● vi Theat uscire di scena; Comput uscire

exonerate /ɪg'zɒnəreɪt/ vt esonerare

exorbitant /ɪg'zɔːbɪtənt/ a esorbitante

exorcize /'eksɔːsaɪz/ vt esorcizzare

exotic /ɪg'zɒtɪk/ a esotico

expand /ɪk'spænd/ vt espandere ● vi espandersi; Comm svilupparsi; ⟨metal:⟩ dilatarsi; **~ on** (fig: explain better) approfondire

expans|e /ɪk'spæns/ n estensione f. **~ion** /-ænʃn/ n espansione f; Comm sviluppo m; (of metal) dilatazione f. **~ive** /-ɪv/ a espansivo

expatriate /eks'pætrɪət/ n espatriato, -a mf

expect /ɪk'spekt/ vt aspettare ⟨letter, baby⟩; (suppose) pensare; (demand) esigere; **I ~ so** penso di sì; **be ~ing** essere in stato interessante

expectan|cy /ɪk'spektənsɪ/ n aspettativa f. **~t** a in attesa; **~t mother** donna f incinta. **~tly** adv con impazienza

expectation /ekspek'teɪʃn/ n aspettativa f, speranza f

expedient /ɪk'spiːdɪənt/ a conveniente ● n espediente m

expedition /ekspɪ'dɪʃn/ n spedizione f. **~ary** a Mil di spedizione

expel /ɪk'spel/ vt (pt/pp expelled) espellere

expend /ɪk'spend/ vt consumare. **~able** /-əbl/ a sacrificabile

expenditure /ɪk'spendɪtʃə(r)/ n spesa f

expense /ɪk'spens/ n spesa f; **business ~s** pl spese fpl; **at my ~** a mie spese; **at the ~ of** fig a spese di

expensive /ɪk'spensɪv/ a caro, costoso. **~ly** adv costosamente

experience /ɪk'spɪərɪəns/ n esperienza f ● vt provare ⟨sensation⟩; avere ⟨problem⟩. **~d** a esperto

experiment /ɪk'sperɪmənt/ n esperimento ● /-'mentl/ vi sperimentare. **~al** /-'mentl/ a sperimentale

expert /'ekspɜːt/ a & n esperto, -a mf. **~ly** adv abilmente

expertise /ekspɜː'tiːz/ n competenza f

expire /ɪk'spaɪə(r)/ vi scadere

expiry /ɪk'spaɪərɪ/ n scadenza f. **~ date** n data f di scadenza

explain /ɪk'spleɪn/ vt spiegare

explana|tion /eksplə'neɪʃn/ n spiegazione f. **~tory** /ɪk'splænətərɪ/ a esplicativo

expletive /ɪkˈspliːtɪv/ n imprecazione f
explicit /ɪkˈsplɪsɪt/ a esplicito. ~ly adv
esplicitamente
explode /ɪkˈspləʊd/ vi esplodere ● vt
fare esplodere
exploit[1] /ˈeksplɔɪt/ n impresa f
exploit[2] /ɪkˈsplɔɪt/ vt sfruttare. ~ation
/eksplɔrˈteɪʃn/ n sfruttamento m
explora|tio| /ekspləˈreɪʃn/ n esplora-
zione f. ~tory /ɪkˈsplɒrətərɪ/ a esplora-
tivo
explore /ɪkˈsplɔː(r)/ vt esplorare; fig
studiare ⟨implications⟩. ~r n esploratore, -trice mf
explos|ion /ɪkˈspləʊʒn/ n esplosione f.
~ive /-sɪv/ a & n esplosivo m
exponent /ɪkˈspəʊnənt/ n esponente
mf
export /ˈekspɔːt/ n esportazione f ● vt
/-ˈspɔːt/ esportare. ~er n esportatore,
-trice mf
expos|e /ɪkˈspəʊz/ vt esporre; ⟨reveal⟩
svelare; smascherare ⟨traitor etc⟩. ~ure
/-ʒə(r)/ n esposizione f; Med esposizione
f prolungata al freddo/caldo; ⟨of crimes⟩
smascheramento m; **24 ~ures** Phot 24
pose
expound /ɪkˈspaʊnd/ vt esporre
express /ɪkˈspres/ a espresso ● adv
⟨send⟩ per espresso ● n ⟨train⟩ espresso
m ● vt esprimere; ~ **oneself** esprimersi. ~ion /-ʃn/ n espressione f. ~ive /-ɪv/
a espressivo. ~ly adv espressamente
expulsion /ɪkˈspʌlʃn/ n espulsione f
exquisite /ekˈskwɪzɪt/ a squisito
ex-ˈserviceman n ex-combattente m
extend /ɪkˈstend/ vt prolungare ⟨visit,
road⟩; prorogare ⟨visa, contract⟩; am-
pliare ⟨building, knowledge⟩; ⟨stretch
out⟩ allungare; tendere ⟨hand⟩ ● vi
⟨garden, knowledge:⟩ estendersi
extension /ɪkˈstenʃn/ n prolungamen-
to m; ⟨of visa, contract⟩ proroga f; ⟨of
treaty⟩ ampliamento m; ⟨part of
building⟩ annesso m; ⟨length of cable⟩
prolunga f; Teleph interno m; ~ **226** interno 226
extensive /ɪkˈstensɪv/ a ampio, vasto.
~ly adv ampiamente
extent /ɪkˈstent/ n ⟨scope⟩ portata f; **to
a certain ~** fino a un certo punto; **to
such an ~ that...** fino al punto che...
extenuating /ɪkˈstenjʊeɪtɪŋ/ a ~
circumstances attenuanti f pl
exterior /ɪkˈstɪərɪə(r)/ a & n esterno m
exterminat|e /ɪkˈstɜːmɪneɪt/ vt ster-
minare. ~ion /-ˈneɪʃn/ n sterminio m

external /ɪkˈstɜːnl/ a esterno; **for ~
use only** Med per uso esterno. ~ly adv
esternamente
extinct /ɪkˈstɪŋkt/ a estinto. ~ion
/-ɪŋkʃn/ n estinzione f
extinguish /ɪkˈstɪŋgwɪʃ/ vt estinguere.
~er n estintore m
extort /ɪkˈstɔːt/ vt estorcere. ~ion
/-ɔːʃn/ n estorsione f
extortionate /ɪkˈstɔːʃənət/ a esorbitante
extra /ˈekstrə/ a in più; ⟨train⟩ straordinario; **an ~ £10** 10 sterline extra, 10
sterline in più ● adv in più; ⟨especially⟩
più; **pay ~** pagare in più, pagare extra;
~ **strong/busy** fortissimo/occupatissi-
mo ● n Theat comparsa f; ~**s** pl extra
mpl
extract[1] /ˈekstrækt/ n estratto m
extract[2] /ɪkˈstrækt/ vt estrarre ⟨tooth,
oil⟩; strappare ⟨secret⟩; ricavare ⟨truth⟩.
~or [fan] n aspiratore m
extradit|e /ˈekstrədaɪt/ Jur vt
estradare. ~ion /-ˈdɪʃn/ n estradizione f
extraˈmarital a extraconiugale
extraordinar|y /ɪkˈstrɔːdɪnərɪ/ a stra-
ordinario. ~ily /-ɪlɪ/ adv straordinariamente
extravagan|ce /ɪkˈstrævəgəns/ n
⟨with money⟩ prodigalità f; ⟨of
behaviour⟩ stravaganza f. ~t a spendac-
cione; ⟨bizarre⟩ stravagante; ⟨claim⟩
esagerato
extrem|e /ɪkˈstriːm/ a estremo ● n
estremo m; **in the ~e** al massimo. ~ely
adv estremamente. ~ist n estremista
mf
extremity /ɪkˈstremətɪ/ n ⟨end⟩ estremità f inv
extricate /ˈekstrɪkeɪt/ vt districare
extrovert /ˈekstrəvɜːt/ n estroverso, -a
mf
exuberant /ɪgˈzjuːbərənt/ a esuberan-
te
exude /ɪgˈzjuːd/ vt also fig trasudare
exult /ɪgˈzʌlt/ vi esultare
eye /aɪ/ n occhio m; ⟨of needle⟩ cruna f;
keep an ~ on tener d'occhio; **see ~ to
~** aver le stesse idee ● vt ⟨pt/pp eyed,
pres p ey[e]ing⟩ guardare
eye: ~**ball** n bulbo m oculare. ~ **brow**
n sopracciglio m ⟨pl sopracciglia f⟩.
~**lash** n ciglio m ⟨pl ciglia f⟩. ~**lid** n
palpebra f. ~**-opener** n rivelazione f.
~**-shadow** n ombretto m. ~**sight** n vista f. ~**sore** n fam pugno m nell'occhio.
~**witness** n testimone mf oculare

Ff

fable /'feɪbl/ n favola f

fabric /'fæbrɪk/ n also fig tessuto m

fabrication /ˌfæbrɪ'keɪʃn/ n invenzione f; (manufacture) fabbricazione f

fabulous /'fæbjʊləs/ a fam favoloso

façade /fə'sɑːd/ n (of building, person) facciata f

face /feɪs/ n faccia f, viso m; (grimace) smorfia f; (surface) faccia f; (of clock) quadrante m; **pull ~s** far boccacce; **in the ~ of** di fronte a; **on the ~ of it** in apparenza ● vt (confront) affrontare; **~ north** (house:) dare a nord; **~ the fact that** arrendersi al fatto che. **face up to** vt accettare (facts); affrontare (person)

face: **~-flannel** n guanto m di spugna. **~less** a anonimo. **~-lift** n plastica f facciale

facet /'fæsɪt/ n sfaccettatura f; fig aspetto m

facetious /fə'siːʃəs/ a spiritoso. **~ remarks** spiritosaggini mpl

'face value n (of money) valore m nominale; **take sb/sth at ~** fermarsi alle apparenze

facial /'feɪʃl/ a facciale ● n trattamento m di bellezza al viso

facile /'fæsaɪl/ a semplicistico

facilitate /fə'sɪlɪteɪt/ vt rendere possibile; (make easier) facilitare

facilit|y /fə'sɪlətɪ/ n facilità f; **~ies** pl (of area, in hotel etc) attrezzature fpl

facing /'feɪsɪŋ/ prep **~ the sea** (house) che dà sul mare; **the person ~ me** la persona di fronte a me

facsimile /fæk'sɪməlɪ/ n facsimile m

fact /fækt/ n fatto m; **in ~** infatti

faction /'fækʃn/ n fazione f

factor /'fæktə(r)/ n fattore m

factory /'fæktərɪ/ n fabbrica f

factual /'fæktʃʊəl/ a **be ~** attenersi ai fatti. **~ly** adv (inaccurate) dal punto di vista dei fatti

faculty /'fækəltɪ/ n facoltà f inv

fad /fæd/ n capriccio m

fade /feɪd/ vi sbiadire; (sound, light:) affievolirsi; (flower:) appassire. **fade in** vt cominciare in dissolvenza (picture).

fade out vt finire in dissolvenza (picture)

fag /fæg/ n (chore) fatica f; (fam: cigarette) sigaretta f; (Am sl: homosexual) frocio m. **~ end** n fam cicca f

fagged /fægd/ a **~ out** fam stanco morto

Fahrenheit /'færənhaɪt/ a Fahrenheit

fail /feɪl/ n **without ~** senz'altro ● vi (attempt:) fallire; (eyesight, memory:) indebolirsi; (engine, machine:) guastarsi; (marriage:) andare a rotoli; (in exam:) essere bocciato; **~ to do sth** non fare qcsa; **I tried but I ~ed** ho provato ma non ci sono riuscito ● vt non superare (exam); bocciare (candidate); (disappoint) deludere; **words ~ me** mi mancano le parole

failing /'feɪlɪŋ/ n difetto m ● prep **~ that** altrimenti

failure /'feɪljə(r)/ n fallimento m; (mechanical) guasto m; (person) incapace mf

faint /feɪnt/ a leggero; (memory:) vago; **feel ~** sentirsi mancare ● n svenimento m ● vi svenire

faint: **~-'hearted** a timido. **~ly** adv (slightly) leggermente. **~ness** n (physical) debolezza f

fair¹ /feə(r)/ n fiera f

fair² a (hair, person) biondo; (skin) chiaro; (weather) bello; (just) giusto; (quite good) discreto; Sch abbastanza bene; **a ~ amount** abbastanza ● adv **play ~** fare un gioco pulito. **~ly** adv con giustizia; (rather) discretamente, abbastanza. **~ness** n giustizia f. **~ play** n fair play m inv

fairy /'feərɪ/ n fata f; **~ story**, **~-tale** n fiaba f

faith /feɪθ/ n fede f; (trust) fiducia f; **in good/bad ~** in buona/mala fede

faithful /'feɪθfl/ a fedele. **~ly** adv fedelmente; **yours ~ly** distinti saluti. **~ness** n fedeltà f

'faith-healer n guaritore, -trice mf

fake /feɪk/ a falso ● n falsificazione f;

(*person*) impostore *m* ● *vt* falsificare; (*pretend*) fingere

falcon /ˈfɔːlkən/ *n* falcone *m*

fall /fɔːl/ *n* caduta *f*; (*in prices*) ribasso *m*; (*Am: autumn*) autunno *m*; **have a ~** fare una caduta ● *vi* (*pt* **fell**, *pp* **fallen**) cadere; ⟨*night*:⟩ scendere; **~ in love** innamorarsi. **fall about** *vi* (*with laughter*) morire dal ridere. **fall back on** *vi* ritornare su. **fall for** *vt fam* innamorarsi di ⟨*person*⟩; cascarci ⟨*sth, trick*⟩. **fall down** *vi* cadere; ⟨*building*:⟩ crollare. **fall in** *vi* caderci dentro; (*collapse*) crollare; *Mil* mettersi in riga; **~ in with** concordare con ⟨*suggestion, plan*⟩. **fall off** *vi* cadere; (*diminish*) diminuire. **fall out** *vi* (*quarrel*) litigare; **his hair is ~ing out** perde i capelli. **fall over** *vi* cadere. **fall through** *vi* ⟨*plan*:⟩ andare a monte

fallacy /ˈfæləsɪ/ *n* errore *m*

fallible /ˈfæləbl/ *a* fallibile

'fall-out *n* pioggia *f* radioattiva

false /fɔːls/ *a* falso; **~ bottom** doppio fondo *m*; **~ start** *Sport* falsa partenza *f*. **~hood** *n* menzogna *f*. **~ness** *n* falsità *f*

false 'teeth *npl* dentiera *f*

falsify /ˈfɔːlsɪfaɪ/ *vt* (*pt/pp* **-ied**) falsificare

falter /ˈfɔːltə(r)/ *vi* vacillare; (*making speech*) esitare

fame /feɪm/ *n* fama *f*

familiar /fəˈmɪljə(r)/ *a* familiare; **be ~ with** ⟨*know*⟩ conoscere. **~ity** /-lɪˈærɪtɪ/ *n* familiarità *f*. **~ize** *vt* familiarizzare; **~ize oneself with** familiarizzarsi con

family /ˈfæməlɪ/ *n* famiglia *f*

family: **~ al'lowance** *n* assegni *mpl* familiari. **~ 'doctor** *n* medico *m* di famiglia. **~ 'life** *n* vita *f* familiare. **~ 'planning** *n* pianificazione *f* familiare. **~ 'tree** *n* albero *m* genealogico

famine /ˈfæmɪn/ *n* carestia *f*

famished /ˈfæmɪʃt/ *a* **be ~** *fam* avere una fame da lupo

famous /ˈfeɪməs/ *a* famoso

fan¹ /fæn/ *n* ventilatore *m*; (*handheld*) ventaglio *m* ● *vt* (*pt/pp* **fanned**) far vento a; **~ oneself** sventagliarsi; *fig* **~ the flames** soffiare sul fuoco. **fan out** *vi* spiegarsi a ventaglio

fan² *n* (*admirer*) ammiratore, -trice *mf*; *Sport* tifoso *m*; (*of Verdi etc*) appassionato, -a *mf*

fanatic /fəˈnætɪk/ *n* fanatico, -a *mf*. **~al** *a* fanatico. **~ism** /-sɪzm/ *n* fanatismo *m*

'fan belt *n* cinghia *f* per ventilatore

fanciful /ˈfænsɪfl/ *a* fantasioso

fancy /ˈfænsɪ/ *n* fantasia *f*; **I've taken a real ~ to him** mi è molto simpatico; **as the ~ takes you** come ti pare ● *a* [a] fantasia ● *vt* (*pt/pp* **-ied**) (*believe*) credere; (*fam: want*) aver voglia di; **he fancies you** *fam* gli piaci; **~ that!** ma guarda un po'! **~ 'dress** *n* costume *m* (*per maschera*)

fanfare /ˈfænfeə(r)/ *n* fanfara *f*

fang /fæŋ/ *n* zanna *f*; (*of snake*) dente *m*

fan: **~ heater** *n* termoventilatore *m*. **~light** *n* lunetta *f*

fantas|ize /ˈfæntəsaɪz/ *vi* fantasticare. **~tic** /-ˈtæstɪk/ *a* fantastico. **~y** *n* fantasia *f*

far /fɑː(r)/ *adv* lontano; (*much*) molto; **by ~** di gran lunga; **~ away** lontano; **as ~ as the church** fino alla chiesa; **how ~ is it from here?** quanto dista da qui?; **as ~ as I know** per quanto io sappia ● *a* ⟨*end, side*⟩ altro; **the F~ East** l'Estremo Oriente *m*

farc|e /fɑːs/ *n* farsa *f*. **~ical** *a* ridicolo

fare /feə(r)/ *n* tariffa *f*; (*food*) vitto *m*. **~-dodger** /-dɒdʒə(r)/ *n* passeggero, -a *mf* senza biglietto

farewell /feəˈwel/ *int liter* addio! ● *n* addio *m*

far-'fetched *a* improbabile

farm /fɑːm/ *n* fattoria *f* ● *vi* fare l'agricoltore ● *vt* coltivare ⟨*land*⟩. **~er** *n* agricoltore *m*

farm: **~house** *n* casa *f* colonica. **~ing** *n* agricoltura *f*. **~yard** *n* aia *f*

far: **~-'reaching** *a* di larga portata. **~-'sighted** *a* *fig* prudente; (*Am: long-sighted*) presbite

fart /fɑːt/ *fam* *n* scoreggia *f* ● *vi* scoreggiare

farther /ˈfɑːðə(r)/ *adv* più lontano ● *a* **at the ~ end of** all'altra estremità di

fascinat|e /ˈfæsɪneɪt/ *vt* affascinare. **~ing** *a* affascinante. **~ion** /-ˈneɪʃn/ *n* fascino *m*

fascis|m /ˈfæʃɪzm/ *n* fascismo *m*. **~t** *n* fascista *mf* ● *a* fascista

fashion /ˈfæʃn/ *n* moda *f*; (*manner*) maniera *f* ● *vt* modellare. **~able** /-əbl/ *a* di moda; **be ~able** essere alla moda. **~ably** *adv* alla moda

fast¹ /fɑːst/ *a* veloce; ⟨*colour*⟩ indelebile; **be ~** ⟨*clock*:⟩ andare avanti ● *adv* velocemente; (*firmly*) saldamente; **~er!** più in fretta!; **be ~ asleep** dormire profondamente

fast² *n* digiuno *m* ● *vi* digiunare

fasten /ˈfɑːsn/ *vt* allacciare; chiudere ⟨*window*⟩; (*stop flapping*) mettere un fermo a ● *vi* allacciarsi. ~**er** *n*, ~**ing** *n* chiusura *f*

fastidious /fə'stɪdɪəs/ *a* esigente

fat /fæt/ *a* (**fatter, fattest**) ⟨*person, cheque*⟩ grasso ● *n* grasso *m*

fatal /'feɪtl/ *a* mortale; ⟨*error*⟩ fatale. ~**ism** /-təlɪzm/ *n* fatalismo *m*. ~**ist** /-təlɪst/ *n* fatalista *mf*. ~**ity** /fə'tæləti/ *n* morte *f*. ~**ly** *adv* mortalmente

fate /feɪt/ *n* destino *m*. ~**ful** *a* fatidico

'**fat-head** *n fam* zuccone, -a *mf*

father /'fɑːðə(r)/ *n* padre *m*; F~ **Christmas** Babbo *m* Natale ● *vt* generare ⟨*child*⟩

father: ~**hood** *n* paternità *f*. ~**-in-law** *n* (*pl* ~**s-in-law**) suocero *m*. ~**ly** *a* paterno

fathom /'fæð(ə)m/ *n Naut* braccio *m* ● *vt* ~ [**out**] comprendere

fatigue /fə'tiːg/ *n* fatica *f*

fatten /'fætn/ *vt* ingrassare ⟨*animal*⟩. ~**ing** *a* **cream is** ~**ing** la panna fa ingrassare

fatty /'fætɪ/ *a* grasso ● *n fam* ciccione, -a *mf*

fatuous /'fætjʊəs/ *a* fatuo

faucet /'fɔːsɪt/ *n Am* rubinetto *m*

fault /fɔːlt/ *n* difetto *m*; *Geol* faglia *f*; *Tennis* fallo *m*; **be at** ~ avere torto; **find** ~ **with** trovare da ridire su; **it's your** ~ è colpa tua ● *vt* criticare. ~**less** *a* impeccabile

faulty /'fɔːltɪ/ *a* difettoso

fauna /'fɔːnə/ *n* fauna *f*

favour /'feɪvə(r)/ *n* favore *m*; **be in ~ of** **sth** essere a favore di qcsa; **do sb a** ~ fare un piacere a qcno ● *vt* (*prefer*) preferire. ~**able** /-əbl/ *a* favorevole

favourit|e /'feɪv(ə)rɪt/ *a* preferito ● *n* preferito, -a *mf*; *Sport* favorito, -a *mf*. ~**ism** *n* favoritismo *m*

fawn /fɔːn/ *a* fulvo ● *n* (*animal*) cerbiatto *m*

fax /fæks/ *n* (*document, machine*) fax *m inv*; **by** ~ per fax ● *vt* faxare. ~ **machine** *n* fax *m inv*. ~**-modem** *n* modem-fax *m inv*, fax-modem *m inv*

fear /fɪə(r)/ *n* paura *f*; **no** ~! *fam* vai tranquillo! ● *vt* temere ● *vi* ~ **for sth** temere per qcsa

fear|ful /'fɪəfl/ *a* pauroso; (*awful*) terribile. ~**less** *a* impavido. ~**some** /-səm/ *a* spaventoso

feas|ibility /fiːzɪ'bɪlɪtɪ/ *n* praticabilità *f*. ~**ible** *a* fattibile; (*possible*) probabile

feast /fiːst/ *n* festa *f*; (*banquet*) banchetto *m* ● *vi* banchettare. ~ **on** godersi

feat /fiːt/ *n* impresa *f*

feather /'feðə(r)/ *n* piuma *f*

feature /'fiːtʃə(r)/ *n* (*quality*) caratteristica *f*; *Journ* articolo *m*; ~**s** (*pl: of face*) lineamenti *mpl* ● *vt* ⟨*film:*⟩ avere come protagonista ● *vi* (*on a list etc*) comparire. ~ **film** *n* lungometraggio *m*

February /'februərɪ/ *n* febbraio *m*

fed /fed/ *see* **feed** ● *a* **be** ~ **up** *fam* essere stufo (**with** di)

federal /'fed(ə)rəl/ *a* federale

federation /fedə'reɪʃn/ *n* federazione *f*

fee /fiː/ *n* tariffa *f*; (*lawyer's, doctor's*) onorario *m*; (*for membership, school*) quota *f*

feeble /'fiːbl/ *a* debole; ⟨*excuse*⟩ fiacco

feed /fiːd/ *n* mangiare *m*; (*for baby*) pappa *f* ● *v* (*pt/pp* **fed**) ● *vt* dar da mangiare a ⟨*animal*⟩; (*support*) nutrire; ~ **sth into sth** inserire qcsa in qcsa ● *vi* mangiare

'**feedback** *n* controreazione *f*; (*of information*) reazione *f*, feedback *m*

feel /fiːl/ *v* (*pt/pp* **felt**) ● *vt* sentire; (*experience*) provare; (*think*) pensare; (*touch: searching*) tastare; (*touch: for texture*) toccare ● *vi* ~ **soft/hard** essere duro/morbido al tatto; ~ **hot/hungry** aver caldo/fame; ~ **ill** sentirsi male; **I don't** ~ **like it** non ne ho voglia; **how do you** ~ **about it?** (*opinion*) che te ne pare?; **it doesn't** ~ **right** non mi sembra giusto. ~**er** *n* (*of animal*) antenna *f*; **put out** ~**ers** *fig* tastare il terreno. ~**ing** *n* sentimento *m*; (*awareness*) sensazione *f*

feet /fiːt/ *see* **foot**

feign /feɪn/ *vt* simulare

feline /'fiːlaɪn/ *a* felino

fell[1] /fel/ *vt* (*knock down*) abbattere

fell[2] *see* **fall**

fellow /'feləʊ/ *n* (*of society*) socio *m*; (*fam: man*) tipo *m*

fellow: ~**-'countryman** *n* compatriota *m*. ~**men** *npl* prossimi *mpl*. ~**ship** *n* cameratismo *m*; (*group*) associazione *f*; *Univ* incarico *m* di ricercatore, -trice

felony /'felənɪ/ *n* delitto *m*

felt[1] /felt/ *see* **feel**

felt[2] *n* feltro *m*. ~**[-tipped] 'pen** /[-tɪpt]/ *n* pennarello *m*

female /'fiːmeɪl/ *a* femminile; **the** ~ **antelope** l'antilope femmina ● *n* femmina *f*

femin|ine /'femɪnɪn/ *a* femminile ● *n* *Gram* femminile *m*. ~**inity** /-'nɪnətɪ/ *n* femminilità *f*. ~**ist** *a* & *n* femminista *mf*

fenc|e /fens/ *n* recinto *m*; (*fam: person*) ricettatore *m* ● *vi Sport* tirar di scherma. **fence in** *vt* chiudere in un recinto. **~er** *n* schermidore *m*. **~ing** *n* steccato *m*; *Sport* scherma *f*

fend /fend/ *vi* **~ for oneself** badare a se stesso. **fend off** *vt* parare; difendersi da ⟨*criticisms*⟩

fender /'fendə(r)/ *n* parafuoco *m inv*; ⟨*Am: on car*⟩ parafango *m*

fennel /'fenl/ *n* finocchio *m*

ferment[1] /'fɜ:ment/ *n* fermento *m*

ferment[2] /fə'ment/ *vi* fermentare ● *vt* far fermentare. **~ation** /fɜ:men'teɪʃn/ *n* fermentazione *f*

fern /fɜ:n/ *n* felce *f*

ferol|ious /fə'rəʊʃəs/ *a* feroce. **~ity** /-'rɒsətɪ/ *n* ferocia *f*

ferret /'ferɪt/ *n* furetto *m* ● **ferret out** *vt* scovare

ferry /'ferɪ/ *n* traghetto *m* ● *vt* traghettare

fertil|e /'fɜ:taɪl/ *a* fertile. **~ity** /fɜ:'tɪlətɪ/ *n* fertilità *f*

fertilize /'fɜ:tɪlaɪz/ *vt* fertilizzare ⟨*land, ovum*⟩. **~r** *n* fertilizzante *m*

fervent /'fɜ:vənt/ *a* fervente

fervour /'fɜ:və(r)/ *n* fervore *m*

fester /'festə(r)/ *vi* suppurare

festival /'festɪvl/ *n* Mus, Theat festival *m*; *Relig* festa *f*

festiv|e /'festɪv/ *a* festivo; **~e season** periodo *m* delle feste natalizie. **~ities** /fe'stɪvətɪz/ *npl* festeggiamenti *mpl*

festoon /fe'stu:n/ *vt* **~ with** ornare di

fetch /fetʃ/ *vt* andare/venire a prendere; ⟨*be sold for*⟩ raggiungere [il prezzo di]

fetching /'fetʃɪŋ/ *a* attraente

fête /feɪt/ *n* festa *f* ● *vt* festeggiare

fetish /'fetɪʃ/ *n* feticcio *m*

fetter /'fetə(r)/ *vt* incatenare

fettle /'fetl/ *n* **in fine ~** in buona forma

feud /fju:d/ *n* faida *f*

feudal /'fju:dl/ *a* feudale

fever /'fi:və(r)/ *n* febbre *f*. **~ish** *a* febbricitante; *fig* febbrile

few /fju:/ *a* pochi; **every ~ days** ogni due o tre giorni; **a ~ people** alcuni; **~er reservations** meno prenotazioni; **the ~est number** il numero più basso ● *pron* pochi; **~ of us** pochi di noi; **a ~** alcuni; **quite a ~** parecchi; **~er than last year** meno dell'anno scorso

fiancé /fɪ'ɒnseɪ/ *n* fidanzato *m*. **~e** *n* fidanzata *f*

fiasco /fɪ'æskəʊ/ *n* fiasco *m*

fib /fɪb/ *n* storia *f*; **tell a ~** raccontare una storia

fibre /'faɪbə(r)/ *n* fibra *f*. **~glass** *n* fibra *f* di vetro

fickle /'fɪkl/ *a* incostante

fiction /'fɪkʃn/ *n* **[works of] ~** narrativa *f*; ⟨*fabrication*⟩ finzione *f*. **~al** *a* immaginario

fictitious /fɪk'tɪʃəs/ *a* fittizio

fiddle /'fɪdl/ *n fam* violino *m*; ⟨*cheating*⟩ imbroglio *m* ● *vi* gingillarsi (**with** con) ● *vt fam* truccare ⟨*accounts*⟩

fiddly /'fɪdlɪ/ *a* intricato

fidelity /fɪ'delətɪ/ *n* fedeltà *f*

fidget /'fɪdʒɪt/ *vi* agitarsi. **~y** *a* agitato

field /fi:ld/ *n* campo *m*

field: ~ events *npl* atletica *fsg* leggera. **~-glasses** *npl* binocolo *msg*. **F~ 'Marshal** *n* feldmaresciallo *m*. **~work** *n* ricerche *fpl* sul terreno

fiend /fi:nd/ *n* demonio *m*

fierce /fɪəs/ *a* feroce. **~ness** *n* ferocia *f*

fiery /'faɪərɪ/ *a* (**-ier, -iest**) focoso

fifteen /fɪf'ti:n/ *a & n* quindici *m*. **~th** *a & n* quindicesimo, -a *mf*

fifth /fɪfθ/ *a & n* quinto, -a *mf*

fiftieth /'fɪftɪɪθ/ *a & n* cinquantesimo, -a *mf*

fifty /'fɪftɪ/ *a & n* cinquanta *m*

fig /fɪg/ *n* fico *m*

fight /faɪt/ *n* lotta *f*; ⟨*brawl*⟩ zuffa *f*; ⟨*argument*⟩ litigio *m*; ⟨*boxing*⟩ incontro *m* ● *v* (*pt/pp* **fought**) ● *vt* also *fig* combattere ● *vi* combattere; ⟨*brawl*⟩ azzuffarsi; ⟨*argue*⟩ litigare. **~er** *n* combattente *mf*; *Aeron* caccia *m inv*. **~ing** *n* combattimento *m*

figment /'fɪgmənt/ *n* **it's a ~ of your imagination** questo è tutta una tua invenzione

figurative /'fɪgjərətɪv/ *a* ⟨*sense*⟩ figurato; ⟨*art*⟩ figurativo

figure /'fɪgə(r)/ *n* ⟨*digit*⟩ cifra *f*; ⟨*carving, sculpture, illustration, form*⟩ figura *f*; ⟨*body shape*⟩ linea *f*; **~ of speech** modo *m* di dire ● *vi* ⟨*appear*⟩ figurare ● *vt* ⟨*Am: think*⟩ pensare. **figure out** *vt* dedurre; capire ⟨*person*⟩

figure: ~-head *n* figura *f* simbolica. **~ skating** *n* pattinaggio *m* artistico

file[1] /faɪl/ *n* scheda *f*; ⟨*set of documents*⟩ incartamento *m*; ⟨*folder*⟩ cartellina *f*; *Comput* file *m inv* ● *vt* archiviare ⟨*documents*⟩

file[2] *n* ⟨*line*⟩ fila *f*; **in single ~** in fila

file[3] *n Techn* lima *f* ● *vt* limare

filing cabinet /'faɪlɪŋkæbɪnət/ *n* schedario *m*, classificatore *m*

filings /'faɪlɪŋz/ *npl* limatura *fsg*

fill /fɪl/ *n* **eat one's ~** mangiare a

sazietà ● *vt* riempire; otturare *‹tooth›* ● *vi* riempirsi. **fill in** *vt* compilare *‹form›*. **fill out** *vt* compilare *‹form›*. **fill up** *vi* *‹room, tank:›* riempirsi; *Auto* far il pieno ● *vt* riempire

fillet /'fɪlɪt/ *n* filetto *m* ● *vt* (*pt/pp* **filleted**) disossare

filling /'fɪlɪŋ/ *n Culin* ripieno *m*; (*of tooth*) piombatura *f*. **~ station** *n* stazione *f* di rifornimento

filly /'fɪlɪ/ *n* puledra *f*

film /fɪlm/ *n Cinema* film *m inv*; *Phot* pellicola *f*; **[cling] ~** pellicola *f* per alimenti ● *vt/i* filmare. **~ star** *n* star *f inv*, divo, -a *mf*

filter /'fɪltə(r)/ *n* filtro *m* ● *vt* filtrare. **filter through** *vi* *‹news:›* trapelare. **~ tip** *n* filtro *m*; (*cigarette*) sigaretta *f* col filtro

filth /fɪlθ/ *n* sudiciume *m*. **~y** *a* (**-ier, -iest**) sudicio; *‹language›* sconcio

fin /fɪn/ *n* pinna *f*

final /'faɪnl/ *a* finale; (*conclusive*) decisivo ● *n Sport* finale *f*; **~s** *pl Univ* esami *mpl* finali

finale /fɪ'nɑːlɪ/ *n* finale *m*

final|ist /'faɪnəlɪst/ *n* finalista *mf*. **~ity** /-'næləti/ *n* finalità *f*

final|ize /'faɪnəlaɪz/ *vt* mettere a punto *‹text›*; definire *‹agreement›*. **~ly** *adv* (*at last*) finalmente; (*at the end*) alla fine; (*to conclude*) per finire

finance /'faɪnæns/ *n* finanza *f* ● *vt* finanziare

financial /faɪ'nænʃl/ *a* finanziario

finch /fɪntʃ/ *n* fringuello *m*

find /faɪnd/ *n* scoperta *f* ● *vt* (*pt/pp* **found**) trovare; (*establish*) scoprire; **~ sb guilty** *Jur* dichiarare qcno colpevole. **find out** *vt* scoprire ● *vi* (*enquire*) informarsi

findings /'faɪndɪŋz/ *npl* conclusioni *fpl*

fine[1] /faɪn/ *n* (*penalty*) multa *f* ● *vt* multare

fine[2] *a* bello; (*slender*) fine; **he's ~** (*in health*) sta bene; **~ arts** belle arti *fpl* ● *adv* bene; **that's cutting it ~** non ci lascia molto tempo ● *int* [va] bene. **~ly** *adv* *‹cut›* finemente

finery /'faɪnərɪ/ *n* splendore *m*

finesse /fɪ'nes/ *n* finezza *f*

finger /'fɪŋɡə(r)/ *n* dito *m* (*pl* dita *f*) ● *vt* tastare

finger: ~-mark *n* ditata *f*. **~-nail** *n* unghia *f*. **~-print** *n* impronta *f* digitale. **~tip** *n* punta *f* del dito; **have sth at one's ~tips** sapere qcsa a menadito;

(*close at hand*) avere qcsa a portata di mano

finicky /'fɪnɪkɪ/ *a* (*person*) pignolo; *‹task›* intricato

finish /'fɪnɪʃ/ *n* fine *f*; (*finishing line*) traguardo *m*; (*of product*) finitura *f*. **have a good ~** *‹runner:›* avere un buon finale ● *vt* finire; **~ reading** finire di leggere ● *vi* finire

finite /'faɪnaɪt/ *a* limitato

Finland /'fɪnlənd/ *n* Finlandia *f*

Finn /fɪn/ *n* finlandese *mf*. **~ish** *a* finlandese ● *n* (*language*) finnico *m*

fiord /fjɔːd/ *n* fiordo *m*

fir /fɜː(r)/ *n* abete *m*

fire /'faɪə(r)/ *n* fuoco *m*; (*forest, house*) incendio *m*; **be on ~** bruciare; **catch ~** prendere fuoco; **set ~ to** dar fuoco a; **under ~** sotto il fuoco ● *vt* cuocere *‹pottery›*; sparare *‹shot›*; tirare *‹gun›*; (*fam: dismiss*) buttar fuori ● *vi* sparare (**at** a)

fire: ~ alarm *n* allarme *m* antincendio. **~ arm** *n* arma *f* da fuoco. **~ brigade** *n* vigili *mpl* del fuoco. **~-engine** *n* autopompa *f*. **~-escape** *n* uscita *f* di sicurezza. **~ extinguisher** *n* estintore *m*. **~man** *n* pompiere *m*, vigile *m* del fuoco. **~place** *n* caminetto *m*. **~side** *n* **by** or **at the ~side** accanto al fuoco. **~ station** *n* caserma *f* dei pompieri. **~wood** *n* legna *f* (*da ardere*). **~work** *n* fuoco *m* d'artificio; **~works** *pl* (*display*) fuochi *mpl* d'artificio

'firing squad *n* plotone *m* d'esecuzione

firm[1] /fɜːm/ *n* ditta *f*, azienda *f*

firm[2] *a* fermo; *‹soil›* compatto; (*stable, fixed*) solido; (*resolute*) risoluto. **~ly** *adv* *‹hold›* stretto; *‹say›* con fermezza

first /fɜːst/ *a & n* primo, -a *mf*; **at ~** all'inizio; **who's ~?** chi è il primo?; **from the ~** [fin] dall'inizio ● *adv* *‹arrive, leave›* per primo; (*beforehand*) prima; (*in listing*) prima di tutto, innanzitutto

first: ~ 'aid *n* pronto soccorso *m*. **~-'aid kit** *n* cassetta *f* di pronto soccorso. **~-class** *a* di prim'ordine; *Rail* di prima classe ● *adv* *‹travel›* in prima classe. **~ 'floor** *n* primo piano *m*; (*Am: ground floor*) pianterreno *m*. **~ly** *adv* in primo luogo. **~ name** *n* nome *m* di battesimo. **~-rate** *a* ottimo

fish /fɪʃ/ *n* pesce *m* ● *vt/i* pescare. **fish out** *vt* tirar fuori

fish: ~bone *n* lisca *f*. **~erman** *n* pescatore *m*. **~-farm** *n* vivaio *m*. **~ 'finger** *n* bastoncino *m* di pesce

fishing /ˈfɪʃɪŋ/ n pesca f. ~ **boat** n peschereccio m. ~**-rod** n canna f da pesca

fish: ~**monger** /-mʌŋɡə(r)/ n pescivendolo m. ~**-slice** n paletta f per fritti. ~**y** a ⟨fam: suspicious⟩ sospetto

fission /ˈfɪʃn/ n Phys fissione f

fist /fɪst/ n pugno m

fit¹ /fɪt/ n ⟨attack⟩ attacco m; ⟨of rage⟩ accesso m; ⟨of generosity⟩ slancio m

fit² a ⟨fitter, fittest⟩ ⟨suitable⟩ adatto; ⟨healthy⟩ in buona salute; Sport in forma; **be ~ to do sth** essere in grado di fare qcsa; **~ to eat** buono da mangiare; **keep ~** tenersi in forma

fit³ n ⟨of clothes⟩ taglio m; **it's a good ~** ⟨coat etc:⟩ ti/le sta bene ● v ⟨pt/pp **fitted**⟩ ● vi ⟨be the right size⟩ andare bene; **it won't ~** ⟨no room⟩ non ci sta ● vt ⟨fix⟩ applicare ⟨to a⟩; ⟨install⟩ installare; **it doesn't ~ me** ⟨coat etc:⟩ non mi va bene; **~ with** fornire di. **fit in** vi ⟨person:⟩ adattarsi; **it won't ~ in** ⟨no room⟩ non ci sta ● vt ⟨in schedule, vehicle⟩ trovare un buco per

fit|ful /ˈfɪtfl/ a irregolare. ~**fully** adv ⟨sleep⟩ a sprazzi. ~**ments** npl ⟨in house⟩ impianti mpl fissi. ~**ness** n ⟨suitability⟩ capacità f; [**physical**] ~**ness** forma f, fitness m

fitted: ~ '**carpet** n moquette f inv. ~ '**cupboard** n armadio m a muro; ⟨smaller⟩ armadietto m a muro. ~ '**kitchen** n cucina f componibile. ~ '**sheet** n lenzuolo m con angoli

fitter /ˈfɪtə(r)/ n installatore, -trice mf

fitting /ˈfɪtɪŋ/ a appropriato ● n ⟨of clothes⟩ prova f; Techn montaggio m; ~**s** pl accessori mpl. ~ **room** n camerino m

five /faɪv/ a & n cinque m. ~**r** n fam biglietto m da cinque sterline

fix /fɪks/ n ⟨sl: drugs⟩ pera f; **be in a ~** fam essere nei guai ● vt fissare; ⟨repair⟩ aggiustare; preparare ⟨meal⟩. **fix up** vt fissare ⟨meeting⟩

fixation /fɪkˈseɪʃn/ n fissazione f

fixed /fɪkst/ a fisso

fixture /ˈfɪkstʃə(r)/ n Sport incontro m; ~**s and fittings** impianti mpl fissi

fizz /fɪz/ vi il frizzare

fizzle /ˈfɪzl/ vi ~ **out** finire in nulla

fizzy /ˈfɪzɪ/ a gassoso. ~ **drink** n bibita f gassata

flabbergasted /ˈflæbəɡɑːstɪd/ a **be ~** rimanere a bocca aperta

flabby /ˈflæbɪ/ a floscio

flag¹ /flæɡ/ n bandiera f ● **flag down** vt ⟨pt/pp **flagged**⟩ far segno di fermarsi a ⟨taxi⟩

flag² vi ⟨pt/pp **flagged**⟩ cedere

'**flag-pole** n asta f della bandiera

flagrant /ˈfleɪɡrənt/ a flagrante

'**flagship** n Naut nave f ammiraglia; fig fiore m all'occhiello

'**flagstone** n pietra f da lastricare

flair /fleə(r)/ n ⟨skill⟩ talento m; ⟨style⟩ stile m

flake /fleɪk/ n fiocco m ● vi ~ [**off**] cadere in fiocchi

flaky /ˈfleɪkɪ/ a a scaglie. ~ **pastry** n pasta f sfoglia

flamboyant /flæmˈbɔɪənt/ a ⟨personality⟩ brillante; ⟨tie⟩ sgargiante

flame /fleɪm/ n fiamma f

flammable /ˈflæməbl/ a infiammabile

flan /flæn/ n ⟨fruit⟩ ~ crostata f

flank /flæŋk/ n fianco m ● vt fiancheggiare

flannel /ˈflæn(ə)l/ n flanella f; ⟨for washing⟩ guanto m di spugna; ~**s** ⟨trousers⟩ pantaloni mpl di flanella

flannelette /flænəˈlet/ n flanella f di cotone

flap /flæp/ n ⟨of pocket, envelope⟩ risvolto m; ⟨of table⟩ ribalta f; **in a ~** fam in grande agitazione ● v ⟨pt/pp **flapped**⟩ ● vi sbattere; fam agitarsi ● vt ~ **its wings** battere le ali

flare /fleə(r)/ n fiammata f; ⟨device⟩ razzo m ● **flare up** vi ⟨rash:⟩ venire fuori; ⟨fire:⟩ fare una fiammata; ⟨person, situation:⟩ esplodere. ~**d** a ⟨garment⟩ svasato

flash /flæʃ/ n lampo m; **in a ~** fam in un attimo ● vi lampeggiare; ~ **past** passare come un bolide ● vt lanciare ⟨smile⟩; ~ **one's head-lights** lampeggiare; ~ **a torch at** puntare una torcia su

flash: ~**back** n scena f retrospettiva. ~**bulb** n Phot flash m inv. ~**er** n Auto lampeggiatore m. ~**light** n Phot flash m inv; ⟨Am: torch⟩ torcia f [elettrica]. ~**y** a vistoso

flask /flɑːsk/ n fiasco m; ⟨vacuum ~⟩ termos m inv

flat /flæt/ a ⟨flatter, flattest⟩ piatto; ⟨refusal⟩ reciso; ⟨beer⟩ sgassato; ⟨battery⟩ scarico; ⟨tyre⟩ a terra; **A ~** Mus la bemolle ● n appartamento m; Mus bemolle m; ⟨puncture⟩ gomma f a terra

flat: ~ '**feet** npl piedi mpl piatti. ~**-fish** n pesce m piatto. ~**ly** adv ⟨refuse⟩ categoricamente. ~ **rate** n tariffa f unica

flatten /ˈflætn/ vt appiattire

flatter /ˈflætə(r)/ vt adulare. ~**ing** a

⟨comments⟩ lusinghiero; ⟨colour, dress⟩ che fa sembrare più bello. **~y** n adulazione f

flat 'tyre n gomma f a terra

flaunt /flɔ:nt/ vt ostentare

flautist /'flɔ:tɪst/ n flautista mf

flavour /'fleɪvə(r)/ n sapore m ● vt condire; **chocolate ~ed** al sapore di cioccolato. **~ing** n condimento m

flaw /flɔ:/ n difetto m. **~less** a perfetto

flax /flæks/ n lino m. **~en** a ⟨hair⟩ biondo platino

flea /fli:/ n pulce f. **~ market** n mercato m delle pulci

fleck /flek/ n macchiolina f

fled /fled/ see **flee**

flee /fli:/ vt/i (pt/pp **fled**) fuggire (**from** da)

fleec|e /fli:s/ n pelliccia f ● vt fam spennare. **~y** a ⟨lining⟩ felpato

fleet /fli:t/ n flotta f; ⟨of cars⟩ parco m

fleeting /'fli:tɪŋ/ a **catch a ~ glance of sth** intravedere qcsa; **for a ~ moment** per un attimo

flesh /fleʃ/ n carne f; **in the ~** in persona. **~y** a carnoso

flew /flu:/ see **fly²**

flex¹ /fleks/ vt flettere ⟨muscle⟩

flex² n Electr filo m

flexib|ility /fleksɪ'bɪlətɪ/ n flessibilità f. **~le** a flessibile

'flexitime /'fleksɪ-/ n orario m flessibile

flick /flɪk/ vt dare un buffetto a; **~ off sth** togliere qcsa da qcsa con un colpetto. **flick through** vt sfogliare

flicker /'flɪkə(r)/ vi tremolare

flier /'flaɪə(r)/ n = **flyer**

flight¹ /flaɪt/ n ⟨fleeing⟩ fuga f; **take ~** darsi alla fuga

flight² n ⟨flying⟩ volo m; **~ of stairs** rampa f

flight: ~ path n traiettoria f di volo. **~ recorder** n registratore m di volo

flighty /'flaɪtɪ/ a (-ier, -iest) frivolo

flimsy /'flɪmzɪ/ a (-ier, -iest) ⟨material⟩ leggero; ⟨shelves⟩ poco robusto; ⟨excuse⟩ debole

flinch /flɪntʃ/ vi ⟨wince⟩ sussultare; ⟨draw back⟩ ritirarsi; **~ from a task** fig sottrarsi a un compito

fling /flɪŋ/ n **have a ~** ⟨fam: affair⟩ aver un'avventura ● vt (pt/pp **flung**) gettare

flint /flɪnt/ n pietra f focaia; ⟨for lighter⟩ pietrina f

flip /flɪp/ v (pt/pp **flipped**) ● vt dare un colpetto a; buttare in aria ⟨coin⟩ ● vi

fam uscire dai gangheri; ⟨go mad⟩ impazzire. **flip through** vt sfogliare

flippant /'flɪpənt/ a irriverente

flipper /'flɪpə(r)/ n pinna f

flirt /flɜ:t/ n civetta f ● vi flirtare

flirtat|ion /flɜ:'teɪʃn/ n flirt m inv. **~ious** /-ʃəs/ a civettuolo

flit /flɪt/ vi (pt/pp **flitted**) volteggiare

float /fləʊt/ n galleggiante m; ⟨in procession⟩ carro m; ⟨money⟩ riserva f di cassa ● vi galleggiare; Fin fluttuare

flock /flɒk/ n gregge m; ⟨of birds⟩ stormo m ● vi affollarsi

flog /flɒg/ vt (pt/pp **flogged**) bastonare; ⟨fam: sell⟩ vendere

flood /flʌd/ n alluvione f; ⟨of river⟩ straripamento m; ⟨fig: of replies, letters, tears⟩ diluvio m; **be in ~** ⟨river:⟩ essere straripato ● vt allagare ● vi ⟨river:⟩ straripare

'floodlight n riflettore m ● vt (pt/pp **floodlit**) illuminare con riflettori

floor /flɔ:(r)/ n pavimento m; ⟨storey⟩ piano m; ⟨for dancing⟩ pista f ● vt ⟨baffle⟩ confondere; ⟨knock down⟩ stendere ⟨person⟩

floor: ~ board n asse f del pavimento. **~-polish** n cera f per il pavimento. **~ show** n spettacolo m di varietà

flop /flɒp/ n fam ⟨failure⟩ tonfo m; Theat fiasco m ● vi ⟨pt/pp **flopped**) ⟨fam: fail⟩ far fiasco. **flop down** vi accasciarsi

floppy /'flɒpɪ/ a floscio. **~ 'disk** n floppy disk m inv. **~ [disk] drive** n lettore di floppy m

flora /'flɔ:rə/ n flora f

floral /'flɔ:rəl/ a floreale

florid /'flɒrɪd/ a ⟨complexion⟩ florido; ⟨style⟩ troppo ricercato

florist /'flɒrɪst/ n fioriao, -a mf

flounce /flaʊns/ n balza f ● vi **~ out** uscire con aria melodrammatica

flounder¹ /'flaʊndə(r)/ vi dibattersi; ⟨speaker:⟩ impappinarsi

flounder² n ⟨fish⟩ passera f di mare

flour /'flaʊə(r)/ n farina f

flourish /'flʌrɪʃ/ n gesto m drammatico; ⟨scroll⟩ ghirigoro m ● vi prosperare ● vt brandire

floury /'flaʊərɪ/ a farinoso

flout /flaʊt/ vt fregarsene di ⟨rules⟩

flow /fləʊ/ n flusso m ● vi scorrere; ⟨hang loosely⟩ ricadere

flower /'flaʊə(r)/ n fiore m ● vi fiorire

flower: ~-bed n aiuola f. **~ed** a a fiori. **~pot** n vaso m [per i fiori]. **~y** a fiorito

flown /fləʊn/ see **fly²**

flu /flu:/ n influenza f

fluctuat|e /'flʌktjʋeɪt/ vi fluttuare. **~ion** /-'eɪʃn/ n fluttuazione f

fluent /'fluːənt/ a spedito; **speak ~ Italian** parlare correntemente l'italiano. **~ly** adv speditamente

fluff /flʌf/ n peluria f. **~y** a (**-ier, -iest**) vaporoso; ⟨toy⟩ di peluche

fluid /'fluːɪd/ a fluido ● n fluido m

fluke /fluːk/ n colpo m di fortuna

flung /flʌŋ/ see **fling**

flunk /flʌŋk/ vt Am fam essere bocciato in

fluorescent /flʋə'resnt/ a fluorescente

fluoride /'flʋəraɪd/ n fluoruro m

flurry /'flʌrɪ/ n ⟨snow⟩ raffica f; fig agitazione f

flush /flʌʃ/ n ⟨blush⟩ [vampata f di] rossore m ● vi arrossire ● vt lavare con un getto d'acqua; **~ the toilet** tirare l'acqua ● a a livello (**with** di); ⟨fam: affluent⟩ a soldi

flustered /'flʌstəd/ a in agitazione; **get ~** mettersi in agitazione

flute /fluːt/ n flauto m

flutter /'flʌtə(r)/ n battito m ● vi svolazzare

flux /flʌks/ n **in a state of ~** in uno stato di flusso

fly[1] /flaɪ/ n (pl **flies**) mosca f

fly[2] v (pt **flew**, pp **flown**) ● vi volare; ⟨go by plane⟩ andare in aereo; ⟨flag:⟩ sventolare; ⟨rush⟩ precipitarsi; **~ open** spalancarsi ● vt pilotare ⟨plane⟩; trasportare [in aereo] ⟨troops, supplies⟩; volare con ⟨Alitalia etc⟩

fly[3] n & **flies** pl ⟨on trousers⟩ patta f

flyer /'flaɪə(r)/ n aviatore m; ⟨leaflet⟩ volantino m

flying /'flaɪɪŋ/: **~ 'buttress** n arco m rampante. **~ 'colours: with ~ colours** a pieni voti. **~ 'saucer** n disco m volante. **~ 'start** n get off to a **~ start** fare un'ottima partenza. **~ 'visit** n visita f lampo

fly: **~ leaf** n risguardo m. **~over** n cavalcavia m inv

foal /fəʋl/ n puledro m

foam /fəʋm/ n schiuma f; ⟨synthetic⟩ gommapiuma® f ● vi spumare; **~ at the mouth** far la bava alla bocca. **~ 'rubber** n gommapiuma® f

fob /fɒb/ vt (pt/pp **fobbed**) **~ sth off** affibbiare qcsa (**on sb** a qcno); **~ sb off** liquidare qcno

focal /'fəʋkl/ a focale

focus /'fəʋkəs/ n fuoco m; **in ~** a fuoco; **out of ~** sfocato ● v (pt/pp **focused** or

focussed) ● vt fig concentrare (**on** su) ● vi Phot **~ on** mettere a fuoco; fig concentrarsi (**on** su)

fodder /'fɒdə(r)/ n foraggio m

foe /fəʋ/ n nemico, -a mf

foetus /'fiːtəs/ n (pl **-tuses**) feto m

fog /fɒg/ n nebbia f

fogey /'fəʋgɪ/ n old **~** persona f antiquata

foggy /'fɒgɪ/ a (**foggier, foggiest**) nebbioso; **it's ~** c'è nebbia

'fog-horn n sirena f da nebbia

foil[1] /fɔɪl/ n lamina f di metallo

foil[2] vt ⟨thwart⟩ frustrare

foil[3] n ⟨sword⟩ fioretto m

foist /fɔɪst/ vt appioppare (**on sb** a qcno)

fold[1] /fəʋld/ n ⟨for sheep⟩ ovile m

fold[2] n piega f ● vt piegare; **~ one's arms** incrociare le braccia ● vi piegarsi; ⟨fail⟩ crollare. **fold up** vt ripiegare ⟨chair⟩ ● vi essere pieghevole; ⟨fam: business:⟩ collassare

fold|er /'fəʋldə(r)/ n cartella f. **~ing** a pieghevole

foliage /'fəʋlɪdʒ/ n fogliame m

folk /fəʋk/ npl gente f; **my ~s** ⟨family⟩ i miei; **hello there ~s** ciao a tutti

folk: **~dance** n danza f popolare. **~lore** n folclore m. **~song** n canto m popolare

follow /'fɒləʋ/ vt/i seguire; **it doesn't ~** non è necessariamente così; **~ suit** fig fare lo stesso; **as ~s** come segue. **follow up** vt fare seguito a ⟨letter⟩

follow|er /'fɒləʋə(r)/ n seguace mf. **~ing** a seguente ● n seguito m; ⟨supporters⟩ seguaci mpl ● prep in seguito a

folly /'fɒlɪ/ n follia f

fond /fɒnd/ a affezionato; ⟨hope⟩ vivo; **be ~ of** essere appassionato di ⟨music⟩; **I'm ~ of...** ⟨food, person⟩ mi piace moltissimo...

fondle /'fɒndl/ vt coccolare

fondness /'fɒndnɪs/ n affetto m; ⟨for things⟩ amore m

font /fɒnt/ n fonte f battesimale; Typ carattere m di stampa

food /fuːd/ n cibo m; ⟨for animals, groceries⟩ mangiare m; **let's buy some ~** compriamo qualcosa da mangiare

food: **~ mixer** n frullatore m. **~ poisoning** n intossicazione f alimentare. **~ processor** n tritatutto m inv elettrico

fool[1] /fuːl/ n sciocco, -a mf; **she's no ~** non è una stupida; **make a ~ of**

oneself rendersi ridicolo ● *vt* prendere in giro ● *vi* ~ **around** giocare; ‹*husband, wife*:› avere l'amante

fool[2] *n Culin* crema *f*

'fool|hardy *a* temerario. **~ish** *a* stolto. **~ishly** *adv* scioccamente. **~ishness** *n* sciocchezza *f*. **~proof** *a* facilissimo

foot /fʊt/ *n* (*pl* feet) piede *m*; (*of animal*) zampa *f*; (*measure*) piede *m* (= 30,48 *cm*); on ~ a piedi; on one's feet in piedi; put one's ~ in it *fam* fare una gaffe

foot: **~-and-'mouth disease** *n* afta *f* epizootica. **~ball** *n* calcio *m*; (*ball*) pallone *m*. **~baller** *n* giocatore *m* di calcio. **~ball pools** *npl* totocalcio *m*. **~brake** *n* freno *m* a pedale. **~bridge** *n* passerella *f*. **~hills** *npl* colline *fpl* pedemontane. **~hold** *n* punto *m* d'appoggio. **~ing** *n* lose one's **~ing** perdere l'appiglio; **on an equal ~ing** in condizioni di parità. **~man** *n* valletto *m*. **~note** *n* nota *f* a piè di pagina. **~path** *n* sentiero *m*. **~print** *n* orma *f*. **~step** *n* passo *m*; **follow in sb's ~steps** *fig* seguire l'esempio di qcno. **~stool** *n* sgabellino *m*. **~wear** *n* calzature *fpl*

for /fə(r)/, accentato /fɔː(r)/ *prep* per; ~ **this reason** per questa ragione; **I have lived here** ~ **ten years** vivo qui da dieci anni; ~ **supper** per cena; ~ **all that** nonostante questo; **what ~?** a che scopo?; **send** ~ **a doctor** chiamare un dottore; **fight** ~ **a cause** lottare per una causa; **go** ~ **a walk** andare a fare una passeggiata; **there's no need** ~ **you to go** non c'è bisogno che tu vada; **it's not** ~ **me to say** no sta a me dirlo; **now you're** ~ **it** ora sei nei pasticci ● *conj* poiché, perché

forage /'fɒrɪdʒ/ *n* foraggio *m* ● *vi* ~ **for** cercare

forbade /fə'bæd/ *see* forbid

forbear|ance /fɔː'beərəns/ *n* pazienza *f*. **~ing** *a* tollerante

forbid /fə'bɪd/ *vt* (*pt* forbade, *pp* forbidden) proibire. **~ding** *a* ‹*prospect*› che spaventa; (*stern*) severo

force /fɔːs/ *n* forza *f*; in ~ in vigore; (*in large numbers*) in massa; come into ~ entrare in vigore; the [armed] ~s le forze armate ● *vt* forzare; ~ sth on sb ‹*decision*› imporre qcsa a qcno; ‹*drink*› costringere qcno a fare qcsa

forced /fɔːst/ *a* forzato

force: **~-'feed** *vt* (*pt/pp* -fed) nutrire a forza. **~ful** *a* energico. **~fully** *adv* ‹*say, argue*› con forza

forceps /'fɔːseps/ *npl* forcipe *m*

forcible /'fɔːsɪbl/ *a* forzato

ford /fɔːd/ *n* guado *m* ● *vt* guadare

fore /fɔː(r)/ *n* to the ~ in vista; come to the ~ salire alla ribalta

fore: **~arm** *n* avambraccio *m*. **~boding** /-'bəʊdɪŋ/ *n* presentimento *m*. **~cast** *n* previsione *f* ● *vt* (*pt/pp* ~cast) prevedere. **~court** *n* cortile *m* anteriore. **~fathers** *npl* antenati *mpl*. **~finger** *n* [dito *m*] indice *m*. **~front** *n* be in the **~front** essere all'avanguardia. **~gone** *a* be a **~gone conclusion** essere una cosa scontata. **~ground** *n* primo piano *m*. **~head** /'fɒrɪd, 'fɔːhed/ *n* fronte *f*. **~hand** *n Tennis* diritto *m*

foreign /'fɒrən/ *a* straniero; ‹*trade*› estero; (*not belonging*) estraneo; he is ~ è uno straniero. ~ **currency** *n* valuta *f* estera. **~er** *n* straniero, -a *mf*. ~ **language** *n* lingua *f* straniera

Foreign: ~ **Office** *n* ministero *m* degli [affari] esteri. ~ **'Secretary** *n* ministro *m* degli esteri

fore: **~man** *n* caporeparto *m*. **~most** *a* principale ● *adv* first and **~most** in primo luogo. **~name** *n* nome *m* di battesimo

forensic /fə'rensɪk/ *a* ~ **medicine** medicina *f* legale

'forerunner *n* precursore *m*

fore'see *vt* (*pt* -saw, *pp* -seen) prevedere. **~able** /-əbl/ *a* in the **~able future** in futuro per quanto si possa prevedere

'foresight *n* previdenza *f*

forest /'fɒrɪst/ *n* foresta *f*. **~er** *n* guardia *f* forestale

fore'stall *vt* prevenire

forestry /'fɒrɪstrɪ/ *n* silvicoltura *f*

'foretaste *n* pregustazione *f*

fore'tell *vt* (*pt/pp* -told) predire

forever /fə'revə(r)/ *adv* per sempre; he's ~ **complaining** si lamenta sempre

fore'warn *vt* avvertire

foreword /'fɔːwɜːd/ *n* prefazione *f*

forfeit /'fɔːfɪt/ *n* (*in game*) pegno *m*; *Jur* penalità *f* ● *vt* perdere

forgave /fə'geɪv/ *see* forgive

forge[1] /fɔːdʒ/ *vi* ~ **ahead** ‹*runner*:› lasciarsi indietro gli altri; *fig* farsi strada

forge[2] *n* fucina *f* ● *vt* fucinare; (*counterfeit*) contraffare. **~r** *n* contraffattore *m*. **~ry** *n* contraffazione *f*

forget /fə'get/ *vt/i* (*pt* -got, *pp* -gotten, *pres p* -getting) dimenticare; dimenticarsi di ‹*language, skill*›. **~table** /-əbl/

a ⟨*day, film*⟩ da dimenticare. **~ful** *a* smemorato. **~fulness** *n* smemoratezza *f*. **~-me-not** *n* non-ti-scordar-dimé *m inv*

forgive /fə'gɪv/ *vt* (*pt* **-gave**, *pp* **-given**) **~ sb for sth** perdonare qcno per qcsa. **~ness** *n* perdono *m*

forgo /fɔː'gəʊ/ *vt* (*pt* **-went**, *pp* **-gone**) rinunciare a

forgot(ten) /fə'gɒt(n)/ *see* **forget**

fork /fɔːk/ *n* forchetta *f*; (*for digging*) forca *f*; (*in road*) bivio *m* ● *vi* ⟨*road:*⟩ biforcarsi; **~ right** prendere a destra. **fork out** *vt fam* sborsare

fork-lift 'truck *n* elevatore *m*

forlorn /fə'lɔːn/ *a* ⟨*look*⟩ perduto; ⟨*place*⟩ derelitto: **~ hope** speranza *f* vana

form /fɔːm/ *n* forma *f*; (*document*) modulo *m*; *Sch* classe *f* ● *vt* formare; formulare ⟨*opinion*⟩ ● *vi* formarsi

formal /'fɔːml/ *a* formale. **~ity** /-'mælətɪ/ *n* formalità *f inv*. **~ly** *adv* in modo formale; (*officially*) ufficialmente

format /'fɔːmæt/ *n* formato *m* ● *vt* formattare ⟨*disk, page*⟩

formation /fɔː'meɪʃn/ *n* formazione *f*

formative /'fɔːmətɪv/ *a* **~ years** anni *mpl* formativi

former /'fɔːmə(r)/ *a* precedente; ⟨*PM, colleague*⟩ ex; **the ~, the latter** il primo, l'ultimo. **~ly** *adv* precedentemente; (*in olden times*) in altri tempi

formidable /'fɔːmɪdəbl/ *a* formidabile

formula /'fɔːmjʊlə/ *n* (*pl* **-ae** /-liː/ *or* **-s**) formula *f*

formulate /'fɔːmjʊleɪt/ *vt* formulare

forsake /fə'seɪk/ *vt* (*pt* **-sook** /-sʊk/, *pp* **-saken**) abbandonare

fort /fɔːt/ *n* Mil forte *m*

forte /'fɔːteɪ/ *n* [pezzo *m*] forte *m*

forth /fɔːθ/ *adv* **back and ~** avanti e indietro; **and so ~** e così via

forth: **~'coming** *a* prossimo; (*communicative*) comunicativo; **no response was ~** non arrivava nessuna risposta. **~right** *a* schietto. **~'with** *adv* immediatamente

fortieth /'fɔːtɪɪθ/ *a* & *n* quarantesimo, -a *mf*

fortification /fɔːtɪfɪ'keɪʃn/ *n* fortificazione *f*

fortify /'fɔːtɪfaɪ/ *vt* (*pt/pp* **-ied**) fortificare; *fig* rendere forte

fortnight /'fɔːt-/ *Br n* quindicina *f*. **~ly** *a* bimensile ● *adv* ogni due settimane

fortress /'fɔːtrɪs/ *n* fortezza *f*

fortuitous /fɔː'tjuːɪtəs/ *a* fortuito

fortunate /'fɔːtʃənət/ *a* fortunato;

that's **~!** meno male!. **~ly** *adv* fortunatamente

fortune /'fɔːtʃuːn/ *n* fortuna *f*. **~-teller** *n* indovino, -a *mf*

forty /'fɔːtɪ/ *a* & *n* quaranta *m*

forum /'fɔːrəm/ *n* foro *m*

forward /'fɔːwəd/ *adv* avanti; (*towards the front*) in avanti ● *a* in avanti; (*presumptuous*) sfacciato ● *n* Sport attaccante *m* ● *vt* inoltrare ⟨*letter*⟩; spedire ⟨*goods*⟩. **~s** *adv* avanti

fossil /'fɒsl/ *n* fossile *m*. **~ized** *a* fossile; ⟨*ideas*⟩ fossilizzato

foster /'fɒstə(r)/ *vt* allevare ⟨*child*⟩. **~-child** *n* figlio, -a *mf* in affidamento. **~-mother** *n* madre *f* affidataria

fought /fɔːt/ *see* **fight**

foul /faʊl/ *a* ⟨*smell, taste*⟩ cattivo; ⟨*air*⟩ viziato; ⟨*language*⟩ osceno; ⟨*mood, weather*⟩ orrendo; **~ play** *Jur* delitto *m* ● *n* Sport fallo *m* ● *vt* inquinare ⟨*water*⟩; *Sport* commettere un fallo contro; ⟨*nets, rope:*⟩ impigliarsi in. **~-smelling** *a* puzzo

found¹ /faʊnd/ *see* **find**

found² *vt* fondare

foundation /faʊn'deɪʃn/ *n* (*basis*) fondamento *m*; (*charitable*) fondazione *f*; **~s** *pl* (*of building*) fondamenta *fpl*; **lay the ~-stone** porre la prima pietra

founder¹ /'faʊndə(r)/ *n* fondatore, -trice *mf*

founder² *vi* ⟨*ship:*⟩ affondare

foundry /'faʊndrɪ/ *n* fonderia *f*

fountain /'faʊntɪn/ *n* fontana *f*. **~-pen** *n* penna *f* stilografica

four /fɔː(r)/ *a* & *n* quattro *m*

four: **~-'poster** *n* letto *m* a baldacchino. **~some** /'fɔːsəm/ *n* quartetto *m*. **~'teen** *a* & *n* quattordici *m*. **~'teenth** *a* & *n* quattordicesimo, -a *mf*

fourth /fɔːθ/ *a* & *n* quarto, -a *mf*

fowl /faʊl/ *n* pollame *m*

fox /fɒks/ *n* volpe *f* ● *vt* (*puzzle*) ingannare

foyer /'fɔɪeɪ/ *n* Theat ridotto *m*; (*in hotel*) salone *m* d'ingresso

fraction /'frækʃn/ *n* frazione *f*

fracture /'fræktʃə(r)/ *n* frattura *f* ● *vt* fratturare ● *vi* fratturarsi

fragile /'frædʒaɪl/ *a* fragile

fragment /'frægmənt/ *n* frammento *m*. **~ary** *a* frammentario

fragran|ce /'freɪgrəns/ *n* fragranza *f*. **~t** *a* fragrante

frail /freɪl/ *a* gracile

frame /freɪm/ *n* (*of picture, door, window*) cornice *f*; (*of spectacles*) montatura *f*; *Anat* ossatura *f*; (*structure, of bike*) telaio *m*; ~ **of mind** stato *m* d'animo ● *vt* incorniciare (*picture*); *fig* formulare; (*sl: incriminate*) montare. ~**work** *n* struttura *f*

franc /fræŋk/ *n* franco *m*

France /frɑːns/ *n* Francia *f*

franchise /'fræntʃaɪz/ *n Pol* diritto *m* di voto; *Comm* franchigia *f*

frank¹ /fræŋk/ *vt* affrancare (*letter*)

frank² *a* franco. ~**ly** *adv* francamente

frankfurter /'fræŋkfɜːtə(r)/ *n* würstel *m inv*

frantic /'fræntɪk/ *a* frenetico; **be ~ with worry** essere agitatissimo. ~**ally** *adv* freneticamente

fraternal /frə'tɜːnl/ *a* fraterno

fraud /frɔːd/ *n* frode *f*; (*person*) impostore *m*. ~**ulent** /-jʊlənt/ *a* fraudolento

fraught /frɔːt/ *a* ~ **with** pieno di

fray¹ /freɪ/ *n* mischia *f*

fray² *vi* sfilacciarsi

frayed /freɪd/ *a* (*cuffs*) sfilacciato; (*nerves*) a pezzi

freak /friːk/ *n* fenomeno *m*; (*person*) scherzo *m* di natura; (*fam: weird person*) tipo *m* strambo ● *a* anormale. ~**ish** *a* strambo

freckle /'frekl/ *n* lentiggine *f*. ~**d** *a* lentigginoso

free /friː/ *a* (**freer, freest**) libero; (*ticket, copy*) gratuito; (*lavish*) generoso; ~ **of charge** gratuito; **set** ~ liberare ● *vt* (*pt/pp* **freed**) liberare

free: ~**dom** *n* libertà *f*. ~**hand** *adv* a mano libera. ~**hold** *n* proprietà *f* (*fondiaria*) assoluta. ~ **kick** *n* calcio *m* di punizione. ~**lance** *a* & *adv* indipendente. ~**ly** *adv* liberamente; (*generously*) generosamente; **I ... admit that...** devo ammettere che.... **F~mason** *n* massone *m*. ~**-range** *a* ~**-range egg** uovo *m* di gallina ruspante. ~'**sample** *n* campione *m* gratuito. ~**style** *n* stile *m* libero. ~**way** *n* *Am* autostrada *f*. ~**-'wheel** *vi* (*car:*) (*in neutral*) andare in folle; (*with engine switched off*) andare a motore spento; (*bicycle:*) andare a ruota libera

freez|e /friːz/ *vt* (*pt* **froze**, *pp* **frozen**) gelare; bloccare (*wages*) ● *vi* (*water:*) gelare; **it's** ~**ing** si gela; **my hands are** ~**ing** ho le mani congelate

freez|er /'friːzə(r)/ *n* freezer *m inv*, congelatore *m*. ~**ing** *a* gelido ● *n* **below** ~**ing** sotto zero

freight /freɪt/ *n* carico *m*. ~**er** *n* nave *f* da carico. ~ **train** *n Am* treno *m* merci

French /frentʃ/ *a* francese ● *n* (*language*) francese *m*; **the ~** *pl* i francesi *mpl*

French: ~ '**beans** *npl* fagiolini *mpl* [verdi]. ~ '**bread** *n* filone *m* (*di pane*). ~ '**fries** *npl* patate *fpl* fritte. ~**man** *n* francese *m*. ~ '**window** *n* porta-finestra *f*. ~**woman** *n* francese *f*

frenzied /'frenzɪd/ *a* frenetico

frenzy /'frenzɪ/ *n* frenesia *f*

frequency /'friːkwənsɪ/ *n* frequenza *f*

frequent¹ /'friːkwənt/ *a* frequente. ~**ly** *adv* frequentemente

frequent² /frɪ'kwent/ *vt* frequentare

fresco /'freskəʊ/ *n* affresco *m*

fresh /freʃ/ *a* fresco; (*new*) nuovo; (*Am: cheeky*) sfacciato. ~**ly** *adv* di recente

freshen /'freʃn/ *vi* (*wind:*) rinfrescare. **freshen up** *vt* dare una rinfrescata a ● *vi* rinfrescarsi

freshness /'freʃnɪs/ *n* freschezza *f*

'**freshwater** *a* a acqua dolce

fret /fret/ *vi* (*pt/pp* **fretted**) inquietarsi. ~**ful** *a* irritabile

'**fretsaw** *n* seghetto *m* da traforo

friar /'fraɪə(r)/ *n* frate *m*

friction /'frɪkʃn/ *n* frizione *f*

Friday /'fraɪdeɪ/ *n* venerdì *m inv*

fridge /frɪdʒ/ *n* frigo *m*

fried /fraɪd/ *see* **fry** ● *a* fritto; ~ **egg** uovo *m* fritto

friend /frend/ *n* amico, -a *mf*. ~**ly** *a* (**-ier, -iest**) (*relations, meeting, match*) amichevole; (*neighbourhood, smile*) piacevole; (*software*) di facile uso; **be** ~**ly with** essere amico di. ~**ship** *n* amicizia *f*

frieze /friːz/ *n* fregio *m*

fright /fraɪt/ *n* paura *f*; **take** ~ spaventarsi

frighten /'fraɪtn/ *vt* spaventare. ~**ed** *a* spaventato; **be** ~**ed** aver paura (**of** di). ~**ing** *a* spaventoso

frightful /'fraɪtfʊl/ *a* terribile

frigid /'frɪdʒɪd/ *a* frigido. ~**ity** /-'dʒɪdətɪ/ *n* freddezza *f*; *Psych* frigidità *f*

frill /frɪl/ *n* volant *m inv*. ~**y** *a* (*dress*) con tanti volant

fringe /frɪndʒ/ *n* frangia *f*; (*of hair*) frangetta *f*; (*fig: edge*) margine *m*. ~ **benefits** *npl* benefici *mpl* supplementari

frisk /frɪsk/ *vt* (*search*) perquisire

frisky /'frɪskɪ/ *a* (**-ier, -iest**) vispo

fritter /'frɪtə(r)/ *n* frittella *f* ● **fritter away** *vt* sprecare

frivol|ity /frɪ'vɒlətɪ/ *n* frivolezza *f*. ~**ous** /'frɪvələs/ *a* frivolo

frizzy /ˈfrɪzɪ/ a crespo

fro /frəʊ/ see **to**

frock /frɒk/ n abito m

frog /frɒg/ n rana f. **~man** n uomo m rana

frolic /ˈfrɒlɪk/ vi (pt/pp **frolicked**) ⟨lambs:⟩ sgambettare; ⟨people:⟩ folleggiare

from /frɒm/ prep da; **~ Monday** da lunedì; **~ that day** da quel giorno; **he's ~ London** è di Londra; **this is a letter ~ my brother** questa è una lettera di mio fratello; **documents ~ the 16th century** documenti del XVI secolo; **made ~** fatto con; **she felt ill ~ fatigue** si sentiva male dalla stanchezza; **~ now on** d'ora in poi

front /frʌnt/ n parte f anteriore; (fig: organization etc) facciata f; (of garment) davanti m; (sea~) lungomare m; Mil, Pol, Meteorol fronte m; **in ~ of** davanti a; **in** or **at the ~** davanti; **to the ~** avanti ● a davanti; ⟨page, row, wheel⟩ anteriore

frontal /ˈfrʌntl/ a frontale

front: **~ 'door** n porta f d'entrata. **~ 'garden** n giardino m d'avanti

frontier /ˈfrʌntɪə(r)/ n frontiera f

front-wheel 'drive n trazione f anteriore

frost /frɒst/ n gelo m; (hoar~) brina f. **~bite** n congelamento m. **~bitten** a congelato

frost|ed /ˈfrɒstɪd/ a **~ed glass** vetro m smerigliato. **~ily** adv gelidamente. **~ing** n Am Culin glassa f. **~y** a also fig gelido

froth /frɒθ/ n schiuma f ● vi far schiuma. **~y** a schiumoso

frown /fraʊn/ n cipiglio m ● vi aggrottare le sopraciglia. **frown on** vt disapprovare

froze /frəʊz/ see **freeze**

frozen /ˈfrəʊzn/ see **freeze** ● a ⟨corpse, hand⟩ congelato; ⟨wastes⟩ gelido; Culin surgelato; **I'm ~** sono gelato. **~ food** n surgelati mpl

frugal /ˈfruːgl/ a frugale

fruit /fruːt/ n frutto m; (collectively) frutta f; **eat more ~** mangia più frutta. **~ cake** n dolce m con frutta candita

fruit|erer /ˈfruːtərə(r)/ n fruttivendolo, -a mf. **~ful** a fig fruttuoso

fruition /fruːˈɪʃn/ n **come to ~** dare dei frutti

fruit: **~ juice** n succo m di frutta. **~less** a infruttuoso. **~ machine** n

macchinetta f mangiasoldi. **~ 'salad** n macedonia f ⟨di frutta⟩

frumpy /ˈfrʌmpɪ/ a scialbo

frustrat|e /frʌˈstreɪt/ vt frustrare; rovinare ⟨plans⟩. **~ing** a frustrante. **~ion** /-eɪʃn/ n frustrazione f

fry[1] vt/i (pt/pp **fried**) friggere

fry[2] /fraɪ/ n inv **small ~** fig pesce m piccolo

frying pan n padella f

fuck /fʌk/ vulg vt/i scopare ● int cazzo. **~ing** a del cazzo

fuddy-duddy /ˈfʌdɪdʌdɪ/ n fam matusa mf inv

fudge /fʌdʒ/ n caramella f a base di zucchero, burro e latte

fuel /ˈfjuːəl/ n carburante m; fig nutrimento m ● vt fig alimentare

fugitive /ˈfjuːdʒɪtɪv/ n fuggiasco, -a mf

fugue /fjuːg/ n Mus fuga f

fulfil /fʊlˈfɪl/ vt (pt/pp **-filled**) soddisfare ⟨conditions, need⟩; realizzare ⟨dream, desire⟩; **~ oneself** realizzarsi. **~ling** a soddisfacente. **~ment** n **sense of ~ment** senso m di appagamento

full /fʊl/ a pieno (**of** di); (detailed) esauriente; ⟨bus, hotel⟩ completo; ⟨skirt⟩ ampio; **at ~ speed** a tutta velocità; **in ~ swing** in pieno fervore ● n **in ~** per intero

full: **~ 'moon** n luna f piena. **~-scale** a ⟨model⟩ in scala reale; ⟨alert⟩ di massima gravità. **~ 'stop** n punto m. **~-time** a & adv a tempo pieno

fully /ˈfʊlɪ/ adv completamente; (in detail) dettagliatamente; **~ booked** ⟨hotel, restaurant⟩ tutto prenotato

fumble /ˈfʌmbl/ vi **~ in** rovistare in; **~ with** armeggiare con; **~ for one's keys** rovistare alla ricerca delle chiavi

fume /fjuːm/ vi (be angry) essere furioso

fumes /fjuːmz/ npl fumi mpl; (from car) gas mpl di scarico

fumigate /ˈfjuːmɪgeɪt/ vt suffumicare

fun /fʌn/ n divertimento m; **for ~** per ridere; **make ~ of** prendere in giro; **have ~** divertirsi

function /ˈfʌŋkʃn/ n funzione f; (event) cerimonia f ● vi funzionare; **~ as** (serve as) funzionare da. **~al** a funzionale

fund /fʌnd/ n fondo m; fig pozzo m; **~s** pl fondi mpl ● vt finanziare

fundamental /fʌndəˈmentl/ a fondamentale

funeral /ˈfjuːnərəl/ n funerale m

funeral: **~ directors** n impresa f di pompe funebri. **~ home** Am, **~**

parlour *n* camera *f* ardente. **~ march** *n* marcia *f* funebre. **~ service** *n* rito *m* funebre

'funfair *n* luna park *m inv*

fungus /'fʌŋgəs/ *n* (*pl* **-gi** /-gaɪ/) fungo *m*

funicular /fjuː'nɪkjʊlə(r)/ *n* funicolare *f*

funnel /'fʌnl/ *n* imbuto *m*; (*on ship*) ciminiera *f*

funnily /'fʌnɪlɪ/ *adv* comicamente; (*oddly*) stranamente; **~ enough** strano a dirsi

funny /'fʌnɪ/ *a* (**-ier, -iest**) buffo; (*odd*) strano. **~ business** *n* affare *m* losco

fur /fɜː(r)/ *n* pelo *m*; (*for clothing*) pelliccia *f*; (*in kettle*) deposito *m*. **~ 'coat** *n* pelliccia *f*

furious /'fjʊərɪəs/ *a* furioso

furnace /'fɜːnɪs/ *n* fornace *f*

furnish /'fɜːnɪʃ/ *vt* ammobiliare (*flat*); fornire (*supplies*). **~ed** *a* **~ed room** stanza *f* ammobiliata. **~ings** *npl* mobili *mpl*

furniture /'fɜːnɪtʃə(r)/ *n* mobili *mpl*

furred /fɜːd/ *a* (*tongue*) impastato

furrow /'fʌrəʊ/ *n* solco *m*

furry /'fɜːrɪ/ *a* (*animal*) peloso; (*toy*) di peluche

further /'fɜːðə(r)/ *a* (*additional*) ulteriore; **at the ~ end** all'altra estremità; **until ~ notice** fino a nuovo avviso ● *adv* più lontano; **~,...** inoltre,...; **~ off** più lontano ● *vt* promuovere

further: ~ edu'cation *n* ≈ formazione *f* parauniversitaria. **~'more** *adv* per di più

furthest /'fɜːðɪst/ *a* più lontano ● *adv* più lontano

furtive /'fɜːtɪv/ *a* furtivo

fury /'fjʊərɪ/ *n* furore *m*

fuse¹ /fjuːz/ *n* (*of bomb*) detonatore *m*; (*cord*) miccia *f*

fuse² *n Electr* fusibile *m* ● *vt* fondere; *Electr* far saltare ● *vi* fondersi; *Electr* saltare; **the lights have ~d** sono saltate le luci. **~-box** *n* scatola *f* dei fusibili

fuselage /'fjuːzəlɑːʒ/ *n Aeron* fusoliera *f*

fusion /'fjuːʒn/ *n* fusione *f*

fuss /fʌs/ *n* storie *fpl*; **make a ~** fare storie; **make a ~ of** colmare di attenzioni ● *vi* fare storie

fussy /'fʌsɪ/ *a* (**-ier, -iest**) (*person*) difficile da accontentare; (*clothes etc*) pieno di fronzoli

fusty /'fʌstɪ/ *a* che odora di stantio; (*smell*) di stantio

futil|e /'fjuːtaɪl/ *a* inutile. **~ity** /-'tɪlətɪ/ *n* futilità *f*

future /'fjuːtʃə(r)/ *a & n* futuro; **in ~** in futuro. **~ perfect** futuro *m* anteriore

futuristic /fjuːtʃə'rɪstɪk/ *a* futuristico

fuzz /fʌz/ *n* **the ~** (*sl: police*) la pula

fuzzy /'fʌzɪ/ *a* (**-ier, -iest**) (*hair*) crespo; (*photo*) sfuocato

Gg

gab /gæb/ *n fam* **have the gift of the ~** avere la parlantina

gabble /'gæb(ə)l/ *vi* parlare troppo in fretta

gad /gæd/ *vi* (*pt/pp* **gadded**) **~ about** andarsene in giro

gadget /'gædʒɪt/ *n* aggeggio *m*

Gaelic /'geɪlɪk/ *a & n* gaelico *m*

gaffe /gæf/ *n* gaffe *f inv*

gag /gæg/ *n* bavaglio *m*; (*joke*) battuta *f* ● *vt* (*pt/pp* **gagged**) imbavagliare

gaily /'geɪlɪ/ *adv* allegramente

gain /geɪn/ *n* guadagno *m*; (*increase*) aumento *m* ● *vt* acquisire; **~ weight** aumentare di peso; **~ access** accedere

● *vi* (*clock:*) andare avanti. **~ful** *a* **~ful employment** lavoro *m* remunerativo

gait /geɪt/ *n* andatura *f*

gala /'gɑːlə/ *n* gala *f*; **swimming ~** manifestazione *f* di nuoto ● *attrib* di gala

galaxy /'gæləksɪ/ *n* galassia *f*

gale /geɪl/ *n* bufera *f*

gall /gɔːl/ *n* (*impudence*) impudenza *f*

gallant /'gælənt/ *a* coraggioso; (*chivalrous*) galante. **~ry** *n* coraggio *m*

'gall-bladder *n* cistifellea *f*

gallery /'gælərɪ/ *n* galleria *f*

galley /'gælɪ/ *n* (*ship's kitchen*) cambusa *f*; **~** [**proof**] bozza *f* in colonna

gallivant /'gælɪvænt/ *vi fam* andare in giro

gallon /'gælən/ n gallone m (= 4,5 l; Am = 3,7 l)

gallop /'gæləp/ n galoppo m ● vi galoppare

gallows /'gæləuz/ n forca f

'gallstone n calcolo m biliare

galore /gə'lɔ:(r)/ adv a bizzeffe

galvanize /'gælvənaɪz/ vt Techn galvanizzare; fig stimolare (**into** a)

gambit /'gæmbɪt/ n prima mossa f

gambl|e /'gæmbl/ n (risk) azzardo m ● vi giocare; (on Stock Exchange) speculare; **~e on** (rely) contare su. **~er** n giocatore, -trice mf [d'azzardo]. **~ing** n gioco m [d'azzardo]

game /geɪm/ n gioco m; (match) partita f; (animals, birds) selvaggina f; **~s** Sch ginnastica f ● a (brave) coraggioso; **are you ~?** ti va?; **be ~ for** essere pronto per. **~keeper** n guardacaccia m inv

gammon /'gæmən/ n coscia f di maiale

gamut /'gæmət/ n fig gamma f

gander /'gændə(r)/ n oca f maschio

gang /gæŋ/ n banda f; (of workmen) squadra f ● **gang up** vi far comunella (**on** contro)

gangling /'gæŋglɪŋ/ a spilungone

gangrene /'gæŋgri:n/ n cancrena f

gangster /'gæŋstə(r)/ n gangster m inv

gangway /'gæŋweɪ/ n passaggio m; Naut, Aeron passerella f

gaol /dʒeɪl/ n carcere m ● vt incarcerare. **~er** n carceriere m

gap /gæp/ n spazio m; (in ages, between teeth) scarto m; (in memory) vuoto m; (in story) punto m oscuro

gap|e /geɪp/ vi stare a bocca aperta; (be wide open) spalancarsi; **~e at** guardare a bocca aperta. **~ing** a aperto

garage /'gæra:ʒ/ n garage m inv; (for repairs) meccanico m; (for petrol) stazione f di servizio

garbage /'ga:bɪdʒ/ n immondizia f; (nonsense) idiozie fpl. **~ can** n Am bidone m dell'immondizia

garbled /'ga:bld/ a confuso

garden /'ga:dn/ n giardino m; [**public**] **~s** pl giardini mpl pubblici ● vi fare giardinaggio. **~ centre** n negozio m di piante e articoli da giardinaggio. **~er** n giardiniere, -a mf. **~ing** n giardinaggio m

gargle /'ga:gl/ n gargarismo m ● vi fare gargarismi

gargoyle /'ga:gɔɪl/ n gargouille f inv

garish /'geərɪʃ/ a sgargiante

garland /'ga:lənd/ n ghirlanda f

garlic /'ga:lɪk/ n aglio m. **~ bread** n pane m condito con aglio

garment /'ga:mənt/ n indumento m

garnish /'ga:nɪʃ/ n guarnizione f ● vt guarnire

garrison /'gærɪsn/ n guarnigione f

garter /'ga:tə(r)/ n giarrettiera f; (Am: on man's sock) reggicalze m inv da uomo

gas /gæs/ n gas m inv; (Am fam: petrol) benzina f ● v (pt/pp **gassed**) ● vt asfissiare ● vi fam blaterare. **~ cooker** n cucina f a gas. **~ 'fire** n stufa f a gas

gash /gæʃ/ n taglio m ● vt tagliare

gasket /'gæskɪt/ n Techn guarnizione f

gas: ~ mask n maschera f antigas. **~-meter** n contatore m del gas

gasoline /'gæsəli:n/ n Am benzina f

gasp /ga:sp/ vi avere il fiato mozzato

'gas station n Am distributore m di benzina

gastric /'gæstrɪk/ a gastrico. **~ 'flu** n influenza f gastro-intestinale. **~ 'ulcer** n ulcera f gastrica

gastronomy /gæ'strɒnəmɪ/ n gastronomia f

gate /geɪt/ n cancello m; (at airport) uscita f

gâteau /'gætəu/ n torta f

gate: ~crash vt entrare senza invito a. **~crasher** n intruso, -a mf. **~way** n ingresso m

gather /'gæðə(r)/ vt raccogliere; (conclude) dedurre; (in sewing) arricciare; **~ speed** acquistare velocità; **~ together** radunare (people, belongings); (obtain gradually) acquistare ● vi (people:) radunarsi. **~ing** n family **~ing** ritrovo m di famiglia

gaudy /'gɔ:dɪ/ a (**-ier, -iest**) pacchiano

gauge /geɪdʒ/ n calibro m; Rail scartamento m; (device) indicatore m ● vt misurare; fig stimare

gaunt /gɔ:nt/ a (thin) smunto

gauze /gɔ:z/ n garza f

gave /geɪv/ see give

gawky /'gɔ:kɪ/ a (**-ier, -iest**) sgraziato

gawp /gɔ:p/ vi **~ [at]** fam guardare con aria da ebete

gay /geɪ/ a gaio; (homosexual) omosessuale; (bar, club) gay

gaze /geɪz/ n sguardo m fisso ● vi guardare; **~ at** fissare

GB abbr (**Great Britain**) GB

gear /gɪə(r)/ n equipaggiamento m; Techn ingranaggio m; Auto marcia f; **in ~** con la marcia innestata; **change ~** cambiare marcia ● vt finalizzare (**to** a)

gear: ~box n Auto scatola f del cambio

~-lever *n*, *Am* **~-shift** *n* leva *f* del cambio

geese /giːs/ *see* **goose**

geezer /'giːzə(r)/ *n sl* tipo *m*

gel /dʒel/ *n* gel *m inv*

gelatine /'dʒelətiːn/ *n* gelatina *f*

gelignite /'dʒelɪgnaɪt/ *n* gelatina *f* esplosiva

gem /dʒem/ *n* gemma *f*

Gemini /'dʒemɪnaɪ/ *n Astr* Gemelli *mpl*

gender /'dʒendə(r)/ *n Gram* genere *m*

gene /dʒiːn/ *n* gene *m*

genealogy /dʒiːnɪˈælədʒɪ/ *n* genealogia *f*

general /'dʒenrəl/ *a* generale ● *n* generale *m*; **in ~** in generale. **~ e'lection** *n* elezioni *fpl* politiche

generaliz|ation /dʒenrəlaɪˈzeɪʃn/ *n* generalizzazione *f*. **~e** /'dʒenrəlaɪz/ *vi* generalizzare

generally /'dʒenrəlɪ/ *adv* generalmente

general prac'titioner *n* medico *m* generico

generate /'dʒenəreɪt/ *vt* generare

generation /dʒenəˈreɪʃn/ *n* generazione *f*

generator /'dʒenəreɪtə(r)/ *n* generatore *m*

generic /dʒɪˈnerɪk/ *a* **~ term** termine *m* generico

generosity /dʒenəˈrɒsɪtɪ/ *n* generosità *f*

generous /'dʒenərəs/ *a* generoso. **~ly** *adv* generosamente

genetic /dʒɪˈnetɪk/ *a* genetico. **~ engineering** *n* ingegneria *f* genetica. **~s** *n* genetica *f*

Geneva /dʒɪˈniːvə/ *n* Ginevra *f*

genial /'dʒiːnɪəl/ *a* gioviale

genitals /'dʒenɪtlz/ *npl* genitali *mpl*

genitive /'dʒenɪtɪv/ *a* & *n* **[case]** genitivo *m*

genius /'dʒiːnɪəs/ *n* (*pl* **-uses**) genio *m*

genocide /'dʒenəsaɪd/ *n* genocidio *m*

genre /'ʒɒrə/ *n* genere *m* [letterario]

gent /dʒent/ *n fam* signore *m*; **the ~s** *sg* il bagno per uomini

genteel /dʒenˈtiːl/ *a* raffinato

gentle /'dʒentl/ *a* delicato; ‹*breeze*, *tap*, *slope*› leggero

gentleman /'dʒentlmən/ *n* signore *m*; (*well-mannered*) gentiluomo *m*

gent|leness /'dʒentlnɪs/ *n* delicatezza *f*. **~ly** *adv* delicatamente

genuine /'dʒenjʊm/ *a* genuino. **~ly** *adv* ‹*sorry*› sinceramente

geograph|ical /dʒɪəˈgræfɪkl/ *a* geografico. **~y** /dʒɪˈɒgrəfɪ/ *n* geografia *f*

geological /dʒɪəˈlɒdʒɪkl/ *a* geologico

geolog|ist /dʒɪˈɒlədʒɪst/ *n* geologo, **-a** *mf*. **~y** *n* geologia *f*

geometr|ic[al] /dʒɪəˈmetrɪk(l)/ *a* geometrico. **~y** /dʒɪˈɒmətrɪ/ *n* geometria *f*

geranium /dʒəˈreɪnɪəm/ *n* geranio *m*

geriatric /dʒerɪˈætrɪk/ *a* geriatrico; **~ ward** *n* reparto *m* geriatria. **~s** *n* geriatria *f*

germ /dʒɜːm/ *n* germe *m*; **~s** *pl* microbi *mpl*

German /'dʒɜːmən/ *n* & *a* tedesco, **-a** *mf*; (*language*) tedesco *m*

Germanic /dʒəˈmænɪk/ *a* germanico

German: ~ 'measles *n* rosolia *f*. **~ 'shepherd** *n* pastore *m* tedesco

Germany /'dʒɜːmənɪ/ *n* Germania *f*

germinate /'dʒɜːmɪneɪt/ *vi* germogliare

gesticulate /dʒeˈstɪkjʊleɪt/ *vi* gesticolare

gesture /'dʒestʃə(r)/ *n* gesto *m*

get /get/ *v* (*pt/pp* **got**, *pp Am also* **gotten**, *pres p* **getting**) ● *vt* (*receive*) ricevere; (*obtain*) ottenere; trovare ‹*job*›; (*buy*, *catch*, *fetch*) prendere; (*transport*, *deliver to airport etc*) portare; (*reach on telephone*) trovare; (*fam: understand*) comprendere; preparare ‹*meal*›; **~ sb to do sth** far fare qcsa a qcno ● *vi* (*become*) **~ tired/bored/angry** stancarsi/annoiarsi/arrabbiarsi; **I'm ~ting hungry** mi sta venendo fame; **~ dressed/married** vestirsi/sposarsi; **~ sth ready** preparare qcsa; **~ nowhere** non concludere nulla; **this is ~ting us nowhere** questo non ci è di nessun aiuto; **~ to** (*reach*) arrivare a. **get at** *vi* (*criticize*) criticare; **I see what you're ~ting at** ho capito cosa vuoi dire; **what are you ~ting at?** dove vuoi andare a parare?. **get away** *vi* (*leave*) andarsene; (*escape*) scappare. **get back** *vi* tornare ● *vt* (*recover*) riavere; **~ one's own back** rifarsi. **get by** *vi* passare; (*manage*) cavarsela. **get down** *vi* scendere; **~ down to work** mettersi al lavoro ● *vt* (*depress*) buttare giù. **get in** *vi* entrare ● *vt* mettere dentro ‹*washing*›; far venire ‹*plumber*›. **get off** *vi* scendere; (*from work*) andarsene; *Jur* essere assolto; **~ off the bus/one's bike** scendere dal pullman/dalla bici ● *vt* (*remove*) togliere. **get on** *vi* salire; (*be on good terms*) andare d'accordo; (*make progress*) andare avanti; (*in life*) riuscire; **~ on the bus/one's bike** salire sul pullman/sulla bici; **how are you**

~ting on? come va?. **get out** *vi* uscire; ⟨*of car*⟩ scendere; **~ out!** fuori!; **~ out of** ⟨*avoid doing*⟩ evitare ● *vt* togliere ⟨*cork, stain*⟩. **get over** *vi* andare al di là ● *vt fig* riprendersi da ⟨*illness*⟩. **get round** *vt* aggirare ⟨*rule*⟩; rigirare ⟨*person*⟩ ● *vi* **I never ~ round to it** non mi sono mai deciso a farlo. **get through** *vi* ⟨*on telephone*⟩ prendere la linea. **get up** *vi* alzarsi; ⟨*climb*⟩ salire; **~ up a hill** salire su una collina

get: **~away** *n* fuga *f*. **~-up** *n* tenuta *f*

geyser /'giːzə(r)/ *n* scaldabagno *m*; *Geol* geyser *m inv*

ghastly /'gɑːstlɪ/ *a* (**-ier, -iest**) terribile; **feel ~** sentirsi da cani

gherkin /'gɜːkɪn/ *n* cetriolino *m*

ghetto /'getəʊ/ *n* ghetto *m*

ghost /gəʊst/ *n* fantasma *m*. **~ly** *a* spettrale

ghoulish /'guːlɪʃ/ *a* macabro

giant /'dʒaɪənt/ *n* gigante *m* ● *a* gigante

gibberish /'dʒɪbərɪʃ/ *n* stupidaggini *fpl*

gibe /dʒaɪb/ *n* malignità *f inv*

giblets /'dʒɪblɪts/ *npl* frattaglie *fpl*

giddiness /'gɪdɪnɪs/ *n* vertigini *fpl*

giddy /'gɪdɪ/ *a* (**-ier, -iest**) vertiginoso; **feel ~** avere le vertigini

gift /gɪft/ *n* dono *m*; ⟨*to charity*⟩ donazione *f*. **~ed** /-ɪd/ *a* dotato. **~-wrap** *vt* impacchettare in carta da regalo

gig /gɪg/ *n Mus fam* concerto *m*

gigantic /dʒaɪ'gæntɪk/ *a* gigantesco

giggle /'gɪgl/ *n* risatina *f* ● *vi* ridacchiare

gild /gɪld/ *vt* dorare

gills /gɪlz/ *npl* branchia *fsg*

gilt /gɪlt/ *a* dorato ● *n* doratura *f*. **~-edged stock** *n* investimento *m* sicuro

gimmick /'gɪmɪk/ *n* trovata *f*

gin /dʒɪn/ *n* gin *m inv*

ginger /'dʒɪndʒə(r)/ *a* rosso fuoco *inv*; ⟨*cat*⟩ rosso ● *n* zenzero *m*. **~ ale** *n*, **~ beer** *n* bibita *f* allo zenzero. **~bread** *n* panpepato *m*

gingerly /'dʒɪndʒəlɪ/ *adv* con precauzione

gipsy /'dʒɪpsɪ/ *n* = **gypsy**

giraffe /dʒɪ'rɑːf/ *n* giraffa *f*

girder /'gɜːdə(r)/ *n Techn* trave *f*

girl /gɜːl/ *n* ragazza *f*; ⟨*female child*⟩ femmina *f*. **~friend** *n* amica *f*; ⟨*of boy*⟩ ragazza *f*. **~ish** *a* da ragazza

giro /'dʒaɪərəʊ/ *n* bancogiro *m*; ⟨*cheque*⟩ sussidio *m* di disoccupazione

girth /gɜːθ/ *n* circonferenza *f*

gist /dʒɪst/ *n* **the ~** la sostanza

give /gɪv/ *n* elasticità *f* ● *v* (*pt* **gave**, *pp* **given**) ● *vt* dare; ⟨*as present*⟩ regalare ⟨**to** *a*⟩; fare ⟨*lecture, present, shriek*⟩; donare ⟨*blood*⟩; **~ birth** partorire ● *vi* ⟨*to charity*⟩ fare delle donazioni; ⟨*yield*⟩ cedere. **give away** *vt* dar via; ⟨*betray*⟩ tradire; ⟨*distribute*⟩ assegnare; **~ away the bride** portare la sposa all'altare. **give back** *vt* restituire. **give in** *vt* consegnare ● *vi* ⟨*yield*⟩ arrendersi. **give off** *vt* emanare. **give over** *vi* **~ over!** piantala!. **give up** *vt* rinunciare a; **~ oneself up** arrendersi ● *vi* rinunciare. **give way** *vi* cedere; *Auto* dare la precedenza; ⟨*collapse*⟩ crollare

given /'gɪvn/ *see* **give** ● *a* **~ name** nome *m* di battesimo

glacier /'glæsɪə(r)/ *n* ghiacciaio *m*

glad /glæd/ *a* contento (**of** di). **~den** /'glædn/ *vt* rallegrare

glade /gleɪd/ *n* radura *f*

gladly /'glædlɪ/ *adv* volentieri

glamor|ize /'glæməraɪz/ *vt* rendere affascinante. **~ous** *a* affascinante

glamour /'glæmə(r)/ *n* fascino *m*

glance /glɑːns/ *n* sguardo *m* ● *vi* **~ at** dare un'occhiata a. **glance up** *vi* alzare gli occhi

gland /glænd/ *n* glandola *f*

glandular /'glændjʊlə(r)/ *a* ghiandolare. **~ fever** *n* mononucleosi *f*

glare /gleə(r)/ *n* bagliore *m*; ⟨*look*⟩ occhiataccia *f* ● *vi* **~ at** dare un'occhiataccia a

glaring /'gleərɪŋ/ *a* sfolgorante; ⟨*mistake*⟩ madornale

glass /glɑːs/ *n* vetro *m*; ⟨*for drinking*⟩ bicchiere *m*; **~es** *pl* ⟨*spectacles*⟩ occhiali *mpl*. **~y** *a* vitreo

glaze /gleɪz/ *n* smalto *m* ● *vt* mettere i vetri a ⟨*door, window*⟩; smaltare ⟨*pottery*⟩; *Culin* spennellare. **~d** *a* ⟨*eyes*⟩ vitreo

glazier /'gleɪzɪə(r)/ *n* vetraio *m*

gleam /gliːm/ *n* luccichio *m* ● *vi* luccicare

glean /gliːn/ *vt* racimolare ⟨*information*⟩

glee /gliː/ *n* gioia *f*. **~ful** *a* gioioso

glen /glen/ *n* vallone *m*

glib /glɪb/ *a pej* insincero

glid|e /glaɪd/ *vi* scorrere; ⟨*through the air*⟩ planare. **~er** *n* aliante *m*

glimmer /'glɪmə(r)/ *n* barlume *m* ● *vi* emettere un barlume

glimpse /glɪmps/ *n* occhiata *f*; **catch a ~ of** intravedere ● *vt* intravedere

glint /glɪnt/ n luccichio m ● vi luccicare

glisten /'glɪsn/ vi luccicare

glitter /'glɪtə(r)/ vi brillare

gloat /gləʊt/ vi gongolare (**over** su)

global /'gləʊbl/ a mondiale

globe /gləʊb/ n globo m; (map) mappamondo m

gloom /gluːm/ n oscurità f; (sadness) tristezza f. **~ily** adv (sadly) con aria cupa

gloomy /'gluːmɪ/ a (-**ier, -iest**) cupo

glorif|y /'glɔːrɪfaɪ/ vt (pt/pp -**ied**) glorificare; **a ~ied waitress** niente più che una cameriera

glorious /'glɔːrɪəs/ a splendido; ⟨deed, hero⟩ glorioso

glory /'glɔːrɪ/ n gloria f; (splendour) splendore m; (cause for pride) vanto m ● vi (pt/pp -**ied**) **~ in** vantarsi di

gloss /glɒs/ n lucentezza f. **~ paint** n vernice f lucida ● **gloss over** vt sorvolare su

glossary /'glɒsərɪ/ n glossario m

glossy /'glɒsɪ/ a (-**ier, -iest**) lucido; **~ [magazine]** rivista f femminile

glove /glʌv/ n guanto m. **~ compartment** n Auto cruscotto m

glow /gləʊ/ n splendore m; (of cheeks) rossore m; (of candle) luce f soffusa ● vi risplendere; ⟨candle:⟩ brillare; ⟨person:⟩ avvampare. **~ing** a ardente; ⟨account⟩ entusiastico

'glow-worm n lucciola f

glucose /'gluːkəʊs/ n glucosio m

glue /gluː/ n colla f ● vt (pres p gluing) incollare

glum /glʌm/ a (**glummer, glummest**) tetro

glut /glʌt/ n eccesso m

glutton /'glʌtən/ n ghiottone, -a mf. **~ous** /-əs/ a ghiotto. **~y** n ghiottoneria f

gnarled /nɑːld/ a nodoso

gnash /næʃ/ vt **~ one's teeth** digrignare i denti

gnat /næt/ n moscerino m

gnaw /nɔː/ vt rosicchiare

gnome /nəʊm/ n gnomo m

go /gəʊ/ n (pl goes) energia f; (attempt) tentativo m; **on the go** in movimento; **at one go** in una sola volta; **it's your go** tocca a te; **make a go of it** riuscire ● vi (pt went, pp gone) andare; (leave) andar via; (vanish) sparire; (become) diventare; (be sold) vendersi; **go and see** andare a vedere; **go swimming/ shopping** andare a nuotare/fare spese; **where's the time gone?** come ha fatto il tempo a volare così?; **it's all gone** è fi-

nito; **be going to do** stare per fare; **I'm not going to** non ne ho nessuna intenzione; **to go** ⟨Am: hamburgers etc⟩ da asporto; **a coffee to go** un caffè da portar via. **go about** vi andare in giro. **go away** vi andarsene. **go back** vi ritornare. **go by** vi passare. **go down** vi scendere; ⟨sun:⟩ tramontare; ⟨ship:⟩ affondare; ⟨swelling:⟩ diminuire. **go for** vt andare a prendere; andare a cercare ⟨doctor⟩; (choose) optare per; (fam: attack) aggredire; **he's not the kind I go for** non è il genere che mi attira. **go in** vi entrare. **go in for** vt partecipare a ⟨competition⟩; darsi a ⟨tennis⟩. **go off** vi andarsene; ⟨alarm:⟩ scattare; ⟨gun, bomb:⟩ esplodere; ⟨food, milk:⟩ andare a male; **go off well** riuscire. **go on** vi andare avanti; **what's going on?** cosa succede? **go on at** vt fam scocciare. **go out** vi uscire; ⟨light, fire:⟩ spegnersi. **go over** vi andare ● vt (check) controllare. **go round** vi andare in giro; (visit) andare; (turn) girare; **is there enough to go round?** ce n'è abbastanza per tutti? **go through** vi ⟨bill, proposal:⟩ passare ● vt (suffer) subire; (check) controllare; (read) leggere. **go under** vi passare sotto; ⟨ship, swimmer:⟩ andare sott'acqua; (fail) fallire. **go up** vi salire; ⟨Theat: curtain:⟩ aprirsi. **go with** vt accompagnare. **go without** vt fare a meno di ⟨supper, sleep⟩ ● vi fare senza

goad /gəʊd/ vt spingere (**into** a); (taunt) spronare

'go-ahead a ⟨person, company⟩ intraprendente ● n okay m

goal /gəʊl/ n porta f; (point scored) gol m inv; (in life) obiettivo m; **score a ~** segnare. **~ie** fam, **~keeper** n portiere m. **~-post** n palo m

goat /gəʊt/ n capra f

gobble /'gɒbl/ vt **~ [down, up]** trangugiare

'go-between n intermediario, -a mf

God, god /gɒd/ n Dio m, dio m

god: ~child n figlioccio, -a mf. **~-daughter** n figlioccia f. **~dess** n dea f. **~-father** n padrino m. **~-fearing** a timorato di Dio. **~-forsaken** a dimenticato da Dio. **~mother** n madrina f. **~parents** npl padrino m e madrina f. **~send** n manna f. **~son** n figlioccio m

go-getter /'gəʊgetə(r)/ n ambizioso, -a mf

goggle /'gɒgl/ vi fam **~ at** fissare con gli occhi sgranati. **~s** npl occhiali mpl;

(*of swimmer*) occhialini *mpl* [da piscina]; (*of worker*) occhiali *mpl* protettivi

going /'gəʊɪŋ/ *a* (*price, rate*) corrente; **~ concern** azienda *f* florida ● *n* **it's hard ~** è una faticaccia; **while the ~ is good** finché si può. **~s-'on** *npl* avvenimenti *mpl*

gold /gəʊld/ *n* oró *m* ● *a* d'oro

golden /'gəʊldn/ *a* dorato. **~ 'handshake** *n* buonuscíta *f* (*al termine di un rapporto di lavoro*). **~ mean** *n* giusto mezzo *m*. **~ 'wedding** *n* nozze *fpl* d'oro

gold: ~fish *n inv* pesce *m* rosso. **~-mine** *n* miniera *f* d'oro. **~-plated** *a* placcato d'oro. **~smith** *n* orefice *m*

golf /gɒlf/ *n* golf *m*

golf: ~-club *n* circolo *m* di golf; (*implement*) mazza *f* da golf. **~-course** *n* campo *m* di golf. **~er** *n* giocatore, -trice *mf* di golf

gondo|la /'gɒndələ/ *n* gondola *f*. **~lier** /-'lɪə(r)/ *n* gondoliere *m*

gone /gɒn/ *see* go

gong /gɒŋ/ *n* gong *m inv*

good /gʊd/ *a* (**better, best**) buono; ‹*child, footballer, singer*› bravo; ‹*holiday, film*› bello; **~** at bravo in; **a ~ deal of anger** molta rabbia; **as ~ as** (*almost*) quasi; **~ morning, ~ afternoon** buon giorno; **~ evening** buona sera; **~ night** buonanotte; **have a ~ time** divertirsi ● *n* bene *m*; **for ~** per sempre; **do ~** far del bene; **do sb ~** far bene a qcno; **it's no ~** è inutile; **be up to no ~** combinare qualcosa

goodbye /gʊd'baɪ/ *int* arrivederci

good: ~-for-nothing *n* buono, -a *mf a* nulla. **G~ 'Friday** *n* Venerdì *m* Santo

good: ~-'looking *a* bello. **~-'natured** *a* **be ~-natured** avere un buon carattere

goodness /'gʊdnɪs/ *n* bontà *f*; **my ~!** santo cielo!; **thank ~!** grazie al cielo!

goods /gʊdz/ *npl* prodotti *mpl*. **~ train** *n* treno *m* merci

good'will *n* buona volontà *f*; *Comm* avviamento *m*

goody /'gʊdɪ/ *n* (*fam: person*) buono *m*. **~-goody** *n* santarellino, -a *mf*

gooey /'gu:ɪ/ *a fam* appiccicaticcio; *fig* sdolcinato

goof /gu:f/ *vi fam* cannare

goose /gu:s/ *n* (*pl* **geese**) oca *f*

gooseberry /'gʊzbərɪ/ *n* uva *f* spina

goose /gu:s/: **~-flesh** *n*, **~-pimples** *npl* pelle *fsg* d'oca

gore¹ /gɔ:(r)/ *n* sangue *m*

gore² *vt* incornare

gorge /gɔ:dʒ/ *n Geog* gola *f* ● *vt* **~ oneself** ingozzarsi

gorgeous /'gɔ:dʒəs/ *a* stupendo

gorilla /gə'rɪlə/ *n* gorilla *m inv*

gormless /'gɔ:mlɪs/ *a fam* stupido

gorse /gɔ:s/ *n* ginestrone *m*

gory /'gɔ:rɪ/ *a* (**-ier, -iest**) cruento

gosh /gɒʃ/ *int fam* caspita

gospel /'gɒspl/ *n* vangelo *m*. **~ truth** *n* sacrosanta verità *f*

gossip /'gɒsɪp/ *n* pettegolezzi *mpl*; (*person*) pettegolo, -a *mf* ● *vi* pettegolare. **~y** *a* pettegolo

got /gɒt/ *see* get; **have ~** avere; **have ~ to do sth** dover fare qcsa

Gothic /'gɒθɪk/ *a* gotico

gotten /'gɒtn/ *Am see* get

gouge /gaʊdʒ/ *vt* **~ out** cavare

gourmet /'gʊəmeɪ/ *n* buongustaio, -a *mf*

gout /gaʊt/ *n* gotta *f*

govern /'gʌv(ə)n/ *vt/i* governare; (*determine*) determinare

government /'gʌvnmənt/ *n* governo *m*. **~al** /-'mentl/ *a* governativo

governor /'gʌvənə(r)/ *n* governatore *m*; (*of school*) membro *m* de consiglio di istituto; (*of prison*) direttore, -trice *mf*; (*fam: boss*) capo *m*

gown /gaʊn/ *n* vestito *m*; *Univ, Jur* toga *f*

GP *n abbr* **general practitioner**

grab /græb/ *vt* (*pt/pp* **grabbed**) **~ [hold of]** afferrare

grace /greɪs/ *n* grazia *f*; (*before meal*) benedicite *m inv*; **with good ~** volentieri; **three days' ~** tre giorni di proroga. **~ful** *a* aggraziato. **~fully** *adv* con grazia

gracious /'greɪʃəs/ *a* cortese; (*elegant*) lussuoso

grade /greɪd/ *n* livello *m*; *Comm* qualità *f*; *Sch* voto *m*; (*Am Sch: class*) classe *f*; *Am* = **gradient** ● *vt Comm* classificare; *Sch* dare il voto a. **~ crossing** *n Am* passaggio *m* a livello

gradient /'greɪdɪənt/ *n* pendenza *f*

gradual /'grædʒʊəl/ *a* graduale. **~ly** *adv* gradualmente

graduate¹ /'grædʒʊət/ *n* laureato, -a *mf*

graduate² /'grædʒʊeɪt/ *vi Univ* laurearsi

graduation /grædʒʊ'eɪʃn/ *n* laurea *f*

graffiti /grə'fi:tɪ/ *npl* graffiti *mpl*

graft /grɑ:ft/ *n* (*Bot, Med*) innesto *m*; (*Med: organ*) trapianto *m*; (*fam: hard work*) duro lavoro *m*; (*fam: corruption*) corruzione *f* ● *vt* innestare; trapiantare ⟨*organ*⟩

grain /greɪn/ *n* (*of sand, salt*) granello *m*; (*of rice*) chicco *m*; (*cereals*) cereali *mpl*; (*in wood*) venatura *f*; **it goes against the ~** *fig* è contro la mia/sua natura

gram /græm/ *n* grammo *m*

grammar /ˈgræmə(r)/ *n* grammatica *f*. **~ school** *n* liceo *m*

grammatical /grəˈmætɪkl/ *a* grammaticale

granary /ˈgrænərɪ/ *n* granaio *m*

grand /grænd/ *a* grandioso; *fam* eccellente

grandad /ˈgrændæd/ *n fam* nonno *m*

ˈgrandchild *n* nipote *mf*

ˈgranddaughter *n* nipote *f*

grandeur /ˈgrændʒə(r)/ *n* grandiosità *f*

ˈgrandfather *n* nonno *m*. **~ clock** *n* pendolo *m* (*che poggia a terra*)

grandiose /ˈgrændɪəʊs/ *a* grandioso

grand: **~mother** *n* nonna *f*. **~parents** *npl* nonni *mpl*. **~ piˈano** *n* pianoforte *m* a coda. **~son** *n* nipote *m*. **~stand** *n* tribuna *f*

granite /ˈgrænɪt/ *n* granito *m*

granny /ˈgrænɪ/ *n fam* nonna *f*

grant /grɑːnt/ *n* (*money*) sussidio *m*; *Univ* borsa *f* di studio ● *vt* accordare; (*admit*) ammettere; **take sth for ~ed** dare per scontato qcsa·

granulated /ˈgrænjʊleɪtɪd/ *a* **~ sugar** zucchero *m* semolato

granule /ˈgrænjuːl/ *n* granello *m*

grape /greɪp/ *n* acino *m*; **~s** *pl* uva *fsg*

grapefruit /ˈgreɪp-/ *n inv* pompelmo *m*

graph /grɑːf/ *n* grafico *m*

graphic /ˈgræfɪk/ *a* grafico; (*vivid*) vivido. **~s** *n* grafica *f*

ˈgraph paper *n* carta *f* millimetrata

grapple /ˈgræpl/ *vi* **~ with** *also fig* essere alle prese con

grasp /grɑːsp/ *n* stretta *f*; (*understanding*) comprensione *f* ● *vt* afferrare. **~ing** *a* avido

grass /grɑːs/ *n* erba *f*; **at the ~ roots** alla base. **~hopper** *n* cavalletta *f*. **~land** *n* prateria *f*

grassy /ˈgrɑːsɪ/ *a* erboso

grate¹ /greɪt/ *n* grata *f*

grate² *vt* *Culin* grattugiare ● *vi* stridere

grateful /ˈgreɪtfl/ *a* grato. **~ly** *adv* con gratitudine

grater /ˈgreɪtə(r)/ *n* *Culin* grattugia *f*

gratif|y /ˈgrætɪfaɪ/ *vt* (*pt/pp* -**ied**) appa-

gare. **~ied** *a* appagato. **~ying** *a* appagante

grating /ˈgreɪtɪŋ/ *n* grata *f*

gratis /ˈgrɑːtɪs/ *adv* gratis

gratitude /ˈgrætɪtjuːd/ *n* gratitudine *f*

gratuitous /grəˈtjuːɪtəs/ *a* gratuito

gratuity /grəˈtjuːɪtɪ/ *n* gratifica *f*

grave¹ /greɪv/ *a* grave

grave² *n* tomba *f*

gravel /ˈgrævl/ *n* ghiaia *f*

grave: **~stone** *n* lapide *f*. **~yard** *n* cimitero *m*

gravitate /ˈgrævɪteɪt/ *vi* gravitare

gravity /ˈgrævɪtɪ/ *n* gravità *f*

gravy /ˈgreɪvɪ/ *n* sugo *m* della carne

gray /greɪ/ *a* *Am* = grey

graze¹ /greɪz/ *vi* ⟨*animal:*⟩ pascolare

graze² *n* escoriazione *f* ● *vt* (*touch lightly*) sfiorare; (*scrape*) escoriare; sbucciarsi ⟨*knee*⟩

grease /griːs/ *n* grasso *m* ● *vt* ungere. **~-proof ˈpaper** *n* carta *f* oleata

greasy /ˈgriːsɪ/ *a* (-**ier**, -**iest**) untuoso; ⟨*hair, skin*⟩ grasso

great /greɪt/ *a* grande; (*fam: marvellous*) eccezionale

great: **~-ˈaunt** *n* prozia *f*. **G~ ˈBritain** *n* Gran Bretagna *f*. **~-ˈgrandchildren** *npl* pronipoti *mpl*. **~-ˈgrandfather** *n* bisnonno *m*. **~-ˈgrandmother** *n* bisnonna *f*

great|ly /ˈgreɪtlɪ/ *adv* enormemente. **~ness** *n* grandezza *f*

great-ˈuncle *n* prozio *m*

Greece /griːs/ *n* Grecia *f*

greed /griːd/ *n* avidità *f*; (*for food*) ingordigia *f*

greedily /ˈgriːdɪlɪ/ *adv* avidamente; ⟨*eat*⟩ con ingordigia

greedy /ˈgriːdɪ/ *a* (-**ier**, -**iest**) avido; (*for food*) ingordo

Greek /griːk/ *a* & *n* greco, -a *mf*; (*language*) greco *m*

green /griːn/ *a* verde; (*fig: inexperienced*) immaturo ● *n* verde *m*; **~s** *pl* verdura *f*; **the G~s** *pl Pol* i verdi. **~ belt** *n* zona *f* verde intorno a una città. **~ card** *n* *Auto* carta *f* verde

greenery /ˈgriːnərɪ/ *n* verde *m*

green fingers *npl* **have ~ ~** avere il police verde

ˈgreenfly *n* afide *m*

green: **~grocer** *n* fruttivendolo, -a *mf*. **~house** *n* serra *f*. **~house effect** *n* effetto *m* serra. **~ light** *n fam* verde *m*

greet /griːt/ *vt* salutare; (*welcome*) accogliere. **~ing** *n* saluto *m*; (*welcome*) ac-

coglienza f. **~ings card** n biglietto m
d'auguri

gregarious /grɪˈgeərɪəs/ a gregario;
(*person*) socievole

grenade /grɪˈneɪd/ n granata f

grew /gru:/ *see* **grow**

grey /greɪ/ a grigio; (*hair*) bianco ● n
grigio m. **~hound** n levriero m

grid /grɪd/ n griglia f; (*on map*) reticolato m; *Electr* rete f

grief /gri:f/ n dolore m; **come to ~**
(*plans:*) naufragare

grievance /ˈgri:vəns/ n lamentela f

grieve /gri:v/ vt addolorare ● vi essere
addolorato

grill /grɪl/ n graticola f; (*for grilling*)
griglia f; **mixed ~** grigliata f mista
● vt/i cuocere alla griglia; (*interrogate*)
sottoporre al terzo grado

grille /grɪl/ n grata f

grim /grɪm/ a (**grimmer, grimmest**)
arcigno; (*determination*) accanito

grimace /grɪˈmeɪs/ n smorfia f ● vi
fare una smorfia

grime /graɪm/ n sudiciume m

grimy /ˈgraɪmɪ/ a (**-ier, -iest**) sudicio

grin /grɪn/ n sorriso m ● vi (*pt/pp*
grinned) fare un gran sorriso

grind /graɪnd/ n (*fam: hard work*)
sfacchinata f ● vt (*pt/pp* **ground**) macinare; affilare (*knife*); (*Am: mince*) tritare; **~ one's teeth** digrignare i denti

grip /grɪp/ n presa f; *fig* controllo m;
(*bag*) borsone m; **get a ~ of oneself**
controllarsi ● vt (*pt/pp* **gripped**) afferrare; (*tyres:*) far presa su; tenere avvin-
to (*attention*)

gripe /graɪp/ vi (*fam: grumble*) lagnarsi

gripping /ˈgrɪpɪŋ/ a avvincente

grisly /ˈgrɪzlɪ/ a (**-ier, -iest**) raccapricciante

gristle /ˈgrɪsl/ n cartilagine f

grit /grɪt/ n graniglia f; (*for roads*) sabbia f; (*courage*) coraggio m ● vt (*pt/pp*
gritted) spargere sabbia su (*road*); **~
one's teeth** serrare i denti

grizzle /ˈgrɪzl/ vi piagnucolare

groan /grəʊn/ n gemito m ● vi gemere

grocer /ˈgrəʊsə(r)/ n droghiere, -a mf;
~'s [shop] drogheria f. **~ies** npl generi
mpl alimentari

groggy /ˈgrɒgɪ/ a (**-ier, -iest**) stordito;
(*unsteady*) barcollante

groin /grɔɪn/ n *Anat* inguine m

groom /gru:m/ n sposo m; (*for horse*)
stalliere m ● vt strigliare (*horse*); *fig*
preparare; **well-~ed** ben curato

groove /gru:v/ n scanalatura f

grope /grəʊp/ vi brancolare; **~ for** cercare a tastoni

gross /grəʊs/ a obeso; (*coarse*) volgare;
(*glaring*) grossolano; (*salary, weight*)
lordo ● n inv grossa f. **~ly** adv (*very*)
enormemente

grotesque /grəʊˈtesk/ a grottesco

grotto /ˈgrɒtəʊ/ n (*pl* **-es**) grotta f

grotty /ˈgrɒtɪ/ a (**-ier, -iest**) (*fam: flat,
street*) squallido

ground¹ /graʊnd/ *see* **grind**

ground² n terra f; *Sport* terreno m;
(*reason*) ragione f; **~s** pl (*park*) giardini
mpl; (*of coffee*) fondi mpl ● vi (*ship:*) arenarsi ● vt bloccare a terra (*aircraft*);
Am Electr mettere a terra

ground: ~ floor n pianterreno m.
~ing n base f. **~less** a infondato.
~sheet n telone m impermeabile.
~work n lavoro m di preparazione

group /gru:p/ n gruppo m ● vt raggrup-
parè ● vi raggrupparsi

grouse¹ /graʊs/ n inv gallo m cedrone

grouse² vi *fam* brontolare

grovel /ˈgrɒvl/ vi (*pt/pp* **grovelled**)
strisciare. **~ling** a leccapiedi inv

grow /grəʊ/ v (*pt* **grew**, *pp* **grown**) ● vi
crescere; (*become*) diventare; (*unemployment, fear:*) aumentare; (*town:*) in-
grandirsi ● vt coltivare; **~ one's hair**
farsi crescere i capelli. **grow up** vi crescere; (*town:*) svilupparsi

growl /graʊl/ n grugnito m ● vi ringhiare

grown /grəʊn/ *see* **grow** ● a adulto.
~-up a & n adulto, -a mf

growth /grəʊθ/ n crescita f; (*increase*)
aumento m; *Med* tumore m

grub /grʌb/ n larva f; (*fam: food*) mangiare m

grubby /ˈgrʌbɪ/ a (**-ier, -iest**) sporco

grudg|e /grʌdʒ/ n rancore m; **bear sb
a ~e** portare rancore a qcno ● vt dare a
malincuore. **~ing** a reluttante. **~ingly**
adv a malincuore

gruelling /ˈgru:əlɪŋ/ a estenuante

gruesome /ˈgru:səm/ a macabro

gruff /grʌf/ a burbero

grumble /ˈgrʌmbl/ vi brontolare (**at**
contro)

grumpy /ˈgrʌmpɪ/ a (**-ier, -iest**)
scorbutico

grunt /grʌnt/ n grugnito m ● vi fare un
grugnito

guarant|ee /gærənˈti:/ n garanzia f
● vt garantire. **~or** n garante mf

guard /gɑ:d/ n guardia f; (*security*)
guardiano m; (*on train*) capotreno m;

Techn schermo *m* protettivo; **be on ~** essere di guardia ● *vt* sorvegliare; (*protect*) proteggere. **guard against** *vt* guardarsi da. **~-dog** *n* cane *m* da guardia

guarded /'gɑ:dɪd/ *a* guardingo

guardian /'gɑ:dɪən/ *n* (*of minor*) tutore, -trice *mf*

guerrilla /gə'rɪlə/ *n* guerrigliero, -a *mf*. **~ warfare** *n* guerriglia *f*

guess /ges/ *n* supposizione *f* ● *vt* indovinare ● *vi* indovinare; (*Am: suppose*) supporre. **~work** *n* supposizione *f*

guest /gest/ *n* ospite *mf*; (*in hotel*) cliente *mf*. **~-house** *n* pensione *f*

guffaw /gʌ'fɔ:/ *n* sghignazzata *f* ● *vi* sghignazzare

guidance /'gaɪdəns/ *n* guida *f*; (*advice*) consigli *mpl*

guide /gaɪd/ *n* guida *f*; [**Girl**] **G~** giovane esploratrice *f* ● *vt* guidare. **~book** *n* guida *f* turistica

guided /'gaɪdɪd/ *a* **~ missile** missile *m* teleguidato; **~ tour** giro *m* guidato

guide: ~-dog *n* cane *m* per ciechi. **~lines** *npl* direttive *fpl*

guild /gɪld/ *n* corporazione *f*

guile /gaɪl/ *n* astuzia *f*

guillotine /'gɪləti:n/ *n* ghigliottina *f*; (*for paper*) taglierina *f*

guilt /gɪlt/ *n* colpa *f*. **~ily** *adv* con aria colpevole

guilty /'gɪltɪ/ *a* (**-ier, -iest**) colpevole; **have a ~ conscience** avere la coscienza sporca

guinea-pig /'gɪnɪ-/ *n* porcellino *m* d'India; (*in experiments*) cavia *f*

guise /gaɪz/ *n* **in the ~ of** sotto le spoglie di

guitar /gɪ'tɑ:(r)/ *n* chitarra *f*. **~ist** *n* chitarrista *mf*

gulf /gʌlf/ *n* *Geog* golfo *m*; *fig* abisso *m*

gull /gʌl/ *n* gabbiano *m*

gullet /'gʌlɪt/ *n* esofago *m*; (*throat*) gola *f*

gullible /'gʌlɪbl/ *a* credulone

gully /'gʌlɪ/ *n* burrone *m*; (*drain*) canale *m* di scolo

gulp /gʌlp/ *n* azione *f* di deglutire; (*of food*) boccone *m*; (*of liquid*) sorso *m* ● *vi*

deglutire. **gulp down** *vt* trangugiare ⟨*food*⟩; scolarsi ⟨*liquid*⟩

gum¹ /gʌm/ *n Anat* gengiva *f*

gum² *n* gomma *f*; (*chewing-gum*) gomma *f* da masticare, chewing-gum *m inv* ● *vt* (*pt/pp* **gummed**) ingommare (**to** a)

gummed /gʌmd/ *see* **gum²** ● *a* ⟨*label*⟩ adesivo

gumption /'gʌmpʃn/ *n fam* buon senso *m*

gun /gʌn/ *n* pistola *f*; (*rifle*) fucile *m*; (*cannon*) cannone *m* ● **gun down** *vt* (*pt/pp* **gunned**) freddare

gun: ~fire *n* spari *mpl*; (*of cannon*) colpi *mpl* [di cannone]. **~man** uomo *m* armato

gun: ~powder *n* polvere *f* da sparo. **~shot** *n* colpo *m* [di pistola]

gurgle /'gɜ:gl/ *vi* gorgogliare; ⟨*baby:*⟩ fare degli urletti

gush /gʌʃ/ *vi* sgorgare; (*enthuse*) parlare con troppo entusiasmo (**over** di). **gush out** *vi* sgorgare. **~ing** *a* eccessivamente entusiastico

gust /gʌst/ *n* (*of wind*) raffica *f*

gusto /'gʌstəʊ/ *n* **with ~** con trasporto

gusty /'gʌstɪ/ *a* ventoso

gut /gʌt/ *n* intestino *m*; **~s** *pl* pancia *f*; (*fam: courage*) fegato *m* ● *vt* (*pt/pp* **gutted**) *Culin* svuotare delle interiora; **~ted by fire** sventrato da un incendio

gutter /'gʌtə(r)/ *n* canale *m* di scolo; (*on roof*) grondaia *f*; *fig* bassifondi *mpl*

guttural /'gʌtərəl/ *a* gutturale

guy /gaɪ/ *n fam* tipo *m*, tizio *m*

guzzle /'gʌzl/ *vt* ingozzarsi con ⟨*food*⟩; **he's ~d the lot** si è sbafato tutto

gym /dʒɪm/ *n fam* palestra *f*; (*gymnastics*) ginnastica *f*

gymnasium /dʒɪm'neɪzɪəm/ *n* palestra *f*

gymnast /'dʒɪmnæst/ *n* ginnasta *mf*. **~ics** /-'næstɪks/ *n* ginnastica *f*

gym: ~ shoes *npl* scarpe *fpl* da ginnastica. **~-slip** *n Sch* grembiule *m* (*da bambina*)

gynaecolog|ist /gaɪnɪ'kɒlədʒɪst/ *n* ginecologo, -a *mf*. **~y** *n* ginecologia *f*

gypsy /'dʒɪpsɪ/ *n* zingaro, -a *mf*

gyrate /dʒaɪ'reɪt/ *vi* roteare

Hh

haberdashery /hæbə'dæʃərɪ/ *n* merceria *f*; *Am* negozio *m* d'abbigliamento da uomo

habit /'hæbɪt/ *n* abitudine *f*; *(Relig: costume)* tonaca *f*; **be in the ~ of doing sth** avere l'abitudine di fare qcsa

habitable /'hæbɪtəbl/ *a* abitabile

habitat /'hæbɪtæt/ *n* habitat *m inv*

habitation /hæbɪ'teɪʃn/ *n* **unfit for human ~** inagibile

habitual /hə'bɪtjʊəl/ *a* abituale; *‹smoker, liar›* inveterato. **~ly** *adv* regolarmente

hack[1] /hæk/ *n (writer)* scribacchino, -a *mf*

hack[2] *vt* tagliare; **~ to pieces** tagliare a pezzi

hackneyed /'hæknɪd/ *a* trito [e ritrito]

'hacksaw *n* seghetto *m*

had /hæd/ *see* **have**

haddock /'hædək/ *n inv* eglefino *m*

haemorrhage /'hemərɪdʒ/ *n* emorragia *f*

haemorrhoids /'hemərɔɪdz/ *npl* emorroidi *fpl*

hag /hæg/ *n* **old ~** vecchia befana *f*

haggard /'hægəd/ *a* sfatto

haggle /'hægl/ *vi* contrattare **(over per)**

hail[1] /heɪl/ *vt* salutare; far segno a *‹taxi›* ● *vi* **~ from** provenire da

hail[2] *n* grandine *f* ● *vi* grandinare. **~stone** *n* chicco *m* di grandine. **~storm** *n* grandinata *f*

hair /heə(r)/ *n* capelli *mpl*; *(on body, of animal)* pelo *m*

hair: **~brush** *n* spazzola *f* per capelli. **~cut** *n* taglio *m* di capelli; **have a ~cut** farsi tagliare i capelli. **~do** *n fam* pettinatura *f*. **~dresser** *n* parrucchiere, -a *mf*. **~-dryer** *n* fon *m inv*; *(with hood)* casco *m* [asciugacapelli]. **~-grip** *n* molletta *f*. **~-pin** *n* forcina *f*. **~-pin 'bend** *n* tornante *m*, curva *f* a gomito. **~-raising** *a* terrificante. **~-style** *n* acconciatura *f*

hairy /'heərɪ/ *a* (**-ier, -iest**) peloso; *(fam: frightening)* spaventoso

hale /heɪl/ *a* **~ and hearty** in piena forma

half /hɑːf/ *n (pl* **halves**) metà *f inv*; **cut in ~** tagliare a metà; **one and a ~** uno e mezzo; **~ a dozen** mezza dozzina; **~ an hour** mezz'ora ● *a* mezzo; **[at] ~ price** [a] metà prezzo ● *adv* a metà, **~ past two** le due e mezza

half: **~ board** *n* mezza pensione *f*. **~-'hearted** *a* esitante. **~-'hourly** *a & adv* ogni mezz'ora. **~ 'mast** *n* **at ~ mast** a mezz'asta. **~ measures** *npl* mezze misure *fpl*. '**~-open** *a* socchiuso. **~-'term** *n* vacanza *f* di metà trimestre. **~-'time** *n Sport* intervallo *m*. **~'way** **the ~way mark/stage** il livello intermedio ● *adv* a metà strada; **get ~way** *fig* arrivare a metà. **~wit** *n* idiota *mf*

hall /hɔːl/ *n (entrance)* ingresso *m*; *(room)* sala *f*; *(mansion)* residenza *f* di campagna; **~ of residence** *Univ* casa *f* dello studente

'hallmark *n* marchio *m* di garanzia; *fig* marchio *m*

hallo /hə'ləʊ/ *int* ciao!; *(on telephone)* pronto!; **say ~ to** salutare

Hallowe'en /hæləʊ'iːn/ *n* vigilia *f* d'Ognissanti e notte delle streghe, celebrata soprattutto dai bambini

hallucination /həluːsɪ'neɪʃn/ *n* allucinazione *f*

halo /'heɪləʊ/ *n (pl* **-es**) aureola *f*; *Astr* alone *m*

halt /hɔːlt/ *n* alt *m inv*; **come to a ~** fermarsi; *‹traffic:›* bloccarsi ● *vi* fermarsi; **~!** alt! ● *vt* fermare. **~ing** *a* esitante

halve /hɑːv/ *vt* dividere a metà; *(reduce)* dimezzare

ham /hæm/ *n* prosciutto *m*; *Theat* attore, -trice *mf* da strapazzo

hamburger /'hæmbɜːgə(r)/ *n* hamburger *m inv*

hamlet /'hæmlɪt/ *n* paesino *m*

hammer /'hæmə(r)/ *n* martello *m* ● *vt* martellare ● *vi* **~ at/on** picchiare a

hammock /'hæmək/ *n* amaca *f*

hamper[1] /'hæmpə(r)/ *n* cesto *m*; **[gift] ~** cestino *m*

hamper² *vt* ostacolare

hamster /'hæmstə(r)/ *n* criceto *m*

hand /hænd/ *n* mano *f*; (*of clock*) lancetta *f*; (*writing*) scrittura *f*; (*worker*) manovale *m*; **at ~, to ~** a portata di mano; **on the one ~** da un lato; **on the other ~** d'altra parte; **out of ~** incontrollabile; (*summarily*) su due piedi; **give sb a ~** dare una mano a qcno ● *vt* porgere. **hand down** *vt* tramandare. **hand in** *vt* consegnare. **hand out** *vt* distribuire. **hand over** *vt* passare; (*to police*) consegnare

hand: **~bag** *n* borsa *f* (*da signora*). **~book** *n* manuale *m*. **~brake** *n* freno *m* a mano. **~cuffs** *npl* manette *fpl*. **~ful** *n* manciata *f*; **be [quite] a ~ful** *fam* essere difficile da tenere a freno

handicap /'hændɪkæp/ *n* handicap *m* *inv.* **~ped** *a* **mentally/physically ~ped** mentalmente/fisicamente handicappato

handi|craft /'hændɪkrɑːft/ *n* artigianato *m.* **~work** *n* opera *f*

handkerchief /'hæŋkətʃɪf/ *n* (*pl* **~s** & **-chieves**) fazzoletto *m*

handle /'hændl/ *n* manico *m*; (*of door*) maniglia *f*; **fly off the ~** *fam* perdere le staffe ● *vt* maneggiare; occuparsi di (*problem, customer*); prendere (*difficult person*); trattare (*subject*). **~bars** *npl* manubrio *m*

hand: **~-luggage** *n* bagaglio *m* a mano. **~made** *a* fatto a mano. **~-out** *n* (*at lecture*) foglio *m* informativo; (*fam: money*) elemosina *f*. **~rail** *n* corrimano *m*. **~shake** *n* stretta *f* di mano

handsome /'hænsəm/ *a* bello; (*fig: generous*) generoso

hand: **~stand** *n* verticale *f*. **~writing** *n* calligrafia *f*. **~-'written** *a* scritto a mano

handy /'hændɪ/ *a* (**-ier, -iest**) utile; (*person*) abile; **have/keep ~** avere/tenere a portata di mano. **~man** *n* tuttofare *m inv*

hang /hæŋ/ *vt* (*pt/pp* hung) appendere (*picture*); (*pt/pp* hanged) impiccare (*criminal*); **~ oneself** impiccarsi ● *vi* (*pt/pp* hung) pendere; (*hair:*) scendere ● *n* **get the ~ of it** *fam* afferrare. **hang about** *vi* gironzolare. **hang on** *vi* tenersi stretto; (*fam: wait*) aspettare; *Teleph* restare in linea. **hang on to** *vt* tenersi stretto a; (*keep*) tenere. **hang out** *vi* spuntare; **where does he usually ~ out?** *fam* dove bazzica di solito? ● *vt* stendere (*washing*). **hang up** *vt* appen-

dere; *Teleph* riattaccare ● *vi* essere appeso; *Teleph* riattaccare

hangar /'hæŋə(r)/ *n* hangar *m inv*

hanger /'hæŋə(r)/ *n* gruccia *f*. **~-on** *n* leccapiedi *mf*

hang: **~-glider** *n* deltaplano *m*. **~-gliding** *n* deltaplano *m*. **~man** *n* boia *m*. **~over** *n* *fam* postumi *mpl* da sbornia. **~-up** *n* *fam* complesso *m*

hanker /'hæŋkə(r)/ *vi* **~ after sth** smaniare per qcsa

hanky /'hæŋkɪ/ *n* *fam* fazzoletto *m*

hanky-panky /'hæŋkɪ'pæŋkɪ/ *n* *fam* qualcosa *m* di losco

haphazard /hæp'hæzəd/ *a* a casaccio

happen /'hæpn/ *vi* capitare, succedere; **as it ~s** per caso; **I ~ed to meet him** mi è capitato di incontrarlo; **what has ~ed to him?** cosa gli è capitato?; (*become of*) che fine ha fatto? **~ing** *n* avvenimento *m*

happi|ly /'hæpɪlɪ/ *adv* felicemente; (*fortunately*) fortunatamente. **~ness** *n* felicità *f*

happy /'hæpɪ/ *a* (**-ier, -iest**) contento, felice. **~-go-'lucky** *a* spensierato

harass /'hærəs/ *vt* perseguitare. **~ed** *a* stressato. **~ment** *n* persecuzione *f*; **sexual ~ment** molestie *fpl* sessuali

harbour /'hɑːbə(r)/ *n* porto ● *vt* dare asilo a; nutrire (*grudge*)

hard /hɑːd/ *a* duro; (*question, problem*) difficile; **~ of hearing** duro d'orecchi; **be ~ on sb** (*person:*) essere duro con qcno ● *adv* (*work*) duramente; (*pull, hit, rain, snow*) forte; **~ hit by unemployment** duramente colpito dalla disoccupazione; **take sth ~** non accettare qcsa; **think ~!** pensaci bene!; **try ~** mettercela tutta; **try ~er** metterci più impegno; **~ done by** *fam* trattato ingiustamente

hard: **~back** *n* edizione *f* rilegata. **~-boiled** *a* (*egg*) sodo. **~ copy** *n* copia *f* stampata. **~ disk** *n* hard disk *m inv*, disco *m* rigido

harden /'hɑːdn/ *vi* indurirsi

hard: **~-'headed** *a* (*businessman*) dal sangue freddo. **~-'hearted** *a* dal cuore duro. **~ line** *n* linea *f* dura; **~ lines!** che sfortuna!. **~line** *a* duro. **~liner** *n* fautore, -trice *mf* della linea dura. **~ luck** *n* sfortuna *f*

hard|ly /'hɑːdlɪ/ *adv* appena; **~ly ever** quasi mai. **~ness** *n* durezza *f*. **~ship** *n* avversità *f* *inv*

hard: **~ 'shoulder** *n* *Auto* corsia *f* d'emergenza. **~ up** *a* *fam* a corto di sol-

di; ~ **up for sth** a corto di qcsa. **~ware**
n ferramenta fpl; Comput hardware m
inv. **~-'wearing** a resistente.
~-'working a **be ~-working** essere un
gran lavoratore

hardy /'hɑːdɪ/ a (**-ier, -iest**) dal fisico
resistente; ⟨plant⟩ che sopporta il gelo

hare /heə(r)/ n lepre f. **~-brained** a
fam ⟨scheme⟩ da scervellati

hark /hɑːk/ vi ~ **back to** fig ritornare
su

harm /hɑːm/ n male m; ⟨damage⟩ danni
mpl; **out of ~'s way** in un posto sicuro;
it won't do any ~ non farà certo male
● vt far male a; ⟨damage⟩ danneggiare.
~ful a dannoso. **~less** a innocuo

harmonica /hɑːˈmɒnɪkə/ n armonica f
[a bocca]

harmonious /hɑːˈməʊnɪəs/ a armo-
nioso. **~ly** adv in armonia

harmon|ize /'hɑːmənaɪz/ vi fig armo-
nizzare. **~y** n armonia f

harness /'hɑːnɪs/ n finimenti mpl; ⟨of
parachute⟩ imbracatura f ● vt bardare
⟨horse⟩; sfruttare ⟨resources⟩

harp /hɑːp/ n arpa f ● **harp on** vi fam
insistere ⟨about su⟩. **~ist** n arpista mf

harpoon /hɑːˈpuːn/ n arpione m

harpsichord /'hɑːpsɪkɔːd/ n clavicem-
balo m

harrowing /'hærəʊɪŋ/ a straziante

harsh /hɑːʃ/ a duro; ⟨light⟩ abbaglian-
te. **~ness** n durezza f

harvest /'hɑːvɪst/ n raccolta f; ⟨of
grapes⟩ vendemmia f; ⟨crop⟩ raccolto m
● vt raccogliere

has /hæz/ see **have**

hash /hæʃ/ n **make a ~ of** fam fare un
casino con

hashish /'hæʃɪʃ/ n hascish m

hassle /'hæsl/ n fam rottura f ● vt rompere le scatole a

haste /heɪst/ n fretta f

hast|y /'heɪstɪ/ a (**-ier, -iest**) frettoloso;
⟨decision⟩ affrettato. **~ily** adv frettolo-
samente

hat /hæt/ n cappello m

hatch[1] /hætʃ/ n ⟨for food⟩ sportello m
passavivande; Naut boccaporto m

hatch[2] vi ~[**out**] rompere il guscio;
⟨egg:⟩ schiudersi ● vt covare; tramare
⟨plot⟩

'hatchback n tre/cinque porte m inv;
⟨door⟩ porta f del bagagliaio

hatchet /'hætʃɪt/ n ascia f

hate /heɪt/ n odio m ● vt odiare. **~ful** a
odioso

hatred /'heɪtrɪd/ n odio m

haught|y /'hɔːtɪ/ a (**-ier, -iest**) altezzo-
so. **~ily** adv altezzosamente

haul /hɔːl/ n ⟨fish⟩ pescata f; ⟨loot⟩ bottino m; ⟨pull⟩ tirata f ● vt tirare; trasportare ⟨goods⟩ ● vi ~ **on** tirare. **~age**
/-ɪdʒ/ n trasporto m. **~ier** /-ɪə(r)/ n
autotrasportatore m

haunt /hɔːnt/ n ritrovo m ● vt frequentare; ⟨linger in the mind⟩ perseguitare;
this house is ~ed questa casa è abita-
ta da fantasmi

have /hæv/ vt (3 sg pres tense **has**; pt/pp
had) avere; fare ⟨breakfast, bath, walk
etc⟩; ~ **a drink** bere qualcosa; ~
lunch/dinner pranzare/cenare; ~ **a
rest** riposarsi; **I had my hair cut** mi
sono tagliata i capelli; **we had the
house painted** abbiamo fatto
tinteggiare la casa; **I had it made** l'ho
fatto fare; ~ **to do sth** dover fare qcsa;
~ **him telephone me tomorrow** digli
di telefonarmi domani; **he has or he's
got two houses** ha due case; **you've
got the money, ~n't you?** hai i soldi,
no? ● v aux avere; ⟨with verbs of motion
& some others⟩ essere; **I ~ seen him**
l'ho visto; **he has never been there**
non ci è mai stato. **have on** vt ⟨be
wearing⟩ portare; ⟨dupe⟩ prendere in
giro; **I've got something on tonight**
ho un impegno stasera. **have out** vt ~
it out with sb chiarire le cose con qcno
● npl **the ~s and the ~-nots** i ricchi e
i poveri

haven /'heɪvn/ n fig rifugio m

haversack /'hævə-/ n zaino m

havoc /'hævək/ n strage f; **play ~ with**
fig scombussolare

haw /hɔː/ see **hum**

hawk /hɔːk/ n falco m

hay /heɪ/ n fieno m. ~ **fever** n raffreddore m da fieno. **~stack** n pagliaio m

'haywire a fam **go ~** dare i numeri;
⟨plans:⟩ andare all'aria

hazard /'hæzəd/ n ⟨risk⟩ rischio m ● vt
rischiare; ~ **a guess** azzardare un'ipotesi. **~ous** /-əs/ a rischioso. ~
[**warning**] **lights** npl Auto luci fpl
d'emergenza

haze /heɪz/ n foschia f

hazel /'heɪz(ə)l/ n nocciolo m; ⟨colour⟩
[color m] nocciola m. **~-nut** n nocciola f

hazy /'heɪzɪ/ a (**-ier, -iest**) nebbioso;
⟨fig: person⟩ confuso; ⟨memories⟩ vago

he /hiː/ pron lui; **he's tired** è stanco;
I'm going but he's not io vengo, ma
lui no

head /hed/ n testa f; ⟨of firm⟩ capo m; ⟨of

primary school) direttore, -trice *mf*; (*of secondary school*) preside *mf*; (*on beer*) schiuma *f*; **be off one's ~** essere fuori di testa; **have a good ~ for business** avere il senso degli affari; **have a good ~ for heights** non soffrire di vertigini; **10 pounds a ~** 10 sterline a testa; **20 ~ of cattle** 20 capi di bestiame; **~ first** a capofitto; **~ over heels in love** innamorato pazzo; **~s or tails?** testa o croce? ● *vt* essere a capo di; essere in testa a ⟨*list*⟩; colpire di testa ⟨*ball*⟩ ● *vi* **~ for** dirigersi verso.

head: **~ache** *n* mal *m* di testa. **~-dress** *n* acconciatura *f*. **~er** /'hedə(r)/ *n* rinvio *m* di testa; (*dive*) tuffo *m* di testa. **~hunter** *n* cacciatore, -trice *mf* di teste. **~ing** *n* (*in list etc*) titolo *m*. **~lamp** *n* Auto fanale *m*. **~land** *n* promontorio *m*. **~light** *n* Auto fanale *m*. **~line** *n* titolo *m*. **~long** *a* & *adv* a capofitto. **~'master** *n* (*of primary school*) direttore *m*; (*of secondary school*) preside *m*. **~'mistress** *n* (*of primary school*) direttrice *f*; (*of secondary school*) preside *f*. **~ office** *n* sede *f* centrale. **~-on** *a* frontale ● *adv* frontalmente. **~phones** *npl* cuffie *fpl*. **~quarters** *npl* sede *fsg*; Mil quartier *m* generale *msg*. **~-rest** *n* poggiatesta *m inv*. **~room** *n* sottotetto *m*; (*of bridge*) altezza *f* libera di passaggio. **~scarf** *n* foulard *m inv*, fazzoletto *m*. **~strong** *a* testardo. **~ 'waiter** *n* capocameriere *m*. **~way** *n* progresso *m*. **~wind** *n* vento *m* di prua

heady /'hedɪ/ *a* che dà alla testa

heal /hi:l/ *vt/i* guarire

health /helθ/ *n* salute *f*

health: **~ farm** *n* centro *m* di rimessa in forma. **~ foods** *npl* alimenti *mpl* macrobiotici. **~-food shop** *n* negozio *m* di macrobiotica. **~ insurance** *n* assicurazione *f* contro malattie

health|y /'helθɪ/ *a* (**-ier, -iest**) sano. **~ily** *adv* in modo sano

heap /hi:p/ *n* mucchio *m*; **~s of** *fam* un sacco di ● *vt* **~ [up]** ammucchiare; **~ed teaspoon** un cucchiaino abbondante

hear /hɪə(r)/ *vt/i* (*pt/pp* **heard**) sentire; **~, ~!** bravo! **~ from** *vi* aver notizie di. **hear of** *vi* sentir parlare di; **he would not ~ of it** non ne ha voluto sentir parlare

hearing /'hɪərɪŋ/ *n* udito *m*; Jur udienza *f*. **~-aid** *n* apparecchio *m* acustico

'hearsay *n* **from ~** per sentito dire

hearse /hɜ:s/ *n* carro *m* funebre

heart /hɑ:t/ *n* cuore *m*; **~s** *pl* (*in cards*) cuori *mpl*; **by ~** a memoria

heart: **~ache** *n* pena *f*. **~ attack** *n* infarto *m*. **~beat** *n* battito *m* cardiaco. **~-break** *n* afflizione *f*. **~-breaking** *a* straziante. **~-broken** *a* **be ~-broken** avere il cuore spezzato. **~burn** *n* mal *m* di stomaco. **~en** *vt* rincuorare. **~felt** *a* di cuore

hearth /hɑ:θ/ *n* focolare *m*

heart|ily /'hɑ:tɪlɪ/ *adv* di cuore; ⟨*eat*⟩ con appetito; **be ~ily sick of sth** non poterne più di qcsa. **~less** *a* spietato. **~-searching** *n* esame *m* di coscienza. **~-to~** *n* conversazione *f* a cuore aperto ● *a* a cuore aperto. **~y** *a* caloroso; ⟨*meal*⟩ copioso; ⟨*person*⟩ gioviale

heat /hi:t/ *n* calore *m*; Sport prova *f* eliminatoria ● *vt* scaldare ● *vi* scaldarsi. **~ed** *a* ⟨*swimming pool*⟩ riscaldato; ⟨*discussion*⟩ animato. **~er** *n* (*for room*) stufa *f*; (*for water*) boiler *m inv*; Auto riscaldamento *m*

heath /hi:θ/ *n* brughiera *f*

heathen /'hi:ðn/ *a* & *n* pagano, -a *mf*

heather /'heðə(r)/ *n* erica *f*

heating /'hi:tɪŋ/ *n* riscaldamento *m*

heat: **~-stroke** *n* colpo *m* di sole. **~ wave** *n* ondata *f* di calore

heave /hi:v/ *vt* tirare; (*lift*) tirare su; (*fam: throw*) gettare; emettere ⟨*sigh*⟩ ● *vi* tirare

heaven /'hevn/ *n* paradiso *m*; **~ help you if...** Dio ti scampi se...; **H~s!** santo cielo! **~ly** *a* celeste; *fam* delizioso

heav|y /'hevɪ/ *a* (**-ier, -iest**) pesante; ⟨*traffic*⟩ intenso; ⟨*rain, cold*⟩ forte; **be a ~y smoker/drinker** essere un gran fumatore/bevitore. **~ily** *adv* pesantemente; ⟨*smoke, drink etc*⟩ molto. **~yweight** *n* peso *m* massimo

Hebrew /'hi:bru:/ *n* ebreo

heckle /'hekl/ *vt* interrompere di continuo. **~r** *n* disturbatore, -trice *mf*

hectic /'hektɪk/ *a* frenetico

hedge /hedʒ/ *n* siepe *f* ● *vi fig* essere evasivo. **~hog** *n* riccio *m*

heed /hi:d/ *n* **pay ~ to** prestare ascolto a ● *vt* prestare ascolto a. **~less** *a* noncurante

heel[1] /hi:l/ *n* tallone *m*; (*of shoe*) tacco *m*; **take to one's ~s** *fam* darsela a gambe

heel[2] *vi* **~ over** Naut inclinarsi

hefty /'heftɪ/ *a* (**-ier, -iest**) massiccio

heifer /'hefə(r)/ *n* giovenca *f*

height /haɪt/ n altezza f; (of plane) altitudine f; (of season, fame) culmine m. ~**en** vt fig accrescere

heir /eə(r)/ n erede mf. ~**ess** n ereditiera f. ~**loom** n cimelio m di famiglia

held /held/ see **hold**²

helicopter /'helɪkɒptə(r)/ n elicottero m

hell /hel/ n inferno m; **go to ~**! sl va' al diavolo! ● int porca miseria!

hello /hə'ləʊ/ int & n = **hallo**

helm /helm/ n timone m; **at the ~** fig al timone

helmet /'helmɪt/ n casco m

help /help/ n aiuto m; (employee) aiuto m domestico; **that's no ~** non è d'aiuto ● vt aiutare; **~ oneself to sth** servirsi di qcsa; **~ yourself** (at table) serviti pure; **I could not ~ laughing** non ho potuto trattenermi dal ridere; **it cannot be ~ed** non c'è niente da fare; **I can't ~ it** non ci posso far niente ● vi aiutare

help|er /'helpə(r)/ n aiutante mf. ~**ful** a ⟨person⟩ di aiuto; ⟨advice⟩ utile. ~**ing** n porzione f. ~**less** a (unable to manage) incapace; (powerless) impotente

helter-skelter /heltə'skeltə(r)/ adv in fretta e furia ● n scivolo m a spirale nei luna park

hem /hem/ n orlo m ● vt (pt/pp **hemmed**) orlare. **hem in** vt intrappolare

hemisphere /'hemɪ-/ n emisfero m

hemp /hemp/ n canapa f

hen /hen/ n gallina f; (any female bird) femmina f

hence /hens/ adv (for this reason) quindi. ~**'forth** adv d'ora innanzi

henchman /'hentʃmən/ n pej tirapiedi m

'hen: ~-**party** n fam festa f di addio al celibato per sole donne. ~**pecked** a tiranneggiato dalla moglie

her /hɜ:(r)/ poss a il suo m, la sua f, i suoi mpl, le sue fpl; ~ **mother/father** sua madre/suo padre ● pers pron (direct object) la; (indirect object) le; (after prep) lei; **I know** ~ la conosco; **give** ~ **the money** dalle i soldi; **give it to** ~ daglielo; **I came with** ~ sono venuto con lei; **it's** ~ è lei; **I've seen** ~ l'ho vista; **I've seen** ~, **but not him** ho visto lei, ma non lui

herald /'herəld/ vt annunciare

herb /hɜ:b/ n erba f

herbal /'hɜ:b(ə)l/ a alle erbe; ~ **tea** tisana f

herbs /hɜ:bz/ npl (for cooking) aromi mpl [da cucina]; (medicinal) erbe fpl

herd /hɜ:d/ n gregge m ● vt (tend) sorvegliare; (drive) far muovere; fig ammassare

here /hɪə(r)/ adv qui, qua; **in ~** qui dentro; **come/bring ~** vieni/porta qui; ~ **is..., ~ are...** ecco...; ~ **you are!** ecco qua!. ~**'after** adv in futuro. ~**'by** adv con la presente

heredit|ary /hə'redɪtərɪ/ a ereditario. ~**y** n eredità f

here|sy /'herəsɪ/ n eresia f. ~**tic** n eretico, -a f

here'with adv Comm con la presente

heritage /'herɪtɪdʒ/ n eredità f

hermetic /hɜ:'metɪk/ a ermetico. ~**ally** adv ermeticamente

hermit /'hɜ:mɪt/ n eremita mf

hernia /'hɜ:nɪə/ n ernia f

hero /'hɪərəʊ/ n (pl -**es**) eroe m

heroic /hɪ'rəʊɪk/ a eroico

heroin /'herəʊɪn/ n eroina f (droga)

hero|ine /'herəʊɪn/ n eroina f. ~**ism** n eroismo m

heron /'herən/ n airone m

herring /'herɪŋ/ n aringa f

hers /hɜ:z/ poss pron il suo m, la sua f, i suoi mpl, le sue fpl; **a friend of** ~ un suo amico; **friends of** ~ dei suoi amici; **that is** ~ quello è suo; (as opposed to mine) quello è il suo

her'self pers pron (reflexive) si; (emphatic) lei stessa; ⟨after prep⟩ sé, se stessa; **she poured** ~ **a drink** si è versata da bere; **she told me so** ~ me lo ha detto lei stessa; **she's proud of** ~ è fiera di sé; **by** ~ da sola

hesitant /'hezɪtənt/ a esitante. ~**ly** adv con esitazione

hesitat|e /'hezɪteɪt/ vi esitare. ~**ion** /-'teɪʃn/ n esitazione f

het /het/ a ~ **up** fam agitato

hetero'sexual /hetərəʊ-/ a eterosessuale

hexagon /'heksəgən/ n esagono m. ~**al** /hek'sægənl/ a esagonale

hey /heɪ/ int ehi

heyday /'heɪ-/ n tempi mpl d'oro

hi /haɪ/ int ciao!

hiatus /haɪ'eɪtəs/ n (pl -**tuses**) iato m

hibernat|e /'haɪbəneɪt/ vi andare in letargo. ~**ion** /-'neɪʃn/ n letargo m

hiccup /'hɪkʌp/ n singhiozzo m; (fam: hitch) intoppo m ● vi fare un singhiozzo

hid /hɪd/, **hidden** /'hɪdn/ see **hide**²

hide¹ /haɪd/ n (leather) pelle f (di animale)

hide² *vt* (*pt* **hid**, *pp* **hidden**) nascondere ● *vi* nascondersi. **~-and-'seek** *n* play **~-and-seek** giocare a nascondino

hideous /'hɪdɪəs/ *a* orribile

'hide-out *n* nascondiglio *m*

hiding¹ /'haɪdɪŋ/ *n* (*fam: beating*) bastonata *f*; (*defeat*) batosta *f*

hiding² *n* **go into ~** sparire dalla circolazione

hierarchy /'haɪəraːkɪ/ *n* gerarchia *f*

hieroglyphics /haɪərə'glɪfɪks/ *npl* geroglifici *mpl*

hi-fi /'haɪfaɪ/ *n fam* stereo *m*, hi-fi *m inv* ● *a fam* ad alta fedeltà

higgledy-piggledy /'hɪgldɪ'pɪgldɪ/ *adv* alla rinfusa

high /haɪ/ *a* alto; (*meat*) che comincia ad andare a male; (*wind*) forte; (*on drugs*) fatto; **it's ~ time we did something about it** è ora di fare qualcosa in proposito ● *adv* in alto; **~ and low** in lungo e in largo ● *n* massimo *m*; (*temperature*) massima *f*; **be on a ~** *fam* essere fatto

high: **~brow** *a & n* intellettuale *mf*. **~ chair** *n* seggiolone *m*. **~er education** *n* formazione *f* universitaria. **~'-handed** *a* dispotico. **~-'heeled** *a* coi tacchi alti. **~ heels** *npl* tacchi *mpl* alti. **~ jump** *n* salto *m* in alto

highlight /'haɪlaɪt/ *n fig* momento *m* clou; **~s** *pl* (*in hair*) mèche *fpl* ● *vt* (*emphasize*) evidenziare. **~er** *n* (*marker*) evidenziatore *m*

highly /'haɪlɪ/ *adv* molto; **speak ~ of** lodare; **think ~ of** avere un'alta opinione di. **~-'strung** *a* nervoso

Highness /'haɪnɪs/ *n* altezza *f*; **Your ~** Sua Altezza

high: **~-rise** *a* (*building*) molto alto ● *n* edificio *m* molto alto. **~ school** *n* scuola *f* superiore. **~ season** *n* alta stagione *f*. **~ street** *n* strada *f* principale. **~ tea** *n* pasto *m* pomeridiano servito insieme al tè. **~ 'tide** *n* alta marea *f*. **~way code** *n* codice *m* stradale

hijack /'haɪdʒæk/ *vt* dirottare ● *n* dirottamento *m*. **~er** *n* dirottatore, -trice *mf*

hike /haɪk/ *n* escursione *f* a piedi ● *vi* fare un'escursione a piedi. **~r** *n* escursionista *mf*

hilarious /hɪ'leərɪəs/ *a* esilarante

hill /hɪl/ *n* collina *f*; (*mound*) collinetta *f*; (*slope*) altura *f*

hill: **~side** *n* pendio *m*. **~y** *a* collinoso

hilt /hɪlt/ *n* impugnatura *f*; **to the ~**

(*fam: support*) fino in fondo; (*mortgaged*) fino al collo

him /hɪm/ *pers pron* (*direct object*) lo; (*indirect object*) gli; (*with prep*) lui; **I know ~** lo conosco; **give ~ it to ~** dagli i soldi; **give it to ~** daglielo; **I spoke to ~** gli ho parlato; **it's ~** è lui; **she loves ~** lo ama; **she loves ~, not you** ama lui, non te. **~'self** *pers pron* (*reflexive*) si; (*emphatic*) lui stesso; (*after prep*) sé, se stesso; **he poured ~ a drink** si è versato da bere; **he told me so ~self** me lo ha detto lui stesso; **he's proud of ~self** è fiero di sé; **by ~self** da solo

hind /haɪnd/ *a* posteriore

hind|er /'hɪndə(r)/ *vt* intralciare. **~rance** /-rəns/ *n* intralcio *m*

hindsight /'haɪnd-/ *n* **with ~** con il senno del poi

Hindu /'hɪnduː/ *n* indù *mf inv* ● *a* indù. **~ism** *n* induismo *m*

hinge /hɪndʒ/ *n* cardine *m* ● *vi* **~ on** *fig* dipendere da

hint /hɪnt/ *n* (*clue*) accenno *m*; (*advice*) suggerimento *m*; (*indirect suggestion*) allusione *f*; (*trace*) tocco *m* ● *vt* **~ that...** far capire che... ● *vi* **~ at** alludere a

hip /hɪp/ *n* fianco *m*

hippie /'hɪpɪ/ *n* hippy *mf inv*

hippo /'hɪpəʊ/ *n* ippopotamo *m*

hip 'pocket *n* tasca *f* posteriore

hippopotamus /hɪpə'pɒtəməs/ *n* (*pl* **-muses** *or* **-mi** /-maɪ/) ippopotamo *m*

hire /'haɪə(r)/ *vt* affittare; assumere (*person*); **~ [out]** affittare ● *n* noleggio *m*; **'for ~'** 'affittasi'. **~ car** *n* macchina *f* a noleggio. **~ purchase** *n* acquisto *m* rateale

his /hɪz/ *poss a* il suo *m*, la sua *f*, i suoi *mpl*, le sue *fpl*; **~ mother/father** sua madre/suo padre ● *poss pron* il suo *m*, la sua *f*, i suoi *mpl*, le sue *fpl*; **a friend of ~** un suo amico; **friends of ~** dei suoi amici; **that is ~** questo è suo; (*as opposed to mine*) questo è il suo

hiss /hɪs/ *n* sibilo *m*; (*of disapproval*) fischio *m* ● *vt* fischiare ● *vi* sibilare; (*in disapproval*) fischiare

historian /hɪ'stɔːrɪən/ *n* storico, -a *mf*

historic /hɪ'stɒrɪk/ *a* storico. **~al** *a* storico. **~ally** *adv* storicamente

history /'hɪstərɪ/ *n* storia *f*; **make ~** passare alla storia

hit /hɪt/ *n* (*blow*) colpo *m*; (*fam: success*) successo *m*; **score a direct ~** (*missile:*) colpire in pieno ● *vt/i* (*pt/pp* **hit**, *pres p*

hitting) colpire; **~ one's head on the table** battere la testa contro il tavolo; **the car ~ the wall** la macchina ha sbattuto contro il muro; **~ the roof** *fam* perdere le staffe. **hit off** *vt* **~ it off** andare d'accordo. **hit on** *vt fig* trovare

hitch /hɪtʃ/ *n* intoppo *m*; **technical ~** problema *m* tecnico ● *vt* attaccare; **~ a lift** chiedere un passaggio. **hitch up** *vt* tirarsi su ‹*trousers*›. **~-hike** *vi* fare l'autostop. **~-hiker** *n* autostoppista *mf*

hit-or-'miss *a* on a very **~ basis** all'improvvisata

hither /'hɪðə(r)/ *adv* **~ and thither** di qua e di là. **~'to** *adv* finora

hive /haɪv/ *n* alveare *m*; **~ of industry** fucina *f* di lavoro ● **hive off** *vt Comm* separare

hoard /hɔːd/ *n* provvista *f*; ‹*of money*› gruzzolo *m* ● *vt* accumulare

hoarding /'hɔːdɪŋ/ *n* palizzata *f*; ‹*with advertisements*› tabellone *m* per manifesti pubblicitari

hoarse /hɔːs/ *a* rauco. **~ly** *adv* con voce rauca. **~ness** *n* raucedine *f*

hoax /həʊks/ *n* scherzo *m*; ‹*false alarm*› falso allarme *m*. **~er** *n* burlone, -a *mf*

hob /hɒb/ *n* piano *m* di cottura

hobble /'hɒbl/ *vi* zoppicare

hobby /'hɒbɪ/ *n* hobby *m inv*. **~-horse** *n fig* fissazione *f*

hockey /'hɒkɪ/ *n* hockey *m*

hoe /həʊ/ *n* zappa *f*

hog /hɒg/ *n* maiale *m* ● *vt* (*pt/pp* **hogged**) *fam* monopolizzare

hoist /hɔɪst/ *n* montacarichi *m inv*; (*fam:* push) spinta *f* in su ● *vt* sollevare; innalzare ‹*flag*›; levare ‹*anchor*›

hold[1] /həʊld/ *n Naut, Aeron* stiva *f*

hold[2] *n* presa *f*; (*fig: influence*) ascendente *m*; **get ~ of** trovare; procurarsi ‹*information*› ● *v* (*pt/pp* **held**) ● *vt* tenere; ‹*container*› contenere; essere titolare di ‹*licence, passport*›; trattenere ‹*breath, suspect*›; mantenere vivo ‹*interest*›; ‹*civil servant etc*:› occupare ‹*position*›; (*retain*) mantenere; **~ sb's hand** tenere qcno per mano; **~ one's tongue** tenere la bocca chiusa; **~ sb responsible** considerare qcno responsabile; **~ that** (*believe*) ritenere che ● *vi* tenere; ‹*weather, luck*:› durare; ‹*offer*:› essere valido; *Teleph* restare in linea; **I don't ~ with the idea that** *fam* non sono d'accordo sul fatto che. **hold back** *vt* rallentare ● *vi* esitare. **hold down** *vt* tenere a bada ‹*sb*›. **hold on** *vi* (*wait*) attendere; *Teleph* restare in

linea. **hold on to** *vt* aggrapparsi a; (*keep*) tenersi. **hold out** *vt* porgere ‹*hand*›; *fig* offrire ‹*possibility*› ● *vi* (*resist*) resistere. **hold up** *vt* tenere su; (*delay*) rallentare; (*rob*) assalire; **~ one's head up** *fig* tenere la testa alta

'hold: **~all** *n* borsone *m*. **~er** *n* titolare *mf*; (*of record*) detentore, -trice *mf*; (*container*) astuccio *m*. **~ing** *n* (*land*) terreno *m* in affitto; *Comm* azioni *fpl*. **~-up** *n* ritardo *m*; (*attack*) rapina *f* a mano armata

hole /həʊl/ *n* buco *m*

holiday /'hɒlɪdeɪ/ *n* vacanza *f*; (*public*) giorno *m* festivo; (*day off*) giorno *m* di ferie; **go on ~** andare in vacanza ● *vi* andare in vacanza. **~-maker** *n* vacanziere *m*

holiness /'həʊlɪnɪs/ *n* santità *f*; **Your H~** Sua Santità

Holland /'hɒlənd/ *n* Olanda *f*

hollow /'hɒləʊ/ *a* cavo; ‹*promise*› a vuoto; ‹*voice*› assente; ‹*cheeks*› infossato ● *n* cavità *f inv*; (*in ground*) affossamento *m*

holly /'hɒlɪ/ *n* agrifoglio *m*

holocaust /'hɒləkɔːst/ *n* olocausto *m*

hologram /'hɒləgræm/ *n* ologramma *m*

holster /'həʊlstə(r)/ *n* fondina *f*

holy /'həʊlɪ/ *a* (**-ier, -est**) santo; ‹*water*› benedetto. **H~ Ghost** *or* **Spirit** *n* Spirito *m* Santo. **H~ Scriptures** *npl* sacre scritture *fpl*. **H~ Week** *n* settimana *f* santa

homage /'hɒmɪdʒ/ *n* omaggio *m*; **pay ~ to** rendere omaggio a

home /həʊm/ *n* casa *f*; (*for children*) istituto *m*; (*for old people*) casa *f* di riposo; (*native land*) patria *f* ● *adv* **at ~** a casa; (*football*) in casa; **feel at ~** sentirsi a casa propria; **come/go ~** venire/andare a casa; **drive a nail ~** piantare un chiodo a fondo ● *a* domestico; ‹*movie, video*› casalingo; ‹*team*› ospitante; *Pol* nazionale

home: **~ ad'dress** *n* indirizzo *m* di casa. **~ com'puter** *n* computer *m inv* da casa. **H~ Counties** *npl* contee *fpl* intorno a Londra. **~ game** *n* gioco *m* in casa. **~ help** *n* aiuto *m* domestico (*per persone non autosufficienti*). **~land** *n* patria *f*. **~less** *a* senza tetto

home: **~-'made** *a* fatto in casa. **H~ Office** *n Br* ministero *m* degli interni. **H~ 'Secretary** *n Br* ministro *m* degli interni. **~sick** *a* be **~sick** avere nostalgia (**for** di). **~sickness** *n* nostalgia *f* di casa. **~ 'town** *n* città *f inv* natia. **~ward** *a* di ritorno ● *adv* verso casa. **~work** *n Sch* compiti *mpl*

homicide /'hɒmɪsaɪd/ *n* (*crime*) omicidio *m*

homoeopath|ic /həʊmɪə'pæθɪk/ *a* omeopatico. **~y** /-'ɒpəθɪ/ *n* omeopatia *f*

homogeneous /hɒmə'dʒiːnɪəs/ *a* omogeneo

homo'sexual *a & n* omosessuale *mf*

honest /'ɒnɪst/ *a* onesto; (*frank*) sincero. **~ly** *adv* onestamente; (*frankly*) sinceramente; **~ly!** ma insomma!. **~y** *n* onestà *f*; (*frankness*) sincerità *f*

honey /'hʌnɪ/ *n* miele *m*; (*fam: darling*) tesoro *m*

honey: ~comb *n* favo *m*. **~moon** *n* luna *f* di miele. **~suckle** *n* caprifoglio *m*

honk /hɒŋk/ *vi Aut* clacsonare

honorary /'ɒnərərɪ/ *a* onorario

honour /'ɒnə(r)/ *n* onore *m* ● *vt* onorare. **~able** /-əbl/ *a* onorevole. **~ably** *adv* con onore. **~s degree** *n* diploma *m* di laurea

hood /hʊd/ *n* cappuccio *m*; (*of pram*) tettuccio *m*; (*over cooker*) cappa *f*; *Am Auto* cofano *m*

hoodlum /'huːdləm/ *n* teppista *m*

'hoodwink *vt fam* infinocchiare

hoof /huːf/ *n* (*pl* **~s** or **hooves**) zoccolo *m*

hook /hʊk/ *n* gancio *m*; (*for fishing*) amo *m*; **off the ~** *Teleph* staccato; *fig* fuori pericolo ● *vt* agganciare ● *vi* agganciarsi

hook|ed /hʊkt/ *a* (*nose*) adunco; **~ed on** (*fam: drugs*) dedito a; **be ~ed on skiing** essere un fanatico dello sci. **~er** *n Am sl* battona *f*

hookey /'hʊkɪ/ *n* **play ~** *Am fam* marinare la scuola

hooligan /'huːlɪgən/ *n* teppista *mf*. **~ism** *n* teppismo *m*

hoop /huːp/ *n* cerchio *m*

hooray /hʊ'reɪ/ *int & n* = **hurrah**

hoot /huːt/ *n* colpo *m* di clacson; (*of siren*) ululato *m*; (*of owl*) grido *m* ● *vi* (*owl:*) gridare; (*car:*) clacsonare; (*siren:*) ululare; (*jeer*) fischiare. **~er** *n* (*of factory*) sirena *f*; *Auto* clacson *m inv*

hoover® /'huːvə(r)/ *n* aspirapolvere *m inv* ● *vt* passare l'aspirapolvere su (*carpet*); passare l'aspirapolvere in (*room*)

hop /hɒp/ *n* saltello *m* ● *vi* (*pt/pp* hopped) saltellare; **~ it!** *fam* tela!. **hop in** *vi fam* saltar su

hope /həʊp/ *n* speranza *f* ● *vi* sperare (**for** in); **I ~ so/not** spero di sì/no ● *vt* **~ that** sperare che

hope|ful /'həʊpfl/ *a* pieno di speranza; (*promising*) promettente; **be ~ful that** avere buone speranze che. **~fully** *adv* con speranza; (*it is hoped*) se tutto va bene. **~less** *a* senza speranze; (*useless*) impossibile; (*incompetent*) incapace. **~lessly** *adv* disperatamente; (*inefficient, lost*) completamente. **~lessness** *n* disperazione *f*

horde /hɔːd/ *n* orda *f*

horizon /hə'raɪzn/ *n* orizzonte *m*

horizontal /hɒrɪ'zɒntl/ *a* orizzontale

hormone /'hɔːməʊn/ *n* ormone *m*

horn /hɔːn/ *n* corno *m*; *Auto* clacson *m inv*

horny /'hɔːnɪ/ *a* calloso; *fam* arrapato

horoscope /'hɒrəskəʊp/ *n* oroscopo *m*

horrib|le /'hɒrɪbl/ *a* orribile. **~y** *adv* spaventosamente

horrid /'hɒrɪd/ *a* orrendo

horrific /hə'rɪfɪk/ *a* raccapricciante; (*fam: accident, prices, story*) terrificante

horrify /'hɒrɪfaɪ/ *vt* (*pt/pp* **-ied**) far inorridire; **I was horrified** ero sconvolto. **~ing** *a* terrificante

horror /'hɒrə(r)/ *n* orrore *m*. **~ film** *n* film *m* dell'orrore

hors-d'œuvre /ɔː'dɜːvr/ *n* antipasto *m*

horse /hɔːs/ *n* cavallo *m*

horse: ~back *n* **on ~back** a cavallo. **~man** *n* cavaliere *m*. **~play** *n* gioco *m* pesante. **~power** *n* cavallo *m* [vapore]. **~-racing** *n* corse *fpl* di cavalli. **~shoe** *n* ferro *m* di cavallo

horti'cultural /hɔːtɪ-/ *a* di orticoltura

'horticulture *n* orticoltura *f*

hose /həʊz/ *n* (*pipe*) manichetta *f* ● **hose down** *vt* lavare con la manichetta

hospice /'hɒspɪs/ *n* (*for the terminally ill*) ospedale *m* per i malati in fase terminale

hospitab|le /hɒ'spɪtəbl/ *a* ospitale. **~y** *adv* con ospitalità

hospital /'hɒspɪtl/ *n* ospedale *m*

hospitality /hɒspɪ'tælətɪ/ *n* ospitalità *f*

host[1] /həʊst/ *n* **a ~ of** una moltitudine di

host[2] *n* ospite *m*

host[3] *n Relig* ostia *f*

hostage /'hɒstɪdʒ/ *n* ostaggio *m*; **hold sb ~** tenere qcno in ostaggio

hostel /'hɒstl/ *n* ostello *m*

hostess /'həʊstɪs/ n padrona f di casa; Aeron hostess f inv

hostile /'hɒstaɪl/ a ostile

hostilit|y /hɒ'stɪlətɪ/ n ostilità f; **~ies** pl ostilità fpl

hot /hɒt/ a (**hotter, hottest**) caldo; (spicy) piccante; **I am** or **feel ~** ho caldo; **it is ~** fa caldo

'hotbed n fig focolaio m

hotchpotch /'hɒtʃpɒtʃ/ n miscuglio m

'hot-dog n hot dog m inv

hotel /həʊ'tel/ n albergo m. **~ier** /-ɪə(r)/ n albergatore, -trice mf

hot: ~head n persona f impetuosa. **~house** n serra f. **~ly** adv fig accanitamente. **~plate** n piastra f riscaldante ~ **tap** n rubinetto m dell'acqua calda. **~-'tempered** a irascibile. **~-'water bottle** n borsa f dell'acqua calda

hound /haʊnd/ n cane m da caccia ● vt fig perseguire

hour /'aʊə(r)/ n ora f. **~ly** a ad ogni ora; (pay, rate) a ora ● adv ogni ora

house¹ /haʊs/ n casa f; Pol camera f; Theat sala f; **at my ~** a casa mia, da me

house² /haʊz/ vt alloggiare (person)

house /haʊs/: **~boat** n casa f galleggiante. **~breaking** n furto m con scasso. **~hold** n casa f, famiglia f. **~holder** n capo m di famiglia. **~keeper** n governante f di casa. **~keeping** n governo m della casa; (money) soldi mpl per le spese di casa. **~plant** n pianta f da appartamento. **~-trained** a che non sporca in casa. **~-warming [party]** n festa f di inaugurazione della nuova casa. **~wife** n casalinga f. **~work** n lavoro m domestico

housing /'haʊzɪŋ/ n alloggio m. **~ estate** n zona f residenziale

hovel /'hɒvl/ n tugurio m

hover /'hɒvə(r)/ vi librarsi; (linger) indugiare. **~craft** n hovercraft m inv

how /haʊ/ adv come; **~ are you?** come stai?; **~ about a coffee/going on holiday?** che ne diresti di un caffè/di andare in vacanza?; **~ do you do?** molto lieto!; **~ old are you?** quanti anni hai?; **~ long** quanto tempo; **~ many** quanti; **~ much** quanto; **~ often** ogni quanto; **and ~!** eccome!; **~ odd!** che strano!

how'ever adv (nevertheless) comunque; **~ small** per quanto piccolo

howl /haʊl/ n ululato m ● vi ululare; (cry, with laughter) singhiozzare. **~er** n fam strafalcione m

HP n abbr **hire purchase**; n abbr (**horse power**) C.V.

hub /hʌb/ n mozzo m; fig centro m

hubbub /'hʌbʌb/ n baccano m

'hub-cap n coprimozzo m

huddle /'hʌdl/ vi **~ together** rannicchiarsi

hue¹ /hju:/ n colore m

hue² n **~ and cry** clamore m

huff /hʌf/ n **be in/go into a ~** fare il broncio

hug /hʌg/ n abbraccio m ● vt (pt/pp hugged) abbracciare; (keep close to) tenersi vicino a

huge /hju:dʒ/ a enorme

hulking /'hʌlkɪŋ/ a fam grosso

hull /hʌl/ n Naut scafo m

hullo /hə'ləʊ/ int = hallo

hum /hʌm/ n ronzio m ● v (pt/pp hummed) ● vt canticchiare ● vi (motor:) ronzare; fig fervere (di attività); **~ and haw** esitare

human /'hju:mən/ a umano ● n essere m umano. **~ 'being** n essere m umano

humane /hju:'meɪn/ a umano

humanitarian /hju:mænɪ'teərɪən/ a & n umanitario, -a mf

humanit|y /hju:'mænətɪ/ n umanità f; **~ies** pl Univ dottrine fpl umanistiche

humbl|e /'hʌmbl/ a umile ● vt umiliare

'humdrum a noioso

humid /'hju:mɪd/ a umido. **~ifier** /-'mɪdɪfaɪə(r)/ n umidificatore m. **~ity** /-'mɪdətɪ/ n umidità f

humiliat|e /hju:'mɪleɪt/ vt umiliare. **~ion** /-'eɪʃn/ n umiliazione f

humility /hju:'mɪlətɪ/ n umiltà f

humorous /'hju:mərəs/ a umoristico. **~ly** adv con spirito

humour /'hju:mə(r)/ n umorismo m; (mood) umore m; **have a sense of ~** avere il senso dell'umorismo ● vt compiacere

hump /hʌmp/ n protuberanza f; (of camel, hunchback) gobba f

hunch /hʌntʃ/ n (idea) intuizione f

'hunch|back n gobbo, -a mf. **~ed** a **~ed up** incurvato

hundred /'hʌndrəd/ a **one/a ~** cento ● n cento m; **~s of** centinaia di. **~th** a centesimo ● n centesimo m. **~weight** n cinquanta chili m

hung /hʌŋ/ see hang

Hungarian /hʌŋ'geərɪən/ a & n ungherese mf; (language) ungherese m

Hungary /'hʌŋgərɪ/ n Ungheria f

hunger /'hʌŋgə(r)/ *n* fame *f*. **~-strike** *n* sciopero *m* della fame *m*

hungr|y /'hʌŋgrɪ/ *a* (**-ier, -iest**) affamato; **be ~y** aver fame. **~ily** *adv* con appetito

hunk /hʌŋk/ *n* [grosso] pezzo *m*

hunt /hʌnt/ *n* caccia *f* ● *vt* andare a caccia di ⟨*animal*⟩; dare la caccia a ⟨*criminal*⟩ ● *vi* andare a caccia; **~ for** cercare. **~er** *n* cacciatore *m*. **~ing** *n* caccia *f*

hurdle /'hɜːdl/ *n* Sport & fig ostacolo *m*. **~r** *n* ostacolista *mf*

hurl /hɜːl/ *vt* scagliare

hurrah /hʊ'rɑː/, **hurray** /hʊ'reɪ/ *int* urrà! ● *n* urrà *m*

hurricane /'hʌrɪkən/ *n* uragano *m*

hurried /'hʌrɪd/ *a* affrettato; ⟨*job*⟩ fatto in fretta. **~ly** *adv* in fretta

hurry /'hʌrɪ/ *n* fretta *f*; **be in a ~** aver fretta ● *vi* (*pt/pp* **-ied**) affrettarsi. **hurry up** *vi* sbrigarsi ● *vt* fare sbrigare ⟨*person*⟩; accelerare ⟨*things*⟩

hurt /hɜːt/ *v* (*pt/pp* **hurt**) ● *vt* far male a; (*offend*) ferire ● *vi* far male; **my leg ~s** mi fa male la gamba. **~ful** *a* fig offensivo

hurtle /'hɜːtl/ *vi* **~ along** andare a tutta velocità

husband /'hʌzbənd/ *n* marito *m*

hush /hʌʃ/ *n* silenzio *m* ● **hush up** *vt* mettere a tacere. **~ed** *a* ⟨*voice*⟩ sommesso. **~-'hush** *a fam* segretissimo

husky /'hʌskɪ/ *a* (**-ier, -iest**) ⟨*voice*⟩ rauco

hustle /'hʌsl/ *vt* affrettare ● *n* attività *f* incessante; **~ and bustle** trambusto *m*

hut /hʌt/ *n* capanna *f*

hybrid /'haɪbrɪd/ *a* ibrido ● *n* ibrido *m*

hydrant /'haɪdrənt/ *n* ⟨*fire*⟩ **~** idrante *m*

hydraulic /haɪ'drɔːlɪk/ *a* idraulico

hydroe'lectric /haɪdrəʊ-/ *a* idroelettrico

hydrofoil /'haɪdrə-/ *n* aliscafo *m*

hydrogen /'haɪdrədʒən/ *n* idrogeno *m*

hyena /haɪ'iːnə/ *n* iena *f*

hygien|e /'haɪdʒiːn/ *n* igiene *m*. **~ic** /haɪ'dʒiːnɪk/ *a* igienico

hymn /hɪm/ *n* inno *m*. **~-book** *n* libro *m* dei canti

hypermarket /'haɪpəmɑːkɪt/ *n* ipermercato *m*

hyphen /'haɪfn/ *n* lineetta *f*. **~ate** *vt* unire con lineetta

hypno|sis /hɪp'nəʊsɪs/ *n* ipnosi *f*. **~tic** /-'nɒtɪk/ *a* ipnotico

hypno|tism /'hɪpnətɪzm/ *n* ipnotismo *m*. **~tist** /-tɪst/ *n* ipnotizzatore, -trice *mf*. **~tize** *vt* ipnotizzare

hypochondriac /haɪpə'kɒndrɪæk/ *a* ipocondriaco ● *n* ipocondriaco, -a *mf*

hypocrisy /hɪ'pɒkrəsɪ/ *n* ipocrisia *f*

hypocrit|e /'hɪpəkrɪt/ *n* ipocrita *mf*. **~ical** /-'krɪtɪkl/ *a* ipocrita

hypodermic /haɪpə'dɜːmɪk/ *a* & *n* [**syringe**] siringa *f* ipodermica

hypothe|sis /haɪ'pɒθəsɪs/ *n* ipotesi *f inv*. **~tical** /-ə'θetɪkl/ *a* ipotetico. **~tically** *adv* in teoria; ⟨*speak*⟩ per ipotesi

hyster|ia /hɪ'stɪərɪə/ *n* isterismo *m*. **~ical** /-'sterɪkl/ *a* isterico. **~ically** *adv* istericamente; **~ically funny** da morir dal ridere. **~ics** /hɪ'sterɪks/ *npl* attacco *m* isterico

I /aɪ/ *pron* io; **I'm tired** sono stanco; **he's going, but I'm not** lui va, ma io no

ice /aɪs/ *n* ghiaccio *m* ● *vt* glassare ⟨*cake*⟩. **ice over/up** *vi* ghiacciarsi

ice: **~ age** *n* era *f* glaciale. **~-axe** *n* piccozza *f* per il ghiaccio. **~-berg** /-bɜːg/ *n* iceberg *m inv*. **~-box** *n Am* frigorifero *m*. **~-'cream** *n* gelato *m*. **~-'cream parlour** *n* gelateria *f*. **~-cube** *n* cubetto *m* di ghiaccio. **~ hockey** *n* hockey *m* su ghiaccio

Iceland /'aɪslənd/ *n* Islanda *f*. **~er** *n* islandese *mf*; **~ic** /-'lændɪk/ *a* & *n* islandese *m*

ice: **~ lolly** *n* ghiacciolo *m*. **~ rink** *n* pista *f* di pattinaggio. **~ skater** pattinatore, -trice *mf* sul ghiaccio. **~ skating** pattinaggio *m* sul ghiaccio

icicle /'aɪsɪkl/ *n* ghiacciolo *m*

icily /'aɪsɪlɪ/ *adv* gelidamente

icing /'aɪsɪŋ/ *n* glassa *f*. **~ sugar** *n* zucchero *m* a velo

icon /'aɪkɒn/ n icona f

icy /'aɪsɪ/ a (**-ier, -iest**) ghiacciato; *fig* gelido

idea /aɪ'dɪə/ n idea f; **I've no ~!** non ne ho idea!

ideal /aɪ'dɪəl/ a ideale ● n ideale m. **~ism** n idealismo m. **~ist** n idealista mf. **~istic** /-'lɪstɪk/ a idealistico. **~ize** vt idealizzare. **~ly** adv idealmente

identical /aɪ'dentɪkl/ a identico

identi|fication /aɪdentɪfɪ'keɪʃn/ n identificazione f; (*proof of identity*) documento m di riconoscimento. **~fy** /aɪ'dentɪfaɪ/ vt (*pt/pp* **-ied**) identificare

identikit® /aɪ'dentɪkɪt/ n identikit m inv

identity /aɪ'dentətɪ/ n identità f inv. **~ card** n carta f d'identità

ideolog|ical /aɪdɪə'lɒdʒɪkl/ a ideologico. **~y** /aɪdɪ'ɒlədʒɪ/ n ideologia f

idiom /'ɪdɪəm/ n idioma f. **~atic** /-'mætɪk/ a idiomatico

idiosyncrasy /ɪdɪə'sɪŋkrəsɪ/ n idiosincrasia f

idiot /'ɪdɪət/ n idiota mf. **~ic** /-'ɒtɪk/ a idiota

idl|e /'aɪd(ə)l/ a (*lazy*) pigro, ozioso; (*empty*) vano; (*machine*) fermo ● vi oziare; (*engine:*) girare a vuoto. **~eness** n ozio m. **~y** adv oziosamente

idol /'aɪdl/ n idolo m. **~ize** /'aɪdəlaɪz/ vt idolatrare

idyllic /ɪ'dɪlɪk/ a idillico

i.e. abbr (**id est**) cioè

if /ɪf/ conj se; **as if** come se

ignite /ɪg'naɪt/ vt dar fuoco a ● vi prender fuoco

ignition /ɪg'nɪʃn/ n Auto accensione f. **~ key** n chiave f d'accensione

ignoramus /ɪgnə'reɪməs/ n ignorante mf

ignoran|ce /'ɪgnərəns/ n ignoranza f. **~t** a (*lacking knowledge*) ignaro; (*rude*) ignorante

ignore /ɪg'nɔ:(r)/ vt ignorare

ill /ɪl/ a ammalato; **feel ~ at ease** sentirsi a disagio ● adv male ● n male m. **~-advised** a avventato. **~-bred** a maleducato

illegal /ɪ'li:gl/ a illegale

illegibl|e /ɪ'ledʒɪbl/ a illeggibile

illegitima|cy /ɪlɪ'dʒɪtɪməsɪ/ n illegittimità f. **~te** /-mət/ a illegittimo

illicit /ɪ'lɪsɪt/ a illecito

illitera|cy /ɪ'lɪtərəsɪ/ n analfabetismo m. **~te** /-rət/ a & n analfabeta mf

illness /'ɪlnɪs/ n malattia f

illogical /ɪ'lɒdʒɪkl/ a illogico

ill-treat /ɪl'tri:t/ vt maltrattare. **~ment** n maltrattamento m

illuminat|e /ɪ'lu:mɪnet/ vt illuminare. **~ing** a chiarificatore. **~ion** /-'neɪʃn/ n illuminazione f

illusion /ɪ'lu:ʒn/ n illusione f; **be under the ~ that** avere l'illusione che

illusory /ɪ'lu:sərɪ/ a illusorio

illustrat|e /'ɪləstreɪt/ vt illustrare. **~ion** /-'streɪʃn/ n illustrazione f. **~or** n illustratore, -trice mf

illustrious /ɪ'lʌstrɪəs/ a illustre

ill 'will n malanimo m

image /'ɪmɪdʒ/ n immagine f; (*exact likeness*) ritratto m

imagin|able /ɪ'mædʒɪnəbl/ a immaginabile. **~ary** /-ərɪ/ a immaginario

imaginat|ion /ɪmædʒɪ'neɪʃn/ n immaginazione f, fantasia f; **it's your ~** è solo una tua idea. **~ive** /ɪ'mædʒɪnətɪv/ a fantasioso. **~ively** adv con fantasia or immaginazione

imagine /ɪ'mædʒɪn/ vt immaginare; (*wrongly*) inventare

im'balance n squilibrio m

imbecile /'ɪmbəsi:l/ n imbecille mf

imbibe /ɪm'baɪb/ vt ingerire

imbue /ɪm'bju:/ vt **~d with** impregnato di

imitat|e /'ɪmɪteɪt/ vt imitare. **~ion** /-'teɪʃn/ n imitazione f. **~or** n imitatore, -trice mf

immaculate /ɪ'mækjʊlət/ a immacolato. **~ly** adv immacolatamente

imma'terial a (*unimportant*) irrilevante

imma'ture a immaturo

immediate /ɪ'mi:dɪət/ a immediato; (*relative*) stretto; **in the ~ vicinity** nelle immediate vicinanze. **~ly** adv immediatamente; **~ly next to** subito accanto a ● conj [non] appena

immemorial /ɪmɪ'mɔ:rɪəl/ a **from time ~** da tempo immemorabile

immense /ɪ'mens/ a immenso

immers|e /ɪ'mɜ:s/ vt immergere; **be ~ed in** fig essere immerso in. **~ion** /-ɜ:ʃn/ n immersione f. **~ion heater** n scaldabagno m elettrico

immigrant /'ɪmɪgrənt/ n immigrante mf

immigrat|e /'ɪmɪgreɪt/ vi immigrare. **~ion** /-'greɪʃn/ n immigrazione f

imminent /'ɪmɪnənt/ a imminente

immobil|e /ɪ'məʊbaɪl/ a immobile. **~ize** /-bɪlaɪz/ vt immobilizzare

immoderate /ɪ'mɒdərət/ a smodato

immodest /ɪ'mɒdɪst/ a immodesto

immoral /ɪ'mɒrəl/ a immorale. **~ity** /ɪmə'rælətɪ/ n immoralità f

immortal /ɪ'mɔːtl/ a immortale. **~ity** /-'tælətɪ/ n immortalità f. **~ize** vt immortalare

immovable /ɪ'muːvəbl/ a fig irremovibile

immune /ɪ'mjuːn/ a immune (**to/from** da). **~ system** n sistema m immunitario

immunity /ɪ'mjuːnətɪ/ n immunità f

immunize /ɪ'mjʊnaɪz/ vt immunizzare

imp /ɪmp/ n diavoletto m

impact /'ɪmpækt/ n impatto m

impair /ɪm'peə(r)/ vt danneggiare

impale /ɪm'peɪl/ vt impalare

impart /ɪm'pɑːt/ vt impartire

im'parti|al a imparziale. **~'ality** n imparzialità f

im'passable a impraticabile

impasse /æm'pɑːs/ n fig impasse f inv

impassioned /ɪm'pæʃnd/ a appassionato

im'passive a impassibile

im'patien|ce n impazienza f. **~t** a impaziente. **~tly** adv impazientemente

impeccabl|e /ɪm'pekəbl/ a impeccabile. **~y** adv in modo impeccabile

impede /ɪm'piːd/ vt impedire

impediment /ɪm'pedɪmənt/ n impedimento m; (in speech) difetto m

impel /ɪm'pel/ vt (pt/pp impelled) costringere; **feel ~led to** sentire l'obbligo di

impending /ɪm'pendɪŋ/ a imminente

impenetrable /ɪm'penɪtrəbl/ a impenetrabile

imperative /ɪm'perətɪv/ a imperativo ● n Gram imperativo m

imper'ceptible a impercettibile

im'perfect a imperfetto; (faulty) difettoso ● n Gram imperfetto m. **~ion** /-'fekʃn/ n imperfezione f

imperial /ɪm'pɪərɪəl/ a imperiale. **~ism** n imperialismo m. **~ist** n imperialista mf

imperious /ɪm'pɪərɪəs/ a imperioso

im'personal a impersonale

impersonat|e /ɪm'pɜːsəneɪt/ vt impersonare. **~or** n imitatore, -trice mf

impertinen|ce /ɪm'pɜːtɪnəns/ n impertinenza f. **~t** a impertinente

imperturbable /ɪmpə'tɜːbəbl/ a imperturbabile

impervious /ɪm'pɜːvɪəs/ a **~ to** fig indifferente a

impetuous /ɪm'petjʊəs/ a impetuoso. **~ly** adv impetuosamente

impetus /'ɪmpɪtəs/ n impeto m

implacable /ɪm'plækəbl/ a implacabile

im'plant[1] vt trapiantare; fig inculcare

'implant[2] n trapianto m

implement[1] /'ɪmplɪmənt/ n attrezzo m

implement[2] /'ɪmplɪment/ vt mettere in atto

implicat|e /'ɪmplɪkeɪt/ vt implicare. **~ion** /-'keɪʃn/ n implicazione f; **by ~ion** implicitamente

implicit /ɪm'plɪsɪt/ a implicito; (absolute) assoluto

implore /ɪm'plɔː(r)/ vt implorare

imply /ɪm'plaɪ/ vt (pt/pp -ied) implicare; **what are you ~ing?** che cosa vorresti insinuare?

impo'lite a sgarbato

import[1] /'ɪmpɔːt/ n Comm importazione f

import[2] /ɪm'pɔːt/ vt importare

importan|ce /ɪm'pɔːtəns/ n importanza f. **~t** a importante

importer /ɪm'pɔːtə(r)/ n importatore, -trice mf

impos|e /ɪm'pəʊz/ vt imporre (**on** a) ● vi imporsi; **~e on** abusare di. **~ing** a imponente. **~ition** /ɪmpə'zɪʃn/ n imposizione f

impossi'bility n impossibilità f

im'possibl|e a impossibile

impostor /ɪm'pɒstə(r)/ n impostore, -trice mf

impoten|ce /'ɪmpətəns/ n impotenza f. **~t** a impotente

impound /ɪm'paʊnd/ vt confiscare

impoverished /ɪm'pɒvərɪʃt/ a impoverito

im'practicable a impraticabile

im'practical a non pratico

impre'cise a impreciso

impregnable /ɪm'pregnəbl/ a imprendibile

impregnate /'ɪmpregneɪt/ vt impregnare (**with** di); Biol fecondare

im'press vt imprimere; fig colpire (positivamente); **~ sth [up]on sb** fare capire qcsa a qcno

impression /ɪm'preʃn/ n impressione f; (imitation) imitazione f. **~able** a (child, mind) influenzabile. **~ism** n impressionismo m. **~ist** n imitatore, -trice mf; (artist) impressionista mf

impressive /ɪm'presɪv/ a imponente

'imprint[1] n impressione f

im'print[2] vt imprimere; **~ed on my mind** impresso nella mia memoria

im'prison vt incarcerare. ~ment n reclusione f

im'probable a improbabile

impromptu /ɪmˈprɒmptjuː/ a improvvisato

im'proper a ⟨use⟩ improprio; ⟨behaviour⟩ scorretto. ~ly adv scorrettamente

impro'priety n scorrettezza f

improve /ɪmˈpruːv/ vt/i migliorare. **improve [up]on** vt perfezionare. ~ment /-mənt/ n miglioramento m

improvis|e /ˈɪmprəvaɪz/ vt/i improvvisare

im'prudent a imprudente

impuden|ce /ˈɪmpjʊdəns/ n sfrontatezza f. ~t a sfrontato

impuls|e /ˈɪmpʌls/ n impulso m; **on [an] ~e** impulsivamente. ~ive /-ˈpʌlsɪv/ a impulsivo

impunity /ɪmˈpjuːnətɪ/ n **with ~** impunemente

im'pur|e a impuro. ~ity n impurità f inv; ~ities pl impurità fpl

impute /ɪmˈpjuːt/ vt imputare (**to** a)

in /ɪn/ prep in; ⟨with names of towns⟩ a; **in the garden** in giardino; **in the street** in or per strada; **in bed/hospital** a letto/all'ospedale; **in the world** nel mondo; **in the rain** sotto la pioggia; **in the sun** al sole; **in this heat** con questo caldo; **in summer/winter** in estate/inverno; **in 1995** nel 1995; **in the evening** la sera; **he's arriving in two hours' time** arriva fra due ore; **deaf in one ear** sordo da un orecchio; **in the army** nell'esercito; **in English/Italian** in inglese/italiano; **in ink/pencil** a penna/matita; **in red** ⟨dressed, circled⟩ di rosso; **the man in the raincoat** l'uomo con l'impermeabile; **in a soft/loud voice** a voce bassa/alta; **one in ten people** una persona su dieci; **in doing this, he...** nel far questo,...; **in itself** in sé; **in that** in quanto ● adv ⟨at home⟩ a casa; ⟨indoors⟩ dentro; **he's not in yet** non è ancora arrivato; **in there/here** li/qui dentro; **ten in all** dieci in tutto; **day in, day out** giorno dopo giorno; **have it in for sb** fam avercela con qcno; **send him in** fallo entrare; **come in** entrare; **bring in the washing** portare dentro i panni ● a ⟨fam: in fashion⟩ di moda ● n **the ins and outs** i dettagli

ina'bility n incapacità f

inac'cessible a inaccessibile

in'accura|cy n inesattezza f. ~te a inesatto

in'ac|tive a inattivo. ~'tivity n inattività f

in'adequate a inadeguato. ~ly adv inadeguatamente

inad'missible a inammissibile

inadvertently /ɪnədˈvɜːtəntlɪ/ adv inavvertitamente

inad'visable a sconsigliabile

inane /ɪˈneɪn/ a stupido

in'animate a esanime

in'applicable a inapplicabile

inap'propriate a inadatto

inar'ticulate a inarticolato

inat'tentive a disattento

in'audibl|e a impercettibile

inaugural /ɪˈnɔːɡjʊrəl/ a inaugurale

inaugurat|e /ɪˈnɔːɡjʊreɪt/ vt inaugurare. ~ion /-ˈreɪʃn/ n inaugurazione f

inau'spicious a infausto

inborn /ˈɪnbɔːn/ a innato

inbred /ɪnˈbred/ a congenito

incalculable /ɪnˈkælkjʊləbl/ a incalcolabile

in'capable a incapace

incapacitate /ɪnkəˈpæsɪteɪt/ vt rendere incapace

incarnat|e /ɪnˈkɑːnət/ a **the devil ~e** il diavolo in carne e ossa

incendiary /ɪnˈsendɪərɪ/ a incendiario

incense[1] /ˈɪnsens/ n incenso m

incense[2] /ɪnˈsens/ vt esasperare

incentive /ɪnˈsentɪv/ n incentivo m

incessant /ɪnˈsesənt/ a incessante

incest /ˈɪnsest/ n incesto m

inch /ɪntʃ/ n pollice m (= 2.54 cm) ● vi ~ **forward** avanzare gradatamente

inciden|ce /ˈɪnsɪdəns/ n incidenza f. ~t n incidente m

incidental /ɪnsɪˈdentl/ a incidentale; ~ **expenses** spese fpl accessorie. ~ly adv incidentalmente; ⟨by the way⟩ a proposito

incinerat|e /ɪnˈsɪnəreɪt/ vt incenerire. ~or n inceneritore m

incision /ɪnˈsɪʒn/ n incisione f

incisive /ɪnˈsaɪsɪv/ a incisivo

incisor /ɪnˈsaɪzə(r)/ n incisivo m

incite /ɪnˈsaɪt/ vt incitare. ~ment n incitamento m

inclination /ɪnklɪˈneɪʃn/ n inclinazione f

incline[1] /ɪnˈklaɪn/ vt inclinare; **be ~d to do sth** essere propenso a fare qcsa

incline[2] /ˈɪnklaɪn/ n pendio m

inclu|de /ɪnˈkluːd/ vt includere. ~ding prep incluso. ~sion /-ˈuːʒn/ n inclusione f

inclusive /ɪnˈkluːsɪv/ a incluso; ~ **of** comprendente; **be ~ of** comprendere ● adv incluso

incognito /ɪnkɒgˈniːtəʊ/ adv incognito

inco'herent a incoerente; (because drunk etc) incomprensibile

income /ˈɪnkʌm/ n reddito m. ~ **tax** n imposta f sul reddito

'incoming a in arrivo. ~ **tide** n marea f montante

in'comparable a incomparabile

incompati'bility n incompatibilità f

incom'patible a incompatibile

in'competen|ce n incompetenza f. ~**t** a incompetente

incom'plete a incompleto

incompre'hensible a incomprensibile

incon'ceivable a inconcepibile

incon'clusive a inconcludente

incongruous /ɪnˈkɒŋgruəs/ a contrastante

inconsequential /ɪnkɒnsɪˈkwenʃl/ a senza importanza

incon'siderate a trascurabile

incon'sistency n incoerenza f

incon'sistent a incoerente; **be ~ with** non essere coerente con. ~**ly** adv in modo incoerente

inconsolable /ɪnkənˈsəʊləbl/ a inconsolabile

incon'spicuous a non appariscente. ~**ly** adv modestamente

incontinen|ce /ɪnˈkɒntɪnəns/ n incontinenza f. ~**t** a incontinente

incon'venien|ce n scomodità f; (drawback) inconveniente m; **put sb to ~ce** dare disturbo a qcno. ~**t** a scomodo; (time, place) inopportuno. ~**tly** adv in modo inopportuno

incorporate /ɪnˈkɔːpəreɪt/ vt incorporare; (contain) comprendere

incor'rect a incorretto. ~**ly** adv scorrettamente

incorrigible /ɪnˈkɒrɪdʒəbl/ a incorreggibile

incorruptible /ɪnkəˈrʌptəbl/ a incorruttibile

increase[1] /ˈɪnkriːs/ n aumento m; **on the ~** in aumento

increase[2] /ɪnˈkriːs/ vt/i aumentare. ~**ing** a (impatience etc) crescente; (numbers) in aumento. ~**ingly** adv sempre più

in'credible a incredibile

incredulous /ɪnˈkredjʊləs/ a incredulo

increment /ˈɪnkrɪmənt/ n incremento m

incriminate /ɪnˈkrɪmɪneɪt/ vt Jur incriminare

incubat|e /ˈɪnkjubeɪt/ vt incubare. ~**ion** /-ˈbeɪʃn/ n incubazione f. ~**ion period** n Med periodo m di incubazione. ~**or** n (for baby) incubatrice f

incumbent /ɪnˈkʌmbənt/ a **be ~ on sb** incombere a qcno

incur /ɪnˈkɜː(r)/ vt (pt/pp incurred) incorrere; contrarre (debts)

in'curable a incurabile

incursion /ɪnˈkɜːʃn/ n incursione f

indebted /ɪnˈdetɪd/ a obbligato (**to** verso)

in'decent a indecente

inde'cision n indecisione f

inde'cisive a indeciso. ~**ness** n indecisione f

indeed /ɪnˈdiːd/ adv (in fact) difatti; **yes ~!** sì, certamente!; ~ **I am/do** veramente!; **very much ~** moltissimo; **thank you very much ~** grazie infinite; ~**?** davvero?

indefatigable /ɪndɪˈfætɪgəbl/ a instancabile

inde'finable a indefinibile

in'definite a indefinito. ~**ly** adv indefinitamente; (postpone) a tempo indeterminato

indelible /ɪnˈdelɪbl/ a indelebile

indemnity /ɪnˈdemnɪtɪ/ n indennità f inv

indent[1] /ˈɪndent/ n Typ rientranza f dal margine

indent[2] /ɪnˈdent/ vt Typ fare rientrare dal margine. ~**ation** /-ˈteɪʃn/ n (notch) intaccatura f

inde'penden|ce n indipendenza f. ~**t** a indipendente. ~**tly** adv indipendentemente

indescribable /ɪndɪˈskraɪbəbl/ a indescrivibile

indestructible /ɪndɪˈstrʌktəbl/ a indistruttibile

indeterminate /ɪndɪˈtɜːmɪnət/ a indeterminato

index /ˈɪndeks/ n indice m

index: ~ **card** n scheda f. ~ **finger** n dito m indice. ~**-'linked** a (pension) legato al costo della vita

India /ˈɪndɪə/ n India f. ~**n** a indiano; (American) indiano [d'America] ● n indiano, -a m/f; (American) indiano, -a m/f [d'America], pellerossa m/f inv

indicat|e /ˈɪndɪkeɪt/ vt indicare;

(*register*) segnare ● *vi Auto* mettere la freccia. **~ion** /-'keɪʃn/ *n* indicazione *f*

indicative /ɪn'dɪkətɪv/ *a* be **~ of** essere indicativo di ● *n Gram* indicativo *m*

indicator /'ɪndɪkeɪtə(r)/ *n Auto* freccia *f*

indict /ɪn'daɪt/ *vt* accusare. **~ment** *n* accusa *f*

in'differen|ce *n* indifferenza *f*. **~t** *a* indifferente; (*not good*) mediocre

indigenous /ɪn'dɪdʒɪnəs/ *a* indigeno

indi'gest|ible *a* indigesto. **~ion** *n* indigestione *f*

indigna|nt /ɪn'dɪgnənt/ *a* indignato. **~ntly** *adv* con indignazione. **~tion** /-'neɪʃn/ *n* indignazione *f*

in'dignity *n* umiliazione *f*

indi'rect *a* indiretto. **~ly** *adv* indirettamente

indi'screet *a* indiscreto

indis'cretion *n* indiscrezione *f*

indiscriminate /ɪndɪ'skrɪmɪnət/ *a* indiscriminato. **~ly** *adv* senza distinzione

indi'spensable *a* indispensabile

indisposed /ɪndɪ'spəʊzd/ *a* indisposto

indisputable /ɪndɪ'spjuːtəbl/ *a* indisputabile

indi'stinct *a* indistinto

indistinguishable /ɪndɪ'stɪŋgwɪʃəbl/ *a* indistinguibile

individual /ɪndɪ'vɪdʒʊəl/ *a* individuale ● *n* individuo *m*. **~ity** /-'ælətɪ/ *n* individualità *f*

indi'visible *a* indivisibile

indoctrinate /ɪn'dɒktrɪneɪt/ *vt* indottrinare

indomitable /ɪn'dɒmɪtəbl/ *a* indomito

indoor /'ɪndɔː(r)/ *a* interno; (*shoes*) per casa; (*plant*) da appartamento; (*swimming pool etc*) coperto. **~s** /-'dɔːz/ *adv* dentro

induce /ɪn'djuːs/ *vt* indurre (**to** a); (*produce*) causare. **~ment** *n* (*incentive*) incentivo *m*

indulge /ɪn'dʌldʒ/ *vt* soddisfare; viziare (*child*) ● *vi* **~ in** concedersi. **~nce** /-əns/ *n* lusso *m*; (*leniency*) indulgenza *f*. **~nt** *a* indulgente

industrial /ɪn'dʌstrɪəl/ *a* industriale; **take ~ action** scioperare. **~ist** *n* industriale *mf*. **~ized** *a* industrializzato

industri|ous /ɪn'dʌstrɪəs/ *a* industrioso. **~y** /'ɪndəstrɪ/ *n* industria *f*; (*zeal*) operosità *f*

inebriated /ɪ'niːbrɪeɪtɪd/ *a* ebbro

in'edible *a* immangiabile

ineffective *a* inefficace

ineffectual /ɪnɪ'fektʃʊəl/ *a* inutile; (*person*) inconcludente

ineffic|iency *n* inefficienza *f*. **~t** *a* inefficiente

in'eligible *a* inadatto

inept /ɪ'nept/ *a* inetto

ine'quality *n* ineguaglianza *f*

inert /ɪ'nɜːt/ *a* inerte. **~ia** /ɪ'nɜːʃə/ *n* inerzia *f*

inescapable /ɪnɪ'skeɪpəbl/ *a* inevitabile

inestimable /ɪn'estɪməbl/ *a* inestimabile

inevitabl|e /ɪn'evɪtəbl/ *a* inevitabile. **~y** *adv* inevitabilmente

ine'xact *a* inesatto

inex'cusable *a* imperdonabile

inexhaustible /ɪnɪg'zɔːstəbl/ *a* inesauribile

inexorable /ɪn'eksərəbl/ *a* inesorabile

inex'pensive *a* poco costoso

inex'perience *n* inesperienza *f*. **~d** *a* inesperto

inexplicable /ɪnɪk'splɪkəbl/ *a* inesplicabile

in'fallible *a* infallibile

infam|ous /'ɪnfəməs/ *a* infame; (*person*) famigerato. **~y** *n* infamia *f*

infan|cy /'ɪnfənsɪ/ *n* infanzia *f*; **in its ~cy** *fig* agli inizi. **~t** *n* bambino, -a *mf* piccolo, -a. **~tile** *a* infantile

infantry /'ɪnfəntrɪ/ *n* fanteria *f*

infatuat|ed /ɪn'fætʃʊeɪtɪd/ *a* infatuato (**with** di). **~ion** *n* infatuazione *f*

infect /ɪn'fekt/ *vt* infettare; **become ~ed** (*wound:*) infettarsi. **~ion** /-'fekʃn/ *n* infezione *f*. **~ious** /-'fekʃəs/ *a* infettivo

infer /ɪn'fɜː(r)/ *vt* (*pt/pp* **inferred**) dedurre (**from** da); (*imply*) implicare. **~ence** /'ɪnfərəns/ *n* deduzione *f*

inferior /ɪn'fɪərɪə(r)/ *a* inferiore; (*goods*) scadente; (*in rank*) subalterno ● *n* inferiore *mf*; (*in rank*) subalterno, -a *mf*

inferiority /ɪnfɪərɪ'ɒrətɪ/ *n* inferiorità *f*. **~ complex** *n* complesso *m* di inferiorità

infern|al /ɪn'fɜːnl/ *a* infernale. **~o** *n* inferno *m*

in'fer|tile *a* sterile. **~'tility** *n* sterilità *f*

infest /ɪn'fest/ *vt* be **~ed with** essere infestato di

infi'delity *n* infedeltà *f*

infighting /'ɪnfaɪtɪŋ/ *n fig* lotta *f* per il potere

infiltrate /'ɪnfɪltreɪt/ *vt* infiltrare; *Pol* infiltrarsi in

infinite /'ɪnfɪnət/ *a* infinito

infinitive /ɪnˈfɪnətɪv/ n Gram infinito m

infinity /ɪnˈfɪnətɪ/ n infinità f

infirm /ɪnˈfɜːm/ a debole. **~ary** n infermeria f. **~ity** n debolezza f

inflame /ɪnˈfleɪm/ vt infiammare. **~d** a infiammato; **become ~d** infiammarsi

in'flammable a infiammabile

inflammation /ɪnfləˈmeɪʃn/ n infiammazione f

inflammatory /ɪnˈflæmətrɪ/ a incendiario

inflatable /ɪnˈfleɪtəbl/ a gonfiabile

inflat|e /ɪnˈfleɪt/ vt gonfiare. **~ion** /-eɪʃn/ n inflazione f. **~ionary** /-eɪʃənərɪ/ a inflazionario

in'flexible a inflessibile

inflexion /ɪnˈflekʃn/ n inflessione f

inflict /ɪnˈflɪkt/ vt infliggere (**on** a)

influen|ce /ˈɪnflʊəns/ n influenza f
● vt influenzare. **~tial** /-ˈenʃl/ a influente

influenza /ɪnflʊˈenzə/ n influenza f

influx /ˈɪnflʌks/ n affluenza f

inform /ɪnˈfɔːm/ vt informare; **keep sb ~ed** tenere qcno al corrente ● vi **~ against** denunziare

in'for|mal a informale; ⟨agreement⟩ ufficioso. **~mally** adv in modo informale. **~'mality** n informalità f inv

informant /ɪnˈfɔːmənt/ n informatore, -trice mf

informat|ion /ɪnfəˈmeɪʃn/ n informazioni fpl; **a piece of ~ion** un'informazione. **~ion highway** n autostrada f telematica. **~ion technology** n informatica f. **~ive** /ɪnˈfɔːmətɪv/ a informativo; ⟨film, book⟩ istruttivo

informer /ɪnˈfɔːmə(r)/ n informatore, -trice mf; Pol delatore, -trice mf

infra-'red /ɪnfrə-/ a infrarosso

infrastructure /ˈɪnfrəstrʌktʃə(r)/ n infrastruttura f

infringe /ɪnˈfrɪndʒ/ vt **~ on** usurpare. **~ment** n violazione f

infuriat|e /ɪnˈfjʊərɪeɪt/ vt infuriare. **~ing** a esasperante

infusion /ɪnˈfjuːʒn/ n ⟨drink⟩ infusione f; ⟨of capital, new blood⟩ afflusso m

ingenious /ɪnˈdʒiːnɪəs/ a ingegnoso

ingenuity /ɪndʒɪˈnjuːətɪ/ n ingegnosità f

ingenuous /ɪnˈdʒenjʊəs/ a ingenuo

ingot /ˈɪŋɡət/ n lingotto m

ingrained /ɪnˈɡreɪnd/ a (in person) radicato; ⟨dirt⟩ incrostato

ingratiate /ɪnˈɡreɪʃɪeɪt/ vt **~ oneself with sb** ingraziarsi qcno

in'gratitude n ingratitudine f

ingredient /ɪnˈɡriːdɪənt/ n ingrediente m

ingrowing /ˈɪnɡrəʊɪŋ/ a ⟨nail⟩ incarnito

inhabit /ɪnˈhæbɪt/ vt abitare. **~ant** n abitante mf

inhale /ɪnˈheɪl/ vt aspirare; Med inalare ● vi inspirare; (when smoking) aspirare. **~r** n (device) inalatore m

inherent /ɪnˈhɪərənt/ a inerente

inherit /ɪnˈherɪt/ vt ereditare. **~ance** /-əns/ n eredità f inv

inhibit /ɪnˈhɪbɪt/ vt inibire. **~ed** a inibito. **~ion** /-ˈbɪʃn/ n inibizione f

inho'spitable a inospitale

in'human a disumano

initial /ɪˈnɪʃl/ a iniziale ● n iniziale f ● vt (pt/pp **initialled**) siglare. **~ly** adv all'inizio

initiat|e /ɪˈnɪʃɪeɪt/ vt iniziare. **~ion** /-ˈeɪʃn/ n iniziazione f

initiative /ɪˈnɪʃətɪv/ n iniziativa f

inject /ɪnˈdʒekt/ vt iniettare. **~ion** /-ekʃn/ n iniezione f

injur|e /ˈɪndʒə(r)/ vt ferire; (wrong) nuocere. **~y** n ferita f; (wrong) torto m

in'justice n ingiustizia f; **do sb an ~** giudicare qcno in modo sbagliato

ink /ɪŋk/ n inchiostro m

inkling /ˈɪŋklɪŋ/ n sentore m

inlaid /ɪnˈleɪd/ a intarsiato

inland /ˈɪnlənd/ a interno ● adv all'interno. **I~ Revenue** n fisco m

in-laws /ˈɪnlɔːz/ npl fam parenti mpl acquisiti

inlay /ˈɪnleɪ/ n intarsio m

inlet /ˈɪnlet/ n insenatura f; Techn entrata f

inmate /ˈɪnmeɪt/ n (of hospital) degente mf; (of prison) carcerato, -a mf

inn /ɪn/ n locanda f

innate /ɪˈneɪt/ a innato

inner /ˈɪnə(r)/ a interno. **~most** a il più profondo. **~ tube** n camera f d'aria

'innkeeper n locandiere, -a mf

innocen|ce /ˈɪnəsəns/ n innocenza f. **~t** a innocente

innocuous /ɪˈnɒkjʊəs/ a innocuo

innovat|e /ˈɪnəveɪt/ vi innovare. **~ion** /-ˈveɪʃn/ n innovazione f. **~ive** /ˈɪnəvətɪv/ a innovativo. **~or** /ˈɪnəveɪtə(r)/ n innovatore, -trice mf

innuendo /ɪnjʊˈendəʊ/ n (pl **-es**) insinuazione f

innumerable /ɪˈnjuːmərəbl/ a innumerevole

inoculat|e /ɪˈnɒkjʊleɪt/ vt vaccinare. **~ion** /-ˈleɪʃn/ n vaccinazione f

inof'fensive a inoffensivo

in'operable a inoperabile

in'opportune a inopportuno

inordinate /ɪˈnɔːdɪnət/ a smodato

inor'ganic a inorganico

'in-patient n degente mf

input /ˈɪnpʊt/ n input m inv, ingresso m

inquest /ˈɪnkwest/ n inchiesta f

inquir|e /ɪnˈkwaɪə(r)/ vi informarsi (about su); **~e into** far indagini su ● vt domandare. **~y** n domanda f; (investigation) inchiesta f

inquisitive /ɪnˈkwɪzətɪv/ a curioso

inroad /ˈɪnrəʊd/ n **make ~s into** intaccare (savings); cominciare a risolvere (problem)

in'sane a pazzo; fig insensato

in'sanitary a malsano

in'sanity n pazzia f

insatiable /ɪnˈseɪʃəbl/ a insaziabile

inscri|be /ɪnˈskraɪb/ vt iscrivere. **~ption** /-ˈskrɪpʃn/ n iscrizione f

inscrutable /ɪnˈskruːtəbl/ a impenetrabile

insect /ˈɪnsekt/ n insetto m. **~icide** /-ˈsektɪsaɪd/ n insetticida m

inse'cur|e a malsicuro; (fig: person) insicuro. **~ity** n mancanza f di sicurezza

insemination /ɪnsemɪˈneɪʃn/ n inseminazione f

in'sensitive a insensibile

in'separable a inseparabile

insert[1] /ˈɪnsɜːt/ n inserto m

insert[2] /ɪnˈsɜːt/ vt inserire. **~ion** /-ɜːʃn/ n inserzione f

inside /ɪnˈsaɪd/ n interno m. **~s** npl fam pancia f ● attrib Aut **~ lane** n corsia f interna ● adv dentro; **~ out** a rovescio; (thoroughly) a fondo ● prep dentro; (of time) entro

insidious /ɪnˈsɪdɪəs/ a insidioso

insight /ˈɪnsaɪt/ n intuito m (into per); **an ~ into** un quadro di

insignia /ɪnˈsɪgnɪə/ npl insegne fpl

insig'nificant a insignificante

insin'cer|e a poco sincero. **~ity** /-ˈserɪtɪ/ n mancanza f di sincerità

insinuat|e /ɪnˈsɪnjʊeɪt/ vt insinuare. **~ion** /-ˈeɪʃn/ n insinuazione f

insipid /ɪnˈsɪpɪd/ a insipido

insist /ɪnˈsɪst/ vi insistere (on per) ● vt **~ that** insistere che. **~ence** n insistenza f. **~ent** a insistente

'insole n soletta f

insolen|ce /ˈɪnsələns/ n insolenza f. **~t** a insolente

in'soluble a insolubile

in'solven|cy n insolvenza f. **~t** a insolvente

insomnia /ɪnˈsɒmnɪə/ n insonnia f

inspect /ɪnˈspekt/ vt ispezionare; controllare (ticket). **~ion** /-ekʃn/ n ispezione f; (of ticket) controllo m. **~or** n ispettore, -trice mf; (of tickets) controllore m

inspiration /ɪnspəˈreɪʃn/ n ispirazione f

inspire /ɪnˈspaɪə(r)/ vt ispirare

insta'bility n instabilità f

install /ɪnˈstɔːl/ vt installare. **~ation** /-stəˈleɪʃn/ n installazione f

instalment /ɪnˈstɔːlmənt/ n Comm rata f; (of serial) puntata f; (of publication) fascicolo m

instance /ˈɪnstəns/ n (case) caso m; (example) esempio m; **in the first ~** in primo luogo; **for ~** per esempio

instant /ˈɪnstənt/ a immediato; Culin espresso ● n istante m. **~aneous** /-ˈteɪnɪəs/ a istantaneo

instant 'coffee n caffè m inv solubile

instantly /ˈɪnstəntlɪ/ adv immediatamente

instead /ɪnˈsted/ adv invece; **~ of doing** anziché fare; **~ of me** al mio posto; **~ of going** invece di andare

'instep n collo m del piede

instigat|e /ˈɪnstɪgeɪt/ vt istigare. **~ion** /-ˈgeɪʃn/ n istigazione f; **at his ~ion** dietro suo suggerimento. **~or** n istigatore, -trice mf

instil /ɪnˈstɪl/ vt (pt/pp instilled) inculcare (into in)

instinct /ˈɪnstɪŋkt/ n istinto m. **~ive** /ɪnˈstɪŋktɪv/ a istintivo

institut|e /ˈɪnstɪtjuːt/ n istituto m ● vt istituire (scheme); iniziare (search); intentare (legal action). **~ion** /-ˈtjuːʃn/ n istituzione f; (home for elderly) istituto m per anziani; (for mentally ill) istituto m per malati di mente

instruct /ɪnˈstrʌkt/ vt istruire; (order) ordinare. **~ion** /-ʌkʃn/ n istruzione f; **~s** (pl: orders) ordini mpl. **~ive** /-ɪv/ a istruttivo. **~or** n istruttore, -trice mf

instrument /ˈɪnstrʊmənt/ n strumento m. **~al** /-ˈmentl/ a strumentale; **be ~al in** contribuire a. **~alist** n strumentista mf

insu'bordi|nate a insubordinato. **~nation** /-ˈneɪʃn/ n insubordinazione f

in'sufferable a insopportabile

insuf'ficient a insufficiente

insular /ˈɪnsjʊlə(r)/ a fig gretto

insulat|e /ˈɪnsjʊleɪt/ vt isolare. **~ing**

tape *n* nastro *m* isolante. **~ion** /-'leɪʃn/ *n* isolamento *m*

insulin /'ɪnsjʊlɪn/ *n* insulina *f*

insult[1] /'ɪnsʌlt/ *n* insulto *m*

insult[2] *my* /ɪnsʌlt/ *vt* insultare

insuperable /ɪn'suːpərəbl/ *a* insuperabile

insur|ance /ɪn'ʃʊərəns/ *n* assicurazione *f*. **~e** *vt* assicurare

insurrection /ɪnsə'rekʃn/ *n* insurrezione *f*

intact /ɪn'tækt/ *a* intatto

'intake *n* immissione *f*; (*of food*) consumo *m*

in'tangible *a* intangibile

integral /'ɪntɪɡrəl/ *a* integrale

integrat|e /'ɪntɪɡreɪt/ *vt* integrare ● *vi* integrarsi. **~ion** /-'ɡreɪʃn/ *n* integrazione *f*

integrity /ɪn'teɡrətɪ/ *n* integrità *f*

intellect /'ɪntəlekt/ *n* intelletto *m*. **~ual** /-'lektjʊəl/ *a* & *n* intellettuale *mf*

intelligen|ce /ɪn'telɪdʒəns/ *n* intelligenza *f*; *Mil* informazioni *fpl*. **~t** *a* intelligente

intelligentsia /ɪntelɪ'dʒentsɪə/ *n* intellighenzia *f*

intelligible /ɪn'telɪdʒəbl/ *a* intelligibile

intend /ɪn'tend/ *vt* destinare; (*have in mind*) aver intenzione di; **be ~ed for** essere destinato a. **~ed** *a* (*effect*) voluto ● *n* **my ~ed** *fam* il mio/la mia fidanzato, -a

intense /ɪn'tens/ *a* intenso; (*person*) dai sentimenti intensi. **~ly** *adv* intensamente; (*very*) estremamente

intensi|fication /ɪntensɪfɪ'keɪʃn/ *n* intensificazione *f*. **~fy** /-'tensɪfaɪ/ *v* (*pt/pp* **-ied**) ● *vt* intensificare ● *vi* intensificarsi

intensity /ɪn'tensətɪ/ *n* intensità *f*

intensive /ɪn'tensɪv/ *a* intensivo. **~ care** (*for people in coma*) rianimazione *f*; **~ care** [**unit**] terapia *f* intensiva

intent /ɪn'tent/ *a* intento; **~ on** (*absorbed in*) preso da; **be ~ on doing sth** essere intento a fare qcsa ● *n* intenzione *f*; **to all ~s and purposes** a tutti gli effetti. **~ly** *adv* attentamente

intention /ɪn'tenʃn/ *n* intenzione *f*. **~al** *a* intenzionale. **~ally** *adv* intenzionalmente

inter'acti|on *n* cooperazione *f*. **~ve** *a* interattivo

intercede /ɪntə'siːd/ *vi* intercedere (**on behalf of** a favore di)

intercept /ɪntə'sept/ *vt* intercettare

'interchange *n* scambio *m*; *Auto* raccordo *m* [autostradale]

inter'changeable *a* interscambiabile

intercom /'ɪntəkɒm/ *n* citofono *m*

'intercourse *n* (*sexual*) rapporti *mpl* [sessuali]

interest /'ɪntrəst/ *n* interesse *m*; **have an ~ in** *Comm* essere cointeressato in; **be of ~** essere interessante; **~ rate** *n* tasso *m* di interesse ● *vt* interessare. **~ed** *a* interessato. **~ing** *a* interessante

interface /'ɪntəfeɪs/ *n* interfaccia *f* ● *vt* interfacciare ● *vi* interfacciarsi

interfere /ɪntə'fɪə(r)/ *vi* interferire; **~ with** interferire con. **~nce** /-əns/ *n* interferenza *f*

interim /'ɪntərɪm/ *a* temporaneo; **~ payment** acconto *m* ● *n* **in the ~** nel frattempo

interior /ɪn'tɪərɪə(r)/ *a* interiore ● *n* interno *m*. **~ designer** *n* arredatore, -trice *mf*

interject /ɪntə'dʒekt/ *vt* intervenire. **~ion** /-ekʃn/ *n* *Gram* interiezione *f*; (*remark*) intervento *m*

interloper /'ɪntələʊpə(r)/ *n* intruso, -a *mf*

interlude /'ɪntəluːd/ *n* intervallo *m*

inter'marry *vi* sposarsi tra parenti; (*different groups:*) contrarre matrimoni misti

intermediary /ɪntə'miːdɪərɪ/ *n* intermediario, -a *mf*

intermediate /ɪntə'miːdɪət/ *a* intermedio

interminable /ɪn'tɜːmɪnəbl/ *a* interminabile

intermission /ɪntə'mɪʃn/ *n* intervallo *m*

intermittent /ɪntə'mɪtənt/ *a* intermittente

intern /ɪn'tɜːn/ *vt* internare

internal /ɪn'tɜːnl/ *a* interno. **~ly** *adv* internamente; (*deal with*) all'interno

inter'national *a* internazionale ● *n* (*game*) incontro *m* internazionale; (*player*) competitore, -trice *mf* in gare internazionali. **~ly** *adv* internazionalmente

Internet /'ɪntənet/ *n* Internet *m*

internist /ɪn'tɜːnɪst/ *n* *Am* internista *mf*

internment /ɪn'tɜːnmənt/ *n* internamento *m*

'interplay *n* azione *f* reciproca

interpret /ɪn'tɜːprɪt/ *vt* interpretare

● *vi* fare l'interprete. **~ation** /-'teɪʃn/ *n* interpretazione *f*. **~er** *n* interprete *mf*

interre'lated *a* (*facts*) in correlazione

interrogat|e /ɪn'terəgeɪt/ *vt* interrogare. **~ion** /-'geɪʃn/ *n* interrogazione *f*; (*by police*) interrogatorio *m*

interrogative /ɪntə'rɒgətɪv/ *a* & *n* ~ [**pronoun**] interrogativo *m*

interrupt /ɪntə'rʌpt/ *vt/i* interrompere. **~ion** /-ʌpʃn/ *n* interruzione *f*

intersect /ɪntə'sekt/ *vi* intersecarsi ● *vt* intersecare. **~ion** /-ekʃn/ *n* intersezione *f*; (*of street*) incrocio *m*

interspersed /ɪntə'spɜːst/ *a* ~ **with** inframmezzato di

inter'twine *vi* attorcigliarsi

interval /'ɪntəvl/ *n* intervallo *m*; **bright ~s** *pl* schiarite *fpl*

interven|e /ɪntə'viːn/ *vi* intervenire. **~tion** /-'venʃn/ *n* intervento *m*

interview /'ɪntəvjuː/ *n Journ* intervista *f*; (*for job*) colloquio *m* [di lavoro] ● *vt* intervistare. **~er** *n* intervistatore, -trice *mf*

intestin|e /ɪn'testɪn/ *n* intestino *m*. **~al** *a* intestinale

intimacy /'ɪntɪməsɪ/ *n* intimità *f*

intimate¹ /'ɪntɪmət/ *a* intimo. **~ly** *adv* intimamente

intimate² /'ɪntɪmeɪt/ *vt* far capire; (*imply*) suggerire

intimidat|e /ɪn'tɪmɪdeɪt/ *vt* intimidire. **~ion** /-'deɪʃn/ *n* intimidazione *f*

into /'ɪntə/, *di fronte a una vocale* /'ɪntʊ/ *prep* dentro, in; **go ~ the house** andare dentro [casa] *o* in casa; **be ~** (*fam: like*) essere appassionato di; **I'm not ~ that** questo non mi piace; **7 ~ 21 goes 3** il 7 nel 21 ci sta 3 volte; **translate ~ French** tradurre in francese; **get ~ trouble** mettersi nei guai

in'tolerable *a* intollerabile

in'toleran|ce *n* intolleranza *f*. **~t** *a* intollerante

intonation /ɪntə'neɪʃn/ *n* intonazione *f*

intoxicat|ed /ɪn'tɒksɪkeɪtɪd/ *a* inebriato. **~ion** /-'keɪʃn/ *n* ebbrezza *f*

intractable /ɪn'træktəbl/ *a* intrattabile; (*problem*) insolubile

intransigent /ɪn'trænzɪdʒənt/ *a* intransigente

in'transitive *a* intransitivo

intravenous /ɪntrə'viːnəs/ *a* endovenoso. **~ly** *adv* per via endovenosa

intrepid /ɪn'trepɪd/ *a* intrepido

intricate /'ɪntrɪkət/ *a* complesso

intrigu|e /ɪn'triːg/ *n* intrigo *m* ● *vt* intrigare ● *vi* tramare. **~ing** *a* intrigante

intrinsic /ɪn'trɪnsɪk/ *a* intrinseco

introduce /ɪntrə'djuːs/ *vt* presentare; (*bring in, insert*) introdurre

introduct|ion /ɪntrə'dʌkʃn/ *n* introduzione *f*; (*to person*) presentazione *f*; (*to book*) prefazione *f*. **~ory** /-tərɪ/ *a* introduttivo

introspective /ɪntrə'spektɪv/ *a* introspettivo

introvert /'ɪntrəvɜːt/ *n* introverso, -a *mf*

intru|de /ɪn'truːd/ *vi* intromettersi. **~der** *n* intruso, -a *mf*. **~sion** /-'uːʒn/ *n* intrusione *f*

intuit|ion /ɪntjʊ'ɪʃn/ *n* intuito *m*. **~ive** /-'tjuːɪtɪv/ *a* intuitivo

inundate /'ɪnəndeɪt/ *vt fig* inondare (**with** di)

invade /ɪn'veɪd/ *vt* invadere. **~r** *n* invasore *m*

invalid¹ /'ɪnvəlɪd/ *n* invalido, -a *mf*

invalid² /ɪn'vælɪd/ *a* non valido. **~ate** *vt* invalidare

in'valuable *a* prezioso; (*priceless*) inestimabile

in'variabl|e *a* invariabile. **~y** *adv* invariabilmente

invasion /ɪn'veɪʒn/ *n* invasione *f*

invective /ɪn'vektɪv/ *n* invettiva *f*

invent /ɪn'vent/ *vt* inventare. **~ion** /-enʃn/ *n* invenzione *f*. **~ive** /-tɪv/ *a* inventivo. **~or** *n* inventore, -trice *mf*

inventory /'ɪnəntrɪ/ *n* inventario *m*

inverse /ɪn'vɜːs/ *a* inverso ● *n* inverso *m*

invert /ɪn'vɜːt/ *vt* invertire; **in ~ed commas** tra virgolette

invest /ɪn'vest/ *vt* investire ● *vi* fare investimenti; **~ in** (*fam: buy*) comprarsi

investigat|e /ɪn'vestɪgeɪt/ *vt* investigare. **~ion** /-'geɪʃn/ *n* investigazione *f*

invest|ment /ɪn'vestmənt/ *n* investimento *m*. **~or** *n* investitore, -trice *mf*

inveterate /ɪn'vetərət/ *a* inveterato

invidious /ɪn'vɪdɪəs/ *a* ingiusto; ⟨*position*⟩ antipatico

invigilat|e /ɪn'vɪdʒɪleɪt/ *vi Sch* sorvegliare lo svolgimento di un esame. **~or** *n* persona *f* che sorveglia lo svolgimento di un esame

invigorate /ɪn'vɪgəreɪt/ *vt* rinvigorire

invigorating /ɪn'vɪgəreɪtɪŋ/ *a* tonificante

invincible /ɪn'vɪnsəbl/ *a* invincibile

inviolable /ɪn'vaɪələbl/ *a* inviolabile

in'visible *a* invisibile

invitation /ɪnvɪ'teɪʃn/ *n* invito *m*

invit|e /ɪn'vaɪt/ *vt* invitare; (*attract*) attirare. **~ing** *a* invitante

invoice /'ɪnvɔɪs/ n fattura f ● vt ~ **sb** emettere una fattura a qcno

invoke /ɪn'vəʊk/ vt invocare

in'voluntar|y a involontario

involve /ɪn'vɒlv/ vt comportare; ⟨affect, include⟩ coinvolgere; ⟨entail⟩ implicare; **get ~d with sb** legarsi a qcno; ⟨romantically⟩ legarsi sentimentalmente a qcno. ~**d** a complesso. ~**ment** n coinvolgimento m

in'vulnerable a invulnerabile; ⟨position⟩ inattaccabile

inward /'ɪnwəd/ a interno; ⟨thoughts etc⟩ interiore; ~ **investment** Comm investimento m di capitali stranieri. ~**ly** adv interiormente. ~**[s]** adv verso l'interno

iodine /'aɪədi:n/ n iodio m

iota /aɪ'əʊtə/ n briciolo m

IOU n abbr (**I owe you**) pagherò m inv

IQ n abbr (**intelligence quotient**) Q.I.

IRA n abbr (**Irish Republican Army**) I.R.A. f

Iran /ɪ'rɑ:n/ n Iran m. ~**ian** /ɪ'reɪnɪən/ a & n iraniano, -a mf

Iraq /ɪ'rɑ:k/ n Iraq m. ~**i** /ɪ'rɑ:kɪ/ a & n iracheno, -a mf

irascible /ɪ'ræsəbl/ a irascibile

irate /aɪ'reɪt/ a adirato

Ireland /'aɪələnd/ n Irlanda f

iris /'aɪrɪs/ n Anat iride f; Bot iris f inv

Irish /'aɪrɪʃ/ a irlandese ● npl **the** ~ gli irlandesi. ~**man** n irlandese m. ~**woman** n irlandese f

iron /'aɪən/ a di ferro. **I~ Curtain** n cortina f di ferro ● n ferro m; ⟨appliance⟩ ferro m [da stiro] ● vt/i stirare. **iron out** vt eliminare stirando; fig appianare

ironic[al] /aɪ'rɒnɪk[l]/ a ironico

ironing /'aɪənɪŋ/ n stirare m; ⟨articles⟩ roba f da stirare; **do the** ~ stirare. ~-**board** n asse f da stiro

'ironmonger /-mʌŋgə(r)/ n ~**'s** [**shop**] negozio m di ferramenta

irony /'aɪrənɪ/ n ironia f

irradiate /ɪ'reɪdɪeɪt/ vt irradiare

irrational /ɪ'ræʃənl/ a irrazionale

irreconcilable /ɪ'rekənsaɪləbl/ a irreconciliabile

irrefutable /ɪrɪ'fju:təbl/ a irrefutabile

irregular /ɪ'regjʊlə(r)/ a irregolare. ~**ity** /-'lærətɪ/ n irregolarità f inv

irrelevant /ɪ'reləvənt/ a non pertinente

irreparabl|e /ɪ'repərəbl/ a irreparabile. ~**y** adv irreparabilmente

irreplaceable /ɪrɪ'pleɪsəbl/ a insostituibile

irrepressible /ɪrɪ'presəbl/ a irrefrenabile; ⟨person⟩ incontenibile

irresistible /ɪrɪ'zɪstəbl/ a irresistibile

irresolute /ɪ'rezəlu:t/ a irresoluto

irrespective /ɪrɪ'spektɪv/ a ~ **of** senza riguardo per

irresponsible /ɪrɪ'spɒnsɪbl/ a irresponsabile

irreverent /ɪ'revərənt/ a irreverente

irreversible /ɪrɪ'vɜ:səbl/ a irreversibile

irrevocabl|e /ɪ'revəkəbl/ a irrevocabile. ~**y** adv irrevocabilmente

irrigat|e /'ɪrɪgeɪt/ vt irrigare. ~**ion** /-'geɪʃn/ n irrigazione f

irritability /ɪrɪtə'bɪlətɪ/ n irritabilità f

irritable /'ɪrɪtəbl/ a irritabile

irritant /'ɪrɪtənt/ n sostanza f irritante

irritat|e /'ɪrɪteɪt/ vt irritare. ~**ing** a irritante. ~**ion** /-'teɪʃn/ n irritazione f

is /ɪz/ see **be**

Islam /'ɪzlɑ:m/ n Islam m. ~**ic** /-'læmɪk/ a islamico

island /'aɪlənd/ n isola f; (in road) isola f spartitraffico. ~**er** n isolano, -a mf

isle /aɪl/ n liter isola f

isolat|e /'aɪsəleɪt/ vt isolare. ~**ed** a isolato. ~**ion** /-'leɪʃn/ n isolamento m

Israel /'ɪzreɪl/ n Israele m. ~**i** /ɪz'reɪlɪ/ a & n israeliano, -a mf

issue /'ɪʃu:/ n (outcome) risultato m; (of magazine) numero m; (of stamps etc) emissione f; (offspring) figli mpl; (matter, question) questione f; **at** ~ in questione; **take** ~ **with sb** prendere posizione contro qcno ● vt distribuire ⟨supplies⟩; rilasciare ⟨passport⟩; emettere ⟨stamps, order⟩; pubblicare ⟨book⟩; **be** ~**d with sth** ricevere qcsa ● vi ~ **from** uscire da

isthmus /'ɪsməs/ n (pl -muses) istmo m

it /ɪt/ pron (direct object) lo m, la f; (indirect object) gli m, le f; **it's broken** è rotto/rotta; **will it be enough?** basterà?; **it's hot** fa caldo; **it's raining** piove; **it's me** sono io; **who is it?** chi è?; **it's two o'clock** sono le due; **I doubt it** ne dubito; **take it with you** prendilo con te; **give it a wipe** dagli una pulita

Italian /ɪ'tæljən/ a & n italiano, -a mf; (language) italiano m

italic /ɪ'tælɪk/ a in corsivo. ~**s** npl corsivo msg

Italy /'ɪtəlɪ/ n Italia f

itch /ɪtʃ/ n prurito m ● vi avere prurito, prudere; **be** ~**ing to** fam avere una voglia matta di. ~**y** a che prude; **my foot is** ~**y** ho prurito al piede

item /'aɪtəm/ n articolo m; (on agenda, programme) punto m; (on invoice) voce f; ~ [of news] notizia f. ~ize vt dettagliare ⟨bill⟩

itinerant /aɪ'tɪnərənt/ a itinerante

itinerary /aɪ'tɪnərərɪ/ n itinerario m

its /ɪts/ poss pron suo m, sua f, suoi mpl, sue fpl; ~ mother/cage sua madre/la sua gabbia

it's = it is, it has

itself /ɪt'self/ pron (reflexive) si; (emphatic) essa stessa; **the baby looked at ~ in the mirror** il bambino si è guardato nello specchio; **by ~** da solo; **the machine in ~ is simple** la macchina di per sé è semplice

ITV n abbr (**Independent Television**) stazione f televisiva privata britannica

ivory /'aɪvərɪ/ n avorio m

ivy /'aɪvɪ/ n edera f

Jj

jab /dʒæb/ n colpo m secco; (fam: injection) puntura f ● vt (pt/pp **jabbed**) punzecchiare

jabber /'dʒæbə(r)/ vi borbottare

jack /dʒæk/ n Auto cric m inv; (in cards) fante m, jack m inv ● **jack up** vt Auto sollevare [con il cric]

jackdaw /'dʒækdɔː/ n taccola f

jacket /'dʒækɪt/ n giacca f; (of book) sopraccoperta f. ~ **po'tato** n patata f cotta al forno con la buccia

'jackpot n premio m (di una lotteria); **win the ~** vincere alla lotteria; **hit the ~** fig fare un colpo grosso

jade /dʒeɪd/ n giada f ● attrib di giada

jaded /'dʒeɪdɪd/ a spossato

jagged /'dʒægɪd/ a dentellato

jail /dʒeɪl/ = gaol

jalopy /dʒə'lɒpɪ/ n fam vecchia carretta f

jam¹ /dʒæm/ n marmellata f

jam² n Auto ingorgo m; (fam: difficulty) guaio m ● v (pt/pp **jammed**) ● vt (cram) pigiare; disturbare ⟨broadcast⟩; inceppare ⟨mechanism, drawer etc⟩; **be ~med** ⟨roads:⟩ essere congestionato ● vi ⟨mechanism:⟩ incepparsi; ⟨window, drawer:⟩ incastrarsi

Jamaica /dʒə'meɪkə/ n Giamaica f. ~**n** a & n giamaicano, -a mf

jam-'packed a fam pieno zeppo

jangle /'dʒæŋgl/ vt far squillare ● vi squillare

janitor /'dʒænɪtə(r)/ n (caretaker) custode m; (in school) bidello, -a mf

January /'dʒænjʊərɪ/ n gennaio m

Japan /dʒə'pæn/ n Giappone m. ~**ese** /dʒæpə'niːz/ a & n giapponese mf; (language) giapponese m

jar¹ /dʒɑː(r)/ n (glass) barattolo m

jar² vi (pt/pp **jarred**) ⟨sound:⟩ stridere

jargon /'dʒɑːgən/ n gergo m

jaundice /'dʒɔːndɪs/ n itterizia f. ~**d** a fig inacidito

jaunt /dʒɔːnt/ n gita f

jaunty /'dʒɔːntɪ/ a (-ier, -iest) sbarazzino

javelin /'dʒævlɪn/ n giavellotto m

jaw /dʒɔː/ n mascella f; (bone) mandibola f

jay-walker /'dʒeɪwɔːkə(r)/ n pedone m indisciplinato

jazz /dʒæz/ n jazz m ● **jazz up** vt ravvivare. ~**y** a vistoso

jealous /'dʒeləs/ a geloso. ~**y** n gelosia f

jeans /dʒiːnz/ npl [blue] jeans mpl

jeep /dʒiːp/ n jeep f inv

jeer /dʒɪə(r)/ n scherno m ● vi schernire; ~ **at** prendersi gioco di ● vt (boo) fischiare

jell /dʒel/ vi concretarsi

jelly /'dʒelɪ/ n gelatina f. ~**fish** n medusa f

jeopar|dize /'dʒepədaɪz/ vt mettere in pericolo. ~**dy** /-dɪ/ n in ~**dy** in pericolo

jerk /dʒɜːk/ n scatto m, scossa f ● vt scattare ● vi sobbalzare; ⟨limb, muscle:⟩ muoversi a scatti. ~**ily** adv a scatti. ~**y** a traballante

jersey /'dʒɜːzɪ/ n maglia f; Sport maglietta f; (fabric) jersey m

jest /dʒest/ n scherzo m; **in ~** per scherzo ● vi scherzare

Jesus /'dʒiːzəs/ n Gesù m f

jet¹ /dʒet/ n (stone) giaietto m

jet² n (of water) getto m; (nozzle) becco m; (plane) aviogetto m, jet m inv

jet: ~-'**black** *a* nero ebano. ~**lag** *n* scombussolamento *m* da fuso orario. ~-**pro'pelled** *a* a reazione

jettison /'dʒetɪsn/ *vt* gettare a mare; *fig* abbandonare

jetty /'dʒetɪ/ *n* molo *m*

Jew /dʒu:/ *n* ebreo *m*

jewel /'dʒu:əl/ *n* gioiello *m*. ~**ler** *n* gioielliere *m*; ~**ler's** [**shop**] gioielleria *f*. ~**lery** *n* gioielli *mpl*

Jew|ess /'dʒu:ɪs/ *n* ebrea *f*. ~**ish** *a* ebreo

jiffy /'dʒɪfɪ/ *n fam* **in a ~** in un batter d'occhio

jigsaw /'dʒɪgsɔ:/ *n* [**puzzle**] puzzle *m inv*

jilt /dʒɪlt/ *vt* piantare

jingle /'dʒɪŋgl/ *n* ⟨*rhyme*⟩ canzoncina *f* pubblicitaria ● *vi* tintinnare

jinx /dʒɪŋks/ *n* ⟨*person*⟩ iettatore, -trice *mf*; **it's got a ~ on it** è iellato

jitter|s /'dʒɪtəz/ *npl fam* **have the ~s** aver una gran fifa. ~**y** *a fam* **in** preda alla fifa

job /dʒɒb/ *n* lavoro *m*; **this is going to be quite a ~** *fam* [questa] non sarà un'impresa facile; **it's a good ~ that...** meno male che.... ~ **centre** *n* ufficio *m* statale di collocamento. ~**less** *a* senza lavoro

jockey /'dʒɒkɪ/ *n* fantino *m*

jocular /'dʒɒkjʊlə(r)/ *a* scherzoso

jog /dʒɒg/ *n* colpetto *m*; **at a ~** in un balzo; *Sport* **go for a ~** andare a fare jogging ● *v* ⟨*pt/pp* **jogged**⟩ ● *vt* ⟨*hit*⟩ urtare; ~ **sb's memory** farlo ritornare in mente a qcno ● *vi Sport* fare jogging. ~**ging** *n* jogging *m*

john /dʒɒn/ *n* ⟨*Am fam: toilet*⟩ gabinetto *m*

join /dʒɔɪn/ *n* giuntura *f* ● *vt* raggiungere, unire; raggiungere ⟨*person*⟩; ⟨*become member of*⟩ iscriversi a; entrare in ⟨*firm*⟩ ● *vi* ⟨*roads:*⟩ congiungersi. **join in** *vi* partecipare. **join up** *vi Mil* arruolarsi ● *vt* unire

joiner /'dʒɔɪnə(r)/ *n* falegname *m*

joint /dʒɔɪnt/ *a* comune ● *n* articolazione *f*; ⟨*in wood, brickwork*⟩ giuntura *f*; *Culin* arrosto *m*; ⟨*fam: bar*⟩ bettola *f*; ⟨*sl:drug*⟩ spinello *m*. ~**ly** *adv* unitamente

joist /dʒɔɪst/ *n* travetto *m*

jok|e /dʒəʊk/ *n* ⟨*trick*⟩ scherzo *m*; ⟨*funny story*⟩ barzelletta *f* ● *vi* scherzare. ~**er** *n* burlone, -a *mf*; ⟨*in cards*⟩ jolly *m inv*. ~**ing** *n* ~**ing apart** scherzi a parte. ~**ingly** *adv* per scherzo

jolly /'dʒɒlɪ/ *a* (-**ier**, -**iest**) allegro ● *adv fam* molto

jolt /dʒəʊlt/ *n* scossa *f*, sobbalzo *m* ● *vt* far sobbalzare ● *vi* sobbalzare

Jordan /'dʒɔ:dn/ *n* Giordania *f*; ⟨*river*⟩ Giordano *m*. ~**ian** /-'deɪnən/ *a* & *n* giordano, -a *mf*

jostle /'dʒɒsl/ *vt* spingere

jot /dʒɒt/ *n* nulla *f* ● **jot down** *vt* ⟨*pt/pp* **jotted**⟩ annotare. ~**ter** *n* taccuino *m*; ⟨*with a spine*⟩ quaderno *m*

journal /'dʒɜ:nl/ *n* giornale *m*; ⟨*diary*⟩ diario *m*. ~**ese** /-ə'li:z/ *n* gergo *m* giornalistico. ~**ism** *n* giornalismo *m*. ~**ist** *n* giornalista *mf*

journey /'dʒɜ:nɪ/ *n* viaggio *m*

jovial /'dʒəʊvɪəl/ *a* gioviale

joy /dʒɔɪ/ *n* gioia *f*. ~**ful** *a* gioioso. ~**ride** *n fam* giro *m* con una macchina rubata. ~**stick** *n Comput* joystick *m inv*

jubil|ant /'dʒu:bɪlənt/ *a* giubilante. ~**ation** /-'leɪʃn/ *n* giubilo *m*

jubilee /'dʒu:bɪli:/ *n* giubileo *m*

judder /'dʒʌdə(r)/ *vi* vibrare violentemente

judge /dʒʌdʒ/ *n* giudice *m* ● *vt* giudicare; ⟨*estimate*⟩ valutare; ⟨*consider*⟩ ritenere ● *vi* giudicare (**by** da). ~**ment** *n* giudizio *m*; *Jur* sentenza *f*

judic|ial /dʒu:'dɪʃl/ *a* giudiziario. ~**iary** /-ʃərɪ/ *n* magistratura *f*. ~**ious** /-ʃəs/ *a* giudizioso

judo /'dʒu:dəʊ/ *n* judo *m*

jug /dʒʌg/ *n* brocca *f*; ⟨*small*⟩ bricco *m*

juggernaut /'dʒʌgənɔ:t/ *n fam* grosso autotreno *m*

juggle /'dʒʌgl/ *vi* fare giochi di destrezza. ~**r** *n* giocoliere, -a *mf*

juice /dʒu:s/ *n* succo *m*

juicy /'dʒu:sɪ/ *a* (-**ier**, -**iest**) succoso; ⟨*fam: story*⟩ piccante

juke-box /'dʒu:k-/ *n* juke-box *m inv*

July /dʒʊ'laɪ/ *n* luglio *m*

jumble /'dʒʌmbl/ *n* accozzaglia *f* ● *vt* ~ [**up**] mischiare. ~ **sale** *n* vendita *f* di beneficenza

jumbo /'dʒʌmbəʊ/ *n* ~ [**jet**] jumbo jet *m inv*

jump /dʒʌmp/ *n* salto *m*; ⟨*in prices*⟩ balzo *m*; ⟨*in horse racing*⟩ ostacolo *m* ● *vi* saltare; ⟨*with fright*⟩ sussultare; ⟨*prices:*⟩ salire rapidamente; ~ **to conclusions** saltare alle conclusioni ● *vt* saltare; ~ **the gun** *fig* precipitarsi; ~ **the queue** non rispettare la fila. **jump at** *vt fig* accettare con entusiasmo ⟨*offer*⟩. **jump up** *vi* rizzarsi in piedi

jumper /'dʒʌmpə(r)/ *n* (*sweater*) golf *m inv*

jumpy /'dʒʌmpɪ/ *a* nervoso

junction /'dʒʌŋkʃn/ *n* (*of roads*) incrocio *m*; (*of motorway*) uscita *f*; *Rail* nodo *m* ferroviario

juncture /'dʒʌŋktʃə(r)/ *n* **at this ~** a questo punto

June /dʒuːn/ *n* giugno *m*

jungle /'dʒʌŋgl/ *n* giungla *f*

junior /'dʒuːnɪə(r)/ *a* giovane; (*in rank*) subalterno; *Sport* junior *inv* ● *npl* the **~s** *Sch* i più giovani. **~ school** *n* scuola *f* elementare

junk /dʒʌŋk/ *n* cianfrusaglie *fpl*. **~ food** *n fam* cibo *m* poco sano, porcherie *fpl*. **~ mail** posta *f* spazzatura

junkie /'dʒʌŋkɪ/ *n sl* tossico, -a *mf*

'junk-shop *n* negozio *m* di rigattiere

jurisdiction /dʒʊərɪs'dɪkʃn/ *n* giurisdizione *f*

juror /'dʒʊərə(r)/ *n* giurato, -a *mf*

jury /'dʒʊərɪ/ *n* giuria *f*; *Jur* giuria *f* [popolare]

just /dʒʌst/ *a* giusto ● *adv* (*barely*) appena; (*simply*) solo; (*exactly*) esattamente; **~ as tall** altrettanto alto; **~ as I was leaving** proprio quando stavo andando via; **I've ~ seen her** l'ho appena vista; **it's ~ as well** meno male; **~ at that moment** proprio in quel momento; **~ listen!** ascolta!; **I'm ~ going** sto andando proprio ora

justice /'dʒʌstɪs/ *n* giustizia *f*; **do ~ to** rendere giustizia a; **J~ of the Peace** giudice *m* conciliatore

justifiabl|e /'dʒʌstɪfaɪəbl/ *a* giustificabile

justi|fication /dʒʌstɪfɪ'keɪʃn/ *n* giustificazione *f*. **~fy** /'dʒʌstɪfaɪ/ *vt* (*pt/pp* **-ied**) giustificare

justly /'dʒʌstlɪ/ *adv* giustamente

jut /dʒʌt/ *vi* (*pt/pp* **jutted**) **~ out** sporgere

juvenile /'dʒuːvənaɪl/ *a* giovanile; (*childish*) infantile; (*for the young*) per i giovani ● *n* giovane *mf*. **~ delinquency** *n* delinquenza *f* giovanile

juxtapose /dʒʌkstə'pəʊz/ *vt* giustapporre

Kk

kangaroo /kæŋgə'ruː/ *n* canguro *m*

karate /kə'rɑːtɪ/ *n* karate *m*

kebab /kɪ'bæb/ *n Culin* spiedino *m* di carne

keel /kiːl/ *n* chiglia *f* ● **keel over** *vi* capovolgersi

keen /kiːn/ *a* (*intense*) acuto; (*interest*) vivo; (*eager*) entusiastico; (*competition*) feroce; (*wind, knife*) tagliente; **~ on** entusiasta di; **she's ~ on him** le piace molto; **be ~ to do sth** avere voglia di fare qcsa. **~ness** *n* entusiasmo *m*

keep /kiːp/ *n* (*maintenance*) mantenimento *m*; (*of castle*) maschio *m*; **for ~s** per sempre ● *v* (*pt/pp* **kept**) ● *vt* tenere; (*not throw away*) conservare; (*detain*) trattenere; mantenere (*family, promise*); avere (*shop*); allevare (*animals*); rispettare (*law, rules*); **~ sth hot** tenere qcsa in caldo; **~ sb from doing sth** impedire a qcno di fare qcsa; **~ sb waiting** far aspettare qcno; **~ sth to oneself** tenere qcsa per sé; **~ sth from sb** tenere nascosto qcsa a qcno ● *vi* (*remain*) rimanere; (*food:*) conservarsi; **~ calm** rimanere calmo; **~ left/right** tenere la sinistra/destra; **~ [on] doing sth** continuare a fare qcsa. **keep back** *vt* trattenere (*person*); **~ sth back from sb** tenere nascosto qcsa a qcno ● *vi* tenersi indietro. **keep in with** *vt* mantenersi in buoni rapporti con. **keep on** *vi fam* assillare (**at sb** qcno). **keep up** *vi* stare al passo ● *vt* (*continue*) continuare

keep|er /'kiːpə(r)/ *n* custode *mf*. **~-fit** *n* ginnastica *f*. **~ing** *n* custodia *f*; **be in ~ing with** essere in armonia con. **~sake** *n* ricordo *m*

keg /keg/ *n* barilotto *m*

kennel /'kenl/ *n* canile *m*; **~s** *pl* (*boarding*) canile *m*; (*breeding*) allevamento *m* di cani

Kenya /'kenjə/ *n* Kenia *m*. **~n** *a & n* keniota *mf*

kept /kept/ *see* keep
kerb /kɜːb/ *n* bordo *m* del marciapiede
kernel /'kɜːnl/ *n* nocciolo *m*
kerosene /'kerəsiːn/ *n Am* cherosene *m*
ketchup /'ketʃʌp/ *n* ketchup *m*
kettle /'ket(ə)l/ *n* bollitore *m*; **put the ~ on** mettere l'acqua a bollire
key /kiː/ *n also Mus* chiave *f*; (*of piano, typewriter*) tasto *m* ● *vt* ~ [in] digitare ‹*character*›; **could you ~ this?** puoi battere questo?
key: ~**board** *n Comput, Mus* tastiera *f*. ~**boarder** *n* tastierista *mf*. ~**ed-up** *a* (*anxious*) estremamente agitato; (*ready to act*) psicologicamente preparato. ~**hole** *n* buco *m* della serratura. ~**ring** *n* portachiavi *m inv*
khaki /'kɑːkɪ/ *a* cachi *inv* ● *n* cachi *m*
kick /kɪk/ *n* calcio *m*; (*fam: thrill*) piacere *m*; **for ~s** *fam* per spasso ● *vt* dar calci a; ~ **the bucket** *fam* crepare ● *vi* ‹*animal*› scalciare; ‹*person*› dare calci.
kick off *vi Sport* dare il calcio d'inizio; *fam* iniziare. **kick up** *vt* ~ **up a row** fare une scenata
'kickback *n* (*fam: percentage*) tangente *f*
'kick-off *n Sport* calcio *m* d'inizio
kid /kɪd/ *n* capretto *m*; (*fam: child*) ragazzino, -a *mf* ● *v* (*pt/pp* **kidded**) ● *vt* *fam* prendere in giro ● *vi fam* scherzare
kidnap /'kɪdnæp/ *vt* (*pt/pp* **-napped**) rapire, sequestrare. ~**per** *n* sequestratore, -trice *mf*, rapitore, -trice *mf*. ~**ping** *n* rapimento *m*, sequestro *m* [di persona]
kidney /'kɪdnɪ/ *n* rene *m*; *Culin* rognone *m*. ~ **machine** *n* rene *m* artificiale
kill /kɪl/ *vt* uccidere; *fig* metter fine a; ammazzare ‹*time*›. ~**er** *n* assassino, -a *mf*. ~**ing** *n* uccisione *f*; (*murder*) omicidio *m*; **make a ~ing** *fig* fare un colpo grosso
'killjoy *n* guastafeste *mf inv*
kiln /kɪln/ *n* fornace *f*
kilo /'kiːləʊ/ *n* chilo *m*
kilo /'kɪlə/: ~**byte** *n* kilobyte *m inv*. ~**gram** *n* chilogrammo *m*. ~**metre** /kɪ'lɒmɪtə(r)/ *n* chilometro *m*. ~**watt** *n* chilowatt *m*
kilt /kɪlt/ *n* kilt *m inv* (*gonnellino degli scozzesi*)
kin /kɪn/ *n* congiunti *mpl*; **next of ~** parente *m* stretto; parenti *mpl* stretti
kind¹ /kaɪnd/ *n* genere *m*, specie *f*; (*brand, type*) tipo *m*; ~ **of** *fam* alquanto; **two of a ~** due della stessa specie
kind² *a* gentile, buono; ~ **to animals** amante degli animali; ~ **regards** cordiali saluti
kindergarten /'kɪndəgɑːtn/ *n* asilo *m* infantile
kindle /'kɪndl/ *vt* accendere
kind|ly /'kaɪndlɪ/ *a* (**-ier, -iest**) benevolo ● *adv* gentilmente; (*if you please*) per favore. ~**ness** *n* gentilezza *f*
kindred /'kɪndrɪd/ *a* **she's a ~ spirit** è la mia/sua/tua anima gemella
kinetic /kɪ'netɪk/ *a* cinetico
king /kɪŋ/ *n* re *m inv*. ~**dom** *n* regno *m*
king: ~**fisher** *n* martin *m inv* pescatore. ~**-sized** *a* ‹*cigarette*› king-size *inv*, lungo; ‹*bed*› matrimoniale grande
kink /kɪŋk/ *n* attricigliamento *m*. ~**y** *n fam* bizzarro
kiosk /'kiːɒsk/ *n* chiosco *m*; *Teleph* cabina *f* telefonica
kip /kɪp/ *n fam* pisolino *m*; **have a ~** schiacciare un pisolino ● *vi* (*pt/pp* **kipped**) *fam* dormire
kipper /'kɪpə(r)/ *n* aringa *f* affumicata
kiss /kɪs/ *n* bacio *m*; ~ **of life** respirazione *f* bocca a bocca ● *vt* baciare ● *vi* baciarsi
kit /kɪt/ *n* equipaggiamento *m*, kit *m inv*; (*tools*) attrezzi *mpl*; (*construction ~*) pezzi *mpl* da montare, kit *m inv* ● **kit out** *vt* (*pt/pp* **kitted**) equipaggiare. ~**bag** *n* sacco *m* a spalla
kitchen /'kɪtʃɪn/ *n* cucina *f* ● *attrib* di cucina. ~**ette** /kɪtʃɪ'net/ *n* cucinino *m*
kitchen: ~ **'garden** *n* orto *m*. ~ **roll** *or* **towel** Scottex® *m inv*. ~**'sink** *n* lavello *m*
kite /kaɪt/ *n* aquilone *m*
kitten /'kɪtn/ *n* gattino *m*
kitty /'kɪtɪ/ *n* (*money*) cassa *f* comune
kleptomaniac /kleptə'meɪnɪæk/ *n* cleptomane *mf*
knack /næk/ *n* tecnica *f*; **have the ~ for doing sth** avere la capacità di fare qcsa
knead /niːd/ *vt* impastare
knee /niː/ *n* ginocchio *m*. ~**cap** *n* rotula *f*
kneel /niːl/ *vi* (*pt/pp* **knelt**) ~ **[down]** inginocchiarsi; **be ~ing** essere inginocchiato
knelt /nelt/ *see* kneel
knew /njuː/ *see* know
knickers /'nɪkəz/ *npl* mutandine *fpl*
knick-knacks /'nɪknæks/ *npl* ninnoli *mpl*
knife /naɪf/ *n* (*pl* **knives**) coltello *m* ● *vt fam* accoltellare

knight /naɪt/ n cavaliere m; (in chess) cavallo m ● vt nominare cavaliere
knit /nɪt/ vt/i (pt/pp **knitted**) lavorare a maglia; ~ **one**, **purl one** un diritto, un rovescio. **~ting** n lavorare m a maglia; (product) lavoro m a maglia. **~ting-needle** n ferro m da calza. **~wear** n maglieria f
knives /naɪvz/ see knife
knob /nɒb/ n pomello m; (of stick) pomo m; (of butter) noce f. **~bly** a nodoso; (bony) spigoloso
knock /nɒk/ n colpo m; **there was a ~ at the door** hanno bussato alla porta ● vt bussare a ⟨door⟩; (fam: criticize) denigrare; ~ **a hole in sth** fare un buco in qcsa; ~ **one's head** battere la testa (**on** contro) ● vi (at door) bussare. **knock about** vt malmenare ● vi fam girovagare. **knock down** vt far cadere; (with fist) stendere con un pugno; (in car) investire; (demolish) abbattere; (fam: reduce) ribassare ⟨price⟩. **knock off** vt (fam: steal) fregare; (fam: complete quickly) fare alla bell'e meglio ● vi (fam: cease work) staccare. **knock out** vt eliminare; (make unconscious) mettere K.O.; (fam: anaesthetize) addormentare. **knock over** vt rovesciare; (in car) investire

knock: ~**-down** a ~**-down price** prezzo m stracciato. ~**er** n battente m. ~**-kneed** /-'ni:d/ a con gambe storte. ~**-out** n (in boxing) knock-out m inv
knot /nɒt/ n nodo m ● vt (pt/pp **knotted**) annodare
knotty /'nɒtɪ/ a (**-ier, -iest**) fam spinoso
know /nəʊ/ v (pt **knew**, pp **known**) ● vt sapere; conoscere ⟨person, place⟩; (recognize) riconoscere; **get to ~ sb** conoscere qcno; ~ **how to swim** sapere nuotare ● vi sapere; **did you ~ about this?** lo sapevi? ● n **in the ~** fam al corrente
know: ~**-all** n fam sapientone, -a mf. ~**-how** n abilità f. ~**ing** a d'intesa. ~**ingly** adv (intentionally) consapevolmente; ⟨smile etc⟩ con un'aria d'intesa
knowledge /'nɒlɪdʒ/ n conoscenza f. ~**able** /-əbl/ a ben informato
known /nəʊn/ see know ● a noto
knuckle /'nʌkl/ n nocca f ● **knuckle down** vi darci sotto (**to** con). **knuckle under** vi sottomettersi
Koran /kə'rɑːn/ n Corano m
Korea /kə'rɪə/ n Corea f. ~**n** a & n coreano, -a mf
kosher /'kəʊʃə(r)/ a kasher inv
kowtow /kaʊ'taʊ/ vi piegarsi
kudos /'kjuːdɒs/ n fam gloria f

lab /læb/ n fam laboratorio m
label /'leɪbl/ n etichetta f ● vt (pt/pp **labelled**) mettere un'etichetta a; fig etichettare ⟨person⟩
laboratory /lə'bɒrətrɪ/ n laboratorio m
laborious /lə'bɔːrɪəs/ a laborioso
labour /'leɪbə(r)/ n lavoro m; (workers) manodopera f; Med doglie fpl; **be in ~** avere le doglie; **L~** Pol partito m laburista ● attrib Pol laburista ● vi lavorare ● vt ~ **the point** fig ribadire il concetto. ~**er** n manovale m
'**labour-saving** a che fa risparmiare lavoro e fatica
labyrinth /'læbərɪnθ/ n labirinto m
lace /leɪs/ n pizzo m; (of shoe) laccio m ● attrib di pizzo ● vt allacciare ⟨shoes⟩; correggere ⟨drink⟩

lacerate /'læsəreɪt/ vt lacerare
lack /læk/ n mancanza f ● vt mancare di; **I ~ the time** mi manca il tempo ● vi **be ~ing** mancare; **be ~ing in sth** mancare di qcsa
lackadaisical /lækə'deɪzɪkl/ a senza entusiasmo
laconic /lə'kɒnɪk/ a laconico
lacquer /'lækə(r)/ n lacca f
lad /læd/ n ragazzo m
ladder /'lædə(r)/ n scala f; (in tights) sfilatura f
laden /'leɪdn/ a carico (**with** di)
ladle /'leɪdl/ n mestolo m ● vt ~ [**out**] versare (col mestolo)
lady /'leɪdɪ/ n signora f; (title) Lady f; **ladies [room]** bagno m per donne

lady: ~**bird** n, Am ~**bug** n coccinella f. ~**like** a signorile

lag¹ /læg/ vi (pt/pp **lagged**) ~ **behind** restare indietro

lag² vt (pt/pp **lagged**) isolare ⟨pipes⟩

lager /'lɑ:gə(r)/ n birra f chiara

lagoon /lə'gu:n/ n laguna f

laid /leɪd/ see **lay³**

lain /leɪn/ see **lie²**

lair /leə(r)/ n tana f

lake /leɪk/ n lago m

lamb /læm/ n agnello m

lame /leɪm/ a zoppo; fig ⟨argument⟩ zoppicante; ⟨excuse⟩ traballante

lament /lə'ment/ n lamento m ● vt lamentare ● vi lamentarsi

lamentable /'læməntəbl/ a deplorevole

laminated /'læmɪneɪtɪd/ a laminato

lamp /læmp/ n lampada f; (in street) lampione m. ~**post** n lampione m. ~**shade** n paralume m

lance /lɑ:ns/ n lancia f ● vt Med incidere. ~·**corporal** n appuntato m

land /lænd/ n terreno m; (country) paese m; (as opposed to sea) terra f; plot of ~ pezzo m di terreno ● vt Naut sbarcare; ⟨fam: obtain⟩ assicurarsi; **be** ~**ed with sth** fam ritrovarsi fra capo e collo qcsa ● vi Aeron atterrare; ⟨fall⟩ cadere. **land up** vi fam finire

landing /'lændɪŋ/ n Naut sbarco m; Aeron atterraggio m; (top of stairs) pianerottolo m. ~**stage** n pontile m da sbarco. ~ **strip** n pista f d'atterraggio

land: ~**lady** n proprietaria f; (of flat) padrona f di casa. ~**locked** a privo di sbocco sul mare. ~**lord** n proprietario m; (of flat) padrone m di casa. ~**mark** n punto m di riferimento; fig pietra f miliare. ~**owner** n proprietario, -a mf terriero, -a f. ~**scape** -skeɪp/ n paesaggio m. ~**slide** n frana f; Pol valanga f di voti

lane /leɪn/ n sentiero m; Auto, Sport corsia f

language /'læŋgwɪdʒ/ n lingua f; (speech, style) linguaggio m. ~ **laboratory** n laboratorio m linguistico

languid /'læŋgwɪd/ a languido

languish /'læŋgwɪʃ/ vi languire

lank /læŋk/ a ⟨hair⟩ diritto

lanky /'læŋkɪ/ a ⟨-ier, -iest⟩ allampanato

lantern /'læntən/ n lanterna f

lap¹ /læp/ n grembo m

lap² n (of journey) tappa f; Sport giro m

● v (pt/pp **lapped**) ● vi ⟨water:⟩ ~ **against** lambire ● vt Sport doppiare

lap³ vt (pt/pp **lapped**) ~ **up** bere avidamente; bersi completamente ⟨lies⟩; credere ciecamente a ⟨praise⟩

lapel /lə'pel/ n bavero m

lapse /læps/ n sbaglio m; (moral) sbandamento m [morale]; (of time) intervallo m ● vi (expire) scadere; (morally) scivolare; ~ **into** cadere in

laptop /'læptɒp/ n ~ [**computer**] computer m inv portabile, laptop m inv

larceny /'lɑ:sənɪ/ n furto m

lard /lɑ:d/ n strutto m

larder /'lɑ:də(r)/ n dispensa f

large /lɑ:dʒ/ a grande; ⟨number, amount⟩ grande, grosso; **by and** ~ in complesso; **at** ~ in libertà; (in general) ampiamente. ~**ly** adv ampiamente. ~**ly because of** in gran parte a causa di

lark¹ /lɑ:k/ n (bird) allodola f

lark² n (joke) burla f ● **lark about** vi giocherellare

larva /'lɑ:və/ n (pl -**vae** /-vi:/) larva f

laryngitis /lærɪn'dʒaɪtɪs/ n laringite f

larynx /'lærɪŋks/ n laringe f

lascivious /lə'sɪvɪəs/ a lascivo

laser /'leɪzə(r)/ n laser m inv. ~ [**printer**] n stampante f laser

lash /læʃ/ n frustata f; (eyelash) ciglio m ● vt (whip) frustare; (tie) legare fermamente. **lash out** vi attaccare; (spend) sperperare (**on** in)

lashings /'læʃɪŋz/ npl ~ **of** fam una marea di

lass /læs/ n ragazzina f

lasso /lə'su:/ n lazo m

last /lɑ:st/ a (final) ultimo; (recent) scorso; ~ **year** l'anno scorso; ~ **night** ieri sera; **at** ~ alla fine; **at** ~! finalmente!; **that's the** ~ **straw** fam questa è l'ultima goccia ● n ultimo, -a mf; **the** ~ **but one** il penultimo ● adv per ultimo; (last time) l'ultima volta ● vi durare. ~**ing** a durevole. ~**ly** adv infine

late /leɪt/ a (delayed) in ritardo; (at a late hour) tardo; (deceased) defunto; **it's** ~ (at night) è tardi; **in** ~ **November** alla fine di Novembre ● adv tardi; **stay up** ~ stare alzati fino a tardi. ~**comer** n ritardatario, -a mf; (to political party etc) nuovo, -a arrivato, -a mf. ~**ly** adv recentemente. ~**ness** n ora f tarda; (delay) ritardo m

latent /'leɪtnt/ a latente

later /'leɪtə(r)/ a ⟨train⟩ che parte più tardi; ⟨edition⟩ più recente ● adv più tardi; ~ **on** più tardi, dopo

lateral /'lætərəl/ a laterale

latest /'leɪtɪst/ a ultimo; (most recent) più recente: **the ~ [news]** le ultime notizie ● **n six o'clock at the ~** alle sei al più tardi

lathe /leɪð/ n tornio m

lather /'lɑːðə(r)/ n schiuma f ● vt insaponare ● vi far schiuma

Latin /'lætɪn/ a latino ● n latino m. **~ A'merica** n America f Latina. **~ A'merican** a & n latino-americano, -a mf

latitude /'lætɪtjuːd/ n Geog latitudine f; fig libertà f d'azione

latter /'lætə(r)/ a ultimo ● n **the ~** quest'ultimo. **~ly** adv ultimamente

lattice /'lætɪs/ n traliccio m

Latvia /'lætvɪə/ n Lettonia f. **~n** a & n lettone mf

laudable /'lɔːdəbl/ a lodevole

laugh /lɑːf/ n risata f ● vi ridere (**at/about** di): **~ at sb** (mock) prendere in giro qcno. **~able** /-əbl/ a ridicolo. **~ing-stock** n zimbello m

laughter /'lɑːftə(r)/ n risata f

launch[1] /lɔːntʃ/ n (boat) lancia f

launch[2] n lancio m; (of ship) varo m ● vt lanciare (rocket, product); varare (ship); sferrare (attack)

launder /'lɔːndə(r)/ vt lavare e stirare; **~ money** fig riciclare denaro sporco. **~ette** /-'dret/ n lavanderia f automatica

laundry /'lɔːndrɪ/ n lavanderia f; (clothes) bucato m

laurel /'lɒrəl/ n lauro m; **rest on one's ~s** fig dormire sugli allori

lava /'lɑːvə/ n lava f

lavatory /'lævətrɪ/ n gabinetto m

lavender /'lævəndə(r)/ n lavanda f

lavish /'lævɪʃ/ a copioso; (wasteful) prodigo; **on a ~ scale** su vasta scala ● vt **~ sth on sb** ricoprire qcno di qcsa. **~ly** adv copiosamente

law /lɔː/ n legge f; **study ~** studiare giurisprudenza, studiare legge; **~ and order** ordine m pubblico

law: ~-abiding a che rispetta la legge. **~court** n tribunale m. **~ful** a legittimo. **~less** a senza legge. **~ school** n facoltà f di giurisprudenza

lawn /lɔːn/ n prato m [all'inglese]. **~-mower** n tosaerba m inv

'law suit n causa f

lawyer /'lɔːjə(r)/ n avvocato m

lax /læks/ a negligente; (morals etc) lassista

laxative /'læksətɪv/ n lassativo m

laxity /'læksətɪ/ n lassismo m

lay[1] /leɪ/ a laico; fig profano

lay[2] see **lie**[2]

lay[3] vt (pt/pp **laid**) porre, mettere; apparecchiare (table) ● vi (hen:) fare le uova. **lay down** vt posare; stabilire (rules, conditions). **lay off** vt licenziare (workers) ● vi (fam: stop) **~ off!** smettila! **lay out** vt (display, set forth) esporre; (plan) pianificare (garden); (spend) sborsare; Typ impaginare

lay: ~about n fannullone, -a mf. **~-by** n piazzola f di sosta

layer /'leɪə(r)/ n strato m

lay: ~man n profano m. **~out** n disposizione f; Typ impaginazione f, layout m inv

laze /leɪz/ vi **~ [about]** oziare

laziness /'leɪzɪnɪs/ n pigrizia f

lazy /'leɪzɪ/ a (**-ier**, **-iest**) pigro. **~-bones** n poltrone, -a mf

lb abbr (**pound**) libbra

lead[1] /led/ n piombo m; (of pencil) mina f

lead[2] /liːd/ n guida f; (leash) guinzaglio m; (flex) filo m; (clue) indizio m; Theat parte f principale; (distance ahead) distanza f (**over** su); **in the ~** in testa ● v (pt/pp **led**) vt condurre; dirigere (expedition, party etc); (induce) indurre; **~ the way** mettersi in testa ● vi (be in front) condurre; (in race, competition) essere in testa; (at cards) giocare (per primo). **lead away** vt portar via. **lead to** vt portare a. **lead up to** vt preludere; **what's this ~ing up to?** dove porta questo?

leaded /'ledɪd/ a con piombo

leader /'liːdə(r)/ n capo m; (of orchestra) primo violino m; (in newspaper) articolo m di fondo. **~ship** n direzione f, leadership f inv; **show ~ship** mostrare capacità di comando

lead-'free a senza piombo

leading /'liːdɪŋ/ a principale; **~ lady/man** attrice f/attore m principale; **~ question** domanda f tendenziosa

leaf /liːf/ n (pl **leaves**) foglia f; (of table) asse f ● **leaf through** vt sfogliare. **~let** n dépliant m inv; (advertising) dépliant m inv pubblicitario; (political) manifestino m

league /liːg/ n lega f; Sport campionato m; **be in ~ with** essere in combutta con

leak /liːk/ n (hole) fessura f; Naut falla f; (of gas & fig) fuga f ● vi colare; (ship:) fare acqua; (liquid, gas:) fuoriuscire ● vt **~ sth to sb** fig far trapelare qcsa a qcno. **~y** a che perde; Naut che fa acqua

lean | leotard

lean¹ /liːn/ *a* magro

lean² *v* (*pt/pp* **leaned** *or* **leant** /lent/) ● *vt* appoggiare (**against/on** contro/su) ● *vi* appoggiarsi (**against/on** contro/su); (*not be straight*) pendere; **be ~ing against** essere appoggiato contro; **~ on sb** (*depend on*) appoggiarsi a qcno; (*fam: exert pressure on*) stare alle calcagne di qcno. **lean back** *vi* sporgersi indietro. **lean forward** *vi* piegarsi in avanti. **lean out** *vi* sporgersi. **lean over** *vi* piegarsi

leaning /ˈliːnɪŋ/ *a* pendente; **the L~ Tower of Pisa** la torre di Pisa, la torre pendente ● *n* tendenza *f*

leap /liːp/ *n* salto *m* ● *vi* (*pt/pp* **leapt** /lept/ *or* **leaped**) saltare; **he leapt at it** *fam* l'ha preso al volo. **~-frog** *n* cavallina *f*. **~ year** *n* anno *m* bisestile

learn /lɜːn/ *v* (*pt/pp* **learnt** *or* **learned**) ● *vt* imparare; **~ to swim** imparare a nuotare; **I have ~ed that...** (*heard*) sono venuto a sapere che... ● *vi* imparare

learn|ed /ˈlɜːnɪd/ *a* colto. **~er** *n also* Auto principiante *mf*. **~ing** *n* cultura *f*

lease /liːs/ *n* contratto *m* d'affitto; (*rental*) affitto *m* ● *vt* affittare

leash /liːʃ/ *n* guinzaglio *m*

least /liːst/ *a* più piccolo; ⟨*amount*⟩ minore; **you've got ~ luggage** hai meno bagagli di tutti ● *n* **the ~** il meno; **at ~** almeno; **not in the ~** niente affatto ● *adv* meno; **the ~ expensive wine** il vino meno caro

leather /ˈleðə(r)/ *n* pelle *f*; (*of soles*) cuoio *m* ● *attrib* di pelle/cuoio. **~y** *a* ⟨*meat, skin*⟩ duro

leave /liːv/ *n* (*holiday*) congedo *m*; Mil licenza *f*; **on ~** in congedo/licenza ● *v* (*pt/pp* **left**) ● *vt* lasciare; uscire da ⟨*house, office*⟩; (*forget*) dimenticare; **there is nothing left** non è rimasto niente ● *vi* andare via; ⟨*train, bus:*⟩ partire. **leave behind** *vt* lasciare; (*forget*) dimenticare. **leave out** *vt* omettere; (*not put away*) lasciare fuori

leaves /liːvz/ *see* **leaf**

Leban|on /ˈlebənən/ *n* Libano *m* **~ese** /-ˈniːz/ *a* & *n* libanese *mf*

lecherous /ˈletʃərəs/ *a* lascivo

lectern /ˈlektɜːn/ *n* leggio *m*

lecture /ˈlektʃə(r)/ *n* conferenza *f*; Univ lezione *f*; (*reproof*) ramanzina *f* ● *vi* fare una conferenza (**on** su); Univ insegnare (**on sth** qcsa) ● *vt* **~ sb** rimproverare qcno. **~r** *n* conferenziere, -a *mf*; Univ docente *mf* universitario, -a

led /led/ *see* **lead²**

ledge /ledʒ/ *n* cornice *f*; (*of window*) davanzale *m*

ledger /ˈledʒə(r)/ *n* libro *m* mastro

leech /liːtʃ/ *n* sanguisuga *f*

leek /liːk/ *n* porro *m*

leer /lɪə(r)/ *n* sguardo *m* libidinoso ● *vi* **~ [at]** guardare in modo libidinoso

leeway /ˈliːweɪ/ *n fig* libertà *f* di azione

left¹ /left/ *see* **leave**

left² *a* sinistro ● *adv* a sinistra ● *n also* Pol sinistra *f*; **on the ~** a sinistra; **left: ~-handed** *a* mancino. **~-'luggage [office]** *n* deposito *m* bagagli. **~overs** *npl* rimasugli *mpl*. **~-'wing** *a Pol* di sinistra

leg /leg/ *n* gamba *f*; (*of animal*) zampa *f*; (*of journey*) tappa *f*; Culin (*of chicken*) coscia *f*; (*of lamb*) cosciotto *m*

legacy /ˈlegəsɪ/ *n* lascito *m*

legal /ˈliːgl/ *a* legale; **take ~ action** intentare un'azione legale. **~ly** *adv* legalmente

legality /lɪˈgælətɪ/ *n* legalità *f*

legalize /ˈliːgəlaɪz/ *vt* legalizzare

legend /ˈledʒənd/ *n* leggenda *f*. **~ary** *a* leggendario

legib|le /ˈledʒəbl/ *a* leggibile. **~ly** *adv* in modo leggibile

legislat|e /ˈledʒɪsleɪt/ *vi* legiferare. **~ion** /-ˈleɪʃn/ *n* legislazione *f*

legislat|ive /ˈledʒɪslətɪv/ *a* legislativo. **~ure** /-ˈletʃə(r)/ *n* legislatura *f*

legitima|te /lɪˈdʒɪtɪmət/ *a* legittimo; ⟨*excuse*⟩ valido

leisure /ˈleʒə(r)/ *n* tempo *m* libero; **at your ~** con comodo. **~ly** *a* senza fretta

lemon /ˈlemən/ *n* limone *m*. **~ade** /-ˈneɪd/ *n* limonata *f*

lend /lend/ *vt* (*pt/pp* **lent**) prestare; **~ a hand** *fig* dare una mano. **~ing library** *n* biblioteca *f* per il prestito

length /leŋθ/ *n* lunghezza *f*; (*piece*) pezzo *m*; (*of wallpaper*) parte *f*; (*of visit*) durata *f*; **at ~** a lungo; (*at last*) alla fine

length|en /ˈleŋθən/ *vt* allungare ● *vi* allungarsi. **~ways** *adv* per lungo

lengthy /ˈleŋθɪ/ *a* (**-ier, -iest**) lungo

lenien|ce /ˈliːnɪəns/ *n* indulgenza *f*. **~t** *a* indulgente

lens /lenz/ *n* lente *f*; Phot obiettivo *m*; (*of eye*) cristallino *m*

Lent /lent/ *n* Quaresima *f*

lent *see* **lend**

lentil /ˈlentl/ *n* Bot lenticchia *f*

Leo /ˈliːəʊ/ *n* Astr Leone *m*

leopard /ˈlepəd/ *n* leopardo *m*

leotard /ˈliːətɑːd/ *n* body *m inv*

leprosy /'leprəsɪ/ *n* lebbra *f*

lesbian /'lezbɪən/ *a* lesbico ● *n* lesbica *f*

less /les/ *a* meno di; **~ and ~** sempre meno ● *adv & prep* meno ● *n* meno *m*

lessen /'lesn/ *vt/i* diminuire

lesser /'lesə(r)/ *a* minore

lesson /'lesn/ *n* lezione *f*

lest /lest/ *conj liter* per timore che

let /let/ *vt* (*pt/pp* **let**, *pres p* **letting**) lasciare, permettere; (*rent*) affittare; **~ alone** (*not to mention*) tanto meno; '**to ~**' 'affittasi'; **~ us go** andiamo; **~ sb do sth** lasciare fare qcsa a qcno, permettere a qcno di fare qcsa; **~ me know** fammi sapere; **just ~ him try!** che ci provi solamente!; **~ oneself in for sth** *fam* impelagarsi in qcsa. **let down** *vt* sciogliersi ⟨hair⟩; abbassare ⟨blinds⟩; (*lengthen*) allungare; (*disappoint*) deludere; **don't ~ me down** conto su di te. **let in** *vt* far entrare. **let off** *vt* far partire; (*not punish*) perdonare; **~ sb off doing sth** abbonare qcsa a qcno. **let out** *vt* far uscire; (*make larger*) allargare; emettere ⟨scream, groan⟩. **let through** *vt* far passare. **let up** *vi fam* diminuire

'let-down *n* delusione *f*

lethal /'liːθl/ *a* letale

letharg|ic /lɪ'θɑːdʒɪk/ *a* apatico. **~y** /'leθədʒɪ/ *n* apatia *f*

letter /'letə(r)/ *n* lettera *f*. **~-box** *n* buca *f* per le lettere. **~-head** *n* carta *f* intestata. **~ing** *n* caratteri *mpl*

lettuce /'letɪs/ *n* lattuga *f*

'let-up *n fam* pausa *f*

leukaemia /luː'kiːmɪə/ *n* leucemia *f*

level /'levl/ *a* piano; (*in height, competition*) allo stesso livello; ⟨spoonful⟩ raso; **draw ~ with sb** affiancare qcno a un livello *m*; **on the ~** *fam* giusto ● *vt* (*pt/pp* **levelled**) livellare; ⟨aim⟩ puntare (**at** su)

level: ~ 'crossing *n* passaggio *m* a livello. **~-'headed** *a* posato

lever /'liːvə(r)/ *n* leva *f* ● **lever up** *vt* sollevare ⟨con una leva⟩. **~age** /-rɪdʒ/ *n* azione *f* di una leva; *fig* influenza *f*

levy /'levɪ/ *vt* (*pt/pp* **levied**) imporre ⟨tax⟩

lewd /ljuːd/ *a* osceno

liabilit|y /laɪə'bɪlətɪ/ *n* responsabilità *f*; (*fam: burden*) peso *m*; **~ies** *pl* debiti *mpl*

liable /'laɪəbl/ *a* responsabile (**for** di); **be ~ to** ⟨rain, break etc⟩ rischiare di; (*tend to*) tendere a

liaise /lɪ'eɪz/ *vi fam* essere in contatto

liaison /lɪ'eɪzɒn/ *n* contatti *mpl*; *Mil* collegamento *m*; (*affair*) relazione *f*

liar /'laɪə(r)/ *n* bugiardo, -a *mf*

libel /'laɪbl/ *n* diffamazione *f* ● *vt* (*pt/pp* **libelled**) diffamare. **~lous** *a* diffamatorio

liberal /'lɪb(ə)rəl/ *a* ⟨tolerant⟩ di larghe vedute; ⟨generous⟩ generoso. **L~** *a Pol* liberale ● *n* liberale *mf*

liberat|e /'lɪbəreɪt/ *vt* liberare. **~ed** *a* ⟨woman⟩ emancipata. **~ion** /-'reɪʃn/ *n* liberazione *f*; (*of women*) emancipazione *f*. **~or** *n* liberatore, -trice *mf*

liberty /'lɪbətɪ/ *n* libertà *f*; **take the ~ of doing sth** prendersi la libertà di fare qcsa; **be at ~ to do sth** essere libero di fare qcsa

Libra /'liːbrə/ *n Astr* Bilancia *f*

librarian /laɪ'breərɪən/ *n* bibliotecario, -a *mf*

library /'laɪbrərɪ/ *n* biblioteca *f*

Libya /'lɪbɪə/ *n* Libia *f*. **~n** *a & n* libico, -a *mf*

lice /laɪs/ *see* **louse**

licence /'laɪsns/ *n* licenza *f*; (*for TV*) canone *m* televisivo; (*for driving*) patente *f*; (*freedom*) sregolatezza *f*. **~-plate** *n* targa *f*

license /'laɪsns/ *vt* autorizzare; **be ~d** ⟨car:⟩ avere il bollo; ⟨restaurant:⟩ essere autorizzato alla vendita di alcolici

licentious /laɪ'senʃəs/ *a* licenzioso

lick /lɪk/ *n* leccata *f*; **a ~ of paint** una passata leggera di pittura ● *vt* leccare; (*fam: defeat*) battere; leccarsi ⟨lips⟩

lid /lɪd/ *n* coperchio *m*; (*of eye*) palpebra *f*

lie¹ /laɪ/ *n* bugia *f*; **tell a ~** mentire ● *vi* (*pt/pp* **lied**, *pres p* **lying**) mentire

lie² *vi* (*pt* **lay**, *pp* **lain**, *pres p* **lying**) ⟨person:⟩ sdraiarsi; ⟨object:⟩ stare; (*remain*) rimanere; **leave sth lying about** *or* **around** lasciare qcsa in giro. **lie down** *vi* sdraiarsi

'lie: ~-down *n* **have a ~-down** fare un riposino. **~-in** *n fam* **have a ~-in** restare a letto fino a tardi

lieu /ljuː/ *n* **in ~ of** in luogo di

lieutenant /lef'tenənt/ *n* tenente *m*

life /laɪf/ *n* (*pl* **lives**) vita *f*

life: ~-belt *n* salvagente *m*. **~-boat** *n* lancia *f* di salvataggio; (*on ship*) scialuppa *f* di salvataggio. **~-buoy** *n* salvagente *m*. **~-guard** *n* bagnino *m*. **~-insurance** *n* assicurazione *f* sulla vita. **~-jacket** *n* giubbotto *m* di salvataggio. **~less** *a* inanimato. **~-like** *a* realistico. **~-long** *a* di tutta la vita. **~-size[d]** *a* in grandezza naturale. **~-time** *n* vita *f*; **the**

chance of a ~time un'occasione unica

lift /lɪft/ n ascensore m; *Auto* passaggio m ● vt sollevare; revocare ⟨*restrictions*⟩; ⟨*fam: steal*⟩ rubare ● vi ⟨*fog:*⟩ alzarsi. **lift up** vt sollevare

'lift-off n decollo m ⟨di razzo⟩

ligament /'lɪgəmənt/ n *Anat* legamento m

light¹ /laɪt/ a ⟨not dark⟩ luminoso; **~ green** verde chiaro ● n luce f; ⟨lamp⟩ lampada f; **in the ~ of** *fig* alla luce di; **have you got a ~?** ha da accendere?; **come to ~** essere rivelato ● vt ⟨pt/pp **lit** or **lighted**⟩ accendere; ⟨illuminate⟩ illuminare. **light up** vi ⟨face:⟩ illuminarsi

light² a ⟨not heavy⟩ leggero ● adv **travel ~** viaggiare con poco bagaglio

'light-bulb n lampadina f

lighten¹ /'laɪtn/ vt illuminare

lighten² vt alleggerire ⟨load⟩

lighter /'laɪtə(r)/ n accendino m

light: ~-'fingered a svelto di mano. **~-'headed** a sventato. **~-'hearted** a spensierato. **~house** n faro m. **~ing** n illuminazione f. **~ly** adv leggermente; ⟨accuse⟩ con leggerezza; ⟨without concern⟩ senza dare importanza alla cosa; **get off ~ly** cavarsela a buon mercato. **~ness** n leggerezza f

lightning /'laɪtnɪŋ/ n lampo m, fulmine m. **~-conductor** n parafulmine m

light: ~weight a leggero ● n ⟨in boxing⟩ peso m leggero. **~ year** n anno m luce

like¹ /laɪk/ a simile ● prep come; **~ this/that** così; **what's he ~?** com'è? ● conj ⟨fam: as⟩ come; ⟨Am: as if⟩ come se

like² vt piacere, gradire; **I should** or **would ~** vorrei, gradirei; **I ~ him** mi piace; **I ~ this car** mi piace questa macchina; **I ~ dancing** mi piace ballare; **I ~ that!** *fam* questa mi è piaciuta! ● n **~s and dislikes** pl gusti mpl

like|able /'laɪkəbl/ a simpatico. **~lihood** /-lɪhʊd/ n probabilità f. **~ly** a (**-ier**, **-iest**) probabile ● adv probabilmente; **not ~ly!** *fam* neanche per sogno!

like-'minded a con gusti affini

liken /'laɪkən/ vt paragonare (**to** a)

like|ness /'laɪknɪs/ n somiglianza f. **'~wise** adv lo stesso

liking /'laɪkɪŋ/ n gusto m; **is it to your**

~? è di suo gusto?; **take a ~ to sb** prendere qcno in simpatia

lilac /'laɪlək/ n lillà m ● a color lillà

lily /'lɪlɪ/ n giglio m. **~ of the valley** n mughetto m

limb /lɪm/ n arto m

limber /'lɪmbə(r)/ vi **~ up** sciogliersi i muscoli

lime¹ /laɪm/ n ⟨fruit⟩ cedro m; ⟨tree⟩ tiglio m

lime² n calce f. **'~light** n **be in the ~light** essere molto in vista. **'~stone** n calcare m

limit /'lɪmɪt/ n limite m; **that's the ~!** *fam* questo è troppo! ● vt limitare (**to** a). **~ation** /-'teɪʃn/ n limite m. **~ed** a ristretto; **~ed company** società f inv a responsabilità limitata

limousine /'lɪməziːn/ n limousine f inv

limp¹ /lɪmp/ n andatura f zoppicante; **have a ~** zoppicare ● vi zoppicare

limp² a floscio

line¹ /laɪn/ n linea f; ⟨length of rope, cord⟩ filo m; ⟨of writing⟩ riga f; ⟨of poem⟩ verso m; ⟨row⟩ fila f; ⟨wrinkle⟩ ruga f; ⟨of business⟩ settore m; ⟨Am: queue⟩ coda f; **in ~ with** in conformità con ● vt segnare; fiancheggiare ⟨street⟩. **line up** vi allinearsi ● vt allineare

line² vt foderare ⟨garment⟩

linear /'lɪnɪə(r)/ a lineare

lined¹ /laɪnd/ a ⟨face⟩ rugoso; ⟨paper⟩ a righe

lined² a ⟨garment⟩ foderato

linen /'lɪnɪn/ n lino m; ⟨articles⟩ biancheria f ● attrib di lino

liner /'laɪnə(r)/ n nave f di linea

'linesman n *Sport* guardalinee m inv

linger /'lɪŋɡə(r)/ vi indugiare

lingerie /'lõʒərɪ/ n biancheria f intima ⟨da donna⟩

linguist /'lɪŋɡwɪst/ n linguista mf

linguistic /lɪŋ'gwɪstɪk/ a linguistico. **~s** n linguistica f sg

lining /'laɪnɪŋ/ n ⟨of garment⟩ fodera f; ⟨of brakes⟩ guarnizione f

link /lɪŋk/ n ⟨of chain⟩ anello m; *fig* legame m ● vt collegare. **link up** vi unirsi (**with** a); *TV* collegarsi

lino /'laɪnəʊ/ n, **linoleum** /lɪ'nəʊlɪəm/ n linoleum m

lint /lɪnt/ n garza f

lion /'laɪən/ n leone m. **~ess** n leonessa f

lip /lɪp/ n labbro m ⟨pl labbra f⟩; ⟨edge⟩ bordo m

lip: ~-read vi leggere le labbra; **~-reading** n lettura f delle labbra. **~-service** n **pay ~-service to** approvare soltanto a parole. **~salve** n burro m [di] cacao. **~stick** n rossetto m

liqueur /lɪˈkjʊə(r)/ n liquore m

liquid /ˈlɪkwɪd/ n liquido m ● a liquido

liquidat|e /ˈlɪkwɪdeɪt/ vt liquidare. **~ion** /-ˈdeɪʃn/ n liquidazione f; **go into ~ion** Comm andare in liquidazione

liquidize /ˈlɪkwɪdaɪz/ vt rendere liquido. **~r** n Culin frullatore m

liquor /ˈlɪkə(r)/ n bevanda f alcoolica

liquorice /ˈlɪkərɪs/ n liquirizia f

liquor store n Am negozio m di alcolici

lisp /lɪsp/ n pronuncia f con la lisca ● vi parlare con la lisca

list¹ /lɪst/ n lista f ● vt elencare

list² vi ⟨ship:⟩ inclinarsi

listen /ˈlɪsn/ vi ascoltare; **~ to** ascoltare. **~er** n ascoltatore, -trice mf

listings /ˈlɪstɪŋz/ npl TV programma m tv

listless /ˈlɪstlɪs/ a svogliato

lit /lɪt/ see **light¹**

literacy /ˈlɪtərəsɪ/ n alfabetizzazione f

literal /ˈlɪtərəl/ a letterale. **~ly** adv letteralmente

literary /ˈlɪtərərɪ/ a letterario

literate /ˈlɪtərət/ a **be ~** saper leggere e scrivere

literature /ˈlɪtrətʃə(r)/ n letteratura f

Lithuania /lɪθjʊˈeɪnɪə/ n Lituania f. **~n** a & n lituano, -a mf

litigation /lɪtɪˈgeɪʃn/ n causa f [giudiziaria]

litre /ˈliːtə(r)/ n litro m

litter /ˈlɪtə(r)/ n immondizie fpl; Zool figliata f ● vt **be ~ed with** essere ingombrato di. **~-bin** n bidone m della spazzatura

little /ˈlɪtl/ a piccolo; ⟨not much⟩ poco ● adv & n poco m; **a ~** un po'; **a ~ water** un po' d'acqua; **a ~ better** un po' meglio; **~ by ~** a poco a poco

liturgy /ˈlɪtədʒɪ/ n liturgia f

live¹ /laɪv/ a vivo; ⟨ammunition⟩ carico; **~ broadcast** trasmissione f in diretta; **be ~** Electr essere sotto tensione; **~ wire** n fig persona f dinamica ● adv ⟨broadcast⟩ in diretta

live² /lɪv/ vi vivere; ⟨reside⟩ abitare; **~ with** convivere con. **live down** vt far dimenticare. **live off** vt vivere alle spalle di. **live on** vt vivere di ● vi sopravvivere. **live up** vt **~ it up** far la bella vita. **live up to** vt essere all'altezza di

liveli|hood /ˈlaɪvlɪhʊd/ n mezzi mpl di sostentamento. **~ness** n vivacità f

lively /ˈlaɪvlɪ/ a (**-ier, -iest**) vivace

liven /ˈlaɪvn/ vt **~ up** vivacizzare ● vi vivacizzarsi

liver /ˈlɪvə(r)/ n fegato m

lives /laɪvz/ see **life**

livestock /ˈlaɪv-/ n bestiame m

livid /ˈlɪvɪd/ a fam livido

living /ˈlɪvɪŋ/ a vivo ● n **earn one's ~** guadagnarsi da vivere; **the ~** pl i vivi. **~-room** n soggiorno m

lizard /ˈlɪzəd/ n lucertola f

load /ləʊd/ n carico m; **~s of** fam un sacco di ● vt caricare. **~ed** a carico; ⟨fam: rich⟩ ricchissimo

loaf¹ /ləʊf/ n (pl **loaves**) pagnotta f

loaf² vi oziare

loan /ləʊn/ n prestito m; **on ~** in prestito ● vt prestare

loath /ləʊθ/ a **be ~ to do sth** essere restio a fare qcsa

loath|e /ləʊð/ vt detestare. **~ing** n disgusto m. **~some** a disgustoso

loaves /ləʊvz/ see **loaf**

lobby /ˈlɒbɪ/ n atrio m; Pol gruppo m di pressione, lobby m inv

lobster /ˈlɒbstə(r)/ n aragosta f

local /ˈləʊkl/ a locale; **I'm not ~** non sono del posto ● n abitante mf del luogo; ⟨fam: public house⟩ pub m inv locale. **~ au'thority** n autorità f locale. **~ call** n Teleph telefonata f urbana. **~ government** n autorità f inv locale

locality /ləʊˈkælətɪ/ n zona f

localized /ˈləʊkəlaɪzd/ a localizzato

locally /ˈləʊkəlɪ/ adv localmente; ⟨live, work⟩ nei paraggi

'local network n Comput rete f locale

locat|e /ləʊˈkeɪt/ vt situare; trovare ⟨person⟩; **be ~ed** essere situato. **~ion** /-ˈkeɪʃn/ n posizione f; **filmed on ~ion** girato in esterni

lock¹ /lɒk/ n ⟨of hair⟩ ciocca f

lock² n ⟨on door⟩ serratura f; ⟨on canal⟩ chiusa f ● vt chiudere a chiave; bloccare ⟨wheels⟩ ● vi chiudersi. **lock in** vt chiudere dentro. **lock out** vt chiudere fuori. **lock up** vt ⟨in prison⟩ mettere dentro ● vi chiudere

locker /ˈlɒkə(r)/ n armadietto m

locket /ˈlɒkɪt/ n medaglione m

lock: **~-out** n serrata f. **~smith** n fabbro m

locomotive /ləʊkəˈməʊtɪv/ n locomotiva f

locum /ˈləʊkəm/ n sostituto, -a mf

locust /ˈləʊkəst/ n locusta f

lodge /lɒdʒ/ n ⟨porter's⟩ portineria f; ⟨masonic⟩ loggia f ● vt presentare ⟨claim, complaint⟩; ⟨with bank, solicitor⟩

depositare; **be ~d** esserci conficcato ●*vi* essere a pensione (**with** da); (*become fixed*) conficcarsi. **~r** *n* inquilino, -a *mf*

lodgings /'lɒdʒɪŋz/ *npl* camere *fpl* in affitto

loft /lɒft/ *n* soffitta *f*

lofty /'lɒftɪ/ *a* (**-ier, -iest**) alto; (*haughty*) altezzoso

log /lɒg/ *n* ceppo *m*; *Auto* libretto *m* di circolazione; *Naut* giornale *m* di bordo ●*vt* (*pt/pp* **logged**) registrare. **log on to** *vt Comput* connettersi a

logarithm /'lɒgərɪðm/ *n* logaritmo *m*

'log-book *n Naut* giornale *m* di bordo; *Auto* libretto *m* di circolazione

loggerheads /'lɒgə-/ *npl* **be at ~** *fam* essere in totale disaccordo

logic /'lɒdʒɪk/ *n* logica *f*. **~al** *a* logico. **~ally** *adv* logicamente

logistics /lə'dʒɪstɪks/ *npl* logistica *f*

logo /'ləʊgəʊ/ *n* logo *m inv*

loin /lɔɪn/ *n Culin* lombata *f*

loiter /'lɔɪtə(r)/ *vi* gironzolare

loll|ipop /'lɒlɪpɒp/ *n* lecca-lecca *m inv*. **~y** *n* lecca-lecca *m inv*; (*fam: money*) quattrini *mpl*

London /'lʌndən/ *n* Londra *f*. ●*attrib* londinese, di Londra. **~er** *n* londinese *mf*

lone /ləʊn/ *a* solitario. **~liness** *n* solitudine *f*

lonely /'ləʊnlɪ/ *a* (**-ier, -iest**) solitario; (*person*) solo

lone|r /'ləʊnə(r)/ *n* persona *f* solitaria. **~some** *a* solo

long¹ /lɒŋ/ *a* lungo; **a ~ time** molto tempo; **a ~ way** distante; **in the ~ run** a lungo andare; (*in the end*) alla fin fine ●*adv* a lungo, lungamente; **how ~ is it?** quanto è lungo?; (*in time*) quanto dura?; **all day ~** tutto il giorno; **not ~ ago** non molto tempo fa; **before ~** fra breve; **he's no ~er here** non è più qui; **as** *or* **so ~as** finché; (*provided that*) purché; **so ~!** *fam* ciao!; **~ out!** atten ~?** [ti] ci vuole molto?

long² *vi* **~ for** desiderare ardentemente

long-'distance *a* a grande distanza; *Sport* di fondo; (*call*) interurbano

'longhand *n* **in ~** in scrittura ordinaria

longing /'lɒŋɪŋ/ *a* desideroso ●*n* brama *f*. **~ly** *adv* con desiderio

longitude /'lɒŋgɪtjuːd/ *n Geog* longitudine *f*

long: ~ jump *n* salto *m* in lungo. **~-life 'milk** *n* latte *m* a lunga conservazione.

~-lived /-'lɪvd/ *a* longevo. **~-range** *a Mil, Aeron* a lunga portata; (*forecast*) a lungo termine. **~-sighted** *a* presbite. **~-sleeved** *a* a maniche lunghe. **~-suffering** *a* infinitamente paziente. **~ wave** *n* onde *fpl* lunghe. **~-winded** /-'wɪndɪd/ *a* prolisso

loo /luː/ *n fam* gabinetto *m*

look /lʊk/ *n* occhiata *f*; (*appearance*) aspetto *m*; [**good**] **~s** *pl* bellezza *f*; **have a ~ at** dare un'occhiata a ●*vi* guardare; (*seem*) sembrare; **~ here!** mi ascolti bene!; **~ at** guardare; **~ for** cercare; **~ like** (*resemble*) assomigliare a. **look after** *vt* badare a. **look down** *vi* guardare in basso; **~ down on sb** *fig* guardare dall'alto in basso qcno. **look forward to** *vt* essere impaziente di. **look in on** *vt* passare da. **look into** *vt* (*examine*) esaminare. **look on to** *vt* (*room:*) dare su. **look out** *vi* guardare fuori; (*take care*) fare attenzione; **~ out for** cercare; **~ out!** attento! **look round** *vi* girarsi; (*in shop, town etc*) dare un'occhiata. **look through** *vt* dare un'occhiata a (*script, notes*). **look up** *vi* guardare in alto; **~ up to sb** *fig* rispettare qcno ●*vt* cercare [nel dizionario] (*word*); (*visit*) andare a trovare

'look-out /'lʊkaʊt/ *n* guardia *f*; (*prospect*) prospettiva *f*; **be on the ~ for** tenere gli occhi aperti per

loom /luːm/ *vi* apparire; *fig* profilarsi

loony /'luːnɪ/ *a & n fam* matto, -a *mf*. **~ bin** *n* manicomio *m*

loop /luːp/ *n* cappio *m*; (*on garment*) passante *m*. **~hole** *n* (*in the law*) scappatoia *f*

loose /luːs/ *a* libero; (*knot*) allentato; (*page*) staccato; (*clothes*) largo; (*morals*) dissoluto; (*inexact*) vago; **be at a ~ end** non sapere cosa fare; **come ~** (*knot:*) sciogliersi; **set ~** liberare. **~ 'change** *n* spiccioli *mpl*. **~ly** *adv* scorrevolmente; (*defined*) vagamente

loosen /'luːsn/ *vt* sciogliere

loot /luːt/ *n* bottino *m* ●*vt/i* depredare. **~er** *n* predatore, -trice *mf*. **~ing** *n* saccheggio *m*

lop /lɒp/ **~ off** *vt* (*pt/pp* **lopped**) potare

lop'sided *a* sbilenco

lord /lɔːd/ *n* signore *m*; (*title*) Lord *m*; **House of L~s** Camera *f* dei Lords; **the L~'s Prayer** il Padrenostro; **good L~!** Dio mio!

lore /lɔː(r)/ *n* tradizioni *fpl*

lorry /'lɒrɪ/ *n* camion *m inv*; **~ driver** camionista *mf*

lose /luːz/ *v* (*pt/pp* **lost**) ●*vt* perdere ●*vi* perdere; (*clock:*) essere indietro; **get lost** perdersi; **get lost!** *fam* va a quel paese! **~r** *n* perdente *mf*

loss /lɒs/ n perdita f; **~es** pl Comm perdite fpl; **be at a ~** essere perplesso; **be at a ~ for words** non trovare le parole

lost /lɒst/ see **lose** ● a perduto. **~ 'property office** n ufficio m oggetti smarriti

lot[1] /lɒt/ (at auction) lotto m; **draw ~s** tirare a sorte

lot[2] n the **~** il tutto; **a ~ of, ~s of** molti; **the ~ of you** tutti voi; **it has changed a ~** è cambiato molto

lotion /ˈləʊʃn/ n lozione f

lottery /ˈlɒtərɪ/ n lotteria f. **~ ticket** n biglietto m della lotteria

loud /laʊd/ a sonoro, alto; ⟨colours⟩ sgargiante ● adv forte; **out ~** ad alta voce. **~ 'hailer** n megafono m. **~ly** adv forte. **~'speaker** n altoparlante m

lounge /laʊndʒ/ n salotto m; (in hotel) salone m ● vi poltrire. **~ suit** n vestito m da uomo, completo m da uomo

louse /laʊs/ n (pl **lice**) pidocchio m

lousy /ˈlaʊzɪ/ a (**-ier, -iest**) fam schifoso

lout /laʊt/ n zoticone m. **~ish** a rozzo

lovable /ˈlʌvəbl/ a adorabile

love /lʌv/ n amore m; Tennis zero m; **in ~** innamorato (**with** di) ● vt amare ⟨person, country⟩; **I ~ watching tennis** mi piace molto guardare il tennis. **~-affair** n relazione f [sentimentale]. **~ letter** n lettera f d'amore

lovely /ˈlʌvlɪ/ a (**-ier, -iest**) bello; (in looks) bello, attraente; (in character) piacevole; ⟨meal⟩ delizioso; **have a ~ time** divertirsi molto

lover /ˈlʌvə(r)/ n amante mf

love: ~ song n canzone f d'amore. **~ story** n storia f d'amore

loving /ˈlʌvɪŋ/ a affettuoso

low /ləʊ/ a basso; ⟨depressed⟩ giù inv ● adv basso; **feel ~** sentirsi giù ● n minimo m; Meteorol depressione f; **at an all-time ~** ⟨prices etc⟩ al livello minimo

low: ~brow a di scarsa cultura. **~-cut** a ⟨dress⟩ scollato

lower /ˈləʊə(r)/ a & adv see **low** ● vt abbassare; **~ oneself** abbassarsi

low: ~-'fat a magro. **~-'grade** a di qualità inferiore. **~-key** fig moderato. **~lands** /-ləndz/ npl pianure fpl. **~ 'tide** n bassa marea f

loyal /ˈlɔɪəl/ a leale. **~ty** n lealtà f

lozenge /ˈlɒzɪndʒ/ n losanga f; (tablet) pastiglia f

LP n abbr **long-playing record**

Ltd abbr (**Limited**) s.r.l.

lubricant /ˈluːbrɪkənt/ n lubrificante m

lubricat|e /ˈluːbrɪkeɪt/ vt lubrificare. **~ion** /-ˈkeɪʃn/ n lubrificazione f

lucid /ˈluːsɪd/ a ⟨explanation⟩ chiaro; (sane) lucido. **~ity** /-ˈsɪdətɪ/ n lucidità f; (of explanation) chiarezza f

luck /lʌk/ n fortuna f; **bad ~** sfortuna f; **good ~!** buona fortuna! **~ily** adv fortunatamente

lucky /ˈlʌkɪ/ a (**-ier, -iest**) fortunato; **be ~** essere fortunato; ⟨thing:⟩ portare fortuna. **~ 'charm** n portafortuna m inv

lucrative /ˈluːkrətɪv/ a lucrativo

ludicrous /ˈluːdɪkrəs/ a ridicolo. **~ly** adv ⟨expensive, complex⟩ eccessivamente

lug /lʌg/ vt (pt/pp **lugged**) fam trascinare

luggage /ˈlʌgɪdʒ/ n bagaglio m; **~-rack** n portabagagli m inv. **~ trolley** n carrello m portabagagli. **~-van** n bagagliaio m

lukewarm /ˈluːk-/ a tiepido; fig poco entusiasta

lull /lʌl/ n pausa f ● vt **~ to sleep** cullare

lullaby /ˈlʌləbaɪ/ n ninnananna f

lumbago /lʌmˈbeɪgəʊ/ n lombaggine f

lumber /ˈlʌmbə(r)/ n cianfrusaglie fpl; (Am: timber) legname m ● vt fam **~ sb with sth** affibbiare qcsa a qcno. **~ jack** n tagliaboschi m inv

luminous /ˈluːmɪnəs/ a luminoso

lump[1] /lʌmp/ n (of sugar) zolletta f; (swelling) gonfiore m; (in breast) nodulo m; (in sauce) grumo m ● vt **~ together** ammucchiare

lump[2] vt **~ it** fam **you'll just have to ~ it** che ti piaccia o no è così

lump sum n somma f globale

lumpy /ˈlʌmpɪ/ a (**-ier, -iest**) grumoso

lunacy /ˈluːnəsɪ/ n follia f

lunar /ˈluːnə(r)/ a lunare

lunatic /ˈluːnətɪk/ n pazzo, -a mf

lunch /lʌntʃ/ n pranzo m ● vi pranzare

luncheon /ˈlʌntʃn/ n (formal) pranzo m. **~ meat** n carne f in scatola. **~ voucher** n buono m pasto

lunch: ~-hour n intervallo m per il pranzo. **~-time** n ora f di pranzo

lung /lʌŋ/ n polmone m. **~ cancer** n cancro m al polmone

lunge /lʌndʒ/ vi lanciarsi (**at** su)

lurch[1] /lɜːtʃ/ n **leave in the ~** fam lasciare nei guai

lurch[2] vi barcollare

lure /lʊə(r)/ n esca f; fig lusinga f ● vt adescare

lurid /'lʊərɪd/ a (gaudy) sgargiante; (sensational) sensazionalistico

lurk /lɜːk/ vi appostarsi

luscious /'lʌʃəs/ a saporito; fig sexy inv

lush /lʌʃ/ a lussureggiante

lust /lʌst/ n lussuria f ● vi ~ **after** desiderare [fortemente]. **~ful** a lussurioso

lusty /'lʌsti/ a (-ier, -iest) vigoroso

lute /luːt/ n liuto m

luxuriant /lʌg'ʒʊərɪənt/ a lussureg-giante

luxurious /lʌg'ʒʊərɪəs/ a lussuoso

luxury /'lʌkʃərɪ/ n lusso m ● attrib di lusso

lying /'laɪɪŋ/ see lie[1] & [2] ● n mentire m

lymph gland /'lɪmf/ n linfoghiandola f

lynch /lɪntʃ/ vt linciare

lynx /lɪŋks/ n lince f

lyric /'lɪrɪk/ a lirico. **~al** a lirico; (fam: enthusiastic) entusiasta. **~s** npl parole fpl

Mm

mac /mæk/ n fam impermeabile m

macabre /mə'kɑːbr/ a macabro

macaroni /mækə'rəʊnɪ/ n maccheroni mpl

mace[1] /meɪs/ n (staff) mazza f

mace[2] n (spice) macis m o f

machinations /mækɪ'neɪʃnz/ npl macchinazioni fpl

machine /mə'ʃiːn/ n macchina f ● vt (sew) cucire a macchina; Techn lavorare a macchina. **~-gun** n mitragliatrice f

machinery /mə'ʃiːnərɪ/ n macchinario m

machinist /mə'ʃiːnɪst/ n macchinista mf; (on sewing machine) lavorante mf adetto, -a alla macchina da cucire

machismo /mə'tʃɪzməʊ/ n machismo m

macho /'mætʃəʊ/ a macho inv

mackerel /'mækr(ə)l/ n inv sgombro m

mackintosh /'mækɪntɒʃ/ n impermeabile m

mad /mæd/ a (**madder, maddest**) pazzo, matto; (fam: angry) furioso (**at** con); **like ~** fam come un pazzo; **be ~ about** sb/sth (fam: keen on) andare matto per qcno/qcsa

madam /'mædəm/ n signora f

madden /'mædən/ vt (make angry) far diventare matto

made /meɪd/ see make; **~ to measure** [fatto] su misura

Madeira cake /mə'dɪərə/ n dolce m di pan di Spagna

mad|ly /'mædlɪ/ adv fam follemente. **~ly in love** innamorato follemente. **~man** n pazzo m. **~ness** n pazzia f

madonna /mə'dɒnə/ n madonna f

magazine /mægə'ziːn/ n rivista f; Mil, Phot magazzino m

maggot /'mægət/ n verme m

Magi /'meɪdʒaɪ/ npl **the ~** i Re Magi

magic /'mædʒɪk/ n magia f; (tricks) giochi mpl di prestigio ● a magico; (trick) di prestigio. **~al** a magico

magician /mə'dʒɪʃn/ n mago, -a mf; (entertainer) prestigiatore, -trice mf

magistrate /'mædʒɪstreɪt/ n magistrato m

magnanim|ity /mægnə'nɪmətɪ/ n magnanimità f. **~ous** /-'nænɪməs/ a magnanimo

magnet /'mægnɪt/ n magnete m, calamita f. **~ic** /-'netɪk/ a magnetico. **~ism** n magnetismo m

magnification /mægnɪfɪ'keɪʃn/ n ingrandimento m

magnificen|ce /mæg'nɪfɪsəns/ n magnificenza f. **~t** a magnifico

magnify /'mægnɪfaɪ/ vt (pt/pp -ied) ingrandire; (exaggerate) ingigantire. **~ing glass** n lente f d'ingrandimento

magnitude /'mægnɪtjuːd/ n grandezza f; (importance) importanza f

magpie /'mægpaɪ/ n gazza f

mahogany /mə'hɒgənɪ/ n mogano m ● a di mogano

maid /meɪd/ n cameriera f; old ~ pej zitella f

maiden /'meɪdn/ n liter fanciulla f ● a (speech, voyage) inaugurale. **~ 'aunt** n zia f zitella. **~ name** n nome m da ragazza

mail /meɪl/ n posta f ● vt impostare

mail: ~-bag n sacco m postale. **~box** n

Am cassetta *f* delle lettere; (*e-mail*) casella *f* di posta elettronica. **~ing list** *n* elenco *m* d'indirizzi per un mailing. **~man** *n Am* postino *m*. **~ order** *n* vendita *f* per corrispondenza. **~-order firm** *n* ditta *f* di vendita per corrispondenza

mailshot /'meɪlʃɒt/ *n* mailing *m inv*

maim /meɪm/ *vt* menomare

main[1] /meɪm/ *n* (*water, gas, electricity*) conduttura *f* principale

main[2] *a* principale; **the ~ thing is to...** la cosa essenziale è di... ● *n* **in the ~** in complesso

main: ~land /-lənd/ *n* continente *m*. **~ly** *adv* principalmente. **~stay** *n fig* pilastro *m*. **~ street** *n* via *f* principale

maintain /meɪn'teɪn/ *vt* mantenere; (*keep in repair*) curare la manutenzione di; (*claim*) sostenere

maintenance /'meɪntənəns/ *n* mantenimento *m*; (*care*) manutenzione *f*; (*allowance*) alimenti *mpl*

maisonette /meɪzə'net/ *n* appartamento *m* a due piani

majestic /mə'dʒestɪk/ *a* maestoso

majesty /'mædʒəstɪ/ *n* maestà *f inv*; **His/Her M~** Sua Maestà

major /'meɪdʒə(r)/ *a* maggiore; **~ road** strada *f* con diritto di precedenza ● *n Mil, Mus* maggiore *m* ● *vi Am* **~ in** specializzarsi in

Majorca /mə'jɔːkə/ *n* Maiorca *f*

majority /mə'dʒɒrətɪ/ *n* maggioranza *f*; **be in the ~** avere la maggioranza

make /meɪk/ *n* (*brand*) marca *f* ● *v* (*pt/pp* **made**) ● *vt* fare; (*earn*) guadagnare; rendere ‹*happy, clear*›; prendere ‹*decision*›; **~ sb laugh** far ridere qcno; **~ sb do sth** far fare qcsa a qcno; **~ it** (*to party, top of hill etc*) farcela; **what time do you ~ it?** che ore fai? ● *vi* **~ as if to** fare do *vi* arrangiarsi. **make for** *vt* dirigersi verso. **make off** *vi* fuggire. **make out** *vt* (*distinguish*) distinguere; (*write out*) rilasciare ‹*cheque*›; compilare ‹*list*›; (*claim*) far credere. **make over** *vt* cedere. **make up** *vt* (*constitute*) comporre; (*complete*) completare; (*invent*) inventare; (*apply cosmetics to*) truccare; fare ‹*parcel*›; **~ up one's mind** decidersi; **~ it up** (*after quarrel*) riconciliarsi ● *vi* (*after quarrel*) fare la pace; **~ up for** compensare; **~ up for lost time** recuperare il tempo perso

'make-believe *n* finzione *f*

maker /'meɪkə(r)/ *n* fabbricante *mf*; **M~** *Relig* Creatore *m*

make: ~ shift *a* di fortuna ● *n* espediente *m*. **~-up** *n* trucco *m*; (*character*) natura *f*

making /'meɪkɪŋ/ *n* **have the ~s of** aver la stoffa di

maladjust|ed /mælə'dʒʌstɪd/ *a* disadattato

malaise /mə'leɪz/ *n fig* malessere *m*

malaria /mə'leərɪə/ *n* malaria *f*

Malaysia /mə'leɪzɪə/ *n* Malesia *f*

male /meɪl/ *a* maschile ● *n* maschio *m*. **~ nurse** *n* infermiere *m*

malevolen|ce /mə'levələns/ *n* malevolenza *f*. **~t** *a* malevolo

malfunction /mæl'fʌŋkʃn/ *n* funzionamento *m* imperfetto ● *vi* funzionare male

malice /'mælɪs/ *n* malignità *f*; **bear sb ~** voler del male a qcno

malicious /mə'lɪʃəs/ *a* maligno

malign /mə'laɪn/ *vt* malignare su

malignan|cy /mə'lɪgnənsɪ/ *n* malignità *f*. **~t** *a* maligno

malinger /mə'lɪŋgə(r)/ *vi* fingersi malato. **~er** *n* scansafatiche *mf inv*

malleable /'mælɪəbl/ *a* malleabile

mallet /'mælɪt/ *n* martello *m* di legno

malnu'trition /mæl-/ *n* malnutrizione *f*

mal'practice /mæl-/ *n* negligenza *f*

malt /mɔːlt/ *n* malto *m*

Malta /'mɔːltə/ *n* Malta *f*. **~ese** /-iːz/ *a* & *n* maltese *mf*

mal'treat /mæl-/ *vt* maltrattare. **~ment** *n* maltrattamento *m*

mammal /'mæml/ *n* mammifero *m*

mammoth /'mæməθ/ *a* mastodontico ● *n* mammut *m inv*

man /mæn/ *n* (*pl* **men**) uomo *m*; (*chess, draughts*) pedina *f* ● *vt* (*pt/pp* **manned**) equipaggiare; essere di servizio a ‹*counter, telephones*›

manage /'mænɪdʒ/ *vt* dirigere; gestire ‹*shop, affairs*›; (*cope with*) farcela; **~ to do sth** riuscire a fare qcsa ● *vi* riuscire; (*cope*) farcela (**on** con). **~able** /-əbl/ *a* ‹*hair*› docile; ‹*size*› maneggevole. **~ment** /-mənt/ *n* gestione *f*; **the ~ment** la direzione

manager /'mænɪdʒə(r)/ *n* direttore *m*; (*of shop, bar*) gestore *m*; *Sport* manager *m inv*. **~ess** /-'res/ *n* direttrice *f*. **~ial** /-'dʒɪərɪəl/ *a* **~ial staff** personale *m* direttivo

managing /'mænɪdʒɪŋ/ *a* **~ director** direttore, -trice *mf* generale

mandarin /'mændərɪn/ *n* **~ [orange]** mandarino *m*

mandat|e /'mændeɪt/ *n* mandato *m*.
~ory /-dətrɪ/ *a* obbligatorio

mane /meɪn/ *n* criniera *f*

mangle /'mæŋgl/ *vt* (*damage*)
maciullare

mango /'mæŋgəʊ/ *n* (*pl* **-es**) mango *m*

mangy /'meɪndʒɪ/ *a* (*dog*) rognoso

man: **~'handle** *vt* malmenare. **~hole** *n*
botola *f*. **~hole cover** *n* tombino *m*.
~hood *n* età *f* adulta; (*quality*) virilità *f*.
~-hour *n* ora *f* lavorativa. **~-hunt** *n*
caccia *f* all'uomo

man|ia /'meɪnɪə/ *n* mania *f*. **~iac** /-ɪæk/
n maniaco, -a *mf*

manicure /'mænɪkjʊə(r)/ *n* manicure *f*
inv ● *vt* fare la manicure a

manifest /'mænɪfest/ *a* manifesto ● *vt*
~ itself manifestarsi. **~ly** *adv* palese-
mente

manifesto /mænɪ'festəʊ/ *n* manifesto *m*

manifold /'mænɪfəʊld/ *a* molteplice

manipulat|e /mə'nɪpjʊleɪt/ *vt* manipo-
lare. **~ion** /-'leɪʃn/ *n* manipolazione *f*

man'kind *n* genere *m* umano

manly /'mænlɪ/ *a* virile

'man-made *a* artificiale. **~ fibre** *n* fibra *f* sintetica

manner /'mænə(r)/ *n* maniera *f*; **in
this ~** in questo modo; **have no ~s**
avere dei pessimi modi; **good/bad ~s**
buone/cattive maniere *fpl*. **~ism** *n* affettazione *f*

manœuvre /mə'nu:və(r)/ *n* manovra *f*
● *vt* fare manovra con (*vehicle*); manovrare (*person*)

manor /'mænə(r)/ *n* maniero *m*

'manpower *n* manodopera *f*

mansion /'mænʃn/ *n* palazzo *m*

'manslaughter *n* omicidio *m* colposo

mantelpiece /'mæntl-/ *n* mensola *f* di
caminetto

manual /'mænjʊəl/ *a* manuale ● *n* manuale *m*

manufacture /mænjʊ'fæktʃə(r)/ *vt*
fabbricare ● *n* manifattura *f*. **~r** *n* fabbricante *m*

manure /mə'njʊə(r)/ *n* concime *m*

manuscript /'mænjʊskrɪpt/ *n* mano-
scritto *m*

many /'menɪ/ *a* & *pron* molti; **there
are as ~ boys as girls** ci sono tanti
ragazzi quante ragazze; **as ~ as 500**
ben 500; **as ~ as that** così tanti; **as ~**
altrettanti; **very ~, a good/great ~**
moltissimi; **~ a time** molte volte

map /mæp/ *n* carta *f* geografica; (*of*
town) mappa *f* ● **map out** *vt* (*pt/pp*
mapped) *fig* programmare

maple /'meɪpl/ *n* acero *m*

mar /mɑ:(r)/ *vt* (*pt/pp* **marred**) rovinare

marathon /'mærəθən/ *n* maratona *f*

marble /'mɑ:bl/ *n* marmo *m*; (*for game*)
pallina *f* ● *attrib* di marmo

March /mɑ:tʃ/ *n* marzo *m*

march *n* marcia *f*; (*protest*) dimostrazione *f* ● *vi* marciare ● *vt* far marciare;
~ sb off scortare qcno fuori

mare /meə(r)/ *n* giumenta *f*

margarine /mɑ:dʒə'ri:n/ *n* margarina *f*

margin /'mɑ:dʒɪn/ *n* margine *m*. **~al**
a marginale. **~ally** *adv* marginalmente

marigold /'mærɪgəʊld/ *n* calendula *f*

marijuana /mærʊ'wɑ:nə/ *n* marijuana *f*

marina /mə'ri:nə/ *n* porticciolo *m*

marinade /mærɪ'neɪd/ *n* marinata *f*
● *vt* marinare

marine /mə'ri:n/ *a* marino ● *n* (*sailor*)
soldato *m* di fanteria marina

marionette /mærɪə'net/ *n* marionetta *f*

marital /'mærɪtl/ *a* coniugale. **~
status** stato *m* civile

maritime /'mærɪtaɪm/ *a* marittimo

mark[1] /mɑ:k/ *n* (*currency*) marco *m*

mark[2] *n* (*stain*) macchia *f*; (*sign*,
indication) segno *m*; *Sch* voto *m* ● *vt* segnare; (*stain*) macchiare; *Sch* correggere; *Sport* marcare; **~ time** *Mil* segnare
il passo; *fig* non far progressi; **~ my
words** ricordati quello che dico. **mark
out** *vt* delimitare; *fig* designare

marked /mɑ:kt/ *a* marcato. **~ly** /-kɪdlɪ/
adv notevolmente

marker /'mɑ:kə(r)/ *n* (*for highlighting*)
evidenziatore *m*; *Sport* marcatore *m*; (*of
exam*) esaminatore, -trice *mf*

market /'mɑ:kɪt/ *n* mercato *m* ● *vt* vendere al mercato; (*launch*) commercializzare; **on the ~** sul mercato. **~ing**
n marketing *m*. **~ re'search** *n* ricerca *f*
di mercato

marksman /'mɑ:ksmən/ *n* tiratore *m*
scelto

marmalade /'mɑ:məleɪd/ *n* marmellata *f* d'arance

maroon /mə'ru:n/ *a* marrone rossastro

marooned /mə'ru:nd/ *a* abbandonato

marquee /mɑ:'ki:/ *n* tendone *m*

marquis /'mɑ:kwɪs/ *n* marchese *m*

marriage /'mærɪdʒ/ *n* matrimonio *m*

married /'mærɪd/ *a* sposato; (*life*) coniugale

marrow /'mærəʊ/ n Anat midollo m; (vegetable) zucca f

marr|y /'mærɪ/ vt (pt/pp -ied) sposare; **get ~ied** sposarsi ● vi sposarsi

marsh /mɑːʃ/ n palude f

marshal /'mɑːʃl/ n (steward) cerimoniere m ● vt (pt/pp **marshalled**) fig organizzare ⟨arguments⟩

marshy /'mɑːʃɪ/ a paludoso

marsupial /mɑːˈsuːpɪəl/ n marsupiale m

martial /'mɑːʃl/ a marziale

martyr /'mɑːtə(r)/ n martire mf ● vt martirizzare. **~dom** /-dəm/ n martirio m. **~ed** a fam da martire

marvel /'mɑːvl/ n meraviglia f ● vi (pt/pp **marvelled**) meravigliarsi (at di). **~lous** /-vələs/ a meraviglioso

Marxis|m /'mɑːksɪzm/ n marxismo m. **~t** a & n marxista mf

marzipan /'mɑːzɪpæn/ n marzapane m

mascara /mæˈskɑːrə/ n mascara m inv

mascot /'mæskət/ n mascotte f inv

masculin|e /'mæskjʊlɪn/ a maschile ● n Gram maschile m. **~ity** /-'lɪnətɪ/ n mascolinità f

mash /mæʃ/ vt impastare. **~ed potatoes** npl purè m inv di patate

mask /mɑːsk/ n maschera f ● vt mascherare

masochis|m /'mæsəkɪzm/ n masochismo m. **~t** /-ɪst/ n masochista mf

mason /'meɪsn/ n muratore m

Mason n massone m. **~ic** /məˈsɒnɪk/ a massonico

masonry /'meɪsnrɪ/ n massoneria f

masquerade /mæskəˈreɪd/ n fig mascherata f ● vi **~ as** (pose) farsi passare per

mass¹ /mæs/ n Relig messa f

mass² n massa f. **~es of** fam un sacco di ● vi ammassarsi

massacre /'mæsəkə(r)/ n massacro m ● vt massacrare

massage /'mæsɑːʒ/ n massaggio m ● vt massaggiare; fig manipolare ⟨statistics⟩

masseu|r /mæˈsɜː(r)/ n massaggiatore m. **~se** /-ˈsɜːz/ n massaggiatrice f

massive /'mæsɪv/ a enorme

mass: ~ media npl mezzi mpl di comunicazione di massa, mass media mpl. **~-pro'duce** vt produrre in serie. **~-pro'duction** n produzione f in serie

mast /mɑːst/ n Naut albero m; (for radio) antenna f

master /'mɑːstə(r)/ n maestro m, padrone m; (teacher) professore m; (of ship) capitano m; M**~** (boy) signorino m

master: ~-key n passe-partout m inv. **~ly** a magistrale. **~-mind** n cervello m ● vt ideare e dirigere. **~-piece** n capolavoro m. **~-stroke** n colpo m da maestro. **~y** n (of subject) padronanza f

masturbat|e /'mæstəbeɪt/ vi masturbarsi. **~ion** /-'beɪʃn/ n masturbazione f

mat /mæt/ n stuoia f; (on table) sottopiatto m

match¹ /mætʃ/ n Sport partita f; (equal) uguale mf; (marriage) matrimonio m; (person to marry) partito m; **be a good ~** ⟨colours:⟩ intonarsi bene; **be no ~ for** non essere dello stesso livello di ● vt (equal) uguagliare; (be like) andare bene con ● vi intonarsi

match² n fiammifero m. **~box** n scatola f di fiammiferi

matching /'mætʃɪŋ/ a intonato

mate¹ /meɪt/ n compagno, -a mf; (assistant) aiuto m; Naut secondo m; (fam: friend) amico, -a mf ● vi accoppiarsi ● vt accoppiare

mate² n (in chess) scacco m matto

material /məˈtɪərɪəl/ n materiale m; (fabric) stoffa f; **raw ~s** pl materie fpl prime ● a materiale

material|ism /məˈtɪərɪəlɪzm/ n materialismo m. **~istic** /-'lɪstɪk/ a materialistico. **~ize** /-laɪz/ vi materializzarsi

maternal /məˈtɜːnl/ a materno

maternity /məˈtɜːnətɪ/ n maternità f. **~ clothes** npl abiti mpl pre-maman. **~ ward** n maternità f inv

matey /'meɪtɪ/ a fam amichevole

mathematic|al /mæθəˈmætɪkl/ a matematico. **~ian** /-məˈtɪʃn/ n matematico, -a mf

mathematics /mæθˈmætɪks/ n matematica fsg

maths /mæθs/ n fam matematica fsg

matinée /'mætɪneɪ/ n Theat matinée f inv

mating /'meɪtɪŋ/ n accoppiamento m; **~ season** stagione f degli amori

matriculat|e /məˈtrɪkjʊleɪt/ vi immatricolarsi. **~ion** /-'leɪʃn/ n immatricolazione f

matrix /'meɪtrɪks/ n (pl **matrices** /-siːz/) n matrice f

matted /'mætɪd/ a **~ hair** capelli mpl tutti appiccicati tra loro

matter /'mætə(r)/ n (affair) faccenda f; (question) questione f; (pus) pus m; (phys: substance) materia f; **as a ~ of fact** a dire la verità; **what is the ~?** che cosa c'è? ● vi importare; **~ to sb**

essere importante per qcno; **it doesn't ~** non importa. **~-of-fact** *a* pratico

mattress /'mætrɪs/ *n* materasso *m*

matur|e /mə'tʃʊə(r)/ *a* maturo; *Comm* in scadenza ● *vi* maturare ● *vt* far maturare. **~ity** *n* maturità *f*; *Fin* maturazione *f*

maul /mɔːl/ *vt* malmenare

Maundy /'mɔːndɪ/ *n* **~ Thursday** giovedì *m* santo

mauve /məʊv/ *a* malva

maxim /'mæksɪm/ *n* massima *f*

maximum /'mæksɪməm/ *a* massimo; **ten minutes ~** dieci minuti al massimo ● *n* (*pl* **-ima**) massimo *m*

May /meɪ/ *n* maggio *m*

may /meɪ/ *v aux* (*solo al presente*) potere; **~ I come in?** posso entrare?; **if I ~ say so** se mi posso permettere; **~ you both be very happy** siate felici; **I ~ as well stay** potrei anche rimanere; **it ~ be true** potrebbe esser vero; **she ~ be old, but...** sarà anche vecchia, ma...

maybe /'meɪbi/ *adv* forse, può darsi

'May Day *n* il primo maggio

mayonnaise /meɪə'neɪz/ *n* maionese *f*

mayor /'meə(r)/ *n* sindaco *m*. **~ess** *n* sindaco *m*; (*wife of mayor*) moglie *f* del sindaco

maze /meɪz/ *n* labirinto *m*

me /mi:/ *pron* (*object*) mi; (*with preposition*) me; **she called me** mi ha chiamato; **she called me, not you** ha chiamato me, non te; **give me the money** dammi i soldi; **give it to me** dammelo; **he gave it to me** me lo ha dato; **it's ~** sono io

meadow /'medəʊ/ *n* prato *m*

meagre /'mi:gə(r)/ *a* scarso

meal[1] /mi:l/ *n* pasto *m*

meal[2] *n* (*grain*) farina *f*

mealy-mouthed /mi:lɪ'maʊðd/ *a* ambiguo

mean[1] /mi:n/ *a* avaro; (*unkind*) meschino

mean[2] *a* medio ● *n* (*average*) media *f*; **Greenwich ~ time** ora *f* media di Greenwich

mean[3] *vt* (*pt/pp* **meant**) voler dire; (*signify*) significare; (*intend*) intendere; **I ~ it** lo dico seriamente; **~ well** avere buone intenzioni; **be ~t for** ⟨*present:*⟩ essere destinato a; ⟨*remark:*⟩ essere riferito a

meander /mɪ'ændə(r)/ *vi* vagare

meaning /'mi:nɪŋ/ *n* significato *m*. **~ful** *a* significativo. **~less** *a* senza senso

means /mi:nz/ *n* mezzo *m*; **~ of transport** mezzo *m* di trasporto; **by ~ of** per mezzo di; **by all ~!** certamente!; **by no ~** niente affatto ● *npl* (*resources*) mezzi *mpl*

meant /ment/ *see* **mean**[3]

'meantime *n* **in the ~** nel frattempo ● *adv* intanto

'meanwhile *adv* intanto

measles /'mi:zlz/ *nsg* morbillo *m*

measly /'mi:zlɪ/ *a fam* misero

measurable /'meʒərəbl/ *a* misurabile

measure /'meʒə(r)/ *n* misura *f* ● *vt/i* misurare. **measure up to** *vt fig* essere all'altezza di. **~d** *a* misurato. **~ment** /-mənt/ *n* misura *f*

meat /mi:t/ *n* carne *f*. **~ ball** *n Culin* polpetta *f* di carne. **~ loaf** *n* polpettone *m*

mechan|ic /mɪ'kænɪk/ *n* meccanico *m*. **~ical** *a* meccanico; **~ical engineering** ingegneria *f* meccanica. **~ically** *adv* meccanicamente. **~ics** *n* meccanica *f* ● *npl* meccanismo *msg*

mechan|ism /'mekənɪzm/ *n* meccanismo *m*. **~ize** *vt* meccanizzare

medal /'medl/ *n* medaglia *f*

medallion /mɪ'dælɪən/ *n* medaglione *m*

medallist /'medəlɪst/ *n* vincitore, -trice *mf* di una medaglia

meddle /'medl/ *vi* immischiarsi (**in** di); (*tinker*) armeggiare (**with** con)

media /'mi:dɪə/ *npl* **the ~** i mass media. **~ studies** *npl* scienze *fpl* della comunicazione

median /'mi:dɪən/ *a* **~ strip** *Am* banchina *f* spartitraffico

mediat|e /'mi:dɪeɪt/ *vi* fare da mediatore. **~ion** /-'eɪʃn/ *n* mediazione *f*. **~or** *n* mediatore, -trice *mf*

medical /'medɪkl/ *a* medico ● *n* visita *f* medica. **~ insurance** *n* assicurazione *f* sanitaria. **~ student** *n* studente, -essa *mf* di medicina

medicat|ed /'medɪkeɪtɪd/ *a* medicato. **~ion** /-'keɪʃn/ *n* (*drugs*) medicinali *mpl*

medicinal /mɪ'dɪsɪnl/ *a* medicinale

medicine /'medsən/ *n* medicina *f*

medieval /medɪ'i:vl/ *a* medievale

mediocr|e /mi:dɪ'əʊkə(r)/ *a* mediocre. **~ity** /-'ɒkrətɪ/ *n* mediocrità *f*

meditat|e /'medɪteɪt/ *vi* meditare (**on** su). **~ion** /-'teɪʃn/ *n* meditazione *f*

Mediterranean /medɪtə'reɪnɪən/ *n* **the ~ [Sea]** il [mare] Mediterraneo ● *a* mediterraneo

medium /'mi:dɪəm/ *a* medio; *Culin* di media cottura ● *n* (*pl* **media**) mezzo *m*; (*pl* **-s**) (*person*) medium *mf inv*

medium: ~-**sized** *a* di taglia media. ~ **wave** *n* onde *fpl* medie

medley /'medlɪ/ *n* miscuglio *m*; *Mus* miscellanea *f*

meek /miːk/ *a* mite, mansueto. ~**ly** *adv* docilmente

meet /miːt/ *v* (*pt/pp* met) ● *vt* incontrare; (*at station, airport*) andare incontro a; (*for first time*) far la conoscenza di; pagare (*bill*); soddisfare (*requirements*) ● *vi* incontrarsi; (*committee:*) riunirsi; ~ **with** incontrare (*problem*); incontrarsi con (*person*) ● *n* raduno *m* [sportivo]

meeting /'miːtɪŋ/ *n* riunione *f*, meeting *m inv*; (*large*) assemblea *f*; (*by chance*) incontro *m*

megabyte /'megəbaɪt/ *n* megabyte *m*

megalomania /megələ'meɪnɪə/ *n* megalomania *f*

megaphone /'megəfəʊn/ *n* megafono *m*

melancholy /'melənkəlɪ/ *a* malinconico ● *n* malinconia *f*

mellow /'meləʊ/ *a* (*wine*) generoso; (*sound, colour*) caldo; (*person*) dolce ● *vi* (*person:*) addolcirsi

melodic /mɪ'lɒdɪk/ *a* melodico

melodrama /'melə-/ *n* melodramma *m*. ~**tic** /-drə'mætɪk/ *a* melodrammatico

melody /'melədɪ/ *n* melodia *f*

melon /'melən/ *n* melone *m*

melt /melt/ *vt* sciogliere ● *vi* sciogliersi. **melt down** *vt* fondere. ~**ing-pot** *n fig* crogiuolo *m*

member /'membə(r)/ *n* membro *m*; ~ **countries** paesi *mpl* membri; **M~ of Parliament** deputato, -a *mf*; **M~ of the European Parliament** eurodeputato, -a *mf*. ~**ship** *n* iscrizione *f*; (*members*) soci *mpl*

membrane /'membreɪn/ *n* membrana *f*

memo /'meməʊ/ *n* promemoria *m inv*

memoirs /'memwɑːz/ *npl* ricordi *mpl*

memorable /'memərəbl/ *a* memorabile

memorandum /memə'rændəm/ *n* promemoria *m inv*

memorial /mɪ'mɔːrɪəl/ *n* monumento *m*. ~ **service** *n* funzione *f* commemorativa

memorize /'meməraɪz/ *vt* memorizzare

memory /'memərɪ/ *n also Comput* memoria *f*; (*thing remembered*) ricordo *m*; **from** ~ a memoria; **in** ~ **of** in ricordo di

men /men/ *see* **man**

menace /'menəs/ *n* minaccia *f*; (*nuisance*) piaga *f* ● *vt* minacciare. ~**ing** *a* minaccioso

mend /mend/ *vt* riparare; (*darn*) rammendare ● *n* **on the** ~ in via di guarigione

'**menfolk** *n* uomini *mpl*

menial /'miːnɪəl/ *a* umile

meningitis /menɪn'dʒaɪtɪs/ *n* meningite *f*

menopause /'menə-/ *n* menopausa *f*

menstruat|e /'menstrʊeɪt/ *vi* mestruare. ~**ion** /-'eɪʃn/ *n* mestruazione *f*

mental /'mentl/ *a* mentale; (*fam: mad*) pazzo. ~ **a'rithmetic** *n* calcolo *m* mentale. ~ '**illness** *n* malattia *f* mentale

mental|ity /men'tælətɪ/ *n* mentalità *f inv*. ~**ly** *adv* mentalmente; ~**ly ill** malato di mente

mention /'menʃn/ *n* menzione *f* ● *vt* menzionare; **don't** ~ **it** non c'è di che

menu /'menju:/ *n* menu *m inv*

MEP *n abbr* **Member of the European Parliament**

mercenary /'mɜːsɪnərɪ/ *a* mercenario ● *n* mercenario *m*

merchandise /'mɜːtʃəndaɪz/ *n* merce *f*

merchant /'mɜːtʃənt/ *n* commerciante *mf*. ~ **bank** *n* banca *f* d'affari. ~ '**navy** *n* marina *f* mercantile

merci|ful /'mɜːsɪfl/ *a* misericordioso. ~**fully** *adv fam* grazie a Dio. ~**less** *a* spietato

mercury /'mɜːkjʊrɪ/ *n* mercurio *m*

mercy /'mɜːsɪ/ *n* misericordia *f*; **be at sb's** ~ essere alla mercé di qcno, essere in balia di qcno

mere /mɪə(r)/ *a* solo. ~**ly** *adv* solamente

merest /'mɪərɪst/ *a* minimo

merge /mɜːdʒ/ *vi* fondersi

merger /'mɜːdʒə(r)/ *n* fusione *f*

meringue /mə'ræŋ/ *n* meringa *f*

merit /'merɪt/ *n* merito *m*; (*advantage*) qualità *f inv* ● *vt* meritare

mermaid /'mɜːmeɪd/ *n* sirena *f*

merri|ly /'merɪlɪ/ *adv* allegramente. ~**ment** /-mənt/ *n* baldoria *f*

merry /'merɪ/ *a* (**-ier, -iest**) allegro; ~ **Christmas!** Buon Natale!

merry: ~-**go-round** *n* giostra *f*. ~-**making** *n* festa *f*

mesh /meʃ/ *n* maglia *f*

mesmerize /'mezməraɪz/ *vt* ipnotizzare. ~**d** *a fig* ipnotizzato

mess /mes/ *n* disordine *m*, casino *m fam*; (*trouble*) guaio *m*; (*something spilt*) sporco *m*; *Mil* mensa *f*; **make a** ~ **of**

(*botch*) fare un pasticcio di ● **mess about** *vi* perder tempo; ~ **about with** armeggiare con ● *vt* prendere in giro (*person*). **mess up** *vt* mettere in disordine, incasinare *fam*; (*botch*) mandare all'aria

message /'mesɪdʒ/ *n* messaggio *m*

messenger /'mesɪndʒə(r)/ *n* messaggero *m*

Messiah /mɪ'saɪə/ *n* Messia *m*

Messrs /'mesəz/ *npl* (*on letter*) ~ **Smith** Spett. ditta Smith

messy /'mesɪ/ *a* (**-ier, -iest**) disordinato; (*in dress*) sciatto

met /met/ *see* **meet**

metal /'metl/ *n* metallo ● *a* di metallo. ~**lic** /mɪ'tælɪk/ *a* metallico

metamorphosis /metə'mɔ:fəsɪs/ *n* (*pl* **-phoses** /-si:z/) metamorfosi *f inv*

metaphor /'metəfə(r)/ *n* metafora *f*. ~**ical** /-'fɒrɪkl/ *a* metaforico

meteor /'mi:tɪə(r)/ *n* meteora *f*. ~**ic** /-'ɒrɪk/ *a fig* fulmineo

meteorological /mi:tɪərə'lɒdʒɪkl/ *a* meteorologico

meteorolog|ist /mi:tɪə'rɒlədʒɪst/ *n* meteorologo, -a *mf*. ~**y** *n* meteorologia *f*

meter[1] /'mi:tə(r)/ *n* contatore *m*

meter[2] *n Am* = **metre**

method /'meθəd/ *n* metodo *m*

methodical /mɪ'θɒdɪkl/ *a* metodico. ~**ly** *adv* metodicamente

Methodist /'meθədɪst/ *n* metodista *mf*

meths /meθs/ *n fam* alcol *m* denaturato

methylated /'meθɪleɪtɪd/ *a* ~ **spirit[s]** alcol *m* denaturato

meticulous /mɪ'tɪkjʊləs/ *a* meticoloso. ~**ly** *adv* meticolosamente

metre /'mi:tə(r)/ *n* metro *m*

metric /'metrɪk/ *a* metrico

metropolis /mɪ'trɒpəlɪs/ *n* metropoli *f inv*

metropolitan /metrə'pɒlɪtən/ *a* metropolitano

mew /mju:/ *n* miao *m* ● *vi* miagolare

Mexican /'meksɪkən/ *a & n* messicano, -a *mf*. '**Mexico** *n* Messico *m*

miaow /mɪ'aʊ/ *n* miao *m* ● *vi* miagolare

mice /maɪs/ *see* **mouse**

mickey /'mɪkɪ/ *n* **take the** ~ **out of** prendere in giro

microbe /'maɪkrəʊb/ *n* microbo *m*

micro /'maɪkrəʊ/: ~**chip** *n* microchip *m inv*. ~**computer** *n* microcomputer *m inv* . ~**film** *n* microfilm *m inv*. ~**phone** microfono *m*. ~**processor** *n* microprocessore *m*. ~**scope** *n* microscopio *m*. ~**scopic** /-'skɒpɪk/ *a* microscopico

~**wave** *n* microonda *f*; (*oven*) forno *m* a microonde

mid /mɪd/ *a* ~ **May** metà maggio; **in** ~ **air** a mezz'aria

midday /mɪd'deɪ/ *n* mezzogiorno *m*

middle /'mɪdl/ *a* di centro; **the M~ Ages** il medioevo; **the** ~ **class[es]** la classe media; **the' M~ East** il Medio Oriente ● *n* mezzo *m*; **in the** ~ **of** (*room, floor etc*) in mezzo a; **in the** ~ **of the night** nel pieno della notte, a notte piena

middle: ~-**aged** *a* di mezza età. ~-**class** *a* borghese. ~**man** *n Comm* intermediario *m*

middling /'mɪdlɪŋ/ *a* discreto

midge /mɪdʒ/ *n* moscerino *m*

midget /'mɪdʒɪt/ *n* nano, -a *mf*

Midlands /'mɪdləndz/ *npl* **the** ~ l'Inghilterra *fsg* centrale

'**midnight** *n* mezzanotte *f*

midriff /'mɪdrɪf/ *n* diaframma *m*

midst /mɪdst/ *n* **in the** ~ **of** in mezzo a; **in our** ~ fra di noi, in mezzo a noi

mid: ~**summer** *n* mezza estate *f* ~**way** *adv* a metà strada. ~**wife** *n* ostetrica *f*. ~**wifery** /-wɪfrɪ/ *n* ostetricia *f*. ~'**winter** *n* pieno inverno *m*

might[1] /maɪt/ *v aux* **I** ~ potrei; **will you come? - I** ~ vieni? - può darsi; **it** ~ **be true** potrebbe essere vero; **I** ~ **as well stay** potrei anche restare; **you** ~ **have drowned** avresti potuto affogare; **you** ~ **have said so!** avresti potuto dirlo!

might[2] *n* potere *m*

mighty /'maɪtɪ/ *a* (**-ier, -iest**) potente ● *adv fam* molto

migraine /'mi:greɪn/ *n* emicrania *f*

migrant /'maɪgrənt/ *a* migratore ● *n* (*bird*) migratore, -trice *mf*; (*person: for work*) emigrante *mf*

migrat|e /maɪ'greɪt/ *vi* migrare. ~**ion** /-'greɪʃn/ *n* migrazione *f*

mike /maɪk/ *n fam* microfono *f*

Milan /mɪ'læn/ *n* Milano *f*

mild /maɪld/ *a* (*weather*) mite; (*person*) dolce; (*flavour*) delicato; (*illness*) leggero

mildew /'mɪldju:/ *n* muffa *f*

mild|ly /'maɪldlɪ/ *adv* moderatamente; (*say*) dolcemente; **to put it** ~**ly** a dire poco, senza esagerazione. ~**ness** *n* (*of person, words*) dolcezza *f*; (*of weather*) mitezza *f*

mile /maɪl/ *n* miglio *m* (= *1,6 km*); ~**s nicer** *fam* molto più bello

mile|age /-ɪdʒ/ n chilometraggio m.
~stone n pietra f miliare

militant /'mɪlɪtənt/ a & n militante mf

military /'mɪlɪtrɪ/ a militare. **~
service** n servizio m militare

militate /'mɪlɪteɪt/ vi **~ against** opporsi a

militia /mɪ'lɪʃə/ n milizia f

milk /mɪlk/ n latte m ● vt mungere

milk: ~man n lattaio m. **~ shake** n
frappé m inv

milky /'mɪlkɪ/ a (-ier, -iest) latteo; ⟨tea
etc⟩ con molto latte. **M~ Way** n Astr Via
f Lattea

mill /mɪl/ n mulino m; ⟨factory⟩ fabbrica
f; ⟨for coffee etc⟩ macinino m ● vt macinare ⟨grain⟩. **mill about, mill around**
vi brulicare

millennium /mɪ'lenɪəm/ n millennio m

miller /'mɪlə(r)/ n mugnaio m

milli|gram /'mɪlɪ-/ n milligrammo m.
~metre n millimetro m

million /'mɪljən/ a & n milione m; **a ~
pounds** un milione di sterline. **~aire**
/-'neə(r)/ n miliardario, -a mf

'millstone n fig peso m

mime /maɪm/ n mimo m ● vt mimare

mimic /'mɪmɪk/ n imitatore, -trice mf
● vt (pt/pp **mimicked**) imitare. **~ry** n
mimetismo m

mimosa /mɪ'məʊzə/ n mimosa f

mince /mɪns/ n carne f tritata ● vt
Culin tritare; **not ~ one's words** parlare senza mezzi termini

mince: ~meat n miscuglio m di frutta
secca; **make ~meat of** fig demolire.
~'pie n pasticcino m a base di frutta secca

mincer /'mɪnsə(r)/ n tritacarne m inv

mind /maɪnd/ n mente f; ⟨sanity⟩ ragione f; **to my ~** a mio parere; **give sb a
piece of one's ~** dire chiaro e tondo a
qcno quello che si pensa; **make up
one's ~** decidersi; **have sth in ~** avere
qcsa in mente; **bear sth in ~** tenere
presente qcsa; **have something on
one's ~** essere preoccupato; **have a
good ~ to** avere una grande voglia di; **I
have changed my ~** ho cambiato
idea; **in two ~s** indeciso; **are you out
of your ~?** sei diventato matto? ● vt
⟨look after⟩ occuparsi di; **I don't ~ the
noise** il rumore non mi dà fastidio; **I
don't ~ what we do** non mi importa
quello che facciamo; **~ the step!** attenzione al gradino! ● vi **I don't ~** non mi
importa; **never ~!** non importa!; **do**

you ~ if...? ti dispiace se...? **mind out**
vi **~ out!** [fai] attenzione!

minder /'maɪndə(r)/ n (Br: bodyguard)
gorilla m inv; ⟨for child⟩ baby-sitter mf
inv

mind|ful a **~ful of** attento a. **~less** a
noncurante

mine¹ /maɪn/ poss pron il mio m, la mia
f, i miei mpl, le mie fpl; **a friend of ~** un
mio amico; **friends of ~** dei miei amici;
that is ~ questo è mio; ⟨as opposed to
yours⟩ questo è il mio

mine² n miniera f; ⟨explosive⟩ mina f
● vt estrarre; Mil minare. **~ detector**
n rivelatore m di mine. **~field** n campo
m minato

miner /'maɪnə(r)/ n minatore m

mineral /'mɪnərəl/ n minerale m ● a
minerale. **~ water** n acqua f minerale

minesweeper /'maɪn-/ n dragamine
m inv

mingle /'mɪŋgl/ vi **~ with** mescolarsi a

mini /'mɪnɪ/ n ⟨skirt⟩ mini f

miniature /'mɪnɪtʃə(r)/ a in miniatura
● n miniatura f

mini|bus /'mɪnɪ-/ n minibus m inv, pulmino m. **~cab** n taxi m inv

minim /'mɪnɪm/ n Mus minima f

minim|al /'mɪnɪməl/ a minimo. **~ize** vt
minimizzare. **~um** n (pl **-ima**) minimo
m ● a minimo; **ten minutes ~um** minimo dieci minuti

mining /'maɪnɪŋ/ n estrazione f ● a
estrattivo

miniskirt /'mɪnɪ-/ n minigonna f

minist|er /'mɪnɪstə(r)/ n ministro m;
Relig pastore m. **~erial** /-'stɪərɪəl/ a
ministeriale

ministry /'mɪnɪstrɪ/ n Pol ministero m;
the ~ Relig il ministero sacerdotale

mink /mɪŋk/ n visone m

minor /'maɪnə(r)/ a minore ● n minorenne mf

minority /maɪ'nɒrətɪ/ n minoranza f;
⟨age⟩ minore età f

minor road n strada f secondaria

mint¹ /mɪnt/ n fam patrimonio m ● a in
~ condition in condizione perfetta

mint² n ⟨herb⟩ menta f

minus /'maɪnəs/ prep meno; ⟨fam:
without⟩ senza ● n — **[sign]** meno m

minute¹ /'mɪnɪt/ n minuto m; **in a ~**
⟨shortly⟩ in un minuto; **~s** pl ⟨of meeting⟩ verbale msg

minute² /maɪ'njuːt/ a minuto; ⟨precise⟩
minuzioso

miracle /'mɪrəkl/ n miracolo m.
~ulous /-'rækjʊləs/ a miracoloso

mirage /'mırɑːʒ/ n miraggio m

mirror /'mırə(r)/ n specchio m ● vt rispecchiare

mirth /mɜːθ/ n ilarità f

misad'venture /mıs-/ n disavventura f

misanthropist /mɪ'zænθrəpɪst/ n misantropo, -a mf

misappre'hension n malinteso m; **be under a ~** avere frainteso

misbe'have vi comportarsi male

mis'calcu|late vt/i calcolare male. **~'lation** n calcolo m sbagliato

'miscarriage n aborto m spontaneo; **~ of justice** errore m giudiziario. **mis'carry** vi abortire

miscellaneous /mɪsə'leɪnɪəs/ a assortito

mischief /'mɪstʃɪf/ n malefatta f; (harm) danno m

mischievous /'mɪstʃɪvəs/ a (naughty) birichino; (malicious) dannoso

miscon'ception n concetto m erroneo

mis'conduct n cattiva condotta f

misde'meanour n reato m

miser /'maɪzə(r)/ n avaro m

miserabl|e /'mɪzrəbl/ a (unhappy) infelice; (wretched) miserabile; (fig: weather) deprimente. **~y** adv (live, fail) miseramente; (say) tristemente

miserly /'maɪzəlɪ/ a avaro; (amount) ridicolo

misery /'mɪzərɪ/ n miseria f; (fam: person) piagnone, -a mf

mis'fire vi (gun:) far cilecca; (plan etc:) non riuscire

'misfit n disadattato, -a mf

mis'fortune n sfortuna f

mis'givings npl dubbi mpl

mis'guided a fuorviato

mishap /'mɪshæp/ n disavventura f

misin'terpret vt fraintendere

mis'judge vt giudicar male; (estimate wrongly) valutare male

mis'lay vt (pt/pp -laid) smarrire

mis'lead vt (pt/pp -led) fuorviare. **~ing** a fuorviante

mis'manage vt amministrare male. **~ment** n cattiva amministrazione f

misnomer /mɪs'nəʊmə(r)/ n termine m improprio

'misprint n errore m di stampa

mis'quote vt citare erroneamente

misrepre'sent vt rappresentare male

miss /mɪs/ n colpo m mancato ● vt (fail to hit or find) mancare; perdere (train, bus, class); (feel the loss of) sentire la mancanza di; **I ~ed that part** (failed to

notice) mi è sfuggita quella parte ● vi **but he ~ed** (failed to hit) ma l'ha mancato. **miss out** vt saltare, omettere

Miss n (pl **-es**) signorina f

misshapen /mɪs'ʃeɪpən/ a malformato

missile /'mɪsaɪl/ n missile m

missing /'mɪsɪŋ/ a mancante; (person) scomparso; Mil disperso; **be ~** essere introvabile

mission /'mɪʃn/ n missione f

missionary /'mɪʃənrɪ/ n missionario, -a mf

mis'spell vt (pt/pp **-spelled, -spelt**) sbagliare l'ortografia di

mist /mɪst/ n (fog) foschia f ● **mist up** vi appannarsi, annebbiarsi

mistake /mɪ'steɪk/ n sbaglio m; **by ~** per sbaglio ● vt (pt **mistook**, pp **mistaken**) sbagliare (road, house); fraintendere (meaning, words); **~ for** prendere per

mistaken /mɪ'steɪkən/ a sbagliato; **be ~** sbagliarsi; **~ identity** errore m di persona. **~ly** adv erroneamente

mistletoe /'mɪsltəʊ/ n vischio m

mistress /'mɪstrɪs/ n padrona f; (teacher) maestra f; (lover) amante f

mis'trust n sfiducia f ● vt non aver fiducia in

misty /'mɪstɪ/ a (**-ier, -iest**) nebbioso

misunder'stand vt (pt/pp **-stood**) fraintendere. **~ing** n malinteso m

misuse¹ /mɪs'juːz/ vt usare male

misuse² /mɪs'juːs/ n cattivo uso m

mite /maɪt/ n (child) piccino, -a mf

mitigat|e /'mɪtɪgeɪt/ vt attenuare. **~ing** a attenuante

mitten /'mɪtn/ n manopola f, muffola f

mix /mɪks/ n (combination) mescolanza f; Culin miscuglio m; (ready-made) preparato m ● vt mischiare ● vi mischiarsi; (person:) inserirsi; **~ with** (associate with) frequentare. **mix up** vt mescolare (papers); (confuse, mistake for) confondere

mixed /mɪkst/ a misto; **~ up** (person) confuso

mixer /'mɪksə(r)/ n Culin frullatore m, mixer m inv; **he's a good ~** è un tipo socievole

mixture /'mɪkstʃə(r)/ n mescolanza f; (medicine) sciroppo m; Culin miscela f

'mix-up n (confusion) confusione f; (mistake) pasticcio m

moan /məʊn/ n lamento m ● vi lamentarsi; (complain) lagnarsi

moat /məʊt/ n fossato m

mob /mɒb/ n folla f; (*rabble*) gentaglia f; (*fam: gang*) banda f ● vt (*pt/pp* **mobbed**) assalire

mobile /'məʊbaɪl/ a mobile ● n composizione f mobile. ~ 'home n casa f roulotte. ~ [**phone**] n [telefono m] cellulare m

mobility /mə'bɪlətɪ/ n mobilità f

mock /mɒk/ a finto ● vt canzonare. ~ery n derisione f

'**mock-up** n modello m in scala

mode /məʊd/ n modo m; *Comput* modalità f

model /'mɒdl/ n modello m; [**fashion**] ~ indossare, -trice mf, modello, -a mf ● a ⟨yacht, plane⟩ in miniatura; ⟨pupil, husband⟩ esemplare, modello ● v (*pt/pp* **modelled**) ● vt indossare ⟨clothes⟩ ● vi fare l'indossatore, -trice mf; (*for artist*) posare

modem /'məʊdem/ n modem m inv

moderate¹ /'mɒdəreɪt/ vt moderare ● vi moderarsi

moderate² /'mɒdərət/ a moderato ● n Pol moderato, -a mf. ~ly adv ⟨drink, speak etc⟩ moderatamente; ⟨good, bad etc⟩ relativamente

moderation /mɒdə'reɪʃn/ n moderazione f; **in ~** con moderazione

modern /'mɒdn/ a moderno. ~ize vt modernizzare

modest /'mɒdɪst/ a modesto. ~y n modestia f

modicum /'mɒdɪkəm/ n **a ~ of** un po' di

modification /mɒdɪfɪ'keɪʃn/ n modificazione f. ~y /'mɒdɪfaɪ/ vt (*pt/pp* **-fied**) modificare

module /'mɒdjuːl/ n modulo m

moist /mɔɪst/ a umido

moisten /'mɔɪsn/ vt inumidire

moisture /'mɔɪstʃə(r)/ n umidità f. ~izer n ⟨crema f⟩ idratante

molar /'məʊlə(r)/ n molare m

molasses /mə'læsɪz/ n Am melassa f

mole¹ /məʊl/ n (*on face etc*) neo m

mole² n Zool talpa f

molecule /'mɒlɪkjuːl/ n molecola f

molest /mə'lest/ vt molestare

mollycoddle /'mɒlɪkɒdl/ vt tenere nella bambagia

molten /'məʊltən/ a fuso

mom /mɒm/ n Am fam mamma f

moment /'məʊmənt/ n momento m; **at the ~** in questo momento. ~**arily** adv momentaneamente. ~**ary** a momentaneo

momentous /mə'mentəs/ a molto importante

momentum /mə'mentəm/ n impeto m

monarch /'mɒnək/ n monarca m. ~y n monarchia f

monastery /'mɒnəstrɪ/ n monastero m. ~**ic** /mə'næstɪk/ a monastico

Monday /'mʌndeɪ/ n lunedì m inv

monetary /'mʌnɪtrɪ/ a monetario

money /'mʌnɪ/ n denaro m

money: ~-**box** n salvadanaio m. ~-**lender** n usuraio m

mongrel /'mʌŋgrəl/ n bastardo m

monitor /'mɒnɪtə(r)/ n Techn monitor m inv ● vt controllare

monk /mʌŋk/ n monaco m

monkey /'mʌŋkɪ/ n scimmia f. ~-**nut** n nocciolina f americana. ~-**wrench** n chiave f inglese a rullino

mono /'mɒnəʊ/ n mono m

monogram /'mɒnəgræm/ n monogramma m

monologue /'mɒnəlɒg/ n monologo m

monopolize /mə'nɒpəlaɪz/ vt monopolizzare. ~y n monopolio m

monosyllabic /mɒnəsɪ'læbɪk/ a monosillabico

monotone /'mɒnətəʊn/ n **speak in a ~** parlare con tono monotono

monotonous /mə'nɒtənəs/ a monotono. ~y n monotonia f

monsoon /mɒn'suːn/ n monsone m

monster /'mɒnstə(r)/ n mostro m

monstrosity /mɒn'strɒsətɪ/ n mostruosità f

monstrous /'mɒnstrəs/ a mostruoso

month /mʌnθ/ n mese m. ~**ly** a mensile ● adv mensilmente ● n (*periodical*) mensile m

monument /'mɒnjʊmənt/ n monumento m. ~**al** /-'mentl/ a fig monumentale

moo /muː/ n muggito m ● vi (*pt/pp* **mooed**) muggire

mooch /muːtʃ/ vi ~ **about** fam gironzolare (**the house** per casa)

mood /muːd/ n umore m; **be in a good/bad** ~ essere di buon/cattivo umore; **be in the** ~ **for** essere in vena di

moody /'muːdɪ/ a (-ier, -iest) (*variable*) lunatico; (*bad-tempered*) di malumore

moon /muːn/ n luna f; **over the** ~ fam al settimo cielo

moon: ~-**light** n chiaro m di luna ● vi fam lavorare in nero. ~-**lit** a illuminato dalla luna

moor¹ /mʊə(r)/ n brughiera f

moor² *vt Naut* ormeggiare

moose /mu:s/ *n* (*pl* **moose**) alce *m*

moot /mu:t/ *a* **it's a ~ point** è un punto controverso

mop /mɒp/ *n* mocio® *m* ; **~ of hair** zazzera *f* ● *vt* (*pt/pp* **mopped**) lavare con il mocio. **mop up** *vt* (*dry*) asciugare con lo straccio; (*clean*) pulire con lo straccio

mope /məʊp/ *vi* essere depresso

moped /'məʊped/ *n* ciclomotore *m*

moral /'mɒrəl/ *a* morale ● *n* morale *f*. **~ly** *adv* moralmente. **~s** *pl* moralità *f*

morale /mə'rɑːl/ *n* morale *m*

morality /mə'ræləti/ *n* moralità *f*

morbid /'mɔːbɪd/ *a* morboso

more /mɔː(r)/ *a* più; **a few ~ books** un po' più di libri; **some ~ tea?** ancora un po' di tè?; **there's no ~ bread** non c'è più pane; **there are no ~ apples** non ci sono più mele; **one ~ word and...** ancora una parola e... ● *pron* di più; **would you like some ~?** ne vuoi ancora?; **no ~, thank you** non ne voglio più, grazie ● *adv* più; **~ interesting** più interessante; **~ [and ~] quickly** [sempre] più veloce; **~ than** più di; **I don't love him any ~** no lo amo più; **once ~** ancora una volta; **~ or less** più o meno; **the ~ I see him, the ~ I like him** più lo vedo, più mi piace

moreover /mɔːr'əʊvə(r)/ *adv* inoltre

morgue /mɔːg/ *n* obitorio *m*

moribund /'mɒrɪbʌnd/ *a* moribondo

morning /'mɔːnɪŋ/ *n* mattino *m*, mattina *f*; **in the ~** del mattino; (*tomorrow*) domani mattina

Morocc|o /mə'rɒkəʊ/ *n* Marocco *m* ● *a* **~an** *a* & *n* marocchino, -a *mf*

moron /'mɔːrɒn/ *n fam* deficiente *mf*

morose /mə'rəʊs/ *a* scontroso

morphine /'mɔːfiːn/ *n* morfina *f*

Morse /mɔːs/ *n* **~ [code]** [codice *m*] Morse *m*

morsel /'mɔːsl/ *n* (*food*) boccone *m*

mortal /'mɔːtl/ *a* & *n* mortale *mf*. **~ity** /mɔː'tælətɪ/ *n* mortalità *f*. **~ly** *adv* ⟨wounded, offended⟩ a morte; ⟨afraid⟩ da morire

mortar /'mɔːtə(r)/ *n* mortaio *m*

mortgage /'mɔːgɪdʒ/ *n* mutuo *m*; (*on property*) ipoteca *f* ● *vt* ipotecare

mortuary /'mɔːtjʊərɪ/ *n* camera *f* mortuaria

mosaic /məʊ'zeɪɪk/ *n* mosaico *m*

Moscow /'mɒskəʊ/ *n* Mosca *f*

Moslem /'mɒzlɪm/ *a* & *n* musulmano, -a *mf*

mosque /mɒsk/ *n* moschea *f*

mosquito /mɒs'kiːtəʊ/ *n* (*pl* **-es**) zanzara *f*

moss /mɒs/ *n* muschio *m*. **~y** *a* muschioso

most /məʊst/ *a* (*majority*) la maggior parte di; **for the ~ part** per lo più ● *adv* più, maggiormente; (*very*) estremamente, molto; **the ~ interesting day** la giornata più interessante; **a ~ interesting day** una giornata estremamente interessante; **the ~ beautiful woman in the world** la donna più bella del mondo; **~ unlikely** veramente improbabile ● *pron* **~ of them** la maggior parte di loro; **at [the] ~** al massimo; **make the ~ of** sfruttare al massimo; **~ of the time** la maggior parte del tempo. **~ly** *adv* per lo più

MOT *n Br* revisione *f* obbligatoria di autoveicoli

motel /məʊ'tel/ *n* motel *m inv*

moth /mɒθ/ *n* falena *f*; [**clothes-**] ~ tarma *f*

moth: **~ball** *n* pallina *f* di naftalina. **~-eaten** *a* tarmato

mother /'mʌðə(r)/ *n* madre *f*; **M~'s Day** la festa della mamma ● *vt* fare da madre a

mother: **~board** *n Comput* scheda *f* madre. **~hood** *n* maternità *f*. **~-in-law** *n* (*pl* **~s-in-law**) suocera *f*. **~ly** *a* materno. **~-of-pearl** *n* madreperla *f*. **~-to-be** *n* futura mamma *f*. **~ tongue** *n* madrelingua *f*

mothproof /'mɒθ-/ *a* antitarmico

motif /məʊ'tiːf/ *n* motivo *m*

motion /'məʊʃn/ *n* moto *m*; (*proposal*) mozione *f*; (*gesture*) gesto *m* ● *vt/i* **~ [to] sb to come in** fare segno a qcno di entrare. **~less** *a* immobile. **~lessly** *adv* senza alcun movimento

motivat|e /'məʊtɪvert/ *vt* motivare. **~ion** /-'veɪʃn/ *n* motivazione *f*

motive /'məʊtɪv/ *n* motivo *m*

motley /'mɒtlɪ/ *a* disparato

motor /'məʊtə(r)/ *n* motore *m*; (*car*) macchina *f* ● *a* a motore; *Anat* motore ● *vi* andare in macchina

Motorail /'məʊtəreɪl/ *n* treno *m* per trasporto auto

motor: **~ bike** *n fam* moto *f inv*. **~ boat** *n* motoscafo *m*. **~cade** /-keɪd/ *n Am* corteo *m* di auto. **~ car** *n* automobile *f*. **~ cycle** *n* motocicletta *f*. **~-cyclist** *n* motociclista *mf*. **~ing** *n* automobilismo *m*. **~ist** *n* automobilista *mf*. **~ racing** *n* corse *fpl* automobilistiche. **~ ~**

vehicle *n* autoveicolo *m*. **~way** *n* autostrada *f*

mottled /'mɒtld/ *a* chiazzato

motto /'mɒtəʊ/ *n* (*pl* -es) motto *m*

mould¹ /məʊld/ *n* (*fungus*) muffa *f*

mould² *n* stampo *m* ● *vt* foggiare; *fig* formare. **~ing** *n Archit* cornice *f*

mouldy /'məʊldɪ/ *a* ammuffito; (*fam: worthless*) ridicolo

moult /məʊlt/ *vi* (*bird:*) fare la muta; (*animal:*) perdere il pelo

mound /maʊnd/ *n* mucchio *m*; (*hill*) collinetta *f*

mount /maʊnt/ *n* (*horse*) cavalcatura *f*; (*of jewel, photo, picture*) montatura *f* ● *vt* montare a (*horse*); salire su (*bicycle*); incastonare (*jewel*); incorniciare (*photo, picture*) ● *vi* aumentare. **mount up** *vi* aumentare

mountain /'maʊntɪn/ *n* montagna *f*. **~ bike** *n* mountain bike *f inv*

mountaineer /maʊntɪ'nɪə(r)/ *n* alpinista *mf*. **~ing** *n* alpinismo *m*

mountainous /'maʊntɪnəs/ *a* montagnoso

mourn /mɔːn/ *vt* lamentare ● *vi* **~ for** piangere la morte di. **~er** *n* persona *f* che partecipa a un funerale. **~ful** *a* triste. **~ing** *n* **in ~ing** in lutto

mouse /maʊs/ *n* (*pl* **mice**) topo *m*; *Comput* mouse *m inv*. **~trap** *n* trappola *f* [per topi]

mousse /muːs/ *n Culin* mousse *f inv*

moustache /məˈstɑːʃ/ *n* baffi *mpl*

mousy /'maʊsɪ/ *a* (*colour*) grigio topo

mouth¹ /maʊð/ *vt* **~ sth** dire qcsa silenziosamente muovendo solamente le labbra

mouth² /maʊθ/ *n* bocca *f*; (*of river*) foce *f*

mouth: ~ful *n* boccone *m*. **~-organ** *n* armonica *f* [a bocca]. **~piece** *n* imboccatura *f*; (*fig: person*) portavoce *m inv*. **~wash** *n* acqua *f* dentifricia. **~watering** *a* che fa venire l'acquolina in bocca

movable /'muːvəbl/ *a* movibile

move /muːv/ *n* mossa *f*; (*moving house*) trasloco *m*; **on the ~** in movimento; **get a ~ on** *fam* darsi una mossa ● *vt* muovere; (*emotionally*) commuovere; spostare (*car, furniture*); (*transfer*) trasferire; (*propose*) proporre; **~ house** traslocare ● *vi* muoversi; (*move house*) traslocare. **move along** *vi* andare avanti ● *vt* muovere in avanti. **move away** *vi* allontanarsi; (*move house*) trasferirsi ● *vt* allontanare. **move forward** *vi* avanzare ● *vt* spostare avanti. **move in**

vi (*to a house*) trasferirsi. **move off** *vi* (*vehicle:*) muoversi. **move out** *vi* (*of house*) andare via. **move over** *vi* spostarsi ● *vt* spostare. **move up** *vi* muoversi; (*advance, increase*) avanzare

movement /'muːvmənt/ *n* movimento *m*

movie /'muːvɪ/ *n* film *m inv*; **go to the ~s** andare al cinema

moving /'muːvɪŋ/ *a* mobile; (*touching*) commovente

mow /məʊ/ *vt* (*pt* **mowed**, *pp* **mown** or **mowed**) tagliare (*lawn*). **mow down** *vt* (*destroy*) sterminare

mower /'məʊə(r)/ *n* tosaerba *m inv*

MP *n abbr* **Member of Parliament**

Mr /'mɪstə(r)/ *n* (*pl* **Messrs**) Signor *m*

Mrs /'mɪsɪz/ *n* Signora *f*

Ms /mɪz/ *n* Signora *f* (*modo m formale di rivolgersi ad una donna quando non si vuole connotarla come sposata o nubile*)

much /mʌtʃ/ *a, adv & pron* molto; **as per quanto; I love you just as ~ as before/him** ti amo quanto prima/lui; **as ~ as £5 million** ben cinque milioni di sterline; **as ~ as that** così tanto; **very ~** tantissimo, moltissimo; **~ the same** quasi uguale

muck /mʌk/ *n* (*dirt*) sporcizia *f*; (*farming*) letame *m*; (*fam: filth*) porcheria *f*. **muck about** *vi fam* perder tempo; **~ about with** trafficare con. **muck up** *vt fam* rovinare; (*make dirty*) sporcare

mucky /'mʌkɪ/ *a* (-ier, -iest) sudicio

mucus /'mjuːkəs/ *n* muco *m*

mud /mʌd/ *n* fango *m*

muddle /'mʌdl/ *n* disordine *m*; (*mix-up*) confusione *f* ● *vt* **~ [up]** confondere (*dates*)

muddy /'mʌdɪ/ *a* (-ier, -iest) (*path*) fangoso; (*shoes*) infangato

'mudguard *n* parafango *m*

muesli /'muːzlɪ/ *n* muesli *m inv*

muffle /'mʌfl/ *vt* smorzare (*sound*). **muffle [up]** *vt* (*for warmth*) imbacuccare

muffler /'mʌflə(r)/ *n* sciarpa *f*; *Am Auto* marmitta *f*

mug¹ /mʌg/ *n* tazza *f*; (*for beer*) boccale *m*; (*fam: face*) muso *m*; (*fam: simpleton*) pollo *m*

mug² *vt* (*pt/pp* **mugged**) aggredire e derubare. **~ger** *n* assalitore, -trice *mf*. **~ging** *n* aggressione *f* per furto

muggy /'mʌgɪ/ *a* (-ier, -iest) afoso

mule /mjuːl/ *n* mulo *m*

mull /mʌl/ *vt* **~ over** rimuginare su

mulled /mʌld/ a ~ **wine** vin brûlé m inv

multi /'mʌltɪ/: **~coloured** a variopinto. **~lingual** /-'lɪŋgwəl/ a multilingue inv. **~media** n multimedia mpl ● a multimediale. **~'national** a multinazionale ● n multinazionale f

multiple /'mʌltɪpl/ a multiplo

multiplication /mʌltɪplɪ'keɪʃn/ n moltiplicazione f

multiply /'mʌltɪplaɪ/ v (pt/pp -ied) ● vt moltiplicare (**by** per) ● vi moltiplicarsi

multi'storey a ~ **car park** parcheggio m a più piani

mum[1] /mʌm/ a **keep** ~ fam non aprire bocca

mum[2] n fam mamma f

mumble /'mʌmbl/ vt/i borbottare

mummy[1] /'mʌmɪ/ n fam mamma f

mummy[2] n Archaeol mummia f

mumps /mʌmps/ n orecchioni mpl

munch /mʌntʃ/ vt/i sgranocchiare

mundane /mʌn'deɪn/ a (everyday) banale

municipal /mju'nɪsɪpl/ a municipale

mural /'mjʊərəl/ n dipinto m murale

murder /'mɜːdə(r)/ n assassinio m ● vt assassinare; (fam: ruin) massacrare. **~er** n assassino, -a mf. **~ous** /-rəs/ a omicida

murky /'mɜːkɪ/ a (-ier, -iest) oscuro

murmur /'mɜːmə(r)/ n mormorio m ● vt/i mormorare

muscle /'mʌsl/ n muscolo m ● **muscle in** vi sl intromettersi (**on** in)

muscular /'mʌskjʊlə(r)/ a muscolare; (strong) muscoloso

muse /mjuːz/ vi meditare (**on** su)

museum /mju:'zɪəm/ n museo m

mushroom /'mʌʃrʊm/ n fungo m ● vi fig spuntare come funghi

music /'mju:zɪk/ n musica f; (written) spartito m.

musical /'mju:zɪkl/ a musicale; ⟨person⟩ dotato di senso musicale ● n commedia f musicale. ~ **box** n carillon m inv. ~ **instrument** n strumento m musicale

music: ~ **box** n carillon m inv. ~ **centre** n impianto m stereo; '~-**hall** n teatro m di varietà

musician /mju:'zɪʃn/ n musicista mf

Muslim /'mʊzlɪm/ a & n musulmano, -a mf

mussel /'mʌsl/ n cozza f

must /mʌst/ v aux (solo al presente) dovere; **you ~ not be late** non devi essere in ritardo; **she ~ have finished by now** (probability) deve aver finito ormai ● n a ~ fam una cosa da non perdere

mustard /'mʌstəd/ n senape f

musty /'mʌstɪ/ a (-ier, -iest) stantio

mutation /mju:'teɪʃn/ n Biol mutazione f

mute /mju:t/ a muto

muted /'mju:tɪd/ a smorzato

mutilat|e /'mju:tɪleɪt/ vt mutilare. **~ion** /-'leɪʃn/ n mutilazione f

mutin|ous /'mju:tɪnəs/ a ammutinato. **~y** n ammutinamento m ● vi (pt/pp -ied) ammutinarsi

mutter /'mʌtə(r)/ vt/i borbottare

mutton /'mʌtn/ n carne f di montone

mutual /'mju:tjʊəl/ a reciproco; (fam: common) comune. **~ly** adv reciprocamente

muzzle /'mʌzl/ n (of animal) muso m; (of firearm) bocca f; (for dog) museruola f ● vt fig mettere il bavaglio a

my /maɪ/ poss a il mio m, la mia f, i miei mpl, le mie fpl; **my mother/father** mia madre/mio padre

myself /maɪ'self/ pers pron (reflexive) mi; (emphatic) me stesso; (after prep) me; **I've seen it** ~ l'ho visto io stesso; **by** ~ da solo; **I thought to** ~ ho pensato tra me e me; **I'm proud of** ~ sono fiero di me

mysterious /mɪ'stɪərɪəs/ a misterioso. **~ly** adv misteriosamente

mystery /'mɪstərɪ/ n mistero m; ~ [**story**] racconto m del mistero

mysti|c[al] /'mɪstɪk[l]/ a mistico. **~cism** /-sɪzm/ n misticismo m

mystified /'mɪstɪfaɪd/ a disorientato

mystify /'mɪstɪfaɪ/ vt (pt/pp -ied) disorientare

mystique /mɪ'sti:k/ n mistica f

myth /mɪθ/ n mito m. **~ical** a mitico

mythology /mɪ'θɒlədʒɪ/ n mitologia f

Nn

nab /næb/ *vt* (*pt/pp* **nabbed**) *fam* beccare

naff /næf/ *a Br fam* banale

nag¹ /næg/ *n* (*horse*) ronzino *m*

nag² *v* (*pt/pp* **nagged**) ● *vt* assillare ● *vi* essere insistente ● *n* (*person*) brontolone, -a *mf*. **~ging** *a* (*pain*) persistente

nail /neɪl/ *n* chiodo *m*; (*of finger, toe*) unghia *f* ● **nail down** *vt* inchiodare; **~ sb down to a time/price** far fissare a qcno un'ora/un prezzo

nail: ~-brush *n* spazzolino *m* da unghie. **~-file** *n* limetta *f* da unghie. **~ polish** *n* smalto *m* [per unghie]. **~ scissors** *npl* forbicine *fpl* da unghie. **~ varnish** *n* smalto *m* [per unghie]

naïve /naɪˈiːv/ *a* ingenuo. **~ty** /-ətɪ/ *n* ingenuità *f*

naked /ˈneɪkɪd/ *a* nudo; **with the ~ eye** a occhio nudo

name /neɪm/ *n* nome *m*; **what's your ~?** come ti chiami?; **my ~ is Matthew** mi chiamo Matthew; **I know her by ~** la conosco di nome; **by the ~ of Bates** di nome Bates; **call sb ~s** *fam* insultare qcno ● *vt* (*to position*) nominare; chiamare ⟨*baby*⟩; (*identify*) citare; **be ~d after** essere chiamato col nome di. **~less** *a* senza nome. **~ly** *adv* cioè

name: ~-plate *n* targhetta *f*. **~sake** *n* omonimo, -a *mf*

nanny /ˈnænɪ/ *n* bambinaia *f*. **~-goat** *n* capra *f*

nap /næp/ *n* pisolino *m*; **have a ~** fare un pisolino ● *vi* (*pt/pp* **napped**) **catch sb ~ping** cogliere qcno alla sprovvista

nape /neɪp/ *n* **~ [of the neck]** nuca *f*

napkin /ˈnæpkɪn/ *n* tovagliolo *m*

Naples /ˈneɪplz/ *n* Napoli *f*

nappy /ˈnæpɪ/ *n* pannolino *m*

narcotic /nɑːˈkɒtɪk/ *a & n* narcotico *m*

narrat|e /nəˈreɪt/ *vt* narrare. **~ion** /-eɪʃn/ *n* narrazione *f*

narrative /ˈnærətɪv/ *a* narrativo ● *n* narrazione *f*

narrator /nəˈreɪtə(r)/ *n* narratore, -trice *mf*

narrow /ˈnærəʊ/ *a* stretto; ⟨*fig: views*⟩ ristretto; ⟨*margin, majority*⟩ scarso ● *vi* restringersi. **~ly** *adv* **~ly escape death** evitare la morte per un pelo. **~-'minded** *a* di idee ristrette

nasal /ˈneɪzl/ *a* nasale

nastily /ˈnɑːstɪlɪ/ *adv* (*spitefully*) con cattiveria

nasty /ˈnɑːstɪ/ *a* (**-ier, -iest**) ⟨*smell, person, remark*⟩ cattivo; ⟨*injury, situation, weather*⟩ brutto; **turn ~** ⟨*person:*⟩ diventare cattivo

nation /ˈneɪʃn/ *n* nazione *f*

national /ˈnæʃənl/ *a* nazionale ● *n* cittadino, -a *mf*

national: ~ 'anthem *n* inno *m* nazionale. **N~ 'Health Service** *n* servizio *m* sanitario britannico. **N~ In'surance** *n* Previdenza *f* sociale

nationalism /ˈnæʃənəlɪzm/ *n* nazionalismo *m*

nationality /næʃəˈnælətɪ/ *n* nazionalità *f inv*

national|ization /næʃənəlaɪˈzeɪʃn/ *n* nazionalizzazione. **~ize** /ˈnæʃənəlaɪz/ *vt* nazionalizzare. **~ly** /ˈnæʃənəlɪ/ *adv* a livello nazionale

'nation-wide *a* su scala nazionale

native /ˈneɪtɪv/ *a* nativo; (*innate*) innato ● *n* nativo, -a *mf*; (*local inhabitant*) abitante *mf* del posto; (*outside Europe*) indigeno, -a *mf*; **she's a ~ of Venice** è originaria di Venezia

native: ~ 'land *n* paese *m* nativo. **~ 'language** *n* lingua *f* madre

Nativity /nəˈtɪvətɪ/ *n* **the ~** la Natività *f*. **~ play** *n* rappresentazione *f* sulla nascita di Gesù

natter /ˈnætə(r)/ *vi fam* chiacchierare

natural /ˈnætʃrəl/ *a* naturale

natural: ~ 'gas *n* metano *m*. **~ 'history** *n* storia *f* naturale

naturalist /ˈnætʃ(ə)rəlɪst/ *n* naturalista *mf*

natural|ization /nætʃ(ə)rəlaɪˈzeɪʃn/ *n* naturalizzazione *f*. **~ize** /ˈnætʃ(ə)rəlaɪz/ *vt* naturalizzare

naturally /ˈnætʃ(ə)rəlɪ/ *adv* (*of course*) naturalmente; (*by nature*) per natura

nature /'neɪtʃə(r)/ n natura f; **by ~** per natura. **~ reserve** n riserva f naturale

naughtily /'nɔ:tɪlɪ/ adv male

naughty /'nɔ:tɪ/ a (**-ier, -iest**) monello; (slightly indecent) spinto

nausea /'nɔ:zɪə/ n nausea f

nause|ate /'nɔ:zɪeɪt/ vt nauseare. **~ating** a nauseante. **~ous** /-ɪəs/ a **I feel ~ous** ho la nausea

nautical /'nɔ:tɪkl/ a nautico. **~ mile** n miglio m marino

naval /'neɪvl/ a navale

nave /neɪv/ n navata f centrale

navel /'neɪvl/ n ombelico m

navigable /'nævɪgəbl/ a navigabile

navigat|e /'nævɪgeɪt/ vi navigare; Auto fare da navigatore ● vt navigare su ⟨river⟩. **~ion** /-'geɪʃn/ n navigazione f. **~or** n navigatore m

navy /'neɪvɪ/ n marina f ● **~ [blue]** a blu scuro inv ● n blu m inv scuro

Neapolitan /nɪə'pɒlɪtən/ a & n napoletano, -a mf

near /nɪə(r)/ a vicino; ⟨future⟩ prossimo; **the ~est bank** la banca più vicina ● adv vicino; **draw ~** avvicinarsi; **~ at hand** a portata di mano ● prep vicino a; **he was ~ to tears** aveva le lacrime agli occhi ● vt avvicinarsi a

near: ~by a & adv vicino. **~ly** adv quasi; **it's not ~ly enough** non è per niente sufficiente. **~ness** n vicinanza f. **~ side** a Auto ⟨wheel⟩ (left) sinistro; (right) destro. **~-sighted** a Am miope

neat /ni:t/ a (tidy) ordinato; (clever) efficace; (undiluted) liscio. **~ly** adv ordinatamente; (cleverly) efficacemente. **~ness** n (tidiness) ordine m

necessarily /nesə'serɪlɪ/ adv necessariamente

necessary /'nesəsərɪ/ a necessario

necessit|ate /nɪ'sesɪteɪt/ vt rendere necessario. **~y** n necessità f inv

neck /nek/ n collo m; (of dress) colletto m; **~ and ~** testa a testa

necklace /'neklɪs/ n collana f

neck: ~line n scollatura f. **~tie** n cravatta f

neé /neɪ/ a **~ Brett** nata Brett

need /ni:d/ n bisogno m; **be in ~ of** avere bisogno di; **if ~ be** se ce ne fosse bisogno; **there is a ~ for** c'è bisogno di; **there is no ~ for that** non ce n'è bisogno; **there is no ~ for you to go** non c'è bisogno che tu vada ● vt aver bisogno di; **I ~ to know** devo saperlo; **it ~s to be done** bisogna farlo ● v aux

you ~ not go non c'è bisogno che tu vada; **~ I come?** devo [proprio] venire?

needle /'ni:dl/ n ago m; (for knitting) uncinetto m; (of record player) puntina f ● vt (fam: annoy) punzecchiare

needless /'ni:dlɪs/ a inutile

'needlework n cucito m

needy /'ni:dɪ/ a (**-ier, -iest**) bisognoso

negation /nɪ'geɪʃn/ n negazione f

negative /'negətɪv/ a negativo ● n negazione f; Phot negativo m; **in the ~** Gram alla forma negativa

neglect /nɪ'glekt/ n trascuratezza f; **state of ~** stato m di abbandono ● vt trascurare; **he ~ed to write** non si è curato di scrivere. **~ed** a trascurato. **~ful** a negligente; **be ~ful of** trascurare

négligée /'neglɪʒeɪ/ n négligé m inv

negligen|ce /'neglɪdʒəns/ n negligenza f. **~t** a negligente

negligible /'neglɪdʒəbl/ a trascurabile

negotiable /nɪ'gəʊʃəbl/ a ⟨road⟩ transitabile; Comm negoziabile; **not ~** ⟨cheque⟩ non trasferibile

negotiat|e /nɪ'gəʊʃɪeɪt/ vt negoziare; Auto prendere ⟨bend⟩ ● vi negoziare. **~ion** /-'eɪʃn/ n negoziato m. **~or** n negoziatore, -trice mf

Negro /'ni:grəʊ/ a & n (pl **-es**) negro, -a mf

neigh /neɪ/ vi nitrire

neighbour /'neɪbə(r)/ n vicino, -a mf. **~hood** n vicinato m; **in the ~hood of** nei dintorni di; fig circa. **~ing** a vicino. **~ly** a amichevole

neither /'naɪðə(r)/ a & pron nessuno dei due, né l'uno né l'altro ● adv **~... nor** né... né ● conj nemmeno, neanche; **~ do/did I** nemmeno io

neon /'ni:ɒn/ n neon m. **~ light** n luce f al neon

nephew /'nevju:/ n nipote m

nerve /nɜ:v/ n nervo m; (fam: courage) coraggio m; (fam: impudence) faccia f tosta; **lose one's ~** perdersi d'animo. **~-racking** a logorante

nervous /'nɜ:vəs/ a nervoso; **he makes me ~** mi mette in agitazione; **be a ~ wreck** avere i nervi a pezzi. **~ 'breakdown** n esaurimento m nervoso. **~ly** adv nervosamente. **~ness** n nervosismo m; (before important event) tensione f

nervy /'nɜ:vɪ/ a (**-ier, -iest**) nervoso; (Am: impudent) sfacciato

nest /nest/ n nido m ● vi fare il nido. **~-egg** n gruzzolo m

nestle /'nesl/ *vi* accoccolarsi

net¹ /net/ *n* rete *f* ● *vt* (*pt/pp* netted) (*catch*) prendere (*con la rete*)

net² *a* netto ● *vt* (*pt/pp* netted) incassare un utile netto di

'netball *n* sport *m inv* femminile, simile a pallacanestro

Netherlands /'neðələndz/ *npl* the ~ i Paesi Bassi

netting /'netɪŋ/ *n* (*wire*) ~ reticolato *m*

nettle /'netl/ *n* ortica *f*

'network *n* rete *f*

neuralgia /njʊəˈrældʒə/ *n* nevralgia *f*

neurolog|ist /njʊəˈrɒlədʒɪst/ *n* neurologo, -a *mf*

neur|osis /njʊəˈrəʊsɪs/ *n* (*pl* -oses /-siːz/) nevrosi *f inv*. ~otic /-ˈrɒtɪk/ *a* nevrotico

neuter /'njuːtə(r)/ *a Gram* neutro ● *n Gram* neutro ● *vt* sterilizzare

neutral /'njuːtrəl/ *a* neutro; (*country, person*) neutrale ● *n* in ~ *Auto* in folle. ~ity /-'trælətɪ/ *n* neutralità *f*. ~ize *vt* neutralizzare

never /'nevə(r)/ *adv* (*non...*) mai; (*fam: expressing disbelief*) ma va; ~ again mai più; well I ~! chi l'avrebbe detto!. ~-ending *a* interminabile

nevertheless /nevəðə'les/ *adv* tuttavia

new /njuː/ *a* nuovo

new: ~born *a* neonato. ~comer *n* nuovo, -a arrivato, -a. *mf*. ~fangled /-ˈfæŋgld/ *a pej* modernizzante. ~-laid *a* fresco

'newly *adv* (*recently*) di recente; ~-built costruito di recente. ~-weds *npl* sposini *mpl*

new: ~ 'moon *n* luna *f* nuova. ~ness *n* novità *f*

news /njuːz/ *n* notizie *fpl*; *TV* telegiornale *m*; *Radio* giornale *m* radio; piece of ~ notizia *f*

news: ~agent *n* giornalaio, -a *mf*. ~bulletin *n* notiziario *m*. ~caster *n* giornalista *mf* televisivo, -a/radiofonico, -a. ~flash *n* notizia *f* flash. ~letter *n* bollettino *m* d'informazione. ~paper *n* giornale *m*; (*material*) carta *f* di giornale. ~reader *n* giornalista *mf* televisivo, -a/radiofonico, -a

new: ~ year *n* (*next year*) anno *m* nuovo; N~ Year's Day *n* Capodanno *m*. N~ Year's 'Eve *n* vigilia *f* di Capodanno. N~ Zealand /'ziːlənd/ *n* Nuova Zelanda *f*. N~ Zealander *n* neozelandese *mf*

next /nekst/ *a* prossimo; (*adjoining*) vi-

cino; who's ~? a chi tocca?; ~ door accanto; ~ to nothing quasi niente; the ~ day il giorno dopo; ~ week la settimana prossima; the week after ~ fra due settimane ● *adv* dopo; when will you see him ~? quando lo rivedi la prossima volta?; ~ to accanto a ● *n* seguente *mf*; ~ of kin parente *m* prossimo

NHS *n abbr* National Health Service

nib /nɪb/ *n* pennino *m*

nibble /'nɪbl/ *vt/i* mordicchiare

nice /naɪs/ *a* ⟨*day, weather, holiday*⟩ bello; ⟨*person*⟩ gentile, simpatico; ⟨*food*⟩ buono; it was ~ meeting you è stato un piacere conoscerla. ~ly *adv* gentilmente; (*well*) bene. ~ties /ˈnaɪsətɪz/ *npl* finezze *fpl*

niche /niːʃ/ *n* nicchia *f*

nick /nɪk/ *n* tacca *f*; (*on chin etc*) taglietto *m*; (*fam: prison*) galera *f*; (*fam: police station*) centrale *f* [di polizia]; in the ~ of time *fam* appena in tempo ● *vt* intaccare; (*fam: steal*) fregare; (*fam: arrest*) beccare; ~ one's chin farsi un taglietto nel mento

nickel /'nɪkl/ *n* nichel *m*; *Am* moneta *f* da cinque centesimi

'nickname *n* soprannome *m* ● *vt* soprannominare

nicotine /'nɪkətiːn/ *n* nicotina *f*

niece /niːs/ *n* nipote *f*

Nigeria /naɪˈdʒɪərɪə/ *n* Nigeria *f*. ~n *a* & *n* nigeriano, -a *mf*

niggling /'nɪglɪŋ/ *a* ⟨*detail*⟩ insignificante; ⟨*pain*⟩ fastidioso; ⟨*doubt*⟩ persistente

night /naɪt/ *n* notte *f*; (*evening*) sera *f*; at ~ la notte, di notte; (*in the evening*) la sera, di sera; Monday ~ lunedì notte/sera ● *a* di notte

night: ~cap *n* papalina *f*; (*drink*) bicchierino *m* bevuto prima di andare a letto. ~club *n* locale *m* notturno, night[-club] *m inv*. ~dress *n* camicia *f* da notte. ~fall *n* crepuscolo *m*. ~-gown, *fam* ~ie /'naɪtɪ/ *n* camicia *f* da notte

nightingale /'naɪtɪŋgeɪl/ *n* usignolo *m*

night: ~-life *n* vita *f* notturna. ~ly *a* di notte, di sera ● *adv* ogni notte, ogni sera. ~mare *n* incubo *m*. ~-school *n* scuola *f* serale. ~-time *n* at ~-time di notte, la notte. ~-'watchman *n* guardiano *m* notturno

nil /nɪl/ *n* nulla *m*; *Sport* zero *m*

nimb|e /'nɪmbl/ *a* agile. ~y *adv* agilmente

nine /naɪn/ a nove inv ●n nove m.
~'teen a diciannove inv ●n diciannove
m. **~'teenth** a & n diciannovesimo, -a
mf
ninetieth /'naɪntɪθ/ a & n novantesimo, -a mf
ninety /'naɪntɪ/ a novanta inv ●n novanta m
ninth /naɪnθ/ a & n nono, -a mf
nip /nɪp/ n pizzicotto m; (bite) morso m
●vt pizzicare; (bite) mordere; **~ in the
bud** fig stroncare sul nascere ●vi (fam:
run) fare un salto
nipple /'nɪpl/ n capezzolo m; (Am: on
bottle) tettarella f
nippy /'nɪpɪ/ a (-ier, -iest) fam (cold)
pungente; (quick) svelto
nitrogen /'naɪtrədʒn/ n azoto m
nitwit /'nɪtwɪt/ n fam imbecille mf
no /nəʊ/ adv no ●n (pl noes) no m inv
●a nessuno; **I have no time** non ho
tempo; **in no time** in un baleno; **'no
parking'** 'sosta vietata'; **'no smoking'**
'vietato fumare'; **no one** = **nobody**
nobility /nəʊ'bɪlətɪ/ n nobiltà f
noble /'nəʊbl/ a nobile. **~man** n nobile m
nobody /'nəʊbədɪ/ pron nessuno; **he
knows ~** non conosce nessuno ●n
he's a ~ non è nessuno
nocturnal /nɒk'tɜ:nl/ a notturno
nod /nɒd/ n cenno m del capo ●v (pt/pp
nodded) ●vi fare un cenno col capo; (in
agreement) fare di sì col capo ●vt **~
one's head** fare di sì col capo. **nod off**
vi assopirsi
nodule /'nɒdjuːl/ n nodulo m
noise /nɔɪz/ n rumore m; (loud) rumore
m, chiasso m. **~less** a silenzioso.
~lessly adv silenziosamente
noisy /'nɔɪzɪ/ a (-ier, -iest) rumoroso
nomad /'nəʊmæd/ n nomade mf. **~ic**
/-'mædɪk/ a nomade
nominal /'nɒmɪnl/ a nominale
nominat|e /'nɒmɪneɪt/ vt proporre
come candidato; (appoint) designare.
~ion /-'neɪʃn/ n nomina f; (person
nominated) candidato, -a mf
nominative /'nɒmɪnətɪv/ a & n Gram
~ [case] nominativo m
nominee /nɒmɪ'niː/ n persona f nominata
nonchalant /'nɒnʃələnt/ a disinvolto
non-com'missioned /nɒn-/ a **~
officer** sottufficiale m
non-com'mittal a che non si sbilancia
nondescript /'nɒndɪskrɪpt/ a qualunque

none /nʌn/ pron (person) nessuno;
(thing) niente; **~ of us** nessuno di noi;
~ of this niente di questo; **there's ~
left** non ce n'è più ●adv **she's ~ too
pleased** non è per niente soddisfatta;
I'm ~ the wiser non ne so più di prima
nonentity /nɒ'nentətɪ/ n nullità f inv
non-event n delusione f
non-ex'istent a inesistente
non-'fiction n saggistica f
non-'iron a che non si stira
nonplussed /nɒn'plʌst/ a perplesso
nonsens|e /'nɒnsəns/ n sciocchezze
fpl. **~ical** /-'sensɪkl/ a assurdo
non-'smoker n non fumatore, -trice
mf; (compartment) scompartimento m
non fumatori
non-'stick a antiaderente
non-'stop a **~ 'flight** volo m diretto
●adv senza sosta; (fly) senza scalo
non-'violent a non violento
noodles /'nuːdlz/ npl taglierini mpl
nook /nʊk/ n cantuccio m
noon /nuːn/ n mezzogiorno m; **at ~** a
mezzogiorno
noose /nuːs/ n nodo m scorsoio
nor /nɔː(r)/ adv & conj né; **~ do I** neppure io
Nordic /'nɔːdɪk/ a nordico
norm /nɔːm/ n norma f
normal /'nɔːml/ a normale. **~ity**
/-'mælətɪ/ n normalità f. **~ly** adv
(usually) normalmente
north /nɔːθ/ n nord m; **to the ~ of** a
nord di ●a del nord, settentrionale
●adv a nord
north: N~ America n America f del
Nord. **~-bound** a Auto in direzione
nord. **~-east** a di nord-est,
nordorientale ●n nord-est m ●adv a
nord-est; (travel) verso nord-est
norther|ly /'nɔːðəlɪ/ a (direction) nord;
(wind) del nord. **~n** a del nord, settentrionale. **N~n Ireland** n Irlanda f del
Nord
north: N~ 'Pole n polo m nord. **N~
'Sea** n Mare m del Nord. **~ward[s]**
/-wəd[z]/ adv verso nord. **~-west** a di
nord-ovest, nordoccidentale ●n nord-
ovest m ●adv a nord-ovest; (travel) verso nord-ovest
Nor|way /'nɔːweɪ/ n Norvegia f.
~wegian /-'wiːdʒn/ a & n norvegese mf
nose /nəʊz/ n naso m
nose: ~bleed n emorragia f nasale.
~dive n Aeron picchiata f
nostalg|ia /nɒ'stældʒɪə/ n nostalgia f.
~ic a nostalgico

nostril /'nɒstrəl/ n narice f

nosy /'nəʊzɪ/ a (**-ier, -iest**) fam ficcanaso inv

not /nɒt/ adv non; **he is ~ Italian** non è italiano; **I hope ~** spero di no; **~ all of us have been invited** non siamo stati tutti invitati; **if ~** se no; **~ at all** niente affatto; **~ a bit** per niente; **~ even** neanche; **~ yet** non ancora; **~ only... but also...** non solo... ma anche...

notabl|e /'nəʊtəbl/ a (remarkable) notevole. **~y** adv (in particular) in particolare

notary /'nəʊtərɪ/ n notaio m; **~ 'public** notaio m

notch /nɒtʃ/ n tacca f ● **notch up** vt (score) segnare

note /nəʊt/ n nota f; (short letter, banknote) biglietto m; (memo, written comment etc) appunto m; **of ~** (person) di spicco; (comments, event) degno di nota; **make a ~ of** prendere nota di; **take ~ of** (notice) prendere nota di ● vt (notice) notare; (write) annotare. **note down** vt annotare

'notebook n taccuino m; Comput notebook m inv

noted /'nəʊtɪd/ a noto, celebre (**for** per)

note: ~paper n carta f da lettere. **~worthy** a degno di nota

nothing /'nʌθɪŋ/ pron niente, nulla ● adv niente affatto; **for ~** (free, in vain) per niente; (with no reason) senza motivo; **~ but** nient'altro che; **~ much** poco o nulla; **~ interesting** niente di interessante; **it's ~ to do with you** non ti riguarda

notice /'nəʊtɪs/ n (on board) avviso m; (review) recensione f; (termination of employment) licenziamento m; [advance] **~** preavviso m; **two months' ~** due mesi di preavviso; **at short ~** con breve preavviso; **until further ~** fino nuovo avviso; **give [in one's] ~** (employee:) dare le dimissioni; **give an employee ~** dare il preavviso a un impiegato; **take no ~ of** non fare caso a; **take no ~!** non farci caso! ● vt notare. **~able** /-əbl/ a evidente. **~ably** adv sensibilmente. **~-board** n bacheca f

noti|fication /nəʊtɪfɪ'keɪʃn/ n notifica f. **~fy** /'nəʊtɪfaɪ/ vt (pt/pp -ied) notificare

notion /'nəʊʃn/ n idea f, nozione f; **~s** pl (Am: haberdashery) merceria f

notoriety /nəʊtə'raɪətɪ/ n notorietà f

notorious /nəʊ'tɔːrɪəs/ a famigerato; **be ~ for** essere tristemente famoso per

notwith'standing prep malgrado ● adv ciononostante

nougat /'nuːgɑː/ n torrone m

nought /nɔːt/ n zero m

noun /naʊn/ n nome m, sostantivo m

nourish /'nʌrɪʃ/ vt nutrire. **~ing** a nutriente. **~ment** n nutrimento m

novel /'nɒvl/ a insolito ● n romanzo m. **~ist** n romanziere, -a mf. **~ty** n novità f; **~ties** pl (objects) oggettini mpl

November /nəʊ'vembə(r)/ n novembre m

novice /'nɒvɪs/ n novizio, -a mf

now /naʊ/ adv ora, adesso; **by ~** ormai; **just ~** proprio ora; **right ~** subito; **~ and again, ~ and then** ogni tanto; **~, ~!** su! ● conj **~ [that]** ora che, adesso che

'nowadays adv oggigiorno

nowhere /'nəʊ-/ adv in nessun posto, da nessuna parte

noxious /'nɒkʃəs/ a nocivo

nozzle /'nɒzl/ n bocchetta f

nuance /'njuːōs/ n sfumatura f

nuclear /'njuːklɪə(r)/ a nucleare

nucleus /'njuːklɪəs/ n (pl **-lei** /-lɪaɪ/) nucleo m

nude /njuːd/ a nudo ● n nudo m; **in the ~** nudo

nudge /nʌdʒ/ n colpetto m di gomito ● vt dare un colpetto col gomito a

nudism /'njuːdɪzm/ n nudismo m

nud|ist /'njuːdɪst/ n nudista mf. **~ity** n nudità f

nugget /'nʌgɪt/ n pepita f

nuisance /'njuːsns/ n seccatura f; (person) piaga f; **what a ~!** che seccatura!

null /nʌl/ a **~ and void** nullo

numb /nʌm/ a intorpidito; **~ with cold** intirizzito dal freddo

number /'nʌmbə(r)/ n numero m; **a ~ of people** un certo numero di persone ● vt numerare; (include) annoverare. **~-plate** n targa f

numeral /'njuːmərəl/ n numero m, cifra f

numerate /'njuːmərət/ a **be ~** saper fare i calcoli

numerical /njuː'merɪkl/ a numerico; **in ~ order** in ordine numerico

numerous /'njuːmərəs/ a numeroso

nun /nʌn/ n suora f

nurse /nɜːs/ n infermiere, -a mf; **children's ~** bambinaia f ● vt curare

nursery /'nɜːsərɪ/ n stanza f dei bambini; (for plants) vivaio m; **[day] ~** asilo *m.* **~ rhyme** *n* filastrocca *f.* **~ school** *n* scuola *f* materna

nursing /'nɜ:sɪŋ/ *n* professione *f* d'infermiere. **~ home** *n* casa *f* di cura per anziani

nurture /'nɜ:tʃə(r)/ *vt* allevare; *fig* coltivare

nut /nʌt/ *n* noce *f; Techn* dado *m;* ⟨*fam: head*⟩ zucca *f;* **~s** *npl* frutta *f* secca; **be ~s** *fam* essere svitato. **~crackers** *npl*

schiaccianoci *m inv.* **~meg** *n* noce *f* moscata

nutrit|ion /njuː'trɪʃn/ *n* nutrizione *f.* **~ious** /-ʃəs/ *a* nutriente

'nutshell *n* **in a ~** *fig* in parole povere

nuzzle /'nʌzl/ *vt* ⟨*horse, dog:*⟩ strofinare il muso contro

nylon /'naɪlɒn/ *n* nailon ,*m;* **~s** *pl* calze *fpl* di nailon ● *a* di nailon

---

O /əʊ/ *n Teleph* zero *m*

oaf /əʊf/ *n* (*pl* **oafs**) zoticone, -a *mf*

oak /əʊk/ *n* quercia *f* ● *attrib* di quercia

OAP *n abbr* (**old-age pensioner**) pensionato, -a *mf*

oar /ɔ:(r)/ *n* remo *m.* **~sman** *n* vogatore *m*

oasis /əʊ'eɪsɪs/ *n* (*pl* **oases** /-si:z/) oasi *f inv*

oath /əʊθ/ *n* giuramento *m;* ⟨*swearword*⟩ bestemmia *f*

oatmeal /'əʊt-/ *n* farina *f* d'avena

oats /əʊts/ *npl* avena *fsg; Culin* [**rolled**] **~** fiocchi *mpl* di avena

obedien|ce /ə'bi:dɪəns/ *n* ubbidienza *f.* **~t** *a* ubbidiente

obes|e /ə'bi:s/ *a* obeso. **~ity** *n* obesità *f*

obey /ə'beɪ/ *vt* ubbidire a; osservare ⟨*instructions, rules*⟩ ● *vi* ubbidire

obituary /ə'bɪtjʊərɪ/ *n* necrologio *m*

object¹ /'ɒbdʒɪkt/ *n* oggetto *m; Gram* complemento *m* oggetto; **money is no ~** i soldi non sono un problema

object² /əb'dʒekt/ *vi* (*be against*) opporsi (**to** a); **~ that...** obiettare che...

objection /əb'dʒekʃn/ *n* obiezione *f;* **have no ~** non avere niente in contrario. **~able** /-əbl/ *a* discutibile; ⟨*person*⟩ sgradevole

objectiv|e /əb'dʒektɪv/ *a* oggettivo ● *n* obiettivo *m.* **~ely** *adv* obiettivamente. **~ity** /-'tɪvətɪ/ *n* oggettività *f*

obligation /ɒblɪ'geɪʃn/ *n* obbligo *m;* **be under an ~** avere un obbligo; **without ~** senza impegno

obligatory /ə'blɪgətrɪ/ *a* obbligatorio

oblig|e /ə'blaɪdʒ/ *vt* (*compel*) obbligare;

much ~ed grazie mille. **~ing** *a* disponibile

oblique /ə'bli:k/ *a* obliquo; *fig* indiretto ● *n* **~** [**stroke**] barra *f*

obliterate /ə'blɪtəreɪt/ *vt* obliterare

oblivion /ə'blɪvɪən/ *n* oblio *m*

oblivious /ə'blɪvɪəs/ *a* **be ~** essere dimentico (**of, to** di)

oblong /'ɒblɒŋ/ *a* oblungo ● *n* rettangolo *m*

obnoxious /əb'nɒkʃəs/ *a* detestabile

oboe /'əʊbəʊ/ *n* oboe *m inv*

obscen|e /əb'si:n/ *a* osceno; ⟨*profits, wealth*⟩ vergognoso. **~ity** /-'senətɪ/ *n* oscenità *f inv*

obscur|e /əb'skjʊə(r)/ *a* oscuro ● *vt* oscurare; (*confuse*) mettere in ombra. **~ity** *n* oscurità *f*

obsequious /əb'si:kwɪəs/ *a* ossequioso

observa|nce /əb'zɜ:vəns/ *n* (*of custom*) osservanza *f.* **~nt** *a* attento. **~tion** /ɒbzə'veɪʃn/ *n* osservazione *f*

observatory /əb'zɜ:vətrɪ/ *n* osservatorio *m*

observe /əb'zɜ:v/ *vt* osservare; (*notice*) notare; (*keep, celebrate*) celebrare. **~r** *n* osservatore, -trice *mf*

obsess /əb'ses/ *vt* **be ~ed by** essere fissato con. **~ion** /-eʃn/ *n* fissazione *f.* **~ive** /-ɪv/ *a* ossessivo

obsolete /'ɒbsəli:t/ *a* obsoleto; ⟨*word*⟩ desueto

obstacle /'ɒbstəkl/ *n* ostacolo *m*

obstetrician /ɒbstə'trɪʃn/ *n* ostetrico, -a *mf.* **obstetrics** /əb'stetrɪks/ *n* ostetricia *f*

obstina|cy /'ɒbstɪnəsɪ/ n ostinazione f. **~te** /-nət/ a ostinato

obstreperous /əb'strepərəs/ a turbolento

obstruct /əb'strʌkt/ vt ostruire; (hinder) ostacolare. **~ion** /-ʌkʃn/ n ostruzione f; (obstacle) ostacolo m. **~ive** /-ɪv/ a be **~ive** ⟨person:⟩ creare dei problemi

obtain /əb'teɪn/ vt ottenere. **~able** /-əbl/ a ottenibile

obtrusive /əb'truːsɪv/ a ⟨object⟩ stonato

obtuse /əb'tjuːs/ a ottuso

obvious /'ɒbvɪəs/ a ovvio. **~ly** adv ovviamente

occasion /ə'keɪʒn/ n occasione f; (event) evento m; **on ~** talvolta; **on the ~ of** in occasione di

occasional /ə'keɪʒənl/ a saltuario; he has the **~ glass of wine** ogni tanto beve un bicchiere di vino. **~ly** adv ogni tanto

occult /ɒ'kʌlt/ a occulto

occupant /'ɒkjʊpənt/ n occupante mf; (of vehicle) persona f a bordo

occupation /ɒkjʊ'peɪʃn/ n occupazione f; (job) professione f **~al** a professionale

occupier /'ɒkjʊpaɪə(r)/ n residente mf

occupy /'ɒkjʊpaɪ/ vt (pt/pp **occupied**) occupare; (keep busy) tenere occupato

occur /ə'kɜː(r)/ vi (pt/pp **occurred**) accadere; (exist) trovarsi; it **~red to me that** mi è venuto in mente che. **~rence** /ə'kʌrəns/ n (event) fatto m

ocean /'əʊʃn/ n oceano m

o'clock /ə'klɒk/ adv it's 7 **~** sono le sette; **at 7 ~** alle sette;

octave /'ɒktɪv/ n Mus ottava f

October /ɒk'təʊbə(r)/ n ottobre m

octopus /'ɒktəpəs/ n (pl **-puses**) polpo m

odd /ɒd/ a ⟨number⟩ dispari; (not of set) scompagnato; (strange) strano; **forty ~** quaranta e rotti; **~ jobs** lavoretti mpl; **the ~ one out** l'eccezione f; **at ~ moments** a tempo perso; **have the ~ glass of wine** avere un bicchiere di vino ogni tanto

odd|ity /'ɒdɪtɪ/ n stranezza f. **~ly** adv stranamente; **~ly enough** stranamente. **~ment** n (of fabric) scampolo m

odds /ɒdz/ npl (chances) probabilità fpl; **at ~** in disaccordo; **~ and ends** cianfrusaglie fpl; **it makes no ~** non fa alcuna differenza

ode /əʊd/ n ode f

odour /'əʊdə(r)/ n odore m. **~less** a inodore

of /ɒv/, /əv/ prep di; **a cup of tea/coffee** una tazza di tè/caffè; **the hem of my skirt** l'orlo della mia gonna; **the summer of 1989** l'estate del 1989; **the two of us** noi due; **made of** di; **that's very kind of you** è molto gentile da parte tua; **a friend of mine** un mio amico; **a child of three** un bambino di tre anni; **the fourth of January** il quattro gennaio; **within a year of their divorce** a circa un anno dal loro divorzio; **half of it** la metà; **the whole of the room** tutta la stanza

off /ɒf/ prep da; (distant from) lontano da; **take £10 ~ the price** ridurre il prezzo di 10 sterline; **~ the coast** presso la costa; **a street ~ the main road** una traversa della via principale; (near) una strada vicino alla via principale; **get ~ the ladder** scendere dalla scala; **get ~ the bus** uscire dall'autobus; **leave the lid ~** lasciare la pentola senza il coperchio ● adv ⟨button, handle⟩ staccato; ⟨light, machine⟩ spento; ⟨brake⟩ tolto; ⟨tap⟩ chiuso; **'off'** (on appliance) 'off'; **2 kilometres ~** a due chilometri di distanza; **a long way ~** molto distante; (time) lontano; **~ and on** di tanto in tanto; **with his hat/coat ~** senza il cappello/cappotto; **with the light ~** a luce spenta; **20% ~** 20% di sconto; **be ~** (leave) andar via; Sport essere partito; ⟨food:⟩ essere andato a male; (all gone) essere finito; ⟨wedding, engagement:⟩ essere cancellato; **I'm ~ alcohol** ho smesso di bere; **be ~ one's food** non avere appetito; **she's ~ today** (on holiday) è in ferie oggi; (ill) è malata oggi; **I'm ~ home** vado a casa; **you'd be better ~ doing...** faresti meglio a fare...; **have a day ~** avere un giorno di vacanza; **drive/sail ~** andare via

offal /'ɒfl/ n Culin frattaglie fpl

'off-beat a insolito

'off-chance n possibilità f remota

off-'colour a (not well) giù di forma; ⟨joke, story⟩ sporco

offence /ə'fens/ n (illegal act) reato m; **give ~** offendere; **take ~** offendersi (**at** per)

offend /ə'fend/ vt offendere. **~er** n Jur colpevole mf

offensive /ə'fensɪv/ a offensivo ● n offensiva f

offer /'ɒfə(r)/ n offerta f ● vt offrire; opporre ‹resistance›; ~ **sb sth** offrire qcsa a qcno; ~ **to do sth** offrirsi di fare qcsa; ~ n offerta f

off'hand a ‹casual› spiccio ● adv su due piedi

office /'ɒfɪs/ n ufficio m; ‹post, job› carica f. ~ **hours** pl orario m di ufficio

officer /'ɒfɪsə(r)/ n ufficiale m; ‹police› agente m [di polizia]

official /ə'fɪʃl/ a ufficiale ● n funzionario, -a mf; Sport dirigente m. ~**ly** adv ufficialmente

officiate /ə'fɪʃɪeɪt/ vi officiare

'offing n **in the** ~ in vista

'off-licence n negozio m per la vendita di alcolici

off·load vt scaricare

'off-putting a fam scoraggiante

'offset vt ‹pt/pp -set, pres p -setting› controbilanciare

'offshoot n ramo m; fig diramazione f

'offshore a ‹wind› di terra; ‹company, investment› offshore inv. ~ **rig** n piattaforma f petrolifera, off-shore m inv

off'side a Sport [in] fuori gioco; ‹wheel etc› ‹left› sinistro; ‹right› destro

'offspring n prole m

off'stage adv dietro le quinte

off-'white a bianco sporco

often /'ɒfn/ adv spesso; **how** ~ ogni quanto; **every so** ~ una volta ogni tanto

ogle /'əʊgl/ vt mangiarsi con gli occhi

oh /əʊ/ int oh!; ~ **dear** oh Dio!

oil /ɔɪl/ n olio m; ‹petroleum› petrolio m; ‹for heating› nafta f ● vt oliare

oil: ~**field** n giacimento m di petrolio. ~**-painting** n pittura f a olio. ~ **refinery** n raffineria f di petrolio. ~ **rig** piattaforma f petrolifera. ~**skins** npl vestiti mpl di tela cerata. ~**-slick** n chiazza f di petrolio. ~**-tanker** n petroliera f. ~ **well** n pozzo m petrolifero

oily /'ɔɪlɪ/ a ‹-ier, -iest› unto; fig untuoso

ointment /'ɔɪntmənt/ n pomata f

OK /əʊ'keɪ/ int va bene, o.k. ● a **if that's OK with you** se ti va bene; **she's OK** ‹well› sta bene; **is the milk still OK?** il latte è ancora buono? ● adv ‹well› bene ● vt ‹anche okay› ‹pt/pp **OK'd, okayed**› dare l'o.k. a

old /əʊld/ a vecchio; ‹girlfriend› ex; **how** ~ **is she?** quanti anni ha?; **she is ten years** ~ ha dieci anni

old: ~ **age** n vecchiaia f. ~**-age 'pensioner** n pensionato, -a mf. ~ **boy** n Sch ex-allievo m. ~**'fashioned** a anti-

quato. ~ **girl** n Sch ex-allieva f. ~ **'maid** n zitella f

olive /'ɒlɪv/ n ‹fruit, colour› oliva f; ‹tree› olivo m ● a d'oliva; ‹colour› olivastro. ~ **branch** n fig ramoscello m d'olivo. ~ **'oil** n olio m di oliva

Olympic /ə'lɪmpɪk/ a ‹olimpico; ~**s**, ~ **Games** Olimpiadi fpl

omelette /'ɒmlɪt/ n omelette f inv

omen /'əʊmən/ n presagio m

ominous /'ɒmɪnəs/ a sinistro

omission /ə'mɪʃn/ n omissione f

omit /ə'mɪt/ vt ‹pt/pp **omitted**› omettere; ~ **to do sth** tralasciare di fare qcsa

omnipotent /ɒm'nɪpətənt/ a onnipotente

on /ɒn/ prep su; ‹on horizontal surface› su, sopra; **on Monday** lunedì; **on Mondays** di lunedì; **on the first of May** il primo di maggio; **on arriving** all'arrivo; **on one's finger** ‹cut› nel dito; ‹ring› al dito; **on foot** a piedi; **on the right/left** a destra/sinistra; **on the Rhine/Thames** sul Reno/Tamigi; **on the radio/television** alla radio/televisione; **on the bus/train** in autobus/treno; **go on the bus/train** andare in autobus/treno; **get on the bus/train** salire sull'autobus/sul treno; **on me** ‹with me› con me; **it's on me** fam tocca a me ● adv ‹further on› dopo; ‹switched on› acceso; ‹brake› inserito; ‹in operation› in funzione; **'on'** ‹on machine› 'on'; **he had his hat/coat on** portava il cappello/cappotto; **without his hat/coat on** senza cappello/cappotto; **with/without the lid on** con/senza coperchio; **be on** ‹film, programme, event:› esserci; **it's not on** fam non è giusto; **be on at** fam tormentare ‹**to** per›; **on and on** senza sosta; **on and off** a intervalli; **and so on** e così via; **go on** continuare; **drive on** spostarsi ‹con la macchina›; **stick on** attaccare; **sew on** cucire

once /wʌns/ adv una volta; ‹formerly› un tempo; ~ **upon a time there was** c'era una volta; **at** ~ subito; ‹at the same time› contemporaneamente; ~ **and for all** una volta per tutte ● conj [non] appena. ~**-over** n fam **give sb/sth the** ~**-over** ‹look, check› dare un'occhiata veloce a qcsa/qcsa

'oncoming a che si avvicina dalla direzione opposta

one /wʌn/ a uno, una; **not** ~ **person** nemmeno una persona ● n uno m ● pron uno; ‹impersonal› si; ~ **another**

l'un l'altro; **~ by** [a] uno a uno; **~ never knows** non si sa mai

one: **~-eyed** *a* con un occhio solo. **~-off** *a* unico. **~-parent 'family** *n* famiglia *f* con un solo genitore. **~self** *pron* (*reflexive*) si; (*emphatic*) sé, se stesso; **by ~self** da solo; **be proud of ~self** essere fieri di sé. **~-sided** *a* unilaterale. **~-way** *a* (*street*) a senso unico; (*ticket*) di sola andata

onion /'ʌnjən/ *n* cipolla *f*

'onlooker *n* spettatore, -trice *mf*

only /'əʊnlɪ/ *a* solo; **~ child** figlio, -a *mf* unico, -a ● *adv & conj* solo, solamente; **~ just** appena

on/'off switch *n* pulsante *m* di accensione

'onset *n* (*beginning*) inizio *m*

onslaught /'ɒnslɔːt/ *n* attacco *m*

onus /'əʊnəs/ *n* **the ~ is on me** spetta a me la responsabilità (**to** di)

onward[s] /'ɒnwəd[z]/ *adv* in avanti; **from then ~** da allora [in poi]

ooze /uːz/ *vi* fluire

opal /'əʊpl/ *n* opale *f*

opaque /əʊ'peɪk/ *a* opaco

open /'əʊpən/ *a* aperto; (*free to all*) pubblico; (*job*) vacante; **in the ~ air** all'aperto ● *n* **in the ~** all'aperto; *fig* alla luce del sole ● *vt* aprire ● *vi* aprirsi; (*shop:*) aprire; (*flower:*) sbocciare. **open up** *vt* aprire ● *vi* aprirsi

open: **~-air 'swimming pool** *n* piscina *f* all'aperto. **~ day** *n* giorno *m* di apertura al pubblico

opener /'əʊpənə(r)/ *n* (*for tins*) apriscatole *m inv*; (*for bottles*) apribottiglie *m inv*

opening /'əʊpənɪŋ/ *n* apertura *f*; (*beginning*) inizio *m*; (*job*) posto *m* libero; **~ hours** *npl* orario *m* d'apertura

openly /'əʊpənlɪ/ *adv* apertamente

open: **~-'minded** *a* aperto; (*broadminded*) di vedute larghe. **~-plan** *a* a pianta aperta. **~ 'sandwich** *n* tartina *f*. **~ secret** *n* segreto *m* di Pulcinella. **~ ticket** *n* biglietto *m* aperto. **O~ University** *corsi mpl universitari per corrispondenza*

opera /'ɒpərə/ *n* opera *f*

operable /'ɒpərəbl/ *a* operabile

opera: **~-glasses** *npl* binocolo *msg* da teatro. **~-house** *n* teatro *m* lirico. **~-singer** *n* cantante *mf* lirico, -a

operate /'ɒpəreɪt/ *vt* far funzionare (*machine, lift*); azionare (*lever, brake*); mandare avanti (*business*) ● *vi* *Techn* funzionare; (*be in action*) essere in fun-

zione; *Mil, fig* operare; **~ on** *Med* operare

operatic /ɒpə'rætɪk/ *a* lirico, operistico

operation /ɒpə'reɪʃn/ *n* operazione *f*; *Tech* funzionamento *m*; **in ~** *Techn* in funzione; **come into ~** *fig* entrare in funzione; (*law:*) entrare in vigore; **have an ~** *Med* subire un'operazione. **~al** *a* operativo; (*law etc*) in vigore

operative /'ɒpərətɪv/ *a* operativo

operator /'ɒpəreɪtə(r)/ *n* (*user*) operatore, -trice *mf*; *Teleph* centralinista *mf*

operetta /ɒpə'retə/ *n* operetta *f*

opinion /ə'pɪnjən/ *n* opinione *f*; **in my ~** secondo me. **~ated** *a* dogmatico

opponent /ə'pəʊnənt/ *n* avversario, -a *mf*

opportun|e /'ɒpətjuːn/ *a* opportuno. **~ist** /-'tjuːnɪst/ *n* opportunista *mf*. **~istic** *a* opportunistico

opportunity /ɒpə'tjuːnətɪ/ *n* opportunità *f inv*

oppos|e /ə'pəʊz/ *vt* opporsi a; **be ~ed to sth** essere contrario a qcsa; **as ~ed to** al contrario di. **~ing** *a* avversario; (*opposite*) opposto

opposite /'ɒpəzɪt/ *a* opposto; (*house*) di fronte; **~ number** *fig* controparte *f*; **the ~ sex** l'altro sesso ● *n* contrario *m* ● *adv* di fronte ● *prep* di fronte a

opposition /ɒpə'zɪʃn/ *n* opposizione *f*

oppress /ə'pres/ *vt* opprimere. **~ion** /-eʃn/ *n* oppressione *f*. **~ive** /-ɪv/ *a* oppressivo; (*heat*) opprimente. **~or** *n* oppressore *m*

opt /ɒpt/ *vi* **~ for** optare per; **~ out** dissociarsi (**of** da)

optical /'ɒptɪkl/ *a* ottico; **~ illusion** illusione *f* ottica

optician /ɒp'tɪʃn/ *n* ottico, -a *mf*

optimis|m /'ɒptɪmɪzm/ *n* ottimismo *m*. **~t** /-mɪst/ *n* ottimista *mf*. **~tic** /-'mɪstɪk/ *a* ottimistico

optimum /'ɒptɪməm/ *a* ottimale ● *n* (*pl* -ima) optimum *m*

option /'ɒpʃn/ *n* scelta *f*; *Comm* opzione *f*. **~al** *a* facoltativo; **~al extras** optional *m inv*

opulen|ce /'ɒpjʊləns/ *n* opulenza *f*. **~t** *a* opulento

or /ɔː(r)/ *conj* o, oppure; (*after negative*) né; **or [else]** se no; **in a year or two** fra un anno o due

oracle /'ɒrəkl/ *n* oracolo *m*

oral /'ɔːrəl/ *a* orale ● *n fam* esame *m* orale. **~ly** *adv* oralmente

orange /'ɒrɪndʒ/ *n* arancia *f*; (*colour*)

arancione *m* ● *a* arancione. **~ade** /-'dʒeɪd/ *n* aranciata *f*. **~ juice** *n* succo *m* d'arancia

orator /'ɒrətə(r)/ *n* oratore, -trice *mf*

oratorio /ɒrə'tɔ:rɪəʊ/ *n* oratorio *m*

oratory /'ɒrətərɪ/ *n* oratorio *m*

orbit /'ɔ:bɪt/ *n* orbita *f* ● *vt* orbitare. **~al** *a* **~al road** tangenziale *f*

orchard /'ɔ:tʃəd/ *n* frutteto *m*

orches|tra /'ɔ:kɪstrə/ *n* orchestra *f*. **~tral** /-'kestrəl/ *a* orchestrale. **~trate** *vt* orchestrare

orchid /'ɔ:kɪd/ *n* orchidea *f*

ordain /ɔ:'deɪn/ *vt* decretare; *Relig* ordinare

ordeal /ɔ:'di:l/ *n fig* terribile esperienza *f*

order /'ɔ:də(r)/ *n* ordine *m*; *Comm* ordinazione *f*; **out of ~** ⟨*machine*⟩ fuori servizio; **in ~ that** affinché; **in ~ to** per ● *vt* ordinare

orderly /'ɔ:dəlɪ/ *a* ordinato ● *n Mil* attendente *m*; *Med* inserviente *m*

ordinary /'ɔ:dɪnərɪ/ *a* ordinario

ordination /ɔ:dɪ'neɪʃn/ *n Relig* ordinazione *f*

ore /ɔ:(r)/ *n* minerale *m* grezzo

organ /'ɔ:gən/ *n Anat, Mus* organo *m*

organic /ɔ:'gænɪk/ *a* organico; ⟨*without chemicals*⟩ biologico. **~ally** *adv* organicamente; **~ally grown** coltivato biologicamente

organism /'ɔ:gənɪzm/ *n* organismo *m*

organist /'ɔ:gənɪst/ *n* organista *mf*

organization /ɔ:gənaɪ'zeɪʃn/ *n* organizzazione *f*

organize /'ɔ:gənaɪz/ *vt* organizzare. **~r** *n* organizzatore, -trice *mf*

orgasm /'ɔ:gæzm/ *n* orgasmo *m*

orgy /'ɔ:dʒɪ/ *n* orgia *f*

Orient /'ɔ:rɪənt/ *n* Oriente *m*. **o~al** /-'entl/ *a* orientale ● *n* orientale *mf*

orient|ate /'ɔ:rɪənteɪt/ *vt* **~ate oneself** orientarsi. **~ation** /-'teɪʃn/ *n* orientamento *m*

origin /'ɒrɪdʒɪn/ *n* origine *f*

original /ə'rɪdʒɪn(ə)l/ *a* originario; ⟨*not copied, new*⟩ originale ● *n* originale *m*; **in the ~** in versione originale. **~ity** /-'nælətɪ/ *n* originalità *f*. **~ly** *adv* originariamente

originat|e /ə'rɪdʒɪneɪt/ *vi* **~e in** avere origine in. **~or** *n* ideatore, -trice *mf*

ornament /'ɔ:nəmənt/ *n* ornamento *m*; ⟨*on mantelpiece etc*⟩ soprammobile *m*. **~al** /-'mentl/ *a* ornamentale. **~ation** /-'teɪʃn/ *n* decorazione *f*

ornate /ɔ:'neɪt/ *a* ornato

orphan /'ɔ:fn/ *n* orfano, -a *mf* ● *vt* rendere orfano; **be ~ed** rimanere orfano. **~age** /-ɪdʒ/ *n* orfanotrofio *m*

orthodox /'ɔ:θədɒks/ *a* ortodosso

orthopaedic /ɔ:θə'pi:dɪk/ *a* ortopedico

oscillate /'ɒsɪleɪt/ *vi* oscillare

ostensibl|e /ɒ'stensəbl/ *a* apparente. **~y** *adv* apparentemente

ostentat|ion /ɒsten'teɪʃn/ *n* ostentazione *f*. **~ious** /-ʃəs/ *a* ostentato

osteopath /'ɒstɪəpæθ/ *n* osteopata *mf*

ostracize /'ɒstrəsaɪz/ *vt* bandire

ostrich /'ɒstrɪtʃ/ *n* struzzo *m*

other /'ʌðə(r)/ *a, pron & n* altro, -a *mf*; **the ~** [one] l'altro, -a *mf* **~he ~ two** gli altri due; **two ~s** altri due; **~ people** gli altri; **any ~ questions?** altre domande?; **every ~ day** ⟨*alternate days*⟩ a giorni alterni; **the ~ day** l'altro giorno; **the ~ evening** l'altra sera; **someone/something or ~** qualcuno/ qualcosa ● *adv* **~ than him** tranne lui; **somehow or ~** in qualche modo; **somewhere or ~** da qualche parte

'otherwise *adv* altrimenti; ⟨*differently*⟩ diversamente

otter /'ɒtə(r)/ *n* lontra *f*

ouch /aʊtʃ/ *int* ahi!

ought /ɔ:t/ *v aux* **I/we ~ to stay** dovrei/dovremmo rimanere; **he ~ not to have done it** non avrebbe dovuto farlo; **that ~ to be enough** questo dovrebbe bastare

ounce /aʊns/ *n* oncia *f* (= 28, 35 g)

our /'aʊə(r)/ *poss a* il nostro *m*, la nostra *f*, i nostri *mpl*, le nostre *fpl*; **~ mother/ father** nostra madre/nostro padre

ours /'aʊəz/ *poss pron* il nostro *m*, la nostra *f*, i nostri *mpl*, le nostre *fpl*; **a friend of ~** un nostro amico; **friends of ~** dei nostri amici; **that is ~** quello è nostro; ⟨*as opposed to yours*⟩ quello è il nostro

ourselves /aʊə'selvz/ *pers pron* ⟨*reflexive*⟩ ci; ⟨*emphatic*⟩ noi, noi stessi; **we poured ~ a drink** ci siamo versati da bere; **we heard it ~** l'abbiamo sentito noi stessi; **we are proud of ~** siamo fieri di noi; **by ~** da soli

out /aʊt/ *adv* fuori; ⟨*not alight*⟩ spento; **be ~** ⟨*flower:*⟩ essere sbocciato; ⟨*workers:*⟩ essere in sciopero; ⟨*calculation:*⟩ essere sbagliato; *Sport* essere fuori; ⟨*unconscious*⟩ aver perso i sensi; ⟨*fig: not feasible*⟩ fuori questione; **the sun is ~** è uscito il sole; **~ and about** in piedi; **get ~!** *fam* fuori!; **you should get**

~ more dovresti uscire più spesso; **~ with it!** *fam* sputa il rospo!; ● *prep* **~ of** fuori da; **~ of date** non aggiornato; ⟨*passport*⟩ scaduto; **~ of order** guasto; **~ of print/stock** esaurito; **be ~ of bed/the room** fuori dal letto/dalla stanza; **~ of breath** senza fiato; **~ of danger** fuori pericolo; **~ of work** disoccupato; **nine ~ of ten** nove su dieci; **be ~ of sugar/bread** rimanere senza zucchero/pane; **go ~ of the room** uscire dalla stanza

out'bid *vt* (*pt/pp* **-bid**, *pres p* **-bidding**) **~ sb** rilanciare l'offerta di qcno

'outboard *a* **~ motor** motore *m*

'outbreak *n* (*of war*) scoppio *m*; (*of disease*) insorgenza *f*

'outbuilding *n* costruzione *f* annessa

'outburst *n* esplosione *f*

'outcome *n* risultato *m*

'outcry *n* protesta *f*

out'dated *a* sorpassato

out'do *vt* (*pt* **-did**, *pp* **-done**) superare

'outdoor *a* ⟨*life, sports*⟩ all'aperto; **~ clothes** *pl* vestiti per uscire; **~ swimming pool** piscina *f* scoperta

out'doors *adv* all'aria aperta; **go ~** uscire [all'aria aperta]

'outer *a* esterno

'outfit *n* equipaggiamento *m*; (*clothes*) completo *m*; (*fam: organization*) organizzazione *f*. **~ter** *n* **men's ~ter's** negozio *m* di abbigliamento maschile

'outgoing *a* (*president*) uscente; ⟨*mail*⟩ in partenza; (*sociable*) estroverso ● *npl* **~s** uscite *fpl*

out'grow *vi* (*pt* **-grew**, *pp* **-grown**) diventare troppo grande per

'outhouse *n* costruzione *f* annessa

outing /'aʊtɪŋ/ *n* gita *f*

outlandish /aʊt'lændɪʃ/ *a* stravagante

'outlaw *n* fuorilegge *mf inv* ● *vt* dichiarare illegale

'outlay *n* spesa *f*

'outlet *n* sbocco *m*; *fig* sfogo *m*; *Comm* punto *m* [di] vendita

'outline *n* contorno *m*; (*summary*) sommario *m* ● *vt* tracciare il contorno di; (*describe*) descrivere

out'live *vt* sopravvivere a

'outlook *n* vista *f*; (*future prospect*) prospettiva *f*; (*attitude*) visione *f*

'outlying *a* **~ areas** zone *fpl* periferiche

out'number *vt* superare in numero

'out-patient *n* paziente *mf* esterno, -a; **~s' department** ambulatorio *m*

'output *n* produzione *f*

'outrage *n* oltraggio *m* ● *vt* oltraggiare. **~ous** /-'reɪdʒəs/ *a* oltraggioso; ⟨*price*⟩ scandaloso

'outright[1] *a* completo; ⟨*refusal*⟩ netto

out'right[2] *adv* completamente; (*at once*) immediatamente; (*frankly*) francamente

'outset *n* inizio *m*; **from the ~** fin dall'inizio

'outside[1] *a* esterno ● *n* esterno *m*; **from the ~** dall'esterno; **at the ~** al massimo

out'side[2] *adv* all'esterno, fuori; (*out of doors*) fuori; **go ~** andare fuori ● *prep* fuori da; (*in front of*) davanti a

out'sider *n* estraneo, -a *mf*

'outskirts *npl* sobborghi *mpl*

out'spoken *a* schietto

out'standing *a* eccezionale; ⟨*landmark*⟩ prominente; (*not settled*) in sospeso

out'stretched *a* allungato

out'strip *vt* (*pt/pp* **-stripped**) superare

out'vote *vt* mettere in minoranza

'outward /-wəd/ *a* esterno; (*journey*) di andata ● *adv* verso l'esterno. **~ly** *adv* esternamente. **~s** *adv* verso l'esterno

out'weigh *vt* aver maggior peso di

out'wit *vt* (*pt/pp* **-witted**) battere in astuzia

oval /'əʊvl/ *a* ovale ● *n* ovale *m*

ovary /'əʊvərɪ/ *n* *Anat* ovaia *f*

ovation /əʊ'veɪʃn/ *n* ovazione *f*

oven /'ʌvn/ *n* forno *m*. **~-ready** *a* pronto da mettere in forno

over /'əʊvə(r)/ *prep* sopra; (*across*) al di là di; (*during*) durante; (*more than*) più di; **~ the phone** al telefono; **~ the page** alla pagina seguente; **all ~ Italy** in tutta [l']Italia; ⟨*travel*⟩ per l'Italia ● *adv* Math col resto di; (*ended*) finito; **~ again** un'altra volta; **~ and ~** più volte; **~ and above** oltre a; **~ here/there** qui/là; **all ~** (*everywhere*) dappertutto; **it's all ~** è tutto finito; **I ache all ~** ho male dappertutto; **come/bring ~** venire/portare; **turn ~** girare

over- *pref* (*too*) troppo

overall[1] /'əʊvərɔ:l/ *n* grembiule *m*; **~s** *pl* tuta *fsg* [da lavoro]

overall[2] /əʊvər'ɔ:l/ *a* complessivo; (*general*) generale ● *adv* complessivamente

over'balance *vi* perdere l'equilibrio

over'bearing *a* prepotente

'overboard *adv* Naut in mare

'overcast *a* coperto

over'charge *vt* **~ sb** far pagare più

del dovuto a qcno ● *vi* far pagare più del dovuto

'overcoat *n* cappotto *m*

over'come *vt* (*pt* **-came**, *pp* **-come**) vincere; **be ~ by** essere sopraffatto da

over'crowded *a* sovraffollato

over'do *vt* (*pt* **-did**, *pp* **-done**) esagerare; (*cook too long*) stracuocere; **~ it** (*fam: do too much*) strafare

'overdose *n* overdose *f inv*

'overdraft *n* scoperto *m*; **have an ~** avere il conto scoperto

over'draw *vt* (*pt* **-drew**, *pp* **-drawn**) **~ one's account** andare allo scoperto; **be ~n by** ⟨*account:*⟩ essere [allo] scoperto di

over'due *a* in ritardo

over'estimate *vt* sopravvalutare

'overflow [1] *n* (*water*) acqua *f* che deborda; (*people*) pubblico *m* in eccesso; (*outlet*) scarico *m*

over'flow [2] *vi* debordare

over'grown *a* ⟨*garden*⟩ coperto di erbacce

'overhaul [1] *n* revisione *f*

over'haul [2] *vt Techn* revisionare

over'head [1] *adv* in alto

'overhead [2] *a* aereo; ⟨*railway*⟩ sopraelevato; ⟨*lights*⟩ da soffitto ● *npl* **~s** spese *fpl* generali

over'hear *vt* (*pt/pp* **-heard**) sentire per caso ⟨*conversation*⟩

over'heat *vi Auto* surriscaldarsi ● *vt* surriscaldare

over'joyed *a* felicissimo

'overland *a & adv* via terra; **~ route** via *f* terrestre

over'lap *v* (*pt/pp* **-lapped**) ● *vi* sovrapporsi ● *vt* sovrapporre

over'leaf *adv* sul retro

over'load *vt* sovraccaricare

over'look *vt* dominare; (*fail to see, ignore*) lasciarsi sfuggire

overly /'əʊvəlɪ/ *adv* eccessivamente

over'night [1] *adv* per la notte; **stay ~** fermarsi a dormire

'overnight [2] *a* notturno; **~ bag** piccola borsa *f* da viaggio; **~ stay** sosta *f* per la notte

'overpass *n* cavalcavia *m inv*

over'pay *vt* (*pt/pp* **-paid**) strapagare

over'populated *a* sovrappopolato

over'power *vt* sopraffare. **~ing** *a* insostenibile

over'priced *a* troppo caro

overpro'duce *vt* produrre in eccesso

over'rate *vt* sopravvalutare. **~d** *a* sopravvalutato

over'reach *vt* **~ oneself** puntare troppo in alto

overre'act *vi* avere una reazione eccessiva. **~ion** *n* reazione *f* eccessiva

over'rid|e *vt* (*pt* **-rode**, *pp* **-ridden**) passare sopra a. **~ing** *a* prevalente

over'rule *vt* annullare ⟨*decision*⟩

over'run *vt* (*pt* **-ran**, *pp* **-run**, *pres p* **-running**) invadere; oltrepassare ⟨*time*⟩; **be ~ with** essere invaso da

over'seas [1] *adv* oltremare

'overseas [2] *a* d'oltremare

over'see *vt* (*pt* **-saw**, *pp* **-seen**) sorvegliare

over'shadow *vt* adombrare

over'shoot *vt* (*pt/pp* **-shot**) oltrepassare

'oversight *n* disattenzione *f*; **an ~** una svista

over'sleep *vi* (*pt/pp* **-slept**) svegliarsi troppo tardi

over'step *vt* (*pt/pp* **-stepped**) **~ the mark** oltrepassare ogni limite

overt /əʊ'vɜːt/ *a* palese

over'tak|e *vt/i* (*pt* **-took**, *pp* **-taken**) sorpassare. **~ing** *n* sorpasso *m*; **no ~ing** divieto di sorpasso

over'tax *vt fig* abusare di

'overthrow [1] *n Pol* rovesciamento *m*

over'throw [2] *vt* (*pt* **-threw**, *pp* **-thrown**) *Pol* rovesciare

'overtime *n* lavoro *m* straordinario ● *adv* **work ~** fare lo straordinario

over'tired *a* sovraffaticato

'overtone *n fig* sfumatura *f*

overture /'əʊvətjʊə(r)/ *n Mus* preludio *m*; **~s** *pl fig* approccio *msg*

over'turn *vt* ribaltare ● *vi* ribaltarsi

over'weight *a* sovrappeso

over'whelm /-'welm/ *vt* sommergere (**with** di); (*with emotion*) confondere. **~ing** *a* travolgente; ⟨*victory, majority*⟩ schiacciante

over'work *n* lavoro *m* eccessivo ● *vt* far lavorare eccessivamente ● *vi* lavorare eccessivamente

ow|e /əʊ/ *vt also fig* dovere ([**to**] **sb** a qcno); **~e sb sth** dovere qcsa a qcno. **~ing** *a* **be ~ing** ⟨*money:*⟩ essere da pagare ● *prep* **~ing to** a causa di

owl /aʊl/ *n* gufo *m*

own [1] /əʊn/ *a* proprio ● *pron* **a car of my ~** una macchina per conto mio; **on one's ~** da solo; **hold one's ~ with** tener testa a; **get one's ~ back** *fam* prendersi una rivincita

own [2] *vt* possedere; (*confess*) ammettere;

I don't ~ it non mi appartiene. **own up**
vi confessare (**to sth** qcsa)
owner /'əʊnə(r)/ *n* proprietario, -a *mf*.
~ship *n* proprietà *f*
ox /ɒks/ *n* (*pl* **oxen**) bue *m* (*pl* buoi)
oxide /'ɒksaɪd/ *n* ossido *m*

oxygen /'ɒksɪdʒən/ *n* ossigeno *m*. ~
mask *n* maschera *f* a ossigeno
oyster /'ɔɪstə(r)/ *n* ostrica *f*
ozone /'əʊzəʊn/ *n* ozono *m*. ~-'**friendly**
a che non danneggia l'ozono. ~ **layer** *n*
fascia *f* d'ozono

Pp

PA *abbr* (**per annum**) all'anno
pace /peɪs/ *n* passo *m*; (*speed*) ritmo *m*.
keep ~ with camminare di pari passo
con ● *vi* ~ **up and down** camminare
avanti e indietro. **~-maker** *n Med*
pacemaker *m*; (*runner*) battistrada *m*
Pacific /pə'sɪfɪk/ *a & n* **the ~ [Ocean]**
l'oceano *m* Pacifico, il Pacifico
pacifier /'pæsɪfaɪə(r)/ *n Am* ciuccio *m*,
succhiotto *m*
pacifist /'pæsɪfɪst/ *n* pacifista *mf*
pacify /'pæsɪfaɪ/ *vt* (*pt/pp* **-ied**) placare
⟨*person*⟩; pacificare ⟨*country*⟩
pack /pæk/ *n* (*of cards*) mazzo *m*; (*of
hounds*) muta *f*; (*of wolves, thieves*)
branco *m*; (*of cigarettes etc*) pacchetto *m*;
a ~ of lies un mucchio di bugie ● *vt*
impacchettare ⟨*article*⟩; fare ⟨*suitcase*⟩;
mettere in valigia ⟨*swimsuit etc*⟩; (*press
down*) comprimere; **~ed [out]**
(*crowded*) pieno zeppo ● *vi* fare i bagagli; **send sb ~ing** *fam* mandare qcno a
stendere. **pack up** *vt* impacchettare
● *vi fam* ⟨*machine:*⟩ piantare in asso
package /'pækɪdʒ/ *n* pacco *m* ● *vt* impacchettare. ~ **deal** offerta *f* tutto compreso. ~ **holiday** *n* vacanza *f* organizza-
ta. ~ **tour** viaggio *m* organizzato
packaging /'pækɪdʒɪŋ/ *n* confezione *f*
packed 'lunch *n* pranzo *m* al sacco
packet /'pækɪt/ *n* pacchetto *m*; **cost a
~** *fam* costare un sacco
packing /'pækɪŋ/ *n* imballaggio *m*
pact /pækt/ *n* patto *m*
pad[1] /pæd/ *n* imbottitura *f*; (*for
writing*) bloc-notes *m inv*, taccuino *m*;
(*fam: home*) [piccolo] appartamento *m*
● *vt* (*pt/pp* **padded**) imbottire. **pad out**
vt gonfiare
pad[2] *vi* (*pt/pp* **padded**) camminare con
passo felpato

padded /'pædɪd/ *a* ~ **bra** reggiseno *m*
imbottito
padding /'pædɪŋ/ *n* imbottitura *f*; (*in
written work*) fronzoli *mpl*
paddle[1] /'pæd(ə)l/ *n* pagaia *f* ● *vt* (*row*)
spingere remando
paddle[2] *vi* (*wade*) sguazzare
paddock /'pædək/ *n* recinto *m*
padlock /'pædlɒk/ *n* lucchetto *m* ● *vt*
chiudere con lucchetto
paediatrician /piːdɪə'trɪʃn/ *n* pedia-
tra *mf*
paediatrics /piːdɪ'ætrɪks/ *n* pediatria *f*
page[1] /peɪdʒ/ *n* pagina *f*
page[2] *n* (*boy*) paggetto *m*; (*in hotel*) fat-
torino *m* ● *vt* far chiamare ⟨*person*⟩
pageant /'pædʒənt/ *n* parata *f*. **~ry** *n*
cerimoniale *m*
pager /'peɪdʒə(r)/ *n* cercapersone *m inv*
paid /peɪd/ *see* **pay** ● *a* ~ **employment**
lavoro *m* remunerato; **put ~ to** mettere
un termine a
pail /peɪl/ *n* secchio *m*
pain /peɪn/ *n* dolore *m*; **be in ~** soffrire;
take ~s to fare il possibile per; ~ **in
the neck** *fam* spina *f* nel fianco
pain: **~ful** *a* doloroso; (*laborious*) penoso.. **~-killer** *n* calmante *m*. **~less** *a* in-
dolore
painstaking /'peɪnzteɪkɪŋ/ *a* minuzioso
paint /peɪnt/ *n* pittura *f*; **~s** *pl* colori
mpl ● *vt/i* pitturare; ⟨*artist:*⟩ dipingere.
~brush *n* pennello *m*. **~er** *n* pittore,
-trice *mf*; (*decorator*) imbianchino *m*.
~ing *n* pittura *f*; (*picture*) dipinto *m*.
~work *n* pittura *f*
pair /peə(r)/ *n* paio *m*; (*of people*) coppia
f; ~ **of trousers** paio *m* di pantaloni; ~
of scissors paio *m* di forbici
pajamas /pə'dʒɑːməz/ *npl Am* pigiama
msg

Pakistan /pɑːkɪˈstɑːn/ n Pakistan m. **~i** a pakistano ● n pakistano, -a mf

pal /pæl/ n fam amico, -a mf

palace /ˈpælɪs/ n palazzo m

palatable /ˈpælətəbl/ a gradevole (al gusto)

palate /ˈpælət/ n palato m

palatial /pəˈleɪʃl/ a sontuoso

palaver /pəˈlɑːvə(r)/ n (fam: fuss) storie fpl

pale /peɪl/ a pallido

Palestin|e /ˈpælɪstaɪn/ n Palestina f. **~ian** /pælɪˈstɪnɪən/ a palestinese ● n palestinese mf

palette /ˈpælɪt/ n tavolozza f

pall|id /ˈpælɪd/ a pallido. **~or** n pallore m

palm /pɑːm/ n palmo m; (tree) palma f; P**~ 'Sunday** n Domenica f delle Palme ● **palm off** vt **~ sth off on sb** rifilare qcsa a qcno

palpable /ˈpælpəbl/ a palpabile; (perceptible) tangibile

palpitat|e /ˈpælpɪteɪt/ vi palpitare. **~ions** /-ˈteɪʃnz/ npl palpitazioni fpl

paltry /ˈpɔːltrɪ/ a (-ier, -iest) insignificante

pamper /ˈpæmpə(r)/ vt viziare

pamphlet /ˈpæmflɪt/ n opuscolo m

pan /pæn/ n tegame m, pentola f; (for frying) padella f; (of scales) piatto m ● vt (pt/pp **panned**) (fam: criticize) stroncare

panache /pəˈnæʃ/ n stile m

'pancake n crêpe f inv, frittella f

pancreas /ˈpæŋkrɪəs/ n pancreas m inv

panda /ˈpændə/ n panda m inv. **~ car** n macchina f della polizia

pandemonium /pændɪˈməʊnɪəm/ n pandemonio m

pander /ˈpændə(r)/ vi **~ to sb** compiacere qcno

pane /peɪn/ n **~ [of glass]** vetro m

panel /ˈpænl/ n pannello m; (group of people) giuria f; **~ of experts** gruppo m di esperti. **~ling** n pannelli mpl

pang /pæŋ/ n **~s of hunger** morsi mpl della fame; **~s of conscience** rimorsi mpl di coscienza

panic /ˈpænɪk/ n panico m ● vi (pt/pp **panicked**) lasciarsi prendere dal panico. **~-stricken** a in preda al panico

panoram|a /pænəˈrɑːmə/ n panorama m. **~ic** /-ˈræmɪk/ a panoramico

pansy /ˈpænzɪ/ n viola f del pensiero; (fam: effeminate man) finocchio m

pant /pænt/ vi ansimare

panther /ˈpænθə(r)/ n pantera f

panties /ˈpæntɪz/ npl mutandine fpl

pantomime /ˈpæntəmaɪm/ n pantomima f

pantry /ˈpæntrɪ/ n dispensa f

pants /pænts/ npl (underwear) mutande fpl; (woman's) mutandine fpl; (trousers) pantaloni mpl

'pantyhose n Am collant m inv

papal /ˈpeɪpl/ a papale

paper /ˈpeɪpə(r)/ n carta f; (wallpaper) carta f da parati; (newspaper) giornale m; (exam) esame m; (treatise) saggio m; **~s** pl (documents) documenti mpl; (for identification) documento m [d'identità]; **on ~** in teoria; **put down on ~** mettere per iscritto ● attrib di carta ● vt tappezzare

paper: ~back n edizione f economica. **~-clip** n graffetta f. **~-knife** n tagliacarte m inv. **~weight** n fermacarte m inv. **~work** n lavoro m d'ufficio

par /pɑː(r)/ n (in golf) par m inv; **on a ~ with** alla pari con; **feel below ~** essere un po' giù di tono

parable /ˈpærəbl/ n parabola f

parachut|e /ˈpærəʃuːt/ n paracadute m inv ● vi lanciarsi col paracadute. **~ist** n paracadutista mf

parade /pəˈreɪd/ n (military) parata f militare ● vi sfilare ● vt (show off) far sfoggio di

paradise /ˈpærədaɪs/ n paradiso m

paradox /ˈpærədɒks/ n paradosso m. **~ical** /-ˈdɒksɪkl/ a paradossale. **~ically** adv paradossalmente

paraffin /ˈpærəfɪn/ n paraffina f

paragon /ˈpærəgən/ n **~ of virtue** modello m di virtù

paragraph /ˈpærəgrɑːf/ n paragrafo m

parallel /ˈpærəlel/ a & adv parallelo. **~ bars** npl parallele fpl. **~ port** n Comput porta f parallela ● n Geog, fig parallelo m; (line) parallela f ● vt essere paragonabile a

paralyse /ˈpærəlaɪz/ vt also fig paralizzare

paralysis /pəˈræləsɪs/ n (pl **-ses** /-siːz/) paralisi f inv

parameter /pəˈræmɪtə(r)/ n parametro m

paramount /ˈpærəmaʊnt/ a supremo; **be ~** essere essenziale

paranoia /pærəˈnɔɪə/ n paranoia f

paranoid /ˈpærənɔɪd/ a paranoico

paraphernalia /pærəfəˈneɪlɪə/ n armamentario m

paraphrase /ˈpærəfreɪz/ n parafrasi f inv ● vt parafrasare

paraplegic /ˌpærəˈpliːdʒɪk/ a paraplegico ● n paraplegico, -a mf

parasite /ˈpærəsaɪt/ n parassita mf

parasol /ˈpærəsɒl/ n parasole m

paratrooper /ˈpærətruːpə(r)/ n paracadutista m

parcel /ˈpɑːsl/ n pacco m

parch /pɑːtʃ/ vt disseccare; **be ~ed** ⟨person:⟩ morire dalla sete

pardon /ˈpɑːdn/ n perdono m; Jur grazia f; **~?** prego?; **I beg your ~?** fml chiedo scusa?; **I do beg your ~** ⟨sorry⟩ chiedo scusa! ● vt perdonare; Jur graziare

pare /peə(r)/ vt ⟨peel⟩ pelare

parent /ˈpeərənt/ n genitore, -trice mf; **~s** pl genitori mpl. **~al** /pəˈrentl/ a dei genitori

parenthesis /pəˈrenθəsɪs/ n (pl **-ses** /-siːz/) parentesi m inv

Paris /ˈpærɪs/ n Parigi f

parish /ˈpærɪʃ/ n parrocchia f. **~ioner** /pəˈrɪʃənə(r)/ n parrocchiano, -a mf

Parisian /pəˈrɪzɪən/ a & n parigino, -a mf

parity /ˈpærətɪ/ n parità f

park /pɑːk/ n parco m ● vt/i Auto posteggiare, parcheggiare; **~ oneself** fam installarsi

parka /ˈpɑːkə/ n parka m inv

parking /ˈpɑːkɪŋ/ n parcheggio m, posteggio m; **'no ~'** 'divieto di sosta'. **~-lot** n Am posteggio m, parcheggio m. **~-meter** n parchimetro m. **~ space** n posteggio m, parcheggio m

parliament /ˈpɑːləmənt/ n parlamento m. **~ary** /-ˈmentərɪ/ a parlamentare

parlour /ˈpɑːlə(r)/ n salotto m

parochial /pəˈrəʊkɪəl/ a parrocchiale; fig ristretto

parody /ˈpærədɪ/ n parodia f ● vt (pt/pp **-ied**) parodiare

parole /pəˈrəʊl/ n **on ~** in libertà condizionale ● vt mettere in libertà condizionale

parquet /ˈpɑːkeɪ/ n **~ floor** parquet m inv

parrot /ˈpærət/ n pappagallo m

parry /ˈpærɪ/ vt (pt/pp **-ied**) parare ⟨blow⟩; ⟨in fencing⟩ eludere

parsimonious /pɑːsɪˈməʊnɪəs/ a parsimonioso

parsley /ˈpɑːslɪ/ n prezzemolo m

parsnip /ˈpɑːsnɪp/ n pastinaca f

parson /ˈpɑːsn/ n pastore m

part /pɑːt/ n parte f; ⟨of machine⟩ pezzo m; **for my ~** per quanto mi riguarda; **on the ~ of** da parte di; **take sb's ~** prendere le parti di qcno; **take ~ in** prendere parte a ● adv in parte ● vt **~ one's hair** farsi la riga ● vi ⟨people:⟩ separare; **~ with** separarsi da

part-ex'change n take in **~** prendere indietro

partial /ˈpɑːʃl/ a parziale; **be ~ to** aver un debole per. **~ly** adv parzialmente

particip|ant /pɑːˈtɪsɪpənt/ n partecipante mf. **~ate** /-peɪt/ vi partecipare (in a). **~ation** /-ˈpeɪʃn/ n partecipazione f

participle /ˈpɑːtɪsɪpl/ n participio m; **present/past ~** participio m presente/passato

particle /ˈpɑːtɪkl/ n Phys, Gram particella f

particular /pəˈtɪkjʊlə(r)/ a particolare; ⟨precise⟩ meticoloso; pej noioso; **in ~** in particolare. **~ly** adv particolarmente. **~s** npl particolari mpl

parting /ˈpɑːtɪŋ/ n separazione f; ⟨in hair⟩ scriminatura f ● attrib di commiato

partisan /pɑːtɪˈzæn/ n partigiano, -a mf

partition /pɑːˈtɪʃn/ n ⟨wall⟩ parete f divisoria; Pol divisione f ● vt dividere ⟨in parti⟩. **partition off** vt separare

partly /ˈpɑːtlɪ/ adv in parte

partner /ˈpɑːtnə(r)/ n Comm socio, -a mf; ⟨sport, in relationship⟩ compagno, -a mf. **~ship** n Comm società f inv

partridge /ˈpɑːtrɪdʒ/ n pernice f

part-'time a & adv part time; **be or work ~** lavorare part time

party /ˈpɑːtɪ/ n ricevimento m, festa f; ⟨group⟩ gruppo m; Pol partito m; Jur parte f ⟨in causa⟩; **be ~ to** essere parte attiva in

'party line¹ n Teleph duplex m inv

party 'line² n Pol linea f del partito

pass /pɑːs/ n lasciapassare m inv; ⟨in mountains⟩ passo m; Sport passaggio m; Sch ⟨mark⟩ ⟨voto m⟩ sufficiente m; **make a ~ at** fam fare delle avances a ● vt passare; ⟨overtake⟩ sorpassare; ⟨approve⟩ far passare; fare ⟨remark⟩; Jur pronunciare ⟨sentence⟩; **~ the time** passare il tempo ● vi passare; ⟨in exam⟩ essere promosso. **pass away** vi mancare. **pass down** vt passare; fig trasmettere. **pass out** vi fam svenire. **pass round** vt far passare. **pass through** vt attraversare. **pass up** vt passare; ⟨fam: miss⟩ lasciarsi scappare

passable /ˈpɑːsəbl/ a ⟨road⟩ praticabile; ⟨satisfactory⟩ passabile

passage /ˈpæsɪdʒ/ n passaggio m;

(*corridor*) corridoio m; (*voyage*) traversata f

passenger /'pæsɪndʒə(r)/ n passeggero, -a mf. ~ **seat** n posto m accanto al guidatore

passer-by /pɑ:sə'baɪ/ n (pl ~s-by) passante mf

'**passing place** n piazzola f di sosta per consentire il transito dei veicoli nei due sensi

passion /'pæʃn/ n passione f. ~**ate** /-ət/ a appassionato

passive /'pæsɪv/ a passivo ● n passivo m. ~**ness** n passività f

'**pass-mark** n Sch [voto m] sufficiente m

Passover /'pɑ:səʊvə(r)/ n Pasqua f ebraica

pass: ~**port** n passaporto m. ~**word** n parola f d'ordine

past /pɑ:st/ a passato; (*former*) ex; **in the ~ few days** nei giorni scorsi; **that's all ~** tutto questo è passato; **the ~ week** la settimana scorsa ● n passato m ● prep oltre; **at ten ~ two** alle due e dieci ● adv oltre; **go/come ~** passare

pasta /'pæstə/ n pasta [sciutta] f

paste /peɪst/ n pasta f; (*dough*) impasto m; (*adhesive*) colla f ● vt incollare

pastel /'pæstl/ n pastello m ● attrib pastello

pasteurize /'pɑ:stʃəraɪz/ vt pastorizzare

pastille /'pæstɪl/ n pastiglia f

pastime /'pɑ:staɪm/ n passatempo m

pastoral /'pɑ:stərəl/ a pastorale

pastrami /pæ'strɑ:mɪ/ n carne f di manzo affumicata

pastr|y /'peɪstrɪ/ n pasta f; ~**ies** pl pasticcini mpl

pasture /'pɑ:stʃə(r)/ n pascolo m

pasty¹ /'pæstɪ/ n pasticcio m

pasty² /'peɪstɪ/ a smorto

pat /pæt/ n buffetto m; (*of butter*) pezzetto m ● adv **have sth off ~** conoscere qcsa a menadito ● vt (pt/pp **patted**) dare un buffetto a; ~ **sb on the back** fig congratularsi con qcno

patch /pætʃ/ n toppa f; (*spot*) chiazza f; (*period*) periodo m; **not a ~ on** fam molto inferiore a ● vt mettere una toppa su. **patch up** vt riparare alla bell'e meglio; appianare (*quarrel*)

patchy /'pætʃɪ/ a incostante

pâté /'pæteɪ/ n pâté m inv

patent /'peɪtnt/ a palese ● n brevetto m ● vt brevettare. ~ **leather shoes** npl scarpe fpl di vernice. ~**ly** adv in modo palese

patern|al /pə'tɜ:nl/ a paterno. ~**ity** n paternità f

path /pɑ:θ/ n (pl ~s /pɑ:ðz/) sentiero m; (*orbit*) traiettoria m; fig strada f

pathetic /pə'θetɪk/ a patetico; (*fam: very bad*) penoso

patholog|ical /pæθə'lɒdʒɪkl/ a patologico. ~**ist** /pə'θɒlədʒɪst/ n patologo, -a mf. ~**y** patologia f

pathos /'peɪθɒs/ n pathos m

patience /'peɪʃns/ n pazienza f; (*game*) solitario m

patient /'peɪʃnt/ a paziente ● n paziente mf. ~**ly** adv pazientemente

patio /'pætɪəʊ/ n terrazza f

patriot /'pætrɪət/ n patriota mf. ~**ic** /-'ɒtɪk/ a patriottico. ~**ism** n patriottismo m

patrol /pə'trəʊl/ n pattuglia f ● vt/i pattugliare. ~ **car** n autopattuglia f

patron /'peɪtrən/ n patrono m; (*of charity*) benefattore, -trice mf; (*of the arts*) mecenate mf; (*customer*) cliente mf

patroniz|e /'pætrənaɪz/ vt frequentare abitualmente; fig trattare con condiscendenza. ~**ing** a condiscendente. ~**ingly** adv con condiscendenza

patter¹ /'pætə(r)/ n picchiettìo m ● vi picchiettare

patter² n (*of salesman*) chiacchiere fpl

pattern /'pætn/ n disegno m (*stampato*); (*for knitting, sewing*) modello m

paunch /pɔ:ntʃ/ n pancia f

pause /pɔ:z/ n pausa f ● vi fare una pausa

pave /peɪv/ vt pavimentare; ~ **the way** preparare la strada (**for** a). ~**ment** n marciapiede m

pavilion /pə'vɪljən/ n padiglione m

paw /pɔ:/ n zampa f ● vt fam mettere le zampe addosso a

pawn¹ /pɔ:n/ n (*in chess*) pedone m; fig pedina f

pawn² vt impegnare ● n **in** ~ in pegno. ~**broker** n prestatore, -trice mf su pegno. ~**shop** n monte m di pietà

pay /peɪ/ n paga f; **in the** ~ **of** al soldo di ● v (pt/pp **paid**) ● vt pagare; prestare (*attention*); fare (*compliment, visit*); ~ **cash** pagare in contanti ● vi pagare; (*be profitable*) rendere; **it doesn't** ~ **to...** fig è fatica sprecata...; ~ **for sth** pagare per qcsa. **pay back** vt ripagare. **pay in** vt versare. **pay off** vt saldare (*debt*) ● vi fig dare dei frutti. **pay up** vi pagare

payable /'peɪəbl/ a pagabile; **make** ~ **to** intestare a

payee /peɪ'iː/ n beneficiario m (di una somma)

payment /'peɪmənt/ n pagamento m

pay: ~ **packet** n busta f paga. ~ **phone** n telefono m pubblico

PC n abbr (**personal computer**) PC m inv

pea /piː/ n pisello m

peace /piːs/ n pace f; ~ **of mind** tranquillità f

peace|able /'piːsəbl/ a pacifico. ~**ful** a calmo, sereno. ~**fully** adv in pace. ~**maker** n mediatore, -trice mf

peach /piːtʃ/ n pesca f; (tree) pesco m

peacock /'piːkɒk/ n pavone m

peak /piːk/ n picco m; fig culmine m. ~**ed 'cap** n berretto m a punta. ~ **hours** npl ore fpl di punta

peaky /'piːkɪ/ a malaticcio

peal /piːl/ n (of bells) scampanio m; ~**s of laughter** pl fragore m di risate

'peanut n nocciolina f [americana]; ~**s** pl fam miseria f

pear /peə(r)/ n pera f; (tree) pero m

pearl /pɜːl/ n perla f

peasant /'peznt/ n contadino, -a mf

pebble /'pebl/ n ciottolo m

peck /pek/ n beccata f; (kiss) bacetto m ● vt beccare; (kiss) dare un bacetto a. ~**ing order** n gerarchia f. **peck at** vt beccare

peckish /'pekɪʃ/ a **be** ~ fam avere un languorino [allo stomaco]

peculiar /pɪ'kjuːlɪə(r)/ a strano; (special) particolare; ~ **to** tipico di. ~**ity** /-'ærətɪ/ n stranezza f; (feature) particolarità f inv

pedal /'pedl/ n pedale m ● vi pedalare. ~ **bin** n pattumiera f a pedale

pedantic /pɪ'dæntɪk/ a pedante

pedestal /'pedɪstl/ n piedistallo m

pedestrian /pɪ'destrɪən/ n pedone m ● a fig scadente. ~ **'crossing** n passaggio m pedonale. ~ **'precinct** n zona f pedonale

pedicure /'pedɪkjʊə(r)/ n pedicure f inv

pedigree /'pedɪgriː/ n pedigree m inv; (of person) lignaggio m ● attrib ⟨animal⟩ di razza, con pedigree

pee /piː/ vi (pt/pp **peed**) fam fare [la] pipì

peek /piːk/ vi fam sbirciare

peel /piːl/ n buccia f ● vt sbucciare ● vi ⟨nose etc:⟩ spellarsi; ⟨paint:⟩ staccarsi

peep /piːp/ n sbirciata f ● vi sbirciare

peer[1] /pɪə(r)/ vi ~ **at** scrutare

peer[2] n nobile m; **his** ~**s** pl (in rank) i suoi pari; (in age) i suoi coetanei. ~**age** n nobiltà f

peeved /piːvd/ a fam irritato

peg /peg/ n (hook) piolo m; (for tent) picchetto m; (for clothes) molletta f; **off the** ~ fam prêt-à-porter

pejorative /pɪ'dʒɒrətɪv/ a peggiorativo

pelican /'pelɪkən/ n pellicano m

pellet /'pelɪt/ n pallottola f

pelt /pelt/ vt bombardare ● vi (fam: run fast) catapultarsi; ~ [**down**] ⟨rain:⟩ venir giù a fiotti

pelvis /'pelvɪs/ n Anat bacino m

pen[1] /pen/ n (for animals) recinto m

pen[2] n penna f; (ball-point) penna f a sfera

penal /'piːnl/ a penale. ~**ize** vt penalizzare

penalty /'penltɪ/ n sanzione f; (fine) multa f; (in football) ~ [**kick**] [calcio m di] rigore m; ~ **area** or **box** area f di rigore

penance /'penəns/ n penitenza f

pence /pens/ see **penny**

pencil /'pensl/ n matita f. ~**-sharpener** n temperamatite m inv

pendant /'pendənt/ n ciondolo m

pending /'pendɪŋ/ a in sospeso ● prep in attesa di

pendulum /'pendjʊləm/ n pendolo m

penetrat|e /'penɪtreɪt/ vt/i penetrare. ~**ing** a acuto; (sound, stare) penetrante. ~**ion** /-'treɪʃn/ n penetrazione f

'penfriend n amico, -a mf di penna

penguin /'peŋgwɪn/ n pinguino m

penicillin /penɪ'sɪlɪn/ n penicillina f

peninsula /pɪ'nɪnsjʊlə/ n penisola f

penis /'piːnɪs/ n pene m

peniten|ce /'penɪtəns/ n penitenza f. ~**t** a penitente ● n penitente mf

penitentiary /penɪ'tenʃərɪ/ n Am penitenziario m

pen: ~**knife** n temperino m. ~**name** n pseudonimo m

pennant /'penənt/ n bandiera f

penniless /'penɪlɪs/ a senza un soldo

penny /'penɪ/ n (pl **pence**; single coins **pennies**) penny m; Am centesimo m; **spend a** ~ fam andare in bagno

pension /'penʃn/ n pensione f. ~**er** n pensionato, -a mf

pensive /'pensɪv/ a pensoso

Pentecost /'pentɪkɒst/ n Pentecoste f

pent-up /'pentʌp/ a represso

penultimate /pɪ'nʌltɪmət/ a penultimo

people /'piːpl/ npl persone fpl, gente

fsg; (*citizens*) popolo *msg*; **a lot of ~** una marea di gente; **the ~** la gente; **English ~** gli inglesi; **~ say** si dice; **for four ~** per quattro ● *vt* popolare

pepper /'pepə(r)/ *n* pepe *m*; (*vegetable*) peperone *m* ● *vt* (*season*) pepare

pepper: ~corn *n* grano *m* di pepe. **~ mill** macinapepe *m inv*. **~mint** *n* menta *f* peperita; (*sweet*) caramella *f* alla menta. **~pot** *n* pepiera *f*

per /pɜ:(r)/ *prep* per; **~ annum** all'anno; **~ cent** percento

perceive /pə'si:v/ *vt* percepire; (*interpret*) interpretare

percentage /pə'sentɪdʒ/ *n* percentuale *f*

perceptible /pə'septəbl/ *a* percettibile; (*difference*) sensibile

percept|ion /pə'sepʃn/ *n* percezione *f*. **~ive** /-tɪv/ *a* perspicace

perch /pɜ:tʃ/ *n* pertica *f* ● *vi* (*bird:*) appollaiarsi

percolator /'pɜ:kəleɪtə(r)/ *n* caffettiera *f* a filtro

percussion /pə'kʌʃn/ *n* percussione *f*. **~ instrument** *n* strumento *m* a percussione

peremptory /pə'remptərɪ/ *a* perentorio

perennial /pə'renɪəl/ *a* perenne ● *n* pianta *f* perenne

perfect[1] /'pɜ:fɪkt/ *a* perfetto ● *n Gram* passato *m* prossimo

perfect[2] /pə'fekt/ *vt* perfezionare. **~ion** /-ekʃn/ *n* perfezione *f*; **to ~ion** alla perfezione. **~ionist** *n* perfezionista *mf*

perfectly /'pɜ:fɪktlɪ/ *adv* perfettamente

perforat|e /'pɜ:fəreɪt/ *vt* perforare. **~ed** *a* perforato; (*ulcer*) perforante. **~ion** *n* perforazione *f*

perform /pə'fɔ:m/ *vt* compiere, fare; eseguire (*operation, sonata*); recitare (*role*); mettere in scena (*play*) ● *vi Theat* recitare; *Techn* funzionare. **~ance** *n* esecuzione *f*; (*at theatre, cinema*) rappresentazione *f*; *Techn* rendimento *m*. **~er** *n* artista *mf*

perfume /'pɜ:fju:m/ *n* profumo *m*

perfunctory /pə'fʌŋktərɪ/ *a* superficiale

perhaps /pə'hæps/ *adv* forse

peril /'perɪl/ *n* pericolo *m*. **~ous** /-əs/ *a* pericoloso

perimeter /pə'rɪmɪtə(r)/ *n* perimetro *m*

period /'pɪərɪəd/ *n* periodo *m*; (*menstruation*) mestruazioni *fpl*; *Sch*

ora *f* di lezione; (*full stop*) punto *m* fermo ● *attrib* (*costume*) d'epoca; (*furniture*) in stile. **~ic** /-'ɒdɪk/ *a* periodico. **~ical** /-'ɒdɪkl/ *n* periodico *m*, rivista *f*

peripher|al /pə'rɪfərəl/ *a* periferico. **~y** *n* periferia *f*

periscope /'perɪskəup/ *n* periscopio *m*

perish /'perɪʃ/ *vi* (*rot*) deteriorarsi; (*die*) perire. **~able** /-əbl/ *a* deteriorabile

perjur|e /'pɜ:dʒə(r)/ *vt* **~e oneself** spergiurare. **~y** *n* spergiuro *m*

perk /pɜ:k/ *n fam* vantaggio *m*

perk up *vt* tirare su ● *vi* tirarsi su

perky /'pɜ:kɪ/ *a* allegro

perm /pɜ:m/ *n* permanente *f* ● *vt* **~ sb's hair** fare la permanente a qno

permanent /'pɜ:mənənt/ *a* permanente; (*job, address*) stabile. **~ly** *adv* stabilmente

permeate /'pɜ:mɪeɪt/ *vt* impregnare

permissible /pə'mɪsəbl/ *a* ammissibile

permission /pə'mɪʃn/ *n* permesso *m*

permissive /pə'mɪsɪv/ *a* permissivo

permit[1] /pə'mɪt/ *vt* (*pt/pp* **-mitted**) permettere; **~ sb to do sth** permettere a qcno di fare qcsa

permit[2] /'pɜ:mɪt/ *n* autorizzazione *f*

perpendicular /pɜ:pən'dɪkjulə(r)/ *a* perpendicolare ● *n* perpendicolare *f*

perpetual /pə'petjuəl/ *a* perenne. **~ly** *adv* perennemente

perpetuate /pə'petjueɪt/ *vt* perpetuare

perplex /pə'pleks/ *vt* lasciare perplesso. **~ed** *a* perplesso. **~ity** *n* perplessità *f inv*

persecut|e /'pɜ:sɪkju:t/ *vt* perseguitare. **~ion** /-'kju:ʃn/ *n* persecuzione *f*

perseverance /pɜ:sɪ'vɪərəns/ *n* perseveranza *f*

persever|e /pɜ:sɪ'vɪə(r)/ *vi* perseverare. **~ing** *a* assiduo

Persian /'pɜ:ʃn/ *a* persiano

persist /pə'sɪst/ *vi* persistere; **~ in doing sth** persistere nel fare qcsa. **~ence** *n* persistenza *f*. **~ent** *a* persistente. **~ently** *adv* persistentemente

person /'pɜ:sn/ *n* persona *f*; **in ~** di persona

personal /'pɜ:sənl/ *a* personale. **~ 'hygiene** *n* igiene *f* personale. **~ly** *adv* personalmente. **~ organizer** *n Comput* agenda *f* elettronica

personality /pɜ:sə'nælɪtɪ/ *n* personalità *f inv*; (*on TV*) personaggio *m*

personnel /pɜːsə'nel/ *n* personale *m*

perspective /pə'spektɪv/ *n* prospettiva *f*

persp|iration /pɜːspɪ'reɪʃn/ *n* sudore *m*. **~ire** /-'spaɪə(r)/ *vi* sudare

persua|de /pə'sweɪd/ *vt* persuadere. **~sion** /-eɪʒn/ *n* persuasione *f*; (*belief*) convinzione *f*

persuasive /pə'sweɪsɪv/ *a* persuasivo. **~ly** *adv* in modo persuasivo

pertinent /'pɜːtɪnənt/ *a* pertinente (**to** a)

perturb /pə'tɜːb/ *vt* perturbare

peruse /pə'ruːz/ *vt* leggere

perva|de /pə'veɪd/ *vt* pervadere. **~sive** /-sɪv/ *a* pervasivo

pervers|e /pə'vɜːs/ *a* irragionevole. **~ion** /-ɜːʃn/ *n* perversione *f*

pervert /'pɜːvɜːt/ *n* pervertito, -a *mf*

perverted /pə'vɜːtɪd/ *a* perverso

pessimis|m /'pesɪmɪzm/ *n* pessimismo *m*. **~t** /-mɪst/ *n* pessimista *mf*. **~tic** /-'mɪstɪk/ *a* pessimistico. **~tically** *adv* in modo pessimistico

pest /pest/ *n* piaga *f*; (*fam: person*) peste *f*

pester /'pestə(r)/ *vt* molestare

pesticide /'pestɪsaɪd/ *n* pesticida *m*

pet /pet/ *n* animale *m* domestico; (*favourite*) cocco, -a *mf* ● *a* prediletto ● *v* (*pt/pp* **petted**) ● *vt* coccolare ● *vi* ‹*couple:*› praticare il petting

petal /'petl/ *n* petalo *m*

peter /'piːtə(r)/ *vi* **~ out** finire

petite /pə'tiːt/ *a* minuto

petition /pə'tɪʃn/ *n* petizione *f*

pet 'name *n* vezzeggiativo *m*

petrif|y /'petrɪfaɪ/ *vt* (*pt/pp* **-ied**) pietrificare. **~ied** *a* (*frightened*) pietrificato

petrol /'petrəl/ *n* benzina *f*

petroleum /pɪ'trəʊlɪəm/ *n* petrolio *m*

petrol: **~-pump** *n* pompa *f* di benzina. **~ station** *n* stazione *f* di servizio. **~ tank** *n* serbatoio *m* della benzina

'pet shop *n* negozio *m* di animali [domestici]

petticoat /'petɪkəʊt/ *n* sottoveste *f*

petty /'petɪ/ *a* (**-ier, -iest**) insignificante; (*mean*) meschino. **~ 'cash** *n* cassa *f* per piccole spese

petulant /'petjʊlənt/ *a* petulante

pew /pjuː/ *n* banco *m* (*di chiesa*)

pewter /'pjuːtə(r)/ *n* peltro *m*

phallic /'fælɪk/ *a* fallico

phantom /'fæntəm/ *n* fantasma *m*

pharmaceutical /fɑːmə'sjuːtɪkl/ *a* farmaceutico

pharmac|ist /'fɑːməsɪst/ *n* farmacista *mf*. **~y** *n* farmacia *f* ● *vt* phase

phase /feɪz/ *n* fase *f* ● *vt* **phase in/out** introdurre/eliminare gradualmente

Ph.D. *n abbr* (**Doctor of Philosophy**) dottorato *m* di ricerca

pheasant /'feznt/ *n* fagiano *m*

phenomen|al /fɪ'nɒmɪnl/ *a* fenomenale; (*incredible*) incredibile. **~ally** *adv* incredibilmente. **~on** *n* (*pl* **-na**) fenomeno *m*

philanderer /fɪ'lændərə(r)/ *n* donnaiolo *m*

philanthrop|ic /fɪlən'θrɒpɪk/ *a* filantropico. **~ist** /fɪ'lænθrəpɪst/ *n* filantropo, -a *mf*

philatel|y /fɪ'lætəlɪ/ *n* filatelia *f*. **~ist** *n* filatelico, -a *mf*

philharmonic /fɪlhɑː'mɒnɪk/ *n* (*orchestra*) orchestra *f* filarmonica ● *a* filarmonico

Philippines /'fɪlɪpiːnz/ *npl* Filippine *fpl*

philistine /'fɪlɪstaɪn/ *n* filisteo, -a *mf*

philosoph|er /fɪ'lɒsəfə(r)/ *n* filosofo, -a *mf*. **~ical** /fɪlə'sɒfɪkl/ *a* filosofico. **~ically** *adv* con filosofia. **~y** *n* filosofia *f*

phlegm /flem/ *n* Med flemma *f*

phlegmatic /fleg'mætɪk/ *a* flemmatico

phobia /'fəʊbɪə/ *n* fobia *f*

phone /fəʊn/ *n* telefono *m*; **be on the ~** avere il telefono; (*be phoning*) essere al telefono ● *vt* telefonare a ● *vi* telefonare. **phone back** *vt/i* richiamare. **~book** *n* guida *f* del telefono. **~ box** *n* cabina *f* telefonica. **~ card** *n* scheda *f* telefonica. **~ call** telefonata *f*. **~-in** *n* trasmissione *f* con chiamate in diretta. **~ number** *n* numero *m* telefonico

phonetic /fə'netɪk/ *a* fonetico. **~s** *n* fonetica *f*

phoney /'fəʊnɪ/ *a* (**-ier, -iest**) fasullo

phosphorus /'fɒsfərəs/ *n* fosforo *m*

photo /'fəʊtəʊ/ *n* foto *f*; **~ album** album *m inv* di fotografie. **~copier** *n* fotocopiatrice *f*. **~copy** *n* fotocopia *f* ● *vt* fotocopiare

photogenic /fəʊtəʊ'dʒenɪk/ *a* fotogenico

photograph /'fəʊtəɡrɑːf/ *n* fotografia *f* ● *vt* fotografare

photograph|er /fə'tɒɡrəfə(r)/ *n* fotografo, -a *mf*. **~ic** /fəʊtə'ɡræfɪk/ *a* fotografico. **~y** *n* fotografia *f*

phrase /freɪz/ *n* espressione *f* ● *vt* esprimere. **~-book** *n* libro *m* di fraseologia

physical /'fɪzɪkl/ a fisico. ~ edu'cation n educazione f fisica. ~ly adv fisicamente

physician /fɪ'zɪʃn/ n medico m

physic|ist /'fɪzɪsɪst/ n fisico, -a mf. ~s n fisica f

physiology /fɪzɪ'plədʒɪ/ n fisiologia f

physio'therap|ist /fɪzɪəʊ-/ n fisioterapista mf. ~y n fisioterapia f

physique /fɪ'zi:k/ n fisico m

pianist /'prənɪst/ n pianista mf

piano /pɪ'ænəʊ/ n piano m

pick¹ /pɪk/ n (tool) piccone m

pick² n scelta f; **take your ~** prendi quello che vuoi ● vt (select) scegliere; cogliere ⟨flowers⟩; scassinare ⟨lock⟩; borseggiare ⟨pockets⟩; **~ and choose** fare il difficile; **~ one's nose** mettersi le dita nel naso; **~ a quarrel** attaccar briga; **~ holes in** fam criticare; **~ at one's food** spilluzzicare. **pick on** vt (fam: nag) assillare; **he always ~s on me** ce l'ha con me. **pick out** vt (identify) individuare. **pick up** vt sollevare; (off the ground, information) raccogliere; prendere in braccio ⟨baby⟩; ⟨learn⟩ imparare; prendersi ⟨illness⟩; (buy) comprare; captare ⟨signal⟩; (collect) andare/venire a prendere; prendere ⟨passengers, habit⟩; ⟨police:⟩ arrestare ⟨criminal⟩; fam rimorchiare ⟨girl⟩; **~ oneself up** riprendersi ● vi (improve) recuperare; ⟨weather:⟩ rimettersi

'pickaxe n piccone m

picket /'pɪkɪt/ n picchettista mf ● vt picchettare. **~ line** n picchetto m

pickle /'pɪkl/ n ~s pl sottaceti mpl; **in a ~** fig nei pasticci ● vt mettere sottaceto

pick: ~pocket n borsaiolo m. **~-up** n (truck) furgone m; (on record-player) pickup m inv

picnic /'pɪknɪk/ n picnic m ● vi (pt/pp -nicked) fare un picnic

picture /'pɪktʃə(r)/ n (painting) quadro m; (photo) fotografia f, (drawing) disegno m; (film) film m inv; **put sb in the ~** fig mettere qcno al corrente; **the ~s** il cinema ● vt (imagine) immaginare

picturesque /pɪktʃə'resk/ a pittoresco

pie /paɪ/ n torta f

piece /pi:s/ n pezzo m; (in game) pedina f; **a ~ of bread/paper** un pezzo di pane/carta; **a ~ of news/advice** una notizia/un consiglio; **take to ~s** smontare. **~meal** adv un po' alla volta.

~-work n lavoro m a cottimo ● **piece together** vt montare; fig ricostruire

pier /pɪə(r)/ n molo m; (pillar) pilastro m

pierc|e /pɪəs/ vt perforare; **~e a hole in sth** fare un buco in qcsa. **~ing** a penetrante

pig /pɪg/ n maiale m

pigeon /'pɪdʒɪn/ n piccione m. **~-hole** n casella f

piggy /'pɪgɪ/ **~back** n **give sb a ~back** portare qcno sulle spalle. **~ bank** n salvadanaio m

pig'headed a fam cocciuto

pig: ~skin n pelle f di cinghiale. **~tail** n (plait) treccina f

pile n (heap) pila f ● vt **~ sth on to sth** appilare qcsa su qcsa. **pile up** vt accatastare ● vi ammucchiarsi

piles /paɪlz/ npl emorroidi fpl

'pile-up n tamponamento m a catena

pilfering /'pɪlfərɪŋ/ n piccoli furti mpl

pilgrim /'pɪlgrɪm/ n pellegrino, -a mf. **~age** -ɪdʒ/ n pellegrinaggio m

pill /pɪl/ n pillola f

pillage /'pɪlɪdʒ/ vt saccheggiare

pillar /'pɪlə(r)/ n pilastro m. **~-box** n buca f delle lettere

pillion /'pɪljən/ n sellino m posteriore; **ride ~** viaggiare dietro

pillory /'pɪlərɪ/ vt (pt/pp -ied) fig mettere alla berlina

pillow /'pɪləʊ/ n guanciale m. **~case** n federa f

pilot /'paɪlət/ n pilota mf ● vt pilotare. **~-light** n fiamma f di sicurezza

pimp /pɪmp/ n protettore m

pimple /'pɪmpl/ n foruncolo m

pin /pɪn/ n spillo m; Electr spinotto m; Med chiodo m; **I have ~s and needles in my leg** fam mi formicola una gamba ● vt (pt/pp pinned) appuntare (to/on su); (sewing) fissare con gli spilli; (hold down) immobilizzare; **~ sb down to a date** ottenere un appuntamento da qcno; **~ sth on sb** fam addossare a qcno la colpa di qcsa. **pin up** vt appuntare; (on wall) affiggere

pinafore /'pɪnəfɔ:(r)/ n grembiule m. **~ dress** n scamiciato m

pincers /'pɪnsəz/ npl tenaglie fpl

pinch /pɪntʃ/ n pizzicotto m; (of salt) presa f; **at a ~** fam in caso di bisogno ● vt pizzicare; (fam: steal) fregare ● vi ⟨shoe:⟩ stringere

'pincushion n puntaspilli m inv

pine¹ /paɪn/ n (tree) pino m

pine² vi **she is pining for you** le manchi molto. **pine away** vi deperire

pineapple /'paɪn-/ n ananas m inv
ping /pɪŋ/ n rumore m metallico
'ping-pong n ping-pong m
pink /pɪŋk/ a rosa inv
pinnacle /'pɪnəkl/ n guglia f
PIN number n codice m segreto
pin: ~point vt definire con precisione.
~stripe a gessato
pint /paɪnt/ n pinta f (= 0,571, Am: 0,47 l);
a ~ fam una birra media
'pin-up n ragazza f da copertina, pin-up
f inv
pioneer /paɪə'nɪə(r)/ n pioniere, -a mf
● vt essere un pioniere di
pious /'paɪəs/ a pio
pip /pɪp/ n (seed) seme m
pipe /paɪp/ n tubo m; (for smoking) pipa
f; **the ~s** Mus la cornamusa ● vt far arrivare con tubature (water, gas etc).
pipe down vi fam abbassare la voce
pipe: ~-cleaner n scovolino m.
~-dream n illusione f. **~line** n
conduttura f; **in the ~line** fam in cantiere
piper /'paɪpə(r)/ n suonatore m di cornamusa
piping /'paɪpɪŋ/ a **~ hot** bollente
pirate /'paɪrət/ n pirata m
Pisces /'paɪsiːz/ n Astr Pesci mpl
piss /pɪs/ vi sl pisciare
pistol /'pɪstl/ n pistola f
piston /'pɪstn/ n Techn pistone m
pit /pɪt/ n fossa f; (mine) miniera f; (for
orchestra) orchestra f ● vt (pt/pp
pitted) fig opporre (**against** a)
pitch¹ /pɪtʃ/ n (tone) tono m; (level) altezza f; (in sport) campo m; (fig: degree)
grado m ● vt montare (tent). **pitch in** vi
fam mettersi sotto
pitch² n **~-'black** a nero come la pece.
~-'dark a buio pesto
'pitchfork n forca f
piteous /'pɪtɪəs/ a pietoso
'pitfall n fig trabocchetto m
pith /pɪθ/ n (of lemon, orange) interno m
della buccia
pithy /'pɪθɪ/ a (-ier, -iest) fig conciso
piti|ful /'pɪtɪfl/ a pietoso. **~less** a spie-
tato
pittance /'pɪtns/ n miseria f
pity /'pɪtɪ/ n pietà f; [**what a**] **~!** che
peccato!; **take ~ on** avere compassione
di ● vt aver pietà di
pivot /'pɪvət/ n perno m; fig fulcro m
● vi imperniarsi (**on** su)
pizza /'piːtsə/ n pizza f
placard /'plækɑːd/ n cartellone m
placate /plə'keɪt/ vt placare

place /pleɪs/ n posto m; (fam: house)
casa f; (in book) segno m; **feel out of ~**
sentirsi fuori posto; **take ~** aver luogo;
all over the ~ dappertutto ● vt collocare; (remember) identificare; **~ an
order** fare un'ordinazione; **be ~d** (in
race) piazzarsi. **~mat** n sottopiatto m
placid /'plæsɪd/ a placido
plagiar|ism /'pleɪdʒərɪzm/ n plagio m.
~ize vt plagiare
plague /pleɪg/ n peste f
plaice /pleɪs/ n inv platessa f
plain /pleɪn/ a chiaro; (simple) semplice; (not pretty) scialbo; (not patterned)
normale; (chocolate) fondente; **in ~
clothes** in borghese ● adv (simply)
semplicemente ● n pianura f. **~ly** adv
francamente; (simply) semplicemente;
(obviously) chiaramente
plaintiff /'pleɪntɪf/ n Jur parte f lesa
plaintive /'pleɪntɪv/ a lamentoso
plait /plæt/ n treccia f ● vt intrecciare
plan /plæn/ n progetto m, piano m ● vt
(pt/pp **planned**) progettare; (intend)
prevedere
plane¹ /pleɪn/ n (tree) platano m
plane² n aeroplano m
plane³ n (tool) pialla f ● vt piallare
planet /'plænɪt/ n pianeta m
plank /plæŋk/ n asse f
planning /'plænɪŋ/ n pianificazione f.
~ permission n licenza f edilizia
plant /plɑːnt/ n pianta f; (machinery)
impianto m; (factory) stabilimento m
● vt piantare. **~ation** /plæn'teɪʃn/ n
piantagione f
plaque /plɑːk/ n placca f
plasma /'plæzmə/ n plasma m
plaster /'plɑːstə(r)/ n intonaco m; Med
gesso m; (sticking ~) cerotto m; **~ of
Paris** gesso m ● vt intonacare (wall);
(cover) ricoprire. **~ed** a sl sbronzo. **~er**
n intonacatore m
plastic /'plæstɪk/ n plastica f ● a pla-
stico
Plasticine® /'plæstɪsiːn/ n plastilina® f
plastic: ~ 'surgeon n chirurgo m pla-
stico. **~ surgery** n chirurgia f plastica
plate /pleɪt/ n piatto m; (flat sheet) placca f; (gold and silverware) argenteria f;
(in book) tavola f [fuori testo] ● vt (cover
with metal) placcare
plateau /'plætəʊ/ n (pl **~x** /-əʊz/)
altopiano m
platform /'plætfɔːm/ n (stage) palco m;
Rail marciapiede m; Pol piattaforma f;
~ 5 binario 5

platinum /'plætɪnəm/ n platino m ● a di platino

platitude /'plætɪtjuːd/ n luogo m comune

platonic /pləˈtɒnɪk/ a platonico

platoon /pləˈtuːn/ n Mil plotone m

platter /'plætə(r)/ n piatto m da portata

plausible /'plɔːzəbl/ a plausibile

play /pleɪ/ n gioco m; Theat, TV rappresentazione f; Radio sceneggiato m radiofonico; ~ **on words** gioco m di parole ● vt giocare a; (act) recitare; suonare ⟨instrument⟩; giocare ⟨card⟩ ● vi giocare; Mus suonare; ~ **safe** non prendere rischi. **play down** vt minimizzare. **play up** vi fam fare i capricci

play: ~**boy** n playboy m inv. ~**er** n giocatore, -trice mf. ~**ful** a scherzoso. ~**ground** n Sch cortile m (per la ricreazione). ~**group** n asilo m

playing: ~**-card** n carta f da gioco. ~**-field** n campo m da gioco

play: ~**mate** n compagno, -a mf di gioco. ~**-pen** n box m inv. ~**thing** n giocattolo m. ~**wright** /-raɪt/ n drammaturgo, -a mf

plc n abbr (**public limited company**) s.r.l.

plea /pliː/ n richiesta f; **make a ~ for** fare un appello a

plead /pliːd/ vi fare appello (**for** a); ~ **guilty** dichiararsi colpevole; ~ **with sb** implorare qcno

pleasant /'plez(ə)nt/ a piacevole. ~**ly** adv piacevolmente; ⟨say, smile⟩ cordialmente

pleas|e /pliːz/ adv per favore; ~**e do** prego ● vt far contento; ~**e oneself** fare il proprio comodo; ~**e yourself!** come vuoi!, pej fai come ti pare!. ~**ed** a lieto; ~**ed with/about** contento di. ~**ing** a gradevole

pleasurable /'pleʒərəbl/ a gradevole

pleasure /'pleʒə(r)/ n piacere m; **with ~** con piacere, volentieri

pleat /pliːt/ n piega f ● vt pieghettare. ~**ed 'skirt** n gonna f a pieghe

pledge /pledʒ/ n pegno m; (promise) promessa f ● vt impegnarsi a; (pawn) impegnare

plentiful /'plentɪfl/ a abbondante

plenty /'plentɪ/ n abbondanza f; ~ **of money** molti soldi; ~ **of people** molta gente; **I've got ~** ne ho in abbondanza

pliable /'plaɪəbl/ a flessibile

pliers /'plaɪəz/ npl pinze fpl

plight /plaɪt/ n condizione f

plimsolls /'plɪmsəlz/ npl scarpe fpl da ginnastica

plinth /plɪnθ/ n plinto m

plod /plɒd/ vi (pt/pp **plodded**) trascinarsi; (work hard) sgobbare

plonk /plɒŋk/ n fam vino m mediocre

plot /plɒt/ n complotto m; (of novel) trama f; ~ **of land** appezzamento m [di terreno] ● vt/i (pt/pp **plotted**) complottare

plough /plaʊ/ n aratro m ● vt/i arare. ~**man's [lunch]** piatto m di formaggi e sottaceti, servito con pane. **plough back** vt Comm reinvestire

ploy /plɔɪ/ n fam manovra f

pluck /plʌk/ n fegato m ● vt strappare; depilare ⟨eyebrows⟩; spennare ⟨bird⟩; cogliere ⟨flower⟩. **pluck up** vt ~ **up courage** farsi coraggio

plucky /'plʌkɪ/ a (-**ier**, -**iest**) coraggioso

plug /plʌg/ n tappo m; Electr spina f; Auto candela f; (fam: advertisement) pubblicità f inv ● vt (pt/pp **plugged**) tappare; (fam: advertise) pubblicizzare con insistenza. **plug in** vt Electr inserire la spina di

plum /plʌm/ n prugna f; (tree) prugno m

plumage /'pluːmɪdʒ/ n piumaggio m

plumb /plʌm/ a verticale ● adv esattamente ● **plumb in** vt collegare

plumb|er /'plʌmə(r)/ n idraulico m. ~**ing** n impianto m idraulico

'plumb-line n filo m a piombo

plume /pluːm/ n piuma f

plummet /'plʌmɪt/ vi precipitare

plump /plʌmp/ a paffuto ● **plump for** vt scegliere

plunge /plʌndʒ/ n tuffo m; **take the ~** fam buttarsi ● vt tuffare; fig sprofondare ● vi tuffarsi

plunging /'plʌndʒɪŋ/ a ⟨neckline⟩ profondo

plu'perfect /pluː-/ n trapassato m prossimo

plural /'plʊərəl/ a plurale ● n plurale m

plus /plʌs/ prep più ● a in più; **500** più di 500 ● n più m; (advantage) extra m inv

plush /plʌʃ/ a lussuoso

plutonium /pluːˈtəʊnɪəm/ n plutonio m

ply /plaɪ/ vt (pt/pp **plied**) ~ **sb with drink** continuare a offrire da bere a qcno. ~**wood** n compensato m

p.m. abbr (**post meridiem**) del pomeriggio

PM n abbr **Prime Minister**

pneumatic /njuːˈmætɪk/ a pneumatico. ~ **'drill** n martello m pneumatico

pneumonia /njuːˈməʊnɪə/ n polmonite f

P.O. abbr Post Office

poach /pəʊtʃ/ vt Culin bollire; cacciare di frodo ⟨deer⟩; pescare di frodo ⟨salmon⟩; ~**ed egg** uovo m in camicia. ~**er** n bracconiere m

pocket /ˈpɒkɪt/ n tasca f; **be out of** ~ rimetterci ● vt intascare. ~-**book** n taccuino m; ⟨wallet⟩ portafoglio m. ~-**money** n denaro m per le piccole spese

pod /pɒd/ n baccello m

podgy /ˈpɒdʒɪ/ a (-ier, -iest) grassoccio

poem /ˈpəʊɪm/ n poesia f

poet /ˈpəʊɪt/ n poeta m. ~**ic** /-ˈetɪk/ a poetico

poetry /ˈpəʊɪtrɪ/ n poesia f

poignant /ˈpɔɪnjənt/ a emozionante

point /pɔɪnt/ n punto m; ⟨sharp end⟩ punta f; ⟨meaning, purpose⟩ senso m; Electr presa f [di corrente]; ~**s** pl Rail scambio m; ~ **of view** punto m di vista; **good/bad** ~**s** aspetti mpl positivi/negativi; **what is the** ~? a che scopo?; **the** ~ **is** il fatto è; **I don't see the** ~ non vedo il senso; **up to a** ~ fino a un certo punto; **be on the** ~ **of doing sth** essere sul punto di fare qcsa ● vt puntare (**at** verso) ● vi ⟨with finger⟩ puntare il dito; ~ **at/to** ⟨person:⟩ mostrare col dito; ⟨indicator:⟩ indicare. **point out** vt far notare ⟨fact⟩; ~ **sth out to sb** far notare qcsa a qcno

point-'blank a a bruciapelo

point|ed /ˈpɔɪntɪd/ a appuntito; ⟨question⟩ diretto. ~**ers** npl ⟨advice⟩ consigli mpl. ~**less** a inutile

poise /pɔɪz/ n padronanza f. ~**d** a in equilibrio; ~**d to** sul punto di

poison /ˈpɔɪzn/ n veleno m ● vt avvelenare. ~**ous** a velenoso

poke /pəʊk/ n [piccola] spinta f ● vt spingere; ⟨fire⟩ attizzare; ⟨put⟩ ficcare; ~ **fun at** prendere in giro. **poke about** vi frugare

poker[1] /ˈpəʊkə(r)/ n attizzatoio m

poker[2] n ⟨Cards⟩ poker m

poky /ˈpəʊkɪ/ a (-ier, -iest) angusto

Poland /ˈpəʊlənd/ n Polonia f

polar /ˈpəʊlə(r)/ a polare. ~ '**bear** n orso m bianco. ~**ize** vt polarizzare

Pole /pəʊl/ n polacco, -a mf

pole[1] n palo m

pole[2] n ⟨Geog, Electr⟩ polo m

'pole-star n stella f polare

'pole-vault n salto m con l'asta

police /pəˈliːs/ npl polizia f ● vt pattugliare ⟨area⟩

police: ~**man** n poliziotto m. ~ **state** n stato m militarista. ~ **station** n commissariato m. ~**woman** n donna f poliziotto

policy[1] /ˈpɒlɪsɪ/ n politica f

policy[2] n ⟨insurance⟩ polizza f

polio /ˈpəʊlɪəʊ/ n polio f

Polish /ˈpəʊlɪʃ/ a polacco ● n ⟨language⟩ polacco m

polish /ˈpɒlɪʃ/ n ⟨shine⟩ lucentezza f; ⟨substance⟩ lucido m; ⟨for nails⟩ smalto m; fig raffinatezza f ● vt lucidare; fig smussare. **polish off** vt fam finire; far fuori ⟨food⟩

polished /ˈpɒlɪʃt/ a ⟨manner⟩ raffinato; ⟨performance⟩ senza sbavature

polite /pəˈlaɪt/ a cortese. ~**ly** adv cortesemente. ~**ness** n cortesia f

politic /ˈpɒlɪtɪk/ a prudente

politic|al /pəˈlɪtɪkl/ a politico. ~**ally** adv dal punto di vista politico. ~**ian** /pɒlɪˈtɪʃn/ n politico m

politics /ˈpɒlɪtɪks/ n politica f

poll /pəʊl/ n votazione f; ⟨election⟩ elezioni fpl; [opinion] ~ sondaggio m d'opinione; **go to the** ~**s** andare alle urne ● vt ottenere ⟨votes⟩

pollen /ˈpɒlən/ n polline m

polling /ˈpəʊlɪŋ/: ~-**booth** n cabina f elettorale. ~-**station** n seggio m elettorale

'poll tax n imposta f locale sulle persone fisiche

pollutant /pəˈluːtənt/ n sostanza f inquinante

pollut|e /pəˈluːt/ vt inquinare. ~**ion** /-uːʃn/ n inquinamento m

polo /ˈpəʊləʊ/ n polo m. ~-**neck** n collo m alto. ~ **shirt** n dolcevita f

polyester /pɒlɪˈestə(r)/ n poliestere m

polystyrene® /pɒlɪˈstaɪriːn/ n polistirolo m

polytechnic /pɒlɪˈteknɪk/ n politecnico m

polythene /ˈpɒlɪθiːn/ n politene m. ~ **bag** n sacchetto m di plastica

polyun'saturated a polinsaturo

pomegranate /ˈpɒmɪɡrænɪt/ n melagrana f

pomp /pɒmp/ n pompa f

pompon /ˈpɒmpɒn/ n pompon m

pompous /ˈpɒmpəs/ a pomposo

pond /pɒnd/ n stagno m

ponder /ˈpɒndə(r)/ vt/i ponderare

pong /pɒŋ/ *n fam* puzzo *m*

pontiff /'pɒntɪf/ *n* pontefice *m*

pony /'pəʊnɪ/ *n* pony *m inv*. **~-tail** *n* coda *f* di cavallo. **~-trekking** *n* escursioni *fpl* col pony

poodle /'puːdl/ *n* barboncino *m*

pool[1] /puːl/ *n* (*of water, blood*) pozza *f*; [swimming] ~ piscina *f*

pool[2] *n* (*common fund*) cassa *f* comune; (*in cards*) piatto *m*; (*game*) biliardo *m* a buca. **~s** *npl* totocalcio *msg* ● *vt* mettere insieme

poor /pʊə(r)/ *a* povero; (*not good*) scadente; **in ~ health** in cattiva salute ● *npl* **the ~** i poveri. **~ly** *a* **be ~ly** non stare bene ● *adv* male

pop[1] /pɒp/ *n* botto *m*; (*drink*) bibita *f* gasata ● *v* (*pt/pp* **popped**) ● *vt* (*fam*: *put*) mettere; (*burst*) far scoppiare ● *vi* (*burst*) scoppiare. **pop in/out** *vi fam* fare un salto/un salto fuori

pop[2] *n fam* musica *f* pop ● *attrib* pop *inv*

'**popcorn** *n* popcorn *m inv*

pope /pəʊp/ *n* papa *m*

poplar /'pɒplə(r)/ *n* pioppo *m*

poppy /'pɒpɪ/ *n* papavero *m*

popular /'pɒpjʊlə(r)/ *a* popolare; (*belief*) diffuso. **~ity** /-'lærətɪ/ *n* popolarità *f*

populat|e /'pɒpjʊleɪt/ *vt* popolare. **~ion** /-'leɪʃn/ *n* popolazione *f*

porcelain /'pɔːsəlɪn/ *n* porcellana *f*

porch /pɔːtʃ/ *n* portico *m*; *Am* veranda *f*

porcupine /'pɔːkjʊpaɪn/ *n* porcospino *m*

pore[1] /pɔː(r)/ *n* poro *m*

pore[2] *vi* ~ **over** immergersi in

pork /pɔːk/ *n* carne *f* di maiale.

porn /pɔːn/ *n fam* porno *m*. **~o** *a fam* porno *inv*

pornograph|ic /pɔːnə'græfɪk/ *a* pornografico. **~y** /-'nɒgrəfɪ/ *n* pornografia *f*

porous /'pɔːrəs/ *a* poroso

porpoise /'pɔːpəs/ *n* focena *f*

porridge /'pɒrɪdʒ/ *n* farinata *f* di fiocchi d'avena

port[1] /pɔːt/ *n* porto *m*

port[2] *n* (*Naut: side*) babordo *m*

port[3] *n* (*wine*) porto *m*

portable /'pɔːtəbl/ *a* portabile

porter /'pɔːtə(r)/ *n* portiere *m*; (*for luggage*) facchino *m*

portfolio /pɔːt'fəʊlɪəʊ/ *n* cartella *f*; *Comm* portafoglio *m*

'**porthole** *n* oblò *m inv*

portion /'pɔːʃn/ *n* parte *f*; (*of food*) porzione *f*

portly /'pɔːtlɪ/ *a* (**-ier, -iest**) corpulento

portrait /'pɔːtrɪt/ *n* ritratto *m*

portray /pɔː'treɪ/ *vt* ritrarre; (*represent*) descrivere; (*actor:*) impersonare. **~al** *n* ritratto *m*

Portug|al /'pɔːtjʊgl/ *n* Portogallo *m*. **~uese** /-'giːz/ *a* portoghese ● *n* portoghese *mf*; (*language*) portoghese *m*

pose /pəʊz/ *n* posa *f* ● *vt* porre (*problem, question*) ● *vi* (*for painter*) posare; ~ **as** atteggiarsi a

posh /pɒʃ/ *a fam* lussuoso; (*people*) danaroso

position /pə'zɪʃn/ *n* posizione *f*; (*job*) posto *m*; (*status*) ceto *m* [sociale] ● *vt* posizionare

positive /'pɒzɪtɪv/ *a* positivo; (*certain*) sicuro; (*progress*) concreto ● *n* positivo *m*. **~ly** *adv* positivamente; (*decidedly*) decisamente

possess /pə'zes/ *vt* possedere. **~ion** /pə'zeʃn/ *n* possesso *m*; **~ions** *pl* beni *mpl*

possess|ive /pə'zesɪv/ *a* possessivo. **~iveness** *n* carattere *m* possessivo. **~or** *n* possessore, -ditrice *mf*

possibility /pɒsə'bɪlətɪ/ *n* possibilità *f inv*

possib|le /'pɒsɪbl/ *a* possibile. **~ly** *adv* possibilmente; **I couldn't ~ly accept** non mi è possibile accettare; **he can't ~ly be right** non è possibile che abbia ragione; **could you ~ly...?** potrebbe per favore...?

post[1] /pəʊst/ *n* (*pole*) palo *m* ● *vt* affiggere (*notice*)

post[2] *n* (*place of duty*) posto *m* ● *vt* appostare; (*transfer*) assegnare

post[3] *n* (*mail*) posta *f*; **by ~** per posta ● *vt* spedire; (*put in letter-box*) imbucare; (*as opposed to fax*) mandare per posta; **keep sb ~ed** tenere qcno al corrente

post- *pref* dopo

postage /'pəʊstɪdʒ/ *n* affrancatura *f*. ~ **stamp** *n* francobollo *m*

postal /'pəʊstl/ *a* postale. ~ **order** *n* vaglia *m inv* postale

post: **~-box** *n* cassetta *f* delle lettere. **~card** *n* cartolina *f*. **~code** *n* codice *m* postale. **~-date** *vt* postdatare

poster /'pəʊstə(r)/ *n* poster *m inv*; (*advertising, election*) cartellone *m*

posterior /pɒ'stɪərɪə(r)/ *n fam* posteriore *m*

posterity /pɒ'sterətɪ/ *n* posterità *f*

posthumous /'pɒstjʊməs/ *a* postumo. **~ly** *adv* dopo la morte

post: ~**man** n postino m. ~**mark** n timbro m postale

post-mortem /-'mɔːtəm/ n autopsia f

'**post office** n ufficio m postale

postpone /pəʊst'pəʊn/ vt rimandare. ~**ment** n rinvio m

posture /'pɒstʃə(r)/ n posizione f

post-'war a del dopoguerra

pot /pɒt/ n vaso m; (for tea) teiera f; (for coffee) caffettiera f; (for cooking) pentola f; ~**s of money** fam un sacco di soldi; **go to** ~ fam andare in malora

potassium /pə'tæsıəm/ n potassio m

potato /pə'teɪtəʊ/ n (pl -es) patata f

poten|t /'pəʊtənt/ a potente. ~**tate** n potentato m

potential /pə'tenʃl/ a potenziale ● n potenziale m. ~**ly** adv potenzialmente

pot: ~-**hole** n cavità f inv; (in road) buca f. ~-**holer** n speleologo, -a mf. ~-**luck** n **take** ~-**luck** affidarsi alla sorte. ~ '**plant** n pianta f da appartamento. ~-**shot** n **take** a ~-**shot at** sparare a casaccio a

potted /'pɒtɪd/ a conservato; (shortened) condensato. ~ '**plant** n pianta f da appartamento

potter[1] /'pɒtə(r)/ vi ~ [**about**] gingillarsi

potter[2] n vasaio, -a mf. ~**y** n lavorazione f della ceramica; (articles) ceramiche fpl; (place) laboratorio m di ceramiche

potty /'pɒtɪ/ a (-ier, -iest) fam matto ● n vasino m

pouch /paʊtʃ/ n marsupio m

pouffe /puːf/ n pouf m inv

poultry /'pəʊltrɪ/ n pollame m

pounce /paʊns/ vi balzare; ~ **on** saltare su

pound[1] /paʊnd/ n libbra f (= 0,454 kg); (money) sterlina f

pound[2] vt battere ● vi (heart:) battere forte; (run heavily) correre pesantemente

pour /pɔː(r)/ vt versare ● vi riversarsi; (with rain) piovere a dirotto. **pour out** vi riversarsi fuori ● vt versare (drink); sfogare (troubles)

pout /paʊt/ vi fare il broncio ● n broncio m

poverty /'pɒvətɪ/ n povertà f

powder /'paʊdə(r)/ n polvere f; (cosmetic) cipria f ● vt polverizzare; (face) incipriare. ~**y** a polveroso

power /'paʊə(r)/ n potere m; Electr corrente f [elettrica]; Math potenza f. ~-**cut** n interruzione f di corrente. ~**ed** a ~**ed by electricity** dotato di corrente

[elettrica]. ~**ful** a potente. ~**less** a impotente. ~-**station** n centrale f elettrica

PR n abbr **public relations**

practicable /'præktɪkəbl/ a praticabile

practical /'præktɪkl/ a pratico. ~'**joke** n burla f. ~**ly** adv praticamente

practice /'præktɪs/ n pratica f; (custom) usanza f; (habit) abitudine f; (exercise) esercizio m; Sport allenamento m; **in** ~ (in reality) in pratica; **out of** ~ fuori esercizio; **put into** ~ mettere in pratica

practise /'præktɪs/ vt fare pratica in; (carry out) mettere in pratica; esercitare (profession) ● vi esercitarsi; (doctor:) praticare. ~**d** a esperto

pragmatic /præg'mætɪk/ a pragmatico

praise /preɪz/ n lode f ● vt lodare. ~**worthy** a lodevole

pram /præm/ n carrozzella f

prance /prɑːns/ vi saltellare

prank /præŋk/ n tiro m

prattle /'prætl/ vi parlottare

prawn /prɔːn/ n gambero m. ~ '**cocktail** n cocktail m inv di gamberetti

pray /preɪ/ vi pregare. ~**er** /preə(r)/ n preghiera f

preach /priːtʃ/ vt/i predicare. ~**er** n predicatore, -trice mf

preamble /priː'æmbl/ n preambolo m

pre-ar'range /priː-/ vt predisporre

precarious /prɪ'keərɪəs/ a precario. ~**ly** adv in modo precario

precaution /prɪ'kɔːʃn/ n precauzione f; **as a** ~ per precauzione. ~**ary** a preventivo

precede /prɪ'siːd/ vt precedere

preceden|ce /'presɪdəns/ n precedenza f. ~**t** n precedente m

preceding /prɪ'siːdɪŋ/ a precedente

precinct /'priːsɪŋkt/ n (traffic-free) zona f pedonale; (Am: district) circoscrizione f

precious /'preʃəs/ a prezioso; (style) ricercato ● adv fam ~ **little** ben poco

precipice /'presɪpɪs/ n precipizio m

precipitate /prɪ'sɪpɪteɪt/ vt precipitare

précis /'preɪsiː/ n (pl précis /-siːz/) sunto m

precis|e /prɪ'saɪs/ a preciso. ~**ely** adv precisamente. ~**ion** /-'sɪʒn/ n precisione f

precursor /priː'kɜːsə(r)/ n precursore m

predator /'predətə(r)/ n predatore, -trice mf. ~**y** a rapace

predecessor /'priːdɪsesə(r)/ n predecessore, -a mf

predicament /prɪ'dɪkəmənt/ n situazione f difficile

predicat|e /'predɪkət/ n Gram predicato m. **~ive** /prɪ'dɪkətɪv/ a predicativo

predict /prɪ'dɪkt/ vt predire. **~able** /-əbl/ a prevedibile. **~ion** /-'dɪkʃn/ n previsione f

pre'domin|ant /prɪ-/ a predominante. **~ate** vi predominare

pre-'eminent /prɪ-/ a preminente

preen /priːn/ vt lisciarsi; **~ oneself** fig farsi bello

pre|fab /'priːfæb/ n fam casa f prefabbricata. **~'fabricated** a prefabbricato

preface /'prefɪs/ n prefazione f

prefect /'priːfekt/ n Sch studente, -tessa mf della scuola superiore con responsabilità disciplinari ecc

prefer /prɪ'fɜː(r)/ vt (pt/pp **preferred**) preferire

prefera|ble /'prefərəbl/ a preferibile (to a). **~bly** adv preferibilmente

preferen|ce /'prefərəns/ n preferenza f. **~tial** /-'renʃl/ a preferenziale

prefix /'priːfɪks/ n prefisso m

pregnan|cy /'pregnənsɪ/ n gravidanza f. **~t** a incinta

prehi'storic /priː-/ a preistorico

prejudice /'predʒudɪs/ n pregiudizio m ● vt influenzare (**against** contro); (harm) danneggiare. **~d** a prevenuto

preliminary /prɪ'lɪmɪnərɪ/ a preliminare

prelude /'preljuːd/ n preludio m

pre-'marital a prematrimoniale

premature /'premətjʊə(r)/ a prematuro

pre'meditated /priː-/ a premeditato

premier /'premɪə(r)/ a primario ● n Pol primo ministro m, premier m inv

première /'premɪeə(r)/ n prima f

premises /'premɪsɪz/ npl locali mpl; **on the ~** sul posto

premium /'priːmɪəm/ n premio m; **be at a ~** essere una cosa rara

premonition /premə'nɪʃn/ n presentimento m

preoccupied /priː'ɒkjupaɪd/ a preoccupato

prep /prep/ n Sch compiti mpl

preparation /prepə'reɪʃn/ n preparazione f. **~s** pl preparativi mpl

preparatory /prɪ'pærətrɪ/ a preparatorio ● adv **~ to** per

prepare /prɪ'peə(r)/ vt preparare ● vi prepararsi (**for** per); **~d to** disposto a

pre'pay /priː-/ vt (pt/pp **-paid**) pagare in anticipo

preposition /prepə'zɪʃn/ n preposizione f

prepossessing /priːpə'zesɪŋ/ a attraente

preposterous /prɪ'pɒstərəs/ a assurdo

prerequisite /priː'rekwɪzɪt/ n condizione f sine qua non

prescribe /prɪ'skraɪb/ vt prescrivere

prescription /prɪ'skrɪpʃn/ n Med ricetta f

presence /'prezns/ n presenza f; **~ of mind** presenza f di spirito

present¹ /'preznt/ a presente ● n presente m; **at ~** attualmente

present² n (gift) regalo m; **give sb sth as a ~** regalare qcsa a qcno

present³ /prɪ'zent/ vt presentare; **~ sb with an award** consegnare un premio a qcno. **~able** /-əbl/ a **be ~able** essere presentabile

presentation /prezn'teɪʃn/ n presentazione f

presently /'prezntlɪ/ adv fra poco; (Am: now) attualmente

preservation /prezə'veɪʃn/ n conservazione f

preservative /prɪ'zɜːvətɪv/ n conservante m

preserve /prɪ'zɜːv/ vt preservare; (maintain, Culin) conservare ● n (in hunting & fig) riserva f; (jam) marmellata f

preside /prɪ'zaɪd/ vi presiedere (**over** a)

presidency /'prezɪdənsɪ/ n presidenza f

president /'prezɪdənt/ n presidente m. **~ial** /-'denʃl/ a presidenziale

press /pres/ n (machine) pressa f; (newspapers) stampa f ● vt premere; pressare ⟨flower⟩; (iron) stirare; (squeeze) stringere ● vi (urge) incalzare. **press for** vi fare pressione per; **be ~ed for** essere a corto di. **press on** vi andare avanti

press: ~ conference n conferenza f stampa. **~ cutting** n ritaglio m di giornale. **~ing** a urgente. **~-stud** n [bottone m] automatico m. **~-up** n flessione f

pressure /'preʃə(r)/ n pressione f ● vt = **pressurize**. **~-cooker** n pentola f a pressione. **~ group** n gruppo m di pressione

pressurize /'preʃəraɪz/ vt far pressione su. **~d** a pressurizzato

prestig|e /pre'sti:ʒ/ n prestigio m. **~ious** /-'stɪdʒəs/ a prestigioso

presumably /prɪ'zju:məblɪ/ adv presumibilmente

presume /prɪ'zju:m/ vt presumere; **~ to do sth** permettersi di fare qcsa

presumpt|ion /prɪ'zʌmpʃn/ n presunzione f; (boldness) impertinenza f. **~uous** /-'zʌmptjʊəs/ a impertinente

presup'pose /pri:-/ vt presupporre

pretence /prɪ'tens/ n finzione f; (pretext) pretesto m; **it's all ~** è tutta una scena

pretend /prɪ'tend/ vt fingere; (claim) pretendere ● vi fare finta

pretentious /prɪ'tenʃəs/ a pretenzioso

pretext /'pri:tekst/ n pretesto m

pretty /'prɪtɪ/ a (-ier, -iest) carino ● adv (fam: fairly) abbastanza

prevail /prɪ'veɪl/ vi prevalere; **~ on sb to do sth** convincere qcno a fare qcsa. **~ing** a prevalente

prevalen|ce /'prevələns/ n diffusione f. **~t** a diffuso

prevent /prɪ'vent/ vt impedire; **~ sb [from] doing sth** impedire a qcno di fare qcsa. **~ion** /-enʃn/ n prevenzione f. **~ive** /-ɪv/ a preventivo

preview /'pri:vju:/ n anteprima f

previous /'pri:vɪəs/ a precedente. **~ly** adv precedentemente

pre-'war /pri:-/ a anteguerra

prey /preɪ/ n preda f; **bird of ~** uccello m rapace ● vi **~ on** far preda di; **~ on sb's mind** attanagliare qcno

price /praɪs/ n prezzo m ● vt Comm fissare il prezzo di. **~less** a inestimabile; (fam: amusing) spassosissimo. **~y** a fam caro

prick /prɪk/ n puntura f ● vt pungere. **prick up** vt **~ up one's ears** rizzare le orecchie

prickl|e /'prɪkl/ n spina f; (sensation) formicolio m. **~y** a pungente; (person) irritabile

pride /praɪd/ n orgoglio m ● vt **~ oneself on** vantarsi di

priest /pri:st/ n prete m

prim /prɪm/ a (primmer, primmest) perbenino

primarily /'praɪmərɪlɪ/ adv in primo luogo

primary /'praɪmərɪ/ a primario; (chief) principale. **~ school** n scuola f elementare

prime¹ /praɪm/ a principale, primo; (first-rate) eccellente ● n **be in one's ~** essere nel fiore degli anni

prime² vt preparare (surface, person)

Prime Minister n Primo Ministro m

primeval /praɪ'mi:vl/ a primitivo

primitive /'prɪmɪtɪv/ a primitivo

primrose /'prɪmrəʊz/ n primula f

prince /prɪns/ n principe m

princess /prɪn'ses/ n principessa f

principal /'prɪnsəpl/ a principale ● n Sch preside m

principality /prɪnsɪ'pælətɪ/ n principato m

principally /'prɪnsəplɪ/ adv principalmente

principle /'prɪnsəpl/ n principio m; **in ~** in teoria; **on ~** per principio

print /prɪnt/ n (mark, trace) impronta f; Phot copia f; (picture) stampa f; **in ~** (printed out) stampato; ‹book› in commercio; **out of ~** esaurito ● vt stampare; (write in capitals) scrivere in stampatello. **~ed matter** n stampe fpl

print|er /'prɪntə(r)/ n stampante f; Typ tipografo, -a mf. **~er port** n Comput porta f per la stampante. **~ing** n tipografia f

'printout n Comput stampa f

prior /'praɪə(r)/ a precedente. **~ to** prep prima di

priority /praɪ'ɒrətɪ/ n precedenza f; (matter) priorità f inv

prise /praɪz/ vt **~ open/up** forzare

prison /'prɪz(ə)n/ n prigione f. **~er** n prigioniero, -a mf

privacy /'prɪvəsɪ/ n privacy f

private /'praɪvət/ a privato; ‹car, secretary, letter› personale ● n Mil soldato m semplice; **in ~** in privato. **~ly** adv (funded, educated etc) privatamente; (in secret) in segreto; (confidentially) in privato; (inwardly) interiormente

privation /praɪ'veɪʃn/ n privazione f; **~s** pl stenti mpl

privatize /'praɪvətaɪz/ vt privatizzare

privilege /'prɪvəlɪdʒ/ n privilegio m. **~d** a privilegiato

privy /'prɪvɪ/ a **be ~ to** essere al corrente di

prize /praɪz/ n premio m ● a (idiot etc) perfetto ● vt apprezzare. **~-giving** n premiazione f. **~-winner** n vincitore, -trice mf. **~-winning** a vincente

pro /prəʊ/ n (fam: professional) professionista mf; **the ~s and cons** il pro e il contro

probability /prɒbə'bɪlətɪ/ n probabilità f inv

probabl|e /'prɒbəbl/ *a* probabile. **~y** *adv* probabilmente

probation /prə'beɪʃn/ *n* prova *f*; *Jur* libertà *f* vigilata. **~ary** *a* in prova; **~ary period** periodo *m* di prova

probe /prəʊb/ *n* sonda *f*; (*fig: investigation*) indagine *f* ● *vt* sondare; (*investigate*) esaminare a fondo

problem /'prɒbləm/ *n* problema *m* ● *a* difficile. **~atic** /-'mætɪk/ *a* problematico

procedure /prə'si:dʒə(r)/ *n* procedimento *m*

proceed /prə'si:d/ *vi* procedere ● *vt* **~ to do sth** proseguire facendo qcsa

proceedings /prə'si:dɪŋz/ *npl* (*report*) atti *mpl*; *Jur* azione *fsg* legale

proceeds /'prəʊsi:dz/ *npl* ricavato *msg*

process /'prəʊses/ *n* processo *m*; (*procedure*) procedimento *m*; **in the ~** nel far ciò ● *vt* trattare; *Admin* occuparsi di; *Phot* sviluppare

procession /prə'seʃn/ *n* processione *f*

proclaim /prə'kleɪm/ *vt* proclamare

procure /prə'kjʊə(r)/ *vt* ottenere

prod /prɒd/ *n* colpetto *m* ● *vt* (*pt/pp* **prodded**) punzecchiare; *fig* incitare

prodigal /'prɒdɪɡl/ *a* prodigo

prodigious /prə'dɪdʒəs/ *a* prodigioso

prodigy /'prɒdɪdʒɪ/ *n* [**infant**] **~** bambino *m* prodigio

produce¹ /'prɒdju:s/ *n* prodotti *mpl*; **~ of Italy** prodotto in Italia

produce² /prə'dju:s/ *vt* produrre; (*bring out*) tirar fuori; (*cause*) causare; (*fam: give birth to*) fare. **~r** *n* produttore *m*

product /'prɒdʌkt/ *n* prodotto *m*. **~ion** /prə'dʌkʃn/ *n* produzione *f*; *Theat* spettacolo *m*

productiv|e /prə'dʌktɪv/ *a* produttivo. **~ity** /-'tɪvətɪ/ *n* produttività *f*

profane /prə'feɪn/ *a* profano; (*blasphemous*) blasfemo. **~ity** /-'fænətɪ/ *n* (*oath*) bestemmia *f*

profession /prə'feʃn/ *n* professione *f*. **~al** *a* professionale; (*not amateur*) professionista; (*piece of work*) da professionista; (*man*) di professione ● *n* professionista *mf*. **~ally** *adv* professionalmente

professor /prə'fesə(r)/ *n* professore *m* [universitario]

proficien|cy /prə'fɪʃnsɪ/ *n* competenza *f*. **~t** *a* **be ~t in** essere competente in

profile /'prəʊfaɪl/ *n* profilo *m*

profit /'prɒfɪt/ *n* profitto *m* ● *vi* **~ from** trarre profitto da. **~able** /-əbl/ *a* proficuo. **~ably** *adv* in modo proficuo

profound /prə'faʊnd/ *a* profondo. **~ly** *adv* profondamente

profus|e /prə'fju:s/ *a* **~e apologies** una profusione di scuse. **~ion** /-ju:ʒn/ *n* profusione *f*; **in ~ion** in abbondanza

progeny /'prɒdʒənɪ/ *n* progenie *f inv*

prognosis /prɒɡ'nəʊsɪs/ *n* (*pl* -**oses**) prognosi *f inv*

program /'prəʊɡræm/ *n* programma *m* ● *vt* (*pt/pp* **programmed**) programmare

programme /'prəʊɡræm/ *n* Br programma *m*. **~r** *n* *Comput* programmatore, -trice *mf*

progress¹ /'prəʊɡres/ *n* progresso *m*; **in ~** in corso; **make ~** *fig* fare progressi

progress² /prə'ɡres/ *vi* progredire; *fig* fare progressi

progressive /prə'ɡresɪv/ *a* progressivo; (*reforming*) progressista. **~ly** *adv* progressivamente

prohibit /prə'hɪbɪt/ *vt* proibire. **~ive** /-ɪv/ *a* proibitivo

project¹ /'prɒdʒekt/ *n* progetto *m*; *Sch* ricerca *f*

project² /prə'dʒekt/ *vt* proiettare (*film, image*) ● *vi* (*jut out*) sporgere

projectile /prə'dʒektaɪl/ *n* proiettile *m*

projector /prə'dʒektə(r)/ *n* proiettore *m*

prolific /prə'lɪfɪk/ *a* prolifico

prologue /'prəʊlɒɡ/ *n* prologo *m*

prolong /prə'lɒŋ/ *vt* prolungare

promenade /prɒmə'nɑːd/ *n* lungomare *m inv*

prominent /'prɒmɪnənt/ *a* prominente; (*conspicuous*) di rilievo

promiscu|ity /prɒmɪ'skju:ətɪ/ *n* promiscuità *f*. **~ous** /prə'mɪskjʊəs/ *a* promiscuo

promis|e /'prɒmɪs/ *n* promessa *f* ● *vt* promettere; **~e sb that** promettere a qcno che; **I ~ed to** l'ho promesso. **~ing** *a* promettente

promot|e /prə'məʊt/ *vt* promuovere; **be ~ed** *Sport* essere promosso. **~ion** /-əʊʃn/ *n* promozione *f*

prompt /prɒmpt/ *a* immediato; (*punctual*) puntuale ● *adv* in punto ● *vt* incitare (**to** a); *Theat* suggerire a ● *vi* suggerire. **~er** *n* suggeritore, -trice *mf*. **~ly** *adv* puntualmente

Proms /prɒmz/ *npl* rassegna *f* di concerti estivi di musica classica presso l'Albert Hall a Londra

prone /prəʊn/ a be ~ to do sth essere incline a fare qcsa

prong /prɒŋ/ n dente m (di forchetta)

pronoun /ˈprəʊnaʊn/ n pronome m

pronounce /prəˈnaʊns/ vt pronunciare; (declare) dichiarare. ~d a (noticeable) pronunciato

pronunciation /prənʌnsɪˈeɪʃn/ n pronuncia f

proof /pruːf/ n prova f; Typ bozza f, prova f ● a ~ against a prova di

prop¹ /prɒp/ n puntello m ● vt (pt/pp propped) ~ open tenere aperto; ~ against (lean) appoggiare a. **prop up** vt sostenere

prop² n Theat, fam accessorio m di scena

propaganda /prɒpəˈgændə/ n propaganda f

propel /prəˈpel/ vt (pt/pp propelled) spingere. ~ler n elica f

proper /ˈprɒpə(r)/ a corretto; (suitable) adatto; (fam: real) vero [e proprio]. ~ly adv correttamente. ~ 'name, ~ 'noun n nome m proprio

property /ˈprɒpətɪ/ n proprietà f inv. ~ developer n agente m immobiliare. ~ market n mercato m immobiliare

prophecy /ˈprɒfəsɪ/ n profezia f

prophesy /ˈprɒfɪsaɪ/ vt (pt/pp -ied) profetizzare

prophet /ˈprɒfɪt/ n profeta m. ~ic /prəˈfetɪk/ a profetico

proportion /prəˈpɔːʃn/ n proporzione f; (share) parte f; ~s pl (dimensions) proporzioni fpl. ~al a proporzionale. ~ally adv in proporzione

proposal /prəˈpəʊzl/ n proposta f; (of marriage) proposta f di matrimonio

propose /prəˈpəʊz/ vt proporre; (intend) proporsi ● vi fare una proposta di matrimonio

proposition /prɒpəˈzɪʃn/ n proposta f; (fam: task) impresa f

proprietor /prəˈpraɪətə(r)/ n proprietario, -a mf

prosaic /prəˈzeɪɪk/ a prosaico

prose /prəʊz/ n prosa f

prosecut|e /ˈprɒsɪkjuːt/ vt intentare azione contro. ~ion /-ˈkjuːʃn/ n azione f giudiziaria; the ~ion l'accusa f. ~or n [Public] P~or Pubblico Ministero m

prospect¹ /ˈprɒspekt/ n (expectation) prospettiva f

prospect² /prəˈspekt/ vi ~ for cercare

prospect|ive /prəˈspektɪv/ a (future) futuro; (possible) potenziale. ~or n cercatore m

prospectus /prəˈspektəs/ n prospetto m

prosper /ˈprɒspə(r)/ vi prosperare; (person:) stare bene finanziariamente. ~ity /-ˈsperətɪ/ n prosperità f

prosperous /ˈprɒspərəs/ a prospero

prostitut|e /ˈprɒstɪtjuːt/ n prostituta f. ~ion /-ˈtjuːʃn/ n prostituzione f

prostrate /ˈprɒstreɪt/ a prostrato; ~ with grief fig prostrato dal dolore

protagonist /prəʊˈtægənɪst/ n protagonista mf

protect /prəˈtekt/ vt proteggere (from da). ~ion /-ekʃn/ n protezione f. ~ive /-ɪv/ a protettivo. ~or n protettore, -trice mf

protégé /ˈprɒtɪʒeɪ/ n protetto m

protein /ˈprəʊtiːn/ n proteina f

protest¹ /ˈprəʊtest/ n protesta f

protest² /prəˈtest/ vt/i protestare

Protestant /ˈprɒtɪstənt/ a protestante ● n protestante mf

protester /prəˈtestə(r)/ n contestatore, -trice mf

protocol /ˈprəʊtəkɒl/ n protocollo m

prototype /ˈprəʊtə-/ n prototipo m

protract /prəˈtrækt/ vt protrarre

protrude /prəˈtruːd/ vi sporgere

proud /praʊd/ a fiero (of di). ~ly adv fieramente

prove /pruːv/ vt provare ● vi ~ to be a lie rivelarsi una bugia. ~n a dimostrato

proverb /ˈprɒvɜːb/ n proverbio m. ~ial /prəˈvɜːbɪəl/ a proverbiale

provide /prəˈvaɪd/ vt fornire; ~ sb with sth fornire qcsa a qcno ● vi ~ for (law:) prevedere

provided /prəˈvaɪdɪd/ conj ~ [that] purché

providen|ce /ˈprɒvɪdəns/ n provvidenza f. ~tial /-ˈdenʃl/ a provvidenziale

providing /prəˈvaɪdɪŋ/ conj = provided

provinc|e /ˈprɒvɪns/ n provincia f; fig campo m. ~ial /prəˈvɪnʃl/ a provinciale

provision /prəˈvɪʒn/ n (of food, water) approvvigionamento m (of di); (of law) disposizione f; ~s pl provviste fpl. ~al a provvisorio

proviso /prəˈvaɪzəʊ/ n condizione f

provocat|ion /prɒvəˈkeɪʃn/ n provocazione f. ~ive /prəˈvɒkətɪv/ a provocatorio; (sexually) provocante. ~ively adv in modo provocatorio

provoke /prəˈvəʊk/ vt provocare

prow /praʊ/ n prua f

prowess /ˈpraʊɪs/ n abilità f inv

prowl /praʊl/ vi aggirarsi ● n on the ~ in cerca di preda. **~er** n tipo m sospetto

proximity /prɒkˈsɪmətɪ/ n prossimità f

proxy /ˈprɒksɪ/ n procura f; (person) persona f che agisce per procura

prude /pruːd/ n **be a** ~ essere eccessivamente pudico

pruden|ce /ˈpruːdəns/ n prudenza f. **~t** a prudente; (wise) oculatezza f

prudish /ˈpruːdɪʃ/ a eccessivamente pudico

prune¹ /pruːn/ n prugna f secca

prune² vt potare

pry /praɪ/ vi (pt/pp **pried**) ficcare il naso

psalm /sɑːm/ n salmo m

pseudonym /ˈsjuːdənɪm/ n pseudonimo m

psychiatric /saɪkɪˈætrɪk/ a psichiatrico

psychiatr|ist /saɪˈkaɪətrɪst/ n psichiatra mf. **~y** n psichiatria f

psychic /ˈsaɪkɪk/ a psichico; **I'm not** ~ non sono un indovino

psycho|'analyse /saɪkəʊ-/ vt psicanalizzare. **~a'nalysis** n psicanalisi f. **~'analyst** n psicanalista mf

psychological /saɪkəˈrɒdʒɪkl/ a psicologico

psycholog|ist /saɪˈkɒlədʒɪst/ n psicologo, -a mf. **~y** n psicologia f

psychopath /ˈsaɪkəpæθ/ n psicopatico, -a mf

P.T.O. abbr (**please turn over**) vedi retro

pub /pʌb/ n fam pub m inv

puberty /ˈpjuːbətɪ/ n pubertà f

public /ˈpʌblɪk/ a pubblico ● n **the** ~ il pubblico; **in** ~ in pubblico. **~ly** adv pubblicamente

publican /ˈpʌblɪkən/ n gestore, -trice mf/proprietario, -a mf di un pub

publication /pʌblɪˈkeɪʃn/ n pubblicazione f

public: ~ con'venience n gabinetti mpl pubblici. ~ 'holiday n festa f nazionale. ~ 'house n pub m inv

publicity /pʌbˈlɪsətɪ/ n pubblicità f

publicize /ˈpʌblɪsaɪz/ vt pubblicizzare

public: ~ 'library n biblioteca f pubblica. ~ relations fpl. ~ 'school n scuola f privata; Am scuola f pubblica. **~-'spirited** a be **~spirited** essere dotato di senso civico. ~ 'transport n mezzi mpl pubblici

publish /ˈpʌblɪʃ/ vt pubblicare. **~er** n editore m; (firm) editore m, casa f editrice. **~ing** n editoria f

pudding /ˈpʊdɪŋ/ n dolce m cotto al vapore; (course) dolce m

puddle /ˈpʌdl/ n pozzanghera f

pudgy /ˈpʌdʒɪ/ a (-ier, -iest) grassoccio

puff /pʌf/ n (of wind) soffio m; (of smoke) tirata f; (for powder) piumino m ● vt sbuffare. **puff at** vt tirare boccate da ⟨pipe⟩. **puff out** vt lasciare senza fiato ⟨person⟩; spegnere ⟨candle⟩. **~ed** a (out of breath) senza fiato. ~ **pastry** n pasta f sfoglia

puffy /ˈpʌfɪ/ a gonfio

pull /pʊl/ n trazione f; (fig: attraction) attrazione f; (fam: influence) influenza f ● vt tirare; estrarre ⟨tooth⟩; stirarsi ⟨muscle⟩; ~ **faces** far boccace; ~ **oneself together** cercare di controllarsi; ~ **one's weight** mettercela tutta; ~ **sb's leg** fam prendere in giro qcno. **pull down** vt (demolish) demolire. **pull in** vi Auto accostare. **pull off** vt togliere; fam azzeccare. **pull out** vt tirar fuori ● vi Auto spostarsi; (of competition) ritirarsi. **pull through** vi (recover) farcela. **pull up** vt sradicare ⟨plant⟩; (reprimand) rimproverare ● vi Auto fermarsi

pulley /ˈpʊlɪ/ n Techn puleggia f

pullover /ˈpʊləʊvə(r)/ n pullover m inv

pulp /pʌlp/ n poltiglia f; (of fruit) polpa f; (for paper) pasta f

pulpit /ˈpʊlpɪt/ n pulpito m

pulsate /pʌlˈseɪt/ vi pulsare

pulse /pʌls/ n polso m

pulses /ˈpʌlsɪz/ npl legumi mpl secchi

pulverize /ˈpʌlvəraɪz/ vt polverizzare

pumice /ˈpʌmɪs/ n pomice f

pummel /ˈpʌml/ vt (pt/pp **pummelled**) prendere a pugni

pump /pʌmp/ n pompa f ● vt pompare; ~ **sb for sth** fam cercare di estorcere qcsa da qcno. **pump up** vt (inflate) gonfiare

pumpkin /ˈpʌmpkɪn/ n zucca f

pun /pʌn/ n gioco m di parole

punch¹ /pʌntʃ/ n pugno m; (device) pinza f per forare ● vt dare un pugno a; forare ⟨ticket⟩; perforare ⟨hole⟩

punch² n (drink) ponce m inv

punch: ~ **line** n battuta f finale. **~-up** n rissa f

punctual /ˈpʌŋktjʊəl/ a puntuale. **~ity** /-ˈælətɪ/ n puntualità f. **~ly** adv puntualmente

punctuat|e /ˈpʌŋktjʊeɪt/ vt punteggiare. **~ion** /-ˈeɪʃn/ n punteggiatura f. **~ion mark** n segno m di interpunzione

puncture /ˈpʌŋktʃə(r)/ n foro m; (tyre) foratura f ● vt forare

pungent /'pʌndʒənt/ *a* acre

punish /'pʌnɪʃ/ *vt* punire. **~able** /-əbl/ *a* punibile. **~ment** *n* punizione *f*

punitive /'pju:nɪtɪv/ *a* punitivo

punk /pʌŋk/ *n* punk *m inv*

punnet /'pʌnɪt/ *n* cestello *m* (*per frutta*)

punt /pʌnt/ *n* (*boat*) barchino *m*

punter /'pʌntə(r)/ *n* (*gambler*) scommettitore, -trice *mf*; (*client*) consumatore, -trice *mf*

puny /'pju:nɪ/ *a* (**-ier, -iest**) striminzito

pup /pʌp/ *n* = **puppy**

pupil /'pju:pl/ *n* alluno, -a *mf*; (*of eye*) pupilla *f*

puppet /'pʌpɪt/ *n* marionetta *f*; (*glove ~, fig*) burattino *m*

puppy /'pʌpɪ/ *n* cucciolo *m*

purchase /'pɜ:tʃəs/ *n* acquisto *m*; (*leverage*) presa *f* ● *vt* acquistare. **~r** *n* acquirente *mf*

pure /pjʊə(r)/ *a* puro. **~ly** *adv* puramente

purée /'pjʊəreɪ/ *n* purè *m inv*

purgatory /'pɜ:gətrɪ/ *n* purgatorio *m*

purge /pɜ:dʒ/ *Pol n* epurazione *f* ● *vt* epurare

puri|fication /pjʊərɪfɪ'keɪʃn/ *n* purificazione *f*. **~fy** /'pjʊərɪfaɪ/ *vt* (*pt/pp* **-ied**) purificare

puritan /'pjʊərɪtən/ *n* puritano, -a *mf*. **~ical** *a* puritano

purity /'pjʊərɪtɪ/ *n* purità *f*

purple /'pɜ:pl/ *a* viola *inv*

purpose /'pɜ:pəs/ *n* scopo *m*; (*determination*) fermezza *f*; **on ~** apposta. **~-built** *a* costruito ad hoc. **~ful** *a* deciso. **~fully** *adv* con decisione. **~ly** *adv* apposta

purr /pɜ:(r)/ *vi* (*cat:*) fare le fusa

purse /pɜ:s/ *n* borsellino *m*; (*Am: handbag*) borsa *f* ● *vt* increspare (*lips*)

pursue /pə'sju:/ *vt* inseguire; *fig* proseguire. **~r** /-ə(r)/ *n* inseguitore, -trice *mf*

pursuit /pə'sju:t/ *n* inseguimento *m*; (*fig: of happiness*) ricerca *f*; (*pastime*) attività *f inv*; **in ~** all'inseguimento

pus /pʌs/ *n* pus *m*

push /pʊʃ/ *n* spinta *f*; (*fig: effort*) sforzo *m*; (*drive*) iniziativa *f*; **at a ~** in caso di bisogno; **get the ~** *fam* essere licenziato ● *vt* spingere; premere (*button*); (*pressurize*) far pressione su; **be ~ed for time** *fam* non avere tempo ● *vi* spingere. **push aside** *vt* scostare. **push back** *vt* respingere. **push off** *vt* togliere ● *vi* (*fam: leave*) levarsi dai piedi. **push on** *vi* (*continue*) continuare. **push up** *vt* alzare (*price*)

push: **~-button** *n* pulsante *m*. **~-chair** *n* passeggino *m*. **~-over** *n* fam bazzecola *f*. **~-up** *n* flessione *f*

pushy /'pʊʃɪ/ *a* fam troppo intraprendente

puss /pʊs/ *n*, **pussy** /'pʊsɪ/ *n* micio *m*

put /pʊt/ *vt* (*pt/pp* **put**, *pres p* **putting**) mettere; **~ the cost of sth at** valutare il costo di qcsa ● *vi* **~ to sea** salpare. **put aside** *vt* mettere da parte. **put away** *vt* mettere via. **put back** *vt* rimettere; mettere indietro (*clock*). **put by** *vt* mettere da parte. **put down** *vt* mettere giù; (*suppress*) reprimere; (*kill*) sopprimere; (*write*) annotare; **~ one's foot down** *fam* essere fermo; *Auto* dare un'accelerata; **~ down to** (*attribute*) attribuire. **put forward** *vt* avanzare; mettere avanti (*clock*). **put in** *vt* (*insert*) introdurre; (*submit*) presentare ● *vi* **~ in for** far domanda di. **put off** *vt* spegnere (*light*); (*postpone*) rimandare; **~ sb off** tenere a bada qcno; (*deter*) smontare qcno; (*disconcert*) distrarre qcno; **~ sb off sth** (*disgust*) disgustare qcno di qcsa. **put on** *vt* mettersi (*clothes*); mettere (*brake*); *Culin* mettere su; accendere (*light*); mettere in scena (*play*); mettere in scena (*accent*); **~ on weight** mettere su qualche chilo. **put out** *vt* spegnere (*fire, light*); tendere (*hand*); (*inconvenience*) creare degli inconvenienti a. **put through** *vt* far passare; *Teleph* **I'll ~ you through to him** glielo passo. **put up** *vt* alzare; erigere (*building*); montare (*tent*); aprire (*umbrella*); affiggere (*notice*); aumentare (*price*); ospitare (*guest*); **~ sb up to sth** mettere qcsa in testa a qcno ● *vi* (*at hotel*) stare; **~ up with** sopportare ● *a* **stay ~!** rimani lì!

putty /'pʌtɪ/ *n* mastice *m*

put-up /'pʊtʌp/ *a* **~ job** truffa *f*

puzzl|e /'pʌzl/ *n* enigma *m*; (*jigsaw*) puzzle *m inv* ● *vt* lasciare perplesso ● *vi* **~e over** scervellarsi su. **~ing** *a* inspiegabile

pygmy /'pɪgmɪ/ *n* pigmeo, -a *mf*

pyjamas /pə'dʒɑ:məz/ *npl* pigiama *msg*

pylon /'paɪlən/ *n* pilone *m*

pyramid /'pɪrəmɪd/ *n* piramide *f*

python /'paɪθn/ *n* pitone *m*

quack¹ /kwæk/ *n* qua qua *m inv* ● *vi* fare qua qua

quack² *n* (*doctor*) ciarlatano *m*

quad /kwɒd/ *n* (*fam: court*) = **quadrangle**. **~s** *pl* = **quadruplets**

quadrangle /'kwɒdræŋgl/ *n* quadrangolo *m*; (*court*) cortile *m* quadrangolare

quadruped /'kwɒdruped/ *n* quadrupede *m*

quadruple /'kwɒdrupl/ *a* quadruplo ● *vt* quadruplicare ● *vi* quadruplicarsi. **~s** /-plɪts/ *npl* quattro gemelli *mpl*

quagmire /'kwɒgmaɪə(r)/ *n* pantano *m*

quaint /kweɪnt/ *a* pittoresco; (*odd*) bizzarro

quake /kweɪk/ *n fam* terremoto *m* ● *vi* tremare

qualif|ication /kwɒlɪfɪ'keɪʃn/ *n* qualifica *f*. **~ied** /-faɪd/ *a* qualificato; (*limited*) con riserva

qualify /'kwɒlɪfaɪ/ *v* (*pt/pp* **-ied**) ● *vt* (*course:*) dare la qualifica a (**as** di); (*entitle*) dare diritto a; (*limit*) precisare ● *vi* ottenere la qualifica; *Sport* qualificarsi

quality /'kwɒlətɪ/ *n* qualità *f inv*

qualm /kwɑːm/ *n* scrupolo *m*

quandary /'kwɒndərɪ/ *n* dilemma *m*

quantity /'kwɒntətɪ/ *n* quantità *f inv*; **in ~** in grande quantità

quarantine /'kwɒrəntiːn/ *n* quarantena *f*

quarrel /'kwɒrəl/ *n* lite *f* ● *vi* (*pt/pp* **quarrelled**) litigare. **~some** *a* litigioso

quarry¹ /'kwɒrɪ/ *n* (*prey*) preda *f*

quarry² *n* cava *f*

quart /kwɔːt/ *n* 1.14 *litro*

quarter /'kwɔːtə(r)/ *n* quarto *m*; (*of year*) trimestre *m*; *Am* 25 centesimi *mpl*; **~s** *pl Mil* quartiere *msg*; **at [a] ~ to six** alle sei meno un quarto ● *vt* dividere in quattro. **~-'final** *n* quarto *m* di finale

quarterly /'kwɔːtəlɪ/ *a* trimestrale ● *adv* trimestralmente

quartet /kwɔːˈtet/ *n* quartetto *m*

quartz /kwɔːts/ *n* quarzo *m*. **~ watch** *n* orologio *m* al quarzo

quash /kwɒʃ/ *vt* annullare; soffocare (*rebellion*)

quaver /'kweɪvə(r)/ *vi* tremolare

quay /kiː/ *n* banchina *f*

queasy /'kwiːzɪ/ *a* **I feel ~** ho la nausea

queen /kwiːn/ *n* regina *f*. **~ mother** *n* regina *f* madre

queer /kwɪə(r)/ *a* strano; (*dubious*) sospetto; (*fam: homosexual*) finocchio ● *n fam* finocchio *m*

quell /kwel/ *vt* reprimere

quench /kwentʃ/ *vt* **~ one's thirst** dissetarsi

query /'kwɪərɪ/ *n* domanda *f*; (*question mark*) punto *m* interrogativo ● *vt* (*pt/pp* **-ied**) interrogare; (*doubt*) mettere in dubbio

quest /kwest/ *n* ricerca *f* (**for** di)

question /'kwestʃn/ *n* domanda *f*; (*for discussion*) questione *f*; **out of the ~** fuori discussione; **without ~** senza dubbio; **in ~** in questione ● *vt* interrogare; (*doubt*) mettere in dubbio. **~able** /-əbl/ *a* discutibile. **~ mark** *n* punto *m* interrogativo

questionnaire /kwestʃə'neə(r)/ *n* questionario *m*

queue /kjuː/ *n* coda *f*, fila *f* ● *vi* ~ [**up**] mettersi in coda (**for** per)

quick /kwɪk/ *a* veloce; **be ~!** sbrigati!; **have a ~ meal** fare uno spuntino ● *adv* in fretta ● *n* **be cut to the ~** *fig* essere punto sul vivo. **~ly** *adv* in fretta. **~-tempered** *a* collerico

quid /kwɪd/ *n inv fam* sterlina *f*

quiet /'kwaɪət/ *a* (*calm*) tranquillo; (*silent*) silenzioso; (*voice, music*) basso; **keep ~ about** *fam* non raccontare a nessuno ● *n* quiete *f*; **on the ~** di nascosto. **~ly** *adv* (*peacefully*) tranquillamente; (*say*) a bassa voce

quiet|en /'kwaɪətn/ *vt* calmare. **quieten down** *vi* calmarsi. **~ness** *n* quiete *f*

quilt /kwɪlt/ *n* piumino *m*. **~ed** *a* trapuntato

quins /kwɪnz/ *npl fam* = **quintuplets**

quintet /kwɪn'tet/ *n* quintetto *m*

quintuplets /'kwɪntjʊplɪts/ *npl* cinque gemelli *mpl*

quip /kwɪp/ *n* battuta *f*

quirk /kwɜːk/ *n* stranezza *f*

quit /kwɪt/ *v* (*pt/pp* **quitted, quit**) ● *vt* lasciare; (*give up*) smettere (**doing** di fare) ● *vi* (*fam: resign*) andarsene; *Comput* uscire; **give sb notice to ~** ‹landlord:› dare a qcno il preavviso di sfratto

quite /kwaɪt/ *adv* (*fairly*) abbastanza; (*completely*) completamente; (*really*) veramente; **~ [so]!** proprio così!; **~ a few** parecchi

quits /kwɪts/ *a* pari

quiver /'kwɪvə(r)/ *vi* tremare

quiz /kwɪz/ *n* (*game*) quiz *m inv* ● *vt* (*pt/pp* **quizzed**) interrogare

quota /'kwəʊtə/ *n* quota *f*

quotation /kwəʊ'teɪʃn/ *n* citazione *f*; (*price*) preventivo *m*; (*of shares*) quota *f*. **~ marks** *npl* virgolette *fpl*

quote /kwəʊt/ *n fam* = **quotation; in ~s** tra virgolette ● *vt* citare; quotare ‹price›

Rr

rabbi /'ræbaɪ/ *n* rabbino *m*; (*title*) rabbi

rabbit /'ræbɪt/ *n* coniglio *m*

rabble /'ræbl/ *n* **the ~** la plebaglia

rabies /'reɪbiːz/ *n* rabbia *f*

race[1] /reɪs/ *n* (*people*) razza *f*

race[2] *n* corsa *f* ● *vi* correre ● *vt* gareggiare con; fare correre ‹horse›

race: ~course *n* ippodromo *m*. **~horse** *n* cavallo *m* da corsa. **~track** *n* pista *f*

racial /'reɪʃl/ *a* razziale. **~ism** *n* razzismo *m*

racing /'reɪsɪŋ/ *n* corse *fpl*; (*horse-*) corse *fpl* dei cavalli. **~ car** *n* macchina *f* da corsa. **~ driver** *n* corridore *m* automobilistico

racis|m /'reɪsɪzm/ *n* razzismo *m*. **~t** /-ɪst/ *a* razzista ● *n* razzista *mf*

rack[1] /ræk/ *n* (*for bikes*) rastrelliera *f*; (*for luggage*) portabagagli *m inv*; (*for plates*) scolapiatti *m inv* ● *vt* **~ one's brains** scervellarsi

rack[2] *n* **go to ~ and ruin** andare in rovina

racket[1] /'rækɪt/ *n Sport* racchetta *f*

racket[2] *n* (*din*) chiasso *m*; (*swindle*) truffa *f*; (*crime*) racket *m inv*, giro *m*

radar /'reɪdɑː(r)/ *n* radar *m*

radian|ce /'reɪdɪəns/ *n* radiosità *f*. **~t** *a* raggiante

radiat|e /'reɪdɪeɪt/ *vt* irradiare ● *vi* ‹heat:› irradiarsi. **~ion** /-'eɪʃn/ *n* radiazione *f*

radiator /'reɪdɪeɪtə(r)/ *n* radiatore *m*

radical /'rædɪkl/ *a* radicale ● *n* radicale *mf*. **~ly** *adv* radicalmente

radio /'reɪdɪəʊ/ *n* radio *f inv*

radio'active *a* radioattivo. **~'activity** *n* radioattività *f*

rad'iograph|er /reɪdɪ'ɒɡrəfə(r)/ *n* radiologo, -a *mf*. **~y** *n* radiografia *f*

radio'therapy *n* radioterapia *f*

radish /'rædɪʃ/ *n* ravanello *m*

radius /'reɪdɪəs/ *n* (*pl* **-dii** /-dɪaɪ/) raggio *m*

raffle /'ræfl/ *n* lotteria *f*

raft /rɑːft/ *n* zattera *f*

rafter /'rɑːftə(r)/ *n* trave *f*

rag /ræɡ/ *n* straccio *m*; (*pej: newspaper*) giornalaccio *m*; **in ~s** stracciato

rage /reɪdʒ/ *n* rabbia *f*; **all the ~** *fam* all'ultima moda ● *vi* infuriarsi; ‹storm:› infuriare; ‹epidemic:› imperversare

ragged /'ræɡɪd/ *a* logoro; ‹edge› frastagliato

raid /reɪd/ *n* (*by thieves*) rapina *f*; *Mil* incursione *f*, raid *m inv*; (*police*) irruzione *f* ● *vt Mil* fare un'incursione in; ‹police, burglars:› fare irruzione in. **~er** *n* (*of bank*) rapinatore, -trice *mf*

rail /reɪl/ *n* ringhiera *f*; (*hand~*) ringhiera *f*; *Naut* parapetto *m*; **by ~** per ferrovia

'railroad *n Am* = **railway**

'railway *n* ferrovia *f*. **~man** *n* ferroviere *m*. **~ station** *n* stazione *f* ferroviaria

rain /reɪn/ *n* pioggia *f* ● *vi* piovere

rain: ~bow *n* arcobaleno *m*. **~coat** *n* impermeabile *m*. **~fall** *n* precipitazione *f* [atmosferica]

rainy /'reɪnɪ/ *a* (**-ier, -iest**) piovoso

raise /reɪz/ *n Am* aumento *m* ● *vt* alzare; levarsi ⟨*hat*⟩; allevare ⟨*children, animals*⟩; sollevare ⟨*question*⟩; ottenere ⟨*money*⟩

raisin /'reɪzn/ *n* uva *f* passa

rake /reɪk/ *n* rastrello *m* ● *vt* rastrellare. **rake up** *vt* raccogliere col rastrello; *fam* rivangare

rally /'rælɪ/ *n* raduno *m*; *Auto* rally *m inv*; *Tennis* scambio *m* ● *v* (*pt/pp* **-ied**) ● *vt* radunare ● *vi* radunarsi; (*recover strength*) riprendersi

ram /ræm/ *n* montone *m*; *Astr* Ariete *m* ● *vt* (*pt/pp* **rammed**) cozzare contro

RAM /ræm/ *n* [memoria *f*] RAM *f*

rambl|e /'ræmbl/ *n* escursione *f* ● *vi* gironzolare; (*in speech*) divagare. **~er** *n* escursionista *mf*; (*rose*) rosa *f* rampicante. **~ing** *a* (*in speech*) sconnesso; ⟨*club*⟩ escursionistico

ramp /ræmp/ *n* rampa *f*; *Aeron* scaletta *f* mobile (*di aerei*)

rampage /'ræmpeɪdʒ/ *n* **be/go on the ~** scatenarsi ● *vi* **~ through the streets** scatenarsi per le strade

rampant /'ræmpənt/ *a* dilagante

rampart /'ræmpɑːt/ *n* bastione *f*

ramshackle /'ræmʃækl/ *a* sgangherato

ran /ræn/ *see* **run**

ranch /rɑːntʃ/ *n* ranch *m inv*

rancid /'rænsɪd/ *a* rancido

rancour /'ræŋkə(r)/ *n* rancore *m*

random /'rændəm/ *a* casuale; **~ sample** campione *m* a caso ● *n* **at ~** a casaccio

randy /'rændɪ/ *a* (**-ier, -iest**) *fam* eccitato

rang /ræŋ/ *see* **ring²**

range /reɪndʒ/ *n* serie *f*; *Comm, Mus* gamma *f*; (*of mountains*) catena *f*; (*distance*) raggio *m*; (*for shooting*) portata *f*; (*stove*) cucina *f* economica; **at a ~ of** a una distanza di ● *vi* estendersi; **~ from... to...** andare da... a.... **~r** *n* guardia *f* forestale

rank /ræŋk/ *n* (*row*) riga *f*; *Mil* grado *m*; (*social position*) rango *m*; **the ~ and file** *n* **the ~s** *pl Mil* i soldati semplici ● *vt* (*place*) annoverare (**among** tra) ● *vi* (*be placed*) collocarsi

rankle /'ræŋkl/ *vi fig* bruciare

ransack /'rænsæk/ *vt* rovistare; (*pillage*) saccheggiare

ransom /'rænsəm/ *n* riscatto *m*; **hold sb to ~** tenere qcno in ostaggio (*per il riscatto*)

rant /rænt/ *vi* **~ [and rave]** inveire;

what's he **~ing on about?** cosa sta blaterando?

rap /ræp/ *n* colpo *m* [secco]; *Mus* rap *m* ● *v* (*pt/pp* **rapped**) ● *vt* dare colpetti a ● *vi* **~ at** bussare a

rape /reɪp/ *n* (*sexual*) stupro *m* ● *vt* violentare, stuprare

rapid /'ræpɪd/ *a* rapido. **~ity** /rə'pɪdətɪ/ *n* rapidità *f*. **~ly** *adv* rapidamente

rapids /'ræpɪdz/ *npl* rapida *fsg*

rapist /'reɪpɪst/ *n* violentatore *m*

rapport /ræ'pɔː(r)/ *n* rapporto *m* di intesa

raptur|e /'ræptʃə(r)/ *n* estasi *f*. **~ous** /-rəs/ *a* entusiastico

rare¹ /reə(r)/ *a* raro. **~ly** *adv* raramente

rare² *a Culin* al sangue

rarefied /'reərɪfaɪd/ *a* rarefatto

rarity /'reərətɪ/ *n* rarità *f inv*

rascal /'rɑːskl/ *n* mascalzone *m*

rash¹ /ræʃ/ *n Med* eruzione *f*

rash² *a* avventato. **~ly** *adv* avventatamente

rasher /'ræʃə(r)/ *n* fetta *f* di pancetta

rasp /rɑːsp/ *n* (*noise*) stridio *m*. **~ing** *a* stridente

raspberry /'rɑːzbərɪ/ *n* lampone *m*

rat /ræt/ *n* topo *m*; (*fam: person*) carogna *f*; **smell a ~** *fam* sentire puzzo di bruciato

rate /reɪt/ *n* (*speed*) velocità *f inv*; (*of payment*) tariffa *f*; (*of exchange*) tasso *m*; **~s** *pl* (*taxes*) imposte *fpl* comunali sui beni immobili; **at any ~** in ogni caso; **at this ~** di questo passo ● *vt* stimare; **~ among** annoverare tra ● *vi* **~ as** essere considerato

rather /'rɑːðə(r)/ *adv* piuttosto; **~!** eccome!; **~ too...** un po' troppo...

rati|fication /rætɪfɪ'keɪʃn/ *n* ratifica *f*. **~fy** /'rætɪfaɪ/ *vt* (*pt/pp* **-ied**) ratificare

rating /'reɪtɪŋ/ *n* **~s** *pl Radio, TV* indice *m* d'ascolto, audience *f inv*

ratio /'reɪʃɪəʊ/ *n* rapporto *m*

ration /'ræʃn/ *n* razione *f* ● *vt* razionare

rational /'ræʃənl/ *a* razionale. **~ize** *vt/i* razionalizzare

'rat race *n fam* corsa *f* al successo

rattle /'rætl/ *n* tintinnio *m*; (*toy*) sonaglio *m* ● *vi* tintinnare ● *vt* (*shake*) scuotere; *fam* innervosire. **rattle off** *vt fam* sciorinare

'rattlesnake *n* serpente *m* a sonagli

raucous /'rɔːkəs/ *a* rauco

rave /reɪv/ *vi* vaneggiare; **~ about** andare in estasi per

raven /'reɪvn/ n corvo m imperiale

ravenous /'rævənəs/ a ⟨person⟩ affamato

ravine /rə'viːn/ n gola f

raving /'reɪvɪŋ/ a ~ **mad** fam matto da legare

ravishing /'rævɪʃɪŋ/ a incantevole

raw /rɔː/ a crudo; (not processed) grezzo; ⟨weather⟩ gelido; (inexperienced) inesperto; **get a ~ deal** fam farsi fregare. ~ **ma'terials** npl materie fpl prime

ray /reɪ/ n raggio m; ~ **of hope** barlume m di speranza

raze /reɪz/ vt ~ **to the ground** radere al suolo

razor /'reɪzə(r)/ n rasoio m. ~ **blade** n lametta f da barba

re /riː/ prep con riferimento a

reach /riːtʃ/ n portata f; **within ~** a portata di mano; **out of ~ of** fuori dalla portata di; **within easy ~** facilmente raggiungibile ● vt arrivare a ⟨place, decision⟩; (contact) contattare; (pass) passare; **I can't ~ it** non ci arrivo ● vi arrivare (to a); ~ **for** allungare la mano per prendere

re'act /rɪ-/ vi reagire

re'action /rɪ-/ n reazione f. ~**ary** a & n reazionario, -a mf

reactor /rɪ'æktə(r)/ n reattore m

read /riːd/ vt (pt/pp read /red/) leggere; Univ studiare ● vi leggere; ⟨instrument:⟩ indicare. **read out** vt leggere ad alta voce

readable /'riːdəbl/ a piacevole a leggersi; (legible) leggibile

reader /'riːdə(r)/ n lettore, -trice mf; (book) antologia f

readi|ly /'redɪlɪ/ adv volentieri; (easily) facilmente. ~**ness** n disponibilità f; **in ~ness** pronto

reading /'riːdɪŋ/ n lettura f

rea'djust /riː-/ vt regolare di nuovo ● vi riabituarsi (**to** a)

ready /'redɪ/ a (**-ier, -iest**) pronto; (quick) veloce; **get ~** prepararsi

ready: ~**-'made** a confezionato. ~ **'money** n contanti mpl. ~**-to-'wear** a prêt-à-porter

real /riːl/ a vero; ⟨increase⟩ reale ● adv Am fam veramente. ~ **estate** n beni mpl immobili

realis|m /'rɪəlɪzm/ n realismo m. ~**t** /-lɪst/ n realista mf. ~**tic** /-'lɪstɪk/ a realistico

reality /rɪ'ælətɪ/ n realtà f inv

realization /rɪəlaɪ'zeɪʃn/ n realizzazione f

realize /'rɪəlaɪz/ vt realizzare

really /'rɪəlɪ/ adv davvero

realm /relm/ n regno m

realtor /'rɪəltə(r)/ n Am agente mf immobiliare

reap /riːp/ vt mietere

reap'pear /riː-/ vi riapparire

rear[1] /rɪə(r)/ a posteriore; Auto di dietro; ~ **end** fam didietro m ● n **the ~** (of building) il retro; (of bus, plane) la parte posteriore; **from the ~** da dietro

rear[2] vt allevare ● vi ~ **[up]** ⟨horse:⟩ impennarsi

'rear-light n luce f posteriore

re'arm /riː-/ vt riarmare ● vi riarmarsi

rear'range /riː-/ vt cambiare la disposizione di

rear-view 'mirror n Auto specchietto m retrovisore

reason /'riːzn/ n ragione f; **within ~** nei limiti del ragionevole ● vi ragionare; ~ **with** cercare di far ragionare. ~**able** /-əbl/ a ragionevole. ~**ably** /-əblɪ/ adv (in reasonable way, fairly) ragionevolmente

reas'sur|ance /riː-/ n rassicurazione f. ~**e** vt rassicurare; ~**e sb of sth** rassicurare qcno su qcsa. ~**ing** a rassicurante

rebate /'riːbeɪt/ n rimborso m; (discount) deduzione f

rebel[1] /'rebl/ n ribelle mf

rebel[2] /rɪ'bel/ vi (pt/pp **rebelled**) ribellarsi. ~**lion** /-jən/ n ribellione f. ~**lious** /-jəs/ a ribelle

re'bound[1] /rɪ-/ vi rimbalzare; fig ricadere

'rebound[2] /riː-/ n rimbalzo m

rebuff /rɪ'bʌf/ n rifiuto m

re'build /riː-/ vt (pt/pp **-built**) ricostruire

rebuke /rɪ'bjuːk/ vt rimproverare

rebuttal /rɪ'bʌtl/ n rifiuto m

re'call /rɪ-/ n richiamo m; **beyond ~** irrevocabile ● vt richiamare; riconvocare ⟨diplomat, parliament⟩; (remember) rievocare

recap /'riːkæp/ vt/i fam = **recapitulate** ● n ricapitolazione f

recapitulate /riːkə'pɪtjʊleɪt/ vt/i ricapitolare

re'capture /riː-/ vt riconquistare; ricatturare ⟨person, animal⟩

reced|e /rɪ'siːd/ vi allontanarsi. ~**ing** a ⟨forehead, chin⟩ sfuggente; **have ~ing hair** essere stempiato

receipt /rɪ'siːt/ n ricevuta f; (receiving) ricezione f; ~**s** pl Comm entrate fpl

receive /rɪ'siːv/ vt ricevere. **~r** n
Teleph ricevitore m; Radio, TV apparecchio m ricevente; (of stolen goods)
ricettatore, -trice mf

recent /'riːsnt/ a recente. **~ly** adv recentemente

receptacle /rɪ'septəkl/ n recipiente m

reception /rɪ'sepʃn/ n ricevimento m;
(welcome) accoglienza f; Radio ricezione f; **~ [desk]** (in hotel) reception f inv.
~ist n persona f alla reception

receptive /rɪ'septɪv/ a ricettivo

recess /rɪ'ses/ n rientranza f; (holiday)
vacanza f; Am Sch intervallo m

recession /rɪ'seʃn/ n recessione f

re'charge /riː-/ vt ricaricare

recipe /'resəpɪ/ n ricetta f

recipient /rɪ'sɪpɪənt/ n (of letter)
destinatario, -a mf; (of money)
beneficiario, -a mf

recipro|cal /rɪ'sɪprəkl/ a reciproco.
~cate /-kert/ vt ricambiare

recital /rɪ'saɪtl/ n recital m inv

recite /rɪ'saɪt/ vt recitare; (list) elencare

reckless /'reklɪs/ a (action, decision)
sconsiderato; **be a ~ driver** guidare in
modo spericolato. **~ly** adv in modo scon-
siderato. **~ness** n sconsideratezza f

reckon /'rekən/ vt calcolare; (consider)
pensare. **reckon on/with** vt fare i conti
con

re'claim /rɪ-/ vt reclamare; bonificare
(land)

reclin|e /rɪ'klaɪn/ vi sdraiarsi. **~ing** a
(seat) reclinabile

recluse /rɪ'kluːs/ n recluso, -a mf

recognition /rekəg'nɪʃn/ n riconoscimento m; **beyond ~** irriconoscibile

recognize /'rekəgnaɪz/ vt riconoscere

re'coil /rɪ-/ vi (in fear) indietreggiare

recollect /rekə'lekt/ vt ricordare.
~ion /-ekʃn/ n ricordo m

recommend /rekə'mend/ vt raccomandare. **~ation** /-'deɪʃn/ n raccomandazione f

recompense /'rekəmpens/ n ricompensa f

recon|cile /'rekənsaɪl/ vt riconciliare;
conciliare (facts); **~cile oneself to**
rassegnarsi a. **~ciliation** /-sɪlɪ'eɪʃn/ n
riconciliazione f

recon'dition /riː-/ vt ripristinare.
~ed engine n motore m che ha subito
riparazioni

reconnaissance /rɪ'kɒnɪsns/ n Mil
ricognizione f

reconnoitre /rekə'nɔɪtə(r)/ vi (pres p
-tring) fare una recognizione

recon'sider /riː-/ vt riconsiderare

recon'struct /riː-/ vt ricostruire.
~ion n ricostruzione f

record[1] /rɪ'kɔːd/ vt registrare; (make a
note of) annotare

record[2] /'rekɔːd/ n (file) documenta-
zione f; Mus disco m; Sport record m
inv; **~s** pl (files) schedario msg; **keep a
~ of** tener nota di; **off the ~** in via uffi-
ciosa; **have a [criminal] ~** avere la
fedina penale sporca

recorder /rɪ'kɔːdə(r)/ n Mus flauto m
dolce

recording /rɪ'kɔːdɪŋ/ n registrazione f

'record-player n giradischi m inv

recount /rɪ'kaʊnt/ vt raccontare

re-'count[1] /riː-/ vt ricontare (votes etc)

're-count[2] /'riː-/ n Pol nuovo conteggio m

recoup /rɪ'kuːp/ vt rifarsi di (losses)

recourse /rɪ'kɔːs/ n **have ~ to** ricorrere a

re-'cover /riː-/ vt rifoderare

recover /rɪ'kʌvə(r)/ vt/i recuperare. **~y**
n recupero m; (of health) guarigione f

recreation /rekrɪ'eɪʃn/ n ricreazione
f. **~al** a ricreativo

recrimination /rɪkrɪmɪ'neɪʃn/ n re-
criminazione f

recruit /rɪ'kruːt/ n Mil recluta f; **new
~** (member) nuovo, -a adepto, -a mf;
(worker) neoassunto, -a mf ● vt assumere (staff). **~ment** n assunzione f

rectang|le /'rektæŋgl/ n rettangolo m.
~ular /-'tæŋgjʊlə(r)/ a rettangolare

rectify /'rektɪfaɪ/ vt (pt/pp -ied) rettifi-
care

recuperate /rɪ'kuːpəreɪt/ vi ristabilir-
si

recur /rɪ'kɜː(r)/ vi (pt/pp recurred) ricorrere; (illness:) ripresentarsi

recurren|ce /rɪ'kʌrəns/ n ricorrenza
f; (of illness) ricomparsa f. **~t** a ricor-
rente

recycle /riː'saɪkl/ vt riciclare

red /red/ a (redder, reddest) rosso ● n
rosso m; **in the ~** (account) scoperto.
R~ Cross n Croce f rossa

redd|en /'redn/ vt arrossare ● vi arros-
sire. **~ish** a rossastro

re'decorate /riː-/ vt (paint) ridipin-
gere; (wallpaper) ritappezzare

redeem /rɪ'diːm/ vt **~ing quality** unico aspetto m positivo

redemption /rɪ'dempʃn/ n riscatto m

rede'ploy /riː-/ vt ridistribuire

red: ~**-haired** *a* con i capelli rossi.
~-**'handed** *a* **catch sb** ~-**handed** cogliere qcno con le mani nel sacco. ~
'**herring** *n* diversione *f*. ~-**hot** *a* rovente
red: ~ '**light** *n Auto* semaforo *m* rosso
re'double /rɪ-/ *vt* raddoppiare
redress /rɪ'dres/ *n* riparazione *f* ● *vt*
ristabilire ⟨balance⟩
red 'tape *n fam* burocrazia *f*
reduc|e /rɪ'dju:s/ *vt* ridurre; *Culin* far
consumare. ~**tion** /-'dʌkʃn/ *n* riduzione *f*
redundan|cy /rɪ'dʌndənsɪ/ *n* licenziamento *m*; ⟨payment⟩ cassa *f* integrazione. ~**t** *a* superfluo; **make** ~**t** licenziare;
be made ~ **t** essere licenziato
reed /ri:d/ *n Bot* canna *f*
reef /ri:f/ *n* scogliera *f*
reek /ri:k/ *vi* puzzare (**of** di)
reel /ri:l/ *n* bobina *f* ● *vi* ⟨stagger⟩ vacillare. **reel off** *vt fig* snocciolare
refectory /rɪ'fektərɪ/ *n* refettorio *m*;
Univ mensa *f* universitaria
refer /rɪ'fɜ:(r)/ *v* ⟨pt/pp **referred**⟩ ● *vt*
rinviare ⟨matter⟩ (**to** a); indirizzare
⟨person⟩ ● *vi* ~ **to** fare allusione a;
⟨consult⟩ rivolgersi a ⟨book⟩
referee /refə'ri:/ *n* arbitro *m*; ⟨for job⟩
garante *mf* ● *vt/i* ⟨pt/pp **refereed**⟩ arbitrare
reference /'refərəns/ *n* riferimento *m*;
⟨in book⟩ nota *f* bibliografica; ⟨for job⟩
referenza *f*; *Comm* '**your** ~' 'riferimento'; **with** ~ **to** con riferimento a; **make**
[**a**] ~ **to** fare riferimento a. ~ **book** *n*
libro *m* di consultazione. ~ **number** *n*
numero *m* di riferimento
referendum /refə'rendəm/ *n* referendum *m inv*
re'fill[1] /ri:-/ *vt* riempire di nuovo;
ricaricare ⟨pen, lighter⟩
'**refill**[2] /ri:-/ *n* (for pen) ricambio *m*
refine /rɪ'faɪn/ *vt* raffinare. ~**d** *a* raffinato. ~**ment** *n* raffinatezza *f*; *Techn*
raffinazione *f*. ~**ry** /-ərɪ/ *n* raffineria *f*
reflect /rɪ'flekt/ *vt* riflettere; **be** ~**ed**
in essere riflesso in ● *vi* ⟨think⟩ riflettere (**on** su); ~ **badly on sb** *fig* mettere in
cattiva luce qcno. ~**ion** /-ekʃn/ *n* riflessione *f*; ⟨image⟩ riflesso *m*; **on** ~**ion**
dopo riflessione. ~**ive** /-ɪv/ *a* riflessivo.
~**or** *n* riflettore *m*
reflex /'ri:fleks/ *n* riflesso *m* ● *attrib* di
riflesso
reflexive /rɪ'fleksɪv/ *a* riflessivo
reform /rɪ'fɔ:m/ *n* riforma *f* ● *vt* riformare　● *vi* correggersi. **R**~**ation**
/refə'meɪʃn/ *n Relig* Riforma *f*. ~**er** *n* riformatore, -trice *mf*

refrain[1] /rɪ'freɪn/ *n* ritornello *m*
refrain[2] *vi* astenersi (**from** da)
refresh /rɪ'freʃ/ *vt* rinfrescare. ~**ing** *a*
rinfrescante. ~**ments** *npl* rinfreschi
mpl
refrigerat|e /rɪ'frɪdʒəreɪt/ *vt* conservare in frigo. ~**or** *n* frigorifero *m*
re'fuel /ri:-/ *v* ⟨pt/pp -**fuelled**⟩ ● *vt* rifornire ⟨di carburante⟩ ● *vi* fare rifornimento
refuge /'refju:dʒ/ *n* rifugio *m*; **take** ~
rifugiarsi
refugee /refjʊ'dʒi:/ *n* rifugiato, -a *mf*
'**refund**[1] /ri:-/ *n* rimborso *m*
re'fund[2] /rɪ-/ *vt* rimborsare
refurbish /ri:'fɜ:bɪʃ/ *vt* rimettere a
nuovo
refusal /rɪ'fju:zl/ *n* rifiuto *m*
refuse[1] /rɪ'fju:z/ *vt/i* rifiutare; ~ **to do**
sth rifiutare di fare qcsa
refuse[2] /'refju:s/ *n* rifiuti *mpl*. ~
collection *n* raccolta *f* dei rifiuti
refute /rɪ'fju:t/ *vt* confutare
re'gain /rɪ-/ *vt* riconquistare
regal /'ri:gl/ *a* regale
regalia /rɪ'geɪlɪə/ *npl* insegne *fpl* reali
regard /rɪ'ga:d/ *n* ⟨heed⟩ riguardo *m*;
⟨respect⟩ considerazione *f*; ~**s** *pl* saluti
mpl; **send/give my** ~**s to your**
brother salutami tuo fratello ● *vt*
⟨consider⟩ considerare (**as** come); **as**
~**s** riguardo a. ~**ing** *prep* riguardo a.
~**less** *adv* lo stesso; ~ **of** senza badare a
regatta /rɪ'gætə/ *n* regata *f*
regenerate /rɪ'dʒenəreɪt/ *vt*
rigenerare ● *vi* rigenerarsi
regime /reɪ'ʒi:m/ *n* regime *m*
regiment /'redʒɪmənt/ *n* reggimento
m. ~**al** /-'mentl/ *a* reggimentale.
~**ation** /-mən'teɪʃn/ *n* irreggimentazione *f*
region /'ri:dʒən/ *n* regione *f*; **in the** ~
of *fig* approssimativamente. ~**al** *a* regionale
register /'redʒɪstə(r)/ *n* registro *m* ● *vt*
registrare; mandare per raccomandata
⟨letter⟩; assicurare ⟨luggage⟩; immatricolare ⟨vehicle⟩; mostrare ⟨feeling⟩ ● *vi*
⟨instrument:⟩ funzionare; ⟨student:⟩
iscriversi (**for** a); ~ **with** iscriversi nella lista di ⟨doctor⟩
registrar /redʒɪ'strɑ:(r)/ *n* ufficiale *m*
di stato civile
registration /redʒɪ'streɪʃn/ *n* ⟨of
vehicle⟩ immatricolazione *f*; ⟨of letter⟩
raccomandazione *f*; ⟨of luggage⟩ assicurazione *f*; ⟨for course⟩ iscrizione *f*. ~
number *n Auto* [numero *m* di] targa *f*

registry office /'redʒɪstrɪ-/ n anagrafe f

regret /rɪ'gret/ n rammarico m ● vt (pt/pp **regretted**) rimpiangere; **I ~ that** mi rincresce che. **~fully** adv con rammarico

regrettab|le /rɪ'gretəbl/ a spiacevole. **~ly** adv spiacevolmente; (before adjective) deplorevolmente

regular /'regjʊlə(r)/ a regolare; (usual) abituale ● n cliente mf abituale. **~ity** /-'lærətɪ/ n regolarità f. **~ly** adv regolarmente

regulat|e /'regʊleɪt/ vt regolare. **~ion** /-'leɪʃn/ n (rule) regolamento m

rehabilitat|e /ri:hə'bɪlɪteɪt/ vt riabilitare. **~ion** /-'teɪʃn/ n riabilitazione f

rehears|al /rɪ'hɜ:sl/ n Theat prova f. **~e** vt/i provare

reign /reɪn/ n regno m ● vi regnare

reimburse /ri:ɪm'bɜ:s/ vt ~ **sb for sth** rimborsare qcsa a qcno

rein /reɪn/ n redine f

reincarnation /ri:ɪnkɑ:'neɪʃn/ n reincarnazione f

reinforce /ri:ɪn'fɔ:s/ vt rinforzare. **~d 'concrete** n cemento m armato. **~ment** n rinforzo m

reinstate /ri:ɪn'steɪt/ vt reintegrare

reiterate /ri:'ɪtəreɪt/ vt reiterare

reject /rɪ'dʒekt/ vt rifiutare. **~ion** /-ekʃn/ n rifiuto m; Med rigetto m

rejoic|e /rɪ'dʒɔɪs/ vi liter rallegrarsi. **~ing** n gioia f

rejuvenate /rɪ'dʒu:vəneɪt/ vt ringiovanire

relapse /rɪ'læps/ n ricaduta f ● vi ricadere

relate /rɪ'leɪt/ vt (tell) riportare; (connect) collegare ● vi ~ **to** riferirsi a; identificarsi con (person). **~d** a imparentato (to a); (ideas etc) affine

relation /rɪ'leɪʃn/ n rapporto m; (person) parente mf. **~ship** n rapporto m (blood tie) parentela f; (affair) relazione f

relative /'relətɪv/ n parente mf ● a relativo. **~ly** adv relativamente

relax /rɪ'læks/ vt rilassare; allentare (pace, grip) ● vi rilassarsi. **~ation** /ri:læk'seɪʃn/ n rilassamento m, relax m; (recreation) svago m. **~ing** a rilassante

relay¹ /ri:'leɪ/ vt (pt/pp **-layed**) ritrasmettere; Radio, TV trasmettere

relay² /'ri:leɪ/ n Electr relais m inv; **work in ~s** fare i turni. **~ [race]** n [corsa f a] staffetta f

release /rɪ'li:s/ n rilascio m; (of film) distribuzione f ● vt liberare; lasciare (hand); togliere (brake); distribuire (film); rilasciare (information etc)

relegate /'relɪgeɪt/ vt relegare; **be ~d** Sport essere retrocesso

relent /rɪ'lent/ vi cedere. **~less** a inflessibile; (unceasing) incessante. **~lessly** adv incessantemente

relevan|ce /'reləvəns/ n pertinenza f. **~t** a pertinente (to a)

reliab|ility /rɪlaɪə'bɪlətɪ/ n affidabilità f. **~le** /-'laɪəbl/ a affidabile. **~ly** adv in modo affidabile; **be ~ly informed** sapere da fonte certa

relian|ce /rɪ'laɪəns/ n fiducia f (on in). **~t** a fiducioso (on in)

relic /'relɪk/ n Relig reliquia f; **~s** pl resti mpl

relief /rɪ'li:f/ n sollievo m; (assistance) soccorso m; (distraction) diversivo m; (replacement) cambio m; (in art) rilievo m; **in ~** in rilievo. **~ map** n carta f in rilievo. **~ train** n treno m supplementare

relieve /rɪ'li:v/ vt alleviare; (take over from) dare il cambio a; **~ of** liberare da (burden)

religion /rɪ'lɪdʒən/ n religione f

religious /rɪ'lɪdʒəs/ a religioso. **~ly** adv (conscientiously) scrupolosamente

relinquish /rɪ'lɪŋkwɪʃ/ vt abbandonare; **~ sth to sb** rinunciare a qcsa in favore di qcno

relish /'relɪʃ/ n gusto m; Culin salsa f ● vt fig apprezzare

relo'cate /ri:-/ vt trasferire

reluctan|ce /rɪ'lʌktəns/ n riluttanza f. **~t** a riluttante. **~tly** adv a malincuore

rely /rɪ'laɪ/ vi (pt/pp **-ied**) **~ on** dipendere da; (trust) contare su

remain /rɪ'meɪn/ vi restare. **~der** n resto m. **~ing** a restante. **~s** npl resti mpl; (dead body) spoglie fpl

remand /rɪ'mɑ:nd/ n **on ~** in custodia cautelare ● vt **~ in custody** rinviare con detenzione provvisoria

remark /rɪ'mɑ:k/ n osservazione f ● vt osservare. **~able** /-əbl/ a notevole. **~ably** adv notevolmente

remarry /ri:-/ vi (pt/pp **-ied**) risposarsi

remedial /rɪ'mi:dɪəl/ a correttivo; Med curativo

remedy /'remədɪ/ n rimedio m (**for** contro) ● vt (pt/pp **-ied**) rimediare a

remember /rɪ'membə(r)/ vt ricordare,

ricordarsi; ~ **to do sth** ricordarsi di
fare qcsa; ~ **me to him** salutamelo ● *vi*
ricordarsi

remind /rɪˈmaɪnd/ *vt* ~ **sb of sth** ricordare qcsa a qcno. ~**er** *n* ricordo *m*;
(memo) promemoria *m inv*; *(letter)* lettera *f* di sollecito

reminisce /remɪˈnɪs/ *vi* rievocare il
passato. ~**nces** /-ˈənsɪz/ *npl* remini-
scenze *fpl*. ~**nt** *a* **be** ~**nt of** richiamare
alla memoria

remiss /rɪˈmɪs/ *a* negligente

remission /rɪˈmɪʃn/ *n* remissione *f*; *(of
sentence)* condono *m*

remit /rɪˈmɪt/ *vt* *(pt/pp remitted)* rimettere *(money)*. ~**tance** *n* rimessa *f*

remnant /ˈremnənt/ *n* resto *m*; *(of
material)* scampolo *m*; *(trace)* traccia *f*

remonstrate /ˈremənstreɪt/ *vi* fare
rimostranze **(with sb** a qcno)

remorse /rɪˈmɔːs/ *n* rimorso *m*. ~**ful** *a*
pieno di rimorso. ~**less** *a* spietato.
~**lessly** *adv* senza pietà

remote /rɪˈməʊt/ *a* remoto; *(slight)* minimo. ~ **access** *n Comput* accesso *m*
remoto. ~ **con'trol** *n* telecomando *m*.
~**-con'trolled** *a* telecomandato. ~**ly**
adv lontanamente; **be not** ~**ly...** non
essere lontanamente...

re'movable /rɪ-/ *a* rimovibile

removal /rɪˈmuːvl/ *n* rimozione *f*;
(from house) trasloco *m*. ~ **van** *n* camion *m inv* da trasloco

remove /rɪˈmuːv/ *vt* togliere; togliersi
(clothes); eliminare *(stain, doubts)*

remuneration /rɪmjuːnəˈreɪʃn/ *n* ri-
munerazione *f*. ~**ive** /-ˈmjuːnərətɪv/ *a*
rimunerativo

render /ˈrendə(r)/ *vt* rendere *(service)*

rendering /ˈrend(ə)rɪŋ/ *n Mus* interpretazione *f*

renegade /ˈrenɪɡeɪd/ *n* rinnegato, -a
mf

renew /rɪˈnjuː/ *vt* rinnovare *(contract)*.
~**al** *n* rinnovo *m*

renounce /rɪˈnaʊns/ *vt* rinunciare a

renovate /ˈrenəveɪt/ *vt* rinnovare.
~**ion** /-ˈveɪʃn/ *n* rinnovo *m*

renown /rɪˈnaʊn/ *n* fama *f*. ~**ed** *a* rinomato

rent /rent/ *n* affitto *m* ● *vt* affittare; ~
[out] dare in affitto. ~**al** *n* affitto *m*

renunciation /rɪnʌnsɪˈeɪʃn/ *n* rinuncia *f*

re'open /riː-/ *vt/i* riaprire

re'organize /riː-/ *vt* riorganizzare

rep /rep/ *n Comm fam* rappresentante
mf; *Theat* teatro *m* stabile

repair /rɪˈpeə(r)/ *n* riparazione *f*; **in
good/bad** ~ in buone/cattive condizioni ● *vt* riparare

repatriate /riːˈpætrɪeɪt/ *vt* rimpatria-
re. ~**ion** /-ˈeɪʃn/ *n* rimpatrio *m*

re'pay /riː-/ *vt* *(pt/pp -paid)* ripagare.
~**ment** *n* rimborso *m*

repeal /rɪˈpiːl/ *n* abrogazione *f* ● *vt*
abrogare

repeat /rɪˈpiːt/ *n TV* replica *f* ● *vt/i* ripetere; ~ **oneself** ripetersi. ~**ed** *a* ri-
petuto. ~**edly** *adv* ripetutamente

repel /rɪˈpel/ *vt* *(pt/pp repelled)* respingere; *fig* ripugnare. ~**lent** *a*
ripulsivo

repent /rɪˈpent/ *vi* pentirsi. ~**ance** *n*
pentimento *m*. ~**ant** *a* pentito

repercussions /riːpəˈkʌʃnz/ *npl* ri-
percussioni *fpl*

repertoire /ˈrepətwɑː(r)/ *n* reperto-
rio *m*

repetition /repɪˈtɪʃn/ *n* ripetizione *f*.
~**ive** /rɪˈpetɪtɪv/ *a* ripetitivo

re'place /rɪ-/ *vt* *(put back)* rimettere a
posto; *(take the place of)* sostituire; ~
sth with sth sostituire qcsa con qcsa.
~**ment** *n* sostituzione *f*; *(person)* sostituto, -a *mf*. ~**ment part** *n* pezzo *m* di ricambio

'replay /ˈriː-/ *n Sport* partita *f* ripetuta;
[action] ~ replay *m inv*

replenish /rɪˈplenɪʃ/ *vt* rifornire
(stocks); *(refill)* riempire di nuovo

replica /ˈreplɪkə/ *n* copia *f*

reply /rɪˈplaɪ/ *n* risposta *f* **(to** a) ● *vt/i*
(pt/pp replied) rispondere

report /rɪˈpɔːt/ *n* rapporto *m*; *TV, Radio*
servizio *m*; *Journ* cronaca *f*; *Sch* pagella
f; *(rumour)* diceria *f* ● *vt* riportare; ~
sb to the police denunciare qcno alla
polizia ● *vi* riportare; *(present oneself)*
presentarsi **(to** a). ~**edly** *adv* secondo
quanto si dice. ~**er** *n* cronista *mf*, reporter *mf inv*

repose /rɪˈpəʊz/ *n* riposo *m*

repos'sess /riː-/ *vt* riprendere possesso di

reprehensible /reprɪˈhensəbl/ *a* riprovevole

represent /reprɪˈzent/ *vt* rappresentare

representative /reprɪˈzentətɪv/ *a*
rappresentativo ● *n* rappresentante *mf*

repress /rɪˈpres/ *vt* reprimere. ~**ion**
/-eʃn/ *n* repressione *f*. ~**ive** /-ɪv/ *a* re-
pressivo

reprieve /rɪˈpriːv/ *n* commutazione *f*
della pena capitale; *(postponement)* so-

spensione *f* della pena capitale; *fig* tregua *f* ● *vt* sospendere la sentenza a; *fig* risparmiare

reprimand /'reprɪmɑːnd/ *n* rimprovero *m* ● *vt* rimproverare

'reprint[1] /ˈriː-/ *n* ristampa *f*

re'print[2] /riː-/ *vt* ristampare

reprisal /rɪˈpraɪzl/ *n* rappresaglia *f*; **in ~ for** per rappresaglia contro

reproach /rɪˈprəʊtʃ/ *n* ammonimento *m* ● *vt* ammonire. **~ful** *a* riprovevole. **~fully** *adv* con aria di rimprovero

repro'duc|e /riː-/ *vt* riprodurre ● *vi* riprodursi. **~tion** /-ˈdʌkʃn/ *n* riproduzione *f*. **~tive** /-ˈdʌktɪv/ *a* riproduttivo

reprove /rɪˈpruːv/ *vt* rimproverare

reptile /'reptaɪl/ *n* rettile *m*

republic /rɪˈpʌblɪk/ *n* repubblica *f*. **~an** *a* repubblicano ● *n* repubblicano, -a *mf*

repudiate /rɪˈpjuːdɪeɪt/ *vt* ripudiare; respingere ⟨*view, suggestion*⟩

repugnan|ce /rɪˈpʌgnəns/ *n* ripugnanza *f*. **~t** *a* ripugnante

repuls|ion /rɪˈpʌlʃn/ *n* repulsione *f*. **~ive** /-ɪv/ *a* ripugnante

reputable /'repjʊtəbl/ *a* affidabile

reputation /repjʊˈteɪʃn/ *n* reputazione *f*

repute /rɪˈpjuːt/ *n* reputazione *f*. **~d** /-ɪd/ *a* presunto; **he is ~d to be** si presume che sia. **~dly** *adv* presumibilmente

request /rɪˈkwest/ *n* richiesta *f* ● *vt* richiedere. **~ stop** *n* fermata *f* a richiesta

require /rɪˈkwaɪə(r)/ *vt* ⟨*need*⟩ necessitare di; ⟨*demand*⟩ esigere. **~d** *a* richiesto; **I am ~d to do** si esige che io faccia. **~ment** *n* esigenza *f*; ⟨*condition*⟩ requisito *m*

requisite /'rekwɪzɪt/ *a* necessario ● *n* **toilet/travel ~s** *pl* articoli *mpl* da toilette/viaggio

re'sale /riː-/ *n* rivendita *f*

rescue /'reskjuː/ *n* salvataggio *m* ● *vt* salvare. **~r** *n* salvatore, -trice *mf*

research /rɪˈsɜːtʃ/ *n* ricerca *f* ● *vt* fare ricerche su; *Journ* fare un'inchiesta su ● *vi* **~ into** fare ricerche su. **~er** *n* ricercatore, -trice *mf*

resem|blance /rɪˈzembləns/ *n* rassomiglianza *f*. **~ble** /-bl/ *vt* rassomigliare a

resent /rɪˈzent/ *vt* risentirsi per. **~ful** *a* pieno di risentimento. **~fully** *adv* con risentimento. **~ment** *n* risentimento *m*

reservation /rezəˈveɪʃn/ *n* ⟨*booking*⟩ prenotazione *f*; ⟨*doubt, enclosure*⟩ riserva *f*

reserve /rɪˈzɜːv/ *n* riserva *f*; ⟨*shyness*⟩ riserbo *m* ● *vt* riservare; riservarsi ⟨*right*⟩. **~d** *a* riservato

reservoir /'rezəvwɑː(r)/ *n* bacino *m* idrico

re'shape /riː-/ *vt* ristrutturare

re'shuffle /riː-/ *n Pol* rimpasto *m* ● *vt* *Pol* rimpastare

reside /rɪˈzaɪd/ *vi* risiedere

residence /'rezɪdəns/ *n* residenza *f*; ⟨*stay*⟩ soggiorno *m*. **~ permit** *n* permesso *m* di soggiorno

resident /'rezɪdənt/ *a* residente ● *n* residente *mf*. **~ial** /-ˈdenʃl/ *a* residenziale

residue /'rezɪdjuː/ *n* residuo *m*

resign /rɪˈzaɪn/ *vt* dimettersi da; **~ oneself to** rassegnarsi a ● *vi* dare le dimissioni. **~ation** /rezɪgˈneɪʃn/ *n* rassegnazione *f*; ⟨*from job*⟩ dimissioni *fpl*. **~ed** *a* rassegnato

resilient /rɪˈzɪlɪənt/ *a* elastico; *fig* con buone capacità di ripresa

resin /'rezɪn/ *n* resina *f*

resist /rɪˈzɪst/ *vt* resistere a ● *vi* resistere. **~ance** *n* resistenza *f*. **~ant** *a* resistente

resolut|e /'rezəluːt/ *a* risoluto. **~ely** *adv* con risolutezza. **~ion** /-ˈluːʃn/ *n* risolutezza *f*

resolve /rɪˈzɒlv/ *vt* **~ to do** decidere di fare

resonan|ce /'rezənəns/ *n* risonanza *f*. **~t** *a* risonante

resort /rɪˈzɔːt/ *n* ⟨*place*⟩ luogo *m* di villeggiatura; **as a last ~** come ultima risorsa ● *vi* **~ to** ricorrere a

resound /rɪˈzaʊnd/ *vi* risonare ⟨**with** di⟩. **~ing** *a* ⟨*success*⟩ risonante

resource /rɪˈsɔːs/ *n* **~s** *pl* risorse *fpl*. **~ful** *a* pieno di risorse; ⟨*solution*⟩ ingegnoso. **~fulness** *n* ingegnosità *f*

respect /rɪˈspekt/ *n* rispetto *m*; ⟨*aspect*⟩ aspetto *m*; **with ~ to** per quanto riguarda ● *vt* rispettare

respectability /rɪspektəˈbɪlətɪ/ *n* rispettabilità *f*

respect|able /rɪˈspektəbl/ *a* rispettabile. **~ably** *adv* rispettabilmente. **~ful** *a* rispettoso

respective /rɪˈspektɪv/ *a* rispettivo. **~ly** *adv* rispettivamente

respiration /respɪˈreɪʃn/ *n* respirazione *f*

respite /'respaɪt/ *n* respiro *m*

respond /rɪˈspɒnd/ *vi* rispondere; ⟨*react*⟩ reagire ⟨**to** a⟩; ⟨*patient:*⟩ rispondere ⟨**to** a⟩

response /rɪ'spɒns/ *n* risposta *f*;
⟨*reaction*⟩ reazione *f*

responsibility /rɪspɒnsɪ'bɪlətɪ/ *n* responsabilità *f inv*

responsib|le /rɪ'spɒnsəbl/ *a* respon-
sabile; ⟨*job*⟩ impegnativo

responsive /rɪ'spɒnsɪv/ *a* be ~
⟨*audience etc:*⟩ reagire; ⟨*brakes:*⟩ essere
sensibile

rest[1] /rest/ *n* riposo *m*; *Mus* pausa *f*;
have a ~ riposarsi ● *vt* riposare; ⟨*lean*⟩
appoggiare (**on** su); ⟨*place*⟩ appoggiare
● *vi* riposarsi; ⟨*elbows:*⟩ appoggiarsi;
⟨*hopes:*⟩ riposare

rest[2] *n* the ~ il resto; ⟨*people*⟩ gli altri
● *vi* it ~s with you sta a te

restaurant /'restərɒnt/ *n* ristorante
m. ~ **car** *n* vagone *m* ristorante

restful /'restfl/ *a* riposante

restive /'restɪv/ *a* irrequieto

restless /'restlɪs/ *a* nervoso

restoration /restə'reɪʃn/ *n* ⟨*of
building*⟩ restauro *m*

restore /rɪ'stɔ:(r)/ *vt* ristabilire; re-
staurare ⟨*building*⟩; ⟨*give back*⟩ restituire

restrain /rɪ'streɪn/ *vt* trattenere; ~
oneself controllarsi. **~ed** *a* controllato. ~**t** *n* restrizione *f*; ⟨*moderation*⟩ rite-
gno *m*

restrict /rɪ'strɪkt/ *vt* limitare; ~
oneself to limitarsi a. ~**ion** /-ɪkʃn/ *n*
limite *m*; ⟨*restraint*⟩ restrizione *f*. ~**ive**
/-ɪv/ *a* limitativo

'rest room *n Am* toilette *f inv*

result /rɪ'zʌlt/ *n* risultato *m*; **as a** ~ a
causa (**of** di) ● *vi* ~ **from** risultare da;
~ **in** portare a

resume /rɪ'zju:m/ *vt/i* riprendere

résumé /'rezjʊmeɪ/ *n* riassunto *m*; *Am*
curriculum vitae *m inv*

resumption /rɪ'zʌmpʃn/ *n* ripresa *f*

resurgence /rɪ'sɜ:dʒəns/ *n* rinascita *f*

resurrect /rezə'rekt/ *vt fig* risuscita-
re. ~**ion** /-ekʃn/ *n* the R~**ion** *Relig* la
Risurrezione

resuscitat|e /rɪ'sʌsɪteɪt/ *vt* riani-
mare. ~**ion** /-'teɪʃn/ *n* rianimazione *f*

retail /'ri:teɪl/ *n* vendita *f* al minuto *o* al
dettaglio ● *a & adv* al minuto ● *vt* vendere al minuto ● *vi* ~ **at** essere venduto
al pubblico al prezzo di. ~**er** *n* detta-
gliante *mf*

retain /rɪ'teɪn/ *vt* conservare; ⟨*hold
back*⟩ trattenere

retaliat|e /rɪ'tælɪeɪt/ *vi* vendicarsi.
~**ion** /-'eɪʃn/ *n* rappresaglia *f*; **in** ~**ion
for** per rappresaglia contro

retarded /rɪ'tɑ:dɪd/ *a* ritardato

retentive /rɪ'tentɪv/ *a* ⟨*memory*⟩ buono

rethink /ri:'θɪŋk/ *vt* (*pt/pp* **rethought**)
ripensare

reticen|ce /'retɪsəns/ *n* reticenza *f*. ~**t**
a reticente

retina /'retɪnə/ *n* retina *f*

retinue /'retɪnju:/ *n* seguito *m*

retire /rɪ'taɪə(r)/ *vi* andare in pensione;
⟨*withdraw*⟩ ritirarsi ● *vt* mandare in
pensione ⟨*employee*⟩. ~**d** *a* in pensione.
~**ment** *n* pensione *f*; **since my** ~**ment**
da quando sono andato in pensione

retiring /rɪ'taɪərɪŋ/ *a* riservato

retort /rɪ'tɔ:t/ *n* replica *f* ● *vt* ribattere

re'touch /ri:-/ *vt Phot* ritoccare

re'trace /rɪ-/ *vt* ripercorrere; ~ **one's
steps** ritornare sui propri passi

retract /rɪ'trækt/ *vt* ritirare; ritrattare
⟨*statement, evidence*⟩ ● *vi* ritrarsi

re'train /ri:-/ *vt* riqualificare ● *vi*
riqualificarsi

retreat /rɪ'tri:t/ *n* ritirata *f*; ⟨*place*⟩ ritiro *m* ● *vi* ritirarsi; *Mil* battere in ritirata

re'trial /ri:-/ *n* nuovo processo *m*

retribution /retrɪ'bju:ʃn/ *n* castigo *m*

retrieval /rɪ'tri:vəl/ *n* recupero *m*

retrieve /rɪ'tri:v/ *vt* recuperare

retrograde /'retrəɡreɪd/ *a* retrogrado

retrospect /'retrəspekt/ *n* **in** ~ guar-
dando indietro. ~**ive** /-'spektɪv/ *a* retro-
spettivo; ⟨*legislation*⟩ retroattivo ● *n* retrospettiva *f*

return /rɪ'tɜ:n/ *n* ritorno *m*; ⟨*giving
back*⟩ restituzione *f*; *Comm* profitto *m*;
⟨*ticket*⟩ biglietto *m* di andata e ritorno;
by ~ [**of post**] a stretto giro di posta; **in**
~ in cambio (**for** di); **many happy** ~**s!**
cento di questi giorni! ● *vi* ritornare
● *vt* ⟨*give back*⟩ restituire; ricambiare
⟨*affection, invitation*⟩; ⟨*put back*⟩ rimettere; ⟨*send back*⟩ mandare indietro;
⟨*elect*⟩ eleggere

return: ~ **flight** *n* volo *m* di andata e
ritorno. ~ **match** *n* rivincita *f*. ~ **ticket** *n* biglietto *m* di andata e ritorno

reunion /ri:'ju:njən/ *n* riunione *f*

reunite /ri:jʊ'naɪt/ *vt* riunire

re'us|able /ri:-/ *a* riutilizzabile. ~**e** *vt*
riutilizzare

rev /rev/ *n Auto, fam* giro *m* ⟨*di motore*⟩
● *v* (*pt/pp* **revved**) ~ [**up**] far andare su di giri ● *vi* andare su di giri

reveal /rɪ'vi:l/ *vt* rivelare; ⟨*dress:*⟩ scoprire. ~**ing** *a* rivelatore; ⟨*dress*⟩ osé *inv*

revel /'revl/ *vi* (*pt/pp* **revelled**) ~ **in
sth** godere di qcsa

revelation /revə'leɪʃn/ n rivelazione f
revelry /'revlrɪ/ n baldoria f
revenge /rɪ'vendʒ/ n vendetta f; Sport rivincita f; **take ~** vendicarsi ● vt vendicare
revenue /'revənju:/ n reddito m
reverberate /rɪ'vɜːbəreɪt/ vi riverberare
revere /rɪ'vɪə(r)/ vt riverire. **~nce** /'revərəns/ n riverenza f
Reverend /'revərənd/ a reverendo
reverent /'revərənt/ a riverente
reverse /rɪ'vɜːs/ a opposto; **in ~ order** in ordine inverso ● n contrario m; (back) rovescio m; Auto marcia m indietro ● vt invertire; **~ the car into the garage** entrare in garage a marcia indietro; **~ the charges** Teleph fare una telefonata a carico del destinatario ● vi Auto fare marcia indietro
revert /rɪ'vɜːt/ vi **~ to** tornare a
review /rɪ'vju:/ n (survey) rassegna f; (re-examination) riconsiderazione f; Mil rivista f; (of book, play) recensione f ● vt riesaminare ⟨situation⟩; Mil passare in rivista; recensire ⟨book, play⟩. **~er** n critico, -a mf
revile /rɪ'vaɪl/ vt ingiuriare
revis|e /rɪ'vaɪz/ vt rivedere; (for exam) ripassare. **~ion** /-'vɪʒn/ n revisione f; (for exam) ripasso m
revival /rɪ'vaɪvl/ n ritorno m; (of patient) recupero m; (from coma) risveglio m
revive /rɪ'vaɪv/ vt resuscitare; rianimare ⟨person⟩ ● vi riprendersi; ⟨person:⟩ rianimarsi
revoke /rɪ'vəʊk/ vt revocare
revolt /rɪ'vəʊlt/ n rivolta f ● vi ribellarsi ● vt rivoltare. **~ing** a rivoltante
revolution /revə'lu:ʃn/ n rivoluzione f; Auto **~s per minute** giri mpl al minuto. **~ary** /-ərɪ/ a & n rivoluzionario, -a mf. **~ize** vt rivoluzionare
revolve /rɪ'vɒlv/ vi ruotare; **~ around** girare intorno a
revolv|er /rɪ'vɒlvə(r)/ n rivoltella f, revolver m inv. **~ing** a ruotante
revue /rɪ'vju:/ n rivista f
revulsion /rɪ'vʌlʃn/ n ripulsione f
reward /rɪ'wɔːd/ n ricompensa f ● vt ricompensare. **~ing** a gratificante
re'write /ri:-/ vt (pt rewrote, pp rewritten) riscrivere
rhapsody /'ræpsədɪ/ n rapsodia f
rhetoric /'retərɪk/ n retorica f. **~al** /rɪ'tɒrɪkl/ a retorico

rheuma|tic /ru'mætɪk/ a reumatico. **~tism** /'ru:mətɪzm/ n reumatismo m
Rhine /raɪn/ n Reno m
rhinoceros /raɪ'nɒsərəs/ n rinoceronte m
rhubarb /'ru:bɑːb/ n rabarbaro m
rhyme /raɪm/ n rima f; (poem) filastrocca f ● vi rimare '
rhythm /'rɪðm/ n ritmo m. **~ic[al]** a ritmico. **~ically** adv con ritmo
rib /rɪb/ n costola f
ribald /'rɪbld/ a spinto
ribbon /'rɪbən/ n nastro m; **in ~s** a brandelli
rice /raɪs/ n riso m
rich /rɪtʃ/ a ricco; ⟨food⟩ pesante ● n **the ~** pl i ricchi; **~es** pl ricchezze fpl. **~ly** adv riccamente; ⟨deserve⟩ largamente
rickety /'rɪkɪtɪ/ a malfermo
ricochet /'rɪkəʃeɪ/ vi rimbalzare ● n rimbalzo m
rid /rɪd/ vt (pt/pp rid, pres p ridding) sbarazzare (**of** di); **get ~ of** sbarazzarsi di
riddance /'rɪdns/ n **good ~!** che liberazione!
ridden /'rɪdn/ see ride
riddle /'rɪdl/ n enigma m
riddled /'rɪdld/ a **~ with** crivellato di
ride /raɪd/ n (on horse) cavalcata f; (in vehicle) giro m; (journey) viaggio m; **take sb for a ~** fam prendere qcno in giro ● v (pt rode, pp ridden) ● vt montare ⟨horse⟩; andare su ⟨bicycle⟩ ● vi andare a cavallo; ⟨jockey, showjumper:⟩ cavalcare; ⟨cyclist:⟩ andare in bicicletta; (in vehicle) viaggiare. **~r** n cavallerizzo, -a mf; (in race) fantino m; (on bicycle) ciclista mf; (in document) postilla f
ridge /rɪdʒ/ n spigolo m; (on roof) punta f; (of mountain) cresta f
ridicule /'rɪdɪkjuːl/ n ridicolo m ● vt mettere in ridicolo
ridiculous /rɪ'dɪkjʊləs/ a ridicolo
riding /'raɪdɪŋ/ n equitazione f ● attrib d'equitazione
rife /raɪf/ a **be ~** essere diffuso; **~ with** pieno di
riff-raff /'rɪfræf/ n marmaglia f
rifle /'raɪfl/ n fucile m. **~-range** n tiro m al bersaglio ● vt **~ [through]** mettere a soqquadro
rift /rɪft/ n fessura f; fig frattura f
rig¹ /rɪg/ n equipaggiamento m; (at sea) piattaforma f [per trivellazioni subacquee] ● **rig out** vt (pt/pp rigged) equipaggiare. **rig up** vt allestire

rig[2] vt (pt/pp **rigged**) manovrare ⟨election⟩

right /raɪt/ a giusto; (not left) destro; **be ~** ⟨person:⟩ aver ragione; ⟨clock:⟩ essere giusto; **put ~** mettere all'ora ⟨clock⟩; correggere ⟨person⟩; rimediare a ⟨situation⟩; **that's ~!** proprio così! ● adv (correctly) bene; (not left) a destra; (directly) proprio; (completely) completamente; **~ away** immediatamente ● n giusto m; (not left) destra f; (what is due) diritto m; **on/to the ~** a destra; **be in the ~** essere nel giusto; **know ~ from wrong** distinguere il bene dal male; **by ~s** secondo giustizia; **the R~** Pol la destra ● vt raddrizzare; **a wrong** fig riparare a un torto. **~ angle** n angolo m retto

rightful /'raɪtfl/ a legittimo

right: ~-'handed a che usa la mano destra. **~-hand 'man** n fig braccio m destro

rightly /'raɪtlɪ/ adv giustamente

right: ~ of way n diritto m di transito; (path) passaggio m; Auto precedenza f. **~-'wing** a Pol di destra ● n Sport ala f destra

rigid /'rɪdʒɪd/ a rigido. **~ity** /-'dʒɪdətɪ/ n rigidità f

rigmarole /'rɪgmərəʊl/ n trafila f; (story) tiritera f

rigorous /'rɪgərəs/ a rigoroso

rile /raɪl/ vt fam irritare

rim /rɪm/ n bordo m; (of wheel) cerchione m

rind /raɪnd/ n (on fruit) scorza f; (on cheese) crosta f; (on bacon) cotenna f

ring[1] /rɪŋ/ n (circle) cerchio m; (on finger) anello m; (boxing) ring m inv; (for circus) pista f; **stand in a ~** essere in cerchio

ring[2] n suono m; **give sb a ~** Teleph dare un colpo di telefono a qcno ● v (pt **rang**, pp **rung**) ● vt suonare; **~ [up]** Teleph telefonare a ● vi suonare; Teleph **~ [up]** telefonare. **ring back** vt/i Teleph richiamare. **ring off** vi Teleph riattaccare

ring: ~leader n capobanda m. **~ road** n circonvallazione f

rink /rɪŋk/ n pista f di pattinaggio

rinse /rɪns/ n risciacquo m; (hair colour) cachet m inv ● vt sciacquare

riot /'raɪət/ n rissa f; (of colour) accozzaglia f; **~s** pl disordini mpl; **run ~** impazzare ● vi creare disordini. **~er** n dimostrante mf. **~ous** /-əs/ a sfrenato

rip /rɪp/ n strappo m ● vt (pt/pp **ripped**) strappare; **~ open** aprire con uno strappo. **rip off** vt fam fregare

ripe /raɪp/ a maturo; ⟨cheese⟩ stagionato

ripen /'raɪpn/ vi maturare; ⟨cheese:⟩ stagionarsi ● vt far maturare; stagionare ⟨cheese⟩

ripeness /'raɪpnɪs/ n maturità f

'rip-off n fam frode f

ripple /'rɪpl/ n increspatura f; (sound) mormorio m ●

rise /raɪz/ n (of sun) levata f; (fig: to fame, power) ascesa f; (increase) aumento m; **give ~ to** dare adito a ● vi (pt **rose**, pp **risen**) alzarsi; ⟨sun:⟩ sorgere; ⟨dough:⟩ lievitare; ⟨prices, water level:⟩ aumentare; (to power, position) arrivare (to a). **~r** n **early ~r** persona f mattiniera

rising /'raɪzɪŋ/ a ⟨sun⟩ levante; **~ generation** nuova generazione f ● n (revolt) sollevazione f

risk /rɪsk/ n rischio m; **at one's own ~** a proprio rischio e pericolo ● vt rischiare

risky /'rɪskɪ/ a (-ier, -iest) rischioso

risqué /'rɪskeɪ/ a spinto

rite /raɪt/ n rito m; **last ~s** estrema unzione f

ritual /'rɪtjʊəl/ a rituale ● n rituale m

rival /'raɪvl/ a rivale ● n rivale mf; **~s** pl Comm concorrenti mpl ● vt (pt/pp **rivalled**) rivaleggiare con. **~ry** n rivalità f inv; Comm concorrenza f

river /'rɪvə(r)/ n fiume m. **~-bed** n letto m del fiume

rivet /'rɪvɪt/ n rivetto m ● vt rivettare; **~ed by** fig inchiodato da

Riviera /rɪvɪ'eərə/ n **the Italian ~** la riviera ligure

road /rəʊd/ n strada f, via f; **be on the ~** viaggiare

road: ~-block n blocco m stradale. **~-hog** n fam pirata m della strada. **~-map** n carta f stradale. **~ safety** n sicurezza f sulle strade. **~ sense** n prudenza f (per strada). **~side** n bordo m della strada. **~-sign** cartello m stradale. **~way** n carreggiata f, corsia f. **~-works** npl lavori mpl stradali. **~worthy** a sicuro

roam /rəʊm/ vi girovagare

roar /rɔː(r)/ n ruggito m; **~s of laughter** scroscio msg di risa ● vi ruggire; ⟨lorry, thunder:⟩ rombare; **~ with laughter** ridere fragorosamente. **~ing** a **do a ~ing trade** fam fare affari d'oro

roast /rəʊst/ a arrosto; **~ pork** arrosto

m di maiale ● *n* arrosto *m* ● *vt* arrostire ⟨*meat*⟩ ● *vi* arrostirsi

rob /rɒb/ *vt* (*pt/pp* **robbed**) derubare (**of** di); svaligiare ⟨*bank*⟩. **~ber** *n* rapinatore *m*. **~bery** *n* rapina *f*

robe /rəʊb/ *n* tunica *f*; (*Am: bathrobe*) accappatoio *m*

robin /ˈrɒbɪn/ *n* pettirosso *m*

robot /ˈrəʊbɒt/ *n* robot *m inv*

robust /rəʊˈbʌst/ *a* robusto

rock¹ /rɒk/ *n* roccia *f*; (*in sea*) scoglio *m*; (*sweet*) zucchero *m* candito. **on the ~s** ⟨*ship*⟩ incagliato; ⟨*marriage*⟩ finito; ⟨*drink*⟩ con ghiaccio

rock² *vt* cullare ⟨*baby*⟩; (*shake*) far traballare; (*shock*) scuotere ● *vi* dondolarsi

rock³ *n Mus* rock *m*

rock-ˈbottom *a* bassissimo ● *n* livello *m* più basso

rockery /ˈrɒkərɪ/ *n* giardino *m* roccioso

rocket /ˈrɒkɪt/ *n* razzo ● *vi* salire alle stelle

rocking /ˈrɒkɪŋ/: **~-chair** *n* sedia *f* a dondolo. **~-horse** *n* cavallo *m* a dondolo

rocky /ˈrɒkɪ/ *a* (**-ier, -iest**) roccioso; *fig* traballante

rod /rɒd/ *n* bacchetta *f*; (*for fishing*) canna *f*

rode /rəʊd/ *see* ride

rodent /ˈrəʊdnt/ *n* roditore *m*

roe /rəʊ/ *n* (*pl* roe *or* roes) **~[-deer]** capriolo *m*

rogue /rəʊg/ *n* farabutto *m*

role /rəʊl/ *n* ruolo *m*

roll /rəʊl/ *n* rotolo *m*; (*bread*) panino *m*; (*list*) lista *f*; (*of ship, drum*) rullio *m* ● *vi* rotolare; **be ~ing in money** *fam* nuotare nell'oro ● *vt* spianare ⟨*lawn, pastry*⟩. **roll over** *vi* rigirarsi. **roll up** *vt* arrotolare; rimboccarsi ⟨*sleeves*⟩ ● *vi fam* arrivare

ˈroll-call *n* appello *m*

roller /ˈrəʊlə(r)/ *n* rullo *m*; (*for hair*) bigodino *m*. **~ blind** *n* tapparella *f*. **~-coaster** *n* montagne *fpl* russe. **~-skate** *n* pattino *m* a rotelle

ˈrolling-pin *n* mattarello *m*

Roman /ˈrəʊmən/ *a* romano ● *n* romano, -a *mf*. **Catholic** *a* cattolico ● *n* cattolico, -a *mf*

romance /rəʊˈmæns/ *n* (*love-affair*) storia *f* d'amore; (*book*) romanzo *m* rosa

Romania /rəʊˈmeɪnɪə/ *n* Romania *f*. **~n** *a* rumeno ● *n* rumeno, -a *mf*; (*language*) rumeno *m*

romantic /rəʊˈmæntɪk/ *a* romantico.

~ally *adv* romanticamente. **~ism** /-tɪsɪzm/ *n* romanticismo *m*

Rome /rəʊm/ *n* Roma *f*

romp /rɒmp/ *n* gioco *m* rumoroso ● *vi* giocare rumorosamente. **~ers** *npl* pagliaccetto *msg*

roof /ruːf/ *n* tetto *m*; (*of mouth*) palato *m* ● *vt* mettere un tetto su. **~-rack** *n* portabagagli *m inv*. **~-top** *n* tetto *m*

rook /rʊk/ *n* corvo *m*; (*in chess*) torre *f*

room /ruːm/ *n* stanza *f*; (*bedroom*) camera *f*; (*for functions*) sala *f*; (*space*) spazio *m*. **~y** *a* spazioso; ⟨*clothes*⟩ ampio

roost /ruːst/ *vi* appollaiarsi

root¹ /ruːt/ *n* radice *f*; **take ~** metter radici ● **root out** *vt fig* scovare

root² *vi* **~ about** grufolare; **~ for sb** *Am fam* fare il tifo per qcno

rope /rəʊp/ *n* corda *f*; **know the ~s** *fam* conoscere i trucchi del mestiere ● **rope in** *vt* coinvolgere

rosary /ˈrəʊzərɪ/ *n* rosario *m*

rose¹ /rəʊz/ *n* rosa *f*; (*of watering-can*) bocchetta *f*

rose² *see* rise

rosé /ˈrəʊzeɪ/ *n* [vino *m*] rosé *m inv*

rosemary /ˈrəʊzmərɪ/ *n* rosmarino *m*

rosette /rəʊˈzet/ *n* coccarda *f*

roster /ˈrɒstə(r)/ *n* tabella *f* dei turni

rostrum /ˈrɒstrəm/ *n* podio *m*

rosy /ˈrəʊzɪ/ *a* (**-ier, -iest**) roseo

rot /rɒt/ *n* marciume *m*; (*fam: nonsense*) sciocchezze *fpl* ● *vi* (*pt/pp* **rotted**) marcire

rota /ˈrəʊtə/ *n* tabella *f* dei turni

rotary /ˈrəʊtərɪ/ *a* rotante

rotat|e /rəʊˈteɪt/ *vt* far ruotare; avvicendare ⟨*crops*⟩ ● *vi* ruotare. **~ion** /-eɪʃn/ *n* rotazione *f*; **in ~ion** a turno

rote /rəʊt/ *n* **by ~** meccanicamente

rotten /ˈrɒtn/ *a* marcio; *fam* schifoso; ⟨*person*⟩ penoso

rotund /rəʊˈtʌnd/ *a* paffuto

rough /rʌf/ *a* (*not smooth*) ruvido; (*ground*) accidentato; (*behaviour*) rozzo; (*sport*) violento; (*area*) malfamato; (*crossing, time*) brutto; (*estimate*) approssimativo ● *adv* ⟨*play*⟩ grossolanamente; **sleep ~** dormire sotto i ponti ● *vt* **~ it** vivere senza confort. **rough out** *vt* abbozzare

roughage /ˈrʌfɪdʒ/ *n* fibre *fpl*

rough ˈdraft *n* abbozzo *m*

rough|ly /ˈrʌflɪ/ *adv* rozzamente; (*more or less*) pressappoco. **~ness** *n* ruvidità *f*; (*of behaviour*) rozzezza *f*

rough paper *n* carta *f* da brutta

roulette /ruːˈlet/ *n* roulette *f*

round /raʊnd/ a rotondo ● n tondo m;
(slice) fetta f; (of visits, drinks) giro m;
(of cõmpetition) partita f; (boxing) ripresa f, round m inv; **do one's ~s** (doctor:)
fare il giro delle visite ● prep intorno a;
open ~ the clock aperto ventiquat-
tr'ore ● adv **all ~** tutt'intorno; **ask sb
~** invitare qcno; **go/come ~ to** (a
friend etc) andare da; **turn/look ~** girarsi; **~ about** (approximately) intorno
a ● vt arrotondare; girare (corner).
round down vt arrotondare (per difetto). **round off** vt (end) terminare. **round
on** vt aggredire. **round up** vt radunare;
arrotondare (prices)

roundabout /'raʊndəbaʊt/ a indiretto
● n giostra f; (for traffic) rotonda f

round: **~ 'trip** n viaggio m di andata e
ritorno

rous|e /raʊz/ vt svegliare; risvegliare
(suspicion, interest). **~ing** a di incoraggiamento

route /ruːt/ n itinerario m; Naut, Aeron
rotta f; (of bus) percorso m

routine /ruː'tiːn/ a di routine ● n
routine f inv; Theat numero m

rov|e /rəʊv/ vi girovagare. **~ing** a
(reporter, ambassador) itinerante

row¹ /rəʊ/ n (line) fila f; **three years in
a ~** tre anni di fila

row² vi (in boat) remare

row³ /raʊ/ n fam (quarrel) litigata f;
(noise) baccano m ● vi fam litigare

rowdy /'raʊdɪ/ a (-ier, -iest) chiassoso

rowing boat /'rəʊɪŋ-/ n barca f a remi

royal /'rɔɪəl/ a reale

royalt|y /'rɔɪəltɪ/ n appartenenza f alla
famiglia reale; (persons) i membri della
famiglia reale. **~ies** npl (payments) diritti mpl d'autore

rpm abbr **revolutions per minute**

rub /rʌb/ n **give sth a ~** dare una
sfregata a qcsa ● vt (pt/pp rubbed)
sfregare. **rub in** vt **don't ~ it in** fam
non rigirare il coltello nella piaga. **rub
off** vt mandar via sfregando (stain);
(from blackboard) cancellare ● vi andar via; **~ off on** essere trasmesso a.
rub out vt cancellare

rubber /'rʌbə(r)/ n gomma f; (eraser)
gomma f [da cancellare]. **~ band** n elastico m. **~y** a gommoso

rubbish /'rʌbɪʃ/ n immondizie fpl;
(fam: nonsense) idiozie fpl; (fam: junk)
robaccia f ● vt fam fare a pezzi. **~ bin** n
pattumiera f. **~ dump** n discarica f;
(official) discarica f comunale

rubble /'rʌbl/ n macerie fpl

ruby /'ruːbɪ/ n rubino m ● attrib di ru-
bini; (lips) scarlatta

rucksack /'rʌksæk/ n zaino m

rudder /'rʌdə(r)/ n timone m

ruddy /'rʌdɪ/ a (-ier, -iest) rubicondo;
fam maledetto

rude /ruːd/ a scortese; (improper) spinto. **~ly** adv scortesemente. **~ness** n
scortesia f

rudiment /'ruːdɪmənt/ n **~s** pl rudimenti mpl. **~ary** /-'mentərɪ/ a rudimentale

rueful /'ruːfl/ a rassegnato

ruffian /'rʌfɪən/ n farabutto m

ruffle /'rʌfl/ n gala f ● vt scompigliare
(hair)

rug /rʌg/ n tappeto m; (blanket) coperta f

rugby /'rʌgbɪ/ n **~ [football]** rugby m

rugged /'rʌgɪd/ a (coastline) roccioso

ruin /'ruːɪn/ n rovina f; **in ~s** in rovina
● vt rovinare. **~ous** /-əs/ a estremamente costoso

rule /ruːl/ n regola f; (control) ordina-
mento m; (for measuring) metro m; **~s**
pl regolamento msg; **as a ~** generalmente ● vt governare; dominare (colony, behaviour); **~ that** stabilire che
● vi governare. **rule out** vt escludere

ruled /ruːld/ a (paper) a righe

ruler /'ruːlə(r)/ n capo m di Stato;
(sovereign) sovrano, -a mf; (measure)
righello m, regolo m

ruling /'ruːlɪŋ/ a (class) dirigente;
(party) di governo ● n decisione f

rum /rʌm/ n rum m inv

rumble /'rʌmbl/ n rombo m; (of
stomach) brontolio m ● vi rombare;
(stomach:) brontolare

rummage /'rʌmɪdʒ/ vi rovistare
(in/through in)

rummy /'rʌmɪ/ n ramino m

rumour /'ruːmə(r)/ n diceria f ● vt **it is
~ed that** si dice che

rump /rʌmp/ n natiche fpl. **~ steak** n
bistecca f di girello

rumpus /'rʌmpəs/ n fam baccano m

run /rʌn/ n (on foot) corsa f; (distance to
be covered) tragitto m; (outing) giro m;
Theat rappresentazioni fpl; (in skiing)
pista f; (Am: ladder) smagliatura f (in
calze); **at a ~** di corsa; **~ of bad luck**
periodo m sfortunato; **on the ~** in fuga;
have the ~ of avere a disposizione; **in
the long ~** a lungo termine ● v (pt ran,
pp run, pres p running) ● vi correre;
(river:) scorrere; (nose, makeup:) colare; (bus:) fare servizio; (play:) essere in
cartellone; (colours:) sbiadire; (in

election) presentarsi [come candidato] ● *vt* (*manage*) dirigere; tenere ⟨*house*⟩; (*drive*) dare un passaggio a; correre ⟨*risk*⟩; *Comput* lanciare; *Journ* pubblicare ⟨*article*⟩; (*pass*) far scorrere ⟨*eyes, hand*⟩; **~ a bath** far scorrere l'acqua per il bagno. **run across** *vt* (*meet, find*) imbattersi in. **run away** *vi* scappare [via]. **run down** *vi* scaricarsi; ⟨*clock:*⟩ scaricarsi; ⟨*stocks:*⟩ esaurirsi ● *vt Auto* investire; (*reduce*) esaurire; (*fam: criticize*) denigrare. **run in** *vi* entrare di corsa. **run into** *vi* (*meet*) imbattersi in; (*knock against*) urtare. **run off** *vi* andare via di corsa ● *vt* stampare ⟨*copies*⟩. **run out** *vi* uscire di corsa; ⟨*supplies, money:*⟩ esaurirsi; **~ out of** rimanere senza. **run over** *vi* correre; (*overflow*) traboccare ● *vt Auto* investire. **run through** *vi* scorrere. **run up** *vi* salire di corsa; (*towards*) arrivare di corsa ● *vt* accumulare ⟨*debts, bill*⟩; (*sew*) cucire

'runaway *n* fuggitivo, -a *mf*

run-'down *a* ⟨*area*⟩ in abbandono; ⟨*person*⟩ esaurito ● *n* analisi *f*

rung[1] /rʌŋ/ *n* (*of ladder*) piolo *m*

rung[2] *see* **ring**[2]

runner /'rʌnə(r)/ *n* podista *mf*; (*in race*) corridore, -trice *mf*; (*on sledge*) pattino *m*. **~ bean** *n* fagiolino *m*. **~-up** *n* secondo, -a *mf* classificato, -a

running /'rʌnɪŋ/ *a* in corsa; ⟨*water*⟩ corrente; **four times ~** quattro volte di

seguito ● *n* corsa *f*; (*management*) direzione *f*; **be in the ~** essere in lizza. **~ 'commentary** *n* cronaca *f*

runny /'rʌnɪ/ *a* semiliquido; **~ nose** naso che cola

run: ~-of-the-'mill *a* ordinario. **~-up** *n* *Sport* rincorsa *f*; **the ~-up to** il periodo precedente. **~way** *n* pista *f*

rupture /'rʌptʃə(r)/ *n* rottura *f*; *Med* ernia *f* ● *vt* rompere; **~ oneself** farsi venire l'ernia ● *vi* rompersi

rural /'rʊərəl/ *a* rurale

ruse /ruːz/ *n* astuzia *f*

rush[1] /rʌʃ/ *n* *Bot* giunco *m*

rush[2] *n* fretta *f*; **in a ~** di fretta ● *vi* precipitarsi ● *vt* far premura a;. **~ sb to hospital** trasportare qcno di corsa all'ospedale. **~-hour** *n* ora *f* di punta

rusk /rʌsk/ *n* biscotto *m*

Russia /'rʌʃə/ *n* Russia *f*. **~n** *a & n* russo, -a *mf*; (*language*) russo *m*

rust /rʌst/ *n* ruggine *f* ● *vi* arrugginirsi

rustic /'rʌstɪk/ *a* rustico

rustle /'rʌsl/ *vi* frusciare ● *vt* far frusciare; *Am* rubare ⟨*cattle*⟩. **rustle up** *vt fam* rimediare

'rustproof *a* a prova di ruggine

rusty /'rʌstɪ/ *a* (**-ier, -iest**) arrugginito

rut /rʌt/ *n* solco *m*; **in a ~** *fam* nella routine

ruthless /'ruːθlɪs/ *a* spietato. **~ness** *n* spietatezza *f*

rye /raɪ/ *n* segale *f*

Ss

sabbath /'sæbəθ/ *n* domenica *f*; (*Jewish*) sabato *m*

sabbatical /sə'bætɪkl/ *n* *Univ* anno *m* sabbatico

sabot|age /'sæbətɑːʒ/ *n* sabotaggio *m* ● *vt* sabotare. **~eur** /-'tɜː(r)/ *n* sabotatore, -trice *mf*

saccharin /'sækərɪn/ *n* saccarina *f*

sachet /'sæʃeɪ/ *n* bustina *f*; (*scented*) sacchetto *m* profumato

sack[1] /sæk/ *vt* (*plunder*) saccheggiare

sack[2] *n* sacco *m*; **get the ~** *fam* essere licenziato ● *vt fam* licenziare. **~ing** *n* tela *f* per sacchi; (*fam: dismissal*) licenziamento *m*

sacrament /'sækrəmənt/ *n* sacramento *m*

sacred /'seɪkrɪd/ *a* sacro

sacrifice /'sækrɪfaɪs/ *n* sacrificio *m* ● *vt* sacrificare

sacrilege /'sækrɪlɪdʒ/ *n* sacrilegio *m*

sad /sæd/ *a* (**sadder, saddest**) triste. **~den** *vt* rattristare

saddle /'sædl/ *n* sella *f* ● *vt* sellare; **I've been ~d with...** *fig* mi hanno affibbiato...

sadis|m /'seɪdɪzm/ *n* sadismo *m*. **~t** /-dɪst/ *n* sadico, -a *mf*. **~tic** /sə'dɪstɪk/ *a* sadico

sad|ly /'sædlɪ/ *adv* tristemente; (*unfor-*

tunately) sfortunatamente. **~ness** *n* tristezza *f*

safe /seif/ *a* sicuro; (*out of danger*) salvo; (*object*) al sicuro; **~ and sound** sano e salvo ● *n* cassaforte *f*. **~guard** *n* protezione *f* ● *vt* proteggere. **~ly** *adv* in modo sicuro; (*arrive*) senza incidenti; (*assume*) con certezza

safety /'seifti/ *n* sicurezza *f*. **~-belt** *n* cintura *f* di sicurezza. **~-deposit box** *n* cassetta *f* di sicurezza. **~-pin** *n* spilla *f* di sicurezza *o* da balia. **~-valve** *n* valvola *f* di sicurezza

sag /sæg/ *vi* (*pt/pp* **sagged**) abbassarsi

saga /'sɑːɡə/ *n* saga *f*

sage /seidʒ/ *n* (*herb*) salvia *f*

Sagittarius /sædʒi'teəriəs/ *n* Sagittario *m*

said /sed/ *see* **say**

sail /seil/ *n* vela *f*; (*trip*) giro *m* in barca a vela ● *vi* navigare; *Sport* praticare la vela; (*leave*) salpare ● *vt* pilotare

'sailboard *n* tavola *f* del windsurf. **~ing** *n* windsurf *m inv*

sailing /'seiliŋ/ *n* vela *f*. **~-boat** *n* barca *f* a vela. **~-ship** *n* veliero *m*

sailor /'seilə(r)/ *n* marinaio *m*

saint /seint/ *n* santo, -a *mf*. **~ly** *a* da santo

sake /seik/ *n* **for the ~ of** (*person*) per il bene di; (*peace*) per amor di; **for the ~ of it** per il gusto di farlo

salad /'sæləd/ *n* insalata *f*. **~ bowl** *n* insalatiera *f*. **~ cream** *n* salsa *f* per condire l'insalata. **~-dressing** *n* condimento *m* per insalata

salary /'sæləri/ *n* stipendio *m*

sale /seil/ *n* vendita *f*; (*at reduced prices*) svendita *f*; **for/on ~** in vendita. **'for ~'** 'vendesi'

sales|man /'seilzmən/ *n* venditore *m*; (*traveller*) rappresentante *m*. **~woman** *n* venditrice *f*

salient /'seiliənt/ *a* saliente

saliva /sə'laivə/ *n* saliva *f*

sallow /'sæləʊ/ *a* giallastro

salmon /'sæmən/ *n* salmone *m*

saloon /sə'luːn/ *n* *Auto* berlina *f*; (*Am: bar*) bar *m*

salt /sɔːlt/ *n* sale *m* ● *a* salato; (*fish, meat*) sotto sale ● *vt* salare; (*cure*) mettere sotto sale. **~-cellar** *n* saliera *f*. **~'water** *n* acqua *f* di mare. **~y** *a* salato

salutary /'sæljutəri/ *a* salutare

salute /sə'luːt/ *Mil n* saluto *m* ● *vt* salutare ● *vi* fare il saluto

salvage /'sælvidʒ/ *n* *Naut* recupero *m* ● *vt* recuperare

salvation /sæl'veiʃn/ *n* salvezza *f*. **S~ 'Army** *n* Esercito *m* della Salvezza

salvo /'sælvəʊ/ *n* salva *f*

same /seim/ *a* stesso (**as** di) ● *pron* **the ~** lo stesso; **be all the ~** essere tutti uguali ● *adv* **the ~** nello stesso modo; **all the ~** (*however*) lo stesso; **the ~ to you** altrettanto

sample /'sɑːmpl/ *n* campione *m* ● *vt* testare

sanatorium /sænə'tɔːriəm/ *n* casa *f* di cura

sanctimonious /sæŋkti'məʊniəs/ *a* moraleggiante

sanction /'sæŋkʃn/ *n* (*approval*) autorizzazione *f*; (*penalty*) sanzione *f* ● *vt* autorizzare

sanctity /'sæŋktəti/ *n* santità *f*

sanctuary /'sæŋktjʊəri/ *n Relig* santuario *m*; (*refuge*) asilo *m*; (*for wildlife*) riserva *f*

sand /sænd/ *n* sabbia *f* ● *vt* ~ [**down**] carteggiare

sandal /'sændl/ *n* sandalo *m*

sand: ~bank *n* banco *m* di sabbia. **~paper** *n* carta *f* vetrata ● *vt* cartavetrare. **~-pit** *n* recinto *m* contenente sabbia dove giocano i bambini

sandwich /'sænwidʒ/ *n* tramezzino *m* ● *vt* **~ed between** schiacciato tra

sandy /'sændi/ *a* (**-ier, -iest**) (*beach, soil*) sabbioso; (*hair*) biondiccio

sane /sein/ *a* (*not mad*) sano di mente; (*sensible*) sensato

sang /sæŋ/ *see* **sing**

sanitary /'sænitəri/ *a* igienico; (*system*) sanitario. **~ napkin** *n Am*, **~ towel** *n* assorbente *m* igienico

sanitation /sæni'teiʃn/ *n* impianti *mpl* igienici

sanity /'sænəti/ *n* sanità *f* di mente; (*common sense*) buon senso *m*

sank /sæŋk/ *see* **sink**

sapphire /'sæfaiə(r)/ *n* zaffiro *m* ● *attrib* blu zaffiro *inv*

sarcas|m /'sɑːkæzm/ *n* sarcasmo *m*. **~tic** /-'kæstik/ *a* sarcastico

sardine /sɑː'diːn/ *n* sardina *f*

Sardinia /sɑː'diniə/ *n* Sardegna *f*. **~n** *a* & *n* sardo, -a *mf*

sardonic /sɑː'dɒnik/ *a* sardonico

sash /sæʃ/ *n* fascia *f*; (*for dress*) fusciacca *f*

sat /sæt/ *see* **sit**

satanic /sə'tænik/ *a* satanico

satchel /'sætʃl/ *n* cartella *f*

satellite /'sætəlait/ *n* satellite *m*. **~**

dish n antenna f parabolica. **~ television** n televisione f via satellite

satin /'sætɪn/ n raso m ● attrib di raso

satire /'sætaɪə(r)/ n satira f

satirical /sə'tɪrɪkl/ a satirico

satir|ist /'sætɪrɪst/ n scrittore, -trice mf satirico, -a; (comedian) comico, -a mf satirico, -a. **~ize** vt satireggiare

satisfaction /sætɪs'fækʃn/ n soddisfazione f, be to sb's ~ soddisfare qcno

satisfactor|y /sætɪs'fæktərɪ/ a soddisfacente. **~ily** adv in modo soddisfacente

satisf|y /'sætɪsfaɪ/ vt (pp/pp -ied) soddisfare; (convince) convincere; **be ~ied** essere soddisfatto. **~ying** a soddisfacente

saturat|e /'sætʃəreɪt/ vt inzuppare (**with** di); Chem, fig saturare (**with** di). **~ed** a saturo

Saturday /'sætədeɪ/ n sabato m

sauce /sɔːs/ n salsa f; (cheek) impertinenza f. **~pan** n pentola f

saucer /'sɔːsə(r)/ n piattino m

saucy /'sɔːsɪ/ a (-ier, -iest) impertinente

Saudi Arabia /saʊdɪə'reɪbɪə/ n Arabia f Saudita

sauna /'sɔːnə/ n sauna f

saunter /'sɔːntə(r)/ vi andare a spasso

sausage /'sɒsɪdʒ/ n salsiccia f; (dried) salame m

savage /'sævɪdʒ/ a feroce; ⟨tribe, custom⟩ selvaggio ● n selvaggio, -a mf ● vt fare a pezzi. **~ry** n ferocia f

save /seɪv/ n Sport parata f ● vt salvare (**from** da); (keep, collect) tenere; risparmiare ⟨time, money⟩; (avoid) evitare; Sport parare ⟨goal⟩; Comput salvare, memorizzare ● vi ~ [**up**] risparmiare ● prep salvo

saver /'seɪvə(r)/ n risparmiatore, -trice mf

savings /'seɪvɪŋz/ npl (money) risparmi mpl. **~ account** n libretto m di risparmio. **~ bank** n cassa f di risparmio

saviour /'seɪvjə(r)/ n salvatore m

savour /'seɪvə(r)/ n sapore m ● vt assaporare. **~y** a salato; fig rispettabile

saw¹ /sɔː/ see **see¹**

saw² /sɔː/ n sega f ● vt/i (pt **sawed**, pp **sawn** or **sawed**) segare. **~dust** n segatura f

saxophone /'sæksəfəʊn/ n sassofono m

say /seɪ/ n have one's ~ dire la propria; **have a ~** avere voce in capitolo ● vt/i (pt/pp **said**) dire; **that is to ~** cioè; **that goes without ~ing** questo è ovvio; **when all is said and done** alla fine dei conti. **~ing** n proverbio m

scab /skæb/ n crosta f; pej crumiro m

scaffold /'skæfəld/ n patibolo m. **~ing** n impalcatura f

scald /skɔːld/ vt scottare; (milk) scaldare ● n scottatura f

scale¹ /skeɪl/ n (of fish) scaglia f

scale² n scala f; **on a grand ~** su vasta scale ● vt (climb) scalare. **scale down** vt diminuire

scales /skeɪlz/ npl (for weighing) bilancia fsg

scallop /'skɒləp/ n (shellfish) pettine m

scalp /skælp/ n cuoio m capelluto

scalpel /'skælpl/ n bisturi m inv

scam /skæm/ n fam fregatura f

scamper /'skæmpə(r)/ vi ~ **away** sgattaiolare via

scampi /'skæmpɪ/ npl scampi mpl

scan /skæn/ n Med scanning m inv, scansioscintigrafia f ● vt (pt/pp **scanned**) scrutare; (quickly) dare una scorsa a; Med fare uno scanning di

scandal /'skændl/ n scandalo m; (gossip) pettegolezzi mpl. **~ize** /-d(ə)laɪz/ vt scandalizzare. **~ous** /-əs/ a scandaloso

Scandinavia /skændɪ'neɪvɪə/ n Scandinavia f. **~n** a & n scandinavo, -a mf

scanner /'skænə(r)/ n Comput scanner m inv

scant /skænt/ a scarso

scant|y /'skæntɪ/ a (-ier, -iest) scarso; (clothing) succinto. **~ily** adv scarsamente; (clothed) succintamente

scapegoat /'skeɪp-/ n capro m espiatorio

scar /skɑː(r)/ n cicatrice f ● vt (pt/pp **scarred**) lasciare una cicatrice a

scarc|e /skeəs/ a scarso; fig raro; **make oneself ~e** fam svignarsela. **~ely** adv appena; **~ely anything** quasi niente. **~ity** n scarsezza f

scare /skeə(r)/ n spavento m; (panic) panico m ● vt spaventare; **be ~d** aver paura (**of** di)

'scarecrow n spaventapasseri m inv

scarf /skɑːf/ n (pl **scarves**) sciarpa f; (square) foulard m inv

scarlet /'skɑːlət/ a scarlatto. **~ 'fever** n scarlattina f

scary /'skeərɪ/ a **be ~** far paura

scathing /'skeɪðɪŋ/ a mordace

scatter /'skætə(r)/ vt spargere; (disperse) disperdere ● vi disperdersi. **~-brained** a fam scervellato. **~ed** a sparso

scatty /'skætɪ/ *a* (**-ier, -iest**) *fam* svitato

scavenge /'skævɪndʒ/ *vi* frugare nella spazzatura. **~r** *n persona f che fruga nella spazzatura*

scenario /sɪ'nɑːrɪəʊ/ *n* scenario *m*

scene /siːn/ *n* scena *f*; (*quarrel*) scenata *f*; **behind the ~s** dietro le quinte

scenery /'siːnərɪ/ *n* scenario *m*

scenic /'siːnɪk/ *a* panoramico

scent /sent/ *n* odore *m*; (*trail*) scia *f*; (*perfume*) profumo *m*. **~ed** *a* profumato (**with** di)

sceptic|al /'skeptɪkl/ *a* scettico. **~ism** /-tɪsɪzm/ *n* scetticismo *m*

schedule /'ʃedjuːl/ *n* piano *m*, programma *m*; (*of work*) programma *m*; (*timetable*) orario *m*; **behind ~** indietro; **on ~** nei tempi previsti; **according to ~** secondo i tempi previsti ● *vt* prevedere. **~d flight** *n* volo *m* di linea

scheme /skiːm/ *n* (*plan*) piano *m*; (*plot*) macchinazione *f* ● *vi pej* macchinare

schizophren|ia /skɪtsə'friːnɪə/ *n* schizofrenia *f*. **~ic** /-'frenɪk/ *a* schizofrenico

scholar /'skɒlə(r)/ *n* studioso, -a *mf*. **~ly** *a* erudito. **~ship** *n* erudizione *f*; (*grant*) borsa *f* di studio

school /skuːl/ *n* scuola *f*; (*in university*) facoltà *f*; (*of fish*) branco *m*

school: **~boy** *n* scolaro *m*. **~girl** *n* scolara *f*. **~ing** *n* istruzione *f*. **~-teacher** *n* insegnante *mf*

sciatica /saɪ'ætɪkə/ *n* sciatica *f*

scien|ce /'saɪəns/ *n* scienza *f*; **~ce fiction** fantascienza *f*. **~tific** /-'tɪfɪk/ *a* scientifico. **~tist** *n* scienziato, -a *mf*

scintillating /'sɪntɪleɪtɪŋ/ *a* brillante

scissors /'sɪzəz/ *npl* forbici *fpl*

scoff¹ /skɒf/ *vi* **~ at** schernire

scoff² *vt fam* divorare

scold /skəʊld/ *vt* sgridare. **~ing** *n* sgridata *f*

scone /skɒn/ *n pasticcino m da tè*

scoop /skuːp/ *n* paletta *f*; *Journ* scoop *m inv* ● **scoop out** *vt* svuotare. **scoop up** *vt* tirar su

scoot /skuːt/ *vi fam* filare. **~er** *n* motoretta *f*

scope /skəʊp/ *n* portata *f*; (*opportunity*) opportunità *f inv*

scorch /skɔːtʃ/ *vt* bruciare. **~er** *n fam* giornata *f* torrida. **~ing** *a* caldissimo

score /skɔː(r)/ *n* punteggio *m*; *Mus* partitura *f*; (*for film, play*) musica *f*; **a ~ [of]** (*twenty*) una ventina [di]; **keep [the] ~** tenere il punteggio; **on that ~** a questo proposito ● *vt* segnare ⟨*goal*⟩; (*cut*) incidere ● *vi* far punti; (*in football etc*) segnare; (*keep score*) tenere il punteggio. **~r** *n* segnapunti *m inv*; (*of goals*) giocatore, -trice *mf* che segna

scorn /skɔːn/ *n* disprezzo *m* ● *vt* disprezzare. **~ful** *a* sprezzante

Scorpio /'skɔːpɪəʊ/ *n Astr* Scorpione *m*

scorpion /'skɔːpɪən/ *n* scorpione *m*

Scot /skɒt/ *n* scozzese *mf*

Scotch /skɒtʃ/ *a* scozzese ● *n* (*whisky*) whisky *m* [scozzese]

scotch *vt* far cessare

scot-'free *a* **get off ~** cavarsela impunemente

Scot|land /'skɒtlənd/ *n* Scozia *f*. **~s, ~tish** *a* scozzese

scoundrel /'skaʊndrəl/ *n* mascalzone *m*

scour¹ /'skaʊə(r)/ *vt* (*search*) perlustrare

scour² *vt* (*clean*) strofinare

scourge /skɜːdʒ/ *n* flagello *m*

scout /skaʊt/ *n Mil* esploratore *m* ● *vi* **~ for** andare in cerca di

Scout *n* [**Boy**] **~** [boy]scout *m inv*

scowl /skaʊl/ *n* sguardo *m* torvo ● *vi* guardare [di] storto

Scrabble® /'skræbl/ *n* Scarabeo® *m*

scraggy /'skrægɪ/ *a* (**-ier, -iest**) *pej* scarno

scram /skræm/ *vi fam* levarsi dai piedi

scramble /'skræmbl/ *n* (*climb*) arrampicata *f* ● *vi* (*clamber*) arrampicarsi; **~ for** azzuffarsi per ● *vt Teleph* creare delle interferenze in; (*eggs*) strapazzare

scrap¹ /skræp/ *n* (*fam: fight*) litigio *m*

scrap² *n* pezzetto *m*; (*metal*) ferraglia *f*; **~s** *pl* (*of food*) avanzi *mpl* ● *vt* (*pt/pp* **scrapped**) buttare via

'scrap-book *n* album *m inv*

scrape /skreɪp/ *vt* raschiare; (*damage*) graffiare. **scrape through** *vi* passare per un pelo. **scrape together** *vt* racimolare

scraper /'skreɪpə(r)/ *n* raschietto *m*

scrappy /'skræpɪ/ *a* frammentario

'scrap-yard *n* deposito *m* di ferraglia; (*for cars*) cimitero *m* delle macchine

scratch /skrætʃ/ *n* graffio *m*; (*to relieve itch*) grattata *f*; **start from ~** partire da zero; **up to ~** (*work*) all'altezza ● *vt* graffiare; (*to relieve itch*) grattare ● *vi* grattarsi

scrawl /skrɔːl/ *n* scarabocchio *m* ● *vt/i* scarabocchiare

scrawny /'skrɔːnɪ/ *a* (**-ier, -iest**) *pej* magro

scream /skriːm/ n strillo m ● vt/i strillare

screech /skriːtʃ/ n stridore m ● vi stridere ● vt strillare

screen /skriːn/ n paravento m; Cinema, TV schermo m ● vt proteggere; (conceal) riparare; proiettare (film); (candidates) passare al setaccio; Med sottoporre a visita medica. **~ing** n Med visita f medica; (of film) proiezione f. **~play** n sceneggiatura f

screw /skruː/ n vite f ● vt avvitare. **screw up** vt (crumple) accartocciare; strizzare (eyes); storcere (face); (sl: bungle) mandare all'aria

'screwdriver n cacciavite m inv

screwy /'skruːɪ/ a (-ier, -iest) fam svitato

scribble /'skrɪbl/ n scarabocchio m ● vt/i scarabocchiare

script /skrɪpt/ n scrittura f (a mano); (of film) sceneggiatura f

'script-writer n sceneggiatore, -trice mf

scroll /skrəʊl/ n rotolo m (di pergamena); (decoration) voluta f

scrounge /skraʊndʒ/ vt/i scroccare. **~r** n scroccone, -a mf

scrub¹ /skrʌb/ n (land) boscaglia f

scrub² vt/i (pt/pp **scrubbed**) strofinare; (fam: cancel) cancellare (plan)

scruff /skrʌf/ n **by the ~ of the neck** per la collottola

scruffy /'skrʌfɪ/ a (-ier, -iest) trasandato

scrum /skrʌm/ n (in rugby) mischia f

scruple /'skruːpl/ n scrupolo m

scrupulous /'skruːpjʊləs/ a scrupoloso

scrutin|ize /'skruːtɪnaɪz/ vt scrutinare. **~y** n (look) esame m minuzioso

scuffle /'skʌfl/ n tafferuglio m

sculpt /skʌlpt/ vt/i scolpire. **~or** /'skʌlptə(r)/ n scultore m. **~ure** /-tʃə(r)/ n scultura f

scum /skʌm/ n schiuma f; (people) feccia f

scurrilous /'skʌrɪləs/ a scurrile

scurry /'skʌrɪ/ vi (pt/pp **-ied**) affrettare il passo

scuttle /'skʌtl/ vi (hurry) **~ away** correre via

sea /siː/ n mare m; **at ~** in mare; fig confuso; **by ~** via mare. **~board** n costiera f. **~food** n frutti mpl di mare. **~gull** n gabbiano m

seal¹ /siːl/ n Zool foca f

seal² n sigillo m; Techn chiusura f ermetica ● vt sigillare; Techn chiudere ermeticamente. **seal off** vt bloccare (area)

'sea-level n livello m del mare

seam /siːm/ n cucitura f; (of coal) strato m

'seaman n marinaio m

seamless /'siːmlɪs/ a senza cucitura

seamy /'siːmɪ/ a sordido; (area) malfamato

seance /'seɪɑːns/ n seduta f spiritica

sea: ~plane n idrovolante m. **~port** n porto m di mare

search /sɜːtʃ/ n ricerca f; (official) perquisizione f; **in ~ of** alla ricerca di ● vt frugare (for alla ricerca di); perlustrare (area); (officially) perquisire ● vi **~ for** cercare. **~ing** a penetrante

search: ~light n riflettore m. **~party** n squadra f di ricerca

sea: ~sick a **be/get ~** avere il mal di mare. **~side** n **at/to the ~side** al mare. **~side resort** n stazione f balneare. **~side town** n città f di mare

season /'siːzn/ n stagione f ● vt (flavour) condire. **~able**, **~al** /-əbl/ a, stagionale. **~ing** n condimento m

'season ticket n abbonamento m

seat /siːt/ n (chair) sedia f; (in car) sedile m; (place to sit) posto m [a sedere]; (bottom) didietro m; (of government) sede f; **take a ~** sedersi ● vt mettere a sedere; (have seats for) aver posti [a sedere] per; **remain ~ed** mantenere il proprio posto. **~-belt** n cintura f di sicurezza

sea: ~weed n alga f marina. **~worthy** a in stato di navigare

secateurs /sekə'tɜːz/ npl cesoie fpl

seclu|ded /sɪ'kluːdɪd/ a appartato. **~sion** /-ʒn/ n isolamento m

second¹ /sɪ'kɒnd/ vt (transfer) distaccare

second² /'sekənd/ a secondo; **on ~ thoughts** ripensandoci meglio ● n secondo m; **~s** pl (goods) merce fsg di seconda scelta; **have ~s** (at meal) fare il bis; **John the S~** Giovanni Secondo ● adv (in race) al secondo posto ● vt assistere; appoggiare (proposal)

secondary /'sekəndrɪ/ a secondario. **~ school** n scuola f media (inferiore e superiore)

second: ~-best a secondo dopo il migliore; **be ~-best** pej essere un ripiego. **~ class** adv (travel, send) in seconda classe. **~-class** a di seconda classe

'second hand n (on clock) lancetta f dei secondi

second-'hand *a & adv* di seconda mano

secondly /'sekəndlɪ/ *adv* in secondo luogo

second-'rate *a* di second'ordine

secrecy /'si:krəsɪ/ *n* segretezza *f*; **in** ~ in segreto

secret /'si:krɪt/ *a* segreto ● *n* segreto *m*

secretarial /sekrə'teərɪəl/ *a* ⟨*work, staff*⟩ di segreteria

secretary /'sekrətərɪ/ *n* segretario, -a *mf*

secret|e /sɪ'kri:t/ *vt* secernere ⟨*poison*⟩. **~ion** /-i:ʃn/ *n* secrezione *f*

secretive /'si:krətɪv/ *a* riservato. **~ness** *n* riserbo *m*

secretly /'si:krɪtlɪ/ *adv* segretamente

sect /sekt/ *n* setta *f*. **~arian** *a* settario

section /'sekʃn/ *n* sezione *f*

sector /'sektə(r)/ *n* settore *m*

secular /'sekjʊlə(r)/ *a* secolare; ⟨*education*⟩ laico

secure /sɪ'kjʊə(r)/ *a* sicuro ● *vt* proteggere; chiudere bene ⟨*door*⟩; rendere stabile ⟨*ladder*⟩; ⟨*obtain*⟩ assicurarsi. **~ly** *adv* saldamente

securit|y /sɪ'kjʊərətɪ/ *n* sicurezza *f*; (*for loan*) garanzia *f*. **~ies** *npl* titoli *mpl*

sedate¹ /sɪ'deɪt/ *a* posato

sedate² *vt* somministrare sedativi a

sedation /sɪ'deɪʃn/ *n* somministrazione *f* di sedativi; **be under** ~ essere sotto l'effetto di sedativi

sedative /'sedətɪv/ *a* sedativo ● *n* sedativo *m*

sedentary /'sedəntərɪ/ *a* sedentario

sediment /'sedɪmənt/ *n* sedimento *m*

seduce /sɪ'dju:s/ *vt* sedurre

seduct|ion /sɪ'dʌkʃn/ *n* seduzione *f*. **~ive** /-tɪv/ *a* seducente

see /si:/ *v* (*pt* **saw**, *pp* **seen**) ● *vt* vedere; (*understand*) capire; (*escort*) accompagnare; **go and** ~ andare a vedere; (*visit*) andare a trovare; ~ **you!** ci vediamo!; ~ **you later!** a più tardi!; **~ing that** visto che ● *vi* vedere; (*understand*) capire; ~ **that** ⟨*make sure*⟩ assicurarsi che; ~ **about** occuparsi di. **see off** *vt* veder partire; ⟨*chase away*⟩ mandar via. **see through** *vi* vedere attraverso; *fig* non farsi ingannare da ● *vt* portare a buon fine. **see to** *vi* occuparsi di

seed /si:d/ *n* seme *m*; *Tennis* testa *f* di serie; **go to** ~ fare seme; *fig* lasciarsi andare. **~ed player** *n Tennis* testa *f* di serie. **~ling** *n* pianticella *f*

seedy /'si:dɪ/ *a* (**-ier, -iest**) squallido

seek /si:k/ *vt* (*pt/pp* **sought**) cercare

seem /si:m/ *vi* sembrare. **~ingly** *adv* apparentemente

seen /si:n/ *see* **see¹**

seep /si:p/ *vi* filtrare

see-saw /'si:sɔ:/ *n* altalena *f*

seethe /si:ð/ *vi* ~ **with anger** ribollire di rabbia

'see-through *a* trasparente

segment /'segmənt/ *n* segmento *m*; (*of orange*) spicchio *m*

segregat|e /'segrɪgeɪt/ *vt* segregare. **~ion** /-'geɪʃn/ *n* segregazione *f*

seize /si:z/ *vt* afferrare; *Jur* confiscare. **seize up** *vi Techn* bloccarsi

seizure /'si:ʒə(r)/ *n Jur* confisca *f*; *Med* colpo *m* [apoplettico]

seldom /'seldəm/ *adv* raramente

select /sɪ'lekt/ *a* scelto; (*exclusive*) esclusivo ● *vt* scegliere; selezionare ⟨*team*⟩. **~ion** /-ekʃn/ *n* selezione *f*. **~ive** /-ɪv/ *a* selettivo. **~or** *n Sport* selezionatore, -trice *mf*

self /self/ *n* io *m*

self: **~-ad'dressed** *a* con il proprio indirizzo. **~-ad'hesive** *a* autoadesivo. **~-as'surance** *n* sicurezza *f* di sé. **~-as'sured** *a* sicuro di sé. **~-'catering** *a* in appartamento attrezzato di cucina. **~-'centred** *a* egocentrico. **~-'confidence** *n* fiducia *f* in se stesso. **~-'confident** *a* sicuro di sé. **~-'conscious** *a* impacciato. **~-con'tained** *a* ⟨*flat*⟩ con ingresso indipendente. **~-con'trol** *n* autocontrollo *m*. **~-de'fence** *n* autodifesa *f*; *Jur* legittima difesa *f*. **~-de'nial** *n* abnegazione *f*. **~-determi'nation** *n* autodeterminazione *f*. **~-em'ployed** *a* che lavora in proprio. **~-e'steem** *n* stima *f* di sé. **~-'evident** *a* ovvio. **~-'governing** *a* autonomo. **~-'help** *n* iniziativa *f* personale. **~-in'dulgent** *a* indulgente con se stesso. **~-'interest** *n* interesse *m* personale

self|ish /'selfɪʃ/ *a* egoista. **~ishness** *n* egoismo *m*. **~less** *a* disinteressato

self: **~-made** *a* che si è fatto da sé. **~-pity** *n* autocommiserazione *f*. **~-'portrait** *n* autoritratto *m*. **~-pos'sessed** *a* padrone di sé. **~-preser'vation** *n* istinto *m* di conservazione. **~-re'spect** *n* amor *m* proprio. **~-'righteous** *a* presuntuoso. **~-'sacrifice** *n* abnegazione *f*. **~-'satisfied** *a* compiaciuto di sé. **~-'service** *n* self-service *m inv* ● *attrib*

self-service. **~-sufficient** *a* autosuffi-
ciente. **~-'willed** *a* ostinato

sell /sel/ *v* (*pt/pp* **sold**) ● *vt* vendere; **be
sold out** essere esaurito ● *vi* vendersi.
sell off *vt* liquidare

seller /'selə(r)/ *n* venditore, -trice *mf*

Sellotape® /'seləʊ-/ *n* nastro *m* adesivo, scotch® *m*

'sell-out *n* ⟨*fam: betrayal*⟩ tradimento
m; **be a ~** ⟨*concert:*⟩ fare il tutto esaurito

selves /selvz/ *pl of* **self**

semblance /'sembləns/ *n* parvenza *f*

semen /'si:mən/ *n* Anat liquido *m* se-
minale

semester /sɪ'mestə(r)/ *n* Am semestre *m*

semi /'semɪ/: **~breve** /'semɪbri:v/ *n*
semibreve *f*. **~circle** /'semɪsɜːk(ə)l/ *n*
semicerchio *m*. **~'circular** *a* semi-
circolare. **~'colon** *n* punto e virgola *m*.
~-de'tached *a* gemella ● *n* casa *f* gemella. **~'final** *n* semifinale *f*

seminar /'semɪnɑː(r)/ *n* seminario *m*.
~y /-nərɪ/ *n* seminario *m*

semolina /semə'li:nə/ *n* semolino *m*

senat|e /'senət/ *n* senato *m*. **~or** *n* se-
natore *m*

send /send/ *vt/i* (*pt/pp* **sent**) mandare;
~ for mandare a chiamare ⟨*person*⟩; far
venire ⟨*thing*⟩. **~er** *n* mittente *mf*. **~-off**
n commiato *m*

senil|e /'si:naɪl/ *a* arteriosclerotico, Med
senile. **~ity** /sɪ'nɪlətɪ/ *n* senilismo *m*

senior /'si:nɪə(r)/ *a* più vecchio; (*in
rank*) superiore ● *n* (*in rank*) superiore
mf; (*in sport*) senior *mf*; **she's two
years my ~** è più vecchia di me di due
anni. **~ 'citizen** *n* anziano, -a *mf*

seniority /si:nɪ'ɒrətɪ/ *n* anzianità *f* di
servizio

sensation /sen'seɪʃn/ *n* sensazione *f*.
~al *a* sensazionale. **~ally** *adv* in modo
sensazionale

sense /sens/ *n* senso *m*; (*common .~*)
buon senso *m*; **in a ~** in un certo senso;
make ~ aver senso ● *vt* sentire. **~less**
a insensato; (*unconscious*) privo di sensi

sensibl|e /'sensəbl/ *a* sensato;
(*suitable*) appropriato. **~y** *adv* in modo
appropriato

sensitiv|e /'sensətɪv/ *a* sensibile;
(*touchy*) suscettibile. **~ely** *adv* con sensibilità. **~ity** /-'tɪvɪtɪ/ *n* sensibilità *f inv*

sensory /'sensərɪ/ *a* sensoriale

sensual /'sensjʊəl/ *a* sensuale. **~ity**
/-'ælətɪ/ *n* sensualità *f inv*

sensuous /'sensjʊəs/ *a* voluttuoso

sent /sent/ *see* **send**

sentence /'sentəns/ *n* frase *f*; Jur sentenza *f*; (*punishment*) condanna *f* ● *vt* **~
to** condannare a

sentiment /'sentɪmənt/ *n* sentimento
m; (*opinion*) opinione *f*; (*sentimentality*)
sentimentalismo *m*. **~al** /-'mentl/ *a* sen-
timentale; *pej* sentimentalista. **~ality**
/-'tælətɪ/ *n* sentimentalità *f inv*

sentry /'sentrɪ/ *n* sentinella *f*

separable /'sepərəbl/ *a* separabile

separate¹ /'sepərət/ *a* separato. **~ly**
adv separatamente

separat|e² /'sepəreɪt/ *vt* separare ● *vi*
separarsi. **~ion** /-'reɪʃn/ *n* separazione *f*

September /sep'tembə(r)/ *n* settem-
bre *m*

septic /'septɪk/ *a* settico; **go ~** infettarsi. **~ tank** *n* fossa *f* biologica

sequel /'si:kwəl/ *n* seguito *m*

sequence /'si:kwəns/ *n* sequenza *f*

sequin /'si:kwɪn/ *n* lustrino *m*,
paillette *f inv*

serenade /serə'neɪd/ *n* serenata *f* ● *vt*
fare una serenata a

seren|e /sɪ'ri:n/ *a* sereno. **~ity**
/-'renətɪ/ *n* serenità *f inv*

sergeant /'sɑːdʒənt/ *n* sergente *m*

serial /'sɪərɪəl/ *n* racconto *m* a puntate;
TV sceneggiato *m* a puntate; *Radio* commedia *f* radiofonica a puntate. **~ize** *vt*
pubblicare a puntate; *Radio, TV* trasmettere a puntate. **~ killer** *n* serial killer *mf inv*. **~ number** *n* numero *m* di serie. **~ port** *n* Comput porta *f* seriale

series /'sɪəriːz/ *n* serie *f inv*

serious /'sɪərɪəs/ *a* serio; ⟨*illness,
error*⟩ grave. **~ly** *adv* seriamente; ⟨*ill*⟩
gravemente; **take ~ly** prendere sul serio. **~ness** *n* serietà *f*; (*of situation*) gravità *f*

sermon /'sɜːmən/ *n* predica *f*

serpent /'sɜːpənt/ *n* serpente *m*

serrated /se'reɪtɪd/ *a* dentellato

serum /'sɪərəm/ *n* siero *m*

servant /'sɜːvənt/ *n* domestico, -a *mf*

serve /sɜːv/ *n* Tennis servizio *m* ● *vt*
servire; scontare ⟨*sentence*⟩; **~ its
purpose** servire al proprio scopo; **it
~s you right!** ben ti sta!; **~s two** per
due persone ● *vi* prestare servizio; *Tennis* servire; **~ as** servire da

server /'sɜːvə(r)/ *n* Comput server *m
inv*

service /'sɜːvɪs/ *n* servizio *m*; Relig
funzione *f*; (*maintenance*) revisione *f*;
~s *pl* forze *fpl* armate; (*on motorway*)
area *f* di servizio; **in the ~s** sotto le
armi; **of ~ to** utile a; **out of ~**

⟨*machine:*⟩ guasto ● *vt Techn* revisionare. **~able** /-əbl/ *a* utilizzabile; ⟨*hardwearing*⟩ resistente; ⟨*practical*⟩ pratico

service: **~ area** *n* area *f* di servizio. **~ charge** *n* servizio *m*. **~man** *n* militare *m*. **~ provider** *n* fornitore, -trice *mf* di servizi. **~ station** *n* stazione *f* di servizio

serviette /sɜ:vɪ'et/ *n* tovagliolo *m*

servile /'sɜ:vaɪl/ *a* servile

session /'seʃn/ *n* seduta *f*; *Jur* sessione *f*; *Univ* anno *m* accademico

set /set/ *n* serie *f* inv, set *m* inv; ⟨*of crockery, cutlery*⟩ servizio *m*; *T.V, Radio* apparecchio *m*; *Math* insieme *m*; *Theat* scenario *m*; *Cinema, Tennis* set *m* inv; ⟨*of people*⟩ circolo *m*; ⟨*of hair*⟩ messa *f* in piega ● *a* ⟨*ready*⟩ pronto; ⟨*rigid*⟩ fisso; ⟨*book*⟩ in programma; **be ~ on doing sth** essere risoluto a fare qcsa; **be ~ in one's ways** essere abitudinario ● *v* ⟨*pt/pp* **set**, *pres p* **setting**⟩ ● *vt* mettere, porre; mettere ⟨*alarm clock*⟩; assegnare ⟨*task, homework*⟩; fissare ⟨*date, limit*⟩; chiedere ⟨*questions*⟩; montare ⟨*gem*⟩; assestare ⟨*bone*⟩; apparecchiare ⟨*table*⟩; **~ fire to** dare fuoco a; **~ free** liberare ● *vi* ⟨*sun:*⟩ tramontare; ⟨*jelly, concrete:*⟩ solidificare; **~ about doing sth** mettersi a fare qcsa. **set back** *vt* mettere indietro; ⟨*hold up*⟩ ritardare; ⟨*fam: cost*⟩ costare a. **set off** *vi* partire ● *vt* avviare; mettere ⟨*alarm*⟩; fare esplodere ⟨*bomb*⟩. **set out** *vi* partire; **~ out to do sth** proporsi di fare qcsa ● *vt* disporre; ⟨*state*⟩ esporre. **set to** *vi* mettersi all'opera. **set up** *vt* fondare ⟨*company*⟩; istituire ⟨*committee*⟩

'set-back *n* passo *m* indietro

set 'meal *n* menù *m* inv fisso

settee /se'ti:/ *n* divano *m*

setting /'setɪŋ/ *n* scenario *m*; ⟨*position*⟩ posizione *f*; ⟨*of sun*⟩ tramonto *m*; ⟨*of jewel*⟩ montatura *f*

settle /'setl/ *vt* ⟨*decide*⟩ definire; risolvere ⟨*argument*⟩; fissare ⟨*date*⟩; calmare ⟨*nerves*⟩; saldare ⟨*bill*⟩ ● *vi* ⟨*to live*⟩ stabilirsi; ⟨*snow, dust, bird:*⟩ posarsi; ⟨*subside*⟩ assestarsi; ⟨*sediment:*⟩ depositarsi. **settle down** *vi* sistemarsi; ⟨*stop making noise*⟩ calmarsi. **settle for** *vt* accontentarsi di. **settle up** *vi* regolare i conti

settlement /'setlmənt/ *n* ⟨*agreement*⟩ accordo *m*; ⟨*of bill*⟩ saldo *m*; ⟨*colony*⟩ insediamento *m*

settler /'setlə(r)/ *n* colonizzatore, -trice *mf*

'set-to *n fam* zuffa *f*; ⟨*verbal*⟩ battibecco *m*

'set-up *n* situazione *f*

seven /'sevn/ *a* & *n* sette *m*. **~'teen** *a* & *n* diciassette *m*. **~'teenth** *a* & *n* diciassettesimo, -a *mf*

seventh /'sevnθ/ *a* & *n* settimo, -a *mf*

seventieth /'sevntɪιθ/ *a* & *n* settantesimo, -a *mf*

seventy /'sevntɪ/ *a* & *n* settanta *m*

sever /'sevə(r)/ *vt* troncare ⟨*relations*⟩

several /'sevrəl/ *a* & *pron* parecchi

sever|e /sɪ'vɪə(r)/ *a* severo; ⟨*pain*⟩ violento; ⟨*illness*⟩ grave; ⟨*winter*⟩ rigido. **~ely** *adv* severamente; ⟨*ill*⟩ gravemente. **~ity** /-'verətɪ/ *n* severità *f*; ⟨*of pain*⟩ violenza *f*; ⟨*of illness*⟩ gravità *f*; ⟨*of winter*⟩ rigore *m*

sew /səʊ/ *vt/i* ⟨*pt* **sewed**, *pp* **sewn** or **sewed**⟩ cucire. **sew up** *vt* ricucire

sewage /'su:ɪdʒ/ *n* acque *fpl* di scolo

sewer /'su:ə(r)/ *n* fogna *f*

sewing /'səʊɪŋ/ *n* cucito *m*; ⟨*work*⟩ lavoro *m* di cucito. **~ machine** *n* macchina *f* da cucire

sewn /səʊn/ *see* **sew**

sex /seks/ *n* sesso *m*; **have ~** avere rapporti sessuali. **~ist** *a* sessista. **~ offence** *n* delitto *m* a sfondo sessuale

sexual /'seksjʊəl/ *a* sessuale. **~ 'intercourse** *n* rapporti *mpl* sessuali. **~ity** /-'ælətɪ/ *n* sessualità *f*. **~ly** *adv* sessualmente

sexy /'seksɪ/ *a* (**-ier, -iest**) sexy inv

shabb|y /'ʃæbɪ/ *a* (**-ier, -iest**) scialbo; ⟨*treatment*⟩ mèschino. **~iness** *n* trasandatezza *f*; ⟨*of treatment*⟩ meschinità *f* inv

shack /ʃæk/ *n* catapecchia *f* ● **shack up with** *vt fam* vivere con

shade /ʃeɪd/ *n* ombra *f*; ⟨*of colour*⟩ sfumatura *f*; ⟨*for lamp*⟩ paralume *m*; ⟨*Am: for window*⟩ tapparella *f*; **a ~ better** un tantino meglio ● *vt* riparare dalla luce; ⟨*draw lines on*⟩ ombreggiare. **~s** *npl fam* occhiali *mpl* da sole

shadow /'ʃædəʊ/ *n* ombra *f*; **S~ Cabinet** governo *m* ombra ● *vt* ⟨*follow*⟩ pedinare. **~y** *a* ombroso

shady /'ʃeɪdɪ/ *a* (**-ier, -iest**) ombroso; ⟨*fam: disreputable*⟩ losco

shaft /ʃɑ:ft/ *n Techn* albero *m*; ⟨*of light*⟩ raggio *m*; ⟨*of lift, mine*⟩ pozzo *m*

shaggy /'ʃægɪ/ *a* (**-ier, -iest**) irsuto; ⟨*animal*⟩ dal pelo arruffato

shake /ʃeɪk/ *n* scrollata *f* ● *v* ⟨*pt* **shook**, *pp* **shaken**⟩ ● *vt* scuotere; agitare ⟨*bottle*⟩; far tremare ⟨*building*⟩; **~ hands with** stringere la mano a ● *vi* tremare. **shake off** *vt* scrollarsi di dosso. **~-up** n Pol rimpasto m; Comm ristrutturazione f

shaky /'ʃeɪkɪ/ a (**-ier**, **-iest**) tremante; ⟨table etc⟩ traballante; (unreliable) vacillante

shall /ʃæl/ v aux I **~ go** andrò; **we ~ see** vedremo; **what ~ I do?** cosa faccio?; **I'll come too, ~ I?** vengo anch'io, no?; **thou shalt not kill** liter non uccidere

shallow /'ʃæləʊ/ a basso, poco profondo; ⟨dish⟩ poco profondo; fig superficiale

sham /ʃæm/ a falso ● n finzione f, (person) spaccone, -a mf ● vt (pt/pp **shammed**) simulare

shambles /'ʃæmblz/ n baraonda fsg

shame /ʃeɪm/ n vergogna f; **it's a ~ that** è un peccato che; **what a ~!** che peccato! **~-faced** a vergognoso

shame|ful /'ʃeɪmfl/ a vergognoso. **~less** a spudorato

shampoo /ʃæm'puː/ n shampoo m inv ● vt fare uno shampoo a

shandy /'ʃændɪ/ n bevanda f a base di birra e gassosa

shan't /ʃɑːnt/ = **shall not**

shanty town /'ʃæntɪtaʊn/ n bidonville f inv, baraccopoli f inv

shape /ʃeɪp/ n forma f; (figure) ombra f; **take ~** prendere forma; **get back in ~** ritornare in forma ● vt dare forma a (into di) ● vi ~ **[up]** mettere la testa a posto; **~ up nicely** mettersi bene. **~less** a informe

shapely /'ʃeɪplɪ/ a (**-ier**, **-iest**) ben fatto

share /ʃeə(r)/ n porzione f; Comm azione f ● vt dividere; condividere ⟨views⟩ ● vi dividere. **~holder** n azionista mf

shark /ʃɑːk/ n squalo m, pescecane m; fig truffatore, -trice mf

sharp /ʃɑːp/ a ⟨knife etc⟩ tagliente; ⟨pencil⟩ appuntito; ⟨drop⟩ a picco; ⟨reprimand⟩ severo; ⟨outline⟩ marcato; ⟨alert⟩ acuto; (unscrupulous) senza scrupoli; **~ pain** fitta f ● adv in punto; Mus fuori tono; **look ~!** sbrigati! ● n Mus diesis m inv. **~en** vt affilare ⟨knife⟩; appuntire ⟨pencil⟩

shatter /'ʃætə(r)/ vt frantumare; fig mandare in frantumi; **~ed** (fam: exhausted) a pezzi ● vi frantumarsi

shav|e /ʃeɪv/ n rasatura f; **have a ~e** farsi la barba ● vt radere ● vi radersi. **~er** n rasoio m elettrico. **~ing-brush** n pennello m da barba; **~ing foam** n schiuma f da barba; **~ing soap** n sapone m da barba

shawl /ʃɔːl/ n scialle m

she /ʃiː/ pers pron lei

sheaf /ʃiːf/ n (pl **sheaves**) fascio m

shear /ʃɪə(r)/ vt (pt **sheared**, pp **shorn** or **sheared**) tosare

shears /ʃɪəz/ npl (for hedge) cesoie fpl

sheath /ʃiːθ/ n (pl **~s** /ʃiːðz/) guaina f

shed[1] /ʃed/ n baracca f; (for cattle) stalla f

shed[2] vt (pt/pp **shed**, pres p **shedding**) perdere; versare ⟨blood, tears⟩; **~ light on** far luce su

sheen /ʃiːn/ n lucentezza f

sheep /ʃiːp/ n inv pecora f. **~-dog** n cane m da pastore

sheepish /'ʃiːpɪʃ/ a imbarazzato. **~ly** adv con aria imbarazzata

'sheepskin n [pelle f di] montone m

sheer /ʃɪə(r)/ a puro; (steep) a picco; (transparent) trasparente ● adv a picco

sheet /ʃiːt/ n lenzuolo m; (of paper) foglio m; (of glass, metal) lastra f

shelf /ʃelf/ n (pl **shelves**) ripiano m; (set of shelves) scaffale m

shell /ʃel/ n conchiglia f; (of egg, snail, tortoise) guscio m; (of crab) corazza f; (of unfinished building) ossatura f; Mil granata f ● vt sgusciare ⟨peas⟩; Mil bombardare. **shell out** vi fam sborsare

'shellfish n inv mollusco m; Culin frutti mpl di mare

shelter /'ʃeltə(r)/ n rifugio m; (air raid ~) rifugio m antiaereo ● vt riparare (from da); fig mettere al riparo; (give lodging to) dare asilo a ● vi rifugiarsi. **~ed** a ⟨spot⟩ riparato; ⟨life⟩ ritirato

shelve /ʃelv/ vt accantonare ⟨project⟩

shelves /ʃelvz/ see **shelf**

shelving /'ʃelvɪŋ/ n (shelves) ripiani mpl

shepherd /'ʃepəd/ n pastore m ● vt guidare. **~'s pie** n pasticcio m di carne tritata e patate

sherry /'ʃerɪ/ n sherry m inv

shield /ʃiːld/ n scudo m; (for eyes) maschera f; Techn schermo m ● vt proteggere (from da)

shift /ʃɪft/ n cambiamento m; (in position) spostamento m; (at work) turno m ● vt spostare; (take away) togliere; riversare ⟨blame⟩ ● vi spostarsi; ⟨wind:⟩ cambiare; (fam: move quickly) darsi una mossa

'shift work n turni mpl

shifty /'ʃɪftɪ/ a (**-ier**, **-iest**) pej losco; ⟨eyes⟩ sfuggente

shilly-shally /'ʃɪlɪʃælɪ/ vi titubare

shimmer /'ʃɪmə(r)/ n luccichio m ● vi luccicare

shin /ʃɪn/ n stinco m

shine /ʃaɪn/ n lucentezza f; **give sth a ~** dare una lucidata a qcsa ● v ⟨pt/pp **shone**⟩ ● vi splendere; ⟨reflect light⟩ brillare; ⟨hair, shoes:⟩ essere lucido ● vt **~ a light on** puntare una luce su

shingle /'ʃɪŋgl/ n ⟨pebbles⟩ ghiaia f

shingles /'ʃɪŋglz/ n Med fuochi mpl di Sant'Antonio

shiny /'ʃaɪnɪ/ a ⟨-ier, -iest⟩ lucido

ship /ʃɪp/ n nave f ● vt ⟨pt/pp **shipped**⟩ spedire; ⟨by sea⟩ spedire via mare

ship: **~ment** n spedizione f; ⟨consignment⟩ carico m. **~per** n spedizioniere m. **~ping** n trasporto m; ⟨traffic⟩ imbarcazioni fpl. **~shape** a & adv in perfetto ordine. **~wreck** n naufragio m. **~wrecked** a naufragato. **~yard** n cantiere m navale

shirk /ʃɜːk/ vt scansare. **~er** n scansafatiche mf inv

shirt /ʃɜːt/ n camicia f; **in ~-sleeves** in maniche di camicia

shit /ʃɪt/ vulg n & int merda f ● vi ⟨pt/pp **shit**⟩ cagare

shiver /'ʃɪvə(r)/ n brivido m ● vi rabbrividire

shoal /ʃəʊl/ n ⟨of fish⟩ banco m

shock /ʃɒk/ n ⟨impact⟩ urto m; Electr scossa f [elettrica]; fig colpo m, shock m inv; Med shock m inv; **get a ~** Electr prendere la scossa ● vt scioccare. **~ing** a scioccante; ⟨fam: weather, handwriting etc⟩ tremendo

shod /ʃɒd/ see **shoe**

shoddy /'ʃɒdɪ/ a ⟨-ier, -iest⟩ scadente

shoe /ʃuː/ n scarpa f; ⟨of horse⟩ ferro m ● vt ⟨pt/pp **shod**, pres p **shoeing**⟩ ferrare ⟨horse⟩

shoe: **~horn** n calzante m. **~lace** n laccio m da scarpa. **~maker** n calzolaio m. **~shop** n calzoleria f. **~string** n **on a ~-string** fam con una miseria

shone /ʃɒn/ see **shine**

shoo /ʃuː/ vt **~ away** cacciar via ● int sciò

shook /ʃʊk/ see **shake**

shoot /ʃuːt/ n Bot germoglio m; ⟨hunt⟩ battuta f di caccia ● v ⟨pt/pp **shot**⟩ ● vt sparare; girare ⟨film⟩ ● vi ⟨hunt⟩ andare a caccia. **shoot down** vt abbattere. **shoot out** vi ⟨rush⟩ precipitarsi fuori. **shoot up** vi ⟨grow⟩ crescere in fretta; ⟨prices:⟩ salire di colpo *

'shooting-range n poligono m di tiro

shop /ʃɒp/ n negozio m; ⟨workshop⟩ of-

ficina f; **talk ~** fam parlare di lavoro ● vi ⟨pt/pp **shopped**⟩ far compere; **go ~ping** andare a fare compere. **shop around** vi confrontare i prezzi

shop: **~ assistant** n commesso, -a mf. **~keeper** n negoziante mf. **~lifter** n taccheggiatore, -trice mf. **~lifting** n taccheggio m; **~per** n compratore, -trice mf

shopping /'ʃɒpɪŋ/ n compere fpl; ⟨articles⟩ acquisti mpl; **do the ~** fare la spesa. **~ bag** n borsa f per la spesa. **~ centre** n centro m commerciale. **~ trolley** n carrello m

shop: **~-steward** n rappresentante mf sindacale. **~-'window** n vetrina f

shore /ʃɔː(r)/ n riva f

shorn /ʃɔːn/ see **shear**

short /ʃɔːt/ a corto; ⟨not lasting⟩ breve; ⟨person⟩ basso; ⟨curt⟩ brusco; **a ~ time ago** poco tempo fa; **be ~ of** essere a corto di; **be in ~ supply** essere scarso; fig essere raro; **Mick is ~ for Michael** Mick è il diminutivo di Michael ● adv bruscamente; **in ~** in breve; **~ of doing** a meno di fare; **go ~** essere privato ⟨of di⟩; **stop ~ of doing sth** non arrivare fino a fare qcsa; **cut ~** interrompere ⟨meeting, holiday⟩; **to cut a long story ~** per farla breve

shortage /'ʃɔːtɪdʒ/ n scarsità f inv

short: **~bread** n biscotto m di pasta frolla. **~ 'circuit** n corto m circuito. **~coming** n difetto m. **~ 'cut** n scorciatoia f

shorten /'ʃɔːtn/ vt abbreviare; accorciare ⟨garment⟩

short: **~hand** n stenografia f. **~-'handed** a a corto di personale. **~hand 'typist** n stenodattilografo, -a mf. **~ list** n lista f dei candidati selezionati per un lavoro. **~-lived** /-lɪvd/ a di breve durata

short|ly /'ʃɔːtlɪ/ adv presto; **~ly before/after** poco prima/dopo. **~ness** n brevità f inv; ⟨of person⟩ bassa statura f

short-range a di breve portata

shorts /ʃɔːts/ npl calzoncini mpl corti

short: **~-'sighted** a miope. **~-'sleeved** a a maniche corte. **~-'staffed** a a corto di personale. **~ 'story** n racconto m, novella f. **~-'tempered** a irascibile. **~-term** a a breve termine. **~ wave** n onde fpl corte

shot /ʃɒt/ see **shoot** ● n colpo m; ⟨person⟩ tiratore m; Phot foto f inv; ⟨injection⟩ puntura f; ⟨fam: attempt⟩ prova *f*; **like a ~** *fam* come un razzo. **~gun** *n* fucile *m* da caccia

should /ʃʊd/ *v aux* **I ~ go** dovrei andare; **I ~ have seen him** avrei dovuto vederlo; **I ~ like** mi piacerebbe; **this ~ be enough** questo dovrebbe bastare; **if he ~ come** se dovesse venire

shoulder /'ʃəʊldə(r)/ *n* spalla *f* ● *vt* mettersi in spalla; *fig* accollarsi. **~-bag** *n* borsa *f* a tracolla. **~-blade** *n* scapola *f*. **~-strap** *n* spallina *f*; (*of bag*) tracolla *f*

shout /ʃaʊt/ *n* grido *m* ● *vt/i* gridare. **shout at** *vi* alzar la voce con. **shout down** *vt* azzittire gridando

shouting /'ʃaʊtɪŋ/ *n* grida *fpl*

shove /ʃʌv/ *n* spintone *m* ● *vt* spingere; (*fam: put*) ficcare ● *vi* spingere. **shove off** *vi fam* togliersi di torno

shovel /'ʃʌvl/ *n* pala *f* ● *vt* (*pt/pp* **shovelled**) spalare

show /ʃəʊ/ *n* (*display*) manifestazione *f*; (*exhibition*) mostra *f*; (*ostentation*) ostentazione *f*; *Theat*, *TV* spettacolo *m*; (*programme*) programma *m*; **on ~** esposto ● *v* (*pt* **showed**, *pp* **shown**) ● *vt* mostrare; (*put on display*) esporre; proiettare (*film*) ● *vi* (*film:*) essere proiettato; **your slip is ~ing** ti si vede la sottoveste. **show in** *vt* fare accomodare. **show off** *vi fam* mettersi in mostra ● *vt* mettere in mostra. **show up** *vi* risaltare; (*fam: arrive*) farsi vedere ● *vt* (*fam: embarrass*) far fare una brutta figura a

'show-down *n* regolamento *m* dei conti

shower /'ʃaʊə(r)/ *n* doccia *f*; (*of rain*) acquazzone *m*; **have a ~** fare la doccia ● *vt* ~ **with** coprire di ● *vi* fare la doccia. **~-proof** *a* impermeabile. **~y** *a* da acquazzoni

'show-jumping *n* concorso *m* ippico

shown /ʃəʊn/ *see* **show**

'show-off *n* esibizionista *mf*

showy /'ʃəʊɪ/ *a* appariscente

shrank /ʃræŋk/ *see* **shrink**

shred /ʃred/ *n* brandello *m*; *fig* briciolo *m* ● *vt* (*pt/pp* **shredded**) fare a brandelli; *Culin* tagliuzzare. **~der** *n* distruttore *m* di documenti

shrewd /ʃruːd/ *a* accorto. **~ness** *n* accortezza *f*

shriek /ʃriːk/ *n* strillo *m* ● *vt/i* strillare

shrift /ʃrɪft/ *n* **give sb short ~** liquidare qcno rapidamente

shrill /ʃrɪl/ *a* penetrante

shrimp /ʃrɪmp/ *n* gamberetto *m*

shrine /ʃraɪn/ *n* (*place*) santuario *m*

shrink /ʃrɪŋk/ *vi* (*pt* **shrank**, *pp*

---

shrunk) restringersi; (*draw back*) ritrarsi (**from** da)

shrivel /'ʃrɪvl/ *vi* (*pt/pp* **shrivelled**) raggrinzare

shroud /ʃraʊd/ *n* sudario *m*; *fig* manto *m*

Shrove /ʃrəʊv/ *n* ~ **'Tuesday** martedì *m* grasso

shrub /ʃrʌb/ *n* arbusto *m*

shrug /ʃrʌg/ *n* scrollata *f* di spalle ● *vt/i* (*pt/pp* **shrugged**) ~ [**one's shoulders**] scrollare le spalle

shrunk /ʃrʌŋk/ *see* **shrink**. **~en** *a* rimpicciolito

shudder /'ʃʌdə(r)/ *n* fremito *m* ● *vi* fremere

shuffle /'ʃʌfl/ *vi* strascicare i piedi ● *vt* mescolare (*cards*)

shun /ʃʌn/ *vt* (*pt/pp* **shunned**) rifuggire

shunt /ʃʌnt/ *vt* smistare

shush /ʃʊʃ/ *int* zitto!

shut /ʃʌt/ *v* (*pt/pp* **shut**, *pres p* **shutting**) ● *vt* chiudere ● *vi* chiudersi; (*shop:*) chiudere. **shut down** *vt/i* chiudere. **shut up** *vt* chiudere; *fam* far tacere ● *vi fam* stare zitto; ~ **up!** stai zitto!

'shut-down *n* chiusura *f*

shutter /'ʃʌtə(r)/ *n* serranda *f*; *Phot* otturatore *m*

shuttle /'ʃʌtl/ *n* navetta *f* ● *vi* far la spola

shuttle: **~cock** *n* volano *m*. **~ service** *n* servizio *m* pendolare

shy /ʃaɪ/ *a* (*timid*) timido. **~ness** *n* timidezza *f*

Siamese /saɪə'miːz/ *a* siamese

sibling /'sɪblɪŋ/ *n* (*brother*) fratello *m*; (*sister*) sorella *f*; **~s** *pl* fratelli *mpl*

Sicil|y /'sɪsɪlɪ/ *n* Sicilia *f*. **~ian** *a* & *n* siciliano, -a *mf*

sick /sɪk/ *a* ammalato; (*humour*) macabro; **be ~** (*vomit*) vomitare; **be ~ of sth** *fam* essere stufo di qcsa; **feel ~** aver la nausea

sicken /'sɪkn/ *vt* disgustare ● *vi* **be ~ing for something** covare qualche malanno. **~ing** *a* disgustoso

sick|ly /'sɪklɪ/ *a* (**-ier, -iest**) malaticcio. **~ness** *n* malattia *f*; (*vomiting*) nausea *f*. **~ness benefit** *n* indennità *f* di malattia

side /saɪd/ *n* lato *m*; (*of person, mountain*) fianco *m*; (*of road*) bordo *m*; **on the ~** (*as sideline*) come attività secondaria; **~ by ~** fianco a fianco; **take ~s** immischiarsi; **take sb's ~** prendere le parti di qcno; **be on the safe ~**

andare sul sicuro ● *attrib* laterale ● *vi* ~ **with** parteggiare per

side: ~**board** *n* credenza *f*. ~**burns** *npl* basette *fpl*. ~**-effect** *n* effetto *m* collaterale. ~**lights** *npl* luci *fpl* di posizione. ~**line** *n* attività *f inv* complementare. ~**show** *n* attrazione *f*. ~**step** *vt* schivare. ~**-track** *vt* sviare. ~**walk** *n Am* marciapiede *m*. ~**ways** *adv* obliquamente

siding /'saɪdɪŋ/ *n* binario *m* di raccordo

sidle /'saɪdl/ *vi* camminare furtivamente (**up to** verso)

siege /siːdʒ/ *n* assedio *m*

sieve /sɪv/ *n* setaccio *m* ● *vt* setacciare

sift /sɪft/ *vt* setacciare; ~ [**through**] *fig* passare al setaccio

sigh /saɪ/ *n* sospiro *m* ● *vi* sospirare

sight /saɪt/ *n* vista *f*; (on gun) mirino *m*; **the** ~**s** *pl* le cose da vedere; **at first** ~ a prima vista; **be within/out of** ~ essere/non essere in vista; **lose** ~ **of** perdere di vista; **know by** ~ conoscere di vista. **have bad** ~ vederci male ● *vt* avvistare

'sightseeing *n* **go** ~ andare a visitare posti

sign /saɪn/ *n* segno *m*; (notice) insegna *f* ● *vt/i* firmare. **sign on** *vi* (as unemployed) presentarsi all'ufficio di collocamento; *Mil* arruolarsi

signal /'sɪgnl/ *n* segnale *m* ● *v* (pt/pp **signalled**) ● *vt* segnalare ● *vi* fare segnali; ~ **to sb** far segno a qcno (**to** di). ~**-box** *n* cabina *f* di segnalazione

signature /'sɪgnətʃə(r)/ *n* firma *f*. ~ **tune** *n* sigla *f* [musicale]

signet-ring /'sɪgnɪt-/ *n* anello *m* con sigillo

significan|ce /sɪg'nɪfɪkəns/ *n* significato *m*. ~**t** *a* significativo

signify /'sɪgnɪfaɪ/ *vt* (pt/pp **-ied**) indicare

sign-language *n* linguaggio *m* dei segni

signpost /'saɪn-/ *n* segnalazione *f* stradale

silence /'saɪləns/ *n* silenzio *m* ● *vt* far tacere. ~**r** *n* (on gun) silenziatore *m*; *Auto* marmitta *f*

silent /'saɪlənt/ *a* silenzioso; (film) muto; **remain** ~ rimanere in silenzio. ~**ly** *adv* silenziosamente

silhouette /sɪlu'et/ *n* sagoma *f*, silhouette *f inv* ● *vt* **be** ~**d** profilarsi

silicon /'sɪlɪkən/ *n* silicio *m*. ~ **chip** piastrina *f* di silicio

silk /sɪlk/ *n* seta *f* ● *attrib* di seta. ~**worm** *n* baco *m* da seta

silky /'sɪlkɪ/ *a* (**-ier, -iest**) come la seta

sill /sɪl/ *n* davanzale *m*

silly /'sɪlɪ/ *a* (**-ier, -iest**) sciocco

silo /'saɪləʊ/ *n* silo *m*

silt /sɪlt/ *n* melma *f*

silver /'sɪlvə(r)/ *a* d'argento; (paper) argentato ● *n* argento *m*; (silverware) argenteria *f*

silver: ~**-plated** *a* placcato d'argento. ~**ware** *n* argenteria *f*. ~ **'wedding** *n* nozze *fpl* d'argento

similar /'sɪmɪlə(r)/ *a* simile. ~**ity** /-'lærətɪ/ *n* somiglianza *f*. ~**ly** *adv* in modo simile

simile /'sɪmɪlɪ/ *n* similitudine *f*

simmer /'sɪmə(r)/ *vi* bollire lentamente ● *vt* far bollire lentamente. **simmer down** *vi* calmarsi

simple /'sɪmpl/ *a* semplice; (person) sempliciotto. ~**-minded** *a* sempliciotto

simplicity /sɪm'plɪsətɪ/ *n* semplicità *f*

simpli|fication /sɪmplɪfɪ'keɪʃn/ *n* semplificazione *f*. ~**fy** /'sɪmplɪfaɪ/ *vt* (pt/pp **-ied**) semplificare

simply /'sɪmplɪ/ *adv* semplicemente

simulat|e /'sɪmjʊleɪt/ *vt* simulare. ~**ion** /-'leɪʃn/ *n* simulazione *f*

simultaneous /sɪml'teɪnɪəs/ *a* simultaneo

sin /sɪn/ *n* peccato *m* ● *vi* (pt/pp **sinned**) peccare

since /sɪns/ *prep* da ● *adv* da allora ● *conj* da quando; (because) siccome

sincere /sɪn'sɪə(r)/ *a* sincero. ~**ly** *adv* sinceramente; **Yours** ~**ly** distinti saluti

sincerity /sɪn'serətɪ/ *n* sincerità *f*

sinful /'sɪnfl/ *a* peccaminoso

sing /sɪŋ/ *vt/i* (pt **sang**, pp **sung**) cantare

singe /sɪndʒ/ *vt* (pres p **singeing**) bruciacchiare

singer /'sɪŋə(r)/ *n* cantante *mf*

single /'sɪŋgl/ *a* solo; (not double) semplice; (unmarried) celibe; (woman) nubile; (room) singolo; (bed) a una piazza ● *n* (ticket) biglietto *m* di sola andata; (record) singolo *m*; ~**s** *pl Tennis* singolo *m* ● **single out** *vt* scegliere; (distinguish) distinguere

single: ~**-breasted** *a* a un petto. ~**-handed** *a & adv* da solo. ~**-minded** *a* risoluto. ~ **'parent** *n* genitore *m* che alleva il figlio da solo

singly /'sɪŋglɪ/ *adv* singolarmente

singular /'sɪŋgjʊlə(r)/ *a Gram* singolare ● *n* singolare *m*. ~**ly** *adv* singolarmente

sinister /'sɪnɪstə(r)/ *a* sinistro

sink /sɪŋk/ *n* lavandino *m* ● *v* (*pt* sank, *pp* sunk) ● *vi* affondare ● *vt* affondare ⟨ship⟩; scavare ⟨shaft⟩; investire ⟨money⟩. **sink in** *vi* penetrare; **it took a while to ~ in** (*fam: be understood*) c'è voluto un po' a capirlo

sinner /'sɪnə(r)/ *n* peccatore, -trice *mf*

sinus /'saɪnəs/ *n* seno *m* paranasale. ~**itis** *n* sinusite *f*

sip /sɪp/ *n* sorso *m* ● *vt* (*pt/pp* sipped) sorseggiare

siphon /'saɪfn/ *n* ⟨bottle⟩ sifone *m* ● **siphon off** *vt* travasare ⟨con sifone⟩

sir /sɜː(r)/ *n* signore *m*; S~ ⟨title⟩ Sir *m*; **Dear S~s** Spettabile ditta

siren /'saɪrən/ *n* sirena *f*

sissy /'sɪsɪ/ *n* femminuccia *f*

sister /'sɪstə(r)/ *n* sorella *f*; ⟨nurse⟩ [infermiera *f*] caposala *f*. ~-**in-law** *n* (*pl* ~**s-in-law**) cognata *f*. ~**ly** *a* da sorella

sit /sɪt/ *v* (*pt/pp* sat, *pres p* sitting) ● *vi* essere seduto; ⟨sit down⟩ sedersi; ⟨committee⟩ riunirsi ● *vt* sostenere ⟨exam⟩. **sit back** *vi fig* starsene con le mani in mano. **sit down** *vi* mettersi a sedere. **sit up** *vi* mettersi seduto; ⟨not slouch⟩ star seduto diritto; ⟨stay up⟩ stare alzato

site /saɪt/ *n* posto *m*; *Archaeol* sito *m*; ⟨building ~⟩ cantiere *m* ● *vt* collocare

sit-in /'sɪtɪn/ *n* occupazione *f* ⟨di fabbrica ecc⟩

sitting /'sɪtɪŋ/ *n* seduta *f*; ⟨for meals⟩ turno *m*. ~-**room** *n* salotto *m*

situat|e /'sɪtjʊeɪt/ *vt* situare. ~**ed** *a* situato. ~**ion** /-'eɪʃn/ *n* situazione *f*; ⟨location⟩ posizione *f*; ⟨job⟩ posto *m*

six /sɪks/ *a* & *n* sei *m*. ~**teen** *a* & *n* sedici *m*. ~**teenth** *a* & *n* sedicesimo, -a *mf*

sixth /sɪksθ/ *a* & *n* sesto, -a *mf*

sixtieth /'sɪkstɪɪθ/ *a* & *n* sessantesimo, -a *mf*

sixty /'sɪkstɪ/ *a* & *n* sessanta *m*

size /saɪz/ *n* dimensioni *fpl*; ⟨of clothes⟩ taglia *f*, misura *f*; ⟨of shoes⟩ numero *m*; **what ~ is the room?** che dimensioni ha la stanza? ● **size up** *vt fam* valutare

sizeable /'saɪzəbl/ *a* piuttosto grande

sizzle /'sɪzl/ *vi* sfrigolare

skate¹ /skeɪt/ *n inv* ⟨fish⟩ razza *f*

skate² *n* pattino *m* ● *vi* pattinare

skateboard /'skeɪtbɔːd/ *n* skate-board *m inv*

skater /'skeɪtə(r)/ *n* pattinatore, -trice *mf*

skating /'skeɪtɪŋ/ *n* pattinaggio *m*. ~-**rink** *n* pista *f* di pattinaggio

skeleton /'skelɪtn/ *n* scheletro *m*. ~ '**key** *n* passe-partout *m inv*. ~ '**staff** *n* personale *m* ridotto

sketch /sketʃ/ *n* schizzo *m*; *Theat* sketch *m inv* ● *vt* fare uno schizzo di

sketch|y /'sketʃɪ/ *a* (-**ier**, -**iest**) abbozzato. ~**ily** *adv* in modo abbozzato

skewer /'skjʊə(r)/ *n* spiedo *m*

ski /skiː/ *n* sci *m inv* ● *vi* (*pt/pp* skied, *pres p* **skiing**) sciare; **go ~ing** andare a sciare

skid /skɪd/ *n* slittata *f* ● *vi* (*pt/pp* **skidded**) slittare

skier /'skiːə(r)/ *n* sciatore, -trice *mf*

skiing /'skiːɪŋ/ *n* sci *m*

skilful /'skɪlfl/ *a* abile

'**ski-lift** *n* impianto *m* di risalita

skill /skɪl/ *n* abilità *f inv*. ~**ed** *a* dotato; ⟨worker⟩ specializzato

skim /skɪm/ *vt* (*pt/pp* **skimmed**) schiumare; scremare ⟨milk⟩. **skim off** *vt* togliere. **skim through** *vt* scorrere

skimp /skɪmp/ *vi* ~ **on** lesinare su

skimpy /'skɪmpɪ/ *a* (-**ier**, -**iest**) succinto

skin /skɪn/ *n* pelle *f*; ⟨on fruit⟩ buccia *f* ● *vt* (*pt/pp* **skinned**) spellare

skin: ~-**deep** *a* superficiale. ~-**diving** *n* nuoto *m* subacqueo

skinflint /'skɪnflɪnt/ *n* miserabile *mf*

skinny /'skɪnɪ/ *a* (-**ier**, -**iest**) molto magro

skip¹ /skɪp/ *n* ⟨container⟩ benna *f*

skip² *n* salto *m* ● *v* (*pt/pp* **skipped**) ● *vi* saltellare; ⟨with rope⟩ saltare la corda ● *vt* omettere

skipper /'skɪpə(r)/ *n* skipper *m inv*

skipping-rope /'skɪpɪŋrəʊp/ *n* corda *f* per saltare

skirmish /'skɜːmɪʃ/ *n* scaramuccia *f*

skirt /skɜːt/ *n* gonna *f* ● *vt* costeggiare

skit /skɪt/ *n* bozzetto *m* comico

skittle /'skɪtl/ *n* birillo *m*

skive /skaɪv/ *vi fam* fare lo scansafatiche

skulk /skʌlk/ *vi* aggirarsi furtivamente

skull /skʌl/ *n* cranio *m*

skunk /skʌŋk/ *n* moffetta *f*

sky /skaɪ/ *n* cielo *m*. ~**light** *n* lucernario *m*. ~**scraper** *n* grattacielo *m*

slab /slæb/ *n* lastra *f*; ⟨slice⟩ fetta *f*; ⟨of chocolate⟩ tavoletta *f*

slack /slæk/ *a* lento; ⟨person⟩ fiacco ● *vi* fare lo scansafatiche. **slack off** *vi* rilassarsi

slacken /'slækn/ *vi* allentare; ~ **[off]**

⟨*trade:*⟩ rallentare; ⟨*speed, rain:*⟩ diminuire ● *vt* allentare; diminuire ⟨*speed*⟩

slacks /slæks/ *npl* pantaloni *mpl* sportivi

slag /slæg/ *n* scorie *fpl* ● **slag off** *vt* (*pt/pp* **slagged**) *Br fam* criticare

slain /sleɪn/ *see* **slay**

slam /slæm/ *v* (*pt/pp* **slammed**) ● *vt* sbattere; ⟨*fam: criticize*⟩ stroncare ● *vi* sbattere

slander /'slɑːndə(r)/ *n* diffamazione *f* ● *vt* diffamare. **~ous** /-rəs/ *a* diffamatorio

slang /slæŋ/ *n* gergo *m*. **~y** *a* gergale

slant /slɑːnt/ *n* pendenza *f*; ⟨*point of view*⟩ angolazione *f*; **on the ~** in pendenza ● *vt* pendere; *fig* distorcere ⟨*report*⟩ ● *vi* pendere

slap /slæp/ *n* schiaffo *m* ● *vt* (*pt/pp* **slapped**) schiaffeggiare; ⟨*put*⟩ schiaffare ● *adv* in pieno

slap: **~dash** *a fam* frettoloso. **~-up** *a fam* di prim'ordine

slash /slæʃ/ *n* taglio *m* ● *vt* tagliare; ridurre drasticamente ⟨*prices*⟩

slat /slæt/ *n* stecca *f*

slate /sleɪt/ *n* ardesia *f* ● *vt fam* fare a pezzi

slaughter /'slɔːtə(r)/ *n* macello *m*; ⟨*of people*⟩ massacro *m* ● *vt* macellare; massacrare ⟨*people*⟩. **~house** *n* macello *m*

Slav /slɑːv/ *a* slavo ● *n* slavo, -a *mf*

slave /sleɪv/ *n* schiavo, -a *mf* ● *vi* **~** [**away**] lavorare come un negro. **~-driver** *n* schiavista *mf*

slav|ery /'sleɪvərɪ/ *n* schiavitù *f*. **~ish** *a* servile

Slavonic /slə'vɒnɪk/ *a* slavo

slay /sleɪ/ *vt* (*pt* **slew**, *pp* **slain**) ammazzare

sleazy /'sliːzɪ/ *a* (**-ier, -iest**) sordido

sledge /sledʒ/ *n* slitta *f*. **~-hammer** *n* martello *m*

sleek /sliːk/ *a* liscio, lucente; ⟨*well-fed*⟩ pasciuto

sleep /sliːp/ *n* sonno *m*; **go to ~** addormentarsi; **put to ~** far addormentare ● *v* (*pt/pp* **slept**) ● *vi* dormire ● *vt* **~s** **six** ha sei posti letto. **~er** *n Rail* treno *m* con vagoni letto; ⟨*compartment*⟩ vagone *m* letto; **be a light/heavy ~er** avere il sonno leggero/pesante

sleeping: **~-bag** *n* sacco *m* a pelo. **~-car** *n* vagone *m* letto. **~-pill** *n* sonnifero *m*

sleep: **~less** *a* insonne. **~lessness** *n* insonnia *f*. **~-walker** *n* sonnambulo, -a *mf*. **~-walking** *n* sonnambulismo *m*

sleepy /'sliːpɪ/ *a* (**-ier, -iest**) assonnato; **be ~** aver sonno

sleet /sliːt/ *n* nevischio *m* ● *vi* **it is ~ing** nevischia

sleeve /sliːv/ *n* manica *f*; ⟨*for record*⟩ copertina *f*. **~less** *a* senza maniche

sleigh /sleɪ/ *n* slitta *f*

sleight /slaɪt/ *n* **~ of hand** gioco *m* di prestigio

slender /'slendə(r)/ *a* snello; ⟨*fingers, stem*⟩ affusolato; *fig* scarso; ⟨*chance*⟩ magro

slept /slept/ *see* **sleep**

sleuth /sluːθ/ *n* investigatore *m*, detective *m inv*

slew[1] /sluː/ *vi* girare

slew[2] *see* **slay**

slice /slaɪs/ *n* fetta *f* ● *vt* affettare; **~d bread** pane *m* a cassetta

slick /slɪk/ *a* liscio; ⟨*cunning*⟩ astuto ● *n* (*of oil*) chiazza *f* di petrolio

slid|e /slaɪd/ *n* scivolata *f*; ⟨*in playground*⟩ scivolo *m*; ⟨*for hair*⟩ fermaglio *m* ⟨*per capelli*⟩; *Phot* diapositiva *f* ● *v* (*pt/pp* **slid**) ● *vi* scivolare ● *vt* far scivolare. **~-rule** *n* regolo *m* calcolatore. **~ing** ⟨*door, seat*⟩ scorrevole. **~ing scale** *n* scala *f* mobile

slight /slaɪt/ *a* leggero; ⟨*importance*⟩ poco; ⟨*slender*⟩ esile. **~est** minimo; **not in the ~est** niente affatto ● *vt* offendere ● *n* offesa *f*. **~ly** *adv* leggermente

slim /slɪm/ *a* (**slimmer, slimmest**) snello; *fig* scarso; ⟨*chance*⟩ magro ● *vi* dimagrire

slim|e /slaɪm/ *n* melma *f*. **~y** *a* melmoso; *fig* viscido

sling /slɪŋ/ *n Med* benda *f* al collo ● *vt* (*pt/pp* **slung**) *fam* lanciare

slip /slɪp/ *n* scivolata *f*; ⟨*mistake*⟩ lieve errore *m*; ⟨*petticoat*⟩ sottoveste *f*; ⟨*for pillow*⟩ federa *f*; ⟨*paper*⟩ scontrino *m*; **give sb the ~** *fam* sbarazzarsi di qcno; **~ of the tongue** lapsus *m inv* ● *v* (*pt/pp* **slipped**) ● *vi* scivolare; ⟨*go quickly*⟩ sgattaiolare; ⟨*decline*⟩ retrocedere ● *vt* he **~ped it into his pocket** se l'è infilato in tasca; **~ sb's mind** sfuggire di mente a qcno. **slip away** *vi* sgusciar via; ⟨*time:*⟩ sfuggire. **slip into** *vi* infilarsi ⟨*clothes*⟩. **slip up** *vi fam* sbagliare

slipped 'disc *n Med* ernia *f* del disco

slipper /'slɪpə(r)/ *n* pantofola *f*

slippery /'slɪpərɪ/ *a* scivoloso

slip-road *n* bretella *f*

slipshod /'slɪpʃɒd/ *a* trascurato

'slip-up *n fam* sbaglio *m*

slit /slɪt/ n spacco m; (tear) strappo m; (hole) fessura f ● vt (pt/pp **slit**) tagliare

slither /'slɪðə(r)/ vi scivolare

sliver /'slɪvə(r)/ n scheggia f

slobber /'slɒbə(r)/ vi sbavare

slog /slɒg/ n [hard] ~ sgobbata f ● vi (pt/pp **slogged**) (work) sgobbare

slogan /'sləʊgən/ n slogan m inv

slop /slɒp/ v (pt/pp **slopped**) ● vt versare. **slop over** vi versarsi

slop|e /sləʊp/ n pendenza f; (ski ~) pista f ● vi essere inclinato, inclinarsi. **~ing** a in pendenza

sloppy /'slɒpɪ/ a (-ier, -iest) (work) trascurato; (worker) negligente; (in dress) sciatto; (sentimental) sdolcinato

slosh /slɒʃ/ vi fam (person, feet:) sguazzare; (water:) scrosciare ● vt (fam: hit) colpire

sloshed /slɒʃt/ a fam sbronzo

slot /slɒt/ n fessura f; (time-~) spazio m ● v (pt/pp **slotted**) ● vt infilare. **slot in** vi incastrarsi

'slot-machine n distributore m automatico; (for gambling) slot-machine f inv

slouch /slaʊtʃ/ vi (in chair) stare scomposto

sloven|ly /'slʌvnlɪ/ a sciatto. **~iness** n sciatteria f

slow /sləʊ/ a lento; be ~ (clock:) essere indietro; in ~ motion al rallentatore ● adv lentamente ● slow down/up vt/i rallentare

slow: **~coach** n fam tartaruga f. **~ly** adv lentamente. **~ness** n lentezza f

sludge /slʌdʒ/ n fanghiglia f

slug /slʌg/ n lumacone m; (fam: bullet) pallottola f

sluggish /'slʌgɪʃ/ a lento

sluice /sluːs/ n chiusa f

slum /slʌm/ n (house) tugurio m; **~s** pl bassifondi mpl

slumber /'slʌmbə(r)/ vi dormire

slump /slʌmp/ n crollo m; (economic) depressione f ● vi crollare

slung /slʌŋ/ see **sling**

slur /slɜː(r)/ n (discredit) calunnia f ● vt (pt/pp **slurred**) biascicare

slurp /slɜːp/ vt/i bere rumorosamente

slush /slʌʃ/ n pantano m nevoso; fig sdolcinatezza f. **~ fund** n fondi mpl neri

slushy /'slʌʃɪ/ a fangoso; (sentimental) sdolcinato

slut /slʌt/ n sgualdrina f

sly /slaɪ/ a (-er, -est) scaltro ● n on the ~ di nascosto

smack¹ /smæk/ n (on face) schiaffo m; (on bottom) sculaccione m ● vt (on face) schiaffeggiare; (on bottom) sculacciare; ~ one's lips far schioccare le labbra ● adv fam in pieno

smack² vi ~ of fig sapere di

small /smɔːl/ a piccolo; be out/work until the ~ hours fare le ore piccole ● adv chop up ~ fare a pezzettini ● n the ~ of the back le reni

small: ~ ads npl annunci mpl [commerciali]. ~ 'change n spiccioli mpl. **~-holding** n piccola tenuta f. **~pox** n vaiolo m. ~ talk n chiacchiere fpl

smarmy /'smɑːmɪ/ a (-ier, -iest) fam untuoso

smart /smɑːt/ a elegante; (clever) intelligente; (brisk) svelto; be ~ (fam: cheeky) fare il furbo ● vi (hurt) bruciare

smarten /'smɑːtn/ vt ~ oneself up farsi bello

smash /smæʃ/ n fragore m; (collision) scontro m; Tennis schiacciata f ● vt spaccare; Tennis schiacciare ● vi spaccarsi; (crash) schiantarsi (into contro). ~ [hit] n successo m. **~ing** a fam fantastico

smattering /'smætərɪŋ/ n infarinatura f

smear /smɪə(r)/ n macchia f; Med striscio m ● vt imbrattare; (coat) spalmare (with di); fig calunniare

smell /smel/ n odore m; (sense) odorato m ● v (pt/pp **smelt** or **smelled**) ● vt odorare; (sniff) annusare ● vi odorare (of di)

smelly /'smelɪ/ a (-ier, -iest) puzzolente

smelt¹ /smelt/ see **smell**

smelt² vt fondere

smile /smaɪl/ n sorriso m ● vi sorridere; ~ at sorridere a (sb); sorridere di (sth)

smirk /smɜːk/ n sorriso m compiaciuto

smithereens /smɪðə'riːnz/ npl to/in ~ in mille pezzi

smitten /'smɪtn/ a ~ with tutto preso da

smock /smɒk/ n grembiule m

smog /smɒg/ n smog m inv

smoke /sməʊk/ n fumo m ● vt/i fumare. **~less** a senza fumo; (fuel) che non fa fumo

smoker /'sməʊkə(r)/ n fumatore, -trice mf; Rail vagone m fumatori

'smoke-screen n cortina f di fumo

smoking /'sməʊkɪŋ/ n fumo m; 'no ~' 'vietato fumare'

smoky /'sməʊkɪ/ a (-ier, -iest) fumoso; ⟨taste⟩ di fumo

smooth /smu:ð/ a liscio; ⟨movement⟩ scorrevole; ⟨sea⟩ calmo; ⟨manners⟩ mellifluo ● vt lisciare. **smooth out** vt lisciare. **~ly** adv in modo scorrevole

smother /'smʌðə(r)/ vt soffocare

smoulder /'sməʊldə(r)/ vi fumare; ⟨with rage⟩ consumarsi

smudge /smʌdʒ/ n macchia f ● vt/i imbrattare

smug /smʌg/ a (**smugger, smuggest**) compiaciuto. **~ly** adv con aria compiaciuta

smuggl|e /'smʌgl/ vt contrabbandare. **~er** n contrabbandiere, -a mf. **~ing** n contrabbando m

smut /smʌt/ n macchia f di fuliggine; fig sconcezza f

smutty /'smʌtɪ/ a (-ier, -iest) fuligginoso; fig sconcio

snack /snæk/ n spuntino m. **~-bar** n snack bar m inv

snag /snæg/ n ⟨problem⟩ intoppo m

snail /sneɪl/ n lumaca f; **at a ~'s pace** a passo di lumaca

snake /sneɪk/ n serpente m

snap /snæp/ n colpo m secco; ⟨photo⟩ istantanea f ● attrib ⟨decision⟩ istantaneo ● v (pt/pp **snapped**) ● vi ⟨break⟩ spezzarsi; **~ at** ⟨dog:⟩ cercare di azzannare; ⟨person:⟩ parlare seccamente a ● vt ⟨break⟩ spezzare; ⟨say⟩ dire seccamente; Phot fare un'istantanea di. **snap up** vt afferrare

snappy /'snæpɪ/ a (-ier, -iest) scorbutico; ⟨smart⟩ elegante; **make it ~!** sbrigati!

'snapshot n istantanea f

snare /sneə(r)/ n trappola f

snarl /snɑ:l/ n ringhio m ● vi ringhiare

snatch /snætʃ/ n strappo m; ⟨fragment⟩ brano m; ⟨theft⟩ scippo m; **make a ~ at sth** cercare di afferrare qcsa ● vt strappare [di mano] (**from** a); ⟨steal⟩ scippare; rapire ⟨child⟩

sneak /sni:k/ n fam spia mf ● vi ⟨fam: tell tales⟩ fare la spia ● vt ⟨take⟩ rubare; **~ a look at** dare una sbirciata a. **sneak in/out** vi sgattaiolare dentro/fuori

sneakers /'sni:kəz/ npl Am scarpe fpl da ginnastica

sneaking /'sni:kɪŋ/ a furtivo; ⟨suspicion⟩ vago

sneaky /'sni:kɪ/ a sornione

sneer /snɪə(r)/ n ghigno m ● vi sogghignare; ⟨mock⟩ ridere di

sneeze /sni:z/ n starnuto m ● vi starnutire

snide /snaɪd/ a fam insinuante

sniff /snɪf/ n ⟨of dog⟩ annusata f ● vi tirare su col naso ● vt odorare ⟨flower⟩; sniffare ⟨glue, cocaine⟩; ⟨dog:⟩ annusare

snigger /'snɪgə(r)/ n risatina f soffocata ● vi ridacchiare

snip /snɪp/ n taglio m; ⟨fam: bargain⟩ affare m ● vt/i (pt/pp **snipped**) **~ [at]** tagliare

snipe /snaɪp/ vi **~ at** tirare su; fig sparare a zero su. **~r** n cecchino m

snippet /'snɪpɪt/ n **a ~ of information/news** una breve notizia/informazione

snivel /'snɪvl/ vi (pt/pp **snivelled**) piagnucolare. **~ling** a piagnucoloso

snob /snɒb/ n snob mf inv. **~bery** n snobismo m. **~bish** a da snob

snooker /'snu:kə(r)/ n snooker m

snoop /snu:p/ n spia f ● vi fam curiosare

snooty /'snu:tɪ/ a fam sdegnoso

snooze /snu:z/ n sonnellino m ● vi fare un sonnellino

snore /snɔ:(r)/ vi russare

snorkel /'snɔ:kl/ n respiratore m

snort /snɔ:t/ n sbuffo m ● vi sbuffare

snout /snaʊt/ n grugno m

snow /snəʊ/ n neve f ● vi nevicare; **~ed under with** fig sommerso di

snow: ~ball n palla f di neve ● vi fare a palle di neve. **~-drift** n cumulo m di neve. **~drop** n bucaneve m inv. **~fall** n nevicata f. **~flake** n fiocco m di neve. **~man** n pupazzo m di neve. **~-plough** n spazzaneve m inv. **~storm** n tormenta f. **~y** a nevoso

snub /snʌb/ n sgarbo m ● vt (pt/pp **snubbed**) snobbare

'snub-nosed a dal naso all'insù

snuff /snʌf/ n tabacco m da fiuto

snug /snʌg/ a (**snugger, snuggest**) comodo; ⟨tight⟩ aderente

snuggle /'snʌgl/ vi rannicchiarsi (**up to** accanto a)

so /səʊ/ adv così; **so far** finora; **so am I** anch'io; **I see** così pare; **that is so** è così; **so much** così tanto; **so much the better** tanto meglio; **so it is** proprio così; **if so** se è così; **so as to** in modo da; **so long!** fam a presto! ● pron I hope/think/am afraid so spero/penso/temo di sì; **I told you so** te l'ho detto; **because I say so** perché lo dico io; **I did so!** è vero!; **so saying/doing,...** così dicendo/facendo,...; **or so**

circa; very much so sì, molto; **and so forth** or **on** e così via ● *conj* (*therefore*) perciò; (*in order that*) così; **so that** affinché; **so there!** ecco!; **so what?** e allora?; **so where have you been?** allora, dove sei stato?

soak /səʊk/ *vt* mettere a bagno● *vi* stare a bagno; ~ **into** (*liquid:*) penetrare. **soak up** *vt* assorbire

soaking /'səʊkɪŋ/ *n* ammollo *m* ● *a* & *adv* ~ **[wet]** *fam* inzuppato

so-and-so /'səʊənsəʊ/ *n* Tal dei Tali *mf*; (*euphemism*) specie *f* di imbecille

soap /səʊp/ *n* sapone *m*. ~ **opera** *n* telenovella *f*, soap opera *f inv*. ~ **powder** *n* detersivo *m* in polvere

soapy /'səʊpɪ/ *a* (**-ier, -iest**) insaponato

soar /sɔː(r)/ *vi* elevarsi; (*prices:*) salire alle stelle

sob /sɒb/ *n* singhiozzo *m* ● *vi* (*pt/pp* **sobbed**) singhiozzare

sober /'səʊbə(r)/ *a* sobrio; (*serious*) serio ● **sober up** *vi* ritornare sobrio

'so-called *a* cosiddetto

soccer /'sɒkə(r)/ *n* calcio *m*

sociable /'səʊʃəbl/ *a* socievole

social /'səʊʃl/ *a* sociale; (*sociable*) socievole

socialis|m /'səʊʃəlɪzm/ *n* socialismo *m*. ~**t** /-ɪst/ *a* socialista ● *n* socialista *mf*

socialize /'səʊʃəlaɪz/ *vi* socializzare

socially /'səʊʃəlɪ/ *adv* socialmente; **know sb** ~ frequentare qcno

social: ~ **se'curity** *n* previdenza *f* sociale. ~ **work** *n* assistenza *f* sociale. ~ **worker** *n* assistente *mf* sociale

society /sə'saɪətɪ/ *n* società *f inv*

sociolog|ist /səʊsɪ'ɒlədʒɪst/ *n* sociologo, -a *mf*. ~**y** *n* sociologia *f*

sock¹ /sɒk/ *n* calzino *m*; (*kneelength*) calza *f*

sock² *fam* *n* pugno *m* ● *vt* dare un pugno a

socket /'sɒkɪt/ *n* (*wall plug*) presa *f* [di corrente]; (*for bulb*) portalampada *m inv*

soda /'səʊdə/ *n* soda *f*; *Am* gazzosa *f*. ~ **water** *n* seltz *m inv*

sodden /'sɒdn/ *a* inzuppato

sodium /'səʊdɪəm/ *n* sodio *m*

sofa /'səʊfə/ *n* divano *m*. ~ **bed** *n* divano *m* letto

soft /sɒft/ *a* morbido, soffice; (*voice*) sommesso; (*light, colour*) tenue; (*not strict*) indulgente; (*fam: silly*) stupido; **have a** ~ **spot for sb** avere un debole per qcno. ~ **drink** *n* bibita *f* analcolica

soften /'sɒfn/ *vt* ammorbidire; *fig* attenuare ● *vi* ammorbidirsi

softly /'sɒftlɪ/ *adv* (*say*) sottovoce; (*treat*) con indulgenza; (*play music*) in sottofondo

soft: ~ **toy** *n* pupazzo *m* di peluche. ~**ware** *n* software *m*

soggy /'sɒgɪ/ *a* (**-ier, -iest**) zuppo

soil¹ /sɔɪl/ *n* suolo *m*

soil² *vt* sporcare

solar /'səʊlə(r)/ *a* solare

sold /səʊld/ *see* **sell**

solder /'səʊldə(r)/ *n* lega *f* da saldatura ● *vt* saldare

soldier /'səʊldʒə(r)/ *n* soldato *m* ● **soldier on** *vi* perseverare

sole¹ /səʊl/ *n* (*of foot*) pianta *f*; (*of shoe*) suola *f*

sole² *n* (*fish*) sogliola *f*

sole³ *a* unico, solo. ~**ly** *adv* unicamente

solemn /'sɒləm/ *a* solenne. ~**ity** /sə'lemnətɪ/ *n* solennità *f inv*

solicit /sə'lɪsɪt/ *vt* sollecitare ● *vi* (*prostitute:*) adescare

solicitor /sə'lɪsɪtə(r)/ *n* avvocato *m*

solid /'sɒlɪd/ *a* solido; (*oak, gold*) massiccio ● *n* (*figure*) solido *m*; ~**s** *pl* (*food*) cibi *mpl* solidi

solidarity /sɒlɪ'dærətɪ/ *n* solidarietà *f inv*

solidify /sə'lɪdɪfaɪ/ *vi* (*pt/pp* **-ied**) solidificarsi

soliloquy /sə'lɪləkwɪ/ *n* soliloquio *m*

solitaire /sɒlɪ'teə(r)/ *n* solitario *m*

solitary /'sɒlɪtərɪ/ *a* solitario; (*sole*) solo. ~ **con'finement** *n* cella *f* di isolamento

solitude /'sɒlɪtjuːd/ *n* solitudine *f*

solo /'səʊləʊ/ *n Mus* assolo *m* ● *a* (*flight*) in solitario ● *adv* in solitario. ~**ist** *n* solista *mf*

solstice /'sɒlstɪs/ *n* solstizio *m*

soluble /'sɒljʊbl/ *a* solubile

solution /sə'luːʃn/ *n* soluzione *f*

solve /sɒlv/ *vt* risolvere

solvent /'sɒlvənt/ *a* solvente ● *n* solvente *m*

sombre /'sɒmbə(r)/ *a* tetro; (*clothes*) scuro

some /sʌm/ *a* (*a certain amount of*) del; (*a certain number of*) qualche, alcuni; ~ **day** un giorno o l'altro; **I need** ~ **money/books** ho bisogno di soldi/libri; **do** ~ **shopping** fare qualche acquisto ● *pron* (*a certain amount*) un po'; (*a certain number*) alcuni; **I want** ~ ne voglio

some: ~**body** /-bədɪ/ *pron* & *n* qualcuno *m.* **~how** *adv* in qualche modo; **~how or other** in un modo o nell'altro. **~one** *pron* & *n* = **somebody**

somersault /'sʌməsɔːlt/ *n* capriola *f*; **turn a ~** fare una capriola

something *pron* qualche cosa, qualcosa; **~ different** qualcosa di diverso; **~ like** un po' come; (*approximately*) qualcosa come; **see ~ of sb** vedere qcno un po'

some: ~time *adv* un giorno o l'altro; **~time last summer** durante l'estate scorsa. **~times** *adv* qualche volta. **~what** *adv* piuttosto. **~where** *adv* da qualche parte ● *pron* **~where to eat** un posto in cui mangiare

son /sʌn/ *n* figlio *m*

sonata /sə'nɑːtə/ *n* sonata *f*

song /sɒŋ/ *n* canzone *f*

sonic /'sɒnɪk/ *a* sonico. **~ 'boom** *n* bang *m inv* sonico

'son-in-law *n* (*pl* **~s-in-law**) genero *m*

sonnet /'sɒnɪt/ *n* sonetto *m*

soon /suːn/ *adv* presto; (*in a short time*) tra poco; **as ~ as** [non] appena; **as ~ as possible** il più presto possibile; **~er or later** prima o poi; **the ~er the better** prima è, meglio è; **no ~er had I arrived than...** ero appena arrivato quando...; **I would ~er go** preferirei andare; **~ after** subito dopo

soot /sʊt/ *n* fuliggine *f*

sooth|e /suːð/ *vt* calmare

sooty /'sʊtɪ/ *a* fuligginoso

sophisticated /sə'fɪstɪkeɪtɪd/ *a* sofisticato

soporific /sɒpə'rɪfɪk/ *a* soporifero

sopping /'sɒpɪŋ/ *a* & *adv* **be ~** [**wet**] essere bagnato fradicio

soppy /'sɒpɪ/ *a* (**-ier, -iest**) *fam* svenevole

soprano /sə'prɑːnəʊ/ *n* soprano *m*

sordid /'sɔːdɪd/ *a* sordido

sore /sɔː(r)/ *a* dolorante; (*Am: vexed*) arrabbiato; **it's ~** fa male; **have a ~ throat** avere mal di gola ● *n* piaga *f*. **~ly** *adv* ⟨*tempted*⟩ seriamente

sorrow /'sɒrəʊ/ *n* tristezza *f*. **~ful** *a* tristе

sorry /'sɒrɪ/ *a* (**-ier, -iest**) (*sad*) spiacente; (*wretched*) pietoso; **you'll be ~!** te ne pentirai!; **I am ~** mi dispiace; **be or feel ~ for** provare compassione per; **~! scusa!**; (*more polite*) scusi!

sort /sɔːt/ *n* specie *f*; (*fam: person*) tipo *m*; **it's a ~ of fish** è un tipo di pesce; **be out of ~s** (*fam: unwell*) stare poco bene ● *vt* classificare. **sort out** *vt* sele-

zionare ⟨*papers*⟩; *fig* risolvere ⟨*problem*⟩; occuparsi di ⟨*person*⟩

'so-so *a* & *adv* così così

sought /sɔːt/ *see* **seek**

soul /səʊl/ *n* anima *f*

sound¹ /saʊnd/ *a* sano; (*sensible*) saggio; (*secure*) solido; ⟨*thrashing*⟩ clamoroso ● *adv* **~ asleep** profondamente addormentato

sound² *n* suono *m*; (*noise*) rumore *m*; **I don't like the ~ of it** *fam* non mi suona bene ● *vi* suonare; (*seem*) aver l'aria ● *vt* (*pronounce*) pronunciare; *Med* auscoltare ⟨*chest*⟩. **~ barrier** *n* muro *m* del suono. **~ card** *n Comput* scheda *f* sonora. **~less** *a* silenzioso. **sound out** *vt fig* sondare

soundly /'saʊndlɪ/ *adv* ⟨*sleep*⟩ profondamente; ⟨*defeat*⟩ clamorosamente

'sound: ~proof *a* impenetrabile al suono. **~track** *n* colonna *f* sonora

soup /suːp/ *n* minestra *f*. **~ed-up** *a fam* ⟨*engine*⟩ truccato

soup: ~-plate *n* piatto *m* fondo. **~-spoon** *n* cucchiaio *m* da minestra

sour /'saʊə(r)/ *a* agro; (*not fresh & fig*) acido

source /sɔːs/ *n* fonte *f*

south /saʊθ/ *n* sud *m*; **to the ~ of** a sud di ● *a* del sud, meridionale ● *adv* verso il sud

south: S~ 'Africa *n* Sudafrica *f*. **S~ A'merica** *n* America *f* del Sud. **S~ American** *a* & *n* sud-americano, -a *mf*. **~-'east** *n* sud-est *m*

southerly /'sʌðəlɪ/ *a* del sud

southern /'sʌðən/ *a* del sud, meridionale; **~ Italy** il Mezzogiorno. **~er** *n* meridionale *mf*

South 'Pole *n* polo *m* Sud

'southward[s] /-wəd[z]/ *adv* verso sud

souvenir /suːvə'nɪə(r)/ *n* ricordo *m*, souvenir *m inv*

sovereign /'sɒvrɪn/ *a* sovrano ● *n* sovrano, -a *mf*. **~ty** *n* sovranità *f inv*

Soviet /'səʊvɪət/ *a* sovietico; **~ Union** Unione *f* Sovietica

sow¹ /saʊ/ *n* scrofa *f*

sow² /səʊ/ *vt* (*pt* **sowed**, *pp* **sown** *or* **sowed**) seminare

soya /'sɔɪə/ *n* **~ bean** soia *f*

spa /spɑː/ *n* stazione *f* termale

space /speɪs/ *n* spazio *m* ● *a* ⟨*research etc*⟩ spaziale ● *vt* **~ [out]** distanziare

space: ~craft *n* navetta *f* spaziale. **~ship** *n* astronave *f*

spacious /'speɪʃəs/ *a* spazioso

spade /speɪd/ n vanga f; (for child) paletta f; **~s** pl (in cards) picche fpl. **~work** n lavoro m preparatorio

Spain /speɪn/ n Spagna f

span¹ /spæn/ n spa~ na f; (of arch) luce f; (of time) arco m; (of wings) apertura f ● vt (pt/pp **spanned**) estendersi su

span² see **spick**

Span|iard /'spænjəd/ n spagnolo, -a mf. **~ish** a spagnolo ● n (language) spagnolo m; **the ~ish** pl gli spagnoli

spank /spæŋk/ vt sculacciare. **~ing** n sculacciata f

spanner /'spænə(r)/ n chiave f inglese

spar /spɑː(r)/ vi (pt/pp **sparred**) (boxing) allenarsi; (argue) litigare

spare /speə(r)/ a (surplus) in più; (additional) di riserva ● n (part) ricambio m ● vt risparmiare; (do without) fare a meno di; **can you ~ five minutes?** avresti cinque minuti?; **to ~** (surplus) in eccedenza. **~ part** n pezzo m di ricambio. **~ time** n tempo m libero. **~ wheel** n ruota f di scorta

sparing /'speərɪŋ/ a parco (**with** di). **~ly** adv con parsimonia

spark /spɑːk/ n scintilla f. **~ing-plug** n Auto candela f

sparkl|e /'spɑːkl/ n scintillio m ● vi scintillare. **~ing** a frizzante; ⟨wine⟩ spumante

sparrow /'spærəʊ/ n passero m

sparse /spɑːs/ a rado. **~ly** adv scarsamente; **~ly populated** a bassa densità di popolazione

spartan /'spɑːtn/ a spartano

spasm /'spæzm/ n spasmo m. **~odic** /-'mɒdɪk/ a spasmodico

spastic /'spæstɪk/ a spastico ● n spastico, -a mf

spat /spæt/ see **spit¹**

spate /speɪt/ n (series) successione f; **be in full ~** essere in piena

spatial /'speɪʃl/ a spaziale

spatter /'spætə(r)/ vt schizzare

spatula /'spætjʊlə/ n spatola f

spawn /spɔːn/ n uova fpl (di pesci, rane ecc) ● vi deporre le uova ● vt fig generare

spay /speɪ/ vt sterilizzare

speak /spiːk/ v (pt **spoke**, pp **spoken**) ● vi parlare (**to** a); **~ing!** Teleph sono io! ● vt dire; **~ one's mind** dire quello che si pensa. **speak for** vi parlare a nome di. **speak up** vi parlare più forte; **~ up for oneself** farsi valere

speaker /'spiːkə(r)/ n parlante mf; (in public) oratore, -trice mf; (of stereo) cassa f

spear /spɪə(r)/ n lancia f

spec /spek/ n **on ~** fam senza certezza

special /'speʃl/ a speciale. **~ist** n specialista mf. **~ity** /-ʃɪ'rælɪtɪ/ n specialità f inv

special|ize /'speʃəlaɪz/ vi specializzarsi. **~ly** adv specialmente; (particularly) particolarmente

species /'spiːʃiːz/ n specie f inv

specific /spə'sɪfɪk/ a specifico. **~ally** adv in modo specifico

specifications /spesɪfɪ'keɪʃnz/ npl descrizione f

specify /'spesɪfaɪ/ vt (pt/pp **-ied**) specificare

specimen /'spesɪmən/ n campione m

speck /spek/ n macchiolina f; (particle) granello m

speckled /'spekld/ a picchiettato

specs /speks/ npl fam occhiali mpl

spectacle /'spektəkl/ n (show) spettacolo m. **~s** npl occhiali mpl

spectacular /spek'tækjʊlə(r)/ a spettacolare

spectator /spek'teɪtə(r)/ n spettatore, -trice mf

spectre /spektə(r)/ n spettro m

spectrum /'spektrəm/ n (pl **-tra**) spettro m; fig gamma f

speculat|e /'spekjʊleɪt/ vi speculare. **~ion** /-'leɪʃn/ n speculazione f. **~ive** /-ɪv/ a speculativo. **~or** n speculatore, -trice mf

sped /sped/ see **speed**

speech /spiːtʃ/ n linguaggio m; (address) discorso m. **~less** a senza parole

speed /spiːd/ n velocità f inv; (gear) marcia f; **at ~** a tutta velocità ● vi (pt/pp **sped**) andare veloce; (pt/pp **speeded**) (go too fast) andare a velocità eccessiva. **speed up** (pt/pp **speeded up**) vt/i accelerare

speed: ~boat n motoscafo m. **~ing** n eccesso m di velocità. **~ limit** n limite m di velocità

speedometer /spiː'dɒmɪtə(r)/ n tachimetro m

speed|y /'spiːdɪ/ a (**-ier, -iest**) rapido. **~ily** adv rapidamente

spell¹ /spel/ n (turn) turno m; (of weather) periodo m

spell² v (pt/pp **spelled** or **spelt**) ● vt **how do you ~...?** come si scrive...?; **could you ~ that for me?** me lo può compitare?; **~ disaster** essere disastroso ● *vi* **he can't ~** fa molti errori d'ortografia

spell[3] *n* (*magic*) incantesimo *m*. **~bound** *a* affascinato

spelling /'spelɪŋ/ *n* ortografia *f*

spelt /spelt/ *see* **spell**

spend /spend/ *vt/i* (*pt/pp* **spent**) spendere; passare (*time*)

spent /spent/ *see* **spend**

sperm /spɜːm/ *n* spermatozoo *m*; (*semen*) sperma *m*

spew /spjuː/ *vt/i* vomitare

spher|e /sfɪə(r)/ *n* sfera *f*. **~ical** /'sferɪkl/ *a* sferico

spice /spaɪs/ *n* spezia *f*; *fig* pepe *m*

spick /spɪk/ *a* **~ and span** lindo

spicy /'spaɪsɪ/ *a* piccante

spider /'spaɪdə(r)/ *n* ragno *m*

spik|e /spaɪk/ *n* punta *f*; *Bot*, *Zool* spina *f*; (*on shoe*) chiodo *m*. **~y** *a* (*plant*) pungente

spill /spɪl/ *v* (*pt/pp* **spilt** *or* **spilled**) ● *vt* versare (*blood*) ● *vi* rovesciarsi

spin /spɪn/ *v* (*pt/pp* **spun**, *pres p* **spinning**) ● *vt* far girare; filare (*wool*); centrifugare (*washing*) ● *vi* girare; (*washing machine:*) centrifugare ● *n* rotazione *f*; (*short drive*) giretto *m*. **spin out** *vt* far durare

spinach /'spɪnɪdʒ/ *n* spinaci *mpl*

spinal /'spaɪnl/ *a* spinale. **~ 'cord** *n* midollo *m* spinale

spindl|e /'spɪndl/ *n* fuso *m*. **~y** *a* affusolato

spin-'drier *n* centrifuga *f*

spine /spaɪn/ *n* spina *f* dorsale; (*of book*) dorso *m*; *Bot*, *Zool* spina *f*. **~less** *a* *fig* smidollato

spinning /'spɪnɪŋ/ *n* filatura *f*. **~-wheel** *n* filatoio *m*

'spin-off *n* ricaduta *f*

spiral /'spaɪrəl/ *a* a spirale ● *n* spirale *f* ● *vi* (*pt/pp* **spiralled**) formare una spirale. **~ 'staircase** *n* scala *f* a chiocciola

spire /spaɪə(r)/ *n* guglia *f*

spirit /'spɪrɪt/ *n* spirito *m*; (*courage*) ardore *m*; **~s** *pl* (*alcohol*) liquori *mpl*; **in good ~s** di buon umore; **in low ~s** abbattuto

spirited /'spɪrɪtɪd/ *a* vivace; (*courageous*) pieno d'ardore

spirit: ~-level *n* livella *f* a bolla d'aria. **~ stove** *n* fornellino *m* [da campeggio]

spiritual /'spɪrɪtjʊəl/ *a* spirituale ● *n* spiritual *m*. **~ism** /-ɪzm/ *n* spiritismo *m*. **~ist** /-ɪst/ *n* spiritista *mf*

spit[1] /spɪt/ *n* (*for roasting*) spiedo *m*

spit[2] *n* sputo *m* ● *vt/i* (*pt/pp* **spat**, *pres p* **spitting**) sputare; (*cat:*) soffiare; (*fat:*) sfrigolare; **it's ~ting [with rain]** pioviggina; **the ~ting image of** il ritratto spiccicato di

spite /spaɪt/ *n* dispetto *m*; **in ~ of** malgrado ● *vt* far dispetto a. **~ful** *a* indispettito

spittle /'spɪtl/ *n* saliva *f*

splash /splæʃ/ *n* schizzo *m*; (*of colour*) macchia *f*; (*fam: drop*) goccio *m* ● *vt* schizzare; **~ sb with sth** schizzare qcno di qcsa ● *vi* schizzare. **splash about** *vi* schizzarsi. **splash down** *vi* (*spacecraft:*) ammarare

spleen /spliːn/ *n* *Anat* milza *f*

splendid /'splendɪd/ *a* splendido

splendour /'splendə(r)/ *n* splendore *m*

splint /splɪnt/ *n* *Med* stecca *f*

splinter /'splɪntə(r)/ *n* scheggia *f* ● *vi* scheggiarsi

split /splɪt/ *n* fessura *f*; (*quarrel*) rottura *f*; (*division*) scissione *f*; (*tear*) strappo *m* ● *v* (*pt/pp* **split**, *pres p* **splitting**) ● *vt* spaccare; (*share, divide*) dividere; (*tear*) strappare ● *vi* spaccarsi; (*tear*) strapparsi; (*divide*) dividersi; **~ on sb** *fam* denunciare qcno ● *a* **a ~ second** una frazione di secondo. **split up** *vt* dividersi ● *vi* (*couple:*) separarsi

splutter /'splʌtə(r)/ *vi* farfugliare

spoil /spɔɪl/ *n* **~s** *pl* bottino *msg* ● *v* (*pt/pp* **spoilt** *or* **spoiled**) ● *vt* rovinare; viziare (*person*) ● *vi* andare a male. **~sport** *n* guastafeste *mf inv*

spoke[1] /spəʊk/ *n* raggio *m*

spoke[2], **spoken** /'spəʊkn/ *see* **speak**

'spokesman *n* portavoce *m inv*

sponge /spʌndʒ/ *n* spugna *f* ● *vt* pulire (*con la spugna*) ● *vi* **~ on** *fam* scroccare da. **~-cake** *n* pan *m* di Spagna

spong|er /'spʌndʒə(r)/ *n* scroccone, -a *mf*. **~y** *a* spugnoso

sponsor /'spɒnsə(r)/ *n* garante *mf*; *Radio*, *TV* sponsor *m inv*; (*god-parent*) padrino *m*, madrina *f*; (*for membership*) socio, -a *mf* garante ● *vt* sponsorizzare. **~ship** *n* sponsorizzazione *f*

spontaneous /spɒn'teɪnɪəs/ *a* spontaneo

spoof /spuːf/ *n* *fam* parodia *f*

spooky /'spuːkɪ/ *a* (**-ier**, **-iest**) *fam* sinistro

spool /spuːl/ *n* bobina *f*

spoon /spuːn/ *n* cucchiaio *m* ● *vt* mettere col cucchiaio. **~-feed** *vt* (*pt/pp* **-fed**) *fig* imboccare. **~ful** *n* cucchiaiata *f*

sporadic /spə'rædɪk/ *a* sporadico

sport /spɔːt/ *n* sport *m inv* ● *vt* sfoggia-

re. ~ing a sportivo; ~ing chance possibilità f inv
sports: ~car n automobile f sportiva. ~ coat n, ~ jacket n giacca f sportiva. ~man n sportivo m. ~woman n sportiva f
sporty /'spɔːtɪ/ a (-ier, -iest) sportivo
spot /spɒt/ n macchia f; (pimple) brufolo m; (place) posto m; (in pattern) pois m inv; (of rain) goccia f; (of water) goccio m; ~s pl (rash) sfogo msg; a ~ of fam un po' di; a ~ of bother qualche problema; on the ~ sul luogo; (immediately) immediatamente; in a [tight] ~ fam in difficoltà ● vt (pt/pp spotted) macchiare; (fam: notice) individuare
spot: ~ 'check n (without warning) controllo m a sorpresa; do a ~ check on sth dare una controllata a qcsa. ~less a immacolato. ~light n riflettore m
spotted /'spɒtɪd/ a (material) a pois
spotty /'spɒtɪ/ a (-ier, -iest) (pimply) brufoloso
spouse /spaʊz/ n consorte mf
spout /spaʊt/ n becco m ● vi zampillare (from da)
sprain /spreɪn/ n slogatura f ● vt slogare
sprang /spræŋ/ see spring²
sprawl /sprɔːl/ vi (in chair) stravaccarsi; (city etc:) estendersi; go ~ing (fall) cadere disteso
spray /spreɪ/ n spruzzo m; (preparation) spray m inv; (container) spruzzatore m ● vt spruzzare. ~-gun n pistola f a spruzzo
spread /spred/ n estensione f; (of disease) diffusione f; (paste) crema f; (fam: feast) banchetto m ● v (pt/pp spread) ● vt spargere; spalmare (butter, jam); stendere (cloth, arms); diffondere (news, disease); dilazionare (payments); ~ sth with spalmare qcsa di ● vi spargersi; (butter:) spalmarsi; (disease:) diffondersi. ~sheet n Comput foglio m elettronico. spread out vt sparpagliare ● vi sparpagliarsi
spree /spriː/ n fam go on a ~ far baldoria; go on a shopping ~ fare spese folli
sprig /sprɪg/ n rametto m
sprightly /'spraɪtlɪ/ a (-ier, -iest) vivace
spring¹ /sprɪŋ/ n primavera f ● attrib primaverile
spring² n (jump) balzo m; (water) sor-

gente f; (device) molla f; (elasticity) elasticità f ● v (pt sprang, pp sprung) ● vi balzare; (arise) provenire (from da) ● vt he just sprang it on me me l'ha detto a cose fatte compiuto. **spring up** balzare; fig spuntare
spring: ~board n trampolino m. ~'cleaning n pulizie fpl di Pasqua. ~time n primavera f
sprinkl|e /'sprɪŋkl/ vt (scatter) spruzzare (liquid); spargere (flour, cocoa); ~ sth with spruzzare qcsa di (liquid); cospargere qcsa di (flour, cocoa). ~er n sprinkler m inv; (for lawn) irrigatore m. ~ing n (of liquid) spruzzatina f; (of pepper, salt) pizzico m; (of flour, sugar) spolveratina f; (of knowledge) infarinatura f; (of people) pugno m
sprint /sprɪnt/ n sprint m inv ● vi fare uno sprint; Sport sprintare. ~er n sprinter mf inv
sprout /spraʊt/ n germoglio m; [Brussels] ~s pl cavolini mpl di Bruxelles ● vi germogliare
spruce /spruːs/ a elegante ● n abete m
sprung /sprʌŋ/ see spring² ● a molleggiato
spud /spʌd/ n fam patata f
spun /spʌn/ see spin
spur /spɜː(r)/ n sperone m; (stimulus) stimolo m; (road) svincolo m; on the ~ of the moment su due piedi ● vt (pt/pp spurred) ~ [on] fig spronare [a]
spurious /'spjʊərɪəs/ a falso
spurn /spɜːn/ vt sdegnare
spurt /spɜːt/ n getto m; Sport scatto m; put on a ~ fare uno scatto ● vi sprizzare; (increase speed) scattare
spy /spaɪ/ n spia f ● v (pt/pp spied) ● vi spiare ● vt (fam: see) spiare. **spy on** vi spiare
spying /'spaɪɪŋ/ n spionaggio m
squabble /'skwɒbl/ n bisticcio m ● vi bisticciare
squad /skwɒd/ n squadra f
squadron /'skwɒdrən/ n Mil squadrone m; Aeron, Naut squadriglia f
squalid /'skwɒlɪd/ a squallido
squalor /'skwɒlə(r)/ n squallore m
squander /'skwɒndə(r)/ vt sprecare
square /skweə(r)/ a quadrato; (meal) sostanzioso; (fam: old-fashioned) vecchio stampo; all ~ fam pari ● n quadrato m; (in city) piazza f; (on chessboard) riquadro m ● vt (settle) far quadrare; Math elevare al quadrato ● vi (agree) armonizzare
squash /skwɒʃ/ n (drink) spremuta f;

(*sport*) squash *m*; (*vegetable*) zucca *f* ● *vt* schiacciare; soffocare ⟨*rebellion*⟩

squat /skwɒt/ *a* tarchiato ● *n fam* edificio *m* occupato abusivamente ● *vi* (*pt/pp* **squatted**) accovacciarsi; **~ in** occupare abusivamente. **~ter** *n* occupante *mf* abusivo, -a

squawk /skwɔːk/ *n* gracchio *m* ● *vi* gracchiare

squeak /skwiːk/ *n* squittio *m*; (*of hinge, brakes*) scricchiolio *m* ● *vi* squittire; ⟨*hinge, brakes:*⟩ scricchiolare

squeal /skwiːl/ *n* strillo *m*; (*of brakes*) cigolio *m* ● *vi* strillare; *sl* spifferare

squeamish /ˈskwiːmɪʃ/ *a* dallo stomaco delicato

squeeze /skwiːz/ *n* stretta *f*; (*crush*) pigia pigia *m inv* ● *vt* premere; (*to get juice*) spremere; stringere ⟨*hand*⟩; (*force*) spingere a forza; (*fam: extort*) estorcere (**out of** da). **squeeze in/out** *vi* sgusciare dentro/fuori. **squeeze up** *vi* stringersi

squelch /skweltʃ/ *vi* sguazzare

squid /skwɪd/ *n* calamaro *m*

squiggle /ˈskwɪgl/ *n* scarabocchio *m*

squint /skwɪnt/ *n* strabismo *m* ● *vi* essere strabico

squire /ˈskwaɪə(r)/ *n* signorotto *m* di campagna

squirm /skwɜːm/ *vi* contorcersi; (*feel embarrassed*) sentirsi imbarazzato

squirrel /ˈskwɪrəl/ *n* scoiattolo *m*

squirt /skwɜːt/ *n* spruzzo *m*; (*fam: person*) presuntuoso *m* ● *vt/i* spruzzare

St *abbr* (**Saint**) S; *abbr* **Street**

stab /stæb/ *n* pugnalata *f*, coltellata *f*; (*sensation*) fitta *f*; (*fam: attempt*) tentativo *m* ● *vt* (*pt/pp* **stabbed**) pugnalare, accoltellare

stability /stəˈbɪlətɪ/ *n* stabilità *f inv*

stabilize /ˈsteɪbɪlaɪz/ *vt* stabilizzare ● *vi* stabilizzarsi

stable¹ /ˈsteɪbl/ *a* stabile

stable² *n* stalla *f*; (*establishment*) scuderia *f*

stack /stæk/ *n* catasta *f*; (*of chimney*) comignolo *m*; (*chimney*) ciminiera *f*; (*fam: large quantity*) montagna *f* ● *vt* accatastare

stadium /ˈsteɪdɪəm/ *n* stadio *m*

staff /stɑːf/ *n* (*stick*) bastone *m*; (*employees*) personale *m*; (*teachers*) corpo *m* insegnante; *Mil* Stato *m* Maggiore ● *vt* fornire di personale. **~-room** *n Sch* sala *f* insegnanti

stag /stæg/ *n* cervo *m*

stage /steɪdʒ/ *n* palcoscenico *m*;

(*profession*) teatro *m*; (*in journey*) tappa *f*; (*in process*) stadio *m*; **go on the ~** darsi al teatro; **by** *or* **in ~s** a tappe ● *vt* mettere in scena; (*arrange*) organizzare

stage: ~ door *n* ingresso *m* degli artisti. **~ fright** *n* panico *m* da scena. **~ manager** *n* direttore, -trice *mf* di scena

stagger /ˈstægə(r)/ *vi* barcollare ● *vt* sbalordire; scaglionare ⟨*holidays etc*⟩; **I was ~ed** sono rimasto sbalordito ● *n* vacillamento *m*. **~ing** *a* sbalorditivo

stagnant /ˈstægnənt/ *a* stagnante

stagnat|e /stægˈneɪt/ *vi* fig [ri]stagnare. **~ion** /-ˈneɪʃn/ *n fig* inattività *f*

'stag party *n* addio *m* al celibato

staid /steɪd/ *a* posato

stain /steɪn/ *n* macchia *f*; (*for wood*) mordente *m* ● *vt* macchiare; ⟨*wood*⟩ dare il mordente a; **~ed glass** vetro *m* colorato; **~ed-glass window** vetrata *f* colorata. **~less** *a* senza macchia; ⟨*steel*⟩ inossidabile. **~ remover** *n* smacchiatore *m*

stair /steə(r)/ *n* gradino *m*; **~s** *pl* scale *fpl*. **~case** *n* scale *fpl*

stake /steɪk/ *n* palo *m*; (*wager*) posta *f*; *Comm* partecipazione *f*; **at ~** in gioco ● *vt* puntellare; (*wager*) scommettere

stale /steɪl/ *a* stantio; ⟨*air*⟩ viziato; (*uninteresting*) trito [e ritrito]. **~mate** *n* (*in chess*) stallo *m*; (*deadlock*) situazione *f* di stallo

stalk¹ /stɔːk/ *n* gambo *m*

stalk² *vt* inseguire ● *vi* camminare impettito

stall /stɔːl/ *n* box *m inv*; **~s** *pl Theat* platea *f*; (*in market*) bancarella *f* ● *vi* ⟨*engine:*⟩ spegnersi; *fig* temporeggiare ● *vt* far spegnere ⟨*engine*⟩; tenere a bada ⟨*person*⟩

stallion /ˈstæljən/ *n* stallone *m*

stalwart /ˈstɔːlwət/ *a* fedele

stamina /ˈstæmɪnə/ *n* [capacità *f inv* di] resistenza *f*

stammer /ˈstæmə(r)/ *n* balbettio *m* ● *vt/i* balbettare

stamp /stæmp/ *n* (*postage ~*) francobollo *m*; (*instrument*) timbro *m*; *fig* impronta *f* ● *vt* affrancare ⟨*letter*⟩; timbrare ⟨*bill*⟩; battere ⟨*feet*⟩. **stamp out** *vt* spegnere; *fig* soffocare

stampede /stæmˈpiːd/ *n* fuga *f* precipitosa, fuggi-fuggi *m inv fam* ● *vi* fuggire precipitosamente

stance /stɑːns/ *n* posizione *f*

stand /stænd/ *n* (*for bikes*) rastrelliera *f*; (*at exhibition*) stand *m inv*; (*in market*) bancarella f; (in stadium) gradinata f; fig posizione f ● v (pt/pp **stood**) ● vi stare in piedi; (rise) alzarsi [in piedi]; (be) trovarsi; (be candidate) essere candidato (**for** a); (stay valid) rimanere valido; ~ **still** non muoversi; **I don't know where I** ~ non so qual'è la mia posizione; ~ **firm** fig tener duro; ~ **together** essere solidali; ~ **to lose/ gain** rischiare di perdere/vincere; ~ **to reason** essere logico ● vt (withstand) resistere a; (endure) sopportare; (place) mettere; ~ **a chance** avere una possibilità; ~ **one's ground** tener duro; ~ **the test of time** superare la prova del tempo; ~ **sb a beer** offrire una birra a qcno. **stand by** vi stare a guardare; (be ready) essere pronto ● vt (support) appoggiare. **stand down** vi (retire) ritirarsi. **stand for** vt (mean) significare; (tolerate) tollerare. **stand in for** vt sostituire. **stand out** vi spiccare. **stand up** vi alzarsi [in piedi]. **stand up for** vt prendere le difese di; ~ **up for oneself** farsi valere. **stand up to** vt affrontare

standard /'stændəd/ a standard; **be** ~ **practice** essere pratica corrente ● n standard m inv; Techn norma f; (level) livello m; (quality) qualità f inv; (flag) stendardo m; ~**s** pl (morals) valori mpl; ~ **of living** tenore m di vita. ~**ize** vt standardizzare

'**standard lamp** n lampada f a stelo

'**stand-by** n riserva f; **on** ~ (at airport) in lista d'attesa

'**stand-in** n controfigura f

standing /'stændɪŋ/ a (erect) in piedi; (permanent) permanente ● n posizione f; (duration) durata f. ~ '**order** n addebitamento m diretto. ~**-room** n posti mpl in piedi

stand: ~**-offish** /stænd'ɒfɪʃ/ a scostante. ~**point** n punto m di vista. ~**still** n **come to a** ~**still** fermarsi; **at a** ~**still** in un periodo di stasi

stank /stæŋk/ see **stink**

staple[1] /'steɪpl/ n (product) prodotto m principale

staple[2] n graffa f ● vt pinzare. ~**r** n pinzatrice f, cucitrice f

star /stɑː(r)/ n stella f; (asterisk) asterisco m; Theat, Cinema, Sport divo, -a mf, stella f ● vi (pt/pp **starred**) essere l'interprete principale

starboard /'stɑːbəd/ n tribordo m

starch /stɑːtʃ/ n amido m ● vt inamidare. ~**y** a ricco di amido; fig compito

stare /steə(r)/ n sguardo m fisso ● vi

it's rude to ~ è da maleducati fissare la gente; ~ **at** fissare; ~ **into space** guardare nel vuoto

'**starfish** n stella f di mare

stark /stɑːk/ a austero; (contrast) forte ● adv completamente; ~ **naked** completamente nudo

starling /'stɑːlɪŋ/ n storno m

'**starlit** a stellato

starry /'stɑːrɪ/ a stellato

start /stɑːt/ n inizio m; (departure) partenza f; (jump) sobbalzo m; **from the** ~ [fin] dall'inizio; **for a** ~ tanto per cominciare; **give sb a** ~ Sport dare un vantaggio a qcno ● vi [in]cominciare; (set out) avviarsi; (engine, car:) partire; (jump) trasalire; **to** ~ **with,...** tanto per cominciare,... ● vt [in]cominciare; (cause) dare inizio a; (found) mettere su; mettere in moto (car); mettere in giro (rumour). ~**er** n Culin primo m [piatto m]; (in race: giving signal) starter m inv; (participant) concorrente mf; Auto motorino m d'avviamento. ~**ing-point** n punto m di partenza

startle /'stɑːtl/ vt far trasalire; (news:) sconvolgere

starvation /stɑː'veɪʃn/ n fame f

starve /stɑːv/ vi morire di fame ● vt far morire di fame

stash /stæʃ/ vt fam ~ [**away**] nascondere

state /steɪt/ n stato m; (grand style) pompa f; ~ **of play** punteggio m; **be in a** ~ (person:) essere agitato; **lie in** ~ essere esposto ● attrib di Stato; Sch pubblico; (with ceremony) di gala ● vt dichiarare; (specify) precisare. ~**less** a apolide

stately /'steɪtlɪ/ a (-ier, -iest) maestoso. ~ '**home** n dimora f signorile

statement /'steɪtmənt/ n dichiarazione f; Jur deposizione f; (in banking) estratto m conto; (account) rapporto m

'**statesman** n statista m

static /'stætɪk/ a statico

station /'steɪʃn/ n stazione f; (police) commissariato m ● vt appostare (guard); **be** ~**ed in Germany** essere di stanza in Germania. ~**ary** /-ərɪ/ a immobile

stationer /'steɪʃənə(r)/ n ~'**s** [shop] cartoleria f. ~**y** n cartoleria f

'**station-wagon** n Am familiare f

statistic|al /stə'tɪstɪkl/ a statistico. ~**s** n & pl statistica f

statue /'stætjuː/ n statua f

stature /'stætʃə(r)/ n statura f

status /'steɪtəs/ n condizione f; (high rank) alto rango m. ~ **symbol** n status symbol m inv

statut|e /'stætjuːt/ n statuto m. ~**ory** a statutario

staunch /stɔːntʃ/ a fedele. ~**ly** adv fedelmente

stave /steɪv/ vt ~ **off** tenere lontano

stay /steɪ/ n soggiorno m ● vi restare, rimanere; (reside) alloggiare; ~ **the night** passare la notte; ~ **put** non muoversi ● vt ~ **the course** resistere fino alla fine. **stay away** vi stare lontano. **stay behind** vi non andare con gli altri. **stay in** vi (at home) stare in casa; Sch restare a scuola dopo le lezioni. **stay up** vi stare su; ⟨person:⟩ stare alzato

stead /sted/ n **in his** ~ in sua vece; **stand sb in good** ~ tornare utile a qcno. ~**fast** a fedele; ⟨refusal⟩ fermo

steadily /'stedɪlɪ/ adv (continually) continuamente

steady /'stedɪ/ a (-ier, -iest) saldo, fermo; ⟨breathing⟩ regolare; ⟨job, boyfriend⟩ fisso; (dependable) serio

steak /steɪk/ n (for stew) spezzatino m; (for grilling, frying) bistecca f

steal /stiːl/ v (pt stole, pp stolen) ● vt rubare (from da). **steal in/out** vi entrare/uscire furtivamente

stealth /stelθ/ n **by** ~ di nascosto. ~**y** a furtivo

steam /stiːm/ n vapore m; **under one's own** ~ fam da solo ● vt Culin cucinare a vapore ● vi fumare. **steam up** vi appannarsi

'steam-engine n locomotiva f

steamer /'stiːmə(r)/ n piroscafo m; (saucepan) pentola f a vapore

'steamroller n rullo m compressore

steamy /'stiːmɪ/ a appannato

steel /stiːl/ n acciaio m ● vt ~ **oneself** temprarsi

steep¹ /stiːp/ vt (soak) lasciare a bagno

steep² a ripido; ⟨fam: price⟩ esorbitante. ~**ly** adv ripidamente

steeple /'stiːpl/ n campanile m. ~**chase** n corsa f ippica a ostacoli

steer /stɪə(r)/ vt/i guidare; ~ **clear of** stare alla larga da. ~**ing** n Auto sterzo m. ~**ing-wheel** n volante m

stem¹ /stem/ n stelo m; (of glass) gambo m; (of word) radice f ● vi (pt/pp stemmed) ~ **from** derivare da

stem² vt (pt/pp stemmed) contenere

stench /stentʃ/ n fetore m

step /step/ n passo m; (stair) gradino m; ~**s** pl (ladder) scala f portatile; **in** ~ al passo; **be out of** ~ non stare al passo; ~ **by** ~ un passo alla volta ● vi (pt/pp stepped) ~ **into** entrare in; ~ **out of** uscire da; ~ **out of line** sgarrare. **step down** vi fig dimettersi. **step forward** vi farsi avanti. **step in** vi fig intervenire. **step up** vt (increase) aumentare

step: ~**brother** n fratellastro m. ~**child** n figliastro, -a mf. ~**daughter** n figliastra f. ~**father** n patrigno m. ~**ladder** n scala f portatile. ~**mother** n matrigna f

'stepping-stone n pietra f per guadare; fig trampolino m

step: ~**sister** n sorellastra f. ~**son** n figliastro m

stereo /'sterɪəʊ/ n stereo m; **in** ~ in stereofonia. ~**phonic** /-'fɒnɪk/ a stereofonico

stereotype /'sterɪətaɪp/ n stereotipo m. ~**d** a stereotipato

steril|e /'steraɪl/ a sterile. ~**ity** /stə'rɪlətɪ/ n sterilità f

steriliz|ation /sterəlaɪ'zeɪʃn/ n sterilizzazione f. ~**e** /'ster-/ vt sterilizzare

sterling /'stɜːlɪŋ/ a fig apprezzabile; ~ **silver** argento m pregiato ● n sterlina j

stern¹ /stɜːn/ a severo

stern² n (of boat) poppa f

stethoscope /'steθəskəʊp/ n stetoscopio m

stew /stjuː/ n stufato m; **in a** ~ fam agitato ● vt/i cuocere in umido; ~**ed fruit** frutta f cotta

steward /'stjuːəd/ n (at meeting) organizzatore, -trice mf; (on ship, aircraft) steward m inv. ~**ess** n hostess f inv

stick¹ /stɪk/ n bastone m; (of celery, rhubarb) gambo m; Sport mazza f

stick² v (pt/pp stuck) ● vt (stab) [con]ficcare; (glue) attaccare; (fam: put) mettere; (fam: endure) sopportare ● vi (adhere) attaccarsi (**to** a); (jam) bloccarsi; ~ **to** attenersi a ⟨facts⟩; mantenere ⟨story⟩; perseverare in ⟨task⟩; ~ **at it** fam tener duro; ~ **at nothing** fam non fermarsi di fronte a niente; **be stuck** ⟨vehicle, person:⟩ essere bloccato; ⟨drawer:⟩ essere incastrato; **be stuck with sth** fam farsi incastrare con qcsa. **stick out** vi (project) sporgere; (fam: catch the eye) risaltare ● vt fam fare ⟨tongue⟩. **stick up for** vt fam difendere

sticker /'stɪkə(r)/ n autoadesivo m

'sticking plaster n cerotto m

stick-in-the-mud n retrogrado m

stickler /'stɪklə(r)/ n **be a** ~ **for** tenere molto a

sticky /'stɪkɪ/ a (-ier, -iest) appiccicoso; (adhesive) adesivo; (fig: difficult) difficile

stiff /stɪf/ a rigido; (brush, task) duro; (person) controllato; (drink) forte; (penalty) severo; (price) alto; **bored ~** fam annoiato a morte; **~ neck** torcicollo m. **~en** vt irrigidire ● vi irrigidirsi. **~ness** n rigidità f

stifl|e /'staɪfl/ vt soffocare. **~ing** a soffocante

stigma /'stɪgmə/ n marchio m

stiletto /stɪ'letəʊ/ n stiletto m; **~ heels** tacchi mpl a spillo; **~s** (pl: shoes) scarpe fpl coi tacchi a spillo

still¹ /stɪl/ n distilleria f

still² a fermo; (drink) non gasato; **keep/stand ~** stare fermo ● n quiete f; (photo) posa f ● adv ancora; (nevertheless) nondimeno, comunque; **I'm ~ not sure** non sono ancora sicuro

'stillborn a nato morto

still 'life n natura f morta

stilted /'stɪltɪd/ a artificioso

stilts /stɪlts/ npl trampoli mpl

stimulant /'stɪmjʊlənt/ n eccitante m

stimulat|e /'stɪmjʊleɪt/ vt stimolare. **~ion** /-'leɪʃn/ n stimolo m

stimulus /'stɪmjʊləs/ n (pl -li /-laɪ/) stimolo m

sting /stɪŋ/ n puntura f; (organ) pungiglione m ● v (pt/pp **stung**) ● vt pungere; (jellyfish:) pizzicare ● vi (insect:) pungere. **~ing nettle** n ortica f

stingy /'stɪndʒɪ/ a (-ier, -iest) tirchio

stink /stɪŋk/ n puzza f ● vi (pt **stank**, pp **stunk**) puzzare

stint /stɪnt/ n lavoro m; **do one's ~** fare la propria parte ● vt **~ on** lesinare su

stipulat|e /'stɪpjʊleɪt/ vt porre come condizione. **~ion** /-'leɪʃn/ n condizione f

stir /stɜː(r)/ n mescolata f; (commotion) trambusto m ● v (pt/pp **stirred**) ● vt muovere; (mix) mescolare ● vi muoversi

stirrup /'stɪrəp/ n staffa f

stitch /stɪtʃ/ n punto m; (in knitting) maglia f; (pain) fitta f; **have sb in ~es** fam far ridere qcno a crepapelle ● vt cucire

stock /stɒk/ n (for use or selling) scorta f, stock m inv; (livestock) bestiame m; (lineage) stirpe f; Fin titoli mpl; Culin brodo m; **in ~** disponibile; **out of ~** esaurito; **take ~** fig fare il punto ● a solito ● vt (shop:) vendere; approvvigio-

nare (shelves). **stock up** vi far scorta (**with** di)

stock: ~broker n agente m di cambio. **~ cube** n dado m [da brodo]. **S~ Exchange** n Borsa f Valori

stocking /'stɒkɪŋ/ n calza f

stockist /'stɒkɪst/ n rivenditore m

stock: ~market n mercato m azionario. **~pile** vt fare scorta di ● n riserva f. **~-'still** a immobile. **~-taking** n Comm inventario m

stocky /'stɒkɪ/ a (-ier, -iest) tarchiato

stodgy /'stɒdʒɪ/ a indigesto

stoic /'stəʊɪk/ n stoico, -a mf. **~al** a stoico. **~ism** /-sɪzm/ stoicismo m

stoke /stəʊk/ vt alimentare

stole¹ /stəʊl/ n stola f

stole², stolen /'stəʊln/ see **steal**

stolid /'stɒlɪd/ a apatico

stomach /'stʌmək/ n pancia f; Anat stomaco m ● vt fam reggere. **~-ache** n mal m di pancia

stone /stəʊn/ n pietra f; (in fruit) nocciolo m; Med calcolo m; (weight) 6,348 kg ● a di pietra; (wall, Age) della pietra ● vt snocciolare (fruit). **~-cold** a gelido. **~-'deaf** a fam sordo come una campana

stony /'stəʊnɪ/ a pietroso; (glare) glaciale

stood /stʊd/ see **stand**

stool /stuːl/ n sgabello m

stoop /stuːp/ n curvatura f ● vi stare curvo; (bend down) chinarsi; fig abbassarsi

stop /stɒp/ n (break) sosta f; (for bus, train) fermata f; Gram punto m; **come to a ~** fermarsi; **put a ~ to sth** mettere fine a qcsa ● v (pt/pp **stopped**) ● vt fermare; arrestare (machine); (prevent) impedire; **~ sb doing sth** impedire a qcno di fare qcsa; **~ doing sth** smettere di fare qcsa; **~ that!** smettila! ● vi fermarsi; (rain:) smettere ● int fermo!. **stop off** vi fare una sosta. **stop up** vt otturare (sink); tappare (hole). **stop with** vi (fam: stay with) fermarsi da

stop: ~gap n palliativo m; (person) tappabuchi m inv. **~over** n sosta f; Aeron scalo m

stoppage /'stɒpɪdʒ/ n ostruzione f; (strike) interruzione f; (deduction) trattenute fpl

stopper /'stɒpə(r)/ n tappo m

stop: ~-press n ultimissime fpl. **~-watch** n cronometro m

storage /'stɔːrɪdʒ/ n deposito m; (in

warehouse) immagazzinaggio *m*; *Comput* memoria *f*

store /stɔː(r)/ *n* (*stock*) riserva *f*; (*shop*) grande magazzino *m*; (*depot*) deposito *m*; **in ~** in deposito; **what the future has in ~ for me** cosa mi riserva il futuro; **set great ~ by** tenere in gran conto ● *vt* tenere; (*in warehouse, Comput*) immagazzinare. **~-room** *n* magazzino *m*

storey /ˈstɔːrɪ/ *n* piano *m*

stork /stɔːk/ *n* cicogna *f*

storm /stɔːm/ *n* temporale *m*; (*with thunder*) tempesta *f* ● *vt* prendere d'assalto. **~y** *a* tempestoso

story /ˈstɔːrɪ/ *n* storia *f*; (*in newspaper*) articolo *m*

stout /staut/ *a* (*shoes*) resistente; (*fat*) robusto; (*defence*) strenuo

stove /stəʊv/ *n* stufa *f*; (*for cooking*) cucina *f* [economica]

stow /stəʊ/ *vt* metter via. **~away** *n* passeggero, -a *mf* clandestino, -a

straddle /ˈstrædl/ *vt* stare a cavalcioni su; (*standing*) essere a cavallo su

straggl|e /ˈstrægl/ *vi* crescere disordinatamente; (*dawdle*) rimanere indietro. **~er** *n* persona *f* che rimane indietro. **~y** *a* in disordine

straight /streɪt/ *a* diritto, dritto; (*answer, question, person*) diretto; (*tidy*) in ordine; (*drink, hair*) liscio ● *adv* diritto, dritto; (*directly*) direttamente; **~ away** immediatamente; **~ on** *or* **ahead** diritto; **~ out** *fig* apertamente; **go ~** *fam* rigare diritto; **put sth ~** mettere qcsa in ordine; **sit/stand up ~** stare diritto

straighten /ˈstreɪtn/ *vt* raddrizzare ● *vi* raddrizzarsi; **~ [up]** (*person*:) mettersi diritto. **straighten out** *vt fig* chiarire (*situation*)

straight'forward *a* franco; (*simple*) semplice

strain[1] /streɪn/ *n* (*streak*) vena *f*; *Bot* varietà *f inv*; (*of virus*) forma *f*

strain[2] *n* tensione *f*; (*injury*) stiramento *m*; **~s** *pl* (*of music*) note *fpl* ● *vt* tirare; sforzare (*eyes, voice*); stirarsi (*muscle*); *Culin* scolare ● *vi* sforzarsi. **~ed** *a* (*relations*) teso. **~er** *n* colino *m*

strait /streɪt/ *n* stretto *m*; **in dire ~s** in serie difficoltà. **~jacket** *n* camicia *f* di forza. **~-'laced** *a* puritano

strand[1] /strænd/ *n* (*of thread*) gugliata *f*; (*of beads*) filo *m*; (*of hair*) capello *m*

strand[2] *vt* **be ~ed** rimanere bloccato

strange /streɪndʒ/ *a* strano; (*not*

known) sconosciuto; (*unaccustomed*) estraneo. **~ly** *adv* stranamente; **~ly enough** curiosamente. **~r** *n* estraneo, -a *mf*

strangle /ˈstræŋgl/ *vt* strangolare; *fig* reprimere

strangulation /stræŋgjʊˈleɪʃn/ *n* strangolamento *m*

strap /stræp/ *n* cinghia *f*; (*to grasp in vehicle*) maniglia *f*; (*of watch*) cinturino *m*; (*shoulder ~*) bretella *f*, spallina *f* ● *vt* (*pt/pp* **strapped**) legare; **~ in** *or* **down** assicurare

strapping /ˈstræpɪŋ/ *a* robusto

strata /ˈstrɑːtə/ *npl see* **stratum**

stratagem /ˈstrætədʒəm/ *n* stratagemma *m*

strategic /strəˈtiːdʒɪk/ *a* strategico

strategy /ˈstrætədʒɪ/ *n* strategia *f*

stratum /ˈstrɑːtəm/ *n* (*pl* **strata**) strato *m*

straw /strɔː/ *n* paglia *f*; (*single piece*) fuscello *m*; (*for drinking*) cannuccia *f*; **the last ~** l'ultima goccia

strawberry /ˈstrɔːbərɪ/ *n* fragola *f*

stray /streɪ/ *a* (*animal*) randagio ● *n* randagio *m* ● *vi* andarsene per conto proprio; (*deviate*) deviare (**from** da)

streak /striːk/ *n* striatura *f*; (*fig: trait*) vena *f* ● *vi* sfrecciare. **~y** *a* striato; (*bacon*) grasso

stream /striːm/ *n* ruscello *m*; (*current*) corrente *f*; (*of blood, people*) flusso *m*; *Sch* classe *f* ● *vi* scorrere. **stream in/out** *vi* entrare/uscire a fiotti

streamer /ˈstriːmə(r)/ *n* (*paper*) stella *f* filante; (*flag*) pennone *m*

'streamline *vt* rendere aerodinamico; (*simplify*) snellire. **~d** *a* aerodinamico

street /striːt/ *n* strada *f*. **~car** *n* *Am* tram *m inv*. **~lamp** *n* lampione *m*

strength /streŋθ/ *n* forza *f*; (*of wall, bridge etc*) solidità *f*; **~s** *pl* punti *mpl* forti; **on the ~ of** grazie a. **~en** *vt* rinforzare

strenuous /ˈstrenjʊəs/ *a* faticoso; (*attempt, denial*) energico

stress /stres/ *n* (*emphasis*) insistenza *f*; *Gram* accento *m* tonico; (*mental*) stress *m inv*; *Mech* spinta *f* ● *vt* (*emphasize*) insistere su; *Gram* mettere l'accento [tonico] su. **~ed** *a* (*mentally*) stressato. **~ful** *a* stressante

stretch /stretʃ/ *n* stiramento *m*; (*period*) periodo *m* di tempo; (*of road*) tratto *m*; (*elasticity*) elasticità *f*; **at a ~** di fila; **have a ~** stirarsi ● *vt* tirare; allargare (*shoes, arms etc*); (*person*:) allungare ● *vi* (*become wider*) allargarsi; (*extend*) estendersi; ⟨*person:*⟩ stirarsi. **~er** *n* barella *f*

strew /stru:/ *vt* (*pp* **strewn** *or* **strewed**) sparpagliare

stricken /'strɪkn/ *a* prostrato; **~ with** affetto da ⟨*illness*⟩

strict /strɪkt/ *a* severo; ⟨*precise*⟩ preciso. **~ly** *adv* severamente; **~ly speaking** in senso stretto

stride /straɪd/ *n* [lungo] passo *m*; **take sth in one's ~** accettare qcsa con facilità ● *vi* (*pt* **strode**, *pp* **stridden**) andare a gran passi

strident /'straɪdənt/ *a* stridente; ⟨*colour*⟩ vistoso

strife /straɪf/ *n* conflitto *m*

strike /straɪk/ *n* sciopero *m*; *Mil* attacco *m*; **on ~** in sciopero ● *v* (*pt/pp* **struck**) ● *vt* colpire; accendere ⟨*match*⟩; trovare ⟨*oil, gold*⟩; ⟨*delete*⟩ depennare; (*occur to*) venire in mente a; *Mil* attaccare ● *vi* ⟨*lightning:*⟩ cadere; ⟨*clock:*⟩ suonare; *Mil* attaccare; ⟨*workers:*⟩ scioperare; **~ lucky** azzeccarla. **strike off**, **strike out** *vt* eliminare. **strike up** *vt* fare ⟨*friendship*⟩; attaccare ⟨*conversation*⟩. **~-breaker** *n* persona *f* che non aderisce a uno sciopero

striker /'straɪkə(r)/ *n* scioperante *mf*

striking /'straɪkɪŋ/ *a* impressionante; ⟨*attractive*⟩ affascinante

string /strɪŋ/ *n* spago *m*; ⟨*of musical instrument, racket*⟩ corda *f*; ⟨*of pearls*⟩ filo *m*; ⟨*of lies*⟩ serie *f*; **the ~s** *pl Mus* gli archi; **pull ~s** *fam* usare le proprie conoscenze ● *vt* (*pt/pp* **strung**) ⟨*thread*⟩ infilare ⟨*beads*⟩. **~ed** *a* ⟨*instrument*⟩ a corda

stringent /'strɪndʒnt/ *a* rigido

strip /strɪp/ *n* striscia *f* ● *v* (*pt/pp* **stripped**) ● *vt* spogliare; togliere le lenzuola da ⟨*bed*⟩; scrostare ⟨*wood, furniture*⟩; smontare ⟨*machine*⟩; (*deprive*) privare (**of** di) ● *vi* (*undress*) spogliarsi. **~ cartoon** *n* striscia *f*. **~ club** *n* locale *m* di strip-tease

stripe /straɪp/ *n* striscia *f*; *Mil* gallone *m*. **~d** *a* a strisce

'striplight *n* tubo *m* al neon

stripper /'strɪpə(r)/ *n* spogliarellista *mf*; ⟨*solvent*⟩ sverniciatore *m*

strip-'tease *n* spogliarello *m*, striptease *m inv*

strive /straɪv/ *vi* (*pt* **strove**, *pp* **striven**) sforzarsi (**to** di); **~ for** sforzarsi di ottenere

strode /strəud/ *see* **stride**

stroke¹ /strəuk/ *n* colpo *m*; ⟨*of pen*⟩ tratto *m*; (*in swimming*) bracciata *f*; *Med* ictus *m inv*; **~ of luck** colpo *m* di fortuna; **put sb off his ~** far perdere il filo a qcno

stroke² *vt* accarezzare

stroll /strəul/ *n* passeggiata *f* ● *vi* passeggiare. **~er** *n* (*Am: push-chair*) passeggino *m*

strong /strɒŋ/ *a* (**-er** /-gə(r)/, **-est** /-gɪst/) forte; ⟨*argument*⟩ valido

strong: ~-box *n* cassaforte *f*. **~hold** *n* roccaforte *f*. **~ly** *adv* fortemente. **~-'minded** *a* risoluto. **~-room** *n* camera *f* blindata

stroppy /'strɒpɪ/ *a* scorbutico

strove /strəuv/ *see* **strive**

struck /strʌk/ *see* **strike**

structural /'strʌktʃərəl/ *a* strutturale. **~ly** *adv* strutturalmente

structure /'strʌktʃə(r)/ *n* struttura *f*

struggle /'strʌgl/ *n* lotta *f*; **with a ~** con difficoltà ● *vi* lottare; **~ for breath** respirare con fatica; **~ to do sth** fare fatica a fare qcsa; **~ to one's feet** alzarsi con fatica

strum /strʌm/ *vt/i* (*pt/pp* **strummed**) strimpellare

strung /strʌŋ/ *see* **string**

strut¹ /strʌt/ *n* ⟨*component*⟩ puntello *m*

strut² *vi* (*pt/pp* **strutted**) camminare impettito

stub /stʌb/ *n* mozzicone *m*; ⟨*counterfoil*⟩ matrice *f* ● *vt* (*pt/pp* **stubbed**) **~ one's toe** sbattere il dito del piede (**on** contro). **stub out** *vt* spegnere ⟨*cigarette*⟩

stubble /'stʌbl/ *n* barba *f* ispida. **~ly** *a* ispido

stubborn /'stʌbən/ *a* testardo; ⟨*refusal*⟩ ostinato

stubby /'stʌbɪ/ *a* (**-ier**, **-iest**) tozzo

stucco /'stʌkəu/ *n* stucco *m*

stuck /stʌk/ *see* **stick²**. **~-'up** *a fam* snob *inv*

stud¹ /stʌd/ *n* ⟨*on boot*⟩ tacchetto *m*; ⟨*on jacket*⟩ borchia *f*; ⟨*for ear*⟩ orecchino *m* [a bottone]

stud² *n* ⟨*of horses*⟩ scuderia *f*

student /'stju:dənt/ *n* studente *m*, studentessa *f*; ⟨*school child*⟩ scolaro, -a *mf*. **~ nurse** *n* studente, studentessa infermiere, -a

studied /'stʌdɪd/ *a* intenzionale; ⟨*politeness*⟩ studiato

studio /'stju:dɪəu/ *n* studio *m*

studious /'stju:dɪəs/ *a* studioso; ⟨*attention*⟩ studiato

study /'stʌdɪ/ n studio m ● vt/i (pt/pp **studied**) studiare

stuff /stʌf/ n materiale m; (fam: things) roba f ● vt riempire; (with padding) imbottire; Culin farcire; ~ **sth into a drawer/one's pocket** ficcare qcsa alla rinfusa in un cassetto/in tasca. ~**ing** n (padding) imbottitura f; Culin ripieno m

stuffy /'stʌfɪ/ a (-ier, -iest) che sa di chiuso; (old-fashioned) antiquato

stumbl|e /'stʌmbl/ vi inciampare; ~**e across** or **on** imbattersi in. ~**ing-block** n ostacolo m

stump /stʌmp/ n ceppo m; (of limb) moncone m. ~**ed** a fam perplesso ● **stump up** vt/i fam sganciare

stun /stʌn/ vt (pt/pp **stunned**) stordire; (astonish) sbalordire

stung /stʌŋ/ see **sting**

stunk /stʌŋk/ see **stink**

stunning /'stʌnɪŋ/ a fam favoloso; ⟨blow, victory⟩ sbalorditivo

stunt¹ /stʌnt/ n fam trovata f pubblicitaria

stunt² vt arrestare lo sviluppo di. ~**ed** a stentato

stupendous /stju:'pendəs/ a stupendo. ~**ly** adv stupendamente

stupid /'stju:pɪd/ a stupido. ~**ity** /-'pɪdətɪ/ n stupidità f. ~**ly** adv stupidamente

stupor /'stju:pə(r)/ n torpore m

sturdy /'stɜ:dɪ/ a (-ier, -iest) robusto; ⟨furniture⟩ solido

stutter /'stʌtə(r)/ n balbuzie f ● vt/i balbettare

sty, stye /staɪ/ n (pl **styes**) Med orzaiolo m

style /staɪl/ n stile m; (fashion) moda f; (sort) tipo m; (hair~) pettinatura f; **in ~** in grande stile

stylish /'staɪlɪʃ/ a elegante. ~**ly** adv con eleganza

stylist /'staɪlɪst/ n stilista mf; (hair-~) parrucchiere, -a mf. ~**ic** /-'lɪstɪk/ a stilistico

stylized /'staɪlaɪzd/ a stilizzato

stylus /'staɪləs/ n (on record player) puntina f

suave /swɑ:v/ a dai modi garbati

sub'conscious /sʌb-/ a subcosciente ● n subcosciente m. ~**ly** adv in modo inconscio

subcon'tract vt subappaltare (**to** a). ~**or** n subappaltatore m

'subdivi|de vt suddividere. ~**sion** n suddivisione f

subdue /səb'dju:/ vt sottomettere; (make quieter) attenuare. ~**d** a ⟨light⟩ attenuato; ⟨person, voice⟩ pacato

subhuman /sʌb'hju:mən/ a disumano

subject¹ /'sʌbdʒɪkt/ a ~ **to** soggetto a; (depending on) subordinato a; ~ **to availability** nei limiti della disponibilità ● n soggetto m; (of ruler) suddito, -a mf; Sch materia f

subject² /səb'dʒekt/ vt (to attack, abuse) sottoporre; assoggettare ⟨country⟩

subjective /səb'dʒektɪv/ a soggettivo. ~**ly** adv soggettivamente

subjugate /'sʌbdʒʊgeɪt/ vt soggiogare

subjunctive /səb'dʒʌŋktɪv/ a & n congiuntivo m

sub'let vt (pt/pp **-let**, pres p **-letting**) subaffittare

sublime /sə'blaɪm/ a sublime. ~**ly** adv sublimamente

subliminal /sə'blɪmɪnl/ a subliminale

sub-ma'chine-gun n mitraglietta f

subma'rine n sommergibile m

submerge /səb'mɜ:dʒ/ vt immergere; **be ~d** essere sommerso ● vi immergersi

submiss|ion /səb'mɪʃn/ n sottomissione f. ~**ive** /-sɪv/ a sottomesso

submit /səb'mɪt/ v (pt/pp **-mitted**, pres p **-mitting**) ● vt sottoporre ● vi sottomettersi

subordinate /sə'bɔ:dɪneɪt/ vt subordinare (**to** a)

subscribe /səb'skraɪb/ vi contribuire; ~ **to** abbonarsi a ⟨newspaper⟩; sottoscrivere ⟨fund⟩; fig aderire a. ~**r** n abbonato, -a mf

subscription /səb'skrɪpʃn/ n (to club) sottoscrizione f; (to newspaper) abbonamento m

subsequent /'sʌbsɪkwənt/ a susseguente. ~**ly** adv in seguito

subservient /səb'sɜ:vɪənt/ a subordinato; (servile) servile. ~**ly** adv servilmente

subside /səb'saɪd/ vi sprofondare; ⟨ground:⟩ avvallarsi; ⟨storm:⟩ placarsi

subsidiary /səb'sɪdɪərɪ/ a secondario ● n [company] filiale f

subsid|ize /'sʌbsɪdaɪz/ vt sovvenzionare. ~**y** n sovvenzione f

subsist /səb'sɪst/ vi vivere (**on** di). ~**ence** n sussistenza f

substance /'sʌbstəns/ n sostanza f

sub'standard a di qualità inferiore

substantial /səb'stænʃl/ a solido; ⟨meal⟩ sostanzioso; (considerable) notevole. **~ly** adv notevolmente; (*essentially*) sostanzialmente

substantiate /səb'stænʃɪeɪt/ vt comprovare

substitut|e /'sʌbstɪtjuːt/ n sostituto ●vt ~e **A for B** sostituire B con A ●vi ~e **for sb** sostituire qcno. **~ion** /-'tjuːʃn/ n sostituzione f

subterranean /sʌbtə'reɪnɪən/ a sotterraneo

'subtitle n sottotitolo m

sub|tle /'sʌtl/ a sottile; ⟨*taste, perfume*⟩ delicato. **~tlety** n sottigliezza f. **~tly** adv sottilmente

subtract /səb'trækt/ vt sottrarre. **~ion** /-ækʃn/ n sottrazione f

suburb /'sʌbɜːb/ n sobborgo m; **in the ~s** in periferia. **~an** /sə'bɜːbən/ a suburbano. **~ia** /sə'bɜːbɪə/ n sobborghi mpl

subversive /səb'vɜːsɪv/ a sovversivo

'subway n sottopassagio m; (*Am: railway*) metropolitana f

succeed /sək'siːd/ vi riuscire; (*follow*) succedere a; **~ in doing** riuscire a fare ●vt succedere a ⟨*king*⟩. **~ing** a successivo

success /sək'ses/ n successo m; **be a ~** (*in life*) aver successo. **~ful** a riuscito; ⟨*businessman, artist etc*⟩ di successo. **~fully** adv con successo

succession /sək'seʃn/ n successione f; **in ~** di seguito

successive /sək'sesɪv/ a successivo. **~ly** adv successivamente

successor /sək'sesə(r)/ n successore m

succinct /sək'sɪŋkt/ a succinto

succulent /'sʌkjʊlənt/ a succulento

succumb /sə'kʌm/ vi soccombere (**to** a)

such /sʌtʃ/ a tale; **~ a book** un libro di questo genere; **~ a thing** una cosa di questo genere; **~ a long time ago** talmente tanto tempo fa; **there is no ~ thing** non esiste una cosa così; **there is no ~ person** non esiste una persona così ●pron **as** ~ come tale; **~ as** chi; **and** ~ e simili; **~ as it is** così com'è. **~like** pron fam di tal genere

suck /sʌk/ vt succhiare. **suck up** vt assorbire. **suck up to** vt fam fare il lecchino con

sucker /'sʌkə(r)/ n Bot pollone m; (*fam: person*) credulone, -a mf

suction /'sʌkʃn/ n aspirazione f

sudden /'sʌdn/ a improvviso ●n **all of a ~** all'improvviso. **~ly** adv improvvisamente

sue /suː/ ●v (*pres p* **suing**) ●vt fare causa a (**for** per) ●vi fare causa

suede /sweɪd/ n pelle f scamosciata

suet /'suːɪt/ n grasso m di rognone

suffer /'sʌfə(r)/ vi soffrire (**from** per) ●vt soffrire; subire ⟨*loss etc*⟩; (*tolerate*) subire. **~ing** n sofferenza f

suffice /sə'faɪs/ vi bastare

sufficient /sə'fɪʃənt/ a sufficiente. **~ly** adv sufficientemente

suffix /'sʌfɪks/ n suffisso m

suffocat|e /'sʌfəkeɪt/ vt/i soffocare. **~ion** /-'keɪʃn/ n soffocamento m

sugar /'ʃʊgə(r)/ n zucchero m ●vt zuccherare. **~ basin**, **~-bowl** n zuccheriera f. **~y** a zuccheroso; fig sdolcinato

suggest /sə'dʒest/ vt suggerire; (*indicate, insinuate*) fare pensare a. **~ion** /-estʃən/ n suggerimento m; (*trace*) traccia f. **~ive** /-ɪv/ a allusivo. **~ively** adv in modo allusivo

suicidal /suːɪ'saɪdl/ a suicida

suicide /'suːɪsaɪd/ n suicidio m; (*person*) suicida mf; **commit ~** suicidarsi

suit /suːt/ n vestito m; (*woman's*) tailleur m inv; (*in cards*) seme m; Jur causa f; **follow ~** fig fare lo stesso ●vt andar bene a; (*adapt*) adattare (**to** a); (*be convenient for*) andare bene per; **be ~ed to** or **for** essere adatto a; **~ yourself!** fa' come vuoi!

suitabl|e /'suːtəbl/ a adatto. **~y** adv convenientemente

'suitcase n valigia f

suite /swiːt/ n suite f inv; (*of furniture*) divano m e poltrone fpl assortiti

sulk /sʌlk/ vi fare il broncio. **~y** a imbronciato

sullen /'sʌlən/ a svogliato

sulphur /'sʌlfə(r)/ n zolfo m. **~ic acid** /-'fjuːrɪk/ n acido m solforico

sultana /sʌl'tɑːnə/ n uva f sultanina

sultry /'sʌltrɪ/ a (-**ier**, -**iest**) ⟨*weather*⟩ afoso; fig sensuale

sum /sʌm/ n somma f; Sch addizione f ●**sum up** ●v (*pt/pp* **summed**) ●vi riassumere ●vt valutare

summar|ize /'sʌməraɪz/ vt riassumere. **~y** n sommario m ●a sommario; ⟨*dismissal*⟩ sbrigativo

summer /'sʌmə(r)/ n estate f. **~-house** n padiglione m. **~time** n (*season*) estate f

summery /'sʌmərɪ/ a estivo

summit /'sʌmɪt/ n cima f. **~ conference** n vertice m

summon /'sʌmən/ vt convocare; Jur ci

tare. **summon up** *vt* raccogliere 〈*strength*〉; rievocare 〈*memory*〉

summons /'sʌmənz/ *n Jur* citazione *f* ● *vt* citare in giudizio

sump /sʌmp/ *n Auto* coppa *f* dell'olio

sumptuous /'sʌmptjʊəs/ *a* sontuoso. **~ly** *adv* sontuosamente

sun /sʌn/ *n* sole *m* ● *vt* (*pt/pp* **sunned**) **~ oneself** prendere il sole

sun: ~bathe *vi* prendere il sole. **~-bed** *n* lettino *m* solare. **~burn** *n* scottatura *f* (*solare*). **~burnt** *a* scottato (*dal sole*)

sundae /'sʌndeɪ/ *n* gelato *m* guarnito

Sunday /'sʌndeɪ/ *n* domenica *f*

'sundial *n* meridiana *f*

sundry /'sʌndrɪ/ *a* svariati; **all and ~** tutti quanti

'sunflower *n* girasole *m*

sung /sʌŋ/ *see* **sing**

'sun-glasses *npl* occhiali *mpl* da sole

sunk /sʌŋk/ *see* **sink**

sunken /'sʌŋkn/ *a* incavato

'sunlight *n* [luce *f* del] sole *m*

sunny /'sʌnɪ/ *a* (**-ier, -iest**) assolato

sun: ~rise *n* alba *f*. **~-roof** *n Auto* tettuccio *m* apribile. **~set** *n* tramonto *m*. **~shade** *n* parasole *m*. **~shine** *n* [luce *f* del] sole *m*. **~stroke** *n* insolazione *f*. **~tan** *n* abbronzatura *f*. **~tanned** *a* abbronzato. **~-tan oil** *n* olio *m* solare

super /'su:pə(r)/ *a fam* fantastico

superb /sʊ'pɜ:b/ *a* splendido

supercilious /su:pə'sɪlɪəs/ *a* altezzoso

superficial /su:pə'fɪʃl/ *a* superficiale. **~ly** *adv* superficialmente

superfluous /sʊ'pɜ:flʊəs/ *a* superfluo

super'human *a* sovrumano

superintendent /su:pərɪn'tendənt/ *n* (*of police*) commissario *m* di polizia

superior /su:'pɪərɪə(r)/ *a* superiore ● *n* superiore, -a *mf*. **~ity** /-'ɒrətɪ/ *n* superiorità *f*

superlative /su:'pɜ:lətɪv/ *a* eccellente ● *n* superlativo *m*

'superman *n* superuomo *m*

'supermarket *n* supermercato *m*

'supermodel *n* top model *f inv*

super'natural *a* soprannaturale

'superpower *n* superpotenza *f*

supersede /su:pə'si:d/ *vt* rimpiazzare

super'sonic *a* supersonico

superstiti|on /su:pə'stɪʃn/ *n* superstizione *f*. **~ous** /-'stɪʃəs/ *a* superstizioso

supervis|e /'su:pəvaɪz/ *vt* supervisionare. **~ion** /-'vɪʒn/ *n* supervisione *f*. **~or** *n* supervisore *m*

supper /'sʌpə(r)/ *n* cena *f*

supple /'sʌpl/ *a* slogato

supplement /'sʌplɪmənt/ *n* supplemento *m* ● *vt* integrare. **~ary** /-'mentərɪ/ *a* supplementare

supplier /sə'plaɪə(r)/ *n* fornitore, -trice *mf*

supply /sə'plaɪ/ *n* fornitura *f*; (*in economics*) offerta *f*; **supplies** *pl Mil* approvvigionamenti *mpl* ● *vt* (*pt/pp* **-ied**) fornire; **~ sb with sth** fornire qcsa a qcno

support /sə'pɔ:t/ *n* sostegno *m*; (*base*) supporto *m*; (*keep*) sostentamento *m* ● *vt* sostenere; mantenere 〈*family*〉; (*give money to*) mantenere finanziariamente; *Sport* fare il tifo per. **~er** *n* sostenitore, -trice *mf*; *Sport* tifoso, -a *mf*. **~ive** /-ɪv/ *a* incoraggiante

suppose /sə'pəʊz/ *vt* (*presume*) supporre; (*imagine*) pensare; **be ~d to do** dover fare; **not be ~d to** *fam* non avere il permesso di; **I ~ so** suppongo di sì. **~dly** /-ɪdlɪ/ *adv* presumibilmente

suppress /sə'pres/ *vt* sopprimere. **~ion** /-eʃn/ *n* soppressione *f*

supremacy /su:'preməsɪ/ *n* supremazia *f*

supreme /su:'pri:m/ *a* supremo

surcharge /'sɜ:tʃɑ:dʒ/ *n* supplemento *m*

sure /ʃʊə(r)/ *a* sicuro, certo; **make ~** accertarsi; **be ~ to do it** mi raccomando di farlo ● *adv Am fam* certamente; **~ enough** infatti. **~ly** *adv* certamente; (*Am: gladly*) volentieri

surety /'ʃʊərətɪ/ *n* garanzia *f*; **stand ~ for** garantire per

surf /sɜ:f/ *n* schiuma *f* ● *vt Comput* **~ the Net** surfare in Internet

surface /'sɜ:fɪs/ *n* superficie *f*; **on the ~ fig** in apparenza ● *vi* (*emerge*) emergere. **~ mail** *n* **by ~ mail** per posta ordinaria

'surfboard *n* tavola *f* da surf

surfing /'sɜ:fɪŋ/ *n* surf *m inv*

surge /sɜ:dʒ/ *n* (*of sea*) ondata *f*; (*of interest*) aumento *m*; (*in demand*) impennata *f*; (*of anger, pity*) impeto *m* ● *vi* riversarsi; **~ forward** buttarsi in avanti

surgeon /'sɜ:dʒən/ *n* chirurgo *m*

surgery /'sɜ:dʒərɪ/ *n* chirurgia *f*; (*place, consulting room*) ambulatorio *m*; (*hours*) ore *fpl* di visita; **have ~** subire un'intervento [chirurgico]

surgical /'sɜ:dʒɪkl/ *a* chirurgico

surly /'sɜ:lɪ/ *a* (**-ier, -iest**) scontroso

surmise /sə'maɪz/ *vt* supporre

surmount /sə'maʊnt/ *vt* sormontare

surname /'sɜ:neɪm/ *n* cognome *m*

surpass /sə'pɑːs/ *vt* superare

surplus /'sɜːpləs/ *a* d'avanzo ● *n* sovrappiù *m*

surpris|e /sə'praɪz/ *n* sorpresa *f* ● *vt* sorprendere; **be ~ed** essere sorpreso (**at** da). **~ing** *a* sorprendente. **~ingly** *adv* sorprendentemente

surrender /sə'rendə(r)/ *n* resa *f* ● *vi* arrendersi ● *vt* cedere

surreptitious /sʌrəp'tɪʃəs/ *a & adv* di nascosto

surrogate /'sʌrəgət/ *n* surrogato *m*. **~ 'mother** *n* madre *f* surrogata

surround /sə'raʊnd/ *vt* circondare. **~ing** *a* circostante. **~ings** *npl* dintorni *mpl*

surveillance /sə'veɪləns/ *n* sorveglianza *f*

survey[1] /'sɜːveɪ/ *n* sguardo *m*; (*poll*) sondaggio *m*; (*investigation*) indagine *f*; (*of land*) rilevamento *m*; (*of house*) perizia *f*

survey[2] /sə'veɪ/ *vt* esaminare; fare un rilevamento di (*land*); fare una perizia di (*building*). **~or** *n* perito *m*; (*of land*) topografo, -a *mf*

survival /sə'vaɪvl/ *n* sopravvivenza *f*; (*relic*) resto *m*

surviv|e /sə'vaɪv/ *vt* sopravvivere a ● *vi* sopravvivere. **~or** *n* superstite *mf*; **be a ~or** *fam* riuscire sempre a cavarsela

susceptible /sə'septəbl/ *a* influenzabile; **~ to** sensibile a

suspect[1] /sə'spekt/ *vt* sospettare; (*assume*) supporre

suspect[2] /'sʌspekt/ *a & n* sospetto, -a *mf*

suspend /sə'spend/ *vt* appendere; (*stop, from duty*) sospendere. **~er belt** *n* reggicalze *m inv*. **~ders** *npl* giarrettiere *fpl*; (*Am:* braces) bretelle *fpl*

suspense /sə'spens/ *n* tensione *f*; (*in book etc*) suspense *f*

suspension /sə'spenʃn/ *n Auto* sospensione *f*. **~ bridge** *n* ponte *m* sospeso

suspici|on /sə'spɪʃn/ *n* sospetto *m*; (*trace*) pizzico *m*; **under ~on** sospettato. **~ous** /-ɪʃəs/ *a* sospettoso; (*arousing suspicion*) sospetto. **~ously** *adv* sospettosamente; (*arousing suspicion*) in modo sospetto

sustain /sə'steɪn/ *vt* sostenere; mantenere (*life*); subire (*injury*)

sustenance /'sʌstɪnəns/ *n* nutrimento *m*

swab /swɒb/ *n Med* tampone *m*

swagger /'swægə(r)/ *vi* pavoneggiarsi

swallow[1] /'swɒləʊ/ *vt/i* inghiottire. **swallow up** *vt* divorare; (*earth, crowd:*) inghiottire

swallow[2] *n* (*bird*) rondine *f*

swam /swæm/ *see* **swim**

swamp /swɒmp/ *n* palude *f* ● *vt fig* sommergere. **~y** *a* paludoso

swan /swɒn/ *n* cigno *m*

swap /swɒp/ *n fam* scambio *m* ● *vt* (*pt/pp* **swapped**) *fam* scambiare (**for** con) ● *vi* fare cambio

swarm /swɔːm/ *n* sciame *m* ● *vi* sciamare; **be ~ing with** brulicare di

swarthy /'swɔːðɪ/ *a* (**-ier, -iest**) di carnagione scura

swastika /'swɒstɪkə/ *n* svastica *f*

swat /swɒt/ *vt* (*pt/pp* **swatted**) schiacciare

sway /sweɪ/ *n fig* influenza *f* ● *vi* oscillare; (*person:*) ondeggiare ● *vt* (*influence*) influenzare

swear /sweə(r)/ *v* (*pt* **swore**, *pp* **sworn**) ● *vt* giurare ● *vi* giurare; (*curse*) dire parolacce; **~ at sb** imprecare contro qcno; **~ by** *fam* credere ciecamente in. **~-word** *n* parolaccia *f*

sweat /swet/ *n* sudore *m* ● *vi* sudare

sweater /'swetə(r)/ *n* golf *m inv*

sweaty /'swetɪ/ *a* sudato

swede /swiːd/ *n* rapa *f* svedese

Swed|e *n* svedese *mf*. **~en** *n* Svezia *f*. **~ish** *a* svedese ● *n* (*language*) svedese *m*

sweep /swiːp/ *n* scopata *f*, spazzata *f*; (*curve*) curva *f*; (*movement*) movimento *m* ampio; **make a clean ~** *fig* fare piazza pulita ● *v* (*pt/pp* **swept**) ● *vt* scopare, spazzare ● *vi* (*go swiftly*) andare rapidamente; (*wind:*) soffiare. **sweep away** *vt fig* spazzare via. **sweep up** *vt* spazzare

sweeping /'swiːpɪŋ/ *a* (*gesture*) ampio; (*statement*) generico; (*changes*) radicale

sweet /swiːt/ *a* dolce; **have a ~ tooth** essere goloso ● *n* caramella *f*; (*dessert*) dolce *m*. **~ corn** *n* mais *m*

sweet: **~heart** *n* innamorato, -a *mf*; **hi, ~heart** ciao, tesoro. **~ness** *n* dolcezza *f*. **~ 'pea** *n* pisello *m* odoroso. **~-shop** *n* negozio *m* di dolciumi

swell /swel/ ● *v* (*pt* **swelled**, *pp* **swollen** *or* **swelled**) ● *vi* gonfiarsi; (*increase*) aumentare ● *vt* gonfiare; (*increase*) far salire. **~ing** *n* gonfiore *m*

swelter /'sweltə(r)/ *vi* soffocare [dal caldo]

swept /swept/ *see* **sweep**

swerve /swɜːv/ vi deviare bruscamente

swift /swɪft/ a rapido. **~ly** adv rapidamente

swig /swɪg/ n fam sorso m ● vt (pt/pp **swigged**) fam scolarsi

swill /swɪl/ n (for pigs) brodaglia f ● vt **~ [out]** risciacquare

swim /swɪm/ n **have a ~** fare una nuotata ● v (pt **swam**, pp **swum**) ● vi nuotare; ⟨room:⟩ girare; **my head is ~ming** mi gira la testa ● vt percorrere a nuoto. **~mer** n nuotatore, -trice mf

swimming /'swɪmɪŋ/ n nuoto m. **~-baths** npl piscina fsg. **~ costume** n costume m da bagno. **~-pool** n piscina f. **~ trunks** npl calzoncini mpl da bagno

'swim-suit n costume m da bagno

swindle /'swɪndl/ n truffa f ● vt truffare. **~r** n truffatore, -trice mf

swine /swaɪn/ n fam porco m

swing /swɪŋ/ n oscillazione f; (shift) cambiamento m; (seat) altalena f; Mus swing m; **in full ~** in piena attività ● v (pt/pp **swung**) ● vi oscillare; (on swing, sway) dondolare; (dangle) penzolare; (turn) girare ● vt oscillare; far deviare ⟨vote⟩. **~-'door** n porta f a vento

swingeing /'swɪndʒɪŋ/ a ⟨increase⟩ drastico

swipe /swaɪp/ n fam botta f ● vt fam colpire; (steal) rubare; far passare nella macchinetta ⟨credit card⟩

swirl /swɜːl/ n (of smoke, dust) turbine m ● vi girare ● vt mulinello

swish /swɪʃ/ a fam chic ● vi schioccare

Swiss /swɪs/ a & n svizzero, -a mf; **the ~** pl gli svizzeri. **~ 'roll** n rotolo m di pan di Spagna ripieno di marmellata

switch /swɪtʃ/ n interruttore m; (change) mutamento m ● vt cambiare; (exchange) scambiare ● vi cambiare; **~ to** passare a. **switch off** vt spegnere. **switch on** vt accendere

switch: **~back** n montagne fpl russe. **~board** n centralino m

Switzerland /'swɪtsələnd/ n Svizzera f

swivel /'swɪvl/ v (pt/pp **swivelled**) ● vt girare ● vi girarsi

swollen /'swəʊlən/ see **swell** ● a gonfio. **~-'headed** a presuntuoso

swoop /swuːp/ n (by police) incursione

f ● vi **~ [down]** ⟨bird:⟩ piombare; fig fare un'incursione

sword /sɔːd/ n spada f

swore /swɔː(r)/ see **swear**

sworn /swɔːn/ see **swear**

swot /swɒt/ n fam sgobbone, -a mf ● vt (pt/pp **swotted**) fam sgobbare

swum /swʌm/ see **swim**

swung /swʌŋ/ see **swing**

syllable /'sɪləbl/ n sillaba f

syllabus /'sɪləbəs/ n programma m [dei corsi]

symbol /'sɪmbl/ n simbolo m (of di). **~ic** /-'bɒlɪk/ a simbolico. **~ism** /-ɪzm/ n simbolismo m. **~ize** vt simboleggiare

symmetr|ical /sɪ'metrɪkl/ a simmetrico. **~y** /'sɪmətrɪ/ n simmetria f

sympathetic /sɪmpə'θetɪk/ a (understanding) comprensivo; (showing pity) compassionevole. **~ally** adv con comprensione/compassione

sympathize /'sɪmpəθaɪz/ vi capire; (in grief) solidarizzare; **~ with sb** capire qcno/solidarizzare con qcno. **~r** n Pol simpatizzante mf

sympathy /'sɪmpəθɪ/ n comprensione f; (pity) compassione f; (condolences) condoglianze fpl; **in ~ with** ⟨strike⟩ per solidarietà con

symphony /'sɪmfənɪ/ n sinfonia f

symptom /'sɪmptəm/ n sintomo m. **~atic** /-'mætɪk/ a sintomatico (of di)

synagogue /'sɪnəgɒg/ n sinagoga f

synchronize /'sɪŋkrənaɪz/ vt sincronizzare

syndicate /'sɪndɪkət/ n gruppo m

syndrome /'sɪndrəʊm/ n sindrome f

synonym /'sɪnənɪm/ n sinonimo m. **~ous** /-'nɒnɪməs/ a sinonimo

synopsis /sɪ'nɒpsɪs/ n (pl **-opses** /-siːz/) (of opera, ballet) trama f; (of book) riassunto m

syntax /'sɪntæks/ n sintassi f inv

synthesize /'sɪnθəsaɪz/ vt sintetizzare. **~r** n Mus sintetizzatore m

synthetic /sɪn'θetɪk/ a sintetico ● n fibra f sintetica

Syria /'sɪrɪə/ n Siria f. **~n** a & n siriano, -a mf

syringe /sɪ'rɪndʒ/ n siringa f

syrup /'sɪrəp/ n sciroppo m; Br tipo m di melassa

system /'sɪstəm/ n sistema m. **~atic** /-'mætɪk/ a sistematico

tab /tæb/ n linguetta f; (with name) etichetta f; (list) tavola f; **at [the]** ~ a tavola; ~ **of contents** tavola f delle materie ● vt proporre. ~**-cloth** n tovaglia f. ~**spoon** n cucchiaio m da tavola. ~**spoon[ful]** n cucchiaiata f

tablet /'tæblɪt/ n pastiglia f; (slab) lastra f; ~ **of soap** saponetta f

'**table tennis** n tennis m da tavolo; (everyday level) ping pong m

tabloid /'tæblɔɪd/ n [giornale m formato] tabloid m inv; pej giornale m scandalistico

taboo /tə'bu:/ a tabù inv ● n tabù m inv

tacit /'tæsɪt/ a tacito

taciturn /'tæsɪtɜ:n/ a taciturno

tack /tæk/ n (nail) chiodino m; (stitch) imbastitura f; Naut virata f; fig linea f di condotta ● vt inchiodare; (sew) imbastire ● vi Naut virare

tackle /'tækl/ n (equipment) attrezzatura f; (football etc) contrasto m, tackle m inv ● vt affrontare

tacky /'tækɪ/ a (paint) non ancora asciutto; ⟨glue⟩ appiccicoso; fig pacchiano

tact /tækt/ n tatto m. ~**ful** a pieno di tatto; ⟨remark⟩ delicato. ~**fully** adv con tatto

tactic|al /'tæktɪkl/ a tattico. ~**s** npl tattica fsg

tactless /'tæktlɪs/ a privo di tatto. ~**ly** adv senza tatto. ~**ness** n mancanza f di tatto; (of remark) indelicatezza f

tadpole /'tædpəʊl/ n girino m

tag[1] /tæg/ n (label) etichetta f ● vt (pt/pp tagged) attaccare l'etichetta a. **tag along** vi seguire passo passo

tag[2] n (game) acchiapparello m

tail /teɪl/ n coda f; ~**s** pl (tailcoat) frac m inv ● vt (fam: follow) pedinare. **tail off** vi diminuire

tail: ~**back** n coda f. ~**-end** n parte f finale; (of train) coda f. ~ **light** n fanalino m di coda

tailor /'teɪlə(r)/ n sarto m. ~**-made** a fatto su misura

'**tail wind** n vento m di coda

taint /teɪnt/ vt contaminare

take /teɪk/ n Cinema ripresa f ● v (pt **took**, pp **taken**) ● vt prendere; (to a place) portare ⟨person, object⟩; (contain) contenere ⟨passengers etc⟩; (endure) sopportare; (require) occorrere; (teach) insegnare; (study) studiare ⟨subject⟩; fare ⟨exam, holiday, photograph, walk, bath⟩; sentire ⟨pulse⟩; misurare ⟨sb's temperature⟩; ~ **sb prisoner** fare prigioniero qcno; **be ~n ill** ammalarsi; ~ **sth calmly** prendere con calma qcsa ● vi ⟨plant:⟩ attecchire. **take after** vt assomigliare a. **take away** vt (with one) portare via; (remove) togliere; (subtract) sottrarre; '**to ~ away**' 'da asporto'. **take back** vt riprendere; ritirare ⟨statement⟩; (return) riportare [indietro]. **take down** vt portare giù; (remove) tirare giù; (write down) prendere nota di. **take in** vt (bring indoors) portare dentro; (to one's home) ospitare; (understand) capire; (deceive) ingannare; riprendere ⟨garment⟩; (include) includere. **take off** vt togliersi ⟨clothes⟩; (deduct) togliere; (mimic) imitare; ~ **time off** prendere delle vacanze; ~ **oneself off** andarsene ● vi Aeron decollare. **take on** vt farsi carico di; assumere ⟨employee⟩; (as opponent) prendersela con. **take out** vt portare fuori; togliere ⟨word, stain⟩; (withdraw) ritirare ⟨money, books⟩; ~ **out a subscription to sth** abbonarsi a qcsa; ~ **it out on sb** fam prendersela con qcno. **take over** vt assumere il controllo di ⟨firm⟩ ● vi ~ **over from sb** sostituire qcno; (permanently) succedere a qcno. **take to** vt (as a habit) darsi a; **I took to her** (liked) mi è piaciuta. **take up** vt portare su; accettare ⟨offer⟩; intraprendere ⟨profession⟩; dedicarsi a ⟨hobby⟩; prendere ⟨time⟩; occupare ⟨space⟩; tirare su ⟨floor-boards⟩; accorciare ⟨dress⟩; ~ **sth up with sb** discutere qcsa con qcno ● vi ~ **up with sb** legarsi a qcno

take: ~**-away** n (meal) piatto m da asporto; (restaurant) ristorante m che prepara piatti da asporto. ~**-off** n Aeron decollo m. **~-over** n rilevamento m. **~-over bid** n offerta f di assorbimento

takings /'teɪkɪnz/ npl incassi mpl

talcum /'tælkəm/ n ~ **(powder)** talco m

tale /teɪl/ n storia f; pej fandonia f

talent /'tælənt/ n talento m. **~ed** a [ricco] di talento

talk /tɔːk/ n conversazione f; (lecture) conferenza f; (gossip) chiacchere fpl; **make small ~** parlaré del più e del meno ● vi parlare ● vt parlare di (politics etc); **~ sb into sth** convincere qcno di qcsa. **talk over** vt discutere

talkative /'tɔːkətɪv/ a loquace

'talking-to n sgridata f

talk show n talk show m inv

tall /tɔːl/ a alto. **~boy** n cassettone m. **~ order** n impresa f difficile. **~ 'story** n frottola f

tally /'tælɪ/ n conteggio m; **keep a ~ of** tenere il conto di ● vi coincidere

tambourine /tæmbə'riːn/ n tamburello m

tame /teɪm/ a (animal) domestico; (dull) insulso ● vt domare. **~ly** adv docilmente. **~r** n domatore, -trice mf

tamper /'tæmpə(r)/ vi ~ **with** manomettere

tampon /'tæmpɒn/ n tampone m

tan /tæn/ a marrone rossiccio ● n marrone m rossiccio; (from sun) abbronzatura f ● v (pt/pp tanned) ● vt conciare (hide) ● vi abbronzarsi

tang /tæŋ/ n sapore m forte; (smell) odore m penetrante

tangent /'tændʒənt/ n tangente f

tangible /'tændʒɪbl/ a tangibile

tangle /'tæŋgl/ n groviglio m; (in hair) nodo m ● vt ~ [up] aggrovigliare ● vi aggrovigliarsi

tango /'tæŋgəʊ/ n tango m inv

tank /tæŋk/ n contenitore m; (for petrol) serbatoio m; (fish ~) acquario m; Mil carro m armato

tankard /'tæŋkəd/ n boccale m

tanker /'tæŋkə(r)/ n nave f cisterna; (lorry) autobotte f

tanned /tænd/ a abbronzato

tantaliz|e /'tæntəlaɪz/ vt tormentare. **~ing** a allettante; (smell) stuzzicante

tantamount /'tæntəmaʊnt/ a ~ **to** equivalente a

tantrum /'tæntrəm/ n scoppio m d'ira

tap /tæp/ n rubinetto m; (knock) colpo m; **on ~** fig a disposizione ● v (pt/pp tapped) ● vt dare un colpetto a; sfruttare (resources); mettere sotto controllo

(telephone) ● vi picchiettare. **~-dance** n tip tap m ● vi ballare il tip tap

tape /teɪp/ n nastro m; (recording) cassetta f ● vt legare con nastro; (record) registrare

'tape: ~ backup drive n Comput unità f di backup a nastro. **~-deck** n piastra f. **~-measure** n metro m [a nastro]

taper /'teɪpə(r)/ n candela f sottile ● **taper off** vi assottigliarsi

'tape: ~ recorder n registratore m. **~ recording** n registrazione f

tapestry /'tæpɪstrɪ/ n arazzo m

'tap water n acqua f del rubinetto

tar /tɑː(r)/ n catrame m ● vt (pt/pp tarred) incatramare

tardy /'tɑːdɪ/ a (-ier, -iest) tardivo

target /'tɑːgɪt/ n bersaglio m; fig obiettivo m

tariff /'tærɪf/ n (price) tariffa f; (duty) dazio m

Tarmac® /'tɑːmæk/ n macadam m al catrame. **tarmac** n Aeron pista f di decollo

tarnish /'tɑːnɪʃ/ vi ossidarsi ● vt ossidare; fig macchiare

tarpaulin /tɑː'pɔːlɪn/ n telone m impermeabile

tart¹ /tɑːt/ a aspro; fig acido

tart² n crostata f; (individual) crostatina f; (sl: prostitute) donnaccia f ● **tart up** vt fam ~ **oneself up** agghindarsi

tartan /'tɑːtn/ n tessuto m scozzese, tartan m inv ● attrib di tessuto scozzese

tartar /'tɑːtə(r)/ n (on teeth) tartaro m

tartar 'sauce /tɑːtə-/ n salsa f tartara

task /tɑːsk/ n compito m; **take sb to ~** riprendere qcno. **~ force** n Pol commissione f; Mil task-force f inv

tassel /'tæsl/ n nappa f

taste /teɪst/ n gusto m; (sample) assaggio m; **get a ~ of sth** fig assaporare il gusto di qcsa ● vt sentire il sapore di; (sample) assaggiare ● vi sapere (of di); **it ~s lovely** è ottimo. **~ful** a di [buon] gusto. **~fully** adv con gusto. **~less** a senza gusto. **~lessly** adv con cattivo gusto

tasty /'teɪstɪ/ a (-ier, -iest) saporito

tat /tæt/ see **tit²**

tatter|ed /'tætəd/ a cencioso; (pages) stracciato. **~s** npl **in ~s** a brandelli

tattoo¹ /tæ'tuː/ n tatuaggio m ● vt tatuare

tattoo² n Mil parata f militare

tatty /'tætɪ/ a (-ier, -iest) (clothes, person) trasandato; (book) malandato

taught /tɔːt/ see **teach**

taunt /tɔːnt/ n scherno m ● vt schernire

Taurus /'tɔːrəs/ n Astr Toro m

taut /tɔːt/ a teso

tawdry /'tɔːdrɪ/ a (**-ier, -iest**) pacchiano

tax /tæks/ n tassa f; (on income) imposte fpl; **before ~** ⟨price⟩ tasse escluse; ⟨salary⟩ lordo ● vt tassare; fig mettere alla prova; **~ with** accusare di. **~able** /-əbl/ a tassabile. **~ation** /-'seɪʃn/ n tasse fpl. **~ evasion** n evasione f fiscale. **~-free** a esentasse. **~ haven** n paradiso m fiscale

taxi /'tæksɪ/ n taxi m inv ● vi (pt/pp **taxied**, pres p **taxiing**) ⟨aircraft:⟩ rullare. **~ driver** n tassista mf. **~ rank** n posteggio m per taxi

'taxpayer n contribuente mf

tea /tiː/ n tè m inv. **~-bag** n bustina f di tè. **~-break** n intervallo m per il tè

teach /tiːtʃ/ vt/i (pt/pp **taught**) insegnare; **~ sb sth** insegnare qcsa a qcno. **~er** n insegnante mf; (primary) maestro, -a mf. **~ing** n insegnamento m

tea: ~-cloth n (for drying) asciugapiatti m inv. **~cup** n tazza f da tè

teak /tiːk/ n tek m

'tea-leaves npl tè m inv sfuso; (when infused) fondi mpl di tè

team /tiːm/ n squadra f; fig équipe f inv ● **team up** vi unirsi

'team-work n lavoro m di squadra; fig lavoro m d'équipe

'teapot n teiera f

tear[1] /teə(r)/ n strappo m ● v (pt **tore**, pp **torn**) ● vt strappare ● vi strappare; ⟨material:⟩ strapparsi; (run) precipitarsi. **tear apart** vt (fig: criticize) fare a pezzi; (separate) dividere. **tear away** vt **~ oneself away** andare via; **~ oneself away from** staccarsi da ⟨television⟩. **tear open** vt aprire strappando. **tear up** vt strappare; rompere ⟨agreement⟩

tear[2] /tɪə(r)/ n lacrima f. **~ful** a ⟨person⟩ in lacrime; ⟨farewell⟩ lacrimevole. **~fully** adv in lacrime. **~gas** n gas m lacrimogeno

tease /tiːz/ vt prendere in giro ⟨person⟩; tormentare ⟨animal⟩

tea: ~-set n servizio m da tè. **~ shop** n sala f da tè. **~spoon** n cucchiaino m [da tè]. **~spoon[ful]** n cucchiaino m

teat /tiːt/ n capezzolo m; (on bottle) tettarella f

'tea-towel n strofinaccio m [per i piatti]

technical /'teknɪkl/ a tecnico. **~ity** /-'kælətɪ/ n tecnicismo m; Jur cavillo m giuridico. **~ly** adv tecnicamente; (strictly) strettamente

technician /tek'nɪʃn/ n tecnico, -a mf

technique /tek'niːk/ n tecnica f

technological /teknə'lɒdʒɪkl/ a tecnologico

technology /tek'nɒlədʒɪ/ n tecnologia f

teddy /'tedɪ/ n ~ [**bear**] orsacchiotto m

tedious /'tiːdɪəs/ a noioso

tedium /'tiːdɪəm/ n tedio m

tee /tiː/ n (in golf) tee m inv

teem /tiːm/ vi (rain) piovere a dirotto; **be ~ing with** (full of) pullulare di

teenage /'tiːneɪdʒ/ a per ragazzi; **~ boy/girl** adolescente mf. **~r** n adolescente mf

teens /tiːnz/ npl **the ~** l'adolescenza fsg; **be in one's ~** essere adolescente

teeny /'tiːnɪ/ a (**-ier, -iest**) piccolissimo

teeter /'tiːtə(r)/ vi barcollare

teeth /tiːθ/ see **tooth**

teeth|e /tiːð/ vi mettere i [primi] denti. **~ing troubles** npl fig difficoltà fpl iniziali

teetotal /tiː'təʊtl/ a astemio. **~ler** n astemio, -a mf

telecommunications /telɪkəmjuːnɪ'keɪʃnz/ npl telecomunicazioni fpl

telegram /'telɪgræm/ n telegramma m

telegraph /'telɪgrɑːf/ n telegrafo m. **~ic** /-'græfɪk/ a telegrafico. **~ pole** n palo m del telegrafo

telepathy /tɪ'lepəθɪ/ n telepatia f

telephone /'telɪfəʊn/ n telefono m; **be on the ~** avere il telefono; (be telephoning) essere al telefono ● vt telefonare a ● vi telefonare

telephone: ~ book n elenco m telefonico. **~ booth** n, **~ box** n cabina f telefonica. **~ directory** n elenco m telefonico. **~ number** n numero m di telefono

telephonist /tɪ'lefənɪst/ n telefonista mf

'telephoto /telɪ-/ a **~ lens** tele-obiettivo m

telescop|e /'telɪskəʊp/ n telescopio m. **~ic** /-'skɒpɪk/ a telescopico

televise /'telɪvaɪz/ vt trasmettere per televisione

television /'telɪvɪʒn/ n televisione f; **watch ~** guardare la televisione. **~ set** n televisore m

telex /'teleks/ n telex m inv

tell /tel/ vt (pt/pp **told**) dire; raccontare ⟨story⟩; (distinguish) distinguere (**from** da); **~ sb sth** dire qcsa a qcno; **~ the time** dire l'ora; **I couldn't ~ why...** non sapevo perché... **time will ~** il tempo ce lo dirà; **his age is beginning to**

~ l'età comincia a farsi sentire [per lui]; **you mustn't** ~ non devi dire niente. **tell off** *vt* sgridare

teller /'telə(r)/ *n* (*in bank*) cassiere, -a *mf*

telling /'telɪŋ/ *a* significativo; ⟨*argument*⟩ efficace

telly /'telɪ/ *n fam* telly tv *f inv*

temerity /tɪ'merətɪ/ *n* audacia *f*

temp /temp/ *n fam* impiegato, -a *mf* temporaneo, -a

temper /'tempə(r)/ *n* (*disposition*) carattere *m*; (*mood*) umore *m*; (*anger*) collera *f*; **lose one's** ~ arrabbiarsi; **be in a** ~ essere arrabbiato; **keep one's** ~ mantenere la calma

temperament /'tempramənt/ *n* temperamento *m*. ~**al** /-'mentl/ *a* (*moody*) capriccioso

temperate /'tempərət/ *a* ⟨*climate*⟩ temperato

temperature /'temprətʃə(r)/ *n* temperatura *f*; **have a** ~ avere la febbre

tempest /'tempɪst/ *n* tempesta *f*. ~**uous** /-'pestjʊəs/ *a* tempestoso

temple[1] /'templ/ *n* tempio *m*

temple[2] *n Anat* tempia *f*

tempo /'tempəʊ/ *n* ritmo *m*; *Mus* tempo *m*

temporar|y /'tempərərɪ/ *a* temporaneo; ⟨*measure, building*⟩ provvisorio. ~**ily** *adv* temporaneamente; ⟨*introduced, erected*⟩ provvisoriamente

tempt /tempt/ *vt* tentare; sfidare ⟨*fate*⟩; ~ **sb to** indurre qcno a; **be** ~**ed** essere tentato (**to** di); **I am** ~**ed by the offer** l'offerta mi tenta. ~**ation** /-'teɪʃn/ *n* tentazione *f*. ~**ing** *a* allettante; ⟨*food, drink*⟩ invitante

ten /ten/ *a & n* dieci *m*

tenable /'tenəbl/ *a fig* sostenibile

tenaci|ous /tɪ'neɪʃəs/ *a* tenace. ~**ty** /-'næsətɪ/ *n* tenacia *f*

tenant /'tenənt/ *n* inquilino, -a *mf*; *Comm* locatario, -a *mf*

tend[1] /tend/ *vt* (*look after*) prendersi cura di

tend[2] *vi* ~ **to do sth** tendere a far qcsa

tendency /'tendənsɪ/ *n* tendenza *f*

tender[1] /'tendə(r)/ *n Comm* offerta *f*; **be legal** ~ avere corso legale ● *vt* offrire; presentare ⟨*resignation*⟩

tender[2] *a* tenero; (*painful*) dolorante. ~**ly** *adv* teneramente. ~**ness** *n* tenerezza *f*; (*painfulness*) dolore *m*

tendon /'tendən/ *n* tendine *m*

tenement /'tenəmənt/ *n* casamento *m*

tenner /'tenə(r)/ *n fam* biglietto *m* da dieci sterline

tennis /'tenɪs/ *n* tennis *m*. ~**-court** *n* campo *m* da tennis. ~ **player** *n* tennista *mf*

tenor /'tenə(r)/ *n* tenore *m*

tense[1] /tens/ *n Gram* tempo *m*

tense[2] *a* teso ● *vt* tendere ⟨*muscle*⟩. **tense up** *vi* tendersi

tension /'tenʃn/ *n* tensione *f*

tent /tent/ *n* tenda *f*

tentacle /'tentəkl/ *n* tentacolo *m*

tentative /'tentətɪv/ *a* provvisorio; ⟨*smile, gesture*⟩ esitante. ~**ly** *adv* timidamente; ⟨*accept*⟩ provvisoriamente

tenterhooks /'tentəhʊks/ *npl* **be on** ~ essere sulle spine

tenth /tenθ/ *a* decimo ● *n* decimo, -a *mf*

tenuous /'tenjʊəs/ *a fig* debole

tepid /'tepɪd/ *a* tiepido

term /tɜːm/ *n* periodo *m*; *Sch Univ* trimestre *m*; (*expression*) termine *m*; ~**s** *pl* (*conditions*) condizioni *fpl*; ~ **of office** carica *f*; **in the short/long** ~ a breve/lungo termine; **be on good/bad** ~**s** essere in buoni/cattivi rapporti; **come to** ~**s with** accettare ⟨*past, fact*⟩; **easy** ~**s** facilità *f* di pagamento

terminal /'tɜːmɪn(ə)l/ *a* finale; *Med* terminale ● *n Aeron* terminal *m inv*; *Rail* stazione *f* di testa; (*of bus*) capolinea *m*; (*on battery*) morsetto *m*; *Comput* terminale *m*. ~**ly** *adv* **be** ~**ly ill** essere in fase terminale

terminat|e /'tɜːmɪneɪt/ *vt* terminare; rescindere ⟨*contract*⟩; interrompere ⟨*pregnancy*⟩ ● *vi* terminare; ~**e in** finire in. ~**ion** /-'neɪʃn/ *n* termine *m*; *Med* interruzione *f* di gravidanza

terminology /tɜːmɪ'nɒlədʒɪ/ *n* terminologia *f*

terminus /'tɜːmɪnəs/ *n* (*pl* -**ni** /-naɪ/) (*for bus*) capolinea *m*; (*for train*) stazione *f* di testa

terrace /'terəs/ *n* terrazza *f*; (*houses*) fila *f* di case a schiera; **the** ~**s** *pl Sport* le gradinate. ~**d house** *n* casa *f* a schiera

terrain /te'reɪn/ *n* terreno *m*

terrible /'terəbl/ *a* terribile. ~**y** *adv* terribilmente

terrier /'terɪə(r)/ *n* terrier *m inv*

terrific /tə'rɪfɪk/ *a fam* (*excellent*) fantastico; (*huge*) enorme. ~**ally** *adv fam* terribilmente

terri|fy /'terɪfaɪ/ *vt* (*pt/pp* -**ied**) atterrire; **be** ~**fied** essere terrorizzato. ~**fying** *a* terrificante

territorial /terɪ'tɔːrɪəl/ *a* territoriale

territory /'terɪtərɪ/ *n* territorio *m*

terror /'terə(r)/ *n* terrore *m*. ~**ism**

/-ızm/ n terrorismo m. **~ist** /-ıst/ n terrorista mf. **~ize** vt terrorizzare

terse /tɜːs/ a conciso

test /test/ n esame m; (in laboratory) esperimento m; (of friendship, machine) prova f; (of intelligence, aptitude) test m inv; **put to the ~** mettere alla prova ● vt esaminare; provare ⟨machine⟩

testament /'testəmənt/ n testamento m; **Old/New T~** Antico/Nuovo Testamento m

testicle /'testıkl/ n testicolo m

testify /'testıfaı/ vt/i (pt/pp **-ied**) testimoniare

testimonial /testı'məʊnıəl/ n lettera f di referenze

testimony /'testımənı/ n testimonianza f

'**test: ~ match** n partita f internazionale. **~-tube** n provetta f. **~-tube 'baby** n fam bambino, -a mf in provetta

tetanus /'tetənəs/ n tetano m

tether /'teðə(r)/ n **be at the end of one's ~** non poterne più

text /tekst/ n testo m. **~book** n manuale m

textile /'tekstaıl/ a tessile ● n stoffa f

texture /'tekstʃə(r)/ n (of skin) grana f; (of food) consistenza f; **of a smooth ~** (to the touch) soffice al tatto

Thai /taı/ a n tailandese mf. **~land** n Tailandia f

Thames /temz/ n Tamigi m

than /ðən/, accentato /ðæn/ conj che; (with numbers, names) di; **older ~ me** più vecchio di me

thank /θæŋk/ vt ringraziare; **~ you [very much]** grazie [mille]. **~ful** a grato. **~fully** adv con gratitudine; (happily) fortunatamente. **~less** a ingrato

thanks /θæŋks/ npl ringraziamenti mpl; **~!** fam grazie!; **~ to** grazie a

that /ðæt/ a & pron (pl **those**) quel, quei pl; (before s + consonant, gn, ps and z) quello, quegli pl; (before vowel) quell' mf, quegli mpl, quelle fpl; **~ one** quello; **I don't like those** quelli non mi piacciono; **~ is** cioè; **is ~ you?** sei tu?; **who is ~?** chi è?; **what did you do after ~?** cosa hai fatto dopo?; **like ~** in questo modo, così; **a man like ~** un uomo così; **~ is why** ecco perché; **~'s it!** (you've understood) ecco!; (I've finished) ecco fatto!; (I've had enough) basta così!; (there's nothing more) tutto qui!; **~'s ~!** (with job) ecco fatto!; (with relationship) è tutto finito!; **and ~'s ~!** punto e basta! **all ~ I know** tutto quello che so ● adv così; **it wasn't ~ good** non era poi così buono ● rel pron che; **the man ~ I spoke to**

l'uomo con cui ho parlato; **the day ~ I saw him** il giorno in cui l'ho visto; **all ~ I know** tutto quello che so ● conj che; **I think ~...** penso che...

thatch /θætʃ/ n tetto m di paglia. **~ed** a coperto di paglia

thaw /θɔː/ n disgelo m ● vt fare scongelare ⟨food⟩ ● vi ⟨food:⟩ scongelarsi; **it's ~ing** sta sgelando

the /ðə/, di fronte a una vocale /ðiː/ def art il, la f; i mpl, le fpl; (before s + consonant, gn, ps and z) lo, gli mpl; (before vowel) l' mf, gli mpl, le fpl; **at ~ cinema/station** al cinema/alla stazione; **from ~ cinema/station** dal cinema/dalla stazione ● adv **~ more ~ better** più ce n'è meglio è; (with reference to pl) più ce ne sono, meglio è; **all ~ better** tanto meglio

theatre /'θɪətə(r)/ n teatro m; Med sala f operatoria

theatrical /θɪ'ætrɪkl/ a teatrale; (showy) melodrammatico

theft /θeft/ n furto m

their /ðeə(r)/ poss a il loro m, la loro f, i loro mpl, le loro fpl; **~ mother/father** la loro madre/il loro padre

theirs /ðeəz/ poss pron il loro m, la loro f, i loro mpl, le loro fpl; **a friend of ~** un loro amico; **friends of ~** dei loro amici; **those are ~** quelli sono loro; (as opposed to ours) quelli sono i loro

them /ðem/ pron (direct object) li m, le f; (indirect object) gli, loro fml; (after prep: with people) loro; (after preposition: with things) essi; **we haven't seen ~** non li/le abbiamo visti/viste; **give ~ the money** dai loro or dagli i soldi; **give it to ~** daglielo; **I've spoken to ~** ho parlato con loro; **it's ~** sono loro

theme /θiːm/ n tema m. **~ song** n motivo m conduttore

them'selves pers pron (reflexive) si; (emphatic) se stessi; **they poured ~ a drink** si sono versati da bere; **they said so ~** lo hanno detto loro stessi; **they kept it to ~** se lo sono tenuti per sé; **by ~ da soli**

then /ðen/ adv allora; (next) poi; **by ~** (in the past) ormai; (in the future) per allora; **since ~** sin da allora; **before ~** prima di allora; **from ~ on** da allora in poi; **now and ~** ogni tanto; **there and ~** all'istante ● a di allora

theolog|ian /θɪə'ləʊdʒɪən/ n teologo, -a mf. **~y** /-'ɒlədʒɪ/ n teologia f

theorem /'θɪərəm/ n teorema m

theoretical /θɪə'retɪkl/ a teorico

theory /ˈθɪərɪ/ n teoria f; **in ~** in teoria

therapeutic /θerəˈpjuːtɪk/ a tera-peutico

therap|ist /ˈθerəpɪst/ n terapista mf. **~y** n terapia f

there /ðeə(r)/ adv là, lì; **down/up ~** laggiù/lassù; **~ is/are** c'è/ci sono; **~ he/she is** eccolo/eccola ● int **~**, **~!** dai, su!

there: **~abouts** adv [or] **~abouts** (roughly) all'incirca. **~'after** adv dopo di che. **~by** adv in tal modo. **~fore** /-fɔ:(r)/ adv perciò

thermal /ˈθɜ:m(ə)l/ a termale; **~ 'underwear** n biancheria f che mantiene la temperatura corporea

thermometer /θəˈmɒmɪtə(r)/ n ter-mometro m

Thermos® /ˈθɜ:məs/ n [flask] ter-mos m inv

thermostat /ˈθɜ:məstæt/ n termostato m

thesaurus /θɪˈsɔːrəs/ n dizionario m dei sinonimi

these /ðiːz/ see this

thesis /ˈθiːsɪs/ n (pl **-ses** /-siːz/) tesi f inv

they /ðeɪ/ pron loro; **~ are tired** sono stanchi; **we're going, but ~ are not** noi andiamo, ma loro no; **~ say** (generalizing) si dice; **~ are building a new road** stanno costruendo una nuo-va strada

thick /θɪk/ a spesso; (forest) fitto; (liquid) denso; (hair) folto; (fam: stupid) ottuso; (fam: close) molto unito; **be 5 mm ~** essere 5 mm di spessore ● adv densamente **n in the ~ of** nel mezzo di. **~en** vt ispessire (sauce) ● vi ispessirsi; (fog:) infittirsi. **~ly** adv densamente; (cut) a fette spesse. **~ness** n spessore m

thick: **~set** a tozzo. **~-'skinned** a fam insensibile

thief /θiːf/ n (pl **thieves**) ladro, -a mf

thieving /ˈθiːvɪŋ/ a ladro ● n furti mpl

thigh /θaɪ/ n coscia f

thimble /ˈθɪmbl/ n ditale m

thin /θɪn/ a (**thinner, thinnest**) sottile; (shoes, sweater) leggero; (liquid) liqui-do; (person) magro; (fig: excuse, plot) inconsistente ● adv = **thinly** ● v (pt/pp **thinned**) ● vt diluire (liquid) ● vi diradarsi. **thin out** vi diradarsi. **~ly** adv (populated) scarsamente; (disguised) leggermente; (cut) a fette sottili

thing /θɪŋ/ n cosa f; **~s** pl (belongings) roba fsg; **for one ~** in primo luogo; **the right ~** la cosa giusta; **just the ~!** pro-

prio quel che ci vuole!; **how are ~s?** come vanno le cose?; **the latest ~** fam l'ultima cosa; **the best ~ would be** la cosa migliore sarebbe; **poor ~!** poveretto!

think /θɪŋk/ vt/i (pt/pp **thought**) pensa-re; (believe) credere; **I ~ so** credo di sì; **what do you ~?** (what is your opinion?) cosa ne pensi?; **~ of/about** pensare a; **what do you ~ of it?** cosa ne pensi di questo?. **think over** vt riflet-tere su. **think up** vt escogitare

third /θɜːd/ a & n terzo, -a mf. **~ly** adv terzo. **~-rate** a scadente

thirst /θɜːst/ n sete f. **~ily** adv con sete. **~y** a assetato; **be ~y** aver sete

thirteen /θɜːˈtiːn/ a & n tredici m. **~th** a & n tredicesimo, -a mf

thirtieth /ˈθɜːtɪɪθ/ a & n trentesimo, -a mf

thirty /ˈθɜːtɪ/ a & n trenta m

this /ðɪs/ a (pl **these**) questo; **~ man/ woman** quest'uomo/questa donna; **these men/women** questi uomini/ queste donne; **~ one** questo; **~ morning/evening** stamattina/stasera ● pron (pl **these**) questo; **we talked about ~ and that** abbiamo parlato del più e del meno; **like ~** così; **~ is Peter** questo è Peter; Teleph sono Peter; **who is ~?** chi è?; Teleph chi parla? ● adv così; **~ big** così grande

thistle /ˈθɪsl/ n cardo m

thorn /θɔːn/ n spina f. **~y** a spinoso

thorough /ˈθʌrə/ a completo; (knowledge) profondo; (clean, search, training) a fondo; (person) scrupoloso

thorough: **~bred** n purosangue m inv. **~fare** n via f principale; **'no ~fare'** 'strada non transitabile '

thorough|ly /ˈθʌrəlɪ/ adv (clean, search, know sth) a fondo; (extremely) estremamente. **~ness** n completezza f

those /ðəuz/ see that

though /ðəu/ conj sebbene; **as ~** come se ● adv fam tuttavia

thought /θɔːt/ see think ● n pensiero m; (idea) idea f. **~ful** a pensieroso; (con-siderate) premuroso. **~fully** adv pen-sierosamente; (considerately) premura-samente. **~less** a (inconsiderate) scon-siderato. **~lessly** adv con noncuranza

thousand /ˈθauznd/ a one/a **~** mille m inv ● n mille m invs; **~s of** migliaia fpl di. **~th** a millesimo ● n millesimo, -a mf

thrash /θræʃ/ vt picchiare; (defeat) scon-figgere. **thrash out** vt mettere a punto

thread /θred/ n filo m; (of screw) filetto

m ● *vt* infilare ⟨*beads*⟩; **~ one's way through** farsi strada fra. **~bare** *a* logoro

threat /θret/ *n* minaccia *f*

threaten /'θretn/ *vt* minacciare (**to do** di fare) ● *vi fig* incalzare. **~ing** *a* minaccioso; ⟨*sky, atmosphere*⟩ sinistro

three /θriː/ *a & n* tre *m*. **~fold** *a & adv* triplo. **~some** /-səm/ *n* trio *m*

thresh /θreʃ/ *vt* trebbiare

threshold /'θreʃəʊld/ *n* soglia *f*

threw /θruː/ *see* **throw**

thrift /θrɪft/ *n* economia *f*. **~y** *a* parsimonioso

thrill /θrɪl/ *n* emozione *f*; ⟨*of fear*⟩ brivido *m* ● *vt* entusiasmare; **be ~ed with** essere entusiasta di. **~er** *n* ⟨*book*⟩ [romanzo *m*] giallo *m*; ⟨*film*⟩ [film *m*] giallo *m*. **~ing** *a* eccitante

thrive /θraɪv/ *vi* (*pt* **thrived** *or* **throve**, *pp* **thrived** *or* **thriven** /'θrɪvn/) ⟨*business:*⟩ prosperare; ⟨*child, plant:*⟩ crescere bene; **I ~ on pressure** mi piace essere sotto tensione

throat /θrəʊt/ *n* gola *f*; **sore ~** mal *m* di gola

throb /θrɒb/ *n* pulsazione *f*; ⟨*of heart*⟩ battito *m* ● *vi* (*pt/pp* **throbbed**) ⟨*vibrate*⟩ pulsare; ⟨*heart:*⟩ battere

throes /θrəʊz/ *npl* **in the ~ of** *fig* alle prese con

thrombosis /θrɒm'bəʊsɪs/ *n* trombosi *f*

throne /θrəʊn/ *n* trono *m*

throng /θrɒŋ/ *n* calca *f*

throttle /'θrɒtl/ *n* (*on motorbike*) manopola *f* di accelerazione ● *vt* strozzare

through /θruː/ *prep* attraverso; ⟨*during*⟩ durante; ⟨*by means of*⟩ tramite; ⟨*thanks to*⟩ grazie a; **Saturday ~ Tuesday** *Am* da sabato a martedì incluso ● *adv* attraverso; **~ and ~** fino in fondo; **wet ~** completamente bagnato; **read sth ~** dare una lettura a qcsa; **let ~** lasciar passare ⟨*sb*⟩ ● *a* ⟨*train*⟩ diretto; **be ~** ⟨*finished*⟩ aver finito; *Teleph* avere la comunicazione

throughout /θruː'aʊt/ *prep* per tutto ● *adv* completamente; ⟨*time*⟩ per tutto il tempo

throw /θrəʊ/ *n* tiro *m* ● *vt* (*pt* **threw**, *pp* **thrown**) lanciare; ⟨*throw away*⟩ gettare; azionare ⟨*switch*⟩; disarcionare ⟨*rider*⟩; ⟨*fam: disconcert*⟩ disorientare; *fam* dare ⟨*party*⟩. **throw away** *vt* gettare via. **throw out** *vt* gettare via; rigettare ⟨*plan*⟩; buttare fuori ⟨*person*⟩. **throw up** *vt* alzare ● *vi* ⟨*vomit*⟩ vomitare

throw-away *a* ⟨*remark*⟩ buttato lì; ⟨*paper cup*⟩ usa e getta *inv*

thrush /θrʌʃ/ *n* tordo *m*

thrust /θrʌst/ *n* spinta *f* ● *vt* (*pt/pp* **thrust**) ⟨*push*⟩ spingere; ⟨*insert*⟩ conficcare; **~ [up]on** imporre a

thud /θʌd/ *n* tonfo *m*

thug /θʌg/ *n* delinquente *m*

thumb /θʌm/ *n* pollice *m*; **as a rule of ~** come regola generale; **under sb's ~** succube di qcno ● *vt* **~ a lift** fare l'autostop. **~-index** *n* indice *m* a rubrica. **~tack** *n Am* puntina *f* da disegno

thump /θʌmp/ *n* colpo *m*; ⟨*noise*⟩ tonfo *m* ● *vt* battere su ⟨*table, door*⟩; battere ⟨*fist*⟩; colpire ⟨*person*⟩ ● *vi* battere (**on** su); ⟨*heart:*⟩ battere forte. **thump about** *vi* camminare pesantemente

thunder /'θʌndə(r)/ *n* tuono *m*; ⟨*loud noise*⟩ rimbombo *m* ● *vi* tuonare; ⟨*make loud noise*⟩ rimbombare. **~clap** *n* rombo *m* di tuono. **~storm** *n* temporale *m*. **~y** *a* temporalesco

Thursday /'θɜːzdeɪ/ *n* giovedì *m inv*

thus /ðʌs/ *adv* così

thwart /θwɔːt/ *vt* ostacolare

thyme /taɪm/ *n* timo *m*

Tiber /'taɪbə(r)/ *n* Tevere *m*

tick /tɪk/ *n* ⟨*sound*⟩ ticchettio *m*; ⟨*mark*⟩ segno *m*; ⟨*fam: instant*⟩ attimo *m* ● *vi* ticchettare. **tick off** *vt* spuntare; *fam* sgridare. **tick over** *vi* ⟨*engine:*⟩ andare al minimo

ticket /'tɪkɪt/ *n* biglietto *m*; ⟨*for item deposited, library*⟩ tagliando *m*; ⟨*label*⟩ cartellino *m*; ⟨*fine*⟩ multa *f*. **~-collector** *n* controllore *m*. **~-office** *n* biglietteria *f*

tick|le /'tɪkl/ *n* solletico *m* ● *vt* fare il solletico a; ⟨*amuse*⟩ divertire ● *vi* fare prurito. **~lish** /'tɪklɪʃ/ *a* che soffre il solletico

tidal /'taɪdl/ *a* ⟨*river, harbour*⟩ di marea. **~ wave** *n* onda *f* di marea

tiddly-winks /'tɪdlɪwɪŋks/ *n* gioco *m* delle pulci

tide /taɪd/ *n* marea *f*; ⟨*of events*⟩ corso *m*; **the ~ is in/out** c'è alta/bassa marea ● **tide over** *vt* **~ sb over** aiutare qcno a andare avanti

tidily /'taɪdɪlɪ/ *adv* in modo ordinato

tidiness /'taɪdɪnɪs/ *n* ordine *m*

tidy /'taɪdɪ/ *a* (**-ier, -iest**) ordinato; ⟨*fam: amount*⟩ bello ● *vt* (*pt/pp* **-ied**) [**up**] ordinare; **~ oneself up** mettersi in ordine

tie /taɪ/ *n* cravatta *f*; ⟨*cord*⟩ legaccio *m*; ⟨*fig: bond*⟩ legame *m*; ⟨*restriction*⟩ impedimento *m*; *Sport* pareggio *m* ● *v* (*pres p* **tying**) ● *vt* legare; fare ⟨*knot*⟩; **be ~d**

(*in competition*) essere in parità ● *vi* pareggiare. **tie in with** *vi* corrispondere a. **tie up** *vt* legare; vincolare ⟨*capital*⟩; **be ~d up** (*busy*) essere occupato

tier /tɪə(r)/ *n* fila *f*; (*of cake*) piano *m*; (*in stadium*) gradinata *f*

tiff /tɪf/ *n* battibecco *m*

tiger /'taɪgə(r)/ *n* tigre *f*

tight /taɪt/ *a* stretto; (*taut*) teso; (*fam: drunk*) sbronzo; (*fam: mean*) spilorcio; **~ corner** *fam* brutta situazione *f* ● *adv* strettamente; ⟨*hold*⟩ forte; ⟨*closed*⟩ bene

tighten /'taɪtn/ *vt* stringere; avvitare ⟨*screw*⟩; intensificare ⟨*control*⟩ ● *vi* stringersi

tight: ~-'fisted *a* tirchio. **~-fitting** *a* aderente. **~ly** *adv* strettamente; ⟨*hold*⟩ forte; ⟨*closed*⟩ bene. **~rope** *n* fune *f* (*da funamboli*)

tights /taɪts/ *npl* collant *m inv*

tile /taɪl/ *n* mattonella *f*; (*on roof*) tegola *f* ● *vt* rivestire di mattonelle ⟨*wall*⟩

till[1] /tɪl/ *prep & conj* = **until**

till[2] *n* cassa *f*

tiller /'tɪlə(r)/ *n* barra *f* del timone

tilt /tɪlt/ *n* inclinazione *f*; **at full ~** a tutta velocità ● *vt* inclinare ● *vi* inclinarsi

timber /'tɪmbə(r)/ *n* legname *m*

time /taɪm/ *n* tempo *m*; (*occasion*) volta *f*; (*by clock*) ora *f*; **two ~s four** due volte quattro; **at any ~** in qualsiasi momento; **this ~** questa volta; **at ~s, from ~ to ~** ogni tanto; **~ and again** cento volte; **two at a ~** due alla volta; **on ~** in orario; **in ~** in tempo; (*eventually*) col tempo; **in no ~ at all** velocemente; **in a year's ~** fra un anno; **behind ~** in ritardo; **behind the ~s** antiquato; **for the ~ being** per il momento; **what is the ~?** che ora è?; **by the ~ we arrive** quando arriviamo; **did you have a nice ~?** ti sei divertito?; **have a good ~!** divertiti! ● *vt* scegliere il momento per; cronometrare ⟨*race*⟩; **be well ~d** essere ben calcolato

time: ~ bomb *n* bomba *f* a orologeria. **~-lag** *n* intervallo *m* di tempo. **~less** *a* eterno. **~ly** *a* opportuno. **~-switch** *n* interruttore *m* a tempo. **~-table** *n* orario *m*

timid /'tɪmɪd/ *a* (*shy*) timido; (*fearful*) timoroso

timing /'taɪmɪŋ/ *n* Sport, Techn cronometraggio *m*; **the ~ of the election** il momento scelto per le elezioni

tin /tɪn/ *n* stagno *m*; (*container*) barattolo *m* ● *vt* (*pt/pp* **tinned**) inscatolare. **~ foil** *n* [carta *f*] stagnola *f*

tinge /tɪndʒ/ *n* sfumatura *f* ● *vt* **~d with** *fig* misto a

tingle /'tɪŋgl/ *vi* pizzicare

tinker /'tɪŋkə(r)/ *vi* armeggiare

tinkle /'tɪŋkl/ *n* tintinnio *m*; (*fam: phone call*) colpo *m* di telefono ● *vi* tintinnare

tinned /tɪnd/ *a* in scatola

'tin opener *n* apriscatole *m inv*

tinsel /'tɪnsl/ *n* filo *m* d'argento

tint /tɪnt/ *n* tinta *f* ● *vt* tingersi ⟨*hair*⟩

tiny /'taɪnɪ/ *a* (**-ier, -iest**) minuscolo

tip[1] /tɪp/ *n* punta *f*

tip[2] *n* (*money*) mancia *f*; (*advice*) consiglio *m*; (*for rubbish*) discarica *f* ● *v* (*pt/pp* **tipped**) ● *vt* (*tilt*) inclinare; (*overturn*) capovolgere; (*pour*) versare; (*reward*) dare una mancia a ● *vi* inclinarsi; (*overturn*) capovolgersi. **tip off** *vt* **~ sb off** (*inform*) fare una soffiata a qcno. **tip out** *vt* rovesciare. **tip over** *vt* capovolgere ● *vi* capovolgersi

'tip-off *n* soffiata *f*

tipped /tɪpt/ *a* ⟨*cigarette*⟩ col filtro

tipsy /'tɪpsɪ/ *a fam* brillo

tiptoe /'tɪptəʊ/ *n* **on ~** in punta di piedi

tiptop /tɪp'tɒp/ *a fam* in condizioni perfette

tire /'taɪə(r)/ *vt* stancare ● *vi* stancarsi. **~d** *a* stanco; **~d of** stanco di; **~d out** stanco morto. **~less** *a* instancabile. **~some** /-səm/ *a* fastidioso

tiring /'taɪərɪŋ/ *a* stancante

tissue /'tɪʃuː/ *n* tessuto *m*; (*handkerchief*) fazzolettino *m* di carta. **~-paper** *n* carta *f* velina

tit[1] /tɪt/ *n* (*bird*) cincia *f*

tit[2] *n* **~ for tat** pan per focaccia

title /'taɪtl/ *n* titolo *m*. **~-deed** *n* atto *m* di proprietà. **~-role** *n* ruolo *m* principale

tittle-tattle /'tɪtltætl/ *n* pettegolezzi *mpl*

to /tuː/, *atono* /tə/ *prep* a; (*to countries*) in; (*towards*) verso; (*up to, until*) fino a; **I'm going to John's/the butcher's** vado da John/dal macellaio; **come/go to sb** venire/andare da qcno; **to Italy/ Switzerland** in Italia/Svizzera; **I've never been to Rome** non sono mai stato a Roma; **go to the market** andare al mercato; **to the toilet/my room** in bagno/camera mia; **to an exhibition** a una mostra; **to university** all'università; **twenty/quarter to eight** le otto meno venti/un quarto; **5 to 6 kilos** da 5 a 6 chili; **to the end** alla fine; **to this day** fino a oggi; **to the best of my recollection** per quanto mi possa ricordare; **give/say sth to sb** dare/dire qcsa a qcno; **give it to me** dammelo; **there's nothing to it** è una cosa da niente ● *verbal constructions*

to go andare; **learn to swim** imparare a nuotare; **I want to/have to go** voglio/devo andare; **it's easy to forget** è facile da dimenticare; **too ill/tired to go** troppo malato/stanco per andare; **you have to** devi; **I don't want to** non voglio; **live to be 90** vivere fino a 90 anni; **he was the last to arrive** è stato l'ultimo ad arrivare; **to be honest,...** per essere sincero,... ● *adv* **pull to** chiudere; **to and fro** avanti e indietro

toad /təʊd/ *n* rospo *m*. **~stool** *n* fungo *m* velenoso

toast /təʊst/ *n* pane *m* tostato; (*drink*) brindisi *m inv* ● *vt* tostare ⟨*bread*⟩; (*drink a ~ to*) brindare a. **~er** *n* tostapane *m inv*

tobacco /tə'bækəʊ/ *n* tabacco *m*. **~nist's [shop]** *n* tabaccheria *f*

toboggan /tə'bɒgən/ *n* toboga *m inv* ● *vi* andare in toboga

today /tə'deɪ/ *a* & *adv* oggi *m*; **a week ~** una settimana a oggi; **~'s paper** il giornale di oggi

toddler /'tɒdlə(r)/ *n* bambino, -a *mf* ai primi passi

to-do /tə'du:/ *n fam* baccano *m*

toe /təʊ/ *n* dito *m* del piede; (*of footwear*) punta *f*; **big ~** alluce *m* ● *vt* **~ the line** rigar diritto. **~nail** *n* unghia *f* del piede

toffee /'tɒfɪ/ *n* caramella *f* al mou

together /tə'geðə(r)/ *adv* insieme; (*at the same time*) allo stesso tempo; **~ with** insieme a

toilet /'tɔɪlɪt/ *n* (*lavatory*) gabinetto *m*. **~ paper** *n* carta *f* igienica

toiletries /'tɔɪlɪtrɪz/ *npl* articoli *mpl* da toilette

toilet: ~ roll *n* rotolo *m* di carta igienica. **~ water** *n* acqua *f* di colonia

token /'təʊkən/ *n* segno *m*; (*counter*) gettone *m*; (*voucher*) buono *m* ● *attrib* simbolico

told /təʊld/ *see* **tell** ● *a* **all ~** in tutto

tolerab|le /'tɒl(ə)rəbl/ *a* tollerabile; (*not bad*) discreto. **~y** *adv* discretamente

toleran|ce /'tɒl(ə)r(ə)ns/ *n* tolleranza *f*. **~t** *a* tollerante. **~tly** *adv* con tolleranza

tolerate /'tɒləreɪt/ *vt* tollerare

toll[1] /təʊl/ *n* pedaggio *m*; **death ~** numero *m* di morti

toll[2] *vi* suonare a morto

tom /tɒm/ *n* (*cat*) gatto *m* maschio

tomato /tə'mɑ:təʊ/ *n* (*pl* **-es**) pomodoro *m*. **~ ketchup** *n* ketchup *m*. **~ purée** *n* concentrato *m* di pomodoro

tomb /tu:m/ *n* tomba *f*

tomboy *n* maschiaccio *m*

tombstone *n* pietra *f* tombale

tom-cat *n* gatto *m* maschio

tomfoolery /tɒm'fu:lərɪ/ *n* stupidaggini *fpl*

tomorrow /tə'mɒrəʊ/ *a* & *adv* domani; **~ morning** domani mattina; **the day after ~** dopodomani; **see you ~!** a domani!

ton /tʌn/ *n* tonnellata *f* (= *1,016 kg.*); **~s of** *fam* un sacco di

tone /təʊn/ *n* tono *m*; (*colour*) tonalità *f inv* ● **tone down** *vt* attenuare. **tone up** *vt* tonificare ⟨*muscles*⟩

toner /'təʊnə(r)/ *n* toner *m*

tongs /tɒŋz/ *npl* pinze *fpl*

tongue /tʌŋ/ *n* lingua *f*; **~ in cheek** ⟨*fam: say*⟩ ironicamente. **~-twister** *n* scioglilingua *m inv*

tonic /'tɒnɪk/ *n* tonico *m*; (*for hair*) lozione *f* per i capelli; (*fig* toccasana *m inv*; **~ [water]** acqua *f* tonica

tonight /tə'naɪt/ *adv* stanotte; (*evening*) stasera ● *n* questa notte *f*; (*evening*) questa sera *f*

tonne /tʌn/ *n* tonnellata *f* metrica

tonsil /'tɒnsl/ *n Anat* tonsilla *f*. **~litis** /-sɪ'laɪtɪs/ *n* tonsillite *f*

too /tu:/ *adv* troppo; (*also*) anche; **~ many** troppi; **~ much** troppo; **~ little** troppo poco

took /tʊk/ *see* **take**

tool /tu:l/ *n* attrezzo *m*

toot /tu:t/ *n* suono *m* di clacson ● *vi Auto* clacsonare

tooth /tu:θ/ *n* (*pl* **teeth**) dente *m*

tooth: ~ache *n* mal *m* di denti. **~brush** *n* spazzolino *m* da denti. **~less** *a* sdentato. **~paste** *n* dentifricio *m*. **~pick** *n* stuzzicadenti *m inv*

top[1] /tɒp/ *n* (*toy*) trottola *f*

top[2] *n* cima *f*, *Sch* primo, -a *mf*; (*upper part or half*) parte *f* superiore; (*of page, list, street*) inizio *m*; (*upper surface*) superficie *f*; (*lid*) coperchio *m*; (*of bottle*) tappo *m*; (*garment*) maglia *f*; (*blouse*) camicia *f*, *Auto* marcia *f* più alta; **at the ~** *fig* al vertice; **at the ~ of one's voice** a squarciagola; **on ~/on ~ of** sopra; **on ~ of that** (*besides*) per di più; **from ~ to bottom** da cima a fondo ● *a* in alto; ⟨*official, floor of building*⟩ superiore; ⟨*pupil, musician etc*⟩ migliore; ⟨*speed*⟩ massimo ● *vt* (*pt/pp* **topped**) essere in testa a ⟨*list*⟩; (*exceed*) sorpassare; **~ped with ice-cream** ricoperto di gelato. **top up** *vt* riempire

top: ~ 'floor *n* ultimo piano *m*. **~ hat** *n*

cilindro m. **~-heavy** a con la parte superiore sovraccarica

topic /'tɒpɪk/ n soggetto m; (of conversation) argomento m. **~al** a d'attualità

top: **~less** a & adv topless. **~most** a più alto

topple /'tɒpl/ vt rovesciare ● vi rovesciarsi. **topple off** vi cadere

top-'secret a segretissimo, top secret inv

topsy-turvy /tɒpsɪ'tɜ:vɪ/ a & adv sottosopra

torch /tɔ:tʃ/ n torcia f [elettrica]; (flaming) fiaccola f

tore /tɔ:(r)/ see **tear¹**

torment¹ /'tɔ:ment/ n tormento m

torment² /tɔ:'ment/ vt tormentare

torn /tɔ:n/ see **tear¹** ● a bucato

tornado /tɔ:'neɪdəʊ/ n (pl -es) tornado m inv

torpedo /tɔ:'pi:dəʊ/ n (pl -es) siluro m ● vt silurare

torrent /'tɒrənt/ n torrente m. **~ial** /tə'renʃl/ a (rain) torrenziale

torso /'tɔ:səʊ/ n torso m; (in art) busto m

tortoise /'tɔ:təs/ n tartaruga f

tortuous /'tɔ:tʃʊəs/ a tortuoso

torture /'tɔ:tʃə(r)/ n tortura f ● vt torturare

Tory /'tɔ:rɪ/ a & n fam conservatore, -trice mf

toss /tɒs/ vt gettare; (into the air) lanciare in aria; (shake) scrollare; (horse:) disarcionare; mescolare (salad); rivoltare facendo saltare in aria (pancake); **~ a coin** fare testa o croce ● vi **~ and turn** (in bed) rigirarsi; **let's ~ for it** facciamo testa o croce

tot¹ /tɒt/ n bimbetto, -a mf; (fam: of liquor) goccio m

tot² vt (pt/pp **totted**) **~ up** fam fare la somma di

total /'təʊtl/ a totale ● n totale m ● vt (pt/pp **totalled**) ammontare a; (add up) sommare

totalitarian /təʊtælɪ'teərɪən/ a totalitario

totally /'təʊtəlɪ/ adv totalmente

totter /'tɒtə(r)/ vi barcollare; (government:) vacillare

touch /tʌtʃ/ n tocco m; (sense) tatto m; (contact) contatto m; (trace) traccia f; (of irony, humour) tocco m; **get/be in ~** mettersi/essere in contatto ● vt toccare; (lightly) sfiorare; (equal) eguagliare; (fig: move) commuovere ● vi toccarsi. **touch down** vi Aeron atterrare. **touch**

on vt fig accennare a. **touch up** vt ritoccare (painting)

touch|ing /'tʌtʃɪŋ/ a commovente. **~y** a permaloso; (subject) delicato

tough /tʌf/ a duro; (severe, harsh) severo; (durable) resistente; (resilient) forte

toughen /'tʌfn/ vt rinforzare. **toughen up** vt rendere più forte (person)

tour /tʊə(r)/ n giro m; (of building, town) visita f; Theat, Sport tournée f inv; (of duty) servizio m ● vt visitare ● vi fare un giro turistico; Theat essere in tournée

touris|m /'tʊərɪzm/ n turismo m. **~t** /-rɪst/ n turista mf ● attrib turistico. **~t office** n ufficio m turistico

tournament /'tʊənəmənt/ n torneo m

'tour operator n tour operator mf inv, operatore, -trice mf turistico, -a

tousle /'taʊzl/ vt spettinare

tout /taʊt/ n (ticket ~) bagarino m; (horse-racing) informatore m ● vi **~ for** sollecitare

tow /təʊ/ n rimorchio m; **'on ~'** 'a rimorchio'; **in ~** fam al seguito ● vt rimorchiare. **tow away** vt portare via col carro attrezzi

toward[s] /tə'wɔ:d(z)/ prep verso (with respect to) nei riguardi di

towel /'taʊəl/ n asciugamano m. **~ling** n spugna f

tower /'taʊə(r)/ n torre f ● vi **~ above** dominare. **~ block** n palazzone m. **~ing** a torreggiante; (rage) violento

town /taʊn/ n città f inv. **~ 'hall** n municipio m

tow: **~-path** n strada f alzaia. **~-rope** n cavo m da rimorchio

toxic /'tɒksɪk/ a tossico

toxin /'tɒksɪn/ n tossina f

toy /tɔɪ/ n giocattolo m. **~shop** n negozio m di giocattoli. **toy with** vt giocherellare con

trace /treɪs/ n traccia f ● vt seguire le tracce di; (find) rintracciare; (draw) tracciare; (with tracing-paper) ricalcare

track /træk/ n traccia f; (path, Sport) pista f; Rail binario m; **keep ~ of** tenere d'occhio ● vt seguire le tracce di. **track down** vt scovare

'track: **~ball** n Comput trackball f inv. **~suit** n tuta f da ginnastica

tractor /'træktə(r)/ n trattore m

trade /treɪd/ n commercio m; (line of business) settore m; (craft) mestiere m; **by ~** di mestiere ● vt commerciare; **~ sth for sth** scambiare qcsa per qcsa ● vi commerciare. **trade in** vt (give in**

part exchange) dare in pagamento parziale

'**trade mark** *n* marchio *m* di fabbrica

trader /'treɪdə(r)/ *n* commerciante *mf*

trade: ~**sman** *n* (*joiner etc*) operaio *m*. ~ **union** *n* sindacato *m*. ~ '**unionist** *n* sindacalista *mf*

trading /'treɪdɪŋ/ *n* commercio *m*. ~ **estate** *n* zona *f* industriale

tradition /trə'dɪʃn/ *n* tradizione *f*. ~**al** *a* tradizionale. ~**ally** *adv* tradizionalmente

traffic /'træfɪk/ *n* traffico *m* ● *vi* (*pt/pp* **trafficked**) trafficare

traffic: ~ **circle** *n Am* isola *f* rotatoria. ~ **jam** *n* ingorgo *m*. ~ **lights** *npl* semaforo *msg*. ~ **warden** *n* vigile *m* [urbano]; (*woman*) vigilessa *f*

tragedy /'trædʒədɪ/ *n* tragedia *f*

tragic /'trædʒɪk/ *a* tragico. ~**ally** *adv* tragicamente

trail /treɪl/ *n* traccia *f*; (*path*) sentiero *m* ● *vi* strisciare; (*plant:*) arrampicarsi; ~ [**behind**] rimanere indietro; (*in competition*) essere in svantaggio ● *vt* trascinare

trailer /'treɪlə(r)/ *n Auto* rimorchio *m*; (*Am: caravan*) roulotte *f inv*; (*film*) presentazione *f* (*di un film*)

train /treɪn/ *n* treno *m*; ~ **of thought** filo *m* dei pensieri ● *vt* formare professionalmente; *Sport* allenare; (*aim*) puntare; educare (*child*); addestrare (*animal, soldier*) ● *vi* fare il tirocinio; *Sport* allenarsi. ~**ed** *a* (*animal*) addestrato (**to do** a fare)

trainee /treɪ'niː/ *n* apprendista *mf*

train|er /'treɪnə(r)/ *n Sport* allenatore, -trice *mf*; (*in circus*) domatore, -trice *mf*; (*of dog, race-horse*) addestratore, -trice *mf*. ~**ers** *pl* scarpe *fpl* da ginnastica. ~**ing** *n* tirocinio *m*; *Sport* allenamento *m*; (*of animal, soldier*) addestramento *m*

traipse /treɪps/ *vi* ~ **around** *fam* andare in giro

trait /treɪt/ *n* caratteristica *f*

traitor /'treɪtə(r)/ *n* traditore, -trice *mf*

tram /træm/ *n* tram *m inv*. ~-**lines** *npl* rotaie *fpl* del tram

tramp /træmp/ *n* (*hike*) camminata *f*; (*vagrant*) barbone, -a *mf*; (*of feet*) calpestio *m* ● *vi* camminare con passo pesante; (*hike*) percorrere a piedi

trample /'træmpl/ *vt/i* ~ [**on**] calpestare

trampoline /'træmpəliːn/ *n* trampolino *m*

trance /trɑːns/ *n* trance *f inv*

tranquil /'træŋkwɪl/ *a* tranquillo. ~**lity** /-'kwɪlətɪ/ *n* tranquillità *f*

tranquillizer /'træŋkwɪlaɪzə(r)/ *n* tranquillante *m*

transact /træn'zækt/ *vt* trattare. ~**ion** /-ækʃn/ *n* transazione *f*

transatlantic /trænzət'læntɪk/ *a* transatlantico

transcend /træn'send/ *vt* trascendere

transfer[1] /'trænsfɜː(r)/ *n* trasferimento *m*; *Sport* cessione *f*; (*design*) decalcomania *f*

transfer[2] /træns'fɜː(r)/ *v* (*pt/pp* **transferred**) ● *vt* trasferire; *Sport* cedere ● *vi* trasferirsi; (*when travelling*) cambiare. ~**able** /-əbl/ *a* trasferibile

transform /træns'fɔːm/ *vt* trasformare. ~**ation** /-fə'meɪʃn/ *n* trasformazione *f*. ~**er** *n* trasformatore *m*

transfusion /træns'fjuːʒn/ *n* trasfusione *f*

transient /'trænzɪənt/ *a* passeggero

transistor /træn'zɪstə(r)/ *n* transistor *m inv*; (*radio*) radiolina *f* a transistor

transit /'trænzɪt/ *n* transito *m*; **in** ~ (*goods*) in transito

transition /træn'zɪʃn/ *n* transizione *f*. ~**al** *a* di transizione

transitive /'trænzɪtɪv/ *a* transitivo

transitory /'trænzɪtərɪ/ *a* transitorio

translat|e /trænz'leɪt/ *vt* tradurre. ~**ion** /-'leɪʃn/ *n* traduzione *f*. ~**or** *n* traduttore, -trice *mf*

transmission /trænz'mɪʃn/ *n* trasmissione *f*

transmit /trænz'mɪt/ *vt* (*pt/pp* **transmitted**) trasmettere. ~**ter** *n* trasmettitore *m*

transparen|cy /træn'spærənsɪ/ *n Phot* diapositiva *f*. ~**t** *a* trasparente

transpire /træn'spaɪə(r)/ *vi* emergere; (*fam: happen*) accadere

transplant[1] /'trænsplɑːnt/ *n* trapianto *m*

transplant[2] /træns'plɑːnt/ *vt* trapiantare

transport[1] /'trænspɔːt/ *n* trasporto *m*

transport[2] /træn'spɔːt/ *vt* trasportare. ~**ation** /-'teɪʃn/ *n* trasporto *m*

transvestite /trænz'vestaɪt/ *n* travestito, -a *mf*

trap /træp/ *n* trappola *f*; (*fam: mouth*) boccaccia *f* ● *vt* (*pt/pp* **trapped**) intrappolare; schiacciare (*finger in door*). ~'**door** *n* botola *f*

trapeze /trə'piːz/ *n* trapezio *m*

trash /træʃ/ *n* robaccia *f*; (*rubbish*) spazzatura *f*; (*nonsense*) schiocchezze *fpl*. ~**can** *n Am* secchio *m* della spazzatura. ~**y** *a* scadente

trauma /'trɔːmə/ *n* trauma *m*. ~**tic**

/-'mætɪk/ *a* traumatico. **~tize** /-taɪz/
traumatizzare

travel /'trævl/ *n* viaggi *mpl* ● *v* (*pt/pp*
travelled) ● *vi* viaggiare; (*to work*) andare ● *vt* percorrere ‹*distance*›. **~
agency** *n* agenzia *f* di viaggi. **~ agent**
n agente *mf* di viaggio

traveller /'trævələ(r)/ *n* viaggiatore,
-trice *mf*; *Comm* commesso *m* viaggiatore; **~s** *pl* (*gypsies*) zingari *mpl*. **~'s
cheque** *n* traveller's cheque *m inv*

trawler /'trɔːlə(r)/ *n* peschereccio *m*

tray /treɪ/ *n* vassoio *m*; (*for baking*)
teglia *f*; (*for documents*) vaschetta *f*
sparticarta; (*of printer, photocopier*)
vassoio *m*

treacher|ous /'tretʃərəs/ *a* traditore;
‹*weather, currents*› pericoloso. **~y** *n* tradimento *m*

treacle /'triːkl/ *n* melassa *f*

tread /tred/ *n* andatura *f*; (*step*) gradino *m*; (*of tyre*) battistrada *m inv* ● *v* (*pt*
trod, *pp* **trodden**) ● *vi* (*walk*) camminare. **tread on** *vt* calpestare ‹*grass*›; pe-
stare ‹*foot*›

treason /'triːzn/ *n* tradimento *m*

treasure /'treʒə(r)/ *n* tesoro *m* ● *vt* tenere in gran conto. **~r** *n* tesoriere, -a *mf*

treasury /'treʒərɪ/ *n* **the T~** il Ministero del Tesoro

treat /triːt/ *n* piacere *m*; (*present*) regalo *m*; **give sb a ~** fare una sorpresa a
qcno ● *vt* trattare; *Med* curare; **~ sb to
sth** offrire qcsa a qcno

treatise /'triːtɪz/ *n* trattato *m*

treatment /'triːtmənt/ *n* trattamento
m; *Med* cura *f*

treaty /'triːtɪ/ *n* trattato *m*

treble /'trebl/ *a* triplo ● *n* *Mus* (*voice*)
voce *f* bianca ● *vt* triplicare ● *vi* triplicarsi. **~ clef** *n* chiave *f* di violino

tree /triː/ *n* albero *m*

trek /trek/ *n* scarpinata *f*; (*as holiday*)
trekking *m inv* ● *vi* (*pt/pp* **trekked**) farsi una scarpinata; (*on holiday*) fare
trekking

tremble /'trembl/ *vi* tremare

tremendous /trɪ'mendəs/ *a* (*huge*)
enorme; (*fam: excellent*) formidabile.
~ly *adv* (*very*) straordinariamente; (*a
lot*) enormemente

tremor /'tremə(r)/ *n* tremito *m*; **[earth]
~** scossa *f* [sismica]

trench /trentʃ/ *n* fosso *m*; *Mil* trincea *f*.
~ coat *n* trench *m inv*

trend /trend/ *n* tendenza *f*; (*fashion*)
moda *f*. **~y** *a* (**-ier**, **-iest**) *fam* di or alla
moda

trepidation /trepr'deɪʃn/ *n* trepidazione *f*

trespass /'trespəs/ *vi* **~ on** introdursi
abusivamente in; *fig* abusare di. **~er** *n*
intruso, -a *mf*

trial /'traɪəl/ *n* *Jur* processo *m*; (*test,
ordeal*) prova *f*; **on ~** in prova; *Jur* in
giudizio; **by ~ and error** per tentativi

triangle /'traɪæŋgl/ *n* triangolo *m*.
~ular /-'æŋgjʊlə(r)/ *a* triangolare

tribe /traɪb/ *n* tribù *f inv*

tribulation /trɪbjʊ'leɪʃn/ *n* tribolazio-
ne *f*

tribunal /traɪ'bjuːnl/ *n* tribunale *m*

tributary /'trɪbjʊtərɪ/ *n* affluente *m*

tribute /'trɪbjuːt/ *n* tributo *m*; **pay ~**
rendere omaggio

trice /traɪs/ *n* **in a ~** in un attimo

trick /trɪk/ *n* trucco *m*; (*joke*) scherzo *m*;
(*in cards*) presa *f*; **do the ~** *fam* funzionare; **play a ~ on** fare uno scherzo a
● *vt* imbrogliare

trickle /'trɪkl/ *vi* colare

trick|ster /'trɪkstə(r)/ *n* imbroglione,
-a *mf*. **~y** *a* (**-ier**, **-iest**) ‹*operation*›
complesso; ‹*situation*› delicato

tricycle /'traɪsɪkl/ *n* triciclo *m*

tried /traɪd/ *see* **try**

trifl|e /'traɪfl/ *n* inezia *f*; *Culin* zuppa *f*
inglese. **~ing** *a* insignificante

trigger /'trɪgə(r)/ *n* grilletto *m* ● *vt* **~
[off]** scatenare

trigonometry /trɪgə'nɒmɪtrɪ/ *n* trigo-
nometria *f*

trim /trɪm/ *a* (**trimmer, trimmest**) curato; ‹*figure*› snello ● *n* (*of hair, hedge*)
spuntata *f*; (*decoration*) rifinitura *f*; **in
good ~** in buono stato; ‹*person*› in forma ● *vt* (*pt/pp* **trimmed**) spuntare
‹*hair etc*›; (*decorate*) ornare; *Naut* orientare. **~ming** *n* bordo *m*; **~mings** *pl*
(*decorations*) guarnizioni *fpl*; **with all
the ~mings** *Culin* guarnito

trinket /'trɪŋkɪt/ *n* ninnolo *m*

trio /'triːəʊ/ *n* trio *m*

trip /trɪp/ *n* (*excursion*) gita *f*; (*journey*)
viaggio *m*; (*stumble*) passo *m* falso ● *v*
(*pt/pp* **tripped**) ● *vt* far inciampare ● *vi*
inciampare (**on/over** in). **trip up** *vt* far
inciampare

tripe /traɪp/ *n* trippa *f*; (*sl: nonsense*)
fesserie *fpl*

triple /'trɪpl/ *a* triplo ● *vt* triplicare
● *vi* triplicarsi

triplets /'trɪplɪts/ *npl* tre gemelli *mpl*

triplicate /'trɪplɪkət/ *n* **in ~** in triplice
copia

tripod /'traɪpɒd/ *n* treppiede *m inv*

tripper /'trɪpə(r)/ *n* gitante *mf*

trite /traɪt/ a banale
triumph /'traɪʌmf/ n trionfo m ●vi trionfare (over su). ~ant /-'ʌmf(ə)nt/ a trionfante. ~antly adv ⟨exclaim⟩ con tono trionfante
trivial /'trɪvɪəl/ a insignificante. ~ity /-'ælətɪ/ n banalità f inv
trod, trodden /trɒd, 'trɒdn/ see tread
trolley /'trɒlɪ/ n carrello m; (Am: tram) tram m inv. ~ bus n filobus m inv
trombone /trɒm'bəʊn/ n trombone m
troop /truːp/ n gruppo m; ~s pl truppe fpl ●vi ~ in/out entrare/uscire in gruppo
trophy /'trəʊfɪ/ n trofeo m
tropic /'trɒpɪk/ n tropico m; ~s pl tropici mpl. ~al a tropicale
trot /trɒt/ n trotto m ●vi (pt/pp **trotted**) trottare
trouble /'trʌbl/ n guaio m; ⟨difficulties⟩ problemi mpl; ⟨inconvenience, Med⟩ disturbo m; ⟨conflict⟩ conflitto m; **be in** ~ essere nei guai; ⟨swimmer, climber:⟩ essere in difficoltà; **get into** ~ finire nei guai; **get sb into** ~ mettere qcno nei guai; **take the** ~ **to do sth** darsi la pena di far qcsa ●vt ⟨worry⟩ preoccupare; ⟨inconvenience⟩ disturbare; ⟨conscience, old wound:⟩ tormentare ●vi **don't** ~! non ti disturbare!. ~**-maker** n be a ~**-maker** seminare zizzania. ~**some** /-səm/ a fastidioso
trough /trɒf/ n trogolo m; ⟨atmospheric⟩ depressione f
trounce /traʊns/ vt ⟨in competition⟩ schiacciare
troupe /truːp/ n troupe f inv
trousers /'traʊzəz/ npl pantaloni mpl
trout /traʊt/ n inv trota f
trowel /'traʊəl/ n ⟨for gardening⟩ paletta f; ⟨for builder⟩ cazzuola f
truant /'truːənt/ n **play** ~ marinare la scuola
truce /truːs/ n tregua f
truck /trʌk/ n ⟨lorry⟩ camion m inv
trudge /trʌdʒ/ n camminata f faticosa ●vi arrancare
true /truː/ a vero; **come** ~ avverarsi
truffle /'trʌfl/ n tartufo m
truism /'truːɪzm/ n truismo m
truly /'truːlɪ/ adv veramente; **Yours** ~ distinti saluti
trump /trʌmp/ n ⟨in cards⟩ atout m inv
trumpet /'trʌmpɪt/ n tromba f. ~**er** n trombettista mf
truncheon /'trʌntʃn/ n manganello m
trunk /trʌŋk/ n ⟨of tree, body⟩ tronco m; ⟨of elephant⟩ proboscide f; ⟨for travelling,

storage⟩ baule m; ⟨Am: of car⟩ bagagliaio m; ~s pl calzoncini mpl da bagno
truss /trʌs/ n Med cinto m erniario
trust /trʌst/ n fiducia f; ⟨group of companies⟩ trust m inv; ⟨organization⟩ associazione f, on ~ sulla parola ●vt fidarsi di; ⟨hope⟩ augurarsi ●vi ~ **in** credere in; ~ **to** affidarsi a. ~**ed** a fidato
trustee /trʌs'tiː/ n amministratore, -trice mf fiduciario, ~a
'trust|ful /'trʌstfl/ a fiducioso. ~**ing** a fiducioso. ~**worthy** a fidato
truth /truːθ/ n (pl -s /truːðz/) verità f inv. ~**ful** a veritiero. ~**fully** adv sinceramente
try /traɪ/ n tentativo m, prova f; ⟨in rugby⟩ meta f ●v (pt/pp **tried**) ●vt provare; ⟨be a strain on⟩ mettere a dura prova; Jur processare ⟨person⟩; discutere ⟨case⟩; ~ **to do sth** provare a fare qcsa ●vi provare. **try on** vt provarsi ⟨garment⟩. **try out** vt provare
trying /'traɪɪŋ/ a duro; ⟨person⟩ irritante
T-shirt /'tiː-/ n maglietta f
tub /tʌb/ n tinozza f; ⟨carton⟩ vaschetta f; ⟨bath⟩ vasca f da bagno
tuba /'tjuːbə/ n Mus tuba f
tubby /'tʌbɪ/ a (-ier, -iest) tozzo
tube /tjuːb/ n tubo m; ⟨of toothpaste⟩ tubetto m; Rail metro f
tuber /'tjuːbə(r)/ n tubero m
tuberculosis /tjuːbɜːkjʊ'ləʊsɪs/ n tubercolosi f
tubular /'tjuːbjʊlə(r)/ a tubolare
tuck /tʌk/ n piega f ●vt ⟨put⟩ infilare. **tuck in** vt rimboccare; ~ **sb in** rimboccare le coperte a qcno ●vi ⟨fam: eat⟩ mangiare con appetito. **tuck up** vt rimboccarsi ⟨sleeves⟩; ⟨in bed⟩ rimboccare le coperte a
Tuesday /'tjuːzdeɪ/ n martedì m inv
tuft /tʌft/ n ciuffo m
tug /tʌg/ n strattone m; Naut rimorchiatore m ●v (pt/pp **tugged**) ●vt tirare ●vi dare uno strattone. ~ **of war** n tiro m alla fune
tuition /tjuː'ɪʃn/ n lezioni fpl
tulip /'tjuːlɪp/ n tulipano m
tumble /'tʌmbl/ n ruzzolone m ●vi ruzzolare. ~**down** a cadente. ~**-drier** n asciugabiancheria f
tumbler /'tʌmblə(r)/ n bicchiere m ⟨senza stelo⟩
tummy /'tʌmɪ/ n fam pancia f
tumour /'tjuːmə(r)/ n tumore m
tumult /'tjuːmʌlt/ n tumulto m. ~**uous** /-'mʌltjʊəs/ a tumultuoso
tuna /'tjuːnə/ n tonno m

tune /tju:n/ *n* motivo *m*; out of/in ~ ⟨*instrument*⟩ scordato/accordato; ⟨*person*⟩ stonato/intonato; **to the ~ of** *fam* per la modesta somma di ● *vt* accordare ⟨*instrument*⟩; sintonizzare ⟨*radio, TV*⟩; mettere a punto ⟨*engine*⟩. **tune in** *vt* sintonizzare ● *vi* sintonizzarsi (**to** su). **tune up** *vi* ⟨*orchestra:*⟩ accordare gli strumenti

tuneful /'tju:nfl/ *a* melodioso

tuner /'tju:nə(r)/ *n* accordatore, -trice *mf*; *Radio, TV* sintonizzatore *m*

tunic /'tju:nɪk/ *n* tunica *f*; *Mil* giacca *f*; *Sch* grembiule *m*

Tunisia /tju:'nɪzɪə/ *n* Tunisia *f*. ~**n** *a & n* tunisino, -a *mf*

tunnel /'tʌnl/ *n* tunnel *m inv* ● *vi* (*pt/pp* tunnelled) scavare un tunnel

turban /'tɜ:bən/ *n* turbante *m*

turbine /'tɜ:baɪn/ *n* turbina *f*

turbulen|ce /'tɜ:bjʊləns/ *n* turbolenza *f*. ~**t** *a* turbolento

turf /tɜ:f/ *n* erba *f*; (*segment*) zolla *f* erbosa ● **turf out** *vt fam* buttar fuori

Turk /tɜ:k/ *n* turco, -a *mf*

turkey /'tɜ:kɪ/ *n* tacchino *m*

Turk|ey *n* Turchia *f*. ~**ish** *a* turco

turmoil /'tɜ:mɔɪl/ *n* tumulto *m*

turn /tɜ:n/ *n* (*rotation, short walk*) giro *m*; (*in road*) svolta *f*, curva *f*; (*development*) svolta *f*; *Theat* numero *m*; (*fam: attack*) crisi *f inv*; **a ~ for the better/worse** un miglioramento/peggioramento; **do sb a good ~** rendere un servizio a qcno; **take ~s** fare a turno; **in ~** a turno; **out of ~** ⟨*speak*⟩ a sproposito; **it's your ~** tocca a te ● *vt* girare, voltare ⟨*back, eyes*⟩; dirigere ⟨*gun, attention*⟩ ● *vi* girare; ⟨*person:*⟩ girarsi; ⟨*leaves:*⟩ ingiallire; (*become*) diventare; ~ **right/left** girare a destra/sinistra; ~ **sour** inacidirsi; ~ **to sb** girarsi verso qcno; *fig* rivolgersi a qcno. **turn against** *vi* diventare ostile a ● *vt* mettere contro. **turn away** *vt* mandare via ⟨*people*⟩; girare dall'altra parte ⟨*head*⟩ ● *vi* girarsi dall'altra parte. **turn down** *vt* piegare ⟨*collar*⟩; abbassare ⟨*heat, gas, sound*⟩; respingere ⟨*person, proposal*⟩. **turn in** *vt* ripiegare in dentro ⟨*edges*⟩; consegnare ⟨*lost object*⟩ ● *vi* (*fam: go to bed*) andare a letto; ~ **into the drive** entrare nel viale. **turn off** *vt* spegnere; chiudere ⟨*tap, water*⟩ ● *vi* ⟨*car:*⟩ girare. **turn on** *vt* accendere; aprire ⟨*tap, water*⟩; *fam: attract*) eccitare ● *vi* (*attack*) attaccare. **turn out** *vt* (*expel*) mandar via; spegnere ⟨*light,* *gas*⟩; (*produce*) produrre; (*empty*) svuotare ⟨*room, cupboard*⟩ ● *vi* (*transpire*) risultare; ~ **out well/badly** ⟨*cake, dress:*⟩ riuscire bene/male; ⟨*situation:*⟩ andare bene/male. **turn over** *vt* girare ● *vi* girarsi; **please ~ over** vedi retro. **turn round** *vi* girarsi; ⟨*car:*⟩ girare. **turn up** *vt* tirare su ⟨*collar*⟩; alzare ⟨*heat, gas, sound, radio*⟩ ● *vi* farsi vedere

turning /'tɜ:nɪŋ/ *n* svolta *f*. ~**-point** *n* svolta *f* decisiva

turnip /'tɜ:nɪp/ *n* rapa *f*

turn: ~**-out** *n* (*of people*) affluenza *f*. ~**over** *n Comm* giro *m* d'affari; (*of staff*) ricambio *m*. ~**pike** *n Am* autostrada *f*. ~**stile** *n* cancelletto *m* girevole. ~**table** *n* piattaforma *f* girevole; (*on record-player*) piatto *m* (*di giradischi*). ~**-up** *n* (*of trousers*) risvolto *m*

turpentine /'tɜ:pəntaɪn/ *n* trementina *f*

turquoise /'tɜ:kwɔɪz/ *a* (*colour*) turchese ● *n* turchese *m*

turret /'tʌrɪt/ *n* torretta *f*

turtle /'tɜ:tl/ *n* tartaruga *f* acquatica

tusk /tʌsk/ *n* zanna *f*

tussle /'tʌsl/ *n* zuffa *f* ● *vi* azzuffarsi

tutor /'tju:tə(r)/ *n* insegnante *mf* privato, -a; *Univ* insegnante *mf universitario, -a che segue individualmente un ristretto numero di studenti*. ~**ial** /-'tɔ:rɪəl/ *n* discussione *f* col tutor

tuxedo /tʌk'si:dəʊ/ *n Am* smoking *m inv*

TV *n abbr* (**television**) tv *f inv*, tivù *f inv*

twaddle /'twɒdl/ *n* scemenze *fpl*

twang /twæŋ/ *n* (*in voice*) suono *m* nasale ● *vt* far vibrare

tweed /twi:d/ *n* tweed *m inv*

tweezers /'twi:zəz/ *npl* pinzette *fpl*

twelfth /twelfθ/ *a & n* dodicesimo, -a *mf*

twelve /twelv/ *a & n* dodici *m*

twentieth /'twentɪɪθ/ *a & n* ventesimo, -a *mf*

twenty /'twentɪ/ *a & n* venti *m*

twerp /twɜ:p/ *n fam* stupido, -a *mf*

twice /twaɪs/ *adv* due volte

twiddle /'twɪdl/ *vt* giocherellare con; ~ **one's thumbs** *fig* girarsi i pollici

twig[1] /twɪg/ *n* ramoscello *m*

twig[2] *vt/i* (*pt/pp* twigged) *fam* intuire

twilight /'twaɪ-/ *n* crepuscolo *m*

twin /twɪn/ *n* gemello, -a *mf* ● *attrib* gemello. ~ **beds** *npl* letti *mpl* gemelli

twine /twaɪn/ *n* spago *m* ● *vi* intrecciarsi; ⟨*plant:*⟩ attorcigliarsi ● *vt* intrecciare

twinge /twɪndʒ/ *n* fitta *f*; ~ **of conscience** rimorso *m* di coscienza

twinkle /'twɪŋkl/ n scintillio m ● vi scintillare

twin 'town n città f inv gemellata

twirl /twɜːl/ vt far roteare ● vi volteggiare ● n piroetta f

twist /twɪst/ n torsione f; ⟨curve⟩ curva f; ⟨in rope⟩ attorcigliata f; ⟨in book, plot⟩ colpo m di scena ● vt attorcigliare ⟨rope⟩; torcere ⟨metal⟩; girare ⟨knob, cap⟩; ⟨distort⟩ distorcere; ~ **one's ankle** storcersi la caviglia ● vi attorcigliarsi; ⟨road:⟩ essere pieno di curve

twit /twɪt/ n fam cretino, -a mf

twitch /twɪtʃ/ n tic m inv; ⟨jerk⟩ strattone m ● vi contrarsi

twitter /'twɪtə(r)/ n cinguettio m ● vi cinguettare; ⟨person:⟩ cianciare

two /tuː/ a & n due m

two: ~**-faced** a falso. ~**-piece** a ⟨swimsuit⟩ due pezzi m inv; ⟨suit⟩ completo m. ~**some** /-səm/ n coppia f. ~**-way** a ⟨traffic⟩ a doppio senso di marcia

tycoon /taɪ'kuːn/ n magnate m

tying /'taɪɪŋ/ see **tie**

type /taɪp/ n tipo m; ⟨printing⟩ carattere m [tipografico] ● vt/i scrivere a macchina. ~**writer** n macchina f da scrivere. ~**written** a dattiloscritto

typhoid /'taɪfɔɪd/ n febbre f tifoidea

typical /'tɪpɪkl/ a tipico. ~**ly** adv tipicamente; ⟨as usual⟩ come al solito

typify /'tɪpɪfaɪ/ vt ⟨pt/pp -**ied**⟩ essere tipico di

typing /'taɪpɪŋ/ n dattilografia f

typist /'taɪpɪst/ n dattilografo, -a mf

typography /taɪ'pɒgrəfɪ/ n tipografia f

tyrannical /tɪ'rænɪkl/ a tirannico

tyranny /'tɪrənɪ/ n tirannia f

tyrant /'taɪrənt/ n tiranno, -a mf

tyre /'taɪə(r)/ n gomma f, pneumatico m

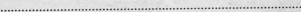

Uu

ubiquitous /juː'bɪkwɪtəs/ a onnipresente

udder /'ʌdə(r)/ n mammella f ⟨di vacca, capra etc⟩

ugl|iness /'ʌglɪnɪs/ n bruttezza f. ~**y** a (-**ier**, -**iest**) brutto

UK n abbr **United Kingdom**

ulcer /'ʌlsə(r)/ n ulcera f

ulterior /ʌl'tɪərɪə(r)/ a ~ **motive** secondo fine m

ultimate /'ʌltɪmət/ a definitivo; ⟨final⟩ finale; ⟨fundamental⟩ fondamentale. ~**ly** adv alla fine

ultimatum /ʌltɪ'meɪtəm/ n ultimatum m inv

ultrasound /'ʌltrə-/ n Med ecografia f

ultra'violet a ultravioletto

umbilical /ʌm'bɪlɪkl/ a ~ **cord** cordone m ombelicale

umbrella /ʌm'brelə/ n ombrello m

umpire /'ʌmpaɪə(r)/ n arbitro m ● vt/i arbitrare

umpteen /ʌmp'tiːn/ a fam innumerevole. ~**th** a fam ennesimo; **for the** ~**th time** per l'ennesima volta

UN n abbr ⟨**United Nations**⟩ ONU f

un'able /ʌn-/ a **be** ~ **to do sth** non potere fare qcsa; ⟨not know how⟩ non sapere fare qcsa

una'bridged a integrale

unac'companied a non accompagnato; ⟨luggage⟩ incustodito

unac'countabl|e a inspiegabile. ~**y** adv inspiegabilmente

unac'customed a insolito; **be** ~ **to** non essere abituato a

una'dulterated a ⟨water⟩ puro; ⟨wine⟩ non sofisticato; fig assoluto

un'aided a senza aiuto

unanimity /juːnə'nɪmətɪ/ n unanimità f

unanimous /juː'nænɪməs/ a unanime. ~**ly** adv all'unanimità

un'armed a disarmato. ~ **combat** n lotta f senza armi

unas'suming a senza pretese

unat'tached a staccato; ⟨person⟩ senza legami

unat'tended a incustodito

un'authorized a non autorizzato

una'voidable a inevitabile

una'ware a **be** ~ **of sth** non rendersi conto di qcsa. ~**s** /-eəz/ adv **catch sb** ~**s** prendere qcno alla sprovvista

un'balanced a non equilibrato; ⟨mentally⟩ squilibrato

un'bearabl|e *a* insopportabile. **~y** *adv* insopportabilmente

unbeat|able /ʌnˈbiːtəbl/ *a* imbattibile. **~en** *a* imbattuto

unbeknown /ʌnbɪˈnəʊn/ *a fam* **~ to me** a mia insaputa

unbe'lievable *a* incredibile

un'bend *vi* (*pt/pp* **-bent**) (*relax*) distendersi

un'biased *a* obiettivo

un'block *vt* sbloccare

un'bolt *vt* togliere il chiavistello di

un'breakable *a* infrangibile

unbridled /ʌnˈbraɪdld/ *a* sfrenato

un'burden *vt* **~ oneself** *fig* sfogarsi (**to** con)

un'button *vt* sbottonare

uncalled-for /ʌnˈkɔːldfɔː(r)/ *a* fuori luogo

un'canny *a* sorprendente; ⟨*silence, feeling*⟩ inquietante

un'ceasing *a* incessante

uncere'monious *a* (*abrupt*) brusco. **~y** *adv* senza tante cerimonie

un'certain *a* incerto; ⟨*weather*⟩ instabile; **in no ~ terms** senza mezzi termini. **~ty** *n* incertezza *f*

un'changed *a* invariato

un'charitable *a* duro

uncle /ˈʌŋkl/ *n* zio *m*

un'comfortabl|e *a* scomodo; imbarazzante ⟨*silence, situation*⟩; **feel ~e** *fig* sentirsi a disagio. **~y** *adv* ⟨*sit*⟩ scomodamente; (*causing alarm etc*) spaventosamente

un'common *a* insolito

un'compromising *a* intransigente

uncon'ditional *a* incondizionato. **~ly** *adv* incondizionatamente

un'conscious *a* privo di sensi; (*unaware*) inconsapevole; **be ~ of sth** non rendersi conto di qcsa. **~ly** *adv* inconsapevolmente

uncon'ventional *a* poco convenzionale

unco'operative *a* poco cooperativo

un'cork *vt* sturare

uncouth /ʌnˈkuːθ/ *a* zotico

un'cover *vt* scoprire; portare alla luce ⟨*buried object*⟩

unde'cided *a* indeciso; (*not settled*) incerto

undeniabl|e /ʌndɪˈnaɪəbl/ *a* innegabile. **~y** *adv* innegabilmente

under /ˈʌndə(r)/ *prep* sotto; (*less than*) al di sotto di; **~ there** lì sotto; **~ repair/construction** in riparazione/costruzione; **~ way** *fig* in corso ● *adv*

(**~ water**) sott'acqua; (*unconscious*) sotto anestesia

'undercarriage *n Aeron* carrello *m*

'underclothes *npl* biancheria *fsg* intima

under'cover *a* clandestino

'undercurrent *n* corrente *f* sottomarina; *fig* sottofondo *m*

under'cut *vt* (*pt/pp* **-cut**) *Comm* vendere a minor prezzo di

'underdog *n* perdente *m*

under'done *a* ⟨*meat*⟩ al sangue

under'estimate *vt* sottovalutare

under'fed *a* denutrito

under'foot *adv* sotto i piedi; **trample ~** calpestare

under'go *vt* (*pt* **-went**, *pp* **-gone**) subire ⟨*operation, treatment*⟩; **~ repair** essere in riparazione

under'graduate *n* studente, -tessa *mf* universitario, -a

under'ground¹ *adv* sottoterra

'underground² *a* sotterraneo; (*secret*) clandestino ● *n* (*railway*) metropolitana *f*. **~ car park** *n* parcheggio *m* sotterraneo

'undergrowth *n* sottobosco *m*

'underhand *a* subdolo

'underlay *n* strato *m* di gomma o feltro posto sotto la moquette

under'lie *vt* (*pt* **-lay**, *pp* **-lain**, *pres p* **-lying**) *fig* essere alla base di

under'line *vt* sottolineare

underling /ˈʌndəlɪŋ/ *n pej* subalterno, -a *mf*

under'lying *a fig* fondamentale

under'mine *vt fig* minare

underneath /ʌndəˈniːθ/ *prep* sotto; **~ it** sotto ● *adv* sotto

under'paid *a* mal pagato

'underpants *npl* mutande *fpl*

'underpass *n* sottopassaggio *m*

under'privileged *a* non abbiente

under'rate *vt* sottovalutare

'underseal *n Auto* antiruggine *m inv*

'undershirt *n Am* maglia *f* della pelle

understaffed /-ˈstɑːft/ *a* a corto di personale

under'stand *vt* (*pt/pp* **-stood**) capire; **I ~ that...** (*have heard*) mi risulta che... ● *vi* capire. **~able** /-əbl/ *a* comprensibile. **~ably** /-əblɪ/ *adv* comprensibilmente

under'standing *a* comprensivo ● *n* comprensione *f*; (*agreement*) accordo *m*; **on the ~ that** a condizione che

'understatement *n* understatement *m inv*

'understudy *n Theat* sostituto, -a *mf*

under'take *vt* (*pt* **-took**, *pp* **-taken**)

intraprendere; ~ **to do sth** impegnarsi a fare qcsa

'**undertaker** n impresario m di pompe funebri; [**firm of**] ~**s** n impresa f di pompe funebri

under'**taking** n impresa f; (promise) promessa f

'**undertone** n fig sottofondo m; **in an** ~ sottovoce

under'**value** vt sottovalutare

'**underwater**[1] a subacqueo

under'**water**[2] adv sott'acqua

'**underwear** n biancheria f intima

'**underweight** a sotto peso

'**underworld** n (criminals) malavita f

'**underwriter** n assicuratore m

unde'**sirable** a indesiderato; (person) poco raccomandabile

undies /'ʌndɪz/ npl fam biancheria fsg intima (da donna)

un'**dignified** a non dignitoso

un'**do** vt (pt -**did**, pp -**done**) disfare; slacciare (dress, shoes); sbottonare (shirt); fig, Comput annullare

un'**done** a (shirt, button) sbottonato; (shoes, dress) slacciato; (not accomplished) non fatto; **leave** ~ (job) tralasciare

un'**doubted** a indubbio. ~**ly** adv senza dubbio

un'**dress** vt spogliare; **get** ~**ed** spogliarsi ● vi spogliarsi

un'**due** a eccessivo

undulating /'ʌndjʊleɪtɪŋ/ a ondulato; (country) collinoso

un'**duly** adv eccessivamente

un'**dying** a eterno

un'**earth** vt dissotterrare; fig scovare; scoprire (secret). ~**ly** a soprannaturale; **at an** ~**ly hour** fam a un'ora impossibile

un'**eas|e** n disagio m. ~**y** a a disagio; (person) inquieto; (feeling) inquietante; (truce) precario

un'**eatable** a immangiabile

uneco'**nomic** a poco remunerativo

uneco'**nomical** a poco economico

unem'**ployed** a disoccupato ● npl **the** ~ i disoccupati

unem'**ployment** n disoccupazione f. ~ **benefit** n sussidio m di disoccupazione

un'**ending** a senza fine

un'**equal** a disuguale; (struggle) impari; **be** ~ **to a task** non essere all'altezza di un compito

une'**quivocal** /ʌnɪ'kwɪvəkl/ a inequivocabile; (person) esplicito

un'**erring** /ʌn'ɜːrɪŋ/ a infallibile

un'**ethical** a immorale

un'**even** a irregolare; (distribution) ineguale; (number) dispari

unex'**pected** a inaspettato. ~**ly** adv inaspettatamente

un'**failing** a infallibile

un'**fair** a ingiusto. ~**ly** adv ingiustamente. ~**ness** n ingiustizia f

un'**faithful** a infedele

unfa'**miliar** a sconosciuto; **be** ~ **with** non conoscere

un'**fasten** vt slacciare; (detach) staccare

un'**favourable** a sfavorevole; (impression) negativo

un'**feeling** a insensibile

un'**finished** a da finire; (business) in sospeso

un'**fit** a inadatto; (morally) indegno; Sport fuori forma; ~ **for work** non in grado di lavorare

un'**flinching** /ʌn'flɪntʃɪŋ/ a risoluto

un'**fold** vt spiegare; (spread out) aprire; fig rivelare ● vi (view:) spiegarsi

unfore'**seen** a imprevisto

unfor'**gettable** /ʌnfə'getəbl/ a indimenticabile

unfor'**givable** /ʌnfə'gɪvəbl/ a imperdonabile

unfor'**tunate** a sfortunato; (regrettable) spiacevole; (remark, choice) infelice. ~**ly** adv purtroppo

un'**founded** a infondato

un'**furl** /ʌn'fɜːl/ vt spiegare

un'**furnished** a non ammobiliato

un'**gainly** /ʌn'geɪnlɪ/ a sgraziato

un'**godly** /ʌn'gɒdlɪ/ a empio; ~ **hour** fam ora f impossibile

un'**grateful** a ingrato. ~**ly** adv senza riconoscenza

un'**happi|ly** adv infelicemente; (unfortunately) purtroppo. ~**ness** n infelicità f

un'**happy** a infelice; (not content) insoddisfatto (**with** di)

un'**harmed** a incolume

un'**healthy** a poco sano; (insanitary) malsano

un'**hook** vt sganciare

un'**hurt** a illeso

unhy'**gienic** a non igienico

unifi'**cation** /juːnɪfɪ'keɪʃn/ n unificazione f

uniform /'juːnɪfɔːm/ a uniforme ● n uniforme f. ~**ly** adv uniformemente

unify /'juːnɪfaɪ/ vt (pt/pp -**ied**) unificare

uni'**lateral** /juːnɪ-/ a unilaterale

uni'**maginable** a inimmaginabile

unim'**portant** a irrilevante

unin'**habited** a disabitato

unin'tentional *a* involontario. **~ly** *adv* involontariamente

union /'juːnɪən/ *n* unione *f*; ⟨*trade ~*⟩ sindacato *m*. **U~ Jack** *n* bandiera *f* del Regno Unito

unique /juːˈniːk/ *a* unico. **~ly** *adv* unicamente

unison /'juːnɪsn/ *n* **in ~** all'unisono

unit /'juːnɪt/ *n* unità *f inv*; ⟨*department*⟩ reparto *m*; ⟨*of furniture*⟩ elemento *m*

unite /juːˈnaɪt/ *vt* unire ● *vi* unirsi

united /juːˈnaɪtɪd/ *a* unito. **U~ 'Kingdom** *n* Regno *m* Unito. **U~ 'Nations** *n* [Organizzazione *f* delle] Nazioni Unite *fpl*. **U~ States [of America]** *n* Stati *mpl* Uniti [d'America]

unity /'juːnətɪ/ *n* unità *f*; ⟨*agreement*⟩ accordo *m*

universal /juːnɪˈvɜːsl/ *a* universale. **~ly** *adv* universalmente

universe /'juːnɪvɜːs/ *n* universo *m*

university /juːnɪˈvɜːsətɪ/ *n* università *f inv* ● *attrib* universitario

unjust *a* ingiusto

unkempt /ʌnˈkempt/ *a* trasandato; ⟨*hair*⟩ arruffato

un'kind *a* scortese. **~ly** *adv* in modo scortese. **~ness** *n* mancanza *f* di gentilezza

un'known *a* sconosciuto

un'lawful *a* illecito, illegale

unleaded /ʌnˈledɪd/ *a* senza piombo

un'leash *vt fig* scatenare

unless /ənˈles/ *conj* a meno che; **~ I am mistaken** se non mi sbaglio

un'like *a* (*not the same*) diversi ● *prep* diverso da; **that's ~ him** non è da lui; **~ me, he...** diversamente da me, lui...

un'likely *a* improbabile

un'limited *a* illimitato

un'load *vt* scaricare

un'lock *vt* aprire (*con chiave*)

un'lucky *a* sfortunato; **it's ~ to...** porta sfortuna...

un'manned *a* senza equipaggio

un'married *a* non sposato. **~ 'mother** *n* ragazza *f* madre

un'mask *vt fig* smascherare

unmistakabl|e /ʌnmɪˈsteɪkəbl/ *a* inconfondibile. **~y** *adv* chiaramente

un'mitigated *a* assoluto

un'natural *a* innaturale; *pej* anormale. **~ly** *adv* in modo innaturale; *pej* in modo anormale

unneces'sarily *adv* inutilmente

un'necessary *a* inutile

un'noticed *a* inosservato

unob'tainable *a* ⟨*products etc*⟩ introvabile; ⟨*telephone number*⟩ non ottenibile

unob'trusive *a* discreto. **~ly** *adv* in modo discreto

unof'ficial *a* non ufficiale. **~ly** *adv* ufficiosamente

un'pack *vi* disfare le valigie ● *vt* svuotare ⟨*parcel*⟩; spacchettare ⟨*books*⟩; **~ one's case** disfare la valigia

un'paid *a* da pagare; ⟨*work*⟩ non retribuito

un'palatable *a* sgradevole

un'paralleled *a* senza pari

un'pick *vt* disfare

un'pleasant *a* sgradevole; ⟨*person*⟩ maleducato. **~ly** *adv* sgradevolmente; ⟨*behave*⟩ maleducatamente. **~ness** *n* ⟨*bad feeling*⟩ tensioni *fpl*

un'plug *vt* (*pt/pp* -**plugged**) staccare

un'popular *a* impopolare

un'precedented *a* senza precedenti

unpre'dictable *a* imprevedibile

unpre'meditated *a* involontario

unpre'pared *a* impreparato

unpre'tentious *a* senza pretese

un'principled *a* senza principi; ⟨*behaviour*⟩ scorretto

unpro'fessional *a* non professionale; **it's ~** è una mancanza di professionalità

un'profitable *a* non redditizio

un'qualified *a* non qualificato; ⟨*fig: absolute*⟩ assoluto

un'questionable *a* incontestabile

un'quote *vi* chiudere le virgolette

unravel /ʌnˈrævl/ *vt* (*pt/pp* -**ravelled**) districare; ⟨*in knitting*⟩ disfare

un'real *a* irreale; *fam* inverosimile

un'reasonable *a* irragionevole

unre'lated *a* ⟨*fact*⟩ senza rapporto (**to** con); ⟨*person*⟩ non imparentato (**to** con)

unre'liable *a* inattendibile; ⟨*person*⟩ inaffidabile, che non dà affidamento

unrequited /ʌnrɪˈkwaɪtɪd/ *a* non corrisposto

unreservedly /ʌnrɪˈzɜːvɪdlɪ/ *adv* senza riserve; ⟨*frankly*⟩ francamente

un'rest *n* fermenti *mpl*

un'rivalled *a* ineguagliato

un'roll *vt* srotolare ● *vi* srotolarsi

unruly /ʌnˈruːlɪ/ *a* indisciplinato

un'safe *a* pericoloso

un'said *a* inespresso

un'salted *a* non salato

unsatis'factory *a* poco soddisfacente

un'savoury *a* equivoco

unscathed /ʌnˈskeɪðd/ *a* illeso

un'screw *vt* svitare

un'scrupulous *a* senza scrupoli

un'seemly *a* indecoroso
un'selfish *a* disinteressato
un'settled *a* in agitazione; ⟨*weather*⟩ variabile; ⟨*bill*⟩ non saldato
unshakeable /ʌnˈʃeɪkəbl/ *a* categorico
unshaven /ʌnˈʃeɪvn/ *a* non rasato
unsightly /ʌnˈsaɪtlɪ/ *a* brutto
un'skilled *a* non specializzato. **~ worker** *n* manovale *m*
un'sociable *a* scontroso
unso'phisticated *a* semplice
un'sound *a* ⟨*building, reasoning*⟩ poco solido; ⟨*advice*⟩ poco sensato; **of ~ mind** malato di mente
unspeakable /ʌnˈspiːkəbl/ *a* indicibile
un'stable *a* instabile; ⟨*mentally*⟩ squilibrato
un'steady *a* malsicuro
un'stuck *a* **come ~** staccarsi; ⟨*fam: project*⟩ andare a monte
unsuc'cessful *a* fallimentare; **be ~** ⟨*in attempt*⟩ non aver successo. **~ly** *adv* senza successo
un'suitable *a* ⟨*inappropriate*⟩ inadatto; ⟨*inconvenient*⟩ inopportuno
unsu'specting *a* fiducioso
unthinkable /ʌnˈθɪŋkəbl/ *a* impensabile
un'tidiness *n* disordine *m*
un'tidy *a* disordinato
un'tie *vt* slegare
until /ənˈtɪl/ *prep* fino a; **not ~** non prima di; **~ the evening** fino alla sera; **~ his arrival** fino al suo arrivo ● *conj* finché, fino a quando; **not ~ you've seen it** non prima che tu l'abbia visto
untimely /ʌnˈtaɪmlɪ/ *a* inopportuno; ⟨*premature*⟩ prematuro
un'tiring *a* instancabile
un'told *a* ⟨*wealth*⟩ incalcolabile; ⟨*suffering*⟩ indescrivibile; ⟨*story*⟩ inedito
unto'ward *a* **if nothing ~ happens** se non capita un imprevisto
un'true *a* falso; **that's ~** non è vero
unused[1] /ʌnˈjuːzd/ *a* non [ancora] usato
unused[2] /ʌnˈjuːst/ *a* **be ~ to** non essere abituato a
un'usual *a* insolito. **~ly** *adv* insolitamente
un'veil *vt* scoprire
un'wanted *a* indesiderato
un'warranted *a* ingiustificato
un'welcome *a* sgradito
un'well *a* indisposto
unwieldy /ʌnˈwiːldɪ/ *a* ingombrante
un'willing *a* riluttante. **~ly** *adv* malvolentieri
un'wind *v* (*pt/pp* **unwound**) ● *vt* svolgere, srotolare ● *vi* svolgersi, srotolarsi; ⟨*fam: relax*⟩ rilassarsi
un'wise *a* imprudente
unwitting /ʌnˈwɪtɪŋ/ *a* involontario; ⟨*victim*⟩ inconsapevole. **~ly** *adv* involontariamente
un'worthy *a* non degno
un'wrap *vt* (*pt/pp* **-wrapped**) scartare ⟨*present, parcel*⟩
un'written *a* tacito
up /ʌp/ *adv* su; ⟨*not in bed*⟩ alzato; ⟨*road*⟩ smantellato; ⟨*theatre curtain, blinds*⟩ alzato; ⟨*shelves, tent*⟩ montato; ⟨*notice*⟩ affisso; ⟨*building*⟩ costruito; **prices are up** i prezzi sono aumentati; **be up for sale** essere in vendita; **up here/there** quassù/lassù; **time's up** tempo scaduto; **what's up?** *fam* cosa è successo?; **up to** ⟨*as far as*⟩ fino a; **be up to** essere all'altezza di ⟨*task*⟩; **what's he up to?** *fam* cosa sta facendo?; ⟨*plotting*⟩ cosa sta combinando?; **I'm up to page 100** sono arrivato a pagina 100; **feel up to it** sentirsela; **be one up on sb** *fam* essere in vantaggio su qcno; **go up** salire; **lift up** alzare; **up against** *fig* alle prese con ● *prep* su; **the cat ran/is up the tree** il gatto è salito di corsa/è sull'albero; **further up this road** più avanti su questa strada; **row up the river** risalire il fiume; **go up the stairs** salire su per le scale; **be up the pub** *fam* essere al pub; **be up on** *or* **in sth** essere bene informato su qcsa ● *n* **ups and downs** *npl* alti *mpl* e bassi
'upbringing *n* educazione *f*
up'date[1] *vt* aggiornare
'update[2] *n* aggiornamento *m*
up'grade *vt* promuovere ⟨*person*⟩; modernizzare ⟨*equipment*⟩
upgradeable /ʌpˈɡreɪdəbl/ *a Comput* upgradabile
upheaval /ʌpˈhiːvl/ *n* scompiglio *m*
up'hill *a* in salita; *fig* arduo ● *adv* in salita
up'hold *vt* (*pt/pp* **upheld**) sostenere ⟨*principle*⟩; confermare ⟨*verdict*⟩
upholster /ʌpˈhəʊstə(r)/ *vt* tappezzare. **~er** *n* tappezziere, -a *mf*. **~y** *n* tappezzeria *f*
'upkeep *n* mantenimento *m*
up-'market *a* di qualità
upon /əˈpɒn/ *prep* su; **~ arriving home** una volta arrivato a casa
upper /ˈʌpə(r)/ *a* superiore ● *n* (*of shoe*) tomaia *f*
upper: **~ circle** *n* seconda galleria *f*. **~ class** *n* alta borghesia *f*. **~ hand** *n* **have the ~ hand** avere il sopravvento.

~**most** *a* più alto; **that's ~most in my mind** è la mia preoccupazione principale

'**upright** *a* dritto; ⟨*piano*⟩ verticale; ⟨*honest*⟩ retto ● *n* montante *m*

'**uprising** *n* rivolta *f*

'**uproar** *n* tumulto *m*; **be in an ~** essere in trambusto

up'root *vt* sradicare

up'set[1] *vt* (*pt/pp* **upset**, *pres p* **upsetting**) rovesciare; sconvolgere ⟨*plan*⟩; ⟨*distress*⟩ turbare; **get ~ about sth** prendersela per qcsa; **be very ~** essere sconvolto; **have an ~ stomach** avere l'intestino disturbato

'**upset**[2] *n* scombussolamento *m*

'**upshot** *n* risultato *m*

upside 'down *adv* sottosopra; **turn ~ ~** capovolgere

up'stairs[1] *adv* [al piano] di sopra

'**upstairs**[2] *a* del piano superiore

'**upstart** *n* arrivato, -a *mf*

up'stream *adv* controcorrente

'**upsurge** *n* ⟨*in sales*⟩ aumento *m* improvviso; ⟨*of enthusiasm, crime*⟩ ondata *f*

'**uptake** *n* **be slow on the ~** essere lento nel capire; **be quick on the ~** capire le cose al volo

up'tight *a* teso

up-to-'date *a* moderno; ⟨*news*⟩ ultimo; ⟨*records*⟩ aggiornato

'**upturn** *n* ripresa *f*

upward /'ʌpwəd/ *a* verso l'alto, in s ~ **slope** salita *f* ● *adv* ~[**s**] verso l'alto; ~**s** of oltre

uranium /jʊ'reɪnɪəm/ *n* uranio *m*

urban /'ɜ:bən/ *a* urbano

urge /ɜ:dʒ/ *n* forte desiderio *m* ● *vt* esortare (**to** a). **urge on** *vt* spronare

urgen|cy /'ɜ:dʒənsɪ/ *n* urgenza *f*. ~**t** *a* urgente

urinate /'jʊərmeɪt/ *vi* urinare

urine /'jʊərɪn/ *n* urina *f*

urn /ɜ:n/ *n* urna *f*; ⟨*for tea*⟩ contenitore *m* munito di cannella che si trova nei self-service, mense ecc

us /ʌs/ *pers pron* ci; ⟨*after prep*⟩ noi; **they know us** ci conoscono; **give us**

the **money** dateci i soldi; **give it to us** datecelo; **they showed it to us** ce l'hanno fatto vedere; **they meant us, not you** intendevano noi, non voi; **it's us** siamo noi; **she hates us** ci odia

US[A] *n[pl] abbr* (**United States [of America]**) U.S.A. *mpl*

usable /'ju:zəbl/ *a* usabile

usage /'ju:sɪdʒ/ *n* uso *m*

use[1] /ju:s/ *n* uso *m*; **be of ~** essere utile; **be of no ~** essere inutile; **make ~ of** usare; ⟨*exploit*⟩ sfruttare; **it is no ~** è inutile; **what's the ~?** a che scopo?

use[2] /ju:z/ *vt* usare. **use up** *vt* consumare

used[1] /ju:zd/ *a* usato

used[2] /ju:st/ *pt* **be ~ to sth** essere abituato a qcsa; **get ~ to** abituarsi a; **he ~ to live here** viveva qui

useful /'ju:sfl/ *a* utile. ~**ness** *n* utilità *f*

useless /'ju:slɪs/ *a* inutile; ⟨*fam: person*⟩ incapace

user /'ju:zə(r)/ *n* utente *mf*. ~-'**friendly** *a* facile da usare

usher /'ʌʃə(r)/ *n Theat* maschera *f*; *Jur* usciere *m*; ⟨*at wedding*⟩ persona *f* che accompagna gli invitati a un matrimonio ai loro posti in chiesa ● **usher in** *vt* fare entrare

usherette ʃə'ret/ *n* maschera *f*

usual /'ju:ʒʊəl/ *a* usuale; **as ~** come al solito. ~**ly** *adv* di solito

usurp /jʊ'zɜ:p/ *vt* usurpare

utensil /jʊ'tensl/ *n* utensile *m*

uterus /'ju:tərəs/ *n* utero *m*

utilitarian /jʊtɪlɪ'teərɪən/ *a* funzionale

utility /jʊ'tɪlɪtɪ/ *n* servizio *m*. ~ **room** *n* stanza *f* in casa privata per il lavaggio, la stiratura dei panni ecc

utilize /'ju:tɪlaɪz/ *vt* utilizzare

utmost /'ʌtməʊst/ *a* estremo ● *n* **one's ~** tutto il possibile

utter[1] /'ʌtə(r)/ *a* totale. ~**ly** *adv* completamente

utter[2] *vt* emettere ⟨*sigh, sound*⟩; proferire ⟨*word*⟩. ~**ance** /-əns/ *n* dichiarazione *f*

U-turn /'ju:-/ *n Auto* inversione *f* a U; *fig* marcia *f* in dietro

Vv

vacan|cy /ˈveɪk(ə)nsɪ/ n ⟨job⟩ posto m vacante; ⟨room⟩ stanza f disponibile. **~t** a libero; ⟨position⟩ vacante; ⟨look⟩ assente

vacate /vəˈkeɪt/ vt lasciare libero

vacation /vəˈkeɪʃn/ n Univ & Am vacanza f

vaccinat|e /ˈvæksɪneɪt/ vt vaccinare. **~ion** /-ˈneɪʃn/ n vaccinazione f

vaccine /ˈvæksiːn/ n vaccino m

vacuum /ˈvækjʊəm/ n vuoto m ● vt passare l'aspirapolvere in/su. **~ cleaner** n aspirapolvere m inv. **~ flask** n thermos® m inv. **~-packed** a confezionato sottovuoto

vagabond /ˈvægəbɒnd/ n vagabondo, -a mf

vagina /vəˈdʒaɪnə/ n Anat vagina f

vagrant /ˈveɪɡrənt/ n vagabondo, -a mf

vague /veɪɡ/ a vago; ⟨outline⟩ impreciso; ⟨absent-minded⟩ distratto; **I'm still ~ about it** non ho ancora le idee chiare in proposito. **~ly** adv vagamente

vain /veɪn/ a vanitoso; ⟨hope, attempt⟩ vano; **in ~** invano. **~ly** adv vanamente

valentine /ˈvæləntaɪn/ n ⟨card⟩ biglietto m di San Valentino

valiant /ˈvæliənt/ a valoroso

valid /ˈvælɪd/ a valido. **~ate** vt ⟨confirm⟩ convalidare. **~ity** /vəˈlɪdətɪ/ n validità f

valley /ˈvælɪ/ n valle f

valour /ˈvælə(r)/ n valore m

valuable /ˈvæljʊəbl/ a di valore; ⟨time⟩ prezioso. **~s** npl oggetti mpl di valore

valuation /væljʊˈeɪʃn/ n valutazione f

value /ˈvæljuː/ n valore m; ⟨usefulness⟩ utilità f ● vt valutare; ⟨cherish⟩ apprezzare. **~ 'added tax** n imposta f sul valore aggiunto

valve /vælv/ n valvola f

vampire /ˈvæmpaɪə(r)/ n vampiro m

van /væn/ n furgone m

vandal /ˈvændl/ n vandalo, -a mf. **~ism** /-ɪzm/ n vandalismo m. **~ize** vt vandalizzare

vanilla /vəˈnɪlə/ n vaniglia f

vanish /ˈvænɪʃ/ vi svanire

vanity /ˈvænətɪ/ n vanità f. **~ bag** or **case** n beauty-case m inv

vantage-point /ˈvɑːntɪdʒ-/ n punto m d'osservazione; fig punto m di vista

vapour /ˈveɪpə(r)/ n vapore m

variable /ˈveərɪəbl/ a variabile; ⟨adjustable⟩ regolabile

variance /ˈveərɪəns/ n **be at ~** essere in disaccordo

variant /ˈveərɪənt/ n variante f

variation /veərɪˈeɪʃn/ n variazione f

varicose /ˈværɪkəʊs/ a **~ veins** vene fpl varicose

varied /ˈveərɪd/ a vario; ⟨diet⟩ diversificato; ⟨life⟩ movimentato

variety /vəˈraɪətɪ/ n varietà f inv

various /ˈveərɪəs/ a vario

varnish /ˈvɑːnɪʃ/ n vernice f; ⟨for nails⟩ smalto m ● vt verniciare; **~ one's nails** mettersi lo smalto

vary /ˈveərɪ/ vt/i ⟨pt/pp **-ied**⟩ variare. **~ing** a variabile; ⟨different⟩ diverso

vase /vɑːz/ n vaso m

vast /vɑːst/ a vasto; ⟨difference, amusement⟩ enorme. **~ly** adv ⟨superior⟩ di gran lunga; ⟨different, amused⟩ enormemente

vat /væt/ n tino m

VAT /viːeɪˈtiː, væt/ n abbr ⟨**value added tax**⟩ I.V.A. f

vault¹ /vɔːlt/ n ⟨roof⟩ volta f; ⟨in bank⟩ caveau m inv; ⟨tomb⟩ cripta f

vault² n salto m ● vt/i ~ **[over]** saltare

VDU n abbr ⟨**visual display unit**⟩ VDU m

veal /viːl/ n carne f di vitello ● attrib di vitello

veer /vɪə(r)/ vi cambiare direzione; Naut, Auto virare

vegetable /ˈvedʒtəbl/ n ⟨food⟩ verdura f; ⟨when growing⟩ ortaggio m ● attrib ⟨oil, fat⟩ vegetale

vegetarian /vedʒɪˈteərɪən/ a & n vegetariano, -a mf

vegetat|e /ˈvedʒɪteɪt/ vi vegetare. **~ion** /-ˈteɪʃn/ n vegetazione f

vehemen|ce /ˈviːəməns/ n veemenza f. **~t** a veemente. **~tly** adv con veemenza

vehicle /ˈviːɪkl/ n veicolo m; ⟨fig: medium⟩ mezzo m

veil /veɪl/ n velo m ● vt velare

vein /veɪn/ n vena f; (mood) umore m; (manner) tenore m. **~ed** a venato

Velcro® /ˈvelkrəʊ/ n **~ fastening** chiusura f con velcro®

velocity /vɪˈlɒsətɪ/ n velocità f

velvet /ˈvelvɪt/ n velluto m. **~y** a vellutato

vendetta /venˈdetə/ n vendetta f

vending-machine /ˈvendɪŋ-/ n distributore m automatico

veneer /vəˈnɪə(r)/ n impiallacciatura f; fig vernice f. **~ed** a impiallacciato

venereal /vɪˈnɪərɪəl/ a **~ disease** malattia f venerea

Venetian /vəˈniːʃn/ a & n veneziano, -a mf. **v~ blind** n persiana f alla veneziana

vengeance /ˈvendʒəns/ n vendetta f; **with a ~** fam a più non posso

Venice /ˈvenɪs/ n Venezia f

venison /ˈvenɪsn/ n Culin carne f di cervo

venom /ˈvenəm/ n veleno m. **~ous** /-əs/ a velenoso

vent[1] /vent/ n presa f d'aria; **give ~ to** fig dar libero sfogo a ● vt fig sfogare ⟨anger⟩

vent[2] n (in jacket) spacco m

ventilat|e /ˈventɪleɪt/ vt ventilare. **~ion** /-ˈleɪʃn/ n ventilazione f; (installation) sistema m di ventilazione. **~or** n ventilatore m

ventriloquist /venˈtrɪləkwɪst/ n ventriloquo, -a mf

venture /ˈventʃə(r)/ n impresa f ● vt azzardare ● vi avventurarsi

venue /ˈvenjuː/ n luogo m (di convegno, concerto, ecc.)

veranda /vəˈrændə/ n veranda f

verb /vɜːb/ n verbo m. **~al** a verbale

verbatim /vɜːˈbeɪtɪm/ a letterale ● adv parola per parola

verbose /vɜːˈbəʊs/ a prolisso

verdict /ˈvɜːdɪkt/ n verdetto m; (opinion) parere m

verge /vɜːdʒ/ n orlo m; **be on the ~ of doing sth** essere sul punto di fare qcsa ● **verge on** vt fig rasentare

verger /ˈvɜːdʒə(r)/ n sagrestano m

verify /ˈverɪfaɪ/ vt (pt/pp -ied) verificare; (confirm) confermare

vermin /ˈvɜːmɪn/ n animali mpl nocivi

vermouth /ˈvɜːməθ/ n vermut m inv

vernacular /vəˈnækjʊlə(r)/ n vernacolo m

versatil|e /ˈvɜːsətaɪl/ a versatile. **~ity** /-ˈtɪlətɪ/ n versatilità f

verse /vɜːs/ n verso m; (of Bible) versetto m; (poetry) versi mpl

versed /vɜːst/ a **~ in** versato in

version /ˈvɜːʃn/ n versione f

versus /ˈvɜːsəs/ prep contro

vertebra /ˈvɜːtɪbrə/ n (pl -brae /-briː/) Anat vertebra f

vertical /ˈvɜːtɪkl/ a & n verticale m

vertigo /ˈvɜːtɪgəʊ/ n Med vertigine f

verve /vɜːv/ n verve f

very /ˈverɪ/ adv molto; **~ much** molto; **~ little** pochissimo; **~ many** moltissimi; **~ few** pochissimi; **~ probably** molto probabilmente; **~ well** benissimo; **at the ~ most** tutt'al più; **at the ~ latest** al più tardi ● a **the ~ first** il primissimo; **the ~ thing** proprio ciò che ci vuole; **at the ~ end/beginning** proprio alla fine/all'inizio; **that ~ day** proprio quel giorno; **the ~ thought** la sola idea; **only a ~ little** solo un pochino

vessel /ˈvesl/ n nave f

vest /vest/ n maglia f della pelle; (Am: waistcoat) gilè m inv. **~ed interest** n interesse m personale

vestige /ˈvestɪdʒ/ n (of past) vestigio m

vestment /ˈvestmənt/ n Relig paramento m

vestry /ˈvestrɪ/ n sagrestia f

vet /vet/ n veterinario, -a mf ● vt (pt/pp **vetted**) controllare minuziosamente

veteran /ˈvetərən/ n veterano, -a mf

veterinary /ˈvetərɪnərɪ/ a veterinario. **~ surgeon** n medico m veterinario

veto /ˈviːtəʊ/ n (pl -es) veto m ● vt proibire

vex /veks/ vt irritare. **~ation** /-ˈseɪʃn/ n irritazione f. **~ed** a irritato; **~ed question** questione f controversa

VHF n abbr (very high frequency) VHF

via /ˈvaɪə/ prep via; (by means of) attraverso

viable /ˈvaɪəbl/ a ⟨life form, relationship, company⟩ in grado di sopravvivere; ⟨proposition⟩ attuabile

viaduct /ˈvaɪədʌkt/ n viadotto m

vibrat|e /vaɪˈbreɪt/ vi vibrare. **~ion** /-ˈbreɪʃn/ n vibrazione f

vicar /ˈvɪkə(r)/ n parroco m (protestante). **~age** /-rɪdʒ/ n casa f parrocchiale

vicarious /vɪˈkeərɪəs/ a indiretto

vice[1] /vaɪs/ n vizio m

vice[2] n Techn morsa f

vice 'chairman n vicepresidente mf

vice 'president n vicepresidente mf

vice versa /vaɪsɪˈvɜːsə/ adv viceversa

vicinity /vɪˈsɪnətɪ/ n vicinanza f; **in the ~ of** nelle vicinanze di

vicious /ˈvɪʃəs/ a cattivo; ⟨attack⟩ bru-

tale; ⟨animal⟩ pericoloso. ~ **'circle** n circolo m vizioso. ~**ly** adv ⟨attack⟩ brutalmente

victim /'vɪktɪm/ n vittima f. ~**ize** vt fare delle rappresaglie contro

victor /'vɪktə(r)/ n vincitore m

victor|ious /vɪk'tɔːrɪəs/ a vittorioso. ~**y** /'vɪktərɪ/ n vittoria f

video /'vɪdɪəʊ/ n video m; ⟨cassette⟩ videocassetta f; ⟨recorder⟩ videoregistratore m ● attrib video ● vt registrare

video: ~ **card** n Comput scheda f video. ~ **cas'sette** n videocassetta f. ~**conference** n videoconferenza f. ~ **game** n videogioco m. ~ **recorder** n videoregistratore m. ~**-tape** n videocassetta f

vie /vaɪ/ vi ⟨pres p vying⟩ rivaleggiare

view /vjuː/ n vista f; ⟨photographed, painted⟩ veduta f; ⟨opinion⟩ visione f; **look at the** ~ guardare il panorama; **in my** ~ secondo me; **in** ~ **of** in considerazione di; **on** ~ esposto; **with a** ~ **to** con l'intenzione di ● vt visitare ⟨house⟩; ⟨consider⟩ considerare ● vi TV guardare. ~ n TV telespettatore, -trice mf; Phot visore m

view: ~**finder** n Phot mirino m. ~**point** n punto m di vista

vigil /'vɪdʒɪl/ n veglia f

vigilan|ce /'vɪdʒɪləns/ n vigilanza f. ~**t** a vigile

vigorous /'vɪgərəs/ a vigoroso

vigour /'vɪgə(r)/ n vigore m

vile /vaɪl/ a disgustoso; ⟨weather⟩ orribile; ⟨temper, mood⟩ pessimo

villa /'vɪlə/ n ⟨for holidays⟩ casa f di villeggiatura

village /'vɪlɪdʒ/ n paese m. ~**r** n paesano, -a mf

villain /'vɪlən/ n furfante m; ⟨in story⟩ cattivo m

vindicate /'vɪndɪkeɪt/ vt ⟨from guilt⟩ discolpare; **you are** ~**d** ti sei dimostrato nel giusto

vindictive /vɪn'dɪktɪv/ a vendicativo

vine /vaɪn/ n vite f

vinegar /'vɪnɪgə(r)/ n aceto m

vineyard /'vɪnjɑːd/ n vigneto m

vintage /'vɪntɪdʒ/ a ⟨wine⟩ d'annata ● n ⟨year⟩ annata f

viola /vɪ'əʊlə/ n Mus viola f

violat|e /'vaɪəleɪt/ vt violare. ~**ion** /-'leɪʃn/ n violazione f

violen|ce /'vaɪələns/ n violenza f. ~**t** a violento

violet /'vaɪələt/ a violetto ● n ⟨flower⟩ violetta f; ⟨colour⟩ violetto m

violin /vaɪə'lɪn/ n violino m. ~**ist** n violinista mf

VIP n abbr ⟨very important person⟩ vip mf

virgin /'vɜːdʒɪn/ a vergine ● n vergine f. ~**ity** /-'dʒɪnətɪ/ n verginità f

Virgo /'vɜːgəʊ/ n Astr Vergine f

viril|e /'vɪraɪl/ a virile. ~**ity** /-'rɪlətɪ/ n virilità f

virtual /'vɜːtjʊəl/ a effettivo. ~ **reality** n realtà f virtuale. ~**ly** adv praticamente

virtue /'vɜːtjuː/ n virtù f inv; ⟨advantage⟩ vantaggio m; **by** or **in** ~ **of** a causa di

virtuoso /vɜːtʊ'əʊzəʊ/ n ⟨pl -si /-ziː/⟩ virtuoso m

virtuous /'vɜːtjʊəs/ a virtuoso

virulent /'vɪrʊlənt/ a virulento

virus /'vaɪərəs/ n virus m inv

visa /'viːzə/ n visto m

vis-à-vis /viːzɑː'viː/ prep rispetto a

viscount /'vaɪkaʊnt/ n visconte m

viscous /'vɪskəs/ a vischioso

visibility /vɪzə'bɪlətɪ/ n visibilità f

visibl|e /'vɪzəbl/ a visibile. ~**y** adv visibilmente

vision /'vɪʒn/ n visione f; ⟨sight⟩ vista f

visit /'vɪzɪt/ n visita f ● vt andare a trovare ⟨person⟩; andare da ⟨doctor etc⟩; visitare ⟨town, building⟩. ~**ing hours** npl orario m delle visite. ~**or** n ospite mf; ⟨of town, museum⟩ visitatore, -trice mf; ⟨in hotel⟩ cliente mf

visor /'vaɪzə(r)/ n visiera f; Auto parasole m

vista /'vɪstə/ n ⟨view⟩ panorama m

visual /'vɪzjʊəl/ a visivo. ~ **aids** npl supporto m visivo. ~ **dis'play unit** n visualizzatore m. ~**ly** adv visualmente; ~**ly handicapped** non vedente

visualize /'vɪzjʊəlaɪz/ vt visualizzare

vital /'vaɪtl/ a vitale. ~**ity** /vaɪ'tælətɪ/ n vitalità f. ~**ly** /'vaɪtəlɪ/ adv estremamente

vitamin /'vɪtəmɪn/ n vitamina f

vivaci|ous /vɪ'veɪʃəs/ a vivace. ~**ty** /-'væsətɪ/ n vivacità f

vivid /'vɪvɪd/ a vivido. ~**ly** adv in modo vivido

vocabulary /və'kæbjʊlərɪ/ n vocabolario m; ⟨list⟩ glossario m

vocal /'vəʊkl/ a vocale; ⟨vociferous⟩ eloquente. ~ **cords** npl corde fpl vocali

vocalist /'vəʊkəlɪst/ n vocalista mf

vocation /və'keɪʃn/ n vocazione f. ~**al** a di orientamento professionale

vociferous /və'sɪfərəs/ a vociante

vodka /'vɒdkə/ n vodka f inv

vogue /vəʊg/ n moda f; **in** ~ in voga

voice /vɔɪs/ n voce f ● vt esprimere. **~mail** n posta f elettronica vocale

void /vɔɪd/ a (not valid) nullo; **~ of** privo di ● n vuoto m

volatile /'vɒlətaɪl/ a volatile; ⟨person⟩ volubile

volcanic /vɒl'kænɪk/ a vulcanico

volcano /vɒl'keɪnəʊ/ n vulcano m

volition /və'lɪʃn/ n **of his own ~** di sua spontanea volontà

volley /'vɒlɪ/ n (of gunfire) raffica f; Tennis volée f inv

volt /vəʊlt/ n volt m inv. **~age** /-ɪdʒ/ n Electr voltaggio m

volubl|e /'vɒljʊbl/ a loquace

volume /'vɒljuːm/ n volume m; (of work, traffic) quantità f inv. **~ control** n volume m

voluntar|y /'vɒləntərɪ/ a volontario. **~y work** n volontariato m. **~ily** adv volontariamente

volunteer /vɒlən'tɪə(r)/ n volontario, -a mf ● vt offrire volontariamente

⟨information⟩ ● vi offrirsi volontario; Mil arruolarsi come volontario

voluptuous /və'lʌptjʊəs/ a voluttuoso

vomit /'vɒmɪt/ n vomito m ● vt/i vomitare

voracious /və'reɪʃəs/ a vorace

vot|e /vəʊt/ n voto m; (ballot) votazione f; (right) diritto m di voto; **take a ~e on** votare su ● vi votare ● vt **~e sb president** eleggere qcno presidente. **~er** n elettore, -trice mf. **~ing** n votazione f

vouch /vaʊtʃ/ vi **~ for** garantire per. **~er** n buono m

vow /vaʊ/ n voto m ● vt giurare

vowel /'vaʊəl/ n vocale f

voyage /'vɔɪdʒ/ n viaggio m [marittimo]; (in space) viaggio m [nello spazio]

vulgar /'vʌlgə(r)/ a volgare. **~ity** /-'gærəti/ n volgarità f inv

vulnerable /'vʌlnərəbl/ a vulnerabile

vulture /'vʌltʃə(r)/ n avvoltoio m

vying /'vaɪɪŋ/ see **vie**

Ww

wad /wɒd/ n batuffolo m; (bundle) rotolo m. **~ding** n ovatta f

waddle /'wɒdl/ vi camminare ondeggiando

wade /weɪd/ vi guadare; **~ through** fam procedere faticosamente in ⟨book⟩

wafer /'weɪfə(r)/ n cialda f, wafer m inv; Relig ostia f

waffle¹ /'wɒfl/ vi fam blaterare

waffle² n Culin cialda f

waft /wɒft/ vt trasportare ● vi diffondersi

wag /wæg/ v (pt/pp **wagged**) ● vt agitare ● vi agitarsi

wage¹ /weɪdʒ/ vt dichiarare ⟨war⟩; lanciare ⟨campaign⟩

wage² n, & **~s** pl salario msg. **~ packet** n busta f paga

waggle /'wægl/ vt dimenare ● vi dimenarsi

wagon /'wægən/ n carro m; Rail vagone m merci

wail /weɪl/ n piagnucolio m; (of wind) lamento m; (of baby) vagito m ● vi piagnucolare; ⟨wind:⟩ lamentarsi; ⟨baby:⟩ vagire

waist /weɪst/ n vita f. **~coat** /'weɪskəʊt/ n gilè m inv; (of man's suit) panciotto m. **~line** n vita f

wait /weɪt/ n attesa f; **lie in ~ for** appostarsi per sorprendere ● vi aspettare; **~ for** aspettare ● vt **~ one's turn** aspettare il proprio turno. **wait on** vt servire

waiter /'weɪtə(r)/ n cameriere m

waiting: **~-list** n lista f d'attesa. **~-room** n sala f d'aspetto

waitress /'weɪtrɪs/ n cameriera f

waive /weɪv/ vt rinunciare a ⟨claim⟩; non tener conto di ⟨rule⟩

wake¹ /weɪk/ n veglia f funebre ● v (pt **woke**, pp **woken**) **~ [up]** ● vt svegliare ● vi svegliarsi

wake² n Naut scia f; **in the ~ of** fig nella scia di

waken /'weɪkn/ vt svegliare ● vi svegliarsi

Wales /weɪlz/ n Galles m

walk /wɔːk/ n passeggiata f; (gait) andatura f; (path) sentiero m; **go for a ~** andare a fare una passeggiata ● vi camminare; (as opposed to drive etc) andare a piedi; ⟨*ramble*⟩ passeggiare ● *vt* portare a spasso ⟨*dog*⟩; percorrere ⟨*streets*⟩. **walk out** *vi* ⟨*husband, employee:*⟩ andarsene; ⟨*workers:*⟩ scioperare. **walk out on** *vt* lasciare

walker /'wɔːkə(r)/ *n* camminatore, -trice *mf*; ⟨*rambler*⟩ escursionista *mf*

walking /'wɔːkɪŋ/ *n* camminare *m*; ⟨*rambling*⟩ fare *m* delle escursioni. **~-stick** *n* bastone *m* da passeggio

'Walkman® *n* Walkman *m inv*

walk: **~-out** *n* sciopero *m*. **~-over** *n fig* vittoria *f* facile

wall /wɔːl/ *n* muro *m*; **go to the ~** *fam* andare a rotoli; **drive sb up the ~** *fam* far diventare matto qcno ● **wall up** *vt* murare

wallet /'wɒlɪt/ *n* portafoglio *m*

wallop /'wɒləp/ *n fam* colpo *m* ● *vt* ⟨*pt/pp* **walloped**⟩ *fam* colpire

wallow /'wɒləʊ/ *vi* sguazzare; ⟨*in self-pity, grief*⟩ crogiolarsi

'wallpaper *n* tappezzeria *f* ● *vt* tappezzare

walnut /'wɔːlnʌt/ *n* noce *f*

waltz /wɔːlts/ *n* valzer *m inv* ● *vi* ballare il valzer

wan /wɒn/ *a* esangue

wand /wɒnd/ *n* ⟨*magic ~*⟩ bacchetta *f* [magica]

wander /'wɒndə(r)/ *vi* girovagare; ⟨*fig: digress*⟩ divagare. **wander about** *vi* andare a spasso

wane /weɪn/ *n* **be on the ~** essere in fase calante ● *vi* calare

wangle /'wæŋgl/ *vt fam* rimediare ⟨*invitation, holiday*⟩

want /wɒnt/ *n* ⟨*hardship*⟩ bisogno *m*; ⟨*lack*⟩ mancanza *f* ● *vt* volere; ⟨*need*⟩ aver bisogno di; **~ [to have]** sth volere qcsa; **~ to do sth** voler fare qcsa; **we ~ to stay** vogliamo rimanere; **I ~ you to go** voglio che tu vada; **it ~s painting** ha bisogno d'essere dipinto; **you ~ to learn to swim** bisogna che impari a nuotare ● *vi* **~ for** mancare di. **~ed** *a* ricercato. **~ing** *a* **be ~ing** mancare; **be ~ing in** mancare di

wanton /'wɒntən/ *a* ⟨*cruelty, neglect*⟩ gratuito; ⟨*morally*⟩ debosciato

war /wɔː(r)/ *n* guerra *f*; *fig* lotta *f* ⟨**on** contro⟩; **at ~** in guerra

ward /wɔːd/ *n* ⟨*in hospital*⟩ reparto *m*; ⟨*child*⟩ minore *m* sotto tutela ● **ward off** *vt* evitare; parare ⟨*blow*⟩

warden /'wɔːdn/ *n* guardiano, -a *mf*

warder /'wɔːdə(r)/ *n* guardia *f* carceraria

wardrobe /'wɔːdrəʊb/ *n* guardaroba *m*

warehouse /'weəhaʊs/ *n* magazzino *m*

war: **~fare** *n* guerra *f*. **~head** *n* testata *f*. **~like** *a* bellicoso

warm /wɔːm/ *a* caldo; ⟨*welcome*⟩ caloroso; **be ~** ⟨*person:*⟩ aver caldo; **it is ~** ⟨*weather:*⟩ fa caldo ● *vt* scaldare. **warm up** *vt* scaldare ● *vi* scaldarsi; *fig* animarsi. **~-hearted** *a* espansivo. **~ly** *adv* ⟨*greet*⟩ calorosamente; ⟨*dress*⟩ in modo pesante

warmth /wɔːmθ/ *n* calore *m*

warn /wɔːn/ *vt* avvertire. **~ing** *n* avvertimento *m*; ⟨*advance notice*⟩ preavviso *m*

warp /wɔːp/ *vt* deformare; *fig* distorcere ● *vi* deformarsi

'war-path *n* **on the ~** sul sentiero di guerra

warped /wɔːpt/ *a fig* contorto; ⟨*sexuality*⟩ deviato; ⟨*view*⟩ distorto

warrant /'wɒrənt/ *n* ⟨*for arrest, search*⟩ mandato *m* ● *vt* ⟨*justify*⟩ giustificare; ⟨*guarantee*⟩ garantire

warranty /'wɒrəntɪ/ *n* garanzia *f*

warring /'wɔːrɪŋ/ *a* in guerra

warrior /'wɒrɪə(r)/ *n* guerriero, -a *mf*

'warship *n* nave *f* da guerra

wart /wɔːt/ *n* porro *m*

'wartime *n* tempo *m* di guerra

war|y /'weərɪ/ *a* ⟨**-ier, -iest**⟩ ⟨*careful*⟩ cauto; ⟨*suspicious*⟩ diffidente. **~ily** *adv* cautamente

was /wɒz/ *see* be

wash /wɒʃ/ *n* lavata *f*; ⟨*clothes*⟩ bucato *m*; ⟨*in washing machine*⟩ lavaggio *m*; **have a ~** darsi una lavata ● *vt* lavare; ⟨*sea:*⟩ bagnare; **~ one's hands** lavarsi le mani ● *vi* lavarsi. **wash out** *vt* sciacquare ⟨*soap*⟩; sciacquarsi ⟨*mouth*⟩. **wash up** *vt* lavare ● *vi* lavare i piatti; *Am* lavarsi

washable /'wɒʃəbl/ *a* lavabile

wash: **~-basin** *n* lavandino *m*. **~ cloth** *n Am* guanto *m* da bagno

washed 'out *a* ⟨*faded*⟩ scolorito; ⟨*tired*⟩ spossato

washer /'wɒʃə(r)/ *n Techn* guarnizione *f*; ⟨*machine*⟩ lavatrice *f*

washing /'wɒʃɪŋ/ *n* bucato *m*. **~-machine** *n* lavatrice *f*. **~-powder** *n* detersivo *m*. **~-'up** *n* do the **~-up** lavare i piatti. **~-'up liquid** *n* detersivo *m* per i piatti

wash: **~-out** *n* disastro *m*. **~-room** *n* bagno *m*

wasp /wɒsp/ *n* vespa *f*

wastage /'weɪstɪdʒ/ *n* perdita *f*

waste /weɪst/ *n* spreco *m*; ⟨*rubbish*⟩ rifiuto m; ~ **of time** perdita f di tempo ● a ‹product› di scarto; ‹land› desolato; **lay** ~ devastare ● vt sprecare. **waste away** vi deperire

waste: ~**-di'sposal unit** n eliminatore m di rifiuti. ~**ful** a dispendioso. ~ **'paper** n carta f straccia. ~**-'paper basket** n cestino m per la carta [straccia]

watch /wɒtʃ/ n guardia f; ‹period of duty› turno m di guardia; ‹timepiece› orologio m; **be on the** ~ stare all'erta ● vt guardare ‹film, match, television›; ‹be careful of, look after› stare attento a ● vi guardare. **watch out** vi ‹be careful› stare attento ‹for a›. **watch out for** vt ‹look for› fare attenzione all'arrivo di ‹person›

watch: ~**-dog** n cane m da guardia. ~**ful** a attento. ~**maker** n orologiaio, -a mf. ~**man** n guardiano m. ~**strap** n cinturino m dell'orologio. ~**word** n motto m

water /'wɔːtə(r)/ n acqua f ● vt annaffiare ‹garden, plant›; ‹dilute› annacquare ● vi ‹eyes:› lacrimare; **my mouth was** ~**ing** avevo l'acquolina in bocca. **water down** vt diluire; fig attenuare

water: ~**-colour** n acquerello m. ~**cress** n crescione m. ~**fall** n cascata f

'watering-can n annaffiatoio m

water: ~**-lily** n ninfea f. ~**logged** a inzuppato. ~**main** n conduttura f dell'acqua. ~ **polo** n pallanuoto f. ~**power** n energia f idraulica. ~**proof** a impermeabile. ~**shed** n spartiacque m inv; fig svolta f. ~**-skiing** n sci m nautico. ~**tight** a stagno; fig irrefutabile. ~**way** n canale m navigabile

watery /'wɔːtərɪ/ a acquoso; ‹eyes› lacrimoso

watt /wɒt/ n watt m inv

wave /weɪv/ n onda f; ‹gesture› cenno m; fig ondata f ● vt agitare; ~ **one's hand** agitare la mano ● vi far segno; ‹flag:› sventolare. ~**length** n lunghezza f d'onda

waver /'weɪvə(r)/ vi vacillare; ‹hesitate› esitare

wavy /'weɪvɪ/ a ondulato

wax[1] /wæks/ vi ‹moon:› crescere; ‹fig: become› diventare

wax[2] n cera f; ‹in ear› cerume m ● vt dare la cera a. ~**works** n museo m delle cere

way /weɪ/ n percorso m; ‹direction› direzione f; ‹manner, method› modo m; ~**s** pl ‹customs› abitudini fpl; **be in the** ~ essere in mezzo; **on the** ~ **to Rome** an-

dando a Roma; **I'll do it on the** ~ lo faccio mentre vado; **it's on my** ~ è sul mio percorso; **a long** ~ **off** lontano; **this** ~ da questa parte; ‹like this› così; **by the** ~ a proposito; **by** ~ **of** come; ‹via› via; **either** ~ ‹whatever we do› in un modo o nell'altro; **in some** ~**s** sotto certi aspetti; **in a** ~ in un certo senso; **in a bad** ~ ‹person› molto grave; **out of the** ~ fuori mano; **under** ~ in corso; **lead the** ~ far strada; fig aprire la strada; **make** ~ far posto ‹for a›; **give** ~ Auto dare la precedenza; **go out of one's** ~ fig scomodarsi ‹to per›; **get one's** ~ ‹own› averla vinta ● adv ~ **behind** molto indietro. ~ **'in** n entrata f

way|lay vt ‹pt/pp -**laid**› aspettare al varco ‹person›

way 'out n uscita f; fig via f d'uscita

way-'out a fam eccentrico

wayward /'weɪwəd/ a capriccioso

WC n abbr WC; **the WC** il gabinetto

we /wiː/ pers pron noi; **we're the last** siamo gli ultimi; **they're going, but we're not** loro vanno, ma noi no

weak /wiːk/ a debole; ‹liquid› leggero. ~**en** vt indebolire ● vi indebolirsi. ~**ling** n smidollato, -a mf. ~**ness** n debolezza f; ‹liking› debole m

wealth /welθ/ n ricchezza f; fig gran quantità f. ~**y** a ‹-ier, -iest› ricco

wean /wiːn/ vt svezzare

weapon /'wepən/ n arma f

wear /weə(r)/ n ‹clothing› abbigliamento m; **for everyday** ~ da portare tutti i giorni; ~ ‹and tear› usura f ● v ‹pt **wore**, pp **worn**› ● vt portare; ‹damage› consumare; ~ **a hole in sth** logorare qcsa fino a fare un buco; **what shall I** ~? cosa mi metto? ● vi consumarsi; ‹last› durare. **wear off** vi scomparire; ‹effect:› finire. **wear out** vt consumare [fino in fondo]; ‹exhaust› estenuare ● vi estenuarsi

wearable /'weərəbl/ a portabile

wear|y /'wɪərɪ/ a ‹-ier, -iest› sfinito ● v ‹pt/pp **wearied**› ● vt sfinire ● vi ~**y of** stancarsi di. ~**ily** adv stancamente

weasel /'wiːzl/ n donnola f

weather /'weðə(r)/ n tempo m; **in this** ~ con questo tempo; **under the** ~ fam giù di corda ‹feel› sopravvivere ‹storm›

weather: ~**-beaten** a ‹face› segnato dalle intemperie. ~**cock** n gallo m segnavento. ~ **forecast** n previsioni fpl del tempo

weave[1] /wiːv/ vi ‹pt/pp **weaved**› ‹move› zigzagare

weave² *n* tessuto *m* ● *vt* (*pt* wove, *pp* woven) tessere; intrecciare ⟨*flowers etc*⟩; intrecciare le fila di ⟨*story etc*⟩. **~r** *n* tessitore, -trice *mf*

web /web/ *n* rete *f*; (*of spider*) ragnatela *f*. **~bed feet** *npl* piedi *mpl* palmati. **~ page** *n* Comput pagina *f* web

wed /wed/ *vt* (*pt/pp* wedded) sposare ● *vi* sposarsi. **~ding** *n* matrimonio *m*

wedding: **~ cake** *n* torta *f* nuziale. **~ day** *n* giorno *m* del matrimonio. **~ dress** *n* vestito *m* da sposa. **~-ring** *n* fede *f*

wedge /wedʒ/ *n* zeppa *f*; (*for splitting wood*) cuneo *m*; (*of cheese*) fetta *f* ● *vt* (*fix*) fissare

wedlock /'wedlɒk/ *n* **born out of ~** nato fuori dal matrimonio

Wednesday /'wenzdeɪ/ *n* mercoledì *m inv*

wee¹ /wiː/ *a fam* piccolo

wee² *vi fam* fare la pipì

weed /wiːd/ *n* erbaccia *f*; (*fam: person*) mollusco *m* ● *vt* estirpare le erbacce da ● *vi* estirpare le erbacce. **weed out** *vt fig* eliminare

'weed-killer *n* erbicida *m*

weedy /'wiːdɪ/ *a fam* mingherlino

week /wiːk/ *n* settimana *f*. **~day** *n* giorno *m* feriale. **~end** *n* fine *m* settimana

weekly /'wiːklɪ/ *a* settimanale ● *n* settimanale *m* ● *adv* settimanalmente

weep /wiːp/ *vi* (*pt/pp* wept) piangere

weigh /weɪ/ *vt/i* pesare; **~ anchor** levare l'ancora. **weigh down** *vt fig* piegare. **weigh up** *vt fig* soppesare; valutare ⟨*person*⟩

weight /weɪt/ *n* peso *m*; **put on/lose ~** ingrassare/dimagrire. **~ing** *n* (*allowance*) indennità *f inv*

weight: **~-lessness** *n* assenza *f* di gravità. **~-lifting** *n* sollevamento *m* pesi

weighty /'weɪtɪ/ *a* (-ier, -iest) pesante; (*important*) di un certo peso

weir /wɪə(r)/ *n* chiusa *f*

weird /wɪəd/ *a* misterioso; (*bizarre*) bizzarro

welcome /'welkəm/ *a* benvenuto; **you're ~!** prego!; **you're ~ to have it/to come** prendilo/vieni pure ● *n* accoglienza *f* ● *vt* accogliere; (*appreciate*) gradire

weld /weld/ *vt* saldare. **~er** *n* saldatore *m*

welfare /'welfeə(r)/ *n* benessere *m*; (*aid*) assistenza *f*. **W~ State** *n* Stato *m* assistenziale

well¹ /wel/ *n* pozzo *m*; (*of staircase*) tromba *f*

well² *adv* (**better, best**) bene; **as ~ anche**; **as ~ as** (*in addition*) oltre a; **~ done!** bravo!; **very ~** benissimo ● *a* **he is ˈnot ~** non sta bene; **get ~ soon!** guarisci presto! ● *int* beh!; **~ I never!** ma va!

well: **~-behaved** *a* educato. **~-being** *n* benessere *m*. **~-bred** *a* beneducato. **~-heeled** *a fam* danaroso

wellingtons /'welɪŋtənz/ *npl* stivali *mpl* di gomma

well: **~-known** *a* famoso. **~-meaning** *a* con buone intenzioni. **~-meant** *a* con le migliori intenzioni. **~-off** *a* benestante. **~-read** *a* colto. **~-to-do** *a* ricco

Welsh /welʃ/ *a & n* gallese; (*language*) gallese *m*; **the ~** *pl* i gallesi. **~man** *n* gallese *m*. **~ rabbit** *n* toast *m inv* al formaggio

went /went/ *see* go

wept /wept/ *see* weep

were /wɜː(r)/ *see* be

west /west/ *n* ovest *m*; **to the ~ of** a ovest di; **the W~** l'Occidente *m* ● *a* occidentale ● *adv* verso occidente; **go ~** *fam* andare in malora. **~erly** *a* verso ovest; occidentale ⟨*wind*⟩. **~ern** *a* occidentale ● *n* western *m inv*

West: **~ Germany** *n* Germania *f* Occidentale. **~ ˈIndian** *a & n* antillese *mf*. **~ ˈIndies** /'ɪndɪz/ *npl* Antille *fpl*

'westward[s] /-wəd[z]/ *adv* verso ovest

wet /wet/ *a* (**wetter, wettest**) bagnato; fresco ⟨*paint*⟩; (*rainy*) piovoso; (*fam: person*) smidollato; **get ~** bagnarsi ● *vt* (*pt/pp* wet, wetted) bagnare. **~ ˈblanket** *n* guastafeste *mf inv*

whack /wæk/ *n fam* colpo *m* ● *vt fam* dare un colpo a. **~ed** *a fam* stanco morto. **~ing** *a* (*fam: huge*) enorme

whale /weɪl/ *n* balena *f*; **have a ~ of a time** *fam* divertirsi un sacco

wham /wæm/ *int* bum

wharf /wɔːf/ *n* banchina *f*

what /wɒt/ *pron* che, [che] cosa; **~ for?** perché?; **~ is it?** (*what do you want*) cosa c'è?; **~ is it for?** a che cosa serve?; **~ is that for?** cosa c'è?; **~ is it like?** com'è?; **~ is your name?** come ti chiami?; **~ is the weather like?** com'è il tempo?; **~ is the film about?** di cosa parla il film?; **~ is he talking about?** di cosa sta parlando?; **he asked me ~ she had said** mi ha chiesto cosa ha detto; **~ about going to the cinema?** e se andassimo al cinema?; ~ **about the children?** (*what will they do*) e i bambini?; ~ **if it rains?** e se piove? ● *a* quale, che; **take ~ books you want** prendi tutti i libri che vuoi; ~ **kind of a** che tipo di; **at ~ time?** a che ora? ● *adv* che; ~ **a lovely day!** che bella giornata! ● *int* ~! [che] cosa!; ~? [che] cosa?

what'ever *a* qualunque ● *pron* qualsiasi cosa; ~ **is it?** cos'è?; ~ **he does** qualsiasi cosa faccia; ~ **happens** qualunque cosa succeda; **nothing ~** proprio niente

whatso'ever *a & pron* = **whatever**

wheat /wi:t/ *n* grano *m*, frumento *m*

wheedle /'wi:d(ə)l/ *vt* ~ **sth out of sb** ottenere qcsa da qualcuno con le lusinghe

wheel /wi:l/ *n* ruota *f*; (*steering ~*) volante *m*; **at the ~** al volante ● *vt* (*push*) spingere ● *vi* (*circle*) ruotare; ~ [**round**] ruotare

wheel: ~**barrow** *n* carriola *f*. ~**chair** *n* sedia *f* a rotelle. ~**-clamp** *n* ceppo *m* bloccaruote

wheeze /wi:z/ *vi* ansimare

when /wen/ *adv & conj* quando; **the day ~** il giorno in cui; ~ **swimming/ reading** nuotando/leggendo

when'ever *adv & conj* in qualsiasi momento; (*every time that*) ogni volta che; ~ **did it happen?** quando è successo?

where /weə(r)/ *adv & conj* dove; **the street ~ I live** la via in cui abito; ~ **do you come from?** da dove vieni?

whereabouts[1] /weərə'baʊts/ *adv* dove

'**whereabouts**[2] *n* **nobody knows his** ~ nessuno sa dove si trova

where'as *conj* dal momento che; (*in contrast*) mentre

where'by *adv* attraverso il quale

whereu'pon *adv* dopo di che

wher'ever *adv & conj* dovunque; ~ **is he?** dov'è mai?; ~ **possible** dovunque sia possibile

whet /wet/ *vt* (*pt/pp* **whetted**) aguzzare ⟨*appetite*⟩

whether /'weðə(r)/ *conj* se; ~ **you like it or not** che ti piaccia o no

which /wɪtʃ/ *a & pron* quale; ~ **one?** quale?; ~ **one of you?** chi di voi?; ~ **way?** (*direction*) in che direzione? ● *rel pron* (*object*) che; ~ **he does frequently** cosa che fa spesso; **after ~** dopo di che; **on/in ~** su/in cui

which'ever *a & pron* qualunque; ~ **it is** qualunque sia; ~ **one of you** chiunque tra voi

whiff /wɪf/ *n* zaffata *f*; **have a ~ of sth** odorare qcsa

while /waɪl/ *n* **a long ~** un bel po'; **a little ~** un po' ● *conj* mentre; (*as long as*) finché; (*although*) sebbene ● **while away** *vt* passare ⟨*time*⟩

whilst /waɪlst/ *conj see* **while**

whim /wɪm/ *n* capriccio *m*

whimper /'wɪmpə(r)/ *vi* piagnucolare; ⟨*dog:*⟩ mugolare

whimsical /'wɪmzɪkl/ *a* capriccioso; ⟨*story*⟩ fantasioso

whine /waɪn/ *n* lamento *m*; (*of dog*) guaito *m* ● *vi* lamentarsi; ⟨*dog:*⟩ guaire

whip /wɪp/ *n* frusta *f*; (*Pol: person*) parlamentare *mf* incaricato, -a di assicurarsi della presenza dei membri del suo partito alle votazioni ● *vt* (*pt/pp* **whipped**) frustare; *Culin* sbattere; (*snatch*) afferrare; (*fam: steal*) fregare. **whip up** *vt* (*incite*) stimolare; *fam* improvvisare ⟨*meal*⟩. ~**ped 'cream** *n* panna *f* montata

whirl /wɜːl/ *n* (*movement*) rotazione *f*; **my mind's in a ~** ho le idee confuse ● *vi* girare rapidamente ● *vt* far girare rapidamente. ~ **pool** *n* vortice *m*. ~ **wind** *n* turbine *m*

whirr /wɜː(r)/ *vi* ronzare

whisk /wɪsk/ *n Culin* frullino *m* ● *vt Culin* frullare. **whisk away** *vt* portare via

whisker /'wɪskə(r)/ *n* ~**s** (*of cat*) baffi *mpl*; (*on man's cheek*) basette *fpl*; **by a ~** per un pelo

whisky /'wɪskɪ/ *n* whisky *m inv*

whisper /'wɪspə(r)/ *n* sussurro *m*; (*rumour*) diceria *f* ● *vt/i* sussurrare

whistle /'wɪsl/ *n* fischio *m*; (*instrument*) fischietto *m* ● *vt* fischiettare ● *vi* fischiettare; ⟨*referee*⟩ fischiare

white /waɪt/ *a* bianco; **go ~** (*pale*) sbiancare ● *n* bianco *m*; (*of egg*) albume *m*; (*person*) bianco, -a *mf*

white: ~ '**coffee** *n* caffè *m inv* macchiato. ~**-collar worker** *n* colletto *m* bianco. ~ '**lie** *n* bugia *f* pietosa

'**Whitehall** *n* strada *f* di Londra, sede degli uffici del governo britannico; *fig* amministrazione *f* britannica

whiten /'waɪtn/ *vt* imbiancare ● *vi* sbiancare

whiteness /'waɪtnɪs/ *n* bianchezza *f*

'**whitewash** *n* intonaco *m*; *fig* copertura *f* ● *vt* dare una mano d'intonaco a; *fig* coprire

Whitsun /'wɪtsn/ *n* Pentecoste *f*

whittle /'wɪtl/ *vt* ~ **down** ridurre

whiz[z] /wɪz/ vi (pt/pp **whizzed**) sibila-re. **~-kid** n fam giovane m prodigio

who /hu:/ inter pron chi ● rel pron che; **the children, ~ were all tired,...** i bambini, che erano tutti stanchi,...

who'ever pron chiunque; **~ he is** chiunque sia; **~ can that be?** chi può mai essere?

whole /həʊl/ a tutto; (not broken) intat-to; **the ~ truth** tutta la verità; **the ~ world** il mondo intero; **the ~ lot** (everything) tutto; (pl) tutti; **the ~ lot of you** tutti voi ● n tutto m; **as a ~** nel-l'insieme; **on the ~** tutto considerato; **the ~ of Italy** tutta l'Italia

whole: **~food** n cibo m macrobiotico. **~-'hearted** a di tutto cuore. **~meal** a integrale

'wholesale a & adv all'ingrosso; fig in massa. **~r** n grossista mf

wholesome /'həʊlsəm/ a sano

wholly /'həʊlɪ/ adv completamente

whom /hu:m/ rel pron che; **the man ~ I saw** l'uomo che ho visto; **to/with ~** a/con cui ● inter pron che; **to ~ did you speak?** con chi hai parlato?

whooping cough /'hu:pɪŋ/ n pertos-se f

whopping /'wɒpɪŋ/ a fam enorme

whore /hɔ:(r)/ n puttana f vulg

whose /hu:z/ rel pron il cui; **people ~ name begins with D** le persone i cui nomi cominciano con la D ● inter pron di chi; **~ is that?** di chi è quello? ● a **~ car did you use?** di chi è la macchina che hai usato?

why /waɪ/ adv (inter) perché; **the reason ~** la ragione per cui; **that's ~** per questo ● int diamine

wick /wɪk/ n stoppino m

wicked /'wɪkɪd/ a cattivo; (mischievous) malizioso

wicker /'wɪkə(r)/ n vimini mpl ● attrib di vimini

wide /waɪd/ a largo; (experience, knowledge) vasto; (difference) profondo; (far from target) lontano; **10 cm ~** lar-go 10 cm; **how ~ is it?** quanto è largo? ● adv (off target) lontano dal bersaglio; **~ awake** del tutto sveglio; **~ open** spalancato; **far and ~** in lungo e in lar-go. **~ly** adv largamente; (known, accepted) generalmente; (different) pro-fondamente

widen /'waɪdn/ vt allargare ● vi allar-garsi

'widespread a diffuso

widow /'wɪdəʊ/ n vedova f. **~ed** a vedo-vo. **~er** n vedovo m

width /wɪdθ/ n larghezza f; (of material) altezza f

wield /wi:ld/ vt maneggiare; esercitare (power)

wife /waɪf/ n (pl **wives**) moglie f

wig /wɪg/ n parrucca f

wiggle /'wɪgl/ vi dimenarsi ● vt dime-nare

wild /waɪld/ a selvaggio; (animal, flower) selvatico; (furious) furibondo; (applause) fragoroso; (idea) folle; (with joy) pazzo; (guess) azzardato; **be ~ about** (keen on) andare pazzo per ● adv **run ~** crescere senza controllo ● n **in the ~** allo stato naturale; **the ~s** pl le zone sperdute

wilderness /'wɪldənɪs/•n deserto m; (fig: garden) giungla f

'wildfire n **spread like ~** allargarsi a macchia d'olio

wild: **~-'goose chase** n ricerca f inuti-le. **~life** n animali mpl selvatici

wilful /'wɪlfl/ a intenzionale; (person, refusal) ostinato. **~ly** adv intenzional-mente; (refuse) ostinatamente

will¹ /wɪl/ v aux he **~ arrive tomorrow** arriverà domani; **I won't tell him** non glielo dirò; **you ~ be back soon, won't you?** tornerai pre-sto, no?; **he ~ be there, won't he?** sarà là, no?; **she ~ be there by now** sarà là ormai; **~ you go?** (do you intend to go) pensi di andare?; **~ you go to the baker's and buy...?** puoi andare dal panettiere a comprare...?; **~ you be quiet!** vuoi stare calmo!; **~ you have some wine?** vuoi del vino?; **the engine won't start** la macchina non parte

will² n volontà f inv; (document) testa-mento m

willing /'wɪlɪŋ/ a disposto; (eager) vo-lonteroso. **~ly** adv volentieri. **~ness** n buona volontà f

willow /'wɪləʊ/ n salice m

'will-power n forza f di volontà

willy-'nilly adv (at random) a casaccio; (wanting to or not) volente o nolente

wilt /wɪlt/ vi appassire

wily /'waɪlɪ/ a (-ier, -iest) astuto

wimp /wɪmp/ n rammollito, -a mf

win /wɪn/ n vittoria f; **have a ~** riporta-re una vittoria ● v (pt/pp **won**; pres p **winning**) ● vt vincere; conquistare (fame) ● vi vincere. **win over** vt convin-cere

wince /wɪns/ vi contrarre il viso

winch /wɪntʃ/ n argano m

wind¹ /wɪnd/ n vento m; (breath) fiato m; (fam: flatulence) aria f; **get/have the ~ up** fam aver fifa; **get ~ of** aver sentore di; **in the ~** nell'aria ● vt ~ **sb** lasciare qcno senza fiato

wind² /waɪnd/ v (pt/pp **wound**) ● vt (wrap) avvolgere; (move by turning) far girare; caricare (clock) ● vi (road:) serpeggiare. **wind up** vt caricare (clock); concludere (proceedings); fam prendere in giro (sb)

wind /wɪnd/: ~**fall** n fig fortuna f inaspettata

winding /'waɪndɪŋ/ a tortuoso

wind: ~ **instrument** n strumento m a fiato. ~**mill** n mulino m a vento

window /'wɪndəʊ/ n finestra f; (of car) finestrino m; (of shop) vetrina f

window: ~**-box** n cassetta f per i fiori. ~**-cleaner** n (person) lavavetri mf inv. ~**-dresser** n vetrinista mf. ~**-dressing** n vetrinistica f; fig fumo m negli occhi. ~**-pane** n vetro m. ~**-shopping** n: **go** ~**-shopping** andare in giro a vedere le vetrine. ~**-sill** n davanzale m

'windscreen n, Am **'windshield** n parabrezza m inv. ~ **washer** n getto m d'acqua. ~**-wiper** n tergicristallo m

wind: ~ **surfing** n windsurf m inv. ~**-swept** a esposto al vento; (person) scompigliato

windy /'wɪndɪ/ a (-ier, -iest) ventoso

wine /waɪn/ n vino m

wine: ~**-bar** n enoteca f. ~**glass** n bicchiere m da vino. ~**-list** n carta f dei vini

winery /'waɪnərɪ/ n Am vigneto m

'wine-tasting n degustazione f di vini

wing /wɪŋ/ n ala f; Auto parafango m; ~**s** pl Theat quinte fpl. ~**er** n Sport ala f

wink /wɪŋk/ n strizzata f d'occhio; **not sleep a ~** non chiudere occhio ● vi strizzare l'occhio; (light:) lampeggiare

winner /'wɪnə(r)/ n vincitore, -trice mf

winning /'wɪnɪŋ/ a vincente; (smile) accattivante. ~**-post** n linea f d'arrivo. ~**s** npl vincite fpl

wint|er /'wɪntə(r)/ n inverno m. ~**ry** a invernale

wipe /waɪp/ n passata f; (to dry) asciugata f ● vt strofinare; (dry) asciugare. **wipe off** vt asciugare; (erase) cancellare. **wipe out** vt annientare; eliminare (village); estinguere (debt). **wipe up** vt asciugare (dishes)

wire /'waɪə(r)/ n fil m di ferro; (electrical) filo m elettrico

wireless /'waɪəlɪs/ n radio f inv

wire 'netting n rete f metallica

wiring /'waɪərɪŋ/ n impianto m elettrico

wiry /'waɪərɪ/ a (-ier, -iest) (person) dal fisico asciutto; (hair) ispido

wisdom /'wɪzdəm/ n saggezza f; (of action) sensatezza f. ~ **tooth** n dente m del giudizio

wise /waɪz/ a saggio; (prudent) sensato. ~**ly** adv saggiamente; (act) sensatamente

wish /wɪʃ/ n desiderio m; **make a ~** esprimere un desiderio; **with best ~es** con i migliori auguri ● vt desiderare; ~ **sb well** fare tanti auguri a qcno; **I ~ you every success** ti auguro buona fortuna; **I ~ you could stay** vorrei che tu potessi rimanere ● vi ~ **for sth** desiderare qcsa. ~**ful** a ~**ful thinking** illusione f

wishy-washy /'wɪʃɪwɒʃɪ/ a (colour) spento; (personality) insignificante

wisp /wɪsp/ n (of hair) ciocca f; (of smoke) filo m; (of grass) ciuffo m

wistful /'wɪstfl/ a malinconico

wit /wɪt/ n spirito m; (person) persona f di spirito; **be at one's ~s' end** non saper che pesci pigliare

witch /wɪtʃ/ n strega f. ~**craft** n magia f. ~**-hunt** n caccia f alle streghe

with /wɪð/ prep con; (fear, cold, jealousy etc) di; **I'm not ~ you** fam non ti seguo; **can I leave it ~ you?** <task> puoi occupartene tu?; ~ **no regrets/money** senza rimpianti/soldi; **be ~ it** fam essere al passo coi tempi; (alert) essere concentrato

with'draw v (pt **-drew**, pp **-drawn**) ● vt ritirare; prelevare (money) ● vi ritirarsi. ~**al** n ritiro m; (of money) prelevamento m; (from drugs) crisi f inv di astinenza; Psych chiusura f in se stessi. ~**al symptoms** npl sintomi mpl da crisi di astinenza

with'drawn see **withdraw** ● a (person) chiuso in se stesso

wither /'wɪðə(r)/ vi (flower:) appassire

with'hold vt (pt/pp **-held**) rifiutare (consent) (**from** a); nascondere (information) (**from** a); trattenere (smile)

with'in prep in; (before the end of) entro; ~ **the law** legale ● adv all'interno

with'out prep senza; ~ **stopping** senza fermarsi

with'stand vt (pt/pp **-stood**) resistere a

witness /'wɪtnɪs/ n testimone mf ● vt autenticare (signature); essere testimone di (accident). ~**-box**, Am ~**-stand** n banco m dei testimoni

witticism /'wɪtɪsɪzm/ *n* spiritosaggine *f*
wittingly /'wɪtɪŋlɪ/ *adv* consapevolmente
witty /'wɪtɪ/ *a* (**-ier, -iest**) spiritoso
wives /waɪvz/ *see* **wife**
wizard /'wɪzəd/ *n* mago *m.* **~ry** *n* stregoneria *f*
wobb|le /'wɒbl/ *vi* traballare. **~ly** *a* traballante
wodge /wɒdʒ/ *n fam* mucchio *m*
woe /wəʊ/ *n* afflizione *f*
woke, woken /wəʊk, 'wəʊkn/ *see* **wake**¹
wolf /wʊlf/ *n* (*pl* **wolves** /wʊlvz/) lupo *m;* (*fam: womanizer*) donnaiolo *m* ● *vt* **~** [**down**] divorare. **~ whistle** *n* fischio *m* ● *vi* **~-whistle at sb** fischiare dietro a qcno
woman /'wʊmən/ *n* (*pl* **women**) donna *f.* **~izer** *n* donnaiolo *m.* **~ly** *a* femmineo
womb /wuːm/ *n* utero *m*
women /'wɪmɪn/ *see* **woman.** **W~'s Libber** /'lɪbə(r)/ *n* femminista *f.* **W~'s Liberation** *n* movimento *m* femminista
won /wʌn/ *see* **win**
wonder /'wʌndə(r)/ *n* meraviglia *f;* (*surprise*) stupore *m;* **no ~!** non c'è da stupirsi!; **it's a ~ that...** è incredibile che... ● *vi* restare in ammirazione; (*be surprised*) essere sorpreso; **I ~** è quello che mi chiedo; **I ~ whether she is ill** mi chiedo se è malata?. **~ful** *a* meraviglioso. **~fully** *adv* meravigliosamente
won't /wəʊnt/ = **will not**
woo /wuː/ *vt* corteggiare; *fig* cercare di accattivarsi (*voters*)
wood /wʊd/ *n* legno *m;* (*for burning*) legna *f;* (*forest*) bosco *m;* **out of the ~** *fig* fuori pericolo; **touch ~!** tocca ferro!
wood: ~ed /-ɪd/ *a* boscoso. **~en** *a* di legno; *fig* legnoso. **~ wind** *n* strumenti *mpl* a fiato. **~work** *n* (*wooden parts*) parti *fpl* in legno; (*craft*) falegnameria *f.* **~worm** *n* tarlo *m.* **~y** *a* legnoso; (*hill*) boscoso
wool /wʊl/ *n* lana *f* ● *attrib* di lana. **~len** *a* di lana. **~lens** *npl* capi *mpl* di lana
woolly /'wʊlɪ/ *a* (**-ier, -iest**) (*sweater*) di lana; *fig* confuso
word /wɜːd/ *n* parola *f;* (*news*) notizia *f;* **by ~ of mouth** a viva voce; **have a ~ with** dire due parole a; **have ~s** bisticciare; **in other ~s** in altre parole. **~ing** *n* parole *fpl.* **~ processor** *n* programma *m* di videoscrittura, word processor *m inv*
wore /wɔː(r)/ *see* **wear**
work /wɜːk/ *n* lavoro *m;* (*of art*) opera *f;* **~s** *pl* (*factory*) fabbrica *fsg;*

(*mechanism*) meccanismo *msg;* **at ~** al lavoro; **out of ~** disoccupato ● *vi* lavorare; (*machine, ruse:*) funzionare; (*study*) studiare ● *vt* far funzionare (*machine*); far lavorare (*employee*); far studiare (*student*). **work off** *vt* sfogare (*anger*); lavorare per estinguere (*debt*); fare sport per smaltire (*weight*). **work out** *vt* elaborare (*plan*); risolvere (*problem*); calcolare (*bill*); **I ~ed out how he did it** ho capito come l'ha fatto ● *vi* evolvere. **work up** *vt* **I've ~ed up an appetite** mi è venuto appetito; **don't get ~ed up** (*anxious*) non farti prendere dal panico; (*angry*) non arrabbiarti
workable /'wɜːkəbl/ *a* (*feasible*) fattibile
workaholic /wɜːkə'hɒlɪk/ *n* staccanovista *mf*
worker /'wɜːkə(r)/ *n* lavoratore, -trice *mf;* (*manual*) operaio, -a *mf*
working /'wɜːkɪŋ/ *a* (*clothes etc*) da lavoro; (*day*) feriale; **in ~ order** funzionante. **~ class** *n* classe *f* operaia. **~-class** *a* operaio
work: ~man *n* operaio *m.* **~manship** *n* lavorazione *f.* **~-out** *n* allenamento *m.* **~shop** *n* officina *f;* (*discussion*) dibattito *m*
world /wɜːld/ *n* mondo *m;* **a ~ of difference** una differenza abissale; **out of this ~** favoloso; **think the ~ of sb** andare matto per qcno. **~ly** *a* materiale; (*person*) materialista. **~-wide** *a* mondiale ● *adv* mondialmente
worm /wɜːm/ *n* verme *m* ● *vt* **~ one's way into sb's confidence** conquistarsi la fiducia di qcno in modo subdolo. **~-eaten** *a* tarlato
worn /wɔːn/ *see* **wear** ● *a* sciupato. **~-out** *a* consumato; (*person*) sfinito
worried /'wʌrɪd/ *a* preoccupato
worr|y /'wʌrɪ/ *n* preoccupazione *f* ● *v* (*pt/pp* **worried**) ● *vt* preoccupare; (*bother*) disturbare ● *vi* preoccuparsi. **~ing** *a* preoccupante
worse /wɜːs/ *a* peggiore ● *adv* peggio ● *n* peggio *m*
worsen /'wɜːsn/ *vt/i* peggiorare
worship /'wɜːʃɪp/ *n* culto *m;* (*service*) funzione *f;* **Your/His W~** (*to judge*) signor giudice/il giudice ● *v* (*pt/pp* **-shipped**) ● *vt* venerare ● *vi* andare a messa
worst /wɜːst/ *a* peggiore ● *adv* peggio [di tutti] ● *n* the **~** il peggio; **get the ~**

of it avere la peggio; **if the ~ comes to the ~** nella peggiore delle ipotesi

worth /wɜ:θ/ n valore m; **£10 ~ of petrol** 10 sterline di benzina ● *a* **be ~** valere; **be ~ it** *fig* valerne la pena; **it's ~ trying** vale la pena di provare; **it's ~ my while** mi conviene. **~less** *a* senza valore. **~while** *a* che vale la pena; ⟨*cause*⟩ lodevole

worthy /'wɜ:ðɪ/ *a* degno; ⟨*cause, motive*⟩ lodevole

would /wʊd/ *v aux* **I ~ do it** lo farei; **~ you go?** andresti?; **~ you mind if I opened the window?** ti dispiace se apro la finestra?; **he ~ come if he could** verrebbe se potesse; **he said he ~n't** ha detto di no; **~ you like a drink?** vuoi qualcosa da bere?; **what ~ you like to drink?** cosa prendi da bere?; **you ~n't, ~ you?** non lo faresti, vero?

wound[1] /wu:nd/ n ferita f ● *vt* ferire

wound[2] /waʊnd/ *see* **wind**[2]

wove, woven /wəʊv, 'wəʊvn/ *see* **weave**[2]

wrangle /'ræŋgl/ n litigio m ● *vi* litigare

wrap /ræp/ n ⟨*shawl*⟩ scialle m ● *vt* (*pt/pp* **wrapped**) **~ [up]** avvolgere; incartare ⟨*present*⟩; **be ~ped up in** *fig* essere completamente preso da ● *vi* **~ up warmly** coprirsi bene. **~per** n ⟨*for sweet*⟩ carta f [di caramella]. **~ping** n materiale m da imballaggio. **~ping paper** n carta f da pacchi; ⟨*for gift*⟩ carta f da regalo

wrath /rɒθ/ n ira f

wreak /ri:k/ *vt* **~ havoc with sth** scombussolare qcsa

wreath /ri:θ/ n (*pl* **~s** /-ðz/) corona f

wreck /rek/ n ⟨*of ship*⟩ relitto m; ⟨*of car*⟩ carcassa f; ⟨*person*⟩ rottame m ● *vt* far naufragare; demolire ⟨*car*⟩. **~age** /-ɪdʒ/ n rottami mpl; *fig* brandelli mpl

wrench /rentʃ/ n ⟨*injury*⟩ slogatura f; ⟨*tool*⟩ chiave f inglese; ⟨*pull*⟩ strattone m ● *vt* ⟨*pull*⟩ strappare; slogarsi ⟨*wrist, ankle etc*⟩

wrest /rest/ *vt* strappare (**from** a)

wrestl|e /'resl/ *vi* lottare corpo a cor-

po; *fig* lottare. **~er** n lottatore, -trice *mf*. **~ing** n lotta f libera; ⟨*all-in*⟩ catch m

wretch /retʃ/ n disgraziato, -a *mf*. **~ed** /-ɪd/ *a* odioso; ⟨*weather*⟩ orribile; **feel ~ed** ⟨*unhappy*⟩ essere triste; ⟨*ill*⟩ sentirsi malissimo

wriggle /'rɪgl/ n contorsione f ● *vi* contorcersi; ⟨*move forward*⟩ strisciare; **~ out of sth** *fam* sottrarsi a qcsa

wring /rɪŋ/ *vt* (*pt/pp* **wrung**) torcere ⟨*sb's neck*⟩; strizzare ⟨*clothes*⟩; **~ one's hands** torcersi le mani; **~ing wet** inzuppato

wrinkle /'rɪŋkl/ n grinza f; ⟨*on skin*⟩ ruga f ● *vt/i* raggrinzire. **~d** *a* ⟨*skin, face*⟩ rugoso; ⟨*clothes*⟩ raggrinzito

wrist /rɪst/ n polso m. **~-watch** n orologio m da polso

writ /rɪt/ n *Jur* mandato m

write /raɪt/ *vt/i* (*pt* **wrote**, *pp* **written**, *pres p* **writing**) scrivere. **write down** *vt* annotare. **write off** *vt* cancellare ⟨*debt*⟩; distruggere ⟨*car*⟩

'write-off n ⟨*car*⟩ rottame m

writer /'raɪtə(r)/ n autore, -trice *mf*; **she's a ~** è una scrittrice

'write-up n ⟨*review*⟩ recensione f

writhe /raɪð/ *vi* contorcersi

writing /'raɪtɪŋ/ n ⟨*occupation*⟩ scrivere m; ⟨*words*⟩ scritte *fpl*; ⟨*handwriting*⟩ scrittura f; **in ~** per iscritto. **~-paper** n carta f da lettera

written /'rɪtn/ *see* **write**

wrong /rɒŋ/ *a* sbagliato; **be ~** ⟨*person:*⟩ sbagliare; **what's ~?** cosa c'è che non va? ● *adv* ⟨*spelt*⟩ in modo sbagliato; **go ~** ⟨*person:*⟩ sbagliare; ⟨*machine:*⟩ funzionare male; ⟨*plan:*⟩ andar male ● n ingiustizia f; **in the ~** dalla parte del torto; **know right from ~** distinguere il bene dal male ● *vt* fare torto a. **~ful** *a* ingiusto. **~ly** *adv* in modo sbagliato; ⟨*accuse, imagine*⟩ a torto; ⟨*informed*⟩ male

wrote /rəʊt/ *see* **write**

wrought'iron /rɔ:t-/ n ferro m battuto ● *attrib* di ferro battuto

wrung /rʌŋ/ *see* **wring**

wry /raɪ/ *a* (**-er, -est**) ⟨*humour, smile*⟩ beffardo

Xx

Xmas /'krɪsməs/ *n fam* Natale *m*
'X-ray *n* (*picture*) radiografia *f*; **have** an ~ farsi fare una radiografia ● *vt* passare ai raggi X

Yy

yacht /jɒt/ *n* yacht *m inv*; (*for racing*) barca *f* a vela. **~ing** *n* vela *f*

Yank /jæŋk/ *n fam* americano, -a *mf*

yank *vt fam* tirare

yap /jæp/ *vi* (*pt/pp* **yapped**) ⟨*dog:*⟩ guaire

yard¹ /jɑːd/ *n* cortile *m*; (*for storage*) deposito *m*

yard² *n* iarda *f* (= 91,44 *cm*). **~stick** *n fig* pietra *f* di paragone

yarn /jɑːn/ *n* filo *m*; (*fam: tale*) storia *f*

yawn /jɔːn/ *n* sbadiglio *m* ● *vi* sbadigliare. **~ing** *a* **~ing gap** sbadiglio *m*

year /jɪə(r)/ *n* anno *m*; (*of wine*) annata *f*; **for ~s** *fam* da secoli. **~book** *n* annuario *m*. **~ly** *a* annuale ● *adv* annualmente

yearn /jɜːn/ *vi* struggersi. **~ing** *n* desiderio *m* struggente

yeast /jiːst/ *n* lievito *m*

yell /jel/ *n* urlo *m* ● *vi* urlare

yellow /'jeləʊ/ *a & n* giallo *m*

yelp /jelp/ *n* (*of dog*) guaito *m* ● *vi* ⟨*dog:*⟩ guaire

yen /jen/ *n* forte desiderio *m* (**for** di)

yes /jes/ *adv* sì ● *n* sì *m inv*

yesterday /'jestədeɪ/ *n & adv* ieri *m inv*; **~'s paper** il giornale di ieri; **the day before ~** l'altroieri

yet /jet/ *adv* ancora; **as ~** fino ad ora; **not ~** non ancora; **the best ~** il migliore finora ● *conj* eppure

yew /juː/ *n* tasso *m* (*albero*)

yield /jiːld/ *n* produzione *f*; (*profit*) reddito *m* ● *vt* produrre; fruttare (*profit*) ● *vi* cedere; *Am Auto* dare la precedenza

yodel /'jəʊdl/ *vi* (*pt/pp* **yodelled**) cantare jodel

yoga /'jəʊgə/ *n* yoga *m*

yoghurt /'jɒgət/ *n* yogurt *m inv*

yoke /jəʊk/ *n* giogo *m*; (*of garment*) carré *m inv*

yokel /'jəʊkl/ *n* zotico, -a *mf*

yolk /jəʊk/ *n* tuorlo *m*

you /juː/ *pers pron* (*subject*) tu, voi *pl*; (*formal*) lei, voi *pl*; (*direct/indirect object*) ti, vi *pl*; (*formal: direct object*) la; (*formal: indirect object*) le; (*after prep*) te, voi *pl*; (*formal: after prep*) lei; **~ are very kind** (*sg*) sei molto gentile; (*formal*) è molto gentile; (*pl & formal pl*) siete molto gentili; **~ can stay, but he has to go** (*sg*) tu puoi rimanere, ma lui deve andarsene; (*pl*) voi potete rimanere, ma lui deve andarsene; **all of ~** tutti voi; **I'll give ~ the money** (*sg*) ti darò i soldi; (*pl*) vi darò i soldi; **I'll give it to ~** (*sg*) te/(*pl*) ve lo darò; **it was ~!** (*sg*) eri tu!; (*pl*) eravate voi!; **~ have to be careful** (*one*) si deve fare attenzione

young /jʌŋ/ *a* giovane ● *npl* (*animals*) piccoli *mpl*; **the ~** (*people*) i giovani. **~ lady** *n* signorina *f*. **~ man** *n* giovanotto *m*. **~ster** *n* ragazzo, -a *mf*; (*child*) bambino, -a *mf*

your /jɔː(r)/ *poss a* il tuo *m*, la tua *f*, i tuoi *mpl*, le tue *fpl*; (*formal*) il suo *m*, la sua *f*, i suoi *mpl*, le sue *fpl*; (*pl & formal pl*) il vostro *m*, la vostra *f*, i vostri *mpl*, le vostre *fpl*; **~ mother/father** tua madre/tuo padre; (*formal*) sua madre/suo padre; (*pl & formal pl*) vostra madre/vostro padre

yours /jɔːz/ *poss pron* il tuo *m*, la tua *f*, i tuoi *mpl*, le tue *fpl*; (*formal*) il suo *m*, la sua *f*, i suoi *mpl*, le sue *fpl*; (*pl & formal pl*) il vostro *m*, la vostra *f*, i vostri *mpl*, le vostre *fpl*; **a friend of ~** un tuo/suo/vostro amico; **friends of ~** dei tuoi/vostri/suoi amici; **that is ~** quello è tuo/vostro/suo; (*as opposed to mine*) quello è il tuo/il vostro/il suo

your'self *pers pron* (*reflexive*) ti; (*formal*) si; (*emphatic*) te stesso; (*formal*) sé, se stesso; **do pour ~ a drink** versati da bere; (*formal*) si versi da bere; **you said so ~** lo hai detto tu stesso; (*formal*) lo ha detto lei stesso; **you can**

be proud of ~ puoi essere fiero di te/di sé; **by ~** da solo

your'selves *pers pron* (*reflexive*) vi; (*emphatic*) voi stessi; **do pour ~ a drink** versatevi da bere; **you said so ~** lo avete detto voi stessi; **you can be proud of ~** potete essere fieri di voi; **by ~** da soli

youth /juːθ/ *n* (*pl* **youths** /-ðːz/) gioventù *f inv*; (*boy*) giovanetto *m*; **the ~** (*young people*) i giovani. **~ful** *a* giovanile. **~ hostel** *n* ostello *m* [della gioventù]

Yugoslav /'juːgəslɑːv/ *a & n* jugoslavo, -a *mf*

Yugoslavia /-'slɑːvɪə/ *n* Jugoslavia *f*

Zz

zany /'zeɪnɪ/ *a* (**-ier, -iest**) demenziale

zeal /ziːl/ *n* zelo *m*

zealous /'zeləs/ *a* zelante. **~ly** *adv* con zelo

zebra /'zebrə/ *n* zebra *f*. **~-'crossing** *n* passaggio *m* pedonale, zebre *fpl*

zero /'zɪərəʊ/ *n* zero *m*

zest /zest/ *n* gusto *m*

zigzag /'zɪgzæg/ *n* zigzag *m inv* ● *vi* (*pt/pp* **-zagged**) zigzagare

zilch /zɪltʃ/ *n fam* zero *m* assoluto

zinc /zɪŋk/ *n* zinco *m*

zip /zɪp/ *n* **~** [**fastener**] cerniera *f* [lam-

po] ● *vt* (*pt/pp* **zipped**) **~** [**up**] chiudere con la cerniera [lampo]

'Zip code *n Am* codice *m* postale

zipper /'zɪpə(r)/ *n Am* cerniera *f* [lampo]

zodiac /'zəʊdɪæk/ *n* zodiaco *m*

zombie /'zɒmbɪ/ *n fam* zombi *mf inv*

zone /zəʊn/ *n* zona *f*

zoo /zuː/ *n* zoo *m inv*

zoolog|ist /zəʊ'ɒlədʒɪst/ *n* zoologo, -a *mf*. **~y** zoologia *f*

zoom /zuːm/ *vi* sfrecciare. **~ lens** *n* zoom *m inv*

ITALIAN VERB TABLES

REGULAR VERBS:

1. in **-are** (*eg* **compr|are**)

    Present ~o, ~i, ~a, ~iamo, ~ate, ~ano
    Imperfect ~avo, ~avi, ~ava, ~avamo, ~avate, ~avano
    Past historic ~ai, ~asti, ~ò, ~ammo, ~aste, ~arono
    Future ~erò, ~erai, ~erà, ~eremo, ~erete, ~eranno
    Present subjunctive ~i, ~i, ~i, ~iamo, ~iate, ~ino
    Past subjunctive ~assi, ~assi, ~asse, ~assimo, ~aste, ~assero
    Present participle ~ando
    Past participle ~ato
    Imperative ~a (*fml* ~i), ~iamo, ~ate
    Conditional ~erei, ~eresti, ~erebbe, ~eremmo, ~ereste, ~erebbero

2. in **-ere** (*eg* **vend|ere**)

    Pres ~o, ~i, ~e, ~iamo, ~ete, ~ono
    Impf ~evo, ~evi, ~eva, ~evamo, ~evate, ~evano
    Past hist ~ei *or* ~etti, ~esti, ~è *or* ~ette, ~emmo, ~este, ~erono *or* ~ettero
    Fut ~erò, ~erai, ~erà, ~eremo, ~erete, ~eranno
    Pres sub ~a, ~a, ~a, ~iamo, ~iate, ~ano
    Past sub ~essi, ~essi, ~esse, ~essimo, ~este, ~essero
    Pres part ~endo
    Past part ~uto
    Imp ~i (*fml* ~a), ~iamo, ~ete
    Cond ~erei, ~eresti, ~erebbe, ~eremmo, ~ereste, ~erebbero

3. in **-ire** (*eg* **dorm|ire**)

    Pres ~o, ~i, ~e, ~iamo, ~ite, ~ono
    Impf ~ivo, ~ivi, ~iva, ~ivamo, ~ivate, ~ivano
    Past hist ~ii, ~isti, ~ì, ~immo, ~iste, ~irono
    Fut ~irò, ~irai, ~irà, ~iremo, ~irete, ~iranno
    Pres sub ~a, ~a, ~a, ~iamo, ~iate, ~ano
    Past sub ~issi, ~issi, ~isse, ~issimo, ~iste, ~issero
    Pres part ~endo
    Past part ~ito
    Imp ~i (*fml* ~a), ~iamo, ~ite
    Cond ~irei, ~iresti, ~irebbe, ~iremmo, ~ireste, ~irebbero

Notes

- Many verbs in the third conjugation take *isc* between the stem and the ending in the first, second, and third person singular and in the third person plural of the present, the present subjunctive, and the imperative: fin|ire **Pres** ~isco, ~isci, ~isce, ~iscono. **Pres sub** ~isca, ~iscano **Imp** ~isci.

- The three forms of the imperative are the same as the corresponding forms of the present for the second and third conjugation. In the first conjugation the forms are also the same except for the second person singular: present *compri*, imperative *compra*. The negative form of the second person singular is formed by putting *non* before the infinitive for all conjugations: *non comprare*. In polite forms the third person of the present subjunctive is used instead for all conjugations: *compri*.

IRREGULAR VERBS:

Certain forms of all irregular verbs are regular (except for *essere*). These are: the second person plural of the present, the past subjunctive, and the present participle. All forms not listed below are regular and can be derived from the parts given. Only those irregular verbs considered to be the most useful are shown in the tables.

accadere   *as* **cadere**

accendere   • **Past hist** accesi, accendesti • **Past part** acceso

affliggere   • **Past hist** afflissi, affliggesti • **Past part** afflitto

ammettere   *as* **mettere**

andare   • **Pres** vado, vai, va, andiamo, andate, vanno • **Fut** andrò *etc* • **Pres sub** vada, vadano • **Imp** va', vada, vadano

apparire   • **Pres** appaio *or* apparisco, appari *or* apparisci, appare *or* apparisce, appaiono *or* appariscono • **Past hist** apparvi *or* apparsi, apparisti, apparve *or* apparì *or* apparse, apparvero *or* apparirono *or* apparsero • **Pres sub** appaia *or* apparisca

aprire   • **Pres** apro • **Past hist** aprii, apristi • **Pres sub** apra • **Past part** aperto

avere   • **Pres** ho, hai, ha, abbiamo, hanno • **Past hist** ebbi, avesti, ebbe, avemmo, aveste, ebbero • **Fut** avrò *etc* • **Pres sub** abbia *etc* • **Imp** abbi, abbia, abbiate, abbiano

bere   • **Pres** bevo *etc* • **Impf** bevevo *etc* • **Past hist** bevvi *or* bevetti, bevesti • **Fut** berrò *etc* • **Pres sub** beva *etc* • **Past sub** bevessi *etc* • **Pres part** bevendo • **Cond** berrei *etc*

cadere   • **Past hist** caddi, cadesti • **Fut** cadrò *etc*

chiedere   • **Past hist** chiesi, chiedesti • **Pres sub** chieda *etc* • **Past part** chiesto *etc*

chiudere   • **Past hist** chiusi, chiudesti • **Past part** chiuso

cogliere   • **Pres** colgo, colgono • **Past hist** colsi, cogliesti • **Pres sub** colga • **Past part** colto

correre   • **Past hist** corsi, corresti • **Past part** corso

crescere   • **Past hist** crebbi • **Past part** cresciuto

cuocere   • **Pres** cuocio, cuociamo, cuociono • **Past hist** cossi, cocesti • **Past part** cotto

dare   • **Pres** do, dai, da, diamo, danno • **Past hist** diedi *or* detti, desti • **Fut** darò *etc* • **Pres sub** dia *etc* • **Past sub** dessi *etc* • **Imp** da' (*fml* dia)

dire
• **Pres** dico, dici, dice, diciamo, dicono • **Impf** dicevo *etc* •
Past hist dissi, dicesti • **Fut** dirò *etc* • **Pres sub** dica,
diciamo, diciate, dicano • **Past sub** dicessi *etc* • *Pres part*
dicendo • **Past part** detto • **Imp** di' (*fml* dica)

dovere
• **Pres** devo *or* debbo, devi, deve, dobbiamo, devono *or*
debbono • **Fut** dovrò *etc* • **Pres sub** deva *or* debba,
dobbiamo, dobbiate, devano *or* debbano • **Cond** dovrei *etc*

essere
• **Pres** sono, sei, è, siamo, siete, sono • **Impf** ero, eri, era,
eravamo, eravate, erano • **Past hist** fui, fosti, fu, fummo,
foste, furono • **Fut** sarò *etc* • **Pres sub** sia *etc* • **Past sub**
fossi, fossi, fosse, fossimo, foste, fossero • **Past part** stato
• **Imp** sii (*fml* sia), siate • **Cond** sarei *etc*

fare
• **Pres** faccio, fai, fa, facciamo, fanno • **Impf** facevo *etc* •
Past hist feci, facesti • **Fut** farò *etc* • **Pres sub** faccia *etc* •
Past sub facessi *etc* • **Pres part** facendo • **Past part** fatto
• **Imp** fa' (*fml* faccia) • **Cond** farei *etc*

fingere
• **Past hist** finsi, fingesti, finsero • **Past part** finto

giungere
• **Past hist** giunsi, giungesti, giunsero • **Past part** giunto

leggere
• **Past hist** lessi, leggesti • **Past part** letto

mettere
• **Past hist** misi, mettesti • **Past part** messo

morire
• **Pres** muoio, muori, muore, muoiono • **Fut** morirò *or*
morrò *etc* • **Pres sub** muoia • **Past part** morto

muovere
• **Past hist** mossi, movesti • **Past part** mosso

nascere
• **Past hist** nacqui, nascesti • **Past part** nato

offrire
• **Past hist** offersi *or* offrii, offristi • **Pres sub** offra • **Past
part** offerto

parere
• **Pres** paio, pari, pare, pariamo, paiono • **Past hist** parvi
or parsi, paresti • **Fut** parrò *etc* • **Pres sub** paia, paiamo *or*
pariamo, pariate, paiano • **Past part** parso

piacere
• **Pres** piaccio, piaci, piace, piacciamo, piacciono • **Past
hist** piacqui, piacesti, piacque, piacemmo, piaceste,
piacquero • **Pres sub** piaccia *etc* • **Past part** piaciuto

porre
• **Pres** pongo, poni, pone, poniamo, ponete, pongono •
Impf ponevo *etc* • **Past hist** posi, ponesti • **Fut** porrò *etc* •
Pres sub ponga, poniamo, poniate, pongano • **Past sub**
ponessi *etc*

potere
• **Pres** posso, puoi, può, possiamo, possono • **Fut** potrò *etc*
• **Pres sub** possa, possiamo, possiate, possano • **Cond**
potrei *etc*

prendere
• **Past hist** presi, prendesti • **Past part** preso

ridere
• **Past hist** risi, ridesti • **Past part** riso

rimanere • **Pres** rimango, rimani, rimane, rimaniamo, rimangono • **Past hist** rimasi, rimanesti • **Fut** rimarrò *etc* • **Pres sub** rimanga • **Past part** rimasto • **Cond** rimarrei

salire • **Pres** salgo, sali, sale, saliamo, salgono • **Pres sub** salga, saliate, salgano

sapere • **Pres** so, sai, sa, sappiamo, sanno • **Past hist** seppi, sapesti • **Fut** saprò *etc* • **Pres sub** sappia *etc* • **Imp** sappi (*fml* sappia), sappiate • **Cond** saprei *etc*

scegliere • **Pres** scelgo, scegli, sceglie, scegliamo, scelgono • **Past hist** scelsi, scegliesti *etc* • **Past part** scelto

scrivere • **Past hist** scrissi, scrivesti *etc* • **Past part** scritto

sedere • **Pres** siedo *or* seggo, siedi, siede, siedono • **Pres sub** sieda *or* segga

spegnere • **Pres** spengo, spengono • **Past hist** spensi, spegnesti • **Past part** spento

stare • **Pres** sto, stai, sta, stiamo, stanno • **Past hist** stetti, stesti • **Fut** starò *etc* • **Pres sub** stia *etc* • **Past part** stato • **Imp** sta' (*fml* stia)

tacere • **Pres** taccio, tacciono • **Past hist** tacqui, tacque, tacquero • **Pres sub** taccia

tendere • **Past hist** tesi • **Past part** teso

tenere • **Pres** tengo, tieni, tiene, tengono • **Past hist** tenni, tenesti • **Fut** terrò *etc* • **Pres sub** tenga

togliere • **Pres** tolgo, tolgono • **Past hist** tolsi, tolse, tolsero • **Pres sub** tolga, tolgano • **Past part** tolto • *Imp fml* tolga

trarre • **Pres** traggo, trai, trae, traiamo, traete, traggono • **Past hist** trassi, traesti • **Fut** trarrò *etc* • **Pres sub** tragga • **Past sub** traessi *etc* • **Past part** tratto

uscire • **Pres** esco, esci, esce, escono • **Pres sub** esca • **Imp** esci (*fml* esca)

valere • **Pres** valgo, valgono • **Past hist** valsi, valesti • **Fut** varrò *etc* • **Pres sub** valga, valgano • **Past part** valso • **Cond** varrei *etc*

vedere • **Past hist** vidi, vedesti • **Fut** vedrò *etc* • **Past part** visto *or* veduto • **Cond** vedrei *etc*

venire • **Pres** vengo, vieni, viene, vengono • **Past hist** venni, venisti • **Fut** verrò *etc*

vivere • **Past hist** vissi, vivesti • **Fut** vivrò *etc* • **Past part** vissuto • **Cond** vivrei *etc*

volere • **Pres** voglio, vuoi, vuole, vogliamo, volete, vogliono • **Past hist** volli, volesti • **Fut** vorrò *etc* • **Pres sub** voglia *etc* • **Imp** vogliate • **Cond** vorrei *etc*

263

English irregular verbs

Infinitive	Past Tense	Past Participle	Infinitive	Past Tense	Past Participle
Infinito	*Passato*	*Participio passato*	*Infinito*	*Passato*	*Participio passato*
arise	arose	arisen	feed	fed	fed
awake	awoke	awoken	feel	felt	felt
be	was	been	fight	fought	fought
bear	bore	borne	find	found	found
beat	beat	beaten	flee	fled	fled
become	became	become	fling	flung	flung
begin	began	begun	fly	flew	flown
behold	beheld	beheld	forbid	forbade	forbidden
bend	bent	bent	forget	forgot	forgotten
beseech	beseeched, besought	beseeched, besought	forgive	forgave	forgiven
			forsake	forsook	forsaken
bet	bet, betted	bet, betted	freeze	froze	frozen
bid	bade, bid	bidden, bid	get	got	got, gotten *Am*
bind	bound	bound	give	gave	given
bite	bit	bitten	go	went	gone
bleed	bled	bled	grind	ground	ground
blow	blew	blown	grow	grew	grown
break	broke	broken	hang	hung, hanged (*vt*)	hung, hanged
breed	bred	bred	have	had	had
bring	brought	brought	hear	heard	heard
build	built	built	hew	hewed	hewed, hewn
burn	burnt, burned	burnt, burned	hide	hid	hidden
burst	burst	burst	hit	hit	hit
bust	busted, bust	busted, bust	hold	held	held
			hurt	hurt	hurt
buy	bought	bought	keep	kept	kept
cast	cast	cast	kneel	knelt	knelt
catch	caught	caught	know	knew	known
choose	chose	chosen	lay	laid	laid
cling	clung	clung	lead	led	led
come	came	come	lean	leaned, leant	leaned, leant
cost	cost, costed (*vt*)	cost, costed	leap	leapt, leaped	leapt, leaped
creep	crept	crept			
cut	cut	cut	learn	learnt, learned	learnt, learned
deal	dealt	dealt			
dig	dug	dug	leave	left	left
do	did	done	lend	lent	lent
draw	drew	drawn	let	let	let
dream	dreamt, dreamed	dreamt, dreamed	lie²	lay	lain
			light	lit, lighted	lit, lighted
drink	drank	drunk			
drive	drove	driven	lose	lost	lost
dwell	dwelt	dwelt	make	made	made
eat	ate	eaten	mean	meant	meant
fall	fell	fallen	meet	met	met

Infinitive	Past Tense	Past Participle	Infinitive	Past Tense	Past Participle
Infinito	*Passato*	*Participio passato*	*Infinito*	*Passato*	*Participio passato*
mow	mowed	mown, mowed	**spend**	spent	spent
			spill	spilt, spilled	spilt, spilled
overhang	overhung	overhung			
pay	paid	paid	**spin**	spun	spun
put	put	put	**spit**	spat	spat
quit	quitted, quit	quitted, quit	**split**	split	split
			spoil	spoilt, spoiled	spoilt, spoiled
read	read /red/	read /red/	**spread**	spread	spread
rid	rid	rid	**spring**	sprang	sprung
ride[2]	rode	ridden	**stand**	stood	stood
ring[2]	rang	rung	**steal**	stole	stolen
rise	rose	risen	**stick**	stuck	stuck
run	ran	run	**sting**	stung	stung
saw	sawed	sawn, sawed	**stink**	stank	stunk
			strew	strewed	strewn, strewed
say	said	said			
see	saw	seen	**stride**	strode	stridden
seek	sought	sought	**strike**	struck	struck
sell	sold	sold	**string**	strung	strung
send	sent	sent	**strive**	strove	striven
set	set	set	**swear**	swore	sworn
sew	sewed	sewn, sewed	**sweep**	swept	swept
			swell	swelled	swollen, swelled
shake	shook	shaken			
shear	sheared	shorn, sheared	**swim**	swam	swum
			swing	swung	swung
shed	shed	shed	**take**	took	taken
shine	shone	shone	**teach**	taught	taught
shit	shit	shit	**tear**	tore	torn
shoe	shod	shod	**tell**	told	told
shoot	shot	shot	**think**	thought	thought
show	showed	shown	**thrive**	thrived, throve	thrived, thriven
shrink	shrank	shrunk			
shut	shut	shut	**throw**	threw	thrown
sing	sang	sung	**thrust**	thrust	thrust
sink	sank	sunk	**tread**	trod	trodden
sit	sat	sat	**understand**	understood	understood
slay	slew	slain	**undo**	undid	undone
sleep	slept	slept	**wake**	woke	woken
slide	slid	slid	**wear**	wore	worn
sling	slung	slung	**weave**[2]	wove	woven
slit	slit	slit	**weep**	wept	wept
smell	smelt, smelled	smelt, smelled	**wet**	wet, wetted	wet, wetted
			win	won	won
sow	sowed	sown, sowed	**wind**[2]	wound	wound
			wring	wrung	wrung
speak	spoke	spoken	**write**	wrote	written
speed	sped, speeded	sped, speeded			
spell	spelled, spelt	spelled, spelt			